A TREATISE

ON THE LAW OF

MONOPOLIES

AND

INDUSTRIAL TRUSTS,

AS ADMINISTERED IN

ENGLAND AND IN THE UNITED STATES OF AMERICA.

BY

CHARLES FISK BEACH, SR.,

COUNSELLOR AT LAW.

AUTHOR OF "COMMENTARIES ON THE LAW OF TRUSTS AND TRUSTEES."

THE LAWBOOK EXCHANGE, LTD.

Clark, New Jersey

2007

ISBN-13: 978-1-58477-752-6
ISBN-10: 1-58477-752-4

The quality of this reprint is equivalent to the quality of the original work.

THE LAWBOOK EXCHANGE, LTD.
33 Terminal Avenue
Clark, New Jersey 07066-1321

Please see our website for a selection of our other publications and fine facsimile reprints of classic works of legal history:
www.lawbookexchange.com

Library of Congress Cataloging-in-Publication Data

Beach, Charles Fisk, 1827-1908.
A treatise on the law of monopolies and industrial trusts, as administered in England and in the United States of America / author, Charles Fisk Beach.
p. cm.
Originally published: St. Louis: Central Law Journal Co., 1898.
Includes bibliographical references and index.
ISBN-13: 978-1-58477-752-6 (alk. paper)
ISBN-10: 1-58477-752-4 (alk. paper)
1. Trusts, Industrial--Great Britain. 2. Trusts, Industrial--Law--United States. 3. Corporation law--Great Britain. 4. Corporation law--United States. 5. Monopolies--Great Britain. 6. Monopolies--United States. I. Title.
KF1649.B4 2007
343.73'072--dc22 2006019396

Printed in the United States of America on acid-free paper

A TREATISE

ON THE LAW OF

MONOPOLIES

AND

INDUSTRIAL TRUSTS,

AS ADMINISTERED IN

ENGLAND AND IN THE UNITED STATES OF AMERICA.

BY

CHARLES FISK BEACH, Sr.,

COUNSELLOR AT LAW.

AUTHOR OF "COMMENTARIES ON THE LAW OF TRUSTS AND TRUSTEES."

ST. LOUIS:

CENTRAL LAW JOURNAL COMPANY.

1898.

St. Louis, Mo.: Printed by Central Law Journal Company

TO

MY WIFE,

HELENE LOUISE LEE,

THIS VOLUME

IS

GRATEFULLY DEDICATED.

CHARLES FISK BEACH, SR.

PREFACE.

This work is an outgrowth of my "Commentaries on the Law of Trusts and Trustees." It was my original intention to write two or three chapters for that work on the subjects discussed in this volume. But the discussion of the law of trusts and trustees assumed such proportions, extending so far beyond the prescribed limits, that it was found altogether impracticable to include in that work even a satisfactory outline of the law of monopolies and industrial trusts.

In offering this treatise to the profession, I flatter myself that there is no call for an apology. To a great extent the law relating to the subjects here treated is either quite new, or of comparatively recent origin. A short time only has elapsed since the decisions of the English courts, which now constitute the law for the British Empire, were rendered, and the most important decisions of the Supreme Court of the United States relating to monopolies and industrial trusts, have been handed down during the past few months. Most of the statutes also of the States of this country have been enacted during a comparatively recent period, and some of them have become law since the writing of this volume had its beginning. In view of these facts, it is not remarkable that no adequate discussion of this subject has heretofore appeared. The only extant treatise relating, even in a general sense, to the subjects here discussed, contains about one-third of the matter of this volume, and it was published before the recent English and American decisions which constitute the law of the present. So far as relates either to the decisions of the courts, or to the statutes of the Federal and State legislatures, this work will be found up to date. It is believed that the chapter devoted to Anti-Trust Legislation will be found of special value.

In the preparation of this work, as of its predecessor, I have had the assistance of Edward Franklin White, Esq., of the Indianapolis bar. In the main, the notes are the product of his labor. For this service Mr. White has qualifications of a high order, and the evidence of his conscientious industry appears on every page. The busy lawyer will find the legal and equitable principles expounded in the text very amply sustained, and very fully and pertinently illustrated by his copious and well chosen notes.

CHARLES FISK BEACH, SR.

Indianapolis, Ind., June 8th, 1898.

TABLE OF CONTENTS.

INTRODUCTION.

		Page.
§ 1.	A recent development	1
2.	Origin of the term	2
3.	A wider significance	4
4.	Some early illustrations	4
5.	Early English monopolies	9
6.	Statutory enactments	12
7.	The doctrine modified	15
8.	An historical review	17
9.	Sustained by popular sentiment	27
10.	The American doctrine	28
11.	The adverse contention	31
12.	Labor organizations	34
13.	Popular sentiment and public policy	35

CHAPTER I.

PUBLIC POLICY AS RELATED TO TRADE AND INDUSTRIAL TRUSTS.

		Page.
§ 14.	Introductory	37
15.	Public policy defined	42
16.	The effect of a change	47
17.	Covenants inconsistent with morality	49
18.	Services in influencing legislation	54
19.	The ground of the rule	58
20.	Where such services may be employed	62
21.	Services in influencing public officials	64
22.	For services in procuring appointments to public offices	68
23.	The subject continued	71
24.	For withdrawal of opposing candidates	72
25.	For services in procuring a pardon	75
26.	For services which are in violation of public duty	77
27.	For services in opposing a public enterprise	80
28.	The subject continued	82

		Page.
§ 29.	Stipulations against liability	85
30.	The rule in New York	91
31.	Contracts in contravention of law	93
32.	For influencing the administration of justice	95
33.	For changing the officers of corporations	99
34.	For renouncing an executorship	101
35.	For assignment of salary not yet due	104

CHAPTER II.

CONTRACTS IN RESTRAINT OF TRADE.

		Page.
§ 36.	Introductory	107
37.	The general rule	110
38.	The rule in England	115
39.	Partial distinguished from general restraint	116
40.	Question of consideration	121
41.	Limitations of time	123
42.	The subject continued	126
43.	Touching territorial limitations	128
44.	The subject continued	131
45.	Territorial limits determined	139
46.	Validity of contracts in restraint of trade as affected by their reasonableness	142
47.	Divisibility of illegal contracts	147
48.	The subject continued	151
49.	Limitations in conveyances	153
50.	The subject continued	157
51.	The grantee restrained by the terms of the conveyance	159
52.	Contracts relating to trade secrets	160
53.	Restraint of trade by patents	165
54.	Where contracts relating to patents are not upheld	169
55.	Restraint in the sale of a trade-mark	171
56.	Restraint in publication contract	174

CHAPTER III.

CONTRACTS RELATING TO PROFESSIONS AND TRADES.

		Page.
§ 57.	Introductory	179
58.	Contract for the sale of a physician's practice	183
59.	The subject continued	185
60.	The rule as applied to attorneys	187
61.	The rule as applied to dentists	190
62.	Application of the rule to the profession of teaching	193
63.	Restraint upon the services of artists and actors	194

Page.
§ 64. As applied to trades and other occupations . . 197
65. In its application to traveling salesmen . . . 202
66. Constraint of trade construed as a limited partnership . 204

CHAPTER IV.

CONTRACTS RELATING TO RESTRICTIONS IN BUSINESS.

Page.
67. Introductory 206
68. Contracts granting an exclusive business privilege . 206
69. Contracts relating to a particular article . . . 209
70. Contracts under which the grantor retains an interest in the business 210
71. Contracts for the sale of a good will . . . 212
72. The subject continued 215
73. Further application of the rule 220
74. Agreement not to buy or sell 221
75. Contract to maintain prices 223
76. Statutory regulations 224

CHAPTER V.

CONSPIRACIES IN RESTRAINT OF TRADE.

Page.
§ 77. Introductory 227
78. Conspiracy defined 228
79. The rule in England 231
80. Conspiracy by a corporation 235
81. Combination to monopolize a particular branch of business 237
82. Combinations for regulating prices 242
83. Conspiracies under the federal anti-trust act . . 246
84. Combination to prevent competition at a judicial sale . 248
85. Combination to destroy competition 252
86. Conspiracy for severing the relation of a minister to his congregation 255
87. Indictment for conspiracy 256
88. Statutory regulations 259

CHAPTER VI.

THE CREATING OF A CORNER.

Page.
§ 89. Introductory 262
90. The corner defined 264
91. The nature of an option 267

		Page.
§ 92.	Modification of the common law doctrine	269
93.	The creation of a corner in necessaries	272
94.	The creation of a corner in stocks	274
95.	Where contracts for future delivery are justifiable	277
96.	Rights and liabilities of third parties	280
97.	Statutory prohibitions	284

CHAPTER VII.

TRADES UNIONS AND LABOR ORGANIZATIONS.

		Page.
§ 98.	Introductory	286
99.	The strike and the lockout	289
100.	The strike as a conspiracy	291
101.	The subject continued	295
102.	Where a strike will be upheld	299
103.	Where a lockout will be held lawful	305
104.	Combination of employees	305
105.	The boycott	311
106.	The nature of the offense	314
107.	Picketing	322
108.	Blacklisting	327
109.	Obligation of carriers as affected by strikes	331
110.	The strike as a violation of the federal anti-trust act	334
111.	The relation of trades unions to a receiver	338
112.	Interference with transportation of the mails	340
113.	Contracts between employers and trades unions	344
114.	Remedy by civil action	348
115.	Remedy by injunction	352
116.	Statutory regulations	356

CHAPTER VIII.

MONOPOLIES FROM MUNICIPAL GRANTS AND CONTRACTS.

		Page.
§ 117.	Introductory	359
118.	Limitation of exclusive privilege	364
119.	Statutory regulations	366
120.	The subject continued	371
121.	How regarded in equity	375
122.	Monopoly in street railways	376
123.	Grant of exclusive gas privilege	381
124.	Exclusive privilege for supplying water	386
125.	The subject continued	390
126.	Exclusive privilege of erecting a toll bridge or of establishing a ferry	392

		Page.
§ 127.	The subject continued	395
128.	Power to impose a ferry license	398
129.	For removal of garbage	400
130.	Municipal grant of a market franchise	404
131.	The subject continued	406
132.	Legislative and business powers distinguished	410

CHAPTER IX.

THE POWER TO REGULATE PRIVATE CORPORATIONS.

		Page.
§ 133.	Introductory	412
134.	Power to regulate the business of a railroad company	419
135.	Power not lost by non-user	424
136.	Power to act through a commission	425
137.	Power to assess damages	429
138.	Power to regulate public warehouses and warehousing	431
139.	Effect of statutory regulations	435
140.	Power to regulate the operations of telegraph companies	437
141.	When subject to congressional control	440
142.	Application of the rule to the telephone	444
143.	Power to regulate in case of patented property	449
144.	Application of the rule to the baking business	451
145.	Application of the rule to the laundry business	453
146.	Immunity from governmental control	456
147.	A business *juris publici* distinguished from a business *juris privati*	458

CHAPTER X.

COMBINATIONS OF RAILWAY COMPANIES FOR THE SUPPRESSION OF COMPETITION.

		Page.
§ 148.	Introductory	464
149.	Combinations for the purpose of suppressing competition	469
150.	The subject continued	473
151.	Purchase of competing lines	476
152.	Lease of competing lines	480
153.	Consolidation of parallel lines	485
154.	The subject continued	490
155.	The rule in case of traffic arrangement	492
156.	Admission to depot grounds	495
157.	General powers of railway corporations	499

CHAPTER XI.

INDUSTRIAL TRUSTS.

		Page.
§ 158.	Introductory	503
159.	Classification of industrial trusts	505
160.	Legality of the "trust,"—class first	507
161.	The subject continued	513
162.	The same subject	517
163.	The legality of the "trust" continued,—class second	525
164.	The rule in England	532
165.	Legality of the "trust" continued,—class third	536
166.	The subject continued	539

CHAPTER XII.

TRUST COMBINATIONS.

		Page.
§ 167.	Introductory	543
168.	The purpose and scope of federal legislation	544
169.	The subject continued	546
170.	Pooling by railroads	552
171.	The pooling of stocks	558
172.	The pooling of products	561
173.	The subject continued	565
174.	Monopoly under patents	568
175.	The subject continued	572
176.	The voting trust	576
177.	The subject continued	580
178.	The same subject	583
179.	Rebates on freight bills	585
180.	The subject continued	589
181.	Combinations of insurance companies	591
182.	Rights of parties under trust combinations	595

CHAPTER XIII.

ANTI-TRUST LEGISLATION.

		Page.
§ 183.	Introductory	600
184.	The federal anti-trust act	601
185.	Alabama insurance act	603
186.	Arkansas anti-trust act	605
187.	California cattle trust	606
188.	Delaware life insurance law	608
189.	Florida legislation relating to trusts and monopolies	609
190.	Georgia anti-monopoly act	611

Page.
§ 191. Illinois act prohibiting pools, trusts and combines . 614
192. Indiana anti-trust act 616
193. Iowa anti-pool and trust law 618
194. Kansas law prohibiting trusts 622
195. Kentucky law prohibiting pools, trusts and conspiracies 626
196. Louisiana law for the prohibition of trusts and combinations in restraint of trade 628
197. Maine anti-trust law 631
198. Michigan anti-trust act 633
199. Minnesota law to prohibit pools and trusts . . 635
200. Mississippi law prohibiting trusts and combines . 636
201. Missouri anti-trust act 639
202. Montana statute against monopolies and trusts . . 646
203. Nebraska statute against trusts and conspiracies against trade and business 648
204. New Mexico law declaring trust combinations illegal . 653
205. New York law to prevent monopolies . . . 654
206. North Carolina law for the prohibition of trusts . . 657
207. North Dakota law declaring certain trusts and combinations unlawful 659
208. Oklahoma law to prevent combinations in restraint of trade 660
209. South Carolina prohibition of trusts and combinations . 662
210. South Dakota anti-trust law 664
211. Tennessee law to prohibit conspiracies and trusts . 666
212. Texas law for the suppression of trusts and the promotion of true competition 670
213. Utah law prohibiting pools and trusts . . . 674
214. Washington law forbidding trusts and monopolies . 677
215. Wisconsin statute prohibiting trusts and combinations in restraint of trade 678

CHAPTER XIV.

REMEDIES BY QUO WARRANTO AND INJUNCTION.

Page.
§ 216. Introductory 680
217. The writ of quo warranto 680
218. The subject continued 684
219. Ground of proceedings against monopolies and industrial combinations 688
220. What courts have jurisdiction 691
221. Who may file an information 697
222. Pleadings and averments 701
223. Judgment under proceedings in quo warranto . . 705
224. Application of the rule to illegal combinations . . 708
225. Remedy by injunction 709
226. The subject continued 713
227. Punishment for contempt 714

CHAPTER XV.

STATUTORY REGULATIONS OF RATES OF TRANSPORTATION.

		Page.
§ 228.	Introductory	717
229.	Statutory enactments subject to judicial investigation	718
230.	Right of railroad corporations to legal protection	719
231.	Right of railway companies to discriminate in rates of transportation	721
232.	Rule for determining what are reasonable rates	723

CHAPTER XVI.

CONCLUDING REFLECTIONS.

TABLE OF CASES.

[The references are to pages.]

A.

Abbott v. Am. Hard Rubber Co. (33 Barb. 578), 710.

Abrams v. Milwaukee, etc. R. Co. (87 Wis. 485; 58 N.W.Rep.780), 86, 93.

Adams v. Adams (25 Minn. 72), 97.

Adams Co. v. Hunter (78 Iowa, 328; 43 N. W. Rep. 208), 65.

Adams Ex. Co. *et al.* v. L. & N. Ry. (117 U. S. 1, 23), 460, 461.

Adams Ex. Co. v. Reagan (29 Ind. 21), 92.

Ainsworth v. Bentley (14 W. R. 630, 632), 175, 211.

Albany Northern Ry.Co. v. Brownell (24 N. Y. 345, 351), 420.

Albert v. Savings Bank (2 Maryl. Dec. 169), 235.

Albright v. Teas (37 N. J. Eq. 171), 115.

Alcock v. Giberton (5 Duer. 76), 161, 162, 193.

Alderman v. People (4 Mich. 414; 51 Am. Dec. 75), 259.

Aldnutt v. Inglis (12 East, 527), 415.

Alexander v. Greer (7 Hill (N. Y.) 533), 92.

Alexander v. Reife (74 Mo. 495), 94.

Alger v. Thatcher (19 Pick. 51; 31 Am. Dec. 119), 108, 115, 129, 138, 215, 218, 538.

Allegheny City v. McClurkan (14 Pa. St. 81), 501.

Allegheny County v. McKeesport Diamond Market (123 Pa. St. 164), 406.

Allen v. Armstrong (16 Iowa, 508), 427.

Allen v. Farnsworth (9 Yerg. 187), 396.

Allen v. Humphries (L. R. 8 P. D. 16), 102.

Allen v. Tarlton (25 La. Ann. 427), 48.

Allen v. Woonsockett Co. (11 R. I. 288), 523.

Allis v. Stowell (16 Fed. Rep. 783), 571.

Allison v. Hubbell (17 Ind. 559), 501.

Allison v. Ry. Co. (10 Bush, 1), 466.

Allsopp v. Wheatcroft (L. L. 15 Eq. 59, 64), 26, 161.

Altgelt v. San Antonio (81 Tex. 436), 386.

Alvord v. Collin (20 Pick. 428), 99.

Ambach v. Baltimore & Ohio B. Co. (30 Ohio L. J. 111), 88.

Amedon v. Gannon (6 Hun. 484), 132, 184.

Ames v. Kansas (111 U. S. 449), 695.

Am. Biscuit, etc. Co. v. Klotz (44 Fed. Rep. 721; 32 Am. & Eng. Corp. Cas. 510), 508, 595.

[The references are to pages.]

Am. Preservers' Trust v. Taylor Mfg. Co. (46 Fed. Rep. 152), 541, 595.

Am. Union Tel. Co. v. Western Union Tel. Co. (67 Ala. 32; 42 Am. Rep. 90), 437.

Am. Rapid Tel. Co. v. Hess (125 N. Y. 641, 646), 438.

Amoskeag Mfg. Co. v. Garner (54 How. Pr. 297), 173.

Amoskeag Mfg. Co. v. Spear (2 Sandf. 607), 173.

Anderson v. Dunn (6 Wheat. 204), 716.

Anderson v. Jett (89 Ky. 375; 12 S. W. Rep. 670), 224, 245.

Angier v. Webber (14 Allen, 211); 92 Am. Dec. 748), 218, 565.

Anheuser-Busch Brewing Assn. v. Houck (27 S. W. Rep. 692; 30 S. W. Rep. 869), 53, 261, 563.

Appleman v. Fisher (34 Md. 540, 549), 268, 277.

Appleton v. Campbell (2 C. & P. 347), 51.

Arbuckle v. Cowhan (3 Bas. & P. 328), 104.

Archer v. Marsh (6 Ad. & E. 959; 2 Nev. & P. 562), 23, 24, 121.

Armas v. Milwaukee, etc. R. Co. (67 Wis. 46), 86.

Armstrong v. Chi., etc. R. Co. (53 Minn. 183; 54 N. W. Rep. 1059), 92.

Armstrong v. Ex. Co. (159 Pa. St. 640), 87.

Armstrong v. United States Express Co. (159 Pa. St. 640; 28 Atl. Rep. 448), 86.

Arnold v. Kreutzer (67 Iowa, 214), 110, 129, 132.

Arnot v. Pittston & Elmira Coal Co. (68 N. Y. 558, 565; 23 Am. Rep. 190), 243, 244, 568, 541.

Arthur v. Oakes (63 Fed. Rep. 310, 318, 321, 324, 327; L. R. A. 414), 297, 301, 305, 322, 341.

Asbestos Felting Co. v. U. S. & F. Salamander Felting Co. (13 Blatchf. 453), 570.

Ash v. People (11 Mich. 349), 456.

Ashburner v. Parrish (81 Pa. St. 52), 46.

Ashton v. Dakin (4 H. & N. 867), 283.

Aston's Estate (5 Whart. 228), 102.

Asylum v. New Orleans (105 U. S. 362), 361.

Atcheson v. Mallon (43 N. Y. 147; 3 Am. Rep. 706), 249.

Atchison & Neb. Ry. Co. v. Baty (6 Neb. 37), 431.

Atchison & N. R. Co. v. Washburn (5 Neb. 117), 88.

Atchison, etc. R. Co. v. Denver, etc. R. Co. (110 U. S. 667; 4 Sup. Ct. Rep. 185), 491, 590.

Atchison, etc. R. Co. v. Lawler (40 Neb. 356, 374; 58 N. W. Rep. 968), 93.

Atchison St. Ry. Co. v. Mo. Pac. Ry. Co. (31 Kan. 660; 3 Pac. Rep. 284), 362.

Atkins v. Busby (25 Ark. 176), 48.

Atkins v. Kinnier (4 Excheq. 776; 19 L. J. Excheq. 132), 120, 132, 141, 184.

Atlantic City Water Works Co. v. Atlantic City (39 N. J. Eq. 367), 366.

Atlantic City Water Works Co. v. Consumers' Water Co. (44 N. J. Eq. 427), 386.

Atlantic City Water Works Co. v. Read (50 N. J. L. 665; 24 Am. & Eng. Corp. Cas. 562), 386.

Atty.-Gen. v. Bank of Niagara (Hopkins, 354), 376.

Atty.-Gen. v. Birmingham (4 Kay & J. 528), 712.

Atty.-Gen. v. Cockermough Local Board (L. R. 18 Eq. Cas. 172), 712.

Atty.-Gen. v. Collins (72 Mo. 13), 99.

[The references are to pages]

Atty.-Gen. v. Del. & B. B. R. R. Co. (12 C. E. Green, 631, 633), 710.
Atty.-Gen. v. Delaware, etc. R. Co. (38 N. J. L. 282, 286), 700.
Atty.-Gen. v. Forbes (2 Myl. & Cr. 123), 712.
Atty.-Gen. v. Gt. Eastern Ry. Co. (L. R. 11 Ch. D. 449), 712.
Atty.-Gen. v. Gt. Northern Ry. Co. (1 Drew & S. 184; 6 Jur. (N. S.) 1006), 539, 712.
Atty.-Gen. v. Hunter (1 Dev. Eq. 12), 713.
Atty.-Gen. v. Jamaica Pond Aqueduct Corp. (133 Mass. 361), 354.
Atty.-Gen. v. Johnson (2 Wils. Ch. 87), 712.
Atty.-Gen. v. Metropolitan R. Co. (125 Mass. 515; 28 Am. Rep. 264), 379.
Atty.-Gen. v. Railroad Companies (35 Wis. 524, 525), 710, 712.
Atty.-Gen. v. Railroad Co. 9 Vroom. 282), 698.
Atty. Gen. v. Salem, (103 Mass. 138), 707.
Atty.-Gen. v. Shrewsbury Bridge Co. (L. R. 21 Ch. D. 752), 712.
Atty.-Gen. v. Stevens (1 N. J. Eq. 369), 376.
Atty.-Gen. v. Terry (L. R. 9 Ch. App. 423), 712.
Atty.-Gen. v. Tudor Ice Co. (104 Mass. 239), 354, 376.
Atty.-Gen. v. Utica Ins. Co. (2 Johns. Ch. 371), 376.
Atty.-Gen. v. Woods (108 Mass. 436), 354.
Aubin v. Holt (2 K. & J. 66), 188.
Aub. & Cato Plank Rd. v. Douglass (9 N. Y. 444), 376.
Audenried v. Phila., etc. Ry. Co. (68 Pa. St. 370), 589.
Austin v. Sandel (19 La. Ann. 309), 48.
Averbeck v. Hall (14 Bush, 505), 97.
Ayers v. Chicago, etc. Ry. Co. (71 Wis. 372; 37 N. W. Rep. 432), 86.
Ayer v. Hutchins (4 Mass. 370), 46 64, 79.

B.

Badger v. Williams (1 D. Chip. 137), 79.
Badische Anilin und Soda Fabrik v. Schott (L. R. 3 Ch. 447, 453), 143, 181.
Baehr v. Wolff (59 Ill. 470), 97.
Baggs' Case (11 Rep. 98), 683.
Bagshaw v. Eastern Union R. W. Co. (2 Mcn. & G. 389), 502.
Bailey v. City of New York (3 Hill, 538), 382.
Baines v. Geary (L. R. 35 Ch. D. 154), 145.
Baker v. Baston (12 Pick. 184), 409.
Baker v. Cordon (86 N. Car. 116), 201.
Baker v. Drake (66 N. Y. 518), 283.
Baker v. Farris (61 Mo. 389), 79, 97.
Bald Eagle Val. Ry. Co. v. Nittany Val. Ry. Co. (171 Pa. St. 284; 33 Atl. Rep. 239; 37 W. N. C. 89), 494.
Baldwin v. Flagg (36 N. J. Eq. 48), 283.
Baldwin v. U. S. Tel. Co. (1 Lans. 125, 132, 136), 437, 439.
Baldy v. Stratton (11 Pa. St. 316), 51.
Ballou v. Earl (17 R. I. 441; 22 Atl. Rep. 1113), 93.
Balto. & Ohio Tel. Co. v. Bell Teleph. Co. (24 Am. Law Reg. 573), 446.
Balto. & Ohio Tel. Co. v. W. Union Tel. Co. (24 Fed. Rep. 319), 222.
Balto. & P. Ry. Co. v. Fifth Baptist Church (108 U. S. 317), 323.

[The references are to pages.]

Balto., etc. R. Co. v. Ragsdale (14 Ind. App. 406; 42 N. E. Rep. 1106), 86.
Bangs v. Dunn (66 Cal. 72; 18 Rep. 572), 105, 106.
Bank v. Agency Co. (24 Conn. 159), 488.
Bank v. Bank (92 U. S. 122, 128), 488.
Bank v. Earle (13 Pet. 519), 488.
Bank, etc. v. Edgerton (30 Vt. 190), 501.
Bank v. King (44 N. Y. 87), 115.
Bank v. Sprague (20 N. J. Eq. 32), 46.
Bank v. Stegal (41 Miss. 142), 94.
Banking Co. v. Smith (128 U. S. 174, 179; 9 Sup. Ct. Rep. 47), 720.
Barber Asphalt Paving Co. v. Brand (7 N. Y. Supl. 744).
Barber v. Conn. Mut. Life Ins. Co. (15 Fed. Rep. 312), 215.
Barber v. Connolly (113 U. S. 27, 31), 454.
Barden v. Improvement Co. (157 U. S. 327, 330; 15 Sup. Ct. Rep. 650), 718.
Bargate v. Shortridge (5 H. L. Cas. 297), 501.
Barker v. Huntingdon (2 Gray, 124), 228.
Barker v. Midland Ry. Co. (18 Com. B. 46), 496.
Barley v. Maguire (22 Wall. 215), 491.
Barnard v. Backhaus (52 Wis. 593), 265, 277, 280.
Barnes v. Barnes (104 N. Car. 613; 10 S. E. Rep. 304), 78.
Barnes v. Brown (80 N. Y. 527, 536), 560.
Barnes v. McAllister (18 How. Pr. 534), 194.
Barnum v. Gilman (27 Minn. 466), 697.
Barwick v. Eng. Stock Bank (L. R. 2 Excheq. 259), 236.
Barr v. Essex Trades Council (53 N. J. Eq. 101; 3 Atl. Rep. 881), 318.
Barrell v. Hanrick. (42 Ala. 60), 94.
Barrington v. Neuse River (69 N. Car. 105), 396.
Barron v. Tucker (53 Vt. 338), 80.
Barrow v. Richard (8 Paige, 351), 156.
Bartheld v. City of New Orleans (24 Fed. Rep. 563; 9 Am. & Eng. Corp. Cas. 509), 409.
Bartlett v. Pitts., etc. Ry. Co. (94 Ind. 281), 333.
Bartlett v. Smith (13 Fed. Rep. 263; 4 McCrary, 388), 265, 279.
Barwick v. Read (1 H. Bl. 627), 104.
Bassett v. Miller (8 Ind. 548), 104.
Bate v. Bate (11 Bush, 639), 101.
Baughman v. Louisville, E. & St. Louis R. R. Co. (94 Ky. 150; 21 S. W. Rep. 757), 88, 93.
Baumgarten v. Broadaway (77 N. Car. 8), 129, 132, 201.
Baxondale v. Ry. Co. (5 C. B. (N. S.) 336), 588.
Bayles v. Kan. Pac. Ry. Co. (13 Colo. 181; 22 Pac. Rep. 341; 40 Am. & Eng. Cas. 42; 5 L. R. A. 480; 2 Int. Com. 643), 586.
Beadel v. Perry (L. R. 3 Eq. 465), 302.
Beadell v. Eastern Counties Ry. Co. (5 Com. B. (N. S.) 509), 496.
Beadle v. Kan. City, etc. R. Co. (51 Kan. 248; 32 Pac. Rep. 910), 590.
Beadles v. Owing (16 Lea, 424), 280.
Beal v. Chase (31 Mich. 490), 115, 132, 133, 178, 219, 221.
Beal v. McVicker (8 Mo. App. 202), 105.
Beal v. Polhemus (67 Mich. 337; 34 N. W. Rep. 532), 63, 68.

[The references are to pages.]

Bean v. Am. Loan & Trust Co. (122 N. Y. 622), 596.
Beard v. Dennis (6 Ind. 200; 63 Am. Dec. 380, 383), 122, 129.
Beaty v. Knowler's Lessee (4 Pet. 152), 488.
Beaty v. Lessee of Knowler (4 Pet. 152), 370.
Begein v. Anderson (28 Ind. 79), 402.
Bedford R. R. Co. v. Bowser (48 Pa. St. 29), 502.
Beekman v. Saratoga & Schen. Ry. Co. (3 Paige, 45), 466, 467, 469.
Beer Co. v. Massachusetts (97 U. S. 25), 452.
Beeman v. Rufford (1 Sim. (N. S.) 550), 502.
Belden v. Munger (5 Minn. 211), 97.
Belger v. Dinsmore (51 N. Y. 166), 93.
Bell v. Clegg (25 Ark. 26), 392.
Bell Teleph. Co. v. Com. (3 Atl. Rep. 825), 446.
Bellsdyke, etc. Co. v. North British R. W. Co. (2 Nev. & McN. R. W. Cas. 105), 588.
Belmont Bridge v. Wheeling Bridge (138 U. S. 287, 684, 685), 491.
Benton v. Hope (19 La. Ann. 463), 94.
Benton v. Pratt (2 Wend. 385), 301.
Benwell v. Inns (24 Beav. 307), 161.
Berlin Machine Works v. Perry (71 Wis. 495, 499, 501; 38 N. W. Rep. 82), 139, 169, 170.
Berry v. Gates (24 Barb. 200), 527.
Bestor v. Wathen (60 Ill. 138), 84.
Betts' Appeal (10 W. N. C. 431), 132, 184.
Betts v. Farmers,' etc. Trust Co. (21 Wis. 80), 86, 93.
Beveridge v. Hewitt (8 Ill. App. 467), 264.
Bigelow v. Benedict (9 Hun, 429; 70 N. Y. 202; 26 Am. Rep. 537), 265, 267.
Bigony v. Tyson (75 Pa. St. 157), 132, 184.
Billings v. Ames (32 Mo. 265), 166.
Billings v. O'Brien (14 Abb. Pr. (N. S.) 238), 106.
Billingsley v. Clelland (41 W. Va. 234; 23 S. E. Rep. 812), 53.
Bird v. Breedlove (24 Ga. 623), 76.
Birdsell v. Hagerstown Agrl. Mfg. Co. (1 Hughes, 64), 571.
Birmingham, etc. Ry. Co, v. Birmingham Ry. Co. (78 Ala. 465), 377, 380.
Birt's Case (48 L. T. 67), 102.
Bishop v. Am. Preservers' Co. (157 Ill. 284, 311; 51 Fed. Rep 272), 510, 597, 598.
Bishop v. Palmer (146 Mass. 469, 475; 16 N. E. Rep. 299), 138, 152.
Bi-Spool Sewing Machine Co. v. Acme Mfg. Co. (15 Mass. 404), 542.
Bissell v. Mich. So. & North. Ind. Ry. Co. (22 N. Y. 258, 299, 305, 309), 235, 501, 520.
Bixby v. Dunlap (56 N. H. 456; 22 Am. Rep. 475), 348.
Blackford v. Preston (8 T. R. 95), 46.
Black v. Del., etc. Canal Co. (22 N. J. Eq. 130; 24 N. J. Eq. 455), 502, 710.
Black v. Goodrich Trans. Co. (55 Wis. 319; 13 N. W. Rep. 244), 86.
Black v. Oliver (1 Ala. 449), 94.
Blackstock v. N. Y., etc. Ry. Co. (20 N. Y. 48; 75 Am. Dec. 372, 373), 331.
Blake v. Layton (6 T. R. 221), 349.
Blasdell v. Fowle (120 Mass. 447), 46, 94.
Bliss v. Kraus (16 Ohio St. 155), 401.

[The references are to pages.]

Bliss v. Lawrence (58 N. Y. 442, 445), 46, 105, 106.
Blisset v. Hart (Willes, 508), 392.
Bloodgood v. Mohawk, etc. R. Co. (18 Wend. 9, 10), 235, 466.
Bloodgood v. Mohawk & Hudson R. R. Co. (18 Wend. 1), 467.
Blossom v. Van Amringe (1 Phil. Eq. 133), 94.
Board, etc. v. Cutler (6 Ind. 354), 501.
Board of Railroad Commissioners v. Ore. Ry., etc. Co. (17 Ore. 65; 35 Am. & Eng. Ry. Cas. 542), 426.
Board, etc. Tipp. Co. v. Lafayette, etc. Ry. Co. (50 Ind. 85, 108, 112), 501.
Board v. Verbarg (63 Ind. 107), 471.
Bodine v. Trenton (36 N. J. L. 198), 368.
Boehl v. Chi., M. & St. P. R. R. Co. (44 Minn. 191; 46 N. W. Rep. 333), 89.
Boehm v. Mayor, etc. of Baltimore (61 Md. 259, 263), 403.
Bogert v. Ind. (13 Ind. 134), 402.
Bohn Mfg. Co. v. Hollis (54 Minn. 233; 21 L. R. A. 337; 40 Am. St. Rep. 319; 55 N. W. Rep. 1119), 24, 253, 304.
Boies v. Blake (13 Me. 381), 94.
Bolt v. Stennett (8 T. R. 606), 415.
Booe v. Junction R. R. Co. (9 Ind. 358), 502.
Booth v. Robinson (55 Md. 419, 439), 488, 535, 536.
Booth v. Seevers (19 Pat. Off. Gaz. 1140), 571.
Borda v. Phila., etc. R. Co. (141 Pa. St, 484; 21 Atl. Rep. 665), 589.
Boston Cham. of Com. v. Lake Shore, etc. Ry. Co. (32 Am. & Eng. Ry. Cas. 618), 470.
Boston Diatite Co. v. Florence Mfg. Co. (114 Mass. 69; 19 Am. Rep. 31), 352.
Boston Glass Manufactory v. Binney (4 Pick. 425), 295, 349.
Boston & L. Ry. Co. v. Salem & L. Ry. Co. (2 Gray, 1), 361, 375, 501.
Boston Water Power Co. v. B. & W. Ry. Co. (23 Pick. 360), 361.
Bosworth v. Hearne (Andr. 91), 120.
Boutelle v. Smith (116 Mass. 111), 110, 218.
Bowen v. Buck (28 Vt. 308), 97.
Bowen v. Hall (62 B. D. 333; 50 L. J. Q. B. 305; 44 L. S. 75; 29 W. R. 367), 254, 301, 318, 348.
Bowen v. Masterson (14 Allen, 499), 242, 295.
Bowers v. Bowers (26 Pa. St. 74), 68, 101, 103, 104.
Bowey v. Bennett (1 Camp. 348), 51.
Bowling v. Taylor (40 Fed. Rep. 404), 161.
Bowling Green v. Carson (10 Bush, 64), 456.
Bowman v. Phillips (41 Kan. 364; 21 Pac. Rep. 230), 52.
Bowman v. Waltham (2 McLean, 376), 398.
Bowser v. Bliss (7 Blackf. 344, 346), 110, 115, 124, 125, 210.
Boyce v. Tabb (18 Wall. 546), 48.
Boyce v. Watson (52 Ill. App. 361).
Boyle v. Adams (50 Minn. 255; 52 N. W. Rep. 860), 99.
Brace v. Evans (3 Ry. & Corp. L. J. 561), 313, 322, 324.
Bradley v. Basley (1 Barb. Ch. 125), 194.
Bradley v. Pierson (148 Pa. St. 502; 24 Atl. Rep. 65), 330.
Bradley v. So. New Eng. Teleph. Co. (66 Conn. 559; 34 Atl. Rep. 499), 446.
Brady v. N. W. Ins. Co. (11 Mich. 425), 455.
Breck v. Cole (4 Sandf. 83), 95.

[The references are to pages.]

Brechbill v. Randall (102 Ind. 582; 52 Am. Rep. 695), 432, 452.
Brewer v. Lamar (69 Ga. 656), 171, 174.
Brewer v. Marshall (19 N. J. Eq. 537, 546, 547), 115, 132, 155, 182, 186.
Brick Presbyterian Church v. New York City (5 Cow. 538, 540), 402, 411.
Bridge Prop'r v. Hoboken (1 Wall. 116), 384.
Brisbane v. Adams (3 N. Y. 129), 249.
Brislin v. Brown (24 Ohio St. 565; 15 Am. Rep. 627), 249.
Britton v. Mayor (21 How. Pr. 251), 369.
Broad v. Jollyfe (Cro. Jac. 596), 19, 118, 122.
Brocaw v. Gibson Co. (73 Ind. 543), 466.
Brokaw v. N. J. R. & Trans. Co. (32 N. J. L. 328, 329), 237.
Brooklyn v. City Ry. Co. (49 N. Y. 475), 369.
Brooks v. Cooper (50 N. J. Eq. 761; 26 Atl. Rep. 978, 981), 45. 66.
Broome v. Telephone Co. (42 N. J. Eq. 131; 7 Atl. Rep. 851), 302.
Brotherline v. Swires (48 Pa. St. 68), 249.
Brou v. Becnel (22 La. Ann. 189), 48.
Brouwer v. Jones (23 Barb. 153), 156.
Brown v. Brina (L. R. 1 Excheq. D. 5), 97.
Brown v. Brown (34 Barb. 333), 62, 55.
Brown v. First Nat. Bank (137 Ind. 655, 668), 95, 98.
Brown v. Great Eastern R. Co. (L. R. 2 Q. B. D. 406), 157.
Brown v. Hall (L. R. 9 Q. B. D. 333), 231.
Brown v. Hess (21 Neb. 113), 318.
Brown v. King (101 Cal. 295; 35 Pac. Rep. 995), 219.
Brown v. Langford (3 Bibb, 497), 51.
Brown v. Pac. Mail Steamship Co. (5 Blatchf. 525), 583, 584.
Brown v. Rounsavell (78 Ill. 589), 207.
Brown v. Steamship Co. (5 Blatchf. 525; Fed. Cas. No. 2325), 582.
Brown v. Stewart (4 Md. Ch. 368), 102.
Bruffet v. Gt. Western R. R. Co. (25 Ill. 310), 501.
Bruine v. Sasser (25 La. Ann. 224), 48.
Brunner v. Boston (102 Mass. 19), 369.
Bryan v. Reynolds (5 Wis. 200), 55, 62.
Bryson v. Philadelphia (47 Pa. St. 329), 369.
Bryson v. Whitehall (1 Sim. & St. 74), 161.
Buchanan v. Kerr (159 Pa. St. 433), 305.
Buck v. Bank (27 Mich. 293), 97.
Buck v. Pa. R. R. Co. (150 Pa. St. 170; 24 Atl. Rep. 678), 85.
Buckeye Marble, etc. Co. v. Harvey (92 Tenn. 115), 528.
Budd v. New York (143 U. S. 517; 12 Sup. Ct. Rep. 468), 432, 435, 721.
Buffalo Lub'g. Oil Co. v. Stand. Oil Co. (106 N. Y. 669; 25 Cent. L. J.), 235, 236, 349.
Buffalo v. Webster (10 Wend. 99), 456.
Buford v. Keokuk Co. (3 Mo. App. 159), 491, 527.
Bull v. Conroe (13 Wis. 233, 244), 431.
Bumgardner v. Leavitt (35 W. Va. 194; 13 S. E. Rep. 67), 579.
Bunn v. Guy (4 East, 190), 22, 112, 118, 124, 189, 190.
Bunts v. Cole (7 Blackf. 265), 470.
Burbank v. Pillsbury (48 N. H. 475), 157.

[The references are to pages.]

Burgess v. Burgess (3 De G., M. & G. 896, 904), 173.
Burke v. Cassin (45 Cal. 467; 13 Am. Rep. 204), 173.
Burke v. Concord Ry. Co. (61 N. H. 160), 470.
Burkham v. Beaver (17 Ind. 367), 501.
Burlington Water Works Co. v. Burlington (43 Kan. 725), 386.
Burlington & Henderson Co. Ferry Co. v. Davis (48 Iowa, 133), 375.
Burlington, etc. Ry. Co. v. Dey (82 Iowa, 312; 45 Am. & Eng. Ry. Cas. 391), 430.
Burlington, C. R. & N. R. Co. v. N. W. Fuel Co. (31 Fed. Rep. 651), 555.
Burney's Heirs v. Ludeling (47 La. Ann. 73; 16 So. Rep. 507), 55.
Burney v. Ludeling (47 La. Ann. 73; 16 So. Rep. 507; 47 La. Ann. 1434; 17 So. Rep. 877), 85.
Burns v. Seep (8 Am. Law Rec. (Ohio) 425), 51.
Burrill v. Daggett (77 Me. 545), 201.
Burt v. Place (6 Cow. 431), 243.
Bury v. Bedford (33 L. J. Ch. 465), 173.
Bush v. Seabury (8 Johns. 418), 456.
Bush v. Thornton (25 Hun, 466), 105.
Bush v. Wéstern (Prec. in Chan. 530), 376.
Butchers' Union, etc. Co. v. Crescent City, etc. Co. (111 U. S. 746; 4 Sup. Ct. Rep. 652), 370.
Butler v. Burleson (16 Vt. 176), 115, 124, 128, 184.
Butler v. Chambers (36 Minn. 69), 455.
Butler v. Galletti (21 How. Pr. 465), 197.
Butler v. Marshall (4 Gill, 487), 197.
Butterfield v. Ashley (2 Gray, 254; 6 Cush. 249), 349.
Byron v. Whitehead (1 Sim. & Stu. 74), 164.
B., C. R. & N. Ry. Co. v. Dey (82 Iowa, 312), 427.

C.

Calder v. Bull (3 Dall. 386, 388), 431.
Cal. Steam Nav. Co. v. Wright (6 Cal. 258), 207.
Callaghan v. Donnolly (45 Cal. 152), 115, 128, 130, 139, 565.
Callan v. Wilson (127 U. S. 540, 545; 8 Sup. Ct. Rep. 1301), 322.
Camblos v. Phila., etc. Ry. Co. (4 Brewst. 563), 465, 597.
Camblos v. Ry. Co. (9 Phila. 411), 496.
Camden, etc. Ry. Co. v. Elkins (37 N. J. Eq. 273), 583.
Cameron v. Hasemeyer (12 N. Y. Supl. 126), 595.
Campbell v. Cooper (34 N. H. 49), 349.
Campbell v. Talbott (132 Mass. 174, 177), 707.
Canada Life Assn. Co. v. Peel Mfg. Co. (26 Grant's Ch. 477, 486).
Canal, etc. St. Ry. Co. v. Crescent City Ry. Co. (41 La. Ann. 561, 566), 379.
Canal Co. v. St. Louis (2 Dillon, 84), 368.
Candee v. West. Union Tel. Co. (34 Wis. 471), 86.
Canfield v. Baltimore, etc. R. Co. (93 N. Y. 352, 532), 86, 92.
Cannon v. Cannon (26 N. J. Eq. 316), 46, 94, 95.
Cantur v. Bennett (39 Tex. 303), 94.
Card v. Hope (2 B. & C. 661), 583.
Carew v. Rutherford (106 Mass. 1), 253, 295, 309, 323, 349.
Carleton v. Whitcher (5 N. H. 196), 68.

[The references are to pages.]

Carleton v. Woods (28 N. H. 290), 148.
Carll v. Snyder (26 Atl. Rep. 977. 978), 125.
Carrigan v. Lycoming F. Ins. Co. (53 Vt. 418), 148.
Carroll v. Giles (30 S. Car. 412; 9 S. E. Rep. 422), 205.
Carroll v. Hickes (10 Phila. 308), 184.
Carrothers v. Russell (53 Iowa, 350), 73.
Carter v. Alling (43 Fed. Rep. 208, 214), 204.
Carter v. Williams (18 W. R. 593), 156.
Carton v. Ill. Central Ry. Co. (59 Iowa, 148; 44 Am. Rep. 676), 423.
Cartwright's Case (114 Mass. 230, 238), 715.
Case of Broderick's Will (21 Wall. 503, 520), 718.
Case v. Cleveland, etc. R. Co. (11 Ind. App. 517: 39 N. E. Rep. 426), 92.
Case v. Gerrish (15 Pick. 49), 94, 100.
Casey v. Cin. Typl. Union No. 3 (45 Fed. Rep. 135, 143, 144; 12 L. R. A. 193), 314, 320, 322, 356.
Casey v. Gunnison (17 N. W. Rep. 881), 215.
Cassard v. Hinman (1 Bosw. 207), 265, 277.
Castile v. Offutt (25 La. Ann. 430), 48.
Cates v. Allen (149 U. S. 451: 13 Sup. Ct. Rep. 883, 977), 719.
Caton v. Stewart (76 N. Car. 357), 46, 76.
Catskill Bank v. Gray (14 Barb. 471. 479), 520, 523, 595.
Catskill Bank v. Hooper (5 Gray, 574), 520.
Catt v. Towle (L. R. 4 Ch. App. 654; 38 L. J. Ch. 665; 21 L. T. 188), 124.
Caughey v. Smith (49 N. Y. 244), 349.
Celluloid Mfg. Co. v. Goodyear Dental Vulcanite Co. (13 Blatchf. 384), 569.
Cent. District Teleph. Co. v. Com. (114 Pa. St. 593), 446.
Cent. Ohio Salt Co. v. Guthrie (35 Ohio St. 666, 672), 242, 245, 470, 541.
Cent. R. Co. v. Collins (40 Ga. 582), 240, 488, 491, 530, 555, 710.
Cent. R., etc. Co. v. Smith (76 Ala. 572, 579; 52 Am. Rep. 353), 520, 523.
Cent., etc. Ry. Co. v. Penn. Ry. Co. (31 N. J. Eq. 475), 527, 530.
Cent. Shade Roller Co. v. Cushman (143 Mass. 353: 9 N. E. Rep. 629), 168, 211, 216, 245, 353, 542.
Cent. Teleph. Co. v. State (118 Ind. 194, 207), 432.
Cent. Trust, etc. Co. v. Ohio Cent. R. R. Co. (23 Am. & Eng. Ry. Cas. 666), 470.
Cent. Union Teleph. Co. v. Bradbury (106 Ind. 1), 447.
Cent. Union Tel. Co. v. Fehring (146 Ind. 189: 45 N. E. Rep. 64), 446.
Cent. Union Teleph. Co. v. State (118 Ind. 194, 205: 123 Ind. 113), 446, 448.
Chadwick v. Knox (31 N. H. 226, 234), 77.
Chambers v. Seay (73 Ala. 372), 209.
Chandler v. Johnson (39 Ga. 85), 79, 97.
Chapin v. Brown (83 Iowa, 156: 32 Am. St. Rep. 297: 48 N. W. Rep. 1074), 210, 215, 223, 541.
Chappell v. Brockway (21 Wend. 157), 110, 112, 132, 136, 189.
Charles River Bridge Co. v. Warren Bridge Co. (11 Pet. 420; 7 Pick. 344; 6 Pick. 376), 458, 467, 469.

[The references are to pages.]

Charlotte, etc. Co. v. Gibbs (27 S. Car. 385; 31 Am. & Eng. Ry. Cas. 464; 142 U. S. 386, 393), 426, 429.
Charlton v. New Castle & Carlisle R. Co. (7 W. R. 735; 5 Jur. (N. S.) 1096), 520, 555.
Chartered Gas Co. v. Great Cent. Consumers' Gas Co. (1 Gas J. 322), 383.
Chemical Works v. Hecker (11 Blatchf. 552), 570.
Chenango Bridge Co. v. Binghampton Bridge Co. (27 N. Y. 87; 3 Wall. 51), 369.
Chenango Bridge Co. v. Paige (83 N. Y. 178), 400.
Chesapeake, etc. Co. v. Baltimore, etc. R. Co. (4 Gill & J. 1), 690.
Chesapeake & Ohio Ry. Co. v. Miller (114 U. S. 176; 5 Sup. Ct. Rep. 813), 370.
Chesapeake & Potomac Teleph. Co. v. Balto. & Ohio Tel. Co. (66 Md. 339, 399, 414), 448.
Chesebrough v. Conover (140 N. Y. 382; 35 N. E. Rep. 633), 62, 63.
Chesman v. Nainby (2 Ld. Raym. 1456 (4th ed.); 1 Bro. P. C. 234), 19, 22, 108, 118, 124.
Chestnut Hill Turnpike Co. v. Rutter (4 S. & R. 6), 236.
Chicago v. Rumpff (45 Ill. 90), 378.
C. & A. Ry. Co. v. Clampit (63 Ill. 95), 427.
C. & A. Ry. Co. v. People (67 Ill. 11), 427.
C. & A. Ry. Co. v. Quaintance (58 Ill. 389), 427.
C., B. R. R. Co. v. Baab (9 Watts, 458), 84.
C., B. & Q. R. R. Co. v. Jones (149 Ill. 361, 382), 426.
Chi., B. & Q. R. Co. v. City of Chicago (166 U. S. 226, 241; 17 Sup. Ct. Rep. 581), 721.
Chi. Gas Light Co. v. People's Gas Light Co. (121 Ill. 530), 240, 532, 542.
Chi., etc. Co. v. Becker (35 Fed. Rep. 883), 423.
Chi., etc. Ry. v. Dey (35 Fed. Rep. 866, 875), 423, 426.
Chi., etc. Ry. Co. v. Iowa (94 U. S. 154, 155, 161, 162), 424, 425.
Chi., etc. Ry. Co. v. Jones (149 Ill. 361; 37 N. E. Rep. 247; 24 L. R. A. 141), 426.
Chi., etc. Ry. Co. v. Minnesota (134 U. S, 418, 458; 10 Sup. Ct. Rep. 462, 702), 421, 428.
Chi., etc. Ry. Co. v. Moss (60 Miss. 641), 431.
Chi., etc. R. Co. v. Osborne (52 Fed. Rep. 912), 590.
Chi., etc. Ry. Co. v. People (67 Ill. 1), 589.
Chi., etc. Co. v. People's, etc. Co. (121 Ill. 330; 13 N. E. Rep. 169), 470.
Chi., etc. Ry. Co. v. Wabash, etc. Co. (61 Fed. Rep. 993), 470.
Chi., D. & V. R. Co. v. Smith (62 Ill. 268; 6 Am. Ry. Rep. 221), 555.
Chi. & Grand Trunk Ry. v. Wellman (143 U. S. 339), 421.
Chi., M. & St. P. R. Co. v. Wabash, St. L. & Pac. R. Co. (61 Fed. Rep. 993; 58 Am. & Eng. R. Cas. 703), 555.
Chi., R. I. & P. R. Co. v. Witty (32 Neb. 275), 88.
Chi., St. L. & N. O. R. Co. v. Abels (60 Miss. 1017), 89.
Chi., St. L. & N. O. Ry. Co. v. Pullman So. Car Co. (139 U. S. 79; 11 Sup. Ct. Rep. 490), 547.
Chiapella v. Brown (14 La. Ann. 189), 398.
Chicot Co. v. Sherwood (148 U. S. 529; 13 Sup. Ct. Rep. 695), 719.

[The references are to pages.]

Chip. Val. & D. R. Co. v. Chicago & St. Paul Ry. Co. (75 Wis. 274; 44 N. W. Rep. 17), 62.
Chippewa Falls Lumber Co. v. Tremper (75 Mich. 36). 158.
Christie v. Mo. Pac. Ry. Co. (94 Mo. 453), 589.
Christopher & Tenth St. R. R. Co. v. Central Crosstown Ry. Co. (67 Barb. 315), 377.
Churchill v. Perkins (5 Mass. 385), 79.
Churchill v. Walker (68 Ga. 681), 697.
Churton v. Douglas (Johns. Ch. 174), 214.
Cin., N. O., etc. Ry. Co. v. Int. Com. Com. (162 U. S. 184), 712.
Cin. St. Ry. Co. v. Smith (29 Ohio St. 291), 378.
Citizens' Gas & Ming. Co. v. Elwood (114 Ind. 332, 333; 20 Am. & Eng. Corp. Cas. 263), 384.
Citizens' St. Ry. Co. v. Jones (34 Fed. Rep. 579), 380.
Citizens' Water Co. v. Bridgeport Hydraulic Co. (55 Conn. 1), 366, 372.
City Carpet Beating Works v. Jones (102 Cal. 506; 36 Pac. Rep. 841). 219, 225.
City Council v. Baptist Ch. (4 Strobh. 306). 401.
City of Brenham v. Brenham Water Co., (67 Tex. 542; 4 S. W. Rep. 143), 367. 383.
City of Burlington v. Burlington St. Ry. Co. (49 Iowa, 144). 375.
City of Davenport v. Kelly (7 Iowa, 102), 375.
City of Dubuque v. Stout (32 Iowa, 80), 375.
City of Colo. Spgs. v. Smith (19 Colo. 554; 36 Pac. Rep. 540), 499.
City of Indianapolis v. Indianapolis, etc. Co. (66 Ind. 396), 411.
City of Laredo v. International Bridge & T. Co. (66 Fed. Rep. 246, 248), 394.
City of Louisville v. Weible (84 Ky. 290, 295; 1 S. W. Rep. 605), 370.
City of Memphis v. Water Co. (Heisk. 495), 365, 383.
City of Newport v. Newport Light Co. (84 Ky. 166, 183), 376.
City of N. Y. v. Miln (11 Pet. 103), 410.
City of Palestine v. Barnes (50 Tex. 538). 406.
City of St. Louis v. Bell Teleph. Co. (96 Mo. 623), 446.
City of Valparaiso v. Gardner (97 Ind. 1), 365, 411.
City of Vincennes v. Citizens' Gas Light Co. (132 Ind. 114, 126; 31 N. E. Rep. 573, 577), 365.
Clancey v. Onondaga Fine Salt Co. (62 Barb. 395), 541. 596.
Clark v. Constantine (3 Bush, 652), 102, 103.
Clark v. Crosby (37 Vt. 188), 110, 192.
Clark v. Foxcraft (6 Greenl. 296), 78.
Clark v. Spencer (14 Kan. 399, 404), 99.
Clay v. Allen (63 Miss. 426), 264, 277, 378.
Clearwater v. Meredith (1 Wall. 29), 520.
Cleary v. Dehesseline (1 McCord, 35), 697.
Clemmitt v. Watson (14 Ind. App. 38, 42; 42 N. E. Rep. 367), 346.
Clerke v. Comer (Cas. *t.* Hardwicke, 53), 19, 108, 118.
Cleve., C. C. & I. R. Co. v. Closser (126 Ind. 348; 26 N. E. Rep. 159; 45 Am. & Eng. R. Cas. 275), 470, 555, 587.
Cleve. Paper Co. v. Courier Co. (67 Mich. 152, 158), 523.
Clippenger v. Hepbaugh (5 W. & S. 315, 319), 55, 59, 60.

[The references are to pages.]

Coates v. Blush (1 Cush. 564), 94.
Coates v. Holbrook (2 Sandf. Ch. 586), 172.
Cobb v. Prell (15 Fed. Rep. 774), 265, 277.
Cockrell v. Thompson (85 Mo. 510), 264.
Cocks v. Izard (7 Wall. 559), 249.
Cockshott v. Bennett (2 T. R. 763). 94.
Coe v. Errol (116 U. S. 517, 525), 549.
Coeur D'Alene Mining Co. v. Miners' Union (51 Fed. Rep. 260; 19 L. R. A. 382, 384), 322, 346.
Coffman v. Young (20 Ill. App. 76), 272.
Cole v. Edwards (93 Iowa. 477; 61 N. W. Rep. 940), 184.
Coleman v. Crump (70 N. Y. 573), 173.
Coleman v. Sec. Ave. Ry. Co. (38 N. Y. 201), 377.
Coles v. Edwards (93 Iowa, 477; 61 N. W. Rep. 940), 133.
Colgate v. Batcheler (Cro. Eliz. 872), 22, 117.
Collins v. Blantern (1 Smith Lead. Cas. pt. 1, p. 680), 45.
Collins v. Hayte. (50 Ill. 337; 99 Am. Dec. 521), 345.
Collins v. Locke (L. R. 4 App. Cas. 674; 48 L. J. P. C. 68, 41; L. T. 292; 28 W. R. 189), 117, 120, 121, 136, 200, 212.
Columbia Bridge Co. v. Geisse (34 N. J. L. 268; 38 N. J. L. 39, 42), 392, 396, 398.
Col. Wire Co. v. Freeman Wire Co. (71 Fed. Rep. 302, 306), 166, 603.
Commercial Bank v. State (6 Sm. & M. 599), 704.
Commiskey v. Williams (20 Mo. App. 606), 277.
Com. v. Alger (7 Cush. 53, 84), 409, 410.
Com. v. Allegheny Bridge Co. (20 Pa. St. 185), 688.
Com. v. Allen (128 Mass. 308). 699.
Com. v. Bacon (76 Ky. 210). 361, 363, 364.
Com. v. Burrell (7 Pa. St. 34). 697.
Com. v. Carlisle (Bright. 36, 40, 41), 287, 311, 557.
Com. v. Corlies (3 Brewst. 575), 257.
Com. v. Cluley (56 Pa. St. 270; 94 Am. Dec. 75. 76). 688.
Com. v. Dyer (128 Mass. 70). 245, 259.
Com. v. East (1 Cush. 189, 224), 257.
Com. v. Eastman (55 Mass. 190; 48 Am. Dec. 596), 259.
Com. v. Hunt (4 Metc. 111, 121, 128, 134; 38 Am. Dec. 346), 244, 287, 294, 295, 309, 321.
Com. v. Judd (2 Mass. 328). 257.
Com. v. Lexington, etc. Turnpike Co. (6 B. Mon. 397), 697, 698.
Com. v. McCarter (98 Pa. St. 604), 698.
Com. v. Murray (11 S. & R. 73; 14 Am. Dec. 614). 684.
Com. v. Phipps (80 Ky. 269). 361.
Com. v. Power (7 Metc. 596). 499.
Com. v. Ry. Co. (20 Pa. St. 518), 688.
Com. v. Sheriff (15 Phila. 393), 345.
Com. v. Shelton (11 Va. L. J. 324), 314.
Com. v. Shedd (7 Cush. 514). 257, 259.
Com. v. Silvers (11 Pa. Co. Rep. 481), 323, 345.
Com. v. Small (26 Pa. St. 31), 684.
Com. v. Smith (10 Allen, 448), 520.
Com. v. Tewksbury (11 Met. 55), 409.
Com. v. Union Ins. Co. (5 Mass. 230, 232), 697, 699.
Com. v. Warren (6 Mass. 74), 257.
Com. v. Williams (6 Gray. 1), 426.

[The references are to pages.]

Commrs. v. Holyoke Water Co. (104 Mass. 446), 366.
Commrs. v. Railroad Co. (50 Ind. 85), 491.
Compagnia Francaise v. West. Union Co. (11 Fed. Rep. 842. 862), 491, 527.
Commercial Union Teleph. Co. v. New Eng. Teleph. Co. (61 Vt. 241; 15 Am. St. Rep. 893). 446.
Condeman v. Trenchard (58 Barb. 165). 79.
Cone v. Russell (48 N. J. Eq. 208; 21 Atl. Rep. 847). 579.
Cone's Exrs. v. Russell (48 N. J. Eq. 208; 21 Atl. Rep. 847). 577.
Conery v. N. O. Water Wks. Co. (41 La. Ann. 910: 7 So. Rep. 8). 386.
Conger v. Hudson Riv. Ry. Co. (6 Duer. 375). 331.
Cong. of Israel v. Peres (2 Cold. 620). 256.
Conklin v. Wash. University (2 Md. Ch. 497). 520.
Connell v. West. Union Tel. Co. (108 Mo. 459; 39 Am. & Eng. Corp Cas. 594). 437.
Conner v. Robertson (37 La. Ann. 814; 55 Am. Rep. 521). 277.
Connor v. Kent (L. R. 2 Q. B. 545), 323, 325.
Conover v. Pac. Ex. Co. (40 Mo. App. 31). 86, 93.
Consumers' Oil Co. v. Nunnemacher (142 Ind. 560. 567, 568; 41 N. E. Rep. 1048), 110, 153.
Continental Ins. Co. v. Board of Underwriters (67 Fed. Rep. 310), 318.
Conway v. Taylor (1 Black, 603), 396, 398.
Cook v. Chi., R. I. & P. R. Co. (81 Iowa, 551: 46 N. W. Rep. 1080; 45 Am. & Eng. Ry. Cas. 291), 591.
Cook v. Johnson (47 Conn. 175; 36 Am. Rep. 64). 115, 142, 192.
Cook v. Shipman (24 Ill. 614), 73.
Cook v. West. & Atl. Ry. Co. (72 Ga. 48), 79, 97.
Cooke v. Davis (53 N. Y. 318). 277.
Copes v. Charleston (10 Rich. L. 502). 401.
Coppack v. Bower (4 Mees. & W. 361). 46, 80.
Corp. of Liverpool v. Wright (5 Jur. (N. S.) 1156, 1157: 28 L. J. Ch. 871). 104, 105.
Costar v. Brush (25 Wend. 628), 369.
Cothran v. Ellis (125 Ill. 496), 277.
Cott v. Towle (L. R. 4 Ch. App. 654), 156.
County of Allegheny v. Gibson (9 Pa. St. 397; 7 W. N. C. 441; 11 L. Bar. 81). 358.
County of Moultrie v. Fairfield (105 U. S. 370), 466.
Coupland v. Housatonic R. Co. (61 Conn. 531: 23 Atl. Rep. 870). 93.
Covington, etc. Ry. Co. v. Covington (9 Bush. 127). 368.
Cowan v. Fairbrother (118 N. Car. 406; 24 S. E. Rep. 212). 146, 178, 220.
Cowles v. Mercer Co. (6 Wall. 118), 719.
Cowley v. R. R. Co. (159 U. S. 569, 583; 16 Sup. Ct. Rep. 127). 719.
Crawford v. Gordon (11 Wkly. L. Bull. 121). 51.
Crawford v. Spencer (92 Mo. 498). 264, 277.
Craft v. McConoughy (79 Ill. 346, 350: 22 Am. Rep. 171). 240. 242, 538, 541. 565, 567.
Cravens v. Rogers (101 Mo. 247, 252; 14 S. W. Rep. 106). 497.
Crescent Gas Co. v. N. O. Gas. Co. (27 La. Ann. 148), 383.
Cronin v. People (82 N. Y. 318; 37 Am. Rep. 564), 401.
Cross v. Cross (58 N. H. 373), 97.
Cross v. W. Va., C. & P. Ry. Co (37 W. Va. 342), 488.

[The references are to pages.]

Croton Turnpike Co. v. Ryder (1 Johns. Ch. 611, 615), 376.
Crump v. Commonwealth (84 Va. 927, 941, 945; 10 Am. St. Rep. 895), 35, 318, 322, 323, 329.
Crutwell v. Lye (17 Ves. 306, 335, 336), 108, 213, 215.
Crystal Ice Mfg. Co. v. San Antonio Brew. Assn. (8 Tex. Civ. App. 1; 27 S. W. Rep. 210), 210, 221.
Cuddon v. Eastwick (Salk. 193), 108.
Cumberland Val. Ry. Co. v. Gettysburg & H. Ry. Co. (177 Pa. St. 564; 35 Atl. Rep. 952), 494.
Cummins v. Barkalow (4 Keyes, 514), 55.
Cummings v. Foss (40 Ill. App. 523, 530, 531; 149 Ill. 353, 359), 272, 273.
Cummings v. Union Blue Stone Co. (44 N. Y. Supl. 787; 15 App. Div. 607), 566.
Cunningham v. Cunningham (18 B. Mon. 24), 102, 104.
Cunningham v. Nat. Bank of Augusta (71 Ga. 400), 265, 280.
Currie v. N. J., etc. R. R. Co. (61 Miss. 725, 731), 83.
Currier v. Concord Ry. Co. (66 N. H. 100; 20 Atl. Rep. 383; 8 Ry. & Corp. L. J. 443), 472.
Currigan's Case (6 Ir. Jur. (N. S.) 116), 104.
Curtis v. Allegheny (1 Phila. 237), 358.
Curtis v. Aspinwall (114 Mass. 187), 100. 249, 252, 577.
Curtis v. Ayrault (47 N. Y. 73), 154.
Curtis v. Bryan (2 Daly, 312; 36 How. Pr. 33), 173.
Curtis v. Gokey (68 N. Y. 300), 110, 219.
Curtis v. Leavitt (15 N. Y. 9. 108), 597.
Cusack v. White (2 Mills, Const. Rep. 279), 51.
Cussan v. Galen (152 N. Y. 33; 46 N. E. Rep. 297, 298), 348.
Cutting v. Fla., R. & N. Co. (48 Fed. Rep. 508), 555.

D.

Dakin v. Williams (11 Wend. 67), 178, 201.
Darcy v. Allen (11 Coke, 84; Noy, 173), 11.
Darley v. The Queen (12 Cl. & Fin. 520), 680.
Darmoth v. Bennett (15 Barb. 601), 243.
Dartsmouth College Case (4 Wheat. 518), 366.
Dartsmouth College v. Woodward (4 Wheat. 518, 536), 488.
Davidson v. Commrs. (18 Minn. 482), 466.
Davies v. Davies (L. R. 36 Ch. D. 359, 364, 396, 397, 398; 35 W. R. 697), 27, 44, 45, 129, 140, 145, 218.
Davies v. Lowen (64 L. T. 655), 150.
Davenport v. Kelley (7 Iowa, 102), 406.
Davenport v. Kleinschmidt (6 Mont. 502, 528; 13 Pac. Rep. 249), 369, 383, 391.
Davis v. Commonwealth (164 Mass. 241; 41 N. E. Rep. 292), 78.
Davis v. Gray (16 Wall. 203, 221), 719.
Davis v. Marlboro (1 Swanst. 79), 104.
Davis v. Mason (5 T. R. 118), 22, 112, 118, 121, 124, 129, 184.
Davis v. Mayor, etc. of New York (14 N. Y. 506, 526; 67 Am. Dec. 186), 377, 713.
Davis v. State (68 Ala. 58), 432.
Davison v. Seymour (1 Bosw. 88), 103.
Dawson v. St. Louis, etc. R. Co. (76 Mo. 514), 92.
Day v. Brownrigg (L. R. 10 Ch. D. 294), 352.

[The references are to pages.]

Dean v. Emerson (102 Mass. 480), 115, 201, 216, 218.
De Begnis v. Armistead (10 Bing. 110), 45.
De Groot v. Vanduzen (20 Wend. 390), 94.
Delaplaine v. Cook (7 Wis. 54), 427.
Del., L. & W. R. R. Co. v. Bowers (58 N. Y. 573, 582), 29, 333.
Del., etc. Ry. Co. v. Cent. Stock Car Co. (45 N. J. Eq. 50, 60), 435.
Del. Railroad Tax (18 Wall. 206, 225), 991.
Del. & R. Canal Co. v. Raritan & Del. Bay Co. (16 N. J. Eq. 321, 378), 376.
Delz v. Winfree (80 Tex. 400; 16 S. W. Rep. 111), 252, 254.
Demarest v. Wickham (63 N. Y. 320), 698.
De Melton v. Mello (12 East. 234), 94.
Dendy v. Henderson (11 Excheq. 194; 24 L. J. Excheq.), 129, 189, 324.
Denny v. Lincoln (5 Mass. 385), 79.
Denny v. Manhattan Co. (2 Denio, 115; 5 Denio, 639), 332.
Dent v. Turpin (2 J. & H. 139), 172.
Denton v. English (2 Mott. & M. 581), 51.
Denver, etc. Ry. Co. v. Denver City Ry. Co. (2 Colo. 673), 377.
Des Moines St. Ry. Co. v. Des Moines Bd. Gauge St. Ry. Co. (73 Iowa, 513; 35 N. W. Rep. 610), 374, 380, 383, 389.
De Sobry v. De Laistre (2 H. & J. 191), 51.
Dethlefs v. Tomsen (7 Daly, 354), 219.
Devlin v. Devlin (67 Barb. 290; 25 Am. Rep. 173), 173.
De Witt Wire Cloth Co. v. N. J. Wire Cloth Co. (14 N. Y. Supl. 777), 243, 562.
Dexter v. Snow (12 Cush. 594), 94, 95.
Diamond Match Co. v. Roeber (106 N. Y. 473), 113, 125, 132, 138, 139, 144, 208, 211, 219.
Dibble v. New Haven (56 Conn. 199; 20 Am. & Eng. Corp. Cas. 174), 392.
Dick v. Cooper (24 Pa. St. 217), 249.
Dick v. Foraker (155 U. S. 404, 415; 15 Supt. Ct. Rep. 124), 718.
Dickson v. Dickson (33 La. Ann. 1261), 349.
Dickson v. Thomas (97 Pa. St. 278), 280.
Dingledein v. Third Ave. R. R. Co. (9 Bosw. 79, 89), 81.
Dingman v. People (51 Ill. 279), 369.
Distilling & Cattle Feeding Co. v. The People (156 Ill. 448, 490; 41 N. E. Rep. 188), 510, 692, 705.
Dixon Crucible Co. v. Guggenheimer (1 Cox's Man. of Trade Mark. Cas. 559), 173.
Dodge v. Council Bluffs (57 Iowa, 560), 386.
Dolph v. Troy Laundry Machinery Co. (28 Fed. Rep. 553, 555), 211, 212, 542.
Donaldson v. Jude (2 Bibb, 57), 49.
Donohue v. County (2 Pa. St. 230), 358.
Doolin v. Ward (6 Johns. 194), 46, 243.
Doremus v. Hennessey (62 Ill. App. 391, 402), 229.
Dorris v. Grace (24 Ark. 326), 48.
Doty v. Martin (32 Mich. 462), 129, 184.

[The references are to pages.]

Dow v. Beidleman (49 Ark. 455; 31 Am. & Eng. Ry. Cas. 14; 125 U. S. 680, 689; 8 Sup. Ct. Rep. 1028), 421, 430, 720.
Downing v. Mt. W. Road Co. (40 N. H. 230, 232), 488.
Downing v. Ringe (7 Mo. 585), 94.
Downs v. Lewis (11 Cush. 76), 94.
Draining Co. v. State (43 Ind. 236), 704.
Drake v. Dodsworth (4 Kan. 159), 201.
Drake v. Siebold (81 Hun, 178), 567.
Drennan v. Douglas (102 Ill. 341), 51.
Drexler v. Tyrrell (15 Neb. 114), 94.
Dubois v. Augusta (Dudley, 30), 401.
Dubowski v. Goldstein (65 L. J. Q. B. 397. 399), 149. 197, 199.
Dubuque & Pac. Ry. v. Litchfield (23 How. 66, 88), 491.
Dudley v. Sudduth (91 Ala. 349; 8 So. Rep. 873), 166.
Duffy v. Shockey (11 Ind. 70), 201.
Dugger v. Mechanics' & Traders' Ins. Co. (95 Tenn. 245; 32 S. W. Rep. 5), 593.
Duignan v. Walker (7 W. R. 562; 5 Jur. (N. S.) 976; 28 L. J. Ch. 867), 141.
Dunkin v. Hodge (46 Ala. 523), 97.
Dunlap v. Gregory (10 N. Y. 241; 61 Am. Dec. 746), 129, 132.
Dunn v. Bell (85 Tenn. 581; 4 S. W. Rep. 41), 283.
Duntley v. Boston & Maine R. Co. (66 N. H. 263), 93.
Dupre v. Thompson (4 Barb. 279), 194.
Durant v. Burt (98 Mass. 161), 283.
Durfee v. Moran (57 Mo. 374), 249.
Durgin v. Am. Ex. Co. (66 N. H. 277; 20 Atl. Rep. 328), 88, 92.
Durkee v. City of Jamesville (28 Wis. 464), 431.
Duvenick v. Mo. Pac. R. Co. (57 Mo. App. 550), 86, 93.
Dwight v. Hamilton (113 Mass. 175), 115, 128, 132, 184, 187, 218.
Dygert v. Schenck (23 Wend. 446), 81.

E.

Earl v. Howell (14 Abb. N. Cas. 474), 283.
Earl of Shrewbury's Case (9 Rep. 50), 683.
Earle v. Seattle, L. S. & E. Ry. Co. (56 Fed. Rep. 909), 493.
East Line & Red River Ry. Co. v. State (75 Tex. 434), 480.
East St. Louis v. East St. Louis G. L. & C. Co. (38 Ill. 424, 425), 392.
Eastern Anglian R. W. Co. v. Eastern Counties R. W. Co. (11 C. B. 795), 502.
Eastern Counties R. W. Co. v. Hawkes (35 Eng. L. & Eq. 32), 501.
Easun v. Buckeye Brew. Co. (51 Fed. Rep. 156), 528.
Eckstein v. Downing (64 N. H. 248; 9 Atl. Rep. 626), 579.
Eclipse Towboat Co. v. Pontchartrain R. Co. (24 La. Ann. 1), 553.
Eddings v. Long (10 Ala. 203, 208), 98.
Eddy v. Capron (4 R. I. 394), 68, 103.
Edison Elec. Light Co. v. Sawyer-Mann Elec. Co. (3 C. C. A. 605; 53 Fed. Rep. 592), 166.
Eels v. St. Louis, K. & N. W. R. Co. (52 Fed. Rep. 903), 88.
Egerton v. Brownlow (4 H. L. Cas. 1), 26, 38, 43.
Eichels v. Evansville St. Ry. Co. (78 Ind. 263; 5 Am. & Eng. R. Cas. 274; 21 Am. Rep. 562), 377.

[The references are to pages.]

Eidman v. Bowman (58 Ill. 444), 502.
Eilenbecker v. Plymouth County (134 U. S. 31, 36), 716.
Eisel v. Hoyt (141 Ind. 41; 40 N. E. Rep. 119), 124.
Eldridge v. Smith (34 Vt. 484), 501.
Elkhart Lodge v. Crary (98 Ind. 238. 240), 65, 84.
Elkins v. Camden & Atl. Ry. Co. (36 N. J. Eq. 5), 491.
Ellerman v. Chicago Junction, etc. Co. (49 N. J. Eq. 217; 23 Atl. Rep. 287), 180.
Ellerman v. Stock Yds. Co. (49 N. J. Eq. 217; 23 Atl. Rep. 287), 219.
Ellicott v. Chamberlain (38 N. J. Eq. 604), 46, 101.
Elliott v. Fairhaven & Westville Ry. Co. (32 Conn. 579), 366.
Elliott v. Richardson (L. R. 5 C. P. 744), 100, 577.
Elliott's Appeal (60 Pa. St. 161).
Ellis v. Jones (56 Ga. 504), 129.
Ellis v. Turner (8 T. R. 531).
Ellis v. Zeilin (42 Ga. 91), 173.
Ely v. Supervisors (36 N. Y. 299, 820), 570.
Elysville Mfg. Co. v. Oskisko Co. (Md. Ch. Dec. 392; 5 Md. 152), 536.
Emack v. Kane (34 Fed. Rep. 47), 322.
Emerson v. Badger (101 Mass. 82), 172, 173.
Emerson v. Com. (108 Pa. St. 111), 384.
Emery v. Ohio Candle Co. (47 Ohio St. 320; 32 Am. & Eng. Corp. Cas. 165), 54, 562, 575.
Enfield Toll Bridge Co. v. H. & N. H. Ry. Co. (17 Conn. 158), 366, 393.
Erie & Pac. Dispatch v. Cecil (112 Ill. 185), 589.
Erwin v. Phila. & Reading R. Co. (7 Ry. & Corp. L. J. 87), 583.
European, etc. R. W. Co. v. Pool (59 Me. 277), 502.
Evans v. Walton (L. R. 2 C. P. 615), 349.
E. & A. R. R. Co. v. Greenwich (25 N. J. Eq. 565), 354.
Evansville & Crawfordsville R. Co. v. Baum (26 Ind. 70), 236.
E. & H. R. R. Co. v. Hunt (20 Ind. 457), 501.
Everhart v. Puckett (73 Ind. 409), 97.
Ewing v. Johnson (34 How. Pr. 202), 132.
Ex parte Clifford (20 Ind. 106), 501.
Ex parte Keeney (84 Col. 304; 24 Pac. Rep. 34), 402.
Ex parte O'Leary (65 Miss. 80), 401.
Ex parte Perham (5 Jur. (N. S.) 1221), 345.
Ex parte Robinson (19 Wall. 505), 716.
Ex parte Rogers (L. R. 15 Ch. D. 207), 283.
Ex parte Sadler (15 Ves. 52), 95.
Ex parte Selma & G. R. Co. (45 Ala. 696), 466.
Ex parte Schrader (3 Cal. 279), 401.
Ex parte Terry (128 U. S. 289), 716.
Ex parte Wolverhampton Banking Co. (L. R. 14 Q. B. Div. 32), 79.
Ex parte Young (6 Biss. C. C. 53), 267, 269.

F.

Fairbank v. Leary (40 Wis. 637, 643), 110, 239, 240.
Fairbank v. Jacobus (14 Blatchf. 337), 173.
Fall River Iron Works Co. v. Old Colony, etc. R. R. Co. (5 Allen, 221), 502.
Fanning v. Gregoire (16 How. 534), 398.

[The references are to pages.]

Fargo v. Mich. (121 U.S. 230, 239), 426.
Fariera v. Campbell (89 Pa. St. 89), 266.
Farmers' Loan & Trust Co. v. N. Pac. Ry. Co. (60 Fed. Rep. 803), 240.
Farrar v. Close (L. R. 4 Q. B. 602), 333.
Fawcett v. Gee (3 Anst. 910), 95.
Fawrie v. Morin's Syndics, (4 Mart. (La.) 39, 49), 71, 72.
Fay, Petitioner (15 Pick. 243), 398.
Fennessy v. Ross (5 App. Div. 342; 39 N. Y. Supl. 323), 579.
Ferrenbach v. Turner (86 Mo. 416; 56 Am. Rep. 439), 401.
Ferris v. Adams (23 Vt. 136), 68.
Fetcher v. Montgomery (33 Beav. 22), 195.
Fidelity & Casualty Co. v. Eickhoff (63 Minn. 170; 65 N. W. Rep. 351), 96.
Field v. Chipley (79 Ky. 260), 106.
Filson v. Hines (5 Pa. St. 452), 62, 68, 69.
Finger v. Hahn (42 N. J. Eq. 606), 215.
First Congl. Church v. Henderson (4 Rob. (La.) 209), 94.
First Nat. Bank v. Hendrie (49 Iowa, 402; 31 Am. Rep. 153), 84.
First Nat. Bank v. Oskaloosa P. Co. (66 Iowa, 41), 264, 277.
Fisher v. Bush (35 Hun, 641), 503, 561, 582, 584.
Fisher v. McGirr (1 Gray, 1), 409.
Fisher v. Schuri (73 Wis. 370; 41 N. W. Rep. 527), 255.
Fitchburg Ry. Co. v. Gage (12 Gray, 393), 589.
Fitchburg, etc. Ry. Co. v. Grand Junction R., etc. Co. (4 Allen, 198), 423.
Fitzgerald v. Grand Trunk R. Co. (63 Vt. 169; 22 Atl. Rep. 76; 49 Am. & Eng. Ry. Cas. 8), 586.
Fivaz v. Nicholls (2 C. B. 501), 79.
Flagg v. Baldwin (38 N. J. Eq. 219), 264, 266.
Flarty v. Odlam (3 T. R. 681), 104.
Fleckner v. Bank (8 Wheat. 351), 489.
Fla. Cent. R. R. Co. v. State (31 Fla. 482), 84.
Fogg v. Griffon (2 Allen, 1), 236.
Foll's Appeal (91 Pa. St. 434), 276.
Foote v. Emerson (10 Vt. 338), 102.
Forbes v. McDonald (54 Cal. 98), 46, 100, 577.
Ford v. Chi. Milk Shippers' Assn. (155 Ill. 166, 179; 39 N. E. Rep. 651), 245, 246, 260.
Forelander v. Hicks (6 Ind. 448), 471.
Foreman v. Berghaus (13 La. Ann. 209), 103.
Forsythe v. State (6 Ohio, 19), 51.
Fort v. Burch (6 Barb. 74), 501.
Fortenbury v. State (47 Ark. 188), 266, 277, 280.
Forward v. Pittard (1 T. R. 27), 331.
Fowle v. Park (131 U. S. 88; 9 Sup. Ct. Rep. 658), 144, 161, 218.
Fox v. Scard (33 Beav. 327), 132, 184, 194.
Fox Solid Pressed Steel Co. v. Schoen (77 Fed. Rep. 29), 566.
Franco v. Bolton (3 Ves. 368), 51.
Frank v. Denver & R. G. Ry. Co. (23 Fed. Rep. 757), 333.
Frankfort Bank v. Johnson (24 Me. 490), 236.
Franklin Bank v. Commercial Bank (36 Ohio St. 350), 491, 527.
Franklin Co. v. Bank (68 Me. 43), 488.
Franklin Co. v. Lewiston Inst. (68 Me. 43), 491, 528, 530.
Fredericks v. Mayor (13 How. Pr. 566), 194.
Freeholders v. State (4 Zab. 718), 398.

[The references are to pages.]

Freemantle v. Company, etc. (1 Lev. 229), 108.
Freemantle v. Silk Throwsters Co. (1 Lev. 229), 120.
Fremont v. Stone (42 Barb. 169. 170), 101, 583.
French v. Buffalo, etc. R. Co. (4 Keyes, 108). 92.
French v. Donohue (29 Minn. 111), 520.
Friend v. Harrison (2 C. & P. 584). 51.
French v. Parker (16 R. I. 219: 14 Atl. Rep. 870). 124, 134.
Freon v. Carriage Co. (42 Ohio St. 30). 581.
Frost v. Belmont (6 Allen. 152), 55. 59.
Frothingham v. Barney (6 Hun, 366). 527.
Fry v. State (63 Ind. 552). 452, 456.
Fuller v. Dame (18 Pick. 472). 84, 100. 250, 577.
Fuller v. Hope (163 Pa. St. 26; 29 Atl. Rep. 779). 123.
Fulton v. Sellers (4 Brewst. 42). 173.
Fuqua v. Pabst Brewing Co. (38 S. W. Rep. 29), 225.

G.

Gage v. Caraher (125 Ill. 451). 427.
Gage v. Censors (63 N. H. 92). 456.
Gage v. Fisher (5 N. Dak. 297; 65 N. W. Rep. 809). 577.
Gaines v. Coates (51 Miss. 335). 455.
Gale v. Cin. (18 Ohio St. 563). 455.
Gale v. Kalamazoo (23 Mich. 344; 9 Am. Rep. 80), 368, 389, 404, 406.
Gale v. Reed (8 East, 80). 121, 215.
Galena, etc. Ry. Co. v. Rae (18 Ill. 488; 68 Am. Dec. 574). 331.
Galesworthy v. Strutt (1 Excheq. 659). 129, 190.
Galt v. Adams Express Co. (McArth. & M. 124; 48 Am. Rep. 742), 86.
Galton v. Chi., etc. R. Co. (95 Iowa, 112; 63 N. W. Rep. 589). 590.
Galveston, H. & S. A. R. Co. v. Ball (80 Tex. 602; 16 S. W. Rep. 441), 88.
Gamewell Fire Alarm Tel. Co. v. Crane (160 Mass. 50; 35 N. E. Rep. 98), 151, 219.
Gandolfo v. Hartman (49 Fed. Rep. 181), 78.
Gardner v. Morse (25 Me. 140), 249.
Garrison v. City of Chicago (7 Biss. 486). 368, 383.
Garton v. Bristol, etc. R. W. Co. (1 B. & S. 112). 588.
Gary v. Frazer (76 Me. 37). 228.
Gas Co. v. City of Saginaw (22 Rep. 578). 384.
Gas Co. v. Parkersburg (30 W. Va. 435. 441: 4 S. E. Rep. 650). 384.
Gaskin v. Balls (L. R. 13 Ch. D. 324). 353.
Gaston v. Drake (14 Nev. 175. 188), 69.
Gaszler v. Georgetown (6 Wheat. 593), 369.
Geismer v. L. S. & M. S. Ry. Co. (102 N. Y. 563: 55 Am. Rep. 837). 333.
Gelpcke v. Dubuque (68 U. S. 175). 148.
Genet v. Hunt (113 N. Y. 158, 172), 559.
Georgia Banking Co. v. Smith (128 U. S. 174. 179). 419, 423.
Georgia, etc. Ry. Co. v. Smith (70 Ga. 694: 9 Am. & Eng. Ry. Cas. 395). 426.
Gibbons v. Ogden (9 Wheat. 203), 410.
Gibbons v. Railroad Co. (36 Ala. 410), 486.
Gibbs v. Balto. Gas. Co. (130 U. S. 396). 240, 532, 542.

[The references are to pages.]

Gibbs v. Smith (115 Mass. 592, 593), 100, 249, 250, 277.
Gibbs v. Somers' Point (49 N. J. L. 515), 697.
Gibbes v. Town Council of Beaufort (20 S. Car. 213). 398.
Gibert v. Peteler (38 Barb. 488; 38 N. Y. 165). 154, 156.
Gibs v. Gas Co. (130 U. S. 396; 9 Sup. Ct. Rep. 553), 38.
Gil v. Davis (12 La. Ann. 219), 55.
Gilbert v. Canal, etc. Co. (8 N. J. Eq. 495), 713.
Gilbert v. Carter (10 Ind. 16), 249, 471.
Gilbert v. Mickle (4 Sand. Ch. 357), 353.
Gill v. Ferris (82 Mo. 156), 115, 129.
Gillett v. Moody (3 N. Y. 479), 597.
Gillis v. Hall (2 Brewst. 341), 161.
Gillis v. Tel. Co. (61 Vt. 461, 464), 439.
Gilman v. Dwight (13 Gray, 356), 114, 218.
Gilman v. Hunnewell (122 Mass. 139). 173.
Girard Storage Co. v. Southwork Co. (105 Pa. St. 248. 252), 432.
Girardy v. Richardson (1 Esp. 13; 1 B. & D. 341*n*), 51.
Gireaud v. Dandelet (32 Md. 561), 110.
Glenn v. So. Ex. Co. (86 Tenn. 594), 8 So. W. Rep. 152), 92.
Glenn, etc. Mfg. Co. v. Hall (61 N. Y. 226; 19 Am. Rep. 278), 173.
Gloucester Isinglass & Glue Co. v. Russia Cement Co. (154 Mass. 92; 27 N. E. Rep. 1005; 12 L. R. A. 563), 116, 216, 542.
Goddard v. Smithett (3 Gray. 116), 697.
Goff v. Great Northern R. Co. (3 E. & E. 672; 30 L. J. Q. B. 140). 235, 236.
Gompers v. Rochester (56 Pa. St. 194), 123.
Goodall v. Thurman (1 Head, 209), 51.
Goodman v. Henderson (58 Ga. 567), 115, 124, 184.
Goodspeed v. East Heddam Bank (22 Conn. 530, 541), 235, 236.
Goodwin v. Clark (65 Me. 280), 148.
Goodwin v. Crowell (56 Ga. 566), 79, 97.
Goodwin v. Goodwin (4 Day, 343), 97.
Goodwin Gas Store Meter Co.'s Appeal (117 Pa. St. 514; 12 Atl. Rep. 736), 579.
Gordon v. Dalby (30 Iowa, 223), 46.
Gordon v. Winchester (12 Bush, 110, 114), 361, 431.
Gorham v. Keyes (137 Mass. 583), 79, 97.
Gosnell v. State (52 Ark. 228; 12 S. W. Rep. 392), 456.
Gosselin v. Womack (21 La. Ann. 757), 48.
Gossigi v. New Orleans (40 So. Rep. 15), 456.
Gott v. Cook (7 Paige, 521; 24 Wend. 641), 559.
Graham v. Cowgill (13 Kan. 114), 695.
Grand Trunk R. Co. v. Stevens (95 U. S. 655), 88.
Grant v. Davenport (36 Iowa, 402), 386.
Grasselli v. Lowden (11 Ohio St. 349), 114.
Grassman v. Dodd (137 N. Y. 599), 93.
Gravelly v. Barnard (L. R. 18 Eq. 518; 47 L. J. Ch. 659; 30 L. T. 863). 121, 128, 184.
Gray v. Hook, (4 N. Y. 449, 457), 46, 73, 74, 103.
Gray v. Mathias (5 Ves. 286), 51.
Gray v. Oxnard Bros. Co. (59 Hun, 387), 595.
Gray v. Swiss (3 Wash. C. C. 276), 94.
Gray v. Wilson (4 Watts, 39), 95.

[The references are to pages.]

Grand Rapids, etc. Light Co. v. Grand Rapids, etc. Co. (21 Am. & Eng. Corp. Cas. 270), 383.
G. E. Ry. Co. v. Turner (L. R. 8 Ch. App. 149), 534.
G. N. Ry. Co. v. E. C. Ry. Co. (21 L. J. Ch. 837), 488.
G. W. Ry. Co. v. Met. Ry. Co. (32 L. J. Ch. 382; 9 Jur. (N. S.) 562), 534.
Gt. Western Ry. Co. v. Sutton (L. R. 4 H. L. 226), 588.
Great Luxembourg R. W. Co. v. Magnay (25 Beav. 586), 502.
Green v. Brooks (81 Cal. 328), 85.
Green v. Creighton (7 R. I. 1), 156.
Green v. Folgham (1 Sim. & Stu. 398), 164.
Green v. London Omnibus Co. (7 C. B. (N. S.) 290), 236.
Green v. Price (13 M. & W. 695), 121.
Greenfield v. Gilman (140 N. Y. 168), 173, 215.
Greensboro v. Ehrenreich (80 Ala. 579; 60 Am. Rep. 130; 18 Am. & Eng. Corp. Cas. 483), 401.
Greenville Water Works Co. v. Greenville (7 So. Rep. 409), 386.
Greenwood v. Curtis (6 Mass. 358, 379), 51.
Greer v. Haughabook (47 Ga. 282), 392.
Greer v. Payne (4 Kan. App. 153; 46 Pac. Rep. 190), 566.
Greer. Mills & Co. v. Stotler (77 Fed. Rep. 1), 713.
Gregory v. Brunswick (6 Man. & G. 205), 318.
Gregory v. Mayor, etc. of N. Y. (40 N. Y. 273), 401.
Gregory v. Wattowa (58 Iowa, 711), 277.
Gregory v. Wendell (40 Mich. 432), 264, 278.
Griffin v. Jewett (15 Wkly. Law Bull. 419), 580.
Griswold v. Gregg (24 Ill. App. 384), 272.
Grogan v. Express Co. (114 Pa. St. 523; 7 Atl. Rep. 134), 85.
Groton v. Waldborough (11 Me. 306), 68.
Grundy v. Edwards (7 J. J. Marsh. 368; 23 Am. Dec. 409), 132.
Guerand v. Dandelet (32 Md. 562), 123, 132.
Guernsey v. Cook (120 Mass. 501, 502), 46, 100, 101, 577, 579, 583.
Guillotte v. New Orleans (12 La. Ann. 432), 455.
Gulf, etc. Ry. Co. v. Ellis (87 Tex. 19; 61 Am. & Eng. Ry. Cas. 357), 430.
Gulf, C. & S. F. Ry. Co. v. Levi (76 Tex. 337), 334.
Gulf, Colo. & S. F. Ry. Co. v. Morris (67 Tex. 692), 478.
Gulf, C. & S. F. R. Co. v. State (72 Tex. 404; 10 S. W. Rep. 81; 36 Am. & Eng. R. Cas. 481; 1 L. R. A. 849; 2 Int. Com. Rep. 335), 470, 555.
Gulicke v. Ward (10 N. J. L. 87), 46.
Gunmakers Co. v. Fell (Willis, 384, 388), 20, 108.
Gunn v. Cent. Ry. etc. Co. (74 Ga. 509), 520, 523.
Gunter v. Astor (4 Moore, 12), 318, 349.

H.

Haas v. Fenlon (8 Kan. 601), 101.
Haas v. K. C., Ft. S. & Gulf Ry. Co. (81 Ga. 792; 7 S. E. Rep. 629), 333.
Hackensack Water Co. v. Hoboken (51 N. J. L. 220; 24 Am. & Eng. Corp. Cas. 511), 386.
Hafer v. N. Y., L. E. & W. Ry. Co. (14 Wkly. Law Bull. 68), 581.
Hagan v. Blindell (54 Fed. Rep. 40; 56 Fed. Rep. 696), 333.
Hagg v. Darby (47 L. J. Ch. 567), 162.

[The references are to pages.]

Haggart v. Morgan (5 N. Y. 422), 95.
Hahn v. Concordia Soc. (42 Md. 460), 196.
Haight v. Gay (8 Cal. 300; 48 Am. Dec. 323), 694.
Hailey v. Hoeffner (19 La. Ann. 518), 48.
Haines v. Lewis (54 Iowa, 301; 6 N. W. Rep. 495), 46, 75, 76.
Harms v. Parsons (32 Beav. 328), 161.
Haithcock v. Swift Island Mfg. Co. (72 N. Car. 410), 392.
Haldman v. Simonton (55 Iowa, 144; 7 N. W. Rep. 493), 132, 133, 184.
Hale v. Haughton (8 Mich. 458), 386.
Hall v. Barrows (33 L. J. Ch. 204), 172, 173.
Hall v. Dyson (16 Jur. 270; L. J. 21 Q. B. 224), 46, 94.
Hall v. Keese (31 Tex. 504), 48.
Hall's Appeal (60 Pa. St. 458), 201.
Hallenback v. Hahn (2 Neb. 379).
Holsapple v. Rome, etc. R. Co. (86 N. Y. 275), 92.
Halthaus v. Kuntz (17 Ill. App. 434).
Hatzfield v. Gulden (7 Watts, 153), 46, 75.
Hamilton v. Savanah, F. & W. R. Co. (52 Am. & Eng. Ry. Cas. 130; 49 Fed. Rep. 412), 502.
Hancock v. Louisville Ry. Co. (145 U. S. 409, 412), 488.
Hand v. Ballou (12 N. Y. 541), 427.
Handforth v. Jackson (150 Mass. 149; 22 N. E. Rep. 634), 218, 245.
Hanks v. Naglee (54 Cal. 51), 51.
Harrell v. Watson (63 N. Car. 454, 460), 49.
Harrington v. Duchatel (1 Bro. Ch. 124), 39.
Hannah v. Fife (27 Mich. 172), 249, 538.
Hannay v. Eve (3 Cr. 241), 94.
Harmison v. City of Lewiston (153 Ill. 313; 38 N. E. Rep. 411), 628.
Harrison v. Baltimore (1 Gill. 264), 401.
Harrison v. Gardner (2 Madd. 198), 108.
Harrison v. Godman (1 Burr. 12), 108, 120.
Harrison v. Greaves (59 Miss. 453), 697.
Harrison v. Lockhart (25 Ind. 112), 129, 201.
Harrison v. Paige (3 Gray, 239), 520.
Hard v. Seeley (47 Barb. 428), 163.
Harding v. Stamford Water Co. (41 Conn. 91), 366.
Harding v. Third Presb. Ch. (20 Ind. 72), 501.
Hare v. London & N. W. Ry. Co. (2 Johns. & H. 80; 30 L. J. Ch. 817; 7 Jur. (N. S.) 1145), 470, 553, 554.
Hare v. Whitmore (49 L. T. (N. S.) 335), 132.
Hargreaves v. Wood (2 Sw. & Tr. 602), 102.
Harlow v. Humiston (6 Cow. 189), 332.
Harms v. Parsons (32 Beav. 328; 9 Jur. (N. S.) 145; 32 L. J. Ch. 247; 7 L. T. 815; 11 W. R. 250), 119, 129.
Harney v. St. Louis (90 Mo. 214), 406.
Harper v. Raymond (3 Bosw. 29), 561.
Harrell v. Walton (63 N. Car. 454), 48.
Harrington v. Du Chastel (1 Bro. Ch. 124; 2 Dick. 581), 68.
Harris v. Cockermough & W. R. Co. (1 Ry. & C. T. Cas. 97), 590.
Harris v. Parsons (32 L. J. Ch. 247), 24.
Harris v. Roof (10 Barb. 489), 55, 60.

[The references are to pages.]

Harris v. Tumbridge (83 N. Y. 92, 95), 268.

Hart v. Aldridge (1 Cowp. 54), 349.

Hart v. Pa. R. Co. (112 U. S. 331: 5 Sup. Ct. Rep. 151), 93.

Hart v. Railroad Co. (112 U. S. 331; 5 Sup. Ct. Rep. 151), 86.

Hartford v. Hartford Bridge Co. (10 How. 534; 17 Conn. 79), 396.

Hartford Fire Ins. Co. v. Chi., M. & St. P. Ry. (70 Fed. Rep. 201: 17 C. C. A. 62), 91.

Hartley v. Cummins (5 C. B. 247), 122.

Harvey v. Improvement Co. (118 N. Car. 692, 698), 561.

Harvey v. Railroad Co. (74 Mo. 538), 93.

Haskins v. Royster (70 N. Car. 603; 16 Am. Rep. 780), 348.

Hastings v. Whitely (2 Excheq. 611), 124, 125, 129, 201.

Hatch v. Douglas (48 Conn. 116; 40 Am. Rep. 154), 275.

Hatch v. Mann (15 Wend. 44), 51.

Havemeyer v. Havemeyer (43 N. Y. Super. Ct. 506, 1213: 86 N. Y. 618), 583, 584.

Hawkeye Ins. Co. v. Brainard (72 Iowa, 130; 33 N. W. Rep. 603), 98.

Hawkins v. N. O. Printing Co. (29 La. Ann. 134), 235.

Hawley v. Kan. & Tex. Coal Co. (48 Kan. 593; 30 Pac. Rep. 14), 586.

Hayes v. Willis (11 Abb. Pr. (N. S.) 167), 196.

Hays v. Penna. Co. (12 Fed. Rep. Rep. 309), 589.

Hayward v. Davidson (41 Ind. 212), 501.

Haywood v. Young (2 Chitty's R. 407), 112, 201.

Hazen v. Boston Bridge Co. (2 Gray, 575), 235.

Hazen v. Commonwealth (23 Pa. St. 363, 364), 228.

Hazlehurst v. Savannah, etc. Ry. Co. (43 Ga. 13), 240, 488, 527, 530.

Health Dept. v. Knoll (70 N. Y. 530), 401.

Hebblewaite v. Hepworth (98 Ill. 126), 51.

Hedge v. Lowe (47 Iowa, 137, 140), 110, 129, 132, 133, 189.

Heichew v. Hamilton (3 G. Greene, 317, 596; 4 G. Greene, 317), 189.

Heine v. Commonwealth (91 Pa. St. 145), 259.

Henderson v. Ogden City Ry. Co. (7 Utah, 199; 26 Pac. Rep. 286), 377.

Henderson v. Palmer (71 Ill. 579), 79, 97.

Hermits of St. Aug. v. County (Bright N. P. 116), 358.

Hersh v. Northern Cent. Ry. Co. (74 Pa. St. 181), 589.

Herreshoff v. Boutimeau (17 R. I. 3, 7), 145, 194.

Hervey v. Smith (1 Kay & J. 392), 302.

Hewett v. Pioneer Press Co. (23 Minn. 178), 235.

Hewitt v. Swift (3 Allen, 420), 236.

Heywood v. Tilson (75 Me. 231), 253.

Hibbard v. Western Union Tel. Co. (33 Wis. 558), 86.

Higgins v. McCrea (116 U. S. 671), 272.

Hill v. Davies (L. R. 21 Ch. D. 798), 353.

Hill v. More (40 Me. 515), 95.

Hill v. Nisbet (100 Ind. 341), 527.

Hill v. Paul (8 Cl. & Fin. 307), 104.

Hilles v. Parrish (14 N. J. Eq. 380), 583.

Hills v. Mittson (8 Excheq. 758), 46, 94.

[The references are to pages.]

Hilton v. Eckersley (6 E. & B. 47), 294, 541.

Hinde v. Gray (1 Scott N. R. 123), 21, 24, 26.

Hiss v. Baltimore & Hampden Pass. Ry. (52 Md. 242; 36 Am. Rep. 371), 379.

Hitchcock v. Coker (6 Ad. & El. 438, 439), 23, 24, 25, 118, 121, 122, 125, 145, 201.

Hitt v. Ormsbeer (14 Ill. 235), 501.

Hoagland v. Seque (38 N. J. L. 230), 110, 180, 201.

Hocker v. Gentry (3 Met. 463), 51.

Hodge v. Sloan (107 N. Y. 244), 113, 144, 157, 208, 222, 560.

Hodsdon v. Wilkins (7 Greenl. 113), 79.

Hockett v. State (105 Ind. 250, 257), 448, 449, 450.

Holbrook v. Waters (9 How. Pr. 335), 129, 132, 184, 187, 189.

Holladay v. Patterson (5 Ore. 176), 83.

Holland v. Challen (110 U. S. 1524; 3 Sup. Ct. Rep. 495), 718.

Holland v. Helm (7 Gratt. 245), 105.

Holman v. Johnson (Cowp. 341, 343), 273.

Holyoke Co. v. Lyman (15 Wall. 500), 366.

Horne v. Rouse (8 Wall. 430), 369.

Honaker v. Board of Education (24 S. E. Rep. 544), 65.

Hood v. Palm (8 Pa. St. 238), 243.

Hooker v. Vandewater (4 Denio, 349; 47 Am. Dec. 258), 243, 470, 538, 565, 568.

Horner v. Graves (7 Bing. 735), 44.

Hoover v. Penna Ry. Co. (156 Pa. St. 220; 27 Atl. Rep. 282), 589.

Hope v. Hope (8 De G., M. & G. 731), 97.

Hopkins v. Oxley Stove Co. (25 Cent. L. J. 494), 317.

Hopkins v. Prescott (4 C. B. 578), 68.

Hoppin v. Buffum (9 R. I. 513; 11 Am. Rep. 291), 583.

Hornby v. Close (L. R. 2 Q. B. 153), 333.

Horner v. Ashford (3 Bing. 319, 322, 326), 19, 22, 108, 114, 118, 182.

Horner v. Graves (7 Bing. 735, 744; 5 Moore & P. 768), 112, 115, 125, 130, 139, 144, 180, 191, 219.

Houlton v. Dunn (60 Minn. 26; 61 N. W. Rep. 898), 55, 61.

Houlton v. Nichol (Wis.), (67 N. W. Rep. 715), 63.

Houston v. Neuse River, etc. Co. (8 Jones, 467), 697.

Howard v. Hodges (1 Selw. N. P. 79), 51.

Howard v. Hopkins (2 Atk. 371), 194.

Howard v. Woodward (10 Jur. (N. S.) 1123), 189.

Howden v. Haigh (11 Ad. & El. 1038), 95.

Howe v. Howe Machine Co. (50 Barb. 236), 173.

Howe Machine Co. v. Louder (58 Ga. 64), 235.

Hoyne v. McClintock (76 Ind. 205), 318.

Hoyt v. Holly (39 Conn. 326; 12 Am. Rep. 390), 132.

Hozier v. Caledonian R. W. Co. (1 Nev. & McN. R. W. Cas. 27), 588.

Hubbard v. Miller (27 Mich. 15), 110, 114, 121, 122, 132, 219.

Hudson v. State (46 Ga. 624), 349.

Huesing v. Rock Island (128 Ill. 465; 27 Am. & Eng. Corp. Cas. 650), 401.

Hull v. Chicago, etc. Ry. Co. (41 Minn. 510; 43 N. W. Rep. 399), 86.

Humes v. Knoxville (1 Humph. 403), 235.

Humphrey v. Pegues (16 Wall. 244), 361.

[The references are to pages.]

Hunlocke v. Blacklowe (2 Wms. Saund. 156*b*), 20.
Hunter v. Gardner (6 Wils. & Shaw, 618), 104.
Hunter v. Peiffer (108 Ind. 199), 250, 470.
Hunter v. Wolf (71 Pa. St. 282), 46, 74.
Hursen v. Gavin (162 Ill. 377; 44 N. E. Rep. 735), 208.
Hurst v. Litchfield (39 N. Y. 377), 95.
Hutchins v. Hutchins (7 Hill, 104), 228.
Hutton v. Parker (7 Dowl. P. C. 739), 121, 123.
Hynds v. Hayt (25 Ind. 31, 36), 148.

I.

Ide v. Ball Engine Co. (31 Fed. Rep. 901), 571.
Ill., etc. Canal Co. v. St. Louis (2 Dill. 70), 383.
Ill. Cent. Ry. Co. v. Crider (91 Tenn. 489; 56 Am. & Eng. Ry. Cas. 157), 430.
Ill. Cent. Ry. Co. v. McLean Co. (17 Ill. 291), 501.
Ill., etc. R. Co. v. Reedy (17 Ill. 580), 235.
Independent Refiners' Assn. v. W., N. Y. & P. Ry. Co. (5 Int. Com. Rep. 415; 4 Int. Com. Rep. 162), 555.
India Bagging Assn. v. Rock (14 La. Ann. 164), 541.
Ind., etc. Ry. Co. v. Gapen (10 Ind. 292), 431.
Indianapolis Cable St. Ry. Co. v. Citizens' St. Ry. Co. (127 Ind. 369, 390), 381.
Indianapolis, D. & S. Ry. Co. v. Davis (32 Ill. App. 67), 586, 590.
Indianapolis, D. & S. Ry. Co. v. Ervin (118 Ill. 250; 8 N. E. Rep. 862; 27 Am. & Eng. Ry. Cas. 8), 586, 590.
Indianapolis, etc. R. R. Co. v. Solomon (23 Ind. 534), 501.
Indianapolis, etc. R. R. Co. v. Warner (35 Ind. 516), 501.
Indianapolis v. Indianapolis Gas Light & Coke Co. (66 Ind. 396), 368, 383.
I. & St. L. Ry. Co. v. Juntgen (10 Ill. App. 295), 333.
In re Acker (66 Fed. Rep. 290), 340.
In re Barnards Banking Co. (L. R. 3 Ch. App. 105), 533, 534.
In re British Life Ins. Assn. (L. R. 8 Ch. D. 679), 527.
In re Citizens' Pass. Ry. Co. (2 Pitts. 10), 377.
In re Debs (158 U. S. 564; s. c., Sup. Ct. Rep. 900, 911), 35, 341, 344, 353, 712, 716.
In re Grand Trunk R. Co. (2 Int. Com. Rep. 96; 3 Int. Com. Com. 89), 587.
In re Green (7 Biss. 338), 280.
In re Greene (52 Fed. Rep. 104), 545, 603.
In re Linehan (72 Cal. 114), 401.
In re Lowe (54 Kan. 757, 762), 39 Pac. Rep. 710), 400, 404.
In re Mayor, etc. of Albany (23 Wend. 277), 369.
In re N. Y. El. R. Co. (70 N. Y. 327), 377.
In re Palmer (L. R. 6 C. P. 194), 406.
In re Parkinson (L. R. 6 C. P. 554), 496.
In re Penna. Hall (5 Pa. St. 204), 358.
In re Quong Foo (13 Fed. Rep. 229), 456.
In re Town of Summerville (33 S. Car. 56; 11 S. E. Rep. 545), 401.
In re Tyler (149 U. S. 164, 190; 13 Sup. Ct. Rep. 785), 719.
In re Wab. Ry. Co. (24 Fed. Rep. 217), 320.
Ingram v. Stiff (5 Jur. (N. S.) 947), 176.

[The references are to pages.]

In the Case of the Earl of Shaftesbury (2 St. Trials, 615; 1 Mod. 144), 714.

In the Case of J. V. N. Yates (4 Johns. 314, 369), 714.

In Rex v. De Berenger (3 M. & S. 67), 244.

Ins. Co. v. State (86 Tex. 250; 24 S. W. Rep. 397), 594.

International & G. N. R. Co. v. Folts (3 Tex. Civ. App. 644; 22 S. W. Rep. 541).

Interstate Com. Com. v. B. & O. R. Co. (145 U. S. 263), 587.

Interstate Com. Com. v. Brimson (154 U. S. 447; 14 Sup. Ct. Rep. 1125), 426, 716.

Interstate Com. Com. v. Cin. & C. Co. (64 Fed. Rep. 981), 426.

Irwin v. Williar (110 U. S. 499; 4 Sup. Ct. Rep. 160), 265, 278, 280.

Isaacs v. State (48 Miss. 234), 259, 260.

Ives v. Smith (8 N. Y. Supl. 46; 3 N. Y. Supl. 645), 555.

J.

Jackson v. Bowman (39 Miss. 671), 369.

Jackson v. Davidson (4 Barn. & Ald. 695), 46, 94.

Jackson v. Foote (12 Fed. Rep. 37), 283.

Jackson v. Lampshire (3 Pet. 289), 373.

Jackson v. McLean (36 Fed. Rep. 213), 53.

Jackson v. Walker (5 Hill, 27), 94.

Jackson Co. Horse Ry. Co. v. Interstate Rapid Transit Ry. Co. (24 Fed. Rep. 306, 308; 32 Am. & Eng. Ry. Cas. 216), 363, 369.

Jacksonville, etc. Ry. Co. v. Prior (34 Fla. 272), 430.

Jacksonville S. E, Ry. Co. v. Rabbitt (29 Ill. App. 288), 586, 590.

Jacobs v. Tobiason (65 Iowa, 245), 96.

Jacoby v. Whitmore (49 L. T. 335; 32 W. R. 18), 124, 132, 215.

Janes v. Reynolds (2 Tex. 250), 431.

Jarvis v. Peck (10 Paige, Ch. 118), 163.

Jenkins v. Fink (30 Cal. 586), 249.

Jenkins v. Fowler (24 Pa. St. 308), 81.

Jenkins v. Temples (39 Ga. 655), 110, 129, 132, 189.

Jenks v. Pawlowski (98 Mich. 110; 56 N. W. Rep. 1105), 158.

Jennings v. Grand Trunk R. Co. (127 N. Y. 438; 28 N. E. Rep. 394), 92.

Jennings v. Throgmorton (Ry. & M. 251), 51.

Jersey City Gas Co. v. Dwight (29 N. J. Eq. 242), 376, 383.

Jersey City Gas Light Co. v. Consumers' Gas Co. (40 N. J. Eq. 427), 431, 694.

Johnson v. Gwinn (100 Ind. 466), 115, 129.

Johnson Harvester Co. v. Meinhardt (9 Abb. N. Cas. 393; 6 How. Pr. 168), 348.

Johnson v. Kanne (21 Mo. App. 22), 264.

Johnson v. Leonhard (Wash. Ter.) (20 Pac. Rep. 591), 95.

Johnson v. Pensacola, etc. Ry. Co. (16 Fla. 623; 26 Am. Rep. 731), 589.

Johnson v. Phila. (60 Pa. St. 445), 369.

Johnson v. Richmond & D. R. Co. (39 S. Car. 55; 17 S. E. Rep. 512), 88, 93.

Johnson v. Simonton (43 Cal. 242), 401.

Johnson v. State (113 Ind. 143), 446, 448.

Johnson v. State (3 Tex. App. 590), 259.

Joint Stock Co. v. Brown (L. R. 8 Eq. 381), 527.

[The references are to pages.]

Jones v. Baker (7 Cow. 445). 228.
Jones v. Blocker (43 Ga. 331). 349, 351.
Jones v. Caswell (3 Johns. Cas. 29), 46, 343.
Jones v. Easton, etc. R. W. Co. (1 Nev. & McN. R. W. Cas. 72), 588.
Jones v. Heavens (L. R. 4 Ch. D. 633). 194.
Jones v. Lees (1 Hurl. & N. 189; 2 Jur. (N. S.), 645; 26 L. J. Excheq. 9), 26, 120, 136, 167, 211, 212.
Jones v. Parker (29 N. H. 31). 520.
Jones v. Randal (Cowp. 39), 46.
Jordan v. Dayton (4 Ohio, 295), 452.
Judd v. Harrington (19 N. Y. Supl. 406; 139 N. Y. 105), 245, 568.

K.

Kalamazoo Hack & Bus Co. v. Sootsma (84 Mich. 194, 201). 496, 499.
Kansas City, St. J. & C. B. R. R. Co. v. Simpson (30 Kan. 645). 89.
Kansas Pac. Ry. Co. v. Mower (16 Kan. 573, 582), 431.
Karst v. St. Paul, etc. Ry. Co. (22 Minn. 118), 369.
Keating v. Hyde (23 Mo. App. 555), 46, 71, 72.
Keeler v. Taylor (53 Pa. St. 194, 467), 110, 186, 215.
Keith v. Herschberg Optical Co. (48 Ark. 138; 2 S. W. Rep. 777). 132, 221.
Kellerman v. Kansas R. Co. (136 Mo. 177; 34 S. W. Rep. 41). 86, 93.
Kelley v. Mfg. Co. (44 Fed. Rep. 19). 570.
Kellogg v. Larkin (3 Pin. 123), 138, 139.
Kelly v. Chicago, Mil. & St. Paul Ry. (93 Iowa, 436; 61 N. W. Rep. 962), 254, 255.
Kelly v. Ypsilanti Dress Stay Mfg. Co. (44 Fed. Rep. 19), 57.
Kemp v. Western Union Tel. Co. (28 Neb. 661), 439.
Kennedy v. Lee (3 Meriv. 452). 213.
Kennedy v. Phelps (10 La. Ann. 227), 401.
Kent v. Miltenberger (13 Mo. App. 503, 507), 269.
Kentucky, etc. Co. v. Louisville, etc. Co. (37 Fed. Rep. 567), 426.
Keppell v. Bailey (2 Myl. & K. 517), 94.
Kergivin v. Drainage Commissioners (115 Ill. 347), 694.
Kettle River Ry. Co. v. Eastern Ry. Co. (41 Minn. 461; 43 N. W. Rep. 469; 40 Am. & Eng. Ry. Cas. 449), 470.
Kick v. Merry (23 Mo. 72). 103.
Kiff v. Atchison, T. & S. F. R. R. Co. (32 Kan. 263; 4 Pac. Rep. 401). 88.
Kilborn v. Field (78 Pa. St. 194), 97.
Kilmer v. New York, etc. Ry. Co. (100 N. Y. 395), 589.
Kimball v. Atchison, T. & S. F. Ry. Co. (46 Fed. Rep. 888, 890). 479.
Kimball v. Harman (34 Md. 407), 231, 349.
Kimbrough v. Lane (11 Bush. 556), 79.
King v. City of London (2 T. R. 522), 706.
King v. Crosby (3 Wils. 188; 2 Bl. Rep. 754), 715.
King v. Davenport (98 Ill. 305; 38 Am. Rep. 89), 455.
Kingsbury v. Kiswan (77 N. Y. 612). 264, 277.
Kirkpatrick v. Adams (20 Fed. Rep. 287), 277, 280.
Kirkpatrick v. Bonsall (72 Pa. St. 158), 263, 267.
Klinger v. Bickel (117 Pa. St. 326), 455.

[The references are to pages.]

Knight v. Hunt (5 Bing. 433). 95.

Knowlton v. Fitch (52 N. Y. 288), 267, 283.

Koehler v. Fearbacher (2 Mo. App. 11), 110.

Kribben v. Haycraft (26 Mo. 396), 46, 77, 103.

Kreigh v. Sherman (105 Ill. 49), 272.

Keulevitz v. Eastern R. Co. (140 Mass. 573; 5 N. E. Rep. 500), 235.

L.

Labouchere v. Dawson (L. R. 13 Eq. 322), 215.

Ladd v. Dillingham (34 Me. 316), 94.

Ladd v. S., C. P. & N. Co. (53 Tex. 172, 188). 459.

Lafever v. Hadel (21 La. Ann. 663), 48.

Lake v. Butler (3 W. R. 458; 5 E. & B. 99), 142.

Lake Erie & Western Ry. Co. v. Bailey (61 Fed. Rep. 494, 496), 298.

Lake Shore, etc. Ry. Co. v. Bennett (89 Ind. 457). 333.

Lamoine Val., etc. Co. v. Bixby (55 Vt. 235), 520.

Land v. Hoffman (12 Am. L. R. (N. S.) 143), 501.

Landrigan v. State (31 Ark. 50), 499.

Landringham v. State (49 Ind. 136), 259, 260.

Lane v. Newdigate (10 Ves. 192), 302.

Lange v. Werke (2 Ohio St. 519, 520), 110, 115, 138, 139, 149.

Langley v. Boston, etc. Ry. (10 Gray, 103), 501.

Langston v. Hughes (1 Maule & Selw. 596), 95.

Laubenheimer v. Mann (17 Wis. 542), 110.

Lawrence v. Kidder (10 Barb. 641), 110, 121, 128, 129.

Lawson v. Bank of London (18 C. B. 84), 172.

Lawson v. Chicago, etc. Ry. Co. (64 Wis. 447; 24 N. W. Rep. 618), 86.

Leather Cloth Co. v. Am. Leather Cloth Co. (11 H. L. Cas. 538), 173.

Leather Cloth Co. v. Lorsont (L. R. 9 Eq. 345, 354; 39 L. J. Ch. 82; 21 L. T. 661; 18 W. R. 572), 24, 44, 114, 136, 140, 161, 182, 212.

Leavenworth Co. v. Miller (7 Kan. 502), 695.

Leavitt v. Palmer (3 N. Y. 19), 148.

Le Claire v. Davenport (13 Iowa, 210), 406, 456.

Ledsinger v. Cent. Line Steamers (75 Ga. 567), 520.

Lee v. West (47 Ga. 311), 349, 351.

Lehigh Water Co.'s Appeal (102 Pa. St. 515), 369.

Leicester v. Rose (4 East, 380), 95.

Leidersdorf v. Flint (8 Biss. 327), 172.

Leigh v. Hinde (9 Bar. & Cr. 774, 779).

Leighton v. Wales (3 Mees. & W. 545, 645), 23, 24, 118.

Leggett v. Hyde (58 N. Y. 272), 523.

Leloup v. Port of Mobile (127 U. S. 640), 442.

Lender v. Caldwell (4 Kan. 339), 94.

Leonard v. Poole (114 N. Y. 371), 565, 568.

Leslie v. Lorillard (110 N. Y. 519, 531; 18 N. E. Rep. 363), 113, 146, 222, 470, 690.

Lewis v. Davidson (4 M. & W. 654; 1 H. & H. 426; 3 Jur. 387), 51.

Lewis v. Gollner (129 N. Y. 227, 236; 29 N. E. Rep. 81), 159, 160.

[The references are to pages.]

Lewis v. Knox (2 Bibb. 453), 68.
Lewis v. Ludwick (6 Colo. 368; 98 Am. Dec. 454), 333.
Lewisville Nat. Gas Co. v. State (135 Ind. 49), 402.
Levi v. Levi (6 Car. & P. 239). 248.
Levy v. Walker (L. R. 10 Ch. D. 436), 215.
License Cases (5 How. 504, 582), 450.
License Tax Cases (5 Wall. 462, 471), 47, 410, 452.
Ledderdale v. Montrose (4 T. R. 248), 104.
Life & Fire Ins. Co. v. Mechanics' Fire Ins. Co. (7 Wend. 31). 235, 501.
Lightner v. Menzie (35 Cal. 468), 110.
Lincoln Co. v. Luning (133 U. S. 529; 10 Sup. Ct. Rep. 363), 719.
Lindsay v. Chicago, etc. Ry. Co. (36 Minn. 539: 33 N. W. Rep. 7), 85.
Lindsay v. Smith (78 N. Car. 328), 79, 97.
Lindsey v. Attorney-General (33 Miss. 509). 684.
Linn v. Sigsbee (67 Ill. 75). 110. 115, 121, 129, 184.
Live Stock Assn. v. Levy (54 N. Y. Sup. Ct. Rep. 32). 210.
Liverpool Steam Co. v. Phœnix Ins. Co. (129 U. S. 397). 85. 91.
Livingston and Fulton v. Van Ingen *et al.* (9 Johns. Rep. 507). 376.
Livingston v. Peppin (31 Ala. 542). 386.
Lloyd v. Johnson (1 B. & P. 340). 51.
Lloyd v. Malone (23 Ill. 43). 249.
Locke v. Fowler (41 Ill. App. 66), 272.
Logan v. Musick (81 Ill. 415). 283.
Logan v. Pyne (43 Iowa. 524: 22 Am. Rep. 261), 389, 398.
London. etc. Ry. Co. v. Commissioners (L. R. 20 Ch. D. 562, 576). 157.
London & N. W. R. Co. v. Evershed (L. R. 3 App. Cas. 1029; 39 L. T. 306), 590.
London & N. W. Ry. Co. v. Lancashire & Y. Ry. Co. (L. R. 4 Eq. 174). 302.
Long v. Duluth (49 Minn. 280). 386.
Long v. Fowl (42 Mo. 545). 113, 144.
Longshore Printing Co. v. Howell (26 Ore. 527. 543; 38 Pac. Rep. 547). 303. 322.
Loog v. Bean (L. R. 26 Ch. D. 306), 353.
Lord v. Oconto (47 Wis. 386). 368.
Loubenheimer v. Mann (17 Wis. 561). 138.
Louisville v. Bank (104 U. S. 47). 466.
Louisville City Ry. Co. v. Louisville (8 Bush, 415). 368.
Louisville Gas Co. v. Citizens' Gas Co. (115 U. S. 683. 694). 360, 361.
Louisville. N. A. & C. R. Co. v. Faylor (156 Ind. 126; 25 N. E. Rep. 869). 88. 93.
Louisville & Nashville Ry. v. Kentucky (161 U. S. 677. 693). 491. 492.
Louisville. etc. R. Co. v. Widman (9 Ind. App. 190; 37 N. E. Rep. 554).
Louisville Transfer Co. v. Am. Dist. Telegraph Co. (24 Abb. L. J. 283). 446.
Louisville & Portland Ry. Co. v. Louisville City Ry. Co. (2 Duv. 175). 377.
Lovatt v. Wingard (1 Jac. & Walk. 394). 164.
Lowry v. Dillman (59 Wis. 197). 265.
Low v. Peers (Wilmot's Op. 364. 378). 41.
Lucas v. Allen (80 Ky. 681). 46. 66.

[The references are to pages.]

Lumley v. Gye (2 El. & Bl. 216), 231, 301, 349.
Lumley v. Wagner (5 De G. & Sm. 485), 196.
Lyon v. Culbertson (83 Ill. 33), 264, 272.
Lyttle v. Whicher (21 La. Ann. 182), 48.

M.

Mackinnon Pen Co. v. Fountain Ink Co. (48 N. Y. Sup. Ct. Rep. 442), 215.
Madan v. Sherard (73 N. Y. 329), 93.
Madison v. Smith (83 Ind. 502), 392.
Madison, etc. Plank Road Co. v. Watertown, etc. Plank Road Co. (7 Wis. 59), 502.
Madison, etc. Ry. Co. v. Whiteneck (8 Ind. 217), 431.
Maffet v. Ijams (103 Pa. St. 266), 249, 251.
Maguire v. Dinsmore (56 N. Y. 168), 92.
Maguire v. Smock (42 Ind. 1), 471.
Mahaska County Ry. Co. v. Des Moines Valley Ry. Co. (28 Iowa, 437), 502.
Mallalien v. Hodgson (16 Ad. & El. 678), 95.
Mallon v. May (11 M. & W. 652, 653; 7 Jur. 536; 12 L. J. Excheq. 376), 23, 25, 119, 124, 125, 139, 148, 191.
Mallory v. Hanaur Oil Wks. (86 Tenn. 598, 798; 20 Am. & Eng. Corp. Cas. 478), 517, 595.
Mallory v. Oil Works (86 Tenn. 598), 510.
Manchester & Lawrence Ry. Co. v. Concord Ry. Co. (66 N. H. 100, 127; 9 L. R. A. 689; 27 Atl. Rep. 383; 47 Am. & Eng. Ry. Cas. 359; 3 Int. Com. Rep. 319), 555.
Mandeville v. Harman (42 N. J. Eq. 185, 194); 7 Atl. Rep. 37), 144, 183, 185, 186.
Manhattan B. & M. Co. v. Sears (45 N. Y. 799), 523.
Manners v. Library Co. (93 Pa. St. 165, 172), 53.
Manning v. Manning (1 Johns. Ch. 533), 103.
Mapstrick v. Ramge (9 Neb. 390; 31 Am. Rep. 415), 297, 349.
March v. People (7 Barb. 391), 259.
March v. Railroad Co. (40 N. H. 548), 95.
Marine Bank v. Ogden (29 Ill. 248), 520, 523.
Markham v. Brown (8 N. H. 523), 496.
Markham v. Jaudon (41 N. Y. 235), 282.
Marriott v. Ry. Co. (1 C. B. (N. S.) 499), 496.
Marsh v. Fairbury (64 Ill. 414), 84.
Marsh v. Russell (66 N. Y. 292), 211.
Marshall v. Baltimore & Ohio Ry. Co. (16 How. 314, 334, 335), 58, 70, 77, 100, 577.
Marshall v. City Bayonne (34 Atl. Rep. 1080), 446.
Marshall v. Grimes (41 Miss. 27), 398.
Martin v. Bartow Iron Works (35 Ga. 320), 94.
Martin v. Mayor (1 Hill, 545), 369.
Martin v. Murphy (129 Ind. 464; 28 N. E. Rep. 1118), 124, 132, 187.
Martin v. Wade (37 Cal. 168), 69.
Martinetti v. Maguire (Deady, 216), 450.
Master Stevedores' Assn. v. Walsh (2 Daly, 1), 345.
Matthews v. Alexandria (68 Mo. 115), 368.
Matthews v. Associated Press (136 N. Y. 333, 340; 32 N. E. Rep. 981), 113, 146, 219, 222.

[The references are to pages.]

Maunsell v. Midland, Gt. Western R. Co. (1 H. & M. 164; 32 L. J. Ch. 513), 555.
Maund v. Monmouthshire Canal Co. (4 Man. & G. 452), 235, 236.
Maxim-Nordenfeldt Co. v. Nordenfeldt (L. R. 1 Ch. 630. 651, 654, 656, 662, 673: App. Cas. 535, 549), 27, 116, 119, 121, 126, 128, 134.
Maxton v. Gheen (75 Pa. St. 166), 267, 277, 283.
Maxwell v. Hogg (L. R. 2 Ch. App. 314), 172.
May v. O'Neill (44 L. J. Ch. 660), 129, 190.
Mayer v. Journeymen Stonecutters' Assn. (47 N. J. Eq. 519; 20 Atl. Rep. 492), 357.
Mayor v. Cabot (28 Ga. 50), 389.
Mayor, etc. v. Colgate (2 Kernan, 146), 501.
Mayor v. Hagan (9 Baxt. 495), 391.
Mayor v. Jersey City & Bergen Ry. Co. (20 N. J. Eq. 360), 380.
Mayor v. Lacy (3 Ala. 618), 94.
Mayor, etc. of Monroe v. Gerspach (33 La. Ann. 1011), 401.
Mayor of Norwich v. Norfolk Ry. Co. (4 E. & B. 397), 534.
Mayor, etc. v. Ohio, etc. Ry. Co. (26 Pa. St. 355), 380.
Mayor v. Rudecke (49 Md. 217), 401.
McAllison v. Howell (42 Ind. 15), 129, 201.
McAndrews v. Bassett (4 De G., J. & S. 386), 172.
McBratney v. Chandler (22 Kan. 692, 695), 56.
McCaull v. Braham (16 Fed. Rep. 37), 196.
McCaw v. Blewit (2 McCord Ch. 90), 101.
McCloskey v. Kreling (76 Cal. 511), 455.
McClure v. Manchester, etc. Ry. Co. (13 Gray. 124), 501.
McClurg's Appeal (58 Pa. St. 51), 110, 121, 128, 132, 184.
McConihay v. Wright (121 U. S. 201, 205; 7 Sup. Ct. Rep. 940), 719.
McConnell v. Pedigo (9 Ky. 465: 18 S. W. Rep. 15; 5 Am. Ry. Corp. Rep. 711), 499.
McCormick v. Nichols (19 Ill. App. 334), 280.
McCulloch v. State of Maryland (4 Wheat. 316), 407.
McCurry v. Gibson (108 Ala. 451: 18 So. Rep. 806, 807, 808), 123, 133, 184.
McDonnell v. Rigney (Mich.) (66 N. W. Rep. 52), 53.
McDuffee v. Portland, etc. R. R. Co. (52 N. H. 430: 13 Am. Rep. 72), 589.
McElvain v. Mudd (44 Ala. 48), 48.
McFadden v. Missouri Pac. Ry. Co. (92 Mo. 343; 4 S. W. Rep. 689), 86, 93.
McGuire v. Corwine (101 U. S. 108), 46, 62.
McGrew v. City Produce Exchange (85 Tenn. 572, 578: 4 S. W. Rep. 38, 39), 265, 283.
McGunn v. Hanlin (29 Mich. 476), 95.
McIlvaine v. Egerton (2 Robt. 422), 277.
McKee v. Cheney (52 How. Pr. 144), 55.
McLean v. Fleming (96 U. S. 245), 172, 173.
McMahon v. Smith (47 Conn. 221), 97.
McMillan v. Carson Min. Co. (12 Phila. 404), 527.
McNutt v. McElwen (1 W. N. C. 552), 132, 184.
McQuilkin v. Doe (8 Blackf. 581), 501.
McRoberts v. Washburne (10 Minn. 8), 392.

[The references are to pages.]

McWilliams v. Bryan (21 La. Ann. 211), 94.

Meacham v. Dow (32 Vt. 721), 46, 71.

Meadville Fuel Gas Co. v. Meadville Nat. Gas Co. (3 Cent. Rep. 921; 2 Dillon Municipal Corp. 693), 369, 383.

Mechanics' Sav. Bank v. Meriden, etc. Co. (24 Conn. 159), 527.

Meguire v. Corwine (101 U. S. 108, 111), 69, 70.

Mell v. Mooney (30 Ga. 413), 115, 132, 184.

Memphis v. Memphis Water Co. (5 Heisk. 495), 386.

Memphis City Ry. Co. v. Memphis (4 Coldw. 406), 378.

Memphis, etc. Gas Co. v. Williams (9 Heisk. 314), 383.

Meneehy v. Meneehy (62 N. Y. 427; 20 Am. Rep. 489).

Mercantile Trust Co. v. Atl. & Pac. Ry. Co. (63 Fed. Rep. 513), 443.

Mercer v. Irving (El., B. & E. 563), 128.

Merchants' Nat. Bank v. State Bank (10 Wall. 604, 650), 101.

Meredith v. Ladd (2 N. H. 517), 68.

Merrill v. Am. Ex. Co. (62 N. H. 514), 92.

Merrill v. Carr (60 N. H. 114), 97.

Merrill v. Tariff Mfg. Co. (10 Conn. 384), 235.

Merritt v. Merritt (25 La. Ann. 257), 48.

Merriwether v. Nixon (2 Smith's Lead. Cas. 297), 81.

Merz Capsule Co. v. U. S. Capsule Co. (67 Fed. Rep. 414), 508, 573.

Messenger v. Pennsylvania R. Co. (37 N. J. L. 531), 590.

Metropolitan Board of Health v. Heister (37 N. Y. 661), 401, 409.

Meyer v. Estes (164 Mass. 457; 41 N. E. Rep. 683), 146.

Midland R. Co. v. London & N. W. R. Co. (L. R. 2 Eq. Cas. 524), 555.

Middlesex Ry. Co. v. Boston & Chelsea Ry. Co. (115 Mass. 347), 710.

Mifflin v. Commonwealth (5 W. & S. 461), 243.

Milbank v. New York, etc. Ry. Co. (64 How. Pr. 20), 527, 530.

Milburn v. Byrne (1 Cranch C. C. 239), 349.

Milhan v. Sharp (27 N. Y. 611), 368, 377, 378, 389.

Mill & Lumber Co. v. Hayes (76 Cal. 386, 393), 153.

Miller v. Baynard (2 Houst. 559), 249.

Miller v. Bensley (20 Ill. App. 528), 277.

Miller v. Craig (11 N. J. Eq. 175), 455.

Miller v. Elliott (1 Ind. 484), 128, 132, 184.

Miller v. Miller (78 Iowa, 177; 42 N. W. Rep. 641.)

Miller v. Palermo (12 Kan. 14), 698.

Miller v. R. & W. R. R. Co. (36 Vt. 490), 501.

Millington v. Fox (3 Myl. & Cr. 338), 172.

Mills v. County Com. (3 Scam. 53), 396.

Mills v. Dunham (L. R. 1 Ch. 576, 587), 180.

Mills v. Mills (40 N. Y. 543), 55, 60.

Mills v. St. Clair Co. (7 Ills. 199), 397.

Milne v. Huber (3 McLean, 212), 94.

Milton v. Haden (32 Ala. 30), 94, 392.

Minturn v. Larue (23 How. 435), 369.

Mississippi Mill v. Cohn (150 U. S. 202, 204; 14 Sup. Ct. Rep. 75), 719.

[The references are to pages.]

Mississippi River Bridge Co. v. Lonergan (91 Ill. 513), 392.
Missouri, etc. R. Co. v. Harris (67 Tex. 166; 2 S. W. Rep. 574), 86.
Mo. Pac. Ry. Co. v. Humes (115 U. S. 512), 430.
Mitchell v. Burlington (4 Wall. 270), 466.
Mitchell v. Reynolds (1 P. Wms. 181, 197), 19, 25, 37, 44, 110, 113, 114, 117, 118, 121.
Mitchell v. Smith (1 Binn. 120), 46.
Mitchell v. Smith (4 Dall. 269), 94.
Mobile & Ohio R. R. Co. v. People (132 Ill. 559; 24 N. E. Rep. 643), 84.
Mobile v. Yuille (3 Ala. 137, 141), 452, 453.
Moenich v. Fenestre (6 L. J. Ch. 737, 740), 199.
Mogul Steamship Co. v. McGregor (L. R. 21 Q. B. D. 544; 23 Q. B. D. 598; L. R. App. Cas. 25), 16, 18, 28, 232, 235, 241, 242, 253, 294.
Mohawk Bridge Co. v. Utica & S. Ry. Co. (6 Paige, 554), 369.
Mollyneaux v. Wittenberg (39 Neb. 549; 58 N. W. Rep. 205), 155.
Mont. Union Ry. Co. v. Langlois (9 Mont. 419; 24 Pac. Rep. 209), 498.
Monroe v. Haffman (29 La. Ann. 651; 29 Am. Rep. 345), 455.
Montague v. Flockton (L. R. 16 Eq. 189, 198), 195.
Montrose v. State (61 Miss. 429), 694.
Moore v. City of Eufaula (97 Ala. 670; 11 So. Rep. 921), 439.
Moore v. Evans (14 Barb. 524), 92.
Moore v. Fitchburg R. Co. (4 Gray, 465), 236.
Moore & Handley Co. v. Towers Hardware Co. (87 Ala. 206), 130, 219.
Moores v. Bricklayers' Union No. 1 (7 Ry. & Corp. L. J. 108; 23 W. L. Bull. 48), 309, 347.
More v. Bennett (140 Ill. 69; 29 N. E. Rep. 888), 224, 253, 573.
More v. Bonnet (40 Cal. 251; 6 Am. Rep. 621, 622), 115, 152.
Morgan v. Perhamus (36 Ohio St. 517; 38 Am. Rep. 607), 129, 200, 220.
Morgan v. Struthers (131 U. S. 246), 561.
Morland v. Cook (L. R. 6 Eq. 252), 157.
Morrill v. Boston & M. R. Co. (55 N. H. 531, 537; 11 Ry. Rep. 484), 472, 555.
Morris v. Coleman (18 Ves. 468), 108.
Morris v. Tuscaloosa Mfg. Co. (83 Ala. 565), 154.
Morris Run Coal Co. v. Barclay Coal Co. (68 Pa. St. 173, 186), 224, 238, 240, 244, 253, 294, 538, 541, 556, 558, 573.
Morris v. Woodward (25 N. J. Eq. 32), 46.
Morrison v. Moat (9 Hare, 241; 21 L. J. Ch. 248), 164.
Morrison v. Phillips' Construction Co. (44 Wis. 405), 88, 89, 93.
Morse v. Morse (103 Mass. 73), 136.
Morse Twist Co. v. Morse (103 Mass. 73, 77), 168, 175, 212, 216, 218, 219.
Morton v. Metropolitan Life Ins. Co. (34 Hun, 367; 103 N. Y. 645), 235.
Moses v. Scott (84 Ala. 608; 4 So. Rep. 742), 582.
Mott v. Mott (11 Barb. 127), 128, 132, 184.
Mouflet v. Cole (21 W. R. 175; 27 L. T. 678; 42 L. J. Excheq. 8; L. R. 8 Excheq. 32), 141.
Mud Creek Draining Co. v. State (43 Ind. 236), 702.
Mugler v. Kansas (123 U. S. 623, 672), 716.

[The references are to pages.]

Mumford v. Gething (7 C. B. (N. S.) 305, 317, 319; 6 Jur. (N.S.) 428), 24, 119, 130, 203.
Municipality v. Cutting (4 La. Ann. 336), 456.
Munn v. Illinois (94 U. S. 125), 414, 422, 432, 435, 437, 448, 460, 461.
Munn v. People (69 Ill. 80, 90), 458.
Munnikhuysen v. Magraw (5 Md. 557), 102.
Murphy v. Farmers' Bank (20 Pa. St. 415), 688, 698, 701.
Murray v. Reeves (8 Barn. & C. 425), 46, 94.
Murray v. Vanderbilt (39 Barb. 140), 471.
Murdock v. Walker (152 Pa. St. 595; 34 Am. St. Rep. 678), 318.
Mutual Sav., etc. Co. v. Meriden Agency Co. (24 Conn. 159, 163), 529.
Mutual Union Tel. Co. v. Chicago (16 Fed. Rep. 309), 437.
Myers v. Croft (13 Wall. 295), 501.
Mynard v. Syracuse, etc. R. Co. (71 N. Y. 180), 92.

N.

Nash v. Page (80 Ky. 539, 542), 433.
Nat. Bank v. St. Joseph (31 Fed. Rep. 216), 369.
Nat. Bank of Augusta v. Cunningham (75 Ga. 366), 280.
Nat. Ben. Co. v. Union Hospital Co. (45 Minn. 272; 47 N. W. Rep. 806), 130, 182.
Nat. Cash. Register Co. v. Boston Cash Indicator Co. (41 Fed. Rep. 51), 571.
Nat. Distilling Co. v. Cream City Importing Co. (86 Wis. 353; 56 N. W. Rep. 864), 546.
Nat. Ex. Co. v. Drew (32 Eng. L. & Eq. 1), 236.
Nat. Harrow Co. v. Hench (76 Fed. Rep. 667, 669), 572, 573, 576.
Nat. Harrow Co. v. Quick (67 Fed. Rep. 130), 546, 575.
Nat. Prov. Bank v. Marshall (L. R. 40 Ch. D. 112), 145, 181.
Nellis v. Nellis (99 N. Y. 505, 516), 559.
Nelson v. Vt., etc. Ry. Co. (26 Vt. 717), 423.
Nester v. Continental Brew. Co. (161 Pa. St. 473, 483; 41 Am. St. Rep. 894; 29 Atl. Rep. 102; 34 W. N. C. 387), 144, 224, 573.
Nessle v. Reese (29 How. Pr. 382), 194.
Neustadt v. Ill. Cent. Ry. Co. (31 Ill. 434), 501.
Newberry v. James (2 Meriv. 446), 163.
Newberry Bank v. Stegall (41 Miss. 142), 148.
Newburgh Turnpike Co. v. Miller (5 Johns. Ch. 101), 388.
Newell v. Meyendorff (9 Mont. 254; 23 Pac. Rep. 333), 207.
New England Ex. Co. v. Maine Central Ry. Co. (57 Me. 188), 589.
New Jersey v. Wilson (7 Cranch, 164), 361.
New Jersey v. Yard (95 U. S. 104), 366, 379.
New Orleans v. Stafford (27 La. Ann. 417), 456.
New Orleans City & L. Ry. Co. v. City of New Orleans (44 La. 728; 11 So. Rep. 78), 377.
New Orleans Co. v. Ocean Dry Dock Co. (28 La. Ann. 173), 528.
New Orleans C. R. Co. v. Crescent City R. Co. (12 Fed. Rep. 308), 369.
New Orleans Gas Co. v. Louisiana Light Co. (115 U. S. 650; 6 Sup. Ct. 252), 366, 375, 385, 386, 387, 542, 552.

[The references are to pages.]

New Orleans Water Works Co. v. Riners (115 U. S. 674, 680), 360, 366, 388.
Newton v. Cubitt (12 C. B. (N. S.) 32; 13 C. B. (N. S.) 864), 398.
New York v. Second Ave., etc. Co., (32 N. Y. 261). 369, 389.
New York Bank Note Co. v. Hamilton, etc. Co. (83 Hun. 593; 31 N. Y. Supl. 1060), 210.
New York C. R. v. Lockwood (17 Wall. 357, 381). 87, 88.
New York & Md. Ry. Co. v. Winans (17 How. 30, 39), 465.
New York & N. H. R. R. Co. v. Schuyler (38 Barb. 534; 7 Tiffany, 30; 34 N. Y. 30, 50). 236.
New York & S. C. Co. v. F. Bank (7 Wend. 412). 520.
New York, etc. Ry. Co. v. Flynn (74 Hun, 124; 26 N. Y. Supl. 859). 499.
Nicol v. Mayor (9 Hun, 268), 386.
Nicoll v. Besse (53 L. T. (N. S.) 659). 132.
Nicholas v. New York Cent. R. Co. (89 N. Y. 370). 92.
Nicholls v. Stretton (11 Jur. 1008), 149.
Nichols v. Mudgett (32 Vt. 546), 46, 71, 73.
Nichols v. Ruggles (3 Day. 145), 79.
Nicholson v. Gt. Western Ry. Co. (7 C. B. (N. S.) 755; 1 Nev. & McN. R. W. Cas. 143). 588.
Nightingale's Case (11 Pick. 168), 456.
Niver v. Rossman (18 Barb. 50), 132, 184.
Nix v. Bell (66 Ga. 664), 94.
Noah v. Webb (1 Edw. Ch. 603), 178.
Noble v. Bates (7 Cow. 307), 110.
Noble v. Vincennes (42 Ind. 125), 392.
Noel v. Drake (28 Kan. 265), 46, 101, 577.
Nordenfeldt v. Maxim-Nordenfeldt Co. (L. R. App. Cas. 533, 535, 540, 554, 575), 27, 116, 144, 211.
Norris v. Beyea (13 N. Y. 273, 289), 559.
Norris v. Moss (25 L. J. Eq. 194), 201.
North v. Phillips (89 Pa. St. 250), 265.
North Balto. Pass. Ry. Co. v. North Ave. Ry. Co. (75 Md. 233; 23 Atl. Rep. 466), 377.
Northern Pac. Ry. Co. v. Roberts (42 Fed. Rep. 734, 746), 466.
Norwich Gas Light Co. v. Norwich City Gas Co. (25 Conn. 18), 368, 383, 389.
Noyes v. Marsh (123 Mass. 286), 101.

O.

Oakdale Mfg. Co. v. Garst (18 R. I. 484; 28 Atl. Rep. 973), 562.
Oakes v. Cattaraugus Water Co. (143 N. Y. 430; 38 N. E. Rep. 461), 78.
Oakland v. Carpentier (13 Cal. 540), 369.
O'Donovan v. Wilkins (24 Fla. 281; 23 Am. & Eng. Corp. Cas. 1), 401.
O'Hara v. Carpenter (23 Mich. 410), 46, 64.
Ohio, etc. Ry. Co. v. Selby (47 Ind. 471), 86.
Ohio & M. Ry. Co. v. State (49 Ohio St. 668; 32 N. E. Rep. 933), 584.
Ohio & Miss. Ry. Co. v. Wheeler (1 Black, 286), 501.
Olcott v. Supervisors (16 Wall. 678, 694), 467.
Old Colony Ry. Co. v. Tripp (147 Mass. 35), 498.
Old Dom. S. S. Co. v. McKenna (30 Fed. Rep. 48), 294, 349, 351.
Olin v. Bate, (98 Ill. 53), 105.

[The references are to pages.]

Olive v. Van Patten (7 Tex. Civ. App. 630; 25 S. W. Rep. 428), 253.
Oliver v. Gilmore (52 Fed. Rep. 562), 219, 545.
Olmstead v. Camp (33 Conn. 532), 366.
Olmstead v. Distg. & Cattle Feeding Co. (77 Fed. Rep. 265), 587.
O'Neil v. Kruger (4 B. & S. 389; 116 E. C. L. 388), 345.
O'Neill v. Longman (4 B. & S. 376; 116 E. C. L. 374), 345.
Ontario Salt Co. v. Merchants' Salt Co. (18 Ontario Ch. 540), 520.
Oppenheimer v. Hirsch (5 App. Div. 232; 38 N. Y. Supl. 311), 201.
Oregon Ry. v. Oregonian Ry. (130 U. S. 1), 491.
Oregon Steam. Nav. Co. v. Winsor (20 Wall. 64, 66, 67, 68, 70), 109, 114, 131, 136, 137, 138, 148, 212, 218.
Ormerod v. Dearman (10 Pa. St. 561; 45 Am. Rep. 391), 62, 97.
Osborn v. Nicholson (13 Wall. 654, 663), 48.
Osborne v. Williams (18 Ves. 379), 46.
Oscanyan v. Arms Co. (103 U. S. 261, 273, 274), 46, 60, 66.
Ouachita Packet Co. v. Aiken (121 U. S. 144), 448.
Outen v. Rhodes (3 A. K. Marsh. 432), 68.
Overby v. Overby (21 La. Ann. 493), 94.
Owen v. Louisville, etc. R. Co. (87 Ky. 629; 9 S. W. Rep. 698), 92.
Owens v. State (16 Lea, 1), 318.
Owings v. Owings (1 Harr. & G. 484), 101, 104.
Oxley Stave Co. v. Coopers' Int. Union (72 Fed. Rep. 695, 699), 316.

P.

Pacific Factor Co. v. Adler (90 Cal. 110; 27 Pac. Rep. 36), 243, 541, 563.
Pacific R. R. Co. v. Seeley (45 Mo. 212), 83.
Page v. Fazackerly (36 Barb. 392), 455.
Page's Estate (57 Cal. 238), 102.
Painter v. London, Brighton & S. C. Ry. Co. (5 Com. B. (N. S.) 70), 496.
Palmer v. Bate (2 Brod. & Bing. 637), 104.
Palmer v. Bishop (146 Mass. 469), 151.
Palmer v. Forbes (23 Ill. 301), 501.
Palmer v. State (39 Ohio St. 236; 48 Am. Rep. 429), 452.
Palmer v. Stebbins (3 Pick. 188), 121, 125, 132, 210, 218.
Parish v. Stone (14 Pick. 198), 152.
Parish v. Wheeler (22 N. Y. 494), 501.
Parker v. Huntington (2 Gray, 124), 242.
Parker v. Nightingale (6 Allen, 341, 344), 156, 160.
Parrott v. City of Lawrence (2 Dill. 332), 284.
Parsons v. Thompson (1 H. Bl. 322), 46, 104.
Partridge v. Menck (2 Barb. Ch. 101; 47 Am. Dec. 281), 172.
Partridge v. Messer (14 Gray, 180), 94.
Patterson v. Commonwealth (11 Bush, 311; 21 Am. Rep. 220), 452.
Patterson v. Donner (48 Cal. 369), 97.
Patterson v. Hubbs (65 N. Car. 119), 697.
Patterson v. Kentucky (97 U. 501), 448, 451.
Payne v. Hook (7 Wall. 425, 430), 719.

[The references are to pages.]

Payne v. Western Ry. (81 Tenn. 507), 253.
Payne v. Western & Atl. R. Co. (13 Lea, 233, 507, 509), 242, 349.
Peabody v. Norfolk (98 Mass. 452, 458), 164.
Pearce v. Atwood (13 Mass. 342). 501.
Pearce v. Foote (113 Ill. 228, 239; 55 Am. Rep. 414), 267, 272, 280.
Pearce v. Wilson (111 Pa. St. 14; 56 Am. Rep. 243), 97.
Pearl v. Harris (121 Mass. 390), 95.
Pearsall v. Gt. Northern Ry. (161 U. S. 646, 676), 486. 490.
Pearson v. Railroad (62 N. H. 537), 488.
Pedrick v. Ripon (73 Wis. 622; 24 Am. & Eng. Corp. Cas. 422), 392.
Peed v. McKee (42 Iowa, 689), 79, 97.
Peik v. Chicago, etc. Ry. Co. (94 U. S. 164), 420.
Peltz v. Eichell (62 Mo. 171), 148, 173.
Pemberton v. Vaughan (L. R. 10 Q. B. 87, 89), 120, 124.
Pennoyer v. McConnaughy (140 U. S. 1, 10; 11 Sup. Ct. Rep. 699), 719.
Pennsylvania v. Wheeling & Belmont Bridge Co. (18 How. 421. 432), 397.
Pennsylvania Co. v. St. L., Alton, etc. Ry. Co. (118 U. S. 290, 291, 294), 481, 491.
Pennsylvania Ry. Co. v. Commonwealth (4 Cent. 501), 495.
Pennsylvania Ry. Co. v. Conn (29 Am. & Eng. Ry. Cas. 145; 7 Atl. Rep. 368), 502.
Pennsylvania Ry. Co. v. Nat. Ry. Co. (23 N. J. Eq. 441), 376.
Pensacola Tel. Co. v. Western, etc. Tel. Co. (96 U. S. 1, 9), 441, 444.
People v. Albany, etc. Ry. Co. (55 Barb. 345), 580, 583.
People v. Arensberg (105 N. Y. 123), 455.
People v. Arnold (46 Mich. 268), 259.
People v. Atty.-Gen. (1 Cal. 85), 693.
People v. B. & O. Ry. Co. (70 N. Y. 569, 570), 420.
People v. Babcock (11 Wend. 558, 586), 397, 398.
People v. Bartlett (6 Wend. 422), 703, 705.
People v. Bingham (82 Cal. 238, 242), 694.
People v. Bowen (30 Barb. 21; 21 N. Y. 517), 383.
People v. Bristol & Rensselaerville Turnpike Co. (23 Wend. 222, 240), 683, 690.
People v. Budd (117 N. Y. 1, 21, 22), 418, 434.
People v. Chi. Gas Trust Co. (130 Ill. 268, 292), 240, 510, 526, 527, 528, 532. 709.
People v. C. & A. R. R. Co. (130 Ill. 175, 182, 184), 83.
People v. Clark (4 Cow. 95), 702.
People v. Cunningham (1 Denio, 524), 81.
People v. Dernille (15 Mich. 164), 697.
People v. Ferry Co. (68 N. Y. 71), 712.
People v. Fisher (14 Wend. 9, 10; 28 Am. Dec. 501). 243, 244, 271, 288, 294, 318, 348, 567.
People v. Gordon (81 Mich. 806; 45 N. W. Rep. 658), 402.
People v. Grand River Bridge Co. (13 Colo. 11; 21 Pac. Rep. 898), 700.
People v. Hall (80 N. Y. 117), 687.
People v. Hills (35 N. Y. 452), 501.
People v. Hud. River Teleph. Co. (19 Abb. N. Cas. 466), 446.
People v. Jones (18 Wend. 604), 687.

[The references are to pages.]

People v. Kostka (4 N. Y. Crim. Rep. 434, 429), 304, 314, 326.
People v. Lambier (5 Denio, 9), 81.
People v. Manhattan Co. (9 Wend. 351), 684.
People v. Mather (4 Wend. 229; 21 Am. Dec. 122), 259.
People v. Mark (99 N. Y. 379), 455.
People v. Maynom (5 Mich. 146), 703.
People v. Melvin (Yate's Sel. Cas. 111; 2 Wheat. Cr. Cas. 262), 288.
People v. Milk Exchange (145 N. Y. 267), 567, 568.
People v. Miner (2 Lans. 396), 712.
People v. Mitchell (35 N. Y. 551), 466.
People v. Mulholland (82 N. Y. 324; 37 Am. Rep. 568), 401.
People v. N. River Sug. Ref. Co. (54 Hun, 354; 121 N. Y. 57, 582, 609, 622), 510, 525, 690.
People v. O'Brien (111 N. Y. 1, 64; 36 Am. & Eng. Ry. Cas. 78), 379, 480, 501.
People v. Perry (79 Cal. 106), 693.
People v. Pres., etc. Manhattan Co. (9 Wend. 337), 687.
People v. Rensselaer, etc. R. Co. (15 Wend. 113; 30 Am. Dec. 33, 37), 705, 707.
People v. Richardson (4 Cow. 113), 687.
People v. Russell (49 Mich. 617; 43 Am. Rep. 478), 452.
People v. Sheldon (139 N. Y. 251; 34 N. E. Rep. 785), 566, 568.
People v. Smith (5 N. Y. Cr. Rep. 513), 347.
People v. Squire (145 U. S. 175; 107 N. Y. 593; 1 Am. St. Rep. 894), 437.
People v. St. Louis (5 Gilman, 351), 713.
People v. St. L., A. & T. H. R. Co. (45 N. E. Rep. 824), 495.
People v. Stanford (77 Cal. 360, 364; 19 Pac. Rep. 694), 703.
People v. Stevens (71 N. Y. 527), 249.
People v. Trequier (1 Wheel. Cr. Cas. 142), 288.
People v. Vanderbilt (28 N. Y. 396; 26 N. Y. 287), 354, 713.
People v. Warden (144 N. Y. 529; 39 N. E. Rep. 686), 357.
People v. Wilzig (4 N. Y. Crim. Rep. 417, 403, 419, 423), 304, 314, 325, 349.
People's Home Sav. Bank v. Superior Court (104 Cal. 649; 38 Pac. Rep. 452), 579.
People's Railroad v. Memphis Railroad (10 Wall. 38), 368.
Peoria, etc. Ry. Co. v. Duggan (109 Ill. 537; 20 Am. & Eng. Ry. Cas. 489), 430.
Perkins v. Clay (58 N. H. 518), 110.
Perkins v. Lyman (9 Mass. 522), 112, 121, 129, 207, 211, 218.
Perkins v. Rogg (28 W. L. Bull. 32), 323.
Perkins v. St. Louis, etc. Ry. Co. (103 Mo. 52), 430.
Perls v. Saalfield (R. L. 2 Ch. 149), 180.
Perrine v. Chesapeake, etc. Co. (9 How. 172), 488, 502.
Perry v. Keene (56 N. H. 514), 466.
Perry v. Truefitt (6 Beav. 86), 173.
Peru v. Gleason (91 Ind. 566), 369.
Peter v. Kendall (6 B. & C. 703), 398.
Peterson v. Humphrey (4 Abb. Pr. 394), 173.
Phelps v. Thomas (6 Gray, 327), 94.
Philadelphia v. Street Ry. Co. (8 Phila. 648), 354.
Philadelphia & Baltimore Ry. Co. v. Quigley (21 How. 209), 236.
Philadelphia & W. & B. R. R. Co. v. Quigley (21 How. 202), 236.
Phillips v. Thorp (10 Ore. 494), 97.
Philpott v. St. George's Hospital (6 H. L. Cas. 338, 347), 45.
Philpotts v. Philpotts (10 C. B. 85), 94.

[The references are to pages.]

Phippen v. Stickney (3 Met. 384, 387), 100, 250, 577.
Piatt v. Oliver (3 McLean C. C. 27), 250.
Pickering v. Case (79 Ill. 328, 398), 264, 267, 272.
Pidcock v. Harrington (64 Fed. Rep. 821), 545, 714.
Pierce v. Bartram (Cowp. 269), 108.
Pierce v. Commonwealth (104 Pa. St. 150; 13 Am. & Eng. Ry. Cas. 74, 79), 465.
Pierce v. Drew (136 Mass. 81), 366.
Pierce v. Fuller (8 Mass. 223, 226), 112, 122, 125, 218.
Pierce v. Kimball (9 Me. 54; 23 Am. Dec. 537), 456.
Pierce v. Maryland (63 Md. 592), 455.
Pierce v. Woodward (6 Pick. 206), 121, 129, 132, 210.
Pilkington v. Scott (15 M. & W. 657; 15 L. J. Excheq. 329), 119, 121.
Piscataqua Bridge v. New Hampshire Bridge (7 N. H. 35, 59, 69), 372.
Pittsburgh Carbon Co. v. McMillan (119 N. Y. 46, 53, 466), 540, 573, 595, 597, 598.
P. C. & St. L. Ry. Co. v. Campbell (86 Ill. 443), 426.
Pittsburgh, etc. Ry. Co. v. Hollowell (65 Ind. 188), 333.
Pittsburgh, etc. R. R. Co. v. Kain (35 Ind. 291), 501.
Pittsburgh, etc. Ry. Co. v. Keokuk, etc. Co. (131 U. S. 371), 470.
Pittsburgh, Ft. W. & C. Ry. Co. v. Hazen (84 Ill. 36, 38), 333.
Pixley v. Boyd (79 Ill. 351), 267.
Pixley v. Boynton (79 Ill. 351), 277, 278.
Place v. Minster (65 N. Y. 89, 95), 228.
Plank Road Co. v. Douglass (9 N. Y. 444), 400.
Plaster v. Burger (5 Ind. 232), 471.
Polinsky v. People (73 N. Y. 65), 401.
Pontchartrain R. R. Co. v. N. O. Ry. Co. (11 La. Ann. 253), 361.
Pope v. Hanke (155 Ill. 617), 277, 280.
Poplett v. Stockdale (Ry. & M. 337; 2 C. & P. 198), 51, 78.
Porter v. Jones (52 Mo. 399, 402), 103.
Porter v. Jones (6 Coldw. 313), 79.
Porter v. Williams (9 N. Y. 142), 597.
Postal Tel. Cable Co. v. Adams (155 U. S. 688; 15 Sup. Ct. Rep. 268), 443.
Postal Tel. Cable Co. v. City of Baltimore (79 Md. 502; 29 Atl. Rep. 819), 446.
Powell v. Daniel (23 La. Ann. 289), 49.
Powell v. Pennsylvania (127 U. S. 678; 114 Pa. St. 265), 455.
Power v. Village of Athens (99 N. Y. 592, 598; 10 Am. & Eng. Corp. Cas. 54), 400.
Powers v. Skinner (34 Vt. 274, 276, 281), 55, 62.
Powers v. Strout (67 Iowa, 341; 25 N. W. Rep. 273), 133.
Pratt v. Draughon (2 La. Ann. 194), 94.
Prescott & A. C. R. R. v. Atchison, T. & S. F. Ry. (73 Fed. Rep. 438), 555, 603.
President, etc. v. Jackson (7 Blackf. 36), 501.
Presbury v. Fisher (18 Mo. 50), 178, 201.
Presbyterian Church v. Mayor, etc. (5 Cow. 538), 368.
Price v. Green (16 M. & W. 346; 16 L. J. Excheq. 108), 148, 201, 215.
Printing, etc. Co. v. Sampson (L. R. 19 Eq. 462, 464, 465), 135, 167, 168, 178, 542.
Proctor v. Sargent (2 Man. & G. 20; 2 Scott, N. R. 289), 21, 23, 24, 119, 128, 198.

[The references are to pages]

Prosser v. Wapello (18 Iowa, 327), 392, 393.
Prost v. More (40 Cal. 347), 243.
Providence Bank v. Billings (4 Pet. 514, 562), 422.
Providence Coal Co. v. Providence & W. R. Co. (1 Int. Com. Rep. 363; 1 Int. Com. Com. 107), 587.
Prudential Assurance Co. v. Knott (L. R. 10 Ch. 142), 352.
Pueblo & A. V. R. Co. v. Taylor (6 Colo. 1; 45 Am. Rep. 512; 6 Am. & Eng. R. Cas. 474), 502.

Q.

Queen v. Paty (2 Ld. Raym. 1105), 715.
Queen's Ins. Co. v. State (86 Tex. 250; 24 S. W. Rep. 397), 261.
Quincy v. White (63 N. Y. 370), 560.

R.

Rackeman v. Riverbank Imp. Co. (167 Mass. 1; 44 N. E. Rep. 990), 157.
Racine, etc. R. R. Co. v. Farmers' Loan & Trust Co. (49 Ill. 331), 501.
Ragan v. Aiken (9 Lea, 609; 42 Am. Rep. 684), 589.
Railroad Commission Cases (116 U. S. 307, 325, 331; 6 Sup. Ct. Rep. 334, 348, 349, 388, 391, 1191), 421, 426, 720.
Railroad Co. v. Collins (48 Ga. 582), 528.
Railroad Co. v. Davis (2 Dev. & Bat. 451, 468), 419.
Railroad Co. v. Gibbes (142 U. S. 386, 391; 12 Sup. Ct. Rep. 255), 720.
Railroad Co. v. Hinsdale (45 Ohio St. 556, 573), 528.
Railroad Co. v. Howard (7 Wall. 413), 501.
Railroad Co. v. Husen (95 U. S. 465), 452.
Railroad Co. v. Maine (96 U. S. 499), 366.
Railroad Co. v. Mayor (1 Hill, 562), 369.
Railroad Co. v. McDonald (53 Miss. 240), 466.
Railroad Co. v. Nicholas (93 Ala. 92; 12 So. Rep. 723), 579.
Railroad Co. v. Railroad Co. (31 N. J. Eq. 475), 528.
Railroad Co. v. Ryan (11 Kan. 602), 101.
Railroad Co. v. Smith (62 Ill. 268), 266.
Railway v. County of Otoe (16 Wall. 667), 466.
Railway Co. v. Broom (6 Excheq. 314), 236.
Railway Co. v. Ellis (165 U. S. 150, 154; 17 Sup. Ct. Rep. 255), 720.
Railway Co. v. Gill (156 U. S. 649, 657; 15 Sup. Ct. Rep. 484), 721.
Railway Co. v. Mayes (58 Ark. 397), 86.
Railway Co. v. Spangler (44 Ohio St. 471), 86.
Railway Co. v. Wellman (143 U. S. 339, 344; 12 Sup. Ct. Rep. 400), 721.
Railway Co. v. Wynn (88 Tenn. 320; 14 S. W. Rep. 311), 86.
Raleigh v. Sorrell (1 Jones, 49), 455.
Ramsdell v. Edgarton (8 Met. 227), 94.
Randal v. C. & D. Canal Co. (1 Harr. 232), 95.
Randall v. Van Vechten (19 Johns. 60), 501.
Ranger v. Great Western Ry. Co. (5 H. L. Cas. 72, 86), 237.
Rannie v. Irvine (7 Man. & G. 676, 969). 23, 119, 161.
Ransome v. Eastern, etc. R. W. Co. (1 C. B. (N. S.) 437), 588.

[The references are to pages]

Rawson v. Pratt (91 Ind. 9, 16), 214.

Raymond v. Leavitt (46 Mich. 447, 450, 452; 41 Am. Rep. 170), 270, 272, 274.

Reagan v. Farmers' Loan & Trust Co. (154 U. S. 362; 14 Sup. Ct. Rep. 1047), 422, 423, 426.

Reed v. Home Savings Bank (13 Mass. 443), 235.

Reed v. Jones (6 Wis. 680), 583.

Reed v. St. L., K. C. & N. Ry. Co. (60 Mo. 199), 333.

Regan v. Trust Co. (154 U. S. 362, 391; 14 Sup. Ct. Rep. 1047), 719, 721.

Reg. v. Archdall (3 N. & P. 696; 8 A. & E. 281), 684.

Reg. v. Barrett (18 L. J. 440), 314.

Reg. v. Bauld (13 Cox Cr. Cas. 282), 323.

Reg. v. Best (2 Ld. Raym. 1167), 259.

Reg. v. Bunn (12 Cox Cr. Cas. 316), 288, 294.

Reg. v. Charlesworth (16 Q. B. 1012), 377.

Reg. v. Druitt (10 Cox Cr. Cas. 592, 593), 288, 294, 318, 323, 325.

Reg. v. Duffield (5 Cox Cr. Cas. 404, 432), 288, 318.

Reg. v. Gompertz (9 Q. B. 824), 259.

Reg. v. Harris (1 Car. & M. 661), 294.

Reg. v. Hewitt (5 Cox Cr. Cas. 162), 345.

Reg. v. Heymann (12 Cox Cr. Cas. 383), 259.

Reg. v. Hibbert (13 Cox Cr. Cas. 82, 404), 288, 323.

Reg. v. Longton Gas Co. (2 El. & El. 651), 377.

Reg. v. O'Connell (11 Cl. & F. 234), 317.

Reg. v. Parnell (14 Cox Cr. Cas. 474, 514), 317, 322.

Reg. v. Rowlands (17 Ad. & El. 670, 671, 687), 294, 345.

Reg. v. Rowlands (5 Cox Cr. Cas. 466, 490), 307.

Reg. v. Rowlands (17 Q. B. 671), 259.

Reg. v. Saffron Walden (9 Q. B. 76), 142.

Reg. v. Selby (5 Cox Cr. Cas. 495), 294, 323.

Reg. v. Seward (1 Ad. & El. 706), 259.

Reg. v. Shepherd (11 Cox Cr. Cas. 325), 323, 326, 345.

Reg. v. Train (2 B. & S. 640; 110 E. C. L. 640), 377.

Reife v. Com. Ins. Co. (5 Mo. App. 173), 94.

Rensington v. Philadelphia (13 Pa. St. 76), 358.

Rensselaer & Saratoga Ry. Co v. Davis (43 N. Y. 137), 487.

Renwick v. Morris (3 Hill, 62; 7 Hill, 575), 81.

Reynolds v. Bridge (6 El. & B. 528), 128.

Reynolds v. Everett (144 N. Y. 189; 39 N. E. Rep. 72), 304, 318.

Rex v. Byerdike (1 M. & S. 179), 244.

Rex v. Carmarthen (2 Burr. 869), 698.

Rex v. City of London (3 Hay. Towns. St. Tr. 545), 705.

Rex v. Berenges (3 M. & S. 67), 270, 276.

Rex v. Eccles (1 Leach Cr. Cas. 274), 294, 317, 320.

Rex v. Harrison (3 Burr. 1323, 1328), 120.

Rex v. Hilbers (2 Chitty, 163), 270.

Rex v. Journeymen Tailors (8 Md. 10), 288.

Rex v. Kinnersley (1 Str. 193), 259.

Rex v. Leigh (4 Burr. 2146, 2143), 687, 702, 703.

Rex v. Marsdon (3 Burr. 1817), 689.

Rex v. Mawbey (6 T. R. 619), 294

[The references are to pages.]

Rex v. Mayor & Alderman of Hartford (1 Ld. Raym. 426; 3 Salk. 374), 707.
Rex v. Mayor of London (1 Show. 274, 280), 707.
Rex v. Newland (Sayres, 96), 687, 702.
Rex v. Trinity House (Gill, 86), 684.
Rex v. Waddington (1 East, 143, 167), 15, 270.
Rex v. Williams (1 Burr. 402), 684, 699.
Rhodes v. Neal (64 Ga. 704), 97.
Rhymney Iron Co. v. Rhymney A. Co. (6 Ry. & T. Cas. 60), 589, 590.
Rice v. Manley (66 N. Y. 82), 301.
Rice v. Rockefeller (134 N. Y. 174), 517, 596.
Rice v. Rock Island, etc. Ry. Co. (21 Ill. 93), 501.
Rice v. Williams (32 Fed. Rep. 437), 51.
Rice v. Wood (113 Mass. 133), 250.
Rich v. Braxton (158 U. S. 375, 405; 15 Sup. Ct. Rep. 1006), 718.
Richards v. Am. Desk & Seating Co. (87 Wis. 503; 58 N. W. Rep. 787, 789), 129, 138, 140.
Richardson v. Buhl (77 Mich. 632, 635, 658; 27 Am. & Eng. Corp. Cas. 256; 43 N. W. Rep. 1102), 510, 538, 541, 575.
Richardson v. Chicago, etc. Ry. Co. (61 Wis. 596; 21 N. W. Rep. 49), 86.
Richardson v. Crandall (38 How. Pr. 142), 243.
Richardson v. Mellish (2 Bligh, 229, 242, 252; 2 Bing. 125), 41, 43, 68.
Richardson v. Peacock (26 N. J. Eq. 40; 28 N. J. Eq. 151; 33 N. J. Eq. 597), 125, 132, 215.
Richardson v. Sibley (11 Allen, 65), 502.
Richmond v. Dubuque & S. C. R. R. Co. (26 Iowa, 191, 201), 43.
Richmond Gas Light Co. v. Middleton (59 N. Y. 228), 383, 389.
Richmond County Gas Light Co. v. Middletown (59 N. Y. 231), 368.
Richmond, etc. Ry. Co. v. Louisa Ry. Co. (13 How. 71), 361.
Richmond, etc. R. R. Co. v. Payne (86 Va. 481), 86.
Richmond, etc. Ry. Co. v. Trammel (53 Fed. Rep. 196), 426.
Richter v. Jour. Tailors' Union (24 W. L. Bull. 189), 323.
Ricker v. Am. Loan & Trust Co. (140 Mass. 346), 518.
Ricketts v. Harvey (106 Ind. 564), 79, 97.
Rider v. Kidder (10 Ves. 366), 51.
Rider Life Raft Co. v. Roach (97 N. Y. 378), 523.
Rio Grande R. R. Co. v. Brownsville (45 Tex. 88), 354.
Ringgold v. Tyson (3 H. & J. 172), 51.
Rives v. Lawrence (41 Ga. 283).
Road Co. v. Sanford (164 U. S. 578, 584, 594, 595, 597; 17 Sup. Ct. Rep. 198), 721.
Robbins v. Webb (68 Ala. 393), 154.
Robert v. Corning (89 N. Y. 225, 235), 559.
Robertson v. Parks (76 Md. 118; 2 Atl. Rep. 411, 413), 231.
Robertson v. Robertson (65 Ala. 610), 68.
Robinson v. Byron (1 Bro. Ch. 588), 302.
Robinson v. Green (3 Met. 159, 161), 152.
Robinson v. Jones (14 Fla. 256), 698.
Rockford, R. I. & St. L. Ry. v. Rogers (62 Ill. 346), 426.
Roderiquez v. Bienvenue (22 La. Ann. 300), 48.

[The references are to pages.]

Rogan v. Wabash Ry. Co. (51 Mo. App. 665), 86, 93.
Rogers v. Burlington (3 Wall. 664), 466.
Rogers v. Evart (17 N. Y. Supl. 264, 268), 304, 326, 327, 356.
Rogers v. Kingston (10 Moore, 102; 2 Bing. 441), 46, 94.
Rogers v. Maddocks (L. R. 3 Ch. 346).
Rogers v. Perry (B. R. trin.; 11 Jac. 1 Rot. 223; 2 Bulst. 136), 19, 22, 118.
Roll v. Raguet (4 Ohio, 400), 79, 97.
Roller v. Ott (14 Kan. 609), 215.
Rool v. Long Island R. Co. (114 N. Y. 300; 21 N. E. Rep. 403; 40 Am. & Eng. R. Cas. 55; 4 L. R. A. 331; 23 N. Y. S. R. 226), 586, 589.
Ropes v. Upton (125 Mass. 258), 129, 218.
Rose v. Truax (21 Barb. 361), 55, 60.
Ross v. Sadgbeer (21 Wend. 116), 113.
Roundtree v. Baker (52 Ill. 241), 48.
Roundtree v. Smith (108 U. S. 269), 278, 283.
Rousillon v. Rousillon (L. R. 14 Ch. D. 351), 44, 25, 136, 140, 145, 198, 204, 212, 215.
Royal Bank of India's Case (L. R. 4 Ch. App. 252, 257), 535.
Rudolf v. Winters (7 Neb. 125), 267.
Ruggles v. Ill. (108 U. S. 526, 538, 531), 456, 458.
Russell v. De Grand (15 Mass. 35), 94.
Ryder v. Alton, etc. Ry. Co. (13 Ill. 516), 583.

S.

Sackett v. New Albany (88 Ind. 473; 2 Am. & Eng. Corp. Cas. 85; 45 Am. Rep. 467), 392.
Saginaw Gas Light Co. v. City of Saginaw (28 Fed. Rep. 529), 369.
St. Joseph & D. R. R. Co. v. Ryan (11 Kan. 602), 83.
St. Joseph Tp. v. Rogers (16 Wall. 664), 466.
St. Louis v. McCoy (18 Mo. 238), 401.
St. Louis v. St. Louis Gas Light Co. (70 Mo. 69), 542.
St. Louis, J. & C. R. R. Co. v. Mathers (104 Ill. 257), 83.
St. Louis, etc. Ry. Co. v. Williams (49 Ark. 492), 431.
St. L. Railroad v. Terre Haute Railroad (145 U. S. 393), 491.
St. L. & San Fran. Ry. v. Gill (156 U. S. 649, 657), 421.
St., L. V. & T. H. R. R. Co. v. Funk (85 Ill. 460).
St. Michael's Ch. v. Co. Bright (N. P. 121; 7 Pa. L. J. 181), 358.
St. Tammany Water Works Co. v. New Orleans Water Works Co. (120 U. S. 6), 386.
Sainter v. Ferguson (7 Com. B. 716; 13 Jur. 828; 18 L. J. Com. P. 217), 121, 128, 132, 184.
Salinas v. Stillman (66 Fed. Rep. 677; 14 C. C. A. 5), 64.
Salt Co. v. Guthrie (35 Ohio St. 672, 666), 538, 565.
Salter v. Howard (43 Ga. 601), 349.
Sampson v. Shaw (101 Mass. 145, 105), 275, 565.
Samuels v. Evening Mail Assn. (9 Hun, 288), 235.
Samuels v. Oliver (130 Ill. 73), 283.
Sanderson v. Goodrich (46 Barb. 611), 94.
San Diego Water Co. v. Flume Co. (108 Cal. 549), 390.
Sandige v. Sanderson (21 La. Ann. 757), 48.
San Francisco Gas Light Co. v. Dunn (62 Cal. 580), 369.

[The references are to pages.]

Santa Clara Co. v. So. Pac. Ry. Co. (118 U. S. 394, 396; 6 Sup. Ct. Rep. 1132), 720.
Santa Clara Val. Mill, etc. Co. v. Hayes (76 Cal. 387; 9 Am. St. Rep. 211), 541, 563.
Saratoga Co. Bank v. King (44 N. Y. 89, 87), 148, 243, 568.
Satterfield v. Spurlock (21 La. Ann. 771), 48.
Satterlee v. Jones (3 Duer, 102), 46.
Sav. Fund v. Phila. (31 Pa. St. 175), 368,
Sawyer v. Taggart (14 Bush, 727, 734), 269.
Saxby v. Easterbrook (L. R. 3 C. P. D. 339), 352.
Sayles v. Sayles (21 N. H. 312), 97.
Schneider v. Turner (130 Ill. 28), 277.
Schofield v. Lake Shore, etc. Ry. Co. (43 Ohio St. 571; 3 N. E. Rep. 907), 589.
Schut v. Chicago, etc. Ry. Co. (70 Mich. 433), 431.
Schwartz v. Tyson (4 H. & J. 288), 94.
Schwenk v. Wyckhoff (46 N. J. Eq. 560; 20 Atl. Rep. 259), 46.
Scott v. Brown (L. R. 2 Q. B. 724), 52.
Scott v. Donald (165 U. S. 58, 68; 17 Sup. Ct. Rep. 265), 719.
Scott v. Neely (140 U. S. 106; 11 Sup. Ct. Rep. 712), 719.
Scudder v. Andrews (2 McLean, 464), 94.
Sedgwick v. Stanton (14 N. Y. 289), 62.
Seeligson v. Lewis (65 Tex. 215; 57 Am. Rep. 593), 265, 277.
Selby v. Wilmington, etc. R. Co. (113 N. Car. 588; 18 S. E. Rep. 88), 92.
Sewell v. Jones (1 W. & S. 129), 250.
Seymour v. Greenwood (6 H. & N. 359), 236.
Shackle v. Baker (14 Ves. 468), 108, 201, 213.
Sharp v. Whitesides (19 Fed. Rep. 156, 160), 463.
Sharpless v. Mayor of Philadelphia (21 Pa. St. 149), 466, 598.
Shaw v. Reed (3 Me. 105, 109), 79, 96.
Shaw v. Spooner (9 N. H. 197, 198), 79, 97.
Shawmut Bank v. P. & M. R. R. Co. (31 Vt. 491), 222.
Shepang Voting Trust Cases (66 Conn. 553; 24 Atl. Rep. 32), 579.
Shepard v. Milwaukee Gas Co. (6 Wis. 539), 542.
Shepherd v. Commissioners (59 Ga. 535), 456.
Sherman v. Barrett (1 McMull. 147), 51.
Sherman v. Wilder (106 Mass. 537), 94.
Sherman, Hall & Co. v. Pa. Ry. Co. (3 Am. & Eng. R. R. Cas. 274), 333.
Sherry v. Perkins (147 Mass. 212; 9 Am. St. Rep. 689; 17 N. E. Rep. 307), 322, 323, 352.
Shiffner v. Gordon (12 East, 296), 94.
Shorter v. Smith (9 Ga. 517), 371.
Shrewsbury & Birmingham R. Co. v. London & N. W. R. C. (L. R. 17 Q. B. 652; 9 Eng. L. & Eq. 394), 553.
Shriver v. Sioux City & St. P. R. Co. (24 Minn. 506), 88.
Siter v. Streets (7 Ind. 132), 94.
Skinner v. Ritch (10 Cox Cr. Cas. 493), 345.
Skinner v. Oakes (10 Mo. App. 45), 173.
Slaughter House Cases (16 Wall. 36), 318, 349, 364, 407, 410.
Sloan v. Mo. Pac. Ry. Co. (61 Mo. 24), 423.
Slocum v. Wooley (43 N. J. Eq. 451; 11 Atl. Rep. 264), 82.

[The references are to pages.]

Sliddell v. Grandjean (111 U. S. 412), 491.
Small v. Minneapolis Electro Matrix Co. (45 Minn. 264, 267), 710.
Smalley v. Green (52 Iowa, 241; 35 Am. Rep. 267), 129, 132, 133.
Smead v. Indianapolis, etc. R. W. Co. (11 Ind. 104), 501.
Smith v. Applegate (23 N. J. L. 352, 358), 46.
Smith v. Barrie (56 Mich. 314; 22 N. W. Rep. 816), 158.
Smith v. Birmingham & Staffordshire Gas Light Co. (1 A. & E. 526), 236.
Smith v. Boubier (7 Pa. St. 325), 277, 283.
Smith v. Bromley (2 Doug. 696), 94.
Smith v. City of Albany (7 Lans. 141), 94.
Smith v. Cuff (6 Maule & Selw. 160), 95.
Smith v. Everett (27 Beav. 446), 215.
Smith v. Freeman (71 Ind. 85), 318.
Smith v. Humphreys (88 Me. 345; 34 Atl. Rep. 166), 78.
Smith v. Louisville, etc. R. Co. (75 Ala. 449), 431.
Smith v. Martin (80 Ind. 260), 215.
Smith v. McWaters (25 La. Ann. 431), 48.
Smith v. Morse (2 Cal. 524), 369.
Smith v. People (25 Ill. 17), 294.
Smith v. San Francisco & N. P. Ry. Co. (115 Cal. 584; 47 Pac. Rep. 582), 582.
Smith v. Sheeley (12 Wall. 358), 501.
Smith v. Smith (4 Wend. 468), 132, 184.
Smith v. Townsend (109 Mass. 500), 100, 579.
Smith v. Ullman (58 Md. 183; 42 Am. Rep. 329, 331), 249, 250.
Smith v. Whyte (L. R. 1 Eq. 626; 35 L. J. Ch. 45; 14 W. R. 510; 14 L. T. (N. S.) 350), 51.
Smith v. Wilcox (19 Barb. 581), 94.
Smith's Appeal (113 Pa. St. 579, 590), 115, 150.
Smith's Case (4 Mod. 53), 705.
Smithson v. Dillon (16 Ind. 169), 501.
Smyth v. Ames (18 Sup. Ct. Rep. 418, 423), 718, 719, 720, 721, 722, 723, 724, 725.
Smyth v. Griffin (14 L. J. Ch. 28; 12 L. J. Ch. 193), 51.
Snider v. Willey (33 Mich. 483), 79, 97.
Snow v. Wheeler (113 Mass. 179, 185, 186), 294, 309, 318, 345.
Soda Fountain Co. v. Green (69 Fed. Rep. 333), 166.
Solomons v. Laing (12 Beav. 339; 6 Eng. Ry. Cas. 289), 491, 527.
Soon Hing v. Crowley (113 U. S. 703, 709), 454, 455.
South, etc. Ry. Co. v. Morris (65 Ala. 193), 431.
Southard v. Boyd (51 N. Y. 177), 55.
Southern Express Co. v. Caperton (44 Ala. 101), 92.
Southern Pacific Co. v. United States (28 Ct. Cl. 77), 598.
Spaulding v. Ewing (145 Pa. St. 375; 24 Atl. Rep. 219), 55, 60.
Spaulding v. Lowell (23 Pick. 71), 455.
Spicer v. Hoop (51 Ind. 305, 365), 178, 201.
Spier v. Lambdin (45 Ga. 319), 193.
Spies v. People (122 Ill. 1; 3 Am. St. Rep. 320), 318, 345.
Spinks v. Davis (32 Miss. 152), 102.
Spofford v. Boston, etc. Ry. (128 Mass. 326), 588.
Sprague v. Mo. Pac. R. Co. (34 Kan. 347; 8 Pac. Rep. 465), 92.
Springfield v. Connecticut River R. R. (4 Cush. 63), 354.

[The references are to pages.]

Springhead Spinning Co. v. Riley (L. R. 6 Eq. 551), 294, 345, 352.
Spring Valley Water Works v. Schottler (110 U. S. 347, 354), 432.
Squire v. Squire (3 Stew. Eq. 627), 102.
Stack v. O'Hara (98 Pa. St. 213), 256.
Stafford v. Shortweed (62 Iowa, 524; 17 N. W. Rep. 756), 132.
Staines v. Wainwright (6 Bing. N. Cas. 174), 45.
Stamford v. Stamford Horse R. R. Co. (56 Conn. 381), 354, 712.
Stanley v. Davenport (54 Iowa, 463; 37 Am. Rep. 216), 379.
Stanton v. Allen (5 Denio, 434), 243, 245, 470, 538, 568.
Stanton v. Parker (19 Hun, 61), 103.
Stanton v. Small (3 Sandf. 230), 277.
Star Brewery Co. v. Primas (163 Ill. 652; 45 N. E. Rep. 145), 159.
State v. Ah Chew (16 Nev. 50), 456.
State v. Am. Cotton Oil Trust (40 La. Ann. 8; 19 Am. & Eng. Corp. Cas. 448), 595.
State v. Ashley (1 Ark. 279), 684.
State v. Atchison & Nebraska Ry. Co. (24 Neb. 143, 162; 32 Am. & Eng. Ry. Cas. 388), 480.
State v. Bartlett (30 Me. 132, 134), 229, 259.
State v. Baughman (38 Ohio St. 455), 694.
State v. Beecher (15 Ohio, 723), 703.
State v. Bell (34 Ohio St. 194), 379.
State v. Bell Telephone Co. (36 Ohio St. 296; 38 Am. Rep. 584; 23 Fed. Rep. 539; 8 Am. & Eng. Corp. Cas. 7), 446.
State v. Bieler (87 Ind. 320), 697.
State v. Bishop (128 Mo. 373; 31 S. W. Rep. 9), 358.
State v. Boston, etc. R. Co. (25 Vt. 433), 695.
State v. Boyd (84 Mo. 198, 201), 699.
State v. Brown (5 R. I. 6), 699.
State v. Buchanan (5 Har. & J. 317), 257.
State v. Burnham (15 N. H. 396), 294, 318.
State v. Burnheim (15 N. H. 401), 321.
State v. Cawood (3 Stew. 360), 260.
State v. Chicago, etc. Ry. Co. (38 Minn. 281; 37 N. W. Rep. 782), 426.
State v. Cincinnati Gas Light & Coke Co. (8 Ohio St. 262), 704, 383.
State v. City of Cincinnati (23 Ohio St. 445, 465), 702.
State v. Claggett (73 Mo. 388), 693.
State v. Collier (72 Mo. 13), 73.
State v. Columbus Gas Co. (34 Ohio St. 572), 383.
State v. Commercial Bank (10 Ohio, 535), 702.
State v. Cook (38 Vt. 439), 269.
State v. Crowley (41 Wis. 271), 318.
State v. Cowan (29 Mo. 330), 401.
State v. Dayton & S. E. Ry. Co. (36 Ohio St. 434), 354, 713.
State v. Debesseline (1 McCord, 52), 697.
State v. Dent (129 U. S. 114; 25 W. Va. 1), 456.
State v. Divine (98 N. Car. 798), 431.
State v. Donaldson (32 N. J. L. 151, 155, 157; 90 Am. Dec. 649), 297, 318, 322, 348.
State v. Douglas Co. Road Co. (10 Ore. 198, 200), 699.
State v. Elting (29 Kan. 397, 401), 74.
State v. Fisher (52 Mo. 174), 456.

[The references are to pages.]

State v. Fremont, etc. Ry. Co. (22 Neb. 313; 35 N. W. Rep. 118; 23 Neb. 113; 36 N. W. Rep. 308), 426.
State v. Gas Co. (34 Ohio St. 572), 383.
State v. Gas Light Co. (18 Ohio St. 262, 291), 368, 704.
State v. Gleason (12 Fla. 265), 703.
State v. Glidden (55 Conn. 46, 74, 77: 3 Atl. Rep. 890), 230, 313, 314, 315, 321, 322, 353.
State v. Goodnight (70 Tex. 682), 355.
State v. Graham (13 Kan. 136), 695.
State v. Haumer (42 N. J. L. 435), 697.
State v. Hartford & N. H. Ry. Co. (29 Conn. 538, 547), 473.
State v. Hurley (54 Me. 562), 426.
State v. Holcomb (68 Iowa, 107; 56 Am. Rep. 852), 401.
State v. Jenkins (25 Mo. 484), 697.
State v. Johnson (52 Ind. 197), 46.
State v. Jones (13 Iowa, 269), 259.
State v. Jones (33 Vt. 443), 259.
State v. Kupferle (44 Mo. 154), 703.
State v. Leiber (11 Iowa, 407), 456.
State v. London (91 Ind. 351), 698.
State v. Lounger (1 Dev. L. 357), 259.
State v. Lowry (49 N. J. L. 391), 401.
State v. Mayberry (48 Me. 218), 257.
State v. Marshall (64 N. H. 549; 15 Atl. Rep. 210), 455.
State v. McConnell (3 Lea, 332), 697, 699.
State v. McDaniel (22 Ohio St. 354, 360, 361), 687, 702.
State v. Miller (3 Mo. 470), 392.
State v. Milwaukee Gas Light Co. (29 Wis. 454), 366, 383.
State v. Minn. Thresher Mfg. Co. (40 Minn. 213, 224), 687.
State v. Morris & Essex R. Co. (3 Zab. 367), 236.
State v. Mott (61 Md. 297; 4 Am. & Eng. Corp. Cas. 334; 48 Am. Rep. 105), 401.
State v. Neb. Distilling Co. (29 Neb. 700; 29 Am. & Eng. Corp. Cas. 656), 510, 541, 542, 575, 708.
State v. New Brunswick (30 N. J. L. 395), 368.
State v. Norton (33 N. J. L. 40, 46), 228.
State v. Noyes (25 Vt. 415), 257, 259, 294, 318.
State v. Olin (23 Wis. 309).
State v. Orr (68 Conn. 101), 403.
State v. Paul (5 Stew. & P. 40), 684.
State v. Phips (50 Kan. 609; 31 Pac. Rep. 1097), 592, 594.
State v. Portland, etc., R. Co. (58 N. H. 113), 684.
State v. Potter (28 Iowa, 256, 554), 257, 258.
State v. Purdy (36 Wis. 213, 222; 17 Am. Rep. 485), 73, 74, 99.
State v. Real Estate Bank (5 Ark. 595; 41 Am. Dec. 109), 684.
State v. Rickey (9 N. J. L. 293), 260.
State v. Ripley (31 Me. 386), 259.
State v. Rowley (12 Conn. 112), 318.
State v. Ruckley (2 Blackf. 249), 501.
State v. Schneirle (5 Rich. 299), 697.
State v. Standard Oil Co. (49 Ohio St. 137, 179, 184; 30 N. E. Rep. 279), 3, 4, 470, 508, 510.
State v. St. Med. Ex. Bd. (32 Minn. 324), 456.
State v. St. Paul & Sioux City Ry. Co. (35 Minn. 222), 695, 697.
State v. Stanley, (52 Ark. 178; 12 S. W. Rep. 327), 52.
State v. Stein (13 Neb. 529), 698.
State v. Stewart (59 Vt. 279, 285), 259, 289, 274, 298, 321, 322, 693.
State v. Straw (42 N. H. 392), 260.

[The references are to pages.]

State v. Teleph. Co. (36 Ohio St. 296, 311; 38 Am. Rep. 583), 450, 452.
State v. Tipton (109 Ind. 73), 698.
State v. Town of Harrison (46 N. J. L. 79), 386.
State v. Vanderbilt (37 Ohio St. 590, 643), 483.
State v. Winston (66 Iowa), 143, 146), 257.
State Bank v. Hasting (15 Wis. 78), 106.
State Bank v. State (1 Blackf. 267, 272, 280), 689, 706.
State *ex rel.* Hequembourg (38 Mo. 535), 699.
State *ex rel.* v. Jones (16 Fla. 306), 702.
State *ex rel.* v. Standard Oil Co. (49 Ohio St. 137), 691.
State *ex rel.* Stewart v. McIlhany, (32 Mo. 382), 699.
State *ex rel.* v. Townley (56 Mo. 107), 699.
State *ex rel.* v. Vail (53 Mo. 97), 699.
State *ex rel.* Young v. Buskirk, (43 Mo. 111), 693.
State Freight-Tax Case (15 Wall. 232, 275), 548.
Steam Nav. Co. v. Weed (17 Barb. 378), 501.
Stearns v. Barrett (1 Pick. 443), 110, 115, 116, 218.
Stearns Co. v. St. Cloud, M. & A. Ry. (36 Minn. 425), 354.
Steers v. Liverpool, etc. Steamship Co. (57 N. Y. 1), 93.
Stein v. Bienville Water Supply Co. (141 U. S. 67), 388.
Steinfeld v. Levy (16 Abb. Pr. (N. S.) 26), 51.
Steinweg v. Erie R. Co. (43 N. Y. 123), 92.
Stephens v. Southern Pacific Co. (109 Cal. 86; 41 Pac. Rep. 783), 49.
Sternberg v. O'Brien (48 N. J. Eq. 370, 372; 22 Atl. Rep. 348), 183, 198.
Stewart v. Challacombe (11 Ill. App. 379), 129.
Stewart v. Erie & W. Transp. Co. (17 Minn. 372), 555, 709.
Stewart v. Lehigh, etc. R. R. Co. (38 N. J. L. 505), 589.
Stewart v. Schall (65 Md. 299; 57 Am. Rep. 327), 280.
Stewart v. Polk Co. (30 Iowa, 9), 466.
Stewart v. Simpson (1 Wend. 376, 379), 349.
Stewart's Appeal, (56 Pa. St. 413), 502.
Stiff v. Cassell (2 Jur. (N.S.) 348), 177.
Stilson v. Stilson (46 Conn. 15), 97.
Stines v. Dorman (25 Ohio St. 580), 201.
Stockdale v. Onwhyn (2 C. & P. 163), 52.
Stockton v. Central R. R. Co. (50 N. J. Eq. 52; 24 Atl. Rep. 964), 538, 712.
Stokes v. Anderson (118 Ind. 533; 21 N. E. Rep. 331), 53.
Stone v. Dennis (3 Port. 231), 95.
Stone v. Farmers', etc. Co. (116 U. S. 307; 6 Sup. Ct. Rep. 334), 423.
Stone v. Lidderdale (2 Anst. 233), 104,
Stone v. Natchez, etc. Ry. Co. (62 Miss. 646; 21 Am. & Eng. Ry. Cas. 6), 426.
Stone v. Yazoo, etc. Ry. Co. (62 Miss. 607; 21 Am. & Eng. Ry. Cas. 6; 52 Am. Rep. 193), 426.
Story v. Solomon (6 Daly, 531).
Stoutenburgh v. Lybrand (13 Ohio St. 228), 97.
Strait v. Harrow Co. (51 Fed. Rep. 819; 18 N. Y. Supl. 224), 166, 538, 569, 572, 575.
Strait v. Nat. Harrow Co. (18 N. Y. Supl. 224), 595.

[The references are to pages.]

Strange v. Hill, etc. Ry. Co. (54 Iowa, 669), 377.
Straus v. Eagle Ins. Co. (5 Ohio St. 59), 528.
St. Ry. Co. v. West Side St. Ry. Co. (48 Mich. 433), 379.
Studebaker v. White (31 Ind. 211), 129, 201.
Sturgis v. Crowninshield (4 Wheat. 197), 373.
Stuyvesant v. Mayor, etc. of New York (7 Cow. 588), 368.
Sugden v. Crossland (3 Sm. & Gif. 193), 102.
Summitt v. State (8 Lea, 413), 498.
Sumner v. Marcy (3 W. & M. 105), 488, 527.
Sumner v. Sumner (54 Mo. 340), 79, 97.
Sun Mut. Ins. Co. v. Mayor, etc. (8 N. Y. 253), 501.
Sutton v. Head (5 S. W. Rep. 410), 158.
Swanger v. Mayberry (59 Cal. 91), 94.
Swanson v. Kirby (98 Ga. 586; 26 S. E. Rep. 71), 209.
Sweeney v. McLeod. (15 Ore. 330; 15 Pac. Rep. 275), 56.
Swift v. Phila., etc. R. Co. (58 Fed. Rep. 59; 64 Fed. Rep. 59), 590.
Sykes v. Sykes (3 B. & C. 541; 10 E. C. L. 176), 173.
Syracuse Water Co. v. City of Syracuse (116 N. Y. 167, 178, 180), 389.

T.

Talcott v. Brackett (5 Bradw. 60), 110.
Tallis v. Tallis, (1 El. & Bl. 391, 411), 21, 24, 25,119, 132, 178, 219.
Talmage v. East River Bank (26 N. Y. 105), 154.
Talmage v. Pell (7 N. Y. 348), 527.
Tappan v. Albany Brewing Co. (80 Cal. 570), 99.
Tatum v. Arnold (42 N. J. Eq. 60), 264.
Taylor v. Blanchard (13 Allen. 370; 90 Am. Dec. 203), 115, 129, 132, 139, 165, 215, 217.
Taylor v. Carpenter (2 Sandf. Ch. 604; 42 Am. Dec. 114), 172.
Taylor v. Earle (8 Hun, 1), 491, 527.
Taylor v. Jaques (106 Mass. 291), 79, 96.
Taylor v. Wait, (54 Vt. 469), 249.
Telegraph Co. v. Texas (105 U. S. 460, 464), 442, 548.
Temperton v. Russell (4 Rep. 376, 383; L. R. 1 Q. B. 435), 254, 325.
Texas Brewing Co. v. Meyer (38 S. W. Rep. 263), 226.
Texas Brewing Co. v. Templeton (38 S. W. Rep. 27), 225.
Texas & P. Ry. v. Int. Com. Commrs. (162 U. S. 197), 712.
Texas & P. Ry. Co. v. Marshall (136 U. S. 393), 84.
Texas & P. R. Co. v. So. Pac. R. Co. (41 La. Ann. 970; 6 South. Rep. 888; 40 Am. & Eng. R. Cas. 475), 470, 555.
Texas Standard Oil Co. v. Adone (83 Tex. 650, 659; 19 S. W. Rep. 274), 565, 566.
Thacker v. Hardy (L. R. 4 Q. B. D. 685), 283.
The Chas. E. Wiswell, (74 Fed. Rep. 802), 603.
The King v. Emery (2 T. R. 515), 705.
The King v. Francis (2 T. R. 484), 689.
The People v. Attorney-General (22 Barb. 117), 699.
The People v. Fairfield (8 Hun, 334; 67 N. Y. 334), 699.
The People v. North Chicago Ry. Co. (88 Ill. 537), 701.

[The references are to pages.]

The People v. Tobacco Co. (42 How. Pr. 162), 699.
The People v. Trustees of Geneva College (5 Wend. 219), 699.
The Poulterer's Case (9 Coke, 55), 259.
The State v. Allen (5 Kan. 213), 695.
The State v. Stewart (32 Mo. 379), 699.
The State v. W. W. Ry. Co. (34 Wis. 197), 695.
Third Nat. Bank v. Harrison (10 Fed. Rep. 243), 267.
Thomas v. Cin., N. O. & T. P. Ry. Co. (62 Fed. Rep. 803, 818, 821), 316, 319, 334.
Thomas v. Edwards (2 Mees. & W. 218), 46.
Thomas v. Mills (3 Ohio St. 274), 110, 149.
Thomas v. Railway Co. (62 Fed. Rep. 822), 342.
Thomas v. Railway Co. (101 U. S. 71, 83), 467, 483.
Thomas v. West Jersey R. Co. (101 U. S. 71), 711.
Thomas v. Williams (L. R. 14 Ch. D. 864), 352.
Thompson v. Catholic Cong. Soc. (7 Pick. 160), 256.
Thompson v. Cummings (68 Ga. 124), 266, 280.
Thompson v. Davies (13 Johns. 112, 115), 46, 249, 251.
Thompson v. Lee Co. (3 Wall. 327), 466.
Thompson v. Means (11 Sm. & M. 604), 132, 184.
Thompson v. People (23 Wend. 538), 703.
Thompson v. Simmons (25 La. Ann. 450), 48.
Thompson v. Staats (15 Wend. 395), 452.
Thompson v. Western Union Tel. Co. (64 Wis. 531; 25 N. W. Rep. 789), 86.
Thompson v. Wharton (70 Ky. 563).
Thorley's Food Co. v. Massam (L. R. 14 Ch. Div. 763), 352.
Thorpe v. Rutland, etc. Ry. Co. (27 Vt. 140, 149), 410, 451.
Thrupp v. Collett (26 Beav. 125), 77.
Tilley v. Savannah, etc. Ry. Co. (5 Fed. Rep. 641).
Timmerman v. Dever (52 Mich. 34; 50 Am. Rep. 240; 23 Am. L. Reg. 50), 115, 132, 141, 184.
Tindal v. Wesley (167 U. S. 204, 220; 17 Sup. Ct. Rep. 770), 719.
Tinsman v. Belvidere Delaware R. R. Co. (1 Dutch. 255), 236.
Tode v. Gross (127 N. Y. 480, 485; 28 N. E. Rep. 469), 140, 165.
Toledo, A., A. & N. M. Ry. v. Penna. Co. (54 Fed. Rep. 730, 740), 301, 322, 351, 356.
Toledo, etc. Ry. Co. v. Elliott (76 Ill. 67), 589.
T., W. & W. R. W. Co. v. Larmon (67 Ill. 68), 426.
Tomblin v. Callen (69 Iowa, 229, 230), 278.
Tool Co. v. Norris (2 Wall. 45, 55), 46, 60, 64, 68, 100.
Touro v. Cassin (1 Not. & M. 172), 94.
Town of Bennington v. Park (50 Vt. 192), 466.
Town of Cromwell v. Conn. Brown Stone Quarry Co. (50 Conn. 470), 81.
Town of Lake View v. Letz (44 Ill. 181), 402.
Town of Pine Grove v. Talcott (19 Wall. 666), 501.
Town of Queensbury v. Culver (19 Wall. 83), 466.
Tracy v. Talmage (14 N. Y. 162), 148.
Train v. Boston Disinfecting Co. (144 Mass. 523; 19 Am. & Eng. Corp. Cas. 548; 59 Am. Rep. 113), 401.
Trans. Co. v. Pipe Line Co. (22 W. Va. 600), 240.

[The references are to pages.]

Trist v. Child (21 Wall. 441), 46, 57, 60, 70.
Trollope v. London Bldg. Trades Federation (W. N. 95; C. A. W. N. 45), 329.
Trotter v. Harris (2 G. & J. 285), 392.
Trovinger v. McBurney (5 Cow. 253), 51.
True v. Houghton (6 Colo. 318), 579.
Truenick v. Smith (63 Pa. St. 18), 465.
Trustees v. Lynch (70 N. Y. 440, 447, 450), 155, 156.
Trustees v. Peaslee (15 N. H. 317), 488.
Tucker v. Aiker (7 N. H. 113), 73, 99.
Tucker v. Finch (66 Wis. 17), 318.
Tulk v. Moxhay (2 Phila. 774), 156.
Turner v. Adams (46 Mo. 95), 249.
Turner v. Hoole (Dowl. & Ryl. N. P. 27), 95.
Turner v. Johnson (7 Dana, 435), 110.
Turner v. Phœnix Ins. Co. (21 N. W. Rep. 326), 235.
Turner v. Schneider (27 Ill. App. 220), 276.
Turnpike Co. v. Sanford (164 U. S. 578, 596, 597; 17 Sup. Ct. Rep. 198), 725.
Tuttle v. Matthews (28 Fed. Rep. 98), 570, 571.
Tyler v. Gates (3 Barb. 222), 243.

U.

Ulery v. Chicago Live Stock Exchange (54 Ill. App. 233, 240), 253.
Union Bank v. Carr (15 Fed. Rep. 438), 267.
Union Ferry Co., *In re* (98 N. Y. 150), 369.
Union Fuel Co. v. A., T. & S. F. R. Co. (43 Pac. Rep. 701), 222.
Union Pac. Ry. v. Goodridge (149 U. S. 680; 13 Sup. Ct. Rep. 970), 589.
Union Pac. Ry. Co. v. U. S. (117 U. S. 355), 589.
U. S. v. Addystone Pipe & Steel Co. (78 Fed. Rep. 712, 718), 551.
U. S. v. Cassidy (67 Fed. Rep. 698, 703), 342.
U. S. v. Debs (63 Fed. Rep. 436; 64 Fed. Rep. 724, 744, 745, 765), 297, 311, 336, 340, 353.
U. S. v. De Witt (9 Wall. 41), 411, 452.
U. S. v. Dustin (2 Bond C. C. 332), 259.
U. S. v. E. C. Knight Co. (156 U. S. 1; 15 Sup. Ct. Rep. 249), 546, 548, 603.
U. S. v. Elliott (62 Fed. Rep. 801; 64 Fed. Rep. 27, 30, 34), 334, 336.
U. S. v. Greenhut (50 Fed. Rep. 462), 603.
U. S. v. Hudson (7 Cranch, 32), 716.
U. S. v. Jellico Mountain Coal & Coke Co. (46 Fed. Rep. 432), 247, 603.
U. S. v. Kane (23 Fed. Rep. 748; 25 Am. & Eng. R. R. Cas. 608), 322, 323.
U. S. v. Kirby (7 Wall. 485), 342.
U. S. v. Martin (4 Cliff. 160, 162), 228.
U. S. v. Patterson (59 Fed. Rep. 280, 283), 258.
U. S. v. Trans-Missouri Freight Assn. (166 U. S. 290, 311, 313, 338, 343; 29 Sup. Ct. Rep. 540, 552, 558, 559; 53 Fed. Rep. 540, 545, 548, 552, 603), 31, 46, 147, 474, 476, 504, 709.
U. S. v. Union Pac. Ry. (160 U. S. 1), 442.
U. S. v. Walsh (5 Dill. 60), 228.
U. S. v. Woolten (29 Fed. Rep. 702), 318.

[The references are to pages.]

U. S. v. Workingmen's Amalgamated Council (54 Fed. Rep. 994), 338, 545, 603.
U. S. Chemical Co. v. Providence, etc. Co. (64 Fed. Rep. 946), 145, 547.
U. S. Express Co. v. Bachman (28 Ohio St. 144), 89.
U. S. Express Co. v. Harris (51 Ind. 127), 86, 92.
Updegraff v. Commonwealth (11 S. & R. 394, 399), 54.
Upton v. Haines (55 N. H. 283), 94.
Urmston v. Whitelegg (63 L. T. 455), 223, 245.
Ushel v. McBratney (3 Dill. 385), 55.

V.

Valley Railway Co. v. Iron Co. (46 Ohio St. 44, 49), 529.
Valley Railway Co. v. Lake Erie Ins. Co. (46 Ohio St. 44), 527.
Valentine v. Stewart (15 Cal. 404), 243.
Valparaiso v. Gardner (97 Ind. 1; 7 Am. & Eng. Corp. Cas. 626; 49 Am. Rep. 416), 392.
Vance v. Erie Ry. Co. (32 N. J. L. 334), 236.
Vanderbilt v. Bennett (2 Ry. & Corp. L. J. 409), 561, 584.
Vandine, Petr. (6 Pick. 187; 7 Am. Dec. 35), 403, 409.
Van Dyck v. Van Buren (1 Johns. 362), 148.
Van Horn v. Van Horn (52 N. J. L. 284, 286), 230.
Van Kuren v. Trenton Co. (13 N. J. Eq 302), 520.
Van Meter v. Jones (2 Green Ch. 520), 102.
Vannini v. Payne (1 Harrington, 65), 452.
Vanover v. Thompson (4 Jones L. 485), 79.
Van Zant v. Waddell (2 Yerg. 260), 431.
Vass v. Wales (129 Mass. 38), 95.
Vegelahn v. Guntner (167 Mass. 92; 44 N. E. Rep. 1077; 43 Cent. L. J. 464), 323.
Vernon v. Hallam (56 L. J. Ch. 115; 35 W. R. 156), 132.
Vickery v. Welch (19 Pick. 523), 162, 215.
Vickroy v. Pratt (7 Kan. 238), 94.
Vicksburg, S. & P. Co. v. Dennis (116 U. S. 665; 6 Sup. Ct. Rep. 625), 369.
Village of Pine City v. Munch (42 Minn. 342), 354.
Viser v. Bertrand (14 Ark. 267), 96.
Von Hoffman v. Quincy (4 Wall. 535), 366.
Vulcan Powder Co. v. Hercules Powder Co. (96 Cal. 510; 31 Pac. Rep. 581), 225, 243.

W.

Wabash, etc. R. Co. v. Black (11 Ill. App. 465), 92.
Wabash R. Co. v. Illinois (118 U. S. 557; 7 Sup. Ct. Rep. 4), 590.
Wadleigh v. Gilman (12 Me. 403; 28 Am. Dec. 188), 455.
Wagner v. Phillips (51 Mo. 117), 249, 250.
Wainwright v. Bridges (19 La. Ann. 234), 48.
Wales Ry. Co. v. Redmond (10 Com. B (N. S.) 674), 522.
Waldo v. Martin (4 Barn. & C. 319), 100, 577.
Walker v. City of Cincinnati (21 Ohio St. 14), 466.
Walker v. Cronin (107 Mass. 555, 564), 228, 301, 349, 351.
Walker v. Ducross (25 La. Ann. 257), 48.
Walker v. Jameson (140 Ind. 591), 401.
Wall v. State (23 Ind. 150), 501.
Wallis v. Day (2 Mees. & W. 273 976), 23, 24, 118.

[The references are to pages.]

Wally v. Kennedy (2 Yerg. 554), 431.
Walsby v. Auley (7 Jur. (N. S.) 465, 466; 3 E. & E. 516), 245, 288, 294, 304.
Walsh v. Fussell (6 Bing. 163, 169), 40.
Walter v. Gernant (13 Pa. St. 515), 249.
Walton v. Crowley (3 Blatchf. 440, 448), 172, 173.
Ward v. Beeton (23 W. R. 533), 178.
Ward v. Byrne (5 Mees. & W. 548, 559, 562, 563, 584; 3 Jur. 1175), 20, 21, 23, 26, 119, 124, 128, 136.
Ward v. Hogan (11 Abb. N. C. 478), 201.
Ward v. Newark & Pompton Turnpike Co. (Spenc. 323), 236.
Ward v. Thompson (6 Gill & J. 349), 102.
Ward v. Vosburgh (31 Fed. Rep. 12, 15), 279.
Warfield v. Booth (33 Md. 63), 124, 132, 184, 215, 219.
Wannel v. Chamberlain (1 Str. 675), 120.
Watch Case Mfg. Co. v. E. Howard Watch & Clock Co. (66 Fed. Rep. 637; 14 C. C. A. 14), 546.
Waterbury v. Newton (50 N. J. Eq. 534), 455.
Waterhouse v. Cornet (55 Fed. Rep. 149, 157, 158), 334, 337, 339.
Watertown v. Mayo (109 Mass. 315, 317), 409.
Watertown Thermometer Co. v. Pool (51 Hun, 157; 4 N. Y. Supl. 861), 132.
Washburn v. Dosch (68 Wis. 436, 440; 32 N. W. Rep. 551), 132, 139, 207.
Watson v. Williams (36 Miss. 331, 341), 715.
Watrous v. Allen (57 Mich. 362; 24 N. W. Rep. 104), 158,
Waugh v. Beck (114 Pa. St. 422, 429, 452), 264, 281.
Webb v. Allington (27 Mo. App. 559), 152.
Webb v. Ridgely (38 Md. 364), 583.
Webb v. Rice (6 Hill, 221), 501.
Webber v. Blunt (19 Wend. 188), 79.
Webber v. Virginia (103 U. S. 344), 452.
Webster v. Dennison (25 Vt. 493), 249.
Webster v. Dillon (3 Jur. (N. S.) 432), 194.
Webster v. French (11 Ill. 254, 268), 252.
Webster v. Sturges (7 Ill. App. 560), 272.
Webster's Telephone Case (17 Neb. 126, 134), 432, 446.
Wedderburn v. Wedderburn (22 Beav. 84, 104), 213.
Weed v. Black (2 MacArthur, 268), 60.
Weeks v. Hill (38 N. H. 199), 97.
Wiel v. Ricord (24 N. J. Eq. 169), 401.
Welch v. Phillips, etc. Windmill Co. (89 Tex. 653; 36 S. W. Rep. 71), 242.
Wellington v. Small (3 Cush. 145), 242.
Wells v. Atlanta (43 Ga. 67), 386.
Wells v. Foster (8 M. & W. 149), 104.
Wells v. McGeoch (71 Wis. 196; 35 N. W. Rep. 769), 272.
Wells v. Steam Navigation Co. (8 N. Y. 375), 92.
Welsh v. Pittsburgh, etc. R. R. Co. (10 Ohio St. 65), 88, 93.
Wertheimer v. Pa. Ry. Co. (3 Am. & Eng. R. R. Cas. 279; 1 Fed. Rep. 232; 17 Blatchf. C. C. 421), 333.
West v. Camden (135 U. S. 507; 10 Sup. Ct. Rep. 838), 577.

[The references are to pages.]

Westcott v. Fargo (61 N. Y. 542), 92.
Western Dist. Warehouse Co. v. Hobson (96 Ky. 550; 29 S. W. Rep. 308), 218.
Western, etc. Assn. v. Starkey (84 Mich. 76; 47 N. W. Rep. 604), 219.
Western News Co. v. Witmarch (33 Kan. 510; 6 Pac. Rep. 786), 235.
Western R. Co. v. Harwell (91 Ala. 340; 8 So. Rep. 649), 92.
Western Saving Fund Society v. City of Philadelphia (31 Pa. St. 175, 183, 185), 381, 382.
Western Union Tel. Co. v. American, etc. Co. (9 Biss. 72; 65 Ga. 160), 222, 470, 541.
Western Union Tel. Co. v. Atlantic & Pacific States Tel. Co. (5 Neb. 102, 109), 442.
Western Union Tel. Co. v. Burlington, etc. R. Co. (11 Fed. Rep. 1), 149.
Western Union Tel. Co. v. Balto., etc. Tel. Co. (23 Fed. Rep. 12), 222.
Western Union Tel. Co. v. B. & S. W. Ry. Co. (3 McCrary, 130), 222.
Western Union Tel. Co. v. Jones (95 Ind. 228), 92.
Western Union Tel. Co. v. Los Angeles Electric Co. (76 Fed. Rep. 178), 443.
Western Union Tel. Co. v. National Tel. Co. (19 Fed. Rep. 660), 222.
Western Union Tel. Co. v. New York (38 Fed. Rep. 552), 437.
Western Union Tel. Co. v. Pendleton (122 U. S. 347; 18 Am. & Eng. Corp. Cas. 18), 437, 441, 452.
Western Union Tel. Co. v. Reynolds (79 Va. 173), 440.
Western Union Tel. Co. v. Scircle (103 Ind. 227), 92.
Western Woodenware Assn. v. Starkey (84 Mich. 76; 47 N. W. Rep. 604), 210.
West River Bridge Co. v. Dix (16 Vt. 466), 369.
West Virginia Transfer Co. v. Ohio River Pipe Line Co. (22 W. Va. 600), 207, 222, 470, 542.
Whatley v. Hughes (53 Miss. 268), 102.
Wheaton v. Ansley (71 Ga. 35), 97.
Wheeler v. McDermitt (36 Ill. App. 179), 272.
Wheeler v. S. F. & A. Ry. Co. (31 Cal. 46), 522.
Wheeling Bridge v. Wheeling & B. Bridge Co. (34 W. Va. 155), 400.
Wheelock v. Looney (15 N. Y. Wkly. Dig. 126), 102.
Whelchel v. State (76 Ga. 644, 648), 702.
Whitaker v. Howe (3 Beav. 383, 384), 129, 136, 188, 189, 212, 219.
Whitchurch v. Hide (2 Atk. 391), 376.
White v. Barber (123 U. S. 392), 272.
White v. Bullock (4 Abb. App. Dec. 578), 102.
White v. Buss (3 Cush. 449), 148.
White v. Howard (38 Conn. 342), 501.
White v. Railroad Co. (135 Mass. 216), 95.
White River T. Co. v. Vermont C. R. Co. (21 Vt. 590), 465.
White v. Fire Co. (52 N. J. Eq. 75), 579.
Whitecar v. Michenor (37 N. J. Eq. 6), 256, 302.
Whitefield v. S. E. Ry. Co. (E. B. & E. 115), 236.
Whitesides v. Hunt (97 Ind. 191; 49 Am. Rep. 441), 264.
Whitmore v. Fourth Cong. Soc. (2 Gray, 306), 256.

[The references are to pages.]

Whitney v. Slayton (40 Me. 224, 231), 110, 121, 129, 132, 219.
Whitney v. Union R. Co. (11 Gray, 359), 155, 156, 159.
Whittaker v. Howe (3 Beav. 383), 24, 25, 26.
Whittenton Mills v. Upton (10 Gray, 582, 595, 596), 510, 520, 522.
Wibert v. N. Y., etc. Ry. Co. (12 N. Y. 245), 331.
Wichita, etc. R. Co. v. Koch (47 Kan. 753; 28 Pac. Rep. 1013), 92.
Wicks v. Hatch (62 N. Y. 535), 283.
Wick China Co. v. Bunn (164 Pa. St. 449), 323.
Wickens v. Evans (3 Younge & Jervis, 318), 124.
Widoe v. Webb (20 Ohio St. 431), 148.
Wiggins Ferry Co. v. East St. Louis (107 U. S. 365), 399.
Wilbur v. Howe (8 Johns. 444), 243.
Wildey v. Collin (7 Md. 273, 278), 62, 75.
Wilder v. Chicago, etc. R. Co. (70 Mich. 382), 431.
Wilder v. McKee (111 Pa. St. 335), 228.
Wiley v. Baumgardner (97 Ind. 66, 69; 49 Am. Rep. 427), 115, 127, 129, 189.
Wilkins v. State (113 Ind. 514), 456.
Wilkinson v. Colley (164 Pa. St. 35; 30 Atl. Rep. 286), 184.
Wilkinson v. Coot (44 Miss. 367), 48.
Willemin v. Bateson (63 Mich. 309), 98.
Williams v. Bullmore (37 L. J. Ch. 461), 51.
Williams v. Ger. Mut. Fire Ins. Co. (68 Ill. 387), 427.
Williams v. Johnson (2 Bosw. 1), 172.
Williams v. Montgomery (148 N. Y. 519, 525; 68 Hun. 416), 560, 561.
Williams v. Tiedman (6 Mo. App. 269), 264, 269.
Williams v. Turner (7 Ga. 348), 392.
Williams v. Williams (3 Meriv. 157), 163.
Williams v. Woodman (8 Pick. 77), 94.
Williamson v. Chicago, R. I. & Pac. Ry. Co. (53 Iowa, 126; 36 Am. Rep. 206), 84.
Williamson v. N. J. So. Ry. Co. (26 N. J. Eq. 398), 482.
Willis v. Beard (6 Ind. 200), 148.
Willis v. Jones (42 Md. 422), 102.
Willis v. Halliburton (25 Ark. 173), 48.
Willoughby v. Chicago, J. R. & U. S. (50 N. J. Eq. 656; 25 Atl. Rep. 277), 587.
Wilstach v. Hawkins (14 Ind. 541), 502.
Winebrinner v. Weisiger (3 T. B. Mon. 32), 51.
Winpenny v. French (18 Ohio St. 469, 475), 67.
Winsmore v. Greenbank (Willes, 577), 349.
Winsor Coal Co. v. Chicago, etc. R. Co. (52 Fed. Rep. 716), 590.
Wis. Cent. Ry. Co. v. Taylor Co. (52 Wis. 77; 1 Am. & Eng. Ry. Cas. 532), 423.
Wolfe v. Frost (4 Sandf. Ch. 72), 156.
Wolfe v. Matthews (L. R. 21 Ch. D. 194), 333.
Wood v. Bowron (L. R. 2 Q. B. 21), 345.
Wood v. McCann (6 Dana, 366, 369), 56.
Wood v. Humphrey (114 Mass. 185), 95.
Woodruff v. Berry (40 Ark. 251 268), 251.

[The references are to pages.]

Woodruff v. Dubuque (30 Fed. Rep. 91), 560, 561, 583.
Woodruff v. Railroad Co. (30 Fed. Rep. 91), 582.
Woods v. Hart (70 N. W. Rep. 53), 209.
Woodstock Iron Co. v. Richmond & D. Extension Co. (129 U. S. 643; 9 Sup. Ct. Rep. 402), 52, 55, 60, 470.
Woodworth v. Bennett (43 N. Y. 273; 3 Am. Rep. 706), 249.
Woodworth v. Wentworth (133 Mass. 309), 577.
Worcester v. Ry. Corp. (4 Metc. 564), 466, 467.
Wortman v. Kleinschmidt (12 Mont. 316), 430.
Woodman v. Philadelphia (33 Pa. St. 202), 455.
Wreford v. People (14 Mich. 41), 401.
Wright v. Allen (2 Tex. 158), 697.
Wright v. Crabbs (78 Ind. 487), 274.
Wright v. Dunham (13 Mich. 414), 427.
Wright v. Nagle (101 U. S. 791), 369.
Wright v. Rider (36 Cal. 342, 347), 115, 129, 207, 565.
Wright v. Rindskopf (43 Wis. 344), 79, 97.

Y.

Yerkes v. Salmon (11 Hun, 471), 279.
York Teleph. Co. v. Keesey (5 Pa. Dist. Rep. 366), 446.
Young v. Timmins (1 Tyrw. 226), 23, 118, 119.

Z.

Zabriskie v. C., C. & C. Ry. Co. (23 How. 381), 501.
Zabriskie v. Hackensack & N. Y. R. Co. (18 N. J. Eq. 178), 710.
Zanesville v. Gas Light Co. (47 Ohio, 1), 432.
Zeisweiss v. James (63 Pa. St. 465, 471), 54.
Ziegler v. South., etc. Ry. Co. (58 Ala. 594), 431.
Zimmer v. N. Y. Cent., etc. R. Co. (137 N. Y. 460), 93.
Zylstra v. Charleston (1 Bail. 382), 401.

MONOPOLIES

AND

INDUSTRIAL TRUSTS.

MONOPOLIES AND INDUSTRIAL TRUSTS.

INTRODUCTION.

THE ORIGIN AND PROGRESS OF INDUSTRIAL "TRUSTS."

§ 1. A Recent Development.
2. Origin of the Term.
3. A Wider Significance.
4. Some Early Illustrations.
5. Early English Monopolies.
6. Statutory Enactments.
7. The Doctrine Modified.
8. An Historical Review.
§ 9. Sustained by Popular Sentiment.
10. The American Doctrine.
11. The Adverse Contention.
12. Labor Organizations.
13. Popular Sentiment and Public Policy.

§ 1. A Recent Development.—Combinations in the form of business or trading and corporate "trusts" are a product of modern enterprise and progress. The idea under which they came into being and have attained their present proportions is not new. It is as old as civilization, if not as old as the race. Before Greece and Rome, Solomon, King of Israel, said: "He that withholdeth corn, the people shall curse him; but blessing shall be upon the head of him that selleth it."[1] It is apparent that even at this early day the thrifty Hebrew was familiar with the modern devices for increasing the price of bread, and it is equally apparent that, in the execution of schemes of this character, he was regarded, both by his countrymen and by the great monarch, with little favor. The motives which

[1] Proverbs, 11:26. See also Job. 29:11-17; Amos, 8:4-10.

prompt to devices of this character have their springs in that corrupt inclination of human nature, under which men, in all ages, have sought to advance their own pecuniary interests by taking advantage of the necessities of their fellows. But while the motives and the ends sought in schemes of this character are not original with modern financiers, the capitalists of the later decades of the nineteenth century have outstripped all the generations of the past in devising new methods for the accomplishment of their purposes. And while their capacity in this direction may be of a higher order than that of the great financiers of earlier periods, the degree of their success is attributable, doubtless, to the industrial conditions which are peculiar to the present age. What they have accomplished would not have been possible at any earlier period.

§ 2. **Origin of the Term.**—The term "trust," as a designation of business or trading and corporate combinations, was first employed by the Standard Oil Trust. As employed by this organization it was a name, not for a corporate body, in the ordinary sense of that term, but for a business association of a new and peculiar character. The compact which was the charter or bond of the Standard Oil Trust was an agreement between the individuals who constitute the association. Under this agreement stockholders in corporations engaged in this branch of business placed their stock in the hands of trustees, for which they received the trust certificates of the new organization. The individuals who held the stock constituted the association, and chose the trustees, each stockholder casting votes proportionate to the amount of his stock. As in the ordinary trust, the trustees hold the legal title to the stock and elect the officers, not only of the association, but, as well, of the corporations by which the stock was issued. They control the entire business. They receive the entire income in the form of dividends on the stock of the corporations, and pay the dividends on the stock certificates. The purpose of the "trust" is to reduce the cost of production, to prevent competition and to regulate the price of their products. Another form of "trust" is that of an unincorporated association of the nature of a joint stock company, and still another is an organization in which a corporation becomes the trustee of a "trust," consisting of a union of other corporations. In this organization the corporation which is vested with trustee powers holds the legal title to the co-partnership property.[1]

[1] For the various agreements upon which the Standard Oil Trust is based, see State *ex rel.* v. Standard Oil Co., 49 Ohio St. 137. "That the nature of the agreement is such as to preclude the defendant from becoming a party to it, is, we think, too clear to require much consideration by us. In the first place, whether the agreement should be regarded as amounting to a partnership between the several companies, limited partnerships and individuals, who are parties to it, it is clear that its observance must subject the defendant to a control inconsistent with its character as a corporation. Under this agreement, all but seven of the shares of the capital stock of the company have been transferred by the real owners to the trustees of the trust, who hold them in trust for such owners; and being enjoined by the terms of the agreement to endeavor to have 'the affairs' of the several companies managed in a manner most conducive to the interest of the holders of the trust certificates issued by the trust, have the right, in virtue of their apparent legal ownership, and by the terms of the agreement, to select such directors of the company as they may see fit: nay, more, may, in fact, select themselves. The law requires that a corporation should be controlled and managed by its directors in the interest of its own stockholders, and conformable to the purpose for which it was created by the laws of its State. By this agreement, indirectly it is true, but none the less effectually, the defendant is controlled and managed by the Standard Oil Trust, an association with its principal place of business in New York City, and organized for a purpose contrary to the policy of our laws. Its object was to establish a virtual monopoly of the business of producing petroleum, and of manufacturing, refining and dealing in it, and all its products, throughout the entire country, and by which it might not merely control the production, but the price at its pleasure. All such contracts are contrary to the policy of our State and void. 'The word "trust," says Mr. Cook, 'was first used to mean an agreement between many stockholders in many corporations to place all their stock in the hands of trustees, and to receive therefor trust certificates from the trustees. The trustees own the stock, vote it, elect the officers of the various corporations, control the business, receive all the dividends on the stock, and use all these dividends to pay dividends on the trust certificates. Their trustees are periodically elected by the trust certificate holders. The purpose of the trust is to control prices, prevent competition, and cheapen the cost of

§ 3. **A Wider Significance.**—In its later use the term "trust" has acquired a broader and more general signification than that above given. It is used to designate any corporation, association or other combination, the object of which is to create a monopoly, either complete or partial, with a view to increasing prices by suppressing competition and obtaining control of the market. It is the claim of combinations of this character, as a rule, that the effect of such "trusts" is to increase the profit of production without an increase of prices, and that, as a direct and necessary result, the public receives a benefit from it. In many instances there is an arrangement between individuals, firms or corporations for the purpose of controlling the market and regulating prices, while the business is continued as it was originally established. Where the object is to maintain prices by limiting the production, a part of the individuals or companies included in the association suspend or close their business operations, and in consideration share the profits of the concerns that continue. Arrangements of this nature, while popularly denominated "trusts," are, strictly and properly, contracts in restraint of trade.

§ 4. **Some Early Illustrations.**—"Trusts" of the character above noticed are not of recent origin. Combinations for increasing or maintaining prices make their appearance under some very ancient forms of civilization. Of the financiering and of the business methods of Assyria and of Egypt, we know little more than is inferable from the inclinations of fallen human nature. But in this form of industrial progress Greece and Rome were no mean rivals of the originators of the modern "trust." One of the problems with which the governments of that period were confronted, was that of the equitable method of suppressing combinations for the control of production and of prices. An illustration of the summary manner in which this class of financiers were some times treated is presented by the following translation of an edict of Zeno, Emperor of the

production.'" State *ex rel.* v. Standard Oil Co., 49 Ohio St. 137, 185. See also Cook on Stock and Stockholders, § 503a.

East, issued to the Prætorian Prefect of Constantinople, A. D. 483: "We command that no one may presume to exercise a monopoly of any kind of clothing, or of fish, or of any other thing serving for food, or for any other use, whatever its nature may be, either of his own authority, or under a rescript of an emperor already procured, or that may hereafter be procured, or under an Imperial decree, or under a rescript signed by Our Majesty; nor may any persons combine or agree in unlawful meetings, that different kinds of merchandise may not be sold at a less price than they may have agreed upon among themselves. Workmen and contractors for buildings, and all who practice other professions, and contractors for baths, are entirely prohibited from agreeing together that no one may complete a work contracted for by another, or that a person may prevent one who has contracted for a work from finishing it; full liberty is given to any one to finish a work begun and abandoned by another without apprehension of loss, and to denounce all acts of this kind without fear and without costs, and if any one shall presume to practice a monopoly, let his property be forfeited and himself condemned to perpetual exile. And in regard to the principals of other professions, if they shall venture in the future to fix a price upon their merchandise, and to bind themselves by agreements not to sell at a lower price, let them be condemned to pay forty pounds of gold. Your court shall be condemned to pay fifty pounds of gold if it shall happen, through avarice, negligence, or any other misconduct, the provisions of this salutary constitution for the prohibition of monopolies and agreements among the different bodies of merchants, shall not be carried into effect."[1] This form of "trust" became a subject of legislation in England at an early period. In the 5th & 6th of Edward VI., we find "An Act against Regrators,[2] Fore-

[1] Code IV., 59. The foregoing translations of this edict is by A. H. Marsh, Q. C., and first appeared in 8 Canadian Law Times, 299, 300. See same also in 23 Am. L. Rev. 261.

[2] "Regrating. In old English law, the offense of buying or getting into one's hands at a fair or market any provisions, corn, or other dead victual, with the inten-

stallers,[1] and Ingrossers."[2] The first six sections of this act are as follows: "Albeit divers good statutes heretofore have been made against forestallers of merchandises and victuals, yet for that good laws and statutes against regrators and ingrossers of the same things have not been heretofore sufficiently made and provided, and also for that it hath not been perfectly known what person should be taken for a forestaller, regrator or ingrosser, the said statutes have not taken good effect, according to the minds of the makers thereof: Therefore be it enacted and declared by the King, our Sovereign Lord, with the assent of the Lords, spiritual and temporal, and the commons in this present parliament assembled, and by the authority of the same, that whatsoever person or persons, that after the first day of May next coming shall buy or cause to be bought any merchandise, victual, or any other thing whatsoever, coming by land or by water toward any market or fair to be sold in the same, or coming toward any city, port, haven, creek or road of

tion of selling the same again in the same fair or market, or in some other within four miles thereof, at a higher price. The offender was termed a regrator." Black. Law Dictionary. "Regrating. In criminal law, every practice or devise, by act, conspiracy, words or news, to enhance the price of victual or other merchandise, is so denominated." Bouvier, Law Dictionary.

[1] "Forestalling the market. The act of buying or contracting for any merchandise or provision on its way to the market with the intention of selling it again at a higher price; or the dissuading persons from bringing their goods or provisions there; or persuading them to enhance the price when there. 4 Blackstone's Comm. 158. This was formerly an indictable offense, but is now abolished by St. 7 & 8 Vict., chap. 24." Black, Law Dictionary. See also Bouvier, tit. Forestalling the Market.

[2] "Engross. In criminal law, to buy up such large quantities of any article as to obtain a monopoly of it for the purpose of selling at an unreasonable price. The tendency of modern English law is very decidedly to restrict the application of the law against engrossing; and it is very doubtful if it applies at all, except to obtaining a monopoly of provisions. 1 East, 143. And now the common law offense of the total engrossing of any commodity is abolished by St. 7 & 8 Vict., chap. 24. Merely buying for the purpose of selling again is not necessarily engrossing. 14 East, 406; 15 East, 511. See 4 Blackstone Comm. 159*n*, for the law upon this subject." Bouvier, Law Dictionary.

this realm or Wales, from any parts beyond the sea to be sold, or make any bargain, contract or promise for the having or buying of the same, or any part thereof, so coming as is aforesaid, before the said merchandise, victuals, or other things, shall be in the market, fair, city, port, haven, creek or road, ready to be sold; or shall make any motion by word, letter, message or otherwise, to any person or persons, for the inhancing of the price or dearer selling of any thing or things above mentioned, or else dissuade, move or stir any person or persons coming to the market or the fair, to abstain or forbear to bring or convey any of the things above rehearsed, to any market, fair, city, port, haven, creek or road, to be sold, as is aforesaid, shall be deemed taken and adjudged a forestaller. II. Further, be it enacted and declared by the authority aforesaid: That whatsoever person or persons, that after the said first day of May shall by any means regrate, obtain, or get into his or their hands or possession, in any fair or market, any corn, wine, fish, butter, cheese, candles, tallow, sheep, lambs, calves, swine, pigs, geese, capons, hens, chickens, pigeons, covies or other dead victual whatsoever, that shall be brought to any fair or market within this realm or Wales to be sold, and do sell the same again in any fair or market holden or kept in the same place, or in any other fair or market within four miles thereof, shall be accepted, reputed and taken for a regrator or regrators. III. And be it also enacted and declared by the authority aforesaid, that whatsoever person or persons, that after the said first day of May shall ingross or get into his or their hands by buying, contracting or promise taking, other than by demise, grant, or lease of land or title, any corn growing in the field, or any other corn or grain, butter, cheese, fish, or other dead victual whatsoever, within the realm of England, to the intent to sell the same again, shall be accepted, reputed and taken for an unlawful ingrosser or ingrossers. IV. And if any person or persons shall at any time after the said first day of May offend in any of the things before recited, and being thereof duly convicted and attainted by the laws of this realm, or after the form hereafter mentioned, shall for his or their first offense have or suffer imprisonment for the space of two months, without bail or mainprise, and shall also lose and forfeit the value of the goods, cattle and victual so by him or them bought or had. V. And if any person lawfully convicted or attainted of or for any of the offenses above said, be thereof eftsoons lawfully convicted or attainted, that then every person or persons, so offending, shall have and suffer for his or their second offense, imprisonment by the space of one-half year, without bail or mainprise, and shall lose double the value of all the goods, cattle and victual so by him bought or had, as is aforesaid. VI. And if any person, being lawfully twice convicted or attainted of or for any of said offenses, shall eftsoons offend the third time, and be thereof lawfully convicted or attainted, that then every such person for the said third offense shall be set on the pillory in the city town or place, where he shall then dwell and inhabit, and lose and forfeit all the goods and cattle that he or they have to their own use, and also be committed to prison, there to remain during the King's majesty's pleasure.[1]

[1] 5 & 6 Edward VI., chap. 14. In 1772, the statute cited was repealed by 12 Geo. III., chap. 71, as follows: "Whereas it hath been found by experience that the restraints laid by several statutes upon the dealing in corn, meal, flour, cattle and sundry other sorts of victuals, by preventing a free trade in said commodities, have a tendency to discourage the growth, and to enhance the price of the same, which statutes, if put into execution, would bring great distress upon the inhabitants of many parts of this kingdom, and in particular upon those of the cities of London and Westminster; be it therefore enacted by the King's most excellent majesty, by and with the advice and consent of the Lords, spiritual and temporal, and commons in this present parliament assembled, and by the authority of the same, that an act made in the third and fourth year of King Edward the Sixth, entitled an act for the buying and selling of butter and cheese; and also an act made in the fifth and sixth year of King Edward the Sixth, entitled an act against regrators, forestallers and engrossers, and also an act made in the third year of Phillip and Mary, entitled an act for keeping milch kine, and for breeding and rearing of calves; and also an act made in the fifth year of Queen Elizabeth, entitled an act touching badgers of corn and drovers of cattle to be licensed; and also an act made in the fifteenth year of King Charles the Second,

§ 5. **Early English Monopolies.**—It appears that at the time of Edward VI., and during the reigns by which his was immediately followed, the sovereign was accustomed to grant special privileges to his favorites, which constituted a practical monopoly. A monopoly is defined by Lord Coke, as follows: "A monopoly is an institution or allowance by the king by his grant, commission or otherwise to any person or persons, bodies politic or corporate, of or for the sole buying, selling, making, working, or using of anything, whereby any person or persons, bodies politic or corporate,

entitled an act to prevent the selling of live, fat cattle by butchers, and so much of an act made in the fifth year of Queen Anne, entitled an act for continuing the laws therein mentioned relating to the poor, and to the buying and selling of cattle in Smithfield, and for suppressing of piracy, as relates to butchers selling cattle alive or dead within the cities of London and Westminster, or within ten miles thereof; and all the acts made for the better enforcement of the same being detrimental to the supply of the laboring and manufacturing poor of this kingdom shall be, and the same are hereby declared to be, repealed. And be it further enacted by the authority aforesaid, that all informations, indictments, suits or prosecutions, already commenced, for the inflicting any punishment, or for the recovery of any fine, penalty or forfeiture under the said former acts, or any of them, shall cease and determine, and no further proceedings shall be had thereon; and that no information, indictment, suit or prosecution shall be commenced or prosecuted against any person or persons whatsoever, under or by virtue of the said acts, or any of them; but that all such proceedings shall be void and of no effect, any law, statute or usage to the contrary notwithstanding." In this connection, see the following statute of 28 George III., chap. 53, § II: And whereas, a certain number of coal buyers have formed themselves into a society and held private meetings at the coal exchange in the city of London, professing to make regulations for the purpose of carrying on the trade in coals, which regulations may have a tendency to prevent the said trade from being free and open; be it further enacted by the authority aforesaid, that from and after the first of June, one thousand seven hundred and eighty-eight, any number of persons united in covenants or partnerships, or in any way whatsoever, consisting of more than five persons, for the purchasing of coals for sale, or for making regulations with respect to the manner of carrying on the said trade in coals, shall be deemed and adjudged to be an unlawful combination to advance the price of coals, and every person concerned therein shall be liable to be punished by the indictment or information for the same in His Majesty's Court of King's Bench at Westminster.

are sought to be restrained of any freedom or liberty that they had before, or hindered in their lawful trade."[1] During the reign of Elizabeth monopolies of this character were granted with great frequency. Favors in this direction were dispensed to her courtiers with a lavish hand. This feature of her administration is described by Hume, as follows: "The active reign of Elizabeth had enabled many persons to distinguish themselves in civil and military employments; and the queen, who was not able from her revenue to give them any rewards proportioned to their services, has made use of an expedient which had been employed by her predecessors, but which had never been carried to such an extreme as under her administration. She granted her servants and courtiers patents for monopolies, and these patents they sold to others, who were thereby enabled to raise commodities to what price they pleased, and who put invincible restraints upon all commerce, industry and emulation in the arts. It is astonishing to consider the number and importance of those commodities which were thus assigned over to patentees. Currants, salt, iron, powder, cards, calfskins, fells, pouldavies, ox-shinbones, train oil, lists of cloth, potashes, anise-seeds, vinegar, sea coals, steel, acqua vitæ, brushes, pots, bottles, saltpetre, lead, accidences, oil, calamine stone, oil of blubber, glasses, paper, starch, tin, sulphur, new drapery, dried pilchards, transportation of iron ordnance, of beer, of horn, of leather, importation of Spanish wool, of Irish yarn. These are but a part of the commodities which had been appropriated to monopolists. When this list was read in the house, a member cried: 'Is not bread in the number?' 'Bread!' said every one with astonishment. 'Yes, I assure you,' replied he, 'if affairs go on at this rate we shall have bread reduced to a monopoly before next parliament.' These monopolists were so exorbitant in their demands that in some places they raised the price of salt from sixteen pence a bushel to fourteen or fifteen shillings. Such high profits naturally begat intruders upon their commerce; and in

[1] Coke, 3 Inst. 181.

order to secure themselves against encroachment, the patentees were armed with high and arbitrary powers from the council, by which they were enabled to oppress the people at pleasure, and to exact money from such as they thought proper to accuse of interfering with their patent. The patentees of saltpetre, having the power of entering into every house, and of committing what havoc they pleased in stables, cellars or wherever they suspected saltpetre might be gathered, commonly extorted money from those who desired to free themselves from this damage or trouble. And while all domestic intercourse was thus restrained, lest any scope should remain for industry, almost every species of foreign commerce was confined to exclusive companies, who bought and sold at any price that they themselves thought proper to offer or exact."[1] It will be observed that monopolies of this character were created, not by a combination of individuals, or of companies, but by royal patents. The legality of such patents was subsequently questioned, and in 1602, in the case of Darcy v. Allen,[2] they were declared void. In this case the court set forth the evils of monopolies in the following propositions, viz.: First. "The price of the same commodity will be raised, for he who has the sole selling of any commodity, may and will make the price as he pleases. * * * The second incident to a monopoly is, that after the monopoly granted the commodity is not so good and merchantable as it was before: for the patentee, having the sole trade, regards only his private benefit, and not the commonwealth. Third. It tends to the impoverishment of divers artificers and others, who before, by the labor of their hands in their art or trade, had maintained themselves and their families, who now will of necessity be constrained to live in idleness and beggary."[3]

[1] Hume, History of England (Harper's Ed.), 335-336.

[2] Darcy v. Allen, 11 Coke, 84; s. c., Noy, 173.

[3] Darcy v. Allen, 11 Coke, 84, 86: s. c., Noy, 173. This case in Coke is entitled, "The Case of the Monopolies." The following is the statement of the case as it appears in the quaint language of the ancient reports, to-wit: "Edward Darcy, Esquire, a groom of the

§ 6. **Statutory Enactments.**—The position of the court in the case above noticed was subsequently confirmed by statute. An Act of 1623, among other things, provided "that all monopolies, and all commissions, grants, licenses,

privy chamber to Queen Elizabeth, brought an action on the case against T. Allein, haberdasher of London, and declared that Queen Elizabeth, *13 Junii Anno*, *30 Eliz.*, intending that her subjects being able men to exercise husbandry, should apply themselves thereunto, and that they should not employ themselves in making playing cards, which had not been any ancient manual occupation within this realm, and that by making such a multitude of cards, card playing was become more frequent, and especially among servants and apprentices, and poor artificers; and to the end her subjects might employ themselves to more lawful and necessary trades, by her letters patent under the great seal of the same date granted to Ralph Bowles, Esquire, full power, license and authority, by himself, his servants, factors and deputies, to provide and buy in any parts beyond the seas, all such playing cards as he thought good, and to import them into this realm, and to sell and utter them within the same, and that he, his servants, factors and deputies should have and enjoy the whole trade, traffic and merchandise of all playing cards; and by the same letters patent further granted, that the said Ralph Bowles, his servants, factors and deputies, and none other, should have the making of playing cards within this realm, to have and to hold for twelve years; and by the same, letters patent the queen charged and commanded, that no person or persons besides the said Ralph Bowles, etc., should bring any cards within the realm during those twelve years, nor should they buy, sell or offer to be sold within the said realm, within the said term, any playing cards, nor should make or cause to be made any playing cards within the said realm, upon pain of the queen's highest displeasure, and of such fine and punishment as offenders, in the case of voluntary contempt, deserve. And afterwards the said queen, 11 Aug. *Anno*, 40 Eliz., by her letters patent reciting the former grants made to Ralph Bowles, granted the plaintiff, his executors and administrators, and their deputies, etc., the same privileges, authorities and other, the said premises, for twenty-one years after the end of the former term, rendering to the queen 100 marks per annum; and further granted to him a seal to mark the cards. And further declared, that after the end of the said term of twelve years, *f.* 30 *Junii Anno*, 42 Eliz., the plaintiff caused to be made 400 grosses of cards for the necessary uses of the subjects, to be sold within this realm, and had expended in making them £5,000, and that the defendants, knowing of the said grant and prohibition in the plaintiff's letters patent, and other, the premises, 15 Martii, *Anno*, 44 Eliz., without the queen's license, or the plaintiff's, etc., at Westminster, caused to be made 80 grosses of playing cards, and as well those, as 100 other grosses of playing charters, and letters patent heretofore made or granted, or hereafter to be made or granted, to any person or persons, bodies politic or corporate whatsoever, of or for the sole buying, selling, making, working or using of anything within this realm, or the dominion of Wales, or of any other monopolies or power, liberty or faculty, to dispense with any others, or to give license or toleration to do, use or exercise anything against the tenor or purport of any law or statute; or to give or make any warrant for any such dispensation, license or toleration, to be had or made; or to agree or compound with any others for any penalty or forfeitures limited by any statute; or of any grant or promise of the benefit, profit or commodity of any forfeiture, penalty or sum of money, that is or shall be

cards, none of which were made within the realm, or imported within the realm by the plaintiff or his servants, factors or deputies, etc., nor marked with his seal, he had imported within the realm, and then had sold and uttered to sundry persons unknown, and showed some in certain, wherefore the plaintiff could not utter his playing cards, etc. *Contra formam prœdict literar patentium, & in contemptum dictœ dominœ reginœ*, whereby the plaintiff was disabled to pay his farm, to the plaintiff's damages. The defendant, except to one-half gross, pleaded not guilty, and as to that pleaded that the city of London is an ancient city, and that within the same, from time whereof, etc., there has been a society of haberdashers, and that within the said city there was a custom, *quod quœlibet persona de societate illa, usus fuit & consuevit emere, vendere & libere merchandizare omnem rem & omnes res merchandizabiles infra hoc regnun angliœ de quocunque, vel quibus cunque personis*, etc., and pleaded that he was *civis & liber homo de civetate & societate illa*, and sold the said half gross of playing cards, being made within the realm, etc., as he lawfully might, and upon which the plaintiff demurred in law." The demurrer was not sustained. The report of the case concludes with these words of the reporter: "And *nota* reader, and well observe the glorious preamble and pretense of this odious monopoly. And it is true, *quod privilegia quœ re vera sunt in prejudicium reipublicœ, magis tamen speciosa habent frontispicia & boni publici pretextum, quaum bonœ & legales concessiones, sed pretexu, liciti non debet admitti illicitum*. And our Lord, the King that now is, in a book which he, in zeal to the law and justice, commanded to be printed *Anno* 1610, entitled, 'A Declaration of his Majesty's Pleasure, etc.,' p. 13, has published, that monopolies are things against the laws of this realm: and therefore expressly commands that no suitor presume to move him to grant any of them."

due by any statute, before judgment thereupon had; and all proclamations, inhibitions, restraints, warrants of assistance, and all other matters and things whatsoever, any way tending to the instituting, erecting, strengthening, furthering or countenancing of the same or any of them, are altogether contrary to the laws of this realm, and so are and shall be utterly void and of none effect, and in no wise to be put in use or execution.[1] A statute of the reign of George III. provided that a combination of five or more persons for the purchase and sale of coals shall be unlawful and punishable by indictment.[2] Combinations of this character were offenses at common law.[3] At a later period the rigor of the statutory enactments against monopolies in restraint of trade were somewhat relaxed, and by a statute of George III., that of the 5th & 6th of Edward VI. was repealed.[4] While this statute indicates a purpose to abrogate the common law offense, by the repeal of the statute of Edward VI., against monopolies, the courts put their own construction upon the enactment and continued to hold that the creation of a monopoly was an offense at common law. It was held that in order to create a monopoly, in the legal sense of that term, it was not necessary to obtain possession of the whole of any product, or even of any large part of it. It was sufficient that their was engrossing to such an extent as to enable the holders to increase the price at a specified time and place. In a case tried in 1800, Lord Kenyon stated the rule, as established at that time, as follows: "Again it is urged that the quantity purchased cannot constitute the offense of engrossing, unless it bear such a proportion to the consumption of the whole kingdom as will affect the general price. This objection is new to me, but if the opinions of Lord Mansfield, Mr. Justice Dennison and Mr. Justice Foster, are deserving of attention, there is as little in that objection as in the rest. I well remember an information moved for before

[1] 20 James I., chap. 2.

[2] 28 Geo. III., chap. 53, § 2.

[3] Thompson's Law Dictionary, tit. "Monopolies."

[4] 12 Geo. III., chap. 71.

them against certain persons for conspiring to monopolize or raise the price of all the salt at Droitwich. They had no doubt of its constituting an offense, although it was not pretended that these persons had endeavored to engross all or any considerable part of the salt of the kingdom. Nor was it questioned but that the monopolizing of salt was an offense at common law."[1]

§ 7. **The Doctrine Modified.**—At a later period, as modern improvements in machinery and manufactures came into use, and under the influence of steam navigation and railway

[1] Rex v. Waddington, 1 East, 143, 156. "Here is a person going into the market who deals in a certain commodity. If he went there for the purpose of making his purchases in the fair course of dealing, with a view of afterwards dispersing the commodity which he collected in proportion to the wants and convenience of the public, whatever profit accrues to him from the transaction. no blame is imputable to him. On the contrary, if the whole of his conduct shows that he did not make his purchases in the market with this view. but that his traffic there was carried on with a view to enhance the price of the commodity, to deprive the people of their ordinary subsistence. or else to compel them to buy it at an exorbitant price: who can deny that this is an offense of the greatest magnitude? It was the peculiar policy of this system of laws to provide for the wants of the poor laboring class of the country. If humanity alone cannot operate to this end, interest and policy must compel our attention to it. Now. this defendant went into the market for the very purpose of tempting the dealers in hops to raise the price of the article. offering them higher terms than they themselves proposed and were contented to take. and urging them to withhold their hops from the market in order to compel the public to pay a higher price. What defense can be made for such conduct? And how is it possible to impute an innocent intention to him? We must judge of a man's motives from his overt acts; and by that rule it cannot be said that the defendant's conduct was fair and honest to the public. It is our duty to take care that persons, in pursuing their own particular interests. do not transgress those laws which were made for the benefit of the whole community. I am perfectly satisfied that the common law remains in force with respect to offenses of this nature; and in considering whether that was intended to be done away by the act of the 12 Geo. III. I cannot regard the resolutions entered on the journal of the Commons House of Parliament, but must look to the statute book. and there I find nothing which touches upon what I have said. but only a repeal of certain statutes, upon none of which is this prosecution founded. but upon the common law. I have said thus much which occurred to me, at present; but I shall consult

transportation many of the statutes against monopolies were repealed, and the decisions of the courts became more tolerant of combinations of capital in business operations. Corporations and joint stock companies, conducting business on a large scale, came to be recognized as legitimate and proper business methods. Courts of equity were somewhat reluctant to conform their decisions to the statutory and common law changes, but the rules established at an earlier day were gradually modified in adaptation to modern industrial conditions. The leading case of The Mogul Steamship Company v. McGregor, before the English Court of Appeal, is recognized as a turning point in the decisions of the courts. It is much more tolerant of "trusts" than the decisions of an earlier period. It sustains as legal certain acts creating monopolies for the increase or the maintaining of prices, that had previously been held illegal and void. In this case the defendants, who were firms of ship owners trading between China and Europe, with a view to obtaining for themselves a monopoly of the homeward tea trade, and thereby keeping up the rate of freight, formed themselves into an association, and offered to such merchants and shippers in China as shipped their tea exclusively in vessels belonging to members of the association, a rebate of 5 per cent. on all freights paid by them. The plaintiffs, who were rival ship owners, trading between China and Europe, were excluded by the defendants from all the benefits of the association, and, in consequence of such exclusion, sustained damage. It was held, affirming the judgment of the lower court, that the association, being formed by the defendants, with the view of keeping the trade in their own hands, and not with the intention of ruining the trade of the plaintiffs, or through any personal malice or ill will toward them, was not unlawful, and that no action for conspiracy was maintainable.[1]

with my brethren, and the case shall be fully considered upon all the objections which have been made before judgment is pronounced." *Ibid.*, 157.

[1] Mogul Steamship Co. v. McGregor, L. R. 23 Q. B. Div. 598. "The next point is whether the means adopted were unlawful. The means adopted were competi-

§ 8. **An Historical Review.**—The opinion in this case, by Lord Justice Bowen, contains a full and instructive discussion of the doctrine on which the decision is based, with a notice of the objections urged in the dissenting opinion of

tion carried to the bitter end. Whether such means were unlawful is in like manner nothing but the old discussion which I have gone through, and which is now revived under a second head of inquiry, except so far as a combination of capitalists differentiates the case of acts jointly done by them from similar acts done by a single man of capital. But I find it impossible myself to acquiesce in the view that the English law places any such restriction on the combination of capital as would be involved in the recognition of such a distinction. If so, one rich capitalist may innocently carry competition to a length which would become unlawful in the case of a syndicate with a joint capital no larger than his own, and one individual merchant may lawfully do that which a firm or partnership may not. What limits, on such a theory, would be imposed by law on the competitive action of a joint stock company limited, is a problem which might well puzzle a casuist. The truth is, that the combination of capital for purposes of trade and competition is a very different thing from such a combination of several persons against one, with a view to harm him, as falls under the head of an indictable conspiracy. There is no just cause or excuse in the latter class of cases. There is such a just cause or excuse in the former. There are cases in which the very fact of a combination is evidence of a design to do that which is hurtful without just cause, is evidence, to use a technical expression, of malice. But it is perfectly legitimate, as it seems to me, to combine capital for all the mere purposes of trade for which capital may, apart from combination, be legitimately used in trade. To limit combinations of capital, when used for purposes of competition, in the manner proposed by the argument of the plaintiffs, would, in the present day, be impossible—would be only another method of attempting to set boundaries to the tides. Legal puzzles, which might well distract a theorist, may easily be conceived of imaginary conflicts between the selfishness of a group of individuals and the obvious well being of other members of the community. Would it be an indictable conspiracy to agree to drink up all the water from a common spring in a time of drought; to buy up, by preconcerted action, all the provisions in a market or district in times of scarcity; to combine to purchase all the shares of a company against a coming settling day, or to agree to give away articles of trade gratis in order to withdraw custom from a trader? May two itinerant match vendors combine to sell matches below their value in order, by competition, to drive a third match vendor from the street? In cases like these, where the elements of intimidation, molestation, or the other kinds of illegality, to which I have alluded, are not present, the question might be decided by the

the Master of the Rolls. In a later case the same jurist enters into a still more extended and exhaustive discussion of this doctrine. His treatment of the historical development of the law, as at present established in England, is very instructive and valuable. The thoughtful student of this subject will deem the following extended extract from his opinion, not too long: "There was an early period in English history when the courts set their face apparently against all restrictions upon trade alike, whether limited or unlimited. This period has long since passed away, but it has been, in my opinion, the doctrine of the courts of common law ever since the reign of Queen Elizabeth that contracts in general restraint of trade are void as being contrary to public policy. Contracts in general restraint of trade may be defined as those by which a person restrains himself from all exercise of his trade in any part of England. A mere limit in time has never been held to convert a covenant in general restraint

application of the test I have indicated. Assume that what is done is intentional, and that it is calculated to do harm to others, then comes the question, Was it done with or without 'just cause or excuse?' If it was *bona fide*, done in the use of a man's own property, in the exercise of a man's own trade, such legal justification would, I think, exist not the less, because what was done might seem to others to be selfish or unreasonable. * * * But such legal justification would not exist when the act was merely done with the intention of causing temporal harm, without reference to one's own lawful gain, or the lawful enjoyment of one's own rights. The good sense of the tribunal which had to decide would have to analyze the circumstances, and to discover on which side of the line each case fell. But if the real object were to enjoy what was one's own, or to acquire for one's self some advantage in one's property or trade, and what was done was done honestly, peaceably, and without any of the illegal acts above referred to, it could not, in my opinion, properly be said that it was done without just cause or excuse. One may, with advantage, borrow for the benefit of traders what was said by Erle, J., in Reg. v. Rowlands (L. R. 17 Q. B. 671, 687*n.*), of workmen and of masters: 'The intention of the law is at present to allow either of them to follow the dictates of their own will, with respect to their own actions and their own property; and either, I believe, has a right to study to promote his own advantage, or to combine with others to promote their mutual advantage.'" Bowen, L. J., in Mogul Steamship Co. v. McGregor, L. R. 23 Q. B. Div., at page 617.

of trade into a covenant of particular or partial restraint of trade. It is necessary to insist on this distinction, which is imbedded in the reports and text books of the last three centuries; since it is through not preserving the exact meaning of the term 'in general restraint of trade,' that some confusion has apparently, at times, arisen. The common law is as precise as it can be on the point; contracts, unlimited in area, although they may be limited in time, are, as a rule, held bad on the ground of public policy. The broad principle is to be found as far back as the year 1614, in Rogers v. Parry,[1] and in Broad v. Jolyfe.[2] It is reaffirmed explicitly by Chief Justice Parker, in the leading case of Mitchell v. Reynolds,[3] where 'general restraint of trade' is explained and defined. The doctrine is assumed to be unquestioned in Chesman v. Nainby,[4] and in Clerke v. Comer.[5] 'Any deed,' says Chief Justice Best, in Homer v. Ashford,[6] 'by which a person binds himself not to employ

[1] Rogers v. Parry, 11 Jac. 1; s. c., Bulstrode, 136.

[2] Broad v. Jollyfe (1620). Cro. Jac. 596.

[3] Mitchell v. Reynolds (1711), 1 P. Wms. 181. "In all restraints of trade, where nothing more appears, the law presumes them bad: but if the circumstances are set forth, that presumption is excluded, and the court is to judge of those circumstances, and determine accordingly, and if, upon them, it appears to be a just and honest contract, it ought to be maintained." *Ibid.* 197.

[4] Chesman v. Nainby (1726), 2 Ld. Raym. 1456 (4th Ed.), by Bayley.

[5] Clerke v. Comer (1734), Cas. *t.* Hardwicke, 53.

[6] Homer v. Ashford (1825), 3 Bing. 322, 326. "But it may often happen (and the present is a strong case of it) that individual interest and general convenience render engagements not to carry on trade or to act in a profession in a particular place proper. Manufactures or dealings cannot be carried on, to any great extent, without the assistance of agents and servants. These must soon acquire a knowledge of the manufactures or dealings of their employers. A merchant or manufacturer would soon find a rival in every one of his servants, if he could not prevent them from using, to his prejudice, the knowledge acquired in his employ. Engagements of this sort between masters and servants are not injurious restraints of trade, but securities necessary for those who are engaged in it. The effect of such contracts is to encourage rather than cramp the employment of capital in trade and the promotion of industry. For partial restraints, however, there must be some consideration, otherwise they are impolitic and oppressive." *Ibid.*

his talents, his industry or his capital, in any useful undertaking in the kingdom would be void.' A note to Hunlocke v. Blacklowe,[1] sufficiently states the reason why a covenant does not cease to be in general restraint of trade merely because the time is limited. 'The principle,' says the learned editor, 'on which restraints of trade, partial in point of space, have been supported, has not been applied to restraints general in point of space, but partial in point of time; for that which the law does not allow is not to be tolerated because it is to last for a short time only.' A similar explanation is given by Mr. Baron Parke, in Ward v. Byrne,[2] where a covenant, indefinite as to the area of restraint, but limited to nine months after the end of the covenantor's employment, was held void in law. 'When,' he says, 'a general restriction, limited only as to time, is imposed, the public are altogether losers, for that time, of the services of the individual, and do not derive any benefit whatever in return,' and looking at the authorities cited upon this subject it does not appear that there is one clear authority in favor of a total restriction on trade limited only as to time.' An ambiguous expression as to limits in respect of time in the case of the Gunmakers Company v. Fell,[3] is explained by Baron Parke, and is due probably to an oversight. Baron Rolfe's judgment is on the same lines as that of Baron Parke. 'Partial restrictions,' he says, 'have always left things in this state, that, when allowed, a portion of

[1] Hunlocke v. Blacklowe, 2 Wms. Saund. (6th Ed.) 156b.

[2] Ward v. Byrne, 5 Mees. & W. 548, 562. "The general policy of the law is against these restrictions, and it is only in deference to the convenience of the trading part of the community that certain exceptions to the general rule have been allowed. These exceptions have always left things in this state; that, when allowed, a portion of the public is not injured at all; that portion of the public to which the restriction does not extend remains exactly as it did before the restriction took place. But in this case the whole of the public is restrained during the period in question, and the only argument is, that this is to endure only for a short time; that is to say, that what the law does not allow is to be tolerated because it is of short duration. I see no principle in favor of such a conclusion; I do not think that is the law." Rolfe, B., in Ward v. Byrne, 5 Mees. & W. 548, 563.

[3] Gunmakers' Company v. Fell, Willes, 384, 388.

the public is not injured at all; that portion of the public to which the restriction does not extend remains exactly as it did before the restriction took place. But in this case,' viz.: in a case of general restraint for a time certain, 'the whole of the public is restrained during the period in question.' Ward v. Byrne,[1] was followed in 1840 by Hinde v. Gray.[2] Chief Justice Tindal repeats the proposition in Proctor v. Sargent.[3] 'Where we once hold a restriction to be unreasonable in point of space, the shortness of the time for which it is imposed will not make it good.' The truth is that the classification which seems to distinguish restraints which are limited in point of space from restraints which are limited in respect of time is a cross division. The antithesis between time and space looks so plausible that some text books and more than one judge in the last few years have lapsed into the mistake of supposing that it corresponds in some way to the line of cleavage upon which general restraints and partial restraints are divided. 'In respect of space,' said Lord Campbell, in Tallis v. Tallis,[4] 'there must be some limit.' Since the reign of Queen Elizabeth the common law authorities are really,—all of them,—one way. Scores of cases have proceeded on this basis; and those who dispute the rule can only do so, as it seems to me, by disregarding the judgments and opinions of an uncounted number of unanimous common law judges. * * * In the history of the application to partial restraints of this test, the courts of common law from time to time have been driven by good sense and by altered social circumstances to make gradual advances in the direction of toleration and indulgence. Judges as far back possibly as the reign of Henry V., and certainly during the reign of Queen Elizabeth, appear, as has been already stated, to have considered that even partial restraints of trade were uniformly bad in law. But as trade progressed it was neces-

[1] Ward v. Byrne, 5 Mees. & W. 584.

[2] Hinde v. Gray, 1 Scott. N. R. 123.

[3] Proctor v. Sargent (1840). 2 Man. & G. 33.

[4] Tallis v. Tallis, 1 Ell. & B. 391, 411.

sarily discovered that a doctrine so rigid must be injurious to the State itself. In the same way and at about the same date, by laws which were in mere regulation of trade, came to be distinguished by the courts from those which were in unlimited restraint of it. Nevertheless, as late as the year 1601, in Colegate v. Bacheler,[1] the court held that it was against law to prohibit or restrain 'any to use a lawful trade at any time or at any place.' This severe view is recorded in a *dictum* of Justice Croke (1613) in Rogers v. Parry,[2] though it was repudiated by Chief Justice Coke and the remainder of the court. One reason for the adoption of a more elastic doctrine appears from a judgment delivered in Broad v. Jolyffe.[3] In London and other large towns it had become usual already for traders to let their shops and wares to their servants when they were out of their apprenticeship, and for the servants to covenant that they would not use that trade in such a shop or in such a street. The courts, yielding to the progress of industry and commerce, finally decided that a man might restrain himself voluntarily and upon valuable consideration, from using his trade in a particular place. The *onus*, however, at this time still lay on the covenantee to show that the covenant on which he was insisting had been made for a good consideration, and that it was reasonable. The law is so expounded in Mitchell v. Reynolds,[4] 'a particular restraint is not good without just reason and consideration.' In 1726[5] the House of Lords affirmed the doctrine and the qualification, and their decision was followed in Clerke v. Comer,[6] Davis v. Marson,[7] and Bunn v. Guy.[8] The reason for favoring such partial restraints is enforced also in Homer v. Ashford.[9] 'It may often happen,' says Chief Justice Best, 'that individual in-

[1] Colgate v. Batcheler, Cro. Eliz. 872.

[2] Rogers v. Parry, 11 Jac. 1; s. c., Bulstrode, 136.

[3] Broad v. Jollyfe, Cro. Jac. 596.

[4] Mitchell v. Reynolds (1711), 1 P. Wms. 181.

[5] Chesman v. Nainby, 1 Bro. P. C. 234; s. c., 2 Ld. Raym. 1456.

[6] Clerke v. Comer (1734), Cas. *t.* Hardw. 53.

[7] Davis v. Mason (1793), 5 T. R. 118.

[8] Bunn v. Guy (1803), 4 East, 190.

[9] Homer v. Ashford (1825), 3 Bing. 322, 326.

terest and general convenience render engagements not to carry on trade or to act in a profession in a particular place proper.' Down to as recent a period as Young v. Timmins[1] it was still, however, considered to be for the person propounding a contract in partial restraint of trade to satisfy the court of the adequacy of the consideration. It was only in 1837, in Hitchcock v. Coker,[2] that a fresh step forward was taken in reference to partial restraints of trade. The Exchequer Chamber there for the first time decided that, in cases of partial restraint, the examination of the adequacy of the consideration was not properly for the court, but for the parties, although the burden remained as before upon the covenantee to show that there was some good and valuable consideration. The cases of Wallis v. Day,[3] Leighton v. Wales,[4] and Archer v. Marsh,[5] were determined on the amended principles. By this date the idea was fully recognized that all partial restraints of trade, which satisfied the conditions of the law as to reasonableness and good considerations, were not an injury, but a benefit to the public. Ward v. Byrne,[6] Proctor v. Sargent,[7] Rannie v. Irvine,[8] Mallan v. May.[9] A further progress in

[1] Young v. Timmins (1831), 1 Tyrw. 226.

[2] Hitchcock v. Coker, 6 A. & E. 438.

[3] Wallis v. Day (1837), 2 Mees. & W. 273.

[4] Leighton v. Wales (1838), 3 Mees. & W. 545.

[5] Archer v. Marsh (1837), 6 A. & E. 959.

[6] Ward v. Byrne (1839), 5 Mees. & W. 548, 559.

[7] Proctor v. Sargent (1840), 2 Scott, N. R. 289.

[8] Rannie v. Irvine (1844), 7 Man. & G. 969.

[9] Mallan v. May (1843), 11 Mees. & W. 653. "The covenant is 'that the defendant should not, without the plaintiffs' consent, carry on the profession of a surgeon dentist, etc., in London, or any of the towns or places in England or Scotland, where the plaintiffs or the defendant, on their account, might have been practicing before the expiration of said service.' According to the terms of this covenant, the defendant is prohibited from carrying on his business, not merely at such place or places as the plaintiffs might be practicing at the time of the expiration of the service, but at any place where they might have been practicing before, though for even so short a time. This covenant goes under beyond what the protection of any interests of the plaintiffs would reasonably require, and it puts into their hands the power of preventing the defendant from practicing

the views with which the law regarded partial restraints was made in Tallis v. Tallis.[1] It was there at last resolved that the *onus* lay upon the person who attacked a covenant in partial restraint of trade to displace the consideration,—a change in the position of the parties which is illustrated by the language of Chief Justice Earle in Mumford v. Gething,[2] 'contracts in partial restraint of trade are beneficial to the public as well as to the immediate parties.' * * * Such is a *resume* of the history of the common law doctrine as to restraint of trade. The first cloud upon the clear sky of the common law narrative comes in the equity decision of Lord Langdale in Whittaker v. Howe,[3]—a decision all the more inexplicable since it was given within three or four years of Hitchcock v. Coker,[4] Wallis v. Day,[5] Leighton v. Wales,[6] Archer v. Marsh,[7] Ward v. Byrne,[8] Hinde v. Gray,[9] and Proctor v. Sargent,[10] from a careful study of which cases alone the broad doctrine of the law as I have above described it may be gathered with perfect ease. * * * In 1869 the case of the Leather Cloth Co. v. Lorsont[11] occurred before Vice-Chancellor James. To the soundness of the actual decision in that case of the illustrious equity lawyer who tried it I have no objection to urge, but his language seems calculated, in several passages, to confuse and not to throw light upon our conceptions of the established common law doctrine. The Vice Chancellor's expressions are at times colored by the same kind of misapprehension of the common law as that which pervades

anywhere. We are, therefore, of opinion that it is an unreasonable restriction, and that the defendant is entitled to our judgment on the demurrer to the second breach for the insufficiency of the declaration in that respect." *Ibid.* 668.

[1] Tallis v. Tallis (1853), 1 E. & B. 391.

[2] Mumford v. Gething (1859), 7 C. B. (N. S.) 305, 319. See also Harris v. Parsons, 32 L. J. Ch. 247.

[3] Whittaker v. Howe (1841), 3 Beav. 383.

[4] Hitchcock v. Coker, 6 A. & E. 438.

[5] Wallis v. Day, 2 Mees. & W. 273.

[6] Leighton v. Wales, 3 Mees. & W. 545.

[7] Archer v. Marsh, 6 A. & E. 959.

[8] Ward v. Byrne, 5 Mees. & W. 548.

[9] Hinde v. Gray, 1 Scott, N. R. 123.

[10] Proctor v. Sargent, 2 Scott, N. R. 289.

[11] Leather Cloth Co. v. Lorsont, L. R. 9 Eq. 345.

the judgment of Lord Langdale in Whittaker v. Howe.[1] * * * Some years later, in Roussillon v. Roussillon,[2] Lord Justice (then Mr. Justice) Fry, in one of the many striking and brilliant judgments for which the profession will long admire him, proclaimed his disbelief in the existence of the rule of the common law, and laid down the proposition that there is no absolute doctrine that a covenant in restraint of trade is void merely because it is unlimited in regard to space. The question in each case he held was whether the restraint extended further than was necessary for the reasonable protection of the covenantee, and, if it did not do so, the performance of the covenant would be enforced even though the restriction was unlimited as to space. This broad negation of the rule appears to me to destroy the distinction (illustrated at length in Mitchel v. Reynolds),[3] which always has subsisted between general and partial restraints of trade. In destroying it Lord Justice Fry appears to me to overlook the importance of the principle which underlies the entire doctrine of the unlawfulness of general restraints of trade,—that the interests of the contracting parties are not necessarily the same as the interests of the commonwealth. Rules which rest upon the foundation of public policy, not being rules which belong to the fixed or customary law, are capable, on proper occasion, of expansion or modification. Circumstances may change and make a commercial practice expedient which formerly was mischievous to commerce. But it is one thing to say that an occasion has arisen upon which to adhere to the letter of the rule would be to neglect its spirit, and another to deny that the rule still exists. The *dicta* which Lord Justice Fry cites from Hitchcock v. Coker,[4] from Tallis v. Tallis,[5] and from Mallan v. May,[6] are all *dicta* in cases of partial restraint, where the reasonableness of the particular contract necessarily came under

[1] Whittaker v. Howe, 3 Beav. 383.

[2] Roussillon v. Roussillon, L. R. 14 Ch. D. 351.

[3] Mitchell v. Reynolds, 1 P. Wms. 181.

[4] Hitchcock v. Coker, 6 A. & E. 348.

[5] Tallis v. Tallis, 1 E. & B. 391.

[6] Mallan v. May, 11 Mees. & W. 653.

consideration. The necessary protection of the individual may, in such cases, be the proper measure of the reasonableness of the bargain. When Lord Justice Fry passes on to examine the question of the existence of the common law rule, he assumes, as it appears to me, without sufficient justification, that complete protection of the individual is the only reason which ought to lie at the root of the doctrine. But the reasonableness of the legal principle which forbids general restraint, altogether, is not the same thing as the reasonableness (as between the parties) of the bargain in any particular case, with regard to the argument that the rule, if it existed, would be an artificial one, and would therefore admit of no exceptions, the judgments of the judges and of the House of Lords in the case of Egerton v. Earl Brownlow,[1] illustrate, I submit, the distinction between a fixed rule of customary law and a rule based on reason and policy. The latter may admit of exceptions, although the former may not. Nor does the Lord Justice, to my mind, sufficiently allow for the weight of a multitude of decided cases when he states that there are 'undoubtedly cases in which it has been said that the restraint must not be universal,' and illustrates this by reference to Ward v. Byrne,[2] Hinde v. Gray[3] and Allsopp v. Wheatcroft.[4] The entire history of the subject of restraint of trade proceeds surely on the basis of the existence of the rule in question. With Whittaker v. Howe[5] I have already dealt. Jones v. Lees[6] was, as I have pointed out, a case of partial restraint in respect of the mode of manu-

[1] Egerton v. Brownlow, 4 H. L. Cas. 1.

[2] Ward v. Byrne, 5 Mees. & W. 548.

[3] Hinde v. Gray, 1 Scott, N. R. 123.

[4] Allsopp v. Wheatcroft, L. R. 15 Eq. 59. "The question in this case is purely legal, viz.: as to the validity of the covenant in restraint of trade. There has been a natural inclination of the courts to bring within reasonable limits the doctrine as to these covenants laid down in the earlier cases, but it has been generally considered in the later as well as in the earlier cases, that a covenant not to carry on a lawful trade, unlimited as to space, is on the face of it void. * * * And the rule, if not obviously just, is at any rate simple and very convenient." *Ibid.* 64.

[5] Whittaker v. Howe, 3 Beav. 383.

[6] Jones v. Lees, 1 H. & N. 189.

facture. 'I consider,' says Lord Justice Fry in conclusion, 'that the cases in which an unlimited prohibition has been spoken of as void, relate only to circumstances in which such a prohibition has been unreasonable.' Is it not a truer view that the courts have never, as a rule, even entered on the consideration of the circumstances of any particular case where the prohibition has been unlimited as to area? In Davies v. Davies[1] opposite opinions on the subject of the common law rule were expressed by Lord Justice Cotton and by Lord Justice Fry; but the matter did not call for decision."[2] The case to which the opinion relates is a *cause celebre.* In 1894 it went to the House of Lords and was affirmed.[3]

§ 9. **Sustained by Popular Sentiment.**—The learned and able review of the progress of the doctrine in England, as above presented, is in harmony with the popular sentiment in that country as it has found expression in its legislative enactments. The repeal of the statute of Edward VI. has already been noticed, and also the circumstance that the common law was not materially changed. But by a statute of the 7th & 8th of Victoria the common law was modified by the abolishing of the offenses of "badgering,

[1] Davies v. Davies, L. R. 36 Ch. D. 359.

[2] Maxim-Nordenfeldt v. Nordenfeldt, L. R. (1893) 1 Ch. 630, 651.

[3] Nordenfeldt v. Maxim-Nordenfeldt Co., L. R. (1894) App. Cas. 535, at page 555, Lord Watson observes: "When the series of cases from the earliest to the present time are carefully considered, I think they will be found to record the history of a protracted struggle between the principle of common honesty in private transactions on the one hand, and the stern rule which forbade all restraints of trade on the other. In my opinion it does not admit of dispute that the ancient rule has had the worst of the encounter, and has been gradually losing ground in all the courts. I do not think that, between the courts of common law and equity, there has been much, if any, real difference of opinion. But I am bound to say that the language used by equity judges is on the whole more in consonance with the commercial policy of the country than some of the favorite *dicta* of the common law courts. I purposely say some of the *dicta*, because I find in the opinions of many common law judges of the highest eminence a clear and liberal recognition of the wider views of policy which have influenced your Lordships in the decision of this appeal."

engrossing, forestalling and regrating."[1] By later statutes there was an enlargement of "the power of combination between workmen and workmen, and between master and master, for the purpose of maintaining and enforcing their respective interests and to remove the objection of being in restraint of trade, to which some of such combinations had been obnoxious."[2]

§ **10. The American Doctrine.**—The law on this subject, as established and administered in England, is accepted in this country only in a general sense. As a rule it may be said that in the consideration of the legality of a combination or covenant in restraint of trade, the decision will turn upon the reasonableness of the restraint. A court of equity will inquire, not whether the restraint extends to an entire State or to the nation, but whether it is a reasonable and proper protection of the party in whose favor the covenant is made, and whether it is prejudicial to the public interest. At present there is a strong tendency to the restricting of the right of restraint. This appears from the latest decisions in equity and from recent legislative enactments. In 1890 an anti-trust act was passed by the national legislature, and in most of the States anti-trust statutes have recently been enacted. In many of these enactments the penalty affixed to a violation of a statute is very severe, and in some instances an attempt to control the price of any commodity or to limit its production is made a criminal conspiracy. The Federal statute makes all contracts, combinations or conspiracies in restraint of trade or commerce between the States, or with foreign nations, and, as well, every attempt to monopolize any part of such trade or commerce a crime. The following extract from the opinion of Mr. Justice Peckham, of the United States Supreme Court, in the case of the United States v. The Trans-Missouri Freight Association, recently decided, is of interest as an indication of the trend

[1] 7 & 8 Vict., chap. XXIV.

[2] Mogul Steamship Co. v. McGregor, L. R. 23 Q. B. Div. 598, 629, 630. See 34 & 35 Vict., chaps. 31 and 39, and 40 Vict., chap. 22.

and scope of legal opinion in this country at the present time: "It is true the results of trusts or combinations of that nature may be different in different kinds of corporations, and yet they all have an essential similarity and have been induced by motives of individual or corporate aggrandizement as against the public interest. In business or trading combinations they may even temporarily, or, perhaps, permanently, reduce the price of the article traded in or manufactured, by reducing the expense inseparable from the running of many different companies for the same purpose. Trade or commerce under those circumstances may, nevertheless, be badly and unfortunately restrained by driving out of business the small dealers and worthy men whose lives have been spent therein and who might be unable to readjust themselves to their altered surroundings. Mere reduction in the price of the commodity dealt in might be dearly paid for by the ruin of such a class and the absorption of control over one commodity by an all powerful combination of capital. In any great and extended change in the manner or method of doing business it seems to be an inevitable necessity that distress, and, perhaps, ruin, shall be its accompaniment, in regard to some of those who were engaged in the old methods. A change from stage coaches and canal boats to railroads threw at once a large number of men out of employment. Changes from hand labor to that of machinery, and from operating machinery by hand to the application of steam for such purpose, leave behind them, for the time, a number of men who must seek other avenues of livelihood. These are misfortunes which seem to be the necessary accompaniment of all great industrial changes. It takes time to effect a readjustment of industrial life so that those who are thrown out of their old employment by reason of such changes as we have spoken of may find opportunities for labor in other departments than those to which they have been accustomed. It is a misfortune, but yet in such cases it seems to be the inevitable accompaniment of change and improvement. It is wholly different, however, when such changes are effected by combinations of capital, whose purpose in combining is to control the production or manufacture of any particular article in the market, and by such control dictate the price at which the article shall be sold,—the effect being to drive out of business all the small dealers in the commodity, and to render the public subject to the decision of the combination as to what price shall be paid for the article. In this light it is not material that the price of an article may be lowered. It is in the power of the combination to raise it, and the result, in any event, is unfortunate for the country, by depriving it of the services of a large number of small but independent dealers, who were familiar with the business, and who had spent their lives in it, and who supported themselves and their families from the small profits realized therein. Whether they be able to find other avenues to earn their livelihood is not so material, because it is not for the real prosperity of any country that such changes should occur which result in transferring an independent business man, the head of his establishment, small though it might be, into a mere servant or agent of a corporation for selling the commodities which he once manufactured or dealt in,—having no voice in shaping the business policy of the company and bound to obey orders issued by others. Nor is it for the substantial interests of the country that any one commodity should be within the sole power and subject to the sole will of one powerful combination of capital. Congress has, so far as its jurisdiction extends, prohibited all contracts or combinations in the form of trusts entered into for the purpose of restraining trade and commerce. The results naturally flowing from a contract or combination in restraint of trade or commerce, when entered into by a manufacturing or trading company, such as above stated, while differing somewhat from those which may follow, a contract to keep up transportation rates by railroads are, nevertheless, of the same nature and kind, and the contracts themselves do not so far differ in their nature that they may not all be treated alike and be condemned in common. It is entirely appropriate, generally, to subject corporations or persons engaged in trading or manufacturing to different rules from those applicable to railroads in their transportation business, but when the evil to be remedied is similar in both kinds of corporations, such as contracts which are unquestionably in restraint of trade, we see no reason why similar rules should not be promulgated in regard to both, and both be covered in the same statute by general language sufficiently broad to include them both. We see nothing either in contemporaneous history, in the legal situation at the time of the passage of the statute, in its legislative history, or in any general difference in the nature or kind of these trading or manufacturing companies from railroad companies, which would lead us to the conclusion that it cannot be supposed the legislature, in prohibiting the making of contracts in restraint of trade, intended to include railroads within the purview of that act."[1]

§ 11. **The Adverse Contention.**—The decision in the case above noticed will serve to settle certain questions in regard to the right of the States to enact anti-trust laws.

[1] United States v. Trans-Missouri Freight Association, 166 U. S. 290; s. c., 17 Sup. Ct. Rep. 552. The report of the committee of the New York Legislature on the sugar trust contains the following: "There has been an enormous speculation in the certificates of the trust and certificates of deposit issued by the Central Trust Company in exchange for the trust certificates. It was plainly one of the chief purposes of this trust to provide for the issue of these certificates, affording thereby an opportunity for great speculation in them, obviously to the advantage of the persons managing the trust, with whom was lodged full and accurate information of its plans and condition, but to the disadvantage of the general public, who were ignorant of the secrets of the trust, its methods and plans, and of the actual value of the certificates in which they dealt. The issue of $50,000,000 of certificates was amply sufficient for a speculation of many hundreds of millions of dollars. It may well be questioned whether the trust was organized more for the purpose of enormous speculations than for the advantages to be obtained by a combination of refineries in the legitimate refining of sugar. That the chief object of the trust was for the purpose of speculation is quite plainly shown by the inflated value placed upon the property of the constituent corporations upon which certificates were issued. Had the aim been solely a more economical and profitable refining

which, in their operation, extend to interstate commerce. Some questions on points of this character have recently come before the Federal courts, and it has been the contention of the advocates of the rights of the great corporations that the modern English rule must be upheld by the American courts. The following extract from a leading law review illustrates this contention: "If some of the modern opinions of judges in trust cases are to be followed, we are relegated at once, by the statutes referred to, to the dark ages, when business was necessarily carried on in defiance of law. For instance, in the Sugar Trust Case in the General Term (6 R. & C. L. J. 142), the court, by Judge Daniels, re-asserted the old doctrines of the common law to their fullest extent. The combination was held to be illegal for the reason, among others, that 'it was intended to bring about and secure ulterior advantages in the way of advanced profits to the associates.' Its affairs 'were to be so managed and carried on as to promote the profit and gain of the associates,' and 'it is no more than just to infer that the control is to be used to avoid competition and enhance prices, and in that manner, as it is the ordinary expedient to that end, promote the interest and profit of the associates.' This is a repetition of the mistake of centuries ago, that business men may not adopt methods which promote their interests and profits, because their desire for profit may cause them to use those methods improperly, and because their advantages may tend to the disadvantage of others. There are four centuries of experience and wisdom between that idea and the language of the judges in Mogul Steamship Co. v. McGregor, to-wit: that 'the instinct of self-advancement and self-protection is the very incentive to all trade;' that 'to say that a man is to trade fairly, but that he is to stop short at any act which is calculated to harm other tradesmen, would be a strange and impossible counsel of perfection;' that 'it is perfectly legiti-

of sugar, this result would have been obtained without an increase of the capitalization of the properties of the constituent corporations."

mate to combine capital for all the mere purposes of trade for which capital may, apart from combination, be legiti mately used in trade;' that 'to limit combination of capital when used for purposes of competition, would be only another method of attempting to set boundaries to the tides;' that 'the object of acquisition of gain is lawful and commendable,' and that as 'competition exists when two or more persons seek to possess or to enjoy the same thing it follows that the success of one must be the failure of another.' "[1]

[1] S. C. T. Dodd in 7 Harvard Law Review, 157, 165. In this connection we also quote the language of Justice White in the dissenting opinion in United States v. Trans-Missouri Freight Association, 166 U. S. 290, 355. Speaking of intent of the Federal anti-trust law, he says: "The plain intention of the law was to protect the liberty of contract and the freedom of trade. Will this intention not be frustrated by a construction which, if it does not destroy, at least gravely impairs both the liberty of the individual to contract and the freedom of trade? If the rule of reason no longer determines the right of the individual to contract, or secures the validity of contracts upon which trade depends and results, what becomes of the liberty of the citizen or of the freedom of trade? Secured no longer by the law of reason all these rights become subject, when questioned, to the mere caprice of judicial authority. Thus, a law in favor of freedom of contract, it seems to me, is so interpreted as to gravely impair that freedom. Progress and not reaction was the purpose of the act of Congress. The construction now given the act disregards the whole current of judicial authority, and tests the right to contract by the conceptions of that right entertained at the time of the Year Books, instead of by the light of reason and the necessity of modern society. To do this violates, as I see it, the plainest conception of public policy: for, as said by Sir G. Jessel, M. R., in Printing Company v. Sampson, L. R. 19 Eq. 465: 'If there is one thing which more than another public policy requires, it is that men of full age and competent understanding shall have the utmost liberty of contracting, and their contracts, when entered into freely and voluntarily, shall be held sacred, and shall be enforced by courts of justice.' The remedy intended to be accomplished by the act of Congress was to shield against the danger of contract or combination by the few against the interest of the many, and to the detriment of freedom. The construction now given, I think, strikes down the interests of the many to the advantage and benefit of the few. It has been held in a case involving a combination among workingmen, that such combinations are embraced in the act of Congress in question, and this view was not doubted by this court. The interpretation of the statute, therefore, which holds that reasonable agreements are within

§ 12. **Labor Organizations.**—Combinations of workmen for increasing or maintaining wages belong to the subject of this work. Though of comparatively recent origin they have already become extended and powerful organizations, and numerous cases involving the rights of such combinations have reached the higher courts. The following extract from the opinion in a leading case of this character is of interest as an indication of the attitude of the courts at the present time: "The right of any laborer or any number of laborers to quit work was not challenged. The scope and purpose of the bill was only to restrain forcible obstructions of the highways along which interstate commerce travels and the mails are carried, and the facts set forth at length are only those facts which tended to show that the defendants were engaged in such obstructions. A most earnest and eloquent appeal was made to us in eulogy of the heroic spirit of those who threw up their employment, and gave up their means of earning a livelihood, not in defense of their own rights, but in sympathy for and to assist others whom they believed to be wronged. We yield to none in our admiration of any act of heroism or self-sacrifice, but we may be permitted to add that it is a lesson which cannot be learned too soon or too thoroughly, that under this government of and by the people the means

its purview, makes it embrace every peaceable organization or combination of the laborer to benefit his condition, either by obtaining an increase of wages or dimininution of the hours of labor. Combinations among labor for this purpose were treated as illegal under the construction of the law which included reasonable contracts within the doctrine of the invalidity of contracts or combinations in restraint of trade, and they were only held not to be embraced within that doctrine, either by statutory exemption therefrom, or by the progress which made reason the controlling factor on the subject. It follows that the construction which reads the rule of reason out of the statute, embraces within its inhibition every contract or combination by which workingmen seek to peaceably better their condition. It is, therefore, as I see it, absolutely true to say that the construction now adopted, which works out such results, not only frustrates the plain purpose intended to be accomplished by Congress, but also makes the statute tend to an end never contemplated, and against the accomplishment of which its provisions were enacted."

of redress of all wrongs are through the courts and at the ballot box, and that no wrong, real or fancied, carries with it legal warrant to invite as a means of redress the co-operation of a mob with its accompanying acts of violence."[1]

§ 13. Popular Sentiment and Public Policy.—From the foregoing it is apparent that the "trust," as a conspiracy or combination for the purpose of creating a monopoly in restraint of trade, for the suppression of competition, for the limitation of production, or for the increase or for the maintaining of prices, or of wages, is in contravention of public policy and illegal. Though the courts of this country are not in full accord with those of England, and though the decisions of the State courts are in a degree

[1] *In re* Debs, 158 U. S. 564; s. c., 15 Sup. Ct. Rep. 900, 911. "It matters little what are the means adopted by combinations formed to intimidate employers, or to coerce other journeymen, if the design or the effect of them is to interfere with the rights or to control the free action of others. No one has a right to be hedged in and protected from competition in business: but he has a right to be free from wanton, malicious and insolent interference, disturbance or annoyance. Every man has the right to work for whom he pleases, and for any price he can obtain; and he has the right to deal with and associate with whom he chooses: or, to let severely alone, arbitrarily and contemptuously, if he will, anybody and everybody upon earth. But this freedom of uncontrolled and unchallenged self-will does not give or imply a right, either by himself or in combination with others, to disturb, injure or obstruct another, either directly or indirectly, in his lawful business or occupation, or in his peace and security of life. Every attempt by force, threat or intimidation, to deter or control an employer in the determination of whom he will employ, or what wages he will pay, is an act of wrong and oppression; and any and every combination for such a purpose is an unlawful conspiracy. The law will protect the victim and punish the movers of any such combination. In law the offense is the combination for the unlawful purpose, and no overt act is necessary to constitute it. * * * A wanton, unprovoked interference by a combination of many with the business of another for the purpose of constraining that other to discharge faithful and long tried servants, or to employ whom he does not wish or will to employ (an interference intended to produce, and likely to produce, annoyance and loss to that business), will be restrained and punished by the criminal law as oppressive to the individual, injurious to the prosperity of the community, and subversive of the peace and good order of society." Crump v. Commonwealth, 84 Va. 927, 941.

divergent, yet on the whole there is a good degree of unanimity in holding that the "trust" is an unlawful organization, and as such void. Moreover, the decisions of the courts have been followed by vigorous and positive statutory enactments. Notwithstanding these facts, however, the "trust" continues to live and prosper. Hitherto it has proved to be stronger than the legislature and the courts. By means of one device or another it has managed to elude the penalties of the law. It has been able to escape the forfeiture of its corporate privileges and the confiscation of its estates. This is due, however, not more to the great strength of these organizations than to the indifference and inertia of the public. When the people of this country are aroused they are stronger than any individual; stronger than any and all business combinations. This is not a prophecy in regard to the future of "trusts," or a discussion of their merits. This work has to do with the law to which these organizations are subject. It will appear in the progress of the discussion that the law is adequate to the control of the "trust," as well as of the individual, and that the remedy for any and all existing evils of this nature, at least, in most of the States, is in an unbiased and faithful administration of the law.

CHAPTER I.

PUBLIC POLICY AS RELATED TO TRADE AND INDUSTRIAL "TRUSTS."

§ 14. Introductory.
15. Public Policy Defined.
16. The Effect of a Change.
17. Covenants Inconsistent with Morality.
18. Services in Influencing Legislation.
19. The Ground of the Rule.
20. Where such Services may be Employed.
21. Services in Influencing Public Officials.
22. For Services in Procuring Appointments.
23. The Subject Continued.
24. The Withdrawal of Opposing Candidate.
25. For Services in Procuring a Pardon.
§ 26. For Services which are in Violation of Public Duty.
27. For Services in Opposing a Public Enterprise.
28. The Subject Continued.
29. Stipulations against Liability.
30. The Rule in New York.
31. Contracts in Contravention of Law.
32. For Influencing the Administration of Justice.
33. For Changing the Offices of Corporations.
34. For Renouncing an Executorship.
35. For Assignment of Salary not yet Due.

§ 14. **Introductory.**—Public policy, as a rule, for the guidance of courts of equity, is of an ancient origin. Its validity and its claim to consideration were recognized at an early day. To go back no farther, it was made the basis of a decision in the leading case of Mitchell v. Reynolds,[1] in 1711, by the the High Court of Chancery of England. The doctrine enunciated in this case has been modified in a degree to adapt it to the changed industrial conditions of later times, but the basal principle is as fully

[1] Mitchell v. Reynolds, 1 P. Wms. 181.

recognized at the present as at any time in the past. With regard to the application of this rule there is not entire harmony between the courts of England and of the United States. But while the courts of the two countries are not in full accord in regard to the extent to which the rule should be applied, and while the courts of the different States are not wholly agreed in their decisions, there is entire unanimity in the recognition of the principles involved. On all sides it is accepted that public policy has a standing in a court of equity, and that whatever is clearly in contravention of its claim is illegal and void. Undoubtedly the application of this rule is attended with grave difficulties, and it should be administered only with great deliberation, and in the exercise of a thoroughly judicial temper. The indefiniteness and uncertainty of the idea on which the rule is based, and which is the ground of the difficulty of its application, renders it especially liable to abuse. A standard text writer uses the following language on this point: "Of late years the principle has been invoked with increasing frequency, and sometimes, at least, seems to be made use of as authority for deciding in whatever way the courts think would, on the whole, be most useful."[1] This

[1] Parsons on Contracts, 249. In the case of Egerton v. Brownlow, in 4 H. L. Cas., at page 237, Lord St. Leonards said: "My Lords, there are just a few remarks that I wish to make upon public policy. I will not add a word to what has been already said by my noble and learned friends, but I will call your attention to what fell from one of the learned judges (Mr. Justice Cresswell), as regards the restraint of trade. That learned judge says that with regard to the restraint of trade, there is a maxim in common law, and he refers to a case in the Year Books to prove it; but the learned judge did not tell your Lordships upon what that maxim was founded. Nobody supposes that there was any statute upon the subject in those times. Upon what, then, was the maxim founded? Why, upon public policy for the good of the realm. It was not good for the realm that men should be prevented from exercising their trades. Now, let us see what this particular case is; it lies in a few words, and remarkable consequences have resulted from it. It was an obligation with a condition that if a man did not exercise his craft of a dyer within a certain town,—that is, where he carried on his business for six months,—then the obligation was to be void; and it was averred that he had used his art there within the time limited; upon which Mr.

may appear an extreme statement, but it is a pertinent suggestion of the liability to the misapplication of the doctrine. This danger has long been recognized by the courts. In a leading English case, Chief

Justice Hull, being uncommonly angry at such a violation of all law, said, according to the book, 'per dieu, if he were here, to prison he should go until he made fine to the king, because he had dared to restrain the liberty of the subject.' I wish to draw your Lordships' attention to this case. Angry as the learned judge was at that infraction of the law, what has been the result of that very rule without any statute intervening? That the common law, as it is called, has adapted itself, upon grounds of public policy, to a totally different and limited rule that would guide us at this day, and the condition which was then so strongly denounced, is just as good a condition now as any that was ever inserted in a contract, because a partial restraint created in that way with a particular object is now perfectly legal. Without any exclamation of the judge, and without any danger of prison, any subject of this realm may sue upon such a condition as Mr. Justice Hull was so very indignant at in that particular case. That shows, therefore, that the rule which the learned judge, whose opinion is now before the House, thought depended upon some rule of common law, regardless of policy, was founded upon public policy, and has been restrained and limited and qualified up to this very hour, and beneficially so, by that very policy which it is supposed had no bearing at all upon the foundation of the rule." In the same case, at page 195, Lord Brougham says: "In considering the question of the legality of the proviso, and the inexpediency of unnecessary restrictions upon the free disposition of property by will or by any other means known to the law, it cannot be denied that such dispositions are subject to some limits and restraints, and that the law will not uphold such as have a tendency prejudicial to the public weal: every man is restricted against using his property to the prejudice of others. * * * It must be superfluous in this House to cite authorities to prove the existence of such a general law. * * * It has been acted upon in a great variety of cases, such as those of marriage brokage bonds, restrictions upon trade, disability of sailors to insure their wages, and sale of offices not within any statute. A case of this last sort was Hanington v. Duchatel, 1 Bro. Ch. 124. That was a case of security given as a consideration for having procured an office in the king's household, and Lord Thurlow expressed himself to the effect that it was 'a matter of public policy similar to marriage brokage bonds, where, though the parties are private, the practice is publicly detrimental.' The same principle has been applied in cases of wagers respecting the public revenue, and numerous other instances. This principle has been expressed in different language, but in all cases to the same import as applying to matters contrary to law because against the public good." In

Justice Sir William Draper Bell, in delivering the opinion of the court, said: "I am not much disposed to yield to arguments of public policy; I think the courts * * * have gone much further than they were warranted in going

Walsh v. Fussell, 6 Bing. 163, 169, Tindal, C. J., observes: "It is not contended that the covenant is illegal on the ground of the breach of any direct rule of law, or the direct violation of any statute; and we think to hold it to be void on the ground of its impolicy or inconvenience, we ought to be clearly satisfied that the performance of it would be necessarily attended with injury or inconvenience to the public. But such is not the case." In Printing Company v. Sampson, Jessel, M. R., says: "Now, it is said on the part of the defendant, that such a contract as that which I have mentioned, a contract by which an inventor agrees to sell what he may invent or acquire a patent for before he has invented it, is against public policy, and it was said to be against public policy, because it would discourage inventions; that if a man knows that he cannot obtain any pecuniary benefit from his invention, having already received the price for it, he will not invent, or if he does invent will keep it secret, and will not take out a patent. It must not be forgotten that you are not to extend arbitrarily those rules which say that a given contract is void as against public policy, because if there is one thing which more than another public policy requires, is that men of full age and competent understanding shall have the utmost liberty of contracting, and that their contracts, when entered into freely and voluntarily, shall be held sacred, and shall be enforced by courts of justice. Therefore, you have this paramount public policy to consider, that you are not likely to interfere with this freedom of contract. Now, there is no doubt public policy may say that a contract to commit a crime is necessarily void. The decisions have gone further, and contracts to commit an immoral offense, or to give money or reward to another to commit an immoral offense, or to induce another to do something against the general rules of morality, though far more indefinite than the previous class, have always been held to be void. I should be sorry to extend the doctrine much further. I do not say there are no other cases to which it does apply, but I should be sorry to extend it much further. However, I am satisfied there is no reason for so extending it in this case. In the first place it is assumed that a man will not invent without pecuniary reward. Experience shows us that that must not be taken as an absolute truth. Some of the greatest inventions which have been of the most benefit to mankind have been invented by those who have given their inventions freely to the world. Again, it is supposed that a man who has obtained money for the future products of his brain will not be ready to produce these products. That must not be assumed. * * * A man who is a needy and struggling inventor may well agree either for a present payment in money down, or for an annual payment, to put his intelin questions of policy; they have taken on themselves, sometimes, to decide doubtful questions of policy, and they are always in danger of so doing, because courts of law look only at the particular case and have not means of bringing before them all those considerations which ought to enter into the judgment of those who decide on questions of policy."[1] In the same case Mr. Justice Burrough said: "I for one, protest, as my Lord has done, against arguing too strongly upon public policy; it is a very unruly horse, and when once you get astride it you never know where it will carry you. It may lead you from sound law. It is never argued at all but when other points fail."[2] The position taken in these opinions is not altogether out of harmony with that of the English courts of the present, but would not be accepted in this country. A better view of public policy as a rule for the guidance of courts of equity is presented by the words of Chief Justice Wilmot: "It is the duty of all courts of justice to keep their eye steadily upon the interest of the public, even in the administration of commutative justice, and when they find an action is founded upon a claim injurious to the public and which has a bad tendency, to give it no countenance or assistance in '*foro civili.*' Upon this principle, turning prosecutions for felony into civil actions for the things stolen, bonds and agreements not to prosecute felonies, and many other cases might be cited which are all governed by that super-eminent and noble principle, the care and protection of the whole community."[3] While this statement must commend itself to the conscientious and unbiased jurist, it is to be admitted, not only that courts of the highest character have

lectual gifts at the service of a purchaser. I see, therefore, not only no rule of public policy against it, but a rule of public policy for it, because it may enable such a man in comparative ease and affluence to devote his attention to scientific research, whereas if such a contract were prohibited he would be compelled to apply himself to some menial or mechanical or lower calling in order to gain a livelihood."

[1] Richardson v. Mellish, 2 Bligh, 229, 242.

[2] Richardson v. Mellish, 2 Bligh 229, 242.

[3] Low v. Peers, Wilmot's Op. (1770) 364, 378.

differed widely in their application of this principle, but also that the position of the earlier courts has been materially modified, at least in England, by the decisions of a recent date. The idea of the rule is not only indefinite but it is subject to change. Certainly, if not of necessity, public policy is modified by the changing usages and maxims of trade and by the revolutions in public sentiment, through which an enlightened people is ever passing. Since the idea on which the rule is based is ever subject to change, the rule itself must change with it. For this reason the decisions of the earlier courts based on public policy have less weight with jurists of the present than those relating to most other equitable rules. Very naturally, and altogether fitly, they inquire, not what rules have been established from the public policy of the past, but what rule is required by a proper regard for the public policy of the present.

§ 15. **Public Policy Defined.**—Public policy, as recognized by courts of equity, is not a hard and fast rule. It admits of no absolute or sharply drawn definition. Nevertheless it is something real and tangible, and admits of being adequately distinguished. In general it may be said, that public policy is that rule or principle of equity under which the individual citizen is restrained from any act, the effect or tendency of which is prejudicial to the interests of the public. Whatever may be the application of the doctrine it is based upon the maxim that the interests of the individual must ever be held subordinate to the public welfare. The citizen must be restrained from any act which is adapted, whether directly or indirectly, to inflict an injury upon the public. But while it is sufficiently plain that what is in conflict with the public weal and, in consequence, in contravention of public policy, is illegal and to be suppressed by courts of equity, the precise requirements of public policy and the extent to which courts are to go in enforcing its requirements, it is not a simple thing to indicate. The following, which is an attempt at explanation rather than at giving a definition, is from Mr. Justice

Story: "Public policy is in its nature so uncertain and fluctuating, varying with the habits and fashions of the day, with the growth of commerce and the usages of trade, that it is difficult to determine its limits with any degree of exactness. It has never been defined by the courts, but has been left loose and free of definition in the same manner as fraud. This rule may, however, be safely laid down that, wherever any contract conflicts with the morals of the time and contravenes any established interest of society, it is void, as being against public policy."[1] In a

[1] 1 Story on Contracts, § 675. "Some criticism has been made in relation to the language in which the principle has been expressed: exceptions have been made to the expression of 'public policy,' and it has been confounded with what may be called political policy, such as whether it is politically wise to have a sinking fund or a paper circulation, or the degree and nature of interference with foreign States, with all which, as applied to the present subject, it has nothing whatever to do. Public policy, in relation to this question, is that principle of the law which holds that no subject can lawfully do that which has a tendency to be injurious to the public or against the public good, which may be termed, as it sometimes has been, the policy of the law, or public policy in relation to the administration of the law." Lord Brougham in Egerton v. Brownlow, 4 H. L. Cas., at page 196: "It is argued by defendant's counsel that this construction of the contract will render it void by reason of being, when thus construed, in contravention of sound public policy; that sound public policy, as also the law maintaining and enforcing it, abhors a monopoly: and that the construction, as above set forth, gives to the elevator a monopoly of handling all the through grain brought on the road of defendants. * * * But further than this, the power of courts to declare a contract void for being in contravention of sound public policy is a very delicate and undefined power, and, like the power to declare a statute unconstitutional, should be exercised only in cases free from doubt." Richmond v. Dubuque & S. C. R. R. Co., 26 Iowa, 191, 201. All authorities, from first to last, concur in one thing, viz.: that the doctrine on this subject is founded on public policy, and I cannot but regard the jarring opinions as exemplifying the well-known *dictum* of Mr. Justice Burrough in Richardson v. Mellish (2 Bing. 229, 252), that public policy 'is a very unruly horse, and when once you get astride it you can never know where it will carry you.' Public policy does not admit of definition, and is not easily explained. If that statement requires authority turn to Egerton v. Brownlow (*supra*), and consult the arguments of counsel and the opinions of judges covering the whole subject, including, in some passages to which I will presently call attention, that part of it which concerns restraints of trade. One thing I take to be

recent leading case before the Court of Errors and Appeals of New Jersey, the court, by Mr. Justice Lippincott, discussed the subject of public policy in the following well considered words: "Turning to the judicial decisions upon this subject, we find them so numerous and of such variety that a consideration of them at any length is not practicable. The general principles governing the matter are well established by a long line of authorities, and in the case now before the court they do not appear to be of difficult application. It has been declared that public policy is a variable quantity, but the principles to be applied have always remained unchanged and unchangeable; and public policy is only variable in so far as the habits, capacities and opportunities of the public have become more varied and complex. The relations of society become from time to time more complex; statutes defining and declaring public and private rights multiply rapidly, and public policy

clear, and it is this, that public policy is a variable quantity; that it must vary and does vary with the habits, capacities and opportunities of the public; that it cannot have been the same when Chief Justice Tindal decided Homer v. Graves (7 Bing. 735) in 1831, as it was when Chief Justice Parker decided Mitchell v. Reynolds (1 P. Wms. 181) in 1711; that it must have changed and did change between 1831 and 1869, when Vice-Chancellor James decided Leather Cloth Co. v. Lorsont (L. R. 9 Eq. 35); and if there had not been a further change before Lord Justice Fry decided Roussillon v. Roussillon (L. R. 14 Ch. D. 351) in 1880, it must have occurred ere now. There are many circumstances familiar to us all, and some of them connected with politics rather than with policy, which have materially altered the relative position of rivals in trade and of the public whom traders supply. Railways, electric telegraphs and telephones have all exercised an influence, and quite recently the parcels post to say nothing of many other novelties, have introduced new elements into competition. I make these remarks because to my mind they go a long way to explain the difference between the earlier and later decisions. Judges have been bound to recognize not merely the old decisions, but the principles on which they were founded, and yet regarding public policy as the principle overriding all, they have struggled to adopt these older decisions to the changed circumstances of the day. There has, I think, been a steady though irregular progress from the stricter rules of the last century, and perhaps it has not yet reached its limit." Kekewich in Davies v. Davies, L. R. 36 Ch. D. 359, 364.

often changes as the laws change, and, therefore, new applications of old principles are required.[1] Whatever tends to injustice or oppression, restraint of liberty, restraint of legal right; whatever tends to the obstruction of justice, a violation of a statute, or the obstruction or perversion of the administration of the law; whatever tends to interfere with or control the administration of the law, as to executive, legislative or other official action,—whenever embodied in, and made the subject of, a contract, the contract is against public policy and therefore void, and not susceptible of enforcement: all contracts prejudicial to the interest of the public, such as contracts tending to prevent competition, whenever the statute or any known rule of law requires it, are void."[2] But, as has already appeared,

[1] Davies v. Davies, L. R. 36 Ch. D. 364.

[2] Brooks v. Cooper, 50 N. J. Eq. 761; s. c., 26 Atl. Rep. 978, 981. "A contract may be illegal, although not in contravention of the specific directions of a statute, if it be opposed to the general policy and intent thereof. Staines v. Wainwright, 6 Bing. N. Cas. 174: Philpott v. St. George's Hospital, 6 H. L. Cas. 338, 347: Collins v. Blantern, 1 Smith Lead. Cas., pt. 1, p. 680. It is not necessary that the statute should contain words of positive prohibition. De Begnis v. Armistead, 10 Bing. 110. The contract here in question between the appellants and respondent, on its face assumes control of the disposition of the selection to publish the laws. It was not within their intention, as appears by the contract and the evidence, that either one of the members of the public body designated by law to make this selection should have the slightest voice in the performance of their duty under the statute. So far as this contract is concerned there might as well have been no existence of any such selecting power, or any statute on the subject. This contract was substituted in the place of the statute, and, so far as the contract is to be considered and interpreted, the statute no longer had any force or effect. The contract was a subversion of the statute. Regardless of the reason of the statute, and the public benefit to be derived from its administration, for the purpose of allaying a personal antagonism between themselves by their agreement, they dictated to the public body provided by law to administer this statute, a course of action without reference to those provisions which designate the objects, purposes and policy of the legislature in its enactment. No grosser form of a contract in contravention of the provisions and policy of the statute could be demonstrated. The contract itself and its tendency are the tests of its illegality. The results which are produced are not the proper tests, although here the results are those

the public policy of one country may differ from that of another, and in the United states the rule established by one court is not necessarily accepted by all others. Moreover, the rule of the same court, at the present time, may differ from that which it sustained at an earlier period. The method of determining what public policy requires at a particular time and place may be of practical importance. But the application of the rule in this regard is well established. Where the public policy of a nation or of a State has been indicated by the fundamental law or by statutory enactments, that is the rule to the courts. In the absence of such a guide the latest decisions in equity will be followed. In a leading case before the Supreme Court of the United States, the rule was stated by Chief Justice Chase, as follows: "The court can know nothing of public policy

which are also interdicted by sound public policy. Its tendency was, and the result was, to influence official action, regardless of the plain provisions of the statute." *Ibid.* See also following cases cited by the court: Gulicke v. Ward, 10 N. J. L. 87; Jones v. Randal, Cowp. 39; Mitchell v. Smith, 1 Binn. 120; Blachford v. Preston, 8 T. R. 95; Coppock v. Bower, 4 Mees. & W. 361; Meacham v. Dow, 32 Vt. 721; Parsons v. Thompson, 1 H. Bl. 322; Jones v. Caswell, 3 Johns. Cas. 29; Doolin v, Ward, 6 Johns. 194; Thompson v. Davies, 13 Johns. 112; Bank v. Sprague, 20 N. J. Eq. 160; Morris v. Woodward, 25 N. J. Eq, 32; Thomas v. Edwards, 2 Mees. & W. 218; Hatzfield v. Gulden, 7 Watts, 153; Kribben v. Haycraft, 26 Mo. 396; State v. Johnson, 52 Ind. 197; Haines v. Lewis, 54 Iowa, 301; s. c., 6 N. W. Rep. 495; Trist v. Child, 21 Wall. 441; McGuire v. Corwine, 101 U. S. 108; Keating v. Hyde, 23 Mo. App. 555; Nichols v. Mudgett, 32 Vt. 546; Guernsey v. Cook, 120 Mass. 501; Noel v. Drake, 28 Kan. 265; Forbes v. McDonald, 54 Cal. 98; Bliss v. Lawrence, 58 N. Y. 442; Schwenk v. Wyckoff, 46 N. J. Eq. 560; s. c., 20 Atl. Rep. 259; Ellicott v. Chamberlain, 38 N. J. Eq. 604; Smith v. Applegate, 23 N. J. L. 352; Jackson v. Davidson, 4 Barn. & Ald. 695; Rogers v. Kingston, 10 Moore, 102; s. c., 2 Bing. 441; Murray v. Reeves, 8 Barn. & C. 425; Hall v. Dyson, 16 Jur. 270; s. c., L. J. 21 Q. B. 224; Hills v. Mitson, 8 Excheq. 758; Cannon v. Cannon, 26 N. J. Eq. 316; Blasdell v. Fowle, 120 Mass. 447; Ayer v. Hutchinson, 4 Mass. 370; Lucas v. Allen, 80 Ky. 681; O'Hara v. Carpenter, 23 Mich. 410; Caton v. Stewart, 76 N. Car. 357; Tool Co. v. Norris, 2 Wall. 45; Oscanyan v. Arms Co., 103 U. S. 261; Gray v. Hook, 4 N. Y. 449; Hunter v. Wolf, 71 Pa. St. 282; Osborne v. Williams, 18 Ves. 379; Ashburner v. Parrish, 81 Pa. St. 52; Gordon v. Dalby, 30 Iowa, 223; Satterlee v. Jones. 3 Duer, 102.

except from the constitution and the laws, and the course of administration and decision. It has no legislative powers. It cannot amend or modify any legislative acts. It cannot examine questions as expedient or inexpedient, as politic or impolitic; considerations of that sort must, in general, be addressed to the legislature. Questions of policy determined there are concluded here. There are cases, it is true, in which arguments drawn from public policy must have large influence; but there are cases in which the course of legislation and administration do not leave any doubt upon the question what the public policy is and in which what would otherwise be obscure or of doubtful interpretation, may be cleared and resolved by reference to what is already received and established."[1] In the recent case of The United States v. The Trans-Missouri Freight Association, we have the following re-statement of the doctrine by Mr. Justice Peckham: "The public policy of the government is to be found in its statutes, and when they have not directly spoken, then in the decisions of the courts and the constant practice of the government officials; but when the law-making power speaks upon a particular subject, over which it has constitutional power to legislate, public policy in such a case is what the statute enacts. If the law prohibit any contract or combination in restraint of trade or commerce, a contract or combination made in violation of such law is void, whatever may have been theretofore decided by the courts to have been the public policy of the country on that subject."[2]

§ 16. **The Effect of a Change.**—It is well established that where a covenant, or agreement of any sort, is conformed to public policy at the time at which it is entered into, it will not be invalidated by any subsequent change of public policy. On the other hand, where a covenant is void, on the ground of public policy, at the time at which it is executed, a change of public policy may render such

[1] License Tax Cases, 5 Wall. 462. 469.

[2] U. S. v. Trans-Missouri Freight Association, 17 Sup. Ct. Rep. 540, 559.

covenant valid, provided the parties renew it subsequently to the change. In a case before the Supreme Court of the United States it was held that it is no defense to a suit brought on a promissory note executed in Louisiana, in February, 1861, by the holder against the maker, to allege and prove that such note was given as the price of slaves sold to the maker. That such sale was at the time lawful in the said State was a sufficient consideration for a note, and the obligation could not be impaired by laws of the State passed subsequently to the date thereof. No law of the United States has impaired such obligation.[1] In a very recent case in California this doctrine was sustained. It

[1] Boyce v. Tabb, 18 Wall. 546. See also Wilkinson v. Coot, 44 Miss. 367; Harrel v. Watson, 63 N. Car. 454; Osborn v. Nicholson, 13 Wall. 654; McElvain v. Mudd, 44 Ala. 48; Roderiquez v. Bienvenu, 22 La. Ann. 300; Hall v. Keese, 31 Tex. 504; Willis v. Halliburton, 25 Ark. 173; Dorris v. Grace, 24 Ark. 326; Roundtree v. Baker, 52 Ill. 241; Atkins v. Busby, 25 Ark. 176; Wainwright v. Bridges, 19 La. Ann. 234; Austin v. Sandel, 19 La. Ann. 309; Hailey v. Hoeffner, 19 La. Ann. 518; Lyttle v. Whicher, 21 La. Ann. 182; Gosselin v. Womack, 21 La. Ann. 193; Sandige v. Sanderson, 21 La. Ann. 757; Satterfield v. Spurlock, 21 La. Ann. 771; Lafever v. Haydel, 21 La. Ann. 663; Brou v. Becnel, 22 La. Ann. 189; Bruin v. Sasser, 25 La. Ann. 224; Allen v. Tarlton, 25 La. Ann. 427; Thompson v. Simmons, 25 La. Ann. 450; Walker v. Ducros, 25 La. Ann. 214; Merritt v. Merritt, 25 La. Ann. 257; Smith v. McWaters, 25 La. Ann. 431; Castile v. Offutt, 25 La. Ann. 430. "Whatever we may think of the institution of slavery, viewed in the light of religion, morals, humanity or a sound political economy, as the obligation here in question was valid when executed, sitting as a court of justice, we have no choice but to give it effect. We cannot regard it as differing in its legal efficacy from any other unexecuted contract to pay money made upon a sufficient consideration at the same time and place, neither in the precedents and principles of the common law, nor in its associated system of equity jurisprudence, nor in the older system known as the civil law is there anything to warrant the result contended for by defendant in error. Neither the rights nor the interests of those of the colored race lately in bondage are affected by the conclusions we have reached." Osborne v. Nicholson, 13 Wall. 654, 663. "In April, 1864, the plaintiff, as administrator, in the county of Hertford which was not within the lines or under the control of the army of the United States, offers for sale, according to the laws of the State, and does sell at auction, a negro man slave. The defendant becomes the purchaser, pays a part of the price, takes the slave and executes his bond for the balance of the price. In what point of view can this transaction be considered against

was held that if a contract conforms to the public policy of the State when made, a change in public policy will not avoid it; and a subsequent statute making it a misdemeanor to start fires in certain localities without first taking certain precautions, whereby the property of an adjoining or contiguous owner is injured, damaged or destroyed, cannot render invalid a covenant in a lease made before its passage exempting the lessor from responsibility for any damage caused by fire.[1] In a case before the Court of Appeals of Kentucky, in 1810, it was held that a writing executed to emancipate slaves before it was lawful to do so would be valid upon re-acknowledgment, after the statute permitting emancipation.[2]

§ 17. **Covenants Inconsistent with Morality.**—It is not the policy of the law to uphold morality by legal sanctions. In the administration of the law courts do not assume any prerogative of omnipotence. Moral obligations consid-

public policy, or as violating good morals, as to authorize a court of justice to refuse to enforce the contract. * * * It was not against the public policy of the State of North Carolina, according to the laws then existing and recognized both by the wrongful government then in power, and the rightful government which was for the time deprived of its power. It was not against the policy of the act of congress of 1862, nor of the proclamation of the president; for, as we have seen, it would not affect that policy, in localities not under the control of the armies of the United States, whether a person was held as a slave by A or B provided, under the circumstances, he was to be the slave of some persons. So far as good morals are involved, the matter is not to be viewed, as we conceive, from a standpoint, where the institution of slavery is deemed wicked and in violation of the laws of God and of the rights of man, but from a standpoint where the institution was considered as established and made lawful by the laws of the State, and recognized and protected by the constitution of the United States, and had been handed down and acted upon from father to son among our people, from the first settlement of the colony of Carolina." Harrell v. Watson, 63 N. Car. 454, 460. A contract to remove slaves and other property to Texas and take care of them, during the late war and before emancipation by the sovereign power, the United States, was legal at the time it was made, and is, therefore, binding on the parties by and between whom it was made. Powell v. Daniel, 23 La. Ann. 289.

[1] Stephens v. Southern Pacific Co., 109 Cal. 86; s. c., 41 Pac. Rep. 783.

[2] Donaldson v. Jude, 2 Bibb, 57.

ered as such are not enforceable by statute or by courts of law or of equity. It is not the province of any legal tribunal to decide questions of morality, *per se*, not simply because such tribunals have no jurisdiction in cases of this character, but, as well, because the decision of such questions, whatever it might be, would deprive the citizen of that freedom of action which is secured by the fundamental law. The obligations of the individual, which are simply moral, are not to any human authority, but to the Sovereign Ruler of the universe. But while this is to be borne in mind it is well established that covenants that are in violation of morality or that relate to transactions which are *contra bonos mores*, will not be enforced by courts of law or of equity. There is an essential and palpable distinction between what is to be tolerated or what is to be left to the retributions of eternity and what is to be upheld by the decisions of courts. An agreement, the fulfillment of which involves a violation of the law of God, or tends to the dissemination of any form of immorality, and, in consequence, is adapted to corrupt the public mind and lower the standard of public morals, is illegal and void. This position was upheld by the civil law. The rule was as follows: "*Pacta quæ contra leges constitutionesque, vel contra bonos mores fiunt, nullam vim habere, indubitate juris est.*[1] This rule is an expression of the natural sense of justice and of the fitness of things entertained by a Pagan court. But the rule, as upheld by the courts of England and of the United States, is a doctrine of the common law, and has its basis in the religion of the Holy Scriptures. The theory of this rule is that the Christian religion is the foundation and the only substantial foundation of public morality. On this ground it is held that any covenant, relating to a business transaction, the effect of which is to corrupt the public morals, or to subvert the Christian religion, is in contravention of public policy and, in consequence, illegal and void.[2] In a late case in Penn-

[1] Cod. Lib. II., tit. 3, 1, 6.

[2] Newland on Contracts, chap. 32, p. 469, *et. seq.* Thus of contracts for illicit sexual intercourse:

sylvania, the court said: "It may be regarded as settled in Pennsylvania that a court of equity will not enforce a trust where its object is the propagation of atheism, infidelity, immorality or hostility to the existing form of government. A man may do many things while living which the law will

Goodale v. Thurman, 1 Head, 209: Baldy v. Stratton, 11 Pa. St. 316: Hanks v. Naglee. 54 Cal. 51: Steinfeld v. Levy, 16 Abb. Pr. (N. S.) 26: Crawford v. Gordon, 11 Wkly. L. Bull. 121: Trovinger v. McBurney, 5 Cow. 253: Denton v. English. 2 Nott. & M. 581: Friend v. Harrison, 2 C. & P. 584: Rider v. Kidder, 10 Ves. 366; De Sobry v. De Laistre, 2 H. & J. 191; Ringgold v. Tyson. 3 H. &. J. 172; Forsythe v. State, 6 Ohio, 19: Williams v. Bullmore, 33 L. J. Ch. 461; Franco v. Bolton, 3 Ves. 368; Smyth v. Griffin. 14 L. J. Ch. 28; s. c., 12 L. J. Ch. 193; Winebrinner v. Weisiger. 3 T. B. Mon. 32; Sherman v. Barrett. 1 McMull. 147; Gray v. Mathias, 5 Ves. 286: Brown v. Langford. 3 Bibb, 497: Cusack v. White, 2 Mills, Const. Rep. 279: Greenwood v. Curtis. 6 Mass. 358, 379. So as to the profits of prostition and leases of houses for the purpose: Bowry v. Bennet. 1 Camp. N. P. 348; Burns v. Seep. 8 Am. Law Rec. (Ohio) 425; Girardy v. Richardson, 1 Esp. 13: s. c., 1 B. & P. 341 *n.*; Appleton v. Campbell, 2 C. & P. 347: Howard v. Hodges, 1 Selw. N. P. 79; Lloyd v. Johnson, 1 B. & P. 340; Jennings v. Throgmorton, Ry. & M. 251; Smith v. Whyte, L. R. 1 Eq. 626; s. c., 35 L. J. Ch. 45; 14 W. R. 510; 14 L. T. (N. S.) 350. So as to recovery for printing an immoral book: Poplett v. Stockdale, Ry. & M. 337; s. c., 2 C. & P. 198. Likewise, contracts which contemplates the commission of a crime: Hocker v. Gentry. 3 Met. 463: Lewis v. Davidson, 4 M. & W. 654; s. c., 1 H. & H. 426; 3 Jur. 387; Hatch v. Mann. 15 Wend. 44; Drennan v. Douglas, 102 Ill. 341; Hebblewaite v. Hepworth, 98 Ill. 126. "Another case may be stated, as within this second exception, in an action on a contract made in a foreign State by a prostitute, to recover the wages of her prostitution. This contract, if lawful where it was made, could not be the legal ground of an action here; for the consideration is confessedly immoral, and a judgment in support of it would be pernicious from its example. And perhaps all cases may be considered as within this second exception, which are founded on moral turpitude, in respect either of the consideration or the stipulation." Greenwood v. Curtis, 6 Mass. 358, 379. A contract by an advertising solicitor to sell to a "specialist" letters written by persons afflicted with diseases, to another person who advertised articles and instruments that it was claimed would cure them, in order that such specialist might send his advertisements to them, is contrary to good morals and void. Rice v. Williams, 32 Fed. Rep. 437. No action can be maintained for pirating a work which professes to be the amours of a courtesan, and it is no answer to the objection that the defendant is also a wrongdoer in publishing them, and that he therefore ought not to set up their immorality. *Semble*, that a person not do for him after he is dead. He may deny the existence of a God and employ his fortune in the dissemination of infidel views, but should he leave his fortune in trust for such purposes the law will strike down the trust as *contra*

being seen correcting the MS. is not sufficient evidence that a copyright of a work is his. Stockdale v. Onwhyn, 2 C. & P. 163. A contract by which a sheriff hires out to another the labor of a convict for twenty-four months to satisfy a fine and costs amounting to $283.90, is contrary to public policy and void. State v. Stanley, 52 Ark. 178; s. c., 12 S. W. Rep. 327. An extension company which had a contract with a railroad company to locate and construct the road "by the nearest, cheapest and most suitable route," between two points, for $20,000 per mile, agreed to locate the road through the town of A in consideration of being paid a bonus by defendant. In locating the road through A it was necessary to deflect from the nearest, cheapest and most natural route a distance of five miles, at an additional cost of $100,000. *Held*, that the contract between the extension company and defendant being an agreement by an employe to violate his obligation to his employer, was against public policy and void. Woodstock Iron Co. v. Richmond & D. Extension Co., 129 U. S. 643; s. c., 9 Sup. Ct. Rep. 402. A contract between certain attorneys and persons engaged in the illegal sale of intoxicating liquors, providing that the attorneys shall, for one year, for the monthly compensation of $80, defend all cases against such persons for violations of the liquor laws, is against public policy and void. Bowman v. Phillips, 41 Kan. 364; s. c., 21 Pac. Rep. 230. An agreement between two or more to purchase shares in a company in order to induce persons who might thereafter purchase shares in such company to believe contrary to the fact, that there was a *bona fide* market for its shares, and that the shares were at a real premium, is an illegal transaction, and no action can be maintained in respect of such agreement or purchase of shares. Scott v. Brown, L. R. (1892) 2 Q. B. 724. A contract between husband and wife, whereby it was agreed to drop all matters of dispute, to refrain from scolding, fault finding and anger, and live together as husband and wife; that the wife should keep her home in a comfortable condition, and that the husband should provide all the necessary expenses of the family, and pay the wife in addition a certain sum per month—is contrary to public policy. Miller v. Miller, 78 Iowa, 177; s. c., 42 N. W. Rep. 641. J and M formed a partnership to build a railroad and to that end caused a corporation to be formed under the general laws of Illinois. J was one director and the clerks of M were the others. It was averred that all the directors acted at the dictation of J and M, and were, in fact, merely their agents. The board awarded the contract for building the road to certain persons, nominally, but in fact, for the benefit of J & M, agreeing to give them all the stock and first mortgage bonds of the company, *bonos mores*"[1] In another leading case in the same State, the court said: "It is in entire consistency with this sacred guarantee of the rights of conscience and religious liberty to hold that even if Christianity is no part of the law of the land, it is the popular religion of the country, an insult to which would be indictable as directly tending to disturb the public peace. The laws and institutions of this State are built on the foundation of reverence for Christianity. To this extent, at least, it must certainly be considered as well settled that the religion revealed in the Bible is not to be openly reviled, ridiculed or blasphemed, to the annoyance of sincere believers, who compose the great mass of the

issued at the rate of $15.000 a mile. On a bill filed by J against the legal representatives of M. to obtain an account of the profits of the partnership growing out of a partial execution of the contract for constructing the road, *held*, that the contract was fraudulent and against public policy, and that equity would not entertain the suit for an accounting, even as to the profits actually realized by M up to the time he abandoned the enterprise. Jackson v. McLean, 36 Fed. Rep. 213. A trust deed, the consideration for which is, that the *cestui que trust* will abandon her real ground of divorce from the grantor, and will attempt to procure the divorce on another ground, in the existence of which she does not, in fact, believe, and that the grantor will make no resistance but will pay her costs and attorney fees, is contrary to public policy and void. Stokes v. Anderson, 118 Ind. 533; s. c., 21 N. E. Rep. 331. A note given to a woman in compromise of a bastardy proceeding is binding and valid, and on sufficient consideration, and the payment thereof cannot be avoided on the ground that the compromise of such proceeding is contrary to public policy, or public morals. Billingsley v. Clelland, 41 W. Va. 234; s. c., 23 S. E. Rep. 812. A combination of persons and firms in a city for the control of the sale of beer and the cessation of competition *inter se* is not void at common law as against public policy, although in restraint of trade, since beer is not an article of prime necessity and its sale is closely restricted by public policy. Anheuser Busch Brewing Ass'n v. Houck (Tex. Civ. App.), 27 S. W. Rep. 692. A contract, whereby one party, for certain commissions, is to attend meetings of persons solicited to buy real estate from the other party, and persuade them to become purchasers, representing himself to them as a purchaser by subscribing for lots, which the owner is to take off his hands if he does not wish to retain them—concealing from the intending buyers his arrangement with such owner—is against public policy, and cannot be enforced. McDonnell v. Rigney (Mich.) (1896), 66 N. W. Rep. 52.

[1] Manners v. Library Company, 93 Pa. St. 165, 172.

good people of the commonwealth. I can conceive of nothing so likely, so sure, indeed, to produce those consequences, as a hall desecrated in perpetuity for the free discussion of religion, politics, etc., under the direction and administration of a society of infidels. Indeed, I would go further, and adopt the sentiment and language of Mr. Justice Duncan (in Updegraff v. Commonwealth).[1] It would prove a nursery of vice, a school of preparation to qualify young men for the gallows and young women for the brothel, and there is not a skeptic of decent manners and good morals who would not consider such a debating club as a common nuisance and disgrace to the city."[2] In a case before the Supreme Court of the United States, Mr. Justice Swayne, in delivering the opinion of the court, said: "In the Roman law it was declared that 'a promise made to effect a base purpose, as to commit homicide or sacrilege, is not binding.' In our jurisprudence a contract may be illegal and void because it is contrary to a constitution or statute or inconsistent with sound policy and good morals. Lord Mansfield said: 'Many contracts which are not against morality are still void as being against the maxims of sound policy.' It is a rule of the common law of universal application that where a contract, express or implied, is tainted with either of the vices last named, as to the consideration or the thing to be done, no alleged right founded upon it can be enforced in a court of justice."[3]

§ 18. **Services in Influencing Legislation.**—The employment of an attorney or other agent to influence members of congress or of a legislature in favor of an act, the object of which is to subserve personal or private ends, is in contravention of public policy and will not be upheld by the courts. Not only public policy but considerations of sound morality require that legislators should act freely and from

[1] Updegraff v. Commonwealth, 11 S. & R. 394, 399.

[2] Zeisweiss v. James, 63 Pa. St. 465, 471.

[3] Trist v. Child, 21 Wall. 441, 448. See also 1 Story, Eq. 294, 303.

sole regard to the interests of their constituents. Any departure from such a course is a betrayal of their high trust and of the nature of treason. Any attempt, therefore, to influence a legislator in that direction is opposed to public policy and inconsistent with common morality. Hence, a contract to perform a service of that character will be treated as illegal and void. In New York it has been held that a contract, the consideration of which is that one of the parties thereto would give "all the aid in his power, spend such reasonable time as may be necessary, and, generally, use his utmost influence and exertions to procure the passage into a law" of a bill introduced into the legislature, is void, as against public policy, and will not be enforced. Such contracts tend to subject the legislature to secret, improper and corrupt influences.[1] In a recent case

[1] Mills v. Mills, 40 N. Y. 543; Frost v. Belmont, 6 Allen, 152; Bryan v. Reynolds, 5 Wis. 200; Usher v. McBratney, 3 Dill. 385; Gil v. Davis, 12 La. Ann. 219; Clippenger v. Hepbaugh, 5 W. & S. 315; Powers v. Skinner, 34 Vt. 274; Harris v. Roof, 10 Barb. 489; Rose v. Truax, 21 Barb. 361; Spalding v. Ewing, 149 Pa. St. 375; s. c., 24 Atl. Rep. 219; Woodstock Iron Co. v. Richmond & D. Extension Co., 129 U. S. 643; s. c., 9 Sup. Ct. Rep. 402; McKee v. Cheney, 52 How. Pr. 144; Cummins v. Barkalow, 4 Keyes, 514; Southard v. Boyd, 51 N. Y. 177; Brown v. Brown, 34 Barb. 533. A contract by which one agreed to procure the passage of a bill by congress declaring certain railroad lands forfeited to the government, so that the other party to the contract might hold a part of such lands as a *bona fide* settlor under the homestead laws is void as against public policy. Houlton v. Dunn, 60 Minn. 26; s. c., 61 N. W. Rep. 898. A contract to pay for professional services in securing additional compensation for defendant as postmaster, where such services consisted in securing special legislation to compel the post office department to pay a claim which had been rejected, is contrary to public policy and cannot be enforced. Spaulding v. Ewing, 149 Pa. St. 375; s. c., 24 Atl. Rep. 219; 30 W. N. Cas. 215. Any agreement which contemplates the use of private influence to secure legislation is void. Burney's Heirs v. Ludeling, 47 La. Ann. 73; s. c. 16 So. Rep. 507. "The contract of an attorney for services as such, whether the services are to be rendered before a court, a department of the government, or a legislative body, is valid, and upon performance of the services a recovery can be had. The contract of a lobbyist, in the sense in which that term is now used, for his services as such, is against public policy and void. Where there is a single contract, and the services contracted for and rendered are partially those of an attorney and

in Oregon it was held that it is against public policy for a person to hire himself out to perform "lobby service" with members of the legislature, and a contract for such services is illegal and invalid.[1] In a leading case before the Supreme Court of the United States, the rule is stated, by Mr. Justice Swayne, as follows: "The theory of our government is that all public stations are trusts, and that those clothed with them are to be animated in the discharge of their duties solely by considerations of right, justice and the public good. They are never to descend to a lower plane. But there is a correlative duty resting upon the citizen. In his intercourse with those in authority, whether executive or legislative, touching the performance of their functions, he is bound to exhibit truth, frankness and integrity. Any departure from the line of rectitude in such cases is not

partially those of a lobbyist, and blended together as part and parcel of a single employment, the entire contract is vitiated—'that which is bad destroys that which is good, and they perish together.' There is no presumption that a contract is illegal. He who denies his liability under a contract, which he admits having made, must make the fact of its illegality apparent. The burden of showing it wrong is on him who seeks to deny his obligation thereon. The presumption is in favor of innocence, and the taint of wrong is matter of defense." McBratney v. Chandler, 22 Kan. 692, 695. "It is certainly all important to just and wise legislation, and therefore to the most essential interests of the public, that the legislature should be perfectly free from any extraneous influence which may either corrupt or deceive the members or any of them, and doubtless there may be among the members themselves enough of personal influences by and upon each other, without inviting the aid of others, by enforcing contracts for compensation for their influence, exerted not from patriotic or public motives, but from those which are altogether mercenary and selfish, and certainly the law should not help to compel the payment of a fee to any man, whether great or of little influence, for his personal solicitations in favor of the enactment of any law whatever. Nothing could be more suicidal or unwise than a contrary doctrine. A lawyer may be entitled to compensation for writing a petition, or even for making a public argument before the legislature, or a committee thereof, but the law should not help him or any other person, to recover a fee for exerting any personal influence, in any way, in any act of legislation. In such a case he must rely on the honorary obligation alone." Wood v. McCann, 6 Dana, 366, 369.

[1] Sweeney v. McLeod, 15 Ore. 330; s. c., 15 Pac. Rep. 275.

only bad in morals, but involves a public wrong. No people can have any higher public interest, except the preservation of their liberties, than integrity in the preservation of their government in all its departments. The agreement in the present case was for the sale of the influence and exertions of the lobby agent to bring about the passage of a law for the payment of a private claim, without reference to its merits, by means which, if not corrupt, were illegitimate, and considered in connection with the pecuniary interest of the agent at stake, contrary to the plainest principles of public policy. No one has a right in such circumstances to put himself in a position of temptation to do what is regarded as so pernicious in its character. The law forbids the inchoate step and puts the seal of its reprobation upon the undertaking."[1] In another leading case before the same court, Mr. Justice Grier said: "Legislators should act with a single eye to the true interest of the whole people, and courts of justice can give no countenance to the use of means which may subject them to be misled by the pertinacious importunity and indirect influences of interested and unscrupulous agents or solicitors. Influences secretly urged under false and covert pretenses must necessarily operate deleteriously on legislative action, whether it be employed to obtain the passage of private or public acts. Bribes, in the shape of high contingent compensation, must necessarily lead to the use of improper means and the exercise of undue influence. Their necessary consequence is the demoralization of the agent who covenants for them; he is soon brought to believe that any means which will produce so beneficial a result to himself are 'proper means;' and that a share of these profits may have the same effect of quickening the perceptions and warming the zeal of influential or 'careless' members in favor of his bill. The use of such agents will have the effect to subject the State government to the combined capital of wealthy corporations, and produce universal corruption, commencing with the representative and ending with the elector. Speculators

[1] Trist v. Child, 21 Wall. 441, 450.

in legislation, public and private, a compact corps of venal solicitors, vending their secret influences, will infest the capital of the Union and of every State, till corruption shall become the normal condition of the body politic, and it will be said of us as of Rome—'*omne Romœ venale.*' "[1]

§ **19. The Ground of the Rule.**—It is not held that the citizens of the States or of the nation are prohibited from making any effort to influence legislation. Such an influence may be for the public good and not in contravention of public policy. Where there is nothing in the end sought or in the methods employed that is illegal, a covenant relating to the consideration for services of this character will be sustained. The ground of the rule, as stated in the preceding section, is the secret and corrupt character of the influence exerted. The end sought is inconsistent with public morality and is in contravention of public policy, and the means employed are in keeping with the object to be accomplished. In a case in Massachusetts, the court said: "The business of 'lobby members' is not to go fairly and openly before the committees and present statements, proofs and arguments that the other side has an opportunity to meet and refute, if they are wrong, but to go secretly to the members and ply them with statements and arguments that the other side cannot openly meet, however erroneous they may be, and to bring illegitimate influences to bear upon them. If the 'lobby member' is selected because of his political or personal influence, it aggravates the wrong. If his business is to unite various interests by means of projects that are called 'log rolling,' it is still worse. The practice of procuring members of the legislature to act under the influence of what they have eaten and drunk at houses of entertainment, tends to render those of them who yield to such influences wholly unfit to act in such cases. They are disqualified from acting fairly towards interested parties, or towards the public. The tendency and object of these influences are to obtain by cor-

[1] Marshall v. Balto. & Ohio R. Co., 16 How. 314. 335.

ruption what it is supposed cannot be obtained fairly."[1] In an important and instructive case before the Supreme Court of Vermont the principle is stated by the court, as

[1] Frost v. Belmont, 6 Allen, 152, 159. "These remarks are not to be understood as having any relation to the case in hand, for no suspicion is entertained that anything out of the ordinary course took place in respect to this bill. Yet, it cannot escape observation, that even here an inducement was not wanting to an improper or at least personal influence, or deceptive acts, to procure the success of the measure. The temptation may be small here, but it has not always been confined within such narrow limits, as there is great reason to fear. We do not say, it is not necessary to the case to say that a certain compensation for such services may not be recovered: but we are clearly of opinion that it would be against sound policy to sanction a practice which may lead to secret, improper and corrupt tampering with legislative action. It is not required that it tends to corruption; if its effect is to mislead, it is decisive against the claim: and that such is its tendency no human being can reasonably doubt. * * * It is, therefore, most erroneous to assume, as is done by plaintiff's counsel, that a practice, leading to such consequences, is not contrary to private interests and public morals. The reverse is too true; for already has a class of persons arisen, at the seat of the general government and elsewhere, who make it a business to push through private claims, for a compensation, greatly, if not entirely dependent on success. How demoralizing this may be it needs not the gift of prophecy to foretell. Nay, more, we feel its effects, for it is impossible to shut our eyes at the consequences of this, with other causes daily developing themselves in the decline of justice and public morals. How easy the transition from private individuals to the members themselves it would not be difficult to divine; but we are not left to conjecture, for we are not without examples, which it would be invidious to mention, but which are too well known. Whatever abuses may exist elsewhere, we hope the judicial tribunals of the country may be kept pure, without suspicion even, that they may never be induced under a pretense to countenance vice, or lend their sanction to a principle, the inevitable effect of which will be to increase, if it does not create fraud and misrepresentation. In the face of many painful examples to the contrary, it is idle to say that individual, extraneous influence, acting secretly, upon the members of the legislature, is not pernicious to the best interests of society. Its direct tendency is to sap the foundations of all morality." Clippenger v. Hepbaugh, 5 W. & S. 315, 319. "The question here involved is a very important one, and we regret that we did not have the benefit of an oral argument by the very able counsel for the plaintiff. If there were services rendered and expenditures incurred by the plaintiff for the defendant, as he alleges, entirely disconnected with the services rendered in procuring

follows: "The principle of the decisions has no respect to the equities between the parties, but is controlled solely by the tendency of the contract, and it matters not that nothing improper was done under it. The law will not

congressional legislation, they would constitute a good cause of action; but, unfortunately for the plaintiff, he has included the value of the whole services and expenditures in one lump sum, and seemingly as though the contract was entire. Evidently the court below so treated the transaction; and from a perusal of the pleadings we do not see how it could have done otherwise. See Trist v. Child, 21 Wall. 441. The courts hold that there are two kinds of agreements relative to the matter of procuring legislation from our State and national legislatures, and our municipal bodies, boards or officers. One is the evil and mischievous agreement which tends to corrupt the law making powers, and is accomplished sometimes by subtle acts of personal importunity and intrigue or by secret and insidious overtures, while at other times corrupt results are reached by startling boldness and daring. Some of the authorities which refuse to enforce this kind of agreements are as follows: Clippenger v. Hepbaugh, 5 Watts & S. 315; Harris v. Roof, 10 Barb. 489; Rose v. Truax, 21 Barb. 361; Mills v. Mills, 36 Barb. 474; Trist v. Child, 21 Wall. 441; Spalding v. Ewing, 149 Pa. St. 375; s. c., 24 Atl. Rep. 219; Oscanyan v. Arms Co., 103 U. S. 261, 274; Tool Co. v. Norris, 2 Wall. 45; Woodstock Iron Co. v. Richmond & D. Extension Co., 129 U. S. 643; s. c., 9 Sup. Ct. Rep. 402. In the case of Clippinger v. Hepbaugh, 5 Watts & S. 315, it was said by the court: 'It matters not that nothing improper was done or was expected to be done by the plaintiff. It is enough that such is the tendency of the contract; that it is contrary to sound morality and public policy, leading, necessarily, in the hands of designing and corrupt men to improper tampering with members and the use of an extraneous, secret influence over an important branch of government. It may not corrupt all, but if it corrupts or tends to corrupt some, or if it deceives or tends to deceive or mislead some, that is sufficient to stamp its character with the seal of reprobation, before a judicial tribunal.' In the case of Rose v. Truax, 21 Barb. 361, the agreement was 'to use his influence, efforts and labor in procuring the passage of a law by the legislature, and the agreement was held void, as against public policy, and that as the contract was entire it was wholly void, and that no recovery could be had for even legitimate services performed under the agreement. In the case of Weed v. Black, 2 MacArthur, 268, the court uses the following language: 'If the terms of the contract be broad enough to cover services of any kind, whether secret or open, honest or dishonest, the law pronounces a ban upon the paper itself.' * * * 'It will be observed that many of the decisions are based upon the corrupt tendency of such contracts, rather than the particular wording of the contract itself. * * * We do concede to any man, however honest he may be, the privilege of making a contract which it would not recognize, when made by designing and corrupt men. A person may, without doubt, be employed to conduct an application to the legislature as well as to conduct a suit at law, and may contract for, and receive, pay for his services in preparing and presenting a petition or other documents, in collecting evidence, in making a statement or exposition of facts, or in preparing and making an oral or written argument, provided all these are used, or designed to be used, either before the legislature itself or some committee thereof as a body; but he cannot with propriety be employed to exert his personal influence, whether it be great or little, with individual members, or to labor privately in any form with them, out of the legislative hall, in favor of or against any

not condemn the attempts to secure legislation for legitimate purposes and in a legitimate manner. Many laws are passed solely for the public good by reason of the presentation of the proper evidence and arguments addressed to legislative bodies or the proper committees by outsiders, done openly, and without corrupting influences having been exercised. Frequently our educational, charitable and humane laws are thus procured. There are also many just and meritorious private claims when, through the neglect or wrongful acts of the government, it would not be improper to present them for allowance and payment and do so by fair argument and legitimate evidence. Many just claims have remained unpaid for years through the neglect of our legislative bodies to give them proper recognition, while corrupt legislation has enabled the lobbyist to succeed, to the injury of the public welfare and deleterious to private morals. In the language of our constitution each person 'ought to obtain justice freely and without purchase, completely and without denial; promptly and without delay, conformably to the laws' (article 1, § 8); but hiring an agent to lobby a large portion of the year during several years, in procuring legislation securing to an individual government lands for a comparatively small sum, worth more than $12,000, does not come within that class of contracts which is sanctioned by the law and does not meet with our approval. The prevalent iniquitous system of lobbying with members of our legislative bodies and public officials is fast becoming a menace to our capacity for self-government. Courts can do but little to stop this most pernicious vice, because it is seldom that such cases come before them, but when they do appear there should go forth from the judicial forum only rebuke and the ban of disapproval." Buck, J., in Houlton v. Dunn, 60 Minn. 26, 2J; s. c., 61 N. W. Rep. 898.

act or subject of legislation. The personal and private nature of the services to be rendered is the point of illegality in this class of cases."[1]

§ **20. Where such Services may be Employed.**— While it is well established that any attempt to influence legislation by private and personal solicitation of the individual members of a legislative body is illegal, and that any covenant relating to services of that character will be treated as opposed to public policy and void, a public address or argument before a legislature or before a committee of such body, if permitted, is not opposed to public policy. This is regarded as a legitimate and proper method of exerting, or of attempting to exert, an influence upon a legislative body. It is presumed that a legislature will not be corrupted or led astray by a public discussion of a bill or measure under consideration, while secret, personal solicitation is presumed to be for an improper and illegal purpose. It is the presumption, also, that the object and effect of such services are not in accord with the public welfare. In Wisconsin it has been held that an agreement to prosecute and superintend, in the capacity of agent and attorney, a private claim before the legislature, is against public policy and void, and no action can be maintained thereon, or for services thus rendered. A person may lawfully make a public argument before a committee of the legislature itself, if permitted to do so, in favor of or against a public or private act, and an agreement by which he was promised to be paid for such service would be enforced.[2] In a recent case plaintiff, a person of large ex-

[1] Powers v. Skinner, 34 Vt. 276, 281. See also Sedgwick v. Stanton, 14 N. Y. 289; Bryan v. Reynolds, 5 Wis. 200; Filson v. Himes, 5 Pa. St. 452; Ormerod v. Dearman, 100 Pa. St. 561; s. c., 45 Am. Rep. 391; McGuire v. Corwine, 101 U. S. 108; Chippewa Valley & D. R. Co. v. Chicago, St. P. R. Co., 75 Wis. 274; s. c., 44 N. W. Rep. 17.

[2] Bryan v. Reynolds, 5 Wis. 200. See also Chesebrough v. Conover, 140 N. Y. 382; s. c., 35 N. E. Rep. 633; Wildey v. Collier, 7 Md. 273; Sedgwick v. Stanton, 14 N. Y. 289; Brown v. Brown, 34 Barb. 333. "The jury could find from the evidence that he was employed by the defendant to draw legislative bills and to explain them to members of the legislature, and to pro-

perience in regard to Federal public lands, because satisfied that a certain class of lands that had been kept out of the market on account of a supposed claim under certain railroad grants could be legally thrown open to settlement, entered into an agreement with defendant, who was desirous of acquiring such lands, to instruct the latter in regard to the manner of procuring the same, and to do all that was necessary to have such lands thrown open to settlement, in consideration of a certain proportion of the value of the land acquired by defendant. It was held that the contract was not *per se* invalid as against public policy as a lobbying contract.[1] In a recent case in Michigan a prominent member and local leader of the political party in control of the general government, contemplating the erection of a costly building, secured from an adjacent property owner a promise of a bonus, conditioned upon the location in the building of the city post office, which was then and had been for fifteen years past on the next street. The promisee went to Washington and induced the United States government to transfer the post office to his building, but there was no testimony tending to show that he used any improper means to gain his point, or that he influenced any senator or representative in congress or any other officer of the government to interfere in his behalf. It was held that the contract was valid, being founded upon a valuable consideration, and according to the evidence in the case not necessarily contrary to public policy.[2] In a case relating to

cure their introduction into the legislature and nothing more. It does not appear that he asked or solicited any member of the legislature to vote for the bills or that he did anything except to explain them and request their introduction; and so much he could do without violating any public policy. It must be the right of every citizen who is interested in any proposed legislation to employ an agent, for compensation payable to him, to draft his bill and explain it to any member of a committee or of the legislature, fairly and openly, and ask to have it introduced; and contracts which do not provide for more, and the services which do not go farther, in our judgment violate no principle of law or public policy." Chesebrough v. Conover, 140 N. Y. 282; s. c., 35 N. E. Rep. 633.

[1] Houlton v. Nichol, 93 Wis. 393; s. c., 67 N. W. Rep. 715.

[2] Beal v. Polhemus, 67 Mich. 337; s. c., 34 N. W. Rep. 532.

the consideration for services of this character, nothing will be presumed in regard to the lawfulness or fitness of the transaction. In a recent case before the Circuit Court of Appeals for the Fifth Circuit, it was held that in the absence of averments to that effect it will not be presumed that services of an agent in securing legislation were of an illegal character, or that there is any objection to a contract to pay them.[1]

§ 21. **Services in Influencing Public Officials.**—The principles and rules relating to the employment of attorneys or other agents for the purpose of influencing legislation are applicable to all covenants relating to services, the object of which is to secure especial favors from public officials. It is well established that all agreements relating to pecuniary consideration for controlling or influencing the business operations of the government, in its administration of justice, and without reference to the character of the means employed, are in contravention of public policy and void. In the case of The Tool Company v. Norris, before the Supreme Court of the United States, Mr. Justice Field, in delivering the opinion of the court, said: "There is no real difference in principle between agreements to procure favors from legislative bodies and agreements to procure favors in the shape of contracts from the heads of departments. The introduction of improper elements to control the action of both is the direct and inevitable result of all such arrangements."[2] In a leading case before the same court, it

[1] Salinas v. Stillman, 66 Fed. Rep. 677; s. c., 14 C. C. A. 5.

[2] Tool Co. v. Norris, 2 Wall. 45, 55. See Ayer v. Hutchins, 4 Mass. 370. A contract in writing, whereby a party, in consideration of five hundred dollars, undertook, under a penalty of two thousand dollars, in case one O'Hara, who was an enrolled citizen of the United States, liable to be drafted into the military service, should be drafted so as to do duty in the United States army, against the late rebellion, within three years from the date of the contract, to "procure for him a substitute or otherwise clear him from said draft, and thus save him harmless from any cost or expense in consequence of the same," is against public policy and void. O'Hara v. Carpenter, 23 Mich. 410. A school commissioner of a district was notified to attend an adjourned meeting of the board of education,

was said: "Independently of the official relation of the plaintiff to his government the personal influence which he stipulated to exert upon another officer of that government was not the subject of bargain and sale. Personal influence, to be exercised over an officer of government in the procurement of contracts, as justly observed by counsel, is not a vendible article in our system of laws and morals, and the courts of the United States will not lend their aid to collect the price of the article. Numerous adjudications to this effect are to be found in the State and Federal courts. This is true when the vendor holds no official relations with the

set to pass upon a proposed contract for the purchase of certain charts for the public schools of their district at the price of $750. He refused to go until the agent selling the charts handed him $2.50 in money to pay him for his time and reimburse him for loss sustained by closing his place of business. Then he attended the meeting of the board at the time and place fixed, and he and the president of the board voted for making the purchase. and signed the contract; but the third commissioner voted against it, and refused to sign the contract. Held. that such contract is against public policy and void for want of the sanction of a competent majority of the board. Honaker v. Board of Education, 42 W. Va. 170; s. c., 24 S. E. Rep. 544. An owner of adjacent property entered into a combination with others, and agreed with the owners of a building in a city, if they would offer their building to the government for a nominal rent, to be used as a post office for ten years, and use their personal influence and "proper persuasion" to secure its acceptance, the former would, in case of success. pay the latter a certain sum annually for ten years. The location was chosen and leased accordingly, one of the owners of the building, who was a personal friend of the postmaster general, having truthfully represented to him that the location was suitable, and their notes were given for the annual instalments. Held, that the consideration of the notes was illegal, the agreement being against public policy, and therefore void. Elkhart County Lodge v. Crary, 98 Ind. 238. Where a storekeeper (under the U. S. Revenue Laws), in charge of a distillery belonging to A, promised to give A a certain sum per month as long as he "continued to carry on the distillery:" Held, in an action by A upon the promise, that the contract was against the policy of the law, and A was not entitled to recover. Caton v. Stewart, 76 N. Car. 357. A contract by a board of supervisors with one who is county treasurer, whereby he is to collect all delinquent personal property taxes, and receive as compensation therefor a certain per cent. of the interest and penalties on such taxes, is against public policy and void. Adams County v. Hunter, 78 Iowa. 328; s. c., 43 N. W. Rep. 208.

government, though the turpitude of the transaction becomes more glaring when he is also its officer."[1] In an important case in Kentucky, the doctrine is stated, as follows: "It is clear that a contract to induce public officers to act partially or corruptly, or to bias them in the discharge of their official duties, is against public policy, and principle, analogy, and authority unite in declaring contracts which have an apparent tendency to corrupt, bias, tempt or draw away public officials from the honest discharge of their duties as void because in contravention of public policy, and we are of the opinion that L, who was an official of the city charged with the custody and power to copy and attest the very ordinance on the authority of which the illegal assessments against the citizens were made, was forbidden by public policy to make the contract whereby, if enforced, he would receive money for the disclosures he made, and the services he rendered against the interest of the city whose employment he was in, and to which the law requires him to be loyal and true so long, at least, as in that employment and in so far as it furnished him, in the course of his duties, information by which he sought or may seek to profit himself."[2] But while the doctrine, as above stated, is established beyond a question, there are circumstances under which a covenant for the employment of an agent to negotiate a contract with the government will be upheld. But there must be a

[1] Oscanyan v. Arms Co., 103 U. S. 261, 273. "In the case of Gulick v. Bailey, 10 N. J. L. 87, the agreement was that Bailey agreed to give Gulick $1,000, on condition that Gulick would forbear to propose or offer himself to the postmaster general to carry the mail on a certain mail route. There was no public auction of a contract, nor was the postmaster general, as the case appeared, bound by statute except, perhaps, by implication, to award the contract to the lowest bidder. He was bound to advertise for bids, and did so. Bailey and another bid in opposition to each other, and the contract was awarded to Bailey. The agreement was held void as contravening the statute of the United States, and against public policy. Any contracts which have for their object the influencing the action of public officials are void as against public policy." Brooks v. Cooper, 50 N. J. Eq. 761; s. c., 26 Atl. Rep. 978, 982.

[2] Lucas v. Allen, 80 Ky. 681, 682.

reason for the act that a court will accept, and the procuring of the contract must be a fair, an open and an honest business transaction. The entire procedure must be of such a character as to bear investigation by the court. In a case before the Supreme Court of Ohio, Mr. Justice Welch, in delivering the opinion of the court, said: "We know of no law forbidding the employment of agents to negotiate contracts with the government. It is an employment which is, in many cases, peculiarly liable to abuse, and which, therefore, should be narrowly watched, but it is not necessarily illegal or against public policy. If fairly and honestly conducted it is in harmony with the public interest and of benefit to both contracting parties. In many cases such agents are indispensable to the contractor on account of his absence or incompetency to transact the business. In such cases they are of benefit to the government also by increasing the number of competitors for its contracts, and by enabling its officials to dispatch public business without unnecessary delay and trouble."[1]

[1] Winpenny v. French, 18 Ohio St. 469, 475. "It is not shown by the findings or the evidence in the case that he used any improper means to gain his point, or even that he influenced any senator or representative in congress, or any officer of the government, to interfere in his behalf. He went to Washington personally, and, while there, secured the location of the office where he wanted it; but there is not the slightest testimony that he used any undue means to accomplish his end. We cannot presume that he used his personal power, which is said to have been very great, in a corrupt or unseemly manner, or in violation of any public policy. For aught we know, he appeared, as any citizen might and has a right to do, before the proper office at Washington, and stated the merits of his claim so convincingly and conclusively that the location desired seemed to be most proper and available one. Certainly there could be nothing wrong in this. It is true there is evidence in relation to some of the contracts not in suit, that B boasted that he could control the senators from his State, and that he must have money to go to Washington to do so, but there is no testimony that either one of them lifted a hand or said a word in his behalf, and there is nothing to show that in the present case he made any such representations to obtain the contract. The defendant agreed to pay a certain sum upon the accomplishment of an object in which he saw a future benefit to his property. That object was attained, and he has had the benefit desired. There is no valid reason why he should not fulfill the contract on

§ 22. For Services in Procuring Appointments to Public Offices.—The principles and rules relating to the employment of agents for the purpose of influencing legislation or of procuring personal favors or advantages from the government, as expounded in the foregoing sections, are applicable to all agreements relating to services for procuring any public office. In the case of The Tool Company v. Norris, the rule was stated by Mr. Justice Field with great clearness and force, as follows: "The same principle has also been applied in numerous instances to agreements for compensation to procure appointments to public offices. These offices are trusts held solely for the public good, and should be conferred from considerations of the ability, integrity, fidelity and fitness for the position of the appointee. No other consideration can properly be regarded by the appointing power. Whatever introduces other elements to control this power must necessarily lower the character of the appointments to the great detriment of the public. Agreements for compensation to procure these appointments tend directly and necessarily to introduce such elements. The law, therefore, from this tendency alone adjudges these agreements inconsistent with sound morals and public policy."[1] In Marshall v. The Baltimore & Ohio

his part. Beal v. Polhemus, 67 Mich. 337; s. c., 34 N. W. Rep. 532.

[1] Tool Company v. Norris, 2 Wall. 45, 55. See also Harrington v. Du Chastel, 1 Bro. Ch. 124; s. c., 2 Dick. 581; Groton v. Waldborough, 11 Me. 306; Robertson v. Robinson, 65 Ala. 610; Bowers v. Bowers, 26 Pa. St. 74; Filson v. Hines, 5 Pa. St. 452; Lewis v. Knox, 2 Bibb, 453; Outen v. Rhodes, 3 A. K. Marsh. 432; Carleton v. Whitcher, 5 N. H. 196; Meredith v. Ladd. 2 N. H. 517; Eddy v. Capron, 4 R. I. 394; Hopkins v. Prescott, 4 C. B. 578; Ferris v. Adams, 23 Vt. 136; Richardson v. Mellish, 2 Bing. 125. An agreement by which a candidate for office receives from another person money to aid him in securing his election, and in consideration thereof agrees to share with such other person a portion of the proceeds and emoluments of the office when elected, is immoral, against public policy, *malum in se*, and is totally void. Whether a contract against public policy be executory or executed, no action can be brought, either on the contract or to recover back the consideration, or to recover judgment on a promissory note made in consideration of a cancellation of such contract. There can be no rescission of a contract against

Railroad Company, the rule is stated by Mr. Justice Grier, as follows: "It is the interest of the State that all places of public trust should be filled by men of capacity and integrity, and that the appointing power should be shielded

public policy. Such contract is void at its inception and there is nothing to rescind. Martin v. Wade, 37 Cal. 168. "So far as plaintiff was concerned the incentive that moved him was self-interest and not the general good: and, too, he was induced to do what he did do by the fact that he was to share the profits, and that defendant's election would increase their business. So in this case, at least, the tendency of the contract stated in the complaint was to induce plaintiff to use all his influence for defendant's election, even though he did not agree to do so, as found by the court, and such was its natural tendency. This arrangement may have induced him to influence ten men, or a hundred, to vote for defendant in opposition to preconceived political principles and fixed ideas of right and duty; and, too, when they may have preferred his opponent as an incumbent of the office. Such a contract cannot be upheld. Its tendency was to corrupt the people upon whose integrity and intelligence the safety of the State and nation depends—to lead voters to work for individual interests rather than the public welfare. * * If there are any contracts upon which courts should 'put the stamp of their disapprobation' it is those curtailing or tending to curtail a free exercise of the elective franchise. The contract stated in the complaint, as well as that found by the court, were of that character and neither can be upheld or enforced." Gaston v. Drake, 14 Nev. 175, 188. On a covenant for a gross sum stated to guarantee on the part of the vendor that a post office should be removed from a neighboring village to the place of business of the vendee, and that he should be appointed to it as postmaster, it was held that the bargain was one, the consideration was one, the covenant was one, and that as the procurement of an appointment to office by private influence was part of the indivisible consideration, and illegal and void on the ground of public policy, the whole was void. Filson v. Himes, 5 Pa. St. 452. "Public offices in this country are created solely for the public good and not for private emolument or benefit, and the tenure of them can in no case be considered or treated as the private property of the incumbent to be bargained for and sold as such, and such being the theory and spirit and constitution of our government, such an agreement as this is incompatible with it and against public policy, and as such no action at law can be maintained upon it." Stroud v. Smith, 4 Houst. (Del.) 448. A contract is contrary to public policy and void, whereby, in consideration of A's procuring B's appointment as special counsel in certain causes against the United States, and aiding him in managing the defense of them, B agrees that he will pay A one-half of the fee which he may receive from the government. Meguire v. Corwine, 101 U. S. 108. In from influences which may prevent the best selection; hence the law annuls every contract for procuring the appointment or election of any person to an office.[1] In a case in Vermont, where the defendant being indebted to the plaintiff, who was a candidate for the office of town representative, the parties agreed that the defendant should use his influence for the plaintiff's election, and do what he could for that purpose, and that if the plaintiff was elected that should be a satisfaction of the plaintiff's claim. The plaintiff was elected, but in violation of his agreement brought suit against the defendant for his debt. The law governing the case was stated by the court, as follows: "The bargain was not only the sale of the defendant's vote, but also his influence and exertions against his convictions and opinions. The defendant, generally, voted for the candidate of the other party, and but for this agreement would not have voted for the plaintiff nor favored his election. This, also, was immoral and against public policy. Every voter is bound to use his influence to promote the

this case, at page 111, the court says: "The law touching contracts like the one here in question has been often considered by this court and is well settled by our adjudications. It cannot be necessary to go over the same ground again. To do so would be a waste of time. The object of this opinion is rather to vindicate the application of our former rulings to this record than to give them new support. They do not need it. Frauds of the class to which the one here disclosed belongs are an unmixed evil. Whether forbidden by a statute or condemned by public policy, the result is the same. No legal right can spring from such a source. They are the sappers and miners of the public welfare and of free government as well. The latter depends for its vitality upon the virtue and good faith of those for whom it exists and of those by whom it is administered. Corruption is always the forerunner of despotism. In Trist v. Child, 21 Wall. 441, while recognizing the validity of an honest claim for services honestly rendered, this court said: 'But they are blended and confused with those which are forbidden; the whole is a unit and indivisible. That which is bad destroys that which is good and they perish together. * * * Where the taint exists it affects fatally in all its parts the entire body of the contract. In all such cases *potior conditio defendentis.* Where there is turpitude, the law will help neither party.'" Meguire v. Corwine, 101 U. S. 108, 111. See also Coppell v. Hall, 7 Wall. 542.

[1] Marshall v. Balto. & Ohio R. Co., 16 How. 314.

public good, according to his own honest opinions and convictions of duty. If for money or other personal profit he agrees to exert his influence against what he believes to be for the public good, he is corrupt, and the agreement void, even though in the actual exercise of his influence against his conscience he resorts to no unlawful means. Such bargains cannot be enforced in law. And the reason why they cannot be enforced is not merely because they are made criminal acts by statute or are opposed to the provisions of the constitution, but because of their own inherent turpitude, because they are corrupt and corrupting, because they are destructive to public virtue and the welfare of the community. In republican governments, especially, whatever tends to destroy the purity of elections should be guarded against with the strictest watchfulness and pursued with the most prompt condemnation by courts and legislators."[1]

§ **23. The Subject Continued.**—While the rule as above stated is well established, it will not apply to any proper expenditures in the conduct of an election. While all contracts relating to the purchase of votes or of political influence will be held void, as plainly in contravention of public policy, covenants for services in setting forth the claims of candidates to the confidence and support of the voter, and all contracts for compensation for printing and distributing the announcements of candidates, or for the discussion of the issues of the election, either by the press or by public addresses, or for the circulation of literature devoted to a discussion of the merits of a candidate, or to the support of the political principle of which he is a representative, will be sustained. In the case of Keating v. Hyde, this distinction is set forth by the court, as follows: "There is a clear distinction between the purchase of services to be devoted only to an advertising of the fact that one is, or desires to be, a candidate, and the purchase of service to be employed in advocating his peculiar merits

[1] Nichols v. Mudgett, 32 Vt. 546. See also Fawrie v. Morin's Syndics, 4 Mart. (La.) 39; Meacham v. Dow, 32 Vt. 721; Keating v. Hyde, 23 Mo. App. 555.

and eligibility, so as to influence the choice of the voter. No public policy forbids the making of compensation, under agreement or otherwise, for printing or distributing announcements, or for the employment of any proper agency which may bring the fact of a person's candidacy more prominently before the public eye. The information thus disseminated is essential to the intelligent determination of the voter's choice. But it becomes a very different thing when money is paid or promised for efforts to control the voter's free agency in selecting the object of his suffrage. In the present case, the promise or agreement shown in the testimony and remarked upon in the instruction belongs to the last mentioned class. The defendant was to 'work for' the plaintiff's nomination; not as an advertiser only, but as an advocate. We think that the circuit court committed no error in holding that the agreement was void, as against public policy."[1]

§ 24. For Withdrawal of Opposing Candidate.— Where two persons are applicants to the president, to a governor, or to any other constitutional appointing power for an office, and they enter into an agreement by which one is to withdraw and to aid the other in securing the appointment, the covenant is not enforceable. In a leading case it was held that: Where two persons apply to the governor of the State to be appointed to the same office,

[1] Keating v. Hyde, 23 Mo. App. 555, 560. A promise, in consideration of the governor being prevailed on by the promisee to appoint the promisor to the office, is not binding. Fawrie v. Morin's Syndics, 4 Mart. (La.) (O. S.) 39, at page 49, the court says: "From the instrument itself, it is manifest that the only consideration on which it rests is the illegal condition on which it is stated that the office was obtained. This condition is contrary to sound policy. Offices are to be granted absolutely without any condition. It is not in the power of the grantor to lessen the emoluments which the law has affixed to the discharge of official duties; it matters not to what use the share of the emolument thus carried out is applied. The public will be ill served, if the circle, within which an officer is to be selected, is narrowed by a reduction of the legal emoluments. If these are withdrawn from the incumbent he may be placed under the temptation of compensating himself by speculation, extortion and fraud."

and it is agreed that one of them shall withdraw his application and aid the other in procuring the appointment, in consideration of which the fees and emoluments of the office are to be divided between them, such contract is illegal and void. Such an agreement, it seems, is not within the statute respecting the sale of offices, but is void by the common law.[1] In the opinion in this case the court said:

[1] Gray v. Hook, 4 Comst. 449. A promise by a candidate to perform the duties of the office for less than the legal salary will avoid the election. State v. Purdy, 36 Wis. 213; State v. Collier, 72 Mo. 13; Carrothers v. Russell, 53 Iowa, 350; Nichols v. Mudgett, 32 Vt. 546; Cook v. Shipman, 24 Ill. 614; Tucker v. Aikin, 7 N. H. 113; State v. Olin, 23 Wis. 309. "The doctrine which we think is established by the foregoing authorities and which we believe to be sound in principle, is, that a vote given for a candidate for a public office in consideration of his promise, in case he shall be elected, to donate a sum of money or other valuable thing to a third party, whether such party be an individual, a county or any other corporation, is void. The power to reject such vote is not vested in the election canvassers, but is vested in the court which is called upon to determine judicially the result of the election. The grounds upon which this doctrine is based are so clearly and fully stated in the above authorities that it seems unnecessary to repeat them. Indeed, every intelligent person knows that free, unbiased and (in the language of some of the books) indifferent elections are absolutely essential to the existence of free institutions. * * * Promises made to the people by candidates for public office that, if elected, they will practice a rigid economy in the expenditures of their several departments, are unobjectionable; and if the successful candidate fulfills his pledges in that behalf he is entitled to commendation. In such case, the candidate only promises to perform a legal and moral duty. For example, should a candidate for governor promise that, if elected, he would discharge all persons employed by the State whose services are not needed, or that he would prevent all unnecessary expenditures of public funds, so far as he may have power to do so, this is only a promise that, if elected, he will, in those respects, faithfully perform the duties of his office. In other words, it is a promise that he will not violate his official oath. But should such candidate propose to the voters and tax payers of the estate, that if they will elect him to the office of governor he will serve the State therein gratuitously or for one-half of the salary allowed by the constitution, and pay the rent of an executive office, and the expenses of fuel, stationery and other incidentals pertaining thereto, out of his own pocket, his proposition has an entirely different aspect. In the one case, the candidate promises that if he is elected he will regard his official duty, while in the other case he proposes to

"I think that this contract was void because it stipulated that H should have a pecuniary compensation for withdrawing his application by which he had probably driven off competition, and contributed to reduce the number of applicants to himself and G. I have no doubt that it is void, because it stipulated that H should have a pecuniary compensation for aiding G to obtain the appointment. And I have no doubt that any agreement between two citizens, by which one stipulates to pay the other a proportion of the fees and emoluments of a public office which he is seeking, in consideration that that other will aid him in obtaining it, is void."[1] In a case in Pennsylvania where plaintiff and defendant being applicants for appointment as United States assessor, plaintiff agreed to withdraw, defendant agreeing if he should be appointed to divide the receipts, it was held that the contract was against public policy and the plaintiff could not recover for services rendered. An alleged agreement after the appointment on the same terms held to be void as being in pursuance of the original contract, which could not be ratified.[2]

buy the office with promises to pay therefor in personal services, or money, or both. The one tends to economy and true reform, but the tendency of the other is to introduce into elections a mischievous element very nearly allied to bribery; an element which never has been tolerated (and never can be with safety) by any free government." State v. Purdy, 36 Wis. 213, 222. "In the closing and degenerate days of Rome's august empire, preceding its immediate downfall, the imperial purple was sold at public auction to the highest bidder. Equally base and equally significant of present decay and impending downfall would be the toleration of the private purchase of electorial votes. That which is wrong when done directly is equally wrong when done indirectly. Salaries are paid by taxation, and when a candidate offers to take less than the stated salary, he offers to reduce *pro tanto* the amount of taxes which each individual must pay. If the candidate went to each elector and offered to pay one dollar of his taxes, that clearly would be direct bribery; and when he offers to take such a salary as will reduce the tax upon each tax payer one dollar, he is indirectly making the same offer of pecuniary gain to the voter, so that those cases rest upon the simple proposition that the election of a candidate for office cannot be secured by personal bribery offered either directly or indirectly to the voter." Brewer, J., in State v. Elting, 29 Kan. 397, 401.

[1] Gray v. Hook, 4 Comst. 449, 457.

[2] Hunter v. Nolf, 71 Pa. St. 282.

§ 25. For Services in Procuring a Pardon.—An agreement to pay for labor expended, or for expense incurred in procuring a pardon for a person convicted of a criminal offense, by procuring signatures to a petition or otherwise, falls under the rule as discussed in the preceding sections. The tendency of such an act is to encourage crime and disobedience of law, and as such is immoral and in contravention of public policy. In the leading case of Hatzfield v. Gulden, before the Supreme Court of Pennsylvania, the court said: "The power to pardon is a constitutional power, to alleviate or remit punishment where perhaps there is doubt of guilt, or where the offense was committed under circumstances extenuating the crime, etc. The general and spontaneous expression of opinion has had, and ought to have, weight with the governor. But if undue means are used to obtain petitioners, it may be a great imposition on the governor. The power to pardon may be considered as a part of the penal code of the State; it operates after trial to be sure, generally, but may be exercised before. It is as important that it should be free from bias, or prejudice, or crime, as that the trial should be so. No man would say that if it were possible to procure a pardon by direct payment to a governor it would be lawful to give one. To bribe others to deceive and impose on him only differs in degree."[1] In a case in England a

[1] Hatzfeld v. Gulden, 7 Watts, 152, 155. See also Haines v. Lewis, 54 Iowa. 301. "Courts of justice are generally open to suitors for the recovery of just claims, but considerations of public policy are often deemed paramount to private rights, and where they are opposed the latter must yield. There is no doctrine better settled than that agreements to obtain executive clemency, by means of pardons or writs of *nolle prosequi*, cannot be enforced. The reasons are obvious. They are designed to protect the exercise of this power from abuse through the intervention of designing persons, and, although, in the particular instance no improper influences may have been resorted to, the public interest in such questions requires that the principle should be enforced in all cases. It may, sometimes, as between the parties, be unjust to a claimant who has rendered valuable services for another in his distress, but rules of law, founded on public policy and the safety of society, will not be set aside to sustain such individual demand." Wildey v. Collier, 7

bequest for purchasing the discharge of poachers, "committed to prison for non-payment of fines, fees or expenses under the game laws," was held void as encouraging

Md. 273, 278. A contract conditioned for the execution and deposit of certain promissory notes by one under sentence for the commission of a crime, to be delivered to the prosecuting witness upon certain conditions, one of which was that the maker should receive a pardon or be acquitted on retrial, was held illegal and void as against public policy. Haines v. Lewis, 54 Iowa, 301. *Contra:* Bird v. Breedlove, 24 Ga. 623. An agreement to procure a pardon from the governor, for a convict in the penitentiary, by the proper use of all legitimate means, is neither immoral nor against the public policy. Formby v. Pryor, 15 Ga. 258. Agreements to procure a pardon tend to obstruct a correct administration of government, and are calculated to induce persons to use their influence in such manner as to defeat public justice. But, otherwise, where an attorney undertook, by the use of his personal influence with the military commander, to save from impending danger of threatened execution, or unauthorized and illegal imprisonment a prisoner who had been convicted by a military court which was unauthorized by law, "such an act cannot be regarded as an agreement to obstruct the proper administration of justice nor to defeat the ends of public justice." Thompson v. Wharton, 70 Ky. 563. It is not at once apparent that it is not lawful and proper for a party who is suffering the punishment of crime, to apply to the pardoning power for a remission of his sentence; and, so far as we are aware, no censure has been regarded as attaching to such an application, either in law or morals. It seems to us equally reasonable for any other person, who believes it his duty to make such application in behalf of another, to present the case to the executive, with such petitions, memorials, statements of facts and evidence as are suitable to satisfy the pardoning power of the propriety of the relief desired, and we think no censure can be justly attached to any person for his exertions in such a case, if the measures adopted are consistent with the facts of the case, and with the truth and honesty of all parties concerned, while any effort to obtain such pardon by falsehood, and misrepresentation, or by any species of fraudulent contrivance, or by prostituting the influence resulting from official station or from personal relation to the pardoning power, is entirely forbidden by law. A person in prison can do little to aid himself in bringing his case to the consideration of the executive. For everything that must be done without the walls of the prison the convict is compelled to rely on the assistance of those who have their liberty. Such assistance may be afforded from motives of charity and compassion, or the motive may be in part kindness and in part an expectation that the party relieved will be ready to afford a suitable compensation for the services and expenses; or the party in prison may employ another to do such acts as may be rightfully and properly done for his relief, and contract to offenses and opposed to public policy.[1] In a case before the Supreme Court of the United States, the court said: "The pardoning power, committed to the executive, should be exercised as free from any improper bias or influence as the trial of the convict before the court; consequently the law will not enforce a contract to pay money for soliciting petitions, or using influence to obtain a pardon."[2] This rule will not be inoperative, and its application will not be in any degree modified where the service is for the purpose of procuring a commutation of a criminal sentence. In Kribben v. Haycraft, the court said: "It is a principle of law dictated by the soundest policy that an agreement cannot be enforced by which one person promises to pay another for obtaining or trying to obtain a pardon. The cases are founded on the obvious reason that such contracts are illegal, inasmuch as they tend to encourage the use of improper means to accomplish the object, and are in conflict with the intelligent and proper exercise of the pardoning power. But it is insisted that the promise in this case is not to obtain a pardon but a commutation of the punishment, and that there is nothing in the contract obnoxious to public policy. The distinction is nominal, for the principle is the same in both cases, and all the considerations that uphold the propriety and wisdom of the rule in the one case apply to the other."[3]

§ 26. For Services which are in Violation of Public Duty.—All agreements to perform any act which is punishable in a criminal sense, or to prevent a criminal prosecution, or to suppress evidence in relation to it, are illegal and void. In England it has been held that a printer cannot recover against a publisher for printing a work which con-

pay him for his services and to repay him his expenses. Such a contract, if the parties contemplate only a resort to legal and proper measures, is free from any just exception, and binding upon the parties." Chadwick v. Knox, 31 N. H. 226, 234.

[1] Thrupp v. Collett, 26 Beav. 125.

[2] Marshall v. Balto. & Ohio R. R. Co., 16 How. 314, 334.

[3] Kribben v. Haycraft, 26 Mo. 396.

tains the life of a prostitute, and the history of her amours with various persons, and it is no answer that the parties are *in pari delicto*.[1] In a case in Georgia it was held that on the trial of an issue whether a promissory note sued on is illegal, because given for the compounding of a felony, it is not necessary that the defendant shall prove that the party charged was actually guilty of the felony; it is sufficient, if there be an act done, of which he is charged to be guilty, which is *prima facie* felony. An offense which may, in the discretion of the court, be punished by confinement in the penitentiary, is so far a felony that compounding of it is illegal. Although one

[1] Poplett v. Stockdale, 2 Carr. & P. 198. A covenant in a deed not to convey or lease land to a Chinaman is void, as contrary to the public policy of the government, in contravention of its treaty with China, and in violation of the fourteenth amendment of the constitution, and is not enforceable in equity. Gandolfo v. Hartman, 49 Fed. Rep. 181. A contract whereby one aided another in obtaining title to land, sold by an administrator at a price much less than its value, to the injury of the creditors and heirs of the intestate, will not support an action. Smith v. Humphreys, 88 Me. 345; s. c., 34 Atl. Rep. 106. A contract by which plaintiff agreed to refrain from forming a corporation for the construction of waterworks in a certain city, and from carrying on or prosecuting such work, in order that defendant might incorporate for that purpose and conduct the business without competition, is not void as against public policy. Oakes v. Cattarangus Water Co., 143 N. Y. 430; s. c., 38 N. E. Rep. 461. A deed, after reciting that differences existed between a husband and wife, and that they desired to adjust such differences and provide an adequate support for the wife, conveyed land to a trustee for the purpose of allowing the husband and wife to have the rents and profits, and to "support the wife in such manner as she has heretofore lived." *Held*, that the deed is not *prima facie* invalid on the ground that it was made in view of a separation of husband and wife. Barnes v. Barnes, 104 N. Car. 613; s. c., 10 S. E. Rep. 304. A contract by a State authorizing a person to prosecute a claim and providing that his compensation should be a certain per cent. of the amount collected by him, to be paid out of the proceeds thereof, is not void as against public policy, because making the payment of compensation contingent on success; the contract being authorized by the legislature, which empowers the governor and council, on behalf of the State, to appoint an agent to prosecute the claim and fix his compensation to be paid out of any amount received therefrom. Davis v. Commonwealth, 164 Mass. 241; s. c., 41 N E. Rep. 292.

may legally take a promissory note as compensation for a personal injury, yet, if the injury was a crime, such as by our law the parties cannot settle between themselves, and if there be any attempt, by giving of the note, to suppress a prosecution for the offense, it vitiates the whole agreement, even though the note be for less than the actual damages received.[1] It is not necessary that there should be an agreement in terms to compound a crime. It is sufficient that that was the intention of the parties, and that the agreement was entered into for the purpose of carrying out that intention. It is not necessary that the person receiving the consideration should agree not to commence proceedings against the person accused.[2] The effect will be the same if he binds himself to release the accused from a pending prosecution. Where a third person makes a promise to indemnify an officer for neglecting his duty in the service of a warrant, the promise is based upon an illegal consideration, and, in consequence, is void.[3] In an English case, a petition having been presented to the House of Commons, against the return of a member, on the ground of bribery, the petitioner entered into an agreement, in consideration of a sum of money, and upon other terms, to proceed no further with the petition. It was held that this

[1] Chandler v. Johnson, 39 Ga. 85; Fivaz v. Nicholls, 2 C. B. 501; Porter v. Jones, 6 Coldw. 313; Gorham v. Keyes, 137 Mass. 583; Kimbrough v. Lane, 11 Bush, 556; Lindsay v. Smith, 78 N. Car. 328; Baker v. Farris, 61 Mo. 389; Shaw v. Reed, 30 Me. 105; Shaw v. Spooner, 9 N. H. 197; Badger v. Williams, 1 D. Chip. 137; Goodwin v. Crowell, 56 Ga. 566; Snider v. Willey, 33 Mich. 483; Sumner v. Sumner, 54 Mo. 340; Wright v. Rindskopf, 43 Wis. 344; Roll v. Raguet, 4 Ohio. 400; Vanover v. Thompson, 4 Jones L. 485; Halthaus v. Kuntz, 17 Ill. App. 434; Henderson v. Palmer, 71 Ill. 579; Taylor v. Jaques, 106 Mass. 291; Peed v. McKee, 42 Iowa, 689; Ricketts v. Harvey, 106 Ind. 564; McMahon v. Smith, 47 Conn. 221; *Ex parte* Wolverhampton Banking Co., L. R. 14 Q. B. Div. 32; Cook v. West & Atl. Ry. Co., 72 Ga. 48.

[2] Couderman v. Trenchard, 58 Barb. 165.

[3] Hodsdon v. Wilkins, 7 Greenl. 113; Ayer v. Hutchins, 4 Mass. 370; Churchill v. Perkins, 5 Mass. 541; Denny v. Lincoln, 5 Mass. 385; Webber v. Blunt, 19 Wend. 188; Clark v. Foxcroft, 6 Greenl. 296. A contract to reprint a book in violation of a copyright belonging to a third party is void. Nichols v. Ruggles, 3 Day, 145.

agreement was illegal. It was held, also, that the written agreement was admissible in evidence, for the purpose of insisting on the illegality of the transaction, in answer to an action for the sum so agreed to be paid, without its being stamped.[1] In Vermont it has been held that the consideration of a contract must not only be valuable, but lawful; hence there can be no recovery by one for his time and service, the purpose and tendency of whose employment was to obstruct the administration of justice, by influencing State witnesses, and by inducing the State's attorney to hold back in the discharge of his official duty in prosecuting the defendant charged with adultery.[2]

§ 27. **For Services in Opposing a Public Enterprise.**— It is well established that all covenants that have as their object the defeat or obstruction of any public enterprise are in contravention of public policy and void. The courts will not lend their aid to the enforcement of any agreement of this nature, and they will not afford relief to any person who has put his property in peril for any purpose of this character. Among cases that fall under this rule are those relating to the opening of a street, or of a public road. In Smith v. Applegate, it was held that a promissory note given by the applicants for a public road to a caveator against such road, in consideration of the caveator's withdrawing his opposition to the road, and permitting the return to be recorded, is void, being founded on an illegal consideration. A contract on the part of the caveator to withdraw his opposition to the laying out of a highway, is against the policy of the law, and, therefore, void. In the opinion in this case, the court said: "The same considerations apply with increased force to a controversy touching the laying out of a public highway. Any one aggrieved is at liberty to caveat against the road. He is under no obligation to do so. He may, at his pleasure, abandon his opposition. But he may not lawfully bind himself to withdraw his opposition, nor may he contract to receive a price

[1] Coppack v. Bower, 4 Mees. & W. 361.

[2] Barron v. Tucker, 53 Vt. 338.

for so doing. The obvious and unavoidable tendency of such a practice to unjust litigation, the lure it would hold out to private cupidity, to the great detriment of public interests, render it necessarily repugnant to the policy, and subversive of the beneficent designs and provisions of the statute."[1] In a recent case before the Court of Chancery of New Jersey, complainant conveyed property to his father-

[1] Smith v. Applegate, 23 N. J. Law, 352, 358. "It is very clear that the contract in question never could have been enforced against the caveator. If the caveator having agreed to withdraw his opposition, and having received a price for so doing, had refused to comply with his contract, and persisted in his opposition to the road, this court surely never could have enforced a compliance with the contract on his part, nor awarded damages for his non-compliance. The contract upon him would have not been obligatory. This consideration, alone, demonstrates that the contract is illegal, as against public policy. The contract, moreover, to be valid, must be binding upon both parties. If not binding upon one it is binding upon neither, and if the contract of the caveator is illegal, and by reason of its illegality forms no valid consideration for the contract of the applicants, the execution of the illegal contract constitutes no better consideration. When the note in question was given there was no consideration for the promise on the part of the makers, but a promise on the part of the payee, illegal, inoperative and not binding upon him. The contract was void. The fact that it had been executed by one of the parties will not authorize the enforcement of an illegal contract as against the other." *Ibid.* A town has no power to agree, for a valuable consideration, to discontinue a highway. The mode of discontinuing highways is fixed by statute with a provision for an appeal by any party aggrieved, and a town cannot, at its mere pleasure, discontinue them. And a town cannot enforce a promise of the other party of which its own promise to destroy a public right was the consideration. Town of Cromwell v. Conn. Brown Stone Quarry Co., 50 Conn. 470. The commission of a lawful act is not actionable though it proceeded from a malicious motive. A public road was laid out along the division line of the unimproved lands of two persons, and the land was afterwards cleared and sown. To save expense, they agreed each to fence to the middle of the road. *Held*, that the agreement to enclose the land was illegal, and either one had the right to remove his portion of the fence, and was not liable for injury sustained by the other in his crop, then ready for harvesting, whether the motive for the removal of the fence was malicious or otherwise. Jenkins v. Fowler, 24 Pa. St. 308. See also Dingledein v. Third Ave. R. R. Co., 9 Bosw. 79, 89; Dygert v. Schenck, 23 Wend. 446; People v. Cunningham, 1 Denio, 524; People v. Lambier, 5 Denio, 9; Renwich v. Morris, 3 Hill, 62; s. c., 7 Hill, 575; Merriwether v. Nixon, 2 Smith's Lead. Cas. 297.

in-law for no other consideration than that the latter was to use his influence in opposition to an extension of a street across the property, with an understanding that it was to be reconveyed to the original owner. The influence was used successfully, but the father-in-law died before the property was reconveyed. It was held that, as the object of the contract was the defeat of a public enterprise, the court would not enforce it.[1]

§ 28. **The Subject Continued.**—The rule, as above stated, is held to apply to the location of a depot by a railroad company. Such company is a public servant or agent, and as such is bound to establish its stations with sole reference to the public convenience and interest. Any agreement to locate a station at a particular place for a consideration is presumptively prejudicial to the interests of the public, and, in consequence, in violation of the duty of the corporation. Such agreements are in contravention of public policy, and will not be enforced by the courts. In a recent and important case in Illinois, the rule is stated by the court, as follows: "It is undoubtedly the rule that railway companies, in the absence of statutory provisions limiting and restricting their powers, are vested with a very broad discretion in the matter of locating and operating their railways, and of locating and maintaining their freight and passenger stations. This discretion, however, is not absolute, but is subject to the condition that it must be exercised in good faith, and with a due regard to the necessities and convenience of the public. Railway companies, though private corporations, are engaged in a business in which the public have an interest, and in which such companies are public servants and amenable as such. This doctrine has been repeatedly announced by this and other courts. * * * It is in recognition of the paramont duty of railway companies to establish and maintain their depots at such points and in such manner as to subserve the public necessities and convenience, that it has been held by all

[1] Slocum v. Wooley, 43 N. J. Eq. 451; s. c., 11 Atl. Rep. 264.

courts, with very few exceptions, that contracts materially limiting their power to locate and relocate their depots are against public policy, and, therefore, void."[1] In another case

[1] People v. C. & A. R. R. Co., 130 Ill. 175, 182, 184. H being a director and president of the Oregon & California R. R. Co., and the owner of a controlling interest in the stock of said company, agreed with P that, in consideration of a certain sum of money, he would cause the line of said railroad to be located on a certain route and a depot to be built at a certain place, instead of adopting another route then surveyed, which was shorter and over which said road could be constructed at less expense. *Held*, that such a contract is contrary to public policy, a railroad being a *quasi* public corporation, and the public has an interest in the location of their lines of road and depots. Holladay v. Patterson, 5 Ore. 176. "With regard to the change of the location in the depot, we would remark that the railroad authorities have unlimited power to fix them for the best interests of the enterprise, even though a money consideration be received therefor, but they cannot make a matter of commerce of them as a punishment to a non-subscribing town, nor establish them for any other purpose that the best interests of the community and of the road." Currie v. N. J. & C. R. R. Co., 61 Miss. 725, 731. A agreed with the Pacific Railroad Company to deed it a certain lot of ground for purposes of speculation in consideration that the company would locate a freight and passenger depot on his land. There was no evidence that the land was to be used for the general business of locating, constructing, managing and using the road. *Held*, that although in one sense the company was a private corporation, yet its chartered privileges were granted, in part, to subserve great public interests; that such an agreement might be superinduced by prospects of mere gain, and thus the general welfare and good of the public might be sacrificed to subserve mere private interest; that for this reason such an agreement was void, as against public policy. Pacific R. R. Co. v. Seeley, 45 Mo. 212. It is the duty of a railroad corporation to furnish reasonable depot facilities for the accommodation of the public in the matter of transportation and travel. A contract in contravention of this duty of furnishing reasonable depot facilities is against public policy and void, and a contract not to have or use a depot within three miles of a given point is such a contract. St. Joseph & D. R. R. Co. v. Ryan, 11 Kan. 602. See also St. L., J. & C. R. R. Co. v. Mathers, 104 Ill. 257. The city of Marshall agreed to give to the Texas & Pacific Railway $300,000 in county bonds and sixty-six acres of land within the city limits, for shops and depots; and "in consideration of the donation" agreed "to permanently establish its eastern terminus and Texas offices at the city of Marshall" and "to establish and construct at said city the main machine shops and car works of said railway company." The city performed its agreement and the company, on its part, made Marshall its eastern terminus and built depots and shops, and established its

in Illinois, the court said: "We cannot admit that an individual is entitled to call for the interference of a court of equity to compel a railroad company to locate unchangeably its depot at a particular spot to subserve the private advantage of such individual. Railroad companies, in order to fulfill one of the ends of their creation,—the promotion of the public welfare,—should be left free to establish and re-establish their depots wheresoever the accommodation of the wants of the public may require."[1] In California it has been held that a written agreement that one party shall purchase a tract of land, and that another party shall share in the profits of the land, and allow the purchaser ten per cent. upon his advances, which agreement is based upon

principal offices there. After the expiration of a few years Marshall ceased to be the eastern terminus of the road and some of the shops were removed. The city filed this bill in equity to enforce the agreement, both as to the terminus and as to the shops. *Held* (1), that the contract on the part of the railway was satisfied and performed when the company had established and kept a depot and offices at Marshall, and had set in operation car works and machine shops there, and had kept them going for eight years and until the interests of the railway company and of the public demanded the removal of some or all of these subjects of contract to some other place. (2) That the word "permanent," in the contract, was to be construed with reference to the subject-matter of the contract, and that under the circumstances of this case it was complied with by the establishment of the terminus, and the offices and shops contracted for, with no intention at the time of removing or abandoning them. (3) That if the contract were to be interpreted as one to forever maintain the eastern terminus, and the shops and Texas offices at Marshall without regard to the convenience of the public, it would become a contract that could not be enforced in equity. Texas & P. Ry. Co. v. Marshall, 136 U. S. 393. Contracts undertaking to obligate a railroad company to establish its depot exclusively at a particular point are void as against public policy. Such companies should be left free to establish and re-establish their depots wherever the public welfare or wants of the public may require. Florida Cent. R. R. Co. v. State, 31 Fla. 482. See, generally, Marsh v. Fairbury, 64 Ill. 414; Fuller v. Dame, 18 Pick. 472; Mobile & Ohio R. R. Co. v. People, 132 Ill. 559; s. c., 24 N. E. Rep. 643; Bestor v. Wathen, 60 Ill. 138; Williamson v. Chicago, R. I. & Pac. R. Co., 53 Iowa, 126; s. c., 36 Am. Rep. 206; First Nat. Bank v. Hendrie, 49 Iowa, 402; s. .c., 31 Am. Rep. 153; Elkhart Lodge v. Crary, 98 Ind. 238, 240; C. B. R. R. Co. v. Baab, 9 Watts, 458.

[1] Marsh v. Fairbury, etc. R. Co., 64 Ill. 414.

the consideration of information to be given as to the location of a railroad depot, making the investment profitable, creates a trust in the land in favor of the party furnishing the information, is founded upon a sufficient consideration and is not void as against public policy, if it does not appear that any rights of the railroad company were affected by the giving of such information, or that it was obtained through a relation to them of trust or confidence, or given in violation of such trust or confidence.[1] In a recent case in Louisiana, it was held that a railroad corporation is *a quasi* public agent, and it is its duty independent of any agreement to secure an advantage to the corporation to establish its stations most convenient for the public interests. An agreement, therefore, by the corporation for a part of the land to establish its depots and hotels at particular points is illegal.[2]

§ 29. **Stipulations Against Liability.**—The rule in regard to the liability of common carriers, and to their stipulations for exemption from liability in case of loss or injury to property in transit, through the carelessness or negligence of their employes, is not uniform. Undoubtedly, the weight of authority favors the rule that a common carrier cannot free himself from responsibility for the faithful discharge of his duty as a public servant. This is the rule of the Supreme Court of the United States, and it is maintained without regard to the *lex loci contractus* of the particular State from which the action may arise. In the leading case of The Liverpool Steam Company v. The Phœnix Insurance Company, it was held that upon a question of the effect of a stipulation exempting a common carrier from responsibility for the negligence of his servants, the courts of the United States are not bound by decisions of the courts of the State in which the contract is made.[3] In this

[1] Green v. Brooks, 81 Cal. 328.

[2] Burney v. Ludeling, 47 La. Ann. 73; s. c., 16 So. Rep. 507: 47 La. Ann. 1434; 17 So. Rep. 877.

[3] Liverpool Steam Co. v. Phoenix Ins. Co., 129 U. S. 397; Grogan v. Express Co., 114 Pa. St. 523; s. c., 7 Atl. Rep. 134: Buck v. Pa. R. R. Co., 150 Pa. St. 170: s. c., 24 Atl. Rep. 678: Lindsley v. Chicago,

case the rule by which the Federal courts are governed is stated by Mr. Justice Gray, as follows: "By the common law of England and America, before the Declaration of Independence, recognized by the weight of English authority

etc. R. Co., 36 Minn. 539; s. c., 33 N. W. Rep. 7; Hull v. Chicago, etc. Ry. Co., 41 Minn. 510; s. c., 43 N. W. Rep. 399; Canfield v. Baltimore, etc. R. Co., 93 N. Y. 352; Railway Co. v. Wynn, 88 Tenn. 320; s. c., 14 S. W. Rep. 311; McFadden v. Missouri Pac. Ry. Co., 92 Mo. 343; s. c., 4 S. W. Rep. 689; Galt v. Adams Express Co., MacArth. & M. 124; s. c., 48 Am. Rep. 742; Abrams v. Milwaukee, etc. R. Co., 87 Wis. 485; s. c., 58 N. W. Rep. 780; Annas v. Milwaukee, etc. R. Co., 67 Wis. 46; Armstrong v. United States Express Co., 159 Pa. St. 640; s. c., 28 Atl. Rep. 448; Atchison, etc. R. Co. v. Grant, 6 Tex. Civ. App. 674; s. c., 26 S. W. Rep. 286; Missouri, etc. R. Co. v. Harris, 67 Tex. 166; s. c., 2 S. W. Rep. 574; Richardson v. Chicago, etc. Ry. Co., 61 Wis. 596; s. c., 21 N. W. Rep. 49; Ayers v. Chicago, etc. Ry. Co., 71 Wis. 372; s. c., 37 N. W. Rep. 432; Black v. Goodrich Transportation Co., 55 Wis. 319; s. c., 13 N. W. Rep. 244; Lawson v. Chicago, etc. Ry. Co., 64 Wis. 447; s. c., 24 N. W. Rep. 618; Thompson v. Western Union Telegraph Co., 64 Wis. 531; s. c., 25 N. W. Rep. 789; Hibbard v. Western Union Telegraph Co., 33 Wis. 558; Candee v. Western Union Telegraph Co., 34 Wis. 471; Railway Co. v. Spangler, 44 Ohio St. 471; Baltimore, etc. R. Co. v. Ragsdale, 14 Ind. App. 406; s. c., 42 N. E. Rep. 1106; Ohio, etc. Ry. Co. v. Selby, 47 Ind. 471; Hart v. Railroad Co., 112 U. S. 331; Railway Co. v. Mayes, 58 Ark. 397; New York, etc. R. Co., 98 Mass. 239; Richmond, etc. R. R. Co. v. Payne, 86 Va. 481; United States Express Co. v. Harris, 51 Ind. 127; McFadden v. Missouri Pacific Ry. Co., 92 Mo. 343; Kellerman v. Kansas City, etc. R. Co., 136 Mo. 177; s. c., 34 S. W. Rep. 41; Rogan v. Wabash Ry. Co., 51 Mo. App. 665; Duvenick v. Missouri Pac. R. Co., 57 Mo. App. 550; Conover v. Pacific Express Co., 40 Mo. App. 31; Betts v. Farmers', etc. Trust Co., 21 Wis. 80. "Conceding, therefore, that special contracts, made by common carriers with their customers, limiting their liability, are good and valid so far as they are just and reasonable, to the extent, for example, of excusing them for all losses happening by accident without any negligence or fraud on their part; when they ask to go still further, and to be excused for negligence—an excuse so repugnant to the law of their foundation and to the public good—they have no longer any plea of justice or reason to support such a stipulation, but the contrary. And then, the inequality of the parties, the compulsion under which the customer is placed and the obligations of the carrier to the public, operate with full force to divest the transaction of validity. On this subject the remarks of Chief Justice Redfield in his recent collection of American railway cases, seem to us eminently just. 'It being clearly established then,' says he, 'that common car-for half a century afterwards, and upheld by decisions of the highest courts of many States of the Union, common carriers could not stipulate for immunity for their own or their servant's negligence. The English Railway and

riers have public duties which they are bound to discharge with impartiality, we must conclude that they cannot, either by notices or special contracts, release themselves from the performance of these public duties, even by the consent of those who employ them; for all extortion is done by the apparent consent of the victim. A public servant or officer who has a monopoly in his department has no just right to impose onerous and unreasonable conditions upon those who are compelled to employ him.' And his conclusion is that, notwithstanding some exceptional decisions, the law of to-day stands substantially as follows: '1. That the exemption claimed by carriers must be reasonable and just, otherwise it will be regarded as extorted from the owners of the goods by duress of circumstances, and, therefore, not binding. 2. That every attempt of carriers, by general notice or special contract, to excuse themselves from responsibility for losses or damages resulting in any degree from their own want of care and faithfulness, is against that good faith which the law requires, as the basis of all contracts or employments; and, therefore, based upon principles and a policy which the law will not uphold.'" Railroad Co. v. Lockwood, 17 Wall. 357, 381. A carrier of live stock cannot by special contract relieve himself from the consequences of his own negligence. In an action against a carrier to recover damages for the loss of a horse, it is proper to submit the case to a jury where there is evidence that the stall in the car in which the horse was being transported was negligently constructed and that the injury happened in consequence thereof. In an action against a carrier a release of liability is properly excluded, where erasures appear on the face of the release and it appears that such erasures were made by the carrier's agent, and there is no evidence that the paper was shown or read to the shipper after the erasures were made. Armstrong v. Express Co., 159 Pa. St. 640. "The counsel for the company in this branch of the case enters into a very able discussion of the validity of the portion of section 4 of article 11 of the constitution of this State, which declares that 'the liability of railroad corporations as common carriers shall never be limited,' contending that this provision is invalid and of no effect, because it conflicts with, as he states it in his argument, 'the exclusive rights of congress to regulate commerce between the States.' Whether he is right in his contention or not, or whether it is settled or established by the weight of authority, or sustained by the best reason, that the States cannot in any manner regulate or legislate so as to effect the portions of such contracts as the one in the case at bar, as would be governed by the above provision, are not necessarily to be determined in reaching a decision of this branch

Canal Traffic Act of 1854, declaring void all notices and conditions made by those classes of common carriers, except such as should be held by the court or judge before whom the case should be tried to be just and reasonable,

of the case. We think they can, and will, more rightfully be decided and determined upon the ground of the invalidity of the contract, as an attempt to limit the common law liability of the company under an agreement in its capacity as a common carrier. In the case of Chicago, R. I. & P. R. Co. v. Witty. 32 Neb. 275, a contract was entered into between the railroad company and Witty for the shipment of a horse from Henry, Illinois, to Jansen, Nebraska, and there was a stipulation therein contained by which the company was only liable for injuries to the horse occurring by reason of its gross negligence, and then for not to exceed the sum of $100. This was held to be invalid under the rule of the common law. Norval, J., in the text of the opinion, states: 'We do not doubt that a carrier may, by a contract fairly entered into, limit, in some respect, its liability as an insurer, or its common law liability, where the restriction imposed is reasonable. But on grounds of public policy, the law has wisely prohibited a common carrier of freight from in any manner contracting against its own negligence.' This doctrine was distinctly held and applied in Atchison & N. R. Co. v. Washburn, 5 Neb. 117. Gantt, J., in the opinion, says: 'The common law fixes the degree of care and diligence due from railroad companies as common carriers, and a failure to exercise this care and diligence is negligence, without any legal distinction as being either gross or ordinary; and the better rule of law, sustained by the weight of authority, is that it is against the policy of the law to allow stipulations which will relieve the company from the exercise of that care and diligence, or which, in other words, will excuse them for negligence in the performance of that duty; decisions are to be found which lay down a contrary doctrine, but the better reason, as well as the current of authority in this country, sustain the rule announced by this court in the case referred to.' and cites, in support of the doctrine announced, New York C. R. v. Lockwood. 17 Wall. 357; Grand Trunk R. Co. v. Stevens, 95 U. S. 655; Shriver v. Sioux City & St. P. R. Co., 24 Minn. 506; Welsh v. Pittsburg. etc. R. R. Co., 10 Ohio St. 65; Kiff v. Atchison, T. & S. F. R. R. Co., 32 Kan. 263; s. c., 4 Pac. Rep. 401; Durgin v. American Express Co., 66 N. H. 277; s. c., 20 Atl. Rep. 328; Morrison v. Phillips Construction Co., 44 Wis. 405; Louisville, N. A. & C. R. Co. v. Faylor, 126 Ind. 126; Eels v. St. Louis, K. & N. W. R. Co., 52 Fed. Rep. 903; Galveston, H. & S. A. R. Co. v. Ball, 80 Tex. 602; s. c., 16 S. W. Rep. 441; International & G. N. R. Co. v. Folts. 3 Tex. Civ. App. 644; s. c., 22 S. W. Rep. 541; Johnstone v. Richmond & D. R. Co., 39 S. Car. 55; s. c., 17 S. E. Rep. 512; Baughman v. Louisville, E. & St. L. R. R. Co., 94 Ky. 150; s. c., 21 S. W. Rep. 757; Ambach v. Baltimore & Ohio R. Co., 30 Ohio L. J. 111.

was substantially a return to the rule of the common law. The only important modification by the Congress of the United States of the previously existing law on this subject is the Act of 1851, to limit the liability of ship owners,[1] and that act leaves them liable without limit for their own negligence, and liable to the extent of the ship and freight for the negligence or misconduct of their master and crew. The employment of a common carrier is a public one, charging him with the duty of accommodating the public in the line of his employment. A common carrier is such by virtue of his occupation, not by virtue of the responsibilities under which he rests. Even if the extent of these responsibilities is restricted by law or by contract the nature of his occupation makes him a common carrier still. A common carrier may become a private carrier, or a bailee for hire, when, as a matter of accommodation or special engagement, he undertakes to carry something which it is not his business to carry. But when a carrier has a regu-

On the subject of limitation as to the amount of damages, it is said in the foregoing opinion: 'It is claimed that the limitation in the contract, as to the amount of damages in case of loss or injury, does not tend to exempt the carrier from liability for negligence. The authorities cited in brief of plaintiff in error so hold, but we are unable to draw such a distinction. If a carrier cannot, by stipulation, be relieved from liability for its negligence, it is equally clear, for the same reason, that it cannot, by contract with the shipper, limit the amount of damages resulting from such negligence. If the plaintiff in error can lawfully stipulate that the damages shall not exceed $100, it could likewise contract that it should not be more than $25, or any smaller sum, thereby practically relieving itself from all responsibility for injuries occasioned by its own negligence. That would be accomplished indirectly what it could not lawfully do directly. The proof fully shows that the horse, when shipped, was worth not less than $400, and to hold that the owner could only recover one-fourth that sum would be to exempt the carrier from a part of the liability assumed by it for injuries resulting from its own negligence. This the law will not sanction,' citing Morrison v. Phillips Construction Co., 44 Wis. 405; Kansas City, St. J. & C. B. R. R. Co. v. Simpson, 30 Kan. 645; Chicago, St. L. & N. O. R. Co. v. Abels, 60 Miss. 1017; United States Express Co. v. Backman, 28 Ohio St. 144; Boehl v. Chicago, M. & St. P. R. R. Co., 44 Minn. 191; s. c., 46 N. W. Rep. 333." Harrison, J., in Atchison, T. & S. F. R. Co. v. Lawler, 40 Neb. 356, 374.

[1] Rev. Stat., §§ 4282-4285.

larly established business for carrying all or certain articles, and, especially, if that carrier is a corporation created for the purpose of the carrying trader, and the carriage of the articles is embraced within the scope of its chartered powers, it is a common carrier, and a special contract about its responsibility does not divest it of that character. The fundamental principles upon which the law of common carriers was established was to secure the utmost care and diligence in the performance of their duties. That end was effected, in regard to goods, by charging the common carrier as an insurer, and, in regard to passengers, by exacting the highest degree of carefulness and diligence. A carrier who stipulates not to be bound to the exercise of care and diligence seeks to put off the essential duties of his employment. Nor can those duties be waived in respect to his agents or servants, especially where the carrier is an artificial being, incapable of acting except by agents and servants. The law demands of the carrier carefulness and diligence in performing the service; not merely an abstract carefulness and diligence in proprietors and stockholders, who take no active part in the business. To admit such a distinction in the law of common carriers, as the business is now carried on, would be subversive of the very object of the law. The carrier and his customer do not stand upon a footing of equality. The individual customer has no real freedom of choice. He cannot afford to higgle or stand out and seek redress in the courts. He prefers rather to accept any bill of lading, or sign any paper, that the carrier presents; and, in most cases, he has no alternative but to do this, or to abandon his business. Special contracts between the carrier and the customer, the terms of which are just and reasonable and not contrary to public policy, are upheld; such as those exempting the carrier from responsibility for losses happening from accident, or from dangers of navigation that no human skill or diligence can guard against; or for money or other valuable articles liable to be stolen or damaged, unless informed of their character or value; or for perishable articles or live animals, when injured without default or negligence of the carrier. But the law does not allow a public carrier to abandon altogether his obligations to the public, and to stipulate for exemptions which are unreasonable and improper, amounting to an abnegation of the essential duties of his employment. It being against the policy of the law to allow stipulations which will relieve the railroad company from the exercise of care or diligence, or which, in other words, will excuse it for negligence in the performance of its duty, the company remains liable for such negligence. The analysis of the opinion in Railroad Company v. Lockwood shows that it affirms and rests upon the doctrine that an express stipulation by any common carrier for hire, in a contract of carriage, that he shall be exempt from liability for losses caused by the negligence of himself or his servants, is unreasonable and contrary to public policy, and, consequently, void. And such has always been the understanding of this court, expressed in several later cases."[1]

§ **30. The Rule in New York.**—In New York the rule of the Supreme Court of the United States has not been fully upheld. It is settled in that State, as the result of numerous decisions, that a common carrier may limit his liability by contract, and his contract may provide for immunity from the consequences of his own negligence or carelessness, and from that of his agents or servants. But, in order to accomplish this end, the terms of the contract must be definite and unequivocal. While the decisions on this point are uniform, it is apparent that the conscience of the eminent jurists of that State is not in full accord with the rule, and, in consequence, all contracts of this character are rigidly construed, and no presumptions are entertained in favor of the carrier. In Mynard

[1] Liverpool Steam Co. v. Phœnix Ins. Co., 129 U. S. 397, 439. A lease by a railroad company of part of its right of way, on condition that the company shall not be liable for damage to property situated thereon caused by fire communicated from locomotives, or resulting from negligence of its employes, is not void as against public policy. Hartford Fire Ins. Co. v. Chicago, M. & St. P. Ry., 70 Fed. Rep. 201; s. c., 17 C. C. A. 62.

v. Syracuse Railroad Company, the court said: "Where general words may operate without including the negligence of the carrier or his servants it will not be presumed that it was intended to include it. Every presumption is against an intention to contract for immunity for not exercising ordinary diligence in the transaction of any business, and hence the general rule is that contracts will not be so construed unless expressed in unequivocal terms."[1] A stipulation on the part of the carrier that the goods are to be transported at the risk of the shipper will not release the carrier from liability for loss, resulting from his failure, or the failure of his servants, to exercise reasonable care and prudence.[2] In a recent case it was held that where a

[1] Mynard v. Syracuse, etc. R. Co., 71 N. Y. 180; Wells v. Steam Nav. Co., 8 N. Y. 375; Steinweg v. Erie R. Co., 43 N. Y. 123; Maguire v. Dinsmore, 56 N. Y. 168; Alexander v. Greer, 7 Hill (N. Y.), 533; Nicholas v. New York Cent. R. Co., 89 N. Y. 370; Holsapple v. Rome, etc. R. Co., 86 N. Y. 275. A carrier may lawfully stipulate a time within which claim for damages must be presented. Case v. Cleveland, etc. R. Co., 11 Ind. App. 517; s. c., 39 N. E. Rep. 426; United States Express Co. v. Harris, 51 Ind. 127; Louisville, etc. R. Co. v. Widman, 9 Ind. App. 190; s. c., 37 N. E. Rep. 554; Westcott v. Fargo, 61 N. Y. 542; Western Union Tel. Co. v. Jones, 95 Ind. 228; Western Union Tel. Co. v. Scircle, 103 Ind. 227; Jennings v. Grank Trunk R. Co., 127 N. Y. 438; s. c., 28 N. E. Rep. 394; Glenn v. Southern Express Co., 86 Tenn. 594; s. c., 8 S. W. Rep. 152; Armstrong v. Chicago, etc. R. Co., 53 Minn. 183; s. c., 54 N. W. Rep. 1059; Sprague v. Missouri Pac. R. Co., 34 Kan. 347; s. c., 8 Pac. Rep. 465; Western R. Co. v. Harwell, 91 Ala. 340; s. c., 8 So. Rep. 649; Selby v. Wilmington, etc. R. Co., 113 N. Car. 588; s. c., 18 S. E. Rep. 88; Wichita, etc. R. Co. v. Koch, 47 Kan. 753; s. c., 28 Pac. Rep. 1013; Owen v. Louisville, etc. R. Co., 87 Ky. 629; s. c., 9 S. W. Rep. 698; Dawson v. St. Louis, etc. R. Co., 76 Mo. 514; Wabash, etc. R. Co. v. Black, 11 Ill. App. 465; Adams Express Co. v. Reagan, 29 Ind. 21; Southern Express Co. v. Caperton, 44 Ala. 101; Western Union Tel. Co. v. Jones, 95 Ind. 228; Merrill v. American Express Co., 62 N. H. 514.

[2] Canfield v. Baltimore, etc. R. Co., 93 N. Y. 532; French v. Buffalo, etc. R. Co., 4 Keyes, 108; Moore v. Evans, 14 Barb. 524. Common carriers may limit their common law liability by express contract against risks not arising from their own negligence. The acceptance, without objection by a shipper, of a receipt for the goods, wherein such limitation is declared, may constitute a contract whereby he will be bound. Durgin v. American Express Co., 66 N. H. 277. Common carriers may, by reasonable regulation, make their notes for transporting live animals

shipper of property enters into a contract with a common carrier, whereby, in consideration of an agreement of the latter to transport the property at reduced rates, it is stipulated that in the event of loss or injury resulting from causes which would make the carrier liable, the liability shall be limited to an amount not exceeding a valuation specified, the shipper, in case of loss or injury, is not entitled to recover more than the sum specified. It is incumbent upon a shipper to acquaint himself with the contents of the contract executed by him, and although he fails to do so, he will be held chargeable with knowledge thereof.[1] In the main the New York rule is sustained in Missouri.[2] In a number of States the common law rule, as upheld by the Supreme Court of the United States, is accepted.[3]

§ 31. Contracts in Contravention of Law.—It is well established that all agreements in contravention of a statute are void, and any engagement to render a service or

to depend on the value of the animals as given by the shipper, and may limit their liability in case of loss to the valuation so given to establish the rates. Duntley v. Boston & Maine R. R. Co., 66 N. H. 263.

[1] Zimmer v. New York Central, etc. R. Co., 137 N. Y. 460; Belger v. Dinsmore, 51 N. Y. 166; Steers v. Liverpool, etc. Steamship Co., 57 N. Y. 1; Madan v. Sherard, 73 N. Y. 329; Grossman v. Dodd, 137 N. Y. 599. See also Kellerman v. Kansas City R. Co., 136 Mo. 177; s. c., 34 S. W. Rep. 41; Harvey v. Railroad Co., 74 Mo. 538; Ballou v. Earle, 17 R. I. 441; s. c., 22 Atl. Rep. 1113; Coupland v. Housatonic R. Co., 61 Conn. 531; s. c., 23 Atl. Rep. 870.

[2] Kellerman v. Kansas City, etc. R. Co., 136 Mo. 177; s. c., 34 S. W. Rep. 41; Hart v. Pennsylvania R. Co., 112 U. S. 331; s. c., 5 Sup. Ct. Rep. 151. See also McFadden v. Missouri Pacific Ry. Co., 92 Mo. 343; Rogan v. Wabash Ry. Co., 51 Mo. App. 665; Duvenick v. Missouri Pacific R. Co., 57 Mo. App. 550; Conover v. Pacific Express Co., 40 Mo. App. 31.

[3] Abrams v. Milwaukee, etc. R. Co., 87 Wis. 485; s. c., 56 N. Y. 780; Betts v. Farmers', etc. Trust Co., 21 Wis. 80; Atchison, etc. R. Co. v. Lawler, 40 Neb. 356; s. c., 58 N. W. Rep. 968; Welsh v. Pittsburg, etc. R. Co., 10 Ohio St. 65; Morrison v. Phillips, etc. Construction Co., 44 Wis. 405; Baughman v. Louisville, etc. R. Co., 94 Ky. 150; s. c., 21 S. W. Rep. 757; Johnstone v. Richmond, etc. R. Co., 39 S. Car. 55; s. c., 17 S. E. Rep. 512; Louisville, etc. R. Co. v. Faylor, 126 Ind. 126; s. c., 25 N. E. Rep. 869. See general note 1 to section 29, *ante*.

to perform an act which is in contravention of the policy of an act of a legislature, though it may not be a literal violation of any of its requirements, will be held illegal, as in contravention of public policy.[1] All instruments made for the purpose of giving effect to an illegal agreement are tainted with the illegality, and cannot be enforced in a court of equity.[2] In a case in Massachusetts, it was held that an agreement by an insolvent debtor to pay some of his creditors a portion of their claims, in consideration that they would not "trouble or oppose his discharge, and would say a good word to other creditors to induce them not to oppose a discharge," is void, as contravening the

[1] Jackson v. Davison, 4 Barn. & Ald. 695; Rogers v. Kingston, 10 Moore. 102; s. c., 2 Bing. 441; Murray v. Reeves, 8 Barn. & Cr. 425; Hall v. Dyson, 16 Jur. 270; s. c., 21 L. J. Q. B. 224; Hills v. Mittson, 8 Excheq. 758; Cannon v. Cannon, 26 N. J. Eq. 316; Keppell v. Bailey, 2 Myl. & K. 517; Smith v. City of Albany, 7 Lans. 14; Philpotts v. Philpotts, 10 C. B. 85; Barrell v. Hanrick, 42 Ala. 60; Blossom v. Van Amringe, 1 Phil. Eq. 133; Black v. Oliver, 1 Ala. 449; Jackson v. Walker, 5 Hill, 27; Cantur v. Bennett, 39 Tex. 303; Pratt v. Draughon, 21 La. Ann. 194; McWilliams v. Bryan, 21 La. Ann. 211; Overby v. Overby, 21 La. Ann. 493; Swanger v. Mayberry, 59 Cal. 91; Scudder v. Andrews, 2 McLean, 464; Downing v. Ringer, 7 Mo. 585; Boies v. Blake, 13 Me. 381; Russell v. De Grand, 15 Mass. 35; Touro v. Cassin, 1 Nott & M. 172; Gray v. Swiss, 3 Wash. C. C. 276; Benton v. Hope, 19 La. Ann. 463; Schwartz v. Tyson, 4 H. & J. 288; Shiffner v. Gordon, 12 East, 296; Williams v. Woodman, 8 Pick. 77; Upton v. Haines, 55 N. H. 283; Milton v. Haden, 32 Ala. 30; De Groot v. Vanduzen, 20 Wend. 390; Mayor v. Lacy, 3 Ala. 618; Bank v. Stegall, 41 Miss. 142; Sanderson v. Goodrich, 46 Barb. 611; Ladd v. Dillingham, 34 Me. 316; Smith v. Wilcox, 19 Barb. 581; Bernard v. Lupping, 32 Mo. 341; Smith v. Foster, 41 N. H. 215; Mitchell v. Smith, 4 Dall. 269; Vickroy v. Pratt, 7 Kan. 238; Nix v. Bell, 66 Ga. 664; Sherman v. Wilder, 106 Mass. 537; Lender v. Caldwell, 4 Kan. 339; Martin v. Bartow Iron Works, 35 Ga. 320; Drexler v. Tyrrell, 15 Nev. 114; Siter v. Streets, 7 Ind. 132; First Cong. Church v. Henderson, 4 Rob. (La.) 209; Reife v. Com. Ins. Co., 5 Mo. App. 173; Alexander v. Reife, 74 Mo. 495; Milne v. Huber, 3 McLean, 212; Hannay v. Eve, 3 Cr. 241; De Melton v. Mello, 12 East, 234.

[2] Blasdell v. Fowle, 120 Mass. 447. See also Cockshott v. Bennett, 2 T. R. 763; Phelps v. Thomas, 6 Gray, 327; Case v. Gerrish, 15 Pick. 49; Coates v. Blush, 1 Cush. 564; Partridge v. Messer, 14 Gray, 180; Dexter v. Snow, 12 Cush. 594; Downs v. Lewis, 11 Cush. 76; Ramsdell v. Edgarton, 8 Met. 227; Smith v. Bromley, 2 Doug. 696.

policy of the insolvent laws.[1] In a case in New Jersey, it has been held that a contract which contravenes either the provisions or policy of a public law is void; but a transaction to be void in law, as a contract, must first have life as a completed treaty between the parties.[2] In an English case, Lord Ellenborough said: "It may be taken as a received rule of law that what is done in contravention of the provisions of an act of Parliament cannot be made the subject-matter of an action."[3]

§ 32. For Influencing the Administration of Justice.— Covenants relating to any service or to any acts the object of which is to influence the administration of justice by the courts are in contravention of public policy and void. It is not necessary that there should be a positive attempt to corrupt the court, or that any actual subversion of justice should result. In a recent case in Indiana, it was held that all agreements for pecuniary consideration to control the regular administration of justice are void as against public policy, regardless of the good faith of the parties, and without reference to the question as to whether improper means are contemplated or used in their execution.[4] In

[1] Dexter v. Snow, 12 Cush. 594.

[2] Cannon v. Cannon, 26 N. J. Eq. 316.

[3] Langston v. Hughes, 1 Maule & Selw. 596. See also Smith v. Cuff, 6 Maule & Selw. 160; Leicester v. Rose, 4 East. 380; Fawcett v. Gee, 3 Anst. 910; *Ex parte* Sadler, 15 Ves. 52; Breck v. Cole, 4 Sandf. 83; Knight v. Hunt, 5 Bing. 433; Howden v. Haigh, 11 Ad. & El. 1038; Mallalieu v. Hodgson, 16 Ad. & El. 678; Turner v. Hoole, Dowl. & Ryl. N. P. 27. When a person has entered as much coal land as the statutes of the United States permit, a contract, whereby another person is to enter additional coal land, obtain the title, and then convey it to the first, is contrary to public policy. Johnson v. Leonhard (Wash. Ter.), 20 Pac. Rep. 591.

[4] Brown v. First Nat'l Bank, 137 Ind. 655; Wood v. Humphrey, 114 Mass. 185; Pearl v. Harris, 121 Mass. 390; Vass v. Wales, 129 Mass. 38; White v. Railroad Co., 135 Mass. 216; Hill v. More, 40 Me. 515; Gray v. Wilson, 4 Watts, 39; Randal v. C. & D. Canal Co., 1 Harr. 233; Stone v. Dennis, 3 Port. (Ala.) 231; Haggart v. Morgan, 5 N. Y. 422; Hurst v. Litchfield, 39 N. Y. 377; McGunn v. Hanlin, 29 Mich. 476; March v. Railroad Co., 40 N. H. 548. An agreement between a fidelity insurance company and the employe whose honesty is guaranteed that the voucher showing payment by the company to the employer of

the opinion in this case, the court said: "'All agreements for pecuniary consideration to control the regular administration of justice are void, as against public policy, without reference to the question whether improper means are contemplated or used in their execution. The law looks to the

loss occasioned through the employe's dishonesty should be conclusive evidence against the employe as to the fact and extent of his liability to the company was void as against public policy. Fidelity & Casualty Co. v. Eickhoff, 63 Minn. 170; s. c., 65 N. W. Rep. 351. Money advanced to the husband at the request of the wife in consideration of his making no opposition to a bill for divorce—being for an illegal and immoral consideration, cannot be recovered against her on her express promise to pay. Viser v. Bertrand, 14 Ark. 267. "If it be the duty of every man it is more especially the duty of persons injured, who have caused criminal prosecutions to be commenced, to appear against offenders, and not to make bargains to allow them to escape conviction, if they or their friends will pay a sum of money to repair the injury. To decide that such bargains might be lawfully made, would be to lend a helping hand to make public justice venal. To procure a compensation to be made to the person injured, is a subordinate object to the State, in causing crimes to be punished. It causes crimes to be punished that they may not be committed with impunity, and, therefore, become more frequent; that the rights of property and the inviolability of the person may not become less secure; that persons may depend upon the execution of the laws, rather than resort to physical force for the preservation and protection of their rights." Shaw v. Reed, 30 Me. 105, 109. Proceedings for the establishment of public highways are essentially public in their character, and are for the benefit of the whole people; and while such proceedings are begun voluntarily by private persons, and while also such persons may not be compelled to prosecute such proceedings to a final result, yet an agreement to abandon such prosecution in consideration of money to be paid for such abandonment, is against public policy, and void in law, and cannot be enforced. Jacobs v. Tobiason, 65 Iowa, 245. The threat of a criminal prosecution, used to compel the giving of a promisory note, may constitute duress, although the amount for which the note is given is actually due to the payee from the maker. A promissory note in settlement of a claim may be void as given under an agreement to suppress a criminal prosecution, although no threats of prosecution are made at the time of the settlement, if they have been made a few days before and not been retracted. Taylor v. Jaques, 106 Mass. 291. Where a note was given in consideration of a promise made by the payee to cause a prosecution for a felony, then pending in the State of Tennessee against the son of the maker of the note to be discontinued, and a mortgage was executed to secure the payment of the note, it was general tendency of such agreements; and it closes the door to temptation by refusing them recognition in any of the courts in the country. Greenhood on Public Policy, p. 5, thus lays down the rule: 'The question of the validity of the contract does not depend upon the circumstance whether it can be shown that the public has in fact suffered any detriment, but whether the contract is in its nature such as might be injurious to the public. It matters not that any particular contract is free from any taint of actual fraud, oppression or corruption. The law looks to the general tendency of such contracts.' The evil tendency of the contract in suit is clearly apparent. The mere statement of it shocks the sense of justice and fair play. By

held that the consideration was illegal and that both note and mortgage could be avoided. Henderson v. Palmer, 71 Ill. 579. An employe of a railroad company may, by contract, waive his right to sue for injuries not arising from criminal negligence on the part of the company, or its other employes: but any negligence, either of omission or commission, on the part of other employes of the road, in connection with their business, from which serious injury results, constitutes criminal negligence, and a contract waiving the right to sue for injuries resulting therefrom is contrary to public policy and void. Cook v. Western & Atlantic R. R., 72 Ga. 48. An agreement to procure witnesses to testify to a certain state of facts, is immoral and against public policy. Patterson v. Donner, 48 Cal. 369. See generally as to agreements for shifting criminal prosecutions: Gorham v. Keyes, 137 Mass. 583; Lindsay v. Smith, 78 N. Car. 328; Baker v. Farris, 61 Mo. 389; Shaw v. Spooner, 9 N. H. 198; Chandler v. Johnson, 39 Ga. 85; Goodwin v. Crowell, 56 Ga. 566: Snider v. Willey, 33 Mich. 483; Summer v. Summer, 54 Mo. 340; Wright v. Rindskopf, 43 Wis. 344: Roll v. Raguet, 4 Ohio, 400: Ricketts v. Harvey, 106 Ind. 564; Peed v. McKee, 42 Iowa, 689; McMahon v. Smith, 47 Conn. 221: Pearce v. Wilson, 111 Pa. St. 14; s. c., 56 Am. Rep. 243; Wheaton v. Ansley, 71 Ga. 35: Ormerod v. Dearman, 100 Pa. St. 561; Rhodes v. Neal, 64 Ga. 704: Averbeck v. Hall, 14 Bush, 505; Baehr v. Wolff, 59 Ill. 470; Dunkin v. Hodge, 46 Ala. 523; Merrill v. Carr, 60 N. H. 114: Buck v. Bank, 27 Mich. 293: Bowen v. Buck, 28 Vt. 308. As to collusion in divorce cases see Stoutenburgh v. Lybrand, 13 Ohio St. 228: Kilborn v. Field, 78 Pa. St. 194; Sayles v. Sayles, 21 N. H. 312; Cross v. Cross, 58 N. H. 373: Goodwin v. Goodwin, 4 Day, 343: Stilson v. Stilson, 46 Conn. 15; Belden v. Munger, 5 Minn. 211; Adams v. Adams, 25 Minn. 72: Everhart v. Puckett, 73 Ind. 409: Phillips v. Thorp, 10 Ore. 494; Hope v. Hope, 8 De G., M. & G. 731: Weeks v. Hill, 38 N. H. 199; Brown v. Brine, L. R. 1 Excheq. D. 5.

virtue of the contract appellant assumed a position where selfish motives might have impelled him to sacrifice the public good for private gain; for there is no greater public good than the right of every person charged with the commission of a crime to have a fair and impartial hearing; and there is no higher security for that right than the preservation of the courts free from corrupting influences."[1] In a recent case it was held that a contract whereby a justice of the peace agrees to charge smaller fees in suits to be brought before him by a certain corporation than prescribed by statute, and that such fees shall not be collected unless paid over by the defendants to the corporation, is contrary to public policy and void.[2] In a case in Michigan, a justice of the peace agreed with an attorney to charge no fees in certain suits brought before him unless the judgments rendered therein were collected. It was held a palpable violation of judicial duty and void as against public policy; and that the justice could not recover from the plaintiff for services *actually* rendered, the whole transaction being beyond the protection of courts of justice.[3] In a recent case in California, it was held that a contract between the

[1] Brown v. First Nat'l Bank, 137 Ind. 655, 668.

[2] Hawkeye Ins. Co. v. Brainard, 72 Iowa, 130; s. c., 33 N. W. Rep. 603. "Here the amount of compensation was to depend upon the success of the party to the suit, in whose favor the witness was to testify, and although there may have been no agreement, or expectation, that the witness would give false testimony, the inevitable tendency of the contract was to give him a bias in favor of the party calling him as a witness, as the promised reward was to be reduced one-half, if the party in whose favor he was to testify was not successful in the suit. This created such an interest in the event of the suit, as would have prevented him from testifying if the contract was valid, and it follows, necessarily, that a promise to compensate a witness for his attendance cannot be enforced, which, if known, would have excluded him from being a witness; as it would be a fraud upon the administration of justice. Such contracts are against sound policy, because their inevitable tendency would be if not to invite to perjury, at least to sway the mind of the witness by giving him the interest of a party to the cause and thus contaminate the stream of justice at its source. It can neither admit of doubt or question, that both morality and sound policy forbid the toleration of such contracts as this." Eddings v. Long, 10 Ala. 203, 208.

[3] Willemin v. Bateson, 63 Mich. 309.

purchaser at a partition sale and one of the parties to the partition suit, who was about to contest the confirmation of the sale for inadequacy of the price bid, to the effect that said party, in consideration of a specified sum to be paid in addition for her interest in the property, would refrain from contesting said confirmation, is a contract for the concealment of a material fact from the court and the other parties to the partition suit, which it was the duty of the contracting party to make known, and is void as against public policy, and neither party should receive the aid of the courts to enforce it.[1] In a case in Missouri, it was held that it is unlawful for a candidate for public office to make offers to the voters to perform the duties of the office, if elected, for less than the legal fees. An election secured by means of such offers is void.[2] In Kansas it has been held that an agreement to withdraw the plea of usury is against public policy and cannot be sustained.[3] In his opinion in this case, Mr. Justice Brewer said: "The agreement to withdraw the plea of usury cannot be sustained. It is no better than an agreement not to plead it, and surely if such an agreement could be sustained a usurious loan would always be accompanied by an agreement not to plead the usury, a very simple if not effectual way of evading the law."[4]

§ 33. **For Changing the Officers of Corporations.**— The appointment and removal of the directors and officers of a corporation cannot be made a matter of bargain and sale. Persons occupying these positions sustain, towards

[1] Tappan v. Albany Brewing Co., 80 Cal. 570. An agreement to withdraw an offer or bid for property of the State offered for sale, to enable one of the parties thereto, by the removal of competition, to buy it cheaper than he otherwise could, is against public policy, and not enforceable, and it is immaterial whether property is offered at public auction or by inviting bids or proposals for its purchase at private sale. Boyle v. Adams 50 Minn. 255; s. c., 52 N. W. Rep. 860.

[2] Attorney-General v. Collin, 72 Mo. 13. See also Alvord v. Collin, 20 Pick. 428; Tucker v. Aiken, 7 N. H. 140; State v. Purdy, 36 Wis. 213; s. c., 17 Am. Rep. 485.

[3] Clark v. Spencer, 14 Kan. 399.

[4] Clark v. Spencer, 14 Kan. 399, 404.

the stockholders, the relation of trust and confidence, and they are bound to act with supreme reference to the interests of those whom they represent. Any agreement into which they may enter, the object of which is to advance their own interests, either at the expense of the stockholders, or irrespective of their interests, is a breach of trust, and will not be enforced in equity. In a case in Massachusetts, it was held that a contract, by which a shareholder in a corporation, in consideration of the purchase of a part of his stock at a price named, agrees to secure to the purchaser the office of treasurer of the corporation, with a fixed salary, and in case of his removal to repurchase the stock at par, is void as against public policy and as a fraud on the other members of the corporation, in the absence of evidence that the transaction was not for the private benefit of the shareholder, or that it was consented to by the other members of the corporation.[1] In the opinion in this case the court said: "It was the purpose and effect of the contract to influence the defendant in the decision of a question affecting the private rights of others by considerations foreign to those rights. The promisee was placed under direct inducement to disregard his duties to other members of the corporation, who had a right to demand his disinterested action in the selection of suitable officers. He was in a relation of trust and confidence which required him to look only to the best interests of the whole, uninfluenced by private gain. The contract operated as a fraud upon his associates."[2] In California it has been held that an agreement of a trustee of a corporation for a pecuniary recompense to resign his trust, is *contra bonos mores*, and a contract based, either wholly or in part, on such an agreement as a consideration, is void.[3] In a case in Kansas N

[1] Guernsey v. Cook, 120 Mass. 501. See also Fuller v. Dame, 18 Pick. 472; Case v. Gerrish, 15 Pick. 49; Smith v. Townsend, 109 Mass. 500; Phippen v. Stickney, 3 Met. 384; Gibbs v. Smith, 115 Mass. 592; Curtis v. Aspinwall, 114 Mass. 187; Waldo v. Martin, 4 Barn. & C. 319; Marshall v. Baltimore & Ohio R. R. Co., 16 How. 314; Elliott v. Richardson, L. R. 5 C. P. 744.

[2] Guernsey v. Cook, 120 Mass. 501, 502.

[3] Forbes v. McDonald, 54 Cal. 98.

entered into a verbal contract with D, a director and the president of a national bank, to buy of the latter one hundred and fourteen shares of stock in the bank, at $140 per share, upon the condition that he should be made cashier of the bank. Subsequently D notified N that he could not and would not fulfill the contract. Thereupon N brought an action for damages for the breach thereof. It was held that the consideration of the contract being against public policy the contract was void, and that N was not entitled to recover damages.[1]

§ 34. **For Renouncing an Executorship.**—A covenant under which an executor engages to retire from his executorship for a consideration, is in contravention of public policy and void. An executor cannot make use of his relations to the trust property to promote his personal interests.[2] In an English case a testator appointed two trustees

[1] Noel v. Drake, 28 Kan. 265. See further Guernsey v. Cook, 120 Mass. 501; Noyes v. Marsh, 123 Mass. 286; Merchants' Nat'l Bank v. State Bank, 10 Wall. 604, 650; Railroad Co. v. Ryan, 11 Kan. 602; Haas v. Fenlon, 8 Kan. 601; Tool Co. v. Norris, 2 Wall. 45. "In the relation of trust and confidence which Drake occupied as a director and president of the bank, which required him to look only to the best interests of the bank and its stockholders, it was improper for him to be influenced by agreements with, or considerations from, a stranger to the association in the selection of a cashier, or in the discharge of any of his other official duties. The appointment of officers by the directors of a national bank ought not to be made a matter of bargain and sale between applicants and members of the board." Noel v. Drake, *supra*. The defendants made an agreement with the plaintiff, by which they stipulated that on the payment by him of $200,000 for a certain number of shares of the capital stock of a railway company, then belonging to them, new directors to be nominated by the plaintiff and his co-purchaser, H, should be substituted in the place of all the other directors, except the plaintiff and H, who were directors at the time. *Held*, that the contract was an attempt improperly to interfere with the rights of others, and was clearly contrary to public policy. And that if the subject-matter of the contract was of that species which would authorize a court of equity to interpose and decree a specific performance, the object and nature of it would forbid any such interposition. Fremont v. Stone, 42 Barb. 169.

[2] Ellicott v. Chamberlain, 38 N. J. Eq. 604; McCaw v. Blewit, 2 McCord Ch. 90; Bate v. Bate, 11 Bush, 639; Bowers v. Bowers, 26 Pa. St. 74; Owings v. Owings, 1

and executors of his will, but by a codicil he excluded them and appointed two other persons. One of them retired in consideration of £75, paid to him by one of the excluded trustees, and executed a deed appointing the excluded trustee to act as trustee in his room. The court directed the new trustee to be removed and the deed to be cancelled;

Harr. & G. 484; Cunningham v. Cunningham, 18 B. Mon. 24; Hargreaves v. Wood, 2 Sw. & Tr. 602; Van Meter v. Jones, 2 Green Ch. 520; Clark v. Constantine, 3 Bush. 652; Wheelock v. Looney, 15 N. Y. Wkly. Dig. 126; Sugden v. Crossland, 3 Sm. & Gif. 193; Whatley v. Hughes, 53 Miss. 268; Spinks v. Davis, 32 Miss. 152; Page's Estate, 57 Cal. 238; Birt's Case, 48 L. T. 67; Foote v. Emerson, 10 Vt. 338; Brown v. Stewart, 4 Md. Ch. 368; Squier v. Squier, 3 Stew. Eq. 627; Aston's Estate, 5 Whart. 228; White v. Bullock, 4 Abb. App. Dec. 578; Allen v. Humphries, L. R. 8 P. D. 16; Willis v. Jones, 42 Md. 422; Ward v. Thompson, 6 Gill & J. 349. On the 14th of October, 1873, the orphan's court of Cecil county passed an order setting aside the alleged will of E W M, and revoking the letters testamentary previously granted to A R M. On the 1st day of November, 1880, H M filed his petition seeking to have the aforesaid order of the orphan's court set aside and annulled. The petitioner alleged "that large property, real and personal, was left to him in trust under the will," and claimed that as trustee under the will he had the right to impeach the validity of said order. The evidence showed that for a pecuniary consideration which he afterwards received, the petitioner agreed to renounce his office of trustee, as well as that of executor. In pursuance thereof he filed a petition in the orphan's court, resigning his office as executor, and praying to be relieved therefrom, and an order was passed by the court accepting his resignation and discharging him from the office of executor. The office of trustee he never, in fact, accepted, except as such acceptance was implied by his assuming the office of executor. It was also in proof that while the petitioner had actual notice in September, 1874, that the will of E W M had been set aside, yet he took no steps to impeach the judgment until the 1st of November, 1880, when he filed his petition. On an appeal from an order of the orphan's court, dismissing his petition, it was held that, in the face of his express agreement to surrender his office as trustee, and after having received and retained a large consideration for entering into the agreement, the petitioner, as trustee, had no interest, under the will, entitling him to maintain his suit, or to impeach the judgment of the orphan's court. Munnikhuysen v. Magraw, 58 Md. 557. "Parties have no right, by agreement, to attempt to control the discretion of the probate court or the clerk in the exercise of this discretion. The law is that the clerk or court, in the contingency named, shall grant letters to any person who shall be considered most suitable. * * * The main purpose of the agreement was to secure the appointment of an declared the conveyance to be void, and directed the £75 to form a part of the assets. It was held farther that a profit derived by a trustee, either from the trust property or from his office of trustee, belongs to the *cestui que trust.*[1] In Staunton v. Parker, the court said: "An executor has the undoubted right to renounce, of his own motion, if he desires. But a renunciation for a consideration,—a renunciation purchased in any manner without the concurrence of the testator, and during his lifetime, is a very different matter. If agreements of this nature are to be enforced, then, surely, testators may well doubt, not only as to who will carry out their wills, but whether they will be carried out at all. * * * The principle is the same whether the difference is small or great: and if the will may be varied by agreement in the lifetime of the testator, in a minor respect in this case, it may be varied in an important one in the next, and the door would be thrown wide open to fraud and corruption on the part of designing men and intriguing descendants, and imposition upon confiding testators."[2] This rule applies to administrators. A contract

administrator. This agreement amounts to a trafficking in this important trust. Although it is not a public office, it is, nevertheless, a private trust just as sacred, and arises from an appointment to be made by a public court or officer. An agreement to procure an appointment to office is against public policy and void. The trust devolved upon an administrator through the appointment of a public functionary, ought to have the same safeguards thrown around it as if it were a public office. The note sued on in this case, and the agreement upon which it was based, must be taken together and viewed as one instrument. As they amounted to a trading in the appointment of an administrator they are void as against public policy. This seems to be well settled by the authorities (see Bowers v. Bowers, 26 Pa. St. 74; Davison v. Seymour, 1 Bosw. 88; Eddy v. Capron, 4 R. I. 394; Foreman v. Berghaus, 13 La. Ann. 209; Gray v. Hook, 4 Comst. 449; Kick v. Merry, 23 Mo. 72; Kribben v. Haycraft, 26 Mo. 396; Comyns, Contracts, 30; Clark v. Constantine, 3 Bush, 652), which seems to intimate a contrary rule in a case somewhat similar to the one under review, does not seem to have been well considered, and is opposed to the principles decided in the very authorities referred by the judge who delivered the opinion." Porter v. Jones, 52 Mo. 399, 402.

[1] Sugden v. Crossland, 3 Sm. & Gif. 192.

[2] Stanton v. Parker, 19 Hun, 61; Manning v. Manning, 1 Johns. Ch. 533.

under which an administrator engages to relinquish the right of administration upon the estate of an intestate for a valuable consideration, is in contravention of public policy and void.[1] But in Ireland a contract of that character was held valid and binding.[2] In a case where the guardian of C made an agreement with C's grandfather by which he was to resign his position as guardian and permit the grandfather to assume it, the consideration being that the grandfather should give C a child's share of his estate, it was held that the contract could not be enforced in equity.[3]

§ 35. **For Assignment of Salary not yet Due.**—It is well settled, both in England and in the United States, that a public officer cannot legally make an assignment of his salary. Such an assignment will be treated as in contravention of public policy and void. In the leading case an agreement between a municipal corporation and its town clerk that he should receive a fixed salary in lieu of the fees to which he was entitled under the statute, and that, to carry out such agreement, he should pay over to the borough fund so much of the amount received for fees as should be in excess of that salary, was held contrary to public policy and invalid.[4] In his opinion in this case Vice-Chancellor Wood said: "It seems to me that there are two plain grounds of public policy which render such

[1] Bowers v. Bowers, 26 Pa. St. 74; Owings v. Owings, 1 Harr. & G. 484.

[2] Currigan's Case, 6 Ir. Jur. (N. S.) 116; Bassett v. Miller, 8 Ind. 548. "While such contracts should not be encouraged, it is far better, in view of public policy and sound morality, that they should be sustained, than that conduct should be tolerated by this court by which solemn engagements may be repudiated, and fraud and deception perpetrated with impunity." Bassett v. Miller, *supra*.

[3] Cunningham v. Cunningham, 18 B. Mon. 24.

[4] Corporation of Liverpool v. Wright, 5 Jur. (N. S.) 1156; s. c., 28 L. J. Ch. 871; Flarty v. Odlam, 3 T. R. 681; Stone v. Lidderdale, 2 Anst. 233; Davis v. Marlboro, 1 Swanst. 79; Lidderdale v. Montrose, 4 T. R. 248; Barwick v. Read, 1 H. Bl. 627; Arbuckle v. Cowhan, 3 Bos. & P. 328; Wells v. Foster, 8 M. & W. 149; Hunter v. Gardner, 6 Wils. & Shaw, 618; Hill v. Paul, 8 Cl. & Fin. 307; Palmer v. Bate, 2 Brod. & Bing. 673; Parsons v. Thompson, 1 H. Bl. 322.

an agreement illegal. * * * There is first the whole class of statutes, agreeing to a great extent with the common law in that respect, although making the common law more forcible and giving additional penalties,—a class of statutes which say that an office of trust of this description is not an office as to which any bargain can be made. * * * Where the statute law uses the word 'corrupt,' I apprehend it does not depend on whether the person does it with a corrupt motive or not, or whether the person having the appointment is a public body or not, but it is considered a corrupt act on the part of such person, however excellent his intention may be. * * * That is the first ground of public policy. The second ground of public policy is this: That, independently of any corrupt bargain with the appointor, nobody can deal with the fees of a person who holds an office of this description, because the law presumes, with reference to an office of trust, that he requires the grant, which the law has assigned him, for the purpose of upholding the dignity, and performing properly the duties of that office. Hence it will not allow the holder of the office to part with any portion of the fees, either to the appointor or to anybody else. He is not allowed to charge or incumber them."[1] In a leading case in New York it was held that an assignment by a public officer of the future salary of his office is contrary to public policy and is void.[2] In his opinion in this case Mr. Justice John-

[1] Corporation of Liverpool v. Wright, 5 Jur. (N. S.) 1156, 1157; s. c., 28 L. J. Ch. 871.

[2] Bliss v. Lawrence, 58 N. Y. 442; Beal v. McVicker, 8 Mo. App. 202; Bangs v. Dunn, 66 Cal. 72; s. c., 18 Reporter, 572; Holland v. Helm, 7 Gratt. 245; Bush v. Thornton, 25 Hun, 466; Olin v. Bate, 98 Ill. 53. "Some misapprehension as to the doctrine involved seems to have arisen from the fact that the modern adjudged cases have often related to the pay of half pay army officers, which, in part, is given as a compensation for past services, and in part with a view to future services. Upon a review of the English cases, it will appear that the general proposition is, upon authority unquestionable, that salary for continuing services could not be assigned, while a pension or compensation for past services might be assigned. The doubt, and the only doubt, in the case of half pay officers, was to which class they were to be taken to belong. It was decided that, inasmuch as their pay was in part in

son said: "The public service is protected by protecting those engaged in performing public duties, and this, not upon the ground of their private interests, but upon that of the necessity of securing the efficiency of the public service, by seeing to it that the funds provided for its maintenance should be received by those who are to perform the work, at such periods as the law has appointed for their payment."[1]

view of future services, it was unassignable." Bliss v. Lawrence, 58 N. Y. 442, 445. "Each of certain deputies and copyists in the office of the clerk of the city and county of San Francisco (in the early part of the month of July, 1881, or before the commencement of that month), delivered to the clerk a writing purporting to be a demand upon the treasury of said city for his compensation or salary as for said July, and having indorsed thereon the words 'received payment,' subscribed with the name of such deputy or copyist. The writing was immediately, and before the salary was due, delivered by the clerk to the petitioner for a valuable consideration. * * * But the plaintiff received the demands 'in the early part of July,' and before the respective salaries for that month were earned. He thus took part in a transaction contrary to public policy, and must be held to have knowingly contravened the law." Bangs v. Dunn (1884), 66 Cal. 72; s. c., 18 Reporter. 752. A contract by which the clerk of the Louisville chancery court transfers and assigns to a trustee for the benefit of appellant, in consideration of a debt due him, all the fees and emoluments of his office in the future, until the debt is paid, with conditions to pay deputies, etc., is void. It is against public policy that such contracts be enforced. Field v. Chipley, 79 Ky. 260. Defendant, a public officer, verbally assigned a share of his pay, to accrue for a certain month, to plaintiff, but subsequently collected the whole, and only paid over to plaintiff a part of the share he had assigned. *Held*, that the sale was void under the statute of frauds. The sale by a public officer of his salary, as such, before it is earned, is void as against public policy. Billings v. O'Brien, 14 Abb. Pr. (N. S.) 238. In Wisconsin, in marked contrast with the foregoing, the court, in State Bank v. Hastings, 15 Wis. 78, says: "We are referred to some English cases which hold that the assignment of the pay of officers in the public service, judges' salaries, pensions, etc., was void as being against public policy; but it was not contended that the doctrine of those cases was applicable to the condition of society, or to the principles of law or public policy in this country. For certainly we can see no possible objection to permitting a judge to assign his salary before it becomes due, if he can find any person willing to take the risk of his living and being entitled to it when it becomes payable."

[1] Bliss v. Lawrence, 58 N. Y. 442, 445.

CHAPTER II.

CONTRACTS IN RESTRAINT OF TRADE.

§ 36. Introductory.
37. The General Rule.
38. The Rule in England.
39. Partial Distinguished from General Restraint.
40. Question of Consideration.
41. Limitations of Time.
42. The Subject Continued.
43. Touching Territorial Limitations.
44. The Subject Continued.
45. Territorial Limits Determined.
46. Validity of Contracts in Restraint of Trade as Affected by their Reasonableness.
47. Divisibility of Illegal Contract.
§ 48. The Subject Continued.
49. Limitations in Conveyances.
50. The Subject Continued.
51. The Grantor Restrained by the Terms of the Conveyance.
52. Contracts Relating to Trade Secrets.
53. Restraint of Trade by Patents.
54. Where Contracts Relating to Patents are not Upheld.
55. Restraint in the Sale of a Trade-Mark.
56. Restraint in Publication Contract.

§ 36. **Introductory.**—The general principle on which contracts in restraint of trade have been held to be in contravention of public policy, and, in consequence, void, is that it is the duty of the law-making power to secure to every citizen the right to pursue his ordinary avocation and to dispose of his labor, or of the product thereof, without restraint, and to protect the public from the evil consequences of an agreement under which it would be deprived of the benefits of competition in skilled labor. The law has regard, on the one hand, to the interests of the person restrained from labor or trade, protecting him from oppression or from the consequences of an injudicious bargain, and, on the other hand, it takes account of the interest of the community in providing that it shall not be deprived of the benefit of his business, or exposed to the burden of his support, as a result of his lack of employment. In a case before the Supreme Judicial Court of Massachusetts, the principle was stated by the court, as follows: "The unreasonableness of contracts in restraint of trade and business is very apparent from several obvious considerations: 1. Such contracts injure the parties making them, because they diminish their means of procuring livelihoods and a competency for their families. They tempt improvident persons, for the sake of present gain, to deprive themselves of the power to make future acquisitions, and they expose such persons to imposition and oppression. 2. They tend to deprive the public of the services of men in the employments and capacities in which they may be most useful to the community as well as to themselves. 3. They discourage industry and enterprise, and diminish the products of ingenuity and skill. 4. They prevent competition and enhance prices. 5. They expose the public to all the evils of monopolies. And this especially is applicable to wealthy companies and large corporations who have the means, unless restrained by law, to exclude rivalry, monopolize business and engross the market. Against evils like these wise laws protect individuals and the public by declaring all such contracts void."[1] The rule under which

[1] Alger v. Thatcher, 19 Pick. 51, 54. See also Clerke v. Comer, Cas. *t.* Hardw. 53; Chesman v. Nainby, 2 Ld. Raym. 1456; s. c., 3 Bro. P. C. 349; Freemantle v. Company of Silk Throwsters, 1 Lev. 229; Cuddon v. Eastwick, Salk. 193; Harrison v. Godman, 1 Burr. 12; Pierce v. Bartram, Cowp. 269; Gunmakers v. Fell, Willes, 384; Harrison v. Gardner, 2 Madd. 198; Shackle v. Baker, 14 Ves. 468; Morris v. Coleman, 18 Ves. 468; Crutwell v. Lye, 17 Ves. 336. "The law will not permit any one to restrain a person from doing what the public and his own interest require that he should do. Any deed, therefore, by which a person binds himself not to employ his talents, his industry or his capital in any useful undertaking in the kingdom, would be void, because no good reason can be imagined for any person imposing such a restraint on himself. But it may often happen that individual interest and general convenience may render engagements not to carry on trade, or to act in a profession in a particular place, proper." Best, C. J., in Homer v. Ashford, 3 Bing.

contracts in restraint of trade were held to be against public policy and void was established in England at an early day, and, with some modifications, by which it has been

319. "In accordance with these principles, it is well settled that a stipulation by a vendee of any trade, business or establishment that the vendor shall not exercise the same trade or business, or erect a similar establishment within a reasonable distance, so as not to interfere with the value of the trade, business or thing purchased, is reasonable and valid. In like manner a stipulation by the vendor of an article to be used in a business or trade in which he is himself engaged, that it shall not be used within a reasonable region or distance so as not to interfere with his said business or trade, is also valid and binding. The point of difficulty in these cases is to determine what is a reasonable distance within which the prohibitory stipulation may lawfully have effect. And it is obvious, at first glance, that this must depend upon the circumstances of the particular case; although, from the uncertain character of the subject, much latitude must be allowed to judgment and discretion of the parties. It is clear that a stipulation that another shall not pursue his trade or employment at such a distance from the business of the person to be protected, as that it could not possibly affect or injure him, would be unreasonable and absurd. On the other hand, a stipulation is unobjectionable and binding which imposes the restraint to only such an extent of territory as may be necessary for the protection of the party making the stipulation, provided it does not violate the two indispensable conditions, that the other party be not prevented from pursuing his calling, and the country be not deprived of the benefit of his exertions." Bradley, J., in Oregon Steam. Nav. Co. v. Winsor, 20 Wall. 64, 68. "It appears, and is conceded by appellant, that the particular business or trade in which appellee was engaged at the time he sold out and executed the contract in controversy was confined to the limits of the city of Hammond. There is no contention that it extended to any other parts of the State beyond these limits. Neither from the nature of the business nor otherwise, does it appear that it was necessary for the protection of the appellant that the appellee should be prohibited from engaging therein at any and all places in the State other than the city of Indianapolis. It is a matter of general knowledge that there are numerous consumers of oil for fuel and illuminating purposes in this great and growing State, and it is manifestly to their interest that there should be competition in the selling of the same, at least, that the price thereof may be reasonable. The enlarged covenant of restraint as to territory, it is obvious, was unnecessary under the circumstances. It could serve no purpose, except as a tendency towards the monopoly of the business. If appellant could buy out appellee and restrict him in this manner, it might proceed to do so to every other person in the whole State engaged in a similar business, and eventually reduce the sale of oils in the State to comparatively few hands, or possibly to its own

adapted to the changed industrial conditions of later times, it continues to be the doctrine of the English and American courts.

§ 37. **The General Rule.**—The general doctrine, as established by very numerous decisions, through a long series of years is, that contracts in restraint of trade are in contravention of public policy and in consequence void. In every case this is the presumption, and the burden of proof is upon the party seeking relief. But this rule is subject to modification by the force of circumstances. A contract in restraint of trade will be held valid where it is limited in its operation, is founded upon a valuable consideration and is reasonable in its provisions. It must not be oppressive to the party restrained from taking an advantage of his necessities; it must not involve a sacrifice of his interests as the result of an injudicious surrender of his rights, and it must not be prejudicial to the interests of the public. All covenants in general restraint of trade, that is, all contracts which restrain a man from carrying on business, or

absolute control, and thus virtually stifle legitimate competition. The law has always been hostile to the creation of monopolies when they tend to impair the interest of the public. It is elementary that whatever is injurious to or against the public good, is void on the ground of public policy. This policy unquestionably favors competition in trade to the end that its commodities may be afforded to the consumer as cheaply as possible, and is opposed to monopolies which tend to advance prices to the injury of the public in general." Jordan, J., in Consumers' Oil Co. v. Nunnemacher, 142 Ind. 560, 567. See generally the following cases: Mitchell v. Reynolds, 1 P. Wms. 181; Whitney v. Slayton, 40 Me. 224; Perkins v. Clay, 58 N. H. 518; Clark v. Crosby, 37 Vt. 188; Hedge v. Lowe, 47 Iowa, 137; Arnold v. Kreutzer, 67 Iowa, 214; Laubenheimer v. Mann, 17 Wis. 542; Fairbank v. Leary, 40 Wis. 637; Keeler v. Taylor, 53 Pa. St. 467; McClurg's Appeal, 58 Pa. St. 51; Koehler v. Fearbacher, 2 Mo. App. 11; Boutelle v. Smith, 116 Mass. 111; Lightner v. Menzel, 35 Cal. 468; Hubbard v. Miller, 27 Mich. 15; Thomas v. Mills, 3 Ohio St. 274; Lange v. Werk, 2 Ohio St. 519; Guerand v. Dandelet, 32 Md. 561; Jenkins v. Temples, 39 Ga. 655; Hoagland v. Segur, 38 N. J. L. 230; Curtis v. Gokey, 68 N. Y. 300; Chappell v. Brockway, 21 Wend. 157; Lawrence v. Kidder, 10 Barb. 641; Bowser v. Bliss, 7 Blackf. 344; Talcott v. Brackett, 5 Bradw. 60; Linn v. Sigsbee, 67 Ill. 75; Stearns v. Barrett, 1 Pick. 443; Turner v. Johnson, 7 Dana, 435.

from the practice of his profession or trade without any limit of time or space, or without a valuable consideration, are void. But all agreements in particular or partial restraint of trade, that is, all agreements which are subject to proper limitations of time and space, if not unreasonable or prejudicial to the public welfare, will be upheld. In a leading case before the Supreme Court of Judicature of the State of New York, the rule is stated by Mr. Justice Bronson, as follows: "The common law will not permit individuals to oblige themselves by a contract where the thing to be done or omitted is injurious to the public. Contracts in restraint of trade are for the most part contrary to sound policy, and are, consequently, held void. This is the general rule. There may be cases where the contract is neither injurious to the public nor to the obligor, and there the law makes an exception, and declares the agreement valid. The general presumption is against all contracts in restraint of trade, and, consequently, it is upon him who seeks to enforce such an obligation to show that it is free from objection. Contracts which go to the total restraint of trade, as that a man will not pursue his occupation or carry on business anywhere in the State, are void upon whatever consideration they may be made. They must be injurious to the public, and no good reason can be shown why one individual should thus better himself or another individual should contract for the restraint. The obligation is injurious to one party without being beneficial to the other. But there may be good reasons for allowing parties to contract for a limited restraint, as that a man will not exercise his trade or carry on business in a particular place, and where such reasons are shown, the contract will be upheld and enforced. The common law on this subject undoubtedly had its origin at a time when there were comparatively very few mechanics and tradesmen, and when there was much more reason for guarding against restraints of this kind than there can be at present. Still, I am unable to say that the reason of the rule has so entirely ceased that the rule itself is at an end. It must be admitted, however, that courts at the present day look upon contracts of this description with much less jealousy than they did at a former period. At one time the contract, however free from objection in other respects, would have been held void if made in the form of a penal obligation. But there is no longer any doubt that the party may bind himself to the performance of such a contract under a penalty, as well as by the covenant or promise. The modern decisions have also allowed a larger restraint than would formerly have been sanctioned, and one or two of the recent cases have gone nearly, if not quite, far enough to give up the principle upon which the courts originally acted, though without professing to do so."[1]

[1] Chappell v. Brockway, 21 Wend. 157, 158. "But it is said that a restraint from Rochester to Buffalo, a distance of about 100 miles, is too large—that it is not confined to a particular place. The objection seems to take it for granted that a valid restraint cannot extend beyond a particular town or city. That is not the rule. A man cannot, for money alone, where he has no other interest in the matter, purchase a valid contract in restraint of trade, however limited may be the circle of its operation. But when a good reason appears for allowing the parties to contract, the restraint may extend far enough to afford a fair protection to the obligee. How far this will be, must depend in a great degree upon the nature of the trade or business to which the contract relates. In Davis v. Mason, 5 Durn. & East, 118, the defendant agreed not to exercise the business of a surgeon, apothecary and man midwife within ten miles of Thetford, and judgment was given for the plaintiff on a breach of the agreement, Lord Kenyon said, he did not see that the limits were necessarily unreasonable. He added what is equally applicable in the case at bar; 'neither are the public likely to be injured by an agreement of this kind, since every other person is at liberty to practice as a surgeon in this town.' In Noble v. Bates, 7 Cow. 307, the restraint extended over a circle of forty miles diameter, and was held good; and in Haywood v. Young, 2 Chitty's R. 407, a restraint of the like extent was upheld. In Pierce v. Fuller, 8 Mass. 223, an agreement not to run a stage between Boston and Providence, and in Perkins v. Lyman, 9 Mass. 522, a contract not to trade from Boston to the northwest coast of America for the period of seven years, were severally held unobjectionable. In Bunn v. Guy, 4 East, 190, a practicing attorney agreed to relinquish his business and recommend his clients to two other attorneys, and that he would not practice within a circle of 300 miles diameter, having London for its center. This, though it certainly was a very large restraint, including a good deal of sea as well as land, was, nevertheless, held valid. In Horner v. Graves, 7

In the case of the Oregon Steam Navigation Company v. Winsor, the rule is stated by Mr. Justice Bradley, as follows: "Cases must be judged according to their circumstances, and can only be rightly judged when the reasons and grounds of the rule are carefully considered. There are two prin-

Bing. 735, the defendant agreed not to practice as a surgeon dentist within 100 miles of the city of York, where the plaintiff carried on that business: and this was held an unreasonable restraint, because it was larger than was necessary to afford a fair protection to the plaintiff in the enjoyment of his trade. The last case to which I have referred gives the true rule on this subject, and is decisive of the question under consideration. The defendant sold out his business of running packet boats between Rochester and Buffalo; and that cannot be an unreasonable restraint, which is only co-extensive with the business which the defendant agreed to relinquish and the purchaser expected to acquire. *Ibid.* 162. "In the celebrated case of Mitchell v. Reynolds, 1 P. Wms. 181, Chief Justice Parker concludes his elaborate argument in these words: 'In all restraints of trade, *where nothing more appears*, the law presumes them bad, but if the circumstances are set forth, that presumption is excluded, and the court is to judge of those circumstances, and determine accordingly, and if upon them it appears to be a just and honest contract, it ought to be maintained.' In this I fully concur. The law starts with the presumption that the contract is void; and it is only by showing that there was an adequate consideration or good reason for entering into it, that the presumption can be destroyed. The rule is, not that a limited restraint is good, but that it may be good. It is valid when the restraint is reasonable: and the restraint is reasonable when it imposes no shackles upon one party which is not beneficial to the other. The facts which prove the restraint reasonable must in some way be made to appear; and as the presumption is against the party setting up the contract, it lies on him to remove the difficulty." Ross v. Sadgbeer, 21 Wend. 166. But see Diamond Match Co. v. Roeber, 106 N. Y. 473. "The latest decisions of courts in this country and in England show a strong tendency to very greatly circumscribe and narrow the doctrine of avoiding contracts in restraint of trade. The courts do not go to the length of saying that contracts which they now would say are in restraint of trade are, nevertheless, valid contracts and to be enforced; they do, however, now hold many contracts not open to the objection that they are in restraint of trade which a few years back would have been avoided on that sole ground both here and in England. The cases in this court which are the latest manifestations of the turn in the tide are cited in the opinion in this case at general term, and are Diamond Match Co. v. Roeber, 106 N. Y. 473; Hodge v. Sloan, 107 N. Y. 244; Leslie v. Lorillard, 107 N. Y. 519." Peckham, J., in Matthews v. Associated Press, 136 N. Y. 333, 340.

cipal grounds on which the doctrine is founded that a contract in restraint of trade is void as against public policy. One is the injury to the public by being deprived of the restricted party's industry; the other is the injury to the party himself by being precluded from pursuing his occupation, and thus being prevented from supporting himself and his family. It is evident that both these evils occur where the contract is general, not to pursue one's trade at all, or not to pursue it in the entire realm or country. The country suffers the loss in both cases, and the party is deprived of his occupation, or is obliged to expatriate himself in order to follow it. A contract that is open to such grave objections is clearly against public policy. But if neither of these evils ensue, and if the contract is founded on a valid consideration and a reasonable ground of benefit to the other party, it is free from objection and may be enforced."[1]

[1] Oregon Steam Nav. Co. v. Winsor, 20 Wall. 64, 68. See also Leather Cloth Co. v. Lorsont, L. R. 9 Eq. 349; Hubbard v. Miller, 27 Mich. 15; Long v. Towl, 42 Mo. 545; Gilman v. Dwight, 13 Gray, 356; Grasselli v. Lowden, 11 Ohio St. 349. "In the second place, it seems to me that this covenant, on which this suit rests, is illegal in itself, and absolutely void. The substance of this covenant is, that neither the former owner of these premises, nor his assigns, shall sell by the quantity any marl taken from these lands. This is not a restriction on the use of the land, for the marl can be dug up and used upon the land; but the restriction is on the sale of the marl after it shall have been dug up. Marl of course is an article of merchandise, and the covenant restrains traffic in that article. It prohibits the sale of it at any time, in any market, either by the owner of the lands or by his assigns. Now, it seems to me, that this is a plain contract 'against trade and traffic, and bargaining and contracting between man and man.' That it is the rule that all general restraints of trade are illegal has never been doubted since the famous opinion of Lord Macclesfield in Mitchel v. Reynolds, reported in 1 P. Wms. 181. And the development in this rule, and its application under a variety of conditions, can be traced in the series of decisions which have been carefully collected and intelligently commented on in the notes to the case just cited in 1 Smith's L. Cas. 182. The reason upon which this rule is founded is thus expressed by Mr. Justice Best in Homer v. Ashford, 3 Bing. 326: 'The law will not permit any one to restrain a person from doing what his own interest and the public welfare require that he should do. Any deed, therefore, by which a person binds himself not to employ his talent,

§ 38. **The Rule in England.**—The rule as upheld by the American courts is based upon the earlier English decisions as they have been modified by those of later times, in adapting the law to the changed industrial conditions of the country at the present day. Similar changes have been effected by the English courts, but they have gone somewhat farther in abrogating or modifying the early doctrine than the courts of this country. There is not entire unanimity in the decisions of the English courts, but they agree in upholding a more liberal rule than that of the courts of the United States. In a recent leading case before the Chancery Division of the Supreme Court of Judicature, which was subsequently sustained by the House of Lords,

his industry, or his capital, in any useful undertaking in the kingdom, would be void.' And so far has this principle been carried, that even in cases in which the restraint sought to be imposed is only partial, it has been repeatedly held that such agreement will be void, unless it be reasonable, and that no such agreement can be reasonable in which the restraint imposed on the one party is larger than is necessary for the protection of the other. Horner v. Graves, 7 Bing. 737. Tested by these principles the covenant in question appears to be destitute of all the essentials of a legal agreement. The restraint it imposes is general both as to time, place and persons. It transcends by far the limits of utility to the covenantee. I cannot say that this covenant is legal, any more than I can say that a covenant on the part of a farmer not to sell, nor permit any of the future owners of his farm to sell, any grain to be grown on his farm, would be legal. I think all such agreements are nugatory as opposed to the valuable rule of law just referred to, and which is designed, and is so well adapted, to promote commerce by preventing the imposition of all unnecessary trammels either on labor or on property." Beasley, C. J., in Brewer v. Marshall, 19 N. J. Eq. 537, 546. See also Alger v. Thatcher, 19 Pick. 51; Albright v. Teas, 37 N. J. Eq. 171; Lange v. Werk, 2 Ohio St. 520; Bank v. King, 44 N. Y. 87; Callahan v. Donnolly, 45 Cal. 152; Taylor v. Blanchard, 13 Allen, 370; More v. Bonnet, 40 Cal. 251; Wright v. Ryder, 36 Cal. 342; Stearns v. Barrett, 1 Pick. 443; Gill v. Ferris, 82 Mo. 156; Wiley v. Baumgardner, 97 Ind. 66: s. c., 49 Am. Rep. 427; Johnson v. Gwinn, 100 Ind. 466; Beal v. Chase, 31 Mich. 490; Dean v. Emerson, 102 Mass. 480; Smith's Appeal, 113 Pa. St. 579; Bowser v. Bliss, 7 Blackf. 344; Goodman v. Henderson, 58 Ga. 567; Cook v. Johnson, 47 Conn. 175; Timmerman v. Dever, 52 Mich. 34; s. c., 50 Am. Rep. 240; 23 Am. Law Reg. 50; Butler v. Burleson, 16 Vt. 176; Linn v. Sigsbee, 67 Ill. 75; Mell v. Mooney, 30 Ga. 413; Dwight v. Hamilton, 113 Mass. 175.

Lord Justice Bowen stated the rule, as follows: "Contracts in general restraint of trade may be defined as those by which a person restrains himself from all exercise of his trade in any part of England. A mere limit in time has never been held to convert a covenant in general restraint of trade into a covenant of particular or partial restraint of trade. It is necessary to insist on this distinction, which is imbedded in the reports and text books of the last three centuries, since it is through not preserving the exact meaning of the term 'in general restraint of trade,' that some confusion has, apparently, at times arisen. The common law is as precise as it can be on the point. Contracts unlimited in area, although they may be limited in time, are, as a rule, held bad on the ground of public policy."[1]

§ 39. Partial Distinguished from General Restraint. —The distinction between general and partial restraint of

[1] Maxim-Nordenfeldt v. Nordenfeldt, L. R. (1893) 1 Ch. 651. In the House of Lords on appeal in Nordenfeldt v. Maxim-Nordenfeldt Co., L. R. (1894) App. Cas. 535, 575, Lord Morris said: "My Lords, I entirely concur in the judgment and the reasons for it given by the Lord Chancellor. But I desire to express my opinion that without going through the numerous cases which have been so exhaustively dealt with in the court of appeal and by your Lordships, the weight of authority up to the present time is with the proposition that general restraints of trade were necessarily void. It appears, however, to me that the time for a new departure has arisen, and that it should be now authoritatively decided that there should be no difference in the legal considerations which would invalidate an agreement whether in general or partial restraint of trading. These considerations, I consider, are whether the restraint is reasonable and is not against the public interest. In olden times all restraints of trading were considered *prima facie* void. An exception was introduced when the agreement only to restrain from trading in a particular place and upon reasonable consideration, leaving still invalid agreements to restrain trading at all. Such a general restraint was in the then state of things considered to be of no benefit even to the covenantee himself; but we have now reached a period when it may be said that science and invention have almost annihilated both time and space. Consequently, there should no longer exist any cast iron rule making void any agreement not to carry on a trade anywhere. The generality of time and space must always be a most important factor in the consideration of reasonableness though not *per se* a decisive test. If the consideration of reasonableness or of public interest is the rule, the appellant, in my opinion, has no case."

trade is recognized by the English courts. The following statement of the rule in relation to this point, as sustained in England, is from the opinion of Lord Justice Bowen, as cited in the preceding section, viz.: "Distinguished from these general restraints, which the English law discountenances, are partial or limited restraints, or, as they are sometimes termed, particular restraints, which, upon certain conditions, the English law permits and enforces. An agreement in 'particular' or 'partial' restraint of trade may be defined as one in which the area of restriction is not absolute, but in which the covenantor retains for himself the right still to carry on his trade, either in some place, or for the benefit of some persons, or in some limited or prescribed manner. Particular restraints, according to the language employed in Mitchell v. Reynolds,[1] are those in which there is some limitation in respect of places or persons short of an absolute and total restriction. But there is also a third kind of limitation which the law will sanction under reasonable conditions, namely, a limitation in respect of the mode or manner in which a trade is to be carried on. The above are the three kinds of partial restraint recognized by the law. The English rule, which strikes indifferently at all general restraints in trade, makes the validity of a partial restraint depend on the circumstances of each case. A partial restraint will be binding in law if made on good consideration and if it is reasonable.[2] * * *

[1] Mitchell v. Reynolds, 1 P. Wms. 181.

[2] Collins v. Locke, L. R. 4 App. Cas. 674, 686. "In the history of the application to partial restraints of this test, the courts of common law from time to time have been driven by good sense and by altered social circumstances to make gradual advances in the direction of toleration and indulgence. Judges as far back possibly as the reign of Henry V., and certainly during the reign of Queen Elizabeth, appear, as has been already stated, to have considered that even partial restraints of trade were uniformly bad in law. But as trade progressed it was necessarily discovered that a doctrine so rigid must be injurious to the State itself. In the same way and at about the same date by-laws which were in mere regulation of trade came to be distinguished by the courts from those which were in unlimited restraint of it. Nevertheless, as late as the year 1601, in Colgate v. Bacheler (Cro. Eliz. 872), the court held that it was against law to

Cases where the contract still leaves to the covenantor a right to trade with particular persons fall, as has been pointed out, under the same head as those where the restraint is partial in respect of space. In both instances

prohibit or restrain 'any to use a lawful trade at any time or at any place.' This severe view is recorded in a *dictum* of Justice Croke (1613) in Rogers v. Parry (B. R. trin.; s. c., 11 Jac. 1 Rot. 223; 2 Bulst. 136), though it was repudiated by Justice Coke and the remainder of the court. One reason for the adoption of a more elastic doctrine appears from a judgment delivered in Broad v. Jollyffe (1620) (Cro. Jac. 596). In London and other large towns it had become usual already for traders to let their shops and wares to their servants when they were out of their apprenticeship; and for the servants to covenant that they would not use that trade in such a shop or in such a street. The courts yielding to the progress of industry and commerce, finally decided that a man might restrain himself voluntarily, and upon valuable consideration from using his trade in a particular place. The *onus*, however, at this time, still lay on the covenantee to show that the covenant on which he was insisting had been made for good consideration and that it was reasonable. The law is so expounded in Mitchel v. Reynolds (1711) (1 P. Wms. 181). "A particular restraint is not good without just reason and consideration." In 1726, Chesman v. Nainby (2 Ld. Raym. 1456; s. c., 1 Bro. P. C. 234), the House of Lords affirmed the doctrine and the qualification, and their decision was followed in Clerke v. Comer (1734) (Cas. *t.* Hardw. 53); Davis v. Mason (1793) (5 T. R. 118), and Bunn v. Guy (1803) (4 East, 190). The reason for favoring such partial restraints is enforced also in Homer v. Ashford (1825) (3 Bing. 322, 326). 'It may often happen' says Chief Justice Best, 'that individual interest and general convenience, render engagements not to carry on trade or act in a profession in a particular place, proper.' Down to as recent a period as Young v. Timmins (1831) (1 Tyrw. 226), it was still, however, considered to be for the person propounding a contract in partial restraint of trade to satisfy the court of the adequacy of the consideration. It was only in 1837, in Hitchcock v. Coker (6 A. & E. 438), that a fresh step forward was taken in reference to partial restraints of trade. The exchequer chamber there for the first time decided that in cases of partial restraint, the examination of the adequacy of the consideration was not properly for the court, but for the parties, although the burden remained as before upon the covenantee to show that there was some good and valuable consideration. The cases of Wallis v. Day (1837) (2 M. & W. 273), Leighton v. Wales (1838) (3 M. & W. 645), and Archer v. Marsh (1837) (6 A. & E. 959), were determined on the amended principle. By this date the idea was fully recognized, that all partial restraints of trade which satisfied the conditions of the law as to reasonableness and good consideration were not an injury, but a benefit to the public.

alike, the restriction upon the trade is not general but limited in area, and such contracts, if reasonable and for good consideration, will be supported by the law. The trader, it is true, is prohibited in such cases from serving a portion of the public, but trade in another quarter is still left open to him, 'Where one party,' says Lord Lyndhurst, in Young v. Timmins,[1] 'agrees to employ another in the way of his trade, and the other undertakes to work exclusively for him, that is a particular restraint of trade which may be supported by proof of adequate consideration.' The covenant in Wallis v. Day,[2] was of this description, and was pronounced good by the court, although its validity was not in fact a necessary condition to the plaintiff's success in that description of action. 'It cannot be said,' according to Lord Abinger,[3] 'to be a contract in absolute restraint of trade, when he' (the contractor) 'contracts to serve another for his life in the same trade.' Instances where one trader covenants not to supply the customers of another, such as in Rannie v. Irvine,[4] fall within this category. 'It is to be observed,' says Chief Justice Tindal,[5] 'that this is not a general restraint of trade, but only restricts the defendant from trading with a very limited number of persons.' So also Pilkington v. Scott.[6] Lastly, a covenant ceases to be referable to the class of general restraints of trade when it

Ward v. Byrne (1839) (5 M. & W. 548, 559); Proctor v. Sargent (1840) (2 Scott, N. R. 289); Rannie v. Irvine (1844) (7 Man. & G. 969), per Maule, J.; Mallan v. May (1843) (11 M. & W. 653). A further progress in the views with which the law regarded partial restraints was made in Tallis v. Tallis (1853) (1 E. & B. 391). It was then at last resolved that the *onus* lay upon the person who attached a covenant in partial restraint of trade to displace the consideration—a change in the position of the parties which is illustrated by the language of Chief Justice Erle, in Mumford v. Gething (1859), 7 C. B. (N. S.) 305, 319). 'Contracts in partial restraint of trade are beneficial to the public as well as to the immediate parties.' See also Harms v. Parsons, 32 L. J. Ch. 247." Bowen, J., in Maxim-Nordenfelt Co. v. Nordenfelt, L. R. (1893) 1 Ch. at page 654.

[1] Young v. Timmins, 1 Tyrw. 226, 236.

[2] Wallis v. Day, 2 M. & W. 273.

[3] *Ibid.*, 976.

[4] Rannie v. Irvine, 7 Man. & G. 969.

[5] *Ibid.*, 976.

[6] Pilkington v. Scott, 15 M. & W. 657.

only regulates or confines the manner in which the trade is to be worked. Such contracts are contracts in partial restraint of trade only, and are recognized accordingly as valid if reasonable and for good consideration.[1] Jones v. Lees,[2] is an illustration of this branch of partial restraints. The plaintiff, who was the owner of a patent, had sold to the defendant a license to use a patented invention, the defendant covenanting in turn that he would not make any machines in future without applying the invention to what he so made. If the defendant covenanted, on the one hand, not to sell the machine without the patented invention, he obtained the privilege, on the other hand, of selling the same machine with that improvement to all England. This, as pointed out in Wms. Saunders,[3] is a restraint which affects the mode of exercising the trade, and which, therefore, is partial. The only real question that remained on such a view of that particular bargain, was whether it was a reasonable one, as to which point the remark that the privilege was commensurate with the restraint appears conclusive. The case is similar to those in which rules regulating trade have been distinguished from rules made in restraint of it.[4] The inquiry as to the reasonableness of the restraint in any particular instance is, however, one that appertains only to the case of partial restraints. It is no objection necessarily to such partial restraints that they are sometimes to continue during the life of the covenantor, who may possibly survive the covenantee, for such an arrangement enables the good will of the business to become the object of purchase and sale.[5] * * * The result seems to me to be as follows: General restraints, or, in other words, restraints wholly unlimited in area, are not, as a rule, permitted by the law, although the rule admits

[1] Collins v. Locke, L. R. 4 App. Cas. 674.

[2] Jones v. Lees, 1 H. & N. 189.

[3] 2 Wms. Saunders, 156a, *n.*

[4] Freemantle v. Silk Throwsters Company, 1 Lev. 229; Wannel v. Chamberlain of London, 1 Str. 675; Bosworth v. Hearne, Andr. 91; Harrison v. Godman, 1 Burr. 12; Rex v. Harrison, 3 Burr. 1323, 1328.

[5] Atkyns v. Kinnier, 4 Ex. 776, 782; Pemberton v. Vaughan, L. R. 10 Q. B. 87, 89.

of exceptions. Partial restraints, or, in other words, restraints which involve only a limit of places at which, of persons with whom, or of modes in which the trade is to be carried on, are valid when made for a good consideration, and where they do not extend further than is necessary for the reasonable protection of the covenantee. A limit in time does not, by itself, convert a general restraint into a partial one. 'That which the law does not allow is not to be tolerated because it is to last for a short time only.' In considering, however, the reasonableness of a partial restraint, the time for which it is to be imposed may be a material element to consider."[1]

§ **40. Questions of Consideration.**—It is well established that a contract in restraint of trade is valid only as it is based on a valuable consideration. Moreover, the consideration must not be a mere form intended simply to answer the demands of the law. Where there is no consideration, or it appears that the consideration named is of no real value, the contract will be treated either as a fraud upon the rights of the party restrained or as a mere voluntary agreement, *nudum pactum*, and, in consequence, invalid. But where it is in evidence that the contract was a *bona fide* transaction the court will not inquire into the adequacy of the consideration. The question whether the party restrained made an injudicious bargain will not be considered.[2] But while the court will not consider the ques-

[1] Maxim-Nordenfelt Co. v. Nordenfelt, L. R. (1893) 1 Ch. 630, 654. 656, 662.

[2] Hitchcock v. Coker. 6 Ad. & El. 438; Mitchel v. Reynolds, 1 P. Wms. 181; Davis v. Mason, 5 T. R. 118; Hutton v. Parker. 7 Dowl. P. C. 739; Gale v. Reed, 8 East, 80; Archer v. Marsh. 6 Ad. & E. 959; s. c., 2 Nev. & P. 562; Pilkington v. Scott, 15 M. & W. 657; s. c.. 15 L. J. Excheq. 329; Sainter v. Ferguson, 7 Com. B. 716; s. c.. 13 Jur. 828; 18 L. J. Com. P. 217; Gravelly v. Barnard. L. R. 18 Eq. 518; s. c.. 47 L. J. Ch. 659: 30 L. T. 863; Collins v. Locke. L. R. 4 App. Cas. 674: s. c.. 48 L. J. P. C. 68: 41 L. T. 292; 28 W. R. 189; Linn v. Sigsbee, 67 Ill. 75; Hubbard v. Miller, 27 Mich. 15, 21; s. c., 15 Am. Rep. 153; Lawrence v. Kidder, 10 Barb. 641; McClurg's Appeal, 58 Pa. St. 51; Perkins v. Lyman, 9 Mass. 522; Palmer v. Stebbins, 3 Pick. 188; Whitney v. Slayton, 40 Me. 231; Green v. Price, 13 M. & W. 695; Pierce v. Woodward, 6 Pick. 206:

tion of the adequacy of the consideration, a *bona fide* consideration must be shown. It must appear on the face of the contract. This has been held to be an exception, and the only exception to the rule that a seal imports a con-

Hartley v. Cummins, 5 C. B. 247. "The circumstances of the present, the nature of the business, the situation, objects and interests of the parties, are precisely of the character which brings the case within these principles as recognized by all the authorities for the last one hundred and fifty years at least. The fact that complainant paid no more than the cost of the articles at Grand Haven can make no difference. Where a consideration, recognized by law as being valuable, is paid, the law very properly allows the parties to judge for themselves of the sufficiency in value of such consideration for their contracts. We cannot, therefore, enter into the question whether the consideration was commensurate in value with the restraint imposed." Hubbard v. Miller, 27 Mich. 15; s. c., 15 Am. Rep. 153, 158. "Such contract must be, like contracts generally, upon a consideration; but that the parties may agree upon what it shall be, so that it is legal; and that the mere purchase of the stock in trade of a party, is a sufficient consideration for that party's agreement to abstain from carrying on the particular trade in the place where the purchaser is to engage in it." Beard v. Dennis, 6 Ind. 200; s. c., 63 Am. Dec. 380, 383. "The consideration of one dollar is, in law, a valuable consideration. It would be sufficient to pass by sale the defendant's stage and stage horses, where no fraud or imposition was practiced. The parties have considered it as reasonable and adequate, and the defendant, by honestly fulfilling his agreement, might have protected himself from the forfeiture. But he has broken it, and he shall not be admitted to say, that although the contract was fairly and honestly made, and for a valuable consideration, to which he consented, the consideration was inadequate; that he made a bad bargain, and that, when the plaintiff has suffered by the breach of it, he shall be relieved from the terms to which he had voluntarily submitted. There is an old case determined when contracts in restraint of trade were confined to narrow limits, in which the apparent consideration was as inadequate as that in the present case is supposed to be. It is the case of Bragg v. Turner, cited in Broad v. Jollyffe, in Cro. Jac. 597. There the defendant, in consideration of ten shillings, promised the plaintiff to pay him a hundred pounds if thenceforward he kept any draper's shop in Newgate Market, and the contract was adjudged good, and the plaintiff had judgment." Pierce v. Fuller, 8 Mass. 223; s. c., 5 Am. Dec. 102, 104. "It was, at an early day, supposed that the consideration in such cases must be adequate—that is, equal in value to the restraint imposed; but this idea has been exploded ever since the decision in Hitchcock v. Coker, 6 Adol. & E. 438, which has been repeatedly approved and followed, and in which Chief Justice Tindal said:

sideration.[1] Contracts restraining the exercise of a trade or branch of business, in a designated locality, where there is a valid consideration, will be sustained. The restraint, however, must not go beyond a reasonable limit.[2]

§ 41. **Limitations of Time.**—Where the conditions of a contract in restraint of trade are such as not to be in contravention of public policy the duration of the restraint is immaterial. A contract binding a person not to follow a trade, to pursue a branch of business or to practice a profession within definitely prescribed limits will not be held void on the ground that the duration of the restraint is not limited. But where the restraint is general, and, on that ground, invalid, as against public policy, it will not be rendered valid by any limitations of time. What is, in itself, bad, will not be legalized by limiting its duration. The ground of this rule is stated by Sir James Parke, in Ward v. Byrne, as follows: "Now, where a limit as to space is imposed, the public, on the one hand, do not lose altogether the services of the party in the particular trade, he will carry it on in the same way elsewhere; nor within the limited space will they be deprived of the benefit of the

'If, by adequacy of consideration, more is intended, and that the court must weigh whether the consideration is equal in value to that which the party gives up or loses by the restraint under which he places himself, we feel ourselves bound to differ from that doctrine. A duty would thereby be imposed upon the court in every particular case, which it has no means whatever to execute. It is impossible for the court to say whether, in any particular case, the party restrained has made an improvident bargain or not.'" McCurry v. Gibson (1895), 108 Ala. 451; s. c., 18 So. Rep. 806, 808.

[1] Gompers v. Rochester, 56 Pa. St. 194; Hutton v. Parker, Dowl. P. C. 739.

[2] Guerand v. Dandelet, 32 Md. 562. A cattle broker, having received cattle at certain stock yards, and then charged fees by the proprietors, made out an account of the fees and demanded them back, on the ground that the proprietors had furnished him nothing, and the landing place was the railroad's. The same day he bought of them cattle, and offered his account in part payment. A settlement was made by which said offer was accepted, the broker agreeing, and giving his bond, to do his business for a year through said yards. *Held*, that the restraint of trade was not unreasonable nor without consideration. Fuller v. Hope, 163 Pa. St. 62, 29 Atl. Rep. 779.

trade being carried on, because the party with whom the contract is made will most probably within those limits exercise it himself. But where a general restriction, limited only as to time, is imposed, the public are altogether losers for that time of the services of the individual, and do not derive any benefit whatever in return; and looking at the authorities cited upon this subject it does not appear that there is one clear authority in favor of a total restriction on trade limited only as to time."[1] The following ex-

[1] Ward v. Byrne, 5 M. & W. 548, 561. See also French v. Parker, 16 R. I. 219; Warfield v. Booth, 33 Md. 63; Mell v. Mooney, 30 Ga. 414; Goodman v. Henderson, 58 Ga. 567; Martin v. Murphy, 129 Ind. 464; s. c., 28 N. E. Rep. 1118; Hastings v. Whitely, 2 Exchеq. 611; Jacoby v. Whitmore, 49 L. T. 335; s. c., 32 W. R. 18; Pemberton v. Vaughan, 10 Q. B. 87; Catt v. Towle, L. R. 4 Ch. App. 654; s. c., 38 L. J. Ch. 665; 21 L. T. 188; Bunn v. Guy, 4 East, 190; Davis v. Mason, 5 T. R. 118; Mallon v. May, 11 M. & W. 652; Butler v. Burleson, 16 Vt. 176. A contract not to engage in a certain business in a certain town while another carries on the same business there, is not invalid as indefinite as to its duration. Eisel v. Hays, 141 Ind. 41; s. c., 40 N. E. Rep. 119. "The circumstance that the restraint is indefinite in point of time, does not invalidate the contract. This objection,—the want of limit as to time,—has been recently very fully discussed in the English courts. In the King's Bench the objection was sustained, but the decision was reversed in the exchequer chamber. In the last named court Tindal, C. J., said that in many of the cases cited, the restriction had been held good, though it continued for the life of the party restrained. On the other hand, no case had been referred to where the contrary doctrine had been laid down. He cited the cases of Bunn v. Guy, 4 East, 190; Chesman v. Nainby, 2 Str. 739, and Wickens v. Evans, 3 Younge & Jervis, 318, to support the position that the agreement was not void merely on the ground that the restriction was indefinite as to duration, the same in other respects being a reasonable restriction." Bowser v. Bliss, 7 Blackf. 344, 346. "I am equally well satisfied that the insistment that the restraint is indefinite as to time, and therefore unreasonable, ought not to prevail. I think a careful study of the case of Mitchel v. Reynolds, reported in 1 Smith, Lead. Cas. (9th Ed.) 694, *et seq.*, with the various annotations, both by the English and American editors, will satisfy the mind as to the principle upon which contracts of this nature not only may well be, but really ought to be, supported, when indefinite as to time. The purchaser of such good will may fairly be supposed to purchase, not only for his own immediate use or benefit, but for the use of his personal representatives, in the same sense that he purchases personal property or real estate. I can see no just reason for his not being able, in the law, to make such an investment which

position of the doctrine is by Lord Justice Smith, in the Maxim-Nordenfelt Case: "Now arise these questions: First, are the limits of time and space in the covenant sued on reasonable for the covenantee? Secondly, is the covenant so large as to interfere with the interests of the public? It is argued that as the defendant was forty-six years of age when he entered into the covenant, a twenty-five years' restriction would probably continue during his lifetime; and it was suggested that it was no limit at all, was wholly un-

shall pass to his assigns, executors or administrators. It cannot be said, when it is limited to a particular district, that this in any manner interferes with sound public policy. It would not be a violation of the rule which required such contracts to be in harmony with the interests of the community at large, in case the stipulations were to be that the covenantee should not carry on the trade in question for twenty or thirty years: and if not for that period of time, then certainly it would not be if the covenant extended to a lifetime. With this in mind when the object of the prohibition put upon such contracts, in view of a sound public policy. is considered, it will be still more apparent that this contract ought to be upheld. Sound public policy requires that every individual shall be employed. The community is entitled to his honest toil, whether manual, mechanical or purely intellectual. This being so, and such policy upholding contracts for a definite period of time, it is not to be presumed that the covenantee, in any such case, will spend the time, which the law regards (supposing that there must be a period limited in the contract), in idleness or in indifference to the demands of such public policy, waiting the time when the period fixed by the contract shall have expired, in order that he may engage once more in the employment which he had agreed to abandon. In such matters the public welfare which the law regards is an essential element of consideration; but the interest of the individual in his own welfare is infinitely more efficacious and potential in securing the public good, although that may not be in his mind. He who has energy and integrity enough to establish a business which is worthy of the name, and for which others will bid a fair price, will not wait for the protection of the paternal hand to make his footprints in other quarters. In the following cases there was no limit as to time, and it will be observed that in many of them resistance was made to their enforcement on this account, but without success: Richardson v. Peacock, 26 N. J. Eq. 40; s. c., 28 N. J. Eq. 151: 33 N. J. Eq. 597; Hitchcock v. Coker, 6 Ad. & El. 439; Hastings v. Whiteley, 2 Excheq. 611; Mallan v. May, 11 M. & W. 653; Bowser v. Bliss, 7 Blackf. 344: Pierce v. Fuller, 8 Mass. 223; Palmer v. Stebbins, 3 Pick. 188: Diamond Match Co. v. Roeber, 106 N. Y. 473; s. c., 13 N. E. Rep. 419, 423." Bird, V. C., in Carll v. Snyder (N. J. Eq.). 26 Atl. Rep. 977, 978.

reasonable and merely delusive. I do not agree with these suggestions. It will be remembered that if the plaintiffs and their successors cease to trade the restraint comes to an end. The £287,500 which the plaintiffs or their predecessors paid to the defendant for the business must obviously take many years before it can be recouped by trading; and why am I to hold that twenty-five years is more than a fair protection to the plaintiff? No facts have been given in evidence from which I can draw such an inference. Indeed, what facts have been proved tend in the contrary direction. In considering this it does not seem to me that the age of the covenantor is the matter to be considered, but what is the fair protection of the covenantee; and I may say that my own opinion is that if the limit here had been the covenantor's life, in the special circumstances of the case, it would not have been unreasonable."[1]

§ 42. **The Subject Continued.**—While it is well settled, as above shown, that where a contract in restraint of trade is properly limited in regard to space, indefiniteness of time is not material, it does not follow that a contract in general restraint of trade is rendered valid by a limitation in time. In the leading case of Wiley v. Baumgardner, the rule on this point is stated by Mr. Justice Black, as follows: "A contract in restraint of trade is void, if the restraint be unreasonable, and the question as to the reasonableness of the restriction is one of law, to be determined by the court, and the contract is supported or avoided on grounds of public policy. 'Whatever restraint is larger than the necessary protection of the party with whom the contract is made is unreasonable and void, as being injurious to the interests of the public, on the ground of public policy.' In the contracts now before us the transaction was not expressed as a sale of the good will of the business, or as a sale of the business. But it would have made no difference if there had been an express sale of the good will. Where a person carrying on any business sells his stock in trade,

[1] Maxim-Nordenfelt v. Nordenfelt, L. R. (1893) 1 Ch. 630, 673, per A. L. Smith, L. J.

or his business and his good will, and in the transaction agrees not to carry on the same business with a limitation as to the time, but none as to space, the agreement as to such restraint is wholly void. This must be so if the test be that the contract is to be supported or avoided on the ground of public policy. If it be prejudicial to the public interests for a citizen to be debarred from pursuing anywhere the calling in which he has acquired skill or proficiency, or to encourage the establishment of monopolies by preventing competition, it must be for definite as well as indefinite periods of time. A contract that would put it in the power of one party to prevent the other from carrying on his calling anywhere whatever is unreasonable."[1] In an English case the rule is stated, as follows:

[1] Wiley v. Baumgardner. 97 Ind. 66: s. c., 49 Am. Rep. 427, 429. As this is the leading case on this point in this country, the following statement of the case, taken from the opinion, may be of interest: "The action was upon a contract in writing by which the appellant sold to the appellees the former's entire stock of dry goods, boots and shoes, merchandise and fixtures in his store in Bluffton at cost, less a certain per cent., and agreed to transfer to them his lease on the building occupied by him for his storeroom, and his unexpired insurance on said stock, and agreed 'not to engage in the dry goods business for a term of five years from' the date of the agreement, being the 29th day of December, 1881, the appellees agreeing on their part, by way of payment, to transfer to the appellant a certain farm, which was to represent $6,000, to execute to him their promissory note for $1,000, and for the balance to execute their promissory notes, secured by mortgage on certain lands of one of the appellees. And it was agreed by all the parties, that 'for the faithful performance of the above contract, we hereby bind ourselves to each other in the sum of $1,000 liquidated damages.' It was alleged that the appellees intending to engage in the dry goods business in said town, the contract was entered into by them and the appellant for such purpose; that immediately after the purchase the appellees engaged in said business in said town, and that they were still continuing the same. The breach alleged was that in September, 1882, the appellant purchased a large stock of dry goods of the value of $10,000, and with them opened a dry goods store in said town within a few doors of the place of business of the appellees, and engaged in the dry goods business in said town and still continued the same; that during the time he had been thus engaged in business he had sold a large amount of dry goods in said town, the amount of $10,000, thereby taking away from the appellees

"A limit in time does not by itself convert a general restraint into a partial one. 'That which the law does not allow is not to be tolerated because it is to last for a short time only.' In considering, however, the reasonableness of a partial restraint, the time for which it is to imposed may be a material element to consider."[1]

§ 43. **Touching Territorial Limitations.**—It is the rule that a contract in restraint of trade is valid only as it is limited as to space. If it is without limit it must be shown, in order to render it valid, that the peculiar circumstances render it a fit and reasonable agreement. Where this question is raised it will be settled by the court, not according to any hard and fast rule, but by an investigation of all the circumstances of the case, and by what, in view of the circumstances, appears to be reasonable and just. In a case before the Supreme Court of California, it was held that a contract in restraint of trade to be upheld must be restricted as to territory, and it must appear to the court in considering the nature of the business in connection with the territorial limits assigned that the limits designated are not unreasonable in extent.[2] In the opinion in this case the

said trade, to their damage, $1,500, for which they demanded judgment." See also Ward v. Byrne, 5 M. & W. 548; s. c., 3 Jur. 1175; Lawrence v. Kidder, 10 Barb. 647. However, in Proctor v. Sargent, 2 Man. & G. 20; s. c., 2 Scott, N. R. 289, Tindal, C. J., uses this language: "I think that when we are deciding upon the unreasonableness of a contract of this kind, we cannot leave out of consideration the duration of the restraint; for although I admit that where we once hold a restriction to be unreasonable in point of space, the shortness of time for which it is imposed will not make it good, yet where the question is whether the restraint is unreasonable or not in point of space, that which would be unreasonable, were it to continue for any length of time, may not be so when it is to last only for a day or two."

[1] Maxim-Nordenfelt Co. v. Nordenfelt, L. R. (1893) 1 Ch. 630, 662.

[2] Callahan v. Donnolly, 45 Cal. 152. See also generally the following cases involving questions of space where contracts were upheld: Butler v. Burleson, 16 Vt. 176; Miller v. Elliott, 1 Ind. 484; McClurg's Appeal, 58 Pa. St. 51; Mott v. Mott, 11 Barb. 127; Dwight v. Hamilton, 113 Mass. 175; Gravelly v. Barnard, L. R. 18 Eq. 518; s. c., 43 L. J. Ch. 649; 30 L. T. 863; Mercer v. Irving, El., B. & E. 563; Reynolds v. Bridge, 6 El. & B. 528; Sainter v. Ferguson, 7 Com. B. 716; s. c., 13 Jur. 828; 18 L. J.

court said: "A contract in restraint of trade and which is not by its terms limited as to the territory embraced in its operation is not to be supported. 'It is to be remembered, however (said Tindal, C. J., in Horner

Com. P. 217; Hastings v. Whiteley, 2 Excheq. 611; Davis v. Mason, 5 T. R. 118; Whittaker v. Howe, 3 Beav. 383; Dendy v. Henderson, 11 Excheq. 194; s. c., 24 L. J. Excheq. 324; May v. O'Neill, 44 L. J. Ch. 660; Galsworthy v. Strutt, 1 Excheq. 659; Smalley v. Green, 52 Iowa, 241; s. c., 35 Am. Rep. 267; Doty v. Martin, 32 Mich. 462; Linn v. Sigsbee, 67 Ill. 75; Holbrook v. Waters, 9 How. Pr. 335; Harms v. Parsons, 32 Beav. 328; s. c., 9 Jur. (N. S.) 145; 32 L. J. Ch. 247; 7 L. T. 815; 11 W. R. 250; Whitney v. Slayton, 40 Me. 224; Gill v. Ferris, 82 Mo. 156; Stewart v. Challacombe, 11 Ill. App. 379; Beard v. Dennis, 6 Ind. 200; s. c., 63 Am. Dec. 380; Hedge v. Lowe, 47 Iowa, 137; Ropes v. Upton, 125 Mass. 258; Johnson v. Gwinn, 100 Ind. 466; Baumgarten v. Broadaway, 77 N. Car. 8; Arnold v. Kreutzer, 67 Iowa, 214; s. c., 25 N. W. Rep. 139; Morgan v. Perhamus, 36 Ohio St. 517; s. c., 38 Am. Rep. 607; Harrison v. Lockhart, 25 Ind. 112; McAllister v. Howell, 42 Ind. 15; Studebaker v. White, 31 Ind. 211; Pierce v. Woodward, 6 Pick. 206; Jenkins v. Temples, 39 Ga. 655; Ellis v. Jones, 56 Ga. 504; Dunlop v. Gregory, 10 N. Y. 241; s. c., 61 Am. Dec. 746; Perkins v. Lyman, 9 Mass. 522. *Contra:* Horner v. Graves, 7 Bing. 735; s. c., 5 Moore & P. 768; Taylor v. Blanchard, 13 Allen, 370; s. c., 90 Am. Dec. 203; Lawrence v. Kidder, 10 Barb. 641; Alger v. Thacher, 19 Pick. 51; s. c., 31 Am. Dec. 119; Wiley v. Baumgardner, 97 Ind. 66; Wright v. Ryder, 36 Cal. 347. A covenant in restraint of trade which is unlimited in regard to space, except by the words "so far as the law allows," is not void either as being against public policy or as being too uncertain in its terms to be capable of being enforced. Such a covenant is to be construed as providing for a restraint to the full extent that the doctrine of law as interpreted by the courts will allow a person to contract himself out of the privilege of trading in a particular business, and will be enforced so as to secure to the covenantee the full benefit of that which he has purchased from the covenantor. Davies v. Davies, 56 L. J. Ch. 481; s. c., 35 W. R. 697. Defendant agreed to purchase $200,000 worth of goods from plaintiff, who agreed not to sell like articles in some thirty States and territories of the United States. In an action for goods sold and delivered, defendant set up this contract, and alleged breaches of it as a counterclaim. There was nothing to show the ordinary amount of manufacture and sale by either party, or that defendant had established a trade in more than one State out of the thirty. *Held*, that the pleading was demurrable in not affirmatively showing that the restraint was reasonably necessary to protect defendant's interest under the contract. Richards v. American Desk & Seating Co., 87 Wis. 503, 58 N. W. Rep. 787. Plaintiff and defendant were corporations engaged in selling "benefit certificates" entitling

v. Graves),[1] that contracts in restraint of trade are in themselves, if nothing more appears to show them reasonable, bad in the eye of the law.' A contract in restraint of trade must designate the space within which it is to operate and must not be unreasonably extended. Such contracts, when upheld, are only in cases where the parties have restricted the territory in which they are to operate, and where the court, in considering the nature of the business in connection with the territorial limits assigned, is of opinion that the designated limits are not unreasonable in extent."[2] In a case in Alabama the rule is stated, as follows: "It is true that such contracts must be limited as to the space they are intended to cover, or they cannot be supported. The meaning of a contract of this character is not to be found solely from a consideration of its expressed terms. Courts look to all the circumstances surrounding the parties and attendant upon the transaction, and from a consideration of these circumstances in connection with the expressions of the undertaking, they will first construe the contract and then proceed to pass upon its reasonableness as thus construed."[3] This rule, so far as it can be termed a rule, relating to territorial limitations, is stated by the Supreme Court of the United States, in the case of the Oregon Steam Navigation Company, as follows: "In accordance with these principles it is well settled that a stipulation by a vendee of any trade, business or establishment, that the vendor shall not exercise the same trade or busi-

the holders, in case of sickness or injury, to maintenance and treatment in hospitals provided by the company. The plaintiff had established a lucrative business in Wisconsin, Minnesota and the northern peninsula of Michigan, and had acquired valuable hospital contracts. The plaintiff agreed to refrain for three years from selling certificates in the territory named, except to railroad employes, and to turn over its hospital contracts, in consideration of which the defendant promised to make certain payments, and also to refrain for three years from selling certificates to railroad employes within said territory. *Held*, that the contract was not void as an unreasonable restraint of trade. Nat'l Ben. Co. v. Union Hospital Co., 45 Minn. 272; s. c., 47 N. W. Rep. 806.

[1] Horner v. Graves, 7 Bing. 744.

[2] Callahan v. Donnolly, 45 Cal. 152.

[3] Moore & Handley Co. v. Towers Hardware Co., 87 Ala. 206.

ness, or erect a similar establishment within a reasonable distance, so as not to interfere with the value of the trade, business or thing purchased, is reasonable and valid. In like manner a stipulation by the vendor of an article to be used in a business or trade in which he is himself engaged, that it shall not be used within a reasonable region or distance so as not to interfere with his said business or trade, is also valid and binding. The point of difficulty in these cases is to determine what is a reasonable distance within which the statutory prohibition may lawfully have effect, and it is obvious at first glance, that this must depend upon the circumstances of the particular case, although, from the uncertain character of the subject, much latitude must be allowed to the judgment and discretion of the parties. It is clear that a stipulation that another shall not pursue his trade or employment at such a distance from the business of the person to be protected, as that it could not possibly affect or injure him, would be absurd. On the other hand, a stipulation is unobjectionable and binding which imposes the restraint to only such extent of territory as may be necessary for the protection of the party making the stipulation, provided it does not violate the two indispensable conditions, that the other party be not prevented from pursuing his calling, and that the country be not deprived of the benefit of his exertions."[1]

§ **44. The Subject Continued.**—In some of the States the courts have manifested a disposition to relax, or to modify, in some degree, the rule in regard to territorial limitations as set forth in the foregoing section. In the leading case of the Diamond Match Company v. Roeber, the court said: "In the present state of the authorities we think it cannot be said that the early doctrine that contracts in general restraint of trade are void without regard to circumstances has been abrogated. But it is manifest that it has been much weakened and that the foundation upon which it was originally placed has, to a considerable

[1] Oregon Steam Navigation Co. v. Winsor, 20 Wall. 64, 68.

extent at least, by the change of circumstances, been removed."[1] It will be observed that it is here conceded that

[1] Diamond Match Co. v. Roeber, 106 N. Y. 473. 484. See also Hubbard v. Miller, 27 Mich. 15; Guerand v. Dandelet, 32 Md. 562; Beal v. Chase, 31 Mich. 490; Ewing v. Johnson, 34 How. Pr. 202; Pierce v. Woodward, 6 Pick. 206; Hedge v. Lowe, 47 Iowa, 137, 140; Chappel v. Brockway, 21 Wend. 157; Jenkins v. Temples, 39 Ga. 655; Smalley v. Greene, 52 Iowa, 241; Arnold v. Kreutzer, 67 Iowa, 214; Baumgarten v. Broadaway, 77 N. Car. 8; Tallis v. Tallis, 1 El. & Bl. 391; Dunlop v. Gregory, 10 N. Y. 241; Washburn v. Dosch, 68 Wis. 436; Keith v. Hirschberg Optical Co., 48 Ark. 138; Richardson v. Peacock, 33 N. J. Eq. 597; Brewer v. Marshall, 19 N. J. Eq. 537; Taylor v. Blanchard, 13 Allen, 370; Vernon v. Hallam, 56 L. J. Ch. 115; s. c., 35 W. R. 156; Nicoll v. Beere, 53 L. T. (N. S.) 659; Hare v. Whitmore, 49 L. T. (N. S.) 335; Jacoby v. Whitmore, 40 L. J. (N. S.) 335; Palmer v. Stebbins, 3 Pick. 188; s. c., 15 Am. Dec. 204; Grundy v. Edwards, 7 J. J. Marsh. 368; s. c., 23 Am. Dec. 409; McClurg's Appeal, 58 Pa. St. 51; Haldeman v. Simonton, 55 Iowa, 144; Amedon v. Gannon, 6 Hun, 384; Warfield v. Booth, 33 Md. 63; Hoyt v. Holly, 39 Conn. 326; s. c., 12 Am. Rep. 390; Smith v. Smith, 4 Wend. 468; Dwight v. Hamilton, 113 Mass. 175; Whitney v. Slayton, 40 Me. 224; McNutt v. McEwen, 1 W. N. C. 552; Stafford v. Shortreed, 62 Iowa, 524; s. c., 17 N. W. Rep. 756; Timmerman v. Dever, 52 Mich. 34; Thompson v. Means, 11 Sm. & M. 604; Mott v. Mott, 11 Barb. 127; Niver v. Rossman, 18 Barb. 50; Bigony v. Tyson, 75 Pa. St. 157; Betts' Appeal, 10 W. N. C. 431; Martin v. Murphy, 129 Ind. 464; Sainter v. Ferguson, 7 C. B. 716; Atkyns v. Kinnier, 4 Excheq. 776; Fox v. Scard, 33 Beav. 327; Mell v. Mooney, 30 Ga. 413; Miller v. Elliott, 1 Ind. 484; Holbrook v. Waters, 9 How. Pr. 335; Whitney v. Slayton, 40 Me. 224. An agreement "not to engage in the manufacture of any thermometers of any kind or description, nor of any storm glasses, at any place within the United States at any time within a period of ten years from date," is not a general restriction of trade, and is not void on the ground of public policy. Watertown Thermometer Co. v. Pool, 51 Hun, 157; s. c., 4 N. Y. Supl. 861. In this case, at page 163, the court says: "The cases cited seem to sustain the doctrine that a restriction which is no greater than the interest of the vendee requires, and by giving which the vendor has obtained an increased price for what he sold, is valid, though it extended through the whole kingdom or country. In this case the defendants, by their demurrer, admit that the business of the plaintiff in the manufacture and sale of thermometers and storm glasses required for its full and proper development the entire territory embraced within the United States, and that one of the considerations that induced the plaintiff to make such purchase and pay the consideration named was such restriction, which would enable it to fully develop its business throughout the whole United States, without interference on the part of the defendant. Assuming this, as we

what is termed "the early doctrine" has not been abrogated, and that under that rule "contracts in general restraint of trade are void, without regard to circumstances." But the holding of the court is that, notwithstanding that rule

must, and it seems quite clear that the restraint, though general, is at the same time co-extensive only with the interest to be protected, and with the benefit meant to be conferred by this agreement; and it imposes no restriction upon the defendants which is not beneficial to the plaintiff, or which was unnecessary for its reasonable protection: and that it was induced by a consideration which made it reasonable for the parties to enter into it." A provision in a contract for the sale, upon a full and adequate consideration, of a printing and publishing establishment and business and good will together with a newspaper and the copyrights of certain books, that the vendor should not engage in the business in the State so long as the vendee should continue in the business at the place of sale, is held not an unreasonable restraint of trade where the business so sold extended over substantially the whole territory of the State, and is sustained against objections that it was void as being against public policy. Beal v. Chase, 31 Mich. 490. "Contracts by professional men, such as physicians, surgeons, dentists and lawyers when coming within the rule stated, not to practice their professions in competition with another pursuing the same calling, have time and again been enforced; and no distinction is made between their contracts and those of tradesmen. The suggestion, that while valid in a court of law, the agreement of a person not to pursue a profession involving the exercise of skill and learning will not be specifically performed in equity, is not tenable. The doubt expressed in an early English case has long since been resolved in favor of the jurisdiction of the chancery court, and numerous instances are to be found of its exercise to restrain by injunction the breach of a valid contract not to practice law or medicine in competition with the complaining party." McCurry v. Gibson (1895), 108 Ala. 451; s. c., 18 So. Rep. 806, 807. "It is contended that the contract is against public policy and ought not to be enforced. The question as to the validity of a contract whereby one agrees for a consideration, to thereafter refrain from prosecuting a business in a certain locality, is no longer an open one in this State. Such contracts are valid. Hedge v. Lowe, 47 Iowa, 137; Smalley v. Greene, 52 Iowa, 241; s. c., 3 N. W. Rep. 78; Haldeman v. Simonton, 55 Iowa, 144; s. c., 7 N. W. Rep. 493; Powers v. Strout, 67 Iowa, 341; s. c., 25 N. W. Rep. 273. As the question has been so fully considered in these cases it needs no further discussion." Coles v. Edwards (1895), 93 Iowa, 477; s. c., 61 N. W. Rep. 940. "The tendency in later cases has certainly been to allow a restriction in point of space which formerly would have been thought unreasonable, manifestly because of the improved means of communication. A radius of 150 is still the law, it has been "much weakened" by recent decisions, and that to a considerable extent the foundation on which the rule was based has been removed. As the question is one of vital importance, the opinion of the court by Mr. Justice Andrews is here quoted at length, as follows: "When the restraint is general but at the same time is co-extensive only with the interest to be protected, and with the benefit meant to be conferred, there seems to be no good reason why, as between the parties, the contract is not as reasonable as when the interest is partial and there is a corresponding partial restraint, and is there any real public interest which necessarily condemns the one and not the other? It is an encouragement to industry and to enterprise in building up a trade that a man shall be allowed to sell the good will of the business and the fruits of his industry upon the best terms he can obtain. If his business extends over a continent, does public policy forbid his accompanying the sale with a stipulation for restraint co-extensive with the business which he sells? If such a contract is permitted, is the seller any more likely to become a burden on the public than a man who, having built up a local trade only, sells it, binding himself not to carry it on in the locality? Are the opportunities for employment and for the exercise of useful talents so shut up and hemmed in that the public is likely to lose a useful member of society in the one case and not in the other? Indeed, what public policy requires is often a vague and difficult inquiry. It is clear that public policy and the interests of society favor the utmost freedom of contract, within the law, and require that business transactions should not be trammeled by unnecessary restrictions. 'If,' says Sir George Jessell,

or even 200 miles has not been held too much in some cases. For the same reason I think a restriction applying to the entire kingdom may in other cases be requisite and justifiable." Maxim-Nordenfelt Co. v. Nordenfelt, L. R. (1894) App. Cas. 535, 549. A contract not to practice medicine within certain limits. is not void simply because the duration of the restraint is not limited. French v. Parker (R. I.) (1888), 14 Atl. Rep. 870. An agreement not to practice a particular trade in a particular place for a limited time is valid. Boyce v. Watson, 52 Ill. App. 361.

in Printing Company v. Sampson,[1] 'there is one thing more than any other which public policy requires, it is that men of full age and competent understanding shall have the utmost liberty of contracting, and that contracts, when entered into freely and voluntarily, shall be held good and shall be enforced by courts of justice.' It has been sometimes suggested that the doctrine that contracts in general restraint of trade are void, is founded in part upon the policy of preventing monopolies, which are opposed to the liberty of the subject, and the granting of which by the king, under claim of royal prerogative led to conflicts memorable in English history. But covenants of the character of the one now in question, operate simply to prevent the covenantor from engaging in the business which he sells so as to protect the purchaser in the enjoyment of what he has purchased. To the extent that the contract prevents the vendor from carrying on the particular trade, it deprives the community of any benefit it might derive from his entering into competition. But the business is open to all others, and there is little danger that the public will suffer harm from lack of persons to engage in a profitable industry. Such contracts do not create monopolies. They confer no special or exclusive privilege. If contracts in general restraint of trade, where the trade is general, are void as tending to monopolies, contracts in partial restraint where the trade is local are subject to the same objection, because they deprive the local community of the services of the covenantor in the particular trade or calling, and prevent his becoming a competitor with the covenantee. We are not aware of any rule of law which makes the motive of the covenantee the test of the validity of such a contract. On the contrary, we suppose a party may legally purchase the trade and business of another for the very purpose of preventing competition, and the validity of the contract, if supported by a consideration, will depend upon its reasonableness as between the parties. Combinations between producers to limit production and to enhance prices are or may be unlawful, but

[1] Printing Co. v. Sampson, L. R. 19 Eq. 462.

they stand on a different footing. We cite some of the cases showing the tendency of recent judicial opinions on the general subject.[1] In Whittaker v. Howe,[2] a contract made by a solicitor not to practice as a solicitor 'in any part of Great Britain,' was held valid. In Rousillon v. Rousillon,[3] a general contract not to engage in the sale of champaigne, without limit as to space, was enforced as being, under the circumstances, a reasonable contract. In Jones v. Lees,[4] a covenant by the defendant, a licensee under a patent, that he would not during the license make or sell any slubbing machines without the invention of the plaintiff applied to them, was held valid. Bramwell, J., said: 'It is objected that the restraint extends to all England, but so does the privilege.' In Oregon Steam Nav. Co. v. Windsor,[5] the cour enforced a covenant by the defendant made on the purchase of a steamship that it should not be run or employed in the freight or passenger business upon any waters in the State of California for the period of ten years. * * * The covenant in the present case is partial and not general. It is practically unlimited as to time, but this, under the authorities, is not an objection, if the contract is otherwise good.[6] It is limited as to space since it excepts the State of Nevada and the territory of Montana from its operation, and, therefore, is a partial and not a general restraint, unless, as claimed by the defendant, the fact that the covenant applies to the whole of the State of New York, constitutes a general restraint within the authorities. In Chappell v. Brockway,[7] Benson, J., in stating the general doctrine as to contracts in restraint of trade, remarks that

[1] Whittaker v. Howe, 3 Beav. 383; Jones v. Lees, 1 Hurl. & N. 189; Rousillon v. Rousillon, L. R. 14 Ch. D. 351; Leather Co. v. Lorsont, L. R. 9 Eq. 345; Collins v. Locke, L. R. 4 App. Cas. 674; Oregon Steam Nav. Co. v. Winsor, 20 Wall. 64; Morse v. Morse, 103 Mass. 73.

[2] Whittaker v. Howe, 3 Beav. 383.

[3] Rousillon v. Rousillon, L. R. 14 Ch. D. 351.

[4] Jones v. Lees, 1 Hurl. & N. 189.

[5] Oregon Steam Nav. Co. v. Winsor, 20 Wall. 64.

[6] Ward v. Byrne, 5 M. & W. 548; Mumford v. Gething, 7 C. B. (N. S.) 305, 317.

[7] Chappell v. Brockway, 21 Ward, 157.

'contracts which go to the total restraint of trade, as that a man will not pursue his occupation anywhere in the State, are void.' The contract under consideration in that case was one by which the defendant agreed not to run or be interested in a line of packet boats on the canal between Rochester and Buffalo. The attention of the court was not called to the point whether a contract was partial, which related to a business extending over the whole country, and which restrained the carrying on of business in the State of New York, but excepted other States from its operation. The remark relied upon was *obiter*, and in reason cannot be considered a decision upon the point suggested. We are of the opinion that the contention of the defendant is not sound in principle and should not be sustained. The boundaries of the States are not those of trade and commerce, and business is restrained within no such limit. The country as a whole is that of which we are citizens, and our duty and allegiance are due both to the State and nation. Nor is it true, as a general rule, that a business established here cannot extend beyond the State, or that it may not be successfully established outside of the State. There are trades and employments which, from their nature, are localized; but this is not true of manufacturing industries in general. We are unwilling to say that the doctrine as to what is a general restraint of trade depends upon State lines, and we cannot say that the exceptions of Nevada and Montana was colorable merely. The rule itself is arbitrary, and we are not disposed to put such a construction upon this contract as will make it a contract in general restraint of trade, when upon its face it is only partial. The case of the Oregon Steam Nav. Co. v. Winsor,[1] supports the view that a restraint is not necessarily general which embraces an entire State. The defendant entered into the covenant as a consideration in part of the purchase of his property by Swift & Courtney & Beacher Company, presumably, because he considered it for his advantage to make the sale. He realized a large sum in money, and on the completion of

[1] Oregon Steam Nav. Co. v. Winsor. 20 Wall. 64.

the transaction became interested as a stockholder in the very business which he had sold. We are of opinion that the covenant being supported by a good consideration, and constituting a partial and not a general restraint, and being, in view of the circumstances disclosed, reasonable, is valid and not void."[1] It will be observed that the view here presented is, substantially, that of the English courts, and that the authorities by which it is supported are largely English. The rule, as here stated, has not been generally accepted by the courts of this country. Whether the trend in this direction is strong enough to secure its universal or general acceptance is yet to appear. In a recent case in Wisconsin, defendant agreed to purchase $200,000 worth of goods from plaintiff, who agreed not to sell like articles in some thirty States and territories of the United States. In an action for goods sold and delivered, defendant set up this contract, and alleged breaches of it as a counterclaim. There was nothing to show the ordinary amount of manufacture and sale by either party, or that defendant had established a trade in more than one State out of the thirty. It was held that the pleading was demurrable in not affirmatively showing that the restraint was reasonably necessary to protect defendants under the contract. For a full statement of the doctrine, as administered in Wisconsin, see the accompanying note.[2]

[1] Diamond Match Co. v. Roeber, 106 N. Y. 473, 482.

[2] Richards v. American Desk Co., 87 Wis. 503; s. c., 58 N. W. Rep. 787. "That any agreement in restraint of trade of one of the parties to a contract is void as being against public policy, unless founded upon a valuable consideration, and limited as regards time, space and the extent of the trade, to what is reasonable under the circumstances of the case, is well settled, for the reason that such contracts tend to deprive the public of the services of parties in the employments and capacities in which they are most useful, and that they tend to expose the public to the evils of monopoly. Kellogg v. Larkin, 3 Pin. 123; Laubenheimer v. Mann, 17 Wis. 561; Alger v. Thacher, 19 Pick. 51; Bishop v. Palmer, 146 Mass. 469, 473; s. c., 16 N. E. Rep. 299; Oregon Steam Navigation Co. v. Winsor, 20 Wall. 66, 67; Gibbs v. Gas Co., 130 U. S. 396; s. c., 9 Sup. Ct. Rep. 553; Lange v. Werke, 2 Ohio St. 519; Gamewell, etc. Tel. Co. v. Crane. 160 Mass. 50; s. c., 35 N. E. Rep. 98. These cases show and many others

§ 45. **Territorial Limits Determined.**—There is a class of cases in which the court is called upon to construe or to define the provisions of a contract relating to territorial limitations. In a case in Michigan, an agreement between

might be cited to the same effect, that it is essential, in order not to be unreasonable, that the restraint imposed must not be larger than is plainly required for the protection of the party with whom the contract is made, and whether it is reasonable in a given case is a question not of fact but of law for the court. Pollock, Contracts, 366, 368; Washburn v. Dosch, 68 Wis. 440; s. c., 32 N. W. Rep. 551. The test as to whether the restraint is reasonable or not is well expressed in the often cited case of Horner v. Graves, 7 Bing. 735, 743, where it is said: 'The question is whether the restraint is such only as to afford a fair protection to the interests of the party in favor of whom it is given, and not so large as to interfere with the interests of the public. Whatever restraint is larger than the necessary protection of the party can be of no benefit to either. It can only be oppressive, and, if oppressive, it is, in the eye of the law, unreasonable.' It is said, in substance, in many cases, that all restraints are presumed to be bad, but if the circumstances are set forth, that presumption may be excluded, and the court is to judge of these circumstances whether the contract be valid or not. Taylor v. Blanchard, 13 Allen, 373; Callahan v. Donnolly, 45 Cal. 152; s. c., 13 Am. Rep. 172; Mallan v. May, 11 Mees. & W. 853; Lange v. Werke, 2 Ohio St. 519; Kellogg v. Larkin, 3 Pin. 123; Berlin Machine Works v. Perry, 71 Wis. 495, 499, 501; s. c., 38 N. W. Rep. 82. It is held, in substance, in these cases, that the pleading will be bad on demurrer if it does not appear from the contract or averments of extrinsic facts that the restraint was reasonable. This is in accordance with the great weight of authority and seems to be the necessary result of the rule as to the validity of such restraint. The great diffusion of wealth, the wonderful advances made in the methods and facilities for manufacturing and carrying on commerce, the manifold improvements in machinery and in the adaptation of steam and electricity as motive power, have enlarged or opened numerous fields of industry and wrought marvelous changes, and the tendency of the later cases has been in relaxation of the earlier rule in relation to contracts in restraint of trade. The most liberal and advanced doctrine on the subject in this country is found in the case of the Diamond Match Co. v. Roeber, 106 N. Y. 473; s. c., 13 N. E. Rep. 419, in which the history of the law is elaborately considered, and a covenant excluding a manufacturer of matches, who had sold his property, stock, etc., from engaging in the manufacture and sale of matches for a period of ninety-nine years within any of the States and territories except Nevada and Montana, was sustained; but it appeared in that case that before such sale he had carried on the business of manufacturing friction matches, 'and of selling the same in the several physicians that one would not practice in a specified city and vicinity, was construed as excluding him from all territory within ten miles of the city limits. In the opinion, the court said: "The decree restrains the defendant from practicing his profession 'in the city of Hastings and vicinity.' This clause of the decree is somewhat indefinite as to the extent of the territory to which it applies, and may give rise to further misunderstanding between the parties. For the purpose of obviating any difficulty of this kind, the decree made by the circuit judge should be so modified as to make certain the limits of its operation. Of course, the extent of territory included in the term 'vicinity of the city' must necessarily depend in a great measure

States and territories of the United States, and in the District of Columbia,' and so the case really came within the rule under consideration, and the restraint was reasonably necessary to protect the other party in his purchase. Tode v. Gross, 127 N. Y. 485; s. c., 28 N. E. Rep. 469, was in relation to a restraint imposed upon the vendor of a business founded on a secret process, but it recognizes and sustains the general rule. A manufacturing business founded upon the use of a secret process, or the use of patented processes or means, is not understood to be within the rule. The cases of Leather Cloth Co. v. Larsont, L. R. 9 Eq. 345, and Rousillon v. Rousillon, L. R. 14 Ch. Div. 351, are understood to represent the more modern views of the law on this subject. In the former case it was said: 'All restraints upon trade are bad as being in violation of public policy, unless they are actually and not unreasonably for the protection of parties in dealing legally with some subject-matter of contract.' The same subject was considered in the somewhat recent case of Davies v. Davies, L. R. 36 Ch. D. 359, in which Cotton, L. J., held the law to be 'that a limited restraint may be good, provided the restraint is reasonable and such as was required for the protection of parties with whom the covenant is entered into; and that the rule ought not to be altered but by the House of Lords; and Bowen, L. J., held substantially the same view, and notices that in that case the court had no material for deciding that the covenant in question was beneficial to the public or reasonably necessary for the protection of the covenantee, and in substance, that to sustain it would be 'leaping into the dark,' while Fry, L. J., was inclined to adhere to his decision in Rousillon v. Rousillon, *supra*, and to hold that the burden of proof as to the validity of the restraint is shifted by showing that it has been entered into for the protection of the interests of one of the contracting parties." Pinney, J., in Richards v. American Desk & Seating Co. (1894), 87 Wis. 503 s. c., 58 N. W. Rep. 787, 789.

upon the size of the city, its location and particular surroundings; and under all the circumstances as they appear upon this record, I think the territory surrounding the city for the distance of ten miles from its corporate boundaries a reasonable limitation, and one which may be safely regarded within the contemplation of the parties when they made the contract."[1] In a case in Connecticut, the plaint-

[1] Timmerman v. Dever, 52 Mich. 34; s. c., 50 Am. Rep. 240; 23 Am. Law Reg. 50. A declaration in covenant, after stating that the defendant and the plaintiff had agreed to enter into partnership as surgeons, etc., stated that the defendant covenanted that he would not, at any time, practice in the profession of a surgeon at No. 28 Dorset Cresent, or within the distance of two miles and a half thereof, measuring by the usual streets or ways of approach thereto, nor reside within the distance of two miles and a half of No. 28 Dorset Cresent, without the plaintiff's consent, nor would attempt to prevail on any of the patients of the defendant or of the partnership to withdraw from the plaintiff, or to employ any other medical attendant in prejudice of the plaintiff, but would in all things endeavor to promote the business and advantage of the plaintiff in the profession of a surgeon as far as it was in the power of the defendant, and he could reasonably and properly be required to do, and that if the defendant should, in any respect, break or infringe this stipulation he should pay the plaintiff £1,000 as liquidated damages and not by way of penalty. *Held*, first, that the distance was to be measured not by the most frequented public ways, but by any of the usual public ways; secondly, that the stipulation as to residence was not void as being in restraint of trade or contrary to public policy. Atkyns v. Kinnier, 4 Excheq. 776; s. c., 19 L. J. Excheq. 132. Under an agreement not to carry on business within seven miles of a certain place, the distance must be measured in a straight line, upon a horizontal plane, and not by the nearest practicable mode of access. Duignan v. Walker, 7 W. R. 562; s. c., 5 Jur. (N. S.) 976; 28 L. J. Ch. 867. The defendant having covenanted with the plaintiff not to carry on the business of a publican within the distance of half a mile from a certain tavern, afterwards carried on such business in premises distant from the tavern less than half a mile in a straight line, but more by the nearest mode of access. *Held*, that the defendant had committed a breach of his covenant, and that the right way of measuring the distance was on a map. Moutlet v. Cole, 21 W. R. 175; s. c., 27 L. T. 678; 42 L. J. Excheq. 8; L. R. 8 Excheq. 32. In Leigh v. Hinde, 9 Bar. & Cr. 774, 779, Parke, J., says: "I should have thought that the proper mode of admeasuring the distance would be to take a straight line from house to house, in common parlance, as the crow flies. The defendant agrees not to keep a public house within the distance of half a

iff, for a sufficient consideration, bought of the defendant his business as a dentist, and the latter executed a contract not to practice dentistry "within a radius of ten miles of Litchfield." The town of Litchfield has an extensive territory and an irregular outline, and contains the village of Litchfield, in which the defendant dwelt and had his office at the time, and where the contract was drawn and executed. It was held that the above expression meant "within ten miles of the center of the village of Litchfield."[1]

§ 46. Validity of Contracts in Restraint of Trade as Affected by Their Reasonableness.—A contract providing for a general restraint of trade is contrary to public policy and, in consequence, void. The ground of this rule is that the restraint being greater than is necessary for the adequate protection of the covenantee is unreasonable, and that what is palpably unreasonable is not to be upheld by a court of equity. But where a contract is based on a valuable consideration and is limited by time or space, then the question whether it is valid is simply the question whether it is reasonable. The court will consider the question of the reasonableness of the limitation in time or space. It will inquire whether the restraint imposed is greater than is essential to the proper protection of the covenantee, and where this appears the contract will be held unreasonable and invalid. In deciding this question the nature and extent of the business or occupation will come under consideration. This examination will extend to all the circumstances of the case, and it must include the question whether the restraint imposed is of such an extent as to conflict with the interests of the public. In a leading English case it

mile; the plain and ordinary sense of these words is, the actual distance, and I think they ought to be so understood unless we can collect from the context that they were meant to be used in a different sense; and here the context raises no such inference." See also Lake v. Butler, 3 W. R. 458; s. c., 5 E. & B. 99; Reg. v. Saffron Walden, 9 Q. B. 76.

[1] Cook v. Johnson, 47 Conn. 175; s. c., 36 Am. Rep. 64.

was held that where a covenant in restraint of trade is general, that is, without qualification, it is bad, as being unreasonable and contrary to public policy. Where it is partial, that is, subject to some qualification either as to time or space, then the question is whether it is reasonable, and if it is reasonable, it is good in law. In considering the question of reasonableness, the points to which the attention of the court is especially directed are the limits of time and space, and the protection required for the trade of the covenantee, this latter point involving the examination of the nature and extent of the trade. The reasonableness depends on all the circumstances, which must be duly weighed in each case. If the restraint is greater than can be possibly required for the protection of the covenantee, the covenant is unreasonable; but, if the restraint is not greater than can possibly be required for the protection of the covenantee, it is not unreasonable; and where the covenant is qualified as to time the burden lies on the covenantee of showing that the restraint is unreasonable.[1]

[1] Badische Anilin und Soda Fabrik v. Schott, L. R. (1892) 3 Ch. 447. "The circumstances which may be legitimately inquired into on this question of reasonableness appear to me to include the general circumstances under which the trade is carried on at the time when the covenant is entered into. The improvements in the means of communication which have taken place in recent times by reason of railways, steamships, postal facilities, the telegraph, and the telephone, are, I think, within the scope of the inquiry, and bear particularly on the question of space; they are relevant more or less in proportion to the greater or lesser area within which the trade sought to be protected is carried on and to the varying nature of the trade itself. Such matters would have little or no relevancy if the question related to the protection of a small local business such as that of a village baker or cobbler, and if the restraint sought to be imposed on a journeyman baker or cobbler, though limited as to time, extended to the whole of England—such restraint would be unreasonable and vexatious. But they would be relevant in reference to the large trade of a merchant and a widely extended news collecting agency, or to any trade covering a great portion of the globe. What might in former ages have been considered an unreasonable restriction would not necessarily be so held in the altered circumstances of the present time." *Ibid.*, 452. "We do not see how a better test can be applied to the question, whether reasonable or not, than by considering whether the restraint is such only

In a case in New Jersey it was held that "contracts in restraint of trade are invalid, and this is so even when the restraint imposed is partial, unless the restraint be reasonable. And the test to be applied in determining whether a restraint is reasonable or not, is to consider whether the restraint is only such as is necessary to afford a fair protection to the interest of the party in whose favor it is given, and not so large as to interfere with the interest of the public."[1] Where contracts in restraint of trade are ren-

as to afford a fair protection to the interests of the party in favor of whom it is given, and not so large as to interfere with the interests of the public. Whatever restraint is larger than the necessary protection of the party can be of no benefit to either, it can only be oppressive, and if oppressive it is, in the eye of the law, unreasonable." Tindal, C. J., in Horner v. Graves, 7 Bing. 735, 743. "No one of the noble and learned lords before whom this appeal was heard has had the least difficulty in holding that the injunction granted was reasonably necessary in order to protect the respondent company's business from the aggressive acts threatened and commenced by the appellant. Nor, so far as I understand, have the noble and learned lords had any hesitation in coming to the conclusion, with the learned judges of the appeal court, that there is no existing rule of public policy which can be effectively pleaded in bar of the injunction. For my own part, I am very clearly of opinion that no violence is done to the canons laid down by the common law courts in affirming that a restraint which is absolutely necessary in order to protect a transaction which the law permits in the interest of the public, ought to be regarded as reasonable, and cannot, in deference to political ideas which are now obsolete, be regarded as in contravention of public policy. Were it necessary I should be prepared to affirm that, in the year 1888, there was not, and there does not now exist, any imperial rule of policy which requires that a restraint having that effect only shall be treated as a nullity, because it is unlimited in space, in circumstances such as occur in the present case. I venture to doubt whether it be now, or ever has been, an essential part of the policy of England to encourage unfettered competition in the sale of arms of precision to tribes who may become our antagonists in warfare. I also doubt whether at any period of time an English court would have allowed a foreigner to break his contract with an English subject in order to foster such competition." Lord Watson, in Nordenfelt v. Maxim-Nordenfelt Co., L. R. (1894) App. Cas. 533, 554.

[1] Mandeville v. Harmon, 42 N. J. Eq. 185; s. c., 7 Atl. Rep. 37. See also Fowle v. Park, 131 U. S. 88; s. c., 9 Sup. Ct. Rep. 658; Long v. Towl, 42 Mo. 545; Diamond Match Co. v. Roeber, 106 N. Y. 473; s. c., 13 N. E. Rep. 419; Hodge v. Sloan, 106 N. Y. 244; Nester v. Continental Brewing Co., 161 Pa. St. 473; s. c., 41 Am. St. Rep. 894;

dered invalid by a statutory provision, the question of reasonableness will not be considered. Public policy and the obligation of the citizen are determined by the legislative enactments. Wherever a contract in restraint of trade falls under a statutory provision, the law thus created

United States Chemical Co. v. Providence, etc. Co., 64 Fed. Rep. 946; Hitchcock v. Coker, 6 Ad. & El. 438; Baines v. Geary, L. R. 35 Ch. D. 154; Davies v. Davies, L. R. 36 Ch. D. 359, 396, 397, 398; Rousillon v. Rousillon, L. R. 14 Ch. D. 363; Nat'l Prov. Bank v. Marshall, L. R. 40 Ch. D. 112. Contracts which impose an unreasonable restraint upon the exercise of a business, trade or profession are void; but contracts in reasonable restraint thereof are valid. Ellerman v. Chicago Junction, etc. Co., 49 N. J. Eq. 217; s. c., 23 Atl. Rep. 287. "Is the contract unreasonable? Courts should be slow to set aside as unreasonable a restriction which has formed a part of the consideration of a contract. Yet when it is a restriction upon individual and common rights, which only oppress one party without benefiting the other, all courts agree that it should not be enforced. In determining the reasonableness of a contract, regard must be had to the nature and circumstances of the transaction. For example, if one has sold the good will of a mercantile enterprise, receiving pay for it upon an agreement not to engage in the same business in the same State for a certain time, such a stipulation would stand upon quite a different footing from the similar stipulation of a mere servant in an ordinary local business. In many undertakings with modern methods of advertising and facilities for ordering by telegraph or mail, and sending goods by railroad or express, it would matter little whether one was located in Providence or Boston, or some other place. In such cases, a restriction embracing the State, or even a larger territory, could not be said on that account to be unreasonable, for without it the seller might immediately destroy the value of what he sold and was paid for. But it is unreasonable to ask courts to enforce a greater restriction than is needed. So it has been uniformly held that restrictions which go too far are void. As was said in the note of the Law Quarterly Review above cited: 'Covenantees desiring the maximum of protection have no doubt a difficult task. When they fail it is commonly because, like the dog in the fable, they grasp at too much, and so lose all.' Beside the matter of protection, the hardship of the restriction upon the party and the public should also be considered." Herreshoff v. Boutineau, 17 R. I. 3, 7. "At the present day there is not that danger, or at least it does not seem to exist to an appreciable extent, except, possibly, as suggested in the case of corporations. In their supervision and in their restriction within the limits of their chartered powers, the government and the public are directly interested. Corporations are great engines for the promotion of the public convenience and for the development of public wealth, and so long as settles all questions of public policy and of reasonableness. In the recent leading case of The United States v. The Trans-Missouri Freight Association, before the Supreme Court of the United States, Mr. Justice Peckham, in delivering the opinion of the court, said: "The arguments which have been addressed to us against the inclusion of all contracts in restraint of trade, as provided for by the language of the act, have been based upon the alleged presumption that congress, notwithstanding the language of the act, could not have intended to embrace all contracts, but only such contracts as were in unreasonable restraint of trade. Under these circumstances we are therefore asked to hold that the act of congress excepts contracts which are not in unreasonable restraint of trade, and which only keep rates up to a reasonable price, notwithstanding the language

they are conducted for the purposes for which organized, they are a public benefit. * * * When, therefore, the provisions of agreements in restraint of competition tend beyond measures for self-protection, and threaten the public good in a distinctly appreciable manner, they should not be sustained. The apprehension of danger to the public interests, however, should rest on evident grounds, and courts should refrain from the exercise of their equitable powers in interfering with and restraining the conduct of individuals or of corporations unless their conduct, in some tangible form, threatens the welfare of the public." Leslie v. Lorillard, 110 N. Y. 533. F and wife sold a newspaper in D county, and agreed that F "shall not edit, print or conduct a newspaper, nor be in anywise connected with one printed anywhere in the State of North Carolina, and that for a like period Mrs. F shall not edit, print or conduct a newspaper or magazine, nor be in anywise connected with one in the county of D, said State, without the consent of such purchaser or his assignees." *Held*, that such contract was not void as an unreasonable restraint on trade. Cowan v. Fairbrother, 118 N. Car. 406; s. c., 24 S. E. Rep. 212. Where electrotype plates are sold so that the absolute title passes to the buyers, a clause in the contract of sale, providing that the buyers will not sell the plates to other parties, or multiply them for the purpose of sale, is a contract in restraint of trade, but is reasonable in view of the nature of the property, and will be enforced between the parties. Meyer v. Estes, 164 Mass. 457; s. c., 41 N. E. Rep. 683. By-law 25, of the Associated Press of New York, which provides that no member "shall receive or publish the regular news dispatches of any other news association covering a like territory and organized for a like purpose," is not void as unreasonable as in restraint of trade. Matthews v. Associated Press, 136 N. Y. 333; s. c., 32 N. E. Rep. 981.

of the act makes no such exception. In other words, we are asked to read into the act, by way of judicial legislation, an exception that is not placed there by the law-making branch of the government, and this is to be done upon the theory that the impolicy of such legislation is so clear that it cannot be supposed congress intended the natural import of the language it used. This we cannot and ought not to do. That impolicy is not so clear nor are the reasons for the exception so potent, as to permit us to interpolate an exception into the language of the act, and thus materially to alter its meaning and effect. It may be that the policy evidenced by the passage of the act itself will, if carried out, result in disaster to the roads, and in a failure to secure the advantages sought from such legislation. Whether that will be the result or not we do not know and cannot predict. These considerations are, however, not for us. If the act ought to read as contended for by defendants, congress is the body to amend it and not this court, by a process of judicial legislation wholly unjustifiable. Large numbers do not agree that the view taken by defendants is sound or true in substance, and congress may, and very probably did, share in that belief in passing the act. The public policy of the government is to be found in its statutes, and, when they have not spoken directly, then in the decisions of the courts and the constant practice of the government officials, but when the law-making power speaks upon a particular subject over which it has constitutional power to legislate, public policy in such a case is what the statute enacts. If the law prohibit any contract or combination in restraint of trade or commerce, a contract or combination made in violation of such law is void, whatever may have been theretofore decided by the courts to have been the public policy of the country on the subject."[1]

§ 47. **Divisibility of Illegal Contract.**—It is well established that where a contract in restraint of trade contains

[1] United States v. Trans-Missouri Freight Association (1897), 166 U. S. 290; s. c., 17 Sup. Ct. Rep. 540, 558.

two or more stipulations, a part of which are valid and the remainder void, the contract may be divided and the valid portion sustained, If the agreement is of such a character as to admit of division, it will be held void only to the extent to which it is illegal, or in contravention of public policy. In a leading case before the Supreme Court of the United States, the rule is stated by Mr. Justice Bradley, as follows: "It is laid down by Chitty as the result of the cases, and his authorities support the statement, 'that agreements in restraint of trade, whether under seal or not, are divisible; and, accordingly, it has been held that when such an agreement contains a stipulation which is capable of being construed divisibly, and one part thereof is void as being in restraint of trade, whilst the other is not, the court will give effect to the latter, and will not hold the agreement to be void altogether.'"[1] In a case in Pennsyl-

[1] Oregon Steam Nav. Co. v. Winsor, 20 Wall. 64, 70. See also Price v. Green, 16 M. & W. 346; s. c., 16 L. J. Excheq. 108; Mallan v. May, 11 M. & W. 653; s. c., 7 Jur. 536; 12 L. J. Excheq. 376; Willis v. Beard, 6 Ind. 200; Gelpcke v. Dubuque, 68 U. S. 175; Goodwin v. Clark, 65 Me. 280; Carleton v. Woods, 28 N. H. 290; Van Dyck v. Van Buren, 1 Johns. 362; Saratoga County Bank v. King, 44 N. Y. 89; Leavitt v. Palmer, 3 N. Y. 19; Newberry Bank v. Stegall, 41 Miss. 142; Tracy v. Talmage, 14 N. Y. 162; Carrigan v. Lycoming F. Ins. Co., 53 Vt. 418; Widoe v. Webb, 20 Ohio St. 431; Hynds v. Hays, 25 Ind. 31, 36; White v. Buss, 3 Cush. 449. A contract not to engage in a particular trade for a specified time "in the city of St. Louis, or at any other place," is divisible, and as to the restriction in St. Louis is not void as in restraint of trade. Peltz v. Eichell, 62 Mo. 171. Declaration in covenant on an indenture, which, after reciting that defendant had for four years been plaintiff's salaried clerk, and requested plaintiff to accept him as articled clerk without payment of any premiums, which plaintiff consented to do on defendant entering into the covenants thereinafter contained, and that defendant had bound himself clerk to plaintiff for five years, to the intent that he might become entitled to make application to be admitted attorney and solicitor, defendant covenanted that he would not, during said term of five years, nor at any time after the expiration of such term, either directly or indirectly, interfere or intermeddle with, or be concerned as attorney, agent or otherwise for any person who had already been, or should thereafter become or be, the client or correspondent in business of, or with, plaintiff, or any partner he might admit to a share with him, or to any person to whom he might sell or assign the whole, or any part of his business or profession, and that

vania, A, for a valuable consideration, covenanted with B, not to engage in the manufacture of ochre "in the county of Lehigh or elsewhere." He afterwards did engage in said business in said county. B filed his bill in equity, praying that A might be enjoined from carrying on said business in said county. It was held: 1. That the contract was reasonable. 2. That it was divisible as to place. 3.

defendant would not act as partner, clerk or assistant with or to any person who should interfere or intermeddle as aforesaid; and in case defendant should commit any breach of his said covenants, he should forfeit £100 for every such breach. *Held*, that the covenant was divisible, and that an action was maintainable against the defendant for being concerned as attorney for persons who were clients of the plaintiff at the date of the deed. Nicholls v. Stretton, 11 Jur. 1008. A and B entered into an indenture in which B covenanted not to be interested in a certain business within a certain county, and also covenanted not to be interested, for five years, in the same business within the United States. *Held*, that B was liable for a breach of the first covenant, although the second covenant might be void as in restraint of trade. Dean v. Emerson, 102 Mass. 480. "Where a contract in restraint of trade embraces several distinct provisions, and is divisible in its nature, the illegality of one provision, which is capable of being construed divisibly, will not necessarily make the entire contract null and void. Western Union Tel. Co. v. Burlington, etc. R. Co., 11 Fed. Rep. 1. L covenanted with W that he would not, for a specified time, be connected, either directly or indirectly, with the manufacture of stearin or star candles in the county of Hamilton, in the State of Ohio, or at any other place in the United States, or give his assistance or communicate his knowledge of his said business to any person whatever, under forfeiture of four thousand dollars as liquidated damages." *Held*, first, that all that part of the covenant which bound L not to pursue the business, or give his assistance, at any other place in the United States, was void, being in general restraint of trade. Second, that it was divisible, and if attended with other necessary requisites, might be good for Hamilton county. Lange v. Werk, 2 Ohio St. 519. Followed in Thomas v. Miles, 3 Ohio St. 274. The defendant entered into an agreement to serve the plaintiff in his business of dairyman as a milk carrier. By the agreement the defendant agreed that he would not, during the continuance of the service, nor at any time thereafter, serve for his own benefit, or for the benefit of any other person, or solicit, or in any way interfere with any of the customers who should at any time be served by the plaintiff in his business. *Held*, that the clause was severable, and that an injunction could properly be granted restraining the defendant from serving persons who were customers of the plaintiff during the employment of the defendant by the plaintiff. Dubowski v. Goldstein (1896), 65 L. J. Q. B. Div. 397.

That an injunction was the proper remedy to enforce it.[1] In the opinion in this case, the court said: "The covenant as to place, 'in the county of Lehigh or elsewhere,' is divisible, and valid as to the county; for the present it is conceded to be void elsewhere. * * * Where a county or city or borough is named as a limit, and an unreasonable extent of territory in addition is also named, the covenant is divisible and may be valid as to the particular place, which is a reasonable limit."[2] In an English case, L was engaged as clerk by D & Co. of London, foreign carriers, by agreement containing the following covenant: "L agrees that he will not within twelve calendar months after the termination of this agreement, from whatever cause, carry on, or be engaged in, or interested directly or indirectly in the cities of" London, Birmingham, Liverpool and New York, "or within fifty miles thereof of each of the above named places, either as principal, clerk, agent or otherwise, in any business similar to the business now or hereafter to be carried on by the employers." Defendant, on leaving plaintiff's service, entered into the service of a rival firm in London. Plaintiff had not any trade with Birmingham, but a considerable business with the other places mentioned. It was held that the limit of time was reasonable; also, that of space, with the exception of Birmingham; that the words "principal, clerk, agent or otherwise" were not too wide; that the words "now or hereafter" were not reasonable.[3] In a recent case in Massachusetts, it was held that a stipulation by a manufacturer of fire alarm and telegraph apparatus, on a sale of all his machinery, stock, letters patent and inventions, that he will not for ten years engage in the manufacture and sale of such apparatus, or enter into competition with the purchaser, while valid in so far as the patents and inventions agreed to be sold are concerned, is void, as against public policy, in so far as it prohibits the seller from engaging in the manufacture and sale of

[1] Smith's Appeal, 113 Pa. St. 579.

[2] Smith's Appeal, 113 Pa. St. 579, 655.

[3] Davies v. Lowen. 64 L. T. 590.

such apparatus under other patents, or under no patents at all.[1]

§ 48. **The Subject Continued.**—In order that a covenant in restraint of trade may be held divisible, and that one part of it may be upheld, the agreement must be of such a character that the part that would otherwise have been valid is not vitiated by that which is void. In a case in Massachusetts, a purchaser promised to pay in installments for a business plant and property, in consideration of its sale and delivery, and the performance of three particular covenants and agreements by the seller, the first of which was a general agreement, without any limitation of space, that for and during the period of five years he would not either directly or indirectly continue in, carry on or engage in that business or any business of which that might form any part; it was held that the covenant was void as being in restraint of trade, and that, not being severable from the rest of the consideration, no action would lie on the promise for installments of the price.[2] In the

[1] Gamewell Fire Alarm Tel. Co. v. Crane, 160 Mass. 50; s. c., 35 N. E. Rep. 98.

[2] Palmer v. Bishop, 146 Mass. 469. "It is contended that the contract restrains the exercise of the business within two distinct areas,—that the contract is severable. The one part restraining the exercise of the business within the city and county of San Francisco, and the other part restraining its exercise within the State, and that, while the latter is void, the former is valid, because the limits are not unreasonable. But we are of the opinion that the contract is, in that respect, entire. No precise rule can be laid down for the solution of the question, whether a contract is entire or separable; but it must be solved by considering both the language and the subject-matter of the contract. There were not two distinct areas, for the one included the other. The defendant's business was not carried on in the two distinct areas as two separate occupations, but the complaint avers that the defendant was carrying on the business in the State, and that he sold such business to the plaintiff. When the price is expressly apportioned by the contract, or the apportionment may be implied by law to each item to be performed, the contract will generally be held to be severable, but no such apportionment can be made of this contract. When the contract provides for the restraint of the business within the State, if the mention of any subdivision of the State will make the contract severable, then it would be easy to defeat the rule prohibiting con-

opinion in this case the court said: "It is contended that the defendants, by being unable to enforce the stipulation in question, only lose what they knew or were bound to know was legally null; that they have all that they supposed they were getting, namely, a promise which might be kept, though incapable of legal enforcement; and that if they were content to accept such promise, and if there is another good and sufficient consideration, they may be held upon their promise. But this argument cannot properly extend to a case where a part of an entire and inseparable consideration is positively vicious, however it might be where it was simply invalid as in Parish v. Stone.[1] The law visits a contract founded on such a consideration with a positive condemnation, which it makes effectual by refusing to support it, in whole or in part, where the consideration cannot be severed."[2] In a leading case before the Supreme Court of Indiana it was held that a contract by

tracts in total restraint of trade by mentioning in the contract each subdivision of the State; and when it is objected that the limits are unreasonable, it will be answered that the plaintiff seeks to enjoin the defendant from pursuing the business in only one of the cities or towns mentioned in the contract." More v. Bonnet, 40 Cal. 251; s. c., 6 Am. Rep. 621, 622. "Where an entire promise is made on one entire consideration, and part of that consideration is illegal, it may avoid the entire contract." Robinson v. Green, 3 Met. 159, 161. Where there are several considerations recited as the ground of a promise, and any of them be frivolous and insufficient or illegal, and the others are good and sufficient, then the good may be severed from the bad and the promise upheld. But if the bad be so connected with the good as to make the consideration an entirety and incapable of severance, the whole promise is void. Webb v. Allington, 27 Mo. App. 559.

[1] Parish v. Stone, 14 Pick. 198. "All the cases put are those of failure of consideration, where the consideration was single and entire, and went to the whole note, and was good and sufficient at the time the note was given, but by some breach of contract, mistake or accident, had afterwards failed. There the rule is, if the consideration has wholly failed or the contract been wholly rescinded, it shall be a good defense to the note. But if he have partially failed only, it would tend to an inconvenient mode of trial, and to a confusion of rights, to try such question in the suit on the note as a partial defense, and, therefore, the party complaining shall be left to his cross-action." *Ibid.*, p. 210.

[2] Bishop v. Palmer, 146 Mass. 469, 475.

which one formerly dealing in oil in the city of H, agreed not to prosecute such business within the State of Indiana, the city of Indianapolis excepted, for the period of five years, is not divisible, and being void as to the restriction within the State, is void as to the restriction in the city of H.[1] In an elaborate and well considered opinion by Chief Justice Jordan, the court said: "It is a recognized principle that when a contract is or can be so separated in parts as to constitute two agreements, one illegal and the other legal, the latter may be enforced and the transaction *pro tanto* sustained. But it is otherwise where the contract in its nature is not divisible. The contract before us is not of this character and does not come within the provisions of the rule stated, and it must either stand or fall as an entirety. The restraint of the trade or business as therein stipulated as to territory, was manifestly too large and is, therefore, in violation of the principles of public policy to which we have referred, and, consequently, void, and cannot in any respect be enforced."[2] In a leading case in California, the court said: "The very essence and mainspring of the agreement, the illegal object 'was to form a combination among all the manufacturers of lumber at or near F, for the sole purpose of increasing the price of lumber, limiting the amount thereof to be manufactured, and to give plaintiff control of all lumber manufactured,' etc. This being the inducement to the agreement, and the sole object in view, it cannot be separated and leave any subject-matter capable of enforcement. * * * The good cannot be separated from the bad, or rather the bad enters into and permeates the whole contract so that none of it can be said to be good, and, therefore, the subject of an action."[3]

§ 49. **Limitations in Conveyances.**—It is well established that a stipulation in a deed that the land conveyed shall not be used for a specified purpose or purposes, or

[1] Consumers' Oil Co. v. Nunnemacher, 142 Ind. 560; s. c., 41 N. E. Rep. 1048.

[2] Consumers' Oil Co. v. Nunnemacher, 142 Ind. 560, 568; s. c., 41 N. E. Rep. 1048.

[3] Mill & Lumber Co. v. Hayes, 76 Cal. 386, 393.

that it shall be used only for the particular purpose specified, is valid, and will be upheld in equity. In a leading case in Alabama, it was held that an express stipulation and reservation in a conveyance of land, part of a larger tract owned in fee by the vendor, that it shall be used as a residence only, and not for carrying on any trading or mercantile business, is not contrary to public policy, nor otherwise illegal; and a court of equity will enforce it against the purchaser, or a subpurchaser with notice, in favor of the vendor, or of a private corporation which has succeeded to his estate, although it may have no power to engage in a mercantile business.[1] In a case before the New York

[1] Morris v. Tuscaloosa Mfg. Co., 83 Ala. 565. See also Curtis v. Ayrault, 47 N. Y. 73; Talmage v. East River Bank, 26 N. Y. 105; Gibert v. Peteler, 38 Barb. 488, affirmed 38 N. Y. 165. Contracts restraining the exercise of any trade, profession or business are legal when they are confined to a limited locality, not unreasonably large or extensive, and there is a fair and reasonable ground for the restriction. Where the owner and proprietor of a public warehouse on a navigable river conveys a tract of land adjoining that on which his warehouse is situated, taking from the purchaser a penal bond containing a covenant not to allow or permit a warehouse or place for shipping or receiving goods upon the conveyed premises, such covenant is not void as against public policy. Robbins v. Webb, 68 Ala. 393. "The purpose of inserting them in the deed is manifest. It was to prevent such a use of the premises by the grantee, and those claiming under him, as might diminish the value of the residue of the land belonging to the grantor, or impair its eligibility as sites for private residences. That such a purpose is a legitimate one, and may be carried out, consistently with the rules of law, by reasonable and proper covenants, conditions or restrictions, cannot be doubted. Every owner of real property has the right so to deal with it as to restrain its use by his grantees within such limits as to prevent its appropriation to purposes which will impair the value or diminish the pleasure of the enjoyment of the land which he retains. The only restriction on this right is, that it shall be exercised reasonably, with a due regard to public policy, and without creating any unlawful restraint of trade. Nor can there be any doubt that in whatever form such a restraint is placed on real estate by the terms of a grant, whether it is in the technical form of a condition or covenant, or of a reservation or exception in the deed, or by words which give to the acceptance of the deed by the grantee the force and effect of a parol agreement, it is binding as between the grantor and the immediate grantee, and can be enforced against him by suitable process, both in law and equity." Bigelow, J., in Whitney

Court of Appeals, the court said: "The right sought to be enforced here is an easement, or, as it is sometimes called, an amenity, and consists in restraining the owner from doing that with and upon his property which he might lawfully have done, and hence is called a negative easement, as distinguished from that class of easements which compels the owner to suffer something to be done upon his property by another. Easements of all kinds may be created and exist in favor of any third person, irrespective of any privity of estate or community of interest between the parties, and in this respect there is no distinction between negative easements and those rights that are more generally known as easements, as a way, etc."[1] It is the rule also

v. Union Ry. Co., 11 Gray, 359. G & G, as partners, owned and operated a livery stable in the town of R, as did H and also J Bros. The last named sold for merely the value thereof the personal property used in the business, a part to G & G and the remainder to H, but did not sell or lease the stable, and, in consideration of the purchase, made a written contract with them, agreeing not to engage in the business in the stable of J Bros., nor to permit others to do so, for a period of five years, and that $2,500 should be paid as liquidated damages for breach of the contract. There was a breach by act of one of the sellers, but H, having quit the business, refused to join G & G as plaintiffs, and, therefore, they made him a defendant. *Held*, that the written contract was upon sufficient consideration, and was valid. Johnson v. Gwin, 100 Ind. 466. Where real estate, consisting of certain lots and the buildings thereon, is sold, and in the granting portion of the deed conveying the same a clause is inserted, stating that the property is not to be used for hotel purposes for two years, it was held that such restriction as to use of the property, being a limited one, was valid, and not an unreasonable restraint of trade. Mollyneaux v. Wittenberg, 39 Neb. 547; s. c., 58 N. W. Rep. 205. A covenant made by a vendor of real estate, that neither he nor his assigns will sell any marl from off the premises adjoining the tract conveyed, will not be enforced in equity against the alienee of the land intended to be burthened by such covenant. Such covenant should not be sustained on the ground that the principle on which alone it could rest would sanction the annexation to the land of any stipulation which human caprice might contrive. Such covenant is also illegal and void as being in general restraint of trade. Equity will enforce covenants connected with land in the hands of alienees, in some cases in which there is no legal remedy against such alienees; but such cases should not be unnecessarily multiplied. Brewer v. Marshall, 19 N. J. Eq. 537.

[1] Trustees v. Lynch, 70 N. Y. 440, 447. "It would be unreasonable and unconscientious to hold

that where a limitation in a conveyance is valid, as between the original parties, the covenant is binding upon a grantor of the covenantor, who has taken the title with notice of the restriction, and this will hold, although the assignees of the covenantor are not mentioned in the conveyance. It is not necessary that the agreement should be a covenant, technically, running with the land; it is sufficient that the purchaser has notice of it. In the leading and instructive case of Hodge v. Sloan, the court said: "Many other instances of restraint might be referred to, and where it is of such a nature as concerns the mode of occupying or dealing with the property purchased in the way of business operations, or even the omission of all business or certain kinds of business, or the erection or non-erection of buildings upon the property, we see no reason to doubt the validity of an agreement fair and valid in other

the grantees absolved from the covenant in equity for the technical reason assigned, that it did run with the land so as to give an action at law. A distinguished judge answered a like objection in a similar case by saying, in substance, that if an action at law could not be maintained, that was an additional reason for entertaining jurisdiction in equity and preventing injustice. The action can be maintained for the establishment and enforcement of a negative easement, created by the deed of the original proprietor, affecting the use of the premises now owned and occupied by the defendants, of which they had notice, and subject to which they took title. There is no equity or reason for making a servitude of the character of that claimed by the plaintiffs in the lands of the defendant, an exception to the general rule which charges lands in the hands of a purchaser with notice with all existing equities, easements and servitudes. The rule and its application does not depend upon the character or classification of the equities claimed, but upon the position and equitable obligation of the purchaser. The language of courts and of judges has been very uniform and very decided upon this subject, and all agree that whoever purchases lands upon which the owner has imposed an easement of any kind, or created a charge which would be enforced in equity against him, takes the title subject to all easements, equities and charges, however created, of which he has notice. *Ibid.*, 450; citing Parker v. Nightingale, 6 Allen, 341; Cott v. Towle, L. R. 4 Ch. App. 654; Carter v. Williams, 18 W. R. 593, before V. C. James; Wolfe v. Frost, 4 Sandf. Ch. 72; Tulk v. Moxhay, 2 Phil. 774; Whiting v. Union R. Co., 11 Gray, 359; Gilbert v. Peteler, 38 Barb. 488; Barrow v. Richard, 8 Paige, 351; Greene v. Creighton, 7 R. I. 1; Brouwer v. Jones, 23 Barb. 153.

respects, which secures that restraint. Indeed, it seems well settled by authority that a personal obligation so insisted upon by a grantor, and assumed by a grantee, which is a restriction as to the use of the land, may be enforced in equity against the grantee and subsequent purchasers with notice."[1]

§ **50. The Subject Continued.**—A familiar example of the application of this rule, as set forth in the preceding section, is that of a restriction upon the right of the grantor to make use of the land conveyed for the sale of intoxicating liquors. Restrictions of this character are upheld upon two grounds. It is well established that in the disposal of property the grantor has the right to restrain the grantee from such a use of the land conveyed as would diminish the value of what remained, or conflict with its sale or use for other purposes. But in addition to this right it is the policy of the law to restrain the sale of intoxicating drinks. The evil of the traffic, both in itself and in its influence, is recognized by the courts. The theory of the law is that it is to be tolerated only; never to be encouraged. In consequence, it is well established that a covenant in a conveyance restricting the right of a grantor to use the property conveyed for the sale of intoxicants will be held valid. In a case in Michigan, it was held that the right of a grantor to convey land on condition that the grantee shall not sell liquor upon the premises, coupled with a provision that in case of such sale the land shall revert to the

[1] Hodge v. Sloan, 107 N. Y. 244, 251. See also Burbank v. Pillsbury, 48 N. H. 475; Morland v. Cook, L. R. 6 Eq. 252; Brown v. Great Eastern R. Co., L. R. 2 Q. B. Div. 406; London, etc. Ry. Co. v. Comrs., L. R. 20 Ch. D. 562, 576. Where an agent procures a sale of land by promising, without authority, that the vendor will not sell adjoining lots at a less price, the mere fact that the vendee takes possession of the land, and has the benefit of such unauthorized promise for nearly a year, will not prevent him from rescinding the sale for non-performance of the promise. An agreement by a vendor not to sell other lots in the same plat at a less price than that paid by the vendee for his lot, will be construed as limited to a reasonable time, and as such is not against public policy. Rackeman v. Riverbank Imp. Co. (1896), 167 Mass. 1; s. c., 44 N. E. Rep. 990.

grantor, who shall at once take possession thereof, cannot be denied, and is within the public policy of this State, but courts will not enforce such condition if inserted for a dishonest purpose, and to enable the grantor to obtain a monopoly of the prohibited business.[1] In Jenks v. Pawlowski, it was held that restrictions in a deed upon the right of the grantee to sell intoxicating liquors on the premises are sustained upon the theory that a party has the right in disposing of his property to prevent such a use by the grantee as might diminish the value of remaining land, or impair its eligibility for other uses.[2] In a case where a deed contained the clause "no intoxicating liquors are to be sold on said premises in less quantities than five gallons," it was held that the restriction was not such a restraint on trade as to make it invalid.[3]

[1] Chippewa Falls Lumber Co. v. Tremper, 75 Mich. 36. "Liquor is not a necessity, like bread, and is generally regarded as of damage to the general community; but I know of no good reason why a person should be permitted to have a monopoly in selling poison to a community any more than food, unless it can be that no other person can be found fit to handle and dispense it. I do not believe, however, that any man or company should be permitted by the law, and aided by the courts, to create a monopoly in himself either in the sale of bread or whisky. The right to insert such a condition as the one in this case for an honest and beneficial purpose cannot be denied, and is within the public policy of this State. Smith v. Barrie, 56 Mich. 314; s. c., 22 N. W. Rep. 816; Watrous v. Allen, 57 Mich. 362; s. c., 24 N. W. Rep. 104. But courts will not enforce such a condition inserted for a dishonest purpose, and to the end that the grantor may thereby obtain a monopoly in any business, and all others restrained therefrom; and there can be no difference in this regard whether the business so sought to be centered in one person in a community is one acknowledged by every one to be of great benefit to mankind, or one regarded by many good people of detriment to the community, provided both are lawful; and certainly one cannot ask a court of justice to enforce such a condition as this against a person selling liquor otherwise lawfully, that he may reap the benefit of unlawful sales. Courts will not enforce forfeitures of estates for any such purposes." *Ibid.*, p. 41. A covenant in restraint of trade is not necessarily invalid, so far as the covenantee has in his own business an interest in enforcing it; and where the business is the selling of liquor, such a condition is not, in Michigan at least, opposed to public policy. Watrous v. Allen, 57 Mich. 362.

[2] Jenks v. Pawlowski, 98 Mich. 110; s. c., 56 N. W. Rep. 1105.

[3] Sutton v. Head (Ky.), 5 S. W. Rep. 410. A provision in a deed

§ 51. **The Grantor Restrained by the Terms of the Conveyance.**—Where a grantor, by the conditions of the sale and conveyance of land, is restricted in the pursuit of his business, the covenant will be upheld, and if violated will be enforced by injunction. In the city of Brooklyn, G obtained a contract for the purchase of a lot situated in a section of the city occupied by residences of people of wealth and social standing, and in which there were no tenement houses. On his announcement of his intention to erect a seven-story flat in close proximity to plaintiff's residence, plaintiff bought his contract and obtained possession of the lot. One of the conditions of the purchase was that G should not "construct or erect any flats in plaintiff's immediate neighborhood." Soon after the sale G commenced the erection of a flat opposite the lot sold, but before the completion of the work sold the lot to his wife, who had knowledge of the contract with plaintiff, for about one-third of its value, and continued the building of the flat as her agent. It was held that the erection of the flat would be enjoined, inasmuch as the wife bought the land subject to the plaintiff's equities, which attached as soon as he acquired title to the same.[1] In the opinion in this case, the court said: "It is true and should be noted, that in

that the premises conveyed "are not to be used for saloon or dram-shop purposes," merely prevents the use of a particular piece of property in a certain way, and is not void as in restraint of trade. Star Brewery Co. v. Primas, 163 Ill. 652; s. c., 45 N. E. Rep. 145.

[1] Lewis v. Gollner, 129 N. Y. 227; s. c., 29 N. E. Rep. 81. "If the contract remains technically a personal one, I think the reasonable and settled doctrine is that the contract equity is so attached to the use of the land, which is the subject-matter, as to follow the land itself into the hands of a purchaser with a full knowledge of all the facts, who buys with his eyes open to the existing equity, and more especially when he buys for the express purpose of defeating and evading that equity. It has been held that the equity resulting from a valid agreement, although the latter was not a covenant running with the land, or a legal exception or reservation out of it, but stood solely upon the ground of a personal contract, dictating the mode of a user, would, nevertheless, go with the land into the hands of a purchaser, with notice, and who did not buy innocently or in good faith." *Ibid.*, p. 236. See also Whitney v. Union Ry. Co., 11 Gray, 363.

these cases the restrictions followed the line of title and were imposed by the original owners and vendors of the land, while here they were not so imposed, but came from one never an owner of the land, but deriving his right from a contract with one who did become such owner. But why should that difference change the result? The original owner's right rests upon one consideration and that of the stranger to the title upon another, but each are equally good and worthy of equitable regard. In Parker v. Nightingale,[1] it is declared not to be in the least material that the restrictive stipulations should be binding at law, or that any privity of estate should subsist between parties in order to render them obligatory and to warrant equitable relief in case of their infraction. I think that doctrine is sound and just. The source of the restriction would seem to be immaterial if itself binding and founded upon sufficient consideration, and a breach is no greater wrong to a privy in estate than to a stranger validly contracting about its use. Nor can the vendee in bad faith stand upon such a difference. Equity has no compassion for a fraud, and he who buys in aid of one with full knowledge of what is right, but with purpose to defeat it, should not escape the hand of equity by a criticism upon the origin of the restriction violated.''[2]

§ 52. **Contracts Relating to Trade Secrets.**—It is a well established principle of public policy that useful and valuable discoveries and inventions are to be encouraged. They are afforded all necessary protection by the law on the ground that the discoverer or inventor is entitled to a proper recompense for the labor and expense incurred in bringing his discovery or invention to perfection, and for the farther reason that it is for the public interest that work of this character should be done. In other words, the protection afforded is a matter of justice and for the promotion of the public welfare. A valuable discovery, before it is divulged, is the property of the discoverer. It

[1] Parker v. Nightingale, 6 Allen, 344.

[2] Lewis v. Gollner, 129 N. Y. 227, 236.

is his privilege to keep his secret and to avail himself, as far as practicable, of its benefits; or, if that promises a larger measure of profit, to dispose of it. Since the sale of the secret is, presumptively, not in restraint of trade but for its extension, it is not in contravention of public policy, and any contract relating to it will be enforced. In a recent leading case before the Supreme Court of the United States, relating to a proprietary medicine, the court said: "Relating as these contracts did to a compound involving a secret in its preparation; based as they were upon a valuable consideration, and limited as to the space within which, though unlimited as to the time for which, the restraint was to operate, we are unable to perceive how they could be regarded as so unreasonable as to justify the court in declining to enforce them. The vendors were entitled to sell to the best advantage, and in so doing to exercise the right to preclude themselves from entering into competition with those who purchased, and to prevent competition between purchasers; and the purchasers were entitled to such protection as was reasonably necessary for their benefit. W had and transferred property in the secret process of manufacturing the article he had discovered, and he and his grantees could claim relief as against breaches of trust in respect to it. The policy of the law is to encourage useful discoveries by securing their fruits to those who make them. If the public found the balsam efficacious, they were interested in not being deprived of its use, but by whom it was sold was unimportant."[1] In a recent case

[1] Fowle v. Parke, 131 U. S. 88, 97. See also Bryson v. Whitehead, 1 Sim. & St. 74, and cases cited; Leather Cloth Co. v. Lorsont, L. R. 9 Eq. 345; s. c., 39 L. J. Ch. 82; 21 L. T. 661; 18 W. R. 572; Alcock v. Giberton, 5 Duer, 76; Gillis v. Hall, 2 Brewst. 341; Bowling v. Taylor, 40 Fed. Rep. 404; Benwell v. Inns, 24 Beav. 307; Harms v. Parsons, 32 Beav. 328; Rannie v. Irvine, 7 Man. & G. 969; Allsopp v. Wheatcroft, L. R. 15 Eq. 59. Under a bond to convey to the obligee the obligor's chocolate mill, "together with his exclusive right and art or secret manner of making chocolate and all information pertaining to his said manner of making chocolate," it is incumbent on the obligor, to convey such exclusive right, with a covenant that he will communicate all the information

relating to this point, before the Court of Appeals of the State of New York, the court said: "The business carried on by the defendant was founded on a secret process known only to herself and her agents. She had the right to continue the business and, by keeping her secret, to enjoy its

necessary to enable the obligee to use the right or secret art, and that he will not divulge the secret to any other person. Such a contract is not in restraint of trade. Vickery v. Welch, 19 Pick. 523. An instrument under seal was executed, upon a sale made by the plaintiff to the defendants, by which the former sold to the latter all his interest in the manufacture of porcelain teeth in the city of New York, with his stock on hand, and the good will of the business. The plaintiff covenanted to instruct one of the defendants in the art of manufacturing porcelain and incorruptible teeth, and to furnish him with his recipes therefor. The agreement also contained the following clause "and the party of the first part will not carry on or cause to be carried on by any person with whom he shall be interested, the manufacture of porcelain teeth, or impart the knowledge of manufacturing the same to any person, other than as aforesaid." It was alleged in the complaint, that the said art of manufacturing porcelain teeth, in which the defendant was to be instructed, was a secret of the plaintiff, and known to be such by the defendant. It was held on demurrer, that the covenant in question was valid, and not one in restraint of trade. Alcock v. Giberton, 5 Duer, 76. The defendant sold to the plaintiff a business of manufacturing and selling the "Government Carbolic Disinfectants," the process of manufacturing which was a secret in his possession, and covenanted not to carry on the business of a manufacturer or seller of the "Government Carbolic Disinfectants" or of any other article or thing of a disinfectant nature for fourteen years, and not to disclose the secret for the same period. The plaintiff brought this action, alleging that the defendant was infringing those covenants and seeking to restrain him. The defendant delivered a statement of defense, whereby he specifically denied that he was infringing the covenants, and further demurred on the ground that the covenant not to carry on such business was in restraint of trade and too general in its provisions. *Held*, that having regard to the subject-matter the covenant was not too general, and that the demurrer must be overruled. Hagg v. Darley, 47 L. J. Ch. 567. In a contract for the sale of the art and mystery of compounding and manufacturing an article of medicine and the exclusive right to make, use and vend the same, the vendor covenanted not to impart the art to any other person and not to make or vend the article himself; in consideration whereof the vendee covenanted to pay a certain sum of money in installments, at specified times. *Held*, that the covenants were independent, and that the vendor need not allege performance of the contract, on his part, in order to recover the money due. *Held*, also that it was benefits to any practicable extent. She also had the right to sell the business, including, as an essential part thereof, the secret process, and, in order to place the purchasers in the same position that she occupied, to promise to divulge

not necessary for the vendor to allege that there was in fact such an art or secret as was mentioned in the contract; or that it was in his exclusive possession. Such a contract is valid, and does not fall under the rule prohibiting a general restraint of trade. Hard v. Seeley, 47 Barb. 428. The principle upon which a contract in general restraint of trade is held to be void as against public policy, is that such a contract deprives the public of the enterprise and skill of one of the parties to the contract, and injures him, without any corresponding benefit to the party contracting for such restriction. Although the policy of the law does not permit general agreements in restraint of trade, a person who is engaged in a particular business which he is carrying on by means of a secret process which he has discovered, may sell the secret to another and may lawfully contract with the purchaser that he will not thereafter use that secret in such business without the consent of the purchaser and will will not disclose the secret to others. Jarvis v. Peck, 10 Paige Ch. 118. "If he invents or discovers, and keeps secret a process of manufacture whether a proper subject for a patent or not, he has not, indeed, an exclusive right to it as against the public or against those who in good faith acquire knowledge of it; but he has a property in it which a court of chancery will protect against one who in violation of contract and breach of confidence undertakes to apply it to his own use or to disclose it to third persons. The jurisdiction in equity to interfere by injunction to prevent such a breach of trust, when the injury would be irreparable and the remedy at law inadequate, is well established by authority. In the earliest reported case of this kind, Lord Eldon, indeed, refused to grant an injunction against imparting, in violation of an agreement, the secret, not only of a patent which had been obtained and had expired, and which the whole public was, therefore, entitled to use, but also that of making a certain kind of pills, for which no patent had been procured, and stated, as a reason for the latter, that if the art and method of preparing them was a secret, the court could not, without having it disclosed, ascertain whether it had been infringed. Newberry v. James, 2 Meriv. 446. But the same learned chancellor afterwards considered the general question as still an open one, whether a court of equity would restrain a party from divulging a secret in medicine, which was not protected by patent, but which he had promised to keep, and in such a case dissolved an injunction of the vice-chancellor, upon the sole ground that the defendant made affidavit that the secret was not derived from the plaintiff. Williams v. Williams, 3 Meriv. 157. And in a later case he unhesitatingly granted an injunction against one who, by the terms of his agreement with the secret to them alone and to keep it from every one else. In no other way could she sell what she had and get what it was worth. Having the right to make this promise she also had the right to make it good to her vendees and to protect them by covenants with proper safeguards against the consequences of any violation. Such a contract simply left matters substantially as they were before the sale, except that the seller of the secret had agreed that she would not destroy its value after she had received full value for it. The covenant was not in general restraint of trade, but was a reasonable measure of mutual protection to the parties, as it enabled the one to sell at the highest

the plaintiff, was not to be instructed in the secret, and who obtained a knowledge of it by a breach of trust. Lovatt v. Winyard, 1 Jac. & Walk. 394. Sir John Leach decreed, in one case, specific performance of an agreement by a trader to sell the good will of a business, and the exclusive secret of dyeing; and, in another, an account of the profits of a secret for making a medicine against a son of the inventor, holding it in trust for his brothers and sisters. Byron v. Whitehead, 1 Sim. & Stu. 74; Green v. Folgham, 1 Sim. & Stu. 398. In a more recent case, Morrison, the inventor and sole proprietor of a medicine, for which no patent had been obtained, entered into partnership with Moat, to whom he communicated the secret of making the medicine, but did not make the secret a part of the assets of the partnership, and reserved it to himself as against all other persons, and Moat covenanted not to reveal it to any person whomsoever. By subsequent agreement Morrison's sons and a son of Moat were admitted as partners in the business, and the secret was surreptitiously obtained from Moat by his son. After the death of both the original parties, on a bill brought by Morrison's sons, who were also legatees of the secret, against Moat's son, Vice-Chancellor Turner, in an elaborate judgment, reviewing all the English authorities, granted an injunction restraining the defendant from using the secret in any manner in compounding the medicine, and refused to restrain him from communicating the secret, simply for want of any allegation or evidence of any intention to communicate it. Morrison v. Moat, 9 Hare, 241. The defendant appealed, but the order was affirmed (21 L. J. Ch. 248), and Lord Cranworth, delivering the opinion of the Court of Appeal, said: 'The principles that were argued in this case, are principles really not to be called in controversy. There is no doubt whatever, that when a party who has a secret in trade employs persons under a contract, express or implied, those persons cannot gain the knowledge of the secret, and then set it up against their employer.'" Gray, J., in Peabody v. Norfolk, 98 Mass. 452, 458.

price and the other to get what they paid for. It imposed no restriction upon either that was not beneficial to the other by enhancing the price to the seller or protecting the purchaser. Recent cases make it clear that such an agreement is not opposed to public policy, even if the restriction was unlimited as to both time and territory."[1] Where a contract relating to a trade secret is of such a character that the effect of it will be prejudicial to the public interest it will not be sustained. In a case in Massachusetts it was held that a contract made between citizens of this commonwealth, by which one of them agreed for a good consideration, never to "set up, exercise or carry on the trade or business of manufacturing and selling shoe-cutters at any place within the commonwealth of Massachusetts," is illegal as being in restraint of trade, although the manufacture of shoe-cutters is an art which can only be carried on by persons instructed in the same, and at the time of making the above contract the person so promising was ignorant of said art, and his said promise was made as a part of an agreement of partnership with one who was skilled and actually engaged in carrying on the same, and to take effect at the expiration of the partnership, and although at that time only three other persons were engaged in the business.[2]

§ 53. **Restraint of Trade by Patents.**—It is public policy to encourage useful inventions by granting the inventor a monopoly in the manufacture and sale of the article invented for a limited period. In a recent case before the United States Circuit Court for the Eastern District of Missouri, the rule is stated, as follows: "The entire theory and purpose of our patent laws is to create a limited monopoly. In consideration that a patentee will give his invention to the public, with full drawings and specifications so as to enable the public to freely use it at the expiration of seventeen years, a grant is made to him of an exclusive right to the monopoly of the patented article or device

[1] Tode v. Gross, 127 N. Y. 480, 485.

[2] Taylor v. Blanchard, 13 Allen, 370.

during that time. The rights so acquired by the patentee under a grant from the United States are entirely inconsistent with the patentee's being made subject to the provisions of the anti-trust laws of the several States. Under his grant he has been given, and for the consideration alluded to, is entitled to maintain a monopoly in the disposition or use of the patented article or device."[1] Public

[1] Columbia Wire Co. v. Freeman Wire Co., 71 Fed. Rep. 302, 306. See also Edison Electric Light Co. v. Sawyer-Mann Electric Co., 3 C. C. A. 605; s. c., 53 Fed. Rep. 592; Strait v. Harrow Co., 51 Fed. Rep. 819; Soda Fountain Co. v. Green, 69 Fed. Rep. 333; Billings v. Ames, 32 Mo. 265. "The objection that the covenants are void as being in restraint of trade, cannot be supported, admitting that all the patents are void. Agreements to restrain trade in particular places, founded on a reasonable consideration, are valid in law, and may be enforced. Here was a sufficient consideration, whether the patents were valid or not. Being the inventors of these machines, the parties may obtain valid patents for them; or, without thus securing a monopoly, they might reasonably expect to enjoy it, in fact, by means of their superior skill. For a time, at least, they would have little to fear from the competition of others. It was, therefore, lawful and reasonable for them to share in the profits of their invention, either by uniting in a joint concern, or by a more convenient arrangement, whereby each one might have the benefit of his own capital, industry and activity." Stearns v. Barrett, 1 Pick. 443; s. c., 11 Am. Dec. 223, 227. The invalidity of a patent does not destroy the consideration for a contract, based on its supposed validity, to settle litigation under it, and fix the respective rights of the parties, especially where the contract includes mutual covenants as to the conduct of their business, and is partly executed before the invalidity is discovered. Gloucester Isinglass & Glue Co. v. Russia Cement Co., 154 Mass. 92; s. c., 12 L. R. A. 563. The grant of the right to make, use and vend a patented article "within the southern half of Alabama, less C county," is not void for uncertainty in defining the boundaries of the territory. Dudley v. Suddoth (1891), 91 Ala. 349; s. c., 8 So. Rep. 873. "Considerations which might obtain, if the agreement were in regard to other articles, cannot be of any weight in the decision of a question arising upon an agreement as to patented articles. If an owner of a patent should choose to refuse to manufacture the article covered by his patent, could anyone else claim such right? His simple neglect or refusal to manufacture would stand as a conclusive reason why it was not manufactured. An owner might sometimes make more money by not manufacturing than by doing so, but of that question he is the sole and absolute judge." Good v. Daland, 121 N. Y. 1, 8; s. c., 24 N. E. Rep. 15, 16. Complainants, who were manufacturing, under patents. stays which consisted of a stiffening blade having a sheet of rubber on each side,

policy so far favors the inventor that it not only upholds his monopoly, but also legalizing any proper sale of his patents, whether already acquired or prospective. In a recent English case, it was held that an agreement by the vendor of a patent to assign to the purchaser all future patent rights which the vendor may hereafter acquire of a like nature to the patent sold, is not contrary to public policy.[1] In his opinion in this case, Sir George Jessel, M. R., said: "Now, nothing is better known than this, that when persons have turned their attention to a particular class of invention they are likely to go on and invent, and likely to continuously improve the nature of their invention, and continuously to discover new modes of attaining the end desired. Persons, therefore, who buy patents of inventors are in the habit of protecting themselves from the utter destruction of the value of the thing purchased by bargaining with the seller that he shall not use any new invention of his for producing that product in which they are about to deal at a cheaper rate, because if he were allowed to do so he might, the day after he had sold his patent, produce something which, without being technically an improvement, might accomplish the desired object in some other way, and utterly destroy the value of that which they

and an outer layer of cloth over each sheet, and defendant, who was making two kinds of stays, the "Bridgeport" and the "Self-Attaching," both of which complainants claimed to be infringements on their patent, entered into an agreement by which complainants licensed defendant to make the "The Self-Attaching," providing that he would not make the "Bridgeport" stay, and defendant agreed to make no stays consisting of a steel, a layer of gutta percha, and two outer layers of fabric. By a supplemental agreement they confined themselves to the manufacture of the "Self-Attaching" by the defendant, and the "Ypsilanti No. 1" by complainants, the latter being a stay of the double layer kind; but it was agreed that complainants might put a cheaper double layer stay on the market, provided they would furnish defendant, at a certain price, the same quantity of such cheaper stay as should be sold by themselves. *Held*, that this contract was not in restraint of trade. Bowling v. Taylor, 40 Fed. Rep. 404.

[1] Printing, etc. Co. v. Sampson, L. R. 19 Eq. 462. See also Jones v. Lees, 1 Hurl. & N. 189; s. c., 2 Jur. (N. S.), 645; 26 L. J. Excheq. 9.

had purchased. They, therefore, not unreasonably, and not unusually, make it a part of their bargain that whatever the man discovers of the same kind in the shape of machinery or apparatus which will produce the product in which they are about to deal shall belong to them. They say 'we cannot buy on any other terms, because otherwise we are exposed to the instantaneous, or almost instantaneous, competition of the inventor with the benefit of his previous experience.' That, as I said before, is not an unusual, nor is it an unreasonable bargain."[1] In a similar case in Massachusetts, it was held that a covenant made by the patentee of a process of manufacture in a business not local in its character, for the purpose of selling the patent to better advantage, and as a part of the transaction of sale, and for one and the same consideration received by him for the patent, to use his best efforts to invent improvements in the process and to transfer them to the buyer, to do no act which may injure the buyer or business, and "at no time to aid, assist or encourage in any manner any competition against the same," is not necessarily void as in restraint of trade.[2]

[1] Printing, etc. Co. v. Sampson, L. R. 19 Eq. 462, 464.

[2] Morse Twist & Drill Co. v. Morse, 103 Mass. 73. Three manufacturers of a certain kind of curtain fixture, under different letters patent owned by them severally, desiring to avoid competition, formed a corporation in which they were the only stockholders, and an agreement was executed by the corporation, of the one part, and the three manufacturers, of the other part, by the terms of which the manufacturers gave the corporation the sole right to sell said curtain fixtures for three years, the corporation agreeing to buy at a specified price all that the manufacturers might make, and the manufacturers, acting as the selling agents of the corporation, and receiving a commission on goods sold by them. The agreement further provided, that during the term of the contract the manufacturers should not dispose of their patents, except upon such terms that a transferee should be bound by the agreement, and that they should not dispose of their stock in the corporation without the written assent of a majority of the stockholders. *Held*, that the agreement was not void as against public policy, and that the court would restrain, by injunction, one of the manufacturers from selling goods on his own account, in violation of the agreement. Central Shade Roller Co. v. Cushman, 143 Mass. 353.

§ 54. Where Contracts Relating to Patents are not Upheld.—The general principle that the restriction provided for by a contract must not be greater than is reasonable, or is essential to the protection of the purchaser, applies to all covenants relating to patents. As has already appeared, a patentee may dispose of his patents and any reasonable contract relating to such sale will be enforced, but it is valid only as the restraint of trade is not unnecessary or unreasonable. In a leading case in Wisconsin, the defendant, a carpenter and joiner, and inventor of sand papering machines, sold his interest in certain patents upon such machines and the business of a firm engaged in the manufacture and sale thereof. In the contract of sale he covenanted that he would not thereafter "manufacture, sell or cause to be sold any sand papering machines of any description," unless with the consent of the purchaser of said patents, etc. It was held, the restriction being greater than is reasonably necessary to protect the purchaser in the enjoyment of the patents and business purchased, and prohibiting the defendant from pursuing his trade or profession of inventing sand papering machines, is void as against public policy, although it affects only a single class of machines.[1] In the well considered opinion in this case, by

[1] Berlin Machine Works v. Perry, 71 Wis. 495; s. c., 38 N. W. Rep. 82. This case arose under the following circumstances. In February. 1884. and previously. the defendant, James Perry. and one Charles A. Mather. were engaged at Berlin. Wis., as partners in the manufacture and sale of wood polishing and sand papering machines of which Perry. either solely or jointly with others, was the inventor. and upon which he then held and owned five letters patent issued to such inventors by the United States. These machines were bulky and expensive. a large capital was required to carry on the successful manufacture and sale of them. and they were only sold and used in large cities. It is not alleged that the business extends beyond the United States. In February. 1884, Perry sold his interest in such business. with the good will thereof. also in all the property of the firm, in the letters patent before mentioned. and in an application for another patent then pending before the United States commissioner of patents. for the sum of $20,000. The contract of sale contained a stipulation by Perry to apply for letters patent on another invention of his, being "improvements in sand paper machines and planer combined for cleaning sashes, doors and blinds,

Mr. Justice Lyon, the court said: "An alleged rule to the effect that restrictions of the character under consideration if made as incidental to the sale of patents and a business thereunder, are valid, no matter how general and unlimited such restrictions may be, is invoked to uphold this covenant. But the cases cited to sustain such a rule do not sustain it as broadly as claimed. They hold that such restriction is valid only when, in the judgment of the court, it is not unreasonable, due regard being had to the subject-matter of the covenant. Tested by that rule, we have seen that the restriction in this case is not a reasonable one, because not necessary to the protection of the covenantee. In other words, this restriction is not in any correct sense of the term incidental to the sale of patents and a business thereunder, but reaches far beyond the point of just and lawful protection to such business. It is also argued that because the restriction affects only a single class of machines and does not cover the trade of a machinist, it is not within the rule which vitiates contracts in restraint of trade. The position cannot be sustained. While the restriction only relates to sand papering machines, the defendant is an inventor of such machines, and the covenant unreasonably and unnecessarily prohibits him from pursuing his trade or profession. It is, therefore, within the rule that such covenants are void."[1]

etc., and, when obtained, to assign such letters patent to Mather. The material stipulation in the contract of sale is to the effect that Perry 'will not hereafter manufacture, sell or cause to be sold any sand papering machines of any description,' unless with the consent of Mather. The plaintiff corporation has acquired by mesne assignments and transfers, the whole interest in the business, including the interest thus sold by Perry to Mather, and the benefit of the stipulation last above mentioned, and is now carrying on the business under the same letters patent, at Berlin aforesaid. Perry is a carpenter and joiner by education and trade, and formerly carried on a certain business in that line. He is the inventor, solely in some cases, and jointly with another person in others, of the devices and machines covered by the letters patent above mentioned.

[1] Berlin Machine Works v. Perry, 71 Wis. 495, 501; s. c., 38 N. W. Rep. 82.

§ 55. Restraint in the Sale of a Trade-Mark.—The general principles under which the sale of patents is upheld are applicable to the sale of trade-marks. A trade-mark under which a profitable business in the manufacture and sale of any article has been established is of value, and any reasonable contract relating to it will be sustained. The idea of a trade-mark, like that of a patent, is to protect a monopoly or a restraint of trade, and the sale of a trade-mark, where the restraint imposed is not greater than necessary and reasonable, will be upheld. In the leading case on this point, where B, the proprietor of a medicine known as "Brewer's Lung Restorer," sold the same with the exclusive right to manufacture and sell it, surrendered his trade-mark to the purchaser, and agreed "never to use or permit my name to be used on any preparation which would be recommended and sold for the same purposes as Brewer's Lung Restorer is used and sold for," such contract is in partial, not general, restraint of trade; and being for a valuable consideration is not unreasonable. Such contract does not limit the skill of the vendor in compounding medicines for the cure of throat and lung diseases, but stipulates that his name shall not appear with his consent on such medicines. The publishing and offering for sale of "Brewer's Sarsaparilla Syrup, professing to be a permanent cure for all diseases of the lungs and throat" is a violation of the contract; and the vendor being insolvent, equity will enjoin such action.[1] In the opinion in this case,

[1] Brewer v. Lamar, 69 Ga. 656. "Within a month subsequent to the death of the senior partner of the firm, his executors sold and conveyed all the interest of the decedent in the business to the surviving partner and complainant whereby they, under the firm name of Fleming Brothers, acquired not only the title to the receipt and the right to make the pills, but also the right to use the labels and trade-marks used by the former owners. Possessed of the whole interest, they (the firm Fleming Brothers) prosecuted the business, with some changes in the individual partners, until July 1st, 1865, when the present complainant sold out his whole interest to his brother, John Fleming, who, as sole proprietor of what the firm owned, continued the business until the 2d day of November, 1870, when he died, leaving a last will and testament. * * * In such cases, the question is not whether the complainant was the original in-

the court said: "But are the covenants of this contract in general restraint of trade? The stipulation which it is alleged is void for this cause is in these words: 'I agree never to use or permit my name to be used on any prepara-

ventor or proprietor of the article made by him, and on which he puts his trade-mark, nor whether the article made and sold under his trade-mark by the respondent is equal to his own in value or quality; but the court proceeds on the ground that the complainant has a valuable interest in the good will of his trade or business, and having a particular label, sign or trade-mark, indicating to his customers that the article bearing it is made or sold by him or by his authority, or that he carries on business at a particular place, he is entitled to protection against one who attempts to deprive him of his trade or customers by using such labels, signs or trade-mark without his knowledge or consent. Coats v. Holbrook, 2 Sandf. Ch. 586; Partridge v. Menck, 2 Barb. Ch. 101; s. c., 47 Am. Dec. 281. Everywhere courts of justice proceed upon the ground that a party has a valuable interest in the good will of his trade, and in the labels or trade-mark which he adopts to enlarge and perpetuate it. Hence, it is held that he, as proprietor, is entitled to protection as against one who attempts to deprive him of the benefit resulting from the same, by using his labels and trade-mark without his consent and authority. Decided cases to that effect are quite numerous, and it is doubtless correct to say that a person may have a right in his own name as a trade-mark as against a trader or dealer of a different name; but the better opinion is, that such a party is not, in general, entitled to the exclusive use of a name merely as such without more. Millington v. Fox, 3 Myl. & Cr. 338; Dent v. Turpin, 2 J. & H. 139; Meneely v. Meneely, 62 N. Y. 427; s. c., 20 Am. Rep. 489. * * * Such a proprietor, if he owns or controls the goods which he exposes to sale, is entitled to the exclusive use of any trade-mark adopted and applied, by him to the goods, to distinguish them as being of a particular manufacture and quality, even though he is not the manufacturer and the name of the real manufacturer is used as part of the device. Walton v. Crowley, 3 Blatchf. 440; Emerson v. Badger, 101 Mass. 82." Clifford, J., in McLean v. Fleming, 96 U. S. 245. See also Williams v. Johnson, 2 Bosw. 1; Leidersdorf v. Flint, 8 Biss. 327; Taylor v. Carpenter, 2 Sandf. Ch. 604; s. c., 42 Am. Dec. 114; Hall v. Barrows, 4 De G., J. & S. 158; McAndrews v. Bassett, 4 De G., J. & S. 386; Maxwell v. Hogg, L. R. 2 Ch. App. 314; Lawson v. Bank of London, 18 C. B. 84. "The principle on which all cases on the subject of trade-marks unite is, that one man will not be permitted, by imitating the distinctive name or mark used by another to designate articles of the latter's manufacture to impose articles of his own manufacture upon the public as the articles of the former. The cases so holding rest upon two considerations: First, that it would be a fraud on the rights of the former person thus to permit his trade-mark to be imition which could be recommended and sold for the same purpose.' Defendant below had already stipulated and did sell all his interest with trade-mark, etc., in the 'Lung Restorer,' to the defendants in error. Then in the stipulation above he agrees further 'never to use or permit his name to be used on any preparation which could be recommended and sold for the same purpose.' This stipulation does not forbid him to manufacture or sell such preparation as he

tated. Second, that it would also be a fraud on the public. See Gilman v. Hunnewell, 122 Mass. 139; McLean v. Fleming, 96 U. S. 245, 251; Coleman v. Crump, 70 N. Y. 573; Fairbanks v. Jacobus, 14 Blatchf. 337; Devlin v. Devlin, 67 Barb. 290; s. c., 25 Am. Rep. 173; Amoskeak Mfg. Co. v. Garner, 54 How. Pr. 297; Curtis v. Bryan, 2 Daly, 312; s. c., 36 How. Pr. 33; Amoskeag Mfg. Co. v. Spear, 2 Sandf. 607; Peterson v. Humphrey, 4 Abb. Pr. 394; Howe v. Howe Machine Co., 50 Barb. 236; Sykes v. Sykes, 3 B. & C. 541; s. c., 10 E. C. L. 176; Burgess v. Burgess, 3 De G., M. & G. 896, 904; Burke v. Cassin, 45 Cal. 467; s. c., 13 Am. Rep. 204; Emerson v. Badger, 101 Mass. 82; Ellis v. Zeilin, 42 Ga. 91; Lord Kingsdown in Leather Cloth Co. v. American Leather Cloth Co., 11 H. L. Cas. 538; Perry v. Truefitt, 6 Beav. 66; Walton v. Crowley, 3 Blatchf. 448; Dixon Crucible Co. v. Guggenheimer, 1 Cox's Man. of Trade-Mark Cases, 559. * * * There are some *quasi* proprietary rights, such as an elective franchise, which are incapable of assignment. But it would be obviously unjust to restrict the right to use a trade-mark. The advantages which accrue from the use of a particular trade-mark or advertising device are often the result of a lifetime of integrity, skill, perseverance and business capacity. Ought it to be held that a right so valuable should die with the person who created it, it being incapable of assignment, when, by reason of age, or other considerations, he might desire to cease using it? The custom of trade, which solves many questions in advance of the courts, has declared that this should not be, and the courts in adopting the view that the right to use a trade-mark is assignable, did no more than declare a result which followed from the concession that it was property; for the *jus disponendi* is embodied in the very idea of property. It is, hence, settled law that the right to use a trade-mark is not a mere personal privilege, but that, within certain limits, it is capable of being bought and sold as other property. 'A trade-mark,' says Strong, J., 'like the good will of a store or manufacturing establishment, is a subject of commerce, and it has been many times held entitled to protection at the suit of vendees.' Fulton v. Sellers, 4 Brewst. 42. See also Bury v. Bedford, 33 L. J. Ch. 465; Hall v. Barrows, 33 L. J. Ch. 204; Glenn, etc. Mfg. Co. v. Hall, 61 N. Y. 226; s. c., 19 Am. Rep. 278; Peltz v. Eichele, 62 Mo. 171." Thompson, J., in Skinner v. Oakes, 10 Mo. App. 45.

may compound, or either, but that he will not himself use his name or permit his name to be used on any such preparation. The only restraint the covenant imposes on him is that his name shall not appear by his consent on such preparation. Can this stipulation be said to be in general restraint of trade, or is it not rather a partial restraint, and is it at all unreasonable? The absence of his name may limit the sales of any new preparation he may compound; the preparation may be wanting in the magic word, but for its absence he contracted and received a consideration therefor. He may compound and sell a score of other nostrums to cure the diseases for which the Lung Restorer is fitted; the only inhibition is he must not put on them the cabalistic word 'Brewer,' and thus violate the contract which he has entered into. That he has done this, the evidence abundantly shows, when he published and offered upon the market 'Brewer's Sarsaparilla Syrup, professing to be a permanent cure for all diseases of the lungs and throat.'"[1]

§ 56. **Restriction in Publication Contract.**—In covenants relating to the sale of periodical publications by publishers, or to the sale of articles written for such publications by the authors, such restrictions as constitute a necessary and reasonable protection to the vendee will be upheld. In Ainsworth v. Bentley, the plaintiff had purchased of the defendant a well established magazine. The contract relating to the sale provided that the defendant should not publish another periodical of a similar nature. Fourteen years later the defendant entered into an arrangement to become the publisher of "Temple Bar," a publication of a like character and within the restriction of the contract. On the trial it was claimed by counsel for the defendant that the agreement was void as in restraint of trade and unlimited, and also that magazine publishing was a trade of itself. It was held that an agreement by a publisher not to publish in future a magazine of a particular

[1] Brewer v. Lamar, 69 Ga. 656, 660.

description, is analogous to an agreement by a tradesman not to deal in a particular article, and, like this latter agreement, is not void as a too general restraint of trade.[1] In a case in Massachusetts, the court said: "In this country there are periodical publications that have a very wide circulation, and it is obvious that a purchaser of the proprietorship cannot afford to pay the full value, unless he can obtain from the vendor a valid restriction against competition, which restriction shall be so extensive as his interest requires, although it may cover the whole of a State, or the whole country. The same would be true as to some books. For example, the author of a popular school book could not sell its proprietorship for its full value unless he could bind himself not to prepare another book which should be used in competition with it."[2] In October, 1857, A, being the proprietor of a weekly publication called "The London Journal," the price of which was 1d., assigned his copyright and interest therein to B for value, and entered into a covenant with B not to publish either alone or in partnership with any other person any weekly periodical of a nature similar to "The London Journal." In May, 1859, he issued an advertisement announcing the publication by him on the 1st June following of a daily newspaper to be called "The Daily London

[1] Ainsworth v. Bentley, 14 W. R. 630. The chief defenses that had been raised were—first, that the agreement was illegal as being too general a restraint of trade; and, secondly, that the agreement was so vague and uncertain that the court could not restrain an infringement of it. As to the first defense, it had never been decided that a person could not be compelled to observe and keep an undertaking not to sell or deal in a particular article of trade. On the contrary, it had often been held that the proprietor of an article might dispose of it to another and legally bind himself never again to deal in that article, or in any article professing to be similar to or identical with it. This was the case here. Mr. Bentley had disposed of his Miscellany to the plaintiff and had undertaken to publish nothing of the kind afterwards. By being bound to abide by that agreement he would be no worse a publisher than he was before; he would only be precluded from publishing anything of a particular kind." *Ibid.*, p. 632.

[2] Morse Twist Co. v. Morse, 103 Mass. 73, 77.

Journal," and to be sold at 1d. B thereupon filed his bill against A for an injunction to restrain A from publishing "The Daily London Journal," and Sir W. P. Wood, V. C., made an order for an injunction. Upon appeal, Sir J. L. Knight Bruce, L. J., confirmed the order for an injunction, upon B undertaking to abide by any order the court might make as to damages, and to bring an action against A within one week.[1] In a case relating to the sale of articles for

[1] Ingram v. Stiff, 5 Jur. (N. S.) 947. This was an appeal by the defendant from an order of Sir W. P. Wood, V. C., for an injunction to restrain the defendant from printing, publishing or selling any newspaper or other periodical under the name of "The Daily London Journal," or under any other name or style of which the words "London Journal" should form part, and from doing or committing any act or default that might tend to lessen or diminish the sale or circulation of the plaintiff's periodical called "The London Journal." The following were the facts of the case: Prior to September, 1857, the defendant was the proprietor and publisher of a well-known periodical called "The London Journal," which was published by him at his office, No. 334 Strand. The publication was not a newspaper, but it contained tales and romances, which were illustrated with wood engravings, and a portion of each week's number was devoted to answers to correspondents. Its circulation then amounted to nearly 500,000 per week. In September, 1857, the plaintiff, Mr. Herbert Ingram, entered into an agreement for the purchase from the defendant of the copyright in "The London Journal" for the sum of £20,000, and also the plant thereof from the defendant for the further sum of £4,000. By the deed of assignment, which bore date the 8th of October, 1857, the defendant covenanted that he would not, directly or indirectly, alone or in partnership with any other person or persons, engage himself or be concerned in bringing out or publishing any weekly periodical of a nature similar to "The London Journal" selling at 1d. per copy, or commit any act or default which might tend to lessen or diminish the sale or circulation of the said periodical, or the profit to be derived by the plaintiff from the future printing or publishing thereof. The assignment was duly registered at Stationer's Hall. The plaintiff continued for some months after the date of the deed of assignment to publish "The London Journal" in defendant's office, No. 334 Strand; but in April, 1858, the the plaintiff removed the publication of that periodical to premises which he took at Nos. 140 and 141 Strand, nearly opposite to the defendant's office. Shortly after such removal, a new publication was published at No. 334 Strand, by a Mr. George Smith, which was, in appearance, nature of contents and style of illustration, precisely similar to "The London Journal." The day of publication and the price were also the same as those of "The London Journal," and the

a periodical, S. proprietor of a weekly newspaper, by a letter to F, an author, agreed that F should write two tales extending over one year, at £10 per week for each number, to contain about the same quantity as was sent under a former similar engagement and to receive the first number on the 22d April, 1855, and to continue to receive one number weekly during one year, conditionally that F should not write for any other newspaper published at less than 6d. F accepted, received £20 deposit and wrote regularly for some weeks, then went to Paris, sent an abrupt conclusion of the then current tale in a small quantity of manuscript, refused to proceed with his engagement with S. and entered into another engagement with C. S thereupon stopped his payment to F, and employed another author to conclude the half finished tale. It was held on demurrer by F (1) that the above engagement was a yearly engagement and could not be closed by F as a weekly engagement. (2) That the condition as to F not engaging elsewhere was valid.[1]

title of the new publication was, "The Guide to Literature and Art." Towards the close of the month of May, in the present year, the attention of the plaintiff was called to advertisements issued by the defendant announcing the publication, on the 1st of June, then next, of a daily newspaper, price 1d., to be called "The London Daily Journal," to be published at No. 334 Strand, and of which the defendant was the sole registered proprietor. The plaintiff thereupon filed the present bill, praying for an injunction to restrain the defendant from publishing "The London Daily Journal." Upon the hearing of the motion, before Sir W. P. Wood, V. C., his Honor made an order for an injunction in the terms stated, being of opinion that it was a case of gross fraud on the part of the defendant, and on that account he refused to put the plaintiff on any terms as to damages. The defendant appealed from that decision. From the evidence it appeared that the plaintiff had already been frequently put to great inconvenience by the delivery at the defendant's office of letters intended for the plaintiff.

[1] Stiff v. Cassell, 2 Jur. (N. S.) 348. A bond or agreement which creates a partial or particular restraint of trade is good, if formed upon an adequate consideration; and specific performance will be decreed. Where N sells out a newspaper establishment to W and T, and by bond and covenant stipulates not to set up another paper within a certain time and distance, and N afterwards buys out T's moiety and becomes joint proprietor with W, the remedy at law against N upon the bond and cove-

nant is gone. Noah v. Webb, 1 Edw. Ch. 603. "Again it is supposed that a man who has obtained money for the future products of his brain will not be ready to produce these products. That must not be assumed. Nothing is more common in intellectual pursuits than for men to sell beforehand, the future intellectual product before it is made, or even conceived. Does any one imagine that it is against public policy for the artist to sell the picture which he has never painted or designed, or for the sculptor to sell the statue, the subject of which is hereafter to be given to him, or for the author to sell the copyright of the book, the title of which is even as yet unknown, or, more than that, that a contributor to a periodical may agree that he will devote himself to the exclusive service of a certain periodical for a given time for a given reward? These examples are, to my mind, entirely repugnant to the argument that there is any public policy in prohibiting such contract. * * * A man who is a needy and struggling inventor may well agree either for a present payment in money down, or for an annual payment to put his intellectual gifts at the service of a purchaser. I see, therefore, not only no rule of public policy against it, but a rule of public policy for it, because it may enable such a man in comparative ease and affluence to devote his attention to scientific research, whereas, if such a contract were prohibited, he would be compelled to apply himself to some menial or mechanical or lower calling in order to gain a livelihood." Jessell, M. R., in Printing, etc. Co. v. Sampson, L. R. 19 Eq. 462, 465. See also Tallis v. Tallis, 1 El. & Bl. 391; Ward v. Beeton, 23 W. R. 533; Spicer v. Hoop, 51 Ind. 365; Presbury v. Fisher, 18 Mo. 50; Dakin v. Williams, 11 Wend. 67; Beal v. Chase, 31 Mich. 490. See also Cowan v. Fairbrother, 118 N. Car. 406; s. c., 24 S. E. Rep. 212.

CHAPTER III.

CONTRACTS RELATING TO PROFESSIONS AND TRADES.

§ 57. Introductory.
58. Contract for the Sale of a Physician's Practice.
59. The Subject Continued.
60. The Rule as Applied to Attorneys.
61. The Rule as Applied to Dentists.
62. Application of the Rule to the Profession of Teaching.
§ 63. Restraint upon the Services of Artists and Actors.
64. As Applied to Trades and other Occupations.
65. In its Application to Traveling Salesmen.
66. Constraint of Trade Construed as a Limited Partnership.

§ 57. **Introductory.**—It is well established that a covenant under which one of the parties, for a valuable consideration, binds himself not to continue the practice of a profession or the pursuit of a trade is valid, provided the limitations are not unreasonable. The reasonableness and fairness of the contract is the test of its validity. If there is a good consideration and the restraint imposed is not greater than is essential to the adequate protection of the vendee, and in consequence is not in contravention of public policy, it will be upheld. This is the rule in England and it is sustained by the American courts. In the leading English case of Horner v. Graves, Chief Justice Tindal stated the rule, as follows: "We do not see how a better test can be applied to the question whether this is or not a reasonable restraint of trade, than by considering whether the restraint is such only as to afford a fair protection to the interests of the party in favor of whom it is given and not so large as to interfere with the interests of the public.

Whatever restraint is larger than the necessary protection of the party requires, can be of no benefit to either; it can only be oppressive, and if oppressive, it is in the eye of the law unreasonable. Whatever is injurious to the interests of the public is void on the grounds of public policy."[1]

[1] Horner v. Graves, 7 Bing. 735, 743. "An agreement not to engage in or pursue a particular business or profession, when made on a good consideration, with one whose business interest it is to prevent competition is valid, if restrained within reasonable limits, is too well settled to be regarded as an open question. The agreement also belongs to that class with respect to which it is competent for the parties, by agreement, to liquidate the damages which should be recoverable on a breach." Hoagland v. Segur, 38 N. J. L. 230, 235. Contracts restraining the exercise of a trade or profession in a particular locality, are good and valid, if there be a fair and reasonable ground for the restriction. The restraint, however, to be lawful, must be confined within reasonable limits. Guerand v. Dandelet, 32 Md. 561. The defendant entered into an agreement with the plaintiff, as his employer, that he would not accept another situation, or establish himself in any business, within fifteen miles of London without the written consent of the plaintiff, for a period of three years after leaving the plaintiff's service; but such permission was not to be withheld if it could be proved to the satisfaction of the plaintiff that the situation sought or the business established, was not for the sale of the same class of goods as those sold by the plaintiff. *Held*, on a motion for an injunction to restrain the defendant from breaking the agreement, that the clause providing that the plaintiff's permission was not to be withheld unless the business in which the defendant engaged was in the same class of goods as the plaintiffs, showed that the restrictive clause was intended to apply to all kinds of business whatsoever, and was, therefore, wider than was necessary for the protection of the plaintiff, and void. Perls v. Saalfield, L. R. (1892) 2 Ch. 149. The test to be applied in determining whether a restraint upon the exercise of a business, trade or profession is reasonable or not is to consider whether the restraint is only such as is necessary to afford a fair protection to the interests of the party in whose favor it is given, and not so large as to interfere with the interests of the public. Ellerman v. Chicago Junction, etc. Co., 49 N. J. Eq. 217; s. c., 23 Atl. Rep. 287. "The principle deducible from all the cases is that the question to be determined is, whether the restraint, having regard to all the circumstances of the case and the nature of the employment, is greater than necessary for the protection of the person in whose favor it is imposed." Lopes, L. J., in Mills v. Dunham, L. R. (1891) 1 Ch. 576, 587. The defendant on entering the service of the plaintiffs, a banking company, executed a bond in the penal sum of £1,000, the condition of which was that it should be void if he should perform his duties in

This rule, announced in 1831, is the law of the present, and in this country as well as in England. In a case in Minnesota the court said: "Formerly in England the courts frowned with great severity upon every contract of this kind. The reasons for this partly grew out of the English law of apprenticeship, by which, in its original severity, no person could exercise any regular trade or handicraft except after having served a long apprenticeship. Hence, if a person was prevented from pursuing his particular trade, he was practically deprived of all means of earning a liveli-

the manner therein mentioned, and also if he should, at any time within two years after his leaving the service of the plaintiffs accept any employment in any other bank within two miles of the plaintiffs' bank. The defendant resigned his employment in the plaintiffs' bank and immediately entered the service of a rival bank in the same town. The plaintiffs brought an action claiming an injunction to restrain the defendant from holding employment in any rival bank. The defendant was willing and offered to pay the penal sum of £1,000. *Held*, that the defendant could not satisfy his obligation by paying the penal sum; but that there was an agreement, between the parties, to be implied from the bond, that the defendant should not enter into the service of the rival bank, which could be enforced in a court of equity, and that the plaintiffs were entitled to an injunction. Nat'l Provincial Bank v. Marshall, L. R. 40 Ch. D. 112. "Although not conclusive on the subject, the opinion of mercantile men, manifested by their acts, is not to be disregarded on the question of reasonableness. In my opinion the clause is not unreasonable for the protection of the plaintiffs' trade. It amounts to this: The defendants say, 'for the limited period of three years you' (the plaintiffs) 'shall have a breathing spell, during which we will abstain from using the knowledge we have acquired in your employ against you by setting up a rival trade.' This is far remote from the case of an attempt to debar during a limited time a handicraftsman from plying his craft anywhere in the world; it is in effect a sale by the defendants of their interest in the good will of a large business built up by the capital, skill and industry of the contracting parties. The defendants have received a large remuneration, and, what is more, that which they themselves considered to be an adequate price for the contract on their part. To hold the stipulation void would tend to deprive persons in the position of the defendants of the advantage of making their own bargains for their remuneration, and would, in my opinion, unnecessarily interfere with their freedom of contract to their detriment and to an extent not required by law." Badisch Anilin Co. v. Schott, L. R. (1892) 3 Ch. 447, 453.

hood, and the State was deprived of his services. No such reason now obtains in this country, where every citizen is at liberty to change his occupation at will. Moreover, as cheaper and more rapid facilities for travel and transportation gradually changed the manner of doing business, so as to enable parties to conduct it over a vastly greater territory than formerly, the courts were necessarily compelled to readjust the standard of reasonableness of restrictions as to place.''[1] In the recent case of Sternberg v. O'Brien, the rule is stated by Vice-Chancellor Van Fleet, as follows: "The law is settled, that a contract in restraint of labor, which seeks to prevent one of the contracting parties from exercising his skill or labor generally, without limitation as to place or time, or which attempts to put a restraint upon his right to labor or to exercise his skill greater than is necessary for the fair protection of the other party to the contract, is void. 'Public policy,' said Vice-Chancellor James, afterwards one of the lord justices of the Court of Appeal of England, in Leather Cloth Co. v. Lorsont,[2] 'requires that every man shall be at liberty to work for himself, and shall not be at liberty to deprive himself or the State of his labor, skill or talent by any contract that he enters into.' 'The law,' said Best, C. J., in Homer v. Ashford,[3] 'will not permit any one to restrain a person from doing what the public welfare and his own interest require that he should do. Any deed, therefore, by which a person binds himself not to employ his talents, his industry or his capital in any useful undertaking in the kingdom would be void, because no good reason can be imagined for any person imposing such a restraint on himself.' 'So far has this principle been carried,' said Chief Justice Beasley, in Brewer v. Marshall,[4] 'that even in cases in which the restraint sought to be imposed is only partial, it has been repeatedly held that such agreement will be void, unless it be

[1] Nat'l Benefit Co. v. Union Hosp. Co., 45 Minn. 272, 275.

[2] Leather Cloth Co. v. Lorsont. L. R. 9 Eq. 345, 354.

[3] Homer v. Ashford, 3 Bing. 322. 326.

[4] Brewer v. Marshall, 4 C. E. Green, 537, 547.

reasonable, and that no such agreement can be reasonable in which the restraint imposed on the one party is larger than is necessary for the protection of the other.' The test which the law prescribes in all such cases is this: The restraint, in order to be valid, must be only such as is necessary to afford a fair protection to the party in favor of whom it is given, and not so large as to interfere with the interest of the public."[1]

§ 58. **Contract for the Sale of a Physician's Practice.** —The practice of a successful physician is recognized by the profession and by the law as a thing of value, and as such a proper subject for a contract for sale. There is a sense in which the practice of a physician belongs to him, and to that extent he may dispose of it for a consideration. In order to a valid sale he must devest himself of his right in it by a transfer to the vendee. He must bind himself not to continue a business which he has transferred to another for a consideration. A contract by which he is restrained from the continued practice of his profession, if the limitations are reasonable, will be upheld by a court of equity. In Butler v. Burleson, the court gave the rule as follows: "The contract between the parties is plain, clear and explicit, and according to the terms of it, the defendant agreed that, at the expiration of the partnership, if he did not purchase of the plaintiff, he would not settle within ten miles of the plaintiff without his consent; and a similar stipulation was entered into by the complainant, if the defendant did purchase. The intention of the parties, in relation to the term 'settle,' is sufficiently explicit by referring to the subject about which they were contracting; that is, they were not to settle in the practice of medicine within the limited distances. This contract is not forbidden by any principle of policy or law. Dr. B can be as useful to the public at any other town as at Berkshire, and the lives and health of persons in other villages are as important as they are there. Community are, therefore, not in-

[1] Sternberg v. O'Brien, 48 N. J. Eq. 370, 372; s. c., 22 Atl. Rep. 348. See also Mandeville v. Harman, 42 N. J. Eq. 185.

jured by any stipulation of this kind between two practicing and eminent physicians."[1] The rule relating to territorial limitations is stated in a recent case as follows: A contract by a physician: "Received of C $262 for my share of office fixtures and proceeds of practice for the month of March, and good will of business in town of W, and agree not to practice therein," is sufficiently definite to be enforced. Where in such a case it appears that it was the understanding of the parties that defendant should not practice within W or vicinity, defendant's chief practice having been in the surrounding country, the contract will be so construed. A contract whereby a physician agrees not to practice medicine within a certain town or vicinity is not void as against public policy.[2]

[1] Butler v. Burleson, 16 Vt. 176, 178. See also the following cases involving physicians' contracts: Davis v. Mason, 5 T. R. 118; Saniter v. Ferguson, 7 C. B. 716; Atkyns v. Kinnier, 4 Excheq. 776; Fox v. Scard, 33 Beav. 327; Gravelley v. Barnard, 43 L. J. Ch. 659; s. c., L. R. 18 Eq. 518; Mell v. Mooney, 30 Ga. 413; Goodman v. Henderson, 58 Ga. 567; Linn v. Sigsbee, 67 Ill. 75; Miller v. Elliott, 1 Ind. 484; Haldeman v. Simonton, 55 Iowa, 144; Warfield v. Booth, 33 Md. 63; Dwight v. Hamilton, 113 Mass. 175; Doty v. Martin, 32 Mich. 462; Timmerman v. Dever, 52 Mich. 34; Carroll v. Hickes, 10 Phila. 308; McNutt v. McEwen, 1 W. N. C. 552; Betts' Appeal, 10 W. N. C. 431; Bigony v. Tyson, 75 Pa. St. 157; McClurg's Appeal, 58 Pa. St. 51; Niver v. Rossman, 18 Barb. 50; Amedon v. Gannon, 6 Hun. 384; Holbrook v. Waters, 9 How. Pr. 335; Mott v. Mott, 11 Barb. 127; Smith v. Smith, 4 Wend. 468; Thompson v. Means, 11 Sm. & M. 604; Wilkinson v. Colley, 164 Pa. St. 35; s. c., 30 Atl. Rep. 286. "Contracts by professional men, such as physicians, surgeons, dentists and lawyers, when coming within the rule stated, not to practice their professions in competition with another pursuing the same calling, have time and again been enforced; and no distinction is made between their contracts and those of tradesmen. The suggestion that, while valid in a court of law, the agreement of a person not to pursue a profession involving the exercise of skill and learning will not be specifically performed in equity, is not tenable. The doubt expressed in an early English case has long since been resolved in favor of the jurisdiction of the chancery court, and numerous instances are to be found of its exercise when invoked to restrain by injunction the breach of a valid contract not to practice law or medicine in competition with the complaining party." McCurry v. Gibson (1895), 108 Ala. 451; s. c., 18 So. Rep. 806, 807.

[2] Cole v. Edwards, 93 Iowa, 477; s. c., 61 N. W. Rep. 940.

§ 59. **The Subject Continued.**—With regard to limitations in time there is some conflict of authorities. On the one hand it is held that a contract in restraint of the practice of a profession that is greater than is essential to the adequate protection of the grantor is unreasonable and void. On the other hand it is held that where there is a proper territorial limitation the limitation in time may be indefinite. In a recent case in New Jersey, it was held that in that State the rule as to contracts in restraint of trade is that a contract imposing a restraint larger than the necessary protection of the party requires, is void, and, hence, a covenant that a physician shall not, "at any time hereafter," engage in practice at Newark is void, since it would prevent such physician from practicing there though the other party to the covenant should die.[1] In the opinion in this case, the court said: "Professional skill, experience and reputation are things which cannot be bought or sold. They constitute part of the individuality of the particular person and die with him. There can be no doubt, I think, that if the complainant was the most distinguished physician of the city of Newark, and had by far the most lucrative practice in that city, and he should be so unfortunate as to die next month or next year, it would be impossible for his personal representative to sell his good will or practice as a thing of property, distinct from the office which he had occupied prior to his death, for any price, and, I think, it is equally obvious that if it were sold in connection with his office, the only possible value which could be ascribed to it would be the slight possibility that some of the persons who had been his patients might, when they needed the services of a physician, go or send there for the next occupant of the office. The practice of a physician is a thing so purely personal, depending so absolutely on the confidence reposed in his personal skill and ability, that when he ceases to exist it necessarily ceases also, and after his death can have neither an intrinsic nor a market value. And if the complainant should make sale of his practice in his lifetime it is

[1] Mandeville v. Harman, 42 N. J. Eq. 185; s. c., 7 Atl. Rep. 37.

manifest all the purchaser could possibly get would be immunity from competition with him, and, perhaps, his implied approval that the purchaser was fit to be his successor, but it would be impossible for him to transfer his professional skill and ability to his successor, or to induce anybody to believe that he had."[1] In support of the opposite view, the court, in the case of Martin v. Murphy, said:

[1] Mandeville v. Harman, 42 N. J. Eq. 185, 194; s. c., 7 Atl. Rep. 37. "These considerations make it apparent. I think, that the reason which induced the court of exchequer chamber to hold a like restraint valid in Hitchcock v. Coker, does not exist in this case. There a right or interest existed which, according to the law of Great Britain, would, on the death of its possessor, pass to his personal representative. No such right or interest exists here, at least its existence is as yet unrecognized in this State by law. No court of law of this State has as yet decided that a covenant between professional gentlemen, so extensive in duration as the one under consideration, is valid. There is strong reason to doubt its validity. It is one of the natural rights of every citizen of this State to use his skill and labor in any useful employment, not only to get food, raiment and shelter, but to acquire property, and I think it may be regarded as very certain that the courts will never deprive anyone of this right, or even abridge it, except in obedience to the sternest demands of justice. Chief Justice Beasley, in speaking of the covenant on trial in Brewer v. Marshall, 4 C. E. Green, 537, said that the restraint which it imposed was general both as to time, place and person, and it, therefore, transcended by far the limits of utility to the covenantee, and must, for that reason, be declared void. And Chief Justice Woodward, in Keeler v. Taylor, 53 Pa. St. 467, declared that such contracts, if they were not limited to a reasonable time as well as confined to a reasonable space, were void at law. He said, also, that if the terms they imposed were at all hard, equity would not enforce them. Vice-Chancellor Shadwell had previously given expression to the same view in Kimberley v. Jennings, 6 Sim. 340. Besides, no one can fail to see that if this covenant is valid and enforceable in equity, then it is competent for every merchant and trader, when he employs a clerk or shop girl, to require them, although the compensation he agrees to pay is no greater than that which is customarily paid for such service, to enter into a covenant that on quitting his service they will not, at any time afterwards, accept like employment from any other merchant or trader in the same town or city, and that if such covenants are made and subsequently broken, it will be the duty of this court to enforce them, though the consequence may be that a citizen will thereby be deprived of his only means of supporting himself and his family. It may well be doubted, I think, whether legal rules producing such consequences will ever be established merely by force of judicial action." *Ibid.*, 194.

"The objection that it is not sufficiently specific as to time is not tenable. M agrees 'to practice medicine no more in Salem after January 1st, 1888.' This is an agreement that he will never again practice medicine in Salem, and covers all time thereafter. This, appellee says, however, is unreasonable, and is a greater restraint than is necessary for the protection of the party, and is for that reason void. A contract for the general restraint of any business is illegal, but is otherwise if the restraint is reasonable and partial. Whether in a given case a restraint is reasonable is a question for the court. A contract reasonably limited as to territory in which the specific business is not to be carried on is not rendered invalid, because the restriction as to time is indefinite or general.[1] In Holbrook v. Waters, defendant bound himself with plaintiff by agreement in writing, in consideration of $500, not to practice medicine nor in any manner to do business as a physician in the county of Oswego at any time after the 1st day of May, 1851.[2] It was held that the contract was valid.[3]

§ 60. **The Rule as Applied to Attorneys.**—In general the sale of a practice by an attorney is subject to the rule as set forth in the foregoing section as applied to that of a physician. As in the latter case the question of legality

[1] Martin v. Murphy, 129 Ind. 464, 467.

[2] Holbrook v. Waters, 9 How. Pr. 335. Where, by a written contract, the defendant, a physician, sold his medical practice to the plaintiff and agreed not to "resettle" in the same town, it was held that he was bound thereby not to again take up his residence in such town for the practice of his profession, but that he might practice in that locality while residing elsewhere. Haldeman v. Simonton, 55 Iowa, 144. A executed a bond to B, conditioned to convey to him for a certain sum his land and buildings, and his practice and good will as a physician. To carry out the agreement, the money was paid by B's wife, and the real estate conveyed to her. In a suit brought by B to restrain A from practicing as a physician in violation of his agreement, *Held*, that as the money was paid by, and the real estate conveyed to, the wife, by consent of the parties, A could not object that B had failed to perform his part of the agreement. A contract by a physician for the sale of his "practice and good will" in a specified town, is not void as against public policy. Dwight v. Hamilton, 113 Mass. 175.

[3] Holbrook v. Waters, 9 How. Pr. 335.

turns upon that of the reasonableness of the restraint imposed. Where it appears that the restraint required is not unreasonable, or is not greater than is essential to the proper protection of the grantee, the contract will be held valid. In the case of an attorney the territorial limitations necessary to the proper protection of the grantor may be greater than in that of a physician. In an English case, Lord Langdale, M. R., in his opinion, said: "The question, therefore, is whether the restraint ought to be considered as reasonable in this particular case. The business is that of attorney and solicitor, which, to a large extent, may be carried on by correspondence or by agents, and as to which it has been already decided that a restraint of practice within a distance of 150 miles was not an unreasonable restraint."[1] In May

[1] Whittaker v. Howe, 3 Beav. 383, 394. A, on being articled to B, covenanted not to be concerned for any of B's clients, and to forfeit £100 for any such breach. A, after being admitted, acted in contravention of this covenant. He was restrained by injunction. Nichols v. Stretton, 7 Beav. 42. An agreement between two solicitors in partnership together, that one of them should continue to carry on the business under their joint names, and should be entitled to all the profits thereof, and should grant to the other partner an annuity of £300 during the life of his mother, and in the event of his dying in the lifetime of his mother, should pay to his widow an annuity of £100 during the remainder of his mother's life, and should indemnify him against all liability in respect of his name being used, and that the partnership should cease on the death of the mother of the retiring partner. *Held*, not to be void as against public policy, but to be a valid and binding agreement. Aubin v. Holt, 2 K. & J. 66. By agreement between the plaintiff, a solicitor, and the defendant, after reciting that the plaintiff, being manager of certain estates at T, and finding it expedient to establish an office there for the transaction of law and other business, had proposed to appoint the defendant as resident clerk there, it was agreed that the defendant should reside at T, and that in consideration of his services the plaintiff should pay him a certain salary, and that either party might determine the agreement by a certain notice, and that the defendant would not, for the space of twenty-one years, notwithstanding the decease of the plaintiff, reside in the parish of T, or within twenty-one miles thereof, or carry on therein or within the distance aforesaid, during the period of twenty-one years, any business of the description of that carried on under the agreement. *Held*, per Pollock, C. B., Alderson, B., and Platt, B., that the restriction was not unreasonable, and was good in law; per Martin, that the agreement was valid, for if the restriction as to residence was void,

v. O'Neill, the defendant bound himself to a London solicitor by articles for a term, and covenanted that he would not at the expiration of the term, or at any time thereafter, either solely or jointly, or as agent for, any other person or persons, directly or indirectly, practice the business of attorney or solicitor within the city of London or the counties of Middlesex or Essex, nor directly or indirectly act as such attorney or solicitor for any client or clients of the plaintiff, or any partner or partners of plaintiff, or for any person or persons who should have been a client or clients of the plaintiff or any partner or partners of the plaintiff, at any time during the term. At the expiration of the term, the defendant having commenced business on his own account in Southwark, it was held that the restriction was not un-

that as to not carrying on the business was good. Dendy v. Henderson, 11 Excheq. 194. The condition of a bond contained a recital that T W had agreed to become the managing clerk of R H, a solicitor at W, and it was thereupon agreed that T W should enter into a bond not to practice as a solicitor at or within fifty miles of W; and provided that if he did so, then, if he should pay to R H the sum of £1,000 as liquidated damages, the bond should be void. On breach by T W, held on the whole scope of the agreement, that it was not intended to be satisfied by the payment of the sum named, and that the court would, therefore, interfere by injunction. Howard v. Woodward. 10 Jur. (N. S.) 1123. Appellee insists that defendant's agreement not to engage again in the practice of law in Adel, is against public policy and void. The defendant did not agree generally not to engage in the practice of law, but simply not to engage in the practice of the law at Adel. A contract in restraint of trade as to particular places is valid. Hedge v. Lowe, 47 Iowa, 137, and cases cited. Jenkins v. Temples, 39 Ga. 655; Chappel v. Brockway, 21 Wend. 157. In Holbrook v. Waters, 9 How. Pr. 335, it was held that an agreement upon sufficient consideration not to practice medicine, nor in any manner to do business as a physician in the county of Oswego at any time after the first of May, 1851, was valid. In Bunn v. Guy, 4 East, 190, a contract entered into by a practicing attorney to relinquish his business, and recommended his clients to two other attorneys for a valuable consideration, and that he would not himself practice in such business within one hundred and fifty miles of London, was held to be valid. See also Heichew v. Hamilton, 3 G. Greene, 596; s. c., 4 G. Greene, 317. "Whittaker v. Howe, 3 Beav. 383," it is said by Mr. Benjamin (Benj., Sales, Sec. 525), "has been practically overruled in the later cases." Wiley v. Baumgardner, 97 Ind. 66, 69.

reasonable, and that the defendants acting for a petitioner in the London court of bankruptcy was a breach of the covenant.[1] In the leading case of Bunn v. Guy, a contract entered into by a practicing attorney to relinquish his business and recommend his clients to two other attorneys for a valuable consideration, and that he would not himself practice in such business within certain limits, and would permit them to make use of his name in their firm for a certain time, but without his interference, etc., was holden to be valid in law.[2] In another English case, by a deed for the dissolution of partnership between the plaintiff and defendant, it was covenanted by the defendant that he would not at any time or times thereafter, within the next seven years, directly or indirectly, either by himself or in co-partnership with another or others, carry on the business of an attorney or solicitor within the distance of fifty miles from a place named, nor interfere with, solicit or influence the clients of the late co-partnership; and that if he should in any respect infringe covenant then he should immediately thereupon pay the plaintiff the sum of £1,000 as and for liquidated damages and not by way of penalty. It was held that the sum of £1,000 was upon the construction of this covenant to be considered by way of liquidated damages and not as a penalty.[3]

§ 61. **The Rule as Applied to Dentists.**—In determining the application of this rule to the practice of dentistry the court will be governed as in relation to the practice of the other professions by a regard for the reasonableness of the contract. It will take into consideration the peculiar character of the profession and determine what, in view of such character, is a fair and just restraint. In the leading case of Mallan v. May, by articles of agreement under seal, it was agreed that the defendant should become assistant to the plaintiffs in their business of surgeon dentists for four years, that the plaintiffs should instruct him in the business of a surgeon dentist, and that after the expiration

[1] May v. O'Neill, L. J. 44 Ch. 660. Bunn v. Guy, 4 East, 190.

[3] Galsworthy v. Strutt, 1 Exchеq. 659.

of the term the defendant should not carry on that business in London, or in any of the towns or places in England or Scotland where the plaintiffs might have been practicing before the expiration of said service. The declaration alleged as breaches: First, that after the term the defendant carried on the said business in London; secondly, that the plaintiffs had, during the said term, carried on business in Great Russell street, Bloomsburg, yet the defendant, after the term, carried on the said business in the same place. Plea to the first breach that London was a large and populous district containing 1,500,000 inhabitants, and that the stipulation in the agreement was an undue, unreasonable and unlawful restriction of trade. Plea to the second breach that before the expiration of the service the plaintiff had practiced in very many towns in England, and, amongst others, London, Preston, Oswestry, etc., and that divers of said towns were distant from each other 150 miles; wherefore the said stipulation was an unreasonable restriction of trade, and the said agreement as to so much was wholly void. It was held that the first plea was bad, as the covenant not to practice in London was valid, the limit of London not being too large for the profession in question. Held, secondly, that the stipulation as to not practicing in towns where the plaintiff might have been practicing during the service was an unreasonable restriction, and, therefore, illegal and void. But that the stipulation as to not practicing in London was not affected by the illegality of the other part.[1] In another English case it was held that an agreement that defendant, a moderately skillful dentist, would abstain from practicing over a district 200 miles in diameter in consideration of receiving instructions and a salary from the plaintiff, determinable at three months' notice, was held unreasonable and void.[2] In a leading case in Connecticut, the plaintiff, for a sufficient consideration, bought of the defendant his business as a dentist and the latter executed a contract not to practice dentistry "within a radius of ten miles of Litchfield." The town of Litch-

[1] Mallan v. May, 11 M. & W. 653. [2] Horner v. Graves, 7 Bing. 735.

field has an extensive territory and an irregular outline, and contains the village of Litchfield in which the defendant dwelt and had his office at the time and where the contract was drawn and executed. It was held that the contract was not void in not fixing a period within which the defendant was not to practice dentistry within those limits. It seems that where a contract is reasonable when made, subsequent circumstances, such as the covenantee's ceasing to do business, do not affect its operation.[1] In Clark v. Crosby, where upon consideration that the plaintiff, a dentist, would keep himself supplied with mineral teeth by purchases of the defendant, the latter agreed not to sell such teeth to any other person in the place where the plaintiff resided, it was held that the contract, being only in partial restraint of trade, was not illegal.[2]

[1] Cook v. Johnson, 47 Conn. 175. "As this belongs to the class of contracts in restraint of trade, three requisites are essential to its validity: 1st. It must be partial or restricted in its operation in respect either to time or place. 2d. It must be on some good consideration. 3d. It must be reasonable, that is, it should afford only a fair protection to the interests of the party in whose favor it is made, and must not be so large in its operation as to interfere with the interests of the public. The motion does not disclose that it was claimed in the court below that the contract was lacking in any of these elements, but only that it was too indefinite and uncertain in its language to be enforced. The respondent admits the making of the contract, and full performance on the part of the petitioner, but concedes that he has paid no attention to it whatever, except to keep the money paid under it. This is not very creditable, to say the least, and the excuse given does not at all relieve him in a moral point of view. He says, in effect, that inasmuch as he did not understand, by the language which he used in the contract, where the circle with its ten mile radius would be drawn, he will locate within the town of Litchfield, where he can do the other party the most injury, and appropriate to himself the good will of the business he had sold, knowing absolutely such conduct to be contrary even to his own understanding of the contract. Such a position might well excuse a court of equity from giving any construction to the contract merely for his future guidance." *Ibid.*, 176.

[2] Clark v. Crosby, 37 Vt. 188. An instrument under seal was executed upon a sale made by the plaintiff to the defendants, by which the former sold to the latter all his interest in the manufacture and sale of porcelain teeth in the city of New York, with his stock on hand, and the good will of the business. The plaintiff covenanted to instruct one of the defendants in the art of manufacturing porcelain and in-

§ 62. Application of the Rule to the Profession of Teaching.—Where a school building, or the privilege of conducting a school at an established rate of tuition, is sold by one teacher to another, a contract binding the grantor not to open a school within a fixed territorial limit, if reasonable, will be sustained. Where A, a school teacher, was induced by B, another school teacher, to purchase of B the lease of an academy under inducements held out by B that, if he could sell, he would quit teaching in the locality, and on these inducements the purchase was made, it was held that equity would enjoin B from teaching a school in the locality during the lease.[1]

corruptible teeth, and to furnish him with his recipes therefor. The agreement also contained the following clause: And the party of the first part will not carry on, or cause to be carried on, by any person with whom he shall be interested, the manufacture of porcelain teeth, or impart the knowledge of manufacturing the same to any person other than as aforesaid." It was alleged in the complaint. that the said art of manufacturing porcelain teeth in which the defendant was to be instructed was a secret of the plaintiff and known to be such by the defendant. *Held*, on demurrer, that the covenant in question was valid, and not one in restraint of trade. Alcock v. Gilberton, 5 Duer, 76.

[1] Spier v. Lambdin, 45 Ga. 319. "In the present case, we think the restriction is unreasonable. Not as a rule of law, because it extends throughout the State, but because it extends beyond any apparently necessary protection which the complainant might reasonably require, and thus without benefiting him it oppresses the respondent, and deprives people in other places of the chance which might be offered them to learn the French and German languages of the respondent. The complainant urges that he has established a school in Providence, at great expense, to teach languages by a new method, where scholars come from all parts of the State; and that, by reason of the small extent of the State and the case of passing to and fro within it, such a restriction is reasonable and necessary to keep teachers from setting up similar schools and enticing away his scholars. All this may be true with reference to Providence and its vicinity. But while, as is averred, many pupils. from all parts of the State, may come to Providence as a center, for the same reason few would go to other places. For example, a school in Westerly or Newport would not be likely to draw scholars from Providence, or places from which Providence is more easily reached. Indeed, the complainant says he offered, after the contract was made, and now offers to allow the respondent to teach in Newport, thereby admitting that the restriction is greater than the necessity. The people of Newport, Westerly and other

§ 63. **Restraint upon the Services of Artists and Actors.**—An engagement on the part of an artist or an actor under which the party is prohibited from entering the service of a rival concern, during a designated period, if the restraint is not unreasonable, will be sustained. In Fredericks v. Mayer, it was held that an artist who has entered into a written agreement to perform his professional services for a party, for a limited time, at a stipulated price, and binds himself not to work for any other house or person during said time, and the agreement is mutual that the party who engages shall employ and pay him according to the agreement, may be restrained by injunction from performing such services, during the term, for any other person than the party to the agreement, without the consent of the latter. The principle is this: That services which involve the exercise of powers of mind which, in many cases, as of writers and performers, are purely and largely intellectual, may form a class in which the court will interfere. Such services are generally individual and peculiar. They exist in nature, or in degree, with some modification of character or expression in the one person. This element of mind exhibited in the subject of the contract, as distinguished from what is mechanical and material, furnishes a rule of distinction and decision.[1]

places have the right to provide for education in languages without coming to Providence. It is hard to believe, and the bill does not aver, that losing the few, if any, from such place, who might leave the complainant, if the respondent were to teach there, would seriously affect the complainant's school. Teaching in Providence, or in any place from which the complainant receives a considerable number of pupils, might affect it, and a restriction limited accordingly might be reasonable; but we think it unreasonable to go further." Herreshoff v. Boutineau, 17 R. I. 3, 7.

[1] Fredericks v. Mayer, 13 How. Pr. 566. See also Webster v. Dillon, 3 Jur. (N. S.) 432; Howard v. Hopkins, 2 Atk. 371; Fox v. Scard, 33 Beav. 327; Jones v. Heavens, L. R. 4 Ch. D. 633; Barnes v. McAllister, 18 How. Pr. 534; Nessle v. Reese, 29 How. Pr. 382; Bradley v. Bosley, 1 Barb. Ch. 125; Dupre v. Thompson, 4 Barb. 279. "It appears to me, on the plainest ground, that an engagement to perform for nine months at theater A, is a contract not to perform at theater B, or at any other theater whatever. How is a man to perform his duty to the proprietor of

In the leading English case a lady, not of age, and her father, by writing signed in a foreign country, agreed with a theatrical manager to sing at his theater for a definite period. By a clause subsequently acceded to and signed

a theater if, when he has engaged himself to perform for him, he is to go away any night that he may be wanted to another theater? I must treat Mr. Flockton as if he were the greatest actor in the world, and as if wherever he went the public would run after him; and according to this, if a proprietor engages an actor to perform for him, he is not, because he is only wanted three nights in the week, to be at liberty to go and perform at any other theater during the other three nights, and thereby take away the advantage of the contract which he has entered into with his employer. That, in my opinion, is utterly inconsistent with the proper construction of the contract. There is no doubt whatever, that the proper construction of these contracts is, that where a man or woman engages to perform or sing at a particular theater for a particular period, that involves the necessity of his or her not performing or singing at any other during that period." Montague v. Flockton, L. R. 16 Eq. 189, 198. The plaintiff, the manager of a London theater, engaged the defendant, a provincial actor, desirous of appearing on the London stage for two years. Though there was nothing expressed on the subject, the court inferred an engagement on the part of the plaintiff to employ the defendant for a reasonable time, and on the part of the defendant not to perform elsewhere. The plaintiff (under these circumstances) delayed the defendant's appearance for five months, the defendant broke his engagement and went to another theater. *Held*, that he had a right to do so, and that the plaintiff was not entitled to an interlocutory injunction to prevent his performing there. Fetcher v. Montgomery, 33 Beav. 22. The defendant agreed with a theatrical company to give them his services as an actor for a specified time, and agreed not to give his services elsewhere without their written permission. The engagement contained a stipulation to the effect that if he should break his engagement, he obligated himself to pay to the company a conventional fine of $200, to be forfeited by any violation of the contract; and then provides as follows: "This sum is already forfeited by any violation of the contract, and requires *no particular legal proceedings* for its execution." On a bill for an injunction filed by the company against the defendant to restrain him from performing at another theater, it was held that the complainants, having fixed by their own estimate the extent of injury they would suffer from a non-observance of this condition in the contract, and having indicated that the only form in which they could seek redress, and recover the stipulated penalty or forfeiture, was a court of law, were precluded from resorting to a court of equity for relief by way of injunction, on the ground that a violation of this part of the conby her agent, and to which she and her father afterwards assented, she engaged "not to use her talents at any other theater nor in any concert or reunion, public or private, without the written authorization of" the manager. The lady engaged with the manager of a rival theater to sing at his theater within the defined period, and her debut was announced in the usual public advertisements. Upon motion, in a suit by the manager against the lady, her father and the manager of the rival theater, it was objected that the positive and negative terms formed but one agreement; and that, as it had been settled that the court could not by injunction enforce the positive term that the lady should sing, it could not enforce the negative stipulation; but held notwithstanding (Kemble v. Kean), that the court would prevent the violation of the negative term, and restrain the lady from singing at the rival theater, though the positive term of the agreement could not be enforced.[1] In a case in Maryland it was held that upon a contract made by a husband for himself and his wife, that his wife should perform at the theater of the manager named therein during a certain period, for a certain salary, a court of equity will not enjoin the wife from performing at any other theater, during the same period; nor the husband from permitting her to change her residence; nor another manager from

tract would result in irreparable damage and injury to them. Hahn v. Concordia Society, 42 Md. 460. Defendant having contracted to perform at plaintiff's theater, at a fixed compensation, for a certain time, and not to perform elsewhere during that time, made an agreement to perform in another theater before the expiration of the contract. *Held*, that he might be restrained by injunction from carrying out that agreement, there being no demand in the complaint for a decree of specific performance, and no uncertainty in the contract as to time, place or substance. In such a case a writ of *ne exeat*, if necessary to carry out the injunctions, will issue. Hayes v. Willis, 11 Abb. Pr. (N. S.) 167. Contracts for the exclusive services of distinguished artists in theatrical representations are not capable of definite determination, and violations of them may be properly restrained by injunction. Where damages for the violation of a covenant are liquidated by agreement, *semble*, an injunction will not be allowed. McCaull v. Braham, 16 Fed. Rep. 37.

[1] Lumley v. Wagner, 5 De G. & Sm. 485.

giving her employment within the term as an actress; neither can specific execution of such a contract, as against the husband or wife, be decreed.[1]

§ 64. **As Applied to Trades and other Occupations.**—In all cases relating to laborers and employees of any class, the general rules, as expounded in the foregoing sections, are applicable. Contracts in restraint of trade or of employment will be upheld, if there is a valuable consideration and the restraint is reasonable and fit. In a recent English case of more than ordinary interest, the defendant entered into an agreement to serve the plaintiff in his business of dairyman as a milk carrier. By the agreement the defendant agreed that he would not, during the continuance of the service, nor at any time thereafter serve, for his own benefit or for the benefit of any other person, or solicit, or in any way interfere with any of the customers who should at any time be served by the plaintiff in his business. It was held that the clause was severable and that an injunction could properly be granted restraining the defendant from serving persons who were customers of the plaintiff during the employment of the defendant by the plaintiff. It was held also, that without any severance, the restrictive clause was valid, as it did not go beyond what was reasonably necessary for the protection of the plaintiff's business.[2] In his opin-

[1] Butler v. Marshall, 4 Gill, 487. Under an agreement by the defendant, a *danseuse*, to dance at the plaintiff's theater, or where he shall prescribe, with no negative or restrictive clauses, the plaintiff, on an alleged breach of the agreement by the defendant, cannot have an injunction restraining the defendant from a violation thereof. Butler v. Galletti, 21 How. Pr. 465.

[2] Dubowski v. Goldstein, 65 L. J. Q. B. 397. "It is said that, over and above the rule, that the contract shall be reasonable, there exists another rule, viz.: that the contract shall be limited as to space, and that this contract being in its terms unlimited as to space, and, therefore, extending to the whole of England and Wales, must be void. Now, in the first place, let me consider whether such a rule would be reasonable. There are many trades which are carried on all over the kingdom, which, by their very nature, are extensive and widely diffused. There are others which, from their nature and necessities, are local. If this rule existed it would afford a complete protection to the latter class of trade, whilst it would prohibit complete protection of the former

ion in this case Lord Justice Rigby said: "The law on this subject has now gone far beyond what it was in the time of Chief Justice Tindal and Lord Denman. Lord Watson, in Nordenfeldt v. Maxim-Nordenfeldt Co., points

class, and an injury which ought not to be wrought without good reason would arise. In the next place the rule, if it existed, would apply in two classes of cases. It would apply where the want of a limitation of space was unreasonable, and also where it was reasonable. Now, in the former class of cases, those in which the universality was unreasonable, the rule would operate nothing, because the ground is already covered by the rule that the restraint must be reasonable. It would, therefore, only operate in cases in which the universality of the prohibition was reasonable; that is, it would only operate where it ought not. For the existence of such a rule I should require clear authority." Fry, J., in Rousillon v. Rousillon, L. R. 14 Ch. D. 351, 366. A contract by which one, in consideration of employment by a merchant engaged in the instalment clothing business, agrees for one year after the employment ceases not to engage in, or be concerned or interested in, the instalment clothing business in a certain city on his own account, or as the agent or employe of any other person "in any capacity," only prevents his accepting employment in the instalment clothing business, and is not objectionable as imposing a restraint on the employe greater than is necessary for the fair protection of the employer, or as interfering with the interest of the public in the employer's labor. Sternberg v. O'Brien, 48 N. J. Eq. 370; s. c., 22 Atl. Rep. 348. The declaration set out a contract whereby the plaintiff agreed to employ the defendant in his service, and the defendant agreed to serve the plaintiff in his business for one month certain and until the expiration of a month's notice, to be given by either party. In consideration whereof the defendant did thereby agree that he would not, during the continuance of such service, nor within the space of twenty-four months after quitting or being discharged from the same, commence, etc., the business of a cow keeper within five miles from Northampton Square, in the county of Middlesex; and if, at any time during such service, or within twenty-four months after the determination thereof, the defendant should commence, etc., such business, that he would pay 10s. for every day that he should act contrary to the agreement. *Held*, that the agreement was valid, being limited both in time and space, and not appearing to be an unreasonable restraint of trade. Proctor v. Sargent, 2 Man. & Gr. 20. "There are two canons of construction to be considered where questions of this kind arise. One is, that you must examine whether the restraint, having regard to the circumstances of the case, the business of the employer and the nature of the employment, is greater than is reasonably required for the protection of the employer in his trade or business. The other is that you must construe the agreement according to the out that the opinions of judges as to public policy must vary at different times. It appears to me that the only test which can be applied in cases of this kind is to consider whether the agreement is reasonably necessary for the protection of the person entering into it. If it is not reasonably necessary for that purpose it is against public policy."[1] In a case in Ohio, M, a married woman engaged in carrying on the business of millinery and dressmaking with her separate property, and, on her own account, in the town of F, sold her stock of goods, together with the good will of the business, and engaged not to carry on the business at any time in the future at the town of F, or at any

reasonable meaning of the words used, without regard to what may be the effect of such construction. The first question to be considered is, who is the employer? He is described as a commission merchant, and as such he may be supposed to deal in anything in the world. If that is his business, what is the object of this agreement? Its object is to protect the plaintiff, not from ordinary retail dealers, but from any competition which might arise from the defendant entering into the employment of other commission agents carrying on a business like that of the plaintiff, and getting profit in a similar way. * * * I think that the words 'any trade or business' mean only any trade or business of the kind which the plaintiff was carrying on, and I do not think the words 'in connection with' carry the matter much further. I also think that the words 'at any time previously to such determination,' mean at any time during the employment of the defendant in the plaintiff's service. The objection was taken that this clause was too wide because it extended over the United Kingdom. That objection fails for this reason: In considering the validity of this agreement, we must have regard to the business of the plaintiff. But the plaintiff's business is one which extends from one end of the United Kingdom to the other. Therefore the restraint is not unreasonable, because it is necessary for the protection of the plaintiff's business, so construed the agreement is neither unreasonable or oppressive." Lopes, L. J., in Moenich v. Fenestre, 61 L. J. Ch. 737, 740. An employer is entitled to the labor and skill of an employe in the pursuit of the business which he was employed to transact during business hours, but has no claim to his labor or earnings before or after such hours. A person employed by a firm as a book-keeper and accountant, may recover for services rendered to another person at his request out of business hours, and also for services during business hours performed by him with the consent and permission of the firm employing him. Wallace v. DeYoung, 98 Ill. 638.

[1] Dubowski v. Goldstein, 65 L. J. Q. B. 397, 399.

place within such distance of said town as would interfere with such business, whether the same was carried on by the purchasers or their successors. It was held that such agreement in equity is binding, and that in an action brought by the successors of the purchasers, M will be enjoined from carrying on such business in violation of the agreement.[1] In the case of Burrill v. Daggett, the court said: "Although there may not have been more than two other shops of the kind in the village, as the case shows, at the time the defendant sold to the plaintiff, it may well be inferred that it was the understanding of the parties, from the language of the bond, viewed in the light of the attendant circumstances as disclosed in the case, that defendant was not again to engage in the business by keeping a barber shop. He sold to the plaintiff not only his shop, tools, etc., but also his good will in the business. It was against the competition of the defendant that the plaintiff intended to provide; and whether the defendant bought out and kept another barber shop, or opened and kept one independently of any in operation at the time, still continuing the business and working at his trade, it would be a violation of the bond."[2] In an English case, where the object of an agreement was to parcel out the stevedoring business of a particular port amongst the parties to it, and so prevent competition, at least, amongst themselves, and also, it may be, to keep up the price to be paid for the work, it was held that such agreement is not invalid if carried into effect by provisions reasonably necessary for the purpose, though the effect of them might be to create a partial restraint upon the power of the parties to exercise their trades.[3] In a very recent case in New York, it was held that an agreement entered into by a person hired as a salesman to make sales of merchandise of his employer to the effect that, after leaving his employer's service, he will not engage in a similar busi-

[1] Morgan v. Perhamus, 36 Ohio St. 517.

[2] Burrill v. Daggett, 77 Me. 545, 548.

[3] Collins v. Locke, L. R. 4 App. Cas. 674.

ness for a period of three years in sixteen States and territories of the United States nor in the Dominion of Canada, will not be enforced by a court of equity where it does not appear that there were trade secrets connected with the business that came to the servant's knowledge or proof that his employer's customers have been diverted by the action of the servant in engaging in a similar business. Such an agreement is unreasonable where it is based upon no increase of wages, because of its having been made, being calculated to deprive the servant of his ability to earn his livelihood.[1]

[1] Oppenheimer v. Hirsch, 5 App. Div. 232; s. c., 38 N. Y. Supl. 311. "The only thing undisputed before the court is, that the defendant made an agreement by which he contracted not to engage in a particular line of business in sixteen States and territories, and the Dominion of Canada, for three years after he should leave the plaintiffs' employment, which, according to the terms of that agreement, would have enabled the plaintiffs to discharge him within a week after he entered their service, and would have tied his hands for a period of three years afterwards, such a stipulation is unreasonable, and should not be enforced, under the situation of the parties to this action, by injunction, and the plaintiffs having failed to show that there was any reason for coupling such a condition with a simple employment of the defendant to sell their wares in a part of one State of the Union, or that they have in reality suffered any loss by reason of the acts of the defendant, or that they are in any way actually prejudiced by such acts, or that he is using any knowledge acquired from them in an illegitimate way, or that the enforcement of the stipulation of the agreement, pending suit, is necessary for their protection, we must hold that the injunction should not have been continued." *Ibid.*, 236. See also following cases: Norris v. Moss, 25 L. J. Eq. 194; Shackle v. Baker, 14 Ves. 468: Drake v. Dodsworth, 4 Kan. 159; Spicer v. Hoop, 51 Ind. 305; Presbury v. Fisher, 18 Mo. 50: Dakin v. Williams, 11 Wend. 67; Burrill v. Daggett, 77 Me. 545; Dean v. Emerson, 102 Mass. 480; Baumgarten v. Broadaway, 77 N. Car. 8; Heichew v. Hamilton, 3 Greene (Iowa), 596; s. c., 4 Greene (Iowa), 317; Harrison v. Lockhart, 25 Ind. 112; Studebaker v. White, 31 Ind. 211; McAllister v. Howell, 42 Ind. 15; Stines v. Dorman, 25 Ohio St. 580; Elliott's Appeal, 60 Pa. St. 161; Hoagland v. Segur, 38 N. J. L. 230; Duffy v. Shockey, 11 Ind. 70; Hall's Appeal, 60 Pa. St. 458; Hastings v. Whitley, 2 Excheq. 611; Hitchcock v. Coker, 6 Ad. & El. 438; Hayward v. Young, 2 Chit. 407: Price v. Green, 16 M. & W. 346: Ward v. Hogan, 11 Abb. N. C. 478; Baker v. Cordon, 86 N. Car. 116.

§ 65. In Its Application to Traveling Salesmen.—It has been held that the rule, as stated in the preceding sections, is applicable to contracts relating to service by this class of employes. In the leading case of Mumford v. Gething, a mercantile house in London, dealing in lace, employed travelers to obtain orders and sell for them, in England, each in a particular district or journey. A vacancy having occurred in the travelership of the M journey, the plaintiffs acquainted the defendant with the fact, he being then in their employ in another occupation, and it was verbally agreed with him that he should fill the place, the understanding being that a contract in writing should be afterwards drawn up and signed. The defendant started on the M journey and sometime afterwards the following form of contract was sent down to him, and he signed it: "In consideration of my entering upon your employ at a salary of, etc., I herewith agree to do so with the understanding that in the event of my wishing to travel, and doing so for any other house in the same trade, on any part of the same ground, to pay you the sum of £50." The defendant, after having traveled for the plaintiffs on the M journey for about a year, quitted their service, and commenced traveling for a rival house of business over the M journey. In an action for the penalty by the plaintiffs it was held that the plaintiffs were entitled to recover, for that a good consideration for the defendant's undertaking appeared on the face of the writing; that the circumstances under which the defendant became traveler to the plaintiffs showed a good consideration, in fact, that the contract meant to engage the entire services of the defendant so long as he was in the plaintiffs' employ, and that it would have been a breach of it to travel for anyone else in the absence of the prohibitory part; and that, therefore, the contract intended the penalty to attach in case the defendant traveled over the same ground for any other house in the same trade after he left the plaintiffs' employ; that extrinsic evidence was properly admitted to identify the particular service in which the defendant was to be employed, viz.: that of traveler, and the ground over which he was to travel, viz.: the M journey; that the contract was not unlimited in point of space and so void as in restraint of trade.[1] In the recent case of Mills v. Dunham, plaintiffs engaged defendant as their traveler and assistant in the business of anti-septic manufacturers, "to call upon and solicit orders from" customers for the said business, defendant agreeing that he would not after the termination of the agreement, for or on account of any employer or on his own account "call upon, or directly or indirectly solicit orders from, or in any way deal or transact business with," any one who during such agreement was a customer of plaintiffs. It was held that, notwithstanding the generality of the language, the true intent of the parties was to bind the defendant not to engage in any competing business; that the agreement was not in restraint of trade; and that plaintiffs were entitled to an injunction restraining the defendant from soliciting orders for a rival firm.[2]

[1] Mumford v. Gething, 6 Jur. (N. S.) 428.

[2] Mills v. Dunham, L. R. (1891) 1 Ch. 576. "It seems to me that the rule, clearly deducible from all these authorities, is that an employer has the right to bind an employe not to go into the employ of a competitor, for a reasonable time after his employment terminates, within the territory where the employer seeks his market; and whether such covenant is reasonable and binding is a judicial question which must depend in each case upon its peculiar facts and circumstances. It has been well said that trade has obliterated State lines. The modern agencies of commerce have enlarged the field for the manufacturer and salesman to, or even beyond, the limit of the continent; and to whatever extent a manufacturer or dealer has, by his energy and enterprise, made a market for his wares, to that extent he has the right to protect his business from piratical competition by contracts like the one under consideration. In the case now under consideration the complainants were manufacturers of inks and similar commodities, and their business extended throughout the entire United States and Canadas. The defendant Alling was employed to canvass for purchasers, and to advertise the products of complainants' business. Prior to making the contract now under consideration, he had been for several years employed in a similar capacity by the complainants, and it must be presumed that he had acquired an extensive knowledge not only of the complainants' business methods, but of their trade secrets, and this knowledge he had acquired while under the pay of complain-

§ 66. Constraint of Trade Construed as a Limited Partnership.—It has been held that a contract in restraint of trade, under which the parties agree to divide the profits of the business established by the agreement, may be construed as a limited partnership, and that, as such, it is subject to the rules by which partnerships are governed. In Carroll v. Giles, it was held that barbering is such a business as will support a sale of its "good will" for a definite time and within a defined territory; but where G, a barber, who had no shop or patronage of his own, entered into an agreement with C, the proprietor of a barber shop, that C

ants and acting for them. It does not, therefore, seem to me unreasonable that the complainants should exact from him a covenant that he would not reveal their trade secrets, and would not enter the employ of any competitor of complainants for the time specified in his covenant after his employment by complainants should terminate. In the wine dealers case just quoted [Rousillon v. Rousillon, L. R. 14 Ch. D. 351] the restriction was for a term of ten years after the employment ceased, and the court held that, under the circumstances, not unreasonable. Here the restriction is for three years only which, it seems to me, was entirely proper for defendant to agree to and for complainants to exact." Carter v. Alling, 43 Fed. Rep. 208, 214. R, a brewer, engaged M as a traveler for procuring orders for and selling malt liquors, and also, if required by R, ærated waters, to the class known as wholesale purchasing agents in a certain district. M agreed that for two years after the determination of his employment he would not be concerned in selling malt liquors or ærated waters within a certain district. R never dealt in ærated waters, nor required M to obtain orders for them. M, after leaving R's employment became traveler to rival brewers within the prescribed district. R brought an action and applied for an injunction. M insisted that the restriction was too wide, and, therefore, void. Stirling, J., construed the restriction as only prohibiting M from selling wholesale, and held that the stipulation as to ærated waters was severable, and granted an injunction limited to selling malt liquors wholesale. *Held*, on appeal, that the agreement must be construed as prohibiting M from selling wholesale or retail within the limit, and that the restraint was not greater than was reasonably necessary for the reasonable protection of R, for that selling wholesale and retail were not two distinct businesses, but only different modes of carrying on the one business of selling malt liquors, that the selling malt liquors, either wholesale or retail, within the district, might affect R's business, and that R was entitled to restrain M from selling malt liquors in any way within the district. Rogers v. Maddocks, L. R. (1892) 3 Ch. 346.

should keep the shop and pay all its expenses, and G was to manage it, and "not to do any work, now or hereafter, outside of the shop owned by C, or hire to any party or open a shop of any kind to carry on the barber business in" that town, and to "convey all patronage extended to him heretofore to the business owned by C," "the gross receipts to be divided equally," such agreement was only a contract of indefinite partnership, and G's stipulation never to do any barbering business outside of C's shop was unreasonable, and will not be specifically enforced or its violation enjoined.[1] In the opinion in this case, the court said: "It is true that the defendant was a barber, going about the town and county barbering, but had no shop, patronage or good will to sell. The plaintiff did not purchase his outfit from the defendant, giving him a liberal price in consideration of his unusual stipulation to stay with him or go out of the business. It seems to us that the contract was really nothing more than one of a partnership indefinite in duration, in which one party stipulated to furnish the capital or outfit, and the other to contribute his labor and skill, 'dividing the gross receipts equally,' and that the stipulation on the part of the defendant never to do any barbering in B, outside of plaintiff's shop, 'now or hereafter,' was 'unreasonable,' and not of such a character as to call for the exercise of the equitable jurisdiction in requiring it to be specifically performed."[2]

[1] Carroll v. Giles, 30 S. Car. 412: s. c., 9 S. E. Rep. 422.

[2] Carroll v. Giles, 30 S. Car. 412, 418: s. c., 9 S. E. Rep. 422.

CHAPTER IV.

CONTRACTS RELATING TO RESTRICTIONS IN BUSINESS.

§ 67. Introductory.
68. Contracts Granting an Exclusive Business Privilege.
69. Contracts Relating to a Particular Article.
70. Contracts under which the Grantor Retains an Interest in the Business.
§ 71. Contracts for the Sale of a Good Will.
72. The Subject Continued.
73. Farther Application of the Rule.
74. Agreement not to Buy or Sell.
75. Contract to Maintain Prices.
76. Statutory Regulations.

§ **67. Introductory.**—The general principles by which contracts in restraint of trade are governed, as expounded in the preceding chapters, are applicable to all contracts between individuals, firms or corporations for the limitation or regulation of any branch of business. The object of this chapter is to discuss the application of these general principles, not to monopolies or to extensive combinations, the object of which is to control prices, but to transactions of a general and limited character. It is proposed to consider that class of contracts that relate to the restriction of business operations on a smaller scale. Business men, business firms and corporations of limited resources attempt to effect, in a narrow sphere, essentially the same thing that is accomplished by the great combinations in a broader field. To this class of restrictions our attention for the present is to be directed.

§ **68. Contracts Granting an Exclusive Business Privilege.**—A contract binding an individual or company not to engage in business at a particular place and for a limited time, is not in contravention of public policy, and if not otherwise in violation of equitable rules will be upheld. But a contract for an exclusive privilege must relate to a single individual, firm or corporation. There must be a valuable consideration; there must be a reason for the contract that the court will accept, and there must be no restraint upon one party that is not beneficial to the other. A contract of this character is in no sense a monopoly. As it relates to a single individual or business association, all other persons are at liberty to engage in the business.[1] In Illinois, it has been held that a contract to furnish a party with sewing machines at a discount and upon a credit, which provides that such party shall deal exclusively in the machine sold by the party agreeing to furnish, and to purchase the same of him exclusively, contains no such restraint of trade as to render it void.[2] In New York, a

[1] California Steam Navigation Co. v. Wright, 6 Cal. 258. See also Washburn v. Dosch, 68 Wis. 436; Wright v. Ryder. 36 Cal. 342; West Va. Transportation Co. v. Ohio Riv. P. L. Co., 22 W. Va. 600; Perkins v. Lyman, 9 Mass. 522.

[2] Brown v. Rounsavell, 78 Ill. 589. In Newell v. Meyendorff, 9 Mont. 254; s. c., 23 Pac. Rep. 333, it was held that a contract to sell a brand of cigars to no one in the State but defendant, and to give him the exclusive agency for such sale, is not in restraint of trade. The court said: "The contract is not general; it is limited as to place and person. The public is not deprived of the alleged restricted party's industry. On the contrary, the contract provides for the placing upon the Montana market the product of the plaintiff's industry, by the selection and services of a local Montana agent, interested in the success of sales, and to be rewarded by such success. Nor is there any injury to the party himself, the plaintiffs, by their being precluded from pursuing their occupation. Rather by the contract, they seem to have sought a means of extending the field of their operations, and not of restricting them. In the light of the authorities, the rules and the reasons therefor, and the facts, we are clearly of the opinion that the contract was not in restraint of trade, and not void. It was simply a contract, for a consideration, for the enlistment of the services of an agent for the plaintiffs in their business." A contract between several companies, under which it is agreed not to sell goods within certain territorial limits for a specified time, and that no company shall sell more than a certain per cent. of the whole amount sold by all the companies, is void under Civil Code, §§ 1673-1675, which provide that every contract, by which one is restrained from exercising a business or calling, is void to that extent, except that one who

person whose only business was that of selling sand from land which he owned, having refused to sell a piece of the land, on the ground that such a sale would be an injury to his business, was finally persuaded to sell on the agreement of the vendee that he would not sell sand from the land purchased. It was held that the stipulation of the vendee was not such a restraint of trade as to be in contravention of public policy.[1] In New York, it has been held that a contract not to sell asphalt for pavements and blocks, except to certain persons in certain cities, is not void as tending to create a monopoly, or to enhance the price of asphalt pavements.[2] In a recent case in Illinois, it was held that a contract not to engage in the livery and undertaking business in the city of Chicago for the period of five years, is not invalid as being in restraint of trade.[3] In a recent case in Georgia, it was held that an agreement of a seller

has sold the good will of a business may agree not to carry on a similar business within a specified county or town, and that, in anticipation of dissolution of a partnership, a partner may agree not to carry on a similar business in the town or city where the partnership was located. Vulcan Powder Co. v. Hercules Powder Co., 96 Cal. 510; s. c., 31 Pac. Rep. 581. A contract made by a seller with the purchaser, that he will not, at any time within 99 years, directly or indirectly, engage in the manufacture or sale of friction matches, excepting in the capacity of agent or employe of said purchaser, within any of the several States of the United States of America, or the territories thereof, or within the District of Columbia, excepting and reserving, however, the right to manufacture and sell friction matches in the State of Nevada, and in the territory of Montana, is not void as a covenant in restraint of trade. Diamond Match Co. v. Roeber, 106 N. Y. 473; s. c. 13 N. E. Rep. 419.

[1] Hodge v. Sloan, 107 N. Y. 244; s. c., 17 N. E. Rep. 335.

[2] Barber Asphalt Pav'g Co. v. Brand, 7 N. Y. Supl. 744.

[3] Hursen v. Gavin (1896), 162 Ill. 377; s. c., 44 N. E. Rep. 735. "One element of the value of the business transferred by appellant to appellee was the probability that the customers of the former would continue to trade with the latter, and this probability was increased and the value of the purchase enhanced, by the agreement of the appellant not to engage in the same business in Chicago for five years. Such an agreement was in part an inducement to appellee to make the purchase, and was based upon a sufficient consideration. Appellant was at liberty to engage in any other business or in the same business in any other place than Chicago. There was, therefore, only a limited restraint upon him as a tradesman, and not upon

not to carry on a certain business, which is limited as to place, and is based on a sufficient consideration, is valid, though unlimited as to time.[1] In Nebraska, it has been held that a stipulation in a contract giving one the exclusive agency to sell another's goods for an indefinite period, does not render the contract void as against public policy.[2]

§ 69. Contracts Relating to a Particular Article.— The principle discussed in the foregoing section applies to contracts in which the grantor binds himself not to manufacture or to trade in a specified article. It is well established that a covenant not to manufacture a particular article, or to engage in trade in such article, if there is a proper limitation in regard to space and a valuable consideration, is not in restraint of trade, and, in consequence, is valid.[3] In a leading case in Indiana, it was held that a contract in restraint of the right of making, selling and trading fanning mills south of the Wabash river, within thirty miles of Marion, in Grant county, is not objection

trade generally. Where one person is restrained from doing a particular business in a particular place competition is left open to all others, and there is no injury to the public. The person restrained in such case merely yields to another the use of what he has disposed of to that other for value. The limitation here did not go beyond what was necessary for the protection of appellee in the prosecution of the business purchased by him, and was, therefore, reasonable." *Ibid.*

[1] Swanson v. Kirby (1896). 98 Ga. 586; s. c., 26 S. E. Rep. 71.

[2] Woods v. Hart (1897) (Neb.), 70 N. W. Rep. 53. "The next contention is that the contract is void as being against public policy, in that it provides that 'W should have the exclusive agency for the sale of the lots.' Such provision did not, in the least operate against the interests of the public, nor yet against those of the defendant, since the appointment as agent was not for a fixed or definite period. The power or right of revocation of the agency remained in H and he could have exercised the same at any time, or sold the property himself. Chambers v. Seay, 73 Ala. 372. Not one of the cases cited by appellant supports the doctrine that the clause under consideration renders the contract void. Suffice it to say that they merely hold that contracts in restraint of trade, or those made for the purpose of preventing competition at auction and other public sales, are contrary to public policy, and therefore void." *Ibid.*, 55.

[3] Gillis v. Hall, 2 Brewst. 342.

able on account of the extent of space prescribed, nor because the restriction is indefinite in regard to time.[1]

§ 70. Contracts under which the Grantor Retains an Interest in the Business.—Where a person engaged in business makes a sale of his property' to a competitor, but retains an interest in the business, an agreement as a part of the transaction by which a definite price of the goods to

[1] Bowser v. Bliss, 7 Blackf. 344. In Crystal Ice Mfg. Co. v. San Antonio Brewing Ass'n, 8 Tex. Civ. App. 1; s. c., 27 S. W. Rep. 210, a contract between an ice manufacturer and a brewer whereby the former agrees to sell to the latter all the ice he needs, the brewer not to retail ice nor sell to retailers, is held not invalid, there being nothing in it to show that the brewer did, or intended to, make and sell ice. The court said: "The contract is not upon its face one necessarily in restraint of trade. It contains nothing which indicates that the brewing association was a manufacturer of or engaged in the pursuit of selling ice or intended entering upon the business, and a manufacturer ordinarily has the right to select his customers, and may sell his goods to a person at a reduced price, to be used by the customer and not sold by him. There is nothing pernicious in such an arrangement if the restraint is such only as affords a fair protection to the interests of the party in favor of whom it is granted, and not so large as to interfere with the interests of the public. Pierce v. Woodward, 6 Pick. 206; Palmer v. Stebbins, 3 Pick. 188. If the brewing association did not deal in ice, nor contemplate doing so, we do not perceive any detriment arising to the public from the restriction in this contract." An agreement between two traders in live stock that the first will sell the other all his commodities and the second will buy from the first alone, is not in violation of law or public policy nor in restraint of trade, where made for a limited time and confined to one locality. Live Stock Ass'n v. Levy, 54 N. Y. Sup. Ct. 32. The grocers in a certain town agreed with a firm which was about to open a butter store that they would not buy any butter for the term of two years. *Held*, that such contract is void as being in restraint of trade. Chapin v. Brown, 83 Iowa, 156; s. c., 48 N. W. Rep. 1074. An agreement by the manufacturer of printing presses not to sell any presses which could be used for certain kinds of printing is valid. New York Bank Note Co. v. Hamilton, etc. Co., 83 Hun, 593; s. c., 31 N. Y. Supl. 1060. A contract between a domestic firm and a foreign corporation, both engaged in the manufacture and sale of woodenware, whereby the former sells its stock, materials, tools and machinery to the latter, and agrees not to manufacture or sell woodenware in seven named States for five years, nor to permit to be used for that purpose during the time limited, is in restraint of trade and void. Western Woodenware Ass'n v. Starkey, 84 Mich. 76; s. c., 47 N. W. Rep. 604.

be sold is fixed, is not void as in restraint of trade, unless the product of the business is an article of necessity, or the sale amounts to an attempt to control prices. In a late case it was held that a contract under which two rival manufacturers agree upon a scale of selling prices for their goods, one of them discontinuing his business and becoming a partner with the other for a specified term, is not void as in restraint of trade, provided the goods manufactured were not articles of necessity, and the transaction did not amount to a conspiracy between the parties to control prices by creating a monopoly.[1] In the opinion in this

[1] Dolph v. Troy Laundry Machinery Co., 28 Fed. Rep. 553. See also Jones v. Lees, 1 Hurl. & N. 189; Ainsworth v. Bentley, 14 W. R. 630; Marsh v. Russell, 66 N. Y. 292: Perkins v. Lyman, 9 Mass. 522. Where several parties severally engaged in the business of manufacturing and selling balance shade rollers, for the purpose of avoiding competition, organize themselves into a corporation, and severally enter into an agreement with the corporation so organized, that all sales of the shade roller shall be made in the name of the corporation, and at once reported to it: that when either party shall establish an agency in any city for the sale of a roller made exclusively for that purpose, no other party shall take orders for the same roller in the same place; and that the prices for rollers of the same grade, made by the different parties, shall be according to an agreed schedule, subject to changes upon recommendation of three-fourths of the stockholders, the agreement is valid and not void as in restraint of trade. Central Shade Roller Co. v. Cushman, 143 Mass. 353; s. c., 9 N. E. Rep. 629. "The defendant entered into the covenant, as a consideration in part of the purchase of his property, by the Swift & Courtney & Beecher Company, presumably because he considered it for his advantage to make the sale. He realized a large sum in money, and on the completion of the transaction became interested as a stockholder in the very business which he had sold. We are of opinion that the covenant, being supported by a good consideration, and constituting a partial and not a general restraint, and being, in view of the circumstances disclosed, reasonable, is valid and not void." Diamond Match Co. v. Roeber, 106 N. Y. 473, 486. "The respondents were incorporated on the 17th of July, 1888, and on the 8th of August the agreement of the 3d of July was adopted by the company. It is to be noted that at the time when this agreement was entered into, to which the Nordenfelt Company was a party, the appellant was managing director of that company, and that in the memorandum of association of the amalgamated company, which was signed by the appellants, the objects of the company were stated to be, *inter alia*, not only the adoption of the agree-

case, the court said: "It is not obnoxious to good morals, or to the rights of the public, that two rival traders agree to consolidate their concerns, and that one shall discontinue business and become a partner with the other for a specified term. It may happen as the result of such an arrangement that the public have to pay more for the commodity in which the parties deal, but the public are not obliged to buy of them. Certainly, the public have no right to complain, so long as the transaction falls short of a conspiracy between the parties to control prices by creating a monopoly."[1]

§ 71. **Contracts for the Sale of a Good Will.**—From an early period the good will of a business establishment, and, to a limited extent, that of a profession or trade, has been regarded as a thing of value, and of the nature of property. As such it may be sold or bartered, and contracts relating to such sales or transfers, if not illegal, will be upheld. Where a person engaged in any branch of business or in a profession, disposes of his stock in trade or of his professional practice, he may enter into an agreement

ment of the 3d of July, but also 'to acquire, undertake and carry on, as successors to the Maxim Gun Company and the Nordenfelt Guns & Ammunition Company, the good will of the trade and businesses heretofore carried on by such companies, and each of them, and the property and rights belonging to or held in connection therewith respectively.' This is of importance, because the appellant, in a forcible argument, pointed out that the judgment of the court of appeal was largely founded on the fact that the covenant in question was entered into in connection with the sale of the good will of the appellants' business, and was designed for the protection of the good will so sold, and he contended that this was an error, inasmuch as there was no sale by him of the good will on that occasion, he having already parted with it to the Nordenfelt Company, the later sale being by that company, and not by him. I think it is impossible to accede to this contention." Lord Herschel, in Nordenfelt v. Maxim-Nordenfelt Company, L. R. (1894) App. Cas. 535, 540.

[1] Dolph v. Troy Laundry Machinery Co., 28 Fed. Rep. 553, 555. See also Whittaker v. Howe, 3 Beav. 383; Jones v. Lees, 1 Hurl. & N. 189; Rousillon v. Rousillon, L. R. 14 Ch. D. 351; Leather Cloth Co. v. Lorsont, L. R. 9 Eq. 345; Collins v. Locke, L. R. 4 App. Cas. 674; Oregon Steam Co. v. Winsor, 20 Wall. 64; Morse, etc. Co. v. Morse, 103 Mass. 73.

with the vendee not to engage in the same business or profession within a designated territorial limit, and for a fixed period, and such covenant will be held valid. In such cases the position of the vendor is somewhat stronger than where there is a simple contract that the vendee shall discontinue his business or profession with a valid consideration. In a leading English case, Sir John Romilly, M. R., defined the legal idea of a good will, as follows: "The good will of a trade, although inseparable from the business, is an appreciable part of the assets of a concern, both in fact and in the estimation of a court of equity. Accordingly, in reported cases, Lord Eldon held, that a share of it properly and as of right belonged to the estate of the deceased partner. It does not survive to the remaining partners, unless by express agreement, but it may by agreement, as it may be agreed that any particular portion of the partnership assets shall so survive. Good will manifestly forms a portion of the subject-matter which produces profits, which constitutes partnership property, and which is to be divided between the surviving partners and the estate of the deceased partner, according to the terms of the contract, and when that is silent, according to their shares in the concern. There is considerable difficulty in defining accurately what is included under this term *good will;* it seems to be that species of connection in trade which induces customers to deal with a particular firm. It varies almost in every case, but it is a matter distinctly appreciable, which may be preserved (at least to some extent) if the business be sold as a going concern, but which is wholly lost if the concern is wound up, its liabilities discharged and its assets got in and distributed. I am of opinion, then, that both on principle, on the authority of the decided cases, and on the ordinary rules of common sense, I must, whenever there is a reputation and connection in business, constituting good will, treat that as part of the assets of the concern."[1] Mr.

[1] Wedderburn v. Wedderburn, 22 Beav. 84, 104. "It was argued that. In Shakle v. Baker, 14 Ves. 468; Crutwell v. Lye, 17 Ves. 335, and Kennedy v. Lee, 3 Meriv. 452, Lord Eldon has laid down the

Justice Story, defines good will, as follows: "Good will may be properly enough described to be the advantage or benefit which is acquired by an establishment beyond the mere value of the capital, stock, funds or property

principle that an assignment of the good will of a trade simpliciter, carries no more with it than the advantage of occupying the premises which were occupied by the former firm, and the chance you thereby have of the customers of the former firm being attracted to those premises. But it would be taking too narrow a view of what is there laid down by Lord Eldon, to say that it is confined to that. Good will, I apprehend, must mean every advantage, every positive advantage, if I may so express it, as contrasted with the negative advantage of the late partner not carrying on the business himself, that has been acquired by the old firm in carrying on its business, whether connected with the premises in which the business was previously carried on, or with the name of the late firm, or with any other matter carrying with it the benefit of the business. When Lord Eldon, in speaking of a nursery garden, or a locality which the customers must frequent to look at the flowers and other things, and when Sir Thomas Plumer, in another case, in speaking of a retail shop which a person must enter in order to buy the goods there exposed—they are only, as it appears to me, giving those as illustrations of what good will is. But it would be absurd to say that, where a large wholesale business is conducted, the public are mindful whether it is carried on at one end of the Strand or the other, or in Fleet street, or in the Strand or any place adjoining, and that they regard that, and do not regard the identity of the house or business, namely, the firm." Churton v. Douglas, Johns. [Eng.] Ch. 174. "Now, what good will did he sell? It was not that of his own stall in the same market where he continued to pursue his occupation. During his *quasi* management of the stall, formerly Journe's, for the brief period of three months, without having posted his name over the stall, as required by the city ordinance, and never occupying it himself in person, he could not have acquired, on his own account, any appreciable amount of additional patronage or good will for that stall. But it is said that upon the death of Journe, the good will that appertained to his stall ceased, and that nothing of the kind could have gone to his heirs. This position is not tenable. It is not exclusively to the person that what is termed the 'good will' is attached, but it is chiefly to the place." Succession of Journe, 21 La. Ann. 391, 393. " 'Good will,' as property, is intangible, and merely an incident of other property. It was not, in this case, an incident of the stock of hardware, tools and machinery which seems to have been the only tangible property purchased by the appellants from the appellees. As a rule, it may be said that 'good will' is never an incident of a stock of merchandise; but, generally speaking, it is an incident of locality or place of the store room or place of business." Rawson v.

employed therein, in consequence of the general public patronage and encouragement, which it receives from constant or habitual customers, on account of its local position or common celebrity, or reputation for skill or affluence, or punctuality, or from other accidental circumstances or necessities, or even from ancient partialities or prejudices."[1]

§ 72. **The Subject Continued.**—In a recent case in New York, the rule was stated by the court, as follows: "While the law, to a certain extent, tolerates contracts in restraint of trade or business, when made between vendor and purchaser, and will uphold them, they are not treated with special indulgence. They are intended to secure to the purchaser of the good will of a trade or business a guaranty against the competition of the former proprietor. When this object is accomplished it will not be presumed that more was intended,"[2] Where a contract of this character

Pratt. 91 Ind. 9, 16. The "good will" connected with any trade or occupation is a valuable right, and may be made the subject of barter and sale. If unlawfully taken away or destroyed, the law will award compensation to the injured party. Where customers, who resort to a particular locality, are driven therefrom by reason of an attachment having been levied, the trade loses what is known as "good will," and suffers not merely a loss of profits. Carey v. Gunnison (Iowa), 17 N. W. Rep. 881. The good will of an established business is a common subject of contract, although it is nothing but the chance of being able to keep the business which has been established, yet the rights of a purchaser of such good will will be enforced in equity, and recognized at law as effectual between the parties to the contract. Barber v. Conn. Mut. Life Ins. Co., 15 Fed. Rep. 312.

[1] Story on Partnership, § 99. See also Smith v. Everett, 27 Beav. 446; Lindley on Partnership, 842.

[2] Greenfield v. Gilman, 140 N. Y. 168, 173. See also Chapin v. Brown, 83 Iowa, 156; s. c., 32 Am. St. Rep. 297; Keeler v. Taylor, 53 Pa. St. 467; Rousillon v. Rousillon, L. R. 14 Ch. D. 351; Jacoby v. Whitmore, 48 L. T. 335; Smith v. Martin, 80 Ind. 260; Vickery v. Welch, 19 Pick. 523; Taylor v. Blanchard, 13 Allen, 370; Roller v. Ott, 14 Kan. 609; Warfield v. Booth, 33 Md. 63; Alger v. Thacher, 19 Pick. 51; Mackinnon Pen Co. v. Fountain Ink Co., 48 N. Y. Sup. Ct. 442; Richardson v. Peacock, 33 N. J. Eq. 597; Finger v. Hahn, 42 N. J. Eq. 606; Levy v. Walker, L. R. 10 Ch. D. 436; Labouchere v. Dawson, L. R. 13 Eq. 322; Cruttwell v. Lye, 17 Ves. 306; Price v. Green, 16 M. & W. 346; Gale v. Reed, 8 East, 80.

is violated by the resumption of business on the part of the grantor, he will not only be restrained by injunction, but he will also be held responsible for the injury that he may do to the business of the purchaser. In a case in Massachusetts, the defendant, having covenanted with the plaintiff, on the dissolution of a firm for the manufacture of daguerreotype materials, of which they had been members, "not, directly or indirectly, to enter into, or carry on, or in any way be interested in, or furnish to any person or persons information in regard to," that business within certain limits, nevertheless formed with a third person a new partnership within said limits for that business, had the whole financial charge of the new partnership, traveled about the country, visiting the customers of the old firm and introducing the goods of the new partnership, and received a commission on all sales. It was held that these facts warranted a finding that the defendant was liable for all the injury occasioned to the plaintiff by the establishment of the new partnership.[1] In a late case

[1] Dean v. Emerson, 102 Mass. 480. "The plaintiff contends that the agreement is not void as being in restraint of trade. First, because it is an agreement pertaining to property and business protected by patents; secondly, because the restraint is so extensive only with the business sold, and is necessary to enable the company to enjoy fully what it has bought and paid for; and thirdly, because it relates to a single commodity, not of prime necessity, and not a staple of commerce. See Central Roller Co. v. Cushman, 143 Mass. 353; s. c., 9 N. E. Rep. 629; Morse Twist Co. v. Morse, 103 Mass. 73; Gloucester Isinglass Co. v. Russia Cement Co., 154 Mass. 92; s. c., 27 N. E. Rep. 1005. There seems to be no reason why the defendant Crane should not assign the patents and inventions which he agreed to assign, if there are any, and no serious objection has been raised by the defendant on this part of the case. The defendant contends that he has a right to assist in forming a corporation, and to act as one of its officers, the business of which is to manufacture and sell fire alarm and police telegraph machines which are not made under any patents owned by the plaintiff, or under any patents which he has agreed to assign to the plaintiff, or which the plaintiff has elected to purchase, under the option given in the contract, even although by so doing he enters into competition with the plaintiff in its business. He, in effect, concedes that, so far as the business is protected by patents which he has assigned, or agreed to assign, the restraint is valid. It appears that there are 'a dozen or fifteen concerns in the United

in Alabama, it was held that a contract by which a partnership, engaged in the business of selling hardware, and selling out their stock of plow blades and plow stocks to a rival

States engaged in a somewhat similar business.' The defendant testified that he looked up the number of patents pertaining to this branch of the art in 1881, and that there were then about 500. The defendant contends that he ought to be able to use his own patents for subsequent improvements, applicable to such apparatus, if the plaintiff does not elect to purchase them; that he was previously a manufacturer of fire alarm and police telegraph apparatus, and not a seller thereof; that the good will which attached to his business was that of a manufacturer who did not sell his manufactures in the market, and that it is against public policy that he should be restrained from exercising his peculiar skill anywhere in the United States, or in the world, for the period of ten years. The apparatus, as the defendant contends, which he has a right to manufacture and sell, is not secret machinery, and is not protected by any patents which the plaintiff owns or has a right to control, but is apparatus either not protected by patents at all, or by patents of his own, or of some other persons who may choose to employ the defendant. The only ground upon which this restriction can be maintained, is that it is reasonably necessary for the beneficial enjoyment by the plaintiff of the property it bought of the defendant, or if this is not so, that the law in modern times does not regard such an agreement as against public policy. So far as we are aware in every modern case in this commonwealth, except one, where a contract in restraint of trade has been held valid, the restriction has been limited as to space. In Taylor v. Blanchard, 13 Allen, 370, the parties entered into a partnership for carrying on 'the trade or business of manufacturing shoe cutters,' and it was provided that 'at whatever time the said co-partnership shall be determined and ended,' the defendant 'shall not, nor will, at any time or times thereafter, either alone or jointly with, or as agent for any person or persons whomsoever, set up, exercise, or carry on the said trade or business of manufacturing and selling shoe cutters within the aforesaid commonwealth of Massachusetts, and shall not, nor will, set up, make or encourage any opposition to the said trade or business hereafter to be carried on by the plaintiff. The manufacture of shoe cutters was an art which could be carried on only by persons instructed in it, and the business was confined to the plaintiff and three other persons, but the court held the agreement void. In Bishop v. Palmer, 146 Mass. 469; s. c., 16 N. E. Rep. 299, the plaintiff, being engaged in the manufacture and selling of bed quilts and comfortables, conveyed to the defendant his 'entire business plant and enterprise as a manufacturer of and dealer in bed quilts and comfortables,' together with the good will of the business and all the machinery, implements and utensils used by him in said business, and agreed 'that for and during the period of five years from the date hereof, he will company, agreed "not to handle any more plow blades or plow stocks," construed, in connection with the attendant circumstances, showing the extent of country over which

not, either directly or indirectly, in his own name or in the name of any other person or persons, continue in, carry on, or engage in the business of manufacturing or dealing in bed quilts or comfortables, or of any business of which that may form a part.' It was held that this was clearly illegal and void as being in restraint of trade, because not limited as to space. See also Alger v. Thacher, 19 Pick. 51; Pierce v. Fuller, 8 Mass. 223; 226; Perkins v. Lyman, 9 Mass. 522; Stearns v. Barrett, 1 Pick. 443; Palmer v. Stebbins, 3 Pick. 188; Gilman v. Dwight, 13 Gray, 356; Angier v. Webber, 14 Allen, 211; Dean v. Emerson, 102 Mass. 480; Dwight v. Hamilton, 113 Mass. 175; Boutelle v. Smith, 116 Mass. 111; Ropes v. Upton, 125 Mass. 258; Handforth v. Jackson, 150 Mass. 149; s. c., 22 N. E. Rep. 634. The case of Morse, etc. Machine Co. v. Morse, 103 Mass. 73, is the case referred to as an exception. The question arose upon demurrer. The agreement of the defendant was only to transfer his patents, machinery, etc., and all improvements and inventions, but 'that he will use his best efforts for the perfecting of improvements in the business and manufacture, and for such alterations and combinations as may tend to insure the success of the same and of the company,' and that he 'will do no act that may injure the company or its business, and that he will at no time aid, assist or encourage, in any manner, any competition against the same.' He also agreed 'to serve as the superintendent of the company for three years,' etc. The plaintiff company was formed by the defendant and others, and the defendant's business was transferred to it. He was a stockholder and was made superintendent. The plaintiff agreed to employ the defendant for three years, and he was actually employed as superintendent up to the time he entered upon a competing business. The case seems to have been decided on the ground that the defendant had agreed to give to the plaintiff his exclusive services with reference to his mechanical skill and ingenuity in all improvements, alterations and combinations which would tend to insure the success of the plaintiff in manufacturing twist drills and collets. The court say that 'the same principle that enables a partner to bind himself to do nothing in competition with the business of the firm ought to apply to him.' The opinion proceeds to consider the English cases where the restriction was held not to extend beyond the good will of the business which was the subject of the sale, or was not greater than the interests of the vendee required, and was not unreasonable in view of all the circumstances. This doctrine, in England, has been carried very far. See Davies v. Davies, L. R. 36 Ch. D. 359. In this country the courts generally have not gone so far, but the old law has been a good deal modified in some jurisdictions in view of modern methods of doing business. See Oregon Steam Navigation Co.

the rivalry in business extended, is not an unreasonable restriction or restraint of trade.[1] In a case in Ohio, M, a married woman, engaged in the business of millinery and dressmaking with her separate funds, and on her own account, in the town of F, sold her stock of goods, together

v. Winsor, 20 Wall. 64; Fowle v. Park, 131 U. S. 88; s. c., 9 Sup. Ct. Rep. 658; Ellerman v. Stockyards Co., 49 N. J. Eq. 217; s. c., 23 Atl. Rep. 287; Western, etc. Association v. Starkey, 84 Mich. 76; s. c., 47 N. W. Rep. 604; Matthews v. Associated Press, 136 N. Y. 333; s. c., 32 N. E. Rep. 981; Oliver v. Gilmore, 52 Fed. Rep. 562; Diamond Match Co. v. Roeber, 106 N. Y. 473; s. c., 13 N. E. Rep. 419; Whitney v. Slayton, 40 Me. 224." Field, C. J., in Gamewell, etc. Tel. Co. v. Crane, 160 Mass. 50; s. c., 35 N. E. Rep. 98.

[1] Moore Hardware Co. v. Towers Hardware Co., 87 Ala. 206. See also Hubbard v. Miller, 27 Mich. 15; Curtis v. Gokey, 68 N. Y. 300; Warfield v. Booth, 33 Md. 63; Dethlefs v. Tomsen, 7 Daly, 354; Beal v. Chase, 31 Mich. 490; Horner v. Graves, 7 Bing. 735; Whittaker v. Howe, 3 Beav. 383; Tallis v. Tallis, 1 El. & Bl. 391; Morse Machine Co. v. Morse, 103 Mass. 73. Under Sec. 1674, Civ. Code, a contract for the sale of the good will of a business and agreeing not to do a similar business in several counties is void as to all but the county in which the business is carried on. City Carpet Beating Works v. Jones, 102 Cal. 506; s. c., 36 Pac. Rep. 841. Civ. Code, § 1673, provides that a contract in restraint of trade otherwise than provided in the next two sections, "is to that extent void," and section 1674 provides that the seller of "the good will of a business may agree with the buyer to refrain from carrying on a similar business within a specified territory, so long as the buyer or any person deriving title to the good will from him carries on the business." *Held*, that a provision, on sale of a good will, that the seller shall not engage in the business for three years in a certain city, is not void, but the contract will be limited to such time, not exceeding three years, as the buyer or his assignee carries on the business. Brown v. Kling, 101 Cal. 295; s. c., 35 Pac. Rep. 995. Defendants were the owners of a tobacco warehouse, and had built up quite a trade in the vicinity. Plaintiff purchased the property and good will of their business from them, defendants executing a deed of conveyance which contained a clause to the effect that defendants were selling "also all our good will in said warehouse business, as members of" the firm "or as individuals; and we agree with said company not to engage in said business, directly or indirectly, for a period of ten years from this date." One of defendants engaged in the same business in the same city within less than five years from the sale. *Held*, that it was error to sustain a demurrer to the petition asking for an order restraining defendants from continuing such business. Western Dist. Warehouse Co. v. Hobson, 96 Ky. 550; s. c., 29 S. W. Rep. 308.

with the good will of the business, and engaged not to carry on the business at any time in the future, at the town of F, or at any place within such distance of said town, as would interfere with such business, whether the same was carried on by the purchasers or by their successors. It was held that such agreement in equity is binding, and that in an action brought by the successors of the purchasers, M will be enjoined from carrying on such business in violation of the agreement.[1]

§ 73. **Farther Application of the Rule.**—The value of a good will is largely determined by the peculiar circumstances under which the business to which it relates has been established and developed. It may be of special value and importance in the sale and transfer of an establishment for the publication of a newspaper, and such sale, if the limitations are reasonable, will be upheld. In a recent case in North Carolina, F and his wife sold a newspaper owned by them in D county, and agreed that F "would not edit, print or conduct a newspaper, nor be in anywise connected with one, printed anywhere in the State of North Carolina, and that, for a like period, Mrs. F should not edit, print or conduct a newspaper or magazine, and be in anywise connected with one anywhere in the county of D, said State, without the consent of such purchaser or his assignees. It was held that such contract was not void as an unreasonable restraint of trade.[2]

[1] Morgan v. Perhamus, 36 Ohio St. 517.

[2] Cowan v. Fairbrother, 118 N. Car. 406; s. c. 24 S. E. Rep. 212. "Where a person acquires a reputation for skill and learning in his profession, as a lawyer or a physician, he often creates an intangible but valuable property, by winning the confidence of his patrons and securing immunity from successful competition for their business. So, where an editor by reason of his style, his power, his pathos, his humor, his learning, or of any gift or attainment, attracts subscribers solely by such personal qualities, he imparts a peculiar value to the good will and property of a newspaper, which goes with him, to its injury when he leaves it and lends the talent and accomplishments that have given it patronage and popularity to a rival journal in the same vicinity. Where he owns the press and plant the enhanced value so imparted by him becomes an element of his

§ 74. Agreement not to Buy or to Sell.—Contracts under which one of the parties is bound not to buy or to sell a particular article, if there is a valid consideration and the restraint is not unreasonable, will be upheld. In a recent case it was held that a contract between an ice manufacturer and a brewer, whereby the former agreed to sell the latter all the ice he needed, the brewer not to retail nor to sell to retailers, is not invalid, there being nothing in the contract to show that the brewer either did, or intended to, make and sell ice.[1] In a recent case in New York, defend-

property, with the same incidental power to dispose of it as attaches to any other of his acquisitions which has a market value. Beal v. Chase, 31 Mich. 529. But it is not like other property which ordinarily passes by delivery or assignment to the purchaser. Neither an editor, a lawyer nor a physician can transfer to another his style, his learning or his manners. Either, however, can add to the chances of success and profits of another who embarks in the same business in the same field, by withdrawing as a competitor. So that the one sells and the other buys something valuable, and the policy of the law limits the right to enter into such contract of sale only to the extent that they are held to injure the public by restraining trade. The one sells his prospective patronage and the other buys the right to compete with all others for it, and to be protected against competition from his vendor. The law intends that the one shall have the lawful authority to dispose of his right to compete, but restricts his power of disposition territorially so as to make it only co-extensive with the right of protection on the part of the purchaser. To the extent that the contract covers territory from which the vendor has derived, and will probably in future derive, no profit or patronage, it needlessly deprives the public of the benefit of open competition in useful business, and of the services of him who sells without any possible advantage to his successor. When the reason upon which a law is founded ceases, the rule itself ceases to operate. The older cases in which the courts attempted to fix arbitrarily geographical bounds, beyond which a contract to forbear competition would not be enforced, have given away to the more rational idea of making every case dependent upon the surrounding circumstances, showing the extent as to time and territory of the protection needed." *Ibid.* 411.

[1] Crystal Ice Mfg. Co. v. San Antonio Brewing Ass'n, 8 Tex. Civ. App. 1; s. c., 27 S. W. Rep. 210. An agreement made by a traveling man with a purchaser not to sell a certain kind of goods to any one else in the same town is not contrary to public policy. Keith v. Herschberg Optical Co., 48 Ark. 138; s. c., 2 S. W. Rep. 777. As to exclusive telegraph grants by railroad companies there is a

ant, a corporation organized under the act "to incorporate the Associated Press of the State of New York," adopted a by-law prohibiting its members from receiving or publishing "the regular news dispatches of any other news association covering a like territory and organized for a like purpose." A suspension of all the rights and privileges of the association was provided as a penalty for a violation of said provision. In an action to restrain defendant from enforcing this penalty, it was held that the association had power to enact the by-law; that it was not objectionable either as unreasonable and oppressive, as tending to restrain trade and competition and to create a monopoly, or as an unlawful interference with vested property rights, at least in the absence of evidence that the alleged violation for which the penalty was sought to be enforced grew out of acts in the performance of a contract entered into before the passage of the by-law, nor did it create a restriction upon the liberty of the press.[1] A contract of this character will be enforced only as there is a valuable consideration and as there is no unreasonable restraint of trade. In a certain town in Iowa, the grocers agreed with a firm, which was about to open a butter store, that they would not buy any butter for the term of two years. The firm did not purchase any established business, and paid nothing to the grocers as a consideration for their agreement not to purchase butter for the time specified. It was held that the contract was void for

general holding that they tend to monopoly, and are, therefore, void. See Western Union Tel. Co. v. American Union Tel. Co., 65 Ga. 160; Western Union Tel. Co. v. B. & S. W. R. Co., 3 McCrary, 130; Western Union Tel. Co. v. American Union Tel. Co., 9 Biss. 72; Western Union Tel. Co. v. Balto., etc. Tel. Co., 23 Fed. Rep. 12; Western Union Tel. Co. v. Nat. Tel. Co., 19 Fed. Rep. 660. See further West Virginia Transp. Co. v. Pipe Line Co., 22 W. Va. 600; Balto. & Ohio Tel. Co. v. Western Union Tel. Co., 24 Fed. Rep. 319. A contract whereby a railroad company grants to a particular telegraph company the exclusive right to establish lines of communication along its right of way is void as a restraint of trade. Union Trust Co. v. Atchison, T. & S. F. R. Co., 43 Pac. Rep. 701.

[1] Matthews v. Associated Press of New York, 136 N. Y. 333; s. c., 32 N. E. Rep. 981. See also Hodge v. Sloan, 107 N. Y. 244; Leslie v. Lorillard, 110 N. Y. 519.

lack of a consideration, and that it was also void as being in restraint of trade.[1]

§ 75. **Contract to Maintain Prices.**—An agreement between two or more individuals to maintain prices, where there is no transfer of property and no valid consideration, will not be sustained. It is in restraint of trade in such a sense as to be invalid. It is not necessary that the contract should amount to a conspiracy or that there should be any attempt to create anything more than a very limited monopoly. Such contract must attempt something that is of the nature of a monopoly in order to accomplish the end sought. It must be an actual restraint of trade. In a recent English case, it was held that a contract by which the members of a mineral water association bound themselves not to sell mineral waters at a less price than 9d. per dozen, or such other price, not being less than 9d. per dozen, as the committee might from time to time direct, is a contract in restraint of trade for which there is no consideration, and which cannot, therefore, be enforced in a court of law.[2] In a recent case in Kentucky this rule was upheld.

[1] Chapin v. Brown, 83 Iowa, 156; s. c., 32 Am. St. Rep. 297; 48 N. W. Rep. 1074.

[2] Urmston v. Whitelegg, 63 L. T. 455. "The conclusions of fact found by the learned court below were amply justified by the record: 'It cannot be gainsaid that the object of this combination is to enable the forty-five brewers of Philadelphia, individuals firms and corporations, who have entered into it, to regulate and control the sale and price of beer within the city of Philadelphia, and the county of Camden. N. J. It certainly is a combination, in restraint of trade, tending to destroy competition and create a monopoly in an article of daily consumption.' The appellants, however, conceding these to be the facts, insist that the contract was not within the prohibition of public policy, because the restraint was but partial. 'Contracts in partial restraint of trade, which the law sustains, are those which are entered into, by a vendor of a business and its good will, with his vendee, by which the vendor agrees not to engage in the same business within a limited territory; and the restraint to be valid must be no more extensive than is reasonably necessary for the protection of the vendee in the enjoyment of the business purchased. But, in the present case, there is no purchase or sale of any business, nor any other analogous

It was held that an agreement between owners of two rival steamboats on the Kentucky river, that, in order to prevent rivalry and consequent reduction of charges, the net profits of each should be shared in a certain proportion, each bearing its own expenses, and that, if the owners of either boat should sell with a view of going out of the trade, notice should be given to the owners of the other boat, and the owners so selling should not enter the trade again within one year, is void as against public policy, and the owner so selling may start a new boat within the year.[1]

§ 76. **Statutory Regulations.**—In some of the States the common law doctrine has been materially modified by statute. In California it has been held that a contract in restraint of trade, otherwise than as expressly excepted in the Civil Code, is against public policy and void by the terms of the same code. A contract for a term of three years

circumstances giving to one party a just right to be protected against competition from the other. All the members of the association are engaged in the same business within the same territory: and the object of the association is, purely and simply, to silence and stifle all competition as between its members. No equitable reason for such restraint exists. * * * The appellants insist that restraint of trade in the necessaries of life only, is within the prohibition of public policy. No standard has been furnished by which to ascertain what constitutes these with reference to the general public. But assuming that beer is not among them, it is equally within the reach of the rule. The law recognizes it as a commodity; regulates its sales; it is 'an article of daily consumption.' and the court should refuse to aid in any attempted imposition upon the public by means of illegal combinations. The fact that coal was 'an article of prime necessity,' was not mentioned as an essential to the illegality of the combination which was involved in Morris Run Coal Co. v. Barclay Coal Co., 68 Pa. St. 173, but was suggested, *arguendo*, as an aggravation of the injury done the public. The whole course of discussion there shows that injury to the public was regarded as the true test of illegality." Sterrett, C. J., in Nester v. Continental Brewing Co., 161 Pa. St. 473; s. c., 41 Am. St. Rep. 894; 29 Atl. Rep. 102; 34 W. N. C. 387. See also More v. Bennett, 140 Ill. 69; s. c., 29 N. E. Rep. 888.

[1] Anderson v. Jett, 89 Ky. 375; s. c., 12 S. W. Rep. 670.

between several powder companies, providing that neither of the parties thereto shall make any shipment of dynamite powder to any part of the United States, east of certain boundaries, and regulating the manufacture and sale of it by parties in the territory west of those boundaries, under certain specified restrictions, and giving power to a standing committee to fix prices, regulate the manufacturing cost, and impose fines for violations of the contract, and providing for a termination of the contract, if any other party or parties shall begin to manufacture and sell dynamite in competition with the parties to the contract, is in restraint of trade, and void as against public policy.[1] In a recent case in the same State, it was held that where the good will of a business has accrued from customers residing in several contiguous counties, though the business was conducted in one alone, a sale of the business and good will, with a covenant restricting the vendor from engaging in business in any of such contiguous counties for a period of years, is not at common law an illegal contract, and is void under the code only as to the counties other than the one in which the business was conducted, but is valid as to that county, the covenant being divisible as regards space, and void only to the extent to which it departs from the provisions of the code.[2] In a recent case in Texas, it was held that a contract of sale between a brewing company and a dealer, whereby the company grants exclusive territory to the dealer for the sale of its products, and further agrees to furnish the dealer with a delivery wagon and ice vault, which were to remain its property, and the dealer agrees not to sell the product of any other company, is a combination in restraint of trade, as prohibited by the statute.[3]

[1] Vulcan Powder Co. v. Hercules Powder Co., 96 Cal. 510.

[2] City Carpet. etc. Co. v. Jones, 102 Cal. 506.

[3] Texas Brewing Co. v. Templeman (1896) (Tex.), 38 S. W. Rep. 27. A contract for the sale of beer, which provides that the purchaser shall handle only the beer named in the contract, and that the manufacturer shall sell to no other dealer in that town or vicinity, creates a trust and conspiracy against trade, within the prohibition of the Act of 1889. Fuqua v. Pabst Brewing Co.

(1896) (Tex.), 38 S. W. Rep. 29. A contract to sell an unlimited quantity of goods, prohibiting the vendee from dealing in the product of any other person, and requiring him to give prompt notice to the vendor of any competition which might arise in the traffic and sale of such goods at the place where the vendee was engaged in business, is void under the anti-trust statute. Texas Brewing Co. v. Meyer (1896) (Tex. Civ. App.), 38 S. W. Rep. 263.

CHAPTER V.

CONSPIRACIES IN RESTRAINT OF TRADE.

§ 77. Introductory.
78. Conspiracy Defined.
79. The Rule in England.
80. Conspiracy by a Corporation.
81. Combination to Monopolize a Particular Branch of Business.
82. Combinations for Regulating Prices.
83. Conspiracies under the Federal Anti-Trust Act.
§ 84. Combination to Prevent Competition at a Judicial Sale.
85. Combination to Destroy Competition.
86. Conspiracy for Severing the Relation of a Minister to His Congregation.
87. Indictment for Conspiracy.
88. Statutory Regulations.

§ 77. **Introductory.**—The object of this chapter is to discuss a single phase only of the subject of conspiracies. An exhaustive or comprehensive treatment of the law relating to conspiracies would not be germane to the subject of this work. But during the past few years conspiracies in restraint of trade have assumed new and very formidable proportions. Since the rise and phenomenal development of the trade and corporate "trust," the attempt to avoid the dangers of that method by adopting others more limited in their operations, but designed to accomplish the same ends, has become of very common occurrence. The dangerous character of many of these methods has attracted the attention of the courts and of legislators, and where the common law has proved inadequate to the correction of the evil, it has been met by legislative enactments. The United States statute, known as "The Anti-Trust Act," with many acts of similar nature by the various State legislatures, are examples of recent legislation on this subject. These enactments indicate a tendency of the present time and provide remedies for the growing evil. To the application of statutory and equitable rules to business methods, held and treated as conspiracies, the following sections are devoted.

§ 78. **Conspiracy Defined.**—In general a conspiracy is an agreement between two or more persons to perform an unlawful act. The essential points are two or more persons combined to do an illegal thing. It may be an agreement to do a thing criminal or unlawful, *per se*, or to do a thing which is, *per se*, lawful, in an unlawful manner. An agreement to accomplish a lawful end by unlawful means constitutes a conspiracy. In order that a combination should amount to a conspiracy there must be an agreement on the part of the parties to the combination to attempt to do an unlawful act. The crime or the offense is determined by the motive by which the act is prompted. The gist of the offense is in the combination and in the purpose to accomplish a criminal or illegal object. It is the power of combination that renders the purpose dangerous to the public or to an individual, and it is this that constitutes the forming of the plan a conspiracy. At common law the gravamen of the offense is the agreement. An overt act is not essential to the completion of the offense. The unexecuted purpose constitutes the crime. In some cases where the matter is regulated by statute an overt act is essential to the offense, but the legal character of the offense is not changed by the execution of the agreement.[1] Where the

[1] United States v. Walsh, 5 Dill. 60; State v. Norton, 33 N. J. L. 40, 46; Hazen v. Commonwealth, 23 Pa. St. 363, 364; United States v. Martin, 4 Cliff. 160, 162; Wilder v. McKee, 111 Pa. St. 335; Place v. Minster, 65 N. Y. 89, 95; Walker v. Cronin, 107 Mass. 555; Gary v. Frazer, 76 Me. 37; Hutchins v. Hutchins, 7 Hill, 104; Jones v. Baker, 7 Cow. 445; Barker v. Huntingdon, 2 Gray, 124. "A conspiracy at common law consists in the unlawful agreement of two or more persons to compass or promote some criminal or illegal purpose, or in the unlawful agreement to compass or promote a purpose not in itself criminal nor unlawful, by criminal and unlawful means. If the crime consists in the illegal object, the purpose must be clearly

offense is of a civil character, exposing the conspirators only to the payment of damages for an injury inflicted, the gist of the wrong is not in the agreement, but in the act by which the injury was effected. The only effect of the con-

and fully stated in the indictment. When the act is itself illegal there is no occasion to state the means by which the conspiracy was effected. When an indictment charged that the defendant conspired by divers false pretenses, and subtle means and devices, to obtain from another large sums of money, and to cheat and defraud him thereof, it was held that the gist of the offense being the conspiracy, it was quite sufficient to state only that fact and its object, and not set out the specified pretenses." State v. Bartlett, 30 Me. 132, 134. "The essence of a conspiracy, so far as it justifies a civil action for damages, is a concert or combination to defraud, or to cause other injury to persons or property, which, because of acts done in pursuance of such conspiracy, actually results in damages to the person or property of the person injured or defrauded. A civil action will not lie for a mere conspiracy. It is the damage done in pursuance of the conspiracy which gives the right of action. It is now well established that, in civil actions, the conspiracy is not the gravamen of the charge, but may be pleaded and proved in aggravation of the wrong of which the plaintiff complains, and as enabling him to recover against all the conspirators, as joint tort-feasors. If a plaintiff fail in the proof of a conspiracy, or concerted design, he may yet recover damages against such of the defendants as are shown to be guilty of a tort, directly resulting in damages to the plaintiff." Doremus v. Hennessey, 62 Ill. App. 391, 402. "It has often been said that a conspiracy to effect an unlawful purpose, or a lawful purpose by unlawful means, is an offense. But this is said to be a limitation rather than a definition. It certainly lacks definiteness. Many acts are said to be unlawful which would not be a subject of a criminal conspiracy. Other acts are unlawful because they are in violation of the criminal law or of some penal statute. If the ends or means are criminal in themselves, or contrary to some penal statute, the conspiracy is clearly an offense. Between these two extremes a great variety of cases may arise, many of which ought not to be regarded as criminal. Suppose two or more boys, for instance, agree to go upon another's land; the proposed act, is, or may be, a trespass, and, therefore, unlawful. If they do not go no harm is done; if they do go they are or may be civilly liable, but no one would seriously contend that in either case they would be liable criminally for conspiracy. But suppose two or more conspire unjustly and wrongfully to deprive another of his liberty or property; then, as we shall hereafter see, the criminal law may take cognizance of the act. Of course, it is difficult if not impossible to define accurately and clearly in advance what would and what would not be an offense. Hence, the difficulty of regulating spiracy in a civil offense is the aggravation of the injury inflicted. In a recent case in New Jersey, the rule was stated by the court, as follows: "It is not necessary to consider the office of the ancient writ of conspiracy, and the process by which, in time, it was superseded by the later and more efficacious action on the case for conspiracy, and the still more modern action for malicious prosecution. Nor will it now be advantageous to show how long and difficult it was to separate the idea of a criminal conspiracy at common law, where the agreement or conspiracy was the gravamen of the offense, from the real complaint in a civil action, that the combination of two or more persons has enabled them to inflict a great wrong on the plaintiff. The combination or conspiracy in the latter case was, therefore, a matter of aggravation or inducement only, of which one or all might be found guilty, while in the former it was essential to show two or more had joined in an agreement to do an unlawful act, or to do a lawful act in an unlawful manner. The distinction is now well established that in civil actions the conspiracy is not the gravamen of the charge, but may be both pleaded and proved as aggravating the wrong of which the plaintiff complains, and enabling him to recover against all as joint tort-feasors. If he fails in the proof of a conspiracy or concerted design, he may still recover damages against such as are shown to be guilty of the tort without such agreement."[1] In a recent case in Mary-

by statute in all cases the law of criminal conspiracy. But this difficulty is not confined to these cases. There are other offenses at common law that are not defined by any statute. The statute prescribes a penalty for such cases without attempting to define in advance the acts which shall constitute an offense. It is left for the court to determine in each particular case whether it is or is not an offense. * * * If we were to attempt to give a rule applicable to this branch of the subject, we should say that it is a criminal offense for two or more persons, corruptly or maliciously, to confederate and agree together to deprive another of his liberty or property. Such a rule is proximately correct and practically just." State v. Glidden, 55 Conn. 46, 70.

[1] Van Horn v. Van Horn, 52 N. J. L. 284, 286. "We have not presented for determination in this pleading the vexed question, whether an action will lie against a third person for the malicious

land, the court said: "It is a general rule that a conspiracy cannot be made the subject of a civil action unless something is done, which, without the conspiracy, would give a right of action. The damage done is the gist of the action, not the conspiracy. Where the mischief contemplated is accomplished, the conspiracy becomes important, as it may affect the means and measures of redress. The party wronged may look beyond the actual participants in committing the injury and join with them as defendants all who conspired to accomplish it, and the fact of conspiracy may aggravate the wrong: but the simple act of conspiracy does not furnish a substantive ground of action."[1]

§ 79. **The Rule in England.**—The rule, as established by the recent decisions of the English courts, is somewhat more tolerant of agreements in restraint of trade than the American decisions. In the recent leading case of the Mogul Steamship Company v. McGregor, the defendants, who were firms of shipowners, trading between China and Europe, with a view to obtaining for themselves a monopoly of the homeward tea trade, and thereby keeping up the rate of freight, formed themselves into an association, and offered to such merchants and shippers in China as shipped their tea exclusively in vessels belonging to members of the association a rebate of 5 per cent. on all freights paid by them. The plaintiffs, who were rival shipowners trading between China and Europe, were excluded by the defendants from all the benefits of the association, and, in consequence of such exclusion, sustained damages. It was held that the association, being formed by the defendants with the view of keeping the trade in their own hands, and not with

procurement of the breach of a contract, if by such procurement damage was intended to result, and did result, to the plaintiff. Lumley v. Gye, 2 El. & Bl. 216: Brown v. Hall, L. R. 9 Q. B. Div. 333. In the opinion of Mr. Pollock (*ubi supra*), the difficulties in such cases disappear, or are greatly reduced, when the cause of action is considered as belonging to the class in which malice, in the sense of actual ill will, is a necessary element." *Ibid.*

[1] Robertson v. Parks, 76 Md. 118; s. c., 24 Atl. Rep. 411, 413. See also Kimball v. Harman, 34 Md. 407: Cooley on Torts, 125.

the intention of ruining the trade of the plaintiffs, or through any personal malice or ill will towards them, was not unlawful and that no action for conspiracy was maintainable.[1] In the opinion in this case, Lord Justice

[1] Mogul Steamship Co. v. McGregor, L. R. 23 Q. B. Div. 598. This case was taken to the House of Lords and there affirmed. The opinions of Lords are elaborate, and state most fully the position of English courts upon this question. The case is reported in L. R. (1892) App. Cas. 25. At page 49, Lord Morris says: "My Lords, the facts of this case demonstrate that the defendants had no other, or further object, than to appropriate the trade of the plaintiffs. The means used were: Firstly, a rebate to those who dealt exclusively with them; secondly, the sending of ships to compete with the plaintiffs' ships; thirdly, the lowering of the freights; fourthly, the indemnifying other vessels that would compete with the plaintiffs'; fifthly, the dismissal of agents who were acting for them and the plaintiffs. The object was a lawful one. It is not illegal for a trader to aim at driving a competitor out of trade, provided the motive be his own gain by appropriation of the trade, and the means he uses be lawful weapons. Of the first four of the means used by the defendants, the rebate to customers and the lowering of the freights are the same in principle, being a bonus by the defendants to customers to come and deal exclusively with them. The sending of ships to compete, and the indemnifying other ships, was the 'competition' entered on by the defendants with the plaintiffs. The fifth means used, viz.: the dismissal of agents might be questionable according to the circumstances; but in the present case, the agents filled an irreconcilable position in being agents for the two rivals, the plaintiffs and the defendants. Dismissal under such circumstances became, perhaps, a necessary incident of the warfare in trade. All the acts done and the means used, by the defendants, were acts of competition for the trade. There was nothing in the defendants' acts to disturb any existing contract of the plaintiffs or induce any one to break such. Their action was aimed at making it unlikely that any one would enter into contracts with the plaintiffs, the defendants offering such competitive inducements as would probably prevent them. The use of rhetorical phrases in the correspondence cannot affect the real substance and meaning of it. Again, what one trader may do in respect of competition, a body or set of traders can lawfully do; otherwise, a large capitalist could do what a number of small capitalists, combining together, could not do, and thus a blow would be struck at the very principle of co-operation and joint stock enterprise. I entertain no doubt that a body of traders, whose motive object is to promote their own trade, can combine to acquire, and thereby in so far to injure the trade of competitors, provided they do no more than is incident to such motive object, and use no unlawful means. And the defendants' case clearly comes within the

Bowen said: "To say that a man is to trade freely, but that he is to stop short at any act which is calculated to harm other tradesmen, and which is designed to attract business to his own shop, would be a strange and impossible counsel of perfection. But we were told that competition ceases to be the lawful exercise of trade, and so to be a lawful excuse for what will harm another, if carried to a length which is

principle I have stated. Now, as to the contention that the combination was in restraint of trade, and, therefore, illegal: In the first place, was it in restraint of trade? It was a voluntary combination. It was not to continue for any fixed period, nor was there any penalty attached to a breach of the engagement. The operation of attempting to exclude others from the trade might be, and was, in fact, beneficial to freighters. Whenever a monopoly was likely to arise with a consequent rise of rates, competition would naturally arise. I cannot see why judges should be considered specially gifted with prescience of what may hamper or what may increase trade, or what is to be the test of adequate remuneration. In these days of instant communication with almost all parts of the world, competition is the life of trade, and I am not aware of any stage of competition called 'fair' intermediate between lawful and unlawful. The question of 'fairness' would be relegated to the idiosyncrasies of individual judges. I can see no limit to competition, except that you shall not invade the rights of another. But suppose the combination in this case was such as might be held to be in restraint of trade, what follows? It could not be enforced. None of the parties to it could sue each other. It might be held void, because its tendency might be held to be against the public interests. Does that make *per se* the combination illegal? What a fallacy would it be that what is void and not enforceable becomes a crime; and cases abound of agreements which the law would not enforce, but which are not illegal; which you may enter into, if you like, but which you will not get any assistance to enforce." Lord Hannen, at page 60, says: "In considering the question, however, of what was the motive of the combination, whether it was for the purpose of injuring others, or merely to benefit those combining, the fact of several agreeing to a common course of action may be important. There are some forms of injury which can only be effected by the combination of many. Thus, if several persons agree not to deal at all with a particular individual, as this could not, under ordinary circumstances, benefit the persons so agreeing, it might well lead to the conclusion that their real object was to injure the individual. But it appears to me that in the present case there is nothing indicating an intention to injure the plaintiffs except in so far as such injury would be the result of the defendants obtaining for themselves the benefits of the carrying trade, by giving better terms to customers than their rivals, the plaintiffs, were willing to offer."

not fair or reasonable. The offering of reduced rates by the defendants in the present case is said to have been 'unfair.' This seems to assume that, apart from fraud, intimidation, molestation or obstruction, of some other personal right *in rem* or *in personam*, there is some natural standard of 'fairness,' or 'reasonableness' (to be determined by the internal consciousness of judges and juries), beyond which competition ought not in law to go. There seems to be no authority, and I think, with submission, that there is no sufficient reason for such a proposition. It would impose a novel fetter upon trade. The defendants, we are told by the plaintiffs' counsel, might lawfully lower rates, provided they did not lower them beyond a 'fair freight,' whatever that may mean. But where is it established that there is any such restriction upon commerce? And what is to be the definition of a 'fair freight?' It is said that it ought to be a normal rate of freight, such as is reasonably remunerative to the shipowner. But over what period of time is the average of this reasonable remunerativeness to be calculated? All commercial men with capital are acquainted with the ordinary expedient of sowing one year a crop of apparently unfruitful prices, in order by driving competition away to reap a fuller harvest of profit in the future; and until the present argument at the bar it may be doubted whether shipowners or merchants were ever deemed to be bound by law to conform to some imaginary 'normal' standard of freights or prices, or that law courts had a right to say to them, in respect to their competitive tariffs, 'thus far shall thou go and no farther.' To attempt to limit English competition in this way would probably be as hopeless an endeavor as the experiment of King Canute. But on ordinary principles of law no such fetter on freedom of trade can, in my opinion, be warranted. A man is bound not to use his property so as to infringe upon another's rights. *Sic utere tuo ut alienium non lœdas.* If engaged in actions which may involve danger to others he ought, speaking generally, to take reasonable care to avoid endangering them. But there is surely no doctrine of law which compels him to use his property in a way that judges and juries may consider reasonable. If there is no such fetter upon the use of property known to English law, why should there be any such a fetter upon trade?"[1]

§ 80. **Conspiracy by a Corporation.**—It is well settled that an action may be maintained against a corporation to recover damages caused by a conspiracy. The leading case on this subject was an action brought against several defendants, some of whom were bodies corporate and some individuals, for the recovery of damages caused by an alleged conspiracy. The defendant demurred to the complaint on the ground that it did not state facts sufficient to constitute a cause of action in this particular, to-wit: that a corporation is not capable of being a party to a conspiracy.[2] In the opinion in this case, the court said: "We

[1] Mogul Steamship Co. v. McGregor. L. R. 23 Q. B. Div. 598. 615.

[2] Buffalo Lubricating Oil Co. v. Standard Oil Co., 106 N. Y. 669; s. c., 25 Cent. L. J. 587. See also Morton v. Metropolitan Life Ins. Co., 34 Hun, 367: affirmed in 103 N. Y. 645; Reed v. Home Sav. Bank, 130 Mass. 443; Krulevitz v. Eastern R. Co., 140 Mass. 573; s. c., 5 N. E. Rep. 500; Western News Co. v. Wilmarch. 33 Kan. 510; s. c., 6 Pac. Rep. 786; Samuels v. Evening Mail Ass'n, 9 Hun. 288; Howe Machine Co. v. Louder. 58 Ga. 64; Hawkins v. New Orleans Printing Co., 29 La. Ann. 134; Hewitt v. Pioneer Press Co., 23 Minn. 178: Turner v. Phœnix Ins. Co., 21 N. W. Rep. 326; Merrills v. Tariff Mfg. Co., 10 Conn. 384: Humes v. Knoxville. 1 Humph. 403; Illinois, etc. R. Co. v. Reedy, 17 Ill. 580; Hazen v. Boston Bridge Co., 2 Gray. 575; Bloodgood v. Mohawk, etc. R. Co., 18 Wend. 9; Goff v. Great Northern R. Co., 3 E. & E. 672; s. c., 30 L. J. Q. B. 140; Maund v. Monmouthshire Canal Co., 4 Man. & G. 452. "Another important legal proposition in the case is so clear upon principle, and so distinctly settled by authority, that nothing but confusion can flow from its discussion. It will bear no more than plain enumeration. A corporation is liable to the same extent and under the same circumstances as a natural person for the consequences of its wrongful acts, and will be held to respond, in a civil action at the suit of an injured party, for every grade and description of forcible, malicious or negligent tort or wrong which it commits, however foreign to its nature or *beyond its granted powers* the wrongful transaction or act may be. Life & Fire Ins. Co. v. Mechanics' Fire Ins. Co., 7 Wend. 31; Angell on Corp., §§ 382, 388. 391; Albert v. Savings Bank, 2 Maryl. Dec. 169; Goodspeed v. East Haddam Bank, 22 Conn. 541; Bissell v. Michigan Southern & Northern Indiana R. R. Co., 22 N. Y. 305. 309, per Selden,

entertain no doubt that an action against a corporation may be maintained to recover damages caused by conspiracy. If actions can be maintained against corporations for malicious prosecution, libel, assault and battery and other torts, we

J.; Wendell's Blackstone. [note] 476; Green v. London Omnibus Co., 7 C. B. (N. S.) 290; Frankfort Bank v. Johnson, 24 Me. 490; Philadelphia & Baltimore Ry. Co. v. Quigley, 21 How. (U. S.) 209, and cases cited by Campbell, J." New York & N. H. R. R. Co. v. Schuyler, 34 N. Y. 30, 50. "In the earlier cases, it was held that an action of trespass could not be maintained against a corporation aggregate, for the technical reason that a *capias* and *exigent*, the proper process in actions of trespass, would not be against a corporation; but this technical objection was not uniformly yielded to, as instances of actions of trespass against corporations are to be met with as early as the year books A and A. Corp., § 385; notes to Maund v. Monmouthshire Canal Co., 4 Man. & G. 454. As corporations became more numerous and were multiplied, until aggregated capital, seeking investment for the purposes of business, is generally invested under acts of incorporation to protect individuals from personal liability, technical objections which stood in the way of subjecting corporations to actions founded on torts have been entirely swept away, and corporations have been held liable for all torts, the same as individuals. That they may be sued in trover, care, trespass *quare clausum fregit*, trespass *vi et armis*, and ejectment, is abundantly established by the cases cited by Green, C. J., in State v. Morris & Essex R. Co., 3 Zab. 367. A corporation is liable for injuries resulting from neglect to repair a bridge, where the obligation to repair lies on them. Ward v. Newark & Pompton Turnpike Co., Spenc. 323; for obstructing the flow of water, whereby lands are overflowed, Tinsman v. Belvidere Delaware R. R. Co., 1 Dutcher, 255; Chestnut Hill Turnpike Co. v. Rutter, 4 S. & R. 6; for making an unlawful distress, Smith v. Birmingham & Staffordshire Gaslight Co., 1 A. & E. 526; for deceit and fraudulent representations, Fogg v. Griffon, 2 Allen, 1; National Exchange Co. v. Drew, 32 Eng. L. & Eq. 1; Barwick v. English Stock Bank, L. R. 2 Excheq. 259; for fraud in issuing spurious stock, N. Y. & N. H. R. R. Co. v. Schuyler, 38 Barb. 534; s. c., 7 Tiffany, 30; for wrongfully and maliciously obstructing a party in his business, Green v. London Omnibus Co., 7 C. B. (N. S.) 290; for maintaining a vexatious suit, Goodspeed v. East Haddam Bank, 22 Conn. 530; for a malicious libel, Whitfield v. S. E. Ry. Co., E., B. & E. 115; Philadelphia & W. & B. R. R. Co. v. Quigley, 21 How. 202; for an assault and battery and false imprisonment, Railway Co. v. Broom, 6 Excheq. 314; Chilton v. London, etc. R. Co., 16 M. & W. 212; Roe v. Railway Co., 7 Excheq. 36; Seymour v. Greenwood, 6 H. & N. 359; Goff v. Great Northern R. Co., 3 E. & E, 672; Moore v. Fitchburg R. Co., 4 Gray, 465; Hewit v. Swift, 3 Allen, 420; Evansville & Crawfordsville R. Co. v. Baum, 26 can perceive no reason for holding that actions may not be maintained against them for conspiracy. It is well settled by the authorities cited that the malice and wicked intent needful to sustain such actions may be imputed to corporations. A careful scrutiny of the complaint in each action has convinced us that sufficient facts are alleged to show that the appellant was a party to the conspiracy set forth, and that sufficient facts are, therefore, alleged in the complaint to show a cause of action against it."[1] The popular assumption that "a corporation has no soul," and, in consequence, no conscience, may be accepted both in law and in equity, but it is the holding of the courts that it is, to such an extent, in possession of the reasoning faculty as to be capable of a business offense for which it is to be held legally if not morally responsible.

§ 81. Combination to Monopolize a Particular Branch of Business.—A combination, the object of which is to obtain control of a particular branch of business, is a conspiracy, and all contracts for the accomplishment of this end are unlawful and void. So far as relates to its legality the extent of the combination is immaterial. It may be confined to a single city or town, or it may extend to a State or to a number of States, or it may include the country. The gist of the offense is the conspiracy or the combination for the purpose of accomplishing the end sought. There is not entire harmony in the decisions of the State courts on

Ind. 70." Brokaw v. N. J. R. & Transp. Co., 32 N. J. L. 328, 329. See also, to the same effect, Vance v. Erie Ry. Co., 32 N. J. L. 334. "Strictly speaking, a corporation cannot, itself, be guilty of fraud. But where a corporation is formed for the purpose of carrying on a trading or other speculation for profit, such as forming a railway, these objects can only be accomplished through the agency of individuals; and there can be no doubt that if the agents employed conduct themselves fraudulently, so that if they had been acting for private employers, the persons for whom they were acting would have been affected by their fraud, the same principles must prevail where the principal under whom the agent acts is a corporation." Ranger v. Great Western Ry. Co., 5 H. L. Cas. 72, 86.

[1] Buffalo Lubricating Oil Co. v. Standard Oil Co., 106 N. Y. 669; s. c., 25 Cent. L. J. 587.

this point, but the rule, as above stated, is generally accepted. In the leading case of the Morris Run Coal Company v. Barclay Coal Company, the doctrine is stated by Mr. Justice Agnew, as follows: "There is a certain freedom which must be allowed to every one in the management of his own affairs. When competition is left free, individual error or folly will generally find a correction in the conduct of others. But here is a combination of all the companies operating the Blossburg and Barclay mining regions, and controlling their entire productions. They have combined together to govern the price and supply of coal in all the markets from the Hudson to the Mississippi rivers, and from Pennsylvania to the lakes. This combination has a power in its confederated form which no individual action can confer. The public interest must succumb to it for it has left no competition free to correct its baleful influence. Where the supply of coal is suspended, the demand for it becomes importunate, and prices must rise. Or if the supply goes forward, the price fixed by the confederates must accompany it. The domestic hearth, the furnaces of the iron master and the fires of the manufacturer, all feel the restraint, while many dependent hands are paralyzed, and hungry mouths are stinted. The influence of a lack of supply or a rise in the price of an article of such prime necessity cannot be measured. It permeates the entire mass of community, and leaves few of its members untouched by its withering blight. Such a combination is more than a contract; it is an offense. 'I take it,' said Gibson, J., 'a combination is criminal whenever the act to be done has a necessary tendency to prejudice the public or to oppress individuals, by unjustly subjecting them to the power of the confederates, and giving effect to the purpose of the latter, whether of extortion or of mischief.' In all such combinations where the purpose is injurious or unlawful, the gist of the offense is the conspiracy. Men can often do by the combination of many what severally no one could accomplish, and even what when done by one would be innocent."[1] Where a combination of this character is kept

[1] Morris Run Coal Co. v. Barclay Coal Co., 68 Pa. St. 173, 186.

secret, and the appearance of competition is kept up, the secrecy of the act constitutes an aggravation of the offense. In a case in Wisconsin, it was held that any number of persons may lawfully form a co-partnership to buy the produce of the country and sell merchandise, at any specified place. If such co-partnership is in fact formed (though not so expressed in the articles) for the purpose of preventing competition in the markets in which the firm may operate, and with the intention of keeping secret from the public the existence of the agreement, and if its existence is thus kept secret and an appearance of competition between the parties maintained by them toward the public, such executed intention of secrecy and deception taints the agreement itself, and renders it illegal and void.[1] In Illinois it has been held

[1] Fairbanks v. Leary, 40 Wis. 637. "Neither is any other express stipulation in the agreement illegal on its face. By the terms of the instrument, a co-partnership between the parties to transact a lawful business in an apparently lawful manner was formed. Of course it does not require argument or citation of authority to show that five, or any other number of men, may lawfully form a co-partnership to buy the produce of the country and sell merchandise at Waupun, or any other place. But it does not necessarily follow that the agreement under consideration is a valid one. Although not expressed therein, if that agreement was in fact made for the purpose of preventing competition in the markets in which the firms might operate, and with the intention of keeping secret from the public the existence of the agreement, and if its existence was thus kept secret, and an appearance of competition between the parties maintained by them towards the public, such executed intention of secrecy and deception tainted the agreement itself, and rendered it illegal and void. In that case, no rights can be enforced under such illegal agreement by any party against another party thereto. The law does not, and did not, require that these parties should compete in the purchase of produce. Individually, each had an undoubted right to bid therefor as low as he pleased. Collectively they had the same right, unless deception was practiced on the public. But if they held themselves out as competing purchasers, and knew that the people who sold in the markets where they operated relied upon such competition (as well they might) as a guaranty that they were obtaining the full market value of their produce, while, at the same time, the purchasers were not in competition, but in secret league to depress the market, the agreement under which the latter operated is illegal and void, and no court will aid to enforce any of its stipulations. The cases which hold that secret agreements between persons attending auction sales not to bid against each other, and to divide the prop-

that a contract entered into by the grain dealers of a town, which on its face indicates that they have formed a partnership for the purpose of dealing in grain, but the true object of which is to form a secret combination, which would stifle all competition, and enable the parties, by secret and fraudulent means, to control the price of grain, costs of storage, and expense of shipment at such town, is in restraint of trade, and, consequently, void on the ground of public policy.[1] A rule, quite out of harmony with the above, has been adopted in Minnesota. A large number of retail

erty bid off by one of them, are illegal, go upon the same principle." *Ibid.*, 643. "The word 'unlawful,' as applied to corporations, is not used exclusively in the sense of *malum in se*, or *malum prohibitum*, it is also used to designate powers which corporations are not authorized to exercise, or contracts which they are not authorized to make, or acts which they are not authorized to do; or, in other words, such acts, powers and contracts as are *ultra vires*. The business of manufacturing and distributing gas by means of pipes laid in the streets of a city, is a business of a public character; it is the exercise of a franchise belonging to the State, the services rendered and to be rendered for such a grant, are of a public nature; the companies engaged in such business owe a duty to the public; any unreasonable restraint upon the performance of such duty is prejudicial to the public interest, and in contravention of public policy. Chicago Gaslight Co. v. People's Gaslight Co., 121 Ill. 530; Gibbs v. Baltimore Gas Co., 130 U. S. 396. Whatever tends to prevent competition between those engaged in a public employment or business impressed with a public character, is opposed to public policy, and therefore unlawful. Whatever tends to create a monopoly is unlawful as being contrary to public policy. 2 Addison on Contracts, 743; Greenhood on Public Policy, pp. 180, 643, 654, 655, 670; Morris Run Coal Co. v. Barclay Coal Co., 68 Pa. St. 173; Craft v. McConoughy, 79 Ill. 346; Central R. R. Co. v. Collins, 40 Ga. 582; Hazelhurst v. Savannah R. R. Co., 43 Ga. 13; Trans. Co. v. Pipe Line Co., 22 Wa. Va. 600." People v. Chicago Gas Trust Co., 130 Ill. 268, 292.

[1] Craft v. McConoughy, 79 Ill. 346. "While these parties were in business, in competition with each other, they had the undoubted right to establish their own rates for grain stored and commissions for shipment and sale. They could pay as high or low a price for grain as they saw proper, and as they could make contracts with the producer, so long as competition was free, the interest of the public was safe. The laws of trade, in connection with the rigor of competition, was all the guaranty the public required, but the secret combination created by the contract destroyed all competition, and created a monopoly against which the public interest had no protection." *Ibid.*, 350.

lumber dealers formed a voluntary association, agreeing that they would not deal with any manufacturer or wholesaler who would sell directly to consumers at any point where a member of the association was retailing, and that, whenever any wholesaler or manufacturer made such sale, their secretary should notify all the members. Plaintiff, having made such a sale, the secretary threatened to send such notice. It was held not actionable, nor ground for an injunction.[1] It has been held that the rule is not to be ap-

[1] Bohn Mfg. Co. v. Hollis, 54 Minn. 223; s. c., 55 N. W. Rep. 1119. "To enable the plaintiff to maintain this action, it must appear that defendants have committed, or are about to commit, some unlawful act which will interfere with, and injuriously affect, some of its legal rights. We advert to this for the reason that counsel for plaintiff devotes much space to assailing this association as one whose object is unlawful because in restraint of trade. We fail to see wherein it is subject to this charge; but even if it were, this would not, of itself, give plaintiff a cause of action. No case can be found in which it was ever held that, at common law, a contract or agreement in general restraint of trade was actionable at the instance of third parties, or could constitute the foundation for such an action. The courts sometimes call such contracts 'unlawful' or 'illegal,' but in every instance it will be found that these terms were used in the sense, merely, of 'void' or 'unenforceable' as between the parties; the law considering the disadvantage so imposed upon the contract a sufficient protection to the public. Mogul Steamship Co. v. McGregor, L. R. 23 Q. B. Div. 598; s. c., L. R. (1892) App. Cas. 25. What one man may lawfully do singly, two or more may lawfully agree to do jointly. The number who unite to do the act cannot change its character from lawful to unlawful. The gist of a private action for the wrongful act of many is not the combination or conspiracy, but the damage done or threatened to the plaintiff by the acts of the defendant. If the act be unlawful, the combination of many to commit it may aggravate the injury, but cannot change the character of the act. In a few cases there may be some loose remarks apparently to the contrary, but they evidently have their origin in a confused and inaccurate idea of the law of original conspiracy, and in failing to distinguish between an unlawful act and a criminal one. It can never be a crime to combine to commit a lawful act, but it may be a crime for several to conspire to commit an unlawful act, which, if done by one individual alone, although unlawful, would not be criminal. Hence, the fact that the defendants associated themselves together to do the act complained of is wholly immaterial in this case. We have referred to this for the reason that counsel has laid great stress upon the fact of the combination of a large number of persons, as if that, of itself, ren-

plied to the relation of principal and agent. In a recent case in Texas it was held that a contract, by which a manufacturer of windmills granted exclusive territory for their sale to a firm, the windmills, after shipment, to remain the property of the maker until sold by the consignees, then to be paid for at a fixed price, was one of agency, and did not create a trust or conspiracy against trade as defined and prohibited by Act March 30, 1889, p. 141, though it fixed the prices at which the windmills were to be sold, and bound the consignees to handle no other kind; the statute having no application to contracts between principal and agent.[1]

§ 82. **Combinations for Regulating Prices.**—An association of business men, of firms or of corporations, the object of which is to control the price of any commodity, is held to be a conspiracy in restraint of trade, and as such illegal. All contracts for the carrying out of the purposes of such associations, as well as the covenant under which they are formed, are in contravention of public policy and void. In a leading case in Ohio, a voluntary association of salt manufacturers was made for the purpose of selling and transporting that commodity. By the articles of association, all salt manufactured or owned by the members, when packed in barrels, became the property of the company, whose committee was authorized and required to regulate the price and grade thereof, and also to control the manner and time of receiving salt from the members, and each member was prohibited from selling any salt during the continuance of the association, except by retail at the factory, and at prices fixed by the company. It was held that such agreement was in restraint of trade, and void as against public policy.[2] In the opinion in this case the

dered their conduct actionable. Bowen v. Matheson, 14 Allen, 499; Mogul Steamship Co. v. McGregor, L. R. 23 Q. B. Div. 598; s. c., L. R. (1892) App. Cas. 25; Parker v. Huntington, 2 Gray, 124; Wellington v. Small, 3 Cush. 145; Payne v. Western & Atlantic R. Co., 13 Lea, 507." *Ibid.*, 233.

[1] Welch v. Phelps, etc. Windmill Co., 89 Tex. 653; s. c., 36 S. W. Rep. 71.

[2] Central Ohio Salt Co. v. Guthrie, 35 Ohio St. 666. See also Craft

court said: "The clear tendency of such an agreement is to establish a monopoly and to destroy competition in trade, and for that reason, on grounds of public policy, courts will not aid in its enforcement. It is no answer to say that

v. McConoughy, 79 Ill. 349; Valentine v. Stewart, 15 Cal. 404; Prost v. More, 40 Cal. 347; People v. Fisher, 14 Wend. 9; Stanton v. Allen, 5 Denio, 434; Saratoga Bank v. King, 44 N. Y. 87; Doolin v. Ward, 6 Johns. 194; Wilbur v. How, 8 Johns. 444; Jones v. Caswell, 3 Johns. Cas. 29; Hood v. Palm, 8 Pa. St. 238; Mifflin v. Commonwealth, 5 W. & S. 461; Pacific Factor Co. v. Adler, 90 Cal. 110; s. c., 27 Pac. Rep. 36; Vulcan Powder Co. v. Hercules Powder Co., 96 Cal. 510; s. c., 31 Pac. Rep. 581; Richardson v. Crandall, 38 How. Pr. 142; Burt v. Place, 6 Cow. 431; Darmoth v. Bennett, 15 Barb. 601; People v. Fisher, 14 Wend. 9; Hooker v. Vandewater, 4 Denio, 349; Tylee v. Yates, 3 Barb. 222; Stanton v. Allen, 5 Denio, 434; De Witt Wire Cloth Co. v. New Jersey Wire Cloth Co., 14 N. Y. Supl. 277. "Bearing in mind the fact found that the product of the Butler company's mines was largely in excess of 2,000 tons per month the object of the agreement is plain. The defendant, without binding himself to take the whole product of the mines of the Butler company, endeavored by this agreement to keep all of the coal of that company out of the market, except the limited amount which it agreed to take, and thus to artificially enhance the price of that necessary commodity. This purpose was the basis of the whole agreement, and as is found by the referee, was understood by both parties at the time of entering into the contract. That a combination to effect such a purpose is inimical to the interests of the public, and that all contracts designed to effect such an end are contrary to public policy, and therefore, illegal, is too well settled by adjudicated cases to be questioned at this day. Every producer or vendor of coal or other commodity has the right to use all legitimate efforts to obtain the best price for the article in which he deals. But when he endeavors to artificially enhance prices by suppressing or keeping out of the market the products of others, and to accomplish that purpose, by means of contracts binding them to withhold their supply, such arrangements are even more mischievous than combinations not to sell under an agreed price. Combinations of that character have been held to be against public policy and illegal. If they should be sustained, the prices of articles of pure necessity, such as coal, flour and other indispensable commodities, might be artificially raised to a ruinous extent far exceeding any naturally resulting from the proportion between supply and demand. No illustration of the mischief of such contracts is, perhaps, more apt than a monopoly of anthracite coal, the region of the production of which is known to be limited. Parties entering into contracts of this description must depend upon each other for their execution, and cannot derive any assistance from the courts." Arnot v. Pittston & El-competition in the salt trade was not, in fact, destroyed, or that the price of the commodity was not unreasonably advanced. Courts will not stop to inquire as to the degree of injury inflicted upon the public; it is enough to know that the inevitable tendency of such contracts is injurious to the

mira Coal Co., 68 N. Y. 558, 565. "In Rex v. De Berenger, 3 M. & S. 67, it was held to be a conspiracy to combine to raise the public funds on a particular day by false rumors. The purpose itself, said Lord Ellenborough, is mischievous—it strikes at the price of a valuable commodity in the market, and if it gives a fictitious price by means of false rumors it is a fraud levelled against the public, for it is against all such as may possibly have anything to do with the funds on that particular day. Every 'corner' in the language of the day, whether it be to affect the price of articles of commerce, such as breadstuffs, or the price of vendible stocks, when accomplished by confederation to raise or depress the price and operate on the markets, is a conspiracy. The ruin often spread abroad by these heartless conspiracies is indescribable, frequently filling the land with starvation, poverty and woe. Every association is criminal whose object is to raise or depress the price of labor beyond what it would bring if it were left without artificial aid or stimulus. Rex v. Byerdike, 1 M. & S. 179. In the case of such associations the illegality consists most frequently in the means employed to carry out the object. To fix a standard of prices among men in the same employment, as a fee bill, is not in itself criminal, but may become so when the parties resort to coercion, restraint or penalties upon the employed or employers; or what is worse, to force of arms. If the means be unlawful the combination is indictable. Commonwealth v. Hunt, 4 Metc. 111. A conspiracy of journeymen of any trade or handicraft to raise the wages by entering into combination to coerce journeymen and master workmen employed in the same branch of industry to conform to rules adopted by such combination for the purpose of regulating the price of labor and carrying such rules into effect by overt acts, is indictable as a misdemeanor. 3 Wharton, C. L., citing The People v. Fisher, 14 Wend. 9. Without multiplying examples, these are sufficient to illustrate the true aspect of the case before us, and to show that a combination, such as these companies entered into, to control the supply and price of the Blossburg and Barclay regions, is illegal, and the contract therefore void." Morris Run Coal Co. v. Barclay Coal Co., 68 Pa. St. 173, 187. In Mill and Lumber Co. v. Hayes, 76 Cal., at page 392, the court says: "In the case at bar the facts are, as we think, even stronger against the plaintiff than in Arnot v. Pittston and Elmira Co., 68 N. Y. 558. Here, it entered into a contract with the object and view to suppress the supply and enhance the price of lumber in four counties of the State. The contract was void as being against public policy, and the defendants, as they had a right to do, repudiated the contract.

public.[1] In the recent leading case of Ford v. Chicago Milk Shippers Association, before the Supreme Court of Illinois, it was held that an association formed for the purpose of regulating the price of milk sold by the members thereof in a particular city to retail dealers, which purpose is carried out by the concurrent action of the members and the association, is within the Act of June 11, 1891, prohibiting pools, trusts and combinations. The incorporation of a body of milk shippers, who have combined to fix the price of milk, in violation of the Act of June 11, 1891, to prevent pools, trusts and combinations, will not render the combination legal on the ground that the corporation cannot alone enter into a trust, as the acts of the corporation are those of the associated persons as individuals. The Act of June 11, 1891, forbidding pools, trusts and combinations to control the price of any commodity, applies to a corporation formed previous to its passage.[2] In the opinion in this case, Mr. Justice Phillips said: "The statute by its terms makes a combination, trust or agreement between corporations, partnerships, associations or individuals to fix the price of any article of merchandise, or to limit the amount

Plaintiff, who has parted with nothing of value, now seeks to recover damages for non-delivery of lumber under this contract. Plaintiff had an undoubted right to purchase any or all of the lumber it chose, and to sell at such prices and places as it saw fit, but when, as a condition of purchase it bound its vendor not to sell to others under a penalty, it transcended a rule the adoption of which has been dictated by the experience and wisdom of ages as essential to the best interests of the community, and as necessary to the protection alike of individuals and legitimate trade. With the results naturally flowing from the laws of demand and supply, the courts have nothing to do, but when agreements are resorted to for the purpose of taking trade out of the realm of competition, and thereby enhancing or depressing prices of commodities, the courts cannot be successfully invoked, and their execution will be left to the volition of the parties thereto."

[1] Central Ohio Salt Co. v. Guthrie, 35 Ohio St. 672.

[2] Ford v. Chicago Milk Shippers Association, 155 Ill. 166; s. c., 39 N. E. Rep. 651. See also Central Shade Roller Co. v. Cushman, 143 Mass. 353; s. c., 9 N. E. Rep. 629; Urmston v. Whitelegg, 63 L. T. 455; Judd v. Harrington, 19 N. Y. Supl. 406; Stanton v. Allen, 5 Denio, 434; Anderson v. Jett, 89 Ky. 375; s. c., 12 S. W. Rep. 670; Handforth v. Jackson, 150 Mass. 149.

to be sold, an offense, which is sought to be prohibited; and it farther provides that a purchaser of any article or commodity from any individual, company or corporation transacting business contrary to the preceding sections of the act shall not be liable for the price or payment of such article or commodity. The purpose of the arrangement between this corporation and the stockholders thereof was to fix the price and control and limit the quantity of milk shipped. The purposes attempted to be accomplished through the corporation were illegal. To carry out such purposes it stands as the active business agent of the members who are stockholders, contracting with it to carry out the purposes of the organization. It is a combination in violation of the statute and in restraint of trade. Any purchaser of any commodity thus sold by such organization is not liable for the price thereof."[1]

§ 83. **Conspiracies under the Federal Anti-Trust Act.**—Section first of the Act of Congress of July 2d, 1890, provides that "every contract, combination in the form of trust or otherwise, or conspiracy, in restraint of trade or commerce among the several States or with foreign nations, is hereby declared to be illegal. Every person who shall make any such contract, or engage in any such combination or conspiracy, shall be deemed guilty of a misdemeanor, and on conviction thereof shall be punished by fine not exceeding five thousand dollars, or by imprisonment not exceeding one year, or by both said punishments, in the discretion of the court." In a recent case before the United States Circuit Court for the Middle District of Tennessee, it was held that an agreement between coal mining companies, operating chiefly in one State, and dealers in coal in a city in another State, creating a coal exchange to advance the interests of the coal business, to treat all parties to the business in a fair and equitable manner, and to establish the price of coal, and change the same from time to

[1] Ford v. Chicago Milk Shippers Association, 155 Ill. 166, 179; S. C., 39 N. E. Rep. 651.

time, by which it was agreed that the price of the coal at the mines should be 4½ cents, the freight being 4 cents, and the margin of the dealer should be 4½ cents, making the price to the consumer 13 cents, and that whenever the price of the coal is advanced beyond an advance in freights, one-half the advance shall go to the mine owner and the other half to the dealer, and a penalty was provided by fine of any member selling coal at a less price than the price fixed by the exchange, and by which it was forbidden for owners or operators of mines to sell coal to any person other than members of the organization, and for dealers to purchase of miners who were not members, but exempting coal used for manufacturing and steamboat purposes from the prices prescribed until all the mines tributary to that market should come into the exchange, or until the exchange could control the prices of coal used by manufacturers, is within the language of the Federal anti-trust act declaring "every contract or combination in the form of a trust or otherwise, or conspiracy in restraint of trade or commerce among the several States," and also the monopolizing or combination with another to monopolize, trade or commerce among the several States, a misdemeanor.[1]

[1] United States v. Jellico Mountain Coal & Coke Co., 46 Fed. Rep. 432. "These provisions, so far as this combination could do so, fixed the lowest price of coal to consumers in and near Nashville at thirteen cents per bushel, and prevented coal being sold there at a cheaper rate, no matter how much less it might cost in an open and unobstructed market. Nor is this all. The exchange ordains that 'owners or operators of mines shall not sell or ship coal to any firm, person or corporation in Nashville or West Nashville or East Nashville, who are not members of this exchange.' The coal trade is confined, so far as the market supply is concerned, to transactions between the miner and dealer, the prices are fixed by them, and the miner and dealer only are eligible to membership. The miners of the concern cannot sell to any dealer in or near Nashville who is not a party to the agreement, nor can such dealer purchase coal of any miner anywhere who is not a member of the body. The operations of both are confined within the membership. So far as Nashville is concerned, they cannot go to cheaper or more favorable markets, or deal with those who would give more favorable terms. The restraint is positive and undeniable. Moreover, in the first section of the by-laws of the exchange it is asserted that 'all coal used for

§ 84. Combination to Prevent Competition at a Judicial Sale.—Bidding at a judicial sale is not a legal obligation. All persons are free to attend judicial sales, or to refrain from attending, and where they attend they may bid, or refrain from bidding. But an agreement between two or more persons, who are in attendance, to refrain from bidding against each other in order to secure the property offered at a price below that which it would otherwise bring, is an offense, and the scheme may be so devised and executed as to be a criminal conspiracy. In an English case, it was held that if brokers agree together before a sale by auction that only one of them shall bid for each article sold, and that all articles thus bought by any of them shall be sold again among themselves at a fair price, and the difference between the auction price and the fair price divided among them; this is a conspiracy for which they are indictable.[1] The doctrine, as here stated, is upheld by the American courts. In a leading case in New York, A and B, having execution against C, of which A's execution was the older lien, and C being indebted to D, it was agreed between A

manufacturing and steamboat purposes shall be exempt from prices made by this exchange until all mines tributary to this market shall become members of the exchange, or until the exchange can control prices to govern coal used by manufacturers.' This clearly indicates the purpose of the association to be to control the price of coal in the Nashville market used in manufacturing and in steamboats whenever it could, that the mines of coal tributary to Nashville were all expected to become members of the exchange, whereupon the prices of coal could be fixed absolutely, and the necessary inference from this declaration and the entire organic structure of the body is that it felt strong enough already to regulate and establish the prices of domestic coal in that market, to a large extent, at least, and that this exchange might now monopolize the business of dealing in domestic coal in the Nashville market, and in the future monopolize by and confine to its membership the entire trade in coal at that point. It seems to me that the purposes and intentions of the association could hardly have been more successfully framed to fall within the provisions of the Act of July 2, 1890, had the object been to organize a combination, the business of which should subject it to the penalties of that statute and that there is no need of authorities to sustain such view of the case. Regarding the act as constitutional, I see no way for the defendants to escape its condemnation." *Ibid.*, 436.

[1] Levi v. Levi, 6 Car. & P. 239.

and D, that A should pay D $225, that, at the sale under execution, A should bid off the personal property of C to the amount of his execution, and that D should bid off the real property of C, to the amount of B's execution, should dispose of the same, and after satisfying his own demands against C should refund A the said sum of $225. A and D at the sale bid off the property of C, in conformity to the agreement, and D disposed of the real estate, and after satisfying his own demands against C there was a sufficient surplus to repay A, and A brought his action to recover the money. It was held that although there was a sufficient consideration to support D's promise, yet the agreement itself was void, being contrary to public policy, as it was an agreement tending to prevent competition at a sale under execution, and thus injurious to the original debtor.[1] In

[1] Thompson v. Davies, 13 Johns. 112. See also Cocks v. Izard, 7 Wall. 559; Webster v. Dennison, 25 Vt. 493; Taylor v. Wait, 54 Vt. 469; Gardner v. Morse, 25 Me. 140; Curtis v. Aspinwall, 114 Mass. 187; Brisbane v. Adams, 3 N. Y. 129; People v. Stephens, 71 N. Y. 527; Dick v. Cooper, 24 Pa. St. 217; Walter v. Gernant, 13 Pa. St. 515; Brotherline v. Swires, 48 Pa. St. 68; Jenkins v. Frink, 30 Cal. 586; Gilbert v. Carter, 10 Ind. 16; Lloyd v. Malone, 23 Ill. 43; Rives v. Lawrence, 41 Ga. 283; Wagner v. Phillips, 51 Mo. 117; Turner v. Adams, 46 Mo. 95; Durfee v. Moran, 57 Mo. 374; Miller v. Baynard, 2 Houst. 559; Smith v. Ullman, 58 Md. 183; s. c., 42 Am. Rep. 329; Maffet v. Ijams, 103 Pa. St. 266. "The whole purpose of the statute is to encourage open, fair competition between responsible bidders, and any secret combination, call it partnership or anything else, the effect of which is to abate honest rivalry or prevent fair competition, is to be condemned as violative of public policy and void. No one can predicate an enforceable right upon such an agreement. Atcheson v. Mallon, 43 N. Y. 147; s. c., 3 Am. Rep. 678; Woodworth v. Bennett, 43 N. Y. 273; s. c., 3 Am. Rep. 706; Gibbs v. Smith, 115 Mass. 592; Hannah v. Fife, 27 Mich. 172; Greenhood, Public Policy, 178, 179 and notes. * * * The purpose, tendency and necessary effect of such a contract was to stifle fair, open, actual competition, and to perpetrate a fraud upon the public officers. If, in letting a contract, such as this, parties without knowledge of the bids of each other submit their bids as the law requires, and afterwards enter into a partnership for the construction of the work with the knowledge of the officers letting the same, a question of a different character is presented. Such a transaction bears some similitude to the contract which was upheld in Breslin v. Brown, 24 Ohio St. 565; s. c., 15 Am. Rep. 627, a case which, on account of the liberal

the opinion in this case, the court, by Mr. Justice Spencer, said: "It has been urged that the plaintiff was not bound to bid on the second execution, and was, therefore, at liberty to enter into this agreement. That is not the test of

view taken of the contract there involved, is not universally endorsed. That case, however, affords no aid to the appellant here." Hunter v. Pfeiffer, 108 Ind. 197, 200. Where evidence shows that by the acts, connivance and representations of a purchaser, bidders were kept away from the sale of certain land; that competition was repressed when the sale took place, and that except for these practices the land would have brought a price greatly in excess of that actually realized, the sale will be set aside. Wagner v. Philllps, 51 Mo. 117. An agreement between two or more persons that one shall bid for the benefit of all upon property about to be sold at public auction, which they desire to purchase together, either because they propose to hold it together, or afterwards to divide it into such parts as they wish individually to hold, neither desiring the whole, or for any similar honest or reasonable purpose, is legal in its character, and will be enforced; but such agreement, if made for the purpose of preventing competition, and reducing the price of the property to be sold below its fair value, is against public policy and in fraud of the just rights of the party offering it, and therefore illegal." Gibbs v. Smith, 115 Mass. 592, 593. See also Phippen v. Stickney, 3 Met. 384, 387; Fuller v. Dame, 18 Pick. 472; Rice v. Wood, 113 Mass. 133. "There is nothing either in law or morals to prevent parties from uniting together in good faith to purchase property, whether it is offered at public auction, or, as in the present case, advertised for sale, and bids from purchasers are invited. In Sewell v. Jones, 1 W. & S. 129, where there was a purchase of property at sheriff's sale by several lienors who united therein, the bid being made by one of their number, and the sale was impeached as for that reason fraudulent and against public policy, Chief Justice Gibson said: 'It is not to be doubted that lien creditors, as well as others, may purchase jointly at sheriff's sale, if all be open and fair; a combination of interests for that purpose is not necessarily corrupt, and if it be forbidden, it must be by some principle of public policy. * * * It is, as we have said, the end to be accomplished which makes such a combination lawful or otherwise. If it be to depress the price of the property by artifice, the purchase would be void; if it be to raise the means of payment by contribution, or to divide the property for the accommodation of the purchasers, it will be valid.' In Piatt v. Oliver, 3 McLean C. C. 27, it was said by Judge McLean: 'To hold that individuals may not associate together for the purpose of purchasing lands of the United States at a public sale, would be a novel doctrine, and contrary to what has been generally practiced by purchasers, and that under the sanction of the government.' " Smith v. Ullman, 58 Md. 183; s. c., 42 Am. Rep. 329, 331. "It is true, a conthe principle. In none of the cases cited was the party bound to bid; but, being at liberty to bid, he suffered himself to be bought off in a way which might prevent a fair competition. The abstaining from bidding, upon concert, and by agreement, under the promise of a benefit for thus abstaining, is the very evil the law intends to repress. A public auction is open to every one; but there must be no combination among persons competent to bid silencing such bidders, for the tendency to sacrifice the debtor's property is inevitable. The principle is of too salutary a nature to permit any refinements which go to sap or subvert it; and in England, the judges have uniformly held a strict hand over every attempt at fraud or circumvention at auctions."[1] In a case in Massachusetts, it was held that by-bidding at an auction sale, advertised "to be positive," of land in lots,

tract not to bid at a sheriff's sale, so as to defraud the defendant in the execution, or his creditors, will be declared void. Here, however, there was evidence which justified submitting to the jury that the defendant in the execution, and all his creditors affected by the sale, had notice of the arrangement between the parties in this case. The verdict removes all pretext that any person interested in the sale was defrauded. The plaintiff in error cannot now invoke the rule, that under many circumstances his contract might have been contrary to public policy, and therefore void." Maffet v. Ijams, 103 Pa. St. 266. "The confederation of bidders being admitted or established by proof, it devolved upon the plaintiff to show that it was for the joint prosecution of a business enterprise, and not a mere desire to shut off or reduce competition. Now they depose that they had no design to get an advantage of the State, or to suppress bidding by which we suppose they mean bidding by persons outside of the combination. For certainly it could never have been contemplated that these dormant partners should be at liberty to put in independent bids of their own if they chose. That would have been an act of bad faith to the partnership. Yet they show no other motive for combining, except the motive, so obvious that it will be inferred, of getting rid of the competition of each other by the surrender of each to the other of a portion of the work and anticipated profits. We cannot presume they united for want of means to undertake the entire job, for they had each proposed to do it singly and alone. * * * The probable effect of the combination was to reduce the competition to zero, and allow the persons concerned to dictate the prices to the board. Woodruff v. Berry, 40 Ark. 251, 268.

[1] Thompson v. Davies, 13 Johns. 112, 115.

will render the sale voidable by a purchaser influenced by such bidding, whether that bidding was upon the lot purchased by him or upon lots previously offered, even though such bidding was instigated by the auctioneer without the seller's knowledge; but if it appears that he was not so influenced the sale is valid.[1] In a case in Illinois, the rule in regard to bids by sealed proposals is stated by the court, as follows: "There is never to be found in the terms of an auction sale a clause prohibiting the bidders from combining together to prevent competition, still it is none the less unlawful for them to do so. The law implies everything which good faith and fair dealing require, and none the less so in the case of sales by sealed proposals than by open bids. In both cases effects and consequences are to be considered, in determining what fair dealing and the true intent of the transaction required. This principle has long been applied to sales by open bids, and we cannot doubt that it ought to be applied where the bids are by sealed proposals."[2]

§ 85. **Combination to Destroy Competition.**—In ordinary business affairs one person may refuse to buy or to sell to another, or in anywise to transact business with him. And what one person may do in this direction, two or more persons may unite in doing. A combination to refuse to buy of a particular individual, or to sell to him, is not a conspiracy or an offense. But a combination to induce a third person to refuse to sell to another, is a conspiracy, and a ground for a civil action. In a recent case it was held that no action for conspiracy will lie by a butcher against several dealers in beef cattle because they have combined to refuse to sell him beeves; but where the petition further alleges that defendants also induced a certain dealer in slaughtered meat likewise to refuse to sell him, such interference with his business is a cause of action, and it is error to sustain a demurrer to the petition.[3] In the opinion

Curtis v. Aspinwall, 114 Mass. 187.

Webster v. French, 11 Ill. 254,

[3] Delz v. Winfree, 80 Tex. 400; s. c., 16 S. W. Rep. 111. "It cannot be held that defendants had the right to prevent plaintiffs from

in this case the court said: "Plaintiff's petition goes further than to charge that each of the defendants refused to sell to him. It charges that they not only did that, but that they induced a third person to refuse to sell to him. It does not appear from the petition that their interference with the business of plaintiff was done to serve some legitimate purpose of their own, but that it was done wantonly

selling to consumers, or that such interference by them (defendants) was serving a legitimate purpose connected with their own business. To break plaintiffs down as competitors for the consumers trade might, it is true, result in benefit to defendants; but such a benefit, obtained in such manner, could not be deemed a legitimate purpose, within the meaning of the opinion quoted. Delz v. Winfree, 80 Tex. 400; s. c., 16 S. W. Rep. 111: Morris Run Coal Co. v. Barclay Coal Co., 68 Pa. St. 173. Plaintiffs had the right to sell at wholesale or retail, or both, to the retail dealer and the actual consumer: and defendants had the same right, as well as the right to solicit and secure trade from plaintiffs' customers by underselling them. This would be legitimate. They could do this, and would not be responsible for the injurious consequences to plaintiffs' business: but they could not, without some legal purpose directly serving their own business, maliciously induce third persons not to trade with plaintiffs, and so injure them. Plaintiffs cannot recover for any injury, except such as results from the wanton and unlawful interference with plaintiffs' business in influencing third persons not to trade with them, and only for the injury that has occurred." Olive v. Van Patten (1894), 7 Tex. Civ. App. 630; s. c., 25 S. W. Rep. 428.

"The plaintiff's action is for an injury resulting from the doing of a lawful act in a lawful manner. A person, with or without reason, may refuse to trade with another, so may ten or fifty persons refuse. An individual may advise his neighbor or friend not to trade with another neighbor: he may even command, when the command amounts only to earnest advice. * * * It is not an unlawful interference with the trade of another to advise people to deal with his competitor, or to decline to do business with him. Nor is it now unlawful to combine to raise the rate of wages. More v. Bennett, 41 Ill. App. 164; Heywood v. Tilson, 75 Me. 231: Payne v. Western Ry. 81 Tenn. 507: Mogul Steamship Co. v. McGregor, L. R. 21 Q. B. Div. 544; s. c., 23 Q. B. Div. 598: L. R. (1892) App. Cas. 25: Bohn Mfg. Co. v. Hollis, 54 Minn. 223: s. c., 55 N. W. Rep. 1119; Carew v. Rutherford, 106 Mass. 1. * * * The fact that such advice is given with a bad or malicious motive, does not render it unlawful or actionable. The law does not ordinarily consider the motive by which people are actuated to lawful acts, while motive plays a very important part when unlawful proceedings are under consideration." Waterman, J., in Ulery v. Chicago Live Stock Exchange, 54 Ill. App. 233, 240.

and maliciously, and that it caused, as they intended it should, pecuniary loss to him. We think the petition stated a cause of action, and that the demurrer should have been overruled."[1] But in a recent case it was held that where the contract between a railroad company and the proprietor of one of its eating houses does not require it to stop its trains at his hotel in order that passengers may take their meals there, it does not constitute an actionable conspiracy, on the part of the company, against such proprietor, for it to induce another to start an eating house a short distance from him by agreeing to stop its trains there for meals.[2] In the opinion in this case the court said: "We see nothing in the petition which charges an actionable conspiracy. Defendant had a right to run its trains as it saw fit, and also had the right to supply meals to its passengers at any place it desired. The lease made between plaintiff and defendant did not obligate defendant to stop its trains for meals at his house. In doing what is charged against it, defendant was neither doing an unlawful act nor a lawful act in an unlawful manner. The motive with which one

[1] Delz v. Winfree, 80 Tex. 400; s. c., 16 S. W. Rep. 111.

[2] Kelly v. Chicago, M. & St. P. Ry., 93 Iowa, 436; s. c., 61 N. W. Rep. 957. "In Bowen v. Hall (6 Q. B. Div. 333; 50 L. J. Q. B. 305; 44 L. T. 75; 29 W. R. 367), the broad principle is laid down that if a man induces one of two parties to a contract to break that contract, with the intent to injure the other party or to do himself a benefit, he thereby commits an actionable wrong. In this case the jury, in answer to the first question put to them, found that the defendants did maliciously induce persons who had entered into contracts with the plaintiff to break those contracts. I think there was abundant evidence to support that finding. The second question in the case is as to inducing persons not to enter into new contracts with the plaintiff. The jury were asked whether the defendants maliciously conspired to induce persons not to enter into such contracts with the plaintiff, and whether such persons were thereby induced not to enter into such contracts; and they answered in the affirmative. Does that answer amount to a finding of an actionable wrong? I think it does. The law appears to me to be that a combination by two or more persons to induce others not to deal with a particular individual or to enter into contracts with him, if it is done with an intent to injure that individual, and if he is thereby injured, is an actionable wrong." Temperton v. Russell, 4 Rep. (English) 376, 383.

does an act furnishes no cause of action unless there be some legal wrong, and not then if it relates to a breach of contract.''[1]

§ 86. Conspiracy for Severing the Relation of a Minister to his Congregation.—The call of a minister to the pastoral charge of a congregation is a free act. There is no law, civil or ecclesiastical, that requires any congregation to call a particular minister. And where the pastoral or ministeral relation has been established and has proved unsatisfactory to the congregation, such proper and orderly steps as are provided for by the constitution of the church may be taken for the severing of such relation. But, while the pastor is amenable to authority, civil and ecclesiastical, he has certain rights, not only as a citizen, but also as a pastor, which the courts will enforce. The contract of a church or congregation is not less binding than that of an individual, and any attempt to break up the pastoral relation that assumes the form of a conspiracy will be held to be an actionable offense. In a recent case in Wisconsin, it was held that a complaint, reciting plaintiff's employment as minister by church officers, and charging defendants with "unlawfully, maliciously and without just cause * * * conspiring, conniving and contriving to injure the plaintiff, and break up his relations with the congregation as their minister, and to drive him from his position as minister, * * * and to deprive him of the support of said congregation," followed by a recital of many acts done by defendants in pursuance of "the purpose aforesaid," is sufficiently definite and certain, and states but one cause of action (unlawful conspiracy), though it also recites that part of the defendants were trustees of the church, who employed plaintiff as minister.[2]

[1] Kelly v. Chicago, M. & St. P. Ry. Co. (1895), 93 Iowa, 436; s. c., 61 N. W. Rep. 957, 962.

[2] Fisher v. Schuri, 73 Wis. 370; s. c., 41 N. W. Rep. 527. "If the defendants had a legal right to rescind their contract on the ground of anterior immorality on his part (a point which need not be decided now), yet we are of opinion that they could not do so by vote without stating that as the reason for rescission, and reciting it in their vote. They gave him no notice of the reason for their vote, and ought not to be permitted

§ 87. **Indictment for Conspiracy.**—An indictment for conspiracy, in order to be valid, must definitely charge the particular offense, stating its peculiar character and setting forth the particular circumstances under which it was committed. It must definitely aver either the criminality of the act, or, if the act is lawful, the criminality of the means employed in accomplishing it. In a leading case in Iowa, an indictment for conspiracy, under the statutes, charged the offense in the following words: "The said J B F and S D P, late of, etc., on etc., at etc., unlawfully and feloniously, did conspire and confederate together, with the fraudulent intent to do an illegal act, injurious to the administration of public justice, to-wit: did conspire and confederate together

to show now for the first time what that reason was." Whitmore v. Fourth Cong. Soc., 2 Gray, 306. The trustees of a Methodist Episcopal church closed the church building against the duly appointed preacher, on the ground that it was not for the interest of the church that he should be its pastor, and that he was appointed against the wish of the majority of the members. *Held*, that they had no right to do so, and after answer a mandatory injunction was issued, requiring them to open the building to the preacher and the church. Whitecar v. Michenor, 37 N. J. Eq. 6. A minister of the gospel, or preacher, who is employed for a given time by his congregation, is entitled to be retained as the minister of the church, unless he loses that right by some fault of his own, and for good cause he may be dismissed by the parish, but they cannot do so arbitrarily, as there is no legal distinction between a contract with a minister and his congregation, and any other civil contract for personal service. Congregation of Israel v. Peres, 2 Cold. 620. Where some of the charges made against a minister and laid before a council furnish ground for a compulsory dissolution of his contract with his society, and others do not, and the result of the council states that several of the charges were proved, but without specifying which, their recommendation of a dissolution of a contract can have no effect. Parol evidence is not admissible to show which charges the council considered to be proved. An *ex parte* council should be composed of men who are presumed to be impartial, and who have not prejudged the case:—so that where some of the members of a council, called by the society alone, had been members of a previous council, which had decided against the minister upon the same charges, a similar result of the *ex parte* council was held to be of no validity. Thompson v. Catholic Cong. Soc., 7 Pick. 160. A priest may be removed from his congregation at the pleasure of the bishop without trial. He cannot, however, be suspended from his priestly functions without specific accusation and trial. Stack v. O'Hara, 98 Pa. St. 213.

with the said intent to defeat the enforcement of the prohibitory liquor law, so called, in said county, wrongfully, to-wit: with money and other unlawful means, to prevent the grand jury, of said county, at, etc., from finding and presenting bills of indictment for violations of said prohibitory liquor law in, etc., contrary, etc. It was held that the indictment was insufficient in failing to state in what manner money was intended to be used, and to specify more particularly the "other unlawful means."[1] In the opinion in this case, the court said: "In order to constitute the crime of conspiracy the accused must confederate together

[1] State v. Potter, 28 Iowa. 554. See also State v. Jones, 13 Iowa. 269; Commonwealth v. East, 1 Cush. 189, 224; Commonwealth v. Shedd, 7 Cush. 514. "The offense of conspiracy may, it is true, be complete without the commission of the overt act at which the conspirators agreed to commit. Commonwealth v. Judd, 2 Mass. 328; Commonwealth v. Warren, 6 Mass. 74; State v. Buchanan, 5 Har. & J. 317; State v. Noyes, 25 Vt. 415. It would seem to follow that, though the overt act may have been committed, it is unnecessary to charge it, unless the indictment is drawn under a statute which requires that it should be charged. In 2 Bishop on Criminal Law, § 203, the author says: 'In conspiracy, the indictment usually sets out the matter aggravating the offense; yet the offense exists without this matter, and, strictly, it need not be stated in the indictment, though some authorities hold otherwise.' On this point we observe that in 3 Greenleaf Evidence, § 95, the learned author seems to regard the rule as different from what Bishop does. He says: 'If the conspiracy was carried out to the full accomplishment of its object, it is necessary to state what was done and the persons who were thereby injured.' In State v. Mayberry, 48 Me. 218, it was held that if the conspirators carry out the object of the conspiracy, that fact may be alleged in aggravation of the offense, and given in evidence to prove the conspiracy. Though the offense of conspiracy, even where the overt act is committed, is complete before the commission of the overt act, in the sense that nothing more is necessary to constitute the crime, yet the conspiracy must be deemed to continue during the commission of the overt act. Commonwealth v. Corlies, 3 Brewst. 575. The conclusion which we reach is that where the overt act is charged, it does not follow, necessarily, that the indictment was designed to charge anything more than conspiracy. If it should be so drawn as to show a design to claim a conviction for the injury committed, though the evidence should fail to sustain the charge of conspiracy, such indictment manifestly could not be sustained, unless the offense could be regarded as a compound offense." State v. Winston, 66 Iowa, 143, 146.

to do a criminal act, or an act that is not criminal by illegal means. In the first case, an indictment for an offense is sufficient, if it be described by the proper name or terms by which it is generally known in the law. In the other instance, the unlawful means by which the act constituting the basis of the offense, under the combination or agreement, is charged to have been intended to be done, must be particularly set forth. The reason of the rule is obvious. To do an act that is not an offense, by means that are not unlawful, cannot constitute a crime; neither can a combination of two or more to do such an act in the same manner be criminal. If such a combination would amount to an offense, we would have the strange and absurd result of an intention being criminal. In the case, then, of a conspiracy to do an act that is not criminal, the gist of the offense is the illegal means. It is plain under the statutory provisions above cited that the acts constituting these means which are 'the particular circumstances of the offense' must be specifically charged."[1] In a case before the United States Circuit Court for the District of Massachusetts, the court said: "Neither the letter of the statute nor the philosophy of pleading conspiracies requires that it should appear that the purpose was to engross, monopolize or grasp into the hands of one of the persons indicted, or that the defendants were interested in behalf of the party for whose benefit they combined to monopolize, engross or grasp, or, indeed, what their relations were to that party. Even if the statute should finally be held to be limited to combinations to engross, monopolize or grasp in behalf of some party to the combination, yet there remains the well known rule of law that it is unnecessary to indict all the persons involved in a conspiracy. Of course, the court would have felt less doubt in meeting this objection if it had been alleged that the corporation named was a party to the conspiracy, or if the relation of the accused to it or some other matter of a kindred character had been set out."[2]

[1] State v. Potter. 28 Iowa. 554, 556.

[2] United States v. Patterson, 59 Fed. Rep. 280, 283. "The claim

§ 88. **Statutory Regulations.**—In many of the States the law relating to conspiracies in restraint of trade is fixed by statute. In a case in Illinois, where the statute of 1891 declares that if any corporation, partnership or individual

that the indictment should negative the ownership of patents by the defendants, and also set out that the commerce carried, or proposed to be carried, on by the National Cash Register Company, was a lawful one, and perhaps some other matters of that character, proved on the hypothesis that its allegations should be certain to every intent, a rule which applies only to pleas in abatement. All such are matters of defense, not to be anticipated by the prosecutor. The claim that these counts left it for the prosecutor, and not for the court, to decide whether they state subject-matters of interstate commerce, and also that it is necessary that they should set out in detail the operations supposed to constitute interstate commerce, are maintainable, because, so far as this feature of the indictment is concerned, it is clearly sufficient, according to numerous decisions of the Supreme Court, which need not be cited, to use the language of the statute. The suggestion of the court, in the opinion passed down February 28th, that the statute is not one of a class where it is sufficient to declare in the words of the enactment related to the particular proposition then under consideration. As to all the propositions touching the existence of commerce in cash registers, or knowledge, or want of allegation of knowledge on the part of the accused, it is sufficient to say that those counts which do allege the existence of such commerce, also allege positively knowledge on the part of the defendants, and those which do not allege such existence are sufficient, because neither the letter of the statute nor its purpose distinguishes between strangling a commerce which has been born, and preventing the birth of a commerce which does not exist. On this point, also, in the opinion of the court, it is sufficient to use the language of the statute." *Ibid.*, 282. See also Commonwealth v. Dyer, 128 Mass. 70; State v. Stewart, 59 Vt. 273; State v. Cook, 38 Vt. 439; State v. Jones, 33 Vt. 443; Reg. v. Rowlands, 17 Q. B. 671. Overt acts need not be alleged when the conspiracy to do the acts is unlawful, as the offense is complete in itself. The Poulterers' Case, 9 Coke, 55; Rex v. Kinnersley, 1 Str. 193; Reg. v. Best, 2 Ld. Raym. 1167; Reg. v. Gompertz, 9 Q. B. 824; Reg. v. Heymann, 12 Cox C. C. 383; Reg. v. Seward, 1 Ad. & El. 706; State v. Bartlett, 30 Me. 132; State v. Ripley, 31 Me. 386; Commonwealth v. Eastman, 55 Mass. 190; s. c., 48 Am. Dec. 596; Commonwealth v. Shedd, 61 Mass. 514; Landringham v. State, 49 Ind. 136; Alderman v. People, 4 Mich. 414; s. c., 51 Am. Dec. 75; Isaacs v. State, 48 Miss. 234; March v. People, 7 Barb. 391; People v. Arnold, 46 Mich. 268; State v. Noyes, 25 Vt. 415; United States v. Dustin, 2 Bond C. C. 332; Johnson v. State, 3 Tex. App. 590; Heine v. Commonwealth, 91 Pa. St. 145; State v. Lounger, 1 Dev. L. 357; People v. Mather, 4 Wend.

shall create or enter into any trust or combination or understanding with any other corporation, partnership or individual to fix the price of any article, or shall become a party to any contract or combination to fix or limit the amount of any article to be manufactured or sold, such corporation, partnership or individual shall be guilty of a conspiracy to defraud. It was held that a corporation, which by combination between its stockholders and itself attempted to regulate the price of milk, came within the purview of said act, although it did not combine with any other corporation or with any person other than its own members.[1] In a case in

229; s. c., 21 Am. Dec. 122; State v. Cawood, 3 Stew. 360; Landringham v. State, 49 Ind. 186; Isaacs v. State, 48 Miss. 234; State v. Straw, 42 N. H. 392; State v. Rickey, 9 N. J. L. 293. "The purpose, which was the object of the conspiracy, as alleged in the third count, not being criminal in itself, if there is any offense charged, it must consist in the means designed to be employed. These must be specifically stated. State v. Ripley, 31 Me. 386. In this count the means are described only as being 'false pretenses.' By this the accused could not be sufficiently informed of the acts, against which they were called to answer. The description of the means are too general and not in accordance with the established rules of criminal pleading." State v. Roberts, 34 Me. 320.

1 Ford v. Chicago Milk Shippers Association, 155 Ill. 166; s. c., 39 N. E. Rep. 651. "It is urged that the corporation cannot alone enter into a trust or combination that would be a violation of this statute. Whilst it is true, as a general proposition, that a corporation may be created and constituted a legal entity, existing separate and apart from the natural persons composing it, yet it cannot act independently, or against the will, or abstain from complying with the direction of the natural persons who constitute the corporate body. A corporation is, in fact, an association of persons united in one body, having perpetual succession vested with political rights conferred upon it by the authority creating it. Morawetz on Corporation, § 227; 1 Kyd on Corporations, 13. Such being the nature of the corporate body, acts done by it are the acts of the associated persons, as corporators or as individuals, and in which capacity the act is done must be determined from the nature and character of the act and the purpose for which the corporation was organized. State *ex rel.* v. Standard Oil Co., 49 Ohio, 137. And when the acts of the corporate body are violative of the statutes of the State and would be a misdemeanor that would subject to punishment in accordance with law, such acts are wholly without the lawful power of the corporation, as the State will create no body with authority to violate its laws. And where, in the organization of the corporate body or

Texas, where the Act of 1889, after defining trusts, provides forfeiture for corporations and punishment for individuals who violate its provisions, declares such violation a conspiracy against trade, and prescribes the necessary allegations of an indictment under the act, and the proof required. It was held that the statute is not a nullity for failure to expressly declare trusts unlawful, nor the acts constituting a trust punishable, nor any act a violation of its provisions, such declarations being clearly implied.[1] In another case, before the same court, where the Act of 1889, relating to conspiracies against trade, forbids combinations of persons or corporations to prevent competition in the purchase, sale or transportation of merchandise, and all agreements not to sell or transport below a certain or graduated price, or to establish "the price of any article or commodity between themselves and others to preclude free competition among themselves or others in its sale or transportation, it was held that a contract between liquor dealers in a city for the control of the beer traffic there and in all markets tributary thereto, each turning "all the beer he or they may handle or control into this co-partnership," violates the above statute, and is void, although the persons so combining are the only dealers in the city, and the price was not increased to the consumers.[2]

the control exercised by the stockholders in determining the agencies selected for managing its business, the business as thus conducted, managed and controlled is against public policy or in contravention of a statute of the State, such acts of the corporate body and of the individual shareholders are the combined acts of all, and courts are not so powerless that they may not prevent the success of ingenious schemes to evade or violate the law. There can be no immunity for evasion of the policy of the State by its own creations." *Ibid.*, 179.

[1] Queen Ins. Co. v. State, 86 Tex. 250; s. c., 24 S. W. Rep. 397.

[2] Anheuser-Busch Brewing Ass'n v. Houck (Tex. Civ. App.), 27 S. W. Rep. 692.

CHAPTER VI.

THE CREATING OF A CORNER.

§ 89. Introductory.
90. The Corner Defined.
91. The Nature of an "Option."
92. Modification of the Common Law Doctrine.
93. The Creation of a Corner in Necessaries.
§ 94. The Creating of a Corner in Stocks.
95. Where Contracts for Future Delivery are Sustained.
96. Rights and Liabilities of Third Parties.
97. Statutory Prohibitions.

§ **89. Introductory.**—The modern idea of cornering the market is closely allied to the early common law offense of engrossing or forestalling. The difference is such as has grown out of the changed industrial conditions of the nineteenth century. Engrossing or forestalling was the buying up or otherwise obtaining possession of a large quantity of grain or of other commodities on its way to market, with a view to selling again, and of increasing the price; or of pursuading any person who held such commodities from offering them in the market, or of inducing any one to increase the price. At common law the complete engrossing of any commodity with the intention of selling it at an unreasonable price was an indictable offense. This rule was abolished by a statute of the 7th & 8th Victoria. As business was conducted at the time that the common law rule was established, a few persons, or even a single individual, might be able to create a monopoly and control the market. The act was dangerous to the public because in many instances the supply was only adequate to the demand, and, in consequence, the creating of a monopoly a comparatively simple matter. On this account the offense was treated by the courts with great severity, and it was only after a great change in business conditions that the law was abrogated by statute. The creating of a "corner" in the produce or stock market is an act similar to that of the early engrossing or forestalling, but in some important respects differing from it. It differs from the earlier methods in that the business is conducted on a larger scale; a large amount of capital is employed and the means employed are adapted to the industrial conditions of the present time.[1]

[1] In Kirkpatrick v. Bonsall. 72 Pa. St. 158, Agnew uses the following pertinent language: "We cannot pronounce this agreement a gambling contract on the face of the writing. A bargain for an option such as it presents may be legitimate and for a proper business object. We can imagine such cases. But it is evident such agreements can be readily prostituted to the worst kind of gambling ventures. and, therefore, its character may be weighed by a jury in connection with other facts in considering whether the bargain was a mere scheme to gamble upon the chances of prices. The form of the venture when aided by evidence may clearly indicate a purpose to wager upon a rise or fall in the price of oil at a future day, and not to deal in the article as men usually do in that business. We must not confound gambling, whether it be in corporation stocks or merchandise. with what is commonly termed speculation. Merchants speculate upon the future prices of that in which they deal. and buy and sell accordingly. In other words. they think of and weigh, that is, speculate upon the coming market, and act upon this lookout into the future in their business transactions; and in this they often exhibit high mental grasp. and great knowledge of business. and of the affairs of the world. Their speculations display talent and forecast. but they act upon their conclusions and buy or sell in a *bona fide* way. Such speculation cannot be denounced. But when ventures are made upon the turn of prices alone, with no *bona fide* intent to deal in the article, but merely to risk the difference between the rise and fall of the price at a given time, the case is changed. The purpose then, is, not to deal in the article, but to stake upon the rise or fall of its price. No money or capital is invested in the purchase, but so much only is required as will cover the difference, a margin. as it is figuratively termed. Then the buyer represents not a transfer of property, but a mere stake or wager upon its future price. The difference requires the ownership of only a few hundreds or thousands of dollars. while the capital to complete an actual purchase or sale may be hundreds of thousands or millions. Hence. ventures upon prices invite men of small means to enter into transactions far beyond their capital which they do not intend to fulfill, and thus the apparent business in the particular trade is inflated and unreal. and like a bubble only needs to be pricked to

§ 90. **The Corner Defined.**—In general the creating of a corner is such a manipulation of any commodity, and, especially, of any article of produce, or of stocks, as to enable the parties conducting the business to control the price. The schemes devised and worked for the accomplishment of this end are too numerous and too intricate to admit of explanation in this work, but the object of each and all of them is an arrangement to force a ficticious rise in the market, for the purpose of obtaining an advantage of dealers who are compelled to buy and of the public to which the commodity cornered is an article of necessity. In a recent case in Missouri, it was held that a sale of goods to be delivered in the future is valid, notwithstanding there is an option as to the time of delivery, and the seller has no other means of getting them than to go into the market and buy them. But if, under the guise of such a contract, valid on its face, the real purpose and intention of the parties is merely to speculate in the rise, or fall, of prices, and the goods are not to be delivered, but the difference between the contract and market price only paid, then the transaction is a wager and the contract void.[1] In a leading case in Illinois, the rule

disappear; often carrying down the *bona fide* dealer in its collapse. Worse even than this, it tempts men of large capital to make bargains of stupendous proportions, and then to manipulate the market to produce the desired price. This, in the language of gambling speculation, is making a corner, that is to say, the article is so engrossed or manipulated as to make it scarce or plenty in the market at the will of the gamblers, and then to place its price within their power. Such transactions are destructive of good morals and fair dealing, and of the best interests of the community. If the article be stocks, corporations are crushed and innocent stockholders ruined to enable the gambler in its price to accomplish his ends. If it be merchandise, *e. g.*, grain, the poor are robbed and misery engendered."

[1] Crawford v. Spencer, 92 Mo. 498. See also Lyon v. Culbertson, 83 Ill. 33; Beveridge v. Hewitt, 8 Ill. App. 467; Pickering v. Case, 79 Ill. 328; Whitesides v. Hunt, 97 Ind. 191; s. c., 49 Am. Rep. 441; First Nat. Bank v. Oskaloosa P. Co., 66 Iowa, 41; Gregory v. Wendell, 40 Mich. 432; Clay v. Allen, 63 Miss. 426; Cockrell v. Thompson, 85 Mo. 510; Tatum v. Arnold, 42 N. J. Eq. 60; Flagg v. Baldwin, 38 N. J. Eq. 219; Kingsbury v. Kirwan, 77 N. Y. 612; Williams v. Tiedeman, 6 Mo. App. 269; Johnson v. Kaune, 21 Mo. App. 22; Waugh v. Beck, 114 Pa. St. 452;

in the case of contracts relating to corners, is stated, as follows: "Although the statutes being considered are highly penal, there is no warrant for construing them with any unreasonable strictness. They ought rather to have a just, if

North v. Phillips, 89 Pa. St. 250; McGrew v. City Produce Exchange, 85 Tenn. 572; Seeligsohn v. Lewis, 65 Tex. 215; Lowry v. Dillman, 59 Wis. 197; Barnard v. Backhaus, 52 Wis. 593; Irwin v. Williar, 110 U. S. 499; Cobb v. Prell, 15 Fed. Rep. 774; Bartlett v. Smith, 13 Fed. Rep. 263; s. c., 4 McCrary, 388; Bigelow v. Benedict, 9 Hun, 429; Cassard v. Hinman, 1 Bosw. 207. "But what is the transaction termed 'futures?' It is this: One person says I will sell you cotton at a certain time in the future for a certain price. You agree to pay that price, knowing that the person you deal with has no cotton to deliver at the time, but with the understanding that, when, the time arrives for delivery, you are to pay him the difference between the market value of that cotton and the price you agreed to pay if cotton declines, and if cotton advances he is to pay you the difference between what you promised to give and the advanced market price, if this is not a speculation on chances—a wagering and betting between the parties—then we are unable to understand the transaction. A betting on a game of faro, brag or poker, cannot be more hazardous or uncertain. Indeed, it may be said that these animals are tame, gentle and submissive, compared to this monster. The law has caged them and driven them to their dens. They have been outlawed, while this ferocious beast has been allowed to stalk about in open mid-day, with gilded signs and flaming advertisements, to lure the unhappy victim to its embrace of death and destruction. What are the consequences of these speculations on 'futures?' The faithful chroniclers of the day have informed us, as growing directly out of these nefarious practices, that there have been bankruptcies, defalcations of public officers, embezzlements, forgeries, larcenies and death. Certainly no one will contend for one moment that a transaction fraught with such evil consequences is not immoral, illegal and contrary to public policy." Cunningham v. National Bank of Augusta, 71 Ga. 400. "Certainly the legislature did not intend to impose any restraints upon legitimate commerce, but only to destroy the parasite that infests it. Contracts for future delivery, if entered into in good faith, and with an actual intention of fulfillment, are as valid as any other species of contract. A farmer may sell and agree to deliver his wheat or his cotton for a stipulated price before it is harvested. Nay, one may sell goods to be delivered at a future day, which he has not in actual or potential possession, but which he intends to go into the market and buy. But this is not what is commonly known as dealing in futures. This phrase has acquired the signification of a mere speculation upon chances, where the grain, cotton or stocks dealt in exist only in the imagination, and where no delivery is connot liberal construction, to the end the legislative intention may be accomplished, to prohibit all dealings in options in grains or other commodities. Nothing is productive of more mischievous results. Considerable fortunes secured by a life of honest industry have been lost in a single venture in 'options.' The evil is all the more dangerous from the fact it seemingly has the sanction of honorable commercial usage in its support. It is a vice that has in recent years grown to enormous proportions. Legitimate transactions on the board of trade are of the utmost importance in commerce. Such contracts, whether for immediate or future delivery, are valid in law, and recieve its sanction and all

templated, but the parties expect to settle upon the difference in the market. When so limited by judicial interpretation, the statute is not inconsistent with public policy. It forbids and punishes wagering contracts; that is, contracts in which they stipulate that they shall gain or lose upon the happening of an uncertain event, in which they have no interest except that arising from the possibility of such gain or loss. Fariera v. Campbell, 89 Pa. St. 89: Thompson v. Cummings, 68 Ga. 124; Flagg v. Baldwin, 38 N. J. Eq. 219." Fortenbury v. State, 47 Ark. 188. "The evidence fully proves that the appellant, Pearce, was operating what is commonly denominated a 'bucket shop,'—in fact, this is established by his own admission on his cross-examination. He was engaged in conducting the illegal business of selling 'futures' or 'options.' The products which he pretended to sell to his customers he did not have at the time, and it was mutually understood and intended by both parties, that the wheat or corn which was claimed to be sold and purchased was not to be delivered, but when the time fixed for its delivery arrived, the market value at Chicago of such cereals should constitute the basis upon which the settlements would be made. As the market would rise or fall there would be a loss or gain to the purchaser. The deals or transactions were understood to be a speculation solely on chances, and were in contravention of, and hostile to, public policy, and therefore illegal. Such transactions are of a like character and akin to bets made on a game of poker or faro, and are equally as uncertain and hazardous. The business or operations of the 'bucket shop' have been the source of much evil. Embezzlements and other crimes on the part of public officers, and bank officials, having the custody of money belonging to others, have been in the past some of the evil fruits directly traceable to dealings in futures in these institutions, and the question of prohibiting such transactions or business as it is generally conducted merits the consideration of the legislation." Jordan, J., in Pearce v. Dill (Ind.), decided Dec. 14, 1897.

the support that can be given to them. It is only against unlawful 'gambling contracts' the penalties of the law are denounced, and no subtle *finesse* of construction ought to be adopted to defeat the end it is to be hoped may be ultimately accomplished."[1]

§ 91. **The Nature of an "Option."**—The term "option," as employed in board of trade transactions, is defined by the court, in Pearce v. Foote, as follows: "As was said by this court in Pixley v. Boynton,[2] the true idea of an option is what are called, in the peculiar language of the dealers, 'puts' and 'calls.' A 'put' is defined to be the 'privilege of delivering or not delivering' the thing sold, and a 'call' is defined to be the 'privilege of calling for or not calling for' the thing bought. 'Optional contracts' in this sense are usually settled by adjusting market values, as the party having the 'option' may elect. It is simply a mode adopted for speculating in differences in market values of grain or other commodities. It must have been in this sense the term 'option' is used in the statute. Such a contract is obviously fictitious, having none of the elements of good faith, as in a contract where both parties are bound, and is defined by statute as a 'gambling contract.' Fictitious purchases or sales, such as were in the contemplation of the parties, were as nothing, and it is a matter of no consequence where it is pretended they were made, whether on the board of trade or elsewhere."[3] In *Ex parte* Young, the

[1] Pearce v. Foote, 113 Ill. 228, 239.

[2] Pixley v. Boyd, 79 Ill. 351.

[3] Pearce v. Foote, 113 Ill. 228, 234; s. c., 55 Am. Rep. 414. See also as to meaning of terms: Maxton v. Gheen, 75 Pa. St. 166; Knowlton v. Fitch, 52 N. Y. 288; Kirkpatrick v. Bonsall, 72 Pa. St. 155; *Ex parte* Young, 6 Biss. C. C. 53; Story v. Solomon, 6 Daly, 531; Union Bank v. Carr, 15 Fed. Rep. 438; Third Nat. Bank v. Harrison, 10 Fed. Rep. 243; Pickering v. Case, 79 Ill. 398; Rudolf v. Winters, 7 Neb. 125; Bigelow v. Benedict, 70 N. Y. 202; s. c., 26 Am. Rep. 537. "The plaintiff bought, through the agency of defendant, a stock option or privilege, known in the language of brokers as a 'straddle.' The word, if not elegant, is at least expressive. It means the double privilege of a 'put' and 'call;' and secures to the holder the right to demand of the seller at a certain price, within a certain time, a certain number of

following definition and statement of the rule were included in the finding of the court: "Puts" or the privilege for a nominal consideration of delivering a large quantity of shares of specified stock, or to require him to take at the same price, within the same time, the same shares of stock. The continuance of the option is fixed by the agreement, and in this case was for sixty days. The value of a 'straddle', it is proven, depends upon the fluctuations of the stock selected. The wider the range ef these fluctuations, whether up or down, the greater the amount which may be realized; and, of course, the longer the option continues, the greater the chance of such fluctuations during the period. The plaintiff swears that she was led into the purchase of the 'straddle' in question by certain printed circulars of the defendant which she produced. Of course, they point out an easy and rapid road to wealth for any one who is careful in his choice of a broker, but the material point in them is that they describe a 'straddle,' explain its dependence for success upon the fluctuations of the selected stock, and offer to any one who will purchase a sixty day 'straddle' of the defendant's selection, paying therefor $400, and $25 more for commission, a guaranty that the aggregate fluctuation in the stock, during the pendency of the contract will amount to eight per cent.; and, further, promise that if the stock does not move to that extent, the cost of the contract, less commissions, shall be refunded." Harris v. Tumbridge, 83 N. Y. 92, 95. "By the evidence offered on the part of the plaintiff, it was shown that a sale of gold short, according to established usage, means a sale of that which the seller has not, but what he expects to buy in at a lower price than that for which he sells. The seller can order the gold to be bought in at any time, and the buyer can call for the delivery of it when he pleases. That the buyer or seller is entitled to a margin for his security, as the gold may rise or fall in the market. This margin must be in money, or its equivalent in securities, and equal to from five to ten per cent. on the price at which the gold is sold, over and above its market price at any time, and such margin must be kept up as the value of gold fluctuates in the market, so that the buyer shall have in hand on a rise in price, an amount in money, or its equivalent, sufficient to cover the loss to the seller caused by such rise in gold above the price at which it was sold short, with from five to ten per cent. on the contract price, added to the amount of such loss. If this margin be not kept up as gold advances, the buyer has the right to buy in the gold for account of the seller, and charge him with the loss." Appleman v. Fisher, 34 Md. 540, 549. "As to the validity of these contracts. From what has been said concerning them, it appears that there is no essential difference between them and the numerous contracts, of the same kind which have been before the courts in England and in this country, and which have been almost uniformly upheld as valid contracts. All these decisions unite upon the proposition that these contracts are presumptively grain within a certain time at a specified price, when taken of parties notoriously running a "corner," are wager contracts, and void as against public policy. Where no delivery of the grain was contemplated by the parties, but they expected simply to settle the differences as established by future prices, the contract is simply a wager, and, therefore, void.[1]

§ 92. Modification of the Common Law Doctrine.— To some extent the common law doctrine in regard to covenants in restraint of trade, as established in England and followed by the courts of this country, has been modified by statute and by the more recent decisions. Where the earlier rule has been found to conflict with modern business methods beyond what is essential to the adequate protection of the parties concerned, it has either been abrogated by statute or materially modified by the courts. Certain transactions which, under the law against engrossing or forestalling, were indictable as misdemeanors, have become simply void, leaving the parties without the means of redress where the contract is violated. In some of the States, as in New York, the late statutes have substituted for the requirements of the earlier certain restraints on combinations, but imposing none on the individual. In England all

valid, but that, though valid on their face, they may be shown by extrinsic evidence to have been intended by the contracting parties, not as commercial transactions, but as mere wagers on the future state of the market: that the one thing which makes them wagers and renders them invalid is an agreement between the contracting parties, made at the time of the contract, and understood as part thereof, that the contract may be discharged by the seller, not by the delivery of the commodity sold, but by paying to the purchaser the difference between the market price on the last day of the performance of the contract and the price at which the sale was made: or, on the other hand, that the purchaser, if the market goes the other way, shall not be bound to receive the commodity purchased, but may settle by the payment of a difference; and that such an agreement will not, if made subsequently to the making of the contract itself, taint the contract and render it invalid in law." Kent v. Miltenberger, 13 Mo. App. 503, 507. See also Sawyer v. Taggart, 14 Bush. 727, 734; Williams v. Tiedeman, 6 Mo. App. 269.

[1] *Ex parte* Young, 6 Biss. 53.

of the earlier statutes relating to this subject have been repealed, but it seems to have been held that the common law is still to such an extent in force as to render combinations to enhance the price of provisions punishable.[1] In the lead-

[1] Rex v. Waddington, 1 East, 143; s. c., 1 East, 167. "There is no doubt that modern ideas of trade have practically abrogated some common law doctrines which are supposed to unduly hamper commerce. At the common law there is no doubt such transactions as were here contemplated, although confined to a single person, were indictable misdemeanors under the law applicable to forestalling and engrossing. Some of our States have abolished the old statutes which were adopted on this subject, and which were sometimes regarded as embodying the whole law of such cases. Where this has been done, as in New York, the statutes have replaced them by restraints or combinations for that purpose, leaving individual action free. In England, there have been several statutes narrowing or repealing all of the ancient statutes, and more recently covering the whole ground. But so long as the early statutes only were repealed, it was considered that enough remained of the common law to punish combinations to enhance values of commodities. And when this doctrine became narrowed, it seems to have been considered that such combinations to enhance the price of provisions remained under the ban. In Rex v. Waddington, 1 East. 143, and s. c., 1 East, 167, it was held, the common law was still in force to punish engrossing the necessaries of life or provisions by single persons. The chief difficulty was in determining whether hops came within that rule, and it was held they did, and that the legislature only could change the law. The defendant was heavily fined. That case has been sharply criticised as not in harmony with modern political economy, and it, no doubt, goes beyond what would be considered proper among us. It has never, so far as the researches of Mr. Bishop have gone,—and he seldom overlooks important cases,—been judicially disapproved, although statutes have been made to change the rule. See Bishop, Criminal Law, §§ 527, 528, and notes to 6th edition. And he intimates that conspiracies for such purposes may, perhaps, be punished, even where the individual offense has been abolished. See also Vol. 2, §§ 202, 206, 216, 220, 230, 231, and notes. In Rex v. Hilbers, 2 Chitty, 163, it was held that there must be a combination of more than one person before an information will be granted for enhancing the price of necessaries. Mr. Russell gives it as his opinion, that in our day, single offenders would not be regarded as punishable unless their offense relates to provisions. 1 Russ. 170. But where there is a conspiracy the law has been given a much wider application, and the case of Rex v. De Berenger, 3 M. & S. 67, has obtained celebrity from the high rank of the offenders who were convicted—(and one of them at least, Lord Cochrane, unjustly)—of conspiring to raise the price of stocks by false rumors." Raymond v. Leavitt, 46 Mich. 447, 450.

ing case of Raymond v. Leavitt, the court, after referring to the cases above cited, said: "We have not referred to these cases to assert the propriety of enforcing common law criminal penalties contrary to the general understanding of the business community. While these offenses have never been abolished in this State by statute, and might theoretically be, therefore, within the possible range of our laws, there would be no toleration of their strict prosecution against single persons to the common law extent as crimes. But the general sentiment has not led to any change in legislation or to any recognition of the legal propriety of allowing every species of produce gambling to be made susceptible of enforcement by contract. We must willfully shut our eyes before we can fail to see that a combination between a man who furnishes money and dealers who manipulate the market, where the money invested is but a trifling percentage of the property to be handled, and where the only intent is to produce unnatural fluctuations in prices, is entirely outside the limits of buying and selling for honest trade purposes. It is the plainest and worst kind of produce gambling, and it is impossible for any but dangerous results to come from it. We do not feel called upon to regard so much of the common law to be obsolete as treats these combinations as unlawful, whether they should now be held punishable as crimes or not. The statute of New York, which is universally conceded to be a limitation of common law offenses, is referred to in the case in 68 N. Y. 558, as rendering such conspiracies unlawful, and this had been previously held in People v. Fisher, 14 Wend. 9, where the subject is discussed at length. There may be difficulties in determining conduct as in violation of public policy, where it has not before been covered by statute or precedents. But in the case before us the conduct of the parties comes within the undisputed censure of the law of the land, and we cannot save the transaction without doing so on the ground that such dealings are so manifestly sanctioned by usage and public approval that it would be absurd to suppose the legislature, if attention were called to them, would not legalize them. We do not think public opinion has become so thoroughly demoralized; and until the law is changed we shall decline enforcing such contracts. If parties see fit to invest money in such ventures they must get it back by some other than legal measure."[1]

§ 93. The Creation of a Corner in Necessaries.—In the rules in regard to corners some distinction is made between different commodities or articles to which the corner relates. In the decisions in cases of this character the courts have regard to the interests of the public. Transactions which in their effects are prejudicial to the interests of the people as a body will not be upheld. In a recent case in Illinois, it was held that an agreement, the object of which is to buy up all cash corn offered and by holding the same create an artificial scarcity, so as to speculate on the market price, is void as against public policy, and an action will not lie to recover money advanced or services rendered thereunder.[2] In the opinion in this case, the court said:

[1] Raymond v. Leavitt, 46 Mich. 447, 452.

[2] Cummings v. Foss, 40 Ill. App. 523. See also Pickering v. Case, 79 Ill. 328; Lyon v. Culbertson, 83 Ill. 33; Webster v. Sturges, 7 Ill. App. 560; Kreigh v. Sherman, 105 Ill. 49; Pearce v. Foote, 113 Ill. 228; Coffman v. Young, 20 Ill. App. 76; Higgins v. McCrea, 116 U. S. 671; White v. Barber, 123 U. S. 392; Griswold v. Gregg, 24 Ill. App. 384; Wheeler v. McDermid, 36 Ill. App. 179; Locke v. Fowler, 41 Ill. App. 66. Rev. St. Ill. 1881, chap. 38, § 130, provides for a penalty against any one cornering the market in certain commodities, or attempting to do so, and that all contracts for that purpose shall be void. Plaintiff and defendant had entered into a speculation to corner the wheat market, which was successful. After the close of the deal, plaintiff's share of the profits was left with the defendant, who, by plaintiff's request, afterwards invested it in a lard deal. *Held*, that defendant must account to plaintiff for the money, although the wheat deal was illegal. Wells v. McGeoch, 71 Wis. 196; s. c., 35 N. W. Rep. 769. "The objection that a contract is immoral or illegal as between plaintiff and defendant sounds at all times very ill in the mouth of the defendant. It is not for his sake, however, that the objection is ever allowed, but it is founded on general principles of policy, which the defendant has the advantage of, contrary to the real justice as between him and the plaintiff, as I may so say. The principle of public policy is this, *ex dolo malo non oritur actio*. No court will lend its aid to a man who founds his cause of action upon an immoral or illegal act. If from the plaintiff's own stating,

"It is manifest in the present case that the clear tendency of the acts of the parties was to unnaturally enhance the price of an article of prime necessity; to create as to it an artificial scarcity, and to compel those whose necessities compelled them to buy to pay, not the price determined by entire freedom of buyers and sellers, but the price to which their combination to buy and to withhold might be able to force the market. Such combination was clearly against public policy, and such conduct of a character that, if it be not now, under the common law, as it existed a century and a half ago, would have been a criminal offense. * * * To the claim of the plaintiffs for moneys advanced and services rendered in aid of this confederacy, so opposed to public interests, so inimical to public welfare, so calculated to make unnaturally dear, food for man and beast, the law answers '*ex turpi causa non oritur actio.*' It is immaterial that the defendants' defense is based upon a confession of their own unlawful conduct. The law will not attempt to adjust differences which arise out of transactions it condemns. It will leave the parties where their own conduct leaves them. It will not compel them to divide the plunder or share the loss of an unlawful enterprise; neither will it require them to remunerate those who, with full cognizance of the character of such undertaking, assist them with money or service."[1] In Raymond v. Leavitt, the court

or otherwise, the cause of action appear to arise *ex turpi causa*, or the transgression of a positive law of this country, there the court says he has no right to be assisted. It is upon that ground the court goes, not for the sake of the defendant, but because they will not lend their aid to such a plaintiff. So if the plaintiff and defendant were to change sides, and the defendant was to bring his action against the plaintiff, the latter would then have the advantage of it; for when both are equally in fault *potior est conditio defendentis.*" Lord Mansfield in Holman v. Johnson, Cowp. 341, 343.

[1] Cummings v. Foss, 40 Ill. App. 523, 530, 531. On error to the Supreme Court, this case was affirmed in Foss v. Cummings, 149 Ill. 353. At page 359, the court says: "Our statute makes it a penal offense to 'corner the market or attempt to do so' in relation to any grain or other commodity, and declares all contracts made for that purpose void. We are unable to distinguish the combination between these parties, as found by the appellate court, from an *attempt* to

said: "The object of the arrangement between these parties was to force a fictitious and unnatural rise in the wheat market for the express purpose of getting the advantage of dealers and purchasers whose necessities compelled them to buy, and necessarily to create a similar difficulty as to all persons who had to obtain or use that commodity, which is an article indispensable to every family in the country. That such transactions are hazardous to the comfort of the community is universally recognized. This alone may not be enough to make them illegal. But it is enough to make them so questionable that very little further is required to bring them within distinct legal prohibition."[1]

§ **94. The Creating of a Corner in Stocks.**—A corner is sometimes created in the stock of a particular corporation, as of a railway or gas company. The object is either speculative or the control of the corporation. The process of creating a corner of this class is termed "the tying up of stocks," and the accomplishment of the object creates what is designated as "a squeeze in the market." Where the object of a transfer of stocks is to create a corner, or to obtain control of a corporation, all contracts in regard to it will be held void. In a case in Massachusetts, it was held that an agreement to make "a corner" in stock, by buying

corner the Chicago market in relation to corn. Practically it is that, and nothing else. But whether it is or not, it was an attempt to advance the price of corn beyond the natural market by a combination between the parties, and that the law condemns, as against public right, and void, and forbids the courts to lend their aid to those engaged therein." In a suit upon a promissory note, it was found specially that the note was given to grain brokers in consideration of commission and advances upon wheat purchased by him for the maker, that the maker of the note had entered into a combination with others to purchase through the plaintiff and other brokers, for delivery during a certain month, more wheat than there was in the market, thereby forcing the price to a high rate with a view to make profit on settling with sellers failing to deliver. Whether the plaintiff was a party to this combination or had knowledge of it was not found. A conclusion of law that the note was valid, and the plaintiff entitled to recover upon it, was held to be correct. Wright v. Crabbs, 78 Ind. 487.

[1] Raymond v. Leavitt, 46 Mich. 447, 450; s. c., 41 Am. Rep. 170.

it up so as to control the market, and then purchasing for future deliveries, is illegal, and the parties thereto are not partners; and one of said parties who has authorized the others to use his funds already in their hands in carrying out the agreement, cannot recover any amount actually expended or appropriated according to its terms, but can recover in an action for money had and received, any balance not so expended or appropriated.[1] In Foll's Ap-

[1] Sampson v. Shaw, 101 Mass. 145. In Hatch v. Douglas, 48 Conn. 116; s. c., 40 Am. Rep. 154, the defendant wrote the plaintiffs, who were stock brokers in the city of New York—"I want to buy, say one hundred shares Union Pacific stock on margin. Will you take $1,000 first mortgage New York & Oswego R. R. and do it?" The plaintiffs replied that they would, and at once bought the stock and soon after sold it by the defendant's order at a profit. Other stocks were afterwards bought and sold by the plaintiffs for the defendant under the same arrangement, resulting in a final loss, exceeding the value of the security held and the plaintiffs sued for the balance. It was held 1, that evidence was admissible on the part of the plaintiffs to show the meaning of the words "on margin," that term being used by stock brokers and having acquired a special and well understood meaning in their business. 2. That the contract not being for the mere payment of differences, but the defendant, having through the plaintiffs as his agents, actually purchased the stock, which was delivered to them and which they were ready to transfer to him on payment of the purchase money, it was not a gaming contract. In the course of the opinion the court uses this language: "Contracts of this nature, however, are distinguishable from speculating contracts. A man may legitimately buy goods or stocks intending to sell in a short time and take an advantage of an advance in the price if there is one. In such a case he takes the risk of a decline, but that does not make it a gambling contract. And he may purchase goods at a fixed price to be delivered at a future day, if the parties intend an actual delivery and acceptance. The actual intention may be difficult to prove or disprove; but when once the fact is established one way or the other, there is no difficulty in applying the law. Now, there are in the transactions between these parties some of the elements which are usually found in a gaming contract. For instance, it is pretty evident that the parties did not contemplate that the stock should be actually transferred to the defendant; but he would have been satisfied with the receipt of the difference between the price paid and the price received, less interest and commissions, if the price advanced, and expected to pay that difference if the price declined. To that extent, it was a contract for the payment of differences. But it was more than that. The defendant, through his agents, the plaintiffs, actually purchased the stock and

peal, before the Supreme Court of Pennsylvania, F, in writing, agreed to sell and G to purchase fifteen shares of the stock of a national bank. G and his friends owned sufficient stock to give them with these fifteen shares the control of the bank. The avowed object of the proposed purchase of the fifteen shares was to obtain control of the bank. F refused to deliver the stock, when G filed a bill in equity to compel its delivery. It was held that for reasons of public policy equity will not enforce such contract by decree for specific performance.[1] In the opinion in this case, the court said: "Were we to affirm this decree, I see no reason why we may not be called upon to use the extraordinary powers of a court of equity to assist in miscellaneous stock jobbing operations. A party who is attempting to make a 'corner' in stock or in any article of merchandise, who had made his contracts with that end in view, might, with equal propriety, call upon us to decree a specific performance thereof. But the decree of a chancellor is the exercise of a sound discretion; it is of grace, not of right, and will never be made where the equity and justice of a case is not clear."[2]

there was an actual delivery—not to the principal, but to the agents for the principal. The plaintiffs advanced the money and held the stocks in their hands as security. The plaintiffs were ready at any time to transfer the stock to the defendant on payment of the purchase money. The import of the finding is, and we must so regard it, that it was an actual and *bona fide* employment of the plaintiffs to purchase stocks, and not a mere formal employment designed to cover a betting operation. It does not appear that the plaintiffs assumed any risk. They were entitled to their commissions and interest on their advancements, whether the stocks went up or down. The most that can be said of them is, that they knew that the defendant was speculating and that they advanced him money for that purpose. But that was neither illegal nor immoral."

[1] Foll's Appeal, 91 Pa. St. 434. See Turner v. Schneider, 27 Ill. App. 220.

[2] Foll's Appeal, 91 Pa. St. 434, 438. In Rex v. Berenger, 3 Maule & Selw. 67, it was held an indictable offense to conspire on a particular day by false rumors to raise the price of the public government funds, with intent to injure the subjects who should purchase on that day, and that the indictment was well enough without specifying the particular persons who purchased as the persons intended to be injured.

§ 95. Where Contracts for Future Delivery are Sustained.—The statutory regulations in regard to contracts for the delivery of grain at a future day, with a fixed price, are not uniform, the difference relating essentially to the burden of proof. Where it appears that a contract for the future delivery of grain, at a fixed price, was a *bona fide* transaction, that is, that it was made with the express understanding that the grain was to be, in fact, delivered and received by the parties, and that the contract was not intended to be a protection of a gambling transaction, it will be sustained. In a case in Wisconsin, it was held that to uphold a contract in writing for the sale and delivery of grain at a future day, for a price certain, it must affirmatively and satisfactorily appear that it was made with an actual view to the delivery and receipt of the grain, and not as a cover for a gambling transaction. Where some of the transactions between the parties which enter into the consideration of a note and mortgage are mere gaming transactions, they render the whole security void.[1] The

[1] Barnard v. Backhaus, 52 Wis. 593. See also Pope v. Hanke, 155 Ill. 617; Crawford v. Spencer, 92 Mo. 498; First Nat. Bank v. Oskaloosa Packing Co., 66 Iowa, 41; Schneider v. Turner, 130 Ill. 28; Cothran v. Ellis, 125 Ill. 496; Fortenbury v. State, 47 Ark. 188; Pixley v. Boynton, 79 Ill. 351; Miller v. Bensley, 20 Ill. App. 528; Clay v. Allen, 63 Miss. 426; Commiskey v. Williams, 20 Mo. App. 606; Kingsbury v. Kirwan, 77 N. Y. 612; Cooke v. Davis, 53 N. Y. 318; Yerkes v. Salomon, 11 Hun, 471; Seeligson v. Lewis, 65 Tex. 215; s. c., 57 Am. Rep. 593; Kirkpatrick v. Adams, 20 Fed. Rep. 287; Bartlett v. Smith, 13 Fed. Rep. 263; s. c., 4 McCrary, 388; Maxton v. Gheen, 75 Pa. St. 166; Appleman v. Fisher, 34 Md. 540; Smith v. Bouvier, 70 Pa. St. 325; Cassard v. Hinman, 1 Bosw. 207; Stanton v. Small, 3 Sandf. 230; McIlvaine v. Egerton, 2 Robt. (N. Y.) 422; Gregory v. Wattowa, 58 Iowa, 711; Cobb v. Prell, 15 Fed. Rep. 774. "A contract for the sale of property which the vendor does not possess, to be delivered in future, is not illegal, unless both parties understood it to be a mere speculation in the future price, with no intention of delivering or accepting, and the burden of proof is on the party alleging the illegality. Conner v. Robertson, 37 La. Ann. 814; s. c., 55 Am. Rep. 521. It is not unlawful to buy or sell commodities to be delivered at a future day, even if at the time of the purchase the seller has none to deliver, and no means of obtaining them, excep to go into the market and buy them, if the parties really intend and agree that the goods are to be delivered and the price paid. Such

rule in Illinois is not in entire accord with that of Wisconsin, as above given. In a leading case before the Circuit Court of the United States for the Eastern District of Wisconsin, it was held that under the Illinois statute, a simple

a proceeding is a wager, and as such void, only when the real intent of the parties is to speculate in the rise and fall of prices, and the goods are not to be delivered, but one party is to pay the other the difference between the contract price and the market price of the goods at the date fixed for executing the contract. The character of such an operation is derived from the intention of the parties, and such party must concur in the vicious intent to bring the transaction under the denunciations of the law against gambling. If either contracts in good faith and contemplates a sale to be followed by the constituents of delivery and payment, he is entitled to the benefit of the contract, no matter what may have been the secret intention or purpose of the other party. Benjamin on Sales (4th Ed.), §§ 82, 83, and 542, and authorities there cited; Irwin v. Williar, 110 U. S. 499; Rountree v. Smith, 108 U. S. 269; Gregory v. Wendell, 40 Mich. 432; Pixley v. Boynton, 79 Ill. 351." Clay v. Allen, 63 Miss. 426, 430. "The plaintiff claims that the transactions out of which T's pretended indebtedness arose were gambling transactions, in that they were not, as they purported to be upon their face, contracts for the sale and delivery of grain, but, virtually, bets in relation to the future market price of grain in Chicago. It is a matter of general information that many ostensible transactions in grain are of a purely gambling and criminal character. The widespread ruin produced shows them to be among the greatest of evils. Where their true character is discovered, courts should promptly condemn them, and hold them void. But they need to proceed with caution. In the movement of the grain of the country, contracts for future delivery are, to some extent, a necessity, and they are as legitimate as any other; and that, too, though the parties may contemplate the possibility of a settlement by a payment of differences. The real intention of the parties, of course, must determine the character of the transaction, and in arriving at the intention we must be governed by the evidence, and not by conjectures based upon our knowledge of other contracts." Tomblin v. Callen, 69 Iowa, 229, 230. "We utterly fail to discover any wrong on the part of the plaintiffs. Their business was a legitimate one, and, so far as appears, their connection with this transaction honest. Their profits were not to be affected by the result, their commissions were not to be increased or diminished by any contingency. It is true they were aware that the defendant, at the time, had no wheat. But the fact itself being immaterial, their knowledge of it is equally so. It is not only common, but perfectly legal, and sometimes necessary, to contract for the sale and future delivery of an article which, at the time, has no existence, but which is afterwards to be purchased, raised or manufactured.

option, reserved by the seller to himself, as to time of delivery of property within certain time, and the settlement of differences upon such a contract, does not render the contract void as a gambling transaction. The burden of proof, in an action on such a contract by a broker for commissions and advances, for settlements made by the "ringing up" process, is, therefore, upon the defendant to show the gambling intent; and it does not follow, from the fact that he himself intended no delivery, that such was the intention of the broker and the other principal, or that deliveries were not made as a matter of fact.[1] In the opinion in this case, the court said: "The weight of authority, therefore, in this circuit, is all one way as applied to Illinois transactions, namely, that a simple option reserved by the seller to himself as to time of delivery of property within certain limits, and the settlement of differences upon such a contract, does not make the contract void as a gambling transaction. The proof must go further, and affirmatively show that it was not the intention of either seller or buyer when the contract was made to deliver any property; and this is not proved by showing merely the intention of one party, even coupled with the intention of his agent representing him in the transaction."[2] In a case before the Supreme Court of the United States, Mr. Justice Matthews,

It does not appear that the defendant had any intention beyond what appears upon the face of the contract, or if he had, that the plaintiffs were cognizant of it. The mischief and illegality arises when the apparent contract is not the real one, when it is a mere cover for ulterior designs, and such as are not authorized by law. A contract for the sale and purchase of wheat, to be delivered in good faith at a future time, is one thing, and is not inconsistent with the law. But such a contract, entered into without an intention of having any wheat pass from one party to the other, but with an understanding that at the appointed time the purchaser is merely to receive or pay the difference between the contract and the market price, is another thing, and such as the law will not sustain. This is what is called a settling of the differences, and as such is clearly and only a betting upon the price of wheat, against public policy, and not only void, but deserving of the severest censure." Rumsey v. Berry, 65 Me. 570, 573.

[1] Ward v. Vosburgh, 31 Fed. Rep. 12.

[2] Ward v. Vosburgh, 31 Fed. Rep. 12, 15.

said: "The generally accepted doctrine in this country is, as stated by Mr. Benjamin, that a contract for the sale of goods to be delivered at a future day is valid, even though the seller has not the goods, nor any other means of getting them than to go into market and buy them; but such a contract is only valid when the parties really intend and agree that the goods are to be delivered by the seller and the price to be paid by the buyer; and if, under the guise of such a contract, the real intent be merely to speculate in the rise and fall of prices, and the goods are not to be delivered, but one party is to pay to the other the difference between the contract price and the market price of the goods at the date fixed for executing the contract, then the whole transaction constitutes nothing more than a wager, and is null and void."[1]

§ 96. **Rights and Liabilities of Third Parties.**—A third party, who acquires an interest in a contract for cornering the market, as an agent or broker, or by advancing money under the contract, stands in the same legal position as the principal parties in interest. In a recent case in Illinois, it was held that a broker, who is privy to the unlawful design of the parties to an option contract, and brings them together for the purpose of making it, cannot recover for any services or losses incurred in the transaction.[2] In the case of Samuels v. Oliver, the rule, relat-

[1] Irwin v. Williar, 110 U. S. 499, 508; s. c., 4 Sup. Ct. Rep. 160.

[2] Pope v. Hanke, 155 Ill. 617. See also Nat'l Bank of Augusta v. Cunningham, 75 Ga. 366; Cunningham v. Nat'l Bank, 71 Ga. 400; Thompson v. Cummings, 68 Ga. 124; McCormick v. Nickols, 19 Ill. App. 334; Stewart v. Schall, 65 Md. 299; s. c., 57 Am. Rep. 327; Fortenbury v. State, 47 Ark. 188; Irwin v. Williar, 110 U. S. 499; *In re* Green, 7 Biss. 338; Kirkpatrick v. Adams, 20 Fed. Rep. 287; Dickson v. Thomas, 97 Pa. St. 278; Beadles v. Owing, 16 Lea, 424; Barnard v. Backhaus, 52 Wis. 593; Pearce v. Foote, 113 Ill. 228; s. c., 55 Am. Rep. 414. "At the argument, the case of Third Nat'l Bank, 10 Fed. Rep. 243, was cited as favoring the position that the rule that money lent knowingly, and for the purpose of furthering an illegal act, cannot be recovered, applies to acts contrary to the statute law, and not to those contrary to the law founded on public policy. That case was upon promissory notes, the plaintiff claiming to be an innocent holder for value. The notes were given for balances

ing to the standing of third parties, is stated, as follows: If a grain broker, in executing the instructions of his principal, is required to pay out money to adjust differences in respect of the purchase and sale of grain, and is guilty of no fraud

on an illegal agreement, unenforceable between the original parties, but it was not within the gaming statute of Missouri, which destroys the negotiable character of a note given for a gaming consideration, within the term of that statute, for it pronounces a gaming contract absolutely void. And it was held that an innocent holder for value would recover. In the opinion it is said that the great weight of authority supports the rule that a broker or agent employed to buy or sell commodities for the purpose of speculating on the rise and fall of prices merely, and the agent buys in his own name, but on his principal's account, and after losses have occurred in such transactions, he advances money at his principal's request to pay such losses, or if he pays such losses, and afterwards his principal gives him a note therefor, may recover against principal the advances so made, or the note so executed, notwithstanding the illegal character of the original venture. Whether such be the rule in this State need not be considered. But it is further remarked: 'If a broker or factor supply his principal with funds for the express purpose of enabling him to engage in illegal transactions, and if he (the agent) conducts the illegal venture in his own name, it seems clear that he becomes a *particeps criminis*, and the law will not aid him to recover moneys advanced for such purposes, nor will it enforce securities taken therefor.' And this makes near approach to the controlling principle and facts, as alleged in the case before us. Where a man lends money to another for the express purpose of enabling him to commit a specific unlawful act, and such act be afterwards committed by means of the aid so received, the lender is a *particeps criminis*." Waugh v. Beck, 114 Pa. St. 422, 429. "The customer employs the broker to buy certain railroad stocks for his account, and to pay for them, and to hold them subject to his order as to the time of the sale. The customer advances ten per cent. of their market value, and agrees to keep good such proportionate advance according to the fluctuations of the market. Waiving, for the moment, all disputed questions, I state the following as the result of this agreement: The broker undertakes and agrees: 1. At once to buy for the customer the stocks indicated. 2. To advance all the money required for the purchase, beyond the ten per cent. furnished by the customer. 3. To carry or hold such stocks for the benefit of the customer so long as the margin of ten per cent. is kept good, or until notice is given by either party that the transaction must be closed. An appreciation in the value of the stocks is the gain of the customer, and not of the broker. 4. At all times to have in his name or under his control, ready for delivery, the shares purchased, or an equal amount of other shares of the same stock. 5.

or violation of law, he will be entitled to be reimbursed by his principal for the outlay. The principal is bound to indemnify his agent or broker for losses incurred in executing his orders. But if one employs a broker to purchase and sell grain with the illegal purpose of "cornering" the market or controlling the price thereof, and this fact is known to the agent or broker, the latter cannot recover of his principal for services or money advanced in the execution of such illegal purpose, nor can the employer recover of his agent for moneys received by him in such illegal dealings upon the market. When parties enter into a contract which is illegal or contrary to public policy, the courts will not assist either of them, but will leave them in the position in which their illegal acts have placed them. The party advancing money or performing services under such a contract cannot recover for the same of his employer, nor will he be liable to his employer for any profits derived by him in the business of his agency. The enhancement of the price of an article of prime necessity, such as wheat or

To deliver such shares to the customer, when required by him, upon the receipt of the advances and commissions accruing to the broker; or, 6. To sell such shares upon the order of the customer, upon payment of the like sums to him. and account to the customer for the proceeds of such sale. Under this contract, the customer undertakes: 1. To pay a margin of ten per cent. on the current market value of the shares. 2. To keep good such margin, according to the fluctuations of the market. 3. To take the shares so purchased on his order whenever required by the broker, and to pay the difference between the percentage advanced by him and the amount paid therefor by the broker. The position of the broker is two-fold. Upon the order of the customer, he purchases the shares of stocks desired by him. This is a clear act of agency. To complete the purchase, he advances from his own funds for the benefit of the customer ninety per cent. of the purchase money. Quite as clearly he does not in this act as agent, but assumes a new position. He also holds or carries the stock for the benefit of the purchaser until a sale is made by the order of the purchaser, or upon his own action. In thus holding or carrying he stands also upon a different ground from that of a broker or agent, whose office is simply to buy and sell. To advance money for the purchase, and to hold and carry stocks, is not the act of a broker as such. In so doing he enters upon a new duty, obtains other rights, and is subject to additional responsibilities." Markham v. Jaudon, 41 N. Y. 235.

other articles, for purposes of extortion, is against public policy, and a combination or agreement to make a "corner" on stock or grain by buying it up, so as to control the market, and then purchasing for future delivery, is illegal, and a party thereto whose funds have been used by his direction in carrying out the agreement cannot recover the same back. A person dealing at a particular market will be taken to have dealt according to the known general custom and usage of that market, and if he employs another to act for him in buying or selling at such market, he will be held as intending that the business shall be conducted according to such general usage and custom, and this has been held the rule whether he in fact knows of the custom or not.[1] In a recent case in Tennessee, it was held that where several confederate together for an unlawful purpose, *e. g.*, stock gambling or dealing in "futures," the acts of one selected to transact the unlawful business are the acts of all, and each confederate is jointly and severally liable therefor.[2] On this point, the court said: "Where it appears that several have unlawfully combined and confederated to gamble with and defraud another through a selected party, each confederate participating is liable for the entire amount received, as the money is received for all, and by all, according to the devised alleged method under which they were all jointly operating."[3]

[1] Samuels v. Oliver, 130 Ill. 73. See also Roundtree v. Smith, 108 U. S. 269; Baldwin v. Flagg, 36 N. J. Eq. 48; Baker v. Drake, 66 N. Y. 518; Wicks v. Hatch, 62 N. Y. 535; Knowlton v. Fitch, 52 N. Y. 288; Earl v. Howell, 14 Abb. N. Cas. 474; Thacker v. Hardy, L. R. 4 Q. B. Div. 685; *Ex parte* Rogers, L. R. 15 Ch. D. 207; Logan v. Musick, 81 Ill. 415; Durant v. Burt, 98 Mass. 161; Maxton v. Gheen, 75 Pa. St. 166; Smith v. Bouvier, 70 Pa. St. 325; Jackson v. Foote, 12 Fed. Rep. 37; Ashton v. Dakin, 4 H. & N. 867.

[2] Dunn v. Bell, 85 Tenn. 581; s. c., 4 S. W. Rep. 41.

[3] McGrew v. City Produce Exchange, 85 Tenn. 572; s. c., 4 S. W. Rep. 38, 39. "Before the passage of this law, such a transaction as dealing in futures, of itself, was not unlawful. Nor was it unlawful unless it was the intent of both parties that there should be no real purchase or delivery. This act was intended to make it unlawful if either had no intention of effectuating a real purchase or sale. It was designed to suppress the evil of dealing in futures, and limit

§ 97. Statutory Prohibition.—In many, if not all of the States, the creating of a corner, or the dealing in futures, with a view to creating a corner, is prohibited by statute. In Illinois, the statute is, as follows: "Whoever contracts to have or give to himself or another the option to sell or buy, at a future time, any grain or other commodity, stock of any railroad or other company, or gold, or forestalls the market by spreading false rumors to influence the price of commodities therein, or corners the market or attempts to do so in relation to any of such commodities, shall be fined not less than $10, nor more than $1,000, or confined in the county jail, not exceeding one year, or both; and all contracts made in violation of this section shall be considered gambling contracts, and shall be void."[1] As Chicago has

such operation to *bona fide* sales and purchases by those who wished to sell to those who wished to buy. In making the seller responsible for the intent of the buyer, and the buyer responsible for the intent of the seller, it intended to suppress gambling by confining the business of buying and selling for future delivery in such limits as would practically preclude the possibility of it. The *bona fide* dealer can still operate, but he cannot do so upon any terms which do not protect the community against the pernicious and ruinous speculation in the rise and fall of prices. He is obliged, for his own safety, as this act provides extreme penalties, to avoid the speculator, and buy only for the legitimate demands of necessity and trade." *Ibid.*, 578.

[1] Starr & Curtis, Ann. Stat. Illinois, ¶ 253, p. 1295. Sec. 3166, of the Code of Tennessee, reads as follows: Any sale, contract or agreement for the sale of bonds, stocks, grain, cotton or other produce, property, commodity, article or thing for future delivery, where either of the contracting parties, buyer or seller, is dealing simply for the margin, or on the prospective rise or fall in the price of the article or thing sold, and where either of the said contracting parties have had no intention or purpose of making actual delivery or receiving the property or thing in specie, shall be deemed and is hereby declared gaming. Section 3168 is as follows: If any person shall buy or sell or contract for the purchase or sale of any property or thing enumerated in section 3166, and in violation of any of the provisions of sections 3166 and 3167, he shall be guilty of a misdemeanor, and, upon conviction thereof, for every such violation shall be punished as provided by law for the punishment of gaming, but he shall not be fined less than twenty-five dollars, nor more than two hundred and fifty dollars, or imprisoned in the county jail not exceeding one year, or both fined and imprisoned within these limits."

been the chief seat of operations of this character, the Illinois statute has been followed by other States. The statute of Missouri is, as follows: "All purchases and sales, or pretended purchases and sales, or contracts and agreements for the purchase and sale of * * * grain, * * * either on margin or otherwise, without any intention of receiving or paying for the property so sold, and all the buying or selling, of such property, on margin or on optional delivery, where the party selling the same or offering to sell the same does not intend to have the full amount of the property on hand or under his control to deliver upon such sale, or when the party buying any of such property, or offering to buy the same, does not intend actually to receive the full amount of the same if purchased, are hereby declared to be gambling and unlawful, and the same are hereby prohibited."[1] The copying of all the statute on this subject would not accord with the plan of this work, but the above will serve as samples. In the details of these statutes there is some divergence, but in general the law is indicated by these illustrations.

[1] § 3931, Rev. Stat. Missouri.

CHAPTER VII.

TRADES UNIONS AND LABOR ORGANIZATIONS.

§ 98. Introductory.
99. The Strike and the Lockout.
100. The Strike as a Conspiracy.
101. The Subject Continued.
102. Where a Strike will be Upheld.
103. Where a Lockout will be Held Lawful.
104. Combination of Employers.
105. The Boycott.
106. The Nature of the Offense.
107. Picketing.
108. Blacklisting.
§ 109. Obligation of Carriers as Affected by Strikes.
110. The Strike as a Violation of the Federal Anti-Trust Act.
111. The Relations of Trades Unions to a Receiver.
112. Interference with Transportation of the Mails.
113. Contracts between Employers and Trades Unions.
114. Remedy by Civil Action.
115. Remedy by Injunction.
116. Statutory Regulations.

§ **98. Introductory.**—In the main the law relating to trades unions and other labor organizations is of very recent origin. The idea of these associations, as the means of securing the ends for which they are organized, and the methods employed, are essentially modern. They are an outgrowth of the civilization and of the industrial conditions of the present age. The law has been determined by the decisions of a recent date, or is the result of such legislation as existing conditions have appeared to demand. A few unimportant English cases of a date anterior to the present century were reported, but we have no report of any case in this country until a later period. The first American case which contributed to the determination of the law as it now stands was that of the Commonwealth v. Carlisle. This case was tried by Mr. Justice Gibson in the Court of *Nisi Prius*, in Philadelphia, in 1821. It was held that a combination is criminal when the act to be done has a necessary tendency to prejudice the public or to oppress individuals by unjustly subjecting them to the power of the confederates.[1] For a considerable period this was the lead-

[1] Commonwealth v. Carlisle, Bright, 36. In Commonwealth v. Hunt, 4 Met. 111; s. c., 38 Am. Dec. 346, 354, decided in 1842, the court says: "The manifest intent of the association is to induce all those engaged in the same occupation to become members of it. Such a purpose is not unlawful. It would give them a power which might be exerted for useful and honorable purposes, or for dangerous and pernicious ones. If the latter were the real and actual object, and susceptible of proof, it should have been specially charged. Such an association might be used to afford each other assistance in times of poverty, sickness and distress; or to raise their intellectual, moral and social condition; or to make improvement in their art; or for other proper purposes. Or the association might be designed for purposes of oppression and injustice. But in order to charge all those, who became members of an association, with the guilt of a criminal conspiracy, it must be averred and proved that the actual, if not the avowed object of the association, was criminal. An association may be formed, the declared objects of which are innocent and laudable, and yet they may have secret articles or an agreement communicated only to the members, by which they are banded together for purposes injurious to the peace of society or the rights of its members. Such would undoubtedly be a criminal conspiracy, on proof of the fact, however meritorious and praiseworthy the declared objects might be. The law is not to be hoodwinked by colorable pretenses. It looks at truth and reality through, whatever disguise it may assume. But to make such an association, ostensibly innocent, the subject of prosecution as a criminal conspiracy, the secret agreement which makes it so is to be averred and proved as the gist of the offense. But when an association is formed for purposes actually innocent, and afterwards its powers are abused, by those who have control and management of it, to purposes of oppression and injustice, it will be criminal in those who thus misuse it or give consent thereto, but not in the other members of the association. In this case no such secret agreement, varying the objects of the association from those avowed, is set forth in the count of the indictment. Nor can we perceive that the objects of this association, whatever they may have been, were to be attained by criminal means. The means which they proposed to employ, as averred in this count, and which we are now to presume were established by the proof were, that they would not work for a person who, after due notice, should employ a journeyman not a member of their society. Supposing the object of the association to be laudable and lawful, or at least not unlawful, are these means criminal? The case supposes that these persons are not bound by contract, but free to

ing case, but in the main the authorities relating to this department of the law belong to a much more recent date. The general theory on which the decisions are based is succinctly and happily stated by the court in the recent case of the State v. Stewart, as follows: "In England and here, it

work for whom they please, or not to work, if they so prefer. In this state of things, we cannot perceive that it is criminal for men to agree together to exercise their own acknowledged rights, in such a manner as best to subserve their own interests. One way to test this is, to consider the effect of such an agreement, where the object of the association is acknowledged on all hands to be a laudable one. Suppose a class of workmen, impressed with the manifold evils of intemperance, should agree with each other not to work in a shop in which ardent spirit was furnished, or not to work in a shop with anyone who used it. or not to work for an employer who should, after notice, employ a journeyman who habitually used it. The consequences might be the same. A workman who still persists in the use of ardent spirit, would find it more difficult to get employment; a master employing such an one might at times experience inconvenience in his work, in losing the services of a skillful but intemperate workman. Still, it seems to us, that as the object would be lawful, and the means not unlawful, such an agreement could not be pronounced a criminal conspiracy." Other early English and American cases are Rex v. Journeymen Tailors, 8 Mod. 10; Reg. v. Duffield, 5 Cox C. C. 404; Reg. v. Druitt, 10 Cox C. C. 593; Reg. v. Bunn, 12 Cox C. C. 316; Reg. v. Hibbert, 13 Cox C. C. 82; People v. Melvin, Yate's Sel. Cas. 111; s. c., 2 Wheel. Cr. Cas. 262; People v. Trequier, 1 Wheel. Cr. Cas. 142; People v. Fisher, 14 Wend. 9; s. c., 28 Am. Dec. 501. "I am decidedly of the opinion that every workman in the service of an employer is entitled to the free and unfettered exercise of his own discretion, whether he will continue in that employment, provided he has not entered into a contract for a specific period of service. It rests with himself whether he will remain in such employment in connection with any other person or persons with whom he may not choose to work. And more than that, if several persons in the employment of a master consider others in that employment obnoxious, either personally or on account of their character or conduct, they have a perfect right to put to their employer the alternative whether he will discharge the obnoxious person or persons and retain their services, or lose them and retain the obnoxious persons. But if men go further than that and do not fairly put the alternative to the master, but seek to coerce him by the threat of doing something which is likely to operate to his injury if he does not discharge from his employment certain other persons against whom they have some objection, I think they properly come within § 3, of Stat. 6, Geo. IV., chap. 129." Cockburn, J., in Walsby v. Auley, 7 Jur. (N. S.) 465.

is lawful, and it may be added commendable, for any body of men to associate themselves together for the purpose of bettering their condition in any respect, financial or social. The very genius of free institutions invites them to higher levels and better fortunes. They may dictate their own wages, fraternize with other associates, chose their own employers, and serve man and mammon according to the dictates of their own conscience. But while the law accords this liberty to one, it accords a like liberty to every other one, and all are bound to so use and enjoy their own liberties and privileges as not to interfere with those of their neighbors. All the legislation in England and America has been progressively in the direction of according to laborers the enjoyment of equal rights with others. The early English statutes, beginning with the middle of the fourteenth century, are to be read in the light of the civilization of that day, and their provisions, to us of the nineteenth century, harsh, illiberal and tyrannical, were but the reflex of the prevalent notions of class distinctions, that shaped and guided the social and political policy of those days. From time to time, however, down to 1875, this legislation has been liberalized and christianized; and to-day in England, as here, workmen stand upon the same broad level of equality before the law with all other vocations, professions or callings whatsoever, respecting the disposition of their labor and the advancement of their associated interests. There, as here, it is unlawful for employers wrongfully to coerce, intimidate or hinder the free choice of workmen in the disposal of their time and talents. There, as here, it is unlawful for workmen wrongfully to coerce, intimidate or hinder employers in the selection of such workmen as they choose to employ. There, as here, no employer can say to a workman he must not work for another employer, nor can a workman say to an employer he cannot employ the service of another workman."[1]

§ 99. The Strike and the Lockout.—A concerted abandonment or discontinuance of their work at an appointed time by

[1] State v. Stewart, 59 Vt. 273, 285.

a number of laboring men is termed a strike. The object of the strike is to secure an increase of wages or to prevent a reduction of wages, or to enforce some demand or request. The strike may be defined as a combination of laboring men or of other persons acting in the capacity of wage earners, designed to enforce some demand or to secure some concession on the part of an employer. The object of the combination may be to secure an increase of wages, or to resist a reduction; or it may be to secure some change in the manner of conducting the business, as the shortening of the time fixed for the labor of a day. Whatever form it may assume, it is an effort to compel an employer to yield to some demand, or to grant some favor that is sought. The lockout is the corresponding act of an employer. Literally, it is the excluding of laborers or other employes from their accustomed place of labor by the locking or closing of the doors. It is the dismission by an employer of persons in his employment, and it may be either a temporary or a permanent dismission. A lockout may be the result of a combination on the part of employes, or a single employe may act on his own responsibility. But whether a concerted or individual action, it is designed as an enforcement, either of some demand, as a reduction of wages or of a refusal to yield to the demand or to the request of the employe. A practical lockout is sometimes effected by striking employes who forcibly prevent the entrance of other workmen who desire to take their places.[1]

[1] "Strike—The act of a body of workmen employed by the same master, in stopping work altogether at a prearranged time, and refusing to continue until higher wages, or shorter time, or some other concession is granted to them by the employer." Black's Law Dictionary. "A combination among laborers, or those employed by others, to compel an increase of wages, a change in the hours of labor, a change in the manner of conducting the business of the principal, or to enforce some particular policy in the character or number of the men employed, or the like." Anderson's Law Dictionary. Strikes of laborers have not been unfrequent, and as well their cause as their consequences, and effects upon business arrangements were well understood by the parties to this contract, and provision was intended to be made against the results, but not against

§ **100. The Strike as a Conspiracy.**—It is the privilege of every employe, except as he may be bound by a contract, to abandon the service of his employer. Unless there is something peculiar in the nature of his employment, or in his relations to his employer, in consequence of which his refusal to continue his work would inflict an injury upon the business, any person is at liberty to discontinue his labor. He is free, also, to enter into a combination with others, the object of which is to promote the interests of the persons constituting such combination, by maintaining or increasing their wages. In itself, associations by tradesmen or other laborers for mutual protection and benefit, is lawful and altogether proper. As long as the acts of such organizations are orderly and in conformity to law they will be favored rather than otherwise by the courts. Whatever is adapted to promote the pecuniary interests of the laboring classes by legitimate and proper means is favored by public policy. But any combination, the object of which is

their occurence: that is, their object was to protect the plaintiff from liability for damages to the defendants, to which it might otherwise be liable, in addition to the losses, which it would necessarily sustain from a strike of its laborers, and a suspension of its business, but not to require from the plaintiff a resort to extraordinary or unusual means to prevent them. A strike is a combination among laborers, those employed by others, to compel an increase of wages, a change in the hours of labor, some change in the mode and manner of conducting the business of the principal, or to enforce some particular policy in the character or number of the men employed or the like. They can always be prevented or arrested whatever be their origin, by a yielding on the part of the employer to the demand of the combination, and if such was the duty of the plaintiff, under the stipulation to make every effort that the contract with the defendants might be performed, the clause providing for an immunity from the consequences of a strike was nugatory and had no meaning. There could be no strike for which the plaintiff would not be responsible, in a way to deprive it of the benefit of the exemption from liability." Delaware, L. & W. R. R. Co. v. Bowns, 58 N. Y. 573, 582. "Lockout—A refusal on the part of an employer to furnish work to his employes in a body, intended as a means of coercion. 'When capitalists refuse to grant so large a proportion of the product for labor as the laborers have heretofore received, and will not continue to supply capital on any terms which laborers will accept, the result is a lockout.' N. A. Rev. CXLIII., 319." Century Dictionary.

to interfere with the freedom of action of other men, whether they are employes or laborers, is an offense. And whether it is simply a civil offense or a criminal conspiracy depends upon the extent to which it is carried. In a recent leading case before the Supreme Court of Vermont, the law to which combinations of this character are subject, is stated by Mr. Justice Powers, as follows: "By the law of the land, these respondents have the most unqualified right to work for whom they please, and at such prices as they please. By the law of the land, O'R and G have the same right. By the same law the Ryegate Granite Company has the right to employ the respondents or O'R on such terms as may be mutually agreed upon, without let, hinderance or dictation from any man or body of men whatever. Suppose the members of a bar association in Caledonia county should combine and declare that the respondents should employ no attorney, not a member of such association, to assist them in their defense in this case, under the penalty of being dubbed a 'scab,' and having his name paraded in the public press as unworthy of recognition among his brethren, and himself brought into hatred, envy and contempt, would the respondents look upon this as an innocent intermeddling with their rights under the law? The proposition has only to be stated to disclose its utter inconsistency with every principle of justice that permeates the law under which we live. If such conspiracies are to be tolerated as innocent, then every farmer in Vermont, now resting in the confidence that he may employ such assistance in carrying on his farm as he thinks he can afford to hire, is exposed to the operations of some secret code of law, in the framing of which he had no voice, and upon the terms of which he has no veto, and every manufacturer is handicapped by a system that portends certain destruction to his industry. If our agricultural and manufacturing industries are sleeping upon the fire of a volcano, liable to eruption at any moment, it is high time our people knew it. But happily such is not the law, and among English speaking people never has been the law. The reports, English and American, are full of illustrations of the doctrine that a combination of two or more persons to effect an illegal purpose, either by legal or illegal means, whether such purpose be illegal at common law or by statute, or to effect a legal purpose by illegal means, whether such means be illegal at common law or by statute, is a common law conspiracy. Such combinations are equally illegal whether they promote objects or adopt means that are *per se* indictable, or promote objects or adopt means that are *per se* oppressive, immoral or wrongfully prejudicial to the rights of others. If they seek to restrain trade, or tend to the destruction of the material prosperity of the country, they work injury to the whole public. These propositions are the clear deduction of the cases cited in argument, and breath a spirit of equality and justice that must commend itself to every intelligent mind. Counsel have cited us to no case in which it has been ruled that this crime of conspiracy does not exist at the common law. We are referred to Mr. Wright's clear monograph upon Criminal Conspiracies, wherein the author, though not denying that conspiracies to injure industries and against the free exercise of one's calling, according to his own choice, were held to be criminal at the common law, still attempts to throw doubt upon the basis upon which the doctrine rests. But when, in 1 Hawkins' Pleas of the Crown, chap. 27, § 2 (a book of great authority; 2 Russell on Crimes, 674), it is laid down 'that all conspiracies whatever, wrongfully to prejudice a third person, are highly criminal at common law,' and in 2 Wharton's Criminal Law, § 2322, it is said that 'a combination is a conspiracy in law whenever the act to be done has a necessary tendency to prejudice the public, or oppress individuals, by unjustly subjecting them to the power of the confederates, and giving effect to the purposes of the latter, whether of extortion or mischief;' and the same proposition in one form of expression and another is laid down in 2 Bishop's Criminal Law, § 172; and in Desty's Criminal Law, § 11; and in 3 Chitty's Criminal Law, 1138; and in Archbold's Crim. Pra. & Pl., 1830; and it was said by Denman, Ch.

J., in Queen v. Kenrick, 5 Q. B. 49: 'It was contended in the first place that the third count was bad by reason of uncertainty, as giving no notice of the offense charged. The whole law of conspiracy, as it has been administered at least for the last hundred years, has been thus called in question; for we have sufficient proof that during that period any combination to prejudice another unlawfully has been considered as constituting the offense so called. The offense has been held to consist in the conspiracy, and not in the acts committed for carrying it into effect; and the charge has been held to be sufficiently made in general terms describing *an unlawful* conspiracy to effect a bad purpose.' "[1]

[1] State v. Stewart, 59 Vt. 273, 285. See also Reg. v. Selsby, 5 Cox Cr. Cas. 495; Reg. v. Harris, 1 Car. & M. 661; Hilton v. Eckersley, 6 E. & B. 47; Rex v. Mawbey, 6 T. R. 619; Rex v. Eccles, 1 Leach Cr. Cas. 274; Walsby v. Anley, 3 E. & E. 516; Reg. v. Rowlands, 17 Ad. & El. 670; Reg. v. Druitt, 10 Cox Cr. Cas. 592; Reg. v. Bunn, 12 Cox Cr. Cas. 316; Springhead Co. v. Riley, L. R. 6 Eq. 551; Mogul S. S. Co. v. McGregor, L. R. 15 Q. B. Div. 476; Commonwealth v. Hunt, 4 Met. 111, 128; Smith v. People, 25 Ill. 17; People v. Fisher, 14 Wend. 9; Snow v. Wheeler, 113 Mass. 186; State v. Noyes, 25 Vt. 415; State v. Burnham, 15 N. H. 396; Morris Run Coal Co. v. Barclay Coal Co., 68 Pa. St. 173. In Mogul S. S. Co. v. McGregor, L. R. (1892) App. Cas., at page 47, Lord Morris says: "There is one thing that is to me decisive. I have always said that a combination of workmen, an agreement among them to cease work except for higher wages, and a strike in consequence, was lawful at common law; perhaps not enforceable *inter se*, but not indictable. The legislature has now so declared. The enactment is express, that agreements among workmen shall be binding, whether they would or not, but for the acts, have been deemed unlawful as in restraint of trade. Is it supposable that it would have done so in the way it has, had the workmen's combination been a punishable misdemeanor?" The procurement of workmen, who are employed upon terms as to wages which are just and satisfactory, to quit work in a body for the purpose of inflicting injury and damage upon the employer by persons who are not in his employ, and until the employer shall accede to demands of such outside persons, which he is under no obligation to grant, constitutes in law a malicious and illegal interference with the employer's business, which is actionable. Old Dominion Steamship Co. v. McKenna, 30 Fed. Rep. 48. "Every man has a right to determine what branch of business he will pursue, and to make his own contracts with whom he pleases, and on the best terms he can. He may change from one occupation to another,

§ 101. The Subject Continued.—The decisions on this subject are based upon the general principle that, while the citizen is engaged in a legitimate calling, he is entitled to the protection of the government, and that the State itself

and pursue as many different occupations as he pleases, and competition in business is lawful. He may refuse to deal with any man or class of men. And it is no crime for any number of persons, without an unlawful object in view, to associate themselves together and agree that they will not work for, or deal with, certain men or classes of men, or work under a certain price, or without certain conditions. Commonwealth v. Hunt, 4 Met. 111; Boston Glass Manufactory v. Binney, 4 Pick. 425: Bowen v. Matheson, 14 Allen, 499. This freedom of labor and business has not always existed. When our ancestors came here, many branches of labor and business were hampered by legal restriction created by English statutes; and it was a long time before the community fully understood the importance of freedom in this respect. Some of our early legislation is of this character. One of the colonial acts entitled 'an act against oppression,' punished by fine and imprisonment, such indisposed persons as may take the liberty to oppress and wrong their neighbors by taking excessive wages for their work, or unreasonable prices for merchandise or other necessaries as may pass from man to man. Anc. Chart. 172. Another required artificers or handicraftsmen meet to labor, to work by the day for their neighbors, in mowing, reaping of corn and the inning thereof. *Ib.* 210. Another act regulated the price of bread. *Ib.* 752. Some of our town records show that, under the power to make by-laws, the towns fixed the prices of labor, provisions and several articles of merchandise, as late as the time of the Revolutionary War. But experience and increasing intelligence led to the abolition of all such restrictions, and to the establishment of freedom for all branches of labor and business; and all persons who have been born and educated here, and are obliged to begin life without property, know that freedom to choose their own occupation and to make their own contracts, not only elevates their condition, but secures to skill and industry and economy their appropriate advantages. Freedom is the policy of this country. But freedom does not imply a right in one person, either alone or in combination with others, to disturb or annoy another, either directly or indirectly, in his lawful business or occupation, or to threaten him with annoyance, or injury, for the sake of compelling him to buy his peace: or in the language of the statute cited above, with intent to extort money or any pecuniary advantage whatever, or to compel him to do any act against his will.'" Carew v. Rutherford, 106 Mass. 1, 14. "There is, perhaps, no crime, an exact definition of which is more difficult to give than the offense of conspiracy. That a combination of persons to effect an end, itself of an indictable nature, will constitute this crime is clear; nor is there any more doubt that, has an interest in the successful prosecution of every legitimate branch of business. The prosperity of the individuals of which it is composed constitutes the prosperity of the commonwealth, and whatever tends to the promotion of

though the purpose the confederacy is designed to accomplish be not criminal, yet, if the means adopted be of an indictable character, this offense is likewise committed. * * * It appears to me that it is not to be denied that the alleged aim of this combination was unlawful; the effort was to dictate to this employer whom he should discharge from his employ. This was an unwarrantable interference with the conduct of his business, and it seems impossible that such acts should not be, in their usual effects, highly injurious. How far is this mode of dictation to be held lawful? If the manufacturer can be compelled in this way to discharge two or more hands, he can by similar means be coerced to retain such workmen as the conspirators may choose to designate. So his customers may be proscribed and his business in other respects controlled. I cannot regard such a course of conduct as lawful. It is no answer to the above considerations to say, that the employer is not compelled to submit to the demand of his employes; that the penalty of refusal is simply that they will leave his service. There is this coercion, the men agree to leave simultaneously, in large numbers, and by preconcerted action. We cannot close our eyes to the fact that the threat of workmen to quit the manufacturer, under these circumstances, is equivalent to a threat, that unless he yield to their unjustifiable demand they will derange his business and thus cast a heavy loss upon him. The workmen who make this threat, understand it in this sense, and so does their employer. In such a condition of affairs, it is idle to suggest that the manufacturer is free to reject the terms which the confederates offer. In the natural position of things, each man acting as an individual there would be no coercion; if a single employe should demand the discharge of a co-employe, the employer would retain his freedom, for he could entertain or repel the requisition without embarrassment to his concerns; but in the presence of a coalition of his employes, it would be but a waste of time to pause to prove that, in most cases, he must submit, under pain of often the most ruinous losses, to the conditions imposed on his necessities. It is difficult to believe that a right exists in law which we can scarcely conceive can produce, in any posture of affairs, other than injurious results. It is simply the right of workmen by concert of action and by taking advantage of their position, to control the business of another. I am unwilling to hold that a right which cannot, in any event, be advantageous to the employe, and which must always be hurtful to the employer, exists in law. In my opinion, this indictment sufficiently shows that the force of the confederates was brought to bear upon their employer for the purpose of oppression and mischief, and that this

this end has a claim upon the protection and favor of its government. This basal principle is stated with great clearness and force in the case above cited, as follows: "The principle upon which the cases, English and American, proceed, is, that every man has the right to employ his talents, industry and capital as he pleases, free from the dictation of others; and if two or more persons combine to coerce his choice in this behalf, it is a criminal conspiracy. The labor and skill of the workman, be it of high or low degree, the plant of the manufacturer, the equipment of the farmer, the investments of commerce, are all in an equal sense property. If men by overt act of violence destroy either they are guilty of crime. The anathemas of a secret organization of men combined for the purpose of controlling the industry of others by a species of intimidation that works upon the mind rather than the body, are quite as

amounts to a conspiracy." Beasley, C. J., in State v. Donaldson, 32 N. J. L. 151, 155. Where two or more men wrongfully and corruptly agree among themselves, either for the purpose of creating sympathy in a threatened strike, or for any other purpose, to cause trains carrying mail or interstate commerce to be stopped or to discharge their employes or to refuse to employ new men, so as to stop such trains, they are guilty of conspiracy. United States v. Debs, 63 Fed. Rep. 436. The defendants, to the number of eighteen, were engaged by the plaintiff as journeymen tailors to do tailoring work for plaintiff by the piece. They conspired together to stop work simultaneously, and return all work in an unfinished condition. On the 31st of March, 1876, they did stop work, and returned to the plaintiff various and numerous pieces or jobs of work (garments) in an unfinished state, which were entirely worthless in such unfinished condition. Plaintiff could not get any workmen to finish said jobs, to plaintiff's damage, etc. *Held*, that a bill of particulars in the county court, setting up the above facts, contained facts sufficient to constitute a cause of action. Mapstrick v. Ramge, 9 Neb. 390. According to the principles of the common law, a conspiracy upon the part of two or more persons with the intent by their combined power to wrong others or to prejudice the rights of the public, is in itself illegal, although nothing be actually done in execution of such conspiracy. This is fundamental in our jurisprudence. So, a combination or conspiracy to procure an employe or body of employes to quit service in violation of the contract of service, would be unlawful, and in a proper case might be enjoined, if the injury threatened would be irremediable at law. Arthur v. Oakes, 63 Fed. Rep. 310.

dangerous and generally altogether more effective than acts of actual violence. And while such conspiracies may give to the individual directly affected by them a private right of action for damages, they at the same time lay a basis for an indictment on the ground that the State itself is directly concerned in the promotion of all legitimate industries and the development of all its resources, and owes the duty of protection to its citizens engaged in the exercise of their callings. The good order, peace and general prosperity of the State are directly involved in the question."[1]

[1] State v. Stewart, 59 Vt. 273. Judge Baker, in Lake Erie & W. Ry. Co. v. Bailey, 61 Fed. Rep. 494, 496, says: "In this case the evidence shows that there are a number of men who belong to a secret labor organization whose ramifications reach not only over the entire extent of the United States, but into Canada as well. It has kindred associations by other names in Europe. All these organizations have the same general aim, and that is by force, violence and terrorism to compel their employers to submit their business, their property and their means of livelihood to the arbitrary demands of these associations. In their secret oath bound assemblies they determine for themselves on what terms they will work for others. They refuse those who are not members of their association the right to labor when they desire to do so. Those who will not submit to their exactions have no more option about carrying on their business than has the belated traveler when a highwayman presents a revolver and bids him submit. As I say, I do not see any difference, either morally or legally, between this sort of business, where an organized body of men combine for the criminal and unlawful purpose of compelling somebody else, against his will, to submit to their demands, than if the same thing were done by a single individual. If they compel submission, it is robbery, because, whoever compels me, by force or terrorism, to give up one dime of my money, or one dime's worth of my property, is equally guilty, whether it be the man who meets me on the street corner in the nighttime, or an organized band of strikers who take possession of my property and deprive me of its use. But these combinations are infinitely worse than isolated violations of the law, in that they teach general disregard and contempt of law. They make people think that human rights are of no value. They teach the fantastic and monstrous doctrine that a man who is hired to labor and is paid for his work, has some sort of equitable right in the property of his employer, together with a right of perpetual employment. It has been said on the floor of the United States Senate that the laborer has a sort of equitable lien on the property of the man for whom he works, whose money bought the property, together with the right of perpetual employ-

§ **102. Where a Strike will be Upheld.**—Under the early English decisions all strikes, that is, all abandonment of service by tradesmen or other laborers, as a body and by previous arrangement, were held to be criminal conspiracies, without regard to the circumstances under which the strike occurred, and the earlier American decisions were in the same general direction. But the doctrine has been gradually modified, and it is now well established that laboring men may abandon the service of an employer, and that they may do so individually or as a body, and by previous agreement. They have the right to combine for the purpose of securing an increase in their wages, of resisting a reduction of wages or of otherwise promoting their pecuniary interest. But they must proceed in an orderly and lawful manner. Any interference with the freedom of their employers, or of that of other workmen, or any infringement upon the

ment. It may do for men who are reckless of the welfare of human society,—who care nothing for its peace and good order,—to imperil life, property and liberty, and the perpetuity of our institutions, by teaching such doctrines, but the judge who tolerates it ought to be stripped of his gown, and be driven from the sacred temple of justice. I think these men have been mislead; I think they have been deceived by false teachers, but still they ought to have known better than to violate the law of the land, and to trample underfoot the solemn processes of the court. * * * If laborers wish to organize to learn the principles of political economy, to learn something about the great laws of supply and demand, or to learn something about the effect immigration and the increase of the number of laborers on the wage market of the country, if they want to organize for the purpose of quitting their employers; in short, if they want to organize to do anything that is recognized as within the pale of the law, I have no word of criticism. I think that such organizations for lawful purposes are to be commended. But when these organizations, as I said on yesterday, combine and confederate for the purpose of seizing other men's property, or when they undertake by force and intimidation to drive other men away from employment, and thus deny them the right of earning a livelihood, they commit a crime that this court cannot suffer to go unpunished. There ought to be blazed on the minds of every one of these men that belongs to a labor organization, as with a hot iron, so that they shall know and understand it, that while it is lawful and commendable to organize for legitimate and peaceful purposes, it is criminal to organize for the invasion of the rights of others to enjoy life, liberty and property."

rights of the public, will render the act an offense. In a recent case before the Circuit Court of Appeals of the Seventh Circuit, which has already become a *cause celebre*, Mr. Justice Harlan stated the rule, as follows: "The rule, we think, is without exception that equity will not compel the actual, affirmative performance by an employe of merely personal services, any more than it will compel an employer to retain in his personal service one who, no matter for what cause, is not acceptable to him for services of that character. The right of an employe engaged to perform personal service to quit that service rests upon the same basis as the right of his employer to discharge him from further personal service. If the quitting in the one case or the discharging in the other is in violation of the contract between the parties, the one injured by the breach has his action for damages; and a court of equity will not, indirectly or negatively, by means of an injunction restraining the violation of the contract, compel the affirmative performance from day to day or the affirmative acceptance of merely personal services. Relief of that character has always been regarded as impracticable. It is supposed that these principles are inapplicable or should not be applied in the case of employes of a railroad company which, under legislative sanction, constructs and maintains a public highway primarily for the convenience of the people, and in the regular operation of which the public are vitally interested. Undoubtedly the simultaneous cessation of work by any considerable number of the employes of a railroad corporation, without previous notice, will have an injurious effect, and for a time inconvenience the public. But these evils, great as they are, and although arising in many cases from the inconsiderate conduct of employes and employers, both equally indifferent to the general welfare, are to be met and remedied by legislation restraining alike employes and employers so far as necessary adequately to guard the rights of the public as involved in the existence, maintenance and safe management of public highways. In the absence of legislation to the contrary, the right of one in the service of a *quasi* public corporation to withdraw therefrom at such time as he sees fit, and the right of the managers of such a corporation to discharge an employe from service whenever they see fit, must be deemed so far absolute that no court of equity will compel him, against his will, to remain in such service, or actually to perform the personal acts required in such employments, or compel such managers, against their will, to keep a particular employe in their service. It was competent for the receivers, in this case, subject to the approval of the court, to adopt a schedule of wages or salaries, and say to employes, 'we will pay according to this schedule, and if you are not willing to accept such wages, you will be discharged.' It was competent for an employe to say, 'I will not remain in your service under that schedule, and if it is to be enforced I will withdraw, leaving you to manage the property as best you may without my assistance.' In the one case, the exercise by the receivers of their right to adopt a new schedule of wages, could not, at least in the case of a general employment without limit as to time, be made to depend upon consideration of hardship and inconvenience to employes. In the other, the exercise by employes of their right to quit in consequence of a proposed reduction of wages, could not be made to depend upon considerations of hardship or inconvenience to those interested in the trust properly or to the public. The fact that employes of railroads may quit under circumstances that would show bad faith upon their part, or a reckless disregard of their contract or of the convenience and interests of both employer and the public, does not justify a departure from the general rule that equity will not compel the actual affirmative performance of merely personal services, or (which is the same thing) require employes, against their will, to remain in the personal service of their employer."[1] The rule in this case in its relation to

[1] Arthur v. Oakes, 63 Fed Rep. 310, 318. See also Toledo, A. A. & N. M. Ry. Co. v. Pennsylvania Co., 54 Fed. Rep. 730, 740; Walker v. Cronin, 107 Mass. 555; Rice v. Manley. 66 N. Y. 82; Benton v. Pratt. 2 Wend. 385; Lumley v. Gye, 2 El. & Bl. 216: Bowen v. Hall. 6 Q. B. Div. 333. 337. As to issuance of mandatory writs before case

the receivers and to the public is farther stated, as follows: "These employes, having taken service first with the company and afterwards with the receivers, under a general contract of employment which did not limit the exercise of

heard on its merits, see Robinson v. Byron, 1 Bro. Ch. 588; Lane v. Newdigate, 10 Ves. 192; Hervey v. Smith, 1 Kay & J. 392; Beadel v. Perry, L. R. 3 Eq. 465; London & N. W. Ry. Co. v. Lancashire & Y. Ry. Co., L. R. 4 Eq. 174; Whitecar v. Michenor, 37 N. J. Eq. 6; Broome v. Telephone Co., 42 N. J. Eq. 141; s. c., 7 Atl. Rep. 851. The English Trades' Union Act of 1871 contains the following provisions: § 2. The purposes of any trade union shall not, by reason merely that they are in restraint of trade, be deemed to be unlawful, so as to render any member of such trade union liable to criminal prosecution for conspiracy or otherwise. § 3. The purposes of any trade union shall not, by reason merely that they are in restraint of trade, be unlawful so as to render void or voidable any agreement or trust. In Cote v. Murphy (1894), 159 Pa. St. 421, 425, the court says: "It is one of the indefeasible rights of a mechanic or laborer in this commonwealth to fix such value on his services as he sees proper, and under the constitution there is no power lodged anywhere to compel him to work for less than he chooses to accept. But in this case the workmen went further; they agreed that no one of them should work for less than the demand, and by all lawful means, such as reasoning and persuasion, they would prevent other workmen from working for less. Their right to do this is also clear. At common law, this last was a conspiracy and indictable, but under the Acts of 1869, 1872, 1876 and 1891, employes, acting together by agreement, may, with a few exceptions, lawfully do all those things which the common law declared a conspiracy. They are still forbidden, in the prosecution of a strike, preventing anyone of their number, who may desire to labor from doing so, by force or menace of harm to person or property; but the strike here was conducted throughout in an orderly and lawful manner. * * * It is not our business to pass on the soundness of the theories which prompt the enactment of statutes. One thing, however, is clear; the moment the legislature relieved one and by far the larger number of the citizens of the commonwealth from the common law prohibitions against combinations to raise the price of labor, and by a combination the price was raised, down went the foundation on which common law conspiracy was based, as to that particular subject. Before any legislation on the question, it was held that a combination of workmen to raise the price of labor, or of employes to depress it, was unlawful, because such combination interfered with the price which would otherwise be regulated by supply and demand; this interference was in restraint of trade or business, and prejudicial to the public at large. Such combinations made an artificial price; workmen, by reason of the combination, were not willing to work for what otherwise they the right to quit the service, their peaceable co-operation as the result of friendly argument, persuasion or conference among themselves, in asserting the right of each and all to refuse further service under a schedule of reduced wages,

would accept: employers would not pay what otherwise they would consider fair wages. Supply and demand consist in the amount of labor for sale, and the needs of the employer who buys. If more men offer to sell labor than are needed, the price goes down and the employer buys cheap; if fewer than required offer, the price goes up and he buys clear: as every seller and buyer is free to bargain for himself. The price is regulated solely by supply and demand. On this reasoning was founded common law conspiracy in this class of cases. But, in this case, the workmen, without regard to the supply of labor or the demand for it, agree upon what, in their judgment, is a fair price, and then combine in a demand for payment of that price: when refused, in pursuance of the combination, they quit work, and agree not to work until the demand is conceded; further, they agree by lawful means to prevent all others, not members of the combination, from going to work until the employers agree to pay the price fixed by the combination. And this, as long as no force was used or menaces to person or property, they had a lawful right to do. And so far as is known to us, the price demanded by them may have been a fair one. But it is nonsense to say that this was a price fixed by supply and demand, it was fixed by a combination of workmen on their combined judgment as to its fairness; and, that the supply might not lessen it, they combined to prevent all other workmen in the market from accepting less. Then followed the combination of employers, not to lower the wages theretofore paid, but to resist the demand of a combination for an advance: not to resist an advance which would naturally follow a limited supply in the market, for the supply, so far as the workmen belonging to the combination was concerned, was by combination wholly withdrawn, and as to workmen other than members, to the extent of their power, they kept them out of the market: by artificial means, the market supply was almost wholly cut off. The combination of the employers, then, was not to interfere with the price of labor as determined by the common law theory, but to defend themselves against a demand made altogether regardless of the price, as regulated by the supply. The element of an unlawful combination to restrain trade because of greed of profit to themselves, or of malice toward plaintiff or others, is lacking, and this is the essential element on which are founded all decisions as to common law conspiracy in this class of cases. And, however unchanged may be the law as to combinations of employers to interfere with wages, when such combinations take the initiative, they certainly do not depress a market price when they combine to resist a combination to artificially advance price." In Longshore Printing Co. v. Howell, 26 Ore. 527, 543; s. c., 38 Pac. Rep.

would not have been illegal or criminal, although they may have so acted in the firm belief and expectation that a simultaneous quitting without notice would temporarily inconvenience the receivers and the public. If in good faith and peaceably they exercise their right of quitting the service,

547, Wolverton, J., uses this language: "If one person can lawfully quit the service of his employer because of the rate of wages paid or the employment of objectionable persons, cannot several or many persons, first agreeing among themselves to the same purpose, likewise lawfully quit? Conspiracy at common law was a combination between two or more persons to do an unlawful thing, or to do a lawful thing by unlawful means. Where not under special contract for a definite time a simultaneous severance of the relation between employer and employes at the instance of the employes, and where there was no preconcerted action of such employes, was never considered unlawful. Coming to the means employed, it is not unlawful for several or many employes to agree between themselves to quit their employer. As we have seen, at one time it was held to be an unlawful conspiracy for laborers to combine for the purpose of quitting simultaneously, with the ultimate purpose of raising their wages, or inducing their employer to confine his employment to certain kinds of labor, or the like; but this is not now the law, the principle underlying it having long since been discarded as inconsistent with liberty and the spirit of our free institutions. After workmen have thus combined it is still not unlawful for them, by use of fair means, to communicate the reasons for their design, and to signify their intention of quitting to their employer. 24 Am. & Eng. Ency. of Law, 123; Bohn Manufacturing Co. v. Hollis, 54 Minn. 233; s. c., 21 L. R. A. 337; 40 Am. St. Rep. 319; 55 N. W. Rep. 1119; Walsby v. Auley, 7 Jur. (N. S.) 466; People v. Kostka, 4 N. Y. Crim. Rep. 434; People v. Wilzig, 4 N. Y. Crim. Rep. 417; Rogers v. Evarts, 17 N. Y. Supl. 268. Within these limits a perfectly legitimate strike may be inaugurated and maintained, the object being to better the condition of workmen. Such an object is not only legitimate and lawful, but is just and praiseworthy. It was not wrongful, therefore, for the Multnomah Typographical Union to adopt a rule limiting the number of apprentices, and seek by fair means to enforce the observance thereof, so that its purpose in that respect was lawful. The claim that a monopoly is thus being promoted surely constitutes no grounds for equitable interference by injunction. This whole controversy has arisen because of the existence of the rule referred to and the efforts of the union to require its observance at the hands of the plaintiff. When, however, unlawful means are used to uphold or maintain a strike, or if the purposes for which it is maintained are unlawful, then it follows, as a matter of course, that the strike is in itself unlawful." See also Reynolds v. Everett, 144 N. Y. 189; s. c., 39 N. E. Rep. 72.

intending thereby only to better their condition by securing such wages as the deem just, but not to injure or interfere with the free action of others, they cannot be legally charged with any loss to the trust property resulting from their cessation of work in consequence of the refusal of the receivers to accede to the terms upon which they were willing to remain in the service. Such a loss under the circumstances stated would be incidental to the situation, and could not be attributed to employes exercising lawful rights in orderly ways, or to the receivers, when, in good faith and in fidelity to their trust, they declare a reduction of wages, and thereby cause dissatisfaction among employes and their withdrawal from service."[1]

§ 103. **Where a Lockout will be Held Lawful.**—The right of the employer to the enjoyment of freedom of action in the management of his business rests upon the same basis as that of the workman in pursuing his calling. As the workman may accept an offer of employment or decline it, according to his pleasure, so the employer may accept the offer of service or refuse it, as shall appear to him to be for his interest. To all intents and purposes, the lockout is simply the refusal of an employer to accept the service of workmen on the terms which they have prescribed. His right to do this is unquestioned. It is simply the right to make a contract, and in this regard the rights of employers are the same as those of other men. Where there is an existing contract it must be fulfilled unless nullified by the act of the other party. But in the absence of a contract the employer may close his doors either permanently or for a limited period. The right of combination among employers suggests other questions which will be considered in a following section.[2]

§ 104. **Combination of Employers.**—It is well established that employers have the same right as employes to combine for mutual protection and support, and that they

[1] Arthur v. Oakes, 63 Fed. Rep. 310, 321.

[2] Buchanan v. Kerr, 159 Pa. St. 433.

are subject in their acts as associations to the same rules. They may do whatever they may deem for the promotion of their interests so long as they do not interfere with the rights of others, or with the interests of the public. But they may not employ their power as a confederation to oppress their employes, or to compel them to accept terms of employment which they would otherwise reject. But while they are not permitted to use their power to the prejudice of the public, or to the oppression of the laborer, they may employ it in resisting an unreasonable demand on the part of employes. Very few cases have been reported in which this was the direct issue, but in some cases relating to the rights of employes the principle has been expounded by the courts. In a leading English case, the court, referring to the Act of Parliament, on which its ruling was based, said: "The object of the legislature manifestly was that all masters and all workmen should be left entirely free to act as they themselves chose with respect to the conduct of their business. The masters should be at liberty to conduct their business in what manner they pleased, and to give what wages they thought right; and the masters should be at liberty to conduct their different establishments as they thought right; that a number of masters might agree among themselves in what manner they would conduct their business respectively, and what wages they would pay. In like manner, the legislature intended to allow that the workmen should meet together and agree and consider, and come to a positive agreement among themselves, on what wages they would work for, what terms they would require for their work; and they were not to be restricted from so doing merely because many of the workmen were in the employment of one person, and, perhaps, others in the employment of others. The legislature having left both parties, therefore, intentionally quite free to make what agreement among themselves they thought fit, foreseeing, nevertheless, that it might be that much violence might be used, or much intimidation might be used, in order to carry into effect such agreement as the parties among themselves might make, enacted positively that no such violence, and no intimidation, and no such molesting, and no obstructing should take place. And by that section of the Act of Parliament, to which the attention of the court has been directed, it is provided, that if any person shall, by violence to the person or property, or by threats or intimidation, or by molesting or in any way obstructing another, force or endeavor to force, any journeyman, manufacturer, workman or other person hired or employed in any manufacture, trade or business to depart from his hiring, employment or work, or to return his work before the same shall be finished: or to prevent, or endeavor to prevent, any journeyman, manufacturer, workman or other person, not being hired or employed, from hiring himself, or from accepting work or employment from any person or persons, therefore, by either of these means, to persuade and endeavor to force any person to leave his employment, or to prevent any person from entering into employment which he would otherwise have been willing to enter into, or by violence or intimidation or molesting, to force, or endeavor to force, any manufacturer or person carrying on trade or business, to make any alteration in his mode of regulating, managing, conducting or carrying on such manufacture, every person so offending or aiding, or abetting or assisting therein, shall be imprisoned for any time not exceeding three calendar months."[1] In the leading American case,

[1] Reg. v. Rowlands, 5 Cox Cr. Cas. 466, 490. "We are dealing in this case with common rights. Every man, be he capitalist, merchant, employer, laborer or professional man, is entitled to invest his capital, to carry on his business, to bestow his labor, or to exercise his calling, if within the law, according to his pleasure. Generally speaking, if, in the exercise of such a right by one, another suffers a loss, he has no ground of action. Thus, if two merchants are in the same business in the same place, and the business of one is injured by the competition, the loss is caused by the other's pursuing his lawful right to carry on business as seems best to him. In this legitimate clash of common rights, the loss which is suffered is *damnum absque injuria*. So it may reduce the employer's profits that his workmen will not work at former prices, and that he is obliged to pay on a higher scale of wages. The loss which he sustains, if it can be called such, arises merely from the exercise of the

the English doctrine is upheld. The rule is stated by the court, as follows: "I take it, then, a combination is criminal wherever the act to be done has a necessary tendency to prejudice the public or to oppress individuals by unjustly

workman's lawful right to work for such wages as he chooses, and to get as high a rate as he can. It is caused by the workman, but it gives no right of action. Again, if a workman is called upon to work with the material of a certain dealer, and it is of such a character as either to make his labor greater than that sold by another, or is hurtful to the person using it, or for any other reason is not satisfactory to the workman, he may lawfully notify his employers of his objection, and refuse to work it. The loss of the material-man in his sales caused by such action of the workman is not a legal injury, and not the subject of action. And so it may be said that in these respects what one workman may do many may do, and many may combine to do without giving the sufferer any right of action against those who cause his loss. But on this common ground of common rights, where every one is lawfully struggling for the mastery, and where losses suffered must be borne, there are losses willfully caused to one by another in the exercise of what otherwise would be a lawful right, from simple motives of malice. * * * The nominal operation of competition in trade is the keeping away or getting away patronage from rivals by inducements offered to the trading public. The nominal operation of the right to labor is the securing of better terms by refusing to contract to labor, except on such terms. * * * If the workmen of an employer refuse to work for him, except on better terms, at a time when their withdrawal will cause great loss to him, and they intentionally inflict such loss to coerce him to come to their terms, they are *bona fide* exercising their lawful rights to dispose of their labor for the purpose of lawful gain. But the dealings between P Bros. and their material-men, or between such material-men and their customers, had not the remotest natural connection either with defendants' wages or their terms of employment. There was no competition or possible contractual relation between plaintiffs and defendants, where their interests were naturally opposed. The right of the plaintiffs to sell their material was not one which, in its exercise, brought them into legitimate conflict with the rights of defendants to dispose of their labor as they chose. The conflict was brought about by the effort of defendants to use plaintiffs' right of trade to injure P Bros., and upon failure of this to use plaintiffs' customers right of trade to injure plaintiffs. Such effort cannot be in the *bona fide* exercise of trade, is without just cause, and is, therefore, malicious. The immediate motive of defendants here was to show to the building world what punishment and disaster necessarily followed a defiance of their demands. The remote motive of wishing to better their condition by the power so acquired, will not, as we think we have shown, make any legal justification for defend-subjecting them to the power of the confederates, and giving effect to the the purposes of the latter, whether of extortion or mischief. According to this view of the law a combination of employers to depress the wages of journeymen below what they would be, if there was no recurrence to artificial means by either side, is criminal. There is between the different parts of the body politic a reciprocity of action on each other, which, like the action of antagonizing muscles in the natural body, not only prescribe to each its appropriate state and condition, but regulates the motion of the whole. The effort of an individual to disturb this equilibrium can never be perceptible, nor carry the operation of his interest on that of any other individual, beyond

ants' acts." Moores v. Bricklayers' Union. 23 Wkly. Cin. Law Bull. 48. "It is insisted that the agreements thus established between the members of the order are in unlawful restraint of trade, and therefore illegal, as being against public policy. But in the opinion of the court the point is not well taken. In the relations existing between labor and capital, the attempt by co-operation on the one side to increase wages by diminishing competition, or on the other to increase the profits due to capital, is within certain limits lawful and proper. It ceases to be so when unlawful coercion is employed to control the freedom of the individual in disposing of his labor or capital. It is not easy to give a definition which shall include every form of such coercion; it is enough that in the compact before us there is no evidence of any purpose to use such unlawful means in any form. In Walker v. Cronin, 107 Mass. 555, 564, it is said that 'every man has a right to enjoy the fruits and advantages of his own enterprise, industry, skill and credit. He has no right to be protected against competition; but he has a right to be free from malicious and wanton interference, disturbance or annoyance. If disturbance or loss come as a result of competition, or the exercise of like rights by others, it is *damnum absque injuria.*' In Carew v. Rutherford, 106 Mass. 1, 14, it is said, 'Every man has a right to determine what branch of business he will pursue, and to make his own contracts with whom he pleases and on the best terms he can.' 'He may refuse to deal with any man or class of men. And it is no crime for any number of persons, without an unlawful object in view, to associate themselves together and agree that they will not work for or deal with certain men or classes of men, or work under a certain price or without certain conditions.' And in Commonwealth v. Hunt, 4 Met. 111, 134, Shaw, C. J., declares that the legality of such association will depend upon the means to be used for the accomplishment of its objects, and whether they be innocent or otherwise." Snow v. Wheeler, 113 Mass. 179, 185.

the limits of fair competition; but the increase of power by combination of means, being in geometrical proportion to the number concerned, any association may be able to give an impulse, not only oppressive to individuals, but mischievous to the public at large; and it is the employment of an engine so powerful and dangerous that gives criminality to an act that would be perfectly innocent, at least in a legal view when done by an individual. The combination of capital for purposes of commerce, or to carry on any other branch of industry, although it may in its consequences indirectly operate on third persons, is unaffected by this consideration, because it is a common means in the ordinary course of human affairs, which stimulates to competition and enables men to engage in undertakings too weighty for an individual. It would, I grant, be impossible for the employers in any branch of manufactures to produce a permanent depression of wages, because others would find it to their interest to embark in the business on more liberal terms; and these, by a just compensation for labor, would have a monopoly of all the journeymen, they would ultimately ruin those who should adhere to the system of depression. The competition of interest must eventually break up every combination of the kind. But though every plan of coercion must recoil on those who put it in practice, it may occasion much temporary mischief to others. The journeymen are compelled to enter, with their employers, into 'the unprofitable contest of who can do the most harm,' or submit to work for such prices as the latter may choose to give. Hence, precisely the same oppressive consequences to the community from a confederacy among the bakers to extort an exorbitant price for bread, which everyone will acknowledge to be indictable. The laboring classes purchase their bread with their labor, or, what is the same thing, they give their labor for the money with which they purchase bread, and it is evident the more labor is depreciated, the more of it will be required to purchase any given quantity of bread. It must be evident, therefore, that an association is criminal where its object is to depress the price of labor below what it would bring, if it were left without artificial excitement by either masters or journeymen, to take its chance in the market. But the motive may also be as important to avoid, as to induce an inference of criminality. The mere act of combining to change the price of labor is, perhaps, evidence of impropriety of intention, but not conclusive; for if the accused can show that the object was not to give an undue value to labor, but to foil their antagonists in an attempt to assign to it, by surreptitious means, a value which it would not otherwise have, they will make out a good defense."[1] The agreement of two or more employers to discharge their employes, or to refuse or to neglect to employ other men in the place of those discharged, or who had abandoned their service in order to create a prejudice against a trades union or to secure public sympathy, is an unlawful conspiracy.[2]

§ **105. The Boycott.**—The boycott, as it is ordinarily conducted, is an attempt on the part of striking or discharged employes to interrupt or to prevent the public

[1] Commonwealth v. Carlisle, Bright, 36, 41.

[2] Of this form of conspiracy, Judge Grosscup, in a charge to the grand jury in United States v. Debs, 63 Fed. Rep. 436, says: "If two or more men, no matter what their position in the railroad company may have been, wrongfully and corruptly agreed among themselves, either for the purpose of creating public sympathy in a threatened strike, or for any other purpose, that they would cause the mail trains and trains carrying interstate commerce to be stopped, and did acts in pursuance of that agreement, they are guilty of conspiracy. If two or more men agreed wrongfully and corruptly among themselves that, for the purpose of creating public sympathy in this strike, they would discharge men from their employ who otherwise would not have been discharged, intending that such discharge should stop the running of the mail or interstate commerce trains, and thereby raise public indignation, they would be guilty of conspiracy. If two or more men, in view of a threatened strike, agreed wrongfully and corruptly that they would not employ men to take the places of the men who had quitted the service, but would allow the trains to stand still for the sake, merely, of creating public sympathy or indignation against the strikers, they would be guilty of conspiracy, unless the circumstances and situations were such that the employment of new men, reasonably viewed, would lead to danger to those men, or danger to the railroad property, or danger to any public interest."

from patronizing a former employer. It is a combination among disaffected workmen or other persons under which they agree to discontinue all business relations with the person or persons against whom their efforts are directed, and to unite in an effort to induce the public to sustain the movement. The object is to compel such person or persons to accede to some demand of the organization. The effort is to interrupt the business thus assailed to such an extent as to force the proprietor to submission. This may be done in a quiet and orderly manner, and in the use only of a moral force, or there may be an effort at intimidation and the threat of physical coercion. In some instances the boycott, practically, extends to the entire community, as many persons as refuse to comply with the demand of the organization are threatened with a withdrawal of patronage and given to understand that a failure to support the movement will mean a serious injury to their own business. The boycott is a comparatively modern device for the coercion of an employer, and the case in which the term had its origin has become historic and famous. An historical notice, as quoted in a recent leading case before the Supreme Court of Connecticut, is here copied. In the opinion, the court said: "We will also notice that it is alleged that the conspiracy contemplated boycotting as a means to the end sought. That word is not easily defined. It is frequently spoken of as passive merely,—a let alone policy,—a withdrawal of all business relations, intercourse and fellowship. If that is its only meaning it will be difficult to find in it anything criminal. We may, however, gather some idea of its real meaning by a reference to the circumstances in which the word originated. Those circumstances are thus narrated by Mr. Justin McCarthy, an Irish gentleman of learning and ability, who will be recognized as good authority. In his work, entitled 'England under Gladstone,' he says: 'The strike was supported by a form of action, or rather inaction, which soon became historical. Captain Boycott was an Englishman, an agent of Lord Earne, and a farmer of Lough

Mark, in the wild and beautiful district of Connemara. In his capacity as agent he had served notice upon Lord Earne's tenants, and the tenantry suddenly retaliated in a most unexpected way by, in the language of schools and society, sending Captain Boycott to Coventry in a very thorough manner. The population of the region for miles around resolved not to have anything to do with him, and, as far as they could prevent it, not to allow anyone else to have anything to do with him. His life appeared to be in danger; he had to claim police protection. His servants fled from him as servants flee from their masters in some plague stricken Italian city. The awful sentence of excommunication could hardly have rendered him more helplessly alone for a time. No one would work for him; no one would supply him with food. He and his wife had to work in their own fields themselves, in most unpleasant imitation of Theocritan shepherd and shepherdesses, and play out their grim eclogue in their deserted fields with the shadows of the armed constabulary ever at their heels. The Orangemen of the north heard of Captain Boycott and his sufferings, and the way in which he was holding his ground, and they organized assistance and sent him down armed laborers from Ulster. To prevent civil war the authorities had to send a force of soldiers and police to Lough Mark, and Captáin Boycott's harvests were brought in and his potatoes dug by the armed Ulster laborers, guarded always by the little army.' "[1]

[1] State v. Glidden, 55 Conn. 46, 77. "The question with which we have to deal is whether this case falls within the rule. That the defendant, the typographical union, set on foot a boycott against the complainant, as stated in the bill, and in the affidavits on file, is not denied. That this boycott was to be enforced by threatening loss of business to those who, having no connection with the union, should continue to advertise with, or in any way patronize, the complainant, is clearly shown. True, it is claimed that no threats were used: but the language of the circulars has no doubtful meaning. The affidavits on file show that it was perfectly understood by those who received them; and the circumstances indicate that it was intended that it should be so understood. In Brace v. Evans, 3 Ry. & Corp. L. J. 561, it was held that the word 'boycott' is in itself a threat. 'In popular acceptation, it is an organized effort to exclude a person

§ 106. **The Nature of the Offense.**—A combination of two or more persons, the object of which is to destroy, to break up or to interrupt the business of any person, is a

from business relations with others by persuasion, intimidation, and other acts which tend to violence, and thereby coerce him, through fear of resulting injury, to submit to dictation in the management of his affairs.' But it is insisted for the defendants that every representation of fact contained in their handbills and circulars is true; that is to say, that the complainant had, in 1888, broken with the typographical union, discharged all union employes, and had since that date employed only those who were not members of the union; and that after repeatedly promising to unionize his office, he had finally, in September, 1890, refused to do so, and declared that he would not employ any person who was connected with the union. All these are conceded facts. Therefore, argue counsel for the defendants, this is only a case of lawful competition. The complainant having declared that he would not employ any member of the union, the union had a right to say that its members would not patronize the complainant. Nobody disputes that proposition. If that were all that is involved in this case, there would be nothing for the court to act upon. But it is not all by any means. Instead of 'fair, although sharp and bitter competition,' as is contended by counsel, it was an attempt by coercion to destroy all competition affecting the union. It was an organized conspiracy to force the complainant to yield his right to select his own workmen, and submit himself to the control of the union, and allow it to regulate prices for him, and to determine whom he should employ and whom discharge. In other words, it was, and is, an organized effort to force printers to come into the union or be driven from their calling for want of employment, and to make the destruction of the complainant's business the penalty for his refusing to surrender to the union. Whatever moral obligation may have been incurred by complainant by reason of his promises to unionize his office, they were wholly without consideration, and they amount to nothing whatever in law or in equity. No case has been cited where, upon a proper showing of facts, an unsuccessful appeal has been made to a court of chancery to restrain a boycott. The authorities are all the other way. At common law, an agreement to control the will of employers by improper molestation is an illegal conspiracy. In New York, it has been held that the 'boycott' is a conspiracy in restraint of trade. People v. Wilzig, 4 N. Y. Crim. R. 403; People v. Kostka, 4 N. Y. Crim. R. 429. So also in Virginia. Commonwealth v. Shelton, 11 Va. Law J. 324. And in Connecticut. State v. Glidden, 55 Conn. 46; s. c., 3 Atl. Rep. 890. And in England. Reg. v. Barrett, 18 L. J. 430." Casey v. Cincinnati Typographical Union No. 3, 45 Fed. Rep. 135, 143. The Century Dictionary defines the word as follows: "Boycott. [From the name of the first prominent victim of the system, Captain Boycott, a farmer at Lough Mark, Connemara, and the agent of Lord criminal conspiracy. In a recent English case, Lord Fitzgerald, in his opinion, said: "If the judgment of the learned judge is correct, and I do not mean to intimate the

Earne, an Irish landlord.] To combine in refusing to work for, buy from, sell to, give assistance to, and in preventing others from working for, buying from, selling to, assisting, or having any kind of dealing with (a person or company), on account of political or other differences, or of disagreements in business matters, as a means of inflicting punishment, or of coercing or intimidating. The word was introduced in Ireland in 1880, and soon became (like the practice) common throughout the English speaking world, and was adopted by the newspapers in nearly every European language." Black's Law Dictionary defines the word, as follows: "A conspiracy formed and intended directly to prevent the carrying on of any lawful business, or to injure the business of anyone by wrongfully preventing those who would be customers from buying anything from, or employing the representatives of said business, by threats, intimidation or other forcible means." "If this is a correct picture, the thing we call a boycott originally signified violence, if not murder. If the defendants, in their handbills and circulars, used the word in its original sense in its application to the Carrington Publishing Company, there can be no doubt of their criminal intent. We prefer, however, to believe that they used it in a modified sense. As an importation from a foreign country, we may presume that they intended it in a milder sense,—in a sense adapted to the laws, institutions and temper of our people. In that sense it may not have been criminal. But even here if it means, as some high in the confidence of the trades union assert, absolute ruin to the business of the person boycotted, unless he yields, then it is criminal. Instances are not wanting in our own country where the boycott has been attended with more or less violence; and it cannot be denied that the natural tendency is, especially when applied by the ignorant and vicious, to attempt to make it successful by force. It too often leads to serious disturbances of the peace, and even murder. We are loth, however, to assume that these defendants intended any such consequences. Nevertheless it is a dangerous instrumentality to use; and if those instigating and resorting to it do not, of their own accord, take notice of its peril and voluntarily abandon its use, as we sincerely hope they will, the courts at no distant day will be called upon to recognize its dangerous tendency, and treat it accordingly." State v. Glidden, *supra*, at p. 74. "But the combination was unlawful without respect to the contract feature. It was a boycott. The employes of the railway companies had no grievance against their employes. Handling and hauling Pullman cars did not render their services any more burdensome. They had no complaint against the use of Pullman cars as cars. They came into no natural relation with Pullman in handling the cars. He paid them no wages. He did not regulate their hours, or in any way slightest doubt as to its correctness,—that a conspiracy to do a thing which has been called by the name of 'boycotting,'—is unlawful, and an indictable offense, and, if so,

determine their services. Simply to injure him in his business, they were incited and encouraged to compel the railway companies to withdraw custom from him by threats of quitting their service. This inflicted an injury on the companies that was very great, and it was unlawful because it was without lawful excuse. All the employes had the right to quit their employment, but they had no right to combine to quit in order thereby to compel their employer to withdraw from a mutually profitable relation with a third person for the purpose of injuring that third person, when the relation thus sought to be broken had no effect whatever on the character or reward of their service. It is the motive for quitting, and the end sought thereby, that make the injury inflicted unlawful, and the combination by which it is effected an unlawful conspiracy. The distinction between an ordinary lawful and peaceable strike, entered upon to obtain concessions in the terms of the strikers' employment, and a boycott, is not a fanciful one, or one which needs the power of fine distinctions to determine which is which. Every laboring man recognizes the one or the other as quickly as the lawyer or the judge." Thomas v. Cin., N. O. & T. P. Ry. Co., 62 Fed. Rep. 803, 818. "The term boycott has acquired a significance in our vocabulary, and in the literature of the law. The resolution of the defendant associations says, unless complainant discontinue the use of said machines on and after January 15, 1896, that Coopers' Union No. 18 would cause a boycott to be placed on all packages hooped by said machines. Just what action would be taken, the resolution does not state. It does not say the defendants could not purchase the packages, or the goods packed in them, but simply says a 'boycott' would issue. That term implies that a general proscription of all articles so manufactured, and the goods packed in them, would be inaugurated and maintained by the power of these assemblies wherever they could reach. It is fair to presume, from the resolution and other testimony, that the defendants were determined to use all means, short of violence, to make the proscription effective. That has been the history of such proceedings in the past, and such is the meaning imputed to the use of the word 'boycott.' It has become a word carrying with it a threat and a menace, and was evidently so intended by this resolution. In Thomas v. Railway Co., 62 Fed. Rep. 818, 821, the court says: 'But the combination was unlawful, without respect to the contract future. It was a boycott.' Again, the court says: 'The combination under discussion was a boycott. It was so termed by Debs, Phelan, and all engaged in it. Boycotts, although unaccompanied by violence, have been pronounced unlawful in every State of the United States where the question has arisen, unless it be in Minnesota, and they are held to be unlawful in England.' " Oxley Stave Co. v. Coopers' International Union, 72 Fed. Rep. 695, 699.

then a thing for which an action will lie, an action may well lie for that which is complained of here."[1] It is well established that whenever an act of a combination has a necessary tendency to prejudice the public or to oppress and injure an individual it is a criminal conspiracy. If the end sought, whatever may be the ulterior object, is to subject the individuals against which the boycott is directed to the power of the combination for the accomplishment of their purpose, the act is an indictable offense.[2] In a recent lead-

[1] Reg. v. Parnell, 14 Cox C. C. 474. The latest case involving the legality of the boycott is that of Hopkins v. Oxley Stave Co., decided Nov. 8th, 1897, by the Circuit Court for the Eighth United States Circuit at St. Louis. In this case it was held that an injunction would be granted to restrain a labor association from boycotting the products of a manufactory which are made by machinery instead of hand labor. The court was composed of Judges Caldwell, Sanborn and Thayer. Caldwell, J., dissented. The majority opinion in 25 Cen L. J. 494, is a very able presentation of the existing law on the subject of "boycotts." The opinion concludes as follows: "We think it is entirely clear, upon the authorities, that the conduct of which the defendants below were accused cannot be justified on the ground that the acts contemplated were legitimate and lawful means to prevent a possible future decline in wages, and to secure employment for a greater number of coopers. No decrease in the rate of wages had been threatened by the Oxley Stave Company, and with one exception the members of the combination were not in the employ of the plaintiff company. The members of the combination undertook to prescribe the manner in which the plaintiff company should manufacture barrels and casks, and to enforce obedience to its orders by a species of intimidation which is no less harmful than actual violence, and which usually ends in violence. The combination amounted, therefore, to a conspiracy to wrongfully deprive the plaintiff of its right to manage its business according to the dictates of its own judgment. Aside from the foregoing consideration, the fact cannot be overlooked that another object of the conspiracy was to deprive the public at large of the benefits to be derived from a labor-saving machine which seems to have been one of great utility. If a combination to that end is pronounced lawful, it follows, of course, that combinations may be organized for the purpose of preventing the use of harvesters, threshers, steam looms and printing presses, type-setting machines, sewing machines and a thousand other inventions which have added immeasurably to the productive power of human labor, and the comfort and welfare of mankind. It results from these views that the injunction was properly awarded, and the order appealed from is accordingly affirmed."

[2] Rex v. Eccles, 1 Leach, 274; Reg. v. O'Connell, 11 Cl. & F. 234;

ing case in Virginia, on a trial for conspiracy, it appeared that defendant and others, members of a typographical union, conspired to compel B Bros. to make their office a "union office," and not to employ any printer who did not belong to the said union. On refusal of B Bros. so to do, defendant and others, composing said union, determined to boycott B Bros. They sent circulars to many customers of B Bros., informing them that they had, with the aid of other labor organizations, boycotted B Bros., and notifying them that the names of all who should, after notification, continue to patronize B Bros., would be published in the Labor Herald, the organ of the union, as a "blacklist," and they, in their turn, "boycotted" until they agreed to withdraw their patronage from B Bros. The employes of B Bros. were denounced for months in the Labor Herald, in order to excite public feeling against them, and prevent them from obtaining even board and shelter. The names, not only of B Bros., their employes and customers, but of the hotels, boarding houses, public schools, railroads and steamboats of the city were listed and published, under the standing head of "blacklist." The conspirators declared it their set purpose to crush B Bros., and used every means short of actual physical force to compel the customers of B Bros. to cease patronizing them. It was held that a conviction for conspiracy was warranted.[1] In a leading case

Reg. v. Druit, 10 Cox Cr. Cas. 593; State v. Donaldson, 32 N. J. L. 157; State v. Crowley, 41 Wis. 271; State v. Rowley, 12 Conn. 112; Reg. v. Duffield, 5 Cox Cr. Cas. 432; Owens v. State, 16 Lea, 1; Spies v. People, 122 Ill. 1; United States v. Wootten, 29 Fed. Rep. 702; Slaughter House Cases, 83 U. S. 16; Bowen v. Hall, L. R. 6 Q. B. Div. 337; Gregory v. Brunswick, 6 Man. & G. 205; Gunter v. Astor, 4 Moore, 12; People v. Fisher, 14 Wend. 9; Snow v. Wheeler, 113 Mass. 186; State v. Noyes, 25 Vt. 415; State v. Burnham, 15 N. H. 396; Brown v. Herr, 21 Neb. 113; Tucker v. Finch, 66 Wis. 17; Smith v. Freeman, 71 Ind. 85; Hoyne v. McClintock, 76 Ind. 205; Reynolds v. Everett, 144 N. Y. 189; s. c., 39 N. E. Rep. 72; Murdock v. Walker, 152 Pa. St. 595; s. c., 34 Am. St. Rep. 678; Barr v. Essex Trades Council, 53 N. J. Eq. 101; s. c., 30 Atl. Rep. 881; Continental Insurance Co. v. Board of Underwriters, 67 Fed. Rep. 310.

[1] Crump v. Commonwealth, 84 Va. 927; s. c., 6 S. E. Rep. 620. The methods of the great strike of 1893 are thus stated by Taft, J., in

already cited, the court said: "If the defendants have the right which they claim, then all business enterprises are alike subject to their dictation. No one is safe in engaging in business, for no one knows whether his business affairs are to be directed by intelligence or ignorance,—whether law and justice will protect the business, or brute

Thomas v. Cincinnati, N. O. & T. P. Ry. Co., 62 Fed. Rep., at page 807: "The plan of the boycott, as shown by the evidence, was this: Pullman cars are used on a large majority of the railways of the country. The members of the American Railway Union, whose duty it was to handle Pullman cars on such railways, were to refuse to do so, with the hope that the railway companies, fearing a strike, would decline further to haul them in their trains, and inflict a great pecuniary injury upon the Pullman Company. In case the railway companies failed to yield to the demand, every effort was to be made to tie up and cripple the doing of any business whatever by them, and particular attention was to be directed to the freight traffic, which it was known was their chief source of revenue. As the lodges of the American Railway Union extended from the Allegheny mountains to the Pacific coast, it will be seen that it was contemplated by those engaged in carrying out this plan that, in case of a refusal of the railway companies to join the union in its attack upon the Pullman Company, there should be a paralysis of all railway traffic of every kind, throughout that vast territory traversed by lines using Pullman cars. It was to be accomplished, not only by the then members of the union, but also by procuring, through persuasion and appeal, all employes not members either to join the union or to strike without joining, by guarantying that, if they would strike, the union would not allow one of its members to return to work until they also were restored." "The editorials in the Bulletin, the organ of the union, December 1st, declares that the boycott is still on, and will be until the proprietor of the rat sheet employs union men. It requests 'all K. of L. assemblies, unions and workingmen to bear in mind that Mr. Casey refused to employ, or in any way recognize, organized labor.' It asks their aid in compelling complainant to recognize the rights of labor by withdrawing their patronage from his paper, and, if possible, let him know why. It calls upon them not to patronize any merchants who advertise in complainant's newspaper, and if they see the paper in any place of business, to refuse to buy goods, unless the merchant immediately stops the 'rat' sheet. The communication sent by the union on the 3d of November to Messrs. Griffin, agents for the sale of complainant's paper, contains the following: 'This union will consider it a great favor for you to give up the agency of the Commonwealth. If you do not do so, we will have to consider you the enemy of organized labor.' These are fair samples, and they indicate the method by which the boycott was to be made effective. Yet counsel force regardless of law will control it: for it must be remembered that the exercise of the power, if conceded, will by no means be confined to the matter of employing help. Upon the same principle and for the same reasons the right to determine what business others shall engage in, when and where it shall be carried, etc., will be demanded and must be conceded. The principle, if it once obtains a foothold, is aggressive, and is not easily checked. It thrives on what it feeds, and is insatiate in its demands. More requires more. If a large body of irresponsible men demand and receive power outside of law and over and above law, it is not to be expected that they will be satisfied

say that there were no threats, that the defendants were only exercising their constitutional right to freely speak and publish their opinion; that what defendants have done is a necessary and natural and proper incident of bitter, but yet lawful, competition, and that this was only fair argument and persuasion. These propositions are in direct conflict with decisions made long ago, and recognized in all subsequent cases. In Rex v. Eccles, 1 Leach. 274, the defendants were indicted for conspiring to impoverish a tailor, and by direct means to prevent him from carrying on his trade. They were convicted, and upon a motion in arrest of judgment it was objected that the indictment ought to have stated the acts that were committed to impoverish the tailor, and to prevent him from carrying on his trade, in order that the defendants might thereby have notice of the particular charges they were called upon to answer. But Lord Mansfield, without hearing the prosecution, said that that was certainly not necessary. 'The offense does not consist in doing the acts by which the mischief is effected, for they may be perfectly indifferent but the conspiring with a view to effect the intended mischief by any means. The illegal combination is the gist of the offense.' See also *In re* Wabash R. Co., 24 Fed. Rep. 217. In that case the following notice was sent to various foremen of the shops of the railroad company, during a strike organized to resist a reduction of wages, the railroad company being at that time in the hands of a receiver appointed by the United States Circuit Court: 'Office of Local Committee, June 17, 1885.—Foreman: You are requested to stay away from the shop until the present difficulty is settled. Your compliance with this will command the protection of the Wabash employes. But in no case are you to consider this as an intimidation.' * * * The court in passing upon the case said: 'The statement in all these notices that they are not to be taken as intimidations goes to show beyond a doubt that the writer knew he was violating the law, and by this subterfuge sought to escape its penalty.'" Casey v. Cincinnati Typographical Union, 45 Fed. Rep. 135, 144.

with a moderate and reasonable use of it. All history proves that abuses and excesses are inevitable. The exercise of irresponsible power by men, like the taste of human blood by tigers, creates an unappeasable appetite for more. Business men have a general understanding of their rights under the law, and have some degree of confidence that the government through the courts will be able to protect those rights. This confidence is the cornerstone of all business. But if their rights are such only as a secret and irresponsible organization is willing to concede to them, and will receive only such protection as such an organization is willing to give, where is that confidence which is essential to the prosperity of the country?"[1]

[1] State v. Glidden, 55 Conn. 46, 72. "The more serious phase of this case, and the one which demands special attention, is the alleged boycott of plaintiff in its business, inaugurated for the purpose of so handicapping it as to compel submission to the rules and regulations of the union. Every person has a right to require that he be protected in his property rights. 'The labor and skill of the workman, or the professional man, be it of high or low degree, the plant of a manufacturer, the equipment of a farmer, the investments of commerce, are all in an equal sense property. If men, by overt acts of violence, destroy either, they are guilty of crime.' Ray on Contractual Limitations, 409; State v. Stewart, 59 Vt. 273; s. c., 59 Am. Rep. 710. Sections 1897 and 1748 of the Code, seem especially designed to prevent and punish acts which are grossly injurious to person or property, and attempts to compel others to do any act against their will. It seems the principle that a combination or conspiracy of two or more persons to injure the rights of others is illegal, although nothing has been done in execution of that intent, has not been embodied in our statutes, but there is no good reason why civil liabilities may not ensue by reason of a conspiracy to commit that which is made unlawful by statute. 'The general rule of the common law is that it is a criminal and indictable offense for two or more to confederate and combine together by concerted means to do that which is unlawful or criminal, to the injury of the public, or portions or classes of a community, or even to the right of an individual.' Commonwealth v. Hunt, 4 Met. 121; s. c., 38 Am. Dec. 346. 'Combinations against law or against individuals are always dangerous to the public peace and to public security.' State v. Burnheim, 15 N. H. 401. 'An agreement to effect an injury or wrong to another by two or more persons is constituted an offense, because the wrong to be effected by a combination assumes a formidable character. When done by one alone, it is but a civil injury, but it assumes a formidable or aggravated character when it is to be

§ 107. **Picketing.**—Closely allied to the boycott, as a means of enforcing a demand, is the device of picketing. This term, as employed in connection with strikes, designates the act of establishing a watch over the actions of workmen not connected with the association by which it is conducted, for the purpose of dissuading them from accepting employment, or of persuading them to abandon it. Pickets are stationed where they will be able to see other workmen as they are going to or returning from their work,

effected by the powers of the combination.' Reg. v. Parnell, 14 Cox Cr. Cas. 514. The entire current of authority for the last century or more is to the same effect. See State v. Donaldson, 32 N. J. L. 151; Crump v. Commonwealth, 87 Va. 927; s. c., 10 Am. St. Rep. 395; 6 S. E. Rep. 620; United States v. Kane, 23 Fed. Rep. 748; Callan v. Wilson, 127 U. S. 540, 545; s. c., 8 Sup. Ct. Rep. 1301. Powers, J., in State v. Stewart, 59 Vt. 286; s. c., 59 Am. Rep. 710; 9 Atl. Rep. 559, says: 'A combination of two or more persons, to effect an illegal purpose, either by legal or illegal means, whether such purpose be illegal at common law or by statute, or to effect a legal purpose by illegal means, whether such purpose be illegal at common law or by statute, or to effect a legal purpose by illegal means, whether such means be illegal at common law or by statute, is a common law conspiracy.' And in State v. Glidden, 55 Conn. 47; s. c., 3 Am. St. Rep. 23; 8 Atl. Rep. 890, an indictment for conspiracy to violate a statute very similar to section 1893, of our code, was sustained by the court. While conspiracy in itself is not an indictable offense under our law, all these authorities show conclusively that such a combination for the purpose of doing injury to the public or to individuals is *per se* wrongful. Civil consequences are not changed by reason of the fact that the combination is not made a statutory offense. Recent decisions sustain the doctrine that in a proper case, where two or more persons conspire and confederate together for the purpose of destroying or injuring the business of another, or doing violence to his property or property rights, and it is clearly made to appear that the injury is threatened and imminent, and will become irreparable to the suitor, an injunction will lie to restrain the conspirators. Brace v. Evans, 3 Ry. & Corp. Law Journal, 561; Cogley on Strikes and Lockouts, 342; Emack v. Kane, 34 Fed. Rep. 47; Sherry v. Perkins, 147 Mass. 212; s. c., 9 Am. St. Rep. 689; 17 N. E. Rep. 307; Coeur d'Alene Mining Co. v. Miners' Union, 51 Fed. Rep. 260; s. c., 19 L. R. A. 382; Casey v. Cincinnati Typographical Union, 45 Fed. Rep. 135; s. c., 12 L. R. A. 193; Toledo, A. A. & N. M. R. R. Co. v. Pennsylvania Co., 54 Fed. Rep. 730; s. c., 19 L. R. A. 387; and Arthur v. Oakes, 63 Fed. Rep. 327; s. c., 25 L. R. A. 414." Longshore Printing Co. v. Howell, 26 Ore. 527, 546.

with a view to the accomplishment of this purpose. Like the boycott, picketing may be conducted in a quiet and orderly manner, or there may be a resort to threats and intimidations. Where the act does not extend beyond inoffensive persuasion it is not necessarily unlawful, but where it amounts to intimidation and coercion it is a criminal conspiracy. In a leading English case, an indictment for conspiracy, to molest and obstruct workmen, with a view to coerce them to quit their employment, and to molest and obstruct employers with a view to coerce them to alter their mode of business, the evidence being that the defendants had continually watched and walked up and down before the prosecutor's premises, and had accosted their workmen, inviting them to quit their employment and promising them money if they did so, and threatening if they refused they would be known as "black sheep," and would not be able to get employment elsewhere, it was held that the question was whether the watching and besetting was carried on in such a manner and to such an extent, that it would operate on the will by giving rise to apprehension or annoyance, and that if the watching and besetting had been done with the intention to coerce, the defendants ought to be found guilty.[1] The rule is the same as that relating to the

[1] Reg. v. Hibbert, 13 Cox Cr. Cas. 82. See also Reg. v. Duffield, 5 Cox Cr. Cas. 404; Reg. v. Shepherd, 11 Cox Cr. Cas. 325; Connor v. Kent, 2 Q. B. 545; Reg. v. Selby, 5 Cox Cr. Cas. 495; Reg. v. Bauld, 13 Cox Cr. Cas. 282; Perkins v. Rogg, 28 Wkly. L. Bull. 32; Commonwealth v. Silvers, 11 Pa. Co. Rep. 481; Crump v. Commonwealth, 84 Va. 927; s. c., 10 Am. St. Rep. 895; U. S. v. Kane, 23 Fed. Rep. 748; s. c., 25 Am. & Eng. R. Cas. 608; Richter v. Journeymen Tailors' Union, 24 Wkly. L. Bull. 189; Sherry v. Perkins, 147 Mass. 212; Carew v. Rutherford, 106 Mass. 1; Baltimore & P. R. Co. v. Fifth Baptist Church, 108 U. S. 317; Wick China Co. v. Brown, 164 Pa. St. 449; Reg. v. Druitt, 10 Cox Cr. C. 592; Temperton v. Russell, L. R. (1893) 1 Q. B. 435. A patrol by strikers in front of a factory, used in combination with social pressure, threats of personal injury or unlawful harm, and persuasion to break existing contracts, is an unlawful interference with the rights of both employer and employe, since it is a means of intimidation indirectly to the employer and directly to persons actually employed or seeking to be employed by him. Vegelahn v. Guntner, 167 Mass. 92; s. c., 44 N. E. Rep. 1077; 43 Cent. L. J. 464. Black's Law Dic-

strike in general or to the boycott. As workmen are free to abandon the service of their employer, and to decline to do any business with him, and as they may by all proper means endeavor to persuade others to join them in the effort to accomplish their purpose, so they may establish a

tionary thus defines the word as here used: "Picketing by members of a trade union on a strike, consists in posting members at all the approaches to the works struck against, for the purpose of observing and reporting the workmen going to or coming from the works, and of using such influence as may be in their power to prevent the workmen from accepting work there." A court of equity has jurisdiction to enjoin the commission of unlawful acts, prejudicial to personal rights where the rights are clear and the injury irreparable. A man's business is property and may be protected against injury by unlawful acts tending to injure or destroy it. The fact that the acts complained of may be the subject of criminal prosecution does not oust equitable jurisdiction to prevent private injury. A bill in equity alleged that a number of persons had combined to proscribe the plaintiff's business by "boycotting" him, and requesting others so to do, by threatening the parties dealing with him that they in turn will be "boycotted" or proscribed, and by following his wagons through the streets with requests to the public to boycott him; and as a result of these acts, plaintiff's business had fallen off greatly and was threatened with entire destruction. *Held*, that a court of equity would enjoin the parties so conspiring to injure plaintiffs from a continuance of these injurious and threatening acts. Brace v. Evans, 3 Ry. & Corp. L. J. 561. "The question remains whether this unlawful demand was sought to be enforced by unlawful means and that depends upon the character of the so-called 'boycott.' Of course, gentlemen, it was unlawful to platoon the street in front of T's place in great numbers, with strange devices, with placards and with circulars denouncing the men inside. That it was unlawful in the sense of the civil law there can be no doubt whatever. It was an unlawful conspiracy within the civil law, for which an appropriate action for damages would lie. Whether the men were amenable to the criminal law is another question, dependent upon intimidation. The essence of the overt act is intimidation. I charge you that it was not necessary that there should be any overt act of violence, nor any direct threat by word of mouth. If those men (parading up and down, dressed as they were, doing what they did, distributing the circulars as they did) presented even to the weak and helpless an attitude of intimidation, that is sufficient. The gentle, the timid and the weak had the right to approach and quietly enter that place of entertainment without being molested, annoyed or disturbed; and if the attitude, conduct and method of these men was such as to deter any of T's customers from entering his place, or to inspire any part of the public with the sense of danger in ignoring picket, as long as they do not resort to acts of violence, or in any manner interfere with the freedom of others. In another English case, where, on an indictment, under 6 Geo. IV., chap. 129, § 3, for conspiracy to force workmen to leave their employment, the evidence being that the defendants merely waited outside the place where the workmen were employed, and tried to induce them not to work there, and that their conduct was civil and peaceable, it was held that the question was whether they had endeavored to control the free action or overcome the free will of the

their appeals, then there was intimidation within the sense of the criminal law." Barrett, J., in People v. Wilzig, 4 N. Y. Crim. Rep. 403, 419. The defendants were members of a trade union of the tailors. The workmen having at the instigation of the union, struck for wages, and the masters having employed work people, men and women, not being members of the union, the defendants, who were members of the managing committees of the union, caused "pickets" to be stationed about the doors of such employers to note work people who went in and out, for the purpose of deterring them from continuing in such employ and inducing them to join the union. Proof was given of the use of insulting expressions and gestures used by "the pickets" to the non-union work people. *Held*, to be "intimidation," "molestation" and "obstruction," within the meaning of the statutes. Reg. v. Druitt, 10 Cox Cr. Cas. 592. "Every person who, with a view to compel any other person to abstain from doing or to do any act which such other person has a legal right to do or abstain from doing, wrongfully and without legal authority: (1) Uses violence to or intimidate such other person or his wife or children, or injures his property; or (2) persistently follows such other person about from place to place; or (3) hides any tools, clothes or other property owned or used by such other person, or deprives him of or hinders him in the use thereof; or (4) watches or besets the house or other place where such other person resides, or works, or carries on business, or happens to be, or the approach to such house or place; or (5) follows such other person with two or more persons in a disorderly manner, in or through any street or road, shall, on conviction thereof, by a court of summary jurisdiction, or on indictment as hereinafter mentioned, be liable either to pay a penalty not exceeding twenty pounds, or to be imprisoned for a term not exceeding three months, with or without hard labor. Attending at or near the house or place where a person resides or works, or carries on business, or happens to be, or the approach to such house or place, in order merely to obtain or communicate information, shall not be deemed a watching or besetting within the meaning of this section." Section 6 of Conspiracy and Protection of Property Act 1875 of England.

workmen by force or intimidation. If there had been merely persuasion, no matter what the consequence of it was, peaceable and unaccompanied by menace or violence, this would not render the defendants amenable to criminal justice on such a charge, they being then protected by 22 Vict. chap. 34.[1] The English doctrine has been accepted at least to some extent in this country, but in some of the States it has been made a misdemeanor, by statute, to persuade employes to abandon their employers. In Rogers v. Evarts, it was held that an injunction will not lie to restrain handicraftsmen from combining, and peaceably and without intimidation, persuading their fellow workmen to leave the service of their employers, in order to compel an advance in wages, on the ground that such persuasion invades the constitutional right of the employer to prosecute his business free from unlawful obstruction. A body of handicraftsmen, combining for the purpose of peaceably and without intimidation persuading their fellow craftsmen to leave their employment in order to obtain an advance in wages, may lawfully pay the expenses of those who leave and post in their places of assembly the names of such persons as have contributed to the fund for the support of those who have surrendered their wages.[2] In the opinion in this case, the court said: "In. People v. Kostka,[3] Justice Barrett says: 'The mere fact that no violence was used in the street is not conclusive. It is for you (the jury) to say whether the attitude of these men was threatening. Nor is it necessary that there should have been a direct threat. If you believe that the attitude actually presented by the distributors of those circulars was an attitude of intimidation, either to the passers by or to the woman inside, considering all the circumstances, then all who participated in it, directly or indirectly, are within the meaning of that word intimidation, as used in the Conspiracy Act.' It stands conceded

[1] Reg. v. Shepherd, 11 Cox Cr. Cas. 325.

[2] Rogers v. Evarts, 17 N. Y. Supl. 264.

[3] People v. Kostka, 4 N. Y. Crim. Rep. 434.

by defendants' counsel that the strikers have not the right to assemble in front of a factory in such numbers as to constitute intimidation. Picketing may be done in such numbers as to constitute intimidation. Jeering and shouting at employes by strikers may constitute intimidation. Persuasion or entreaty may be so persistent as to constitute intimidation. Whenever the strikers assume towards the employes an attitude of menace, their persuasion and entreaty, with words however smooth, may constitute intimidation, which will render those who use them liable to the penalties both of the civil and criminal law. There has been no evidence offered in this case as to circumstances surrounding the acts of persuasion and entreaty, so that the court can hold that they were so used as to constitute intimidation, and thus become unlawful. It may be impossible to lay down a general rule as to what surrounding circumstances will characterize persuasion and entreaty as intimidation. Each case must probably depend upon its own surroundings. But where the evidence presents such a case as to convince the court that the employes are being induced to leave the employer by operating upon their fears rather than upon their judgments or their sympathy, the court will be quick to lend its strong arm to his protection. Rights guaranteed by law will be enforced by the courts, whether invoked by employer or employe."[1]

§ **108. Blacklisting.**—Blacklisting is a device to which employers resort for the purpose of compelling workmen or other employes to accept their terms of employment, and to which trades unions resort in order to compel their fellow workmen to conform to their rules, or to compel an employer to accede to their demands in regard to wages and other conditions of service. Blacklisting may be defined as the preparing and publication of a list of the names of persons, by employers or by employes, for the purpose of compelling the persons so listed to accept some prescribed terms of service or of employment. On the part of employers, it is an attempt to prevent other employers from

[1] Rogers v. Evarts, 17 N. Y. Supl. 264.

giving employment to such persons, and on the part of employes it is an effort to interrupt or to destroy the business of an employer, in order to bring him to an acceptance of their terms of labor. It is designed to coerce the persons listed by rendering them odious to employers or to fellow workmen and their supporters and to the public. Such action is a criminal conspiracy; and, where it has resulted in pecuniary injury, it entitles the persons listed to compensatory damages. In the leading case of Crump v. The Commonwealth, before the Supreme Court of Appeals of Virginia, the offense is described and the law stated, as follows: "Not only B Bros. and their employes and their customers, but the hotels, boarding houses, public schools, railroads and steamboats, conducting the business, travel and transportation of the city, were listed and published under the obloquy and denunciation of the 'blacklist.' One or two specimens willl suffice: 'Boycott B Bros. and all who patronize them.' 'Watch out for B Bros.' "rats," and find out where they board. It is dangerous for honest men to board in the same house with these creatures. They are so mean that the air becomes contaminated in which they breathe.' 'Boycott B Bros. every day in the week.' 'Boycott B Bros. because they are the enemies of honest labor.' 'Boycott B Bros.'s customers whenever you find them.' 'The Lynchburg boys will begin to play their hand on Messrs. B's boycotted goods in a short time. The battle will not be fought in Richmond only, but in all Virginia and North Carolina will be raised the cry, "away with the goods of this tyrannical firm." Let our friends remember it is the patronage of the Chesapeake & Ohio; Richmond, Fredericksburg & Potomac; Richmond & Danville, and Richmond & Allegheny railroads that is keeping B Bros. up.' 'We are sorry to see the Exchange Hotel on the black list. There will be two thousand strangers in this city in October, none of whom will patronize a hotel or boarding house *whose name appears on that list.*' 'The boycott on B Bros. is working so good that a man cannot buy a single bristol board from the *rat* firm without having his name put upon the black list.' 'The old *rat* establishment is about to cave in. Let it fall with a crash that will be a warning to all enemies of labor in the future.' * * * The acts alleged and proven in this case are unlawful and incompatible with the prosperity, peace and civilization of the country, and if they can be perpetrated with impunity by combinations and irresponsible cabals or cliques, there will be an end of government, and of society itself. Freedom, *individual* and *associated*, is the boon and boasted policy and *peculium* of our country; but it is liberty regulated by *law;* and the motto of the law is, '*sic utere tuo, ut alienum non leadas.*'"[1] Where employes fail to obtain work on account of a blacklist by a former employer, but are members of a trades union by which they are paid while out of employment, an action for damages will not be sustained. In a recent case in Pennsylvania, four employes of defendants asked for an increase of wages, and, on being refused, left work. Defendants were members of a manufacturer's association, the by-laws of which provided that, when any hands employed by the members should be on strike, either for wages or disagreement, no member should employ them after receiving due notice thereof, and addressed a circular letter to the other members, giving the names of such employes, and requesting that they should not be employed until the trouble was settled. Plaintiff, one of said employes, failed to get work for a month, and brought an action against defendants for damages. It appeared that plaintiff and the other em-

[1] Crump v. Commonwealth, 84 Va. 927, 945. Where a trades union published a poster headed "T's Blacklist," giving the names of T's non-union workmen: *Held*, by Kekewich, J., that as on the evidence, the principle motive was to injure T and the non-union men, and as the injury was being inflicted from day to day, T and the non-union men were entitled to an injunction against the trades union and their servants, etc., and against the secretary and other officers who were defendants by name without addition. Affirmed on appeal on the ground that a *prima facie* case had been established that defendants had gone beyond what they were entitled to do, and had refused to give an undertaking to desist pending the action. Trollope v. London Building Trades Federation (1895), W. N. 95; s. c., C. A. (1895) W. N. 45.

ployes were members of a union, and that the union paid them while they were out of employment. It was held that a nonsuit was properly granted.[1]

[1] Bradley v. Pierson, 148 Pa. St. 502; s. c., 24 Atl. Rep. 65. "A list of persons marked out for special avoidance, antagonism or enmity on the part of those who prepare the list, or those among whom it is intended to circulate; as where a trades union 'blacklists' workmen who refuse to conform to its rules, or where a list of insolvent or untrustworthy persons is published by a commercial agency or mercantile association." Black's Law Dictionary, tit. Blacklist. The Constitution of North Dakota, § 212, prohibits the exchange of blacklists between corporations. The statute, § 7042, provides: "Every corporation, officer, agent or employe thereof, and every person of any corporation on behalf of such corporation, who exchanges with or furnishes or delivers to any other corporation or any officer, agent, employe or person thereof, any 'backlist,' is guilty of a misdemeanor." The Indiana statute governing the offense is as follows: Section 7076. "That if any person, agent, company or corporation, after having discharged any employe from his or its service, shall prevent, or attempt to prevent, by word or writing of any kind, such discharged employe from obtaining employment with any other person, company or corporation, such person, agent or corporation shall be guilty of a misdemeanor, and shall be punished by a fine not exceeding five hundred dollars, nor less than one hundred dollars, and such person, agent, company or corporation shall be liable in penal damages to such discharged person, to be recovered by civil action; but this section shall not be construed as prohibiting any person or agent of any corporation from informing in writing any other person, company or corporation, to whom such discharged person or employe has applied for employment, a truthful statement of the reasons for such discharge. Section 7077. If any railway company, or any other company, or partnership or corporation in this State, shall authorize or allow any of its or their agents to blacklist any discharged employe, or attempt by word or writing, or any other means, whatever, to prevent such discharged employe, or any employe who may have voluntarily left said company's service, from obtaining employment with any other person or company, except as provided for in section 1, of this act, such company or co-partnership shall be liable in treble damages to such employe so prevented from obtaining employment, to be recovered by him by a civil action. Section 7078. It shall be the duty of any person, agent, company or corporation, after having discharged any employe from his or its service, upon demand by such discharged employe, to furnish him in writing a full, succinct and complete statement of the cause or causes of his discharge, and if such person, agent, company or corporation shall refuse so to do within a reasonable time after such demand, it shall ever after be unlawful for such person, agent, company or corporation to furnish any state-

§ 109. Obligations of Carriers as Affected by Strikes.—Common carriers are subject to very stringent regulations. They must transport and deliver goods committed to their care without unnecessary delay. The former rule was that unless prevented by an act of God or of a public enemy they were responsible for any delay or non-delivery of goods. This is the English rule at the present time.[1]

ment of the cause of such discharge to any person or corporation, or in any way to blacklist or to prevent such discharged person from procuring employment elsewhere, subject to the penalties prescribed in section 1, of this act. *Provided*, that said written cause of discharge, when so made by such person, agent, company or corporation at the request of such discharged employe, shall never be used as the cause for an action for slander or libel, either civil or criminal, against the person, agent, company or corporation so furnishing the same."

[1] Forward v. Pittard, 1 T. R. 27; Galena, etc. R. Co. v. Rae, 18 Ill. 488: s. c., 68 Am. Dec. 574. In Blackstock v. New York, etc. R. R. Co., 20 N. Y. 48; s. c., 75 Am. Dec. 372, 373, Denio, J., says: "It has been repeatedly held, and may be taken as settled law, that a carrier is not under the same absolute obligation to carry the goods intrusted to him at the usual time which he is to deliver them ultimately at their destination. Conger v. Hudson River R. R. Co., 6 Duer. 375; Wibert v. New York, etc. R. R. Co., 12 N. Y. 245. But in the absence of a legal excuse, he is answerable for any delay to forward them in the time which is ordinarily required for transportation, by the kind of conveyance which he uses. In the case of Wibert v. New York, etc. R. R. Co., *supra*, we held that where a railroad was fully equipped with engines and freight carriages, but more property was offered at a particular point than could be sent forward at once, the delay was justifiable, provided no unfair preference was given to other freight over that of the plaintiff. In the present case, the excuse arises wholly out of the misconduct of the defendants' servants who wrongfully refused to perform their duty, and thus deprived the defendants, for the time, of the ability to send forward the property; and the question is, whether the defendants' case can be separated from that of the engineers, so that it can be held that, though the latter were culpable, their employers, the defendants, were without fault, and consequently not responsible to the plaintiff. This involves a consideration of the legal effect of the relations which exist between these several parties. In the first place, there was no privity between the plaintiff and the engineers. The latter owed no duty to the former which the law can recognize. If they had committed a positive tort or trespass upon the property, the owner might pass by the employers and hold them responsible, but for a non-feasance or simple neglect of duty they were only answerable to their employers. The maxim in such cases is *respondeat superior*. Story on

But this rule has been somewhat modified by recent American decisions. Where a common carrier is prevented from delivering goods by a mob consisting of persons not at the time in his employment, he will not be held responsible for the delay. While he is responsible for the acts of his own employes, if he is rendered helpless by strikers and their supporters, he will be held excusable. In a recent case in Illinois, it was held that a common carrier is only required to exercise due care and diligence to guard against delay, and where its servants are overpowered by a mob and prevented from forwarding its trains, it will not be held responsible

Agency, § 309; Denny & Manhattan Co., 2 Denio, 115; s. c., in error, 5 *Id.* 639. Although the nature of the contract between the railroad company and the engineers is not disclosed in the finding, it is quite improbable that it was such that the latter might throw up their employment upon two days' notice without any legal cause. If it were of that character, the liability, moral as well as legal, would rest upon the defendants, for in that case they would have neglected a most ordinary precaution for securing the continuous running of their trains. Assuming, then, that abandoning their work was a breach of contract on the part of the engineers, they, by that act, became responsible to the defendants for all its direct consequences. The case, therefore, is one in which the actual delinquents, through whose fault the injury was sustained, were responsible to the defendants, but were not responsible to the plaintiff. This shows the equity of the rule which holds the master or employer answerable in such cases. Its policy is not less apparent. Those who intrust their goods to carriers have no means of ascertaining the character or disposition of their subordinate agents or servants; they have no agency in their selection, and no control over their actions. In the case of a loss by the misconduct of a servant, the party injured has no means of ascertaining whether due caution was exercised by the master in employing him, or prudence in retaining him; and in the case of a controversy between the master and the servant as to which was the real delinquent, the owner of the property must generally be without the necessary evidence to charge the liability upon the master. The rule which the law has adopted, by which the master is held responsible for the acts of his servants, is the one best calculated to secure the observance of good faith on the part of persons intrusted with the property of others. The motive of self-interest is the only one adequate to secure the highest degree of caution and vigilance by the master. The principle itself is extremely well settled. Story on Agency, § 452; 2 Kent's Commentaries, 259; Harlow v. Humiston, 6 Cow. 189; Ellis v. Turner, 8 T. R. 531."

for the delay, provided it omits no reasonable effort to secure the property in course of transportation. For a delay, occasioned by a refusal of the company's servants to do their duty, the company is responsible; but for a delay resulting solely from the lawless violence of men not in its employ, the company is not responsible.[1] In a case in Illinois, the rule is stated by the court, as follows: "Where employes suddenly refuse to work, and are discharged, and delay results from the failure of the carrier to supply promptly their places, such delay is attributable to the misconduct of the employes in refusing to do their duty, and this misconduct in such case is justly considered the proximate cause of the delay, but where the places of the recusant employes are promptly supplied by other competent men, and the 'strikers' then prevent the new employes from doing duty by lawless and irresistible violence, the delay resulting solely from this cause is not attributable to the misconduct of the employes, but arises from the misconduct of persons for whose acts the carrier is in no manner responsible"[2] In a recent case in Texas, it was held that for failure to carry and deliver, the carrier cannot excuse himself by reason of the fact that through human agency not under his control this was prevented, without fault on his part. When the goods are actually transported and delivered, but the time of delivery was delayed, such delay if caused by mobs, strikes or other causes not under control

[1] Indianapolis & St. L. R. R. Co. v. Juntgen, 10 Ill. App. 295. See also Bartlett v. Pittsburgh, etc. R. Co., 94 Ind. 281; Pittsburgh, etc. R. Co. v. Hollowell, 65 Ind. 188; Lake Shore, etc. R. Co. v. Bennett, 89 Ind. 457; Sherman, Hall & Co. v. Pa. R. R. Co., 3 Am. & Eng. R. R. Cas. 274; Del., Lackawanna & W. R. Co. v. Bowns, 58 N. Y. 573; Lewis v. Ludwick, 6 Colo. 368; s. c., 98 Am. Dec. 454; Haas v. Kansas City, Ft. Scott & Gulf R. Co., 81 Ga. 792; s. c., 7 S. E. Rep. 629; Frank v. Denver & R. G. Ry. Co., 23 Fed. Rep. 757; Hagan v. Blindell, 54 Fed. Rep. 40; s. c., 56 Fed. Rep. 696; Reed v. St. L., K. C. & N. R. Co., 60 Mo. 199; Geismer v. Lake Shore & M. S. R. Co., 102 N. Y. 563; s. c., 55 Am. Rep. 837; Wertheimer v. Pa. R. R. Co., 3 Am. & Eng. R. R. Cas. 279; s. c., 1 Fed. Rep. 232; 17 Blatchf. C. C. 421; Wolfe v. Matthews, L. R. 21 Ch. D. 194; Hornby v. Close, L. R. 2 Q. B. 153; Farrar v. Close, L. R. 4 Q. B. 602.

[2] Pittsburgh, Ft. W. & C. R. Co. v. Hazen, 84 Ill. 36, 38.

of the carrier, may be excused; his duty then remains that he omit no reasonable effort to secure the safety of the goods.[1]

§ **110. The Strike as a Violation of the Federal Anti-Trust Law.**—The refusal of locomotive engineers to handle the cars of a connecting road on account of a strike or disagreement of the engineers of such road with its officers is in violation of the Act of Congress of July 2d, 1890, and renders such engineers obnoxious to the penalties of said statute. In the recent case of Waterhouse v. Comer, before the United States Circuit Court for the Western District of Georgia, it was held that rule 12 of an association of locomotive engineers, styled the "Brotherhood of Locomotive Engineers," which provides "that hereafter when an issue has been sustained by the grand chief, and carried into effect by the Brotherhood of Locomotive Engineers, it shall be recognized as a violation of obligations if a member of the Brotherhood of Locomotive Engineers, who may be employed on a railroad run in connection with or adjacent to said road, to handle the property belonging to said railroad or system in any way that may benefit said company with which the Brotherhood of Locomotive Engineers are at issue, until the grievances or issues or differences of any nature or kind have been amicably settled," is plainly a rule or agreement in restraint of trade or commerce, and violative of section 1 of the Act of Congress of July 2d, 1890. Construing several clauses of the interstate commerce law with section 5440, of the Revised Statutes, it follows that a combination of persons, without regard to their occupation, which will have the effect to defeat the provisions of the interstate commerce law, inhibiting discrimination in the transportation of freight and passengers, and further to restrain the trade or commerce of the country, will be obnoxious to the penalties therein prescribed.[2]

[1] Gulf, Colo. & Santa Fe Ry. Co. v. Levi, 76 Tex. 337.

[2] Waterhouse v. Comer, 55 Fed. Rep. 149. See also United States v. Elliott, 62 Fed. Rep. 801; Thomas v. Cincinnati, N. O. & T. P. Ry. Co., 62 Fed. Rep. 803. "On July 2, 1890, Congress passed the law

In the opinion in this case, the court said: "It is true that in any concievable strike upon the transportation lines of this country, whether main lines or branch roads, there will be interference with and restraint of interstate or foreign commerce. This will be true also of strikes upon telegraph lines for the exchange of telegraphic messages between

entitled, 'An act to protect trade and commerce against unlawful restraints and monopolies,' section 1 of which is as follows: 'Every contract, combination in the form of trust or otherwise, or conspiracy in restraint of trade or commerce among the several States, or with foreign nations, is hereby declared to be illegal.' It may be conceded, that the controlling objective point in the mind of Congress in enacting this statute was to suppress what are known as 'trusts' and 'monopolies.' But, like a great many other enactments, the statute is made so comprehensive and far-reaching in its express terms as to extend to like incidents and acts clearly within the expression and spirit of the law. It declares that every act, combination in the form of trust or otherwise, or conspiracy in restraint of trade or commerce among the States, or with foreign nations, is forbidden. Therefore, any combination or confederation among two or more persons, in restraint of trade or commerce, comes within the express letter of the statute. The term 'restraint of commerce' was used in its ordinary business understanding and acceptation. Among the recognized meanings of the word are 'prohibition of action, holding or pressing back from action, hindrance, confinement, restriction.' It is a restriction or hindrance created by the application of external force. * * * Congress passed the Act of 1890 in response to the public necessities, and as the sequel proved, in the great extremity to which the country was forced last summer, the framers of the law 'builded wiser than they knew.' The furious assaults made on the federal judiciary in connection with this trouble, for grasping jurisdiction, are wholly unwarranted, in view of the express authority given the courts by said act of Congress. The federal courts are the creation of the federal constitution, and the laws made in pursuance thereof. It is their office to execute, and not make, the laws. They possess just such powers, and all the power and jurisdiction as are conferred on them by the supreme law of the land. And when they come in the exercise of the jurisdiction with which they have been clothed by an express act of the federal legislature, and grant injunctions, as they did last summer, against unlawful combinations of men, to restrain and prevent the operations of the unreasoning and unappeasable spirit of the mob, in the protection of the freedom of trade and commerce, to break the blockades on the public highways so as to open up travel and the transportation of the United States mails, and restore, by civil processes, the healthful glow and flow of a nation's commerce, they come as servants, within the meaning of the preamble to the federal constitupeople of different States in interstate commerce. In the presence of these statutes, which we have recited, and in view of the intimate interchange of commodities between people of several States of the Union, it will be practically impossible hereafter for a body of men to combine to hinder and delay the work of the transportation company without

tion, 'to establish justice and to conserve the public welfare.'" Phillips, J., in United States v. Elliott, 64 Fed. Rep. 27, 30, 34. In United States v. Debs, 64 Fed. Rep., at page 747, Woods, J., uses this language: "It is, therefore, the privilege and duty of the court, uncontrolled by considerations drawn from other sources, to find the meaning of the statute in the terms of its provisions, interpreted by the settled rules of construction. That the original design to suppress trusts and monopolies created by contract or combination in the form of trust, which, of course, would be of a 'contractual character,' was adhered to is clear; but it is equally clear that a further and more comprehensive purpose came to be entertained, and was embodied in the final form of the enactment. Combinations are condemned, not only when they take the form of trusts, but in whatever form found, if they be in restraint of trade. That is the effect of the words 'or otherwise.' It may be that those words should be deemed to include only forms of like character,—that is to say, some form of contract as distinguished from tort; but if that be so, it only emphasizes and makes imperative the inference, which otherwise, it seems to me, would be sufficiently clear, that the word 'conspiracy' should be interpreted independently of the preceding words. It is hardly to be believed that the words 'or otherwise' were used simply for the purpose of giving fuller scope to the antecedent words 'contract' and 'combination' and then 'conspiracy' added merely for the same purpose. Construed literally, the terms used in the body of this act forbid all contracts or combinations in restraint of trade or commerce; but that construction is controlled by the title, which shows that only unlawful restraints were intended. But what constitutes an unlawful restraint is not defined; and under the familiar rule that such federal enactments will be interpreted by the light of the common law, I have no doubt but that this statute, in so far as it is directed against contracts or combinations in the form of trusts, or in any form of a 'contractual character,' should be limited to contracts and combinations such, in their general characteristics, as the courts have declared unlawful. But to put any such limitation upon the word conspiracy is neither necessary, nor, as I think, permissible. To do so would deprive the word, as here used, of all significance. It is a word whose meaning is quite as well established in the law as the meaning of the phrase 'in restraint of trade' when used as commonly, if not universally, that phrase has been used in reference to contracts. A conspiracy, to be sure, consists in an agreement to do something; but in the sense of the law, and, there-becoming amenable to the provisions of these statutes. And a combination or agreement of railroad officials or other representative of capital, with the same effect, will be equally under the ban of the penal statutes. It follows, therefore, that a strike or boycott, as it is popularly called, if it was ever effective, can be so no longer. Organized labor, when injustice has been done or threatened to its membership, will find its useful and valuable mission in presenting to the courts of the country a strong and resolute protest and a petition for redress against unlawful trusts and combinations which would do unlawful wrong to it. Its membership need not doubt that their counsel will be heard, nor that speedy and exact justice will be administered wherever the courts have jurisdiction. It will follow, therefore, that in all such controversies it will be competent, as we have done in this case, for the courts to preserve the rights of the operators,—to spare them hardships and at the same time to spare to the public the unmerited hardship which it has suffered from such conflicts in the past. It will also be found that by such methods organized labor will be spared much of the antagonism it now encounters, and in its appeal to the courts it will have the sympathy of thousands, where, in its strikes, it has their opposition and resentment."[1]

fore, in the sense of this statute, it must be an agreement between two or more to do. by concerted action, something criminal or unlawful, or it may be to do something lawful by criminal or unlawful means. A conspiracy, therefore. is in itself unlawful, and in so far as this statute is directed against conspiracies in restraint of trade among the several States, it is not necessary to look for the illegality of the offense in the kind of restraint proposed; and, since it would be unnecessary, it would be illogical to conclude that only conspiracies which are founded upon, or are intended to be accomplished by means of contracts or combinations in restraint of trade are within the purview of the act. It would be to make tautologous, words which have distinctly different meanings, and to deprive the statute, in a large measure, of its just and needful scope. Any proposed restraint of trade, though it be in itself innocent, if it is to be accomplished by conspiracy, is unlawful."

[1] Waterhouse v. Comer, 55 Fed. Rep. 149, 157. A combination of men to secure or compel the employment of none but union men becomes a combination in restraint of interstate commerce within the

§ 111. The Relation of Trades Unions to a Receiver.—Where a railroad is in the hands of a receiver, the relations of the employes to their employers are materially modified. The receiver is an officer of the court, and as such is clothed with authority not possessed by the ordinary officers of an incorporation. The receiver cannot violate or disregard the instructions of the court, and he cannot be compelled by a trades union to do anything inconsistent with his instructions. He is in such a sense the representative of the court that an attempt to coerce him is an attempt to coerce the court. In the case above cited, the rule is stated by the court, as follows: "If there were no statutory enactments upon the subject, no court of equity could justifiably direct its receiver to enter into a contract with a body of men who hold themselves bound to repudiate their contract, and disregard a grave public duty, because of real or alleged grievances, which some other person or corporation not a party to the contract inflicts, or is alleged to inflict, not upon a party to the contract, but upon somebody else. To compel the receiver to do this would be monstrous. The receiver may be wholly just, considerate, humane and even indulgent to the engineers in his employ. They may with reason regard him not only as their kindly employer, but as their friend. The people of Georgia may have afforded to them every needed evidence of sympathy; the compensation may be ample, their future as bright as possible for intelligent, energetic, and courageous manhood; and yet because of a difficulty with or without cause which originates in Maine or Minnesota, they will abandon the service of their kind employer, and forego the realization of their own hopeful anticipation, and bring dismay, and it may be ruin, upon the kindly and sympathetic people among whom they live. This is almost the inevitable consequence of this rule.

meaning of the statute, when, in order to gain its ends, it seeks to enforce, and does enforce, by violence and intimidation, a discontinuance of labor in all departments of business, including the transportation of goods from State to State, and to and from foreign nations. U. S. v. Workingmen's Amalgamated Council, 54 Fed. Rep. 994.

It is in evidence, and is generally known, that almost the entire business of transportation of freight is carried on in cars which, without breaking the bulk of their freight, are forwarded from one railroad to another. This is an absolute necessity. The interests of the public and the economies of cheap and rapid transit demand it. There are 1,200,000 cars upon the railroads of the United States. There are 168,400 miles of railroad, or more than seven cars per mile. The Central Railroad, according to the recent report of the superintendent, has less than two cars per mile. It is, therefore, indispensable that it should use the cars of other lines, but if it were otherwise it would be impossible, under the present system, to deny to the cars and freight of other lines transit over the lines of the Central without violation of the law. The receiver cannot violate the law, and the engineers cannot compel him to do so without themselves becoming obnoxious to the criminal statutes, and the court does not doubt, from their bearing and testimony in the case, that they only needed to be advised of these facts when they will immediately recede from the unlawful and most dangerous attitude in which this rule has placed them. It is, indeed, a rule which, more than all others, has given strength and comfort to the enemies of organized labor."[1]

[1] Waterhouse v. Comer, 55 Fed. Rep. 149, 158. A court of equity having charge of a railroad through its receivers has authority to restrain the formation and execution of a conspiracy among the employes to quit the service in a body with the design and intent of crippling the property in their custody, or embarrassing the operation of the road. A strike is a combination among workmen to compel the master to the concession of a certain demand by preventing the conduct of his business until compliance with the demand. The concerted cessation of work is but one of, and the least effective of, the means to the end, the intimidation of others from engaging in the service, the interference with and the disabling and destruction of property, and resort to actual force and violence when necessary to the accomplishment of the end being the other and more effective means employed. Such a strike is unlawful, and a federal court having charge through its receivers of an interstate railroad, had jurisdiction to enjoin the executive heads of the various organizations of railroad employes from ordering a strike

§ 112. Interference in the Transportation of the Mails.—Under the Constitution of the United States the general government has power to remove any and every obstacle placed upon highways, whether natural or

upon the road. Farmers' Loan & Trust Co. v. Northern Pacific R. Co., 60 Fed. Rep. 803. "My conclusion in the case on the information of the United States implies a like conclusion in the other case tried at the same time and upon the same evidence, wherein, by an information presented by the receivers of the Santa Fe railroad, the defendants were charged with wrongful and violent interference with the operation of that road pending the strike. That they did interfere as alleged is established by the evidence already considered. Though violation of the injunction of July 2d is alleged in the bill, the questions of jurisdiction and of the construction and application of the Act of 1890 are not essentially involved, because, the property being in the custody of the court, any improper interference with its management, it is well settled, constituted a contempt of the court's authority, as exercised in making the order appointing the receivers, and enjoining interference with their control. The decision, or rather letter, of Judge Caldwell, has been referred to, but while that recognized the right of employes to quit the service of the receivers, it contained no warrant for intimidating or abusing those who were willing to take employment, or for otherwise interfering directly, as the defendants and their followers did, with the management and operation of the road." Woods, J., in United States v. Debs, 64 Fed. Rep. 724, 765. The United States court made an order directing a United States marshal to take into his service as many deputies as should be required to afford all necessary protection to the receivers of the N. P. R. Co., appointed by said court, and to the property in their hands, and to attach and bring before the court any persons wrongfully interfering with such property, to show cause why they should not be punished for contempt. Pursuant to said order, a deputy marshal arrested one A, who was confined under such arrest for more than a month without being taken before any magistrate, or examined or held to bail. *Held*, upon *habeas corpus* seeking A's discharge from such confinement, that his detention without examination and regular commitment was illegal, and he should be discharged. *In re* Acker, 66 Fed. Rep. 290. "It seems entirely clear, upon authority, that any combination or conspiracy upon the part of its employes would be unlawful, which has for its object to cripple the property in the hands of the receivers, and to embarrass the operation of the railroads under their management, and thereby disabling or rendering unfit for use engine, cars and other property in their hands, or by interfering with their possession, or by actually obstructing their control and management, or by using force, intimidation, threats, or other unlawful methods against the receivers or other agents, or against employes remaining in artificial, for the purpose of interrupting interstate commerce or the carrying of the mails. While the executive branch of the government may exercise its power for the forceable removal of such obstacles, it is competent also for the proper officer of the government to appeal to the civil courts. He may ask for an inquiry and determination by the proper court as to the existence and character of such obstruction, and if any is found to exist or to threaten to occur, he may ask that they be removed or restrained. In such cases relief will be granted even though the act may be criminal and subject to a penalty as a criminal offense.[1]

their service, or by using like methods to cause the employes to quit, or prevent or deter others from entering the service in place of those leaving it. Combinations of that character disturb the peace of society, and are mischievous in the extreme. They imperil the interests of the public, which may rightfully demand that the free course of trade shall not be unreasonably obstructed. They endanger the personal security and personal liberty of individuals who, in the exercise of their inalienable privilege of choosing the terms upon which they shall labor, enter and attempt to enter the service of those against whom such combinations are specially aimed." Harlan, J., in Arthur v. Oakes, 63 Fed. Rep. 324.

[1] *In re* Debs, 158 U. S. 565. "The second essential element in the offense described by the statute is the purpose of the conspirators to commit an offense against the United States. The indictment charges that the defendants conspired with others to commit two offenses against the United States, one to obstruct and retard the passage of the United States mail, and the carrier carrying the same, and the other, that they engaged in a combination and conspiracy in restraint of trade and commerce among the several States of the United States, and with foreign countries. The first charge is based upon the provisions of section 3995 of the Revised Statutes, which provides as follows: 'Any person who shall knowingly and willfully obstruct and retard the passage of the mail, or any carriage, horse, driver, or carrier carrying the same, shall, for every such offense, be punishable by a fine of not more than one hundred dollars.' This section of the Revised Statutes was originally section 9 of the Act of March 3, 1825 (4 Stat. 104), and, having been passed prior to the introduction into the United States of the method of transporting mail by railroads, the phraseology of the law conformed to the conditions prevailing at that time, but it is equally applicable to the modern system of conveyance, and protects alike the transportation of the mail by the 'limited express,' as it does the carriage by the old fashioned stage coach. There are, however, certain provisions of law directed specifically to the transportation

In this case the rule was stated by the court, Mr. Justice Brewer delivering the opinion, as follows: "We have given to this case the most careful and anxious atten-

of the mail by railroad trains, to which I desire to call your attention. Section 3964 of the Revised Statutes provides as follows: 'The following are established post roads: * * * All railroads, or parts of railroads, which are now or hereafter may be in operation.' Section 3, Act March 3, 1879 (20 Stat. 358), provides 'that the postmaster general shall, in all cases, decide upon what trains and in what manner the mails shall be conveyed.' Section 4000 of the Revised Statutes provides that 'every railway company carrying the mail shall carry on any train which may run over its road, and without extra charge therefor, all mailable matter directed to be carried thereon, with the person in charge of the same.' * * * Recurring now to Section 3995 of the Revised Statutes, making it an offense to obstruct and retard the passage of the mails, and you will observe that the statute applies to those persons who 'knowingly and willfully' obstruct and retard the passage of the mails, or the carrier carrying the same; that is to say, to those who know that the acts performed, however innocent they may otherwise be, will have the effect of obstructing and retarding the passage of the mail, and they perform the acts with the intention that such shall be their operation. United States v. Kirby, 7 Wall. 485. 'It would be no defense under this statute,' said an eminent judge in a recent case, 'that the obstruction was effected by merely quitting employment, where the motive of quitting was to retard the mails, and had nothing to do with the terms of employment.' Thomas v. Railway Co., 62 Fed. Rep. 822. The statute also applies to those persons who, having in view the accomplishment of other purposes, perform unlawful acts, which have the effect of obstructing and retarding the passage of the mails. In such cases, the intention to obstruct and retard the passage of the mails will be imputed to the authors of the unlawful act, although the attainment of other ends may have been their primary object." United States v. Cassidy, 67 Fed. Rep. 698, 703. "The second objection is that the defendants charged with the overt acts of retarding the mail trains are not charged with having known at the time that the trains carried the mails of the United States. It is said that no intent against the mails can be inferred, unless the perpetrators had knowledge that the mails were on board the trains obstructed. I do not concur in this view. The defendants are properly chargeable with an intent to do all the acts that are the reasonable and natural consequence of the acts done. The laws make all the railways post routes of the United States, and it is within every one's knowledge that a large proportion of the passenger trains on these roads carry the mails. There is no stretching either of law or of common sense, to presume that a person obstructing one of these trains contemplates, among other intents, the obstruction of the mails." United States v. Debs, 65 Fed. Rep. 210, 211.

tion, for we realize that it touches closely questions of supreme importance to the people of this country. Summing up our conclusions, we hold that the government of the United States is one having jurisdiction over every foot of soil within its territory, and acting directly upon each citizen; that while it is a government of enumerated powers, it has within the limits of those powers all the attributes of sovereignty; that to it is committed power over interstate commerce and the transmission of the mail; that the powers thus conferred upon the national government are not dormant, but have been assumed and put into practical exercise by the legislation of Congress; that in the exercise of those powers it is competent for the nation to remove all obstructions upon highways, natural or artificial, to the passage of interstate commerce or the carrying of the mail; that while it may be competent for the government (through the executive branch and in the use of the entire executive power of the nation) to forcibly remove all such obstructions, it is equally within its competency to appeal to the civil courts for an inquiry and determination as to the existence and character of any alleged obstruction, and if such are found to exist or threaten to occur to invoke the powers of those courts to remove or restrain such obstruction; that the jurisdiction of courts to interfere in such matters by injunction is one recognized from ancient times and by indubitable authority; that such jurisdiction is not ousted by the fact that the obstructions are accompanied by or consist of acts in themselves violations of the criminal law; that the proceeding by injunction is of a civil character, and may be enforced by proceedings in contempt; that such proceedings are not in execution of the criminal laws of the land; that the penalty for a violation of the injunction is no substitute for and no defense to a prosecution for any criminal offenses committed in the course of such violation; that the complaint filed in this case clearly showed an existing obstruction of artificial highways for the passage of interstate commerce and the transmission of the mail,—an obstruction not only temporarily existing, but threatening to continue; that under such complaint the circuit court had power to issue its process of injunction; that it having been issued and served on these defendants, the circuit court had authority to inquire whether its orders had been disobeyed, and when it found that they had been then to proceed, under section 725, Revised Statutes, which grants power 'to punish by fine or imprisonment * * * disobedience * * * by any party * * * or other person, to an lawful writ, process, order, rule, decree or command,' and enter the order of punishment complained of; and, finally, that the circuit court, having full jurisdiction in the premises, its finding of the fact of disobedience is not open to review on *habeas corpus* in this or any other court. We enter into no examination of the Act of July 2d, 1890, upon which the circuit court relied mainly to sustain its jurisdiction. It must not be understood from this that we dissent from the conclusions of that court in reference to the scope of the act, but simply that we prefer to rest our judgment on the broader ground which has been discussed in this opinion, believing it of importance that the principles underlying it should be fully stated and affirmed."[1]

§ **113. Contracts Between Employers and Trades Unions.**—There is nothing to forbid employers from entering into a contract with the officers of a trades union in regard to any matter properly appertaining to their relations as employers and employes. The fixing of the terms and conditions of the service to be rendered, so far as it involves nothing illegal, is a proper subject for a contract. But a contract under which an employer undertakes to interfere with the rights of third parties is illegal and void. Two parties may enter into an agreement in regard to their own business relations, but a covenant, the oject of which is to control the acts of third parties to their injury, is an unlawful conspiracy, and, as such, in contravention of pub-

[1] *In re* Debs, 158 U. S. 535, 599.

lic policy. In a leading English case, the rule is stated by Sir William Erle, as follows: "The law is clear that workmen have a right to combine for their own protection, and to obtain such wages as they choose to agree to demand. I say nothing at present as to the legality of other persons, not workmen, combining with them to assist in that purpose. As far as I know, there is no objection in point of law, to it: and it is not necessary to go into that matter: but I consider the law to be clear so far, only, as while the purpose of the combination is to obtain a benefit for the parties who combine; a benefit which by law they can claim. I make that remark because a combination for the purpose of injuring another is a combination of a different nature, directed personally against the party to be injured: and the law allowing them to combine for the purpose of obtaining a lawful benefit to themselves gives no sanction to combinations which have for their immediate purpose the hurt of another. The rights of workmen are conceded: but the exercise of a free will and freedom of action, within the limits of the law, is also secured equally to the masters. The intention of the law is at present to allow either of them to follow the dictates of their own will, with respect to their own actions, and their own property; and either, I believe, has a right to study to promote his own advantage, or to combine with others to promote their mutual advantage."[1]

[1] Reg. v. Rowlands, 17 Ad. & El. (N. S.) 671. 687. See also Com. v. Sheriff, 15 Phila. 393: Master Stevedores' Association v. Walsh. 2 Daly. 1: Springhead Spinning Co. v. Riley, L. R. 6 Eq. 551: Reg. v. Shepherd, 11 Cox C. C. 325; O'Neill v. Longman, 4 B. & S. 376: s. c.. 116 E. C. L. 374; O'Neill v. Kruger, 4 B. & S. 389; s. c.. 116 E. C. L. 388; *Ex parte* Perham, 5 Jur. (N. S.) 1221; Reg. v. Hewitt, 5 Cox Cr. Cas. 162: Skinner v. Kitch. 10 Cox Cr. Cas. 493; Wood v. Bowron, L. R. 2 Q. B. 21: Walsby v. Auley, 7 Jur. (N. S.) 465: Connor v. Kent, L. R. (1891) 2 Q. B. 545: Commonwealth v. Dyer, 128 Mass. 70: Spies v. People, 122 Ill. 1: s. c., 3 Am. St. Rep. 320; Collins v. Hayte, 50 Ill. 337; s. c., 99 Am. Dec. 521; Snow v. Wheeler, 113 Mass. 179: Commonwealth v. Silvers, 11 Pa. Co. Ct. Rep. 481. "The evidence justifies the conclusion that defendants are organized into associations wherein submission to stringent and arbitrary rules is required: that by means approaching dictation they have attempted to control employers in the selection of laborers

This rule is sustained by the American courts. In a recent case in New York, the rule was stated by the court, as follows: "In the general consideration of the subject it must be premised that the organization or the co-operation of

and the wages to be paid them, and have discouraged and, as far as they could, prevented those who do not belong to their societies from procuring work; that by force, in one instance, they took complainant's laborers from its mine to their hall, where, upon such laborers refusing to comply with their demands to join them, and abide by their laws, they actually ordered their banishment from the State, and in a manner deserving the most severe condemnation, enforced their lawless decree, and against men who, by reason of their birth, and not through the grace of the government, were entitled to all the rights of American citizenship; that in such numbers, and under such circumstances as were necessary, they have requested non-union men to cease work, and to such have applied in an offensive and threatening manner most opprobious epithets and in other ways have annoyed and vexed laborers who refuse to join their association. I am not unmindful that they meet these charges by alleging in effect that when such things were done it was without their authority and that the meeting referred to was held by citizens; but such defense is too transparent to conceal the truth. Such meeting was held in their hall, was composed largely of miners. and was presided over by defendant who says he was, and now is, the president of the Miners' Union of Burke,' and he also says that 'the meeting voted that they [the men banished] should be marched up the canyon, upon the ground that if they proceeded down the canyon violence might be apprehended from outsiders.' Such explanations cannot be received in exculpation of the wrong done by defendants, but on the contrary they cast a shadow over all their statements." Beatty, J., in Coeur D'Alene Mining Co. v. Miners' Union, 51 Fed. Rep. 260; s. c., 19 L. R. A. 382, 384. "Under our law every workman assumes many risks arising from the incompetency or negligence of his fellow workmen, it would be an anomalous doctrine to hold that after their fellows have concluded that he was not a safe, or even a desirable companion, they must continue to work with him, under the penalty of paying damages, if by their refusal to do so the works are for a time stopped and he thrown out of employment, we cannot believe it to be in accordance with the spirit of our institution or the law of the land to say that a body of workmen must respond in damages because they, without malice or any evil motive, peaceably and quietly quit work, which they are not required to continue, rather than remain at work with one who is for any reason unsatisfactory to them. To hold so would be subversive of their natural and legal rights, and tend to place them in a condition of involuntary servitude." Gavin, J., in Clemmitt v. Watson, 14 Ind. App. 38, 42; s. c., 42 N. E. Rep workingmen is not against any public policy. Indeed, it must be regarded as having the sanction of law when it is for such legitimate purposes as that of obtaining an advance in the rate of wages or compensation, or of maintaining such rate. It is proper and praiseworthy, and, perhaps, falls within that general view of human society which perceives an underlying law, that men should unite to achieve that which each by himself cannot achieve, or can achieve less readily, but the social principle which justifies such organizations is departed from when they are so extended in their operation as either to intend or to accomplish injury to others. Public policy and the interests of society favor the utmost freedom in the citizen to pursue his lawful trade or calling, and if the purpose of an organization or combination of workingmen be to hamper or restrict that freedom, and through contracts or arrangements with employers, to coerce other working men to become members of the organization and to come under its rules and conditions, under the penalty of the loss of their positions and of deprivation of employment, then that purpose seems clearly unlawful, and militates against the spirit of our government and nature of our institutions. The effectuation of such a purpose would conflict with that principle of public policy which prohibits monopolies and exclusive privileges. It would tend to deprive the public of the services of men in useful employments and capacities."[1] It would, to use the language of Mr. Justice Barrett, in People v. Smith, "impoverish and crush a citizen for no reason connected in the slightest degree with the advancement of wages or the maintenance of the rate."[2]

367. A business firm sued a trade union for losses charged to a malicious conspiracy to injure plaintiff's business. *Held*, that an attempt to injure the business as a coercive measure to regulate the employment of workmen constituted an unlawful and actionable conspiracy; and that plaintiffs might show declarations made by their customers at the time they withdrew their trade, as to their reason for its withdrawal. Moores v. Bricklayers' Union No. 1, 7 Ry. & Corp. Law J. 108; s. c., 23 Wkly. Law Bull. 48.

[1] People v. Smith, 5 N. Y. Cr. R. 513.

[2] Curran v. Galen (1897), 152 N. Y. 33; s. c., 46 N. E. Rep. 297.

§ 114. **Remedy by Civil Action.**—An attempt on the part of a combination or of an individual to compel employes to abandon the service of their employer by violence or by intimidation of any sort is unlawful, and constitutes a ground for a civil action for any damage that may be caused by such acts. In the leading English case of Bowen v. Hall, it was held that an action lies against a third person, who maliciously induces another to break his contract of exclusive personal service with an employer, which thereby would naturally cause, and did in fact cause, an injury to such employer, although the relation of master and servant may not strictly exist between the employer and employed. Where, in such an action, the employed was also a defendant, but as against him the plaintiff claimed only an injunction and not damages, it was held that damages might, in the discretion of the court, be given under Lord Cairns' Act, and that the jury, therefore, should be directed by the judge, in the event of the verdict for the plaintiff, to find such damages as should be awarded: first, if the court should think it a proper case both for injunction and damages; and secondly, if the court should think it a proper case for damages only, and not also for an injunction.[1] This doctrine is fully upheld by the

298. All combinations and associations designed to coerce workmen to become members of such combinations or associations, or to obstruct or annoy them in working, or in obtaining work, because they are not members, or in order to induce them to become members, or designed to prevent employers from making a just discrimination in the rate of wages, or to interfere with the perfect freedom of employers in the proper management and control of their lawful business, or to dictate in any particular the terms upon which their business shall be conducted, by means of threats of injury or loss, by interference with their property or traffic, or with their lawful employment of other persons, are *pro tanto* illegal combinations or associations, and all acts done in furtherance of such intention by such means and accompanied by damage are actionable. Old Dominion Steamship Co. v. McKenna, 30 Fed. Rep. 48.

[1] Bowen v. Hall, L. R. 6 Q. B. Div. 333. See also People v. Fisher, 14 Wend. 1; s. c., 28 Am. Dec. 501; State v. Donaldson, 32 N. J. L. 151; s. c., 90 Am. Dec. 649; Johnston Harvester Co. v. Meinhardt, 9 Abb. N. Cas. 393; s. c., 60 How. Pr. 168; Bixby v. Dunlap, 56 N. H. 456; s. c., 22 Am. Rep. 475; Haskins v. Royster, 70 N.

American courts. In a case before the United States Circuit Court for the Southern District of New York, it was held that all combinations and associations designed to coerce workmen to become members of such combinations or associations, or to interfere with, obstruct, vex or annoy

Car. 603; s. c., 16 Am. Rep. 780; People v. Wilzig, 4 N. Y. Crim. Rep. 423; Carew v. Rutherford, 106 Mass. 1; s. c., 6 Am. Rep. 287; Hart v. Aldridge, 1 Cowp. 54; Gunter v. Astor, 4 Moore, 12; Boston Glass Manufactory v. Binney, 4 Pick. 425; Walker v. Cronin, 107 Mass. 555; Salter v. Howard, 43 Ga. 601; Jones v. Blocker, 43 Ga. 331; Dickson v. Dickson, 33 La. Ann. 1261; Mapstrick v. Ramge, 9 Neb. 390; s. c., 31 Am. Rep. 415; Old Dominion Steamship Co. v. McKenna, 30 Fed. Rep. 48; Slaughter House Cases, 16 Wall. 36; Kimball v. Harman, 34 Md. 407; Buffalo Lubricating Oil Co. v. Everest, 30 Hun, 586; Payne v. Western, etc. R. Co., 13 Lea, 509; Lumley v. Gye, 2 El. & Bl. 216; Butterfield v. Ashley, 2 Gray, 254; Campbell v. Cooper, 34 N. H. 49; Evans v. Walton, L. R. 2 C. P. 615; Lee v. West, 47 Ga. 311; Hudson v. State, 46 Ga. 624; Blake v. Lanyon, 6 T. R. 221; Milburn v. Byrne, 1 Cranch C. C. 239; Winsmore v. Greenbank, Willes, 577. In Caughey v. Smith, 47 N. Y. 244, Folger, J., said: "The complaint in this action is for enticing from the service of the plaintiff, his minor son, who still owed service to him. But to maintain an action for enticement from service, it must appear that the child, apprentice or servant, was at the time in the actual service of the parent or master, and that the moving cause of desertion was the inducement held out by the defendant. If before the child, apprentice or servant, had ever met or communicated with the defendant, there had been an abandonment of the services, it cannot be maintained that there was an enticement therefrom by the defendant. Butterfield v. Ashley, 6 Cush. 249. The solicitation to leave must be shown. Stuart v. Simpson, 1 Wend. 376, 379; Blake v. Layton, 6 T. R. 221. And there must be an actual state of service then subsisting. Butterfield v. Ashley, 2 Gray, 254." In Carew v. Rutherford, 106 Mass. 1, 13, Chapman, C. J., says: "We have no doubt that a conspiracy against a mechanic, who is under the necessity of employing workmen in order to carry on his business, to obtain a sum of money from him, which he is under no legal liability to pay, by inducing his workmen to leave him, and by deterring others from entering into his employment, or by threatening to do this, so that he is induced to pay the money demanded, under a reasonable apprehension that he cannot carry on his business without yielding to the illegal demand, is an illegal, if not a criminal conspiracy: that the acts done under it are illegal, and that the money thus obtained may be recovered back, and, if the parties succeed in injuring his business, they are liable to pay all the damage thus done to him. It is a species of annoyance and extortion which the common law has never tolerated." In Walker v.

them in working, or in obtaining work, because they are not members, or in order to induce them to become members, or designed to prevent employers from making a just discrimination in the rate of wages paid to the skillful and the unskillful; to the diligent and to the lazy; to the efficient and to the inefficient; and all associations designed to interfere with the perfect freedom of employers in the proper management and control of their lawful business, or to dictate in any particular the terms upon which their business shall be conducted, by means of threats of injury or loss, by interference with their property or traffic, or

Cronin, 107 Mass. 555, it is held that an action in tort may be maintained upon a count which alleges that a certain shoemaker was in the plaintiff's service and employment on a specified day, and for a valuable consideration on that day agreed to make three cases of shoes for the plaintiff within one month; that the defendant, well knowing this, contriving to defraud the plaintiff of the profit and benefit of said service and of the performance of said contract, did, on another day, specified as being before the expiration of the month, entice and procure, the shoemaker, then being in the plaintiff's service, and before he had performed said contract, as the defendant well knew, to leave the plaintiff's service and refuse to perform the contract, without the plaintiff's leave and against the plaintiff's will, by means of which enticement the shoemaker on the last named day did leave said service and neglect and refuse to perform said contract, without the leave and against the will of the plaintiff, and that the plaintiff thereby lost profits and benefits which would otherwise have accrued to him from said service and by the performance of said contract. "A person who, knowing the premises, entices or persuades one to break a subsisting contract of service, or who retains one in his employ after notice that he owes his services to another, under a contract still existing, or who knowingly persuades or entices a servant to leave the employ of his master, in whose service he then is, although no binding contract to continue to serve him exists, and he is a mere servant at will, or who prevents a person from entering the service of another by menaces, threats or other means is liable for all the damages sustained by the person to whom the services are due, which are the natural and necessary result of his wrongful and tortious acts. An action for enticing and harboring may be joined, and a recovery may be had for harboring even though no enticing away is proved, and employment of one's servant by another is *prima facie* evidence of enticement. But in order to recover upon the latter ground, knowledge or notice must be shown on the part of the defendant that the services of the servant were due to the plaintiff and a retention of the servant after such notice." Wood's Master and Servant, 454.

with their lawful employment of other persons, or designed to abridge any of these rights, are *pro tanto* illegal combinations or associations, and all acts done in furtherance of such intention by such means and accompanied by damage are actionable.[1] The rule, as above stated, is held applicable also where the offense is committed by an individual instead of a combination. In Georgia it has been held that where one man employed a laborer to work on his farm, and another man, knowing of such contract of employment, entices, hires or persuades the laborer to leave the service of his employer during the time for which he was so employed, the law gives to the party injured a right of action to recover damages.[2] In a case in Massachusetts, the rule was stated by Mr. Justice Wells, as follows: "It is a familiar and well established doctrine of the law upon the relation of master and servant, that one who entices away a servant or induces him to leave his master, may be held liable in damages therefor, provided there exists a valid contract for continued service, known to the defendant. It has sometimes been supposed that this doctrine sprang from the English statute of laborers, and was confined to menial service. But we are satisfied that it is founded upon the legal right derived from the contract, and not merely upon the relation of master and servant; and that it applies to all contracts of employment, if not to contracts of every description."[3]

[1] Old Dominion S. S. Co. v. McKenna, 30 Fed. Rep. 48.

[2] Jones v. Blocker, 43 Ga. 331.

[3] Walker v. Cronin, 107 Mass. 555. The measure of damage for enticing away the servant of another, who is hired by the year, is the direct loss suffered, and the average net profits that were made by men of fair business capacity, out of the labor of such servant during the year for which the enticed servant was hired. Lee v. West, 47 Ga. 311. If the common carrier company against whom a combination to induce the officers of a common carrier corporation subject to the provisions of the interstate commerce act, and its locomotive engineers, to refuse to receive, handle and haul interstate freight from another like common carrier is directed, is injured by acts done in furtherance of it, has a cause of action against all of those engaged in the conspiracy. Toledo, A. A. & N. M. Ry. Co. v. Pennsylvania Co., 54 Fed. Rep. 730.

§ **115. Remedy by Injunction.**—It is well settled that any attempt to prevent one person from entering into or continuing in the employment of another by threats or intimidation in any form is unlawful, and where such acts are continuous in their nature, an injunction will issue to restrain them. In a recent case in Massachusetts, the rule was stated by Mr. Justice Allen, as follows: "The act of displaying banners with devices, as a means of threats and intimidation to prevent persons from entering into or continuing in the employment of the plaintiffs, was injurious to the plaintiffs and illegal at common law and by statute. We think that the plaintiffs are not restricted to their remedy by an action at law, but are entitled to relief by injunction. The acts and injury were continuous. The banners were used more than three months before the filing of the plaintiffs' bill, and continued to be used at the time of the hearing. The injury was to the plaintiffs' business, and an adequate remedy could not be given by damages in a suit at law. The wrong is not, as argued by the defendants' counsel, a libel upon the plaintiffs' business. It is not found that the inscription upon the banners were false, nor do they appear to have been in disparagement of the plaintiffs' business. The scheme, in pursuance of which the banners were displayed and maintained, was to injure the plaintiffs' business, not by defaming it to the public, but by intimidating workmen, so as to deter them from keeping or making engagements with the plaintiffs. The banner was a standing menace to all who were or wished to be in the employment of the plaintiffs to deter them from entering the plaintiffs' premises. Maintaining it was a continuous unlawful act, injurious to the plaintiffs' business and property, and was a nuisance such as a court of equity will grant relief against.[1] In its general provisions this rule is

[1] Sherry v. Perkins, 147 Mass. 212. See also Boston Diatite Co. v. Florence Mfg. Co., 114 Mass. 69; s. c., 19 Am. Rep. 31; Springhead Spinning Co. v. Riley, L. R. 6 Eq. 551; Prudential Assurance Co. v. Knott, L. R. 10 Ch. 142; Saxby v. Easterbrook, L. R. 3 C. P. D. 339; Thorley's Food Co. v. Massam, L. R. 14 Ch. D. 763; Thomas v. Williams, L. R. 14 Ch. D. 864; Day v. Brownrigg, L. R. 10 Ch. D. 294;

applicable to the employes of a railroad company or to trades unions, the members of which are railroad employes, and it is farther modified by the requirement of the interstate commerce act. In the recent leading case of the

Gaskin v. Balls. L. R. 13 Ch. D. 324; Hill v. Davies. L. R. 21 Ch. D. 798; Loog v. Bean, L. R. 26 Ch. D. 306: State v. Glidden, 55 Conn. 46: s. c., 3 Am. St. Rep. 23; Gilbert v. Mickle, 4 Sand. Ch. 357. Judge Wood. in U. S. v. Debs. 64 Fed. Rep., at page 745. says: "While. however, the point is not decided. the authorities on the subject have been brought forward so fully because, in part, of their bearing upon the question now to be considered, whether or not the injunction was authorized by the Act of July 2. 1890. It was under that act that the order was asked and granted: but it has been seriously questioned in this proceeding, as well as by an eminent judge. and by lawyers elsewhere, whether the statute is by its terms applicable, or consistently with constitutional guarantees can be applied to cases like this. It is admitted in one of the briefs for the defendant, and the authorities already quoted clearly demonstrates, 'that were Congress to declare that the United States might maintain a bill to enjoin the obstruction of interstate commerce on railroads engaged therein, where such obstructions amounted to what on a public highway would be a public nuisance, such legislation would be admissible.' Such an act, not going beyond the scope of equity jurisdiction in England at the time when the federal constitution was adopted, it is plain would not be obnoxious to the objection that it was an invasion of the field of criminal law which involved interference with the right of trial by jury. The jurisdiction of the courts of equity, and by implication their right to punish for contempt, are established by the constitution equally with the right of trial by jury, and so long as there is no attempt to extend jurisdiction over subjects not properly cognizable in equity, there can be no ground for the assertion that the right of jury trial has been taken away or impaired. The same act may constitute a contempt and a crime. But the contempt is one thing, the crime another; and the punishment for one is not a duplication of the punishment of the other. The contempt can be tried and punished only by the court, while the charge of crime can be tried only by a jury." In the Supreme Court in *In re* Debs, 158 U. S., at page 582. Brewer, J., says: "But passing to the second question, is there no other alternative than the use of force on the part of the executive authorities whenever obstructions arise to the freedom of interstate commerce or the transportation of the mails? Is the army the only instrument by which rights of the public can be enforced and the peace of the nation preserved? Grant that any public nuisance may be forcibly abated, either at the instance of the authorities, or by any individual suffering private damage therefrom, the existence of this right of forcible abatement is not inconsistent with, nor does it destroy, the right of appeal in an orderly

Toledo, Ann Arbor & Northern Michigan Railway Company v. The Pennsylvania Company, before the United States Circuit Court for the Northern District of Ohio, W. D., it was held that circuit courts of the United States have

way to the courts for a judicial determination, and an exercise of their powers by writ of injunction and otherwise to accomplish the same result. In Stamford v. Stamford Horse Railroad Co., 56 Conn. 381, an injunction was asked by the borough to restrain the company from laying down its track in a street of the borough. The right of the borough to forcibly remove the track was insisted upon as a ground for questioning the jurisdiction of a court of equity, but the court sustained the injunction, adding, 'And none the less so because of its right to remove the track by force. As a rule, injunctions are denied to those who have an adequate remedy atlaw. Wh ere the choice is between the ordinary and the extraordinary processes of law, and the former are sufficient, the rule will not permit the use of the latter. In some cases of nuisance, and in some cases of trespass, the law permits an individual to abate the one and prevent the other by force, because such permission is necessary to the complete protection of property and person. When the choice is between redress, or prevention of injury by force, and by peaceful process, the law is well pleased if the individual will consent to waive his right to the use of force and await its action. Therefore, as between force and the extraordinary writ of injunction, the rule will permit the latter.' So in the case before us, the right to use force does not exclude the right of appeal to the courts for a judicial determination, and for the exercise of all their powers of prevention. Indeed, it is more to the praise than to the blame of the government that, instead of determining for itself questions of right and wrong on the part of these petitioners and their associates, and enforcing that determination by the club of the policeman and the bayonet of the soldier, it submitted all those questions to the peaceful determination of judicial tribunals, and invoked their consideration and judgment as to the measure of its rights and powers, and the correlative obligations of those against whom it made complaint. And it is equally to the credit of the latter that the judgment of those tribunals was by the great body of them respected, and the troubles which threatened so much disaster terminated." See also People v. Vanderbilt, 28 N. Y. 396; State v. Dayton & S. E. R. R., 36 Ohio St. 434; Springfield v. Connecticut River R. R., 4 Cush. 63; Atty.-Gen. v. Woods, 108 Mass. 436; Easton & Amboy R. R. Co. v. Greenwich, 25 N. J. Eq. 565; Stearns Co. v. St. Cloud, M. & A. R. R., 36 Minn. 425; Rio Grande R. R. Co. v. Brownsville, 45 Tex. 88; Philadelphia v. Street Ry. Co., 8 Phila. 648; Atty.-Gen. v. Tudor Ice Co., 104 Mass. 239; Atty.-Gen. v. Jamaica Pond Aqueduct Corporation, 133 Mass. 361; Village of Pine City v. Munch, 42 Minn. 342; State v. Goodnight, 70 Tex. 682.

jurisdiction of a bill in equity to restrain violations of the interstate commerce law to the irreparable injury of the complainant, because of the subject-matter, and without regard to the citizenship of the parties. A combination to induce and procure the officers of a common carrier corporation, subject to the provisions of the interstate commerce act, and its locomotive engineers, to refuse to receive, handle and haul interstate freight from another like common carrier in order to injure the latter, is a combination or conspiracy to commit the misdemeanor described by section 10 of the interstate commerce act, and, if any person engaged in it does an act in furtherance thereof, all combining for the purpose are guilty of criminal conspiracy, as denounced by section 5440, Revised Statutes. The injury which will be caused to the common carrier against which such conspiracy is directed will be irreparable, and, in order to prevent this and maintain the *status quo* until full relief can be granted, a preliminary and temporary mandatory injunction will issue against the company and its employes threatening the injury, restraining them from refusing to afford the proper interchange of interstate freight and traffic facilities to complainant. The employes, while in the employ of the defendant company, must obey this mandatory injunction, but may, without contempt of court, avoid or evade obedience thereto by ceasing to be such employes, otherwise the injunction would, in effect, be an order compelling the employes to continue the relation of servant to the complainant,—a kind of order never yet issued by a court of equity. A preliminary injunction may issue against the chief member of such a conspiracy, as that above described, to restrain him from giving the order and signal which will result, and is intended to result, in the unlawful and irreparable injuries to the complainant. Where such chief member has already issued an unlawful, willful and criminal order, the injurious effect of which will be continuing, the court may by mandatory injunction compel him to rescind the same, especially when the necessary effect of the order or signal is to induce and procure flagrant violations of an injunction previously issued by the court.[1]

§ **116. Statutory Regulations.**—In many, perhaps in most of the States, there are statutes designed to determine the rights of trades unions in their relations to their employers, and, especially, with reference to strikes. In some of the States, as Arkansas, California, Maine, Tennesse, etc., it has been made a criminal offense to commit any act that is adapted to injure the public health or morals, or that constitutes an obstruction to trade or commerce, or that tends to the perversion of justice or is an obstruction to the orderly and regular administration of the law. In other States, as Delaware, Maine, Michigan, Wisconsin, etc., statutes have been enacted, the object of which is to restrain trades unions or other combinations from interference with the operations of railroads, or the work of corporations, or with the regular course of business, by firms or individuals. In other States, as Michigan, Rhode Island, etc., it is made a misdemeanor to attempt by force or by any manner of intimidation to prevent any person from entering into or from continuing in any employment. In New Jersey, where it is provided by statute that "it shall not be unlawful for any two or more persons to unite, combine, or bind themselves by oath, covenant, agreement, alliance or otherwise to persuade, advise or encourage, by peaceable means, any person or persons to enter into any combination for or against leaving or entering into the employment of any person or persons or corporations," it was held that under this statute it is not unlawful for the members

[1] Toledo, A. A. & N. M. Ry. Co. v. Penna Co., 54 Fed. Rep. 730. Equity will enjoin the publication and circulation of posters, handbills, circulars, etc., printed and circulated in pursuance of a combination to boycott a newspaper. Casey v. Cincinnati Typographical Union No. 3, 45 Fed. Rep. 135. An injunction will not lie to restrain handicraftsmen from combining, and peaceably and without intimidation persuading their fellow-workmen to leave the service of their employers, in order to compel an advance in wages, on the ground that such persuasion invades the constitutional right of the employer to prosecute his business free from unlawful obstruction. Rogers v. Evarts, 17 N. Y. Supl. 264.

of an association to combine for the purpose of securing the control of the work connected with their trade, and to endeavor to effect such purpose by peaceable means, and equity will not enjoin such acts on the ground that they may be detrimental to trade or injurious to individual business.[1]

[1] Mayer v. Journeymen Stone Cutters' Association, 47 N. J. Eq. 519; s. c., 20 Atl. Rep. 492. 24 United States Statutes at Large, chap. 567, provides "that the term 'National Trade Union,' in the meaning of this act, shall signify any association of working people having two or more branches in the States or territories of the United States for the purpose of aiding its members to become more skillful and efficient workers, the promotion of their general intelligence, the elevation of their character, the regulation of their wages and their hours and conditions of labor, and the protection of their individual rights in the prosecution of their trade or trades, the raising of funds for the benefit of sick, disabled, or unemployed members, or the families of deceased members, or for such other object or objects for which working people may lawfully combine, having in view their mutual protection or benefit." Chap. 114, Illinois Statutes. ¶ 128, provides: "If any locomotive engineer, in furtherance of any combination or agreement, shall willfully and maliciously abandon his locomotive upon any railroad at any other point than the regular schedule destination of such locomotive, he shall be fined not less than $20, nor more than $100, and confined in the county jail not less than twenty days, nor more than ninety days." ¶ 130: "If two or more persons shall willfully and maliciously combine or conspire together to obstruct or impede by any act, or by means of intimidation, the regular operation and conduct of the business of any railroad company, or any other corporation, firm or individual in this State, or to impede, hinder or obstruct, except by due process of law, the regular running of any locomotive engine, freight or passenger train on any railroad, or the labor or business of any such corporation, firm or individual, such persons shall, on conviction thereof, be punished by fine, not less than $20, nor more than $200, and confined in the county jail not less than twenty days, nor more than ninety days." ¶ 131: "This act shall not be construed to apply to cases of persons voluntarily quitting the employment of any railroad company, or such other corporation, firm or individual, whether by concert of action or otherwise, except as provided in section 1 [¶ 128, *supra*] of this act." Laws 1892, chap. 602, which creates a board for the examination of plumbers, and which forbids any person to exercise the calling of a master plumber without passing an examination before said board, is a valid exercise of the police power, since the work of plumbing is essential to the comfort and health of the inhabitants of cities. People v. Warden, 144 N. Y. 529; s. c., 39 N. E. Rep. 686. In Pennsylvania there is a statute which

provides: "In all cases where any dwelling house, or other building or property, real or personal, has been or shall be destroyed within the county of Philadelphia, in consequence of any mob or not, it shall be lawful for the person or persons interested in and owning such property to bring suit against the said county where such property was situated, and being for the recovery of such damages as he or they sustained by reason of the destruction thereof, and the amount which shall be recovered in said action shall be paid out of the county treasury on warrants drawn by the commissioners thereof, who are hereby required to draw the same as soon as said damages are finally fixed and ascertained." The act was afterwards extended to Allegheny county. The validity of the act has been upheld. *In re* Pennsylvania Hall, 5 Pa. St. 204; County of Allegheny v. Gibson, 90 Pa. St. 397; s. c., 7 W. N. C. 441; 11 L. Bar. 81; Donoghue v. The County, 2 Pa. St. 230; Hermits of St. Augustine v. County, Bright. N. P. 116; St. Michael's Church v. County, Bright. N. P. 121; s. c., 7 Pa. L. J. 181; Kensington v. Philadelphia, 13 Pa. St. 76; Curtis v. Allegheny, 1 Phila. 237. The State of Illinois has a general statute covering the same ground. ¶¶ 406-412, chap. 38. Act 1893, p. 260, protecting unions of workingmen in labels adopted by them to show that goods manufactured by persons employing only members of the union were made by such members, does not violate constitution, art. 4, § 53, which prohibits the legislature from granting to any corporation or association any special right, privilege or immunity. State v. Bishop, 128 Mo. 373; s. c., 31 S. W. Rep. 9.

CHAPTER VIII.

MONOPOLIES FROM MUNICIPAL GRANTS AND CONTRACTS.

§ 117. Introductory.
118. Limitation of Exclusive Privilege.
119. Statutory Regulations.
120. The Subject Continued.
121. How Regarded in Equity.
122. Monopoly in Street Railways.
123. Grant of Exclusive Gas Privilege.
124. Exclusive Privilege for Supplying Water.
125. The Subject Continued.
§ 126. Exclusive Privilege of Erecting a Toll Bridge or of Establishing a Ferry.
127. The Subject Continued.
128. Power to Impose a Ferry License.
129. For Removal of Garbage.
130. Municipal Grant of Market Franchise.
131. The Subject Continued.
132. Legislative and Business Powers Distinguished.

§ 117. **Introductory.**—The original idea of a monopoly was that of an exclusive privilege of trade in a particular article or articles within a designated district and for a specified time. It was granted by the king and, ordinarily, without pecuniary consideration, and as an expression of the royal favor. It is defined by Blackstone as "a license or privilege allowed by the king, for the sole buying and selling, making, working or using of anything whatsoever, whereby the subject in general is restrained from that liberty of manufacturing or trading which he had before."[1] Lord Coke defines a monopoly as "an institution by the king, by his grant, commission or otherwise, to any persons or corporations, of or for the sole buying, selling, making, working or using of everything, whereby any persons or corporations are sought to be restrained of any freedom or

[1] 4 Blackstone's Commentaries, 159.

liberty that they had before, or hindered in their lawful trade."[1] It is to be borne in mind in defining a monopoly that, as originally granted and as defined by the early authorities, it was an exclusive privilege of trade, etc., in some branch of business which was not limited to an individual or to a few individuals, but was carried on by a considerable class. It had reference to a branch of business in which all had a right to engage and in which, as a matter of fact, many had previously been engaged. An exclusive privilege is not, necessarily, a monopoly, inasmuch as it does not in all cases relate to a privilege which others had previously enjoyed. The right to operate a ferry, to construct a bridge, or to supply a city with water or gas, is an exclusive privilege, but not a monopoly in the sense of depriving a class of persons of a privilege of which they had previously been in possession. The grant of such a privilege is a contract, and the presumption is that the primary object of the authorities in making it is not to confer a special favor upon the party to whom the grant is made, but to promote the public interest. One of the conditions of the grant is that of rendering to the public a special service, and a failure to render such service invalidates the contract. Such grants of exclusive privileges are not void at common law as monopolies, and they are not in contravention of public policy.[2] In The Commonwealth v. Bacon,

[1] 3 Coke Inst. 181.

[2] New Orleans Water Works Co. v. Riners, 115 U. S. 674; Louisville Gas Co. v. Citizens' Gas Co., 115 U. S. 683. "Permission to keep a tavern or a ferry, to erect a toll bridge over a stream where it is crossed by a public highway, to build a mill dam across a navigable stream, and the like, are special privileges, and being matters in which the public have an interest, may be granted by the legislature to individuals or corporations; but the grantee, upon accepting the grant at once becomes bound to render that service, to secure which the grant was made; and such obligation, on the part of the grantee, is just as necessary to the validity of a legislative grant of an exclusive privilege, as a consideration, either good or valuable, is to the validity of an ordinary contract. Whenever by accepting such privilege, the grantee becomes bound by an express or implied undertaking, to render service to the public, such undertaking will uphold the grant, no matter how inadequate it may be; for, the legislature being vested with

power to make grants of that character, when the public convenience demands it, the legislative judgment is conclusive both as to the necessity for making the grant and the amount of service to be rendered in consideration therefor, and the courts have no power to interfere, however inadequate the consideration or unreasonable the grant may appear to them to be. But when they can see that the grantee of an exclusive privilege has come under no obligation whatever to serve the public in any matter in any way connected with the enjoyment of the grant, it is their duty to pronounce the grant void, as contravening that provision of the bill of rights which prohibits the granting of exclusive privileges, except in consideration of public service." Gordon v. Winchester, 12 Bush, 110, 114. "These [the foregoing] observations were made in a case where it was held that a statute giving a building association the right to receive a greater rate of interest than was allowed by the general law was unconstitutional, in that it conferred exclusive privileges not in consideration of any public services to be performed." Louisville Gas Co. v. Citizens' Gas Co., 115 U. S. 683, 694. See also Commonwealth v. Phipps, 80 Ky. 269; Commonwealth v. Bacon, 13 Bush. 210; Boston & Lowell R. R. Co. v. Salem & Lowell R. R. Co., 2 Gray, 1; Boston Water Power Co. v. Boston & Worcester R. R., 23 Pick. 360; Richmond, etc. R. R. Co. v. Louisa R. R. Co., 13 How. 71. "In the same manner as Congress may reward the discoverer of a new invention or mode of constructing roads, by an exclusive privilege, the legislature may reward those who employ their capital and industry in doubtful enterprises, for the construction of a railway between two points, which may be of great utility to the public, though the success of the enterprise may be precarious." Pontchartrain R. R. Co. v. New Orleans Ry. Co., 11 La. Ann. 253. See also Asylum v. New Orleans, 105 U. S. 362; New Jersey v. Wilson, 7 Cranch, 164; Humphrey v. Pégues, 16 Wall. 244. "The precise question is, had the city of Kansas the power to grant for a term of years the exclusive right to occupy its streets with street railroads? The question must be answered in the negative. Let me in the outset formulate two or three unquestioned propositions: (1) The legislature has, as a general representative of the public, the power, subject to specific constitutional limitations, to grant special privileges; (2) it may, with similar limitations, grant the like power to municipal corporations, as to all matters of purely municipal nature; but (3) as the possession by one individual of a privilege not open to acquisition by others apparently conflicts with that equality of rights which is the underlying principle of social organization and popular government, he who claims such exclusive privilege must show clear warrant of title, if not also probable corresponding benefit to the public. Hence the familiar rule that charters, grants of franchises, privileges, etc., are to be construed in favor of the government. Doubts as to what is granted are resolved in favor of a grantor, or, as often epigrammatically said, a doubt destroys a grant. Now, coming close to the question, the legislature has not in terms given to the city the power of granting an exclusive privilege of occupying the streets with railroads; it has not in terms given to it the right to contract away its continuous control of the streets, and its future judgment of the needs of the public in those streets, by a surrender of their occupation for railroad purposes to individuals for a series of years. Indeed, it has not in terms made any specific grant in respect to the occupation of streets by railroads, and their operation thereon. Upon what, then, can it be claimed that the city has the power to give to an individual, the right to occupy the streets with railroads, secure him that right for a term of years and also the right of debarring, during such term, every other citizen from a like use of the streets. It was held in the Atchison case [Atchison St. Ry. Co. v. Mo. Pac. Ry. Co., 31 Kan. 660; s. c., 3 Pac. Rep. 284], that the city might *permit* a street railroad, and this because the legislature had granted to it a general control and supervision of the streets. In this the current of opinion and authority was followed. Under such power the city may permit any ordinary use of a street as a street. A street railroad comes within the ordinary scope of such use. But power to permit one citizen to use the streets in a given way is a very different thing from power to give such citizen the right to keep every other citizen from a like use of the streets. The one is a mere street regulation—a license; the other rises into the dignity of a contract — a franchise. The one may rest upon the ordinary powers of street management and control, the other requires the support of a special grant. Doubtless, the city may practically secure exclusive occupation to one, and withholding permission from all others, the occupation of that one becomes for the time being, exclusive. But this is an altogether different matter. In the one case, the exclusiveness depends on the continuous will of the city; in the other upon that of the individual company. In the one the full and constant control of the streets is retained; in the other it is partially transferred to the other company. Again, exclusiveness of occupation is not necessary to the full performance of a street railroad company of all its functions. The running of a street railroad on one street is in no manner interfered with by the running of a similar road on a parallel street. Doubtless the profits of the one will be increased if the other is stopped. Monopoly implies increase of profits. But the question of profits is very different from that of the unimpeded facilities for transacting business. The latter may be granted without exclusiveness, and power to grant all facilities for transacting business does not imply power to forbid all others from transacting like business. Even where a charter is granted by the legislature directly, it grants no exclusive right, unless the exclusiveness is expressly named. As said by Judge Dillon, 2 Mun. Corp. § 727: 'But a legislative grant of authority to construct a street railway is not exclusive, unless so declared in terms, and, therefore, the legislature may at will, and without compensation to the first company, authorize a second railway on the same streets or line, unless it has disabled itself by making the first grant irreparable and exclusive.' And if a direct grant from a legislature carries no implication of exclusiveness, it was held that in prohibiting unlicensed persons from keeping a ferry, and in interdicting the establishment of lateral roads, etc., the government exercises public functions, and does not invade the private right of the citizen.[1]

why should it be presumed that the legislature intended to vest in a city the power to give exclusive privileges, when it has in terms granted no such power? Will the power to create monopolies be presumed unless it is expressly withheld? That would reverse the settled rule of construction, which is that nothing in the way of exclusiveness or monopoly passes, unless expressly named. It will not do to say that the grant of general supervision and control of the streets carries with it, by implication, the power to give exclusive privileges; for that grant implies a vesting in the city of continuous control. It is no authority for surrendering its constant supervision and management to any other corporation or individual. It implies that the city to-day, to-morrow, and so long as the grant remains, shall exercise its constant judgment as to the needs of the public in the streets, and not that it may to-day surrender to an individual or a private corporation the right of determining a score of years hence what the public may then need. The city to-day may determine that one street railroad will answer all the wants of the public, and so give the privilege of occupying the streets to but a single company. Ten years hence its judgment may be that two railroads are needed. Where is the language in the charter which restricts it from carrying such judgment into effect by giving a like privilege to a second company? It is doubtless true, as counsel say, that capital is timid, and will not undertake such enterprises without abundant guaranties and undoubtful security. But this suggests matters of policy, and presents considerations for the legislature. It does not aid in determining what powers have been granted or in the construction of charters or ordinances. When the legislature deems that the public interests require that cities should be invested with power to grant exclusive privileges, it will say so in unmistakable terms, as it already has in some instances. Till then, courts must deny the possession of such power." Brewer, J., in Jackson County Horse R. Co. v. Interstate Rapid Transit Ry. Co., 24 Fed. Rep. 306, 308; s. c., 32 Am. & Eng. Ry. Cas. 216.

[1] Commonwealth v. Bacon, 76 Ky. 210. "It is the duty of government to establish and maintain highways. Ferries are parts of highways and the government may perform its duty in establishing through the agency of private individuals or corporations, and such agencies are representatives of the government, and perform for it a part of its functions. And in consideration of the service thus performed for the public, the government may prohibit altogether persons from keeping ferries and competing with those it has licensed. The establishment of public highways being a function of government, no person has a right to establish such a highway

But while special privileges of this character are not illegal, a grant by which the grantor is enabled to create a monopoly, in the proper sense of that term, is in contravention of public policy, and void at common law. Such a grant destroys the freedom of trade, which is the constitutional right of every citizen. It discourages enterprise and industry, and restrains the citizen from an honest effort to obtain a livelihood. Besides, it enables the grantor to enhance the price of the commodity of which he enjoys a monopoly and thus to become a robber and oppressor of the public.[1]

§ 118. **Limitation of Exclusive Privilege.**—In all grants of special privileges there must be a limitation in time. As municipal authorities have no power to grant a monopoly, so they have no right to grant a perpetual franchise. The extent in time to which they may go has not been definitely fixed. It appears that each case must be determined by its peculiar circumstances. In a recent case in Indiana, the court said: "The making of contracts for the supply of gas or water is a matter delegated to the governing powers of municipalities, to be exercised according to their own discretion; and, in the absence of fraud, while acting within the authority delegated to them, their action is not subject to review by the courts. The length of time for which they shall bind, their towns and cities depends upon so many circumstances and conditions as to situation, cost of supply

without the consent of government; and hence in prohibiting unlicensed persons from keeping a ferry the government does not invade the right of even those who own the soil on both sides of the stream. The owner of the soil may, unless his land be regularly condemned for the purpose, prohibit any other person from using it as a landing for a ferry. This he may do, because he is the owner of the soil. So the government, being charged with the duty of establishing and maintaining ferries, has the exclusive right to establish them, and may prohibit any one it chooses from doing so, because the establishment of a ferry without the consent of government is an invasion of its right, just as the use of the soil for a ferry landing, without the consent of the owner, would be an invasion of his right of property. Commonwealth v. Bacon, 76 Ky. 210, 212.

[1] On this point see the very able dissenting opinions of Justices Field, Swayne and Bradley in the Slaughter House Cases, 16 Wall. 83, 130.

and future prospects, that courts can interfere only in extreme cases and upon reasonable application. We cannot say that twenty-five years is an unreasonable time for which to contract for a supply of light or water. Improvements made in the methods and cost of street lighting have in many instances rendered contracts that were fair and equitable when made to seem now to be grinding and oppressive."[1] The rule appears to be that a grant of an exclusive privilege must not to an unreasonable extent restrict the legislative power of succeeding municipal authorities, and it must have regard to the interests of the public. It must not give the grantor a privilege that will enable him at a future time to take advantage of the necessities of the people by fixing exorbitant and oppressive rates. Where the length of time for which a franchise is granted is plainly unreasonable and inconsistent with the public welfare, the grant is not void, but voidable. It is voidable as an *ultra vires* act of the municipal authorities. A grant may be made for a term of years, and a privilege which is not a monopoly at the time at which it is granted does not become a monopoly by the lapse of any reasonable period. In municipal grants there is a necessity for a fixed and somewhat extended time. As the cost of supplying a city with gas or water is large and involves an expensive plant, it would not be undertaken by a private corporation on any temporary or uncertain franchise.[2]

[1] City of Vincennes v. Citizens' Gas Light Co., 132 Ind. 114, 126; s. c., 31 N. E. Rep. 573, 577. See also City of Valparaiso v. Gardner, 97 Ind. 1.

[2] City of Memphis v. Water Co., 5 Heisk. 495. In 1853, the common council of the city of Bridgeport accepted a proposition made by one G to supply the city with water, and granted him (with a right of assignment) the exclusive right to lay pipes in the streets, so long as a full supply of pure water should be furnished. In 1857 the Bridgeport Hydraulic Company was incorporated with power to acquire, and which did acquire, all the rights of G under the vote of the city, and became charged with all his duties; and this company, soon after, expended a large sum of money in acquiring property and establishing its water works. *Held* that, so long as this company supplied the city with an abundance of pure water, the legislature had no power to give another corporation the right to lay its pipes in the streets of the city for the

§ **119. Statutory Regulations.**—There is some conflict of authority in the statutory enactments of the different States touching the right of municipal authorities to grant exclusive privileges. In some of the States an exclusive privilege is treated as a monopoly and illegal. In the case of the City of Brenham v. The Brenham Water Co., the charter of the city provided that it "shall be capable of contracting and being contracted with," and gave it power to provide the city with water for the convenience of the inhabitants, and the extinguishment of fires; while the law under which the water company was organized provided that it should have full power to furnish water to any city where it was located, for public or private buildings, or for other purposes, and to lay pipes through the streets with the consent of the city. A general law also authorized any

purpose of supplying the city with water. Although the State may be no party to, and have no interest in, the subject-matter of a contract, yet if it invests a corporation, otherwise powerless, with a power to make it, the legislature is thereafter concluded in reference to it. It is as a lawful contract, sacred from any interference other than judicial construction. It is the duty of courts to preserve contracts inviolate rather than to destroy monopolies. If the common council had no power to grant the exclusive use of the streets, yet as the charter of the defendant company recognized and confirmed the grant by the city, it became as effective as if the city had had the power to make it, and as if the legislature had made it in the most direct and explicit words. By a clause in the charter of the defendant company, the legislature reserved the power to recall the franchise at its pleasure. *Held*, that this provision did not authorize the legislature to set aside or impair the contract which the city had entered into for the exclusive use of its streets by the defendant company, so long as it should supply the city with water, and which the charter had recognized and confirmed. Citizens' Water Co. v. Bridgeport Hydraulic Co., 55 Conn. 1. See also Dartsmouth College Case, 4 Wheat. 518; Enfield Toll Bridge Co. v. Hartford & N. H. R. R., 17 Conn. 58; New Orleans Gas Co. v. Louisiana Light Co., 115 U. S. 650; Elliott v. Fairhaven & Westville R. R. Co., 32 Conn. 579; Olmstead v. Camp, 33 Conn. 532; Harding v. Stamford Water Co., 41 Conn. 91; State v. Milwaukee Gas Light Co., 29 Wis. 454; Atlantic City Water Works Co. v. Atlantic City, 39 N. J. Eq. 367; Pierce v. Drew, 136 Mass. 81; Von Hoffman v. Quincy, 4 Wall. 535; Holyoke Co. v. Lyman, 15 Wall. 500; New Orleans Water Works Co. v. Rivers, 115 U. S. 674; New Jersey v. Yard, 95 U. S. 104; Railroad Co. v. Maine, 96 U. S. 499; Commissioners v. Holyoke Water Co., 104 Mass. 446.

city in which a water company was organized to contract with it for supplying the city with water. It was held that while these several laws, taken together, undoubtedly authorized the city to make some contract for supplying itself with water, yet they did not confer on the city the express power to make a contract giving the water company the exclusive right to supply the city and inhabitants with water for the period of twenty-five years, at a fixed rate per annum, and, as no such power was necessary or essential to the proper exercise of the powers expressly granted, it could not be implied, and this contract must be considered as unauthorized by the legislature and invalid. Power given to a municipal corporation to contract in relation to a given subject-matter does not carry by implication the power to contract, even with reference to that, so as to embarrass and interfere with its future control over the matter, as the public interest may require. A grant which gives to one or an association of persons an exclusive right to buy, sell, make or use a given thing or commodity, or to pursue a given employment, creates a monopoly. The exclusive right need not continue indefinitely, so as to amount to a perpetuity. It is sufficient that it is an exclusive privilege for a period of time of the character forbidden. So, in this case, the ordinance granting the exclusive right to sell water to a community, for public and private uses, affects all the inhabitants in their common rights directly, and in their individual rights indirectly, and is in conflict with that clause of the Texas constitution which provides that perpetuities and monopolies are contrary to the genius of a free government and shall never be allowed.[1] In a recent case in

[1] City of Brenham v. Brenham Water Co., 67 Tex. 542; s. c., 4 S. W. Rep. 143. "Whether and how a municipal government will exercise a discretionary power conferred upon it, must necessarily depend upon the determination of that question by it in the exercise of whatever legislative power has been conferred upon it. To secure the means to carry out such legislative determination, the making of one or many contracts may become necessary. The validity of every contract a municipal corporation may assume to make, must at last depend upon the validity of the law or municipal ordinance under which it is made. If the legislature had expressly author-

Montana, it was held that the grant by a city council of the exclusive right of selling to the city all the water required by it for sewerage and fire purposes for the period of twenty years at a minimum rate fixed in the contract is a

ized the making of the contract under consideration, it would doubtless be binding, unless there be some constitutional objection to such a law,—a matter which will be considered hereafter,—and the ordinance could not be held to operate, considered with its acceptance as a contract, as a surrender of any power the legislature intended the city government to exercise at all times. The question would then have been determined by a power superior to that of the municipality,—a power from which it derives all the power it has, and even its existence as a corporation. The city having given such a power as we have stated, it must be understood that it was intended not only that it might use it, but that it should use it, if deemed necessary for the public welfare, so long as the power is possessed by it, *i. e.*, until taken away by the legislature. Will not the contract under consideration, if valid, have the effect not only to embarrass the city government in the exercise of the power conferred upon it, but to withdraw from it the right to provide, in any authorized way, water for public purposes, and the use of its inhabitants, which was the sole purpose for which the power to erect, maintain and regulate water works was given to it? It seems so to us, for, as we have before said, the contract in effect assumes to give an exclusive right,—assumes to surrender to a private corporation for a period of twenty-five years the power which the legislature conferred on the municipal government. The power given to a municipal corporation to contract in relation to a given subject-matter does not carry the implication that it may contract, even with reference to that, so as to render it unable, in the future, so to control any municipal matter over which it is given power to legislate as may be deemed best. If the contract relied on is valid, neither the repeal of the charter of the city, nor any other act of the legislature can abrogate it. If it is invalid, the city council had the right to declare it null, and to refuse to comply with it." *Ibid.*, 554. See also Richmond County Gas Light Co. v. Middletown, 59 N. Y. 231; State v. Gas Light Co., 18 Ohio St. 291; Garrison v. City of Chicago, 7 Biss. 486; Canal Company v. St. Louis, 2 Dillon, 84; Norwich Gas Light Co. v. Norwich City Gas Co., 25 Conn. 18; Lord v. Oconto, 47 Wis. 386; Matthews v. Alexandria, 68 Mo. 115; Bodine v. Trenton, 36 N. J. L. 198; State v. New Brunswick, 30 N. J. L. 395; Indianapolis v. Indianapolis Gas Co., 66 Ind. 396; Milhau v. Sharp, 27 N. Y. 611; Gale v. Kalamazoo, 23 Mich. 344; s. c., 9 Am. Rep. 80; Louisville City Railroad Co. v. Louisville, 8 Bush, 415; Covington, etc. R. R. Co. v. Covington, 9 Bush, 127; People's Railroad v. Memphis Railroad, 10 Wall. 38; Presby. Church v. Mayor, etc., 5 Cow. 538; Stuyvesant v. Mayor, etc., of New York, 7 Cow. 588; Sav. Fund v.

monopoly; and this though the grant does not prevent other people from selling water to private citizens.[1] It was held farther in the same case that a city council has no authority to grant to any person a monopoly, even where no express prohibition is found in the charter or other acts of the legislature.[2] The present inclination of the courts is to construe statutory enactments relating to the powers of municipal authorities in favor of the citizen. In a late case before the United States Circuit Court for the Eastern District of Michigan, it was held that authority conferred by act of legislature upon a city council "to cause the streets of a city to be lighted," and to make "reasonable regulations" with reference thereto, does not empower the city government to grant to one company the exclusive right to furnish gas for thirty years, and that the exclusive right to light a city with gas for thirty years is not legally impaired by a subsequent contract with another company to light the streets with electricity.[3] But it has been held that if the

Philadelphia, 31 Pa. St. 175; Lehigh Water Co.'s Appeal, 102 Pa. St. 515; San Francisco Gas Light Co. v. Dunn, 62 Cal. 580; *In re* Mayor, etc., of Albany, 23 Wend. 277; Railroad Co. v. Mayor, 1 Hill, 562; Martin v. Mayor, 1 Hill, 545; Goszler v. Georgetown, 6 Wheat. 593; Bryson v. Philadelphia, 47 Pa. St. 329; Britton v. Mayor, 21 How. Pr. 251; New York v. Second Avenue, etc. Co., 32 N. Y. 261; Dingman v. People, 51 Ill. 277; Brunner v. Boston, 102 Mass. 19; Johnson v. Philadelphia, 60 Pa. St. 445; Jackson v. Bowman, 39 Miss. 671; Oakland v. Carpentier, 13 Cal. 540; Smith v. Morse, 2 Cal. 524; Karst v. St. Paul, etc. R. R. Co., 22 Minn. 118; Peru v. Gleason, 91 Ind. 566; National Bank v. St. Joseph, 31 Fed. Rep. 216; Costar v. Brush, 25 Wend. 628; Brooklyn v. City Railroad Co., 47 N. Y. 475; Home v. Rouse, 8 Wall. 430.

[1] Davenport v. Kleinschmidt, 6 Mont. 502; s. c., 13 Pac. Rep. 249. See also case of Union Ferry Co., 98 N. Y. 150; Mohawk Bridge Co. v. Utica & S. R. Co., 6 Paige, 554; Costar v. Brush, 25 Wend. 628; Chenango Bridge Co. v. Binghampton Bridge Co., 27 N. Y. 87; s. c., 3 Wall. 51; West River Bridge Co. v. Dix, 16 Vt. 446.

[2] Davenport v. Kleinschmidt, 6 Mont. 502; s. c., 13 Pac. Rep. 249. See also Jackson Co. H. R. Co. v. Interstate R. T. Ry. Co., 24 Fed. Rep. 306; New Orleans C. R. Co. v. Crescent City R. Co., 12 Fed. Rep. 308; Meadville Fuel & Gas Co.'s Appeal (Pa.), 4 Atl. Rep. 733.

[3] Saginaw Gas Light Co. v. City of Saginaw, 28 Fed. Rep. 529. See also Minturn v. Larue, 23 How. 435; Wright v. Nagle, 101 U. S. 791; Vicksburg, S. & P. Co. v. Dennis, 116 U. S. 665; s. c., 6 Sup. Ct. Rep. 625; Beaty v. Lessee of

State, or its municipalities, delegate any of its police or sovereign powers to persons or corporations, and the person or corporation in consideration thereof engages in some enterprise which he could not have otherwise done, then such grants or privileges, public and private, become contracts, for a sufficient consideration, and cannot be impaired by any subsequent act of the State or its municipalities capriciously and without just cause.[1] In a case in Georgia, it was held that grants by the public are to be strictly construed and nothing passes by implication. The whole legislative history of this State shows that the understanding of our people has been that exclusive privileges are never conferred, where none such are expressly given by the charter. The legislature, or the inferior court, as its agent, after having chartered a company to make a particular improvement for public accommodation, without any provision that no rival improvement should afterwards be authorized, may grant a charter to another company or individual, to make an improvement of the same or of a different kind to afford the like accommodation, however the work of the junior company might impair or even destroy the profits of the elder. It is competent for the legislature to grant charters with exclusive privileges, but should a change in the business population

Knowler, 4 Pet. 152; Chesapeake & Ohio Ry. Co. v. Miller, 114 U. S. 176; s. c., 5 Sup. Ct. Rep. 813; Butchers' Union, etc. Co. v. Crescent City, etc. Co., 111 U. S. 746; s. c., 4 Sup. Ct. Rep. 652.

[1] City of Louisville v. Weible, 84 Ky. 290; s. c., 1 S. W. Rep. 605. "The power to protect, through her cities and towns and other public agencies, the public health, the public morals, and the public safety, cannot be relinquished or surrendered; for the government is bottomed upon the fundamental principles, promotion of the peace, safety, happiness and security of its citizens. Therefore, any surrender of its power to protect the public health, the public morals, the public safety of the citizen, would violate this fundamental principle, and tend to revolution and anarchy. The power, therefore, cannot be surrendered. The State, however, and its municipalities intrusted with the execution of this power, may provide the means of protecting the public health; it is its duty to do so. Any means may be adopted that will effect that end, such as employing trusty persons to take the matter in charge, under the supervision and control of the State or city." *Ibid.*, 295.

and intercourse of the country require it, new avenues may be opened within the limits of such exclusive grant, by providing just compensation. There is no difference between a franchise and any other property in this respect; all may be made subservient to the public use, provided the public faith be not violated in making adequate remuneration.[1]

§ **120. The Subject Continued.**—The law, as stated in the foregoing section, is not sustained in all the States. In a recent leading case in Connecticut, the view upheld is quite out of harmony with the above stated. In 1853 the common council of the city of Bridgeport accepted a proposition made by one G, to supply the city with water, and granted him (with a right of assignment) the exclusive right to lay pipes in the streets so long as a full supply of pure water should be furnished. In 1857 the Bridgeport Hydraulic Company was incorporated with power to acquire, and which did acquire, all the rights of G, under the vote of the city, and became charged with all his duties; and this company soon after expended a large sum of money in acquiring property and establishing its water works. It was held that, so long as this company supplied the city with an abundance of pure water, the legislature has no power to give another corporation the right to lay its pipes in the streets of the city for the purpose of supplying the city with water. Although the State may be no party to, and have no interest in, the subject-matter of a contract, yet if it invests a corporation, otherwise powerless, with power to make it, the legislature is thereafter concluded in reference to it. It is, as a lawful contract, sacred from any interference other than judicial construction. It is the duty of courts to preserve contracts inviolate rather than to destroy monopolies. If the common council had no power to grant the exclusive use of the streets, yet as the charter of the defendant company recognized and confirmed the grant by the city, it became as effective as if the city had had the power

[1] Shorter v. Smith, 9 Ga. 517.

to make it, and as if the legislature had made it in the most direct and explicit words. By a clause in the charter of the defendant company the legislature reserved the power to recall the franchise at its pleasure. It was held that this provision did not authorize the legislature to set aside or impair the contract which the city had entered into for the exclusive use of its streets by the defendant company so long as it should supply the city with water, and which the charter had recognized and confirmed.[1] A similar view has been upheld in New Hampshire. In a case before the Supreme Court of that State, it was held that this court has jurisdiction in chancery of a complaint by the grantees of an exclusive right of building and maintaining a bridge, setting forth that others are attempting to infringe their rights by the erection of another bridge to their prejudice; and if the right is clear, may, by injunction, restrain the party from proceeding to erect such bridge. The existence of a ferry does not render void an act of the legislature granting an exclusive right to erect a bridge within certain limits which include the place where the ferry is situated; and the extinguishment of the ferry, afterwards, does not give to the legislature a right to grant another bridge within such limits. The legislature have power to grant an exclusive right to erect and maintain a bridge within certain limits, and to take tolls. The grant in such case gives to the grantee a franchise; and the legislature cannot authorize the erection of another bridge within those limits without provision for a compensation to the first grantee. But such franchise is property, and another grant to build a bridge within those limits may afterwards be made if compensation is provided. It is not sufficient, however, to authorize the erection of such other bridge, that the first grantee may obtain compensation, by action, for the wrong done in erecting it; no provision for compensation having been made in the second grant.[2] In a recent leading case before the Supreme Court

[1] Citizens' Water Co. v. Bridgeport Hydraulic Co., 55 Conn. 1.

[2] Piscataqua Bridge v. New Hampshire Bridge, 7 N. H. 35. "If Furbur had had the grant of a ferry, generally, we should pause

of Iowa, it was held that an ordinance which grants a street railroad company the right to lay and operate tracks in a city, and provides that "the right herein granted to said company to operate said railway shall be exclusive for

before holding that the legislature could not grant a bridge, or even another ferry, so near as to be consequently injurious to him. Upon this subject different opinions have been entertained; and it may well be questioned whether the grantee of a ferry, or of a right to erect and maintain a bridge at a particular place, without any terms of exclusion in the grant, can set up that right in avoidance of any other grant which is not directly injurious in its operation, but injurious merely in its remote consequences by diverting travel and tolls. It would seem to have been the understanding, in this State at least, that if the party intended to secure himself from competition of this character, he must obtain a provision to that effect in his grant; and if no such provision is found, it may well be held that the grant was taken with a reliance on the wisdom and discretion of the legislature to protect the grantee from injurious competition by refusing to authorize any other enterprise of a similar character in the immediate vicinity, unless required by an imperious necessity, and with an assent, on the part of the grantee, that whenever the legislature should deem it expedient, they might make other grants remotely affecting the former, so long as the right and privilege conferred by the terms of the grant were not infringed. * * * The grant contains no covenant in terms that the State will never grant another bridge within those limits, nor do we think that any such covenant is to be implied, and, of course, no obligation to that effect is imposed. Sturgis v. Crowninshield, 4 Wheat. 197; Jackson v. Lamphire, 3 Pet. 289. The terms and object of the grant are satisfied without any such stipulation. The grantees have all the State professed to grant,—the exclusive right. They have a property in this, and no part of it can be taken from them, except for public use, and upon adequate compensation being made. If a grant of franchises is like other grants of property, why should a covenant be implied extending the right of property in a franchise of this character beyond the rights of the holders of other property, and enabling the grantees to resist all public improvements, and deny all public wants entirely, or until such compensation as they please to demand shall be made to them? When the legislature shall have granted land, with a covenant that no highway, canal or railroad shall ever be made through it, or a bridge with a stipulation that no other bridge shall ever be erected within a certain distance, it may deserve inquiry whether such contract is within the scope of its constitutional power, whether the right to provide for the public necessities, and to take property for public use whenever those necessities require it, making therefor an adequate compensation, are not inherent rights of sovereignty which no legislature can part with or control by any stipulation, so as thirty years, and that no privilege shall be granted to other persons which may impair the privilege herein granted,'' operates as an exclusive grant of street railway privileges to such corporation, and not merely to secure the corporation the sole use of the tracks it should lay. Under Code, Iowa, § 464, which empowers cities ''to authorize or forbid'' the laying down of a street railroad track, a city council may make provision by contract for present and future street railroad service, and may secure the company contracted with against the impairment of its profits for a term of thirty years, and against interference with its extension during that time by the grant of exclusive privileges, if by such contract a better service can be obtained. Under an ordinance which grants the exclusive right to operate street railways in a city to a certain corporation for a term of years, such corporation has the right to prevent the operation of a competing line, not only on the streets already occupied by its own lines, but on any street. The constitution of the State of Iowa, § 12, art. 8, providing that ''no exclusive privileges, except as in this article provided, shall ever be granted,'' has no application to the case of an exclusive grant to a corporation, where the grant is of such rights as might properly be acquired by an individual by contract.[1]

to bind the people. * * * We conclude, then, that the legislature might lawfully authorize the taking of a portion of the plaintiff's franchise for public use, making a just compensation.'' *Ibid.*, 59, 69, 70. If a State grant no exclusive privileges to one company which it has incorporated, it impairs no contract by incorporating a second one which itself largely manages and profits by, to the injury of the first. In such a case it is no defense to a *scire facias* against the first for non-user or abuser of its franchises, that the State had incorporated the second, was in part managing it, and largely profiting by it, and in consequence of all this, that the revenues of the first company were so far lessened that it could observe its charter no better than it did. If a State injure one incorporated company by the unlawful grant of a charter to another and rival one, the remedy of the first company is by proper proceedings to restrain the second from getting into operation, and not by neglecting its own duties. Turnpike Company v. State, 3 Wall. 210.

[1] Des Moines St. R. Co. v. Des Moines Broad Gauge St. Ry. Co., 73 Iowa, 513; s. c., 33 N. W. Rep. 610. ''In the case at bar, the time limited was thirty years, which

§ 121. How Regarded in Equity.—In the abstract monopolies and special privileges are not favored in equity. It is a very common occurrence, if not the rule, that in controversies between the people and corporations enjoying monopolies or special privileges the right is with the people. So, generally, is this true that the interests of the people will be favored by the courts. But while corporations will not be favored and nothing will be presumed in their inter-

does not seem to be unreasonable. and especially in view of the fact that the lines were operated at a loss for fourteen years. Possibly thirty years. or any shorter time, should be deemed too long in any case, if the contract were such that the street railroad company could not be required to meet the public wants as the same should arise. In the case at bar, two miles only of track were specifically stipulated for, but it is not denied by the plaintiff that the acceptance of the ordinance, which allowed its assignor to lay a track upon all the streets, raised an implied contract upon the part of its assignor to lay so much track as reasonably might be demanded by the public. At the time of the commencement of this controversy, the plaintiff and its assignor had in fact laid ten miles of track, and was contemplating the laying of still more. It may be that neither the plaintiff nor its assignor did all that it should; but such a question is not before us. The ordinance appears to us to be reasonable, and our holding is that, under our statute, which empowers cities to authorize or forbid the laying down of a street railroad track, a city council may make a reasonable provision by contract for the present and future street railroad service, and may secure the company contracted with against the impairment of its profits for a limited time, and against interference with its extension during the time, if a larger and better. or more immediate service can be thus obtained. This question has never before been determined by this court: but the ruling in Burlington & Henderson County Ferry Co. v. Davis, 48 Iowa, 133, goes far towards supporting the views which we have expressed. See also. as having a slight bearing on the case, City of Davenport v. Kelly. 7 Iowa, 102; City of Dubuque v. Stout, 32 Iowa. 80: City of Burlington v. Burlington St. Ry. Co., 49 Iowa, 144. In New Orleans Gas Light Co. v. Louisiana Light Co., 115 U. S. 650; s. c., 6 Sup. Ct. Rep. 252, and in Boston & L. R. Corp. v. Salem & L. R. Co.. 2 Gray, 1. cited by plaintiff, the question was essentially different: but there is much said in the course of the opinion, showing the view which those courts took in regard to the importance, sometimes, of securing a service to the public by contract, even though the contract should, for a limited time. grant an exclusive right. Other courts have held somewhat different views, supported by more or less weight of reasoning. Some of the reasoning. however, we think. cannot be allowed much weight as applied to the condition and policy of Iowa."

ests, it is the province of equity to protect corporations no less than individuals. Where the right is with the corporation it will be sustained against any usurpation of its franchise, and against any effort to put an end to its corporate existence. Public prejudice is not a rule to a court of chancery.[1] In the case of The Jersey City Gas Co. v. Dwight, the court said: "The foundation of the present suit is the invasion of a private right created by statute, and that, I have always understood, it is the undoubted province of a court of equity to protect, whether the injury be committed by an individual or a corporation."[2]

§ 122. **Monopoly in Street Railways.**—It is well established that municipal authorities have no power *virtute officio* to grant any exclusive privilege to a street railway corporation. Such power may be conferred by the legislature, but it must be in direct and express terms. Nothing

[1] Jersey City Gas Co. v. Dwight, 29 N. J. Eq. 242; Atty.-Gen. v. Stevens, 1 N. J. Eq. 369; Pennsylvania R. R. Co. v. National Ry. Co., 23 N. J. Eq. 441; Atty.-Gen. v. Utica Ins. Co., 2 Johns. Ch. 371; Atty.-Gen. v. Bank of Niagara, Hopkins, 354; City of Newport v. Newport Light Co., 84 Ky. 166, 183; Atty.-Gen. v. Tudor Ice Co., 104 Mass. 239; Delaware & R. Canal Co. v. Raritan & Delaware Bay Co., 16 N. J. Eq. 321, 378. "The only question is as to the remedy, and this appears to me to be equally certain. It is settled that an injunction is the proper remedy to secure to a party the enjoyment of a statute privilege, of which he is in the actual possession, and when his legal title is not put in doubt. The English books are full of cases arising under this head of equity jurisdiction. (Bush v. Western, Prec. in Chan. 530; Whitchurch v. Hide, 2 Atk. 391.) But I need not enter into this discussion, for the point has been recently settled in this State in the case of Livingston and Fulton v. Van Ingen and others (9 Johns. Rep. 507), and I shall rest upon the authority of that case, and upon the application of the principles on which it was decided. The equity jurisdiction in such a case is extremely benign and salutary. Without it the party would be exposed to constant and ruinous litigation, as well as to have his right excessively impaired by frauds and evasion. Croton Turnpike Co. v. Ryder, 1 Johns. Ch. 611, 615. Legislative acts granting franchises are to be construed strictly according to their terms, and the grantees in such acts take nothing by implication, either as against the power making the grant, or against other corporations or individuals. Auburn & Cato Plank Road v. Douglass, 9 N. Y. 444.

[2] Jersey City Gas Co. v. Dwight, 29 N. J. Eq. 242.

in favor of such a grant will be presumed, but the charter will be strictly construed. In this direction the courts will recognize such powers only as are clearly and unequivocally expressed in the legislative act. The rule is that a grant of a monopoly by the government of a city is illegal and void, but there are exceptions. The rule applies to all branches of business in which citizens have a common right, but whether it will apply to an enterprise which is essentially a monopoly or of the nature of a monopoly will depend upon the circumstances of the case. It has been denied that a legislature has power to confer upon a municipal corporation the authority to grant to a street railway company an exclusive privilege which is a practical monopoly, but it is now well settled that, in the absence of any prohibition of such a grant by the constitution of the State, a legislature may not only confer upon a city government the power to make such a grant, but it may directly grant to a corporation or to an individual a franchise to construct and operate a street railway within any city, town or village in the State. In a recent case it was held by the Court of Appeals of New York, that the legislature may authorize the construction of a railway upon the streets of New York without farther compensation to the adjoining landowners.[1] In the case of

[1] *In re* New York El. R. Co., 70 N. Y. 327. See also New Orleans City & L. R. R. Co. v. City of New Orleans, 44 La. 728; s. c., 11 So. Rep. 78; *In re* Citizens' Pass. Ry. Co., 2 Pittsb. 10; Henderson v. Ogden City Ry. Co., 7 Utah, 199; s. c., 26 Pac. Rep. 286; Canal & Claiborne St. R. R. Co. v. Crescent City R. R. Co., 41 La. Ann. 561; Christopher & Tenth St. R. R. Co. v. Central Crosstown R. R. Co., 67 Barb. 315; Louisville & Portland R. R. Co. v. Louisville City R. R. Co., 2 Duv. 175; North Balto. Pass. Ry. Co. v. North Ave. R. R. Co., 75 Md. 233; s. c., 23 Atl. Rep. 466; Davis v. Mayor, etc. of N. Y., 14 N. Y. 506; s. c., 67 Am. Dec. 186; Milhau v. Sharp, 27 N. Y. 611; s. c., 84 Am. Dec. 314; Coleman v. Second Ave. R. Co., 38 N. Y. 201; People v. O'Brien, 111 N. Y. 1; s. c., 36 Am. & Eng. R. Cas. 78; Eichels v. Evansville St. R. Co., 78 Ind. 263; s. c., 5 Am. & Eng. R. Cas. 274; 41 Am. Rep. 562; Birmingham, etc. R. Co. v. Birmingham R. Co., 78 Ala. 465; Strange v. Hill, etc. R. Co., 54 Iowa, 669; Stanley v. Davenport, 54 Iowa, 463; s. c., 37 Am. Rep. 216; Denver, etc. R. Co. v. Denver City R. Co., 2 Colo. 673; State v. Bell, 34 Ohio St. 194; Reg. v. Train, 2 B. & S. 640; s. c., 110 E. C. L. 640; Reg. v. Charlesworth, 16 Q. B. 1012; Reg. v. Longton

New Jersey v. Yard, before the Supreme Court of the United States, Mr. Justice Miller, in speaking of the difference in the power of the legislature where there is no constitutional inhibition and where there is such constitu-

Gas Co., 2 E. & El. 651; Chicago v. Rumpff, 45 Ill. 90; Logan v. Pyne, 43 Iowa, 524; Memphis City R. Co. v. Memphis, 4 Coldw. 406. The corporate authorities of the city of New York have no power to confer upon individuals, by contract for an indefinite period, the franchise of constructing and operating a railroad in the public streets for their private advantage. The powers of the corporation, in respect to the control and regulation of the streets, are held in trust for the public benefit, and cannot be abrogated nor delegated to private parties. A resolution of the common council, authorizing private persons to construct and operate a railroad upon certain conditions, without limitation as to time, or reserving a power of revocation, is not a license, nor an act of municipal legislation merely, but a contract which, if valid, it could not abrogate. Such a contract, if valid, conveyed, it seems, an immediate freehold interest in the streets, and a right to the exclusive use of the rails to be laid upon them in perpetuity, and is void because it would deprive the corporation of its power to control and regulate such use. It is no answer to the application for an injunction, that the wrong complained of is a public nuisance if it subjects the plaintiff to a special injury not common to the public. The finding of fact, that a proposed railroad "will be specially injurious to the property of the plaintiffs, and other property similarly situated," construed as showing a special and direct injury to each of the plaintiffs in severalty, not a remote one, and not merely a common or public nuisance. Milhau v. Sharp, 27 N. Y. 611. Under the provisions of the municipal code, the city council is not authorized to pass an ordinance giving to street railroad companies the exclusive right to maintain and operate such railroad upon a street, or to grant the right to construct such railroads on streets, to be designated, to such corporation or company of individuals as will bid "the lowest price of commutation tickets in packages," the law requiring such grants to be let to the one that "will agree to carry passengers at the lowest rate of fare;" and where an ordinance contains such unauthorized provisions, and they are so connected with authorized provisions that their separation is impracticable, the whole ordinance is invalid. Cin. St. R. Co. v. Smith, 29 Ohio St. 291. The city of New Orleans, by delegated power from the legislature, has the paramount control and regulation of the streets of the city, and can grant the use of street railway already constructed to another which she has authorized to be operated. The city council cannot grant the exclusive use of the streets to a street railway, and deprive succeeding councils of the power of performing the duty of regulating the use of the streets in such manner as it may deem best for the public interest. The proprietary right tional inhibition, said: "The case differs from those in which, by the constitution of some of the States, this right to alter, amend and repeal all laws creating corporate privileges, becomes an inalienable legislative power. The power thus conferred cannot be limited or bargained away by any act of the legislature, because the power itself is beyond the legislative control."[1] In some of the States the powers of municipal corporations are fixed by statutes of a general character. In a leading case in Iowa, it was held that before the enactment of the statute giving to cities the power to authorize or forbid the location and laying down of tracks for railways and street railways, the city of Des Moines, by ordinance, granted to plaintiff's assignor the exclusive right to build and operate street railways on its streets for a term of thirty years. Whether without legislative grant, the city had or

which a street railway has on its track is subject to the right of eminent domain. Canal. etc. St. R. Co. v. Crescent City R. Co., 41 La. Ann. 561. Where a regularly incorporated street railway company becomes entitled to the exclusive right to lay its track in certain streets upon the relinquishment or forfeiture of such right by another company, it is thereafter entitled to the same protection against injurious interference to the extent of this right, as the other company would have been. A municipal ordinance gave a street railway company the exclusive right to lay its track in such streets as should be designated by the council, if accepted by the company within a certain time. *Held*, that the company, after forfeiting such right as to specified streets, could not maintain a bill to enjoin another company, upon which the right had been subsequently conferred, from laying its track in streets not so designated to complainant, unless it could show actual injury thereby to its own interests. Where a street railway company has refused to build an additional road lawfully required by the common council, it is discretionary with the council to make such changes in the proposed route as to adapt it to form a junction with the road of some company that will build it, even though, in so doing, a street in which the former company had exclusive rights is used as a connecting link. If such a use infringes the rights of the former company, it is *damnum absque injuria*. A common council cannot properly so multiply street railway tracks in a particular street as to interfere with the rights of the general public in the street. Street Ry. Co. v. West Side Street Ry. Co., 48 Mich. 433. See also Hiss v. Baltimore & Hampden Pass. Ry., 52 Md. 242; s. c., 36 Am. Rep. 371; Atty.-Gen. v. Metropolitan R. Co., 125 Mass. 515; s. c., 28 Am. Rep. 264.

[1] New Jersey v. Yard, 95 U. S. 104, 111.

had not the power to grant such exclusive rights, it was held that under said section it had the right to ratify the grant and to make the privilege practically exclusive by withholding it from others; also that it had power to bind itself by contract to withhold it for a reasonable time from others, if it deemed it necessary to make such contract in order to secure a service to the public which it might not otherwise be able to do.[1] In this case it was farther held that section 12, art. 8, of the constitution, which declares: "No exclusive privileges, except as in this article provided, shall ever be granted," did not apply to the grant by a city to a person or company, of the exclusive right to build and operate street railways on the city streets.[2] In a case in New Jersey, the charter of a street railroad company authorized it to lay rails in the streets of a city, upon first obtaining the consent of the common council. By a supplement, it was positively authorized to construct several tracks specified in the supplement, without any condition or reference to the consent of the common council. It was held that as to such tracks the consent of council was not necessary. The grant of powers of local government to a municipal corporation is not a contract, but an exercise of legislative power, and the legislature may, at any time, take away, resume or limit such power. The rule of construction of statutes is that a provision in a statute inconsistent with a provision in a former statute repeals the first statute *pro tanto*.[3]

[1] Des Moines St. R. R. Co. v. Des Moines Broad Guage St. Ry. Co., 73 Iowa, 513.

[2] Des Moines St. R. R. Co. v. Des Moines Broad Guage St. Ry. Co., 73 Iowa, 513.

[3] Mayor v. Jersey City & Bergen R. Co., 20 N. J. Eq. 360. "Grants of franchises by public corporations to individuals or private corporations are to be strictly construed, and no exclusive privilege passes unless it be plainly conferred by express words or necessary implication. Citizens' St. Ry. Co. v. Jones, 34 Fed. Rep. 579. A grant made by the commonwealth, or by a municipal corporation, under authority from the commonwealth, is to be taken most strongly against the grantee, and nothing is to be taken by implication against the public, except what necessarily flows from the nature of the terms of the grant. Mayor, etc. v. Ohio, etc. R. R. Co., 26 Pa. St. 355; Birmingham, etc. Ry. Co. v. Birmingham, etc. Ry. Co., 79 Ala. 465."

§ 123. Grant of Exclusive Gas Privilege.—The rules relating to the granting of a franchise to a street railway corporation are applicable in the main to the special privileges to a gas company. The right to supply a city with gas may be granted on such terms as to render a practical monopoly. Where the charter of a city empowers the council to contract with a gas company for the lighting of its streets, public buildings, etc., and for the privilege of supplying the people of the city with light, it may exercise such power, as far as conferred by its franchise, according to its discretion. The power conferred by the charter is the power to confer privileges of this nature according to the judgment and sense of fitness of the men intrusted with the administration of the government. And what the municipal corporation may do indirectly, through the instrumentality of a company or individual, it may do directly, as a private corporation, and acting in this capacity it will incur the same responsibility as other private corporations or as a natural person, and such obligations the legislature cannot authorize a municipal corporation to violate.[1] In a

Indianapolis Cable St. R. R. Co. v. Citizens' St. R. R. Co., 127 Ind. 369, 390.

[1] Western Saving Fund Society v. City of Philadelphia. 31 Pa. St. 185. "The restriction upon the power of a municipal corporation to enter into contracts which may prevent it from performing its duty to the public, is nothing more than the application of the principle which avoids the contracts of individuals when they are detrimental to the public rights. But the contract which a municipal corporation may make for the purpose of supplying the inhabitants with gas light in their streets and houses, relate to the 'things of commerce,' as distinguished in the civil law from the 'things public,' which are regulated by the sovereign. Such contracts are not made by the municipal corporation, by virtue of its powers of local sovereignty, but in its capacity of a private corporation. The supply of gas light is no more a duty of sovereignty than the supply of water. Both these objects may be accomplished through the agency of individuals or private corporations, and in very many instances they are accomplished by those means. If this power is granted to a borough or a city, it is a special. private franchise, made as well for the private emolument and advantage of the city as for the public good. The whole investment is the private property of the city, as much so as the lands and houses belonging to it. Blending the two powers in one grant does not destroy the clear and well-settled distinction, and the process of separation is not

leading case in Indiana, it was held that a city incorporated under the general act for the incorporation of cities has power with respect to the lighting of its streets, public buildings, etc., to contract with a gas company upon that subject, and may exercise such power, within the limits of its franchise, according to its own discretion. Such a contract when made, must be regarded as made by such city in the exercise of its power to contract, and not in the exercise of its power to legislate, although the power to make the contract be authorized by an ordinance. And when, by the terms of such a contract, the city is not restricted in any respect from the legitimate exercise of its public power touching the subject-matter thereof, but expressly reserves its administrative authority to keep the posts, lamps and burners in good repair, if the company should fail to do so, and also reserves the right to test the quality of the gas furnished by such company and the capacity of the burners at all times; and is not restricted from extending its streets, establishing an additional number of lamps, obtaining gas from other sources or establishing its own gas works, as the public interests may require; such contracts, not being a restriction upon its legislative power, nor fraudulent, nor against public policy, is valid and binding upon such city, may be enforced in the same manner as the contract of a person or a business corporation, and cannot be repealed,

rendered impossible by the confusion. In separating them, regard must be had to the object of the legislature in conferring them. If granted for public purposes exclusively, they belong to the corporate body in it public, political or municipal character. But if the grant was for purposes of private advantage and emolument, though the public may derive a common benefit therefrom, the corporation *quoad hoc* is to be regarded as a private company. It stands on the same footing as would any indi- or body of persons upon whom the like special franchise had been conferred. These principles are well enforced by Chief Justice Nelson, in delivering the opinion of the Supreme Court of New York, in the case of Bailey v. City of New York, 3 Hill, 538. In that case, the acts of the city had relation to the construction of water works. In this they have relation to gas works. But the principle is precisely the same in both cases." Western Saving Fund Soc. v. Philadelphia, 31 Pa. St. 175, 183.

impaired or changed by the city by ordinance or otherwise.[1] In a case from Louisiana, before the Supreme Court of the United States, it was held that the legislative grant of an exclusive right to supply gas to a municipality and its inhabitants, through pipes and mains laid in the public streets, and upon condition of the performance of the service by

[1] Indianapolis v. Indianapolis Gas Light & Coke Co., 66 Ind. 396. See also State v. Cincinnati Gas Co., 18 Ohio St. 262; State v. Milwaukee Gas Co., 29 Wis. 454; People v. Bowen, 30 Barb. 21; s. c., 21 N. Y. 517; Crescent Gas. Co. v. New Orleans Gas Co., 27 La. Ann. 148; Des Moines Gas Co. v. City of Des Moines, 44 Iowa, 505; Jersey City Gas Co. v. Dwight, 29 N. J. Eq. 242; Chartered Gas Co. v. Great Cent. Consumers' Co., 1 Gas J. 322; Memphis, etc. Gas Co. v. Williams, 9 Heisk. 314; Grand Rapids Electric Light Co. v. Grand Rapids, etc. Co., 21 Am. & Eng. Corp. Cas. 270; State v. Milwaukee Gas Light Co., 27 Wis. 454; State v. Columbus Gas Co., 34 Ohio St. 572; Richmond Gas Light Co. v. Middletown, 59 N. Y. 228. "A municipal corporation cannot grant to any fuel or gas supply company a monopoly of its streets. There is nothing in the nature or business of such a company making its use of the streets necessarily exclusive. The spirit and policy of the law forbid municipal corporations from creating monopolies, by favoring one corporation to the exclusion of others. It is probably true that a municipal corporation may make a contract with a gas company for supplying light to the public lamps for a limited time, even though it be for a number of years; on this point, however, there is some conflict, but there is no conflict on the proposition that, in the absence of express legislative authority, a municipal corporation cannot grant to any corporation the exclusive privilege of using its streets. There is, we know, much conflict among the authorities upon the question of the power of the legislature to grant an exclusive right to a gas company to use the highways of a municipal corporation; and, under our constitution, it is very doubtful whether the legislature possesses such authority. But we are not here concerned with that phase of the question, since the legislature has not attempted to vest an exclusive privilege in any corporation. Upon the direct question before us there is a remarkable uniformity in the decisions of the courts.' City of Indianapolis v. Indianapolis Gas Light, etc. Co., 66 Ind. 396; Norwich Gas Light Co. v. Norwich City Gas Co., 25 Conn. 19: State v. Cincinnati Gas Light, etc. Co., 18 Ohio St. 262; State v. Gas Co., 34 Ohio St. 572; City of Memphis v. Memphis Water Co., 5 Heisk. 495; State v. Milwaukee Gas Light Co., 29 Wis. 454; Garrison v. City of Chicago, 7 Biss. 480; Illinois, etc. Canal Co. v. St. Louis, 2 Dill. 70; City of Brenham v. Brenham Water Co., 67 Tex. 542; Richmond County Gas Light Co. v. Middleton, 59 N. Y. 228; Davenport v. Kleinschmidt, 6 Mont. 502; Meadville Fuel Gas Co. v. Meadville Natural Gas Co., 3 Cent. Rep. 921; s. c., 2 Dillon Munic.

the grantee, is a grant of a franchise vested in the State, in consideration of the performance of a public service, and, after performance by the grantee, is a contract protected by

Corp. (3d ed.), section 693." Elliott, J., in Citizens' Gas & Mining Co. v. Elwood, 114 Ind. 332, 333; s. c., 20 Am. & Eng. Corp. Cas. 263. Upon the question whether an exclusive privilege to furnish gas illumination to a city will exclude other means, the following from the West Virginia Supreme Court is pertinent: "We have already shown that the grant of an exclusive privilege will not be implied. It is equally well settled that such privilege, when legally granted, will not be extended beyond its obvious meaning. Thus, in Parrott v. City of Lawrence, 2 Dill. 332, it was held that the exclusive right to build a bridge at a given point, would not prevent the establishment of a ferry near the same point. In Bridge Prop'r v. Hoboken, 1 Wall. 116, it was decided that an exclusive right to build a bridge at a certain point was not infringed by the establishment of a bridge for the passage of a railway alone. In Emerson v. Com., 108 Pa. St. 111, the court decided that the franchises of two charters, the one, the Fuel Gas Company, incorporated for the purpose of supplying 'heat to the public from gas within the city of Pittsburgh, and the other, the Pennsylvania Fuel Company, incorporated for the purpose of supplying heat to the public within the city of Pittsburgh by means of natural gas, conveyed from such adjoining counties as may be convenient,' were not identical, and, therefore, not necessarily hostile to each other, under the statute granting an exclusive privilege to the company first chartered. The effect of the decision in this case is that the grant of an exclusive right to one company to supply the city of Pittsburgh with manufactured gas is not infringed by the grant of the right to another company to supply the city with natural gas. In 1868 the city of Saginaw made a contract with the gas light company, giving it the exclusive right to light the street lamps and supply the inhabitants with gas for thirty years. In 1886 the city council passed a resolution accepting a proposition from an electric light company for lighting the streets and business houses. Upon a bill filed by the gas company to restrain the city and electric light company from carrying out the contract with the latter, it was decided, in Gas Company v. City of Saginaw, 22 Reporter, 578, that said contract with the gas company, so far as it attempts to give an exclusive right to supply gas for thirty years, was a monopoly, and could not be enforced, and that the plaintiff was not entitled to any relief. Brown, J., in the conclusion of his opinion in that case, says: 'The plaintiff took nothing by its franchises but the privilege of lighting the streets with gas, and this it will continue to enjoy so far as its patrons prefer the use of gas to electricity. But its claim to the exclusive privilege of lighting the city by all methods of illumination cannot be supported on legal principles.'" Gas Company v. Parkersburg, 30 W. Va. 435, 441; s. c., 4 S. E. Rep. 650.

the Constitution of the United States against State legislation to impair it. In granting the exclusive franchise to supply gas to a municipality and its inhabitants, a State legislature does not part with the police power and duty of protecting the public health, the public morals and the public safety, as one or the other may be affected by the exercise of that franchise by the grantee. The prohibition in the Constitution of the United States against the passage of laws impairing the obligation of contracts applies to the constitution as well as the laws of each State.[1] In the opinion in this case, the court said: "The wants of the public are often so imperative that a duty is imposed on the government to provide for them; and, as experience has proved that a State should not directly attempt to do this, it is necessary to confer on others the faculty of doing what the sovereign power is unwilling to undertake. The legislature, therefore, says to public spirited citizens: 'If you will embark with your time, money and skill in an enterprise which will accommodate the public necessities, we will grant to you for a limited period, or in perpetuity, privileges that will justify the expenditure of your money and the employment of your time and skill.' Such a grant is a contract with mutual considerations, and justice and good policy alike require that the protection shall be assured to it. The same principle was declared by the Supreme Court of Louisiana in Pontchartrain Railroad Co. v. Orleans Navigation Co., where Chief Justice Martin said: 'In the same manner as Congress may reward the discoverer of a new invention or mode of constructing roads, by an exclusive privilege, the legislature may reward those who employ their capital and industry in doubtful enterprises, for the construction of a railway between two points which may be of great utility to the public, though the success of the enterprise may be precarious.' And in Crescent City Gas Light Co. v. New Orleans Gas Light Co., the court said: 'As the legislature had the right in 1835 to grant the sole and exclusive privilege to the defendant company to make

[1] New Orleans Gas Co. v. Louisiana Light Co., 115 U. S. 650.

and vend gas in New Orleans for forty years, the legislature of 1870 had the same power to confer on the plaintiff the same privilege for fifty years from the termination of the grant to defendant. We, therefore, conclude that the grant of the monopoly complained of does not violate the constitution and is valid.' "[1]

§ 124. **Exclusive Privilege for Supplying Water.**—The power of a municipal corporation to grant special and exclusive privileges to a water company depends upon the authority conferred upon it by its charter. In some of the States there has been special legislation determining the powers of municipal corporations in this regard. In a recent case in New Jersey, it was held that the power of a municipal corporation to contract with a water company for extinguishing fires, etc., for a term of years, granted by the Act of March 15th, 1881, is expressly limited to a term not exceeding ten years. A contract for twenty years would be without authority, and void. If a municipal corporation, in granting consent to the organization of a company for constructing water works for the purpose of supplying the city with water, under the provisions of the Act of 1876, annex thereto a stipulation for a contract to take the water at a specified price for twenty years, having no authority except that derived from the Act of March 15th, 1881, the stipulation is without authority and void, and the whole proceeding vitiated thereby.[2] Where there is no

[1] New Orleans Gas Co. v. Louisiana Light Co., 115 U. S. 650, 663.

[2] State v. Town of Harrison, 46 N. J. L. 79. See also Burlington Water Works Co. v. Burlington, 43 Kan. 725; Hackensack Water Co. v. Hoboken, 51 N. J. L. 220; s. c., 24 Am. & Eng. Corp. Cas. 511; Atlantic City Water Works Co. v. Read, 50 N. J. L. 665; s. c., 24 Am. & Eng. Corp Cas. 562; Conery v. New Orleans Water Works Co., 41 La. Ann. 910; s. c., 7 So. Rep. 8; Livingston v. Pippin, 31 Ala. 542; Wells v. Atlanta, 43 Ga. 67; Hale v. Houghton, 8 Mich. 458; Nichol v. Mayor, 9 Hun, 268; Grant v. Davenport, 36 Iowa, 402; Greenville Water Works Co. v. Greenville (Miss.), 7 So. Rep. 409; St. Tammany Water Works Co. v. New Orleans Water Works Co., 120 U. S. 64; Atlantic City Water Works Co. v. Consumers' Water Co., 44 N. J. Eq. 427; Memphis v. Memphis Water Co., 5 Heisk. 495; Altgelt v. San Antonio, 81 Tex. 436; Long v. Du-

special legislation upon this point a city government may act under the general powers conferred by its charter to do such things as may be necessary to the security and welfare of the people for preserving the peace, health and good

luth. 49 Minn. 280: Dodge v. Council Bluffs. 57 Iowa. 560. "The New Orleans Water Works Company was in existence before the adoption of the present constitution of Louisiana, one of the articles of which. as we have seen. repeals the monopoly features in the charters of all her then existing corporations other than railroad companies. This case is. therefore. controlled by the decision just rendered in New Orleans Gas Co. v. Louisiana Light Co.. 115 U. S. 650. The two are not to be distinguished upon principle; for. if it was competent for the State before the adoption of her present constitution. as we have held it was. to provide for supplying the city of New Orleans and its people with illuminating gas by means of pipes, mains and conduits placed at the cost of a private corporation. in its public ways. it was equally competent for her to make a valid contract with a private corporation for supplying by the same means pure and wholesome water for like use in the same city. The right to dig up and use the streets and alleys of New Orleans for the purpose of placing pipes and mains to supply the city and its inhabitants with water is a franchise belonging to the State. which she could grant to such persons or corporations, and upon such terms as she deemed best for the public interests. And as the object to be attained was a public one. for which the State could make provision by legislative enactment. the grant of the franchise could be accompanied with such exclusive privileges to the grantee. in respect of the subject of the grant as in the judgment of the legislative department would best promote the public health and the public comfort. or the protection of public and private property. Such was the nature of the plaintiff's grant. which, not being at the time prohibited by the constitution of the State. was a contract. the obligation of which cannot be impaired by subsequent legislation, or by a change in her organic law. It is as much a contract. within the meaning of the Constitution of the United States. as a grant to a private corporation for a valuable consideration. or in consideration of public services to be rendered by it, of the exclusive right to construct and maintain a railroad within certain lines and between given points. or a bridge over a navigable stream within a prescribed distance above and below a designated point. It is idle to insist that this contract was prejudicial either to the public health or to the public safety. as might, perhaps. be said to be the case if the State. after making it. was prevented from exercising any control whatever over the matter of supplying the city and its inhabitants with water. But. notwithstanding the exclusive privileges granted to the plaintiff, the power remains with the State. or with the municipal government of New Orleans. acting under legislative order of the public, and for making such contracts as may be essential to the welfare of the municipality. In Georgia it has been held that under a power conferred by the legislature upon a municipal corporation, to make all contracts

authority, to make such regulations as will secure to the public the uninterrupted use of the streets, as well as prevent the distribution of water unfit for use, and provide for such a continuous supply, in quantity, as protection to property, public and private, may require. In the case just decided we said: 'The constitutional prohibition upon State laws impairing the obligation of contracts does not restrict the power of the State to protect the public health, the public morals, or the public safety, as the one or the other may be involved in the execution of such contracts. Rights and privileges arising from contracts with a State are subject to regulations for the protection of the public health, the public morals, and the public safety, in the same sense as are all contracts and all property, whether owned by natural persons or corporations.' " New Orleans Water Works Co. v. Rivers, 115 U. S. 674, 680. A contract with a municipal corporation, whereby the corporation grants to the contractor the sole privilege of supplying the municipality with water from a designated source for a term of years is not impaired, within the meaning of the contract clause of the constitution, by a grant to another party of a privilege to supply it with water from a different source. Stein v. Bienville Water Supply Co., 141 U. S. 67. "The construction and effect to be given to the contract between the State and the grantee of a franchise have been the subject of much discussion, and the view of Chancellor Kent at one time was that, although 'the creation of the franchise be declared exclusive, yet it is necessarily implied in the grant, as in the case of the grant of a ferry, bridge or turnpike or railroad, that the government will not either directly or indirectly interfere with it, so as to destroy or materially impair its value. All grants or franchises ought to be so construed as to give them due effect by excluding all contiguous competition which would be injurious and operate fraudulently upon the grant.' (3 Kent's Com. 469; Newburgh Turnpike Co. v. Miller, 5 Johns. Ch. 101.) Whatever support that rule may seemingly have in reason or propriety, it is not now available to that extent for the beneficial protection of the grantee in the exercise of his franchise, but, on the contrary, public grants are to be so strictly construed as to operate as a surrender by them of the sovereignty —no farther than is expressly declared by the language employed for the purposes of their creation. The grantee takes nothing in that respect by inference. Such is deemed the legal intent of the State in imparting to its citizens or corporations powers and privileges of public character. And, therefore, except so far as they are by the terms of the grant made exclusive, the power is reserved to grant and permit the exercise of competing and rival powers and in their corporate capacity, which they may deem necessary for the welfare of the city, and which do not conflict with the constitution and laws of the Federal or State government, they have the right to make a contract for the construction of water works.[1] A contract between two corporations, under which one supplies the water to the other, or makes the other a special and exclusive agent, has been upheld. In a recent and very important case, it was held that a contract making a water company the exclusive agent of a flume company for the sale and distribution of water within the corporate limits of a city to consumers of water, all sales of water being subject to the approval of the flume company, is not illegal, nor beyond the powers of either of the corporations, nor is such contract against public policy, as being a combination between the corporations for the purpose of creating a monopoly for the sale of water to the city and its inhabitants, nor as injuriously affecting the interests of the city or its inhabitants. A contract between corporations for a common supply of a city and its inhabitants with water through one distributing system at reasonable rates, whereby the interests of the city is furthered in that its streets are not subjected to the burden of laying

privileges, however injurious they may be to those taken by the prior grantee. * * * The municipal corporation, as such, could bind itself by such contract only as it was authorized by statute to make. It could not grant exclusive privileges, especially to put mains, pipes and hydrants in its streets, nor could it lawfully, by contract, deny to itself the right to exercise the legislative powers vested in its common council. It cannot well be claimed that any express power was delegated to the municipality to grant any exclusive franchises, and public policy will not permit the inference of authority to make a contract inconsistent with the continuously operative duty to make such by-laws, rules and regulations as the public interest or welfare of the city may require. Milhau v. Sharp, 27 N. Y. 611; New York v. Second Ave. R. R. Co., 32 N. Y. 261; Richmond Co. Gas Light Co. v. Middleton, 59 N. Y. 228; Gale v. Village of Kalamazoo, 23 Mich. 344; s. c., 9 Am. Rep. 80; Logan v. Pyne, 43 Iowa, 524; s. c., 22 Am. Rep. 261; Des Moines Gas Co. v. City of Des Moines, 44 Iowa, 505; s. c., 24 Am. Rep. 756; Norwich Gas Light Co. v. Norwich City Gas Co., 25 Conn. 19." Bradley, J., in Syracuse Water Co. v. City of Syracuse, 116 N. Y. 167, 178, 180.

[1] Mayor v. Cabot, 28 Ga. 50.

and keeping in repair an additional system of mains and pipes, is not an unreasonable restriction of competition between the parties; nor does public policy condemn or prohibit an arrangement intended to prevent a competition between corporations which would result in the financial ruin of one or both of them, and which could not in any event benefit the city or its inhabitants. Where water can be supplied more cheaply through one distributing plant by two corporations, the governing body of the city in whom is vested the power to fix water rates is bound to take that fact into consideration, as well as all other facts which enable it to fix reasonable rates and award a just compensation, and an agreement between such corporations for a common supply, through one distributing plant, cannot increase the rate of compensation to be paid by the city or its inhabitants for the water supplied. The agreement between the flume company and the water company, making the latter an exclusive agent for the sale and distribution of water in the city limits, and providing for a distribution of profits, does not create a partnership between the two corporations, but only a limited agency with a mode provided of determining the compensation to be received by the flume company for the water furnished by it to the water company.[1]

§ **125. The Subject Continued.**—It has been held that a committee of a municipal corporation, unless specially authorized, has no power to bind the city by a contract for the introduction of a new and expensive improvement in a system of water works. Such power can be exercised only under a corporate act. In Tennessee it has been held that the power to make a contract for the introduction of a new and expensive improvement in a system of water works, being equivalent in general to the power to levy, collect and disburse taxes, must be exercised in the same manner and by the same authority, that is, by a corporate act. There being no general law or ordinance modifying this rule, a water works

[1] San Diego Water Co. v. Flume Co., 108 Cal. 549.

committee had no power to bind a corporation by a contract of this character.[1] In a case in Minnesota, it was held that, under the statute, the board of water commissioners of St. Paul is invested with authority to make contracts with reference to the water works in its own name, as the representative of the city. This is not the creation of a corporation within the inhibition of the constitution. The contracts which the board is thus authorized to make are, in effect, made with as well as for the city. The statute which requires contractors for doing any work or furnishing any material to or for said city, to enter into a bond with the city for the use of all persons who may do work or furnish materials pursuant to any such contract, is applicable to the case of a contract made by the board of water commisioners in its own name, within the scope of its authority, in reference to water works, and the bond may be taken by the board in its own name.[2] Where a municipal government has entered into a contract that is illegal, as conferring a monopoly, the tax payers of the city may maintain a bill in equity to enjoin it from carrying out the contract. The fact that such contract, if carried out, would increase the burden of taxation, and thus inflict an injury upon the plaintiffs, would be a sufficient ground for the action.[3]

[1] Mayor v. Hagan. 9 Baxt. 495.

[2] Morton v. Power. 33 Minn. 521.

[3] Davenport v. Kleinschmidt. 6 Mont. 502. "The city charter of Helena contains the following provisions: 'The city council shall have power to provide the city with water. erect hydrants and pumps. build cisterns. and dig wells in the streets for the supply of engines and buckets (Sec. 8. page 8), to provide for the prevention and extinguishment of fires.' (Sec. 18. page 9.) Under the powers to provide the city with water. and to erect hydrants. and to provide for the prevention and extinguishment of fires are doubtless included. as necessarily incident thereto. or implied therein and essential thereto. the power to do this by agents employed for that purpose and to make contracts with individuals or other corporations to do the same. The city could scarcely accomplish such objects in any other way: and it is hardly probable that any other method was contemplated in the granting of the charter. Though. doubtless. the city council would cause water works to be built. and own. operate and control them thereafter as the property of the city. the charter does not limit the city corporation to either one method or the other. Any appropriate means necessary to carry

§ 126. Exclusive Privilege of Erecting a Toll Bridge or of Establishing a Ferry.—In England the right to establish and operate a ferry is a privilege granted by the crown, but it has been held that a user of thirty-five years creates a presumption that the establishment of the ferry was legal.[1] In this country the State has power, by its right of eminent domain, to establish ferries wherever it is required by the necessities or convenience of the public. As in the case of land condemned for other public uses, the owners of the soil are entitled to compensation, but they have no special rights or privileges beyond that of personal and private use. In Iowa it has been held that a public ferry franchise can be conferred only by the government, and must be founded on grant, license or prescription. Ownership of

out the objects would be properly within the powers granted to the city council in the charter. East St. Louis v. East St. Louis G. L. & C. Co., 98 Ill. 424, 425. Then, the power to provide the city with water, by making a proper contract with some person to erect water works, and sell water to the city, being conceded, the next question that presents itself is as to the power of the city to make this particular contract. Is the present such a contract as to be beyond the power of the city council to enter into so as to bind the municipal corporation? Does this contract create a monopoly? For, if it does, it goes beyond the power of a city council. Monopolies may be created: but they must be called into being by the sovereign power alone. A city council has no authority to grant to any person a monopoly, even where no express prohibition is found in the charter or other acts of the legislature. Monopolies are contrary to the genius of free government, and ought not to be encouraged by the people or countenanced by the courts, except when expressly authorized by positive law. *Ibid.*, 528. See also Dibble v. New Haven, 56 Conn. 199; s. c., 20 Am. & Eng. Corp. Cas. 174; Valparaiso v. Gardner, 97 Ind. 1; s. c., 7 Am. & Eng. Corp. Cas. 626; 49 Am. Rep. 416; Sackett v. New Albany, 88 Ind. 473; s. c., 2 Am. & Eng. Corp. Cas. 85; 45 Am. Rep. 467; Madison v. Smith, 83 Ind. 502; Noble v. Vincennes, 42 Ind. 125; Pedrick v. Ripon, 73 Wis. 622; s. c., 24 Am. & Eng. Corp. Cas. 422.

[1] Trotter v. Harris, 2 G. & J. 285. See also Williams v. Turner, 7 Ga. 348; Blisset v. Hart, Willes, 508; McRoberts v. Washburne, 10 Minn. 8; Mississippi River Bridge Co. v. Lonergan, 91 Ill. 513; Bell v. Clegg, 25 Ark. 26; Prosser v. Wapello, 18 Iowa, 327; Haithcock v. Swift Island Mfg. Co., 72 N. Car. 410; Stark v. Miller, 3 Mo. 470; Milton v. Haden, 32 Ala. 30; Columbia, etc. Co. v. Geise, 34 N. J. L. 268; Greer v. Haughabook, 47 Ga. 282.

the soil upon each side of the stream does not confer the right to establish thereon, without grant or license, a public ferry at which tolls are charged. The owner may establish a private ferry for the convenience of himself and family, and at which he may ferry for a compensation fixed by contract, expressed or implied, when not forbidden by statute, and when this does not injure or affect any established public ferry. In establishing a ferry, preference should be given in awarding the franchise to the owner of the land on which it is established, if he is a proper person to receive and exercise the same. The granting of a ferry franchise does not authorize the holder thereof to use the land of another without his consent or without making due compensation. Such authority may be secured by contract or by proper proceedings to confirm the right and compensate the owner for it.[1] As the word government is employed in the preceding syllabus, it includes that of a city or of a county. While the grant of a ferry or bridge franchise is a monopoly in a general sense, it is held not to be such in the strict and legal sense, or in any sense that renders it in contravention of public policy and void. In a case in Connecticut, it was held that a grant, by the legislature, in consideration of expenses to be incurred by the grantees, and in contemplation of a public benefit, of the exclusive right of erecting a bridge and taking tolls, to reimburse such expenses, within certain limits, for a limited time, is not a monopoly, in the odious sense of that term. Such a grant is in the nature of a contract, which may not be impaired. The court will give to its stipulations such construction as will carry them into full effect.[2] In a case before the United States Circuit Court of Appeals, the city of Laredo, Tex., owning a ferry franchise over the Rio Grande river, granted to it at an early day by the Spanish government, contracted, by ordinance, with a bridge company to permit the erection

[1] Prosser v. Wapello County, 18 Iowa, 327.

[2] Enfield Toll Bridge v. Hartford & New Haven R. R. Co., 17 Conn. 40.

of the north end of a bridge in certain of its streets, and agreed not to exercise its ferry franchise for a period of twenty-five years, in return for which it was to receive $5,000 per year for the same period. It was held that this ordinance did not create a monopoly, within the meaning of the Texas constitution, which declares that "perpetuities and monopolies are contrary to the genius of a free government, and shall never be allowed." In thus converting its ferry privilege into an equivalent or more beneficial bridge privilege, for a limited period, the city was not exercising a discretion so clearly beyond the purposes of the franchise, as to make the contract void, and the ordinance was within the lawful power of the council to enact.[1]

[1] City of Laredo v. International Bridge & T. Co., 66 Fed. Rep. 246. "There are classes of exclusive privileges which certainly do not amount to 'monopolies,' within the meaning of the common law or of the Texas constitution. Courts of last resort have generally refrained from propounding an authoritative affirmative definition of the 'monopoly' so odious to the common law and to the genius of a free government. It would try the power of expression of most judges, if not of human speech, to frame such a definition outside of which a grant or contract must wholly and clearly rest to escape the stroke of nullity. It has, therefore, generally been deemed wise and safe to use rather the process of exclusion, and determine what is not a monopoly, so far as the case in hand required. From the time of the separation of Texas from Mexico, the provision above quoted has had a place in her constitution. From its first adoption, now nearly sixty years ago, it has been the constant practice to grant exclusive ferry privileges to individuals and to corporations. These grants have been made sometimes directly by the legislature, but commonly by the subordinate municipal bodies. It has also been the practice in that State to grant to individuals and to corporations authority to erect and maintain toll bridges over the larger streams. At one time a general law authorized the securing of such a privilege to be exclusive for a period of not exceeding ten years, on the terms and in the manner prescribed in that statute. Special charters have been passed granting such privileges to individuals and corporations for longer periods than ten years; and the power of the legislature to make such grants has been held to be undoubted by the Supreme Court of Texas. Hudson v. Emigration Co., 47 Tex. 56. It may be safely affirmed that many of these enterprises thus authorized and fostered have been as useful and beneficial to the public, as promotive of the general good, as they have proved profitable to the holders of the privilege; that they have been made successful by means of the enjoyment of the exclusive right; and that, at the time

§ 127. **The Subject Continued.**—As stated in the preceding section, the legislature of a State has the power to establish or to discontinue a ferry wherever it is essential to the convenience of the public. Where the river is a boundary line between two States, each State may grant a franchise for its own territory, and neither can grant a privilege for the opposite shore. In the leading case of Conway v. Taylor, before the Supreme Court of the United States, it was held that a ferry franchise on the Ohio is grantable, under the laws of Kentucky, to a citizen of that State who is a riparian owner on the Kentucky side; and it is not necessary to the validity of the grant that the grantee should have a right of landing on the other side or beyond

and place when and where these bridges were erected, they could have been constructed, maintained and conducted to success only in that way. It is not suggested that the defendant's bridge is not promotive of the general good, or useful and beneficial to the inhabitants of the city of Laredo, or that it is not as useful and beneficial as the ferry which the city had maintained for more than a century under its grants from the Spanish crown and from the State of Texas. It is not shown by the plaintiff's pleading, nor can it be fairly inferred therefrom, that the ferry privilege so early granted, so often recognized by the legislature, and so long enjoyed, was held by the city of Laredo for strictly municipal purposes, rather than bestowed as a source of revenue, to be administered as such for the best interest of the city, in the sound discretion of its constituted authorities, acting in good faith. On the contrary, if the petition does not expressly so aver, it is fairly and clearly to be implied from its allegations that the privilege was originally extended as an endowment for the purpose of providing revenue for the infant town, to be reared in a remote province existing in the state of nature, inhabited chiefly by savage Indians. * * * Considering the grant of the ferry privilege as an endowment for the purpose of producing revenues, and conceding that this franchise, though not alluded to in the defendant's proposition, was a material, if not the chief subject of the contract between the parties, the administration and disposition of it by the ordinance which embodies their contract does not appear to have been or to be reckless or improvident. The discretion to convert the ferry privilege into an equivalent or more beneficial bridge privilege without loss of revenue to the city, does not appear to us to be a dangerous discretion, so clearly beyond the purposes of the franchise as to make the agreement to do so void. In the nature of the case, such a disposition, if made at all, must extend over a period approximating the ordinary lifetime of the bridge structure." *Ibid.*, 248.

the jurisdiction of the State. The concurrent action of two States is not necessary to the grant of a ferry franchise on a river that divides them. A ferry is in respect to the landing, not to the water; the water may be to one, and the ferry to another. After a citizen of Kentucky has become the grantee of a ferry franchise, and his riparian rights have been repeatedly held sufficient to sustain the grant by the highest legal tribunal of the State, the same question is not open here; the adjudications of the State courts are a rule of property and a rule of decision, which this court is bound to recognize. A license to establish a ferry, which does not extend across the river, may be less valuable for that reason, but not less valid as far as it goes. The laws of Kentucky, relating to ferries on the Ohio and Mississippi, are like the laws of most, if not all, the other States bordering on those rivers; they do not leave the rights of the public unprotected, and are not unconstitutional. The franchises which the State grants are confined to the transit from her own shores, and she leaves other States to regulate the same rights on their side. A ferry franchise is property, and as sacred as other property. An injunction to protect the exclusive privilege to a ferry does not conflict or interfere with the right of a boat to carry passengers or goods in the ordinary prosecution of commerce without the regularity or purpose of ferry trips; that remedy applies only to one which is run openly and avowedly as a ferry boat. The authority to establish and regulate ferries is not included in the power of the Federal government to "regulate commerce with foreign nations and among the several States and with the Indian tribes." The authority to regulate ferries has never been claimed by the general government, has always been exercised by the States, never by Congress, and is undoubtedly a part of the immense mass of undelegated powers reserved to the States respectively.[1] While the grant of a

[1] Conway v. Taylor, 1 Black (U. S.), 603. See also Allen v. Farnsworth, 5 Yerg. 187; Barrington v. Neuse River, 69 N. Car. 105; Mills v. County Com., 3 Scam. 53; Hartford v. Hartford Bridge Co., 10 How. 534; s. c., 17 Conn. 79; Columbia, etc. Co. v. Geisse, 38 N.

ferry franchise is, in a sense a monopoly, the legislature has the right to establish another ferry within such a distance of one already in operation as to interfere with its business and to diminish its value, unless the original ferry

J. 39; People v. Babcock, 11 Wend. 586. The legislatures of the several States possess the power within their limits to establish and regulate ferries, and that power is sufficiently extensive to authorize a grant for the construction of a ferry from the Illinois shore, on the waters of the Mississippi, in the manner prescribed by the Act of March 2, 1819, a privilege thus conferred in no way conflicts with the provision of any treaties made by the United States with foreign powers, or with any act or acts of Congress relative to the free navigation of these waters. A ferry franchise is neither more nor less than a right conferred to land at a particular point, and receive toll for the transportation of passengers and property from that point across a stream. The exercise of such a franchise divests no right or privilege which any citizen theretofore enjoyed freely and uninterruptedly to navigate the river. This right of free navigation can, by no manner of means, be construed as conferring upon the citizens the right to appropriate the banks or landing of this river to themselves, or to receive toll for transporting passengers and property from point to point across the same. The grant of a ferry franchise by the legislature of a State, unless limited by some general law, or some restrictive provision in the grant itself, is necessarily exclusive to the extent of the privilege thus conferred. When a grant has once been made by legislative authority, to the extent of the privilege thus conferred, the power which made it is expended, and it cannot be taken back or transferred to another until the public interests and welfare shall demand its resumption, and provision shall have been made for just compensation to the owner in the manner required by law. Mills v. County of St. Clair, 7 Ill. 197. "In respect to those purely internal streams of a State, the public right of navigation is exclusively under the control and regulation of the State legislature; and in cases where these erections or obstructions to the navigation are constructed under a law of the State, or sanctioned by legislative authority, they are neither a public nuisance subject to abatement, nor is the individual who may have sustained special damage from their interference with the public use entitled to any remedy for his loss. So far as the public use of the stream is concerned, the legislature having the power to control and regulate it, the statute authorizing the structure, though it may be a real impediment to the navigation, makes it lawful." Pennsylvania v. Wheeling & Belmont Bridge Co., 18 How. 421, 432. "Neither the fact that the title to the Pennsylvania landing was in another, nor that the exclusive ferry franchise on that shore existed in another will operate to defeat the grant made to Geisse by the legislature of this State. The grant was of a franchise capable of existence in-is protected by the terms of its privilege.[1] The act of Congress by which the State of Mississippi was admitted to the Union, and which recites that "the Mississippi river shall be a common highway, and forever free to the citizens of the United States," without any tax, duty, impost or toll therefor imposed by this State, does not interfere with the police power of the State to grant ferry licenses across the river.[2]

§ 128. **Power to Impose a Ferry License.**—A State legislature has power to levy a license tax upon all ferries subject to its authority. It may do this directly, or it may be done indirectly, through the municipal corporations of the State. In the leading case of the Wiggins Ferry Company v. East St. Louis, it was held that the fourth section of the act of the legislature of Illinois, passed in 1819, touching a ferry across the Mississippi river from a place in Illinois to the city of St. Louis, Missouri, declares: "That the ferry established shall be subject to the same taxes as are now, or hereafter may be, imposed on other ferries

dependent of the title to the land. To enable the owner of such a franchise to exercise it and enjoy its emoluments, he must obtain the right to use the land on both sides of the river, for the purpose of receiving and landing passengers, but he need not have any property in the soil. Peter v. Kendall, 6 B. & C. 703; Newton v. Cubitt, 12 C. B. (N. S.) 32; s. c., 13 C. B. (N. S.) 864; Bowman v. Waltham, 2 McLean, 376; Fay, Petitioner, 15 Pick. 243. The grant by one State of a ferry franchise over a river which is the boundary between it and another State, is valid, and it is not necessary to the validity of such a grant that there be concurrent action by the legislatures of both States, nor that the grantee have the right of a landing on the other side, or beyond the State by which the grant is made. Conway v. Taylor, 1 Black (U. S.), 603; Freeholders v. State, 4 Zab. (N. J.) 718; People v. Babcock, 11 Wend. 558. That by reason of hostile legislation in the other State, the grantee may be unable to exercise his franchises on the other shores, or, because of exclusive rights in others under such legislation, his profits may be diminished, will not defeat his franchise, as far as his own property rights are concerned, or the jurisdiction of his State extends. The franchise may be less valuable for that reason, but it will be valid, as far as it goes." Columbia Bridge Co. v. Geisse, 38 N. J. L. 39, 42.

[1] Gibbes v. Town Council of Beaufort, 20 S. Car. 213.

[2] Marshall v. Grimes, 41 Miss. 27; Fanning v. Gregoire, 16 How. 534; Chiapella v. Brown, 14 La. Ann. 189.

within this State, and under the same regulations and forfeitures." It was held that the section provides for equality of taxation: that is to say, that the property of the ferry company shall be valued and taxed by the same rule as other like property, and be subject to the same exactions and forfeitures, but the company is not exempted from any license tax on its ferry boats, which the State or a municipal corporation thereto authorized might impose. The power to license is a police power, although it may also be exercised for the purpose of raising revenue. The State has the power to impose a license fee, either directly or through one of its municipal corporations, upon the ferry keepers living in the State, for boats which they own and use in conveying from a landing in the State passengers and goods across a navigable river to a landing in another State. The levying of a tax upon such boats, although they are enrolled and licensed under the laws of the United States, or the exaction of a license fee by the State within which the property subject to the exaction has its *situs*, is not a a regulation of commerce within the meaning of the Constitution of the United States, nor is such tax or fee a duty on tonnage, if it be not graduated by the tonnage of the boats or by the number of times they cross the river or land within the limits of the State.[1]

[1] Wiggins Ferry Co. v. East St. Louis, 107 U. S. 365. Long after the license and establishment of a ferry, the legislature, by general law, provided that the county courts should not license a ferry within half a mile in a direct line of one already established. It was held that this general law, so far as it applied to such existing ferry, did not create in it the right to a perpetual monopoly, but was repealable at the will of the legislature. The purchase of said ferry by the W. & B. Bridge Co., under an enabling act authorizing them to make the purchase, could not enlarge nor add to the ferry franchise or privileges, nor convert said monopolistic feature into an irrevocable perpetuity in the hands of the vendee, but left it subject to repeal just as it was held by the vendor: and the legislature having repealed it by general law, the W & B Bridge Co. have no right to complain, and a new bridge may be erected within the restricted territory without any violation of vested rights. One internal improvement company, in the same manner, and generally under the same conditions, that it may take the lands owned by others, provided the lands proposed to be taken are not necessary to the en-

§ 129. **For Removal of Garbage.**—Municipal authorities may require all persons acting in the capacity of scavengers to take out a license for that work, and to pay a license tax, as a condition of the privilege of engaging in this business. But as it is an ordinary branch of business in which a large class of persons may engage, and may desire to engage, no exclusive privilege can be granted. In a recent case in Kansas, it was held that ordinance No. 1718, of the city of Topeka, as amended by ordinance No. 1744, providing that the mayor and council may appoint two or more persons as scavengers, who shall have the exclusive privilege of removing garbage from private premises as well as public, is an attempt to create a monopoly and is void.[1] In the opinion

joyment of its franchise by the defendant company; nor will any mere trivial or temporary use by the defendant company be sufficient to protect its land from such condemnation and appropriation. Wheeling Bridge v. Wheeling & B. Bridge Co., 34 W. Va. 155. "No person can, in this State, establish and operate a public ferry for hire without legislative authority. (Chenango Bridge Co. v. Paige, 83 N. Y. 178.) The legislature having jurisdiction of the whole subject may limit a ferry franchise according to its pleasure. It may confer the right to operate a ferry across a river between two places in both directions, or it may limit the right so that the ferry can be operated from one side of the river only. A legislative grant of a ferry franchise across a river from a place on one side to a place on the other side, standing alone, unexplained, would ordinarily be construed to give the right of a ferry across the river between the two places in both directions. Common sense and public convenience would require such a construction. But to determine whether a legislative grant authorizes a ferry in both directions or only in one, all the language of the grant must be scrutinized, and all legislative acts *in pari materia*, and the user under them, and the circumstances of the particular case must be considered. An act of the legislature merely granting the right to establish and operate a ferry across any water does not confer an exclusive right, so as to deprive the legislature of power to authorize another competing ferry at or near the same place. Whatever doubt there may have been as to this proposition at an early day has been removed, and the law is now well-settled. (3 Kent's Com., 459, and note; Plankroad Co. v. Douglass, 9 N. Y. 444.) Before a ferry franchise can be held to be exclusive, there must be something in the act granting it showing that such was the legislative intention." Power v. Village of Athens, 99 N. Y. 592, 598; s. c., 10 Am. & Eng. Corp. Cas. 54.

[1] *In re* Lowe, 54 Kan. 757; s. c., 39 Pac. Rep. 710. See generally on the power of municipal corporation to pass ordinances on the

in this case the rule was stated, as follows: "It will be observed that the ordinance under consideration authorizes the appointment of two or more persons as scavengers. It, therefore, places it in the power of the mayor to grant to

preservation of public health: Harrison v. Baltimore, 1 Gill. 264; State v. Mott, 61 Md. 297; s. c., 4 Am. & Eng. Corp. Cas. 334; 48 Am. Rep. 105; Mayor v. Radecke, 49 Md. 217; Town of Summerville, 33 S. Car. 56; s. c., 11 S. E. Rep. 545; City Council v. Baptist Church, 4 Strobh. 306; Copes v. Charleston, 10 Rich. L. 502; Zylstra v. Charleston, 1 Bail. 382; Huesing v. Rock Island, 128 Ill. 465; s. c., 27 Am. & Eng. Corp. Cas. 650; State v. Lowery, 49 N. J. L. 391; Weil v. Ricord, 24 N. J. Eq. 169; Gregory v. Mayor, etc. of New York, 40 N. Y. 273; Cronin v. People, 82 N. Y. 318; s. c., 37 Am. Rep. 564; People v. Mulholland, 82 N. Y. 324; s. c., 37 Am. Rep. 568; Metropolitan Board of Health v. Heister, 37 N. Y. 661; Johnson v. Simonton, 43 Cal. 242; *In re* Linehan, 72 Cal. 114; *Ex parte* Shrader, 3 Cal. 279; Bliss v. Kraus, 16 Ohio St. 155; State v. Cowan, 29 Mo. 330; Mayor, etc. of Monroe v. Gerspach, 33 La. Ann. 1011; Kennedy v. Phelps, 10 La. Ann. 227; Wreford v. People, 14 Mich. 41; Dubois v. Augusta, Dudley, 30; St. Louis v. McCoy, 18 Mo. 238; Metcalfe v. St. Louis, 11 Mo. 103; Train v. Boston Disinfecting Co., 144 Mass. 523; s. c., 19 Am. &. Eng. Corp. Cas. 548; 59 Am. Rep. 113; O'Donovan v. Wilkins, 24 Fla. 281; s. c., 23 Am. & Eng. Corp. Cas. 1; Polinsky v. People, 73 N. Y. 65; Health Department v. Knoll, 70 N. Y. 530; Johnson v. Simonton, 43 Cal. 242; *Ex parte* O'Leary, 65 Miss. 80; State v. Holcomb, 68 Iowa, 107; s. c., 56 Am. Rep. 852. A city may abolish wells in its streets as a sanitary measure, without compensation to lot owners. Ferrenbach v. Turner, 86 Mo. 416; s. c., 56 Am. Rep. 437. As to regulation of second-hand clothing dealers see Greensboro v. Ehrenreich, 80 Ala. 579; s. c., 60 Am. Rep. 130; 18 Am. & Eng. Corp. Cas. 483. In Indiana, in Walker v. Jameson, 140 Ind. 591, a different view is taken. In this case the court held an ordinance prohibiting owners or tenants of premises from hauling away garbage from their premises, requiring them to put it into receptacles convenient for removal by a public contractor, requiring such owners or tenants to pay a certain specified amount per pound, but not prohibiting their destruction of such garbage on the premises (taking care not to create a nuisance in so doing) to be valid under and authorized by the provisions of a statute empowering the common council to enact ordinances "to prevent the deposit of any unwholesome substances, either on private or public property; to compel its removal to designated points, and to require slops, garbage, ashes, waste or other material to be removed to designated points, or to require occupants of premises to place them conveniently for removal." In the course of the opinion Daily, J., says: "In view of the great weight of authorities, we are of the opinion that the contract and two persons a monopoly of the scavenger's business within the limits of the city. While monopolies of any ordinary legitimate business are odious, we have seen that monopolies are upheld when deemed necessary in executing a duty

ordinance assailed are both within the long settled and clearly recognized lines of public power, which is as broad as the power of taxation, and being simply a sanitary regulation, they cannot be considered as in the nature of confiscation or an attempt to create a monopoly. The provision for the removal of the garbage at the expense of the property holder is an extreme exercise of this power, but is an incident to its existence. It is a familiar rule that if the power is conferred upon a municipal corporation by the laws of the State, and the law is silent as to the mode of doing such act, the corporate authorities are necessarily clothed with a reasonable discretion to determine the manner in which such act shall be done; all the reasonable methods of executing such power are inferred. Lewisville Natural Gas Co. v. State, 135 Ind. 49." A conviction for removing garbage in an open wagon, contrary to an ordinance of the city of Detroit which provides that all garbage shall be collected in water tight closed carts, will be affirmed, as the restrictions imposed by the ordinance are reasonable, and authorized by the city charter, giving the council power to regulate the handling of garbage. People v. Gordon, 81 Mich. 806; s. c., 45 N. W. Rep. 658. As to regulations governing burials, see Bogert v. Indianapolis, 13 Ind. 134; Begpin v. Anderson, 28 Ind. 79; Town of Lake View v. Letz, 44 Ill. 181; Brick Presbyterian Church v. New York, 5 Cow. 538; *Ex parte* Keeney, 84 Cal. 304; s. c., 24 Pac. Rep. 34. "The validity of these ordinances was not seriously questioned in argument. That they are a lawful and proper exercise of the power 'to preserve the health of the city and to prevent and remove nuisances' does not admit of doubt. Such powers have been universally granted to municipal corporations in this country. In fact, the preservation of the health and safety of the inhabitants is one of the chief purposes of local government, and reasonable by-laws in relation thereto have always been sustained in England as within the incidental authority of such corporations. Under such a power a municipal corporation has the undoubted right to pass ordinances creating boards of health, appointing health commissioners, with other subordinate officials, regulating the removal of house dirt, night soil, refuse, offal and filth, by persons licensed to perform such work, and providing for the prohibition, abatement and suppression of whatever is intrinsically and inevitably a nuisance. * * * The subject-matter dealt with by these ordinances required the adoption of very stringent rules and regulations and such is the character of their provisions. Every person obtaining a license to perform this offensive but necessary work, is very properly subject to orders of the board of health in all matters pertaining to the manner of doing it." Boehm v.

incumbent on the city authorities or the legislature for the protection of the public health. It is sometimes a matter of great nicety and difficulty to determine whether a particular business or calling is in its nature so directly connected with the public welfare that the performance can only be safely intrusted to some one acting under public authority. So much of the business of the scavenger as consists in removing dead animals, it would seem under the authorities, may properly be regarded as a public function, for the discharge of which a monopoly may be created. But this ordinance goes further and gives to the scavengers the exclusive privilege also of cleaning privy vaults and cesspools, and of removing garbage not only from the streets, but from the private premises of the citizens. By its terms it would prohibit the owners from performing these services for themselves, or from employing any one else than the persons appointed. It not only makes a monopoly of the cleaning of vaults and cesspools, which are necessarily offensive to the senses, but it also includes the removal of garbage. * * * The business of a scavenger may not be nice or attractive, but the removal of garbage and filth is a necessary work, which has been ordinarily performed through any agency the party interested might select. If the term 'garbage' includes all refuse from the kitchen, then the waste which ordinarily is used, when practicable, to feed swine, can only be removed from the premises by the person appointed under this ordinance. Privies and cesspools are not ordinarily deemed nuisances *per se*. They are not so regarded by the statute under consideration. They may be permitted or not by the city authorities, according as the circumstances and surroundings of the particular place or portion of the city render it more or less dangerous to the health of the inhabitants. When constructed they are on private property, and in order to remove their contents, or to remove garbage not deposited in the streets or alleys, it would be necessary to

Mayor, etc. of Baltimore, 61 Md. 259, 263. See Vandine, Petr., 6 Pick. 187; s. c., 7 Am. Dec. 35; State v. Orr, 68 Conn. 101.

enter private premises. We are not cited to any case holding that a monopoly of this business may be created."[1] The rule relating to the power of municipal corporations to license and regulate the business of scavengers, is stated, as follows: "The power of the city council to license and regulate the business of scavengers is not now questioned, nor, in view of the express authority contained in the statute above quoted, can there be any question of their power to make and enforce all reasonable rules and regulations for the conduct of this disagreeable business. Under the authorities, and, especially, in view of the constitutional provision quoted, these regulations must have a way open to every person who will comply with the requirements of the ordinance to engage at least in so much of the business of scavengers as relates to entering on private property and removing filth and garbage therefrom. This ordinance clearly authorizes the restriction of this business to two persons, to be selected by the mayor, thereby providing for a monopoly. This the mayor and council had no power to do."[2]

§ **130. Municipal Grant of Market Franchise.**—The rule governing a municipal grant of an exclusive privilege in a market is not uniform. In the leading case in Michigan, the plaintiff contracted with the authorities of a village to build a market house, and to put it under their control for ten years, in consideration that they would pay over the rents thereof to him, appoint a person to superintend it, permit no other public market house to be erected or used, nor certain articles specified to be sold elsewhere in the village during the said ten years. In an action for breach of contract, it was held that the said contract was against public policy and void.[3] The opinion in this case is an able and logical discussion of the principle on which the decision is based. It merits very deliberate consideration.[4] In Iowa

[1] *In re* Lowe, 54 Kan. 757, 762; s. c., 39 Pac. Rep. 710.

[2] *In re* Lowe, 54 Kan. 757, 762; s. c., 39 Pac. Rep. 710.

[3] Gale v. Kalamazoo, 23 Mich. 344; s. c., 9 Am. Rep. 80.

[4] "In each of these particulars, this contract differs widely from

an opposite view has been upheld. It appears that the doctrine of the Michigan court was at one time accepted in Iowa, but at a later period it was overruled. In the case of Leclaire v. The City of Davenport, it was held that

one which should merely put the city in possession of a market house to be controlled and disposed of according as subsequent circumstances should appear to render desirable. Suppose,—in order to illustrate the difference,—that the village, after a year's experiment, should be satisfied that market limits and a market house were not desirable; that it was better that every person be allowed to sell where he could find customers, and to buy where he could procure what he needed, and that a manager or clerk of the market was unnecessary; in the one case the village might have upon its hands a building for which it had no need, but in the other, if this contract possesses any legal validity, it would have obligated itself for a term of years to continue a system which experience had demonstrated was not for the public good. Or, suppose the subsequent growth of the village should demonstrate that the location chosen for the market house was not the proper and suitable one, though the market itself was needful: in the one case, by the proper exercise of legislative authority, a new site might be chosen, but in the other, the village would not only have bound itself to continue a useless market, but would have precluded itself from the establishment of one which would accommodate the public needs. If a municipal corporation can preclude itself in this manner from establishing markets wherever they may be thought desirable, or from abolishing them when found undesirable, it must have the right also to agree that it will not open streets, or grade or pave such as are open, or introduce water for the supply of its citizens, except from some specified source, or buy fire engines of any other than some stipulated kind, or contract for any public work, except with persons named; and if it might do these things, it is easy to perceive that it might not be long before the incorporation itself, instead of being a convenience to its citizens, would have been used in various ways to compel them to submit to unreasonable inconveniences, and would itself constitute a public nuisance of the most serious and troublesome description. Individual citizens, looking only to the furtherance of their private interests, might, in various directions, engage it in permanent contracts which, while ostensibly for the public benefit, would impose obligations, precluding further improvements and depriving the town prospectively of those advantages and conveniences which the municipality was created to supply, and without which it is worthless. For if the village might bind itself to one market house for ten years, it might do so for all time to come; and if it might agree that improvements and conveniences of one class might be confined by contract to one-quarter of the town, a reckless or improvident board might agree with a greedy the council of the city of Davenport has power to authorize an individual to erect a building upon private property, and to lease or rent the rooms or stalls therein for a market; to declare such building a public market place, and to dictate the mode and manner of conducting the markets therein; to exact rates of rent that shall not operate as a restraint upon the trade of the city; and to protect the owner in the exclusive privilege of such market; overruling the City of Davenport v. Kelley.[1] The courts will not construe an ordinance making such a grant as void upon the ground of public policy unless such a construction is clearly deducible from its language.[2] This view has been upheld in Texas. In The City of Palestine v. Barnes, it was held that it is not beyond the authority of a city, acting under the general charter law, to contract for the erection of a market house with a person or corporation, conceding in consideration of such building and the use of a part of the same, exclusive market privileges in such city, with rights to lease stalls, collect rents, and an exemption from city taxes for a term of twenty-one years. That an ordinance for the protection of the exclusive market privileges so granted may not be rigidly enforced is not a violation of such contract authorizing its rescission.[3]

§ **131. The Subject Continued.**—It has been held that a legislature may grant an exclusive privilege of establishing and of carrying on the business of a slaughter house. In the leading case, before the Supreme Court of the United States, where it appeard that the legislature of Louisiana, on the 8th of March, 1869, passed an act, granting to a corporation, created by it, the exclusive right, for twenty-

or unscrupulous proprietor of town lots, that all improvements of every description should be so located or made as to conduce to his benefit, irrespective of the general good." Gale v. Kalamazoo, 23 Mich. 344, 352; s. c., 9 Am. St. Rep. 80.

[1] Davenport v. Kelley, 7 Iowa, 102.

[2] Le Claire v. Davenport, 13 Iowa, 210.

[3] City of Palestine v. Barnes, 50 Tex. 538. See also Harney v. St. Louis, 90 Mo. 214; Allegheny County v. McKeesport Diamond Market, 123 Pa. St. 164.

five years, to have and maintain slaughter houses, landings for cattle and yards for enclosing cattle intended for sale or slaughter within the parishes of Orleans, Jefferson and St. Bernard, in that State (a territory which it was said contained 1,154 square miles, including the city of New Orleans, and a population of between two and three hundred thousand people), and prohibiting all other persons from building, keeping or having slaughter houses, landings for cattle and yards for cattle intended for sale or slaughter, within those limits; and requiring that all cattle and other animals intended for sale or slaughter in that district should be brought to the yards and slaughter houses of the corporation; and authorizing the corporation to exact certain prescribed fees for the use of its wharves, and for each animal landed, and certain prescribed fees for each animal slaughtered, besides the head, feet, gore and entrails, except of swine.[1] It was held that this grant of exclusive right or

[1] Slaughter House Cases, 16 Wall. 36. "It cannot be denied that the statute under consideration is aptly framed to remove from the more densely populated part of the city, the noxious slaughter houses, and large and offensive collections of animals necessarily incident to the slaughtering business of a large city, and to locate them where the convenience, health and comfort of the people require they shall be located. And it must be conceded that the means adopted by the act for this purpose are appropriate, are stringent and effectual. But it is said that in creating a corporation for this purpose, and conferring upon it exclusive privileges,—privileges which it is said constitute a monopoly,—the legislature exceeded its power. If this statute had imposed on the city of New Orleans precisely the same duties, accompanied by the same privileges, which it has on the corporation which it created, it is believed that no question would have been raised as to its constitutionality. In that case the effect on the butchers in pursuit of their occupation and on the public would have been the same as it is now. Why cannot the legislature confer the same powers on another corporation, created for a lawful and useful public object, that it can on the municipal corporation already existing? That wherever a legislature has the right to accomplish a certain result, and that result is best attained by means of a corporation, it has the right to create such a corporation, and to endow it with the powers necessary to effect the desired and lawful purpose, seems hardly to admit of debate. The proposition is ably discussed and affirmed in the case of McCulloch v. State of Maryland (4 Wheat. 316), in relation to the power of Congress to organize the

privilege, guarded by proper limitation of the prices to be charged, and imposing the duty of providing ample conveniences, with permission to all owners of stock to land, and of all butchers to slaughter at those places, was a police

Bank of the United States to aid in the fiscal operations of the government. It can readily be seen that the interested vigilance of the corporation created by the Louisiana legislature will be more efficient in enforcing the limitation prescribed for the stock landing and slaughtering business for the good of the city, than the ordinary efforts of the officers of the law. Unless, therefore, it can be maintained that the exclusive privilege granted by the charter to the corporation is beyond the power of the legislature of Louisiana, there can be no just exception to the validity of the statute. And in this respect we are not able to see that these privileges are especially odious or objectionable. The duty imposed as a consideration for the privilege is well defined, and its enforcement well guarded." *Ibid.*, 64. "The business which the defendant carries on in his slaughter house, without the written consent and permission of the selectmen of Watertown, is in plain violation of the provisions of the St. 1871, chap. 167, which prohibit the use of any building for slaughtering cattle, etc., or for other noxious or offensive trades, without such consent, in any city or town containing more than four thousand inhabitants. * * * All rights to the use and enjoyment of property, secured by the Constitution of the United States, or of this commonwealth, are subject to regulation under that power known as the police power of the State, which, like the power of taxation, is necessary to its existence, and which is implied in the idea of free civil government. It is defined by Blackstone to be that power which concerns 'the due regulation and domestic order of the kingdom, whereby the individuals of the State, like members of a well-governed family, are bound to conform their general behavior to the rules of propriety, good neighborhood and good manners, and to be decent, industrious and inoffensive in their respective stations.' 4 Blackstone's Commentaries, 162. It has its foundation in that maxim of all well-ordered society, which requires everyone to use his own, so as not to injure the equal enjoyments of others having equal rights of property. Laws passed in the legitimate exercise of this power are not obnoxious to constitutional provisions, although in some measure interfering with private rights, merely because they do not provide compensation to the individual whose liberty is restrained. He is presumed to be rewarded by the common benefits secured. It differs from the right of eminent domain, which involves the appropriation of private property to public use, and requires, in its lawful exercise, pecuniary compensation for the loss inflicted on the owner. Familiar instances of its exercise are found in all quarantine and fire regulations; and it has been repeatedly recognized and variously applied in the decisions of this court. Commonwealth v.

regulation, for the health and comfort of the people (the statute locating them where health and comfort required) within the power of the State legislatures, unaffected by the Constitution of the United States previous to the adoption of the thirteenth and fourteenth articles of amendment. In the opinion in this case, the court said: "The wisdom of the monopoly, granted by the legislature, may be open to question, but it is difficult to see a justification for the assertion that the butchers are deprived of the right to labor in their occupation, or the people of their daily service in preparing food, or how this statute, with the duties and guards imposed upon the company, can be said to destroy the business of the butcher or seriously interfere with its pursuit. The power here exercised by the legislature of Louisiana is, in its essential nature, one which has been, up to the present period in the constitutional history of this country, always conceded to belong to the States, however it may be questioned in some of its details. 'Unwholesome trades, slaughter houses, operations offensive to the senses, the deposit of powder, the application of steam power to propel cars, the building with combustible materials and the burial

Alger, 7 Cush. 53; Fisher v. McGirr, 1 Gray, 1: Commonwealth v. Tewksbury, 11 Met. 55; Baker v. Boston, 12 Pick. 184; Vandine, Petitioner, 6 Pick. 187." Watertown v. Mayo, 109 Mass. 315, 317. See also Metropolitan Board v. Heister, 37 N. Y. 661. An ordinance of the city of New Orleans prescribed the place where slaughter houses must be located. Relying upon this designation of such place, complainant secured land within its limits, and proceeded thereon to erect houses and make other improvements for slaughtering purposes, when the city amended the ordinance by making it unlawful to maintain slaughter houses in the prescribed place, "except permission be granted by the council of the city of New Orleans," and proceeded to prevent complainant, who had no such permission, from carrying on his slaughtering business. *Held*, that the amendment is unconstitutional because it would, in effect, deny complainant the equal protection of the laws guaranteed by the XIVth Amendment of the United States Constitution. The prevention by the city of the complainant's exercise of his business is enjoinable in equity as being likely to do him irreparable injury for which damages at law would be no adequate compensation. Barthel v. City of New Orleans, 24 Fed. Rep. 563: S. C., 9 Am. & Eng. Corp. Cas. 509.

of the dead, may all,' says Chancellor Kent, 'be interdicted by law, in the midst of dense masses of population, on the general and rational principle, that every person ought so to use his property as not to injure his neighbors; and that private interests must be made subservient to the general interests of the community.' This is called the public power; and it is declared, by Chief Justice Shaw, that it is much easier to perceive and realize the existence and sources of it than to mark it boundaries, or prescribe limits to its exercise. The power is, and must be, from its very nature, incapable of any very exact definition or limitation. Upon it depends the security of social order, the life and health of the citizen, the comfort of an existence in a thickly populated community, the enjoyment of private and social life and the beneficial use of property. 'It extends,' says another eminent judge, 'to the protection of the lives, limbs, health, comfort and quiet of all persons, and the protection of all the property within the State; * * * and persons and property are subjected to all kinds of restraints and burdens in order to secure the general comfort, health and prosperity of the State. Of the perfect right of the legislature to do this no question ever was, or, upon acknowledged general principles, ever can be made, so far as natural persons are concerned.' The regulation of the place and the manner of conducting the slaughtering of animals, and the business of butchering within a city, and the inspection of the animals to be killed for meat, and of the meat afterwards, are among the most necessary and frequent exercises of the power. It is not, therefore, that we seek for a comprehensive definition, but rather look for the proper source of its exercise."[1]

§ 132. Legislative and Business Powers Distinguished.—There is a well established distinction between

[1] Slaughter House Cases, 16 Wall. 36, 61. See also 2 Kent's Commentaries, 340; Commonwealth v. Alger, 7 Cush. 84; Thorpe v. Rutland, etc. R. R. Co., 27 Vt. 149; Gibbons v. Ogden, 9 Wheat. 203; City of New York v. Miln, 11 Pet. 103; License Tax Cases, 5 Wall.

the ordinary legislative power of a municipal government and its capacity to transact business relating to the affairs of the city. There are cases in which the distinction is of practical and vital importance. In the case of The City of Valparaiso v. Gardner, the court said: "The important and controlling questions which confronts us here is as to the power of the municipal corporation to enter into the contract described in the pleadings. We have no doubt that the corporation had authority to contract for a supply of water for a period of twenty years, and that the contract cannot be overthrown solely on the ground that it is a surrender of legislative power. There is a distinction between powers of a legislative character and powers of a business nature. The power to execute a contract for goods, for houses, for gas, for water and the like, is neither a judicial nor a legislative power, but is purely a business power. The question is, however, so firmly settled by authority that we deem it unnecessary to further discuss it."[1]

471; United States v. DeWitt, 9 Wall. 41; Harmison v. City of Lewiston, 153 Ill. 313; s. c., 38 N. E. Rep. 628.

[1] City of Valparaiso v. Gardner, 97 Ind. 1, 4. See also City of Indianapolis v. Indianapolis, etc. Co., 66 Ind. 396. "The defendants are a corporation, and in that capacity are authorized by their charter, and by laws, to purchase and hold, sell and convey real estate, in the same manner as individuals. They are considered a person in law within the scope of their corporate powers, and are subject to the same liabilities, and entitled to the same remedies, for the violation of contracts, as natural persons. They are also clothed, as well by their charter as by subsequent statutes of the State, with legislative powers, and in the capacity of a local legislature are particularly charged with the care of the public morals and the public health within their own jurisdiction. In ascertaining their rights and liabilities as a corporation, or as an individual, we must not consider their legislative character. They had no power, as a party, to make a contract which should control or embarrass their legislative powers and duties. Their enactments, in their legislative capacity, are to have the same effect upon their individual acts as upon those of any other persons, or the public at large, and no other effect." Presbyterian Church v. City of New York, 5 Cow. 538, 540.

CHAPTER IX.

THE POWER TO REGULATE PRIVATE CORPORATIONS.

§ 133. Introductory.
134. Power to Regulate the Business of a Railway Company.
135. Power not Lost by Non-User.
136. Power to Act Through a Commission.
137. The Power to Assess Damages.
138. Power to Regulate Public Warehouses and Warehousing.
139. Effect of Statutory Regulations.
140. Power to Regulate the Operations of Telegraph Companies.
§ 141. Where Subject to Congressional Control.
142. Application of the Rule to the Telephone.
143. Power to Regulate in Case of Patented Property.
144. Application of the Rule to the Baking Business.
145. Application of the Rule to the Laundry Business.
146. Immunity from Governmental Control.
147. A Business *Juris Publici* Distinguished from a Business *Juris Privati*.

§ **133. Introduction.**—It is well established that private corporations, so far as the public has an interest in their business, are subject to governmental control. In certain branches of business, as that of a railroad corporation or telegraph company, a work of a public character is committed to a private corporation. During the earlier periods of English history, the highways were laid out and constructed directly by the government. The government assumed the direct and sole management and control of the public roads. The carrying on of this business was recognized as an essential function of the government. In the grant of a railroad franchise this prerogative is committed to a private corporation. But in carrying on a work of this character, through the instrumentality of a private corporation, the government does not surrender its power of control of the work. It may make such regulations, including the fixing of a maximum rate of transportation, or of freight, as may be demanded by the interests of the public, and it may do whatever else is required by the public welfare, unless its power in this regard has been surrendered in the grant of a charter. In the leading case of Munn v. Illinois, before the Supreme Court of the United States, the general doctrine relating to governmental control of private corporations is stated at length. It was held that under the powers inherent in every sovereignty, a government may regulate the conduct of its citizens toward each other, and, when necessary for the public good, the manner in which each shall use his own property. It has, in the exercise of these powers, been customary in England, from time immemorial, and in this country, from its first colonization, to regulate ferries, common carriers, hackmen, bakers, millers, wharfingers, innkeepers, etc., and, in so doing, to fix a maximum of charge to be made for services rendered, accommodations furnished and articles sold. Down to the time of the adoption of the fourteenth amendment of the Constitution of the United States, it was not supposed that statutes regulating the use, or even the price of the use, of private property, necessarily deprived an owner of his property without due process of law. Under some circumstances they may, but not under all. The amendment does not change the law in this particular; it simply prevents the States from doing that which will operate as such deprivation. When the owner of property devotes it to a use in which the public has an interest, he, in effect, grants to the public an interest in such use, and must, to the extent of that interest, submit to be controlled by the public, for the common good, as long as he maintains the use. He may withdraw his grant by discontinuing the use. Rights of property, and to a reasonable compensation for its use, created by the common law, cannot be taken away without due process; but the law itself, as a rule of conduct, may, unless constitutional limitations forbid, be changed at the will of the legislature. The great office of statutes is to remedy defects in the common law as they are developed, and to adapt it to the changes of time and circumstances. The limitation by legislative enactment of the rate of charge for services rendered in a public employment, or for the use of property in which the public has an interest, establishes no new principle in the law, but only gives a new effect to an old one.[1] In the case of Railroad Com-

[1] Munn v. Illinois, 94 U. S. 113. In the course of the opinion in this case, Chief Justice Waite uses this language: "This brings us to inquire as to the principles upon which this power of regulation rests, in order that we may determine what is within and what is without its operative effect. Looking, then, to the common law, from whence came the right which the constitution protects, we find that when private property is 'affected with a public interest, it ceases to be *juris privati* only.' This was said by Lord Chief Justice Hale, more than two hundred years ago, in his treatise, *De Portibus Maris*, 1 Harg. Law Tracts, 78, and has been accepted without objection as an essential element in the law of property ever since. Property does become clothed with a public interest when used in a manner to make it of public consequence, and affect the community at large. When, therefore, one devotes his property to a use in which the public has an interest, he, in effect, grants to the public an interest in that use, and must submit to be controlled by the public for the common good, to the extent of the interest he has thus created. He may withdraw his grant by discontinuing its use; but, so long as he maintains its use, he must submit to the control. Thus, as to ferries, Lord Hale says, in his treatise, *De Jure Maris*, 1 Harg. Law Tracts, 6, the king has 'a right of franchise or privilege that no man may set up a common ferry for all passengers without a prescription time out of mind, or a charter from the king. He may make a ferry for his own use, or the use of his family, but not for the common use of all the king's subjects passing that way, because it doth, in consequence, tend to a common charge, and is become a thing of public interest and use, and every man, for his passage, pays a toll, which is a common charge, and every ferry ought to be under a public regulation, viz.: that it give attendance at due times, keep a boat in due order, and take but a reasonable toll, for if he fail in these he is finable.' So if one owns the soil and landing places on both banks of a stream, he cannot use them for the purposes of a public ferry, except upon such terms and conditions as the body politic may from time to time impose, and this because the common good requires that all public ways shall be under the control of the public authorities. This privilege or prerogative of

pany v. Davis, the rule is expounded, as follows: "Upon the supposition that the legislature may take the property to the public use, it is next said that this taking is not legitimate, because the property is bestowed on private persons. It is true that this is a private corporation; its outlays and emoluments being individual property; but it is constituted

the king, who in this connection only represents and gives another name to the body politic, is not primarily for his profit, but for the protection of the people and the promotion of the general welfare. And, again, as to wharves and wharfingers, Lord Hale, in his treatise, *De Portibus Maris*, already cited, says: 'A man, for his own private advantage may, in a port or town, set up a wharf or crane, and may take what rates he and his customers can agree for cranage, wharfage, housellage, pesage, for he doth no more than is lawful for any man to do, viz.: makes the most of his own. * * * If the king or subject have a public wharf, unto which all persons that come to that port must come and unlade or lade their goods as for the purpose, because they are the wharfs only licensed by the queen, * * * or because there is no other wharf in that port, as it may fall out where a port is newly erected; in that case there cannot be taken arbitrary and excessive duties for cranage, wharfage, pesage, etc., neither can they be enhanced to an immoderate rate; but the duties must be reasonable and moderate, though settled by the king's license or charter. For now the wharf and crane and other conveniences are affected with a public interest, and they cease to be *juris privati* only, as if a man set out a street in new building on his own land, it is now no longer bare private interest, but is affected by a public interest.' This statement of the law by Lord Hale was cited with approbation, and acted upon by Lord Kenyon at the beginning of the present century, in Bolt v. Stennett, 8 T. R. 606. And the same has been held as to warehouses and warehousemen. In Aldnutt v. Inglis, 12 East, 527, decided in 1810, it appeared that the London Dock Company had built warehouses in which wines were taken in store at such rate of charge as the company and the owners might agree upon. Afterwards the company obtained authority, under the general warehousing act, to receive wines from importers before the duties upon the importation were paid; and the question was, whether they could charge arbitrary rates for such storage, or must be content with a reasonable compensation. Upon this point Lord Ellenborough said (p. 537): 'There is no doubt that the general principle is favored, both in law and justice, that every man may fix what price he pleases upon his own property, or the use of it; but if for a particular purpose the public have a right to resort to his premises and make use of them, and he have a monopoly in them for that purpose, if he will take the benefit of that monopoly, he must, as an equivalent, perform the duty attached to it on reasonable terms. The question then, is, whether, circumstanced as this to effect a public benefit by means of a road, and that is *publici juris*. In earlier times there seems to have been a necessity upon governments, or at least it was a settled policy with them, to effect everything of this sort by the direct and sole agency of the government. The highways were made by the public, and the use was accordingly free

company is, by the combination of the warehousing act with the act by which they were originally constituted, and with the actually existing state of things in the port of London, whereby they alone have the warehousing of these wines, they be not, according to the doctrine of Lord Hale, obliged to limit themselves to a reasonable compensation for such warehousing. And, according to him, whenever the accident of time casts upon a party the benefit of having a legal monopoly of landing goods in a public port, as where he is the owner of the only wharf authorized to receive goods which happens to be built in a port newly erected, he is confined to take reasonable compensation only for the use of the wharf.' And further on (p. 539): 'It is enough that there exists in the place and for the commodity in question, a virtual monopoly of the warehousing for this purpose, on which the principle of law attaches, as laid down by Lord Hale in the passage referred to [that from *De Portibus Maris* already quoted] which includes the good sense as well as the law on the subject,' and in the same case Le Blanche, J.. said (p. 541): 'Then admitting these warehouses to be private property, and that the company might discontinue the application of them, or that they might have made what terms they pleased in the first instance, yet having, as they now have, this monopoly, the question is, whether the warehouses be not private property clothed with a public right, and, if so, the principle of law attaches upon them. The privilege, then, of bonding these wines being at present confined by the act of Parliament to the company's warehouses, is it not the privilege of the public, and shall not that which is for the good of the public attach on the monopoly, that they shall not be bound to pay an arbitrary but reasonable rent? But upon this record the company resist having their demand for warehouse rent confined within any limit,' and though it does not follow that the rent in fact fixed by them is unreasonable, they do not choose to insist on its being reasonable for the purpose of raising the question. For this purpose, therefore, the question may be taken to be whether they may claim an unreasonable rent. But though this be private property yet the principle laid down by Lord Hale attaches upon it, that when private property is affected with a public interest it ceases to be *juris privati* only; and, in case of its dedication to such a purpose as this, the owners cannot take arbitrary and excessive duties, but the duties must be reasonable.' We have quoted thus largely the words of these eminent expounders of the common law, because, as we think, we find in them the principle which supports the legislation to the public. The government assumed the exclusive direction as well as authority, as if they chose to be seen and felt in everything, and would avoid even a remote connection between private interests and public institutions. An immense and beneficial revolution has been brought

we are now examining. Of Lord Hale, it was once said by a learned American judge: 'In England, even on rights of prerogative, they scan his words with as much care as if they had been found in Magna Charta; and the meaning, once ascertained, they do not trouble themselves to search any further.' 6 Cow. (N. Y.) 536, note." "The power of regulation in these cases does not turn upon the fact that the entities affected by the legislation are corporations deriving their existence from the State, but upon the fact that the corporations are common carriers and, therefore, subject to legislative control. The State in constituting a corporation may prescribe or limit its powers and reserve such control as it sees fit, and the body accepting the charter takes it subject to such limitations and reservations, and is bound by them. The considerations upon which a corporation holds its franchises are the duties and obligations imposed by the act of incorporation. But when a corporation is created it has the same rights and the same duties, within the scope marked out for its action, that a natural person has. Its property is secured to it by same constitutional guaranties, and in the management of its property and business is subject to regulation by the legislature to the same extent only as natural persons, except as the power may be extended by its charter. The mere fact of a corporate character does not extend the power of legislative regulation. For illustration, it could not be justly contended that the Act of 1888 would be a valid exercise of legislative power as to corporations organized for the purpose of elevating grain, although invalid as to private persons conducting the same business. The conceded power of legislation over common carriers is adverse to the claim that the police power does not in any case include the power to fix the price of the uses of private property, and of services connected with such use unless there is a legal monopoly, or special governmental privileges or protection has been bestowed. It is said that the control which the legislature is permitted to exercise over the business of common carriers is a survival of that class of legislation which in former times extended to the details of personal conduct and assumed to regulate the private affairs and business of men in the minutest particulars. This is true. But it has survived because it was entitled to survive. By reason of the changed conditions of society and a truer appreciation of the proper functions of government, many things have fallen out of the range of the police power as formerly recognized, the regulation of which by legislation would now be regarded as invading personal liberty. But society could not safely surrender the power to regulate by law the business of common carriers. Its value has about in modern times, by engaging individual enterprise, industry and economy, in the execution of public works of internal improvement. The general management has been left to individuals, whose private interests prompt them to conduct it beneficially to the public; but it is not entirely confided to them. From the nature of their undertaking and the character of the work, they are under sufficient responsibilities to insure the construction and preservation of the work, which is the great object of the government. The public interests and control are neither destroyed nor suspended. The control continues as far as it is consistent with the interests granted, and in all cases as far as may be necessary to the public use. The road is a highway, although the tolls may be private property, by force of the grant of the franchise to collect them. It is a common nuisance to allow it to become ruinous, or to obstruct it. The government may, upon sufficient cause, claim a forfeiture of the charter, or compel the execution and repairs of the road by those undertaking them by any means applicable to other persons charged with the like duties in respect to other highways. The difference is, that the corporation, in lieu of the sovereign, has the custody and property of the road, and the collection of the tolls in reimbursement of the cost of construction and remuneration for labor and risk of capital. As to the corporation, it is a franchise, like a ferry or any other. As to the public, it is a highway, and, in the strictest sense, *publici juris*. The land needed for its construction is taken by the public for the public

been infinitely increased by the condition of modern commerce, under which the carrying trade of the country is, to a great extent, absorbed by corporations, and, as a check upon the greed of these consolidated interests, the legislative power of regulation is demanded by imperative public interests. The same principle upon which the control of common carriers rest has enabled the State to regulate in the public interest the charges of telephone and telegraph companies, and to make the telephone and telegraph, those important agencies of commerce, subservient to the wants and necessities of society. These regulations in no way interfere with rational liberty—liberty regulated by law." Andrews, J., in People v. Budd, 117 N. Y. 1, 21.

use, and not merely for the private advantage of individuals. It is only vested in the company for the purposes of the act; that is, to make the road."[1]

§ 134. Power to Regulate the Business of a Railroad Company.—It is the rule, and it is well established, that the incorporation of a railway company by a legislature affects the property and employment of such company with a public use, and thus subjects the business of the company to legislative control. This is a result of the special privileges conferred by the charter of a railway company, and, in particular, of the authority, which it confers, to exercise the right of eminent domain to appropriate private property to its uses, and, also, of the obligation assumed by the company in the acceptance of its charter, to transport passengers and freight at reasonable rates. This regulation of rates extends to the prevention of extortion by unreasonable charges, and of any form of favoritism by improper discrimination.[2] In the recent leading case of The Georgia

[1] Railroad Company v. Davis, 2 Dev. & Bat. 451, 468.

[2] Georgia Banking Co. v. Smith, 128 U. S. 174, 179. The Chicago & Northwestern Railway Company was, by its charter and the charters of other companies consolidated with it, authorized "to demand and receive such sum or sums of money for the transportation of persons and property, and for the storage of property, as it shall deem reasonable." The constitution of Wisconsin in force, when the charters were granted, provides that all acts for the creation of corporations within the State "may be altered or repealed by the legislature at any time after their passage." *Held*, that the legislature had power to prescribe a maximum of charges to be made by said company for transporting persons or property within the State, or taken up outside the State and brought within it, or taken up inside and carried without. Certain Wisconsin railroad corporations were consolidated with others of Illinois on terms which, in effect, required that the consolidated company should, when operating in Wisconsin, be subject to its laws. *Held*, that Wisconsin can legislate for the company in that State precisely as it could have legislated for its own original companies, if no consolidation had taken place. The Act of Wisconsin, approved March 11, 1874, entitled "an act relating to railroads, express and telegraph companies, in the State of Wisconsin," is confined to State commerce, or such interstate commerce as directly affects the people of Wisconsin. Until Congress shall act in reference to the relations of this consolidated company to interstate commerce, the regulation of its fares,

Banking Company v. Smith, before the Supreme Court of the United States, the rule was stated by the court, as follows: "It has been adjudged by the court in numerous instances that the legislature of a State has the power to pre-

etc., so far as they are of domestic concern, is within the power of the State. Where property has been clothed with a public interest the legislature may fix a limit to that which shall in law be reasonable for its use. Peik v. Chicago, etc. Ry. Co., 94 U. S. 164. "Railroad corporations hold their property and exercise their functions for the public benefit and they are, therefore, subject to legislative control. The legislature which has created them may regulate the mode in which they shall transact their business, the price which they shall charge for the transportation of freight and passengers, the speed at which they may run their trains, and the way in which they may cross or run upon highways and turnpikes used for public travel. It may make all such regulations as are appropriate to protect the lives of persons carried upon railroads or passing upon highways crossed by railroads. All this is within the domain of legislative power, although the power to alter and amend the charters of such corporations has not been reserved. * * * Such legislation violates no contract, takes away no property, and interferes with no vested right. But the defendant was incorporated under chapter 917, of the Laws of 1869, by the consolidation of other railroad companies, and hence it took its charter under the constitution, and the laws subject to the right of the legislature to alter or amend it. Under this reserved power, the legislature may impose upon railroad corporations such additional restrictions and burdens as the public good requires. It may not confiscate property, but it cannot be doubted that it can do all that is required by the Act of 1874." People v. B. & O. R. R. Co., 70 N. Y. 569, 570. See also Albany Northern R. R. Co. v. Brownell, 24 N. Y. 345, 351. "The plaintiffs in error do not contend that it is always or generally unreasonable to restrict the rate for carrying each passenger to three cents a mile. They argue that it is so in this case by reason of the admitted fact that with the same traffic that their road has now, and charging for transportation at the rate of three cents per mile, the net yearly income will pay less than one and a half per cent. on the original cost of the road, and only a little more than two per cent. on the amount of its bonded debt. But there is no evidence whatever as to how much money the bonds cost, or as to the amount of the capital stock of the corporation as reorganized, or as to the sum paid for the road by that corporation or its trustees. It certainly cannot be presumed that the price paid at the sale under the decree of foreclosure equalled the original cost of the road, or the amount of the outstanding bonded debt. Without any proof of the sum invested by the reorganized corporation or its trustees, the court has no means, if it would under any circumstances have the scribe the charges of a railroad company for the carriage of persons and merchandise within its limits, in the absence of any provision in the charter of the company constituting a contract vesting in it authority over those matters, subject

power, of determining that the rate of three cents a mile fixed by the legislature is unreasonable. Still less does it appear that there has been any such confiscation as amounts to a taking of property without due process of law. It is equally clear that the plaintiffs in error have not been denied the equal protection of the laws. The legislature, in the exercise of its power of regulating fares and freights, may classify the railroads according to the amount of the business which they have done or appear likely to do. Whether the classification shall be according to the amount of passengers and freight carried, or of gross or net earnings during a previous year, or according to the simpler and more constant test of the length of the line of railroad, is a matter within the discretion of the legislature. If the same rule is applied to all railroads of the same class, there is no violation of the constitutional provision securing to all the equal protection of the laws." Dow v. Beidleman, 125 U. S. 680, 690. "We are thus brought to the second proposition relied on by the plaintiff in error, that as the act, when applied to the defendants' railroad, requires the company to do business at a positive loss, it therefore, constitutes a taking of defendants' property without due process of law. Whether, if the power of the State to fix and regulate the passenger and freight charges of a railroad has not been restricted by contract, there can be found, by judicial inquiry, a limit to such power in the practical effect its exercise may have on the earnings of the corporation, presents a question not free from difficulty. Given the case of a general law prescribing rates to all companies, can the courts inquire whether such rates are reasonable, and may they find that as to one company the prescribed rates permit it to do business at a profit, and as to another, whose facilities are inferior, or where expenditures are greater, the rates afford no profit? And will the fate of the law, as to its validity, depend in each case, on the result of such an inquiry? This court has declared, in several cases, that there is a remedy in the courts for relief against legislation establishing a tariff of rates which is so unreasonable as to practically destroy the value of property of companies engaged in the carrying business, and that especially may the courts of the United States treat such a question as a judicial one, and hold such acts of legislation to be in conflict with the Constitution of the United States as depriving the companies of their property without due process of law, and as depriving them of the equal protection of the laws." St. L. & San Francisco Ry. v. Gill, 156 U. S. 649, 657, citing Railroad Commission Cases, 116 U. S. 307, 331; Dow v. Beidleman, 125 U. S. 681; Chicago, Milwaukee, etc. Ry. v. Minnesota, 134 U. S. 418; Chicago & Grand Trunk Ry. v. Wellman, 143 U. S.

to the limitation that the carriage is not required without reward, or upon conditions amounting to the taking of property for public use without just compensation; and that what is done does not amount to a regulation of foreign or interstate commerce. The incorporation of the company, by which numerous parties are permitted to act as a single body for the purposes of its creation, or, as Chief Justice Marshall expresses it, by which 'the character and properties of individuality' are bestowed 'on a collective and changing body of men;' the grant to it of special privileges to carry out the object of its incorporation, particularly the authority to exercise the State's right of eminent domain, that it may appropriate needed property,—a right which can be exercised only for public purposes; and the obligation, assumed by the acceptance of its charter, to transport all persons and merchandise, upon like conditions and upon reasonable rates, affect the property and employment with a public use; and where property is thus affected, the business in which it is used is subject to legislative control. So long as the use continues, the power of regulation remains, and the regulation may extend not merely to provisions for the security of passengers and freight against accidents and for the convenience of the public, but also to prevent extortion by unreasonable charges and favoritism by unjust discriminations. This is not a new doctrine, but old doctrine, always asserted whenever property or business is, by reason of special privileges received from the government, the better to secure the purposes to which the property is dedicated or devoted, affected with a public use. There have been differences of opinion among the judges of this court in some cases as to the circumstances or conditions under which some kinds of property or business may be properly held to be thus affected, as in Munn v. Illinois,[1] but none as to the doctrine that when such use exists the business becomes subject to

339; Reagan v. Farmers' Loan & Trust Co., 154 U. S. 362.

[1] Munn v. Illinois, 94 U. S. 113, 126, 139, 146. See also Providence Bank v. Billings, 4 Pet. 514, 562.

legislative control in all respects necessary to protect the public against danger, injustice and oppression. In almost every case which has been before this court, where the power of the State to regulate the rates of charges of railroad companies for the transportation of persons and freight within its jurisdiction has been under consideration, the question discussed has not been the original power of the State over the subject; but whether that power had not been, by stipulations of the charter or other legislation amounting to a contract, surrendered to the company, or been in some manner qualified. It is only upon the latter point that there have been differences of opinion."[1] In an earlier case, before the same court, the rule is stated by Chief Justice Waite, as follows: "This company, in the transaction of its business, has the same rights and is subject to the same control as private individuals under the same circumstances. It must carry when called upon to do so, and can charge only a reasonable sum for the carriage. In the absence of any legislative regulation upon the subject, the courts must decide for it, as they do for private persons, when controversies arise, what is reasonable. But when the legislature steps in and prescribes a maximum of charge, it operates upon this corporation the same as it does upon individuals engaged in a similar business. It was within the power of the company to call upon the legislature to fix permanently this limit, and make it a part of the charter; and if it was refused to abstain from building the road and establishing the contemplated business. If that had been done, the charter might have presented a contract against future legislative interference. But it was not; and the

[1] Georgia Banking Co. v. Smith, 128 U. S. 174, 179. See also Chicago, etc. R. Co. v. Dey, 35 Fed. Rep. 866; Chicago, etc. R. Co. v. Becker, 35 Fed. Rep. 883; Reagan v. Farmers' Loan & Trust Co., 154 U. S. 362; s. c., 14 Sup. Ct. Rep. 1047; Stone v. Farmers' etc. Co., 116 U. S. 307; s. c., 6 Sup. Ct. Rep. 334; Carton v. Illinois Central R. Co., 59 Iowa, 148; s. c., 44 Am. Rep. 676; Wisconsin Cent. R. Co. v. Taylor Co., 52 Wis. 77; s. c., 1 Am. & Eng. R. Cas. 532; Sloan v. Mo. Pac. R. Co., 61 Mo. 24; Nelson v. Vt., etc. R. Co., 26 Vt. 717; Fitchburg, etc. R. Co. v. Grand Junction R., etc. Co., 4 Allen, 198.

company invested its capital, relying upon the good faith of the people and the wisdom and impartiality of legislators for protection against wrong under the form of legislative regulation."[1]

§ **135. Power not Lost by Non-User.**—The power of the government to regulate the business of railway companies is not acquired by exercise or assumption, and is not lost by any failure to exercise it. This power is inherent to the government; it existed from the beginning, and it will continue to the end. In the case of The Chicago, Burlington & Quincy Railroad Company v. Iowa, before the Supreme Court of the United States, the rule was stated by Mr. Chief Justice Waite, in delivering the opinion of the court, as follows: "It is a matter of no importance that the power of regulation now under consideration was not exercised for more than twenty years after this company was organized. A power of goverment, which actually exists, is not lost by non-user. A good government never puts forth its extraordinary powers, except under circumstances which require it. That government is the best which, while performing all its duties, interferes the least with the lawful pursuits of its people. In 1691, during the third year of the reign of William and Mary, Parliament provided for the regulation of the rates of charges by common carriers. This statute remained in force, with some amendment, until 1827, when it was repealed, and it has never been reenacted. No one supposes that the power to restore its provisions has been lost. A change of circumstances seemed to render such a regulation no longer necessary, and it was abandoned for the time. The power was not surrendered. That remained for future exercise, when required. So here the power of regulation existed from the beginning, but it was not exercised until in the judgment of the body politic the condition of things was such as to render it necessary for the common good. Neither does it affect the case that before the power was exercised the

[1] Chicago, etc. R. R. Co. v. Iowa, 94 U. S. 154, 161.

company had pledged its income as security for the payment of debts incurred, and had leased its road to a tenant that relied upon the earnings for the means of paying the agreed rent. The company could not grant or pledge more than it had to give. After the pledge and after the lease the property remained within the jurisdiction of the State, and continued subject to the same govermental powers that existed before."[1]

§ 136. **Power to Act Through a Commission.**—It is now well settled that the power which a legislature exercises, directly, in the regulation of the business of a railroad, so far as relates to the charges for freight, and the rates of fair for passengers, etc., may be exercised through a board of commissioners. The manner in which this power shall be exercised is within the discretion of the legislature. In the Railroad Commission Cases, before the Supreme Court of the United States, it was held that an act of incorporation, which confers upon the directors of a railroad company the power to make by-laws, rules and regulations touching the disposition and management of the company's property and all matters appertaining to its concerns, confers no right which is violated by the creation of a State railroad commission, charged with the general duty of preventing the exaction of unreasonable or discriminating rates upon transportation done within the limits of the State, and with the enforcement of reasonable police regulations for the comfort, convenience and safety of travelers and persons doing business with the company within the State. A railroad, forming a continuous line in two or more States, and owned and managed by a corporation whose corporate powers are derived from the legislature of each State in which the road is situated, is, as to the domestic traffic in each State, a corporation of that State, subject to State laws not in conflict with the Constitution of the United States. This court agrees with the Supreme Court of Mississippi, that a statute creating a commission, and charging it with the duty

[1] Chicago, etc. R. R. Co. v. Iowa, 94 U. S. 155, 162.

of supervising railroads, is not in conflict with the constitution of that State. The provisions of the statute of Mississippi. creating a railroad commission, are not so inconsistent and uncertain as to necessarily render the entire act void on its face.[1] In the case of The Charlotte, Columbia

[1] Railroad Commission Cases, 116 U. S. 307. See also Interstate Commerce Commission v. Brimson, 154 U. S. 447; s. c., 14 Sup. Ct. Rep. 1125; Fargo v. Michigan, 121 U. S. 230, 239; Interstate Commerce Commission v. Cincinnati, etc. Co., 64 Fed. Rep. 981; Kentucky, etc. Co. v. Louisville, etc. Co., 37 Fed. Rep. 567; Chicago, etc. Co. v. Dey, 35 Fed. Rep. 866, 875; Tilley v. Savannah, etc. R. R. Co., 5 Fed. Rep. 641; Reagan v. Farmers', etc. Co., 154 U. S. 362; s. c., 14 Sup. Ct. Rep. 1047. See also following cases upholding State commissions by State courts: State v. Chicago, etc. R. Co., 38 Minn. 281; s. c., 37 N. W. Rep. 782; State v. Fremont, etc. R. Co., 22 Neb. 313; s. c., 35 N. W. Rep. 118; 23 Neb. 113; 36 N. W. Rep. 308; Charlotte, etc. Co. v. Gibbs, 27 S. Car. 385; s. c., 31 Am. & Eng. R. Cas. 464; Stone v. Natchez, etc. R. Co., 62 Miss. 646; s. c., 21 Am. & Eng. R. Cas. 6; Georgia, etc. R. Co. v. Smith, 70 Ga. 694; s. c., 9 Am. & Eng. R. Cas. 385; Stone v. Yazoo, etc. R. Co., 62 Miss. 607; s. c., 21 Am. & Eng. R. Cas. 6; 52 Am. Rep. 193; Board of R. R. Commissioners v. Oregon R., etc. Co., 17 Ore. 65; s. c., 35 Am. & Eng. R. Cas. 542; Chicago, etc. R. Co. v. Jones, 149 Ill. 361; s. c., 37 N. E. Rep. 247; 24 L. R. A. 141; Richmond, etc. R. Co. v. Trammel, 53 Fed. Rep. 196. In C., B. & Q. R. R. Co. v. Jones, 149 Ill. 361, the supreme court discussing a phase of the Illinois R. R. Commission Law, at page 382, says: "It is argued that the provision of the statute making the schedule of the commissioners *prima facie* evidence that the rates therein fixed are reasonable maximum rates of charges, is unconstitutional and void, not only as depriving the carriers of their property without due process of law, but as infringing upon the right of trial by jury. We do not think that this objection should be sustained. In the first place the act does not deprive the railroad corporations of the right to have a judicial determination of the reasonableness of the rates, if they are not satisfied with the schedule made by the commission. The courts are open to them for a review of the acts of the commissioners in fixing the rates of charges. In the next place, the provision is an exercise by the legislature of its undoubted power to prescribe the rules of evidence. (2 Rice on Evidence, pages 806, 807; Commonwealth v. Williams, 6 Gray, 1; State v. Hurley, 54 Me. 562.) Such provisions are not unusual. Cases have arisen in this State under a statute making the fact of injury, caused by sparks from a locomotive passing along the road, *prima facie* evidence of negligence, and no question has ever been raised as to the validity of the statute. P., C. & St. L. Ry. Co. v. Campbell, 86 Ill. 443; St. L., V. & T. H. R. R. Co. v. Funk, 85 Ill. 460; T., W. & W. R. W. Co. v. Larmon, 67 Ill. 68; Rockford, R.

& Augusta Railroad Company v. Gibbes, the rule was stated by Mr. Justice Field, in delivering the opinion of the court, as follows: "The duties of the railroad commissioners, when properly discharged, must be in the highest

I. & St. L. R. R. v. Rogers, 62 Ill. 346; C. & A. R. R. Co. v. Clampit, 63 Ill. 95; C. & A. R. R. Co. v. Quaintance, 58 Ill. 389. Acts making tax deeds *prima facie* evidence of the regularity of proceedings antecedent to the deed have been held valid. 2 Rice on Evidence, page 607; Hand v. Ballou, 12 N. Y. 541; Delaplaine v. Cook, 7 Wis. 54; Allen v. Armstrong, 16 Iowa, 508; Wright v. Dunham, 13 Mich. 414; Gage v. Caraher, 125 Ill. 451. See also Williams v. German Mut. Fire Ins. Co., 68 Ill. 387. Cases referred to by counsel, which involve the validity of acts providing for references to auditors or referees and making the findings of the facts by them in their reports *prima facie* evidence of facts in trials before juries, will be found to be clearly distinguishable from the case at bar. The Supreme Court of Iowa has decided, that a provision making the schedule of the commission *prima facie* evidence of the reasonableness of the rates of charges, as contained in a statute of that State similar to said Act of 1873, was not obnoxious to the objections here urged against it, saying: 'The provision of the statute, that the rates fixed by the commissioners shall be regarded as reasonable, is not of an unusual character, and was enacted in the exercise of the undoubted power of the State to prescribe rules of evidence in all proceedings under the laws of the State. The law presumes the acts of officers of the State to be rightly done, and gives them faith accordingly. This rule is not unlike the provision of the statute complained of by the plaintiff.' B., C. R. & N. Ry. Co. v. Dey, 82 Iowa, 312. See also C. & A. R. R. Co. v. People, 67 Ill. 11." "Under section 8, of the statute, which the Supreme Court of Minnesota says is the only one which relates to the matter of the fixing by the commission of general schedules of rates, and which section, it says, fully and exclusively provides for that subject, and is complete in itself, all that the commission is required to do is, on the filing with it by a railroad company of copies of its schedules of charges to 'find' that any part thereof is in any respect unequal or unreasonable, and then it is authorized and directed to compel the company to change the same and adopt such charge as the commission 'shall declare to be equal and reasonable,' and to that end, it is required to inform the company in writing in what respect its charges are unequal and unreasonable. No hearing is provided for, no summons or notice to the company before the commission has found what it is to find, and declared what it is to declare, no opportunity provided for the company to introduce witnesses before the commission, in fact nothing which has the semblance of due process of law; and, although in the present case, it appears that, prior to the decision of the commision, the company appeared before it by its agent, and degree beneficial to the public, securing faithful service on the part of the railroad companies, and safety, convenience and comfort in the operation of their roads. That the State has the power to prescribe the regulations mentioned there can be no question. Though railroad corporations are private corporations, as distinguished from those created for municipal and governmental purposes, their uses are public. They are formed for the convenience of the public in the transportation of persons and merchandise, and are invested for that purpose with special privileges. They are allowed to exercise the State's right of eminent domain that they may appropriate for their uses the necessary property of others upon paying just compensation therefor, a right which can only be exercised for public purposes And they assume, by the acceptance of their charters, the obligations to transport all persons and merchandise upon like conditions and at reasonable rates; and they are authorized to charge reasonable compensation for the

the commission investigated the rates charged by the company for transporting milk, yet it does not appear what the character of the investigation was or how the result was arrived at. By the second section of the statute in question, it is provided that all charges made by a common carrier for the transportation of passengers or property shall be equal and reasonable. Under this provision the carrier has a right to make equal and reasonable charges for such transportation. In the present case, the return alleged that the rate of charge fixed by the commission was not equal or unreasonable, and the supreme court held that statute deprived the company of the right to show that judicially. The question of the reasonableness of a rate of charge for transportation by a railroad company, involving as it does the element of reasonableness, both as regards the company and as regards the public, is eminently a question for judicial investigation, requiring due process of law for its determination. If the company is deprived of the power of charging reasonable rates for the use of its property, and such deprivation takes place in the absence of an investigation by judicial machinery, it is deprived of the lawful use of its property, and thus, in substance and effect, of the property itself, without due process of law, and in violation of the Constitution of the United States; and in so far as it is thus deprived, while other persons are permitted to receive reasonable profits upon their invested capital, the company is deprived of the equal protection of the laws." Chicago, etc. Ry. Co. v. Minnesota, 134 U. S. 418, 458.

services they thus perform. Being the recipients of special privileges from the State, to be exercised in the interest of the public, and assuming the obligations thus mentioned, their business is deemed affected with a public use and to the extent of that use is subject to legislative regulation. That regulation may extend to all measures deemed essential not merely to secure the safety of passengers and freight, but to promote the convenience of the public in the transaction of business with them, and to prevent abuses by extortionate charges and unjust discrimination. It may embrace a general supervision of the operation of their roads, which may be exercised by direct legislation, commanding or forbidding, under severe penalties, the doing or omission of particular acts, or it may be exercised through commissioners specially appointed for that purpose. The mode or manner of regulation is a matter of legislative discretion. When exercised through commissioners, their services are for the benefit of the railroad corporations as well as of the public. Both are served by the required supervision over the roads and means of transportation, and there would seem to be no sound reason why the compensation of the commissioners in such case should not be met by the corporations, the operation of whose roads and the exercise of whose franchises are supervised."[1]

§ 137. **The Power to Assess Damages.**—It has been held that where a railway company neglects to erect or to maintain suitable fences, cattle guards, etc., as required by law, and, in consequence, an injury is inflicted upon cattle, horses or other domestic animals, the company shall be held liable for damages to double the sum of the injury occasioned by such neglect. The legislature has power to hold a railway corporation responsible for the gross negligence of its officers or agents. Fines and penalties may be assessed and enforced in addition to a proper satisfaction for the damage actually done. In the case of the Missouri Pacific Railway Company v. Humes, it was held by the

[1] Charlotte, etc. Co. v. Gibbes, 142 U. S. 386, 393.

Supreme Court of the United States, that a statute for a State, requiring every railroad corporation in the State to erect and maintain fences and cattle guards on the sides of its road, and, if it does not, making it liable in double the amount of damages occasioned thereby and done by its agents, cars or engines, to cattle or other animals on its road, does not deprive a railroad corporation, against which such double damages are recovered, of its property without due process of law, or deny it the equal protection of the laws, in violation of the fourteenth article of amendment of the Constitution of the United States. The legislature of a State may fix the amount of damages beyond compensation to be awarded to a party injured by the gross negligence of a railroad company to provide suitable fences and guards of its road, or prescribe the limit within which the jury, in assessing such damages, may exercise their discretion. The additional damages are by way of punishment to the company for its negligence; and it is not a valid objection that the sufferer instead of the State receives them. The mode in which fines and penalties shall be enforced, whether at the suit of a private party or at the suit of the public, and what disposition shall be made of the amounts collected, are matters of legislative discretion.[1]

[1] Missouri Pacific Ry Co. v. Humes, 115 U. S. 512. See also Illinois Cent. R. Co. v. Crider, 91 Tenn. 489; s. c., 56 Am. & Eng. R. Cas. 157; Jacksonville, etc. R. Co. v. Prior, 34 Fla. 271; Wortman v. Kleinschmidt, 12 Mont. 316; Burlington, etc. R. R. Co. v. Dey, 82 Iowa, 312; s. c., 45 Am. & Eng. R. Cas. 391; Gulf, etc. R. Co. v. Ellis, 87 Tex. 19; s. c., 61 Am. & Eng. R. Cas. 357; Peoria, etc. R. Co. v. Duggan, 109 Ill. 537; s. c., 20 Am. & Eng. R. Cas. 489; Perkins v. St. Louis, etc. Ry. Co., 103 Mo. 52; Dow v. Beidleman, 49 Ark. 455; s. c., 31 Am. & Eng. R. Cas. 14. "Again it is said that that portion of section 2 giving to the stock owner the right to recover attorney fees is unconstitutional. The proposition is thus stated by the learned counsel for plaintiff in error. 'Our State Constitution (Bill of Rights, §§ 1, 18), guarantees to all equity of rights, and remedies for injury by due course of law. We contend that a law which gives a successful plaintiff in a civil action his attorney's fees, and denies them to defendant, is a most gross violation of these constitutional provisions.' We do not think the contention of counsel can be sustained. While the law may be harsh and rigorous (and yet its rigor may have seemed to the legislature as essential to its

§ 138. **Power to Regulate Public Warehouses and Warehousing.**—The right of a State to regulate its domestic affairs is not affected by the limitation of the powers of Congress by the Constitution of the United States. And notwithstanding that warehouses are used by persons engaged in interstate commerce, the State legislature may prescribe and enforce regulations as a matter of State concern. In the leading case of Munn v. Illinois, it was held by the Supreme Court of the United States that where wharehouses are situated and their business is carried on exclusively within a State she may, as a matter of domestic concern, prescribe regulations for them, notwithstanding they are used as instruments by those engaged in

value. for, if a claimant for stock killed was compelled to pay his attorney's fees. it might well happen that in all cases the amount of his claim—such amounts, being uniformly small—would be consumed by attorney's fees, and so leave the claimant in no better condition than before), we see no reason to hold it beyond the power of the legislature. It is no uncommon thing for legislatures to provide, in cases where a failure to pay seems to imply more than ordinary wrong, that such failure should carry with it something in the nature of a penalty. Sometimes double or treble damages are given. The Iowa stock law gave double damages. Our trespass act provides for both double and treble damages. Ten per cent. may sometimes be added in the discretion of the court. Other illustrations might be suggested." Kansas Pacific Ry. Co. v. Mower, 16 Kan. 573, 582. *Contra:* See Chicago, etc. R. Co. v. Moss, 60 Miss. 641; South., etc. R. Co. v. Morris. 65 Ala. 193; Wilder v. Chicago, etc. R. Co., 70 Mich. 382; Schut v. Chicago, etc. R. R. Co., 70 Mich. 433; Ziegler v. South., etc. R. R. Co., 58 Ala. 594; Smith v. Louisville, etc. R. Co., 75 Ala. 449; State v. Divine, 98 N. Car. 778; Indiana, etc. R. Co. v. Gapen, 10 Ind. 292; Madison, etc. R. Co. v. Whiteneck, 8 Ind. 217; St. Louis, etc. R. R. Co. v. Williams, 49 Ark. 492. The rights of every individual must stand or fall by the same general law that governs every member of the body politic in the land, under similar circumstances, therefore a partial law which proposes to affect or destroy the rights of particular persons, or a particular class of persons, is not the law of the land. That part of the statute of June 22, 1867, which gives to the owner of live stock "double the value" of his property accidentally injured or destroyed on a railroad track is void. Atchison & Neb. R. R. Co. v. Baty, 6 Neb. 37. See generally: Calder v. Bull, 3 Dall. 386, 388; Bull v. Conroe, 13 Wis. 233, 244; Wally v. Kennedy, 2 Yerg. 554; Gordon v. Winchester, 12 Bush, 110; Durkee v. City of Janesville, 28 Wis. 464; Janes v. Reynolds. 2 Tex. 250; Van Zant v. Waddel, 2 Yerg. 260.

interstate, as well as in State, commerce; and until Congress acts in reference to their interstate relations, such regulations can be enforced, even though they may indirectly operate upon commerce beyond her immediate jurisdiction. The court does not hold that a case may not arise in which it may be found that a State has, under the form of regulating her own affairs, encroached upon the exclusive domain of Congress in respect to interstate commerce. The ninth section of the first article of the Constitution of the United States operates only as a limitation of the powers of Congress, and in no respect affects the States in the regulation of their domestic affairs. The act of the General Assembly of Illinois, entitled "an act to regulate public warehouses and the warehousing and inspection of grain, and to give effect to article 13 of the constitution of this State," is not repugnant to the Constitution of the United States.[1] In a recent case in New York, an act of

[1] Munn v. Illinois, 94 U. S. 113. This case, which is justly considered the leading case on this point, was rendered by a divided court. Its authority was repeatedly attacked and its soundness questioned. However, in the case of Budd v. New York, 143 U. S. 517, Justice Blatchford, in a most convincing decision commencing with these words: "The main question involved in these cases is whether this court will adhere to its decision in Munn v. Illinois, 94 U. S. 113," clearly and finally upholds the case. He cites in support of the late conclusion, among others: Spring Valley Water Works v. Schottler, 110 U. S. 347, 354; Davis v. State, 68 Ala. 58; Girard Storage Co. v. Southwork Co., 105 Pa. St. 248, 252; Brechbill v. Randall, 102 Ind. 528; Webster Telephone Case, 17 Neb. 126; Zanesville v. Gas Light Co., 47 Ohio, 1; Central Union Telephone Co. v. The State, 118 Ind. 194, 207; Chesapeake & Potomac Telephone Co. v. Balto. & Ohio Telegraph Co., 66 Md. 399, 414. "Since the formation of the State government, the sale of this great staple [tobacco] has been fostered and protected by legislation. The rights and duties of the warehouseman, the buyers and sellers and all the officers connected with the warehouses, have been defined by statute, and no commodity has received the same protection in the way of either general or special legislation. Nine-tenths of the tobacco is sold at auction, with the right unquestioned, until the present controversy, of all parties to enter the warehouses as buyers or as sellers, by their warehousemen as their agents, and competition left unrestricted, save the option on the part of the owner to approve or reject the bid. There is no provision, it is true, in any of the statutes now in force, or that existed prior to the law as we now

the legislature of New York provided that the maximum charge for elevating, receiving, weighing and discharging grain should not exceed five-eighths of one cent a bushel; and that, in the process of handling grain by means of float-

find it, compelling the producer of tobacco to take it to the warehouses in the city of Louisville, or to expose it for sale at public auction, but such warehouses have always been regulated by law for the benefit of the producer, as well as those who are the proprietors of these warehouses, and the latter have assumed an obligation to the public that exists so long as they continue public warehousemen. They have assumed a *quasi* public character under the protection of the law, and will not be allowed to exercise all the privileges that have heretofore belonged to warehousemen, and evade all the duties and responsibilities of their position by the passage of a resolution disclaiming that they are operating their houses in the capacity of warehousemen, but as commission merchants." Nash v. Page, 80 Ky. 539, 542. "The power of the legislature to regulate the charge for elevating grain where the business is carried on by individuals upon their own premises, depends upon the question whether the regulation falls within the scope of what is called the police power, which is but another name for that authority which reside in every sovereignty to pass all laws for the internal regulation and government of the State, necessary for the public welfare. The existence of this power is universally recognized. All property, all business, every private interest may be affected by it and be brought within its influence. Under this power the legislature regulates the uses of property, prescribes rules of personal conduct, and in numberless ways, through its pervading and ever present authority, supervises and controls the affairs of men in their relations to each other and the community at large to secure the mutual and equal rights of all, and promote the interests of society. It has limitations; it cannot be arbitrarily exercised so as to deprive the citizen of his liberty or property. But a statute does not work such a deprivation in the constitutional sense, simply because it imposes burdens or abridges freedom of action, or regulates occupations, or subjects individuals or property to restraints in matters indifferent, except as they affect public interests or the rights of others. Legislation under the police power infringes the constitutional guaranty only when it extends to subjects not within its scope and purview, as that power was defined and understood when the constitution was adopted. The generality of the terms employed by jurists and publicists in defining this power, while they show its breadth and the universality of its presence, nevertheless leave its boundaries and limitations indefinite, and impose upon the court the necessity and duty, as each case is presented, to determine whether the particular statute falls within or outside of its appropriate limits. * * * There are elements of publicity in the business of elevating grain which pecuing and stationary elevators, the lake vessels or propellers, the ocean vessels or steamships and canal boats should only be required to pay the actual cost of trimming or shovelling to the leg of the elevator when unloading, and trimming

liarly affect it with a public interest. They are found in the nature and extent of the business, its relation to the commerce of the State and country, and the practical monopoly enjoyed by those engaged in it. The extent of the business is shown by the facts to which we have referred. A large proportion of the surplus cereals of the country passes through the elevators at Buffalo and finds its way through the Erie canal and Hudson river to the seaboard at New York, from whence they are distributed to the markets of the world. The business of elevating grain is an incident to the business of transportation. The elevators are indispensable instrumentalities in the business of the common carrier. It is scarcely too much to say that, in a broad sense, the elevators perform the work of carriers. They are located upon or adjacent to the waters of the State, and transfer from the lake vessels to the canal boats, or from the canal boats to the ocean vessels, the cargoes of grain, and thereby perform an essential service in transportation. It is by means of the elevators that transportation of grain by water from the upper lakes to the seaboard is rendered possible. It needs no argument to show that the business of elevating grain has a vital relation to commerce in one of its most important aspects. Every excessive charge made in the course of the transportation of grain is a tax on commerce, and the public have a deep interest that no exorbitant charges shall be exacted at any point upon the business of transportation." People v. Budd, 117 N. Y. 1, 22. "The defendants' business [stock yards] is of recent origin. Their duties and liabilities are wholly undefined, except as they may be deduced from the application of well-established legal principles to other corporations in analogous cases. No case was cited on the argument, and none is known to exist, in which the duties of a body corporate, like the defendants', have been the subject of judicial consideration. The business of the defendants has no exact counterpart or model in any of the established instruments of commerce, or agencies used by the public in the transaction of business. It bears a closer resemblance to the business carried on by warehousemen than to any other business known to the law. Except in the character of the property, which is the subject of the bailment, the business of the defendants corresponds, in many respects, with that of the warehouseman. That is the only business which can, in my judgment, be safely used, by way of analogy, for the purpose of ascertaining whether or not, according to established principles of general law, the defendants are subject to the duty which the complainants ask the court to compel them to perform. There can be no doubt, I think, that a warehouseman is not required, by any general rule of law, to receive cargo when loading, it was held that the act was a legitimate exercise of the police power of the State over a business affected with a public interest, and did not violate the Constitution of the United States and was valid.[1]

§ **139. Effect of Statutory Regulations.**—The business of conducting a warehouse for the accommodation of the public is subject to legislative control. It is subject not only to any statutory regulations that may have been in force at the time that the business was commenced, but, as well, to any changes that may subsequently be made in the statute by which they are controlled. In Munn v. Illinois, the rule is stated by the court, as follows: "It matters not in this case that these plaintiffs in error had built their warehouses and established their business before the regulations complained of were adopted. What they did was from the beginning subject to the power of the body politic to require them to conform to such regulations as might be established by the proper authorities for the common good. They entered upon their business and provided themselves with the means to carry it on subject to this condition. If they did not wish to submit themselves to such interference, they should not have clothed the public with an interest in their concerns. The same principle applies to them that does to the proprietor of a hackney carriage, and as to him it has never been supposed that he was exempt from regulating statutes or ordinances, because he had purchased his horses and carriage and established his business before the

goods on storage against his will. In Addison on Contracts, p. 630, it is said: 'A man cannot be made a depositary without his consent; he cannot have the possession of another man's property, with its accompanying duties and responsibilities, forced upon him against his will.' This must be so from the very nature of such transactions, for all bailments, not made by force of statutory regulation, rest in contract, and no contract can exist without consent, express or implied. Warehouses for the storage of grain must, however, since the decision of the Elevator Cases, reported under the title of Munn v. Illinois, 94 U. S. 113, be regarded as so far public in their nature as to be subject to legislative control." Delaware, etc. R. R. Co. v. Central Stock Yards Co., 45 N. J. Eq. 50, 60.

[1] Budd v. New York, 143 U. S. 517.

statute or ordinance was adopted. It is insisted, however, that the owner of property is entitled to reasonable compensation for its use, even though it be clothed with a public interest, and that what is reasonable is a judicial and not a legislative question. As has already been shown, the practice has been otherwise. In countries where the common law prevails, it has been customary from time immemorial for the legislature to declare what shall be a reasonable compensation, under such circumstances, or, perhaps, more properly speaking, to fix a maximum beyond which any charge made would be unreasonable. Undoubtedly, in mere private contracts, relating to matters in which the public has no interest, what is reasonable must be ascertained judicially. But this is because the legislature has no control over such a contract. So, too, in matters which do affect the public interest, and as to which legislative control may be exercised, if there are no statutory regulations upon the subject, the courts must determine what is reasonable. The controlling fact is the power to regulate at all. If that exists, the right to establish the maximum of charge, as one of the means of regulation, is implied. In fact, the common law rule, which requires the charge to be reasonable, is itself a regulation as to price. Without it the owner could make his rates at will and compel the public to yield to his terms, or forego the use. But a mere common law regulation of trade or business may be changed by statute. A person has no property, no vested interest in any rule of the common law. That is only one of the forms of municipal law, and is no more sacred than any other. Rights of property which have been enacted by the common law cannot be taken away without due process; but the law itself, as a rule of conduct, may be changed at the will, or even at the whim, of the legislature, unless prevented by constitutional limitations. Indeed, the great office of statutes is to remedy defects in the common law as they are developed, and to adapt it to the changes of time and circumstances. To limit the rate of charge for services rendered in a public employment, or for the use of property in which the public has an interest, is only changing a regulation which existed before. It establishes no new principle in the law, but only gives a new effect to an old one. We know that this is a power which may be abused; but that is no argument against its existence. For protection against abuses by legislatures, the people must resort to the polls, not to the courts."[1]

§ 140. **Power to Regulate the Operations of Telegraph Companies.**—The legal *status* and responsibility of telegraph companies are held to be essentially analogous to that of common carriers. They are not strictly common carriers, and their responsibilities are not identical with those of common carriers. This follows from the diverse character of the two forms of business. But as public servants, and as engaged in branches of business in some respects similar, they are subject to responsibilities of a kindred nature. In a case in New York the court said: "Although telegraph companies are not, strictly speaking, common carriers for the reason that they do not have tangible possession of goods which can be stolen or destroyed, yet from the public nature of their employment, the important matters confided wholly to their care, and the skill and fidelity required in the proper performance of their duties, their legal characteristics become so analogous to those of carriers that the law must consider them as such, subject only to such modifications as the peculiar nature of their business renders absolutely necessary. In this view, no reason appears why a telegraph company should be permitted to limit its liability in any other manner than a common carrier."[2] In a leading case in Vermont the relation

[1] Munn v. Illinois, 94 U. S. 113, 133.

[2] Baldwin v. U. S. Tel. Co., 1 Lans. 125, 136. See generally, on State control: Connell v. Western Union Tel. Co., 108 Mo. 459; s. c., 39 Am. & Eng. Corp. Cas. 594; People v. Squire, 145 U. S. 175, affirming 107 N. Y. 593; s. c., 1 Am. St. Rep. 894; American Union Tel. Co. v. Western Union Tel. Co., 67 Ala. 32; s. c., 42 Am. Rep. 90; Mut. Union Tel. Co. v. Chicago, 16 Fed. Rep. 309; Western Union Tel. Co. v. New York, 38 Fed. Rep. 552; Western Union Tel. Co. v. Pendleton, 122 U. S. 347; s. c., 18 Am. & Eng. Corp. Cas. 18. In

of telegraph companies to common carriers, or the analogy between them, is stated by the court, as follows: "Although there may be no analogy between the business of telegraph companies and that of public carriers of passengers for

this last case. Field, J., says: "The subjects upon which the State may act are almost infinite, yet in its regulations with respect to all of them there is this necessary limitation,—that the State does not thereby encroach upon the free exercise of the power vested in Congress by the constitution. Within that limitation it may undoubtedly make all necessary provisions with respect to the buildings, poles and wires of telegraph companies in its jurisdiction, which the comfort and convenience of the community may require." "In the exercise of its rights under the assumed grant and contract. this corporation was subject to the regulation and control of the legislature. By giving the franchise the State did not abdicate its power over the public streets, nor in any way curtail its police power to be exercised for the general welfare of the people, nor did the State absolve itself from its primary duty to maintain the streets and highways of the State in a safe and proper condition for public travel and other necessary street and highway purposes. The grant, if any, was made in reference to the streets, and their maintenance and regulation forever as streets. The State could at all times regulate the size and location of the poles, the height of the wires from the surface of the ground, and their location in the streets, and when the poles and wires became a serious obstruction and nuisance in the streets from any cause, it could take such action and make such provisions by law as were needful to remove the nuisance and restore the utility of the streets for public purposes. The right of the plaintiff to maintain and operate its wires in the streets could certainly be no greater than the right of railroads which, by public authority, occupy the streets and highways of the State. The State, in the exercise of its police power, and the regulating control which it has over corporations created by its authority, may exercise a general supervision over such corporations. It may prescribe the location of the tracks, the size and character of the rails, the precautions which shall be taken for the protection of the public, and the character and style of highway crossings; and no one has ever questioned that it may do whatever is necessary and proper for the public welfare in the control and regulation of the franchises which such corporations have obtained by statutory authority." American Rapid Telegraph Co. v. Hess, 125 N. Y. 641, 646. Section 12 of the act relating to telegraph companies makes such company "liable for the non-delivery of dispatches intrusted to its care, and for all mistakes in transmitting messages made by any person in its employ," etc., and provides that it shall not be exempted from any such liability by reason of any "clause, condition or agreement contained in its printed blanks." Such require-hire, yet we regard their legal *status* as practically the same. Both are engaged in a business of a public nature; both must serve all who come; neither are insurers nor liable as such, but both are liable for negligence."[1] In a recent case in Virginia it was held that telegraph companies are not public carriers, in the strict sense of the term, yet, on account of the public nature of their employment, they have in many cases been held to a very similar responsibility. The obligation of such companies, upon payment of the usual charges to transmit faithfully and promptly all messages presented for transmission, rests in Virginia not merely on contract, but is imposed by statute. Such companies may make their own regulations for the conduct of their business, but they must be reasonable and not in conflict with any liability imposed by law, and they cannot relieve themselves from liability for the improper or negli-

ments are reasonable, and are binding on all telegraph companies in the State. Kemp v. Western Union Tel. Co., 28 Neb. 661. A city ordinance requiring telegraph companies engaged in business within the State in which such city is located, and which have a place of business in such city, to pay a license tax, is valid, in that it can be enforced without interfering with or violating any rights such companies may have under the interstate commerce law. Moore v. City of Eufaula, 97 Ala. 670; s. c., 11 So. Rep. 921. "This well-founded rule of the joint liability of connecting carriers, upon the contract made at the terminus of the route with the common agent, who receives pay for the whole distance, applies with equal force and good sense to telegraph as to railroad companies. Judge Daly, in his elaborate opinion in the case of De Rutte v. N. Y., Albany & Buffalo Tel. Co., says: 'Where a message is to be transmitted through many connecting lines, it is a matter of convenience to be able to pay the entire charge either at the place from which it is sent, or at the place where it is received; and it is the interest of companies to make arrangements whereby, upon the payment to them of the whole charge, a message may be sent the entire length of telegraphic communication. *It is to be assumed that this is the case*, where a telegraph company is paid for the transmission of a message to a place beyond its own lines, with which it is in connection by the agency of other companies. For their own benefit, telegraph companies should arrange matters of this kind *inter se, and should be taken, each to have made the other their agents.*'" Baldwin v. U. S. Tel. Co., 1 Lans. 125, 132.

[1] Gillis v. Telegraph Co., 61 Vt. 461, 464.

gent conduct of their servants or defective character of their instruments.[1]

§ **141. Where Subject to Congressional Control.**— Under its power to regulate the commercial relations of the States, Congress has control of the business of telegraph companies, so far as relates to their interstate communications. Any statutory regulations of the different States that are adapted to interfere with the interstate operations of telegraph companies will be set aside, as in conflict with the Constitution of the United States. In the leading case of the Pensacola Telegraph Company v. The Western Union Telegraph Company, before the Supreme Court of the United States, it was held that the powers conferred upon Congress to regulate commerce with foreign nations and among the several States, and to establish post offices and post roads, are not confined to the instrumentalities of commerce, or of the postal service known or in use when the constitution was adopted, but keep pace with the progress of the country and adapt themselves to the new developments of time and circumstances. They were intended for the government of the business to which they relate, at all times and under all circumstances, and it is not only the right, but the duty, of Congress to take care that intercourse among the States and the transmission of intelligence are not obstructed or unnecessarily incumbered by State legislation. The Act of Congress, entitled an "act to aid in the construction of telegraph lines, and to secure to the government the use of the same for postal, military and other purposes," so far as it declares that the erection of telegraph lines shall, as against State interference, be free to all who accept its terms and conditions, and that a telegraph company of one State shall not, after accepting them, be excluded by another State from prosecuting its business within her jurisdiction, is a legitimate regulation of commerce and intercourse among the States, and is appropriate legislation to execute the powers of Congress over

[1] Western Union Tel. Co. v. Reynolds, 77 Va. 173.

the postal service. Nor is it limited in its operation to such military and post roads as are upon the public domain. The statute of Florida, so far as it grants to the Pensacola Telegraph Company the exclusive right of establishing and maintaining lines of electric telegraph as therein specified, is in conflict with that act, and, therefore, inoperative against a corporation of another State entitled to the privileges which that act confers. Without deciding whether, in the absence of that act, the legislation of Florida of 1874 would have been sufficient to authorize a foreign corporation to construct and operate a telegraph line within the counties of Escambia and Santa Rosa in that State, the court hold that a telegraph company of another State, which has secured a right of way by private arrangement with the owner of the land and duly accepted the restrictions and obligations required by that act, cannot be excluded by the Pensacola Telegraph Company.[1] This case

[1] Pensacola Tel. Co. v. Western, etc. Tel. Co., 96 U. S. 1. The statute of the State of Indiana, §§ 4176, 4178, Rev. Stat. Ind. 1881, which require telegraph companies to deliver dispatches by messenger to the persons to whom the same are addressed, or to their agents, provided they reside within one mile of the telegraphic station, or within the town or city in which such station is, are in conflict with the clause of the Constitution of the United States, which vests in Congress the power to regulate commerce among the States, in so far as they attempt to regulate the delivery of such dispatches at places situated in other States. The authority of Congress over the subject of commerce by telegraph with foreign countries or among the States being supreme, no State can impose an impediment to its freedom by attempting to regulate he delivery in other States of messages received within its own borders. The reserved police power of a State under the constitution, although difficult to define, does not extend to the regulation of the delivery at points without the State of telegraphic messages received within the State; but the State may, within the reservation that it does not encroach upon the free exercise of the powers vested in Congress, make all necessary provisions in respect of the buildings, poles and wires of telegraph companies within its jurisdiction, which the comfort and convenience of the community may require. W. U. Tel. Co. v. Pendleton, 122 U. S. 347. Where a telegraph company is doing the business of transmitting messages between different States and has accepted and is acting under the telegraph law passed by Congress, July 24th, 1866, no State within which it sees fit to establish an office can impose

was decided in 1877, but the decision is the law of the present. In the opinion the court, Mr. Chief Justice Waite, said: "The electric telegraph marks an epoch in the progress of time. In little more than a quarter of a century

upon it a license tax or require it to take out a license for the transaction of such business. Telegraphic communications are commerce, as well as in the nature of postal service, and if carried on between different States, they are interstate commerce, and within the power of regulation conferred upon Congress, free from the control of State regulations, except such as are of a police character; and any State regulations by way of tax on the occupation or business, or requiring a license to transact such business, are unconstitutional and void. Leloup v. Port of Mobile, 127 U. S. 640. See also Telegraph Co. v. Texas, 105 U. S. 460. "Is telegraphy any branch of commercial intercourse? To ask the question is to answer it. So interwoven has the custom of communication by telegraph become with trade and traffic, that to separate it without serious disturbance of vast trade relations and financial transactions, would be a task as difficult as to cut the pound of flesh without a single drop of blood. It is the life and soul of civilized commercial transactions; many of the most important are daily ruled by telegraph. The banker, the merchant, the farmer, the broker, all traders depend upon the telegraph for speedy information and means of intercourse in their various business and traffic. If the ship that carries the cargo comes within the constitutional power of Congress to regulate commerce, as it confessedly does, as a means of commercial intercourse, certainly the instrumentality through which is directed the lading, sailing and unlading of the ship, the purchase and sale of the cargo, and all the *minutiæ* of the venture and the voyage, is equally a means, only of a higher and more advanced grade. * * * Does the Act of Congress attempt to regulate this branch of commercial intercourse? On the part of appellant it is claimed not, because no specific rules are prescribed for its exercise. The act gives to any telegraph company the right to construct, maintain and operate telegraph lines on the public lands of the United States, and along the post and military roads, upon evidence of acceptance of its terms under specified restrictions, and for certain compensation, which is the priority of government messages, and the privilege of purchase, at option, by the United States, at any time after the expiration of five years. To that extent, then, there is regulation; the right is given by rule, and limited by rule, certainly as much regulated as the licensing or registering of vessels." Western Union Tel. Co. v. Atlantic & Pacific States Tel. Co., 5 Nev. 102, 109. See as to power of Congress to amend and alter franchises, United States v. Union Pacific Railway, 160 U. S. 1. A franchise to operate a telegraph line over any part of the United States' domain or any military or post road, acquired under Act of Congress, July 24. 1866, it has changed the habits of business, and become one of the necessities of commerce. It is indispensable as a means of intercommunication, but especially is it so in commercial transactions. The statistics of the business before the recent reduction in rates show that more than eighty per cent. of all the messages sent by telegraph related to commerce. Goods are sold and money paid upon telegraphic orders. Contracts are made by telegraphic correspondence, cargoes secured and the movement of ships directed. The telegraphic announcement of the markets abroad regulates prices at home, and a prudent merchant rarely enters upon an important transaction without using the telegraph freely to secure information. It is not only important to the people, but to the government. By means of it the heads of the departments in Washington are kept in close communication with all their various agencies at home and abroad, and can know at almost any hour, by inquiry, what is transpiring anywhere that affects the interest they have in charge. Under such circumstances it cannot for a moment be doubted that this powerful agency of commerce and intercommunication comes within the controlling power of Con-

when accompanied by occupancy thereunder, confers rights superior to those of a company subsequently constructing a line for transmitting electricity both for lighting purposes and for propelling machinery, and the latter line must be constructed so as not to interfere with the former. Western Union Tel. Co. v. Los Angeles Electric Co., 76 Fed. Rep. 178. A State privilege tax of a certain amount per mile of wires operated within the State imposed on all telegraph companies therein operating in lieu of all other State, county and municipal taxes and amounting to less than the ordinary *ad valorem* tax, is substantially a mere tax on property, to which a foreign corporation operating within the State is subject, notwithstanding it is engaged in interstate commerce, and has accepted the rights conferred on telegraph companies by the statutes. Postal Telegraph Cable Co. v. Adams, 155 U. S. 688; s. c., 15 Sup. Ct. Rep. 268. Under Rev. Stat. 5263, authorizing telegraph companies to operate lines "through and over any portion of the public domain, and over and along any of the military or post roads," a telegraph company may erect a line on a railroad right of way granted by Congress over public lands, that is declared to be a military and post road. Mercantile Trust Co. v. Atlantic & Pacific R. Co., 63 Fed. Rep. 513.

gress, certainly as against hostile State legislation. In fact from the beginning it seems to have been assumed that Congress might aid in developing the system; for the first telegraph line of any considerable extent ever erected was built between Washington and Baltimore, only a little more than thirty years ago, with money appropriated by Congress for that purpose, and large donations of land and money have since been made to aid in the construction of other lines. It is not necessary now to inquire whether Congress may assume the telegraph as part of the postal service, and exclude all others from its use The present case is satisfied, if we find that Congress has power, by appropriate legislation, to prevent the States from placing obstructions in the way of its usefulness."[1]

§ **142. Application of the Rule to the Telephone.**—It is well established that the rule relating to the power of the government to regulate the business of corporations affected with a public use, as expounded in the preceding sections, applies to the operation of the telephone. Though the decisions are recent and not numerous, they are all to that effect. It is held that the proprietors of a public telephone, like a corporation which operates a telegraph line, is a common carrier of news, and that, as such, it is subject to the rules by which the business of a telegraph company is governed. Though it is a recent invention, it is so nearly allied to the telegraph in the objects for which it is established and in the mode of its operations, that there is an obvious fitness in subjecting the telephone business to the same rules of governmental control as those to which the older institution has been subject. In the Webster Telephone case, before the Supreme Court of Nebraska,—the leading case relating to the subject,—the rule is stated by the court, as follows: "That the telephone by the necessities of commerce and public use has become a public servant, a factor in the commerce of the nation and of a great portion of the civilized world, cannot be questioned. It is to all in-

[1] Pensacola Tel. Co. v. Western Union Tel. Co., 96 U. S. 1, 9.

tents and purposes a part of the telegraphic system of the country, and, in so far as it has been introduced for public use and has been undertaken by the respondent, so far should the respondent be held to the same obligations as the telegraph and other public servants. It has assumed the responsibilities of a common carrier of news. Its wires and poles line our public streets and thoroughfares. It has, and must be held to have taken its place by the side of the telegraph as such common carrier. The views herein expressed are not new, similar questions have arisen in and have been frequently discussed and decided by the courts, and no statute has been deemed necessary to aid the courts in holding that when a person or company undertakes to supply a demand which is 'affected with a public interest,' it must supply all alike who are like situated, and not discriminate in favor of nor against any. This reasoning is not met by saying that the rules laid down by the courts as applicable to railroads, express companies, telegraphs and other older servants of the public, do not apply to telephones, for the reason that they are of recent invention and were not thought of at the time the decisions were made, and hence are not affected by them, and can only be reached by legislation. The principles established and declared by the courts, and which were and are demanded by the highest material interests of the country, are not confined to the instrumentalities of commerce, nor to the particular kinds of service known or in use at the time when those principles were enunciated, 'but they keep pace with the progress of the country, and adapt themselves to the new developments of time and circumstances. They extend from the horse with its rider to the stage coach, from the sailing vessel to the steamboat, from the coach and the steamboat to the railroad, and from the railroad to the telegraph,' and from the telegraph to the telephone, 'as these new agencies are successively brought into use to meet the demands of increasing population and wealth. They were intended for the government of the business to which they relate, at all times and under all circumstances.'''[1] In a recent case in Indiana, it was held that the State has a right to prescribe

[1] Webster Telephone Case, 17 Neb. 126, 134. See also Central Union Telephone Co. v. State, 123 Ind. 113; State v. Bell Telephone Co., 36 Ohio St. 296; s. c., 38 Am. Rep. 584; Bell Teleph. Co. v. Com. (Pa.). 3 Atl. Rep. 825; Central Dist. Teleph. Co. v. Com., 114 Pa. St. 592; Commercial Union Tel. Co. v. New England Teleph. Co., 61 Vt. 241; s. c., 15 Am. St. Rep. 893; State v. Bell Teleph. Co., 23 Fed. Rep. 539; s. c., 8 Am. & Eng. Corp. Cas. 7; Louisville Transfer Co. v. American District Telephone Co., 24 Alb. L. J. 283; People v. Hudson River Telephone Co., 19 Abb. N. Cas. 466; Balto. & Ohio Tel. Co. v. Bell Telephone Co., 24 Am. L. Reg. 573; Johnson v. State, 113 Ind. 143; Bradley v. Southern New England Telephone Co., 66 Conn. 559; s. c., 34 Atl. Rep. 499; Marshall v. City Bayonne, (N. J.), 34 Atl. Rep. 1080; York Telephone Co. v. Keesey, 5 Pa. Dist. Rep. 366; Central Union Tel. Co. v. Fehring, 146 Ind. 189; s. c., 45 N. E. Rep. 64; Postal Tel. Cable Co. v. City of Balto., 79 Md. 502; s. c., 29 Atl. Rep. 819. A telephone company organized under article 5, of chapter 21, of the Revised Statutes of 1879, has all the powers therein conferred upon such corporations among which are the power to own and operate lines of telephone, to make reasonable charges for the use of the same, to erect its poles along and across public roads and streets and to condemn private property for a right of way. Such corporation is subject to public regulations and the State has the power to fix and prescribe a maximum rate for telephone service and it may delegate such power to municipal corporations. The power of the city of St. Louis to regulate the use of its streets extends to new uses as they spring into existence from time to time, as well as to uses common and known at the time of the grant of the power. The erection and maintenance of telephone poles is one of these new uses and is a proper use of the streets. But the power to regulate charges for telephone service is neither included in, nor incidental to, the power to regulate the use of the streets, and an ordinance regulating such charges cannot be upheld upon any such ground. City of St. Louis v. Bell Telephone Co., 96 Mo. 623. "In determining this case it is important to consider the nature of the telephone, how operated, the utility of it, and the rights of the parties in the absence of the statutes enacted by the legislature. The telephone differs from the telegraph very materially, in this, that the transmission of news, the sending and receiving of messages by telegraph, can only be done by those having a knowledge of the business, and having a knowledge of the art and science of telegraphy. To others who are not telegraphists, the telegraph would be useless. It is, therefore, only beneficial to the general public when operated by persons or companies keeping in their employ telegraphists, to send, receive and transmit messages, and messengers to deliver them to persons to whom addressed. A telegraphic instrument in the house or place of business of a patron of the company,

the maximum price which a telephone company shall charge for the use of its telephones, and the statute limiting the rental price of such instruments, and also the amount which shall be collected for conversations between cities and villages is con-

connected with the wires of the company, with facilities for transmitting and receiving messages by telegraph, would be of no use to a patron, unless he was learned in the art of telegraphy. But the telephone is entirely different; a telephone, with proper connections and facilities for use, can be used by any person: it requires no experience to operate it. Webster defines it as 'an instrument for conveying sound to a great distance.' In the case of the Central Union Telephone Co. v. Bradbury, 106 Ind. 1, the word 'telephone,' as used in the Act of April 13th, 1885, was held to mean 'an organized apparatus, or combination of instruments, usually in use in transmitting, as well as in receiving, telephonic messages.' By the use of the telephone persons are enabled to converse with each other while in their respective business houses or residences a great distance apart. Although of recent date, it has become of important use in the transaction of business, and there is no other invention or device to supply its place. While it may not supply and take the place of the telegraph in many instances and for many purposes, yet in others it far surpasses it, and is, and can be, put to many uses for which the telegraph is unfitted, and by persons wholly unable to operate and use the telegraph. It has been held universally by the courts, considering its use and purpose, to be an instrument of commerce and a common carrier of news, the same as the telegraph, and by reason of being a common carrier, it is subject to proper obligations, and to conduct its business in a manner conducive to the public benefit, and to be controlled by law. To conduct the business of the telephone by public telephone stations, and by sending messengers to notify persons with whom a patron of the company desires to converse in other parts of the city, to compel the person desiring to converse with others to remain at the public telephone station until the person with whom they desire to converse can be notified, and so arrange their business as to leave and go to another telephone station, and hold the conversation, renders the use of the telephone almost worthless. It is by reason of the fact that business men can have them in their offices and residences, and, without leaving their homes or their places of business, call up another at a great distance, with whom they have important business, and converse without the loss of valuable time on the part of either, that the telephone is particularly valuable as an instrument of commerce. It being an instrument of commerce, and persons or corporations engaged in the general telephone business being common carriers of news, what are the rights of the public, independent of the statute, as regards discrimination? * * * It is not controverted in the argument, by counsel for the appellant, that the stitutional. In legal contemplation all the instruments and appliances used by a telephone company in the prosecution of its business are devoted to a public use, and property thus devoted to such use becomes a legitimate subject of legislative regulation. Where a statute is one which the legislature had power to enact, the courts cannot sit in judgment upon either its justice or expediency, but relief must be sought of the legislature.[1] In the opinion in this case, the court said: "The telephone is one of the remarkable productions of the present century, and, although its

legislature had the right to regulate the price to be charged and collected for the use of telephones and telephonic connections, facilities and service; and even if it were controverted, it is well-settled by authorities that the legislature has the right to do so, relative to the business connected within the State. Hockett v. State, 105 Ind. 250; Central Union Telephone Co. v. Bradbury, *supra*, and authorities cited in those cases; Johnson v. State, 113 Ind. 143; Munn v. Illinois. 94 U.S. 113; Ouachita Packet Co. v. Aiken, 121 U. S. 144; Patterson v. Kentucky, 97 U. S. 501." Central Union Telephone Co. v. State, 118 Ind. 194, 205. The word "telegraph," which means and includes any apparatus or adjustment of instruments for transmitting messages or other communications by means of electric currents and signals, embraces the "telephone." A company organized as a telegraph company, under the general incorporation law, before the passage of the Act of 1884, chap. 360, is fully authorized to do a general telephone business; and, in doing such business, it is subject to the provisions of the general incorporation law that apply to telegraph companies. The telegraph and telephone are public vehicles of intelligence, and they who own or control them can no more refuse to perform impartially the functions that they have assumed to discharge, than a railway company, as a common carrier, can rightfully refuse to perform its duty to the public. They may make and establish all reasonable and proper rules and regulations for the government of their offices and those who deal with them. but they have no power to discriminate, and while offering to serve some, refuse to serve others; they must serve all alike upon compliance with their reasonable rules and regulations. They cannot be exonerated from the performance of such duty by any conditions or restrictions imposed by contract with the owner of the invention applied in the exercise of the employment. The legislature of the State has full power to regulate the service of telephone companies as to the parties to whom facilities should be furnished, notwithstanding the instruments employed are the product of a patented invention. Chesapeake & Potomac Telephone Co. v. Baltimore & Ohio Tel. Co., 66 Md. 399.

[1] Hockett v. State, 105 Ind. 250.

discovery is of recent date, it has been in use long enough to have attained well defined relations to the general public. It has become as much a matter of public convenience and of public necessity as were the stage coach and sailing vessel a hundred years ago, or as the steamboat, the railroad and the telegraph have become in later years. It has already become an important instrument of commerce. No other known device can supply the extraordinary facilities which it affords. It may, therefore, be regarded, when relatively considered, as an indispensable instrument of commerce. The relations which it has assumed toward the public make it a common carrier of news, a common carrier in the sense in which the telegraph is a common carrier, and impose upon it certain well defined obligations of a public character. All the instruments and appliances used by a telephone company in the prosecution of its business are, consequently, in legal contemplation, devoted to a public use. It is now a well settled legal proposition that property thus devoted to a public use becomes a legitimate subject of legislative regulation and control."[1]

§ **143. Power to Regulate in Case of Patented Property.**—The claim has been set up that the State has no power to regulate a branch of business which is conducted under a right conferred by letters patent. But this position has not been sustained. In a late case in Ohio, the rule was stated by the court, as follows: "It is claimed that the statute above referred to cannot control or invalidate the contract in question, because the exclusive right to make, vend and use these telephone instruments is vested by the assignment of letters patent under an act of Congress in the American Bell Telephone Company; and that it is not within the power of a State to impair the right so secured. In our opinion, this statute is not the subject of constitutional infirmity. While it is true that letters patent secure a monopoly in the thing patented, so that the right to make, vend or use the same is vested exclusively in

[1] Hockett v. State, 105 Ind. 250, 257.

the patentee, his heirs and assigns, for a limited period; it is not true that a right to make, vend or use the same in a manner which would be unlawful except for the letters patent, thereby becomes lawful, under the act of Congress, and beyond the power of the States to regulate or control."[1] In a more recent case in Indiana, it was held that the fact that the telephone and appliances are articles patented under the constitution and laws of the United States, while vesting in the patentee, his heirs and assigns, the exclusive right for a limited time to make, use and vend the tangible property brought into existence by the application of the discovery covered by the letters patent, does not preclude State regulation of the property thus brought into existence.[2]

[1] State v. Telephone Co., 36 Ohio St. 296, 311.

[2] Hockett v. State, 105 Ind. 250. "It is first and most earnestly contended that as the articles used by the company, as above, are patented, under the Constitution and laws of the United States, the legislature of a State has no power to limit the price, use, sale or rental value of such articles, and that, as a consequence, all acts of a State legislature of the class to which the one before us belongs, are inoperative and ineffectual for any practical purpose. Conceding the force as well as the plausibility of many of the arguments and illustrations used by counsel, the ready and, indeed, inevitable answer is, that the question thus presented ought no longer to be regarded as an open question. There is a reserved and, at the same time, well recognized power, affecting their domestic concerns, remaining in all the States, which the government of the United States cannot, and has seldom attempted to invade. This power is so varied and comprehensive that an exact definition, as applicable to all its phases, has so far been found to be impracticable, but all the instances in which the existence of such a power has been judicially recognized, in particular cases, are quite numerous, as well as various, in their application to our complex system of government. This reserved power is usually, though, perhaps, not always, accurately denominated the police power of a State, and embraces the entire system of internal State regulation, having in view not only the preservation of public order and the prevention of offenses against the State, but also the promotion of such intercourse between the inhabitants of the State as is calculated to prevent a conflict of rights, and to promote the interests of all. Cooley Const. Lim. 572. It is a power inherent in every sovereignty, and is, in its broadest sense, nothing more than the power of a State to govern men and things within the limits of its own dominion. License Cases, 5 How. 504, 582. It extends to the protec-

§ 144. Application of the Rule to the Baking Business.—It is well settled that the State has power to regulate the manufacture of bread. It may require all persons engaged in the baking business to take out a license author-

tion of the lives, limbs, health, comfort and convenience, as well as the property of all persons within the State. It authorizes the legislature to prescribe the mode and manner in which every one may so use his own as not to injure others, and to do whatever is necessary to promote the public welfare, not inconsistent with, is our organic law. Thorpe v. R. & B. R. R. Co., 27 Vt. 140. In 1867 letters patent were issued to one De Witt for a discovery in the manufacture of a quality of oil known as 'Aurora Oil,' and one Patterson became the assignee of the right conferred upon De Witt by his letters patent. Under a system of inspection provided by the laws of Kentucky, some casks containing this Aurora oil were branded 'unsafe for illuminating purposes,' and notwithstanding a statute of that State making it penal offense to sell oil thus branded, Patterson sold the casks of oil in question to one Davis. Patterson was thereupon indicted, tried and convicted in one of the Kentucky courts for the alleged unlawful sale of these condemned casks of oil. This judgment convicting Patterson of a criminal offense having been affirmed by the court of appeals of that State, the cause was taken to the Supreme Court of the United States to test the validity of the statute under which Patterson was so convicted, as a restraint upon the sale of a commodity covered by letters patent of the United States. Upon a review of all the questions involved, the validity of the statute was maintained, and the judgment of the court of appeals was in all things affirmed. See Patterson v. Kentucky, 97 U. S. 501. The court held in that case, and as we have no doubt correctly, that all that the letters patent secured was the exclusive right in the discovery, and that the right thus secured was an incorporeal right, and hence without 'tangible evidence;' that the right to sell the oil was not derived from the letters patent, but existed and could have been exercised before the issuing of such letters, unless prohibited by some local statute: that because the patentee acquired a monopoly in his discovery, and was hence secure against interference, it did not follow that the tangible property which came into existence by the application of the discovery was beyond the control of State legislation; that, on the contrary, the right of the property in the physical substance, which is the fruit of the discovery, is altogether distinct from the discovery itself, just as the property in the instruments or plate by which copies of a map are multiplied is distinct from the copyright itself; that hence the right conferred upon the patentee and his assigns to make, use and vend the corporeal article or commodity brought into existence by the application of the patented discovery must be exercised in subordination to the police or local regulations established by the State. The doctrine of that case izing them to engage in this work, and it may fix the weight and price of the baker's loaf. And the power which a legislature may exercise directly, it may grant to a municipal corporation. In the leading case of The Mayor and Alderman of Mobile v. Yuille, it was held by the Supreme Court of Alabama, that a power granted to the corporation of the city of Mobile, "to license bakers and regulate the weight and price of bread, and prohibit the baking for sale, except by those licensed," is not contrary to the constitution of the State.[1] The principle involved in this decision is expounded by the court, as follows: "The regulation in this case seems to combine all these qualities. Where a great number of persons are collected together in a town or city, a regular supply of wholesome bread is a matter of the utmost importance; and whatever doubts may have been thrown over the question by the theories of political economists, it would seem that experience has shown that this great end is better secured by licensing a sufficient number of bakers and by an assize of bread, than by leaving it to the voluntary acts of individuals. By this means a constant

was approved and followed in the more recent case of Webber v. Virginia, 103 U. S. 344, and has the support either in direct terms or in principle, of numerous other carefully considered cases. Patterson v. Commonwealth, 11 Bush, 311; s. c., 21 Am. Rep. 220; State v. Telephone Co., 36 Ohio St. 296; s. c., 38 Am. Rep. 583, and note; Jordan v. Dayton, 4 Ohio, 295; Fry State, 63 Ind. 552; People v. Russell, 49 Mich. 617; s. c., 43 Am. Rep. 478; Thompson v. Staats, 15 Wend. 395; Martinetti v. Maguire, Deady, 216; Vannini v. Payne, 1 Harrington, 65; License Tax Cases, 5 Wall. 462; United States v. De Witt, 9 Wall. 41; Railroad Co. v. Husen, 95 U. S. 465; Beer Co. v. Massachusetts, 97 U. S. 25; Brechbill v. Randall, 102 Ind. 582; s. c., 52 Am. Rep. 695; Palmer v. State, 39 Ohio St. 236; s. c., 48 Am. Rep. 429; Western Union Tel. Co. v. Pendleton, 95 Ind. 12; s. c., 48 Am. Rep. 692; New Orleans Gas Co. v. Louisiana Light Co., 115 U. S. 650. While, therefore, it is true that letters patent confer upon the patentee a monopoly to the extent of vesting in him, his heirs and assigns, the exclusive right to make, use and vend the tangible property brought into existence by a practical application of the discovery covered by the letters patent, for a limited time, it is not true that such exclusive right authorizes the making, using or vending of such tangible property in a manner which would be unlawful, except for such letters patent, and independently of State legislation and State control." *Ibid.*, 254.

[1] Mobile v. Yuille, 3 Ala. 137.

supply is obtained without that fluctuation in quantity which would be the inevitable result of throwing the trade entirely open, and the consequent rise in price, when from accident or design a sufficient supply was not produced. The interest of the city in always having an abundant supply will be a sufficient guaranty against any abuse of the right to regulate the weight, the consequence of which would be to drive the baker from the trade."[1]

§ 145. **Application of the Rule to the Laundry Business.**—It has been held that the business of washing and ironing, as sustained by public patronage, may be regulated by legislative enactments. The legislature has power to fix the territorial limits within which public laundries and washhouses may be established, and it may determine the hours during which the business may be pursued. The granting to a city government of ordinary municipal powers carries with it this right. In the leading case of Soon Hing v. Crowley, before the Supreme Court of the United States, it was held that a municipal ordinance, prohibiting from washing and ironing in public laundries and washhouses within defined territorial limits from 10 o'clock at night to 6 in the morning, is a police regulation within the competency of a municipality possessed of ordinary powers. It is no objection to a municipal ordinance, prohibiting one kind of business within certain hours, that it permits other and different kinds of business to be done within those hours. Municipal restrictions imposed upon one class of persons engaged in a particular business, which are not imposed upon others engaged in the same business and under like conditions, impair the equal rights which all can claim in the enforcement of the laws. When the general security and welfare require that a particular kind of work should be done at certain times or hours, and an ordinance is made to that effect, a person engaged in performing that sort of work has no inherent right to pursue his occupation during the prohibited time. This court cannot inquire into the

[1] Mobile v. Yuille, 3 Ala. 137, 141.

motives of legislators in enacting laws except as they may be disclosed on the face of the acts, or be inferable from their operation, considered with reference to the condition of the country and existing legislation.[1] In the opinion in this case, by Mr. Justice Field, the court said: "However

[1] Soon Hing v. Crowley, 113 U. S. 703. "The fourteenth amendment, declaring that no State 'shall deprive any person of life, liberty, or property without due process of law, nor deny to any person within its jurisdiction the equal protection of the laws,' undoubtedly intended not only that there should be no arbitrary deprivation of life or liberty, or arbitrary spoliation of property, but that equal protection and security should be given to all under like circumstances in the enjoyment of their personal and civil rights; that all persons should be equally entitled to pursue their happiness and acquire and enjoy property; that they should have like access to the courts of the country for the protection of their persons and property, the prevention and redress of wrongs, and the enforcement of contracts; that no impediment should be interposed to the pursuits of any one except as applied to the same pursuits by others under like circumstances; that no greater burdens should be laid upon one than are laid upon others in the same calling and condition, and that in the administration of criminal justice no different or higher punishment should be imposed upon one than such as is prescribed to all for like offenses. But neither the amendment—broad and comprehensive as it is—nor any other amendment, was designed to interfere with the power of the State, sometimes termed its police power, to prescribe regulations to promote the health, peace, morals, education and good order of the people, and to legislate so as to increase the industries of the State, develop its resources, and add to its wealth and prosperity. From the very necessities of society, legislation of a special character, having these objects in view, must often be had in certain districts, such as for draining marshes and irrigating arid plains. Special burdens are often necessary for general benefits,—for supplying water, preventing fires, lighting districts, cleaning streets, opening parks and many other objects. Regulations for these purposes may press with more or less weight upon one than upon another, but they are designed not to impose unequal or unnecessary restrictions upon any one, but to promote with as little individual inconvenience as possible, the general good. Though in many respects, necessarily special in their character, they do not furnish just ground of complaint if they operate alike upon all persons and property under the same circumstances and conditions. Class legislation, discriminating against some and favoring others, is prohibited, but legislation which, in carrying out a public purpose, is limited in its application, if within the sphere of its operation it affects alike all persons similarly situated, is not within the amendment." Field, J., in Barber v. Connolly, 113 U. S. 27, 31.

broad the right of every one to follow such calling and employ his time as he may judge most conducive to his interests, it must be exercised subject to such general rules as are adopted by society for the common welfare. All sorts of restrictions are imposed upon the actions of men, notwithstanding the liberty, which is guaranteed to each. It is liberty regulated by just and impartial laws. Parties for example, are free to make any contracts they choose for a lawful purpose, but society says what contracts shall be in writing, and what may be verbally made, and on what days they may be executed, and how long they may be enforced, if their terms are not complied with. So, too, with the hours of labor. On few subjects has there been more regulation. How many hours shall constitute a day's work in the absence of contract, at what time shops in our cities shall close at night, are constant subjects of legislation. Laws setting aside Sunday as a day of rest are upheld, not from any right of the government to legislate for the promotion of religious observances, but from its right to protect all persons from the physical and moral debasement which comes from uninterrupted labor. Such laws have always been deemed beneficent and merciful laws, especially to the poor and dependent, to the laborers in our factories and workshops and in the heated rooms of our cities, and their validity has been sustained by the highest courts of the States."[1]

[1] Soon Hing v. Crowley, 113 U. S. 703, 709. See generally on the police power of the State: Wadleigh v. Gilman, 12 Me. 403; s. c., 28 Am. Dec. 188; Brady v. Northwestern Ins. Co., 11 Mich. 425; Monroe v. Hoffman, 29 La. Ann. 651; s. c., 29 Am. Rep. 345; King v. Davenport, 98 Ill. 305; s. c., 38 Am. Rep. 89; Klinger v. Bickel, 117 Pa. St. 326; McCloskey v. Kreling, 76 Cal. 511; Miller v. Craig, 11 N. J. Eq. 175. See following cases on oleomargarine laws: Powell v. Pennsylvania, 127 U. S. 678; affirming 114 Pa. St. 265; Butler v. Chambers, 36 Minn. 69; Waterbury v. Newton, 50 N. J. Eq. 534; People v. Mark, 99 N. Y. 377; People v. Arensberg, 105 N. Y. 123; Pierce v. Maryland, 63 Md. 592; State v. Marshall, 64 N. H. 549; s. c., 15 Atl. Rep. 210. As to weights and measures see Gaines v. Coates, 51 Miss. 335; Guillotte v. New Orleans, 12 La. Ann. 432; Page v. Fazackerly, 36 Barb. 392; Raleigh v. Sorrel, 1 Jones (N. Car.), 49; Wortman v. Philadelphia, 33 Pa. St. 202; Spaulding v. Lowell, 23 Pick. 71; Gall v.

§ **146. Immunity from Governmental Control.**—The charter of a corporation is a contract, as that term is employed by the Federal Constitution. In the granting of such charter a legislature may protect the corporation from any subsequent legislative control. It may bind itself not to exercise its power in the regulation of the business of a corporation thus protected. In the case of a railway, of a street railroad, of a telegraph or gas company, etc., it may bind itself not to regulate established rates of fare, or of freight or other charges, as they may be fixed by such corporation. But in the absence of any specific provisions of its charter, nothing will be presumed in favor of the corporation in this regard. It enjoys immunity from governmental control only by being of an express and unequivocal legislative enactment. Without this the right of the legislature, either directly or through the instrumentality of a municipal corporation, to regulate the business of any company acting under a legislative or municipal franchise, is not to be questioned.[1] In the case of Ruggles v. Illinois,

Cincinnati, 18 Ohio St. 563; State v. Fisher, 52 Mo. 174; Municipality v. Cutting, 4 La. Ann. 336. As to prohibiting sales of opium: State v. Ah Chew, 16 Nev. 50. As to market licenses and privileges: Buffalo v. Webster, 10 Wend. 99; Bush v. Seabury, 8 Johns. 418; Ash v. People, 11 Mich. 347; State v. Leiber, 11 Iowa, 407; LeClaire v. Davenport, 13 Iowa, 210; Bowling Green v. Carson, 10 Bush, 64; New Orleans v. Stafford, 27 La. Ann. 417; Nightingale's Case, 11 Pick. 168; Gossigi v. New Orleans (La.), 4 So. Rep. 15. See generally as to State laws governing trades and professions: Pierce v. Kimball, 9 Me. 54; s. c., 23 Am. Dec. 537; Shepherd v. Commissioners, 59 Ga. 535; Fry v. State, 63 Ind. 552; *In re* Quong Foo, 13 Fed. Rep. 229; State v. State Med. Ex. Board, 32 Minn. 324; Gage v. Censors, 63 N. H. 92; Wilkins v. State, 113 Ind. 514; Gosnell v. State, 52 Ark. 228; s. c., 12 S. W. Rep. 392; State v. Dent, 129 U. S. 114; s. c., 25 W. Va. 1.

[1] Ruggles v. Illinois, 108 U. S. 526, 538. "Great stress is laid on the fact that this warehouse was erected in 1862, long anterior to the passage of the law and by this kind of legislation the alternative is presented, either to abandon the use of the property for which it was fitted, or to do business for less compensation than its owners had theretofore and always received. In another part of their argument they say that they, by consent of their customers, have received during the past year higher rates of storage than those specified in the act, and so, in this respect, the act is a plain, palpable violation of the clause of the con-

before the Supreme Court of the United States, the rule was stated by the court, as follows: "Grants of immunity from legitimate governmental control are never to be presumed. On the contrary, the presumptions are all the

stitution relied on,—that depriving them of the value of the use, is depriving them of their property. This argument is answered by what we have already said. It is idle to talk about the consent of their customers to higher rates of charges than this law allows them to receive. Their customers, before this law was enacted, had no protection against these monopolists. They had no consent to give. They were obliged to have their grain taken to these warehouses, and be subjected to such charges as the organized combination, shutting out all competition, might choose to demand. The producer and shipper had no alternative but submission. They were completely in the power of this combination, and it did not fail to demand and exact the highest charges. It is this state of things the law is designed to remedy. One of the first and most imperative duties of the law-making power is, to enact all necessary laws to remedy existing evils, taking care in so doing not to transgress any constitutional limitation. The means by which to do it most effectually is, in the discretion of the legislature, keeping in view the provisions of the organic law. This law in no respect affects the title, possession or use of this warehouse by the plaintiffs in error. It deprives them of nothing they owned and possessed at the time of its enactment. Anticipated profits are not and cannot be held and regarded as property in the ownership or possession of him who owns the article out of which profits are expected to flow. The property is one thing and remains untouched,—the profits are not *in esse*, and cannot be claimed as property. When it is said one is deprived of his property, the understanding is, it has been taken away from him,—he is divested of title and possession. This provision in the bill of rights has never been so construed by the courts of any State, whose constitution has such a provision, as to deny to the legislature the power to make all needful rules and regulations respecting the use and enjoyment of property. Ever since the organization of our State government, the legislature has exercised this power unquestioned. Familiar instances are found in regulating public ferries and public mills, and fixing the compensation in the shape of toll. Another is, in delegating power to municipal bodies to regulate charges of hackmen and draymen, and the weight and price of bread: But in a property the most sought after by nearly all classes of community, and deemed the most valuable of any, as it controls all others, the legislative power of every State in the Union has been brought to bear upon it, and no court has ever questioned the right so to do. We allude to the interest laws,—laws declaring at what rate a man may loan his money. The argument used here, it seems to us, would prove all these laws unconstitutional, for they do regulate the use other way, and unless an exemption is clearly established the legislature is free to act on all subjects within its general jurisdiction as the public interests may seem to require. As was said by Chief Justice Taney, speaking for the court, in Charles River Bridge v. Warren Bridge:[1] 'It can never be assumed that the government intended to diminish its power of accomplishing the end for which it was created.' This is an elementary principle."[2]

§ 147. **A Business Juris Publici Distinguished from a Business Juris Privati.**—A branch of business, not affected by a public use, is not subject to legislative or municipal control and regulation, and a corporation or individual engaged in such business is not bound to conduct it with reference to the convenience or to the necessities of the public. A business that is, essentially, a private business is not affected by a public use by any extension or enlargement of its operations. A business is affected by a public use, and their business subject to governmental regulation, only as, by the terms of its charter or by the nature of the service rendered, the corporation or the individual by which it is conducted becomes a public servant. In a case in Texas, the rule is stated by the court, as follows: "The business of warehousing and compressing cotton is free to every one who wishes to engage in it. No grant or franchise need be obtained from the State to authorize those desiring to do so to embark in this character of business. It is not one of the employments which the common law declares public. Nor is it claimed to have been made so by statute. And we know of no authority, and none has been shown us, for saying that a business strictly *juris privati* will become *juris publici*, merely by reason of its extent. If the magnitude of a particular business is such, and the persons affected by it so

of a man's property, they do fix a value upon its use, and, as all observation shows, in most localities, greatly below its market value." Breese, J., in Munn v. People, 69 Ill. 80, 90.

[1] Charles River Bridge v. Warren Bridge, 11 Pet. 420, 547.

[2] Ruggles v. Illinois, 108 U. S. 526, 531.

numerous, that the interest of society demands that the rules and principles applicable to public employments should be applied to it, this would have to be done by the legislature (if not restrained from doing so by the constitution) before a demand for such an use could be enforced by the courts."[1] In a case before the United States Circuit Court for the Eastern District of Tennessee, the rule is stated by Mr. Justice Key in his opinion, as follows: "The control which courts may have over railroads and business incidental to, and necessary for, their conduct and operation, such as warehousing in our great railroad centers, is based upon public necessity. Railroads do nearly all the business of interior transportation. The public is compelled to use them exclusively. There is scarcely anything to compete with them where they operate. Hence, discriminations or extortion cannot be tolerated in their management. If they refuse like facilities to their shippers, or discriminate in rates or otherwise, courts may compel them to be just. The

[1] Ladd v. S. C. P. & M. Co., 53 Tex. 172, 188. "It will readily be admitted that in many instances combinations may be made by parties engaged in a particular trade, or by those who, at the time, have the control of the market for some article of prime necessity, to make most inconceivable exactions for their services, or demand a most extortionate price for their commodities. But certainly this does not change the nature of the employment in which they are engaged, or authorize the court to say, when the business of the parties is strictly private, that it has become public. If the combination is illegal, the parties to it will subject themselves to such penalties as the law imposes, and if the injury to society to be apprehended from such combinations is of a character demanding it, the legislature may, by adequate provision, regulate or prohibit persons from engaging in them. Nor do we say that there may not be instances where, by combination, or even without it, some particular business, by reason of its extent and magnitude, and the great number of persons affected by it, though strictly *privati juris* under the common law and previous statute, which may be declared *publici juris* by the legislature. This seems, in effect, what was held by the Supreme Court of the United States to have been done by the legislature of Illinois. (Munn v. Illinois, 94 U. S. 125.) But as this is not the character of this case, we are not called upon to express an authoritative opinion on the point. It is sufficient for us to say that in the absence of legislation to that effect, a party who has not subjected his property and services to public use by the character of the

business in which he is engaged, does not do so by reason of combination with others in a like business, though he is enabled thereby to exact from those who employ him unreasonable and extortionate charges for the services rendered. Whether payments made under such circumstances may not be held to have been paid under duress, is another question to be considered hereafter. Nor can it justly be held that the mere extent and magnitude of the business changes a private charge for services into a toll to be regulated by law. Nor, if so, that the court may, in the absence of legislation upon the subject, substitute its judgment as to the proper amount of such toll for the contract of the parties. * * * It is not contended by appellant that, as ordinarily conducted, the business of receiving, storing, compressing and delivering cotton is *privati juris*, which those engaged in it have not the right to fix the rates and conditions upon which it will be conducted. But the argument seems to be that, in view of the necessities of trade, its magnitude and effect upon the interest of the people throughout the State, as well as of those engaged in the business of appellant, it has become of like public interest as other occupations and trades which the law pronounces and holds to be *iuris publici*. The conclusion sought to be maintained rests upon the hypothesis that whenever it is made to appear that any particular business is of so general public interest as that which the law holds to be *juris publici*, the courts have the power to so declare and hold it. The case of Munn v. Illinois, 94 U. S. 125, seems to be the auority mainly relied on to support this position. We cannot regard this case as authority for such a doctrine. It was brought to enforce the statute law of the State. The conclusion to be drawn from it is, as we think, that the legislature may declare a particular business *publici juris*, if the facts and circumstances under which it is conducted justifies and the good of society requires it; but not that the court may so treat it in advance of legislative recognition or declaration. Whether this may be done, even by the legislature, without infringing upon the constitution, need not now be considered. Neither is it necessary for us at present to determine whether the submission of property and service to public use (as there is high authority for holding) is solely dependent upon the fact that those engaged in such business enjoy some franchise, privilege, or immunity from the State, or did so in the early days of the common law when this character was impressed upon their property or service." *Ibid.*, 189, 191. In the Express Cases, 117 U. S. 1, 23, Chief Justice Waite uses this language: "The reason is obvious why special contracts in reference to this business are necessary. The transportation required is of a kind which must, if possible, be had for the most part on passenger trains. It requires not only speed, but reasonable certainty as to the quantity that will be carried at any one time. As the things carried are to be kept in the personal custody of the messenger or other employe of the express company, it is important that a certain amount of car space should be specially set apart for the business, and that this should, as far as practicable, be put in the exclusive possession of the expressman cases of Munn v. Illinois,[1] and Adams Express Co. v. L. & N. R. R.,[2] and other cases referred to, proceed on this theory. There is no such ground for jurisdiction in the case under consideration. There is no necessity, public or other, for people to visit Lookout Point. That is a mere matter

in charge. As the business to be done is 'express,' it implies access to the train for loading at the latest, and for unloading at the earliest convenient moment, all this is entirely inconsistent with the idea of an express business on passenger trains free to all express carriers. Railroad companies are by law carriers of both persons and property. Passenger trains have from the beginning been provided for the transportation primarily of passengers and their baggage. This must be done with reasonable comfort to the passenger. The express business on passenger trains is in a degree subordinate to the passenger business, and it is consequently the duty of a railroad company in arranging for the express to see that there is as little interference as possible with the wants of passengers. This implies a special understanding and agreement as to the amount of car space that will be afforded, and the conditions on which it is to be occupied, the particular trains that can be used, the places at which they shall stop, the price to be paid, and all the varying details of a business which is to be adjusted between two public servants, so that each can perform in the best manner its own particular duties. All this must necessarily be a matter of bargain, and it by no means follows that, because a railroad company can serve one express company in one way, it can as well serve another company in the same way and still perform its other obligations to the public in a satisfactory manner. The car space that can be given to the express business on a passenger train is, to certain extent, limited, and, as has been seen, that which is allotted to a particular carrier must be, in a measure, under his exclusive control. No express company can do a successful business unless it is at all times reasonably sure of the means it requires for transportation. On important lines one company will at all times fill all the space the railroad company can well allow for the business. If this space had to be divided among several companies, there might be occasions when the public would be put to inconvenience by delays which could otherwise be avoided. So long as the public are served to their reasonable satisfaction, it is a matter of no importance who serves them. The railroad company performs its whole duty to the public at large and to each individual when it affords the public all reasonable express accommodations. If this is done the railroad company owes no duty to the public as to the particular agencies it shall select for that purpose. The public require the carriage, but the company may choose its own appropriate means of carriage, always provided they are such as to insure reasonable promptness and security."

[1] Munn v. Illinois, 94 U. S. 125.

[2] Adams Expres Co. et. al. v. L. & N. R. R., 117 U. S. 1.

of taste, pleasure, curiosity. Commerce, the public weal, social order, the public health or comfort, have nothing to do with it. Already the courts have gone 'to the verge of the law' in the direction asked for here, and it is apprehended that no authoritative case can be found which will carry us as far as we are now asked to go. Now, take the case in hand: Miss W, as the owner of the Point and park, or her privies in estate, at one time might have excluded all persons from entering upon either. It, to say the least, has been private property. No legislative act has declared a public use in it. If such use has been impressed upon it, it has been done by her. Holding the absolute title, she could control it as she liked, so long as she did not use it to the injury of others. She could have donated it to a public use generally and absolutely, or to such limited use as she might prescribe, or she could have preserved its private character. As her private property she had the right to inclose it; after its inclosure she had the right to admit as many or as few within the inclosure as she pleased. Because she saw fit to admit some persons upon payment of a given fee gave to others no right to be admitted on the tender of a like fee. They were in no worse or different position than before any admissions were made. No losses have been sustained by them. No consideration had passed from them. Nothing can be found on which to predicate an equity in their favor. The fact that people may have been admitted to such an extent as to make the business of carrying passengers to the Point profitable to the complainant raises no equity in his favor. It was brought about by no use of his property or expenditure of his money. Respondent has as much right to require him to contribute such portions of profits as might be deemed equitable, which she has enabled him to make by the allowance of great numbers to go to the Point, as he has to demand of her the use of her property that his business may prosper. Neither he nor the public has any greater right to the property than she has given them. There is no greater obligation on her part to contribute to the public use, gratification or pleasure than rests upon others. She holds her property subject to her control just as others hold theirs, until it is applied to the public use by an act of the sovereign power through methods known to the law, or until she appropriates it by her voluntary act to the use of the public. A court cannot appropriate to such purpose against her consent. She can determine who shall be admitted within her premises and who shall be refused admission. Of course, this remark has no reference to officers of the law armed with process."[1]

[1] Sharp v. Whitesides, 19 Fed. Rep. 156, 160.

CHAPTER X.

COMBINATIONS OF RAILWAY COMPANIES FOR THE SUPPRESSING OF COMPETITION.

§ 148. Introduction.
149. Combinations for the Purpose of Suppressing Competition.
150. The Subject Continued.
151. Purchase of Competing Lines.
152. Lease of Competing Lines.
§ 153. Consolidation of Parallel Lines.
154. The Subject Continued.
155. Rule in Case of Traffic Arrangement.
156. Admission to Depot Grounds.
157. General Powers of Railway Corporations.

§ **148. Introductory.**—By the conditions of its corporate existence a railroad company is subject to certain public obligations. In accepting its charter and in entering upon its work it undertakes to render a public service. This is the condition of its corporate privileges. These privileges are granted by the legislature, not as a favor to the individuals of which the company is composed,—for it has no power to confer personal favors,—but for the benefit of the public. And the privileges, having been accepted, the obligations involved cannot be escaped. They fasten upon the company, and attach themselves to the property acquired under its charter. In a leading case, before the Supreme Court of the United States, this doctrine is stated by Mr. Justice Campbell, as follows: "The plaintiff complains here of this charge, for that the cars employed were not built by, and did not belong to, the company. That they were the exclusive property of the Maryland corporation; and that the agreement to divide the profits did not constitute a partnership, nor evince a relation of principal or agent to impose a liability. This conclusion implies, that the duties imposed upon the plaintiff by the charter are fulfilled by the construction of the road, and that by alienating its right to use, and its powers of control and supervision, it may avoid further responsibility. But those acts involve an overturn of the relations which the charter has arranged between the corporation and the community. Important franchises were conferred upon the corporation to enable it to provide the facilities to communication and intercourse required for the public convenience. Corporate management and control over these were prescribed, and corporate responsibility for their insufficiency provided, as a remuneration to the community for their grant. The corporation cannot absolve itself from the performance of its obligations without the consent of the legislature."[1] In a more recent

[1] New York & Md. R. R. Co. v. Winans, 17 How. 30. 39. See also White River T. Co. v. Vermont C. R. Co., 21 Vt. 590; Pierce v. Commonwealth, 104 Pa. St. 150: s. c., 13 Am. & Eng. R. Cas. 74. 79: Camblos v. Phila., etc. R. Co., 4 Brewst. 563, 597; Trunick v. Smith, 63 Pa. St. 18. "The owners of railroads are common carriers. They cannot distinguish between different persons. They must carry for all that come, and for reasonable rates controllable by the public. If they refuse to receive freight that is offered, they are liable to an action in damages; and, indeed, in such case the agrieved party would not be confined to the slow remedy by action, but might sue out a *mandamus* to compel the corporation to carry his goods. They must provide adequate and sufficient rolling stock to do the business offered, and cannot excuse themselves for not receiving freight or passengers on the ground of the lack of any of these things which it is in their power to provide. Apply any of these tests to a corporation, the use of whose property is private, and the distinction between a private and public use is apparent. Now the question presents itself something in this shape: Is it clear beyond any reasonable doubt, and by evidence irrefragable, that the use of a railroad is not a public use? If the use is strictly private, then the legislature cannot authorize taxation in its aid, because it cannot take the property or money of one person and hand it over to another with or without compensation, for a mere private purpose. But, if the use be a public use, then it is admitted that the legislature may levy a tax to aid in the construction. It seems almost a self-evident proposition that the use of a railroad is public. It is so as a matter of common knowledge. It has been so adjudged by the United States Supreme Court, and by the highest courts in every State in the Union, for the purpose of invoking the power of eminent

case, before the same court, the doctrine is stated by Mr. Justice Miller, as follows: "That principle is that where a corporation, like a railroad company has granted to it, by charter, a franchise, intended in large measure to be exercised for the public good, the due performance of those

domain in the condemnation of real estate for right of way, depot grounds, round houses, freight yards, etc. Indeed, this power was thoroughly settled in the leading case of Beekman v. Railroad Co., 3 Paige, 45, and has never been questioned since. * * * The State has always exercised the authority to tax the people to build and maintain highways and the authority is not questioned. It may do so itself, or through individuals or corporations, and authorize the establishment of toll gates. It may build a road through the State or any part of it. It may authorize a town or county to build a town or county road, and tax its people for its construction and maintenance. This power has been recognized and practiced from very ancient days, and from the first dawn of civilized life. It was common in the times of the Roman Empire, and has come down to us from immemorial days, and through immemorial usage. It has always been exercised in this country from the first settlement of the colonies. The practice and the principle are older than the common law, or the present nations of the world, and have been transmitted to us from a period now darkened to view by time and distance. Laying aside, then, the question of public policy, of which the State must judge, why should the naked authority be now questioned simply because the necessities of civilization have demanded a more commodious method of travel than the old common highway could afford? The following are some of the leading cases on the subject: Beekman v. Railroad Co., 3 Paige, 45; Brocaw v. Gibson Co., 73 Ind. 543; Allison v. Railway Co., 10 Bush, 1; Town of Bennington v. Park, 50 Vt. 192; Perry v. Keene, 56 N. H. 514; Walker v. City of Cincinnati, 21 Ohio St. 14; Sharpless v. Mayor of Philadelphia, 21 Pa. St. 147; Railroad Co. v. Smith, 62 Ill. 268; Hallenbeck v. Hahn, 2 Neb. 377; *Ex parte* Selma & G. R. Co., 45 Ala. 696; Davidson v. Commissioners, 18 Minn. 482; Railroad Co. v. McDonald, 53 Miss. 240; People v. Mitchell, 35 N. Y. 551; Gibbons v. Railroad Co., 36 Ala. 410; Thompson v. Lee Co., 3 Wall. 327; Bloodgood v. Railroad Co., 18 Wend. 10; Worcester v. Railroad Corp., 4 Metc. 564; Stewart v. Polk Co., 30 Iowa, 9; Town of Queensbury v. Culver, 19 Wall. 83; Railroad v. County of Otoe, 16 Wall. 667; Louisville v. Bank, 104 U. S. 47; County of Moultrie v. Fairfield, 105 U. S. 370; St. Joseph Tp. v. Rogers, 16 Wall. 664; Rogers v. Burlington, 3 Wall. 664; Mitchell v. Burlington, 4 Wall. 270." Northern Pac. R. Co. v. Roberts, 42 Fed. Rep. 734, 746. "That railroads, though constructed by private corporations and owned by them, are public highways, has been the doctrine of nearly all the courts ever since such conveniences for passage and transportation have had any existence. Very early the functions being the consideration of the public grant, any contract which disables the corporation from performing those functions which undertakes, without the consent of the State, to transfer to others the rights and powers conferred by the charter, and to relieve the grantees of the burden which it imposes, is a violation of the contract with the State, and is void as against public policy."[1] In the case of Beekman v. The Saratoga & Schenectady Railroad Company, before the Court of Chancery of the State of New

question arose whether a State's right of eminent domain could be exercised by a private corporation created for the purpose of constructing a railroad. Clearly it could not, unless taking land for such a purpose by such an agency is taking land for public use. The right of eminent domain nowhere justifies property for a private use. Yet it is a doctrine universally accepted that a State legislature may authorize a private corporation to take land for the construction of such a road, making compensation to the owner. What else does this doctrine mean, if not that building a railroad, though it is built by a private corporation, is an act done for a public use? And the reason why the use has always been held a public one, is that such a road is a highway, whether made by the government itself, or by the agency of corporate bodies, or even by individuals, when they obtain their power to construct it from government grant. It would be useless to cite the numerous decisions to this effect which have been made in the State courts. We may, however, refer to two or three which exhibit fully not only the doctrine itself, but the reasons upon which it rests. (Beekman v. Saratoga & Schenectady R. R. Co., 3 Paige, 45; Bloodgood v. Mohawk & Hudson R. R. Co., 18 Wend. 1; Worcester v. R. R. Co., 4 Metc. 564.) Whether the use of a railroad is a public or a private one depends in no measure upon the question who constructed it or who owns it. It has never been considered a matter of any importance that the road was built by the agency of a private corporation. No matter who is the agent, the functions performed is that of the State. Though the ownership is private the use is public. So turnpikes, bridges, ferries and canals, although made by individuals under public grants, or by companies, are regarded as *publici juris*. The right to exact tolls or charge freights is granted for a service to the public. The owners may be private companies, but they are compellable to permit the public to use their works in the manner in which such works can be used. (Charles River Bridge Co. v. Warren, 7 Pick. 495.) That all persons may not put their own cars upon the road, and use their own motive power, has no bearing upon the question whether the road is a public highway. It bears only upon the mode of use of which the legislature is the exclusive judge." Olcott v. Supervisors, 16 Wall. 678, 694.

[1] Thomas v. Railroad Co., 101 U. S. 71, 83.

York, the doctrine is stated by Chancellor Walworth, as follows: "It is objected, however, that a railroad differs from other public improvements, and particularly from turnpikes and canals, because travelers cannot use it with their own carriages, and farmers cannot transport their produce in their own vehicles; that the company in this case are under no obligation to accommodate the public with transportation; and that they are unlimited in the amount of tolls which they are authorized to take. If the making of a railroad will enable the traveler to go from one place to another without the expense of a carriage and horses, he derives a greater benefit from the improvement than if he was compelled to travel with his own conveyance over a turnpike road at the same expense, and if a mode of conveyance has been discovered by which the farmer can procure his produce to be transported to market at half the expense which it would cost him to carry it there with his own wagon and horses, there is no reason why the public should not enjoy the benefit of the discovery. And if any individual is so unreasonable as to refuse to have the railroad made through his lands, for a fair compensation, the legislature may lawfully appropriate a portion of his property for this public benefit, or may authorize an individual or a corporation thus to appropriate it, upon paying a just compensation to the owner of the land for the damage sustained. The objection that the corporation is under no legal obligation to transport produce or passengers upon this road, and at a reasonable expense, is unfounded in fact. The privilege of making a road and taking tolls thereon is a franchise as much as the establishment of a ferry or a public wharf and taking tolls for the use of the same. The public have an interest in the use of the railroad, and the owners may be prosecuted for the damages sustained, if they should refuse to transport an individual or his property, without any reasonable excuse, upon being paid the usual rate of fare. The legislature may also, from time to time, regulate the use of the franchise and limit the amount of toll which it shall be lawful to take, in the same manner as they may regulate the amount of tolls to be taken at a ferry, or for grinding at a mill, unless they have deprived themselves of that power by a legislative contract with the owner of the road."[1] The doctrine appertaining to the relations of railway companies to the public, as above expounded, lies at the basis of all legislation and of all sound decisions of the courts, in regard to the attempts of such companies to create a monopoly or to suppress competition between competing or parallel lines. They are public servants, and their special privileges impose upon them the obligation, not only to serve the public, but also to make only fair and reasonable charges for such service. And, for this reason, the attempt to create a monopoly, by entering into a covenant for the suppression of competition, with a view of increasing or to maintaining either freight or passenger rates, is illegal and void.

§ 149. Combinations for the Purpose of Suppressing Competition.—Any combination of railway companies, the object of which is to restrain competition by establishing and maintaining a uniform charge for the transportation of freight, or of passengers, is illegal and void. Where the agreement provides that any member of the pool or association that shall carry either freight or passengers for less than the rate fixed, shall be subject to a fine, such provision will not be enforced by the courts. It is the rule that contracts or agreements of this character are void as in contravention of public policy, and in many of the States such compacts are rendered nugatory by constitutional or statutory enactments. In a late case in Indiana, it was held that a contract, entered into between competing common carriers for the establishment and maintenance of freight rates, forming what is known as a "pool," being a combination for no other purpose than that of stifling competition, and providing means to accomplish that purpose, is illegal. Such a combination being void, any one of the associated

[1] Beekman v. Saratoga & Schenectady R. R. Co., 3 Paige. 45, 74. See also Charles River Bridge Co. v. Warren Bridge, 11 Pet. 420; s. c., 7 Pick. 344; 6 Pick. 376.

carriers has a right to provide by special contract for a special rate to a shipper, and such contract will be upheld when no element of partiality, oppression or improper favoritism entered into the contract.[1] In delivering the opinion in this case, Mr. Justice Elliott said: "It is, however, both appropriate and necessary to adjudge that a combination between common carriers to prevent competition is, at least, *prima facie*, illegal. The doubt is as to whether any ultimate purpose can save it from the condemnation of the law; there can be no doubt that, unexplained, such a combination for such a purpose is condemned by public policy. If such a combination can, in any event, be admitted to be legal, it can only be so when it is affirmatively shown that its object was to prevent ruinous competition, and that it does not establish unreasonable rates, unjust discrimination or oppressive regulations. If such a contract can stand it must be upon an affirmative showing, and one so full, complete and clear as to remove the presumption (to which its existence, in itself, gives rise), that it was found to do mischief to the public by repressing fair competition. The burden is on the carrier to remove the presumption, and until it is removed the agreement providing for the combination gives way before this presumption, and

[1] Cleveland, C., C. & I. Ry. Co. v. Closser, 126 Ind. 348; s. c., 26 N. E. Rep. 159. See also Texas, etc. Ry. Co. v. Southern Pacific Ry. Co., 41 La. Ann. 970; Woodstock Iron Co. v. Richmond, etc. Extension Co., 129 U. S. 693; Central Trust, etc. Co. v. Ohio Central R. R. Co., 23 Am. & Eng. R. R. Cas. 666; Boston Chamber of Commerce v. Lake Shore, etc. Ry. Co., 32 Am. & Eng. R. R. Cas. 618; Hare v. London, etc. Ry. Co., 2 J. & H. 80; Leslie v. Lorillard, 110 N. Y. 519; Chicago, etc. R. Co. v. Wabash, etc. Co., 61 Fed. Rep. 993; Gulf, etc. R. Co. v. State, 72 Tex. 404; s. c., 10 S. W. Rep. 81; State v. Standard Oil Co., 49 Ohio St. 137; s. c., 30 N. E. Rep. 279; Central, etc. Co. v. Guthrie, 35 Ohio St. 666; Stanton v. Allen, 5 Denio, 434; Hooker v. Vandewater, 4 Denio, 349; Chicago, etc. Co. v. People's, etc. Co., 121 Ill. 330; s. c., 13 N. E. Rep. 169; West Virginia, etc. Co. v. Ohio River, etc. Co., 22 W. Va. 600; Western Union Tel. Co. v. American, etc. Co., 65 Ga. 160; Sayre v. Louisville Assn., 1 Duv. 143; Burke v. Concord R. Co., 61 N. H. 160; Pittsburgh, etc. R. Co. v. Keokuk, etc. Co., 131 U. S. 371; Kettle River R. Co. v. Eastern R. Co., 41 Minn. 461; s. c., 40 Am. & Eng. R. Cas. 449; 43 N. W. Rep. 469.

the agreement must be held to be within the condemnation directed against all contracts which violate public policy."[1]

[1] Cleveland, C., C. & I. Ry. Co. v. Closser, 126 Ind. 348, 360; s. c., 26 N. E. Rep. 159. "Coming to the question which awaits our judgment, and to which we have cleared our path, we affirm that a contract between corporations charged with a public duty, such as is that of common carriers, providing for the formation of a combination having no other purpose than that of stifling competition, and providing means to accomplish that object, is illegal. The purpose to break down competition poisons the whole contract, and there is here no antidote which will rescue it from legal death. The element which destroys the contract is the purpose to stifle competition, for a combination of rival carriers, moved and controlled by that purpose alone, is destructive of public interest, and to the last degree antagonistic to sound public policy. The principle on which this rule rests is a very old one, and its place in the law is very firm. The overshadowing element in this case, and in kindred cases, is the purpose which influences the parties in uniting themselves in a combination, and concerting means to make its purpose effective, for the law abhors a combination which has for its principal object the suppression of competition in matters of commerce in which the public have an interest. Among the early cases establishing and enforcing the general principle which now occupies our attention, are those wherein it is held that an agreement to prevent or hinder competition at public sales is void. Our court has again and again enforced the general principle we have stated. Hunter v. Pfeiffer, 108 Ind. 197; Board v. Verbarg, 63 Ind. 107; Maguire v. Smock, 42 Ind. 1; Gilbert v. Carter, 10 Ind. 16; Forelander v. Hicks, 6 Ind. 448; Plaster v. Burger, 5 Ind. 232; Bunts v. Cole, 7 Blackf. 265." *Ibid.*, 360. In Murray v. Vanderbilt, 39 Barb. 140, an agreement was made between the Pacific Mail Steamship Company and the Accessory Transit Company, by which the former company was to pay to the latter a certain sum per trip, or per month, so long as the boats of the Pacific Company should run without opposition. It was held that in an action brought by the Transit Company against the Pacific Company, although the contract was unusual and in restraint of trade and commerce, the court would not enforce it against the delinquent party, or if the money had been paid, enable the party paying to recover it back but would leave the parties as the law found them: both being *in pari delicto*. Yet this rule did not apply to an action by one of the principals in such a contract, against the agent who had received money thereon. "The allegation of the bill is, that the Boston & Maine Railroad, a corporation chartered by the legislature of this State, and the Eastern Railroad, a Massachusetts corporation, but which, on the first day of May, 1874, and for a long time prior thereto, did, and does now, run, operate and control certain railroads chartered by the legislature of New Hampshire, on or about the first day of May, 1874, entered into a contract,

In a leading case before the Supreme Court of Errors, for the State of Connecticut, the Hartford & New Haven Railroad Company was chartered to construct and operate a railroad from Hartford to the navigable waters of New Haven harbor. A steamboat company was afterwards chartered to run in connection with it to New York and the railroad and line of steamboats constituted a route that was of great convenience to the public. After the construction of the road and the use of it in connection with the steamboat line for several years, the railroad company constructed a track diverging from the original track at a point a mile and a half from its terminus at tide water, and running to the station of the New York & New Haven Railroad Company in the city of New Haven, and discontinued the running of passenger trains to the original terminus at tide water. This change incommoded travelers who wished to pass by the steamboat route, of whom there were many. It was held

agreement, or arrangement, by the terms of which the said Boston & Maine and Eastern railroads should each retain sixty per cent. of its gross earnings between all competing points of their respective routes and the city of Boston, to pay the running expenses of the respective roads, and the balance of said gross earnings, being forty per cent. thereof, should constitute a common fund to be divided equally between said roads. The question is, whether such a contract and arrangement comes within the prohibition of the act? It is argued, on behalf of the defendants, that the latter part of the section quoted is intended to qualify and explain the preceding clauses, and not to establish a new limitation. The whole section together seems to me quite plain, and when so read the last clause appears to be a specification inserted to make more definite and certain the application and effect of what precedes. First, the consolidation of the roads or lines is prohibited in general terms; then the running of one rival road upon an arrangement by another is prohibited; then the running, management and operation of every such railroad by its own officers and agents is enjoined; and then comes the provision that each shall be dependent for support upon its own earnings, etc., that is, shall not be dependent for support upon the earnings of another,—which seems to be little more than a corollary from what comes before, a specification of an act in the nature of consolidation which had been already forbidden. It seems to me not to admit of doubt that the arrangement set up in the bill comes within the prohibition of the statute." Morrill v. Railroad, 55 N. H. 531, 537. See also Currier v. Concord R. Co., 66 N. H. 100; s. c., 20 Atl. Rep. 383; 8 Ry. & Corp. L. J. 443.

that a *mandamus* ought to be issued to compel the railroad company to run passenger trains to the original terminus. The railroad company had discontinued the running of passenger trains over that part of the road under a contract with the New York & New Haven Railroad Company, by which the latter was to prevent the extension of a certain railroad chartered by the legislature which would interfere with the Hartford & New Haven road, was to secure an advantage over the line of steamboats in competing for public travel. It was held that this contract was void as against public policy, and that the *mandamus* was properly applied for by the attorney for the State.[1] The principle on which this decision is based is stated by the court, as follows: "We forbear going into other questions raised on the trial, or commenting on the authorities cited by counsel. We think it unnecessary and prefer to place our decision upon the simple ground of the corporate duty of the respondents. All jurists and judges will at once agree that chartered companies are obliged fairly and fully to carry out the objects for which they are created, and that they can be compelled by *mandamus* to do it; and it will not be questioned that in the case of public highways, whether turnpikes or railroads, they are bound to keep them fit for use, and, in the case of railroads, to keep them furnished with suitable cars, engines and attendants, without which they cannot be used at all."[2]

§ 150. The Subject Continued.—The doctrine, as above expounded, is sustained by the recent decision of the Supreme Court of the United States in the leading case of The United States v. The Trans-Missouri Freight Association. In that case it was held that an agreement between a number of competing railroads, engaged in interstate traffic, "for the purpose of mutual protection by establishing and maintaining reasonable rates, rules and regulations on all freight traffic, both through and local," and forming an association to prescribe rates, which, when agreed to,

[1] State v. Hartford & N. H. R. R. Co., 29 Conn. 538.

[2] State v. Hartford & N. H. R. R. Co., 29 Conn. 538, 547.

are to govern all the companies, and a violation of which subjects the defaulting company to a pecuniary penalty, is an agreement or combination in restraint of trade or commerce, in the meaning of the anti-trust law, though each party to the agreement may withdraw therefrom on giving thirty days' notice.[1] In the opinion the principle on which

[1] United States v. Trans-Missouri Freight Association, 166 U. S. 290; s. c., 17 Sup. Ct. Rep. 540. In the course of the able and well reasoned opinion of Mr. Justice Peckham in this great case, at page 314, he uses the following language: "It is maintained that an agreement like the one in question on the part of the railroad companies is authorized by the Commerce Act, which is a special statute applicable only to railroads, and that a construction of the Trust Act (which is a general act) so as to include within its provisions the case of railroads, carries with it the repeal by implication of so much of the Commerce Act as authorized the agreement. It is added that there is no language in the Trust Act which is sufficiently plain to indicate a purpose to repeal those provisions of the Commerce Act which permit the agreement; that both acts may stand, the special or Commerce Act as relating solely to railroads and their proper regulation and management, while the later and general act will apply to all contracts of the nature therein described, entered into by any one other than competing common carriers by railroad for the purpose of establishing rates of traffic for transportation. On a line with this reasoning it is said that if Congress had intended to in any manner affect the railroad carrier as governed by the Commerce Act, it would have amended that act directly and in terms, and not left it as a question of construction to be determined whether so important a change in the commerce statute had been accomplished by the passage of the statute relating to trusts. The first answer to this argument is that, in our opinion, the Commerce Act does not authorize an agreement of this nature. It may not in terms prohibit, but it is far from conferring either directly or by implication any authority to make it. If the agreement be legal it does not owe its validity to any provisions of the Commerce Act, and if illegal it is not made so by that act. The fifth section prohibits what is termed 'pooling,' but there is no express provision in the act prohibiting the maintenance of traffic rates among competing roads by making such an agreement as this, nor is there any provision which permits it. Prior to the passage of the act the companies had sometimes endeavored to regulate competition and to maintain rates by pooling arrangements, and in the act that kind of an arrangement was forbidden. After its passage other devices were resorted to for the purpose of curbing competition and maintaining rates. The general nature of a contract like the one before us is not mentioned in or provided for by the act. The provisions of that act look to the prevention of discrimination, to the furnishing of

this case was decided is stated and expounded by Mr. Justice Peckham, as follows: "It is matter of common knowledge that agreements as to rates have been continually made of late years, and that complaints of each company in regard to the violation of such agreements by its rivals have been frequent and persistent. Rate wars go on notwithstanding any agreement to the contrary, and the struggle for business among competing roads keeps on, and in the nature of things will keep on, any alleged agreement to the contrary notwithstanding, and it is only by the exercise of good sense and by the presence of a common interest that railroads without entering into any affirmative agreement in regard thereto will keep within the limit of exacting a fair and reasonable return for services rendered. These agreements have never been found really effectual for any extended period. The interstate commerce commission, from whose reports quotations have been quite freely made by counsel for the purpose of proving the views of its learned members in regard to this subject, has never distinctly stated that agreements among competing railroads to maintain prices are to be commended, or that the general effect is to be regarded as beneficial. They have stated in their fourth annual report that competition may degenerate into rate wars, and that such wars are as unsettling to the busi-

equal facilities for the interchange of traffic, to the rate of compensation for what is termed the long and the short haul, to the attainment of a continuous passage from the point of shipment to the point of destination, at a known and published schedule, and in the language of counsel for defendants, 'without reference to the location of those points or the lines over which it is necessary for the traffic to pass,' or to procuring uniformity of rates charged by each company to its patrons, and to other subjects of a similar nature. The act was not directed to the securing of uniformity of rates to be charged by competing companies, nor was there any provision therein as to a maximum or minimum of rates. Competing and non-competing roads are not authorized by this statute to make an agreement like this one. As the Commerce Act does not authorize this agreement, argument against a repeal by implication, of the provisions of the act which it is alleged grant such authority, becomes ineffective. There is no appeal in this case, and both statutes may stand, as neither is inconsistent with the other."

ness of the country as they are mischievous to the carriers, and that the spirit of existing law is against them. They then add: 'Agreements between railroad companies which from time to time they have entered into with a view to prevent such occurrences have never been found effectual, and for the very sufficient reason that the mental reservations in forming them have been quite as numerous and more influential than the written stipulations.' It would seem true, therefore, that there is no guaranty of financial health to be found in entering into agreements for the maintenance of rates, nor is financial ruin or insolvency the necessary result of their absence. The claim that the company has the right to charge reasonable rates, and that, therefore, it has the right to enter into a combination with competing roads to maintain such rates, cannot be admitted. The conclusion does not follow from an admission of the premise. What one company may do in the way of charging reasonable rates is radically different from entering into an agreement with other and competing roads to keep up the rates to that point. If there be any competition, the extent of the charge for the service will be seriously affected by that fact. Competition will itself bring charges down to what may be reasonable, while in the case of an agreement to keep prices up, competition is allowed no play; it is shut out, and the rate is practically fixed by the companies themselves by virtue of the agreement, so long as they abide by it."[1]

§ 151. Purchase of Competing Lines of Transportation.—Under ordinary circumstances the object, and if not the sole object, at least the primary or principal object of such purchases, is the creation of a monopoly for the purpose of suppressing competition. But the creation of such a monopoly is in contravention of public policy at common law, and will not be upheld unless it is accomplished under the provisions of its charter. The legislature may grant

[1] United States v. Trans-Missouri Fre ght Association (1897), 166 U. S. 290, 338; s. c., 17 Sup. Ct. Rep. 540, 558.

such power, unless prohibited by the constitution of the State, and it is only under a legislative grant that it can be exercised. A railway company cannot sell its property to a competing line, and where it is sold at judicial sale the purchaser will acquire no rights or privileges which were not conferred by the charter upon the original company. The new company can do in this direction only what might be done by the original proprietors. In a very recent and leading case before the Supreme Court of Texas, it was held that a corporation, organized for public purposes, cannot, except with the consent of the political authority which created it, render itself incapable of performing its corporate duties to the public, whether this be attempted by contract of lease, sale or otherwise. Any such contract made without legislative sanction is void. Under the statute authorizing a railway company to borrow money to construct, complete, improve or operate its road, and to give mortgages therefor, a purchaser may acquire title to the road by a sale made under a power conferred in such a mortgage, or title may be acquired by purchase under judicial sale to pay such indebtedness. After such a sale the corporate existence continues, and the purchaser becomes, in effect, a stockholder of the corporation. A railway company chartered under general laws cannot purchase the railway of another company; it results that, since the power to make such a purchase could not exist under an original charter of incorporation, it could not be obtained through an amended charter in the absence of legislative permission. Though the statute requires articles of incorporation to be passed on by the attorney-general before they can be filed with the secretary of state, and the incorporation completed, yet that officer cannot judicially determine either the purposes for which a company may be incorporated or what powers it may acquire by the act of incorporation; the law, to be construed by the judicial department, must determine both. The rule that a corporation has only power to do such acts as its charter, considered in relation to the general law, authorizes it to do, applies to every class of corporation. The Gulf, Colorado & Santa Fe Railway Company obtained an amended charter under general law, which provided, among other things, that it might purchase the Central & Montgomery Railroad, and own, operate and equip the same. Certain stockholders of the Gulf, Colorado & Santa Fe Railway Company purchased all the bonds and stocks of the Central & Montgomery Railroad Company, and, after destroying the bonds, attempted to sell the latter road to the Gulf, Colorado & Santa Fe Railway Company. Possession of the road-bed, etc., was taken under the attempted sale, and the road operated and controlled as part of the Gulf, Colorado & Santa Fe Railway Company. It was held: (1) That no title to the road passed by the purchase. (2) The Central & Montgomery Railroad Company continued as an existing corporation, and those holding its stock might complete a reorganization. (3) The Central & Montgomery Railroad Company and its property was liable for any debts incurred in its management, without regard to whose management it was subjected to.[1] In

[1] Gulf, Colorado & Santa Fe R. Co. v. Morris, 67 Tex. 692. "It may be urged however, that if the power of the one corporation to buy the other was not given under the original charters of either corporation, yet that such a power was acquired through the amendment of the charter of the Gulf, Colorado & Santa Fe Railway Company, which provided in effect that it should have the 'right to purchase the Central & Montgomery Railroad and to own, operate, equip and maintain the same under this charter as a part of said Eastern branch.' The law providing for the amendment of railroad charters nowhere intimates that such a corporation may acquire rights or powers through an amendment that it could not have acquired under its original incorporation." *Ibid.*, 701. "The next question I shall consider, with a due appreciation of its importance, is whether the constitutional inhibition contained in sec. 17, art. 12 (of Missouri) is any more comprehensive than the statutory prohibition last considered. According to the view that the court takes of the case it cannot, or at least it ought not, to grant an injunction, unless it clearly appears that the general assembly has failed to give full effect to the constitutional prohibition, nor unless it appears that the purchase of the Frisco stock is in violation of the constitution though not in violation of the statute. It is sufficient to say on this point that the court is not prepared to hold that the general assembly has either misconstrued sec. 17, art. 12 of the constitution, or that it intentionally failed to give it full effect when it enacted section 2569 of the

New Jersey it has been held that where railroad companies were by legislative authority authorized to consolidate their capital stock, and by supplement one of them which had then mortgaged its after-acquired property was authorized

Revised Statutes. On the contrary I have no doubt that the legislature intended to make the statute as broad as the constitution, and good reasons, no doubt, exist for holding that it accomplished its purpose. It is certainly a reasonable view, and one justified by the language employed, that the constitutional inhibition, like the statutory, was aimed at railroad corporations which might at one time own, operate, manage, or secure the right to run trains over roads located in this State, and that the purpose was to prevent such a corporation from purchasing, leasing or controlling another road of the State, or that was parallel to, or that competed with, the road so owned, operated or managed. Such an inhibition would certainly preserve the independence of, and secure competition between, rival lines of railroad crossing the State in all directions, and connecting important commercial centers within the State: and it may fairly be urged that this was the purpose had in view by those who framed the present constitution. On the other hand, it may well be doubted whether the constitutional prohibition in question was intended to have the effect of preventing a great railroad system like the Atchison, occupying as it does an extensive area of country to the westward of this State, from obtaining access to the city of St. Louis by the purchase of, or by consolidation with, one of the four or five trunk lines crossing the State from east to west, merely because the road so purchased touches some points in Kansas which the Atchison system also reaches. The preservation of reasonable rates was the great object in view, and as the proof in this case abundantly shows, the aquisition by the Atchison company of the Frisco stock has had no effect upon rates between points in this State and those points in Kansas which are reached by the Frisco: and it must be apparent to any one familiar with the railroad situation in this State and Kansas that it cannot have any tendency in the future to increase such rates. In what I have thus said on the point now under consideration I would not be understood as deciding definitely that the prohibitions contained in the constitution and the statute are in all respects identical. * * * From the views which I have thus outlined, it follows that I must decline to grant an injunction, because the purchase of the Frisco stock was not, in my judgment, in contravention of the statute, and because it is by no means certain that such purchase was prohibited by the constitution." Kimball v. Atchison, T. & S. F. R. Co., 46 Fed. Rep. 888, 890. A charter power given to a railway corporation to join stocks or consolidate with any other railway company "running in the same general direction," only empowers such consolidation with a railway having a road which might constitute a part of the line between in lieu of consolidation of capital stock, to purchase the stock of the other company, and the purchase, and sale and delivery of the stock were actually made, for the purpose of consolidation and an actual consolidation of the roads was in fact made, and completely recognized, the purchase, and the sale, and delivery of the capital stock was held to be a consolidation in accordance with the provisions of the acts.[1]

§ 152. **Lease of Competing Lines.**—Where a railway company leases or attempts to lease a competing line the presumptive object is the creation of a monopoly for the suppression of competition. But as this is illegal, as opposed to public policy, a lease of this character will be upheld only as it is made under an express provision of its charter. As a rule, the charter of a railway corporation will enable it to lease a branch line, which is in no proper sense

the points designated in the charter for the road which it was authorized to build. The charter power conferred on a railway company to rent, lease, sell or consolidate with another railroad company cannot exist in the absence of some law authorizing it, and cannot be implied from a prohibition extending only to parallel or competing lines. Railway companies, by reason of their relations with or control or management of other lines than their own, may become within the meaning of the law competing lines, though the railways owned by them may not in fact connect. East Line & Red Riv. Ry. Co. v. State, 75 Tex. 434. "The uniform course of legislation in reference to street railroads, shows a policy on the part of the State to facilitate arrangements for the connection of continuous lines, and the transfer of passengers from one road to another, with the view of giving the longest service possible to the public without increase of fare. It can hardly be supposed that the legislature while expressly making provisions for such facilities intended to proscribe companies connecting with another road, which happened to own a line parallel for a certain portion of its length, but which also owned other lines extending beyond the parallel portion, from the benefits to be derived from a traffic contract. It seems to us that the obvious intent of this provision was to avoid the monopoly of parallel lines, and prevent the acquisition by one railroad company of the exclusive possession and control of such lines. It, therefore, prohibits leases to parallel roads. This does not, and, in our judgment, was not intended to preclude such companies from making traffic contracts for the partial use of their respective routes beyond the line of parallelism." People v. O'Brien, 111 N. Y. 1, 64.

[1] Williamson v. N. J. Southern R. R. Co., 26 N. J. Eq. 398.

a competitor, but where the line is parallel and is or may become a competing line, it may lease it only as the power to do so is specifically and unequivocally conferred by the legislature. Provisions of this character in a charter will be most rigidly and strictly construed. Nothing will be presumed in favor of the power. It has been held that where a railway corporation leases its property to another road without such power for a long period the act will be held as an abandonment of the operation of the road, and that such abandonment subjects it to forfeiture.[1] In the case here

[1] State v. Atchison & Neb. R. R. Co., 24 Neb. 143. "To justify the defendant in leasing its line to the B. & M. R. R. Company, it must be able to point to the exact statute granting such authority, which it has failed to do. Penn Co. v. St. Louis, Alton & T. H. Railroad, 118 U. S. 294. In the opinion of the majority of the court in that case it is said: 'We think it may be stated, as the just result of these cases, and on sound principle, that unless specially authorized by its charter or aided by some other legislative action, a railroad company cannot, by lease or any other contract, turn over to another company for a long period of time its road and all its appurtenances, the use of its franchises, and the exercise of its powers, nor can any other railroad company, without similar authority, make a contract to receive and operate such road, franchises and property of the first corporation, and that such a contract is not among the ordinary powers of a railroad company, and it is not to be presumed from the usual grant of powers in a railroad charter. This, in our view, is a correct statement of the law.'" *Ibid.*, 161. "The attorney-general says, and the record supports, the statement, that these roads are 'for sixty miles lying parallel and near to each other.' That they are, indeed, in the largest sense, parallel and competing roads, seems to be beyond dispute, and it may be fairly inferred from the record that a leading object in making the consolidation was to destroy that competition. That being true, the lines of these roads are not, in my judgement, 'so constructed as to admit the passage of burden or passenger cars over two or more of such roads continuously,' within the proper meaning of section 3379. That the mere physical ability to pass cars from one road to the other satisfies the statute is a construction of it,—which is wholly inadmissible, for the provision requiring such connection would be without meaning. In imposing that restriction upon consolidation, the legislature intended, not merely that the physical fact should exist, but that such consolidation should only be made for the very purpose of passing freight and passengers over both lines, or some material parts thereof, not necessarily in a direct or straight line, but *continuously*. * * * Having regard to the language of this statute, in the light of such aids as are here indicated I am satisfied the legislature never intended that railroads,

situated as these are, should be regarded as constructed for the carriage of freight and passengers *continuously*, in the manner contemplated by the section. Indeed, each of these consolidating companies had a line for the carriage of freight and passengers from Cincinnati to Lake Erie, 'continuously, without break or interruption,' and the policy of the country in general, indicated in the constitutional and statutory provisions, has long been opposed to the consolidation of roads bearing such relation to each other, and this strengthens the belief that these companies are not within the section in question. Consolidation for the transportation of freight and passengers continuously is a thing which the legislature might well desire to encourage, as it may be advantageous alike to the public and the companies; but corporations have power only as granted by the general assembly; and where companies, situated as these are, being parallel and competing, claim that authority to consolidate has been granted to them, they must be able to point to words in the statute which admit of no other construction, for it will not be assumed that the law-making power has authorized the creation of a monopoly so detrimental to the public interest. But the statute contains no such words. An examination of the provisions relating to the power of railroad companies to lease does not lead us to a different conclusion. True, by the Act of 1851, it was not provided in express words that the fact that the lines of two companies were parallel and competing should be a bar to a lease by one to the other or to a consolidation of the companies; nor was there any such express provisions in the Act of 1852 (3 Curwen, 1884). or the Act of 1869 (3 Sayler, 1760), with respect to leasing. Express provision, however, prohibiting one company from leasing to another where their lines were competing, was made by the Act of 1873 (4 Sayler, 2950), and that provision was carried in the Rev. Stats. § 3300. From the absence of any such express prohibition with respect to consolidation, it is argued that here is a legislative expression that the fact that lines are competitive is no objection to consolidation, but that conclusion, in my judgment, is altogether erroneous. By the Act of 1852 (3 Curwen, 1877), a consolidation was provided for in section 21, and leasing in section 24. When section 24 was repealed and re-enacted with certain changes in 1869, it was left, in the respect mentioned, unchanged, and such prohibition was introduced, as we have seen, in 1873, when the section was again amended. Perhaps this latter amendment was introduced by reason of some abuse which had no direct relation to consolidation, and hence the propriety of amending the section on that subject was not considered. But, however this may be, it does not follow that such change in the language of the act worked any radical change in the law. The presumption, as we have seen, is the other way, where the purpose to require a change in the construction is not clear. Notwithstanding the Act of 1873, the question still is as to the fair interpretation of the section relating to consolidation previous to that time, which section is still in force in substantially the same form. Rev. Stats. 3379. That it does not authorize a consolidation of lines bearing to cited the rule is stated by the court, as follows: "In Thomas v. Railroad Company,[1] a railroad company in New Jersey had leased its road, franchises and property for a period of twenty years, giving the lessee complete control thereof, and received as rent one-half the gross sum collected by the lessee from the operation of the road. The decision turned upon the power of the company under its corporate authority to make the lease. The lessee insisted that a corporation may, as at common law, do an act which is not either expressly or impliedly prohibited by its charter. To this the court responded: 'We do not concur in this proposition. We take the general doctrine to be in this country, though there may be exceptional cases and some authorities to the contrary, that the powers of corporations organized under legislative statutes are such, and such only, as those statutes confer. Conceding the rule applicable to all statutes, that what is fairly implied is as much granted as what is expressed, it remains that the charter of a corporation is the measure of its powers, and that the enumeration of these powers implies the exclusion of all others.' The doctrine, as above stated, meets our hearty approval. If the allegations of the information are true, and they are to be so considered on demurrer to the information, the defendant induced the people along its line, from the Kansas border to the city of Lincoln, to grant liberal aid for the construction of the road. Every piece of land subject to taxation in the counties along the line of said road is practically mortgaged by the issuing of bonds

each other the relation borne by these roads, is a proposition to which I fully assent. Entertaining these views, the question how far this consolidation may be affected by the clause in the Act of 1873, incorporated into section 3300 of the Revised Statutes, is not with me a vital one. But the policy of the State, as declared in that enactment, cannot be in doubt. Since 1873 at least there can be no lease where the lines of the lessor and lessee are competing, and it is admitted that if there can be no lease, there can be no consolidation of such lines leased since then. The rule upon the subject may be more rigid since 1873 than it was under the former legislation. I do not think it necessary to determine how that was." State v. Vanderbilt, 37 Ohio St. 590, 643.

[1] Thomas v. Railroad Company, 101 U. S. 71.

to aid in building it. The interest has presumably been paid on these bonds to the present time; many of the settlers along such road when the bonds were issued were pioneers, struggling with the hardships, poverty, privations and difficulties incident to a new country. To many of them, no doubt, the taxes necessary to meet the interest and amount required for the sinking fund have been a burden, and by every one the tax was voted to aid in constructing and operating an independent line of railway. That was the contract of the parties, and the State would be derelict in its duties if it did not compel an observance on the part of the defendant of its duties. The defendant, however, having obtained this bonus, sought to surrender all its powers, rights and franchises to another corporation for the period of nine hundred and ninety-nine years. So far as the defendant is concerned, it has ceased to operate a railroad, and the charge of misuser and non-user plainly appears on the face of the record. It is not the policy of the law to allow a railroad company, organized as an independent line, to procure aid on every hand in that character, and after the road is completed sell out to the highest bidder. Honorable and fair dealing are as essential in the dealings of a railroad corporation with individuals and the public in the construction and operation of its road as between individuals in the ordinary affairs of life. A railway company cannot be permitted to act in bad faith with those from whom it has received aid upon certain conditions. Having received the consideration it must perform on its part, and the parties are entitled to a literal compliance. And while a lessee in a proper case, or assignee or purchaser, will take a road burdened with the conditions, obligations and duties assumed by the original corporation, yet there can be no such transfer by lease, assignment or sale without express statutory authority, and as we find no such authority, and the defendant has been guilty of misuser and non-user of its franchises, they are subject to forfeiture."[1]

[1] State v. Atchison & Neb. R. R. Co., 24 Nev. 143, 162; s. c., 32 Am. & Eng. R. Cas. 388.

§ 153. Consolidation of Parallel Lines.—The consolidation of railway corporations which own and operate parallel and competing lines, like the purchase or lease of a parallel line, is invalid at law, but is subject to statutory regulation. The legislature has power to prohibit or to grant the consolidation of competing lines of railway, or of corporations owning and operating such lines. The leading case relating to this subject is that of Pearsall v. The Great Northern Railway. In 1856 the Minneapolis & St. Cloud Railroad Company was incorporated by the territorial legislature of Minnesota with very liberal rights and privileges, and under this charter the road was put in operation. In 1874 the State of Minnesota enacted that "no railroad corporation or the lessees, purchasers or managers of any railroad corporation shall consolidate the stock, property or franchises of such corporation with, or lease or purchase the works or franchises of, or in any way control any other railroad corporation owning or having under its control a parallel or competing line; nor shall any officer of such railroad corporation act as the officer of any other railroad corporation owning or having the control of a parallel or competing line; and the question whether railroads are parallel or competing lines shall, when demanded by the party complainant, be decided by a jury as in other civil issues;" and in 1881 its legislature enacted that "no railroad corporation shall consolidate with, lease or purchase, or in any way become owner of, or control any other railroad corporation, or any stock, franchise, rights of property thereof, which owns or controls a parallel or competing line." In 1889 the company changed its name to the Great Northern Railway Company, and extended its line westward. At the organization of the Northern Pacific Railroad an arrangement was entered into by the two companies, which was a practical consolidation of their lines. In the case of Pearsall v. The Great Northern Railway Company, a stockholder of the Great Northern Company filed his bill against it to restrain it from carrying out such agreement. It was held that the Great Northern Company was subject to the provisions of the Acts of 1874 and 1881, and that the proposed arrangement was in violation of the provisions in those acts, prohibiting railroad corporations from consolidating with, leasing or purchasing, or in any other way becoming the owner of, or controlling any other railroad corporation, or the stock, franchises or rights of property thereof, having a parallel or competing line, and was, therefore, beyond the corporate power of the company to make. Where, by a railway charter, a general power is given to consolidate with, purchase, lease or acquire the stock of other roads which has remained unexecuted, it is within the competency of the legislature to declare, by subsequent acts, that this power shall not extend to the purchase, lease or consolidation with parallel or competing lines. Where a charter authorizes a company in sweeping terms to do certain things which are unnecessary to the main object of the grant, and not directly and immediately within the contemplation of the parties thereto, the power so conferred, so long as it is unexecuted, is within the control of the legislature, and may be treated as a license, and may be revoked if a possible exercise of such power is found to conflict with the interests of the public.[1] In the opinion in this

[1] Pearsall v. Gt. Northern Ry., 161 U. S. 646. "We do not deem it necessary to express an opinion in this case whether the legislature could wholly revoke the power it had given to this company to extend its system by the construction or purchase of branch lines or feeders; since a possibility of an extension of the road even to the Pacific coast may have had an influence upon persons contemplating the purchase of its stock or securities, so that a right to do this might be said to have become vested. But we think it was competent for the legislature, out of due regard for the public welfare, to declare that its charter should not be used for the purpose of stifling competition, and building up monopolies. In short, we cannot recognize a vested right to do a manifest wrong. Nor do we undertake to say that the legislature may not, in the exercise of a wise foresight, and for the purpose of attracting capital to enterprises of doubtful profit, authorize the granting of monopolies for a limited time, irrevocable by a subsequent legislature. To do so would practically ignore or overrule a series of cases to which we have already adverted, wherein corporations have been induced to furnish municipalities with bridges, gas, water and other requirements of modern civilization, by the promise of exclusive privileges for a term of years. Perhaps, too, it might not be beyond the competency of

case, delivered by Mr. Justice Brown, the principle on which the decision is based is expounded, as follows: "Whether the consolidation of competing lines will necessarily result in an increase of rates, or whether such con-

the legislature to authorize a railroad, by a clear and explicit act, to consolidate with a parallel or competing line, since cases may be imagined where it might be for the public welfare to permit such consolidation. But the Act of 1865, upon which the defendant relies, contains no such provision. There is only a general authority to consolidate, which we think the legislature may, by another act, declare shall not apply to cases manifestly not within its original intent. We think the general doctrine requiring grants to corporations to be construed favorably to the public, where there is a reasonable doubt as to the extent of the privilege conferred, may properly be invoked to declare that such privileges shall not be used to the detriment of the public." *Ibid.*, 675. The acquisition of lands for speculation or sale, or to prevent interference by competing lines or methods of transportation, or in aid of collateral enterprises, remotely connected with the running or operating of the road though they may increase its revenue and business, are not such purposes as authorize the condemnation of private property therefor. Accordingly where a railroad company, having one of the *termini* of its road upon a navigable waterway extending into the territory of a foreign power, in its application for the acquisition of certain lands situate on the shore of such waterway near the said terminus, alleges, as a prominent reason for their condemnation, that a charter had been granted by such foreign government for the construction of a ship canal connecting the said waterway with other navigable waters, which, when completed, would greatly increase the business of the railroad, and that the lands were needed for the construction of ships and docks for the accommodation of vessels bringing freight to or taking it from the said road and of tenements for the employes of the railroad and to meet the requirements of the anticipated increased business; and it appeared from the proofs that the company already had, at such terminus, a convenient and accessible water front and docks, which were used but in part, and were capable of extension on its own premises, and it did not appear that the work on the ship canal referred to had been commenced, or that the capital to construct it had been secured, *held*, that it was not sufficiently shown that the lands were required for the present or prospective business of the corporation within the meaning of the statute, and they could not be taken against the will of the owner. Rensselaer & Saratoga R. R. Co. v. Davis, 43 N. Y. 137. "It is enough that by the lease the connected roads form a continuous line, and it is not essential that the leased line be an extension from either terminus of the lessee's road. The evil which was intended to be guarded against by this limitation was the placing of parallel and competing roads solidation has generally resulted in a detriment to the public, is beside the question. Whether it has that effect or not, it certainly puts it in the power of the consolidated corporation to give it that effect,—in short, puts the public at

under one management, and the control by one company of the general railroad affairs of the State through the leasing of roads remote from its own, and with which it has no physical or direct business connection. It was not intended to prevent a company with a long road, like the lessee company, from leasing branches by means of which it establishes continuous lines from their several *termini* to each of its own. By this lease a direct and continuous line from Louisville to Shelbyville was created, and neither the letter nor the spirit of the statute was thwarted." Hancock v. Louisville R. R. Co., 145 U. S. 409, 412. In Pearson v. Railroad, 62 N. H. 537, it is held that a railroad corporation cannot become a stockholder in another railroad corporation for the purpose of controlling the business of the latter, or the election of its officers, unless such power is given by statute. In the opinion the court say: "A corporation cannot become a stockholder in another corporation unless such power is given it by its charter or is necessarily implied in it (Franklin Co. v. Bank, 68 Me. 43; Bank v. Agency Co., 24 Conn. 159; Green's Brice's Ultra Vires, 91, and cases cited; Morawetz on Corporations, § 229, and cases cited), especially if the purchase be for the purpose of controlling or affecting the management of the other corporation. Sumner v. Marcy, 3 W. & M. 105; Central R. R. Co. v. Collins, 40 Ga. 582; Hazlehurst v. Savannah, etc. R. R. Co., 43 Ga. 13; G. N. Ry. Co. v. E. C. Ry. Co., 21 L. J. Ch. 837; Booth v. Robinson, 55 Md. 419, 439. Dealing in stocks is not expressly prohibited in the Act of Congress providing for the organization of national banks (U. S. Rev. St. § 5136, par. 7), but such prohibition is implied from the failure to grant the power. Bank v. Bank, 92 U. S. 122, 128. Corporations are creatures of the legislature, having no other powers than such as are given to them by their charters, or such as are incidental or necessary to carry into effect the purposes for which they were established. Downing v. Mt. W. Road Co., 40 N. H. 230, 232; Trustees v. Peaslee, 15 N. H. 317, 330; Beaty v. Knowler's Lessee, 4 Pet. 152; Perrine v. Company, 9 How. 172; Bank v. Earle, 13 Pet. 519; Dartmouth College v. Woodward, 4 Wheat. 518, 536. Certain classes of corporations, such as religious and charitable corporations, and corporations for literary purposes, may rightfully invest their moneys in the stock of other corporations. The power, if not expressly mentioned in their charters, is necessarily implied, for the preservation of the funds with which such institutions are endowed, and to render their funds productive. So an insurance company or savings bank may rightfully invest its capital or deposits in the stocks of railroad companies, banks, manufacturing companies and similar corporations. The power is nec-the mercy of the corporation. There is and has been, for the past three hundred years, both in England and in this country, a popular prejudice against monopolies in general, which has found expression in innumerable acts of legislation. We cannot say that such prejudice is not well founded. It is a matter upon which the legislature is entitled to pass judgment. At least, there is sufficient doubt of the propriety of such monopolies to authorize the legislature, which may be presumed to represent the views of the public, to say that it will not tolerate them unless the power to establish them be conferred by clear and explicit language. While, in particular cases, two railways by consolidating their interests under a single management, may have been able to so far reduce the expenses of administration as to give their customers the benefit of a lower tariff, the logical effect of all monopolies is an increase of price of the thing produced, whether it be merchandise or transportation. Owing to the greater speed, and cheapness of the service performed by them, railways become necessarily monopolists of all traffic along their lines, but the general sentiment of the public declares that such monopolies must be limited to the necessities of the case, and rebels against the attempt of one road to control all traffic between terminal points, also connected by a competing line. There are, moreover, thought to be other dangers to the moral sense of the community incident to such great aggregations of

essary to enable them to engage in the business for which they are organized, and hence is implied, if not expressly granted, in their charters. Such investments are in the line of their business. On the other hand, a manufacturing or railroad corporation is incorporated to do the business of manufacturing, or transporting passengers and merchandise. Investing their funds in that of other corporations is not in the line of their business. Under extraordinary circumstances it may become necessary for a national bank or a manufacturing corporation, or a railroad corporation, as in satisfaction of a valid debt, or by way of security, but with a view to its subsequent sale or conversion into money so as to make good or redeem an anticipated loss." See also Fleckner v. Bank, 8 Wheat. 351. A joint stock corporation has power by law to declare that no person who is attorney against it in a suit shall be eligible as a director. Cross v. W. Va., C. & P. Ry. Co., 37 W. Va. 342.

wealth, which, though indirect, are even more insidious in their influence, and such as have awakened feelings of hostility which have not failed to find expression in legislative acts. The consolidation of these two great corporations will unavoidably result in giving to the defendant a monopoly of all traffic in the northern half of the State of Minnesota, as well as of all trans-continental traffic north of the line of the Union Pacific, against which public regulation will be but a feeble protection. The acts of the Minnesota legislature of 1874 and 1881 undoubtedly reflected the general sentiment of the public, that their best security is in competition. In conclusion, we hold that where, by a railway charter, a general power is given to consolidate with, purchase, lease or acquire the stock of other roads, which has remained unexecuted, it is within the competency of the legislature to declare, by subsequent acts, that this power shall not extend to the purchase, lease or consolidation with parallel or competing lines."[1]

§ **154. The Subject Continued.**—Where the consolidation of parallel lines cannot be accomplished by direct action an attempt to accomplish it by indirection will not be sustained. In a recent case before the Supreme Court of the United States, it was held that a contemporaneous construction of its charter, which ratified the purchase of a few short local lines, does not justify the company in consolidating with a parallel and competing line between its two *termini* with a view of distroying the competition which had existed between the two lines. If, from reasons of public policy, a legislature declares that a railway company shall not become the purchaser of a parallel or competing line, the purchase is not the less unlawful, because the parties choose to let it take the form of a judicial sale. Whatever is contrary to public policy or inimical to the public interests is subject to the police power of the State, and is within legislative control: and, in the execution of such power, the legislature is vested with a large discretion, which, if

[1] Pearsall v. Gt. Northern Ry., 161 U. S. 646, 676.

exercised *bona fide* for the protection of the public, is beyond the reach of judicial inquiry.[1] In the opinion in this case the rule is stated, as follows: "We do not understand,

[1] Louisville & N. R. R. v. Kentucky, 161 U. S. 677. "By the Act of March 7, 1854, the company was given power to unite their road with any other road connecting therewith upon such conditions as the two companies might agree upon. As we have frequently held that a power to connect or unite with another road refers merely to a physical connection of the tracks, and does not authorize the purchase, or even the lease, of such road, or any union of their franchise, it is evident that this act is no authority for the proposed consolidation. Atchison, Topeka, etc. R. R. v. Denver & New Orleans Railroad, 110 U. S. 667; Pennsylvania Co. v. St. Louis, Alton, etc. R. R., 118 U. S. 290; Oregon Railway v. Oregonian Railway, 130 U. S. 1; St. Louis Railroad v. Terre Haute R. R., 145 U. S. 393; Commissioners v. Railroad Co., 50 Ind. 85. The important power to purchase or consolidate with another line cannot be inferred from such indefinite language as 'to unite or connect with such road.' * * * The company insists that the power to purchase and hold other roads is not only unlimited, and extends to all other roads built, or to be built, although parallel and competing lines, but that it constitutes an irrevocable contract, which a subsequent legislature is powerless to impair. In construing this section, we are bound to bear in mind the general rule, so often affirmed by this court, that all doubts, with regard to the authority granted in a corporate charter, are to be resolved against the corporation, and that a surrender of the power of the legislature in any matter of public concern must never be presumed from uncertain or equivocal expressions. Dubuque & Pacific R. R. v. Litchfield, 23 How. 66, 88; Delaware Railroad Tax, 18 Wall. 206, 225; Bailey v. Maguire, 22 Wall. 215; Slidell v. Grandjean, 111 U. S. 412; Belmont Bridge v. Wheeling Bridge, 138 U. S. 287." *Ibid.*, 684, 685. In Elkins v. Camden & Atlantic R. R. Co., 36 N. J. Eq. 5, the directors of a railroad company, without any authority, either by statute or charter, passed a resolution to assume certain debts, and to buy a majority of the stock and bonds, and the equipment of a rival railroad. The resolution also provided for the calling of a special meeting of the stockholders to vote upon the matter, and it was not to be carried out without their approval. It was held that the proposed purchase was *ultra vires*, and hence could not be executed, even if ratified by the stockholders. That it was void and against public policy, in that its object was to prevent lawful competition. See, as to inability of railroad to become stockholder in another railroad, Central R. R. Co. v. Collins, 40 Ga. 582; Compagnie Francaise v. Western Union Co., 11 Fed. Rep. 842; Solomons v. Laing, 6 Eng. Ry. Cas. 289; Franklin Bank v. Commercial Bank, 36 Ohio St. 350; Franklin Co. v. Lewiston Inst., 68 Me. 43; Taylor v. Earle, 8 Hun, 1; Buford v. Keokuk Co., 3 Mo. App. 159.

however, that the fact that a purchase is made at a judicial sale confers upon the purchaser any right he is forbidden to acquire, if the purchase had been made at a private sale. If, from reasons of public policy, the legislature declares that a railway shall not become the purchaser of a parallel or competing line, the purchase is not the less unlawful, because the parties choose to let it take the form of a judicial sale. A person who, by reason of any statutory disability,—such as infancy, lunacy, marriage or otherwise,—is incompetent to buy at private sale, is not less incompetent from becoming the purchaser at a judicial sale. The prohibition is not upon the power of the court foreclosing the mortgage to order a judicial sale of the property, but upon its power to confirm a sale made to a parallel or competing road."[1]

§ 155. **Rule in Case of Traffic Arrangement.**—The rule relating to the control of parallel lines by a competing railroad applies *mutatis mutandis* to all traffic agreements by which one company obtains control of the property and of the management of the business of a competing line. A railway company cannot purchase the controlling interest in the stock of a competing line, and thus control its business with a view to suppressing competition. In a recent case before the United States Circuit Court for the District of Washington, it was held that a railroad company, organized under the laws of Washington, has no authority to transfer its franchise, except by sale and conveyance or lease made in accordance with the statutes relating to the transfer of titles to such property; and where, by a so-called "traffic agreement," the trustees, without the consent of the minority stockholders, in effect, transfer to another railroad company the entire control and management of the property, for practically the legal lifetime of the corporation, such contract is illegal and void. A controlling interest in the stock of a railway company was purchased by another railway company, which thereby secured the elec-

[1] Louisville & N. R. R. v. Kentucky, 161 U. S. 677, 693.

tion of a board of trustees, consisting of its own officers and employes, who owned no stock in their own right. This board then executed an illegal traffic agreement whereby the entire control of the franchises and property of the former company was surrendered to the latter. It was held that the minority stockholders in the former company could maintain a bill to annul the contract without first applying to the board of trustees for protection.[1] In

[1] Earle v. Seattle, L. S. & E. Ry. Co., 56 Fed. Rep. 909. "The only authority found in the charter of the Northern Pacific Railroad Company for what has been done in absorbing the property and franchise of the Seattle, Lake Shore & Eastern Company, and assuming liability for its bonded indebtedness, is section 17, supplemented by a provision of the laws of this State, authorizing railroad corporations to purchase or lease and operate connecting lines of railway in this State, enacted March 28, 1890. (Laws Wash. 1889-90, p. 527.) The section of the charter referred to reads as follows: 'Sec. 17. And be it further enacted that the said company is authorized to accept to its own use any grant, donation, loan, power, franchise, aid or assistance which may be granted to, or conferred upon, said company by the Congress of the United States, by the legislature of any State, or by any corporation, person or persons; and said corporation is authorized to hold and enjoy such grant, donation, loan, power, franchise, aid or assistance to its own use for the purpose aforesaid.' The statute referred to does not prescribe the manner whereby purchases or leases of railways may be consummated, otherwise than by the general provisions of the several statutes relating to corporations, and to conveyances of property. A railroad corporation cannot lawfully transfer its franchise without authority emanating from the power which granted it. And an unauthorized transfer, made in disguise, as by a traffic contract, will not, in a judicial proceeding, be treated with greater favor than if the contract expressed plainly the real intention of the parties. On the subject of traffic contracts, the text of Green's Brice's Ultra Vires (page 427) concisely and clearly states the law, as follows: 'Corporations may make all necessary arrangements for cheaply and expeditiously developing or carrying on their particular business; but it is another thing, going beyond this, to enter into contracts, for instance, by which the exclusive control or the exclusive right of working the line is handed over to other parties. All such arrangements, whatever their forms, however disguised, are *ultra vires* and void. This applies with peculiar force in the case of those bodies which have been created for what may be conveniently styled public purposes.' Now, assuming that the section of the charter above quoted does authorize the Northern Pacific Railroad Company to take the benefit of rights and privileges, and exercise new powers, granted

Pennsylvania it has recently been held that a railroad company has a right to make a special traffic contract with a connecting railroad which is not parallel or competing; and it may also make such a contract with a special class of shippers to secure business. On a bill in equity, where it appears that the defendant, a furnace company, has agreed for a sufficient consideration to give all of its traffic to the plaintiff, a railroad company, the court will decree specific performance of the contract, but will not enjoin the officers of the defendant company from participating in the construction of a railroad parallel to that of the plaintiff, and to which, the plaintiff alleges, the defendant's traffic was to be given.[1] In another very recent case, before the same court,

and conferred by the State of Washington, the question whether the contracts and proceedings by which it has gained control of the Seattle, Lake Shore & Eastern Company's franchise and business are *ultra vires* or not depends upon whether the requirements of the State laws in this regard have been met. There has been no sale and conveyance, nor lease, of the railroad property, in accordance with the laws of this State relating to the manner of transferring titles to such property. As the parties have not done what the statute authorizes to be done, I do not think that the deal between them has any government sanction whatever. No consolidation has been attempted, and yet the transaction is of such resemblance to a consolidation that the legal principles by which the validity of proceedings to effect a consolidation may be applied." Earle v. Seattle, L. S. & E. Ry. Co., 56 Fed. Rep. 909, 910.

[1] Bald Eagle Valley R. R. Co. v. Nittany Valley R. R. Co., 171 Pa. St. 284; s. c., 33 Atl. Rep. 239; 37 W. N. C. 89. In Cumberland Valley R. Co. v. Gettysburg & H. Ry. Co. (1896), 177 Pa. 564; s. c., 35 Atl. Rep. 952, it is held that a contract between railroad companies whose roads approach their point of connection almost at right angles, so that they cannot become competitors, to interchange traffic and cars, sell coupon passenger tickets, make through bills of lading and apportion their earnings, is not unlawful. In the course of the opinion, Dean, J., says: "We are clear in our conclusions that the South Mountain and Gettysburg & Harrisburg form in no reasonable view a parallel and competing line to the Cumberland Valley, with which they connect. Their line approaches Carlisle, the connecting point, almost at right angles. A glance at any railroad map shows this. From Gettysburg to Carlisle, the traffic along this line, when the contract of 30th September, 1882, was made, was not one for which the Cumberland Valley could compete. The only competitors that these two short roads could have had at that date were country wagons on the ordinary highways. The contract was

a railroad company negotiated through another railroad company for the purchase of a controlling interest in the stock of a parallel or competing line, the legal title of the stock to be held by the other railroad, but the consideration coming from the competing company. A preliminary injunction to restrain the execution of the contract was granted, and a decree entered continuing the injunction until final hearing was affirmed on appeal.[1]

§ 156. Admission to Depot Grounds.—The question whether a railway company may prohibit all solicitations of

not, therefore, forbidden by the constitution. It was, in fact, an advantage to the public, as well as to the contracting parties; for it relieved the public of the inconvenience of transfer of goods and rebilling, provided for traveler's close connections, and necessarily lessened the actual cost of transportation, and there is no evidence that the contract was made with a view to increase charges to the shipper. The profits of the contracting parties were expected to result from a lessening of operating expenses to all of them. Any such contract inevitably tends to the advantage of the public: for the cheaper any product can be delivered at destination, the better able is the producer to meet in the market the same products brought to the same destination by other roads, which last always aim to reach, and do reach, the points where products are marketable. The contract really tends to accomplish the purpose of the general railroad law of 1868, which provides that railroads of a similar character shall have the right to connect, upon such terms as may be agreed upon by those who have the management of such roads, and also of the constitution which declares that they shall have the right to connect, and then avows the purpose that they may receive and transport each the other's passengers, tonnage and cars, loaded or empty, without delay or discrimination.' We conclude, therefore, that the contract was not between parallel and competing roads, nor was it unlawful in its ostensible purpose. Whether any of its provisions are unlawful, or whether because of the indefiniteness of others it is incapable of specific execution, are altogether different questions." *Mandamus* will lie to compel a railroad to run a passenger train. A railroad running through three counties having a population each of from 17,000 to 19,000 inhabitants, and eight towns ranging in population from 200 to 5,000, the country being tributary to St. Louis, should be required to run a daily passenger train. The running of a passenger coach attached to a freight train is not a compliance with its duty to the public, where the revenues of the company are sufficient to pay the operating expenses of a separate train for passengers. People v. St. L., A. & T. H. R. Co. (1896), 45 N. E. Rep. 824.

[1] Penna R. R. Co. v. Commonwealth, 4 Cent. 501.

business on the grounds connected with its stations has not been definitely and finally determined. But it is well settled that in their regulations relating to this matter they cannot discriminate in favor of one person and against another engaged in the same branch of business. They cannot admit the omnibus or hack of one person or company to their grounds and exclude that of another. And they cannot give one person or company any advantage over a competitor. Their treatment of all engaged in this branch of business must be strictly fair and impartial. In the leading case on this subject it was held that a railroad company cannot legally give to one hack and bus company the right to the use and occupancy of a portion of its depot grounds to the exclusion of others engaged in the like business of the carriage of passengers and freight to and from its depot. The statute requiring all railroad companies to grant equal facilities for the transportation of passengers and freight to all persons, companies or corporations does not relate entirely to the mere carriage in the cars of the road, but includes the receiving of such passengers and freight at its depots, and by other "persons, companies or corporations" at the point upon its road where the carriage ends. A railroad company can make all needful, reasonable rules and regulations concerning the use of its depot and grounds, and can exclude all persons therefrom who have no business with the railroad or passengers going to and coming from its trains or depots, and it probably can prohibit all persons from soliciting business for themselves upon its premises; but it cannot, arbitrarily, admit one common carrier of passengers or freight to its depots or grounds and exclude all others, for no other reason than that it is for its own profit or pleasure to do so.[1] In the

[1] Kalamazoo Hack & Bus Co. v. Sootsma, 84 Mich. 194. See also Marriott v. Ry. Co., 1 C. B. (N. S.) 499; *In re* Palmer, L. R. 6 C. P. 194; *In re* Parkinson, L. R. 6 C. P. 554; Camblos v. Railroad Co., 9 Phila. 411; New England Express Co. v. Railroad Co., 57 Me. 188; Beadell v. Eastern Counties Ry. Co., 5 Com. B. (N. S.) 509; Painter v. London, Brighton & S. C. Ry. Co., 5 Com. B. (N. S.) 70; Barker v. Midland Ry. Co., 18 Com. B. 46; Markham v. Brown, 8 N. H.

opinion in this case the doctrine is stated by the court, as follows: "The plea is made that the railway company, owning these grounds, or having the actual occupancy and possession thereof, has the same right of control over them

523. "The exclusive privilege which the plaintiffs claim under their license from the railroad company's station agent of occupying the space beside the railroad platform of easiest approach thereto, next to the station building, the objective point for the discharge of railroad passengers, is a valuable one, giving the plaintiffs an advantage in carrying on their business over the defendants, their rivals in the same line of business. The business of both parties is that of common carriers for hire, on the same line, and, by their connection with the railroad, forming one continuous line by which passengers are transported to the same general destination: the railroad company carrying them to its station near the city, and the plaintiffs and defendants carrying them to their severals destinations in the city. As common carriers it is the duty of each of the parties to transport all persons who offer to take and pay for passage with them; and they are charged with grave and responsible duties to such persons when they have once taken passage. They must make the trip whether they have one or many passengers. As a corollary of this duty to carry all, there ought to be a corresponding right upon the part of each to have the same facilities afforded them to obtain the passage in their respective vehicles of all such passengers as are brought to the point of connection by the connecting carrier, the railroad company on the same general route. In this way the enterprise of each is encouraged, competition is stimulated, the price of transportation is kept within reasonable bounds, the safest, best and most comfortable means of conveyance, a rapid passage, and polite and agreeable service are apt to be secured to the traveling public. On the other hand, if better facilities are afforded to one carrier than another by the connecting carrier competition is discouraged, a monopoly created, and the traveling public are apt to receive a slow, uncomfortable, slovenly, negligent and expensive service. Monopolies are obnoxious to the spirit of our laws, and ought to be discouraged. This is the spirit of our constitutional provision which prohibits 'discrimination in charges, or facilities in transportation * * * between transportation companies and individuals or in favor of either.' Article 12, § 23. And in this case we do not think the railroad company could give the plaintiffs the exclusive privilege of approach to nearly one-half of its platform and that the most desirable and advantageous half for procuring passengers and thereby deny it to the defendants, both being there for the same purpose, and in the same business, of forwarding the railroads passengers to their places of destination from the point where the railroad company landed them." Cravens v. Rodgers, 101 Mo. 247, 252; s. c., 14 S. W. Rep. 106. A railroad

that any citizen would have under similar circumstances, provided only that it discharges its duties to the public, with reference thereto, as a common carrier. This is true. But when the ground is used in its business as common car-

company may not grant to one person the exclusive right to the use of a portion of its depot platform to deliver passengers departing, and to receive and solicit the patronage of incoming passengers, to the exclusion of all other persons from the exercise of such rights, as such grant is against public policy and contrary to the provisions of Article XV., § 7, of the constitution, which provides that 'no discrimination in charges, or facilities for transportation of freight or passengers of the same class shall be made by any railroad or transportation or express company, between persons or places within this State.' Passengers arriving at or departing from the station of a common carrier are entitled to whatever benefit of competition may grow out of the contests of others to supply the public demands and receive the compensation therefor. A rule or regulation as applied to the government of the conduct of persons, or of a class of persons, contemplates uniformity and not discrimination, and the grant by a railroad company of a platform privilege at its depot to one hackman to the exclusion of all others is therefore not such a rule or regulation as applied to the right of a common carrier to make and enforce all reasonable rules and regulations necessary to govern persons coming to its station buildings, platform and grounds. Montana Union Ry. Co. v. Langlois, 9 Mont. 419; s. c., 24 Pac. Rep. 209. A railroad company may make and enforce by its agents reasonable and necessary rules for the transaction of its business, and for the proper and orderly management of its depot and other buildings open to the public. The rules, however, must be reasonable and such as do not unnecessarily infringe upon the rights of the public and others having or carrying on business in connection with railroad traffic and travel. A regulation forbidding hackmen, peddlers, expressmen and loafers from coming within the passenger depot is reasonable. Summitt v. State, 8 Lea (Tenn.), 413. In Massachusetts, in Old Colony Railroad Co. v. Tripp, 147 Mass. 35, a different view is taken. In this case the court held that a railroad corporation may contract with one to furnish the means to carry incoming passengers or their baggage and merchandise from its stations, and may grant to him the exclusive right there to solicit the patronage of such passengers. Such an agreement is not within the Pub. Stats. chap. 112, § 188, which provides that such a corporation "shall give to all persons or companies reasonable and equal terms, facilities and accomodations * * * for the use of its depot and other buildings and grounds. The holding was by a nearly equally balanced bench. In the majority opinion, Allen, J., says: "We have not been referred to any decision or *dictum* in England or in this country, that a common carrier of passengers and their rier, and for the purpose of the standing or 'setting' of hacks and buses to solicit the patronage of incoming passengers, then it must use it for the benefit of all, and not for the privilege of one. It could probably refuse, if such refusal was reasonable in that there was other proper ground for them to stand upon, to permit any hacks or buses to occupy the ground at all; but if it opens the door to one, all must enter and have equal facilities and privileges, one with the other. No doubt one wrongfully creating disorder or disturbance upon this ground, or defrauding or deceiving passengers, could be lawfully ejected therefrom, and, persisting in such conduct, be forever barred therefrom by the railroad company, but that would be a matter for the railroad company, rather than the plaintiff."[1]

§ 157. **General Powers of Railway Corporations.**—In general the powers of a railway company is represented by its board of directors. In the exercise of this power a board of directors is subjected to the restrictions of the charter and by-laws of the company. It must be guided by these rules and by the legal regulations to which such corporations are subject. In a leading case in Indiana, the rule was stated, as follows: "A railroad company is a

baggage to and from a railroad station has any right without the consent of the railroad company, to use the grounds, buildings and platforms of the station for the purpose of soliciting the patronage of passengers, or that a regulation of the company which allows such use by particular persons, and denies it to others, violates any right of the latter. Cases at common law or under statutes to determine whether such railroad companies in particular instances gave equal terms and facilities to different parties to whom they furnished transportation and with whom they dealt as common carriers, have no bearing on the case at bar. The defendant in his business of solicitor of the patronage of passengers held no relations with the plaintiff as a common carrier, and had no right to use its station grounds and buildings."

[1] Kalamazoo Hack & Bus Co. v. Sootsma, 84 Mich. 194, 201. See generally, McConnell v. Pedigo, 92 Ky. 465; s. c., 18 S. W. Rep. 15; 5 Am. R. & Corp. Rep. 711; New York, etc. R. Co. v. Flynn, 74 Hun, 124; s. c., 26 N. Y. Supl. 859; City of Colorado Springs v. Smith, 19 Colo. 554; s. c., 36 Pac. Rep. 540; Landrigan v. State, 31 Ark. 50; Commonwealth v. Power, 7 Metc. 596.

quasi public corporation. It depends on the public for its support, and the public depends upon it for its accommodations. Powers are granted to it which are denied to individuals or partnerships or other corporations, as those for producing, manufacturing, commercial or monetary purposes. It has privileges which are denied to other common carriers, such as lines of ships, steamboats, or stage coaches, or other means of the carrying trade. It exercises the right of eminent domain, which is an attribute of sovereignty. The power of taxation, as in the case before us, is often invoked in its aid. It is, therefore, bound to reciprocal obligations to the State, and owes reciprocal obligations to the public. It must not make contracts beyond its chartered powers, or perform acts injurious to the public, or pursue a course in contravention of public policy. It is created, sustained and protected by the law, and wields power with which private enterprise cannot compete; it must, therefore, obey the law, keep within its powers, and pursue, in its general course, the end and design of its creation. * * * A board of directors represents the general power of a railroad company, subject to the restrictions in the charter and the by-laws of the corporation. Within their general agency their acts will bind the company. They have no power to manage the property or franchises of the road for their own benefit. They may not divert the business of the road, or impair its ability to carry out its duties to the stockholders. Their power, as between themselves and the company, is conferred by the corporators, and must not be exceeded. They cannot subject the capital of the company to risks, or incur liabilities beyond their agency. They cannot sever the road and favor one portion of it to the injury of another, or serve the interests of a part of the stockholders to the injury of other stockholders. They are the agents of the corporation, and are limited in their powers. They cannot change the *termini* of the road, or its general course and direction, but must in all things subserve the original purpose, design and end of the organization. A board of directors of a railroad company stands as a trustee of the stockholders, in the general business and for the property of the roads, and may not violate their trust. It can make no considerable change in the road, as severing its trunk, changing its *termini*, leasing or selling a portion of its track, without their consent. As between the corporation and the stockholders, the latter are not bound by the acts of the board of directors outside of the ordinary business and general purpose of the road. The corporation may become bound by the act of its board of directors, when the stockholders, as between themselves and the corporation, would not be bound by the same act, unless acquiesced in; but if the act is *ultra vires* of the corporation it is void, and no one is bound."[1]

[1] Board, etc. Tippecanoe County v. Lafayette, etc. R. R. Co., 50 Ind. 85, 108, 112. See also McCluer v. Manchester, etc. R. R. Co., 13 Gray, 124; Bissell v. Michigan Southern, etc. R. R. Co., 22 N. Y. 299; Langley v. Boston, etc. R. R., 10 Gray, 103; Life & Fire Insurance Co. v. Mechanic Fire Insurance Co., 7 Wend. 31; Allegheny City v. McClurkan, 14 Pa. St. 81; Bargate v. Shortridge, 5 H. L. Cas. 297; Railroad Company v. Howard, 7 Wall. 413; Zabriskie v. C., C. & C. R. R. Co., 23 How. 381; Randall v. Van Vechten, 19 Johns. 60; Neustadt v. Ill. Cent. R. R. Co., 31 Ill. 484; Illinois Cent. R. R. Co. v. McLean Co., 17 Ill. 291; Rice v. Rock Island, etc. R. R. Co., 21 Ill. 93; Palmer v. Forbes, 23 Ill. 301; Bruffet v. Great Western R. R. Co., 25 Ill. 310; Racine, etc. R. R. Co. v. Farmers' Loan & Trust Co., 49 Ill. 331; Ohio & Miss. R. R. Co. v. Wheeler, 1 Black, 286; Pearce v. Atwood, 13 Mass. 342; Allison v. Hubbell, 17 Ind. 559; Harding v. Third Presb. Church, 20 Ind. 72; *Ex parte* Clifford, 20 Ind. 106; Wall v. State, 23 Ind. 150; Webb v. Rice, 6 Hill. 221; Hitt v. Ormsbee, 14 Ill. 235; McQuilkin v. Doe, 8 Blackf. 581; Fort v. Burch, 6 Barb. 74; Board, etc. v. Culter, 6 Ind. 354; State v. Buckley, 2 Blackf. 249; Smithson v. Dillon, 16 Ind. 169; Mayor, etc. v. Colgate, 2 Kernan, 146; Sun Mut. Ins. Co. v. Mayor, etc., 8 N. Y. 253; People v. Hills, 35 N. Y. 452; People v. O'Brien, 38 N. Y. 195; Smead v. Indianapolis, etc. R. W. Co., 11 Ind. 104; E. & H. R. R. Co. v. Hunt, 20 Ind. 457; President, etc. v. Jackson, 7 Blackf. 36; Burkham v. Beaver, 17 Ind. 367; Indianapolis, etc. R. R. Co. v. Solomon, 23 Ind. 534; Pittsburgh, etc. R. R. Co. v. Kain, 35 Ind. 291; Indianapolis, etc. R. R. Co. v. Warner, 35 Ind. 516; Smith v. Sheeley, 12 Wall. 358; Myers v. Croft, 13 Wall. 295; Land v. Hoffman, 12 Am. L. R. (N. S.) 143; Hayward v. Davidson, 41 Ind. 212; White v. Howard, 38 Conn. 342; Eastern Counties R. W. Co. v. Hawkes, 35 Eng. L. & Eq. 32; Bank, etc. v. Edgerton, 30 Vt. 190; Eldridge v. Smith, 34 Vt. 484; Miller v. R. & W. R. R. Co., 36 Vt. 490; Parish v. Wheeler, 22 N. Y. 494; Town of Pine Grove v. Talcott, 19 Wall. 666; Steam Nav. Co. v. Weed, 17 Barb. 378; Boston, etc.

R. R. Corp. v. Salem, etc. R. R. Co., 2 Gray, 1; Black v. Delaware, etc. Canal Co., 22 N. J. Eq. 130; Fall River Iron Works Co. v. Old Colony, etc. R. R. Co., 5 Allen, 221; Great Luxembourg R. W. Co. v. Magnay, 25 Beav. 586; Beman v. Rufford, 1 Sim. (N. S.) 550; Bagshaw v. Eastern Union R. W. Co., 2 Macn. & G. 389; Eastern Anglian R. W. Co. v. Eastern Counties R. W. Co., 11 C. B. 775; Richardson v. Sibley, 11 Allen, 65; Eidman v. Bowman, 58 Ill. 444; Stewart's Appeal, 56 Pa. St. 413; Madison, etc. Plank Road Co. v. Watertown, etc. Plank Road Co., 7 Wis. 59; Perrine v. Chesapeake, etc. Co., 9 How. 172; Bedford R. R. Co. v. Bowser, 48 Pa. St. 29; European, etc. R. W. Co. v. Poor, 59 Me. 277; Booe v. Junction R. R. Co., 9 Ind. 358; Wilstach v. Hawkins, 14 Ind. 541. Railroads are *quasi* public corporations and agencies, their directors acting in the double capacity as agents for the companies and as trustees for the public. When the public interests are brought in conflict with the private interests of the company, or of private individuals with whom such companies deal, such private interests must yield to those of the public. Pueblo & A. V. R. Co. v. Taylor, 6 Colo. 1; s. c., 45 Am. Rep. 512; 6 Am. & Eng. R. Cas. 474. The directors of a railroad company may thereto authorized by the language of its articles of incorporation, and in the manner therein pointed out, sell and transfer a part of its uncompleted road-bed, estate and franchise connected therewith to another company. Mahaska County R. Co. v. Des Moines Valley R. Co., 28 Iowa, 437. The phrase "a parallel or competing line," as used in Pennsylvania constitution and statutes, includes a projected road surveyed, laid out, and in process of construction, which, when completed and in operation, would actually compete with the other road. Before completion it is a parallel road and when completed it is a competing road. Pennsylvania R. Co. v. Conn, 29 Am. & Eng. R. Cas. 145; s. c., 7 Atl. Rep. 368. Under Georgia Constitution of 1877, art. 4, § 2, par. 2, which forbids one corporation to make any contract with another tending to defeat or lessen competition in their respective businesses, the purchase by defendant of a road which ran parallel to its own road is illegal and void. Hamilton v. Savannah, F. & W. R. Co., 52 Am. & Eng. R. Cas. 130; s. c., 49 Fed. Rep. 412.

CHAPTER XI.

INDUSTRIAL TRUSTS.

§ 158. Introductory.
159. Classification of Industrial Trusts.
160. Legality of the "Trust."—Class First.
161. The Subject Continued.
162. The Same Subject.
§ 163. Legality of the "Trust" Continued.—Class Second.
164. The Rule in England.
165. Legality of the "Trust" Continued,—Class Third.
166. The Subject Continued.

§ 158. **Introductory.**—The term "trust," as applied to business associations, does not admit of an accurate and exhaustive definition. It is employed to designate any combination, the object of which is to control and regulate the production or the traffic in any commodity or article of commerce. The primary design, of course, is to suppress competition, and to increase or to maintain prices. As the word "trust" was originally employed it designated the combination or union of the stockholders of a number of corporations or companies in one new organization. By the terms of this union all the stockholders of the corporations or companies, which were parties to the covenant, placed their stock in the hands of a board of directors or trustees, as they were termed, to which the control and management of the "trust" was committed. In return for their stock the stockholders of the original organizations received the trust certificates of the new corporation. The "trust" was a consolidation of the interests of all the stockholders of the associations which came into the new concern, and the entire control of it was committed to the board of trustees. They held the legal title to all the stock of the original companies; they cast the votes to which the original proprietors were entitled; they chose the officers of the subordinate business associations; they managed the business of the earlier concern and disposed of the profits. The dividends of all the stock came directly into their hands, and from the net proceeds of these dividends they paid the dividends on the trust certificates. These directors or trustees are chosen for a definite period by the holders of the trust certificates. The phenomenal success of The Standard Oil Trust, The Sugar Trust and The American Cotton-Seed Oil Trust, which all belonged to the same general class, gave an extraordinary impetus to this method of creating monopolies, and brought the scheme very prominently before the public. But its rapid extension in the multiplying of combinations of this general character, early, began to awaken the popular apprehension, and to excite wide-spread and determined opposition. This is true especially of the closing decade of the century. The aid of the courts has been invoked, and during the past five years some very drastic statutes, designed to suppress the evil, have been enacted.[1]

[1] In United States v. Trans-Missouri Freight Association, 166 U. S. 290, Mr. Justice Peckham uses this language as illustrative of the text: "Trading, manufacturing and railroad corporations are all engaged in the transaction of business with regard to articles of trade and commerce each in its special sphere, either in manufacturing or trading in commodities or in their transportation by rail. A contract among those engaged in the latter business by which the prices for the transportation of commodities traded in or manufactured by the others is greatly enhanced from what otherwise it would be if free competition were the rule, affects, and to a certain extent restricts, trade and commerce, and affects the price of the commodity. Of this there can be no question. Manufacturing or trading companies may also affect prices by joining together in forming a trust or other combination, and by making agreements in restraint of trade and commerce, which, when carried out, affect the interests of the public. Why should not a railroad company be included in general legislation aimed at the prevention of that kind of agreement made in restraint of trade, which may exist in all companies, which is substantially of the same nature wherever found, and which tends very much toward the same results whether put in practice by a trading and manufacturing or by a railroad company? It is true, the results of trusts or combinations of that nature may be different in different kinds of corporations, and yet they all have an essential

§ 159. Classification of Trusts.—In their general characteristics "trusts" have been divided into three classes: FIRST, such as are created by a union or combination of a number of corporations or companies. In this class all the

similarity, and have been induced by motives of individual or corporate aggrandizement as against the public interest. In business or trading combinations they may even temporarily, or perhaps permanently, reduce the price of the article traded in or manufactured, by reducing the expense inseparable from the running of many different companies for the same purpose. Trade or commerce under those circumstances may, nevertheless, be badly and unfortunately restrained by driving out of business the small dealers and worthy men whose lives have been spent therein, and who might be unable to readjust themselves to their altered surroundings. Mere reductions in the price of the commodity dealt in might be dearly paid for by the ruin of such a class, and the absorption of control over one commodity by an all powerful combination of capital. A change from stage coaches and canal boats to railroads threw at once a large number of men out of employment: changes from hand labor to that of machinery, and from operating machinery by hand to the application of steam for such purpose, leave behind them for the time a number of men who must seek other avenues of livelihood. These are misfortunes which seem to be the necessary accompaniment of all great industrial changes. It takes time to effect a readjustment of industrial life so that those who are thrown out of their old employment, by reason of such changes as we have spoken of, may find opportunities for labor in other departments than those to which they have been accustomed. It is a misfortune, but yet in such cases it seems to be the inevitable accompaniment of change and improvement. It is wholly different, however, when such changes are effected by combinations of capital, whose purpose in combining is to control the production or manufacture of any particular article in the market, and by such control dictate the price at which the article shall be sold, the effect being to drive out of business all the small dealers in the commodity and to render the public subject to the decision of the combination as to what price shall be paid for the article. In this light it is not material that the price of an article may be lowered. It is in the power of the combination to raise it, and the result in any event is unfortunate for the country by depriving it of the services of a large number of small but independent dealers who were familiar with the business and who had spent their lives in it, and who had supported themselves and their families from the small profits realized therein. Whether they be able to find other avenues to earn their livelihood is not so material, because it is not for the real prosperity of any country that such changes should occur which result in transferring an independent business man, the head of his establishment, small though it might be, into a mere stock of the combining corporations is transferred to a board of directors or trustees, as explained in the foregoing section. In lieu of the stock thus surrendered the stockholders receive trust certificates. Under this form of trust the directors or trustees are clothed with absolute control of the entire business of the combination. They receive their appointment from the holders of the stock certificates, and are answerable only to them. A SECOND class of "trusts" consists of corporations that have acquired control of other corporations by purchasing their stock. This organization is of the same general character as the preceding, but the form is changed in order to escape the force of the decisions of the courts relating to corporate partnerships. THE THIRD class of "trusts" consists of corporations which have

servant or agent of a corporation for selling the commodities which he once manufactured or dealt in, having no voice in shaping the business policy of the company and bound to obey orders issued by others. Nor is it for the substantial interests of the country that any one commodity should be within the sole power and subject to the sole will of one powerful combination of capital. Congress has, so far as its jurisdiction extends, prohibited all contracts or combinations in the form of trusts entered into for the purpose of restraining trade and commerce. The results naturally flowing from a contract or combination in restraint of trade or commerce, when entered into by a manufacturing or trading company, such as above stated, while differing somewhat from those which may follow a contract to keep up transportation rates by railroads, are nevertheless of the same nature and kind, and the contracts themselves do not so far differ in their nature that they may not all be treated alike and be condemned in common. It is entirely appropriate generally to subject corporations or persons engaged in trading or manufacturing to different rules from those applicable to railroads in their transportation business, but when the evil to be remedied is similar in both kinds of corporations, such as contracts which are unquestionably in restraint of trade, we see no reason why similar rules should not be promulgated in regard to both, and both be covered in the same statute by general language sufficiently broad to include them both. We see nothing either in contemporaneous history, in the legal situation at the time of the passage of the statute, in its legislative history, or in any general difference in the nature or kind of these trading or manufacturing companies, which would lead us to the conclusion that it cannot be supposed the legislature in prohibiting the making of contracts in restraint of trade intended to include railroads within the purview of that act."

purchased the plants, including the real estate, machinery, stock in trade, good will, etc., of a number of corporations, firms or individuals engaged in a particular branch of business. Payment for this property is made in the stock of the corporation. The work is then carried on by the officers and directors of the corporation with reference to the interests of all the stockholders alike. As the corporation holds both the legal and equitable title to all the property of the associated corporations it conducts the business as it was previously conducted by all, or suspends the operation of one or more of the plants as may be deemed best for the interests of the whole. The object of the combination in this form is to limit production where that can be made profitable, as well as to create a monopoly and control prices.

§ 160. Legality of the "Trust," — Class First.—A union of a number of business associations, engaged in the same branch of business, is not, necessarily, illegal. Both the object sought and the means employed may be altogether unobjectionable from a legal point of view. But upon the character then, that is, upon the nature of the end in view and of the method of accomplishing it, the legality of the union depends. Of "trusts" of the first class, The Standard Oil Trust and The North River Sugar Refining Company, commonly designated , The Sugar Trust, are prominent examples. In an action brought by the State to secure the dissolution of The Standard Oil Company, one of the corporations which constituted The Standard Oil Trust, it was held by the Supreme Court of Ohio that an agreement by which all or a majority of the stockholders of a corporation transfer their stocks to certain trustees, in consideration of the agreement of the stockholders of other companies and of the members of limited partnerships, engaged in the same business, to do likewise; and by which all are to receive in lieu of their stocks and interests so transferred trust certificates to be issued by the trustees equal at par to the par value of their stocks and interests; and by which the trustees are empowered, as apparent owners of the stock, to elect directors of the several companies, and thereby control their affairs in the interests of the trust so created; and are to receive all dividends made by the several companies and limited partnerships, from which, as a common fund, dividends are to be made by the trustees to the holders of the trust certificates, tends to the creation of a monopoly to control production as well as prices, and is against public policy.[1]

[1] State v. Standard Oil Company, 49 Ohio St. 138. Defendant and his partner sold their bakery business to complainant corporation, receiving payment in its stock, and defendant leased to it the premises where the business was conducted, and contracted to carry it on as the purchaser's agent, for a salary. After operating under this arrangement for a time, he repudiated the sale, resumed possession under the old firm name, and refused to account to complainant. The bill was brought to enjoin him from asserting a hostile claim, for an accounting and a receiver. Defendant and his partner, as intervenor, filed a cross-bill for rescission of the sale for fraudulent representations, and tendered back the stock. Complainant was practically a trust, organized to monopolize the business, and had already secured control of thirty-five leading bakeries in twelve different States. *Held*, that while a case was made for a receiver, pending litigation between ordinary parties, the prayer would be denied, as equity would not encourage a combination in restraint of trade. and probably illegal under Federal Anti-Trust Act of 1890, "to protect trade and commerce against unlawful restraints and monopolies," and Act Louisiana, July 5, 1890, for the same purpose. American Biscuit & Manf. Co. v. Klotz, 44 Fed. Rep. 721. A contract by which a Michigan corporation agrees with other persons and corporations to transfer its entire property and business to a new corporation, which is to be organized for the purpose of controlling the business of making and selling a certain article, is void under 3 How. Ann. St. Mich., § 3832, forbidding monopolies and combinations. Merz Capsule Co. v. United States Capsule Co., 67 Fed. Rep. 414. "The agreement recites that it is designed by its signers to form a trust for the purpose of securing co-operation in the business of manufacturing preserves, etc., and of selling and dealing in the same in home and foreign markets. This co-operation, to be secured through the extraordinary powers conferred upon the nine trustees named in the agreement, six of whom are designated by name and authorized to elect three others, could not result otherwise than in a grinding monopoly controlling all trade in the business specified, and raising or depressing prices therein at the will of the trustees. Such trustees are empowered to organize corporations with all or any of the powers specified in the purposes of the agreement; and the stock of such corporation is to be issued to or purchased by said trustees. For this stock the trus-

In the opinion in this case, Mr. Justice Minshall, said: "Applying, then, the principle that a corporation is simply an association of natural persons, united in one body under a special denomination, and vested by the policy of the law

tees are to issue certificates of trust. The agreement is to go into effect within sixty days from the time those holding the majority of the stock in seven specified corporations formed, or to be formed, shall transfer the same to the trustees. Each signer of the agreement agrees to assign and transfer to said trustees absolutely all the shares, which he may own in said corporations formed, or to be formed, and is to receive therefor, not money, but trust certificates, equal to the appraised amount of the earning capacity of his stock as fixed by the trustees and the stockholder. The trustees are authorized to purchase in the same way, by the issue of trust certificates, other stocks of the same companies, and also the property and business of any firm or individual engaged in the business of manufacturing and dealing in said products. The trustees are to exercise supervision over the corporations whose stocks are transferred to them, and are empowered to elect themselves directors and officers in such corporations and procure such management of the same as will be conducive to the interests of the holders of the trust of the trust certificates. These trust certificates are divided into shares of the par value of $100 each, and are prepared by the trustees. They provide that the holders thereof shall be bound by the terms of the trust agreement and of the by-laws passed in pursuance thereof, and are intended to show the interest of each beneficiary in the trust. The trustees hold the stocks transferred to them in trust for the holders of the certificates, and are to receive and hold the dividends or interest upon said stocks, and are to distribute the same by declaring dividends upon the certificates. The stocks so transferred to the trustees are to be held by them for the benefit of all the owners of the trust certificates. The trust is to continue for twenty-five years, subject to the right of 75 per cent. of the holders of the certificates to terminate it after the expiration of one year, and of $66\frac{2}{3}$ per cent. of such holders to terminate it at the end of five years; and the trustees cannot sell or surrender any of the stocks held by them during the continuance of the trust, without the consent of a majority in number and value of the holders of the trust certificates. It will thus be seen, that the agreement in question makes provision for welding together all the interests engaged in the business named in the agreement, into one giant combination or partnership under the absolute dominion and control of a board of nine trustees. Its illegal purpose is apparent upon its face, and, therefore, under the decisions above referred to, it must be held to be void as being injurious to the public interest. The object of the testimony of the defendant, upon the trial below was to show that the plaintiff, The American Preservers' Company, was a party to this illegal combiwith the capacity of acting in several respects as an individual, and disregarding the mere fiction of a separate legal entity, since to regard it in an inquiry like the one before us would be subversive of the purpose for which it was in-

nation, and that the execution of the bill of sale to it was to enable it to carry out the unlawful designs of such combination. If this testimony as offered had been received, it would have tended to show, not only that the plaintiff company was under the control of this board of trustees, but that it was in a partnership with other corporations. The corporators named in plaintiffs' charter and whose names are signed to the agreement therein set out. upon the basis of which they were declared to be a corporation, were trustees in the trust. The court below ruled out the testimony, showing that these trustees held stock in more than a dozen different corporations in the different States of the Union. besides the stock in the plaintiff company transferred to it by the defendant and others. The agreement was illegal as providing for a partnership among corporations. It is a violation of law for corporations to enter into partnership. The provisions of the general incorporation act of Illinois are to the effect that every corporation organized in this State must manage its own affairs separately and exclusively, and cannot enter into any contract or relation, by which it is divested of such power of exclusive management, or by which its franchises are vested in a partner or any outside board, with equal power to direct its business. Whittenton Mills v. Upton, 10 Gray, 582; People v. N. Riv. Sug. Ref. Co., 121 N. Y. 582. The appellee here, a foreign corporation, so far as it was doing business in this State through any control which it assumed to exercise over the business transferred to it by appellant, was subject to the same restrictions and duties as corporations formed in this State and could have no other or greater powers. 1 Starr & Cur. Stat. page 619, chap. 32, § 26. It was, therefore, unlawful for it to be operating in this State as a member of a partnership of corporations. State v. Nebraska Distilling Co., 29 Neb. 700; Mallory v. Oil Works, 86 Tenn. 598; People v. Chicago Gas Trust Co., 130 Ill. 268." Magruder, J., in Bishop v. American Preservers' Co., 157 Ill. 284, 311. In Distilling & Cattle Feeding Co. v. The People, 156 Ill. 448, 490; s. c., 41 N. E. Rep. 188, the court, after commenting on State v. Nebraska Distilling Co., 29 Neb. 700; State v. Standard Oil Co., 49 Ohio St. 137; People v. North River Sugar Refining Co., 54 Hun, 354; s. c., 121 N. Y. 57; Richardson v. Buhl, 77 Mich. 632; People v. Chicago Gas Trust Co., 130 Ill. 268, says, at page 490: "The defendant contends that, while this may all be so, the change in organization from an unincorporated association to a corporation, and the change in the mode of holding the distillery properties of the various corporations formerly belonging to the trust, by surrendering the stock of the corporations, by means of which the control of those properties was formerly maintained and having the propvented, is there, upon an analysis of the agreement, room for doubt, that the act of all the stockholders, officers and directors of the company in signing it, should be imputed to them as an act done in their capacity as a corporation? We think not, since thereby all the property and business of the company is, and was intended to be, virtually transferred to the Standard Oil Trust, and is controlled, through its trustee, as effectually as if a formal transfer had been made by the directors of the company. On a question of this kind, the fact must constantly be kept in view, that

erties themselves transferred and conveyed directly to the defendant corporation, have purged the combination of its illegality it must be admitted that these changes, so far as they have any effect upon the rights or interests of the former stockholders in those corporations or of the public, are formal rather than substantial. The same interests are controlled in substantially the same way and by the same agencies as before. The nine trustees of the trust, who, as the holders of all the capital stock of the corporations and as a majority of the directors of each, controlled such corporate property, became the subscribers for all the stock of the new corporation and its board of directors. The conveyance and transfer of the properties of the constituent companies to the new corporation was merely a transfer by the trustees to themselves, though in a slightly different capacity, and the former stockholders in the constituent companies simply exchanged their trust certificates, share for share, for stock in the new corporation. That corporation thus succeeds to the trust, and its operations are to be carried on in the same way, for the same purposes, and by the same agencies as before. The trust, then, being repugnant to public policy and illegal, it is impossible to see why the same is not true of the corporation which succeeds to it and takes its place. The control exercised over the distillery business of the country—over production and prices—and the virtual monopoly formerly held by the trust, are in no degree changed or relaxed, but the methods and purposes of the trust are perpetuated and carried out with the same persistence and vigor as before the organization of the corporation. There is no magic in a corporate organization which can purge the trust scheme of its illegality, and it remains as essentially opposed to the principles of sound public policy as when the trust was in existence. It was illegal before, and is illegal still, and for the same reasons." A mercantile corporation cannot, by an arrangement with other corporations, place its stock in the hands of trustees, with power to manage the affairs of all the companies as one, for the purpose of increasing its profits, thus substituting the trustees as the governing body of the corporation instead of its officers, as such an act is inconsistent with the purposes of its creation. Gould v. Head, 38 Fed. Rep. 886.

the metaphysical entity has no thought or will of its own; that every act ascribed to it emanates from and is the act of the individuals personated by it; and that it can no more do an act or refrain from doing it, contrary to the will of these natural persons, than a house could be said to act independently of the will of its owner; and where an act is ascribed to it, it must be understood to be the act of the persons associated as a corporation, and whether done in their capacity as corporators or as individuals, must be determined by the nature and tendency of the act. It, therefore, follows, as we think, from the discussion we have given the subject, that where all or a majority of the stockholders, comprising a corporation, do an act which is designed to affect the property and business of the company, and which, through the control their numbers give them over the selection and conduct of the corporate agency, does affect the property and business of the company, in the same manner as if it had been a formal resolution of its board of directors; and the act so done is *ultra vires* of the corporation and against public policy, and was done by them in their individual capacity for the purpose of concealing their real purpose and object, the act should be regarded as the act of the corporation; and, to prevent the abuse of corporate power, may be challenged as such by the State in a proceeding in *quo warranto*. That the nature of the agreement is such as to preclude the defendant from becoming a party to it, is, we think, too clear to require such consideration by us. In the first place, whether the agreement should be regarded as amounting to a partnership between the several companies, limited partnerships and individuals, who are parties to it, it is clear that its observance must subject the defendant to a control inconsistent with its character as a corporation. Under the agreement all but seven of the shares of capital stock of the company have been transferred by the real owners to the trustees of the trust, who hold them in trust for such owners; and being enjoined by the terms of the agreement to endeavor to have 'the affairs' of the several companies managed in a manner most conducive to the interests of the holders of the trust certificates issued by the trust, have the right, in virtue of their apparent ownership, and by the terms of the agreement, to select such directors of the company as they may see fit, nay more, may, in fact, select themselves. The law requires that a corporation should be controlled and managed by its directors in the interest of its own stockholders, and conformable to the purpose for which it was enacted by the laws of its State. By this agreement, indirectly, it is true, but none the less effectually, the defendant is controlled and managed by The Standard Oil Trust, an association, with its principal place of business in New York City, and organized for a purpose contrary to the policy of our laws. Its object was to establish a virtual monopoly of the business of producing petroleum, and of manufacturing, refining and dealing in it and all its products, throughout the entire country, and by which it might not merely control the production, but the price at its pleasure. All such associations are contrary to the policy of our State and void."[1]

§ **161. The Subject Continued.**—Another illustration of this class of "trust" is presented by The North River Sugar Refining Company. In a case before the New York Court of Appeals, where, in an action brought by the attorney-general, in the name of the people, against the defendant, a corporation organized under the General Manufacturing Act, to vacate its charter and annul its corporate existence, it appeared that at a meeting of defendant's stockholders, held April 22d, 1887, at which all its trustees were present, a preamble and resolutions were adopted by a unanimous vote. The preamble recited that it was contemplated by the sugar refineries in the city of New York to consolidate in one large concern and company, and that it was for defendant's interest to participate in the consolidation. By the resolutions a committee named were appointed to perfect the consolidation, with full power to act, and defendant's president and secretary were authorized "to sign

[1] State v. Standard Oil Co., 49 Ohio St. 137, 184.

all contracts, agreements and papers which the above-named committee may make in relation to said consolidation.'' An agreement was thereupon made by and between various corporations engaged in the sugar refining business. To this agreement the name of defendant was signed by its secretary, as he testified, ''by virtue of authority * * * from the stockholders and trustees.'' It was held that the official signature was but the evidence of the agreement entered into by the committee, the authorized agency; and that the making of the agreement was a deliberate corporate act. By the agreement or ''deed,'' as it was termed, so executed, a ''board'' so called was formed, the parties agreed to transfer all their shares of capital stock ''to the names of the board of trustees, to be held by them and their successors as members of the board strictly as joint tenants,'' which board, it was declared, ''shall hold the stock transferred to it with all the rights and powers incident to stockholders in the several corporations.'' The board was authorized to transfer ''to such persons as it may be desired to constitute trustees or directors or other officers of corporations, so many of the shares as may be necessary for that purpose.'' In lieu of the capital stock it was provided that certificates should be issued by the board to the contracting parties in specified proportions. It was provided that each of the parties should maintain a separate organization and carry on and conduct its own business, paying over the profits to the board, ''the aggregate or such amount as shall be designated for dividends,'' to be proportionally distributed by the board to the holders of the certificates. The board was prohibited from taking any action ''which shall create liability by it or by its members,'' but it was provided that the funds necessary to enable the board to make payments as specified ''may be raised by mortgage to be made by the corporation or any, either or all of them upon their property.'' The number and amount of shares to be issued by the board was fixed, with a proviso that they ''may from time to time be increased or diminished by deeds executed by a majority in value of the certificate holders." Defendant's stock was transferred and certificates issued to its stockholders, as provided for. The board elected defendant's officers and board of trustees, having transferred to each a share of the stock to enable him to hold office. It was held that the transaction was not an absolute sale of defendant's stock by its holders; but that a trust was created in the board, to whom as trustee and upon the trusts declared the stock was transferred: that the certificates issued were formal declarations of the trust, and through the operation of which the stockholders retained the beneficial ownership; that by the deed the corporation parties thereto entered into a co-partnership, vesting the partnership power in the board. By the terms of the trust deed it took effect October 1, 1887. At a meeting of defendant's stockholders, held November 4, 1887, a preamble and resolution were adopted, by which, after referring to the former action, alleging that the committee so appointed had failed to make or sign contracts, and that the powers conferred upon the committee and the president and secretary had not been executed, it was resolved that the powers so conferred be revoked. At a subsequent meeting, held November 25th, a preamble and resolution were adopted, by which, after reciting the fact of the signature of the trust deed by the secretary, "under the belief that he was authorized so to do," and that one S had offered to purchase defendant's stock for $325,000, a committee was appointed consisting of the same persons who had been authorized to make the consolidation agreement, to deliver the stock to S or to those persons named as trustees, on receipt of the sum offered, the proceeds to be divided among the stockholders. The stock was transferred on defendant's books and delivered to S, who delivered it to the board, receiving in exchange a certificate for $700,000, less fifteen per cent., as provided for in the deed. S was a member of the board; he was elected defendant's president, and other members were elected trustees. Defendant's share of the regular dividends was allotted to it for the certificate holders, and it wholly ceased to refine sugar. It was held that there was corporate action in making the combination agreement, which bound defendant, and was not revoked by the subsequent proceedings; that such action was in excess of its corporate powers, illegal and tended to the public injury, and so authorized a dissolution of the corporation.[1]

[1] People v. North River Sugar Refining Co., 121 N. Y. 582. "The first question requires us to ascertain what the defendant corporation has done in violation of its duty, or omitted to do in performance of its duty. We find disclosed by the proof that it has become an integral part and constituent element of a combination which possesses over it an absolute control, which has absorbed most of its corporate functions, and dictates the extent and manner and terms of its entire business activity. Into that combination, which drew into its control sixteen other corporations engaged in the refining of sugar, the defendant has gone, in some manner and by some process, for as an unquestionable truth we find it there. All its stock has been transferred to the central association of eleven individuals denominated a 'Board;' in exchange it has taken and distributed to its own stockholders certificates of the board, carrying a proportionate interest in what it describes as its capital stock; the new directors of the defendant corporation have been chosen by the board, made eligible by its gift of single shares, and liable to removal under the terms of their appointment at any moment of independent action. It has lost the power to make a dividend, and is compelled to pay over its net earnings to the master whose servant it has become. Under the orders of that master, it has ceased to refine sugar, and by so much, has lessened the supply upon the market. It cannot stir unless the master approve, and yet is entitled to receive from the earnings of the other refineries, massed as profits in the treasury of the board, its proportionate share for division among its own stockholders holding the substituted certificates. In return for this advantage it has become liable to be mortgaged, not for its own corporate benefit alone, but to supply with funds the controlling board when reaching out for other and coveted refineries. No one can look these facts fairly in the face without being compelled to say that the defendant is in the combination and in to stay. Indeed, so much is with great frankness admitted on the part of the appellant. Its counsel concedes that the stock was transferred 'to the board mentioned in the agreement and on the terms and for the purposes mentioned in the agreement; and that this action effectually lodged the control of the defendant company so far as such control can be secured by the voting power in that board.'" *Ibid.*, 609. The stockholders and members of certain corporations and partnerships engaged in a similar business, by agreement in writing, created a trust, the object of which was to authorize the trustees to control and manage the business of the parties. The trustees issued to

§ **162. The Same Subject.**—In the opinion in the case of The People v. North River Sugar Refining Company, noticed in the preceding section, the doctrine is expounded by Mr. Justice Finch, as follows: "It is quite clear that the

the parties trust certificates transferable on their books. By the terms of the agreement the parties thereto, and the transferees of the certificates, were the beneficiaries under the trust. By the terms of the certificates they were transferable only on the books of the trustees on surrendering the certificates, and it was provided that the holder of a certificate should be subject to all terms of the agreement or the by-laws adopted in pursuance thereof, as fully as if he had signed the same. Upon the back of each was a blank form for a transfer thereof by the terms of which the transferee was appointed attorney with authority to make the necessary transfer upon the books. These certificates were dealt in, in the open market in the city of New York. Plaintiff purchased in said market one of said certificates which was delivered to him with the transfer on the back made out to him by the person to whom it had been issued. Plaintiff presented the certificate to the trustees, with a demand that a transfer be made on the books and a new certificate issued to him, he offering upon receipt thereof to surrender the old certificate. The transfer was refused. *Held*, that an action to compel such transfer was maintainable; that while to give plaintiff the character of transferee for the purposes of recognition by the trust, a transfer on its books was necessary, this was for the benefit and protection of the trust, and as by the agreement and the form of the certificate, the quality of transferability was given to it, this imported the right to make the transfer on the books. Rice v. Rockefeller, 134 N. Y. 174. In Mallory v. Hanaur Oil Works, 86 Tenn. 798; s. c., 20 Am. & Eng. Corp. Cas. 478, where a number of manufacturing corporations entered into a contract whereby a committee composed of representatives selected from each corporation took entire control of the property and machinery of each company, and managed and operated the same for the common benefit, the several corporations sharing the profits and losses in agreed proportions, it was held that such contract was a contract for partnership between the corporations. In the opinion, the court says: "A careful examination of this agreement discloses every essential element to a contract of partnership. The absolute ownership of the corporate property, the mills, machinery, etc., is not conveyed to the partnership, nor is this necessary. The beneficial use of all such property is surrendered to the common purpose. The provisions for the complete possession, control and use of the properties of the several corporations by the partnership or syndicate is perfect. Nothing is left to the several co-partners but the right to receive a share of the profits, and participate in the management and control of the consolidated interest as one of the effect of the defendant's action was to divest itself of the essential and vital elements of its franchise by placing them in trust; to accept from the State the gift of corporate life only to disregard the condition upon which it was

new associations. The contract is both technically and in its essential character a partnership, in so far as it is possible for corporations to form such an association. * * * A partnership and a corporation are incongruous. Such a contract is wholly inconsistent with the scope and tenor of the powers expressly conferred and the duties expressly enjoined upon a corporation, whether it be a strictly business and private corporation, or one owing duties to the public, such as a common carrier. In a partnership each member binds the firm when acting within the scope of the business. A corporation must act through its directors or authorized agents, and no individual member can, as such member, bind the corporation. Now, if a corporation be a member of a partnership, it may be bound by any other member of the association, and in so doing he would act, not as an officer or agent of the corporation, and by virtue of authority received from it, but as a principal in an association in which all are equal, and each capable of binding the society by his acts. The whole policy of the law creating and regulating corporations looks to the exclusive management of the affairs of each corporation by the officers provided for or authorized by its charter. This management must be separate and exclusive, and any arrangement by which the control of the affairs of the corporation should be taken from its stockholders and the authorized officers and agents of the corporation would be hostile to the policy of our general incorporation acts. The decided weight of authority is that a corporation has not the power to enter a partnership either with other corporations or with individuals." The "Car Trust" is thus described by Allen, J., in Ricker v. American Loan & Trust Co., 140 Mass. 346: "The New England Car Trust is a partnership unless, indeed, it is to be considered that there are two or more partnerships under the same name. The essential features are as follows: A number of persons formed an association, by an instrument in writing containing numerous articles, for the purpose of buying, selling and leasing railroad rolling stock, to be sold or leased to the New York and New England Railroad Company, with provisions for admitting other persons to membership. The members of the car trust were to furnish money for the purchase of the rolling stock, and were to have certificates for the amounts so furnished, providing that the principal sum contributed by each member should be repaid in ten annual instalments, with interest; both principal and interest being payable only out of the rentals received for the rolling stock. Instead of the lease being made to the railroad company directly by the car trust, a plan was adopted by which the car trust delivered the property to the American Loan & Trust Company, as trustees, which given; to receive its powers and privileges merely to put them in pawn; and to give away to an irresponsible board its entire independence and self control. When it had passed into the hands of the trust, only a shell of a corporation was left standing, as a seeming obedience to the law, but with its internal structure destroyed or removed. Its stockholders, retaining their beneficial interests, have separated from it their voting power, and so parted with the control which the charter gave them and the State required them to exercise. It has a board of directors nominally and formally in office, but qualified by shares which they do not own, and owing their official life to the board which can end their power at any movement of disobedience. It can make no dividends, whatever may be its net earnings, and must incumber its property at the command of its master, and for purposes wholly foreign to its own corporate interests and duties. At the command of that master it has ceased to refine sugar, and without any doubt for the purpose of so far lessening the market supply as to prevent what is termed 'over production.' In all these respects it has wasted and perverted the privileges conferred by the

trustee issued the certificates to the members of the car trust, and also executed the leases to the railroad company with provisions for a rental sufficient to meet the above payments of principal and interest, in addition to the expenses, including the taxes. In this manner, the railroad company became bound by its covenants in the leases to make payments which in the course of ten years would pay in full for the rolling stock, so that the rolling stock would become the property of the railroad company at the end of that time. All contracts relating to any business of the car trust, involving liabilities for the payment of money, were to be in writing, and made under the direction of the board of managers. The original board of managers was named in the articles of association, but the shareholders were to have the power to remove them and to elect others. At all meetings every shareholder was to have one vote for each share of stock owned by him, and provision was made for the transfer of shares, and the association was not to be dissolved by the death of members. Every owner of one or more shares was to be entitled to a proportionate share of the rentals received. The contemplated profits, to be sure, were limited to six per cent. interest on the money advanced. The losses, if any, must be borne proportionally. This constituted a partnership."

charter, abused its powers and proved unfaithful to its duties. But graver still is the illegal action substituted for the conduct which the State had a right to expect and require. It has helped to create an anomolous trust which is, in substance and effect, a partnership of twenty separate corporations. The State permits in many ways an aggregation of capital, but mindful of the possible dangers to the people, overbalancing the benefits, keeps upon it a restraining hand and maintains over it a prudent supervision, where such aggregation depends upon its permission and grows out of its corporate grants. It is a violation of law for corporations to enter into a partnership. The case last cited [Whittenton Mills v. Upton],[1] furnishes

[1] Whittenton Mills v. Upton, 10 Gray, 582, 596. See also New York & S. C. Co. v. F. Bank, 7 Wend. 412; Clearwater v. Meredith, 1 Wall. 29; Central R. & C. Co. v. Smith, 76 Ala. 572; s. c., 52 Am. Rep. 353; Mallory v. Hanaur Oil Works, 86 Tenn. 598; Charlton v. New Castle & C. Ry. Co., 5 Jur. (N. S.) 297; Commonwealth v. Smith, 10 Allen, 448; Hanson v. Paige, 3 Gray, 239; Bissell v. Michigan Southern & N. I. R. Co., 22 N. Y. 258; Catskill Bank v. Gray, 14 Barb. 471; Catskill Bank v. Hooper, 5 Gray, 574; Marine Bank v. Ogden, 29 Ill. 248; Conklin v. Washington Univ., 2 Md. Ch. 497; Gunn v. Central R., etc. Co., 74 Ga. 509; Jones v. Parker, 29 N. H. 31; Van Kuren v. Trenton Co., 13 N. J. Eq. 302; French v. Donohue, 29 Minn. 111; Lamoine Val., etc. Co. v. Bixby, 55 Vt. 235; Ontario Salt Co. v. Merchants' Salt Co., 18 Ontario Ch. 540; Ledsinger v. Central Line Steamers, 75 Ga. 567. "At the threshold of the cause and of its elaborate discussion is the question. Was this corporation capable of forming a partnership, of entering into the contract? This question presents itself in two forms. The more general one is: Has a corporation, as one of its usual inherent powers, the capacity to form a contract of co-partnership? The narrower question, but for this case the practical and pertinent one is, can a manufacturing corporation in this commonwealth, incorporated since February, 1831, and subject to the provisions of the thirty-eighth and forty-fourth chapters of the Revised Statutes, enter into a contract or society of co-partnership? This corporation was created in March, 1836, as a manufacturing corporation, for the purpose of manufacturing cotton goods in the town of Taunton, and for that purpose was invested with all the powers and privileges and made subject to all the duties, restrictions and liabilities set forth in the thirty-eighth and forty-fourth chapters of the Revised Statutes passed on the 4th of November preceding, but not to take effect till the 1st of May, 1832. Stat. 1836, chap. 19. This charter, with the provisions of the chapters referred to and made part of it, is the origin and source of the powers

the reasons with precission and at length. It shows the utter inconsistency of a double allegiance by those who act for the corporation to two different principles, and demonstrates that the vital characteristics of the corporation are

and functions of the corporation. What powers are granted expressly, or by implication, because necessary or usual for the purposes which this charter was given to effect, the corporation has and no more. There is one obvious and important distinction between such a society as this charter creates and that of a partnership. An act of the corporation, done either by direct vote or by agents authorized for the purpose, is the manifestation of the collected will of the society. No member of the corporation, as such, can bind the society. In a partnership each member binds the society as a principal. If, then, this corporation may enter into partnership with an individual, there would be two principals, the legal person and the natural person, each having, within the scope of the society's business, full authority to manage its concerns including even the disposition of its property. The second section of chapter 38, of the Revised Statutes, provides that the business of every such manufacturing corporation shall be managed and conducted by the president and directors thereof and such other officers, agents and factors as the company shall think proper to authorize for that purpose. It is plain that the provisions of this section cannot be carried into effect where a partnership exists. The partner may manage and conduct the business of the corporation and bind it by his acts. In so doing he does not act as an officer or agent of the corporation by authority received from it, but as a principal, in a society in which all are equals, and each capable of binding the society by the act of its individual will. * * * Indeed, the effect of all our statutes, the settled policy of our legislature, for the regulation of manufacturing corporations is that the corporation is to manage its affairs separately and exclusively; certain power to be exercised by the stockholders, and others by officers who are the servants of the corporation and act in its name and behalf. And the formation of a contract, or the entering into a relation by which the corporation or the officers of its appointment should be divested of that power, or by which its franchises should be vested in a partner with equal power to direct and control its business, is entirely inconsistent with that policy. The power to form a partnership is not only not among the powers granted expressly or by reasonable implication, but is wholly inconsistent with the scope and tenor of the powers expressly conferred, and the duties expressly imposed, upon a manufacturing corporation under the legislation of the commonwealth. The difficulties would be obviously greater in holding such a partnership to be valid, when formed and carried on for the prosecution of a business other than that, if not foreign from that, for which the corporation was created. It is difficult to see how the corporation should engage in of necessity drowned in the paramount authority of the partnership. That the combination of the refineries partakes of the nature of a partnership is not denied. Indeed, in one of the papers added to the appellant's brief, it is not

such business, even when under its own control, still less to enter into co-partnership with third persons for that purpose. By the Stat. of 1852, chap. 195, not adverted to in the argument, corporations created for the manufacture of woolen and cotton goods are authorized to carry on certain other manufactures, but this only when four-fifths of the stockholders shall, by vote at a special meeting called for the purpose, consent to the same. This statute furnishes a pretty strong implication that the power to carry on a different business from that for which the corporation was chartered did not exist before the statute was passed. We are, therefore, all of opinion that in the formation of the alleged partnership the corporation exceeded the powers given by its charter expressly or by implication, and that the contract of co-partnership was illegal and void." Whittenton Mills v. Upton, 10 Gray, 582, 595. "The general rule, that corporations created by an act of the legislature, or organized under general laws, can exercise only the powers expressly granted, the implied powers necessary and proper to carry into effect the express powers, and such incidental powers, as pertain to the purposes of their creation, is not controverted. It may be conceded, that a railroad company, in the absence of express power, is authorized to make traffic arrangements for transportation by water, or may purchase, own and operate steamboats, or other water craft, when such an arrangement or business legitimately pertains to the corporate purposes, or may reasonably be inferred to have been contemplated and intended by the creating power. Such power is incidental to the purposes of the corporation, and such inference is reasonable when a railroad company is incorporated with power to construct a railroad between fixed and designated *termini*, and to effectuate the construction it is necessary to cross navigable rivers, bays or arms of sea, which, on account of their width and depth, or from other causes, cannot be bridged, or when a body of water, lying at the termination of the railroad proper, separates it from the metropolis, to and from which it was contemplated, intended, and is necessary to transport freight and passengers conveyed over the road — 'from the ostensible and substantial *termini* of their route;' or when the act under which the company is organized authorizes it 'to contract for the transportation and delivery of, and to deliver persons and property, conveyed over their road beyond its *termini*.' Wheeler v. S. F. & A. R. R. Co., 31 Cal. 46; Shawmut Bank v. P. & M. R. R. Co., 31 Vt. 491; So. Wales R. R. Co. v. Redmond, 10 Com. B. (N. S.) 674. In such cases the power is implied, as necessary and proper to accomplish the objects of the incorporation; or is incidental, pertaining to its purposes as expressed in the charter or general law, and without which the express only admitted, but asserted and defended. That paper shows quite clearly that, by force of the arrangement, there was a community of interest in the fund created by the corporate earnings before division, and that each member of the trust shared in the profit and loss of all. It is said, however, that a consolidation of manufacturing corporations is permitted by the law, and that the trust or combination or partnership, however it may be described, amounts only to a practical consolidation, which public policy does not forbid, because the statute permits it. The refineries did not avail themselves of that statute. They chose to disregard it, and to reach its practical results without subjection to the prudential restraints with which the State accompanied its permission. If there had been a consolidation under the statute, one single corporation would have

powers are ineffectual. * * * A late decision of the Supreme Court of Georgia has rendered a further discussion of the question unnecessary. In Gunn v. Cent. R. R. & Banking Co., 74 Ga. 509, that court has construed the powers conferred by the charter of the defendant, and held that the corporation has no power to enter into a partnership with a natural person to purchase and run a steamboat on one of the rivers of that State. This decision was made in a suit brought by a passenger on the same steamboat, to recover damages for injuries sustained at the same time and under the same circumstances, as the plaintiff in the present action. If we entertained doubt of the power of the defendant to engage in such business,—when it is said 'to be in doubt is to be resolved,' comity would suggest an acceptance of, and acquiescence in, the construction of the statutes of that State, under which the corporation was organized, by the court of last resort." Central R. R. & Banking Co. v. Smith, 76 Ala. 572, 579. "I do not think it was necessary to establish a co-partnership between the defendants to create the liability claimed against them. A corporation may, in furtherance of the object of its creation, contract with an individual, though the effect of the contract may be to impose upon the company the liability of a partner. And, as to third persons, the liability of a partner is frequently imposed, though it was not the intention of the party sought to be charged to become one, and even though a partnership could not have been made. Field, Corporations, § 263; Manhattan, B. & M. Co. v. Sears, 45 N. Y. 799; Leggett v. Hyde, 58 N. Y. 272; Rider Life Raft Co. v. Roach, 97 N. Y. 378; Catskill Bank v. Gray, 14 Barb. 471; Marine Bank v. Ogden, 29 Ill. 248; Allen v. Woonsocket Co., 11 R. I. 288." Sherwood, J., in Cleveland Paper Co. v. Courier Co., 67 Mich. 152, 158.

taken the place of the others dissolved. They would have disappeared utterly, and not, as under the trust, remained in apparent existence to threaten and menace other organizations, and occupy the ground which otherwise would be left free. Under the statute the resultant combination would itself be a corporation deriving its existence from the State, owing duties and obligations to the State, and subject to the control and supervision of the State, and not, as here, an unincorporated board, a colossal and gigantic partnership, having no corporate functions and owing no corporate allegiance. Under the statute the consolidated company, taking the place of the separate corporation, could have as capital stock only an amount equal to the fair aggregate value of the rights and franchises of the companies absorbed; and not, as here, a capital stock double that value at the outset and capable of an elastic and irresponsible increase. The difference is very great, and serves further to indicate the inherent illegality of the trust combination. And here, I think, we gain a definite view of the injurious tendencies developed by its organization and operation, and of the public interests which are menaced by its action. As corporate grants are always assumed to have been made for the public benefit, any conduct which destroys their normal functions, and maims and cripples their separate activity, and takes away their free and independent action, must so far disappoint the purpose of their creation as to affect unfavorably the public interest; and that to a much greater extent when beyond their own several aggregations of capital they compact them all into one combination which stands outside of the ward of the State, which dominates the range of an entire industry and puts upon the market a capital stock proudly defiant of actual values and capable of an unlimited expansion. It is not a sufficient answer to say that similar results may be lawfully accomplished; that an individual having the necessary wealth might have bought all these refineries, manned them with his own chosen agents, and managed them as a group at his sovereign will; for it is one thing for the State to respect the rights of ownership and protect them out of regard to the business freedom of the citizen, and quite another thing to add to that possibility a further extension of those consequences by creating artificial persons to aid in producing such aggregation. The individuals are few who hold in possession such enormous wealth, and fewer still who peril it all in a manufacturing enterprise; but if corporations can combine, and mass their forces in a solid trust or partnership, with little added risk to the capital already embarked, without limit to the magnitude of the aggregation, a tempting and easy road is opened to enormous combinations, vastly exceeding in number and in strength and in their power over industry any possibilities of individual ownership; and the State, by the creation of the artificial persons, constituting the elements of the combination, and failing to limit and restrain their powers, becomes itself the responsible creator, the voluntary cause of an aggregation of capital which it simply endures in the individual as the product of his free agency. What it may bear is one thing; what it should cause and create is quite another."[1]

§ 163. **Legality of the "Trust" Continued, — Class Second.**—The leading case relating to "trusts" of this class is that of The Chicago Gas Trust Company. This corporation was organized under the General Corporation Law of Illinois.[2] The object of the trust, as set forth in the certificate of corporation, was, as follows: "The object for which it is formed is to build, erect, purchase, lease, establish, maintain, enlarge, extend and operate or demise works in the city of Chicago, in the county of Cook and State of Illinois, and in such other place or places in said State of Illinois as said corporation may, by the vote of the majority of its stockholders, elect, for the manufacture, supply, sale and distribution of gas and electricity, or either, for the furnishing of light, heat, fuel and power for any and all purposes for which gas or electricity may now

[1] People v. North River Sugar Refining Co., 121 N. Y. 582, 622.

[2] Rev. Ill. Code, 32, 1 & 5.

or hereafter be used; and to purchase and hold or sell the capital stock or purchase or lease or operate the property, plant, good will, rights and franchises of any gas works or gas company or gas companies, or any electric company or electric companies in the said city of Chicago, or elsewhere in said State, as said corporation may, by vote of the majority of the stockholders, elect; and to purchase, hold, sell, operate or anywise become interested in coal or other properties productive of material necessary or useful in the supply or manufacture of gas, or other agency or medium of light, heat, power or fuel; and to sell, improve, enlarge, extend, maintain, operate and demise any and all property,—so purchased or leased."[1] In the case of The People v. The Chicago Gas Trust Company, it was held that a corporation formed under the general law for a lawful purpose, such as the manufacture and sale of gas, cannot clothe itself with power to purchase and hold stock in similar corporations merely by naming this as one of the objects of its incorporation in the articles filed with the secretary of state. A corporation cannot become a stockholder in another corporation unless such power is expressly given or is necessarily implied, and this more especially when the object is to obtain the control or effect the management of such other corporation. The General Incorporation Law of this State does not, in express terms, confer upon corporations formed thereunder the power to purchase and hold shares of stock in other corporations, but it is silent on the subject. The only powers granted by it are the ordinary corporate powers, such as the right to be bodies corporate and politic, to sue and be sued, to have a common seal, etc. Section 5 of the General Incorporation Law expressly restricts the powers of a corporation formed under such law to such as are necessary to carry into effect the object for which it was formed. The purchase of stock in other companies not being necessary to enable a gas company to carry its object in making and selling gas into effect, is impliedly prohibited by the statute. Whatever

[1] People v. Chicago Gas Trust Co., 130 Ill. 275.

tends to prevent competition between those engaged in an employment or business impressed with a public character, is opposed to public policy, and, therefore, unlawful; and whatever tends to create a monopoly is unlawful as being contrary to public policy. All grants creating monopolies, and acts tending to prevent proper competition, are by the common law illegal and void. If grants and contracts, the tendency of which is to create monopolies, are void at common law, then, when a corporation is organized under a general statute, a provision in the declaration of its corporate purposes, the necessary effect of which is the creation of a monopoly, will also be void. The Chicago Gas Trust Company, being a corporation formed under the General Incorporation Law, for the purpose of erecting and operating gas works, and the manufacture and sale of gas, has no power to purchase and hold or sell shares of stock in other gas companies as an incident to such purpose of its formation, even though such power is specified in its articles of incorporation. The gas trust company mentioned was incorporated under the general law for two purposes, as expressed in its articles of association: First, for the purpose of erecting and operating gas works for the manufacture and sale of gas in Chicago and other places in this State; and second, "to purchase and hold or sell the capital stock, or purchase or lease or operate the property, plant, good will, rights and franchises of any gas works or gas company or companies, or any electric company or companies, in Chicago or elsewhere," etc.[3] The company

[1] People v. Chicago Gas Trust Co., 130 Ill. 275. See also Talmage v. Pell, 7 N. Y. 348; Berry v. Yates, 24 Barb. 200; Milbank v. New York, etc. R. Co., 64 How. Pr. 20; Mechanics' Sav. Bank v. Meriden, etc. Co., 24 Conn. 159; Central, etc. R. Co. v. Pennsylvania R. R. Co., 31 N. J. Eq. 475; Hazlehurst v. Savannah, etc. R. Co., 43 Ga. 13; Valley R. Co. v. Lake Erie Ins. Co., 46 Ohio St. 44; Hill v. Nisbet, 100 Ind. 341; Compagnie Francaise v. Western Union Co., 11 Fed. Rep. 862; Solomons v. Laing, 12 Beav. 339; Franklin Bank v. Commercial Bank, 36 Ohio St. 350; Buford v. Keokuk Co., 3 Mo. App. 159; McMillan v. Carson Min. Co., 12 Phila. 404; *In re* British Life Ins. Assn., L. R. 8 Ch. D. 679; Taylor v. Earle, 8 Hun. 1; Frothingham v. Barney, 6 Hun. 366; Joint-Stock Co. v. Brown, L. R. 8 Eq. 381; Sumner v. Marcy, 3 W. & M. 105; New Orleans Co.

sought to exercise the powers claimed under the second clause, only, and for that purpose bought a majority of the shares of all the stock of all the gas companies in Chicago, being four in number, whereby it might have the control of all the gas companies in the city, and thus destroy competition and monopolize the gas business. It was held that the corporation so formed was not for a lawful purpose, and that all acts done by it towards the accomplishment of such object were illegal and void.[1] In the opinion in this case,

v. Ocean Dry Dock Co., 28 La. Ann. 173; Easun v. Buckeye Brew. Co., 51 Fed. Rep. 156; Buckeye Marble, etc. Co. v. Harvey, 92 Tenn. 115.

[1] People v. Chicago Gas Trust Co., 130 Ill. 268. A corporation authorized to conduct a lumber business is legally incapable of being a stockholder in a telegraph company. Peshtigo Co. v. Gt. Western Tel. Co., 50 Ill. App. 624. "We think it well settled as a result of the decisions in this State, as well as elswhere, that an incorporated company cannot, unless authorized by statute. make a valid subscription to the capital stock of another, that such subscription is *ultra vires* and void. Mr. Morawetz, in stating this to be the law, observes: 'The right of forming a corporation is conferred by the incorporation laws only upon persons acting individually, and not upon associations; moreover, it would, under ordinary circumstances, be a violation of the charter of an existing company to subscribe for shares in a new company and assume the resulting liabilities.' (Priv. Corp. § 433.) There has been no direct decision upon the question by this court, but such has been the uniform holding elsewhere. Railroad Company v. Railroad Company, 31 N. J. Eq. 475; Franklin Co. v. Lewiston Savings Bank, 68 Me. 43; Railroad Company v. Collins, 48 Ga. 582. These cases all proceed upon the legislative principle that the powers of corporations organized under legislative statute are such, and such only, as those statutes confer, or that may be fairly implied therefrom. This doctrine was clearly announced and applied in Straus v. Eagle Ins. Co., 5 Ohio St. 59, and has been firmly adhered to in this court. Railroad Co. v. Hinsdale, 45 Ohio St. 556, 573. No claim is made by the defendant that the iron company had any express statutory authority to use its capital or assets in aid of the construction of a railroad by subscription to its capital stock or otherwise. The only averment as to this, is, the iron company conceived that it would be benefited by the reduction of the price of coal at Cleveland, its place of business, and the market which the construction of the road would afford for its manufactures, and by these considerations was induced to make the subscription. But all of this can be of no avail in the face, at least, of the prohibition contained in § 3266, of the Revised Statutes, that 'no corporation shall employ its stock, means, assets or other property, directly or indirectly, for any

the court said: "Of what avail is it that any number of gas companies may be formed under the General Incorporation Law, if a giant trust company can be clothed with the power of buying up and holding the stock and property of

other purpose whatever, than to accomplish the legitimate objects of its creation.' There was, then, as we think, no authority whatever in the iron company to make a valid subscription to the capital stock of the railway company, and no recovery can be had upon it." Valley Railway Co. v. Iron Co., 46 Ohio St. 44, 49. "The purpose for which the agency company united, as expressed in their articles of association, was to do a general insurance agency, commission and brokerage business, and such other things as were incidental to, and necessary in, the management of that business. So far as that company was concerned the proper officers of the company had power to act and bind the company. But if they departed from that business, and entered into contracts not authorized by the company, such contracts would not be binding. A subscription to the stock of a building association has no legitimate connection with the business of an insurance agent, commission merchant or broker, and was not, therefore, authorized by the defendants' articles of association. It is said that the defendants had power to borrow money, mortgage their real estate for its security, and, if necessary, to obtain a loan, as in this case, become a stockholder in a building association. We are not disposed to question the right of the defendants to borrow money, and mortgage their real estate for its security. This may be one of the powers incidental to, and necessary in, the prosecution of their business, and the successful management of the same. We are inclined to think the power is implied in their articles of association. But when the directors of the company subscribed for stock in a building association, whatever may have been their motive, whether to obtain a loan of money, or for purposes of speculation, they transcended the powers conferred upon them, and departed from the legitimate business of the company, as much so as if they had subscribed for stock in a manufacturing or steamboat company. Such subscription, in our opinion, is not binding upon the defendants, and any payments made upon it to the plaintiffs would be money received by them without consideration." Mutual Sav., etc. Co. v. Meriden Agency Co., 24 Conn. 159, 163. A railroad company chartered for the purpose of building and maintaining a railroad from Savannah to Macon, with general powers to purchase and hold personal estate, of any character whatever, is not authorized to become a stockholder in a railroad from Savannah to Bainbridge. Such a purchase is wholly beyond the purposes of the charter. It is a part of the public policy of the State, as indicated by the charter of several railroads from the seaboard to the interior to secure a reasonable competition between said roads for public patronage, and it is contrary to that policy such companies, and through the control thereby attained can direct all their operations and weld them into one huge combination? The several privileges or franchises intended to be exercised by a number of companies are thus vested exclusively in a single corporation. To create one corpora-

for one of said roads to attempt to secure a controlling interest in another, and any contract made with that view will be set aside by a court of equity as illegal, beyond the objects of the charter, and contrary to the public policy of the State. Central R. R. v. Collins, 40 Ga. 582. See also Hazlehurst v. Savannah, etc. R. R. Co., 43 Ga. 13. Though a railroad company may take title to all kinds of personal property, including stock of other railroad corporations, to secure debts due it, the investment by a railroad company of its corporate funds in the purchase of the stock of another corporation is not necessary in the exercise of any of its corporate powers, and is unauthorized and in violation of the statute and is consequently *ultra vires*. While a railroad corporation remains the owner of the stock of another corporation, it may collect and receive dividends thereon and has the right to sell and dispose of the same, but has no right to vote thereon; and the stockholders of the company whose stock is thus held, have the right to have the company holding such stock enjoined from so voting, in case it threatened to do so. Milbank v. New York, etc. R. R. Co., 64 How. Pr. 20. A corporation cannot, in its own name, subscribe for stock, or be a corporator, under the general railroad law; nor can it do so by a simulated compliance with the provisions of the law through its agents as pretended corporators and subscribers of stock. Any attempt by a corporation to avail itself unlawfully of the general railroad law to build a railroad, will, on complaint of the party injured, be enjoined as an abuse of the law. Central R. R. Co. of New Jersey v. Pennsylvania R. R. Co., 31 N. J. Eq. 475. The trustees of the Lewiston Institution for Savings subscribed for $50,000 of the capital stock of the Continental Mills, and having no power to pay for it, the Franklin Company, another corporation, paid that amount to the Continental Mills, taking the notes of the savings institution therefor, and a certificate of the stock in their own name as collateral security for the payment of the notes. *Held*, that the action of the trustees of the savings institution was *ultra vires;* that it was not within the authority of savings institutions, at a time when they have no funds for investment, to purchase stocks or other property, not needed for immediate use, on credit, and thus create a debt binding upon the institution; that the Franklin Company, having participated in the illegal transaction, could not claim the privileges of a *bona fide* holder of commercial paper; and that the savings institution, having received no benefit from the transaction, was not estopped to set up the defense of *ultra vires*. Franklin Co. v. Lewiston Savings Bank, 68 Me. 43.

tion for the express purpose of enabling it to control all the corporations engaged in a certain kind of business, and particularly a business of a public character, is not only opposed to the public policy of the State, but is in contravention of the spirit, if not the letter, of the constitution. That the exercise of the power attempted to be conferred upon the appellee company must result in the creation of a monopoly, results from the very nature of the power itself. If the privilege of purchasing and holding all the shares of stock in all the gas companies of Chicago can be lawfully conferred upon appellee, under the General Incorporation Act, it can be lawfully conferred upon any other corporation formed for the purpose of buying and holding all the shares of stock of said gas companies. The design of that act was that any number of corporations might be organized to engage in the same business, if it should be deemed desirable. But the business now under consideration could hardly be exercised by two or three corporations. Suppose that after appellee had purchased and become the holder of the majority of shares of stock of the four companies in Chicago, another corporation had been organized with the same object in view, that is to say, for the purpose of purchasing and holding a majority of the shares of stock of the gas companies in Chicago. There being only four such companies, what would there be for the corporation last formed to do? It would not carry out the object of its creation, because the stock it was formed to buy was already owned by an existing corporation. Hence, to grant to the appellee the privilege of purchasing and holding the capital stock of any gas company in Chicago is to grant to it a privilege which is exclusive in its character. It is making use of the General Incorporation Law to secure a special 'privilege, immunity or franchise;' it is obtaining a special charter, under the cover and through the machinery of that law, for a purpose forbidden by the constitution. To create one corporation that it may destroy the energies of all other corporations of a given kind and suck their life blood out of them is not a lawful purpose' "[1]

§ **164. The Rule in England.**—The rule in England, as determined by the recent decisions, is not in harmony with that of the American courts, as stated in the preceding section. It is held that where the articles of incorporation set forth the general purpose to trade in the stocks of other corporations, a trading company may buy stock in other companies without express legislative authority. In the case, *In re* Barned's Banking Company, it was held by the Court of Appeal in Chancery that a limited company may

[1] People v. Chicago Gas Trust Co., 130 Ill. 268, 297. "Gas companies being engaged in a business of a public character are charged with the performance of public duties. Their use of the streets, whose fee is held by the municipal corporation in trust for the benefit of the public, has been likened to the exercise of the power of eminent domain. Chicago Gas Light & Coke Co. v. People's Gas Light & Coke Co., 121 Ill. 530. In Gibbs v. Baltimore Gas Co., 130 U. S. 396, the Supreme Court of the United States, in an able opinion delivered by Mr. Chief Justice Fuller, uses these words: 'These gas companies entered the streets of Baltimore, under their charters, in the exercise of the equivalent of the power of eminent domain, and are to be held as having assumed an obligation to fulfill the public purposes to subserve which they were incorporated.' The privileges awarded to the four gas companies under their respective charters were given them in return for, and in consideration of, services to be rendered by them to the public. When they entered the streets of Chicago, they assumed the performance of the public duty of furnishing light to the inhabitants. That they should be permitted or required, or forced to abandon the performance of such public duty is against the policy of the law. The public duty is imposed upon each company separately, and not upon the four when combined together. Each for itself, when it accepted its articles of association, assumed an obligation to perform the objects of its incorporation. But the appellee, through the control which it does or may exercise over the four companies by reason of its ownership of a majority of their stock, renders it impossible for them to discharge their public duties except at the dictation of an outside force, and in the manner prescribed by a corporation operating independently of them. They are thus virtually forced to abandon the performance of their duty to the public. The freedom and effectiveness of their action in carrying out the purposes of their creation are seriously interfered with, if not actually destroyed. A power, whose exercise leads to such a result cannot be lawfully intrusted to any corporate body." *Ibid.*, 301.

become a shareholder in another limited company, if authorized by its own memorandum and articles of association to do so.[1] In a later case, before the same court, Lord

[1] *In re* Barned's Banking Co., L. R. 3 Ch. App. 105. "The second argument was, that even assuming that according to the constitution of the Contract Corporation, it was not *ultra vires* to invest their money in shares of another trading company, yet that under the Act of 1862, one trading corporation could not become a member of another trading corporation. Now, if that argument is to prevail, it must be upon the words of the Act of Parliament of 1862, because there is no apparent or *prima facie* objection to a corporation so joining with another corporation in trade. A trading corporation, as we all well know, may enter into trade or partnership along with an individual. There is no reason at common law, so far as I know, why one corporate body should not become a member of another corporate body. Other acts of Parliament relating to companies appear to assume that corporations may become members of and shareholders in companies. For example, the General Act, the Companies Clauses Consolidation Act of 1845, provides, in the interpretation clause, that 'shareholder' in that Act shall include a corporation; and the Chartered Companies Act, 1 Vict., chap. 73, expressly points out that the owner may grant a charter to a trading corporation, the shareholders in which may themselves be corporate bodies, and whose liability under that charter may be limited. Now, looking to the words of the Act of 1862, it is said, no doubt justly, that they appear throughout to point to persons, and to the executors and administrators of persons, as if the shareholders were all to be persons in their natural capacity. But even in this act, there are traces that the term 'shareholder' and the word 'persons' must have been intended to be used in a larger sense, for in the 50th and 51st clauses provision is made for the determination of questions of considerable importance by general meetings, and by votes to be given at those meetings, either in person or by proxy, in cases where, by the regulations of the company, proxies are allowed; and on turning to the forms in the schedule, which may be adopted by any company for its regulation, we find, in the 49th clause of Table A, a provision that the instrument appointing a proxy shall be in writing under the hand of the appointor; 'or if such appointor is a corporation, under their common seal.' Form B contains a similar clause (clause 22), as do also the forms in the schedule to the Act of 1856. It would, therefore, appear to have been in the contemplation of the legislature that the appointor of a proxy might be a corporation; and inasmuch as the appointor was to be a shareholder, that a shareholder might be a corporate body." *Ibid.*, 113. "Another objection was made which does not appear to me to present any serious difficulty; that objection is, that it was *ultra vires* of the defendants to acquire stock in another trading company. There is, I apprehend, no general rule, that one trading corporation can-

Justice Selwyn stated the rule, as follows: "Now, with respect to the first question which has been argued, viz.: as to the capacity of a trading corporation to accept shares in another trading corporation, it is sufficient for me to say that I entirely agree with the judgment of Lord Cairns in the case of Barned's Banking Company,[1] viz.: that there is not, either by the common or statute law, anything to prohibit one trading corporation from taking or accepting

not hold shares in another trading corporation. Where, indeed, the holding of such shares would be incompatable with the purposes for which the company was incorporated, there would be an implied prohibition against holding them. The rule is thus stated by Mr. Brice, in his book on the doctrine of *Ultra Vires*. 'A corporation may deal in the shares of other corporations without express power so to do, provided the nature of its business be such as to render such transactions conducive to its prosperity.' If this be correct we have the statement of the defendants themselves to bring them within the rule; for their answer prefaces their account of the contract of purchase of shares with this allegation. 'That the property and privileges of the said Port Credit Harbor Company being adjacent to the property of the defendants it became important for the defendants to acquire the said property and all the rights, privileges and franchises of the said company; and we find that in 1873, the legislature enabled the two companies to aid one another, and to hold stock in the company of the other—some evidence that the holding of such stock was conducive to the prosperity of each company. Whatever doubt may have existed of the power of one trading company to hold shares in another, and such doubt did exist as is shown by the elaborate judgments in the Mayor of Norwich v. Norfolk Railway Company (4 E. & B. 397), it seems to be now settled that the holding of such shares is not *ultra vires*. The question was discussed very fully by Lord Cairns, in *In re* Barned's Banking Company, *ex parte* contract corporation. L. R. 3 Ch. App. 105." Canada Life Assn. Co. v. Peel Manufacturing Co., 26 Grant's Ch. (Can.) 477, 486. In England, however, there is in the later decision a tendency to modify the older position on this point. In the 3d edition of his work on Ultra Vires, Mr. Brice, at page 133, says: "With regard to railway companies and other semi-public corporations it is quite clear that they cannot, without statutory authority, purchase, take or deal in the shares of other companies; and in the case of such companies, any such power will be construed strictly, whether as to limit of shares in number which may be taken or as to holding shares when taken." See G. E. Ry. Co. v. Turner, L. R. 8 Ch. App. 149; G. W. Ry. Co. v. Met. Ry. Co., 32 L. J. Ch. 382; s. c., 9 Jur. (N. S.) 562.

[1] *In re* Barned's Banking Co., L. R. 3 Ch. App. 105.

shares in another trading corporation. There may, of course, be circumstances which prohibit or render it improper for a company to do so, having regard to its own constitution as defined by its memorandum and articles; but excluding all these considerations, although in the statute of 1862 the words 'person or persons' continually occur, still I think it must be taken to include corporations, and looking at the question as a mere abstract question, in my judgment there is nothing to prevent a corporation from being a shareholder in another trading corporation."[1] This rule, in its essential features, has been adopted in Maryland, and possibly in some of the other States, but so far as the courts of the country are concerned the position is exceptional. The doctrine, as set forth in the preceding sections, is well established. In the case of Booth v. Robinson, before the Supreme Court of Maryland, it was held that there is no legal presumption of illegality or unfairness, in transactions between two corporations, from the mere fact that a portion of the board of directors in the one company constituted a part of the board of directors in the other at the same time, and participated in the dealings between the two corporations. It is only when their dealings are shown to be prejudicial to the one or other of the corporations represented by them, that their conduct will be subject to a strict and severe scrutiny by the courts. A corporation may invest in the stock of other corporations as well as in any other funds, provided it be done *bona fide* and with no sinister or unlawful purpose, and there be nothing in its charter or in the nature of its business that forbids it.[2] In the opinion in this case, the court said: "The first question is, as to the power of the Steam Packet Company to purchase and hold the stock of the Powhatan Company. This, it is contended by the plaintiff, could not be done without express authority by law. But while some courts have so held, the great weight of authority is the other way. There is nothing in

[1] Royal Bank of India's Case, L. R. 4 Ch. App. 252, 257.

[2] Booth v. Robinson, 55 Md. 419.

the charter of the Steam Packet Company, or in the nature of its business, that would, in the slightest manner, forbid the exercise of such power; and having money to loan or invest, there would appear to be no good reason why it might not invest in the stock of other corporations as well as in any other funds, provided it be done *bona fide* and with no sinister or unlawful purpose. The courts of England, at one time, strongly opposed the right of one corporation to deal or invest in the stock of another corporation without express authority for so doing; but that opposition has been entirely overcome, and it is now settled there that one corporation may deal in the shares of another without express authority so to do, unless where expressly prohibited or the nature of its business render it improper so to deal."[1]

§ 165. Legality of the "Trust" Continued, — Class Third.—Trusts of this class, as above shown,[2] are corporations which have purchased or otherwise acquired the plants, including the real estate, machinery, stock in trade, good will, etc., of a number of corporations, firms or individuals engaged in a particular branch of business. Payment for all property thus acquired is made in the stock of the new corporation. The business is then conducted by the officers and directors of the corporation and with reference to the common interests of all the stockholders. They continue the business of all the separate concerns, or suspend the work of a part of them, as is believed to be for the profit of the new organization. The object is the creation of a monopoly and the control of prices, and this may require that the production of the combined interests should be limited. The leading case relating to corporations of this class is that of The Diamond Match Company, before the Supreme Court of Michigan. The legality of this corporation was determined in the case of Richardson v. Buhl. In this suit the corporation was not directly a party. The Diamond Match Company was organized

[1] Booth v. Robinson, 55 Md. 419, 433. See also Elysville Manf. Co. v. Okisko Co., 1 Md. Ch. Dec. 392; s. c., 5 Md. 152.

[2] *Ante*, § 158.

December 3d, 1880, under the laws of the State of Connecticut, for the purpose of uniting in one corporation all the match manufacturers in the United States. Its object was to monopolize and control the business of making all the friction matches in the country, and to establish the price thereof, and it became necessary to buy many plants which had become established in the business or were preparing therefor, and all the property used in connection therewith, and to obtain promises from the owners and manufacturers that they would not engage in the business themselves, or indirectly through others, for ten or more years thereafter; and, for the purpose of obtaining the control and good will of such manufactories and their properties, large powers were given by the legislature to the Diamond Match Company when organized and under the by-laws by which it was controlled. The extent to which it was allowed to go in this direction in the accomplishment of its purposes appears in the articles of incorporation, in which it is stated, among other things, that the business of the company is "to manufacture, buy, sell and deal in friction matches of all kinds, and all articles entering into the composition and manufacture thereof; to manufacture, buy, sell and deal in machines and machinery, whether applicable to the manufacture of friction matches or to other purposes; to purchase, own and sell exclusive rights under letters patent relating to the manufacture of friction matches, and to machines and machinery, whether applicable to the manufacture of friction matches or to other purposes; to manufacture, buy, sell and deal in animal pokes, tobacco pipes, curry combs, brushes, shoe blacking and shoe dressing, and also articles entering into the composition and manufacture thereof; to purchase, own and sell exclusive rights under letters patent relating to the manufacture of all the articles herein enumerated, and to machines and machinery applicable to the manufacture thereof; to buy, sell, own and deal in any real or personal property, necessary or convenient to the prosecution of said business,—and, generally, to do all things incidental to said business and the proper management thereof."[1] In Richardson v. Buhl, it was held that a corporation, organized for the purpose of controlling the manufacture and sale of matches, and by means of which scheme all competition is stifled and opposition crushed, and the whole business of the country in that line engrossed by said corporation, is a menace to the public; its object and direct tendency being to prevent free and fair competition and to control prices throughout the national domain. It is no answer to say that this monopoly has, in fact, reduced the price of friction matches. That policy may have been necessary to crush competition. The fact exists that it rests in the discretion of the corporation at any time to raise the price to an exorbitant degree. Such combinations have frequently been condemned by courts as unlawful, and against public policy.[2]

[1] Richardson v. Buhl, 77 Mich. 632, 635; s. c., 27 Am. & Eng. Corp. Cas. 256.

[2] Richardson v. Buhl, 77 Mich. 632. See also Hooker v. Vandewater, 4 Denio, 349; Stanton v. Allen, 5 Denio, 434; Salt Co. v. Guthrie, 35 Ohio St. 672; Craft v. McConoughy, 79 Ill. 346; Hannah v. Fife, 27 Mich. 172; Alger v. Thacher, 19 Pick. 51; Morris Run Coal Co. v. Coal Co., 68 Pa. St. 186; Strait v. National Harrow Co., 18 N. Y. Supl. 224. In Stockton v. Central R. R. Co., 50 N. J. Eq. 52; s. c., 24 Atl. Rep. 964, it was held that where a railroad company in violation of statute leases all its rights, property and franchises, including 40 auxiliary roads, leased or controlled by it, to foreign railroad corporation for 999 years, making the lessee, with other roads controlled by it, constitute a consolidation of three out of six of the great coal carriers from the coal region of Pennsylvania and adjoining States, the lessor and lessee owning the major portion of the capital stock of corporations which own more than one-half of the anthracite coal fields of Pennsylvania, and the consolidation tending to create a monopoly in coal, and to raise the price of that commodity, equity will, at the suit of the attorney-general, restrain the performance of the lease. In the course of the opinion at page 81, Chancellor McGill says: "There are peculiar features in the transaction now considered that evince a public danger much more serious than appears in the mere transfer of corporate duties to performance by a foreign corporation. The real lessor and lessee here are extensive producers and carriers of anthracite coal. They constitute two of the six great anthracite coal carriers from the coal regions of Pennsylvania to this and adjoining States. It is disclosed that the real lessee has secured a lease of the Lehigh Valley Railroad Company, and that thereby, and by the lease in question, it controls three

§ 166. The Subject Continued.—In the case of Richardson v. Buhl, above cited, the rule relating to trusts of this class is stated, as follows: "Monopoly in trade or in any kind of business in this country is odious to our form

of the six great coal carriers referred to, and also that the alliance thus formed now controls, through the instrumentality of coal companies, the capital stock of which these combined carriers own, more than one-half of all the anthracite coal fields in Pennsylvania. Moreover, as an indication of the tendency of the combination, the attorney-general presents a report by the lessor defendant to its stockholders, in which it congratulates them upon an alliance which, with the co-operation of other large coal producing companies, will insure them 'greater uniformity in the prices of coal' and the 'avoidance of needless and expensive competition between producers.' He urges that, in substance, this report declares the reaching out to a monopoly which will work incestimable disaster to the people of the State. And as a further evidence that monopoly is in view, he points also to an admission by the president of the Philadelphia and Reading Railroad Company that the lease complained of will possibly facilitate the corporation of other coal producers, and, in itself, undoubtedly affect prices of coal in some localities. The proofs show that there are localities in this State which formerly had the advantage of competition between these allied roads but now are subject to the monopoly which this lease affords. It is true co-operation of the remaining coal roads, which is necessary to a complete monopoly, has not yet been secured. By the lease only one competition is silenced and only a little more than one-half of the entire coal region is controlled. It is only the second step in the direction of monopoly, the first being the lease of the Lehigh Valley Railroad. It is to be remembered, however, that the attorney-general may have his injunction when the *ultra vires* act tends or is of a nature to produce public injury. He is not required to wait until all the monopoly possible is created or until all the injury possible is in process of infliction. The present situation may be justly regarded as Vice-Chancellor Kindersley considered that which was presented to him in Attorney-General v. Gt. Northern Ry. Co., 1 Drew & S. 184; s. c., 6 Jur. (N. S.) 1006, where the *ultra vires* act was the mere dealing in coal by a railway company. He comments upon it, as follows: 'Mr. Rolt argued well, but there is no danger of monopoly, because, even if you were to suppose that this company got the entire command of all the coal which comes down that line from the inland districts and the northern part of England, that is not a monopoly; there is all the coal that comes from the northwestern district, the Lancashire district, and all the coal from the Welsh district, Bristol coal and so on, and there is no monopoly. But follow that out, and suppose this company has got the command of all the coal on its line, and from that part of the of government. It is sometimes permitted to aid the government in carrying on a great public enterprise or public work, under government control, in the interest of the public. Its tendency is, however, distructive of free insti-

country from which it starts, and suppose that the London and Northwestern has got the control of all the Lancashire and Northwestern coal country, and suppose the Great Western has got the command of all the Welsh and Bristol coal fields, you have got, then, the whole traffic in coal which is to supply the metropolis and the country in the hands of three companies. Are not the interests of the public most deeply concerned in preventing that? Is it not obvious that the interests of the public must suffer if that state of things is allowed to arise? And yet what this company is doing may just as well be done by each of the other companies I have mentioned, and the result would be, in effect, not a monopoly of one company, but a monopoly of three or four or five companies, and a monopoly most prejudicial.'" In 1887, plaintiff, with other corporations engaged in the manufacturing of carbon, entered into a contract with H, the object of which was, by a combination, to vest in H as a common trustee, the management and control of the business of manufacturing and selling their products. The several companies agreed to lease to such trustee their respective factories, and operate them under his direction. He was to designate the kind of goods to be manufactured, fix the prices at which and the persons to whom they should be sold, and, after paying expenses, divide the net proceeds and profits as provided in the contract. When this contract was made, plaintiff had an outstanding contract to furnish carbons to the B. E. L. Co. from time to time. Plaintiff assigned to H, as such trustee, all existing contracts, and he assumed their performance. Carbons manufactured at plaintiff's factory in April, May and June, 1887, were billed in the name of H and delivered under said contract to the B. E. L. Co. About July, 1887, plaintiff refused to continue in the combination, and an action was commenced against the trustee and the contracting corporations to dissolve the same which resulted in the appointment of defendant as receiver of its property. In an action brought by plaintiff to recover for said carbons, the B. E. L. Co. paid the amount into court. The court found that the contract to combine was made for unlawful purposes and was illegal; that the trust was then insolvent, and its assets, including the claim against the B. E. L. Co., insufficient to pay its creditors. *Held*, that as between the plaintiff and the receiver, the latter was entitled to the fund; that plaintiff stood in the position of a party to an illegal contract claiming a fund which, if the contract was valid, belonged to the trust combination, and to sustain the action would permit it to escape from the operation of the rule which denies affirmative relief to a party to an illegal contract. Pittsburg Carbon Co. v. McMillan, 119 N. Y. 46.

tutions, and repugnant to the instincts of a free people, and contrary to the whole scope and spirit of the Federal Constitution, and is not allowed to exist under express provisions in several of our State constitutions. Indeed, it is doubtful if free government can long exist in a country where such enormous amounts of money are allowed to be accumulated in the vaults of corporations to be used at discretion in controlling the property and business of the country, against the interests of the public and that of the people, for the personal gain and aggrandizement of a few individuals. It is always destructive of individual rights, and of that free competition which is the life of business, and it invites and perpetuates one of the great evils which it was the object of the framers of our form of government to eradicate and prevent. It is alike destructive to both individual enterprise and individual prosperity, whether conferred upon corporations or individuals, and, therefore, public policy is, and ought to be, as well as public sentiment, against it. All combinations among persons or corporations for the purpose of raising or controlling the prices of merchandise, or of any of the necessaries of life, are monopolies and intolerable, and ought to receive the condemnation of all courts."[1]

[1] Richardson v. Buhl, 77 Mich. 632, 658. There is no general rule determining what are articles of necessity. The following are a few of the articles held to be articles of necessity: Lumber, Santa Clara Valley Mill, etc. Co. v. Hayes, 76 Cal. 387; s. c., 9 Am. St. Rep. 211: butter, Chapin v. Brown, 83 Iowa, 156; coal, Morris Run Coal Co. v. Barclay Coal Co., 68 Pa. St. 173: Arnot v. Pittston, etc. Coal Co., 68 N. Y. 568; s. c., 23 Am. Rep. 190: cotton bagging, India Bagging Assoc. v. Kock, 14 La. Ann. 164: grain, Craft v. McConoughy, 79 Ill. 346: s. c., 22 Am. Rep. 171: salt, Central Ohio Salt Co. v. Guthrie, 35 Ohio St. 666; Clancy v. Onondaga Fine Salt Co., 62 Barb. 395; cloth, Hilton v. Eckersley, 6 El. & Bl. 47; grain bags, Pacific Factory Co. v. Adler, 90 Cal. 110; alcohol, State v. Nebraska Distilling Co., 29 Neb. 700: s. c., 29 Am. & Eng. Corp. Cas. 656: candles, Emery v. Ohio Candle Co., 47 Ohio St. 320: s. c., 32 Am. & Eng. Corp. Cas. 165: preserves, American Preservers' Trust v. Taylor Mfg. Co., 46 Fed. Rep. 152. "Alcohol is an article of commerce. It is applied to a thousand uses in arts and manufactures. The amount which is rectified and used as intoxicating drinks forms but a very small part of the quantity actually distilled, and being

an article of commerce any contract creating a monopoly therein is against public policy and void." State v. Nebraska Distilling Co., 29 Neb. 700, 718. "The supplying of illuminating gas is a business of a public nature to meet a public necessity. It is not a business like that of an ordinary corporation engaged in the manufacture of articles that may be furnished by individual effort. New Orleans Gas Co. v. Louisiana Light Co., 115 U. S. 683; Shepard v. Milwaukee Gas Co., 6 Wis. 539; Chicago Gas Light & Coke Co. v. People's Gas Light & Coke Co., 121 Ill. 530; St. Louis v. St. Louis Gas Light Co., 70 Mo. 69. Hence, while it is justly urged that those rules which say that a given contract is against public policy should not be arbitrarily extended so as to interfere with the freedom of contract (Printing, etc. Registering Co. v. Sampson, L. R. 19 Eq. 462), yet in the instance of business of such character that it presumably cannot be restrained to any extent whatever without prejudice to the public interest, courts decline to enforce or sustain contracts imposing such restraint, however partial, because in contravention of public policy. This subject is much considered and the authorities cited in West Virginia Transportation Co. v. Ohio River Pipe Line Co., 22 W. Va. 600; Chicago, etc. Gas Co. v. People's Gas Co., 121 Ill. 530; Western Union Tel. Co. v. American Union Tel. Co., 65 Ga. 160." Gibbs v. Baltimore Gas Co., 130 U. S. 396, 408. The following are held not to be articles of necessity: Sewing machines, Bi-Spool Sewing Machine Co. v. Acme Mfg. Co., 15 Mass. 404; washing machines, Dolph v. Troy Laundry Machine Co., 28 Fed. Rep. 553; curtain fixtures, Central Shade Roller Co. v. Cushman, 143 Mass. 353. An agreement between two manufacturers of glue from fish skins under a supposed valid patent, the object of which is to avoid competition between themselves and secure to each a reasonable profit, is not against public policy, the article in question not being one of prime necessity, nor a a staple commodity ordinarily bought and sold in the market. Gloucester Isinglass & Glue Co. v. Russia Cement Co., 154 Mass. 92; s. c., 27 N. E. Rep. 1005.

CHAPTER XII.

TRUST COMBINATIONS.

§ 167. Introduction.
168. The Purpose and Scope of Federal Legislation.
169. The Subject Continued.
170. Pooling by Railroads.
171. The Pooling of Stocks.
172. The Pooling of Products.
173. The Subject Continued.
174. Monopoly under Patents.
175. The Subject Continued.
§ 176. The Voting Trust.
177. The Subject Continued.
178. The Same Subject.
179. Rebates on Freight Bills.
180. The Subject Continued.
181. Combinations of Insurance Companies.
182. Rights of Parties under Trust Combinations.

§ **167. Introductory.**—The decisions and legislation adverse to the "trust" proper, as examined in the preceding chapter, has led to a variety of combinations which are of the nature of a trust, but are designed to conform to the requirements of the law. The design of these combinations is to secure the ends answered by the trust, while avoiding the methods which have rendered the trust illegal as in contravention of public policy and void. But the numerous schemes of this character have not been largely successful. As the ends sought are essentially illegal, condemnation is not escaped by a change of methods. These combinations have appeared under a variety of forms. But whatever phase they may assume the object is to suppress competition, or to regulate the production and sale of some article of necessity or of some commodity that is in general use. But this is a problem which, in view of recent decisions, presents some very grave difficulties, and the result has been that very many of these combinations have been found illegal and void.

§ 168. The Purpose and Scope of Federal Legislation.—Federal statutes, prohibiting trust combinations, are limited, of course, to contracts relating either directly or indirectly to interstate commerce. But while Federal legislation is, necessarily, limited in this direction, the object, as in the case of State legislation of this character, is to suppress combinations designed to create a monopoly in restraint of trade. The most important statute on this subject is the Act of July 2d, 1890, entitled: "An Act to Protect Trade and Commerce against Unlawful Restraints and Monopolies." The design and scope of this act appears from section 1, which provides that "every contract, combination in the form of trust or otherwise, or conspiracy, in restraint of trade or commerce, among the several States or with foreign nations, is hereby declared to be illegal. Every person who shall make any such contract, or engage in any such combination, or conspiracy, shall be deemed guilty of a misdemeanor, and, on conviction thereof, shall be punished by a fine, not exceeding $5,000, or by imprisonment, not exceeding one year, or by both said punishments, in the discretion of the courts."[1] In the recent leading case of The United States v. The Trans-Missouri Freight Association, we have a construction of this act by the Supreme Court of the United States. In that case it was held that, under this act, all combinations in restraint of trade or commerce are prohibited by the Act of Congress of July 2d, 1890, whether they are in the form of trusts or in any other form whatever. The words, "unlawful restraints and monopolies," in the title of the Act of Congress of July 2d, 1890, do not show that the purpose of the act was to include only contracts which were unlawful at common law, but refer to and include those restraints and monopolies which are made unlawful in the body of the act. The term "contract in restraint of trade," as used in the Act of Congress of July 2d, 1890, does not refer only to contracts which were invalid at common law, but includes every contract in restraint of trade, and is not limited to that kind of

[1] Federal Anti-Trust Act, § 1.

a contract which is in unreasonable restraint of trade. The public policy of the government is to be found in its statutes, and where they have not directly spoken, then, in the decisions of the court and the constant practice of the government officials; but where the law-making power speaks on a particular subject over which it has constitutional power to legislate, public policy in such a case is what the statute enacts. A contract or combination made in violation of a law is void, whatever may have been theretofore decided by the courts to have been the public policy of the country on the subject.[1]

[1] United States v. Trans-Missouri Freight Association, 166 U. S. 290, 20 Stat. 209, declaring illegal "every contract or combination in the form of trust, or otherwise in restraint of trade or commerce among the several States or with foreign nations," applies to combinations of laborers as well as of capitalists. In order to sustain the allegations of a bill for an injunction against a combination in restraint of interstate commerce, complainant may offer in evidence, as matter of history, the official proclamation of the various government officers and also newspapers reports supported by affidavits containing manifestoes and declarations of respondents. United States v. Workingmens' Amalgamated Council, 54 Fed. Rep. 994. A contract between manufacturers, whereby the first party agrees in consideration of a percentage on the sales made by the second party, not to use his plant for the production of strap and T hinges for five years, the contract to be void in case the second party increases his facilities for production of such hinges, is void as against public policy. Oliver v. Gilmore, 52 Fed. Rep. 562. To constitute the offense of "monopolizing, or attempting to monopolize," trade or commerce among the States, within the meaning Act July 2, 1890, § 2, it is necessary to acquire, or attempt to acquire, an exclusive right in such commerce by means which will prevent others from engaging therein. *In re* Greene, 52 Fed. Rep. 104. The act "to protect trade and commerce against unlawful restraints and monopolies" confers no right upon a private individual to sue in equity for the restraint of the acts forbidden by such statute, an action at law for damages being the only remedy provided for private persons, and the right to bring suits in equity being vested in the district-attorneys of the United States. Pidcock v. Harrington, 64 Fed. Rep. 821. An action in a Federal Circuit Court for New York, charging numerous business competitors of complainants in various States with forming a combination and attempting to create a monopoly in 1887, but charging that after the Act of July 2, 1890, defendants ratified and renewed their previous combinations, and demanding treble damages "under and by virtue of the statute," held to be

§ 169. The Subject Continued.—In the opinion in the case of The United States v. The Trans-Missouri Freight Association, we have a farther construction of the purpose and scope of the Federal Anti-Trust Act. In delivering the opinion, Mr. Justice Peckham said: "Coming to the merits of the suit, there are two important questions which demand our examination: They are, first, whether the above-cited

an action founded on the 1890 Act. In an action by a manufacturer of watch cases against numerous other manufacturers thereof in various States to recover treble damages under Act Congress July 2, 1890, prohibiting unlawful restraints and monopolies of interstate commerce, the complaint alleged that plaintiff operated an extensive factory; that previous to Nov. 16, 1887, it sold its goods to a great number of dealers "throughout the United States and Canada;" that prior to that date defendants had agreed with each other to maintain arbitrary and fixed prices for their watch cases; that for the purpose of compelling plaintiff to join with them therein, defendants on said date mutually agreed that they would not thereafter sell any goods to persons who bought or sold goods manufactured by plaintiff; that they caused notice thereof to be served on many dealers in such goods throughout the United States and Canada, who had formerly dealt in plaintiff's goods, whereupon many of such dealers withdrew their patronage from plaintiff; that after the passage of the Act of 1890, defendants ratified, renewed and confirmed their previous agreements, and served notice of such ratification on all said dealers in plaintiff's goods, whereby said dealers were compelled to refuse to purchase plaintiff's watch cases. *Held*, that the complaint failed to state a cause of action under the statute. Dueber Watch Case Mfg. Co. v. E. Howard Watch & Clock Co., 66 Fed. Rep. 637; s. c., 14 C. C. A. 14. A corporation organized to procure assignments of all patents relating to spring tooth harrows, to grant licenses for the use of the same, to regulate the price at which such harrows shall be sold and prosecute all infringements, is an illegal combination, contrary to public policy, whose purposes equity should not aid by entertaining infringement suits. National Harrow Co. v. Quick, 67 Fed. Rep. 130. The purchase of stock of sugar refineries, for the purpose of acquiring control over the business of refining sugar for sale in the United States, does not involve a monopoly or combination in restraint of commerce among the States within the prohibition of Act July 2, 1890. United States v. E. C. Knight Co., 156 U. S. 1; s. c., 15 Sup. Ct. Rep. 249. Where both plaintiff and defendant, in an action for goods sold, were corporations of the State in which the sale was made, the sale was not a transaction within Act July 2, 1890, relating to restraint of trade and commerce between the several States. National Distilling Co. v. Cream City Importing Co., 86 Wis. 352; s. c., 56 N. W. Rep. 864. A lease by one corporation to another, engaged in the same business, of act of Congress,—called herein the Trust Act,—applies to and covers common carriers by railroads; and, if so, second, does the agreement set forth in the bill violate any provision of that act? As to the first question: The language of the act includes every contract, combination in the form of trust or otherwise, or conspiracy in restraint of trade or commerce, among the several States or with foreign nations. So far as the very terms of the statute go, they apply to any contract of the nature described. A contract, therefore, that is in restraint of trade or commerce is by the strict language of the act prohibited, even though such contract is entered into between competing common carriers by railroads and only for the purpose of thereby affecting traffic rates for the transportation of persons and property. If such an agreement restrains trade or commerce, it is prohibited by the statute, unless it can be said that an agreement, no matter what its terms, relating only to transportation, cannot restain trade or commerce. We see no escape from the conclusion that if any agreement of such a nature does restrain it, the agreement is condemned by this act. It cannot be denied that those who are engaged in the transportation of persons or property from one State to another are engaged in interstate commerce, and it would seem to follow that if such persons enter into agreements between themselves in regard to the compensation to be secured from the owners of the articles transported, such agreement would at least relate to the business of commerce, and

its premises and plant, which gives no exclusive privilege but is made to remove the lessor's competition, is not against public policy nor void. United States Chemical Co. v. Provident Chemical Co., 64 Fed. Rep. 946. A stipulation in a contract that a sleeping car company shall have the exclusive right for fifteen years, to furnish drawing rooms and sleeping cars for a railroad company's use, does not render the contract void as being in restraint of trade or as against public policy, as such stipulation does not disable the sleeping car company from furnishing cars to a rival railroad, and the law will imply, from the terms of the contract, that it must furnish the railroad company in question, not only adequate and safe cars, but sufficient in number for the use of the public traveling on the latter's road. Chi., St. L. & N. O. R. Co. v. Pullman So. Car Co., 139 U. S. 79; s. c., 11 Sup. Ct. Rep. 490.

might more or less restrain it. The point urged on the defendant's part is that the statute was not really intended to reach that kind of an agreement relating only to traffic rates entered into by competing common carriers by railroad; that it was intended to reach only those who were engaged in the manufacture or sale of articles of commerce, and who, by means of trusts, combinations and conspiracies were engaged in affecting the supply or the price or the place of manufacture of such articles. The terms of the act do not bear out such construction. Railroad companies are instruments of commerce, and their business is commerce itself. An act which prohibits the making of every contract, etc., in restraint of trade or commerce among the several States would seem to cover by such language a contract between competing railroads, and relating to traffic rates for the transportation of articles of commerce between the States, provided such contract by its direct effect produces a restraint of trade or commerce. What amounts to a restraint within the meaning of the act if thus construed need not now be discussed."[1] After a farther discussion of

[1] United States v. Trans-Missouri Freight Association, 166 U. S. 290, 311, 313. See also State Freight-Tax Case, 15 Wall. 232, 275; Telegraph Co. v. Texas, 105 U. S. 460, 464. The case of United States v. Knight, 156 U. S. 1, makes very clear the distinction between State and Federal jurisdiction on trust subjects. In the course of the opinion, at page 12, Chief Justice Fuller uses this language: "The argument is that the power to control the manufacture of refined sugar is a monopoly over a necessary of life, to the enjoyment of which by a large part of the population of the United States interstate commerce is indispensable, and that, therefore, the general government in the exercise of the power to regulate commerce may repress such monopoly directly and set aside the instruments which have created it. But this argument cannot be confined to necessaries of life merely, and must include all articles of general consumption. Doubtless the power to control the manufacture of a given thing involves in a certain sense the control of its disposition, but this is a secondary and not the primary sense; and although the exercise of that power may result in bringing the operation of commerce into play, it does not control it, and affects it only incidentally and indirectly. Commerce succeeds to manufacture, and is not a part of it. The power to regulate commerce is the power to prescribe the rule by which commerce shall be governed, and is a power independent of the power to suppress monopoly. But it may operate in

the merits of the case and the principles involved, the opinion continues: "The conclusion which we have drawn from the examination above made into the question before us is, that the Anti-Trust Act applies to railroads, and that it renders illegal all agreements which are in restraint of trade or commerce, as we have above defined that expression, and the question then arises whether the agreement before us

repression of monopoly whenever that comes within the rules by which commerce is governed or whenever the transaction is itself a monopoly of commerce. It is vital that the independence of the commercial power and of the police power, and the delimitation between them, however sometimes perplexing, should always be recognized and observed, for while the one furnishes the strongest bond of union, the other is essential to the preservation of the autonomy of the States as required by our dual form of government; and acknowedged evils, however grave and urgent they may appear to be, had better be borne, than the risk be run, in the effort to suppress them, of more serious consequences by resort to expedients of even doubtful constitutionality. It will be perceived how far reaching the proposition is that the power of dealing with a monopoly directly may be exercised by the general goverment whenever interstate or international commerce may be ultimately affected. The regulation of commerce applies to the subjects of commerce and not to matters of internal police. Contracts to buy, sell or exchange goods to be transported among the several States, the transportation and its instrumentalities, and articles bought, sold or exchanged for the purposes of such transit among the States, or put in the way of transit, may be regulated, but this is because they form part of interstate trade or commerce. The fact that an article is manufactured for export to another State does not of itself make it an article of interstate commerce, and the intent of the manufacturer does not determine the time where the article or product passes from the control of the State and belongs to commerce. This was so ruled in Coe v. Errol, 116 U. S. 517, 525, in which the question before the court was, whether certain logs cut at a place in New Hampshire and hauled to a river town for the purpose of transportation to the State of Maine were liable to be taxed like other property in the State of New Hampshire. Mr. Justice Bradley, delivering the opinion of the court, said: 'Does the owner's state of mind in relation to the goods, that is, his interest to export them, and his partial preparation to do so, exempt them from taxation? This is the precise question for solution. * * * There must be a point of time when they cease to be governed exclusively by the domestic law and begin to be governed and protected by the national law of commercial regulation, and that moment seems to us to be a legitimate one for this purpose, in which they commence their final move-is of that nature. Although the case is heard on bill and answer, thus making it necessary to assume the truth of the allegations in the answer, which are well pleaded, yet the legal effect of the agreement itself cannot be altered by the answer, nor can its violation of law be made valid by allegations of good intention or of desire simply to maintain reasonable rates; nor can the plaintiff's allegations as to the intent with which the agreement was entered into be

ment from the state of their origin to that of their destination.' * * * It was in the light of well settled principles that the Act of July 2, 1890, was framed. Congress did not attempt thereby to assert the power to deal with monopoly directly as such; or to limit and restrict the rights of corporations created by the States or the citizens of the States in the acquisition, control or disposition of property; or to regulate or prescribe the price or prices at which such property or the products thereof should be sold; or to make criminal the acts of persons in the acquisition and control of property which the State of their residence or creation sanctioned or permitted. Aside from the provisions applicable where Congress might exercise municipal power, what the law struck at was combinations, contracts and conspiracies to monopolize trade and commerce among the several States or with foreign nations; but the contracts and acts of the defendants related exclusively to the acquisition of the Philadelphia refineries and the business of sugar refining in Pennsylvania, and have no direct relation to commerce between the States or with foreign nations. The object was manifestly private gain in the manufacture of the commodity, but not through the control of interstate or foreign commerce. It is true, that the bill alleged that the products of these refineries were sold and distributed among the several States, and that all the companies were engaged in trade or commerce with the several States and with foreign nations, but this was no more than to say that trade and commerce served manufacture to fulfill its function. Sugar was refined for sale, and sales were probably made at Philadelphia for consumption, and undoubtedly for resale by the first purchasers throughout Pennsylvania and other States, and refined sugar was also forwarded by the companies to other States for sale. Nevertheless, it does not follow that an attempt to monopolize or the actual monopoly of, the manufacture was an attempt, whether executory or consummated, to monopolize commerce, even though in order to dispose of the product the instrumentality of commerce was necessarily invoked. There was nothing in the proofs to indicate any intention to put a restraint upon trade or commerce, and the fact, as we have seen, that trade or commerce might be indirectly affected was not enough to entitle complainants to a decree. The subject-matter of the sale was shares of manufacturing stock, and the relief sought was the surrender regarded, as such intent is denied on the part of defendants; and if the intent alleged in the bill were a necessary fact to be proved in order to maintain the suit, the bill would have to be dismissed. In the view we have taken of

of property which had already passed and the suppression of the alleged monopoly in manufacture by the restoration of the *status quo* before the transfers, yet the Act of Congress only authorized the circuit courts to proceed by way of preventing and restraining violations of the act in respect of contracts, combinations or conspiracies in restraint of interstate or international trade or commerce." "In regard to State legislation, it has been declared from the beginning that, to render such legislation subject to constitutional objection under the commerce clause, the effect of the legislation upon interstate commerce must be direct, and not incidental or indirect. This general statement of the law so often repeated has been illustrated by the varying facts of many cases, but it would extend this opinion beyond reasonable limits to now refer to these. It has often been observed that the line of demarkation between State and federal jurisdiction and regulation is a delicate one, and at times grows dim and shadowy. In considering a question of this delicate nature, proper and practical distinctions become extremely important. A particular business must be distinguished from the mere subjects of the business, and from mere incidents to or instruments by which the business is carried on. It is hardly conceivable that any large industrial or manufacturing establishment could be carried on without shipping products from one State to another, and such would certainly be the course of business contemplated. Nevertheless, the business of such an establishment would be related to interstate commerce only incidentally and indirectly. Commerce would not be the main business, nor within the main purpose of the ordinary manufacturing establishment. Interstate commerce would be altogether an incident. There is no direct relation between the two. It is probably true that every wholesale establishment within the limits of the larger cities is engaged in such mode of business as that it is known that the business can be conducted only by the method of interstate commerce in part. Such commerce is, however, not directly affected, and least of all, impeded or restricted. If every private enterprise which is carried on in part or chiefly by interstate shipments, or by a mode of business which makes this necessary, is to be regarded as thereby so related to interstate commerce as to come within the regulating power of Congress, it is obvious that this power could at once be extended to almost every form of business in the country which is conducted on anything like an extensive scale. So liberal an interpretation as this would obviously in a large sense obliterate the lines between federal and State jurisdiction, and as an act of Congress is paramount in authority, would strike down the autonomy of the States." United States v. Addystone Pipe & Steel Co., 78 Fed. Rep. 712, 718.

the question, the intent alleged by the government is not necessary to be proved. The question is one of law in regard to the meaning and effect of the agreement itself, namely: Does the agreement restrain trade or commerce in any way so as to be a violation of the act? We have no doubt that it does. The agreement on its face recites that it is entered into 'for the purpose of mutual protection by establishing and maintaining reasonable rates, rules and regulations on all freight traffic, both through and local.' To that end the association is formed and a body created which is to adopt rates, which, when agreed to, are to be the governing rates for all the companies, and a violation of which subjects the defaulting company to the payment of a penalty, and, although the parties have a right to withdraw from the agreement on giving thirty days' notice of a desire so to do, yet, while in force and assuming it to be lived up to, there can be no doubt that its direct, immediate and necessary effect is to put a restraint upon trade or commerce, as described in the act. For these reasons the suit of the government can be maintained without proof of the allegation that the agreement was entered into for the purpose of restraining trade or commerce, or for maintaining rates above what was reasonable. The necessary effect of the agreement is to restrain trade or commerce, no matter what the intent was on the part of those who signed it."[1]

§ 170. **Pooling by Railroads.**—A contract between competing lines of railroad, under which their earnings are put into a pool or common fund, and the proceeds divided in proportion to the importance of the roads, in order to prevent competition, is in contravention of public policy and void. Contracts of this general character, of two kinds, have been made by parallel and competing railroad lines. In one class there is a pooling of the traffic or business, and in the other a pooling of receipts or earnings. The traffic pool is an agreement by which a fixed percentage of the business is allotted to each line in the association. In the

[1] United States v. Trans-Missouri Freight Association, 166 U. S. 290, 341, 342.

other class the receipts or earnings are divided in accordance with the proportion or percentage agreed upon in the covenant, not, necessarily, according to the amount of business actually done by each road. In England railroad pooling is not, necessarily, illegal. If there is nothing in the compact that is, essentially, illegal, or in contravention of public policy, it will be sustained by the courts. In a leading English case, two groups of railway companies, being respectively the owners of independent conterminous routes, agreed to divide the profits of the whole traffic in certain fixed proportions, calculated on the experience of the past course of traffic. It was held that such an agreement, being *bona fide*, was not *ultra vires*.[1] Other decisions of the

[1] Hare v. London & N. W. Ry. Co., 2 Johns. & H. 80; s. c., 30 L. J. Ch. 817; 7 Jur. (N. S.) 1145. See also Shrewsbury & Birmingham R. Co. v. London & Northwestern R. Co., L. R. 17 Q. B. 652; 9 Eng. L. & Eq. 394. The defendants, owning a short railway from New Orleans to Lake Pontchartrain and one Morgan, owning a line of steamers plying from the lake terminus to Mobile, and the plaintiffs and other parties owning two other steamers in the same trade, an arrangement was made by defendants with Morgan, and temporarily with the proprietors of the other steamers, respectively, to share *pro rata* the through freight from New Orleans to Mobile. It appeared that this arrangement was unprofitable to the defendants, for the lines of steamers, by competing and lowering rates of freight, greatly reduced the share coming to the railway. The defendants, therefore, entered into an agreement with Morgan by which the latter loaned them $250,000, and the former agreed to prorate with him the through freight from New Orleans to Mobile, and to charge all other steamers the tariff rates paid by the public generally. The plaintiffs immediately laid up their steamers and sued for damages on the ground that this prorating with Morgan and refusing to further prorate with plaintiffs was an illegal combination with Morgan to confer on him an unlawful monopoly and preference. *Held*, that the acts of defendants were not in contravention of any statute of Louisiana or any principle of her jurisprudence; that they might agree or refuse to prorate through freight with anybody, and the plaintiffs could not complain of a refusal to prorate with them; and that as common carriers, in the absence of statutory prohibition, their acts in the premises were not unlawful. Eclipse Towboat Co. v. Pontchartrain R. Co., 24 La. Ann. 1. "The second plea avers, and the demurrer of course admits, that at the time of the making of the contracts between the parties, and of the dealings thereunder, their respective roads 'were rival and competing

English courts are in the same general direction. In this country there is not entire harmony in the decisions on this subject. In some of the States the decisions turn upon the

railroads, by the competition of which the prices of transportation thereon were, and, but for said supposed contracts, dealings, transactions, operation and business would have continued to be materially reduced, and said alleged contracts, dealings, transactions and business were made and had for the purpose of destroying and preventing such competition, and did destroy and prevent it.' It will be noticed that there is no averment in the plea that the purpose of the contracts was to raise the prices of transportation above a reasonable standard, or that they did have this effect, or that the public were prejudiced by their operation in any manner, and the naked question presented then, is, whether all contracts between rival railway corporations which prevent competition are necessarily contrary to public policy, and, therefore, *mala prohibita* and illegal in themselves. To state this question is to answer it in the negative, because it is obvious that the illegality depends upon circumstances. While without doubt contracts which have a direct tendency to prevent a healthy competition are detrimental to the public and, consequently, against public policy, it is equally free from doubt that when such contracts prevent an unhealthy competition, and yet furnish the public with adequate facilities at fixed and reasonable rates, they are beneficial, and in accord with sound principles of public policy. For the lessons of experience, as well as the deductions of reason, amply demonstrate that the public interest is not subserved by competion which reduces the rate of transportation below the standard of fair compensation; and the theory which formerly obtained that the public is benefited by unrestricted competition between railroads has been so emphatically disproved by the results which have generally followed its adoption in practice, that the hope of any permanent relief from excessive rates through the competition of a parallel or rival road may, as a rule, be justly characterized as illusory and fallacious. Upon authority, also, arrangements and contracts between competing railroads, by which unrestrained competition is prevented, do not contravene public policy. Hare v. London & N. W. R. Co., 2 Johns. & H. 80, is directly in point. In that case a bill in chancery had been filed by a stockholder in the defendant company to annul an agreement between two railway companies to divide the profits of the traffic in fixed proportions; and it was admitted there, as it is here, that the purpose of the agreement was to prevent competition. In dismissing the bill, Vice-Chancellor Wood said (p. 103): 'With regard to the argument against the validity of the agreement, I may clear the ground of one objection by saying that I see nothing in the alleged injury to the public arising from the prevention of competion. * * * It is a mistaken notion that the public is benefited by pitting two railway companies against each other till circumstances of the case under consideration.[1] But in most of the States pooling is held illegal, and all contracts relating to it void. The tendency is to a more rigid enforcement of this doctrine. In a leading case in Pennsylvania, five coal corporations of that State entered into an agreement in New York, to divide two coal regions, of which they had the control; to appoint a committee to take charge of their interests, which was to decide all questions and ap-

one is ruined, the result being at last to raise the fares to highest possible standard." Manchester & Lawrence R. Co. v. Concord R. Co., 66 N. H. 100, 127; s. c., 9 L. R. A. 689; 27 Atl. Rep. 383; 47 Am. & Eng. R. Cas. 359; 3 Int. Com. Rep. 319. But see Charlton v. Newcastle & Carlisle R. Co., 7 W. R. 735; s. c., 5 Jur. (N. S.) 1096; Midland R. Co. v. London & N. W. R. Co., L. R. 2 Eq. Cas. 524; Maunsell v. Midland, Gt. Western R. Co., 1 H. & M. 164; s. c., 32 L. J. Ch. 513.

[1] Cleveland, etc. R. Co. v. Closser, 126 Ind. 348; s. c., 45 Am. & Eng. R. Cas. 275. See also Chicago, M. & St. P. R. Co. v. Wabash, St. L. & P. R. Co., 61 Fed. Rep. 993; s. c., 58 Am. & Eng. R. Cas. 703; Central R. Co. v. Collins, 40 Ga. 582; Cutting v. Florida, R. & N. Co., 48 Fed. Rep. 508; Morrill v. Boston & M. R. Co., 55 N. H. 531; s. c., 11 Ry. Rep. 484; Gulf, C. & S. F. R. Co. v. State, 72 Tex. 404; s. c., 10 S. W. Rep. 81; 36 Am. & Eng. R. Cas. 481; 1 L. R. A. 849; 2 Int. Com. Rep. 335; Chicago, D. & V. R. Co. v. Smith, 62 Ill. 268; s. c., 6 Am. Ry. Rep. 221; Texas & P. R. Co. v. Southern Pacific R. Co., 41 La. Ann. 970; s. c., 6 So. Rep. 888; s. c., 40 Am. & Eng. R. Cas. 475; Stewart v. Erie & W. Transp. Co., 17 Minn. 372; Burlington, C. R. & N. R. Co. v. Northwestern Fuel Co., 31 Fed. Rep. 652. A railroad pooling contract, the evident object of which is to stifle competition for the purpose of raising rates, is void, as contrary to public policy. Chicago, M. & St. P. Ry. Co. v. Wabash, etc. Ry. Co., 61 Fed. Rep. 993. A contract by which a railroad company arranges with another, to the exclusion of still others, for the interchange of passengers and freight by through tickets and bills of lading, is not a contract in unlawful restraint of trade, within the meaning of the Act of July 2, 1890. Prescott & A. C. R. Co. v. Atch., T. & S. F. Co., 73 Fed. Rep. 438. The provision of section 5, making any "contract, agreement or combination with any common carrier or carriers for the pooling of freights of different and competing railroads" unlawful, does not apply to a pooling contract between a railroad company and a pipe line company for the transportation of oil. Independent Refiners' Assoc. v. Western, N. Y. & P. R. Co., 5 Int. Com. Com. 415; s. c., 4 Int. Com. Rep. 162. The provisions of section 5, prohibiting freight pooling, does not invalidate a contract for such pooling as a whole, but only the pooling provisions therein. Ives v. Smith, 8 N. Y. Supl. 46; affirming 3 N. Y. Supl. 645.

point a general agent at Watkins, New York; the coal mined to be delivered through him, each corporation to deliver its proportion at its own cost in the different markets at such time and to such persons as the committee might direct; the committee to adjust the prices, rates of freight, etc., enter into agreements with anthracite companies; the five companies might sell their coal themselves only to the extent of their proportion and at prices adjusted by the committee; the agent to suspend shipments by either beyond their proportion; frequent detailed reports to be made by companies, and settlements monthly by the committee, prices to be averaged and payments made to those in arrears by those in excess, neither to sell coal otherwise than as agreed upon, and the regulations of the committee to be carried out faithfully. A statute of New York makes it a misdemeanor for "persons to conspire to commit any act injurious to trade or commerce." It was held that their agreement was in contravention of the statute, and also against public policy, and, therefore, illegal and void.[1]

[1] Morris Run Coal Co. v. Barclay Coal Co., 68 Pa. St. 173. "The referee found, as his conclusion upon the whole case, that the contract was void by the statute, and void at common law, as against public policy. The restraint of the contract upon trade and its injury to the public is thus clearly set forth by the referee: 'These corporations (he says) represented almost the entire body of bituminous coal in the northern part of the State. By combination between themselves they had the power to control the entire market in that district. And they did control it by a contract not to ship and sell coal otherwise than as therein provided. And in order to destroy competition they provided for an arrangement with dealers and shippers of anthracite coal. They were thereby prohibited from selling under prices to be fixed by a committee representing each company. And they were obliged to suspend shipments upon notice from an agent that their allotted share of the market had been forwarded or sold. Instead of regulating the business by the natural laws of trade, to-wit, those of demand and supply, these companies entered into a league by which they could limit the supply below the demand in order to enhance the price. Or if the supply was greater than the demand, they could nevertheless compel the payment of the price arbitrarily fixed by the joint committee. The restraint on the trade in bituminous coal was by this contract as wide and extensive as the market for the article. It already embraced the State of New York, and was intended, and no

In the opinion in this case, Mr. Justice Agnew said: "There is a certain freedom which must be allowed to every one in the management of his own affairs. Where competition is left free, individual error or folly will generally find a correction in the conduct of others. But here is a combination of all the companies operating in the Blossburgh and Barclay mining regions, and controlling their entire productions. They have combined together to govern the supply and the price of coal in all the markets from the Hudson to the Mississippi rivers, and from Pennsylvania to the lakes. This combination has a power in its confederated form which no individual action can confer. The public interest must succumb to it, for it has left no competition free to correct its baleful influence. When the supply of coal is suspended, the demand for it becomes importunate, and prices must rise; or, if the supply goes forward, the price fixed by the confederates must accompany it. The domestic hearth, the furnaces of the iron master and the fires of the manufacturer all feel the restraint, while many dependent hands are paralyzed and hungry mouths are stinted. The influence of a lack of supply, or of a rise in the price of an article of such prime necessity, cannot be measured. It permeates the entire mass of community, and leaves few of its members untouched by its withering blight. Such a combination is more than a contract; it is an offense. 'I take it,' said Gibson, Justice, 'a combination is criminal whenever the act to be done has a necessary tendency to prejudice the public, or to oppose individuals, by unjustly subjecting them to the power of the confederates, and giving effect to the purpose of the latter, whether of extortion or of mischief.'[1] In all such combinations

doubt did, affect the market in the western States. It is expressly stipulated that the parties to this contract shall not be considered as partners. The agreement was not entered into for the purpose of aggregating the capital of the several companies, nor for greater facilities for the transaction of their business, nor for the protection of themselves by a reasonable restraint as to a limited time and space, upon others who might interfere with their business.'" *Ibid.*, 183.

[1] Commonwealth v. Carlisle, Brightley, 40.

where the purpose is injurious or unlawful, the gist of the offense is the conspiracy. Men can often do by the combination of many what, severally, no one could accomplish, and even what when done by one would be innocent."[1]

§ **171. The Pooling of Stocks.**—The putting of stocks into a pool or common fund is not, necessarily, illegal. If the object is not objectionable, a reasonable regulation in regard to the manner of selling corporate stocks, in order to prevent a sacrifice of the interests of the parties concerned, is not in contravention of public policy as in restraint of trade. In the recent and leading case of Williams v. Montgomery, before the New York Court of Appeals, the court said: "After careful study of the agreement in question, we think that it was neither a violation of the statute against accumulations nor a restraint upon trade. What are the facts? Four promoters of a corporation, who owned ninety-nine one-hundredths of its capital stock, as tenants in common, agreed, in writing, to partition their holdings, after first placing in the treasury one-fifth of all the stock, to be sold in order to provide working capital for the company. As the amount of the capital stock was large and they did not wish to glut the market by the sale of treasury stock in competition with individual stock, they provided for the deposit of the latter with a trust company, under the agreement that they would not withdraw the same for six months, except by mutual consent, unless enough treasury stock should be sooner sold to realize the sum of $30,000, in which event any one could withdraw his certificate on five days' notice to the others. No trust was created. The title was not vested in a trustee, unable to sell, with like inability on the part of the beneficiary. No restriction was placed on the power of any stockholder to sell, but he could not deliver the certificates for six months, except in either of the contingencies named. There was no suspension of absolute ownership, because the statute expressly declares that the 'power of alienation is suspended when

[1] Morris Run Coal Co. v. Barclay Coal Co., 68 Pa. St. 173, 186.

there are no persons in being by whom an absolute fee in possession can be conveyed."[1] While this applies, primarily, to real estate, by a subsequent chapter it is made applicable to personal property also.[2] The test of alienability of real or personal property is that there are persons in being who can give a perfect title.[3] Where there are living parties who have, unitedly, the entire right of ownership, the statute has no application.[4] The ownership is absolute whether the power to sell resides in one individual or in general. If there is a present right to dispose of the entire interest, even if its exercise depends upon the consent of many persons, there is no unlawful suspension of the power of alienation. The ownership, although divided, continues absolute. The agreement in question, therefore, which expressly reserved the right to sell by mutual consent, did not violate the statute, because there was no time when an absolute title to the stock or any part of it could not have been transferred by the joint action of the four parties to the contract. Nor was the agreement opposed to public policy, for a reasonable regulation, as to the mode of selling the stock, so as to prevent the sacrifice thereof, was not a restraint upon trade. As an incident to the contract, making partition of the shares, it was competent for the parties to agree that the stock donated to the corporation, in which they had a common interest, should be first offered for sale. This was no restraint upon the business freedom of the parties, but a promotion of the general interest, by temporarily withholding from the market shares owned by individuals, in order to afford a reasonable opportunity to sell shares, indirectly owned by all. The protection of the interests of all concerned by preventing the market from suddenly becoming overcrowded and ruinously depressed, was a reasonable, just and honest purpose, which the law does not condemn. There was no evil tendency in the

[1] 1 Rev. Stat. 723, § 14.

[2] 1 Rev. Stat. 773, § 2.

[3] Genet v. Hunt, 113 N. Y. 158, 172; Nellis v. Nellis, 99 N. Y. 505, 516; Robert v. Corning, 89 N. Y. 225, 235; Gott v. Cook, 7 Paige, 521; affirmed 24 Wend. 641; Bolles on Suspension, 2.

[4] Norris v. Beyea, 13 N. Y. 273, 289.

arrangement, as it simply prevented a course of action that would have brought loss both to the common and to the personal interests.[1]

[1] Williams v. Montgomery, 148 N. Y. 519, 525. See also Hodge v. Sloan, 107 N. Y. 244. "There was nothing in the written contract between the parties which required the plaintiff to transfer the control and management of the corporation to Brown and Seligman; but I will assume that it was the understanding and a part of the scheme that he should do so. Brown and Seligman were attempting to procure the control of the corporation and of its franchises for a legitimate purpose. There is no reason to suppose that they meant to perpetrate any fraud on the stockholders. They were dealing with a person who held a majority of the stock and who, in virtue thereof, had the right and the power to control the corporation within the limits of its chartered powers. He had the right to sell out all his stock and interest in the corporations, and in doing so he perpetrated no wrong upon any one, and when he ceased to have any interest in the corporation, it was certainly legitimate and right that he should cease to control it. It is the general rule sanctioned by the policy of the law, that those who have the largest interest in corporations may control them, as they have the greatest interest that they shall be well managed." Barnes v. Brown, 80 N. Y. 527, 536. The officers of a corporation having taken means to obtain from the stockholders a deposit of their stock, together with powers of attorney, in the hands of such officers or their agents in order to enable them, among other things, to vote on the stock at a stockholders' meeting, *held*, that one stockholder is not entitled to have the officers restrained from voting on the stock of others, upon the theory that the transaction creates a trust for the corporation, unless corporate funds were used in doing what was done. Woodruff v. Dubuque, 30 Fed. Rep. 91. In an action against several persons upon an account arising from stock transactions, claimed by plaintiff to have been joint transactions on the part of the defendants, but claimed by one of the defendants to have been several, *held*, that evidence that said defendant had a private account running at the same time was competent as a circumstance tending to show that the other account was joint and not several. Quincey v. White, 63 N. Y. 370. In the course of the opinion, at page 383, Church, Ch. J., says: "It is not *per se* unlawful for three persons to unite either in a general business, or upon a special venture of dealing in stocks or a particular stock, on speculation. This is not unlawful as against public policy. It is unnecessary to consider whether a combination might not be made to produce results which would not be sustained, nor now to define the nature of such a combination, nor the means which might be deemed unlawful in carrying it out." "Various devices have been resorted to for the purpose of so tying up the stock that no one of the parties to the 'pool' or combination can break the agreement. 'Irrevocable' proxies to vote the stock have been given

§ **172. The Pooling of Products.**—A corporation or other business association, consisting of a number of independent companies or individuals, engaged in the same branch of business, and organized for the purpose of controlling the production and price of a commodity in general use, is in contravention of public policy and void. The claim of one of the parties to such an organization against another will not be enforced by the courts. In the recent

to a designated party who acted as trustee or agent, but the courts held such proxies not irrevocable and that they might be revoked at any time. Cook on Stocks, § 610, 622: Woodruff v. Dubuque, 30 Fed. Rep. 91: Vanderbilt v. Bennett, 2 Ry. & Corp. L. J. 409. Another plan was to place the stock of the various parties in the hands of trustees, with power to transfer the stock to themselves and to hold and vote the same, trustees' certificates being issued to the various parties, specifying the amount of stock so deposited by them and their interest in the pool, but the courts held that any holder of a trustee's certificate might at any time demand back his part of the stock. Another device was that the parties contracted together not to sell their stock for a specified time or only to a purchaser acceptable to them all. It was held that, notwithstanding such contract any one of the parties might sell his stock to any one he pleased and at any time. Fisher v. Bush, 35 Hun. 642; Williams v. Montgomery, 68 Hun, 416. Another plan was to restrict by a by-law the right to transfer stock, but this was held illegal. Morgan v. Struthers, 131 U. S. 246. A provision that a purchaser of a certificate of stock who sold in violation of the agreement should be entitled to the dividends but should receive no right to vote, was likewise held invalid. Harper v. Raymond, 3 Bosw. (N. Y.) 29. Numerous decisions affirm the correctness of the above rulings, which are based upon the illegality, because against public policy, of permitting large blocks of stock to be irrevocably tied up for the purpose of being voted *in solido* for the interest of a clique or section of the stockholders, and not according to the judgment of each individual stockholder for the benefit of the entire corporation. There are some few decisions trenching more or less upon the principles above stated, but we deem them contrary to sound principle of public policy, and hence not authority. In short, all agreements and devices by which stockholders surrender their voting powers are invalid. 5 Thompson, Corporations, § 6604. The power to vote is inherently annexed to and inseparable from the real ownership of each share, and can only be delegated by proxy with power of revocation. The 'pooling' arrangement, admitted to have been entered into by the majority of stockholders in the present case is contrary to public policy and voidable." Harvey v. Improvement Co., 118 N. Car. 692, 698.

case of Emery v. The Ohio Candle Company, the court said: "We are of the opinion that the suit cannot be maintained, for the reason that the objects of the association were contrary to public policy, and in no way to be aided by the courts. No recovery can be had except by giving effect to the terms of the agreement. The action is, in substance, a suit against the association to recover a sum due the plaintiff under the terms on which the association was formed. The committee represents the association, and a judgment against them is a judgment against it. If, as claimed by the defendants, a member could not withdraw from the association until the six years had expired, then the committee, as representing the association, had a defense on which it might have relied, had the objects of the association been perfectly legitimate. But should a court be called on to consider any defense, so long as the claim itself is based upon an agreement to which it can give no countenance? It must be observed that the withdrawal of the plaintiff was not at a time nor under circumstances that could give to it the merit of repentance. It had passed beyond the point at which it might by withdrawal have secured the aid of a court in recovering what it had advanced in furtherance of an illegal object. Its suit is to recover its portion of the ill-gotten gains."[1] In a still

[1] Emery v. Ohio Candle Co., 47 Ohio St. 320 322; s. c., 24 N. E. Rep. 660, 661. An association of manufacturers of wire cloth, formed for the avowed purpose of regulating the price of the commodity; each of the members stipulating, under a heavy penalty, that he will not sell at less than a specified rate, is contrary to public policy and illegal; and one of the members of the association, who has paid the penalty for violation of the stipulation, cannot recover it back. De Witt Wire Cloth Co. v. New Jersey Wire Cloth Co., 14 N. Y. Supl. 277. A contract by which three of four companies engaged in the manufacture of oleomargarine, consolidate as a corporation for the purpose of stopping the sharp competition between them, and agree that none of them shall separately engage in the business for five years, is not invalid as constituting a monopoly. Oakdale Manfg. Co. v. Garst, 18 R. I. 484; s. c., 28 Atl. Rep. 973. Where a contract for the sale of grain bags provides that the vendee shall have the exclusive sale of the same to the amount of 187,500, and the vendor agreed not to sell, or offer the same for sale, to any other person, and if the vendee failed to sell the full amount, the vendor agreed to ac-

more recent case, where plaintiffs, representing four cotton seed mills, and defendants, representing a large number of like mills, all independent dealers in cotton seed and manufacturers or products therefrom, entered into a contract which provided that plaintiffs, in consideration of "covenants" therein, should deliver to defendants the entire yield of their mills, and defendants guaranteed plaintiffs a certain profit per ton. The prices to be paid for seed cotton were established, and were to be changed only "by mutual agreement of the parties." Defendants were authorized to establish from time to time "the minimum prices at which all meal cake and lint produced at plaintiff's mill shall be sold," and that plaintiffs "shall not purchase any seed or ship any from" a certain place, and a specified portion of seed shipped from certain other places to be "subject to be bought by" defendants. In an action to recover the net profits, under the guaranty, it was held that the contract was void as being in restraint of trade, and that plaintiffs could not recover. In the opinion in this

cept the sale of a *pro rata* amount, and such contract is a part of a scheme to gain a monopoly, it is void as against public policy, and there can be no recovery for a breach thereof. Pacific Factor Co. v. Adler, 90 Cal. 110; s. c., 27 Pac. Rep. 36. For the sole purpose of forming a combination among all the manufacturers of lumber at a certain point, increasing the price, limiting the amount and giving plaintiff the control of the supply in four counties for a year, plaintiff, by contracts with the other manufacturers, either by lease of their mills or by purchase of their product for the year, secured control of the product, among which contracts, and similar to the others, was one of defendants to sell plaintiff during the year a specified amount of lumber at a given price; and, further, to manufacture no lumber for sale in said counties during said year except under the contract, and to pay plaintiff $20 per M for any lumber sold to others in that period. *Held*, void as against public policy. Santa Clara Val. M. & L. Co. v. Hayes, 76 Cal. 387; s. c., 18 Pac. Rep. 391. Under Act of March 30, 1889, prohibiting combinations in restraint of trade, a combination of dealers in beer, which secured control, by lease, of "all the cooling room capacity for cooling beer" in a town, so that competition in beer would be kept out, is unlawful; the parties to it cannot recover for a breach of contract, the performance of which would have aided them to carry out their unlawful enterprise. Anheuser-Busch Brewing Assn. v. Houck, 27 S. W. Rep. 692; s. c., 30 S. W. Rep. 869.

case, after referring to the agreement under which that association was organized, the court said: "It thus appears that the above artificial regulations of the value or prices of these staple articles of trade, as well as the arbitrary restrictions imposed by the contract upon the right to deal in them in the usual or customary course of legitimate business, were intended to apply to and control, as far as the contracting parties were able to do, the market in reference to these staples, and the agreement embraces within its operation the chief cities or commercial centers of the State, as well as the cotton producing regions thereof, as we may judicially know. There seems to us to be scarcely anything lacking to characterize the combination between the parties in this case, as evidenced by the language and purpose of their agreement, as a complete monopoly, except the proof that they were the only parties who were engaged at the specified localities in the manufacture referred to in the contract, at the time it was made. It is not improbable that every cotton oil mill in the State was represented in this combination, or was intended to be brought into it eventually; but as this is not alleged in the petition we cannot presume it. We must admit some limit even to judicial knowledge. But to render the contract void it is not necessary that it should create a pure monopoly. It would seem that the agreement may be illegal if the natural or necessary consequences of its operation are to prevent competition and create fictitious prices independently of the law of demand and supply, and to such an extent as injuriously to affect the interests of the public or the interests of any particular class of citizens who may be especially interested either as producers or consumers, in the articles or staples which are the subject of the restrictions imposed by the contract. Likewise the agreement may be in some instances void, because of unreasonable restrictions imposed upon even one of the parties to it. According to the authorities, the extent of the restraint, though sometimes difficult to measure, determines the character of the agreement, whether legal or not. The authorities are too numerous even to cite all of them."[1]

§ **173. The Subject Continued.**—The forming of an association or the entering into an agreement by a number of independent dealers in an article in common use, with a view to controlling the price by suppressing competition, if

[1] Texas Standard Oil Co. v. Adoue, 83 Tex. 650; s. c., 19 S. W. Rep. 274. See also Callaghan v. Donnolly, 45 Cal. 152; Salt Co. v. Guthrie, 35 Ohio St. 666; Sampson v. Shaw, 101 Mass. 145; Wright v. Ryder, 36 Cal. 342, 361; Hooker v. Vandewater, 4 Denio (N. Y.), 349; s. c., 47 Am. Dec. 258; Craft v. McConoughy, 79 Ill. 346; Leonard v. Poole, 114 N. Y. 371; Angier v. Webber, 14 Allen, 211; s. c., 92 Am. Dec. 748. "It will be seen that the Howard Company was given almost an unrestricted field to obtain the raw material for its mills, and the exclusive right to control, free from the competition of the owners of the 'four mills' (who had no doubt up to that time been its rivals) not only the sales and ruling prices of the products of its own mills (which are not disturbed in this respect), but also 'the entire yield' of the mills of the other parties to the contract. It was thus enabled by the confederation of all of the parties to dictate at will the prices at which the public must buy (if at all) the oils or other products of any of the mills. If both of the parties had entered a market open to both under the contract, in order to purchase the raw materials they could not have competed, for no competition was contemplated, and all freedom of action in this particular was forestalled by arbitrary regulations of the price to be paid, which must be observed. In the markets assigned to each they are confronted by the same barrier, and the party cannot buy at all if the market price at that point happens to be greater than the contract price; or if the price prevailing there should even be below the contract price, still the party could not avail himself of this advantage without first obtaining, if he *could*, the consent of the other parties. In other words, neither the parties nor the producers of the raw material are to have the benefit of but *one* price, which has been definitely fixed in advance. These things, as it seems to us, are well calculated to affect the interests of the public detrimentally, and would doubtless have been deemed by the parties as injurious to their own interests had they been contemplating a lawful enterprise. These restrictions, however, were instituted in this instance, not for the purpose of a fair protection to all of the parties, but as suitable means for preventing all competition. If not, then it would have been clearly to the advantage of the Howard Oil Company, in view of its obligations to the 'four mills,' that the raw materials should be bought by all of the parties to the contract at the lowest figures. This company had bound itself to pay or bear the cost of the seed as well as the expense of 'working' the same by 'the four

put into execution, constitutes a conspiracy and will not be enforced. In a recent case in New York, it was held that where there exists in a city an association of retail coal dealers, the object of which is to fix a uniform price of coal sold in the city, in order to prevent competition among the retail dealers in coal, such agreement, followed by overt

mills,' etc. We recur now to the law of the case. We can scarcely conceive how mere territory limits can be the controlling test in all instances of the legality of the restraints imposed upon the ordinary course of trade. This criterion may do very well when applied to the occupation or profession of one man or even a few individuals; for neither their labor, industry, business nor services may be so necessary to the public as not to be dispensed with without inconvenience or injury. It appears to us, however, that the case is very different in regard to trade or commerce in those articles of prime necessity or even of very frequent use among a large number of people in any given locality. Does any one doubt that a combination of a number of the most extensive dealers in flour, meat or oils, etc., in one great city, to sell those commodities at only one price or not at all within the limits of that city, would affect the interests of the public, and, perhaps, also some of the individual dealers, much more extensively and disastrously than a similar agreement extended to a much greater area of country, but in which only a very few people reside or require such articles? It would seem that the injurious effects upon the public interests would be in proportion to the number of people affected by the restrictions, though we are not unaware that this position has not been deemed tenable by some of the authorities in cases where the right to exercise a trade or profession within a particular district or locality has been restricted by the contract. We think that territory cannot be the sole test, though in the present instance the contract embraces such extensive territory and such a number of localities as to bring it even within that rule. In determining the reasonableness of the restraint the effect upon the interest of the public is a better test." Standard Oil Co. v. Adoue, 83 Tex. 650, 659. A contract between manufacturers, whereby, without any sale of the business of one to the other, one party is prohibited from manufacturing of pressed metal any parts of a diamond car truck frame, is void as an unreasonable restraint of trade. Fox Solid Pressed Steel Co. v. Schoen, 77 Fed. Rep. 29. A contract to control the price of a commodity is void as in restraint of trade where the annual sales of such commodity in the State are about $1,500,000, though it is not an article of necessity. Cummings v. Union Blue Stone Co., 44 N. Y. Supl. 787; s. c. 15 App. Div. 607. See also People v. Sheldon, 139 N. Y. 251; s. c., 34 N. E. Rep. 785; Greer v. Payne, 4 Kan. App. 153; s. c., 46 Pac. Rep. 190. In an action brought by the attorney-general to vacate the charter of defendant, a domestic corporation, and to annul its corporate existence, acts, on their part, constitutes a conspiracy within the meaning of the Penal Code, and the members of such association are guilty of a misdemeanor. Ordinarily persons in their dealings may adopt such method as they please to regulate the measure of compensation or prices in the future, through the period of the operation of their contracts, but they cannot effectually do so to accomplish an unlawful purpose. As the business of buying and selling coal is in itself legitimate, the fact that the prices adopted between the vendor and the vendee are in furtherance of a scheme of an association to regulate the price thereof would not deny to the seller all remedy for non-payment of the price of the coal delivered by him under such contract; but the contract, so far as the prices therein provided for, are founded or dependent upon the prices fixed by such association, is ineffectual and void. Where it appears that a contract, which is the subject of an action, is void as against public policy, the court will decline to enforce it by judgment, although such infirmity is not pleaded, if the invalidity of the contract appears in the presentation thereof by the plaintiff upon the trial, but if the contract, as alleged and proved by the plaintiff, is valid on its face, the defense that it is in fact against public policy and illegal is not available, unless specially pleaded.[1]

these facts appeared: In defendant's charter the object of its organization was stated to be the "buying and selling of milk at wholesale and retail." A large majority of the stockholders were milk dealers in the city of New York, and creamery or milk commission men in that vicinity. At the first meeting of its board of directors a by-law was adopted, declaring that said board "shall have the power to make and fix the standard or market price at which milk shall be purchased by the stockholders of the company." Acting under this by-law, the board fixed from time to time the price of milk to be paid by dealers. No milk was purchased by defendant, but it did a commission business, selling milk for farmers to dealers, who would purchase at the price fixed, guaranteeing payment and charging a commission therefor. The prices so fixed largely controlled the market in and about said city. *Held*, that the evidence justified a finding that the corporation was a combination inimical to trade and commerce, and so unlawful, and that a judgment granting the relief sought was proper. People v. Milk Exchange, 145 N. Y. 267.

[1] Drake v. Siebold, 81 Hun, 178. See also Craft v. McConoughy, 79 Ill. 346; People v. Fisher, 14 Wend.

§ 174. Monopoly under Patent.—A patent, for the time for which the special privilege is granted is, essentially, a monopoly. The idea of a patent is the prevention of any manufacture or sale of the article patented by other parties. The patent confers the exclusive privilege of manufacture and sale. This is not a matter of governmental favor, but a consideration for the labor and money

10; Arnot v. P. & E. Coal Co., 68 N. Y. 558. A combination between independent dealers to prevent competition between themselves in the sale of an article of prime necessity is, in the contemplation of law, an act inimical to trade or commerce, without regard to what may be done under and in pursuance of it, and although the object of such a combination was merely the due protection of the parties against ruinous rivalry, and no attempt was made to charge undue or excessive prices. Where it appears that the parties acted under the agreement, an indictment for conspiracy is sustainable upon trial of an indictment for conspiracy to raise the price of coal at retail and to destroy free competition, the court charged the jury that if the defendants entered into an organization agreement for the purpose of controlling the price and managing the business of the sale of coal, so as to prevent competition in price between the members of the organization, the agreement was illegal, and if the jury found this was their intent, and that the price was raised in pursuance of the agreement, the crime of conspiracy was established. *Held*, no error. People v. Sheldon, 139 N. Y. 251. See also Hooker v. Vandewater, 4 Denio, 349; Stanton v. Allen, 5 Denio, 434; Saratoga Co. Bank v. King, 44 N. Y. 87; Leonard v. Poole, 114 N. Y. 371; People v. Milk Exchange, 145 N. Y. 267. An agreement, the real nature and purpose of which is to suppress competition in articles of food, and so tends to enhance the price, is contrary to public policy and is void. Certain parties who were brokers and dealers in sheep and lambs, executed an agreement, by its terms organizing an association for the declared purpose "of guarding and protecting their business interests from loss by unreasonable competition," by which they agreed to pool their commissions, except such as should be agreed to be paid to a certain butchers' association, and the association so formed entered into an agreement with the butchers' association, by the terms of which the brokers were only to sell to the butchers, and the butchers to buy only of the brokers belonging to their respective associations. In an action brought by plaintiff, as treasurer of the brokers' association, against one of its members to recover damages stipulated therein for a breach of the agreement, *held*, that the two agreements were to be taken and considered together; that they were intended to control the markets, fix the price and destroy competition, and so were invalid and not enforceable; that the the public might be prejudiced, and whether they were so, in fact, was not material. Judd v. Harrington, 139 N. Y. 105.

expended in the invention of the patented article. In a monopoly of this character there is no restraint of trade. No right of any other party is abridged or in any way infringed. In order to render a monopoly illegal its operation must depose some person or class of persons of some privilege which they had previously enjoyed. But this is not true of a monopoly under a patent right. The patent simply secures to the patentee the reward or, for a limited time, the sole enjoyment of the fruit of his skill and labor in producing the article patented. Moreover, the protection which is given to an individual as a patentee is extended to a combination of individuals or companies which are in possession of patents relating to the same article, provided the combination is not otherwise illegal. In a recent case before the United States Circuit Court for the Northern District of New York, it was held that the fact that a corporation owning letters patent upon a particular kind of machinery has entered into a combination with other manufacturers thereof to secure a monopoly in its manufacture and sale, and to that end has acquired all the rights of other manufacturers for the exclusive sale and manufacture of such machine under patents, will not entitle a stranger to the combination to enjoin the corporation from bringing any suits for infringement against him or his customers.[1]

[1] Strait v. National Harrow Co., 51 Fed. Rep. 819. "The complaint alleges that the plaintiffs, and other persons threatened with suit, do not infringe any of the patents of the defendant, but, as was said by Mr. Justice Hunt, in Celluloid Manfg. Co. v. Goodyear Dental Vulcanite Co., 13 Blatchf. 384: 'To allow the action is to reverse the proper position of the parties. Whoever receives letters patent from the United States receives thereby a *prima facie* right to maintain an action against every infringer of the right given by such letters. While it is true that such right is *prima facie* only, and that the holder must be prepared to maintain it in the courts when attacked, it is still a right on his part to sue such alleged violators. The present action would convert the right to sue into a liability to be sued, which is quite a different thing. * * * The defendant has a right of action against each one of these individuals. It has the right to sue the whole of them. It has the right to sue any one of them, and to allow the others to go undisturbed. While it would not be a highminded theory, I know of no principle that, as a matter of

It is to be observed that the basis of this decision is that no rights of third parties or of the public are infringed, and that the combination gave the parties concerned no rights and no power which the individuals had not previously possessed. The monopoly was not created by the combination, but was enjoyed by the interested parties before it was

law, would prevent its seeking the feeblest of them all,—the one least able to defend himself,—and to make a victim of him. If that individual shall appear to have infringed upon this defendant's patents, he is liable to the damages, although he may be poor,—unable to defend himself,—although others may have offended in a greater degree, and although we may condemn the spirit which selected him as the particular defendant. On principle, this cannot be doubted. See also Asbestos Felting Co. v. United States & F. Salamander Felting Co., 13 Blatchf. 453; Tuttle v. Matthews, 28 Fed. Rep. 98; Kelley v. Manufacturing Co., 44 Fed. Rep. 19; Chemical Works v. Hecker, 11 Blatchf. 552. If the defendant had brought suit against the plaintiffs for some breach of contract or violation of its alleged rights, founded upon the combination agreement, then it might become pertinent to inquire into the character of the combination and ascertain whether the court would enforce any rights growing out of it. But in a suit brought for the infringement of a patent by the owner, any such inquiry, at the behest of the infringer, would be as impertinent as one in respect to the moral character or antecedents of the plaintiff in an ordinary suit for trespass upon his property. Even a gambler, or the keeper of a brothel, cannot be deprived of his property because he is an obnoxious person or a criminal, and it is no defense to the trespass upon it, unless it was removed or destroyed in the suppression of a nuisance, that it was used in carrying on the unlawful occupation. Ely v. Supervisors, 36 N. Y. 297." *Ibid.*, 820. A defendant in a patent suit, who was the manufacturer of certain articles claimed to be an infringement of plaintiff's patent, sought to obtain an order enjoining the prosecution of three suits begun in other districts against its customers, as well as the commencement of new suits, and the sending of letters and circulars to others engaged in the trade, threatening prosecution for selling articles made by the defendant. *Held*, First, that the prosecution of suits in other districts should not be enjoined, because such suits were begun before this suit, and because comity demanded that application should be made to the court in which such suits were pending. Second, that as the plaintiff might recover substantial damages against the defendant's vendees, in addition to those which he would be entitled to recover against the defendant as manufacturer, the commencement of new suits should not be enjoined, unless irreparable injury was threatened to defendant's business, or there was evidence of malice or bad faith on the part of the plaintiff in commencing such formed. In the opinion in this case, Wallace, Judge, said: "This is a suit wherein the relief demanded is a permanent injunction to restrain the defendant from instituting or prosecuting any action in any court of law or equity against the plaintiffs for the infringement of any letters patent owned by the defendant covering improvements in spring-tooth harrows, or from instituting or prosecuting any such suits against any person using the spring-tooth harrows manufactured by the plaintiffs. The defendant has demurred to the complaint. In substance the complaint shows that the defendant has entered into a combination with various other manufacturers of spring-tooth harrows for the purpose of acquiring a monopoly in this country in the manufacture and sale of the same, and, as an incident thereto, has acquired all the rights of the other manufacturers for the exclusive sale and manufacture of such harrows under patents, or interests in patents, owned by them respectively. Such a combination may be an odious and wicked one, but the proposition that the plaintiffs, while infringing the rights vested in the defendant under letters patent of the United States, is entitled to stop the defendant from bringing or prosecuting any suit therefor, because the defendant is an obnoxious corporation, and is seeking to perpetuate the monopoly which is conferred upon it by its title to the letters patent, is a novel one, and entirely unwarranted. The party having such a patent has a right to bring suit on it, not only against a manufacturer who infringes, but against the dealers and users of the

suits. And third, that plaintiff had a right to notify persons using his device of his claim, and to call attention to the fact that, by selling or using it, they were making themselves liable to prosecution, and that an injunction would not be ordered unless the language of his letters or circulars was false, malicious, offensive or opprobrious, or they were used for the willful purpose of inflicting an injury. Kelly v. Ypsilanti Dress Stay Manufacturing Co., 44 Fed. Rep. 19. See also Allis v. Stowell, 16 Fed. Rep. 783; Booth v. Seevers, 19 Pat. Off. Gaz. 1140; Birdsell v. Hagerstown Agricultural Mfg. Co., 1 Hughes (U. S.), 64; Ide v. Ball Engine Co., 31 Fed. Rep. 901; National Cash Register Co. v. Boston Cash Indicator Co., 41 Fed. Rep. 51; Tuttle v. Matthews, 28 Fed. Rep. 98.

patented article, if he believes the patent is being infringed; and the motive which prompts him to sue is not open to judicial inquiry, because, having a legal right to sue, it is immaterial, whether his motives are good or bad, and he is not required to give his reasons for the attempt to assert his legal rights."[1]

§ **175. The Subject Continued.**—While a patent is the grant of a monopoly for the manufacture and sale of the article patented, it confers upon the patentee no right to enter into an illegal combination for extending or perpetuating such monopoly. With regard to combinations designed to create a monopoly, the proprietor of a patent enjoys no special privileges. He has no right to make an agreement with other manufacturers to pool the products of their manufactories for the purpose of increasing or maintaining prices, and he may not enter into any association with a view to the accomplishment of any similar purpose. In the recent case of The National Harrow Company v. Hench, it was held that a combination among manufacturers of spring-tooth harrows, by which each manufacturer assigns to a corporation, organized for the purpose, the patents under which he is operating, and takes back an exclusive license to make and sell the same style of harrows, previously made by him, and no other, all the parties being bound to sell at uniform prices, was held to be an unlawful combination for the enhancement of prices and in restraint of trade.[2] In the opinion in this case, Acheson, Judge, said: "Now, it is quite evident to me, as well by the papers themselves as from the testimony of witnesses, that this scheme was devised for the purpose of regulating and enhancing prices for float spring-tooth harrows, and for controlling the manufacture thereof throughout the whole country, and that the combination, especially by force of the numbers engaged therein, tends to stifle all competition in an important branch of business. I am not aware that such a far-

[1] Strait v. National Harrow Co., 51 Fed. Rep. 819.

[2] National Harrow Co. v. Hench, 76 Fed. Rep. 667, 669.

reaching combination as is here disclosed has ever been judicially sustained. On the contrary, the courts have repeatedly adjudged combinations between a number of persons engaged in the same general business to prevent competition among themselves, and to maintain prices, to be against sound public policy, and, therefore, illegal.[1] I am

[1] National Harrow Co. v. Hench, 76 Fed. Rep. 667, 669. See also Morris Run Coal Co. v. Barclay Coal Co., 68 Pa. St. 173; Pittsburg Carbon Co. v. McMillan, 119 N. Y. 46; s. c., 23 N. E. Rep. 530; Merz Capsule Co. v. United States Capsule Co., 67 Fed. Rep. 414. A combination or conspiracy among a number of persons engaged in a particular business, to stifle or prevent competition, and thereby to enhance or diminish prices to a point above or below what they would be if left to the influence of unrestricted competition, is contrary to public policy, and the courts will refuse their aid to the enforcement of contracts by which such combinations are sought to be effected. So a contract, entered into by the members of a stenographic association in a city, by which the prices of reporting legal proceedings by shorthand are to be kept up by the prevention of competition, although such association may embrace but a comparatively small part of the stenographic reporters engaged in the business, but which is open for the admission of all reporters who may be induced to join and by which a schedule of prices is fixed, and by which any member violating its rules as to prices is subject to a fine, is void, as tending to prevent a free and unrestricted competition in business. More v. Bennett, 140 Ill. 69. "Appellants insist that restraint of trade in the necessaries of life only is within the prohibition of public policy. No standard has been furnished by which to ascertain what constitute these with reference to the general public. But, assuming that beer is not among them, it is equally within the reach of the rule. The law recognizes it as a commodity, regulates its sales, it is 'an article of daily consumption,' and the court should refuse to aid in any attempted imposition upon the public by means of illegal combinations. The fact that coal was 'an article of prime necessity' was not mentioned as essential to the illegality of the combination which was involved in Morris Run Coal Co. v. Coal Co., 68 Pa. St. 173, but was suggested, *arguendo*, as an aggravation of the injury done the public. The whole course of discussion there shows that injury to the public was regarded as the true test of illegality." Nester v. Brewing Co., 161 Pa. St. 473, 483; s. c., 29 Atl. Rep. 102. Three manufacturers of a certain kind of curtain fixture, under different letters patent, owned by them severally, desiring to avoid competition, formed a corporation in which they were the only stockholders, and an agreement was executed by the corporation, of the one part, by the terms of which the manufacturers gave the corporation the sole right to sell said curtain fixtures for three years, the corporation agreeing to buy, at a specified

not able to concur in the view that the principle of these cases is inapplicable here, because the agreement in question involves patents. It is true that a patentee has the exclusive control of his invention during the life of the patent. He may practice the invention or not, as he sees fit,

price, all that the manufacturers might make, and the manufacturers acting as the selling agents of the corporation, and receiving a commission on goods sold by them. The agreement further provided, that during the term of the contract, the manufacturers should not dispose of their patents except upon such terms that a transferee should be bound by the agreement; and that they should not dispose of their stock in the corporation without the written assent of a majority of the stockholders. *Held*, that the agreement was not void as against public policy, and that the court would restrain by injunction one of the manufacturers from selling goods on his own account, in violation of the agreement. Central Shade Roller Co. v. Cushman, 143 Mass. 353. At page 363, the court says: "The contract does not restrict the sale of the commodity. It does not look toward withholding a supply from the market in order to enhance the price, as in Craft v. McConoughy, 79 Ill. 346, and other cases cited by the defendant. On the contrary, the contract intends that the parties shall make sales, and gives them full power to do so; the only restrictions being that sales not at retail or for export shall be in the name of the plaintiff, and reported to it, and the accounts of them kept by it, and the provisions that, when any party shall establish an agency in any city or town for the sale of a roller made exclusively for that purpose, no other party shall take orders for the same roller in the same place. To these restrictions, clearly valid, is added the one which affords an argument for the invalidity of the contract, the restriction as to price. That restriction is, in substance, that the prices for rollers of the grade made by the different parties shall be the same, and shall be according to a schedule contained in the contract, subject to changes which may be made by the plaintiff upon recommendation of three-fourths of its stockholders. In effect, it is an agreement between three makers of a commodity, that, for three years, they will sell it at a uniform price fixed at the outset, and to be changed only by consent of a majority of them. The agreement does not refer to an article of prime necessity, nor to a staple of commerce, nor to merchandise to be bought and sold in the market, but to a particular curtain fixture of the parties own manufacture. It does not look to affecting competition from outside,—the parties have a monopoly by their patents,—but only to restrict competition in price between themselves. Even if such an agreement tends to raise the price of the commodity, it is one which the parties have a right to make. To hold otherwise would be to impair the right of persons to make contracts, and to put a price on the products of their own industry."

and he may grant to others licenses upon his own terms. But where, as was the case here, a large number of independent manufacturing concerns are engaged in making and selling, under different patents and in various forms, an extensively used article, competition is the natural and inevitable result, and thereby the public interest is promoted. Therefore, a combination between such manufacturers, which imposes a widespread restraint upon the trade, and destroys competition, is as injurious to the community, and as obnoxious to sound public policy, as if the confederates were dealing in unpatented articles. To the present case may well be applied the remarks of the Supreme Court of Pennsylvania, in the case of The Morris Run Coal Company v. The Barclay Coal Company: 'This combination has a power in its confederated form which no individual action can confer.' By the united action of more than a score of different manufacturers, natural and salutary competition is destroyed. To sanction such a result, because accomplished by a combination of patentees, would be, I think, to pervert the patent laws. Moreover, it is to be noted, that under these license contracts, the licensees can only make or sell their own specific form of harrow. All other forms, whether patented or unpatented, are prohibited to them. For this interdiction there is no justification. In the case of The National Harrow Company v. Quick,[1] Judge Baker expressed the opinion that this combina-

[1] National Harrow Co. v. Quick, 67 Fed. Rep. 130. "It seems to me that such a combination is illegal. and that its purposes are violative of sound public policy. The common law forbids the organization of such combinations, composed of numerous corporations and firms. They are dangerous to the peace and good order of society, and they arrogate to themselves the exercise of powers destructive of the right of free competition in the markets of the country. and by their aggregate power and influence imperil the free and pure administration of justice. Strait v. Harrow Co., 18 N. Y. Supl. 224; Richardson v. Buhl. 77 Mich. 632: s. c., 43 N. W. Rep. 1102: Emery v. Candle Co., 47 Ohio St. 320: s. c., 24 N. E. Rep. 660: State v. Nebraska Distilling Co., 29 Neb. 700; s. c., 46 N. W. Rep. 155. Complainant says that its title to the patent in question is valid. and that it has a lawful right to its protection from invasion by a stranger, regardless of the objects and purposes of the combination which it

tion was unlawful and against sound public policy. I am constrained to regard the license contracts sued on as part of an illegal combination, and in unwarrantable restraint of trade. I must, therefore, deny the plaintiff the relief sought."[1]

§ 176. **The Voting Trust.**—A voting trust or an agreement among the shareholders of a corporation under which they unite their votes, with a view to controlling an election, is legal or illegal, as the circumstances and objects are justifiable or unjustifiable. Such an agreement is not, essentially, illegal, but the ends sought and the means employed may render it in contravention of public policy and void. Where the agreement is a bargain by which one or more of the parties is to receive some special benefit which is not shared by other stockholders it will not be sustained. In a leading case in Massachusetts, it was held that a contract, by which a shareholder in a corporation, in consideration of the purchase of a part of his stock at a price

represents. On the other hand, the defendants contend that to give its title protection would be to give aid to the unlawful purposes of the combination. In suits at law it is doubtless true, as a general proposition, that a wrongdoer will not be permitted to dispute the legal title of one in possession of money or property by showing that the title thereto was unlawfully acquired, or that the owner intends to apply it to an unlawful use. I have strong doubts whether this rule ought to apply to a suit in equity, where nothing but clean hands and a good conscience will move the court to act. The combination represented by the complainant is not illegal in any other sense, except that the law will not lend its aid to the accomplishment of its purposes. The common law does not prohibit the making of such combinations. It merely declines, after they have been made, to recognize their validity, by refusing to make any decree or order which will in any way give aid to the purposes of such combinations. It seems to me that the court cannot sustain the present bill without giving aid to the unlawful combination or trust represented by the complainant. The question is not free from doubt, but in a case of doubt I feel it my duty to resolve it in such a way as will not lend the countenance of the court to the creation of combinations, trusts, or monopolies. They have already grown to alarming proportions, and courts, to the full extent of their powers, ought to discountenance and repress them." *Ibid.*, 131.

[1] National Harrow Co. v. Hench, 76 Fed. Rep. 667, 669.

named, agrees to secure to the purchaser the office of treasurer of the corporation, with a fixed salary, and, in case of his removal, to repurchase the stock at par, is void as against public policy, and as a fraud on the other members of the corporation, in the absence of evidence that the transaction was not for the private benefit of the shareholder, or that it was consented to by the other members of the corporation.[1] It is to be observed that under this decision, in a

[1] Guernsey v. Cook, 120 Mass. 501. See also cases cited by the court: Fuller v. Dame, 18 Pick. 472; Smith v. Townsend, 109 Mass. 500; Phippen v. Stickney, 3 Met. 384; Gibbs v. Smith, 115 Mass. 592; Curtis v. Aspinwall, 114 Mass. 187; Waldo v. Martin, 4 B. & C. 319; Marshall v. Baltimore & Ohio R. R., 16 How. 314; Elliott v. Richardson, L. R. 5 C. P. 744. In Gage v. Fisher, 5 N. Dak. 297: s. c., 65 N. W. Rep. 809, it was held that a contract to allow another to control the voting of stock based upon a promise of the one who is to control such stock to secure for the owner of the stock an office in the corporation, is illegal; and the whole contract is void, although the illegal consideration (*i. e.*, the promise to secure for the owner of the stock a corporate office), constitutes only a part of the consideration for the agreement to give such promisee control of the stock. In the opinion the court uses this language: "That a contract relating to the purchase or control of corporate stock founded in whole or in part upon a promise to secure for the person who owns the stock employment in the corporation, and an office therein, is illegal and void, is a doctrine supported by the unanimous voice of the decisions. Woodruff v. Wentworth, 133 Mass. 309; Noel v. Drake, 28 Kan. 265; Guernsey v. Cook, 120 Mass. 501; Forbes v. McDonald, 54 Cal. 98; Cone's Exrs. v. Russell, 48 N. J. Eq. 208; s. c., 21 Atl. Rep. 847; West v. Camden, 135 U. S. 507; s. c., 10 Sup. Ct. Rep. 838. In the case last cited the court, referring to a contract, one element of which was a promise to give one of the parties to it permanent employment as manager of a corporation in which he was a stockholder, said: 'It was a contract, the purpose and effect of which was to influence the defendant as a stockholder and officer of the company, in the decision of a question affecting the private rights of others, by considerations foreign to those rights, and the defendant, by the contract, was placed under direct and very powerful inducement to disregard his duties to other members of the corporation, who had a right to demand his disinterested action in the selection of suitable officers. He was to be in a relation of trust and confidence, which would require him to look only to the best interests of the whole, uninfluenced by private contracts. We think this statutory rule is applicable in this case, notwithstanding the alleged contract was not corruptly made for private gain on the part of the defendant. There were other stockholders in the company. The defendant and the Standard

transaction of this character, the presumption is that the end in view vitiates the act and renders the agreement illegal and void. Unless it is shown, beyond a reasonable doubt, that it was a fair and honest transaction, and adapted to promote the interests of all the shareholders alike, or, at least, that it had the consent of the shareholders, it will not be upheld. In the opinion in the case

Oil Company, for whose benefit it is alleged the contract was made, were not all the stockholders; and it seems to us that it was certainly the right of those other stockholders to have the defendant's judgment, as an officer of the company, exercised with a sole regard to the interests of the company.' " A syndicate purchased a majority of the capital stock of the Shepang Railroad Company, which was placed in a voting trust to continue for five years, or until a consolidation was effected with some other railroad company, or it should be dissolved by agreement. 'A trust company was to act as trustee, and was to take the title and issue certificates to the members of the syndicate of the shares in it held by each, and was to vote on the stock as directed by a committee of the syndicate. The apparent object of the arrangement was simply to extend the railroad to tide water and form a connection there with a certain other road, but there was a secret purpose to make a profit for themselves out of the construction contracts which they, as directors of the railroad company, would be able to make. After they had purchased the majority of the stock, they made themselves directors and officers of the road, and one of their number its president. The syndicate made S one of their number, their financial agent, and. it being necessary to borrow money to pay for the stock purchased, had a large portion of the trust certificates issued directly to him, and they were pledged by him in raising the money. They were, by their terms, transferable, and had powers of attorney printed upon them, which were signed in blank by S. Before the connection at tide water could be effected, S failed and went into insolvency. The loans were not paid and the pledged certificates were sold at public sale, and most of them were bought by the plaintiffs. The certificates thus bought covered 7,000 shares of capital stock. The plaintiffs also purchased 3,300 shares of the stock which had not gone into the trust, making their entire holdings 85 per cent. of the whole capital. After the plaintiffs had acquired these trust certificates and this stock, they notified the trust company that they revoked the powers given by the trust agreement and demanded that the stock represented by the certificate should be transferred to them upon a surrender of the trust certificates, but the trust company refused to make the transfer. *Held*, 1. That the trust agreement was void as in violation of the duties of the directors of the railroad company, and against the policy of our law. 2. That the plaintiffs had the right to revoke the powers given to the trust company by the trust agreement, and to have transferred above cited, the court said: "It was the purpose and effect of the contract to influence the defendant, in the decision of a question affecting the private rights of others, by considerations foreign to those rights. The promisor was placed under direct inducement to disregard his duties to other members of the corporation, who had a right to demand his disinterested action in the selection of suitable officers. He was in a relation of trust and confidence, which required him to look only to the best interests of the whole, uninfluenced by private gain. The contract operated as a fraud upon his associates.[1] But whatever doubt may arise, where the object is plainly illegal or open to question, it is plain that where there is palpable fraud, or any deliberate

to them, on surrender of the trust certificate, as many shares of the stock as the certificates represented. Shepang Voting Trust Cases, 66 Conn. 553; s. c., 24 Atl. Rep. 32. In the opinion in this case the court says: "It is the policy of our law that an untrammeled power to vote shall be incident to the ownership of the stock, and a contract by which the real owner's power is hampered by a provision therein that he shall vote as somebody else dictates is objectionable. I think it against the policy of our law for a stockholder to contract that his stock shall be voted just as some one who has no beneficial interest or title in or to the stock directs: saving to himself simply the title, the right to dividends, and perhaps the right to cast the vote directed, willing or unwilling, whether it be for the interest of other stockholders, or for the interest of the corporation or otherwise. This I conceive to be against the policy of the law, whether the power so to vote be for five years or for all time. It is the policy of our law that ownership of stock shall control the property and the management of the corporation, and this cannot be accomplished, and this good policy is defeated if stockholders are permitted to surrender all their discretion and will, in the important matter of voting, and suffer themselves to be mere passive instruments in the hands of some agent who has no interest in the stock, equitable or legal, and no interest in the general prosperity of the corporation."

[1] Guernsey v. Cook, 120 Mass. 501, 502. See also White v. Tire Co., 52 N. J. Eq. 75; Cone v. Russell, 48 N. J. Eq. 208; s. c., 21 Atl. Rep. 847; Fennessy v. Ross, 5 App. Div. 342; s. c., 39 N. Y. Supl. 323; Railroad Co. v. Nicholas, 98 Ala. 92; s. c., 12 So. Rep. 723; People's Home Sav. Bank v. Superior Court, 104 Cal. 649; s. c., 38 Pac. Rep. 452; Eckstein v. Downing, 64 N. H. 248; s. c., 9 Atl. Rep. 626; Goodwin Gas Stove Meter Co.'s Appeal, 117 Pa. St. 514; s. c., 12 Atl. Rep. 736; True v. Houghton, 6 Colo. 318; Bumgardner v. Leavitt, 35 W. Va. 194; s. c., 13 S. E. Rep. 67.

irregularity in the manner of conducting an election, or of casting any part of the votes, the whole proceeding will be held illegal and void. In a case in New York, where there was a preconceived scheme, combination or conspiracy on the part of a portion of the stockholders in a railroad corporation, to carry an election of directors, and thus get the control of the road, by the use and abuse of legal process and proceedings, and by their efforts and contrivances to prevent a fair election of inspectors, at a preliminary meeting of stockholders, which conspiracy was carried into effect by those means, together with the concurring preoccupation of the room where such meeting was to be, and was, held, by such a number of persons, not stockholders, as utterly precluded a free and fair meeting for such purpose, it was held that an election of directors held under these circumstances, by inspectors so chosen, was irregular, fraudulent and void.[1]

§ 177. **The Subject Continued.**—The voting trust, as we have seen, is not *per se* illegal or void. But the presumption is against its validity and the burden is on the parties interested to show that the transaction is fair and honest, and that it cannot work to the injury of other members of the corporation. In a recent case in Ohio, before a lower court, it was held that an agreement by which the stockholders of a railroad company confer the power to vote upon their shares, for a lawful purpose, is not illegal or against public policy, but such agreement may be revoked at any time by any one of the subscribing shareholders, notwithstanding it is in terms irrevocable.[2] So far as

[1] People v. Albany, etc. Ry. Co., 55 Barb. 345.

[2] Griffith v. Jewett, 15 Wkly. Law Bull. 419. "We can perceive no reason why any number of shareholders, either by means of a proxy or by vesting the legal title in another. may not authorize him to vote upon their stock, and, as such is the substance of this agreement, we consider it not illegal. So long as the parties to it, or their successors in interest, are satisfied with it, no other person may complain, and the 'irrevocable clause' does not affect the rights of any one. But if the equitable owner elects to withdraw the legal title from the holder thereof, the case assumes a different aspect. As we have heretofore seen it is a dry trust—the trustees having no

appears this decision has not been affirmed by any court of last resort, and it may be doubted whether the position is altogether correct. At all events, special emphasis must be placed upon the words "for a lawful purpose," and this is a point to be established by very conclusive proof. Where it is manifest that the transaction is for the interests of all the stockholders of the corporation it will be sustained. In the case of Havemeyer v. Havemeyer, before the Supreme

interest to set up in favor of its continuance; but the parties have agreed that this power to vote, vested in the trustees, shall be irrevocable. Can this provision be sustained as against the demand of certificate holders,—that they be permitted to revoke? If such demand be not complied with, the party holding the entire beneficial interest in the stock cannot cast the vote thereof, while it may be voted upon by one having no interest in it or in the company; and so it may come to pass that the ownership of a majority of the stock of a company may be vested in one set of persons, and the control of the company irrevocably invested in others. It seems clear that such state of affairs would be intolerable, and it is not contemplated by the law, the universal policy of which is that the control of stock companies shall be and remain with the owners of the stock. The right to vote is an incident of the ownership of stock and cannot exist apart from it. Freon v. Carriage Co., 42 Ohio St. 30; Hafer v. N. Y., L. E. & W. Ry. Co., 14 Wkly. Law Bull. 68. The owners of these trust certificates are, in our opinion, the equitable owners of the shares of stock which they represent, and being such, the incidental right to vote upon the stock necessarily pertains to them. They may permit the trustees as holders of the legal title to vote in their stead, if they choose, but when they elect to exercise the power themselves, the law will not permit the trustees to refuse it to them." *Ibid.*, 422. A written agreement between purchasers of stock in a corporation that they will for five years "retain the power to vote the shares in one body, and that the vote which shall be cast by said shares shall be determined by ballot between them or their survivors" is a proxy, authorizing the vote of all the stock to be cast in accordance with the determination of the majority of the parties thereto. It is sufficient consideration for an agreement between purchasers of stock to have it voted in one block for five years, the vote to be determined by ballot between the parties, that in their agreement among themselves to purchase they had stipulated for such a voting agreement; and it is immaterial that the voting agreement was not executed till after their bid for the stock was made, it having been executed before they had completed the purchase and become the owners by paying the purchase money; and it is likewise immaterial that a certificate for part of the stock was issued to each party. Smith v. San Fran-

Court of New York, it was held that an agreement between direct stockholders of a corporation who, together, own a majority of all the shares of the capital stock of said corporation, entered into for the purpose of the election of directors, who would manage the affairs of the company in the interests of the stockholders, and thus improve the value of their stock, is not in conflict with the requirements of law, and in no wise derogates from its policy. There is nothing in it that tends to frustrate or interfere with the legal right of the majority of stockholders to delegate to directors of

cisco & N. P. Ry. Co., 115 Cal. 584; s. c., 47 Pac. Rep. 582. In this case the court says: "In cases of 'voting trusts' where the owners of stock transfer the shares to trustees with authority to vote at elections according to the direction of a majority of those holding trust certificates, and the only consideration for such transfer and agreement is the mutual promises of the several stockholders, it has been held that any stockholder may revoke his agreement and withdraw his stock at will; and it is also held that stockholders who become such after an agreement of this nature is entered into are not bound by its terms, but will hold their shares freed from the limitations of the agreement. Fisher v. Bush, 35 Hun, 641; Woodruff v. Railroad Co., 30 Fed. Rep. 91; Brown v. Steamship Co., 5 Blatchf. 525; Fed. Cas. No. 2325. In Moses v. Scott, 84 Ala. 608; s. c., 4 So. Rep. 742, certain stockholders had formed a voting trust, and placed their stock in the hands of four trustees, with power to vote the stock as a unit at all meetings as three of them should think best, or if they failed to agree, as three-fourths of the stock represented should determine, and had agreed not to sell their stock so pooled for three years. There was no consideration for this agreement other than the mutual promise of the several stockholders, and while the court refused to enforce the agreement concerning the sale, upon the ground that it was in restraint of the free alienation of property, it said: 'We cannot say there is anything *per se* illegal in an agreement entered into by and between certain stockholders in a joint stock company by which they promise to vote together as a unit in all matters pertaining to the government of the corporation. Each member has the clear right to cast his ballot as he pleases, wisely or unwisely, and no other stockholder can control his conduct or gainsay his discretion, and it can make no difference if several stockholders uniformly vote together, or so vote in obedience to a prior agreement that they will do so. The vote, when cast, is but the expressed wish of the stockholder, or, at least, must be so regarded, and no other stockholder can be supposed to be injured thereby. To hold otherwise would greatly abridge the voter's right to cast his ballot as he pleased.'"

its own choice the management of the affairs of the company, nor is an agreement made between a like number of stockholders, in regard to holding their stock or selling the same together, invalid and in contravention of public policy and law. In the opinion in this case, the court said: "I am unable to perceive anything in this combination, or in the agreement therefor, which tends to defeat the rights of stockholders generally, or the interests of the public at large, as defined by that provision of the revised statutes, which declares that the directors of railroad corporations 'shall be chosen annually by the majority of the votes of the stockholders voting at such elections.' Practically, the selection of candidates must precede an election, and it would often be difficult, if not impossible, to make such selections without comparison of views, combination, concession and concerted action. No formidable and effective opposition to an existing board, however obnoxious, could be organized without combination. An agreement to combine stock for the purpose of terminating mismanagement by a change in the directors, through the instrumentality of a majority of votes, at a regular election, is not in conflict with the requirements of the law and in nowise derogates from its policy."[1]

§ **178. The Same Subject.**—Where a voting trust or an agreement in regard to voting is in restraint of trade and against public policy, or forbids voting by proxy, or is not founded upon a valid and proper consideration, it will not be upheld. In a recent and leading case in New York, the complainant alleged that the plaintiff, the defendant and

[1] Havemeyer v. Havemeyer. 43 N. Y. Super. Ct. 506. See also Fremont v. Stone. 42 Barb. 170; Guernsey v. Cook. 120 Mass. 501; People v. Albany & Susquehanna R. Co.. 55 Barb. 344. 381, 382; Card v. Hope. 2 B. & C. 661; Fisher v. Bush, 35 Hun, 641; Camden, etc. R. Co. v. Elkins, 37 N. J. Eq. 273; Hilles v. Parrish. 14 N. J. Eq. 380; Ryder v. Alton. etc. R. Co.. 13 Ill. 516; Woodruff v. Dubuque, 30 Fed. Rep. 91; Brown v. Pacific Mail Steamship Co.. 5 Blatchf. 525; Webb v. Ridgely, 38 Md. 364; Hoppin v. Buffum, 9 R. I. 513; s. c.. 11 Am. Rep. 291; Reed v. Jones, 6 Wis. 680; Erwin v. Philadelphia & Reading R. Co.. 7 Ry. & Corp. L. J. 87.

eight other persons signed the following written sealed instrument: "For value received from and paid to each other, we, the undersigned, stockholders of the Genesee Valley Canal Railroad Company, mutually agreed with the others and to all, that we will not sell, assign, set over, pledge or give power of attorney to vote, or agree to sell, assign, transfer, set over, pledge or give power of attorney to vote, in any way, shape or manner, the stock which we respectively and individually own, hold or possess, in said company, without the concurrent consent of all signers of this instrument. * * * This agreement is made for mutual protection and to prevent the sale of the company's franchise by a majority of the members of the present board of directors, who are, and who represent, a minority of the shares of the capital stock of this company." It was held that the agreement was void, because: FIRST. It was in restraint of trade and against public policy. SECOND. Because the clause providing that none of the signers should vote by proxy was a pernicious and unlawful provision. THIRD. Because it was not founded upon an adequate and sufficient considera tion. Agreements of this character must be supported by a real and special consideration.[1]

[1] Fisher v. Bush, 35 Hun, 641. See also Havemeyer v. Havemeyer, 43 N.Y. Super. Ct. 506, 1213; affirmed 86 N.Y. 618; Vanderbilt v. Bennett, 2 Ry. & Corp. L. J. 409. An agreement by which various owners of stock place their stock in the hands of one person as trustee or agent to hold for a certain period of time, the parties agreeing not to sell their stock without having first offered to sell it to the rest of their associates at a price not above the then current market value, and in case of their declining to take it, without next offering it to the trustee, but any one of the parties to be at liberty to withdraw at any time on those terms is not "contrary to public policy or anywise open to objection." Brown v. Pacific Mail S. Co., 5 Blatchf. 525. In Ohio & M. Ry. Co. v. State, 49 Ohio St. 668; s. c., 32 N. E. Rep. 933, it is held that stockholders may place their stock in the hands of a depositary, with direction to vote it as directed by a committee appointed by themselves and subject to their control. It the opinion the court uses this language: "It does not appear that the ownership of the stock and its voting power were separated by the agreement under which the 'shareholders' committee was appointed and the stock deposited with the depositary therein named * * * and that the agreement does not, therefore, constitute what

§ **179. Rebates on Freight Bills.**—There is a wide divergence in the American decisions in regard to the right of railway companies to make rebates on their freight rates. In some of the States it is held that they may enter into an agreement to refund to a shipper a percentage of their schedule rates as a rebate. It is held that where a contract of this nature is made without reference to rates made to other shippers, it is not to be reckoned as a discrimination between parties. In these States, as a rule, it is held that the presumption is that such contracts may be made and that the burden is on a complainant to establish a charge of unjust or illegal discrimination. In the leading case of Bayles v. The Kansas Pacific Railway Company, it was held that under the constitution of Colorado forbidding "undue or unreasonable discrimination" by railroad companies in freight charges, a contract to carry freight for a party at a specific rate, being less than its published schedule, is not void as being an unjust discrimination and against public policy, in the absence of evidence that such special rate is an exclusive privilege. Freight charges must in all cases be reasonable to shippers, and where the circumstances and conditions are the same they must likewise be equal. The fundamental law prohibits the granting of privileges to one shipper, tending to give him a monopoly to the prejudice of others engaged in like pursuits. Contracts creating such privileges are against public policy and void. A railroad company may contract to refund to a shipper a certain

is known as a 'voting trust.' It was, at most, a convenient method by which distant and widely separated shareholders became enabled, indirectly, to participate in the control and management of the company, and from which each could recede at any time, and demand the return of his stock, without violating any term of the agreement. The depositary is a proxy required to vote the stock as directed by the committee; and he and the committee both derive their power from the shareholders by the same instrument, and in the end effectuate their wishes. Such an arrangement differs widely from an agreement whereby the stock is placed in the hands of trustees, who are invested with the power of voting it as their interests may dictate, irrespective of the wishes or direction of the owners. Such an agreement as the latter would be void as against the policy of our corporation law."

portion of the schedule rates as "rebates" or "drawbacks," and when made without reference to the rates charged other shippers, such contracts make no discrimination between parties.[1] In the States where the common law rule is in force this

[1] Bayles v. Kansas Pac. R. Co., 13 Colo. 181; s. c., 22 Pac. Rep. 341; 40 Am. & Eng. R. Cas. 42; 5 L. R. A. 480; 2 Int. Com. Rep. 643. See also Indianapolis, D. & S. R. Co. v. Ervin, 118 Ill. 250; s. c., 8 N. E. Rep. 862; 27 Am. & Eng. R. Cas. 8; Indianapolis, D. & S. R. Co. v. Davis, 32 Ill. App. 67; Jacksonville S. E. R. Co. v. Rabbitt, 29 Ill. App. 288. Before the passage of the interstate commerce act defendant promised to pay plaintiffs a rebate of $6 a car on 170 car loads of lumber which plaintiffs promised to furnish for transportation. Plaintiffs delivered and defendants transported 73 car loads before and 97 after the act took effect. Defendants paid the rebate on the 73 cars. This suit was to recover it upon the remaining 97. The agreed case was that plaintiffs should have judgment unless their right to recover was "barred" by the interstate commerce act. *Held*, that plaintiffs could not recover; for the contract was void at common law as a discrimination, and, being void, plaintiffs never had any right under it which could be barred. Fitzgerald v. Grand Trunk R. Co., 63 Vt. 169; s. c., 22 Atl. Rep. 76; 49 Am. & Eng. R. Cas. 8. A railroad company may not make any unreasonable or unjust discriminations between its customers in freight charges, but the question whether such discrimination has been made is ordinarily one of fact. So, *held*, where a railroad company gave a rebate on coal in consideration that the favored party erect a dock on the company's land for the use of both parties. Root v. Long Island R. Co., 114 N. Y. 300; s. c., 21 N. E. Rep. 403; 40 Am. & Eng. R. Cas. 55; 4 L. R. A. 331; 23 N. Y. S. R. 226. When a person is engaged in the business of dealing in and furnishing railroad piles, and the railroad company over whose railroad he transports the same has a fixed rate or price for the transportation of such property, but it has favored customers for whom it will transport such property at a lower rate by first charging the full price, and, afterwards, when the transportation is completed, paying back a certain proportion thereof as a rebate, and the owner of the piles procures them, by an agreement with a favored customer, to be transported in the name of such favored customer, who afterwards receives the rebate, *held*, that the whole transaction is in violation of law and public policy, and the owner of the piles, who procured them to be so transported, cannot afterwards recover the amount of the rebate from the favored customer. Hawley v. Kansas & Texas Coal Co., 48 Kan. 593; s. c., 30 Pac. Rep. 14. The interstate commerce act is not violated by an agreement by a railroad with a stockyard company to pay a customer an annual sum, although a large portion of the stock received at its yards is shipped from, and reshipped to, other States, where such payment has no relation to the railway

decision will be sustained. In Indiana this rule has followed. In the leading case of the Cleveland, Columbus, Cincinnati & Indianapolis Railway Company v. Closser, it was held that if a common carrier makes a special contract to repay part of the sum received from the shipper, he must perform his part of the contract, unless he overthrows the presumption of fairness and right by countervailing facts. It is not necessary for the shipper to prove that the rate charged and paid by him, under his contract, was excessive or unjust. His right to recover rests upon the contract providing for a drawback.[1] This rule, somewhat modified,

charges, which are uniform and no rebate is made thereon. Willoughby v. Chicago, J. R. & U. S. Co., 50 N. J. Eq. 656; s. c., 25 Atl. Rep. 277. See also the following interstate commerce cases: Interstate Commerce Commission v. B. & O. R. Co., 145 U. S. 263; *In re* Grand Trunk R. Co., 2 Int. Com. Rep. 496; s. c., 3 Int. Com. Com. 89; Shamberg v. Delaware, L. & W. R. Co., 3 Int. Com. Rep. 502; s. c., 4 Int. Com. Com. 630; Providence Coal Co. v. Providence & W. R. Co., 1 Int. Com. Rep. 363; s. c., 1 Int. Com. Com. 107. The D Co., which manufactured and sold spirits, etc., issued to the purchasers of its goods so-called "rebate vouchers," by which, "for the purpose of securing the continuous patronage" of the customer, it promised to pay him, in six months, a sum equal to five cents per gallon of the goods purchased by him; such voucher providing that it should "be valid and payable only on condition" that the purchaser and his successors should, during such six months, have bought all his supply of such goods from the D Co. or certain persons named as its distributing agents. The D Co., having been placed in the hands of a receiver, certain of these vouchers were presented to him for allowance, by persons who claimed to hold them as equitable assignees from the persons to whom they were issued. It appeared that the condition as to continued purchases from the D Co. had not been complied with. *Held*, that such vouchers did not create a present obligation to pay the rebate, subject to be defeated by a breach of the condition, but that such obligation would arise only on performance of the condition, and, accordingly, that even if the condition were held to be illegal, there would be no obligation without performance. *Held*, further, that such rebate vouchers were not illegal or against public policy. Olmstead v. Distilling & Cattle Feeding Co., 77 Fed. Rep. 265.

[1] Cleveland, C., C. & I. R. Co. v. Closser, 126 Ind. 348; s. c., 26 N. E. Rep. 159; 45 Am. & Eng. R. Cas. 275. "The contract described is valid. It is not different, in any material respect, from the ordinary one in which the carrier stipulates directly to carry goods at a fixed rate, for the agree-

is upheld in Pennsylvania. In a recent case it was held that railroad companies have no right to make any undue discrimination or preference in their charges; and a charge made to one shipper higher than to another, for the same

ment to repay does not of itself change the legal effect of the undertaking to such an extent as to transform it into an an illegal contract. It is, in contemplation of law, nothing more than an agreement to carry the grain at the compensation ultimately agreed upon, inasmuch as the provision binding the carrier to pay back part of the nominal compensation, simply fixes the amount of the actual compensation, although it does provide for a peculiar mode of payment. There is no element of moral or legal wrong in an agreement to repay part of the compensation received; to give an illegal character to such an agreement more must be shown than the mere fact that the parties stipulated for a rebate. In simply making a rebate, or in providing for a drawback, parties violate no law, and their contracts must stand. It cannot be presumed that fraud was intended, or practiced, nor can it be presumed that there was any wrongful combination to secure an undue advantage over other shippers; neither can it be presumed that in stipulating for a rebate the carrier intended to make, in favor of the particular shipper, a discrimination forbidden by law. It is by no means, every favor shown a particular shipper, although it may constitute, in some measure, a discrimination favorable to him and unfavorable to other shippers, that impresses upon a contract for the carriage of goods the seal of condemnation. The common law authorities (and by them this case is ruled) fully support the doctrine that a mere discrimination will not invalidate a contract; to have that effect other elements must enter into the contract; but when such elements are present in such force as to make the discrimination unjust or oppressive the contract will be illegal. It is not necessarily, or *per se*, a legal wrong for a carrier to give better rates to one who ships many car loads of grain than to one who ships a single car load or a single bushel. It is a matter of common knowledge, and, therefore, one of which judicial notice is taken, that an increase in the volume of business is desirable and advantageous, and in the rivalry of business competition it is lawful to favor those whose business is great rather than those whose business is small or inconsiderable." *Ibid.*, 351. See cases cited by the court: Nicholson v. Gt. Western Ry. Co., 7 C. B. (N. S.) 755; s. c., 1 Nev. & McN. R. W. Cas. 143; Garton v. Bristol, etc. R. W. Co., 1 B. & S. 112; Hozier v. Caledonian R. W. Co., 1 Nev. & McN. R. W. Cas. 27; Great Western Ry. Co. v. Sutton, L. R. 4 H. L. 226; Ransome v. Eastern, etc. R. W. Co., 1 C. B. (N S.) 437; Jones v. Easton, etc R. W. Co., 1 Nev. & McN. R. W. Cas. 72; Baxendale v. Railway Co., 5 C. B. (N. S.) 336; Bellsdyke, etc. Co. v. North British R. W. Co., 2 Nev. & McN. R. W. Cas. 105; Spofford v. Boston, etc. Railroad, 128 Mass. 326;

service, under like circumstances, constitutes undue preferences and discrimination, and, consequently, renders the charge unreasonable. The equality, however, which is thus described, is not a strict and literal equality,—under all circumstances, however varying and different. It is rather an equality in the sense of freedom from unreasonable discrimination. The statute of 1883 prohibits only such discrimination as is undue or unreasonable, and the prohibited discrimination is farther limited by the consideration that it must be "for a like service, from the same place, upon like conditions and under similar circumstances."[1]

§ **180. The Subject Continued.**—In other States it has been held that an agreement to make a rebate is void at common law, and in some States there are statutes making such contracts illegal and void. In Illinois it has recently been held that a contract between a railroad company and a shipper, that the latter shall pay the regular and established rates of freight, the same as all other shippers, and that the company shall pay back to him, by way of rebate, a certain portion of the freight so charged and paid, whereby such shipper will pay a less rate for transportation than that paid by others, and the public generally, for like services,

Fitchburg R. R. Co. v. Gage, 12 Gray. 393; Johnson v. Pensacola, etc. R. R. Co., 16 Fla. 623; s. c., 26 Am. Rep. 731; Ragan v. Aiken, 9 Lea. 609; s. c., 42 Am. Rep. 684; McDuffee v. Portland, etc. R. R., 52 N. H. 430; s. c., 13 Am. Rep. 72; Hersh v. Northern Central R. W. Co., 74 Pa. St. 181; Christie v. Missouri Pac. R. W. Co., 94 Mo. 453; Chicago, etc. R. R. Co. v. People, 67 Ill. 1; Toledo, etc. R. W. Co. v. Elliott, 76 Ill. 67; Erie & Pacific Dispatch v. Cecil, 112 Ill. 185; Root v. Long Island R. R. Co., 114 N. Y. 300; Kilmer v. New York, etc. R. R. Co., 100 N. Y. 395; Stewart v. Lehigh, etc. R. R. Co., 38 N. J. L. 505; Union Pacific R. W. Co. v. United States, 117 U. S. 355; Hays v. Pennsylvania Co., 12 Fed. Rep. 309; Rhymney Iron Co. v. Rhymney A. Co., 6 Ry. & T. Cas. 60.

[1] Hoover v. Pennsylvania R. Co., 156 Pa. St. 220; s. c., 27 Atl. Rep. 282, See also Borda v. Philadelphia, etc. R. Co., 141 Pa. St. 484; s. c., 21 Atl. Rep. 665; Sharpless v. Mayor, 21 Pa. St. 147; Audenried v. Philadelphia, etc. R. Co., 68 Pa. St. 370; McDuffee v. Portland, etc. R. Co., 52 N. H. 430; New England Ex. Co. v. Maine Central R. Co., 57 Me. 188; Scofield v. Lake Shore, etc. R. Co., 43 Ohio St. 571; s. c., 3 N. E. Rep. 907; Union Pac. R. Co. v. Goodridge, 149 U. S. 680; s. c., 13 Sup. Ct. Rep. 970.

under similar circumstances and for like distances, is void, as being against public policy at the common law, and in violation of the statute against unjust discriminations.[1] In Iowa it has been held that where a railroad company makes a rebate in favor of one shipper, other shippers, who have paid the regular freight rates over the same line, may collect from the company the same proportionate amount of rebate. In the case of Cook & Wheeler v. The Chicago, Rock Island and Pacific Railway Company, the plaintiffs, who were shippers of cattle, were charged by the defendant from three to ten dollars per car load of cattle shipped over its road in excess of the charges made to other shippers for the same service and under the same conditions, the difference being allowed the favored shippers in the form of a secret rebate, which fact was concealed from the plaintiffs. It was held that at common law a common carrier is entitled to a reason-

[1] Indianapolis, D. & S. R. Co. v. Ervin, 118 Ill. 250; s. c., 8 N. E. Rep. 862; 27 Am. & Eng. R. Cas. 8. See also Indianapolis, D. & S. R. Co. v. Davis, 32 Ill. App. 67; Jacksonville S. E. R. Co. v. Rabbitt, 29 Ill. App. 288; Beadle v. Kansas City, etc. R. Co., 51 Kan. 248; s. c., 32 Pac. Rep. 910; Winsor Coal Co. v. Chicago, etc. R. Co., 52 Fed. Rep. 716; Swift v. Philadelphia, etc. R. Co., 58 Fed. Rep. 59; s. c., 64 Fed. Rep. 59; Gatton v. Chicago, etc. R. Co., 95 Iowa, 112; s. c., 63 N. W. Rep. 589; Atchison, etc. R. Co. v. Denver, etc. R. Co., 110 U. S. 667; s. c., 4 Sup. Ct. Rep. 185; Chicago, etc. R. Co. v. Osborne, 52 Fed. Rep. 912; Wabash R. Co. v. Illinois, 118 U. S. 557; s. c., 7 Sup. Ct. Rep. 4; Messenger v. Pennsylvania R. Co., 37 N. J. L. 531. Under the Railway Clauses Act 1845 and the Railway and Canal Traffic Act 1854, it constitutes an undue preference for a railway company, in order to compete with another line, to give certain advantages as to free cartage and rebate to shippers who have a direct communication by sidings with such other line, and refuse these advantages to others in the same trade not having such direct communication with the other railway. London & N. W. R. Co. v. Evershed, L. R. 3 App. Cas. 1029; s. c., 39 L. T. 306. An agreement between one trader and a railway, which secures to the trader rates unequal when compared with those of another trader having similar traffic, which is carried by the railway to the same place, is, *prima facie*, an undue preference, and the circumstances that the company have offered the same agreement as to rates and rebates to the competing trader will not necessarily justify the unequality. Rhymney Iron Co. v. Rhymney R. Co., 6 Ry. & C. T. Cas. 60. See also Harris v. Cockermouth & W. R. Co., 1 Ry. & C. T. Cas. 97

able charge only for the service rendered; that its discriminations in favor of other shippers were evidence that the charges demanded of the plaintiffs were unreasonable; and that the plaintiffs were entitled to recover the difference between the charges paid by them and the more favorable rates granted to other shippers.[1] It is well established that at common law a common carrier is bound to transport freight for as many shippers as may apply to him, and that he must render such service for a reasonable compensation. If the charge to one shipper is less than to another it is presumptive evidence that the higher charge is unreasonable, and, consequently, illegal. It has been maintained that at common law it is not illegal to transport freight for a favored individual at an exceptionally low rate, or even without consideration; that a simple discrimination in favor of a particular customer is not unlawful, unless the circumstances render it an unjust discrimination. Where there is no statutory regulation relating to the subject, it has been held that common carriers are not absolutely bound to charge all customers the same price for the same service, but it is well established that they must charge only a reasonable price for their service, and this seems to imply that one customer must not be favored at the expense of another. If they can afford to carry freight at the lower price, the higher is an unreasonable charge. Such discrimination is illegal, unless there is a special and satisfactory reason for it.[2]

§ **181. Combination of Insurance Companies.**—In some of the States the combination of insurance companies to control the rates of insurance or the commissions of their agents is prohibited by statute. In Kansas it has been held that foreign insurance companies doing business in that State, that combine to control and increase the rates of insurance on property within a city in that State, violate the provisions

[1] Cook v. Chicago, R. I. & P. R. Co., 81 Iowa, 551; s. c., 46 N. W. Rep. 1080; 45 Am. & Eng. R. Cas. 291.

[2] Story on Bailments, § 508, note 3; 1 Wood Railway Law, 566.

of the statute of 1889, being "an act to declare unlawful trusts and combinations in restraint of trade and products, and to provide penalties therefor;" and their local agents, who attempt to and do enforce such combined rates are subject to prosecution under the provisions of said act.[1] In the

[1] State v. Phipps, 50 Kan. 609; s. c., 31 Pac. Rep. 1097. Act of Feb. 18th, 1897, of Alabama, provides: "That every contract or policy of insurance made or issued after the passage of this act, shall be construed to mean that, in the event of loss or damage thereunder, the assured or beneficiary thereunder may, in addition to the actual loss or damage suffered, recover twenty-five per cent. of the amount of such actual loss, any provision or stipulation in such contract or policy to the contrary notwithstanding: provided, at the time of the making of such contract or policy of insurance, or subsequently before the time of trial the insurer belonged to, or was a member of, or in any way connected with, any tariff association or such like thing by whatever name called, or who had made any agreement or had any understanding with any other person, corporation or association engaged in the business of insurance, as agent or otherwise, about any particular rate of premium which should be charged or fixed for any kind or class of insurance risk; and, provided further, no stipulation or agreement in such contract or policy of insurance to arbitrate loss or damage, nor to give notice or make proofs of loss or damage, shall in any such case be binding on the assured or beneficiary, but right of action accrues immediately upon loss or damage. § 2. That if it is shown to the reasonable satisfaction of the jury by a preponderance of the weight of the testimony that such assurer at the time of the making of such agreement or policy of insurance, or subsequently before the time of trial belonged to, or was a member of, in any way connected with any tariff association or such like thing by whatever name called, either in or out of this State, or had made any agreement or had any understanding either in or out of this State with any other person, corporation or association engaged in the business of insurance as agent or otherwise, about any particular rate of premium which should be charged or fixed for any risk of insurance on any person or property or on any kind or class of insurance risk, they must, if they find for the assured or beneficiary in addition to his actual damages assess, and add twenty-five per cent. of the amount of such actual loss, and judgment shall be rendered accordingly. § 3. That this act shall be liberally construed to accomplish its object. The Missouri Act relating to pools, trusts and conspiracies, Laws of Missouri, 1897, contains this exception as to insurance: "Provided, however, that the provisions of this section shall not apply to agreements of fire insurance companies, or their agent, or boards of fire underwriters, to regulate the price or premium to be paid for insuring property against loss or damage by fire, lightning, or storm, in cities in this State which now

opinion in this case, the court said: "At this writing, it is probable that every State in the Union has passed laws upon this subject, until it may be said that the right of State regulation of the business of insurance is universally recognized and upheld. So it can be confidently said that this court, when it held, in *In re Pinkney*, that insurance was 'trade,' did not contemplate that the term used could be tortured into interstate commerce; and it can be said with equal confidence that the settled law of this country is that the issuing of a policy of insurance is not a transaction of commerce. As we have said, neither the major nor the minor premise of the argument of counsel for the appellants is sound, and the inevitable conclusion,—that Congress alone has power to regulate interstate commerce, and to provide penalties against insurance trusts and combinations,—does not follow. The court did not mean 'trade' as synonymous with interstate commerce. The business of insurance is not interstate commerce. The State has power to regulate and control, and to provide penalties for the transgression of its regulating and controlling statutes, of the business of a foreign insurance company within its boundaries. If the theory of the counsel for the appellants ever ripens into authoritative judicial decision, the power of the State

have or which may hereafter acquire a population of one hundred thousand inhabitants or more; and provided, further, that if such insurance companies or their agents, or the board of fire underwriters doing business in any such city, shall combine in such city, either directly or indirectly, or agree or attempt to agree, directly or indirectly, to fix or regulate the price or premium to be paid for insuring property to be located wholly outside of such city against loss or damage by fire, lightning or storm, such company so violating the provisions of this act either by itself, its agents, or any such board of underwriters, shall be taken and deemed to have forfeited its right to do business in this State, and shall become liable to all the penalties and forfeitures provided for by the provisions of this act." Act 1893, chap. 107, § 1, enacting that all insurance companies shall pay losses in full and prohibiting stipulations to the contrary, and providing that insurance policies upon cotton in bales, shall not be subject to the provisions of the Act, does not conflict with constitution, art. 11, § 8 prohibiting the legislature from granting special immunities or privileges. Dugger v. Mechanics' & Trades Ins. Co., 95 Tenn. 245; s. c., 32 S. W. Rep. 5.

to regulate and control the business of insurance within its limits is gone. The insurance department and every act upon the statute books for the protection of the policy holders, and every line looking to the punishment of the violators of its public policy in this respect, goes with it, except, possibly, as to such companies as may be organized and operated under the laws of the State."[1] In Texas a different rule has been established. While upholding the view that insurance is not commerce, it has been held that the statute, entitled "an act to define trusts, and to provide for penalties and punishment of corporations, persons, firms and association of persons connected with them, and to promote free competition in the State of Texas," did not apply to a combination to fix rates of insurance, or the commissions of the agents of insurance companies. These combinations are not embraced within the provisions of the act. A combination between two or more insurance companies to increase their rates or to diminish the rates to be paid to their agents, is, in a general sense, a combination in restraint of trade. But, I think, that the words, "restrictions in trade," were not intended to receive that construction in the statute.[2]

[1] State v. Phipps, 50 Kan. 609, 619; s. c., 31 Pac. Rep. 1097.

[2] Insurance Company v. State, 86 Tex. 250; s. c., 24 S. W. Rep. 397. "Insurance is a mere contract of indemnity against a contingent loss. Though it is an important aid to commerce, it is not a business of commerce, or one in which the public have any direct right. No franchise is necessary for its prosecution, and no one has a right to demand of an underwriter that his property shall be insured at any rate. Any individual may execute a policy, and so any company incorporated for the purpose of insuring property may refuse to execute one, unless it be so bound by its charter. Forced insurance, for obvious reasons, is detrimental to the public interest, and it is therefore not probable that such restrictions will be found in any charter. Labor is necessary to production and transportation, and therefore it is not merely an aid, but a necessity of commerce. It is advantageous to the public, and in that sense they have an interest in it. The services of professional men are likewise indispensable in most civilized communities, and are presumably likewise advantageous to the public. The public have an interest in them, in the same sense in which they have an interest in the business of insurance. It follows, therefore, that if insurance companies are to be brought within

§ 182. Right of Parties under Trust Combinations.— It is elementary law that the courts will not lend their aid to the enforcement of an illegal contract. The individual or corporation that becomes a party to such a contract assumes the entire responsibility of the act. The courts will leave such persons where it finds them. A corporation which is a member of a trust combination cannot recover its share of the profits of the business, or of any money due the members of the trust, under the agreement. To afford such a party aid would be to enforce an illegal compact. In a recent case in New York, it was held that the receiver of a sugar refining company, appointed under a judgment, in an action brought by the State to dissolve the corporation on account of its having become a party to an illegal combination, formed for the manufacture and sale of sugars, cannot maintain an action to recover the profits of the illegal transaction from another party engaged with the sugar refining company in such illegal combination, where it is necessary, in order to sustain the action, to appeal to and depend upon the terms of the illegal agreement.[1] In another recent case in

the rule that makes agreements to increase the price of merchandise illegal, upon the ground that the public have an interest in their business, agreements among laborers and among professional men not to render services below a stipulated rate should be held contrary to public policy and void, upon the same ground." *Ibid.*, 270.

[1] Gray v. Oxnard Bros. Co., 59 Hun. 387; Pittsburg Carbon Co. v. McMillan, 119 N. Y. 466; American Biscuit, etc. Co. v. Klotz, 44 Fed. Rep. 721; s. c., 32 Am. & Eng. Corp. Cas. 510; Mallory v. Hanaur Oil Works, 86 Tenn. 598; s. c., 20 Am. & Eng. Corp. Cas. 478; American Preservers' Trust v. Taylor Mfg. Co., 46 Fed. Rep. 152; Strait v. National Harrow Co., 18 N. Y. Supl. 224; Cameron v. Havemeyer, 12 N. Y. Supl. 126; State v. American Cotton Oil Trust, 40 La. Ann. 8; s. c., 19 Am. & Eng. Corp. Cas. 448. Act July 2, 1890, which forbids combinations in restraint of interstate commerce, and gives a right of action to any person injured by acts in violation of its provisions, does not authorize suit where the only cause of action is the bringing of two suits which have not been decided. Bishop & American Preservers' Co., 51 Fed. Rep. 272. The stockholders and members of certain corporations and partnerships engaged in a similar business, by agreement in writing, created a trust, the object of which was to authorize the trustees to control and manage the business of the parties. The trustees issued to the parties trust certificates transferable on their books. By the terms of the agree-

New York, a party to an illegal combination withdrew from the trust, and commenced an action against the trustee and the contracting corporations to dissolve the trust. The result was the appointment of a receiver of the property. In

ment the parties thereto and transferees of the certificates, were the beneficiaries under the trust. By the terms of the certificates they were transferable only on the books of the trustees on surrendering the certificates, and it was provided that the holder of a certificate should be subject to all terms of the agreement or the by-laws adopted in pursuance thereof as fully as if he had signed the same. Upon the back of each was a blank form for a transfer thereof by the terms of which the transferee was appointed attorney with authority to make the necessary transfer upon the books. These certificates were dealt in, in the open market in the city of New York. Plaintiff purchased in said market one of said certificates which was delivered to him with the transfer on the back made out to him by the person to whom it had been issued. Plaintiff presented the certificate to the trustees, with a demand that a transfer be made on the books and a new certificate issued to him, by offering upon receipt thereof to surrender the old certificate. The transfer was refused. *Held*, that an action to compel such transfer was maintainable; that while to give plaintiff the character of transferer for the purposes of recognition by the trust, a transfer on its books was necessary, this was for the benefit and protection of the trust, and as by the agreement and form of the certificate, the quality of transferability was given to it, this imported the right to make the transfer effectual by transfer on the books. Rice v. Rockefeller, 134 N. Y. 174. See, also, Bean v. American Loan & T. Co., 122 N. Y. 622. Where the business specified in the charter of a corporation is a perfectly legitimate business, and the corporation is legally created, the subsequent abuse or perversion of its corporate powers, though it may furnish a reason why the legislature or the courts should amend the charter and annul the corporation, will not destroy the body corporate. It is still a legal entity, and bound to answer the claims of creditors, although the intention of those who participated in its creation was to effect illegal purposes. Where the purposes attempted to be accomplished through a corporation are illegal, contracts and agreements entered into to secure the end must be equally so. But as it is possible that a party may enter into contracts which may give effect to the illegal purpose, in ignorance of the unlawful design, it is necessary for those assailing such agreements to show that the agreements were entered into with knowledge of the illegal object. Clancey v. Onondaga Fine Salt Mfg. Co., 62 Barb. 395. In an action under Federal Anti-Trust Law which forbids combinations in restraint of interstate commerce, and gives a right of action to any person injured by acts in violation of its provisions, a declaration which does not aver that the goods manufactured by plaintiff, and in respect of which he claims to be an action brought by said party to recover money due from a debtor of the trust, the money was paid into court by the debtor. The court found that the contract to combine was made for unlawful purposes, and was illegal; that the trust was then insolvent, and its assets, including the claim against the debtor, insufficient to pay its creditors. It was held farther that, as between the plaintiff and the receiver, the latter was entitled to the fund; that the plaintiff stood in the position of a party to an illegal contract claiming a fund which, if the contract was valid, belonged to the trust combination, and to sustain the action would permit it to escape from the operation of the rule which derives affirmative relief to a party to an illegal contract.[1] With regard to the legal position of the receiver in such a case, the court, in the opinion in the case above cited, said: "The general rule is well established that a receiver takes the title of the corporation or individul whose receiver he is, and that any defense which would have been good against the former may be asserted against the latter. But there is a recognized exception which prevents a receiver of an insolvent individual or corporation, in the interests of creditors, to disaffirm dealings of the debtor in fraud of their rights.[2] Assuming that the trustee could not have recovered of the debtor for the reasons suggested, it would be a very strange application of the doctrine that no right of action can spring from an illegal transaction, which should deny to innocent creditors of the combination, or to the receiver who represents them, the right to have the debt collected and applied in satisfaction of their claim. The just rule of the common law, that courts will not lend their aid to enforce illegal transactions at the instance of a party to the illegality,

injured, are a subject of interstate commerce, or that the acts complained of have anything to do with any contract in restraint of trade, or that the parties are citizens of different States, is demurrable. Bishop v. American Preservers' Co., 51 Fed. Rep. 272.

[1] Pittsburg Carbon Co. v. McMillan, 119 N. Y. 46.

[2] Gillett v. Moody, 3 N. Y. 479; Porter v. Williams, 9 N. Y. 142; Curtis v. Leavitt, 15 N. Y. 9, 108.

would be misapplied if permitted to be used to present the application of the fund in question to the payment of creditors of the combination."[1] In Illinois it has been held that a foreign corporation, although abusing the privilege which it enjoys of doing business in this State, is not to be considered as an outlaw, having no right to sue for the property it owns. The organization of a foreign corporation cannot be attacked collaterally for the supposed violation of the law in regard to trusts.[2]

[1] Pittsburg Carbon Co. v. McMillan, 119 N. Y. 46, 53.

[2] Bishop v. American Preservers' Co., 51 Ill. App. 417. See, also, Catskill Bank v. Gray, 4 Barb. 479. Where the government contracts with a railroad corporation, the lessee of several roads, to carry the mail over its leased line, it is no defense to an action for compensation that the leases were void, as operated by a combination intended to neutralize competition. Southern Pac. Co. v. United States, 28 Ct. Cl. 77. One who requests and accepts services of a tug for towage purposes cannot escape paying the reasonable value of the services rendered, on the ground that the tug owners are members of an association which is illegal under the Act of July 2, 1890, relating to trusts and monopolies. The Charles E. Wiswell, 74 Fed. Rep. 802.

CHAPTER XIII.

ANTI-TRUST LEGISLATION.

§ 183. Introductory.
184. The Federal Anti-Trust Act.
185. Alabama Insurance Act.
186. Arkansas Anti-Trust Act.
187. California Cattle Trust.
188. Delaware Life Insurance Law.
189. Florida Legislation Relating to Trusts and Monopolies.
190. Georgia Anti-Monopoly Act.
191. Illinois Act Prohibiting Pools, Trusts and Combines.
192. Indiana Anti-Trust Act.
193. Iowa Anti-Pool and Trust Law.
194. Kansas Law Prohibiting Trusts.
195. Kentucky Law Prohibiting Pools, Trusts and Conspiracies.
196. Louisiana Law for the Prohibition of Trusts and Combinations in Restraint of Trade.
197. Maine Anti-Trust Law.
198. Michigan Anti-Trust Act.
199. Minnesota Law to Prohibit Pools and Trusts.
200. Mississippi Law Prohibiting Trusts and Combines.
201. Missouri Anti-Trust Act.
202. Montana Statute against Monopolies and Trusts.
§ 203. Nebraska Statute against Trusts and Conspiracies against Trade and Business.
204. New Mexico Law Declaring Trust Combinations Illegal.
205. New York Law to Prevent Monopolies.
206. North Carolina Law for the Prohibition of Trusts.
207. North Dakota Law Declaring Certain Trusts and Combinations Unlawful.
208. Oklahoma Law to Prevent Combinations in Restraint of Trade.
209. South Carolina Prohibition of Trusts and Combinations.
210. South Dakota Anti-Trust Law.
211. Tennessee Law to Prohibit Conspiracies and Trusts.
212. Texas Law for the Suppression of Trusts and the Promotion of True Competition.
213. Utah Law Prohibiting Pools and Trusts.
214. Washington Law Forbidding Trusts and Monopolies.
215. Wisconsin Statute Prohibiting Trusts and Combinations in Restraint of Trade.

§ **183. Introductory.**—Legislation relating to illegal combinations of the nature of the modern "trust" is of recent date. Decisions of the courts and legislative acts in regard to monopolies and the contracts in restraint of trade commenced at an early period. The courts and legislators were impressed with the necessity of such decisions and acts, and what was commenced at a remote period has continued to the present time. But the proportions attained by the comparatively recent trust combinations and the threatening attitude assumed by the more powerful of the great "trusts" has excited the apprehensions of thoughtful men, and moved legislators to some vigorous efforts for the protection of the public interests. Many of the States have adopted some very comprehensive and drastic statutes for the regulation or suppression of such combinations. Legislation of this character is not equally important to all of the States. Those States in which the great centers of commercial operations are located or are in a degree under the influence of such cities, have recognized the necessity of vigorous and positive anti-trust legislation, and where the legislatures have not been subject to the control of these combinations or of some great corporation statutes of this character have been enacted. In some of the States laws have been passed that effectually suppress all combinations, the object of which is to create a monopoly, or to increase or to maintain prices, by the suppression of competition, while in others anti-trust legislation has been of the nature of a farce. The design has been to satisfy the popular demand without at all interfering with the operations of the "trust." But the indications are that the time is drawing nigh when the popular indignation against such combinations will find expression in language which mercenary and venal legislators will not deem it prudent to disregard. The following sections contain the Federal Anti-Trust Act of 1890, and the statutes of all the States that have enacted laws on this subject. These statutes are all of comparatively recent date, and a number are as late as the sessions of 1897. In some of the States, where there has been no anti-trust legislation, the rapacity of the combination has been held in check, and the public interests have been protected in a good degree by the decisions of the courts. The judiciary has stood firmly against the machinations, which have proved effective with legislators.

§ 184. **The Federal Anti-Trust Act.**—This act was entitled: "An act to protect trade and commerce against unlawful restraints and monopolies." It was approved July 2d, 1890. The question of the application of this law to railroad combinations was argued before the Supreme Court of the United States in December, 1896, on appeal from the Circuit Court of Appeals for the Eighth Circuit, and in March, 1897, an able and elaborate opinion in the case was delivered by Mr. Justice Peckham, sustaining its constitutionality. The act is as follows: Be it enacted by the Senate and House of Representatives of the United States of America in Congress assembled: § 1. Every contract, combination in the form of trust or otherwise, or conspiracy, in restraint of trade or commerce among the several States or with foreign nations, is hereby declared to be illegal. Every person who shall make any such contract or engage in any such combination or conspiracy shall be deemed guilty of a misdemeanor, and, on conviction thereof, shall be punished by fine not exceeding five thousand dollars, or by imprisonment not exceeding one year, or by both said punishments, in the discretion of the court. § 2. Every person who shall monopolize or attempt to monopolize, or combine or conspire with any other person or persons to monopolize any part of the trade or commerce among the several States or with foreign nations, shall be deemed guilty of a misdemeanor, and, on conviction thereof, shall be punished by fine not exceeding five thousand dollars, or by imprisonment not exceeding one year, or by both said punishments, in the discretion of the court. § 3. Every contract, combination in form of trust or otherwise, or conspiracy, in restraint of trade or commerce, in any territory of the United States or of the District of Columbia, or in restraint of trade or commerce between any such territory and another, or between any such territory or territories, and any State or States or the District of Columbia or with foreign nations, or between the District of Columbia and any State or States or foreign nations, is hereby declared illegal. Every person who shall make any such contract or engage in any such combination or conspiracy shall be deemed guilty of a misdemeanor, and, on conviction thereof, shall be punished by fine not exceeding five thousand dollars, or by imprisonment not exceeding one year, or by both said punishments, in the discretion of the court. § 4. The several circuit courts of the United States are hereby invested with jurisdiction to prevent and restrain violations of this act; and it shall be the duty of the several district attorneys of the United States, in their respective districts, under the direction of the attorney-general, to institute proceedings in equity to prevent and restrain such violations. Such proceedings may be by way of petition setting forth the case, and praying that such violation shall be enjoined or otherwise prohibited.' When the parties complained of shall have been duly notified of such petition the court shall proceed, as soon as may be, to the hearing and determination of the case; and pending such petition and before final decree the court may at any time make such temporary restraining order or prohibition as shall be deemed just in the premises. § 5. Whenever it shall appear to the court, before which any proceeding under section four of this act may be pending, that the ends of justice require that other parties should be brought before the court, the court may cause them to be summoned, whether they reside in the district in which the court is held or not; and subpœnas to that end may be served in any district by the marshal thereof. § 6. Any property owned under any contract or by any combination, or pursuant to any conspiracy (and being the subject thereof mentioned in section one of this act, and being in the course of transportation from one State to another, or to a foreign country, shall be forfeited to the United States, and may be seized and condemned by like proceedings as those provided by law for the forfeiture, seizure and condemnation of property imported into the United States contrary to law. § 7. Any person who shall be injured in his business or property by any other person or corporation by reason of anything forbidden or declared to be unlawful by this act, may sue therefor in any circuit court of the United States in the district in which the defendant resides or is found, without respect to the amount in controversy, and shall recover three-fold the damages by him sustained, and the cost of suit, including a reasonable attorney's fee. § 8. That the word "person" or "persons," wherever used in this act, be deemed to include corporations and associations existing under or authorized by the laws of either the United States, the laws of any of the territories, the laws of any State or the laws of any foreign country.[1]

§ 185. **Alabama Insurance Act.**—The anti-trust legislation of Alabama appears to have been limited to an act relating to illegal combinations of insurance companies for the purpose of establishing and maintaining rates of insurance. This act was approved February 18th, 1897, and is, as follows: An act to more effectively protect the people against combinations, conspiracies and agreements between insurers, whereby rates of insurance are raised or fixed. Whereas existing laws have proved inadequate to protect the people against combinations, conspiracies and agreements between insurers, whereby rate of insurance are raised or fixed by such practices, therefore, in order to suppress such combinations, conspiracies and agreements to the

[1] See, also, United States v. Trans-Missouri Freight Association, 166 U. S. 290; United States v. Jellico Mountain Coal Co., 46 Fed. Rep. 432; United States v. Greenhut, 50 Fed. Rep. 462; *In re* Greene, 52 Fed. Rep. 104; United States v. Trans-Missouri Freight Association, 53 Fed. Rep. 440; United States v. Workingmen's Amalgamated Council, 54 Fed. Rep. 994; Waterhouse v. Comer, 55 Fed. Rep. 149; United States v. E. C. Knight Co., 156 U. S. 1; The Charles E. Wiswell, 74 Fed. 802; Columbia Wire Co. v. Freeman Wire Co., 71 Fed. Rep. 302; Prescott & A. C. R. R. v. Atchison, T. & S. F. Ry., 73 Fed. Rep. 438.

end that competition in business shall alone make such rates: § 1. Be it enacted by the General Assembly of Alabama, that every contract or policy of insurance made or issued after the passage of this act shall be construed to mean that in the event of loss or damage thereunder, the assured or beneficiary thereunder may, in addition to the actual loss or damage suffered, recover twenty-five per cent. of the amount of such actual loss, any provision or stipulation in such contract or policy to the contrary notwithstanding: provided, at the time of the making of such contract or policy of insurance, or subsequently before the time of trial the insurer belonged to, or was a member of, or in any way connected with, any tariff association or such like thing by whatever name called or who had made any agreement or had any understanding with any other person, corporation or association engaged in the business of insurance, as agent or otherwise, about any particular rate of premium, which should be charged or fixed for any kind or class of insurance risk; and, provided, further, no stipulation or agreement in such contract or policy of insurance to arbitrate loss or damage, nor to give notice or make proofs of loss or damage, shall in any such case be binding on the assured or beneficiary, but right of action accrues immediately upon loss or damage. § 2. Be it further enacted that if it is shown to the reasonable satisfaction of the jury by a preponderance of the weight of the testimony that such insurer at the time of the making of such agreement or policy of insurance, or, subsequently, before the time of trial belonged to, or was a member of, or in any way connected with, any tariff association or such like thing by whatever name called, either in or out of this State, or had made any agreement, or had any understanding, either in or out of this State, with any other person, corporation or association engaged in the business of insurance, as agent or otherwise, about any particular rate of premium which should be charged or fixed for any risk of insurance on any person or property or on any class of insurance risk, they must, if they find for the assured or beneficiary, in addition to his actual damages, assess and add twenty-five per cent. of the amount of such actual loss and judgment shall be rendered accordingly. § 3. Be it further enacted that this act shall be liberally construed to accomplish its object.

§ **186. Arkansas Anti-Trust Act.**—An act of the legislature of the State of Arkansas, entitled "An act to prevent combinations of trusts and corporations in the State of Arkansas," was approved March 16th, 1897. It is, as follows: Be it enacted by the General Assembly of the State of Arkansas: § 1. That from and after the passage of this act all arrangements, contracts, agreements, trusts or combinations, between persons or corporations, made with a view to lessen, or which tend to lessen, full and free competition in the importation or sale of articles imported into this State, or in the manufacture or sale of articles of domestic growth or of domestic raw material, and all arrangements, contracts, agreements, trusts or combinations, between persons or corporations, designed, or which tend to advance, reduce or control the price, or the cost to the producer, or to the consumer of any such article or product, are hereby declared to be against public policy, unlawful and void. § 2. Be it further enacted that any corporation chartered under the laws of this State, which shall violate the provisions of this act, shall thereby forfeit its charter and franchise, and its corporate existence shall thereupon cease and determine. Every foreign corporation which shall violate the provisions of this act, is hereby denied the right to do so, and is prohibited from doing business in this State. It is hereby made the duty of the attorney-general of this State to enforce this provision by due process of law. § 3. Be it further enacted that any violation of this act shall be deemed, and is hereby declared, destructive of full and free competition and a conspiracy against trade, and any person or persons who may engage in any such conspiracy, or who shall as principal, manager, director or agent, or in any other capacity, knowingly carry out any of the stipulations, purposes, prices, rates or orders, made in furtherance of such conspiracy, shall, on conviction, be punished by any fine not less than five hundred dollars, nor more than two thousand dollars, or by imprisonment in the penitentiary not less than one, nor more than ten years, or, in the judgment of the court, by either such fine or punishment. § 4. Be it further enacted that the provisions of this act shall not apply to agricultural products or to live stock while in the possession of the producer or raiser. § 5. Be it further enacted that any person or persons, or corporation, that may be injured or damaged by any such arrangements, contracts, agreements, trusts or combinations, described in section one of this act, may sue for and recover in any court of competent jurisdiction in this State, of any person or persons, or corporations, operating such trusts or combinations, the full consideration or sum paid him or them for any goods, wares, merchandise or article of sale of which is controlled by such combination or trust. § 6. Be it further enacted that it shall be the duty of the judges of the circuit courts of this State to specially instruct the juries as to the provisions of this act. § 7. Be it further enacted that all laws and parts of laws in conflict with the provisions of this act be and the same are hereby repealed.

§ **187. California Cattle Trust.**—The anti-trust legislation of California, at the present writing, is limited to "An act to prevent combinations to obstruct the sale of live stock in the State of California." This act was approved February 27th, 1893, and is, as follows: "The people of the State of California, represented in Senate and Assembly, do enact, as follows: § 1. It shall be unlawful for any two or more persons, or corporations, to combine or agree together to do any act which will, in any respect, prevent any person from buying live stock at any place in this State from any person having the same for sale, either for himself or as the representative or agent of the owner of the same. § 2. It shall be unlawful for any corporation, organized under the laws of this State, or any board of directors or trustees, or stockholders or agents, or officers of any corporation, to have, pass or enforce any rule, by law or regulation, whereby any officer, stockholder, member, shareholder, agent, servant thereof, or any other person in any way interested in or connected with such corporation, shall in any respect be prohibited, prevented or enjoined from buying live stock from any other person having such live stock for sale, either as owner thereof or as the agent, representative or assistant of such owner, in any market in this State where live stock is brought to be sold. § 3. Every rule, regulation or by-law of any corporation doing business in this State, which has for its purpose, or which, directly or indirectly, tends to prevent its members or stockholders from freely purchasing live stock from any person, lawfully having the same for sale, upon any live stock market of this State, are hereby declared to be contrary to the public policy of this State, and unlawful and void; and any person or persons who shall attempt, directly or indirectly, to enforce any such rule, regulation or by-law, shall be deemed guilty of a misdemeanor, and, in addition to the penalties prescribed by this act, shall be personally liable for all damages which may arise from the enforcement of such rule, regulation or by-law, to any person damaged thereby. § 4. No trusts, combinations or conspiracies shall be organized or exist in this State, to prevent any person or persons, or corporations, from selling live stock on commission, for such an amount of commission as any person engaged in the business may see fit to charge; and all rules, regulations, by-laws or agreements, of any corporation, association, society or combination of persons, whereby any such corporation, association, society or combination of individuals are required to charge not less than a given sum for commission, or whereby any person or commission merchant is, in any respect, restrained from charging less than a certain fixed sum for his services as such commission merchant in the sale of live stock, are hereby declared to be contrary to the public policy of this State and unlawful. And any person who shall enter into any such trust, combination or conspiracy, or who shall enforce or aid, abet, assist or encourage the enforcement of any such rule, regulation, by-law or agreement, shall be liable to the penalties prescribed by this act, and, also, shall be personally liable to any person, individual, society or corporation who may be injured in his property or business thereby to the full extent of the injury resulting therefrom. § 5. Whoever shall, directly or indirectly, be a party to any combination, conspiracy or association, which attempts, directly or indirectly, to prevent any other person from freely selling live stock at any market in this State, for such persons as see fit to engage his services, or shall endeavor to compel, directly or indirectly, any person to charge not less than a fixed minimum sum for services in the sale of live stock, or shall, in any way, hinder or prevent another from lawfully selling live stock for another, for such rate of commission as may be agreed upon by the owner of the live stock and the commission merchant, shall be deemed guilty of a misdemeanor, and suffer the penalties prescribed by this act, and shall be personally liable to any one aggrieved thereby for the full amount of any damage sustained by such person. § 6. Any one who shall violate the provisions of this act shall be punished by a fine in any sum not less than five hundred dollars and not more than five thousand dollars, or by imprisonment in the county jail not exceeding one year, or by either or both, in the discretion of the court, and shall be liable, in a civil action, to any person aggrieved, in such damages as he or she may have sustained by the violation of this act. § 7. This act shall take effect and be in force from and after its passage.

§ **188. Delaware Life Insurance Law.**—The anti-monopoly legislation of the State of Delaware appears to be limited to a statute relating to the operations of life insurance companies in that State. It is entitled: "An act to prevent any life insurance company or agents thereof, doing business in Delaware, from making or permitting any distinction or discrimination in favor of individuals between insurance of the same class and equal expectations of life in the amount or payment of premiums or rates charged for policies of life or endowment insurance, and providing a penalty for violation thereof." It was passed at Dover, February 15th, 1891, and is, as follows: § 1. That no life insurance company, doing business in this State, shall make or permit any distinction or discrimination in favor of individuals between insurance of the same class and equal expectations of life in the amount or payment of premiums or rates charged for policies of life or endowment insurance, or in the dividends or other benefits payable thereon, or in any other of the terms and conditions of the contracts it makes; nor shall any such company, or agent thereof, make any contract of insurance or agreement as to such contract other than as plainly expressed in the policy issued thereon; nor shall any such company, or agent, pay or allow, or offer to pay or allow, as inducements to insurance, any rebate of premium payable on the policy, or any special favor or advantage in the dividends or other benefits to accrue thereon, or any valuable consideration or inducements whatever not specified in the policy contract of insurance. § 2. Any life insurance company, its agent or agents, violating section one of this act, shall be guilty of a misdemeanor, and upon conviction thereof the offender or offenders shall be sentenced to pay a fine of five hundred dollars on each and every violation, where the amount of insurance is twenty-five thousand dollars or less, and for every additional twenty-five thousand dollars insurance or less there shall be an additional penalty of five hundred dollars.

§ 189. **Florida Legislation Relating to Trusts and Monopolies for the Control of Trade in Cattle.**—The anti-trust statute of Florida, is entitled, "An act to prohibit arrangements, contracts, agreements, trusts or combinations and certain other acts or things intended, or tending to prevent, hinder or obstruct the lawful sale of Florida fed beef or other beef, or fresh meat or cattle, or other edible animal in this State, or tending to monopolize or control the sale or price thereof." This act was approved June 11th, 1897, and is, as follows: Be it enacted by the legislature of the State of Florida: § 1. That every arrangement, contract, agreement, trust or combination, between persons or corporations, or between any person and any corporation, made with a view to, or tending to prevent, hinder or obstruct the lawful sale in this State, or any place therein, of beef or other fresh meat of cattle or any other edible animal raised, fattened or fed, in the State of Florida, or any other beef or fresh meat, or with a view to or tending to prevent, hinder or obstruct the lawful sale of any cattle or other edible animal in this State, or any place therein, or which shall tend to monopolize or control the sale or price of beef or other fresh meat in this State, of any place therein, is hereby declared to be against public policy. § 2. Any corporation chartered under the laws of this State, which shall violate any of the provisions of this act, shall thereby forfeit its charter and franchises, and its corporate existence shall thereupon cease and determine. Every foreign corporation which shall violate any of the provisions of this act is hereby denied the right to do, and is prohibited from doing, business in this State. It is hereby made the duty of the attorney-general of this State to enforce this provision by due process of law. § 3. Any violation of any provision of this act shall be deemed and is hereby declared to be destructive of full and free competition and a conspiracy against trade, and any person or persons who may engage in such conspiracy, or who shall, as principal, manager, director or agent, or in any other capacity, knowingly carry out any of the stipulations, purposes, prices, rates or orders made in furtherance of such conspiracy shall, on conviction, be punished by fine of not more than five thousand dollars, or by imprisonment for not more than one year, or by both such fine and imprisonment, in the discretion of the court. § 4. The circuit courts of this State are hereby given jurisdiction in chancery, and it is hereby made their duty to restrain or enjoin any violation of this act in their respective circuits, and to restrain or enjoin any raising or lowering of the price or prices of beef or other fresh meat in any place or places in such several circuits, with intent to or tending to prevent, hinder or obstruct the sale of beef or other fresh meat of cattle or any other edible animal raised, fattened or fed in the State of Florida, or any other beef or fresh meat, or with intent to or tending to prevent, hinder or obstruct the lawful sale of any cattle or other edible animal in any such place or places. It is hereby made the duty of the State's attorneys to institute and prosecute all proper suits in their respective circuits in the name of the State to enforce this section. Any citizen of this State also may institute and prosecute suit in his own name to enforce this section. In case decree shall be rendered in the circuit court in favor of the complainant, whether the State or an individual, the court may decree that the defendant or defendants pay a reasonable fee in the cause for the State's attorney or complainant's solicitor therein. Nothing herein contained shall operate or be construed to deprive any person of any right to any damages, or of any remedy to recover damages which such person would have without this act, in order about and or from matter mentioned or included in this act. § 5. No person shall be excused from attending and testifying or from producing books, papers, contracts, agreements and documents on subpœna for the State, or as witnesses for the State, or on cross-examination for the State in any prosecution, suit or proceeding, criminal or civil, under, authorized by or based upon this act, or growing out of any violation thereof, when such prosecution, suit or proceeding is in the name of the State, and prosecuted or carried on by the attorney-general or State's attorney, on the ground or for the reason that the testimony or evidence, documentary or otherwise required of him, may tend to criminate him or subject him to a penalty or forfeiture. But no such person shall be prosecuted or subjected to any penalty or forfeiture for, or on account of any transaction, matter or thing, concerning which he may so testify or produce evidence: Provided, that no person so testifying shall be exempt from prosecution and punishment for perjury committed in so testifying.

§ 190. Georgia Anti-Monopoly Act.—An act designed to prevent the creation of monopolies in any branch of trade, whether by individuals, companies or combinations of any sort or kind, passed by the legislature of Georgia, was approved December 23, 1896, and is as follows: An act to declare unlawful and void all arrangements, contracts, agreements, trusts, or combinations made with a view to lessen, or which tend to lessen, free competition in the importation or sale of articles imported into this State, or in the manufacture or sale of articles of domestic growth, or of domestic raw material; to declare unlawful and void all arrangements, contracts, agreements, trusts or combinations between persons or corporations designed, or which tend to advance, reduce or control the price of such product or article to producer or consumer of any such product or article; to provide for forfeiture of the charter and franchise of any corporation organized under the laws of this State, violating any of the provisions of this act; to prohibit every foreign corporation, violating any of the provisions of this act, from doing business in this State; to require the attorney-general of this State to institute legal proceedings against any such corporations violating any of the provisions of this act, and to enforce the penalties prescribed; to prescribe penalties for any violations of this act; to authorize any person or corporation, damaged by any such trust, agreement or combination, to sue for the recovery of such damage, and for other purposes. § 1. Be it enacted by the General Assembly of Georgia, and it is hereby enacted by the authority of the same, that from and after the passage of this act, all arrangements, contracts, agreements, trusts or combinations between persons or corporations made with a view to lessen, or which tend to lessen, full and free competition in the importation or sale of articles imported into this State, or in the manufacture or sale of articles of domestic growth, or of domestic raw material, and all arrangements, contracts, agreements, trusts or combinations between persons or corporations designed, or which tend to advance, reduce or control the price or the cost to the producer or to the consumer of any such product or article, are hereby declared to be against public policy, unlawful and void. § 2. Be it further enacted by the authority aforesaid, that any corporation, chartered under the laws of this State, which shall violate any of the provisions of this act, shall thereby forfeit its charter and its franchise, and its corporate existence shall thereupon cease and determine. Every foreign corporation which shall violate any of the provisions of this act is hereby denied the right to do, and is prohibited from doing, business in this State. It is hereby made the duty of the attorney-general of the State to enforce this provision by due process of law. § 3. Be it further enacted by the authority aforesaid, that any violation of the provision of this act shall be deemed, and is hereby declared to be, destructive of full and free competition, and a conspiracy against trade, and any person or persons who may engage in any such conspiracy, or who shall, as principal, manager, director or agent, or in any other capacity, knowingly carry out any of the stipulations, purposes, prices, rates or orders made in furtherance of such conspiracy, shall, on conviction, be punished by a fine of not less than one hundred dollars nor more than five thousand dollars, and by imprisonment in the penitentiary not less than one year nor more than ten years; or, in the judgment of the court, by either such fine or such imprisonment. § 4. Be it further enacted by the authority aforesaid, that the provisions of this act shall not apply to agricultural products or live stock while in the possession of the producer or raiser. § 5. Be it further enacted by the authority aforesaid, that any person or persons, or corporations that may be injured or damaged by any such arrangement, contract, agreement, trust or combination, described in section one of this act, may sue for and recover, in any court of competent jurisdiction in this State, of any person, persons or corporation operating such trust or combination, the full consideration or sum paid by him or them for any goods, wares, merchandise or articles, the sale of which is controlled by such combination or trust. § 6. Be it further enacted by the authority aforesaid, that it shall be the duty of the judges of the superior courts of this State specially to instruct the grand juries as to the provisions of this act. § 7. Be it further enacted by the authority aforesaid, that all laws and parts of laws in conflict with the provisions of this act be, and the same are hereby repealed.

§ **191. Illinois Act Prohibiting Pools, Trusts and Combines.**—The original act relating to this subject was approved June 11, 1891. This act was amended, and the amendment was approved June 10, 1897. The act as amended is as follows: An act to provide for the punishment of persons, co-partnerships or corporations forming pools, trusts and combines, and mode of procedure and rules of evidence in such cases. § 1. Be it enacted by the people of the State of Illinois, represented in the General Assembly: If any corporation organized under the laws of this or any other State or country, for transacting or conducting any kind of business in this State, or any partnership or individual or other association of persons whosoever, shall create, enter into, become a member of, or a party to, any pool, trust, agreement, combination, confederation or understanding with any other corporations, partnership, individual, or any other person or association of persons, to regulate or fix the price of any article of merchandise or commodity, or shall enter into, become a member of, or party to, any pool, agreement, contract, combination or confederation to fix or limit the amount or quantity of any article, commodity or merchandise to be manufactured, mined, produced or sold in this State, such corporation, partnership or individual or other association of persons, shall be deemed and adjudged guilty of a conspiracy to defraud, and be subject to indictment and punishment as provided in this act: Provided, however, that in the mining, manufacture or production of articles of merchandise, the cost of which is mainly made up of wages, it shall not be unlawful for persons, firms or corporations doing business in this State, to enter into joint arrangements of any sort, the principal object or effect of which is to maintain or increase wages. § 2. It shall not be lawful for any corpora tion to issue or to own trust certificates, or for any corporation, agent, officer or employes, or the directors or stockholders of any corporation, to enter into any combination, contract or agreement with any person or persons, corporation or corporations, or with any stockholder or director thereof, the purpose and effect of which combination, contract or agreement shall be to place the management or control of such combination or combinations, or the manufactured product thereof, in the hands of any trustee or trustees, with the intent to limit or fix the price or lessen the production and sale of any article of commerce, use or consumption, or to prevent, restrict or diminish the manufacture or output of any such article. § 3. If a corporation or a company, firm or association shall be found guilty of a violation of this act, it shall be punished by a fine in any sum not less than five hundred dollars ($500) nor more than two thousand dollars ($2,000) for the first offense, and for the second offense not less than two thousand dollars ($2,000), nor more than five thousand dollars ($5,000), and for the third offense not less than five thousand dollars ($5,000) nor more than ten thousand dollars ($10,000), and for every subsequent offense and conviction thereof, shall be liable to a fine of fifteen thousand dollars ($15,000): Provided, that in all cases under this act, either party shall have the right of trial by jury. § 4. Any president, manager, director or other officer or agent or receiver of any corporation, company, firm or association, or any member of any company, firm or association, or any individual found guilty of a violation of the first section of this act, may be punished by a fine of not less than two hundred dollars ($200), nor to exceed one thousand dollars ($1,000), or be punished by confinement in the county jail not to exceed one year, or both, in the discretion of the court before which such conviction may be had. § 5. Any contract or agreement in violation of any provisions of the preceding sections of this act shall be absolutely void. § 6. Any purchaser of any article or commodity from any individual, company or corporation transacting business contrary to any provision of the preceding sections of this act, shall not be liable for the price or payment of such article or commodity, and may plead this act as a defense to any suit for such price or payment. § 7. The fines hereinbefore provided for may be recovered in an action of debt, in the name of the people of the State of Illinois. If, upon the trial of any cause instituted under this act to recover the penalties, as provided for in section three, the jury shall find for the people, and that the defendant has been before convicted of a violation of the provisions of this act, they shall return such finding with their verdict, stating the number of times they find defendant so convicted, and shall assess and return with their verdict the amount of the fine to be imposed upon the defendant in accordance with said section three: Provided, that in all cases under the provisions of this act, a preponderance of evidence in favor of the people shall be sufficient to authorize a verdict and judgment for the people. § 8. It shall be the duty of the prosecuting attorneys in their respective jurisdictions, and the attorney-general, to enforce the foregoing provisions of this act, and any prosecuting attorney of any county securing a conviction under the provisions of this act shall be entitled to such fee or salary as by law he is allowed for such prosecution. When there is a conviction under this act the informer shall be entitled to one-fifth of the fine recovered, which shall be paid to him when the same is collected. All fines recovered under the provisions of this act shall be paid into the county treasury of the county in which the suit is tried, by the person collecting the same in the manner now provided by law, to be used for county purposes.

§ **192. Indiana Anti-Trust Act.**—The anti-trust statute of Indiana is entitled, "An act to declare unlawful and void all arrangements, contracts, agreements, trusts or combinations made with a view to lessen, or which tend to lessen, free competition in the importation or sale of articles imported into this State, or in the manufacture or sale of articles of domestic growth or of domestic raw material; to declare unlawful and void all arrangements, contracts, agreements, trusts or combinations, between persons and corporations, designed or which tend to advance, reduce or control the price of such product or article to producer or consumer of any such product or article; to provide for the forfeiture of the charter and franchise of any corporation, organized under the laws of this State, violating any of the provisions of this act, from doing business in this State; to require the attorney-general of this State to institute legal proceedings against any such corporation violating the provisions of this act, and to enforce the penalties prescribed; to prescribe penalties for any violation of this act: to authorize any person or corporation damaged by any such trust, agreement or combination to sue for the recovery of such damage and for other purposes." The statute was approved March 5th, 1897, and is, as follows: § 1. Be it enacted by the General Assembly of the State of Indiana, and it is hereby enacted by the authority of the same, that from and after the passage of this act all arrangements, contracts, agreements, trusts or combinations, between persons or corporations, who control the output of any article of merchandise, made with a view to lessen, or which tend to lessen, full and free competition in the importation or sale of articles imported into this State, and all arrangements, contracts, agreements, trusts or combinations, between persons or corporations, who control the output of said article of merchandise, designed, or which tend to advance, reduce or control the price or the cost to the producer or to the consumer of any such product or article, are hereby declared to be against public policy, unlawful and void. § 2. That any corporation, chartered under the laws of this State, which shall violate any of the provisions of this act, shall thereby forfeit its charter and its franchise, and its corporate existence shall thereupon cease and determine. Every foreign corporation which shall violate any of the provisions of this act is hereby denied the right to do, and is prohibited from doing business in this State. It is hereby made the duty of the attorney-general of the State to enforce this provision by due process of law. § 3. That any violation of the provisions of this act shall be deemed and is hereby declared to be destructive of full and free competition and a conspiracy against trade, and any person or persons who may engage in any such conspiracy, or who shall, as principal, manager, director or agent, or in any other capacity, knowingly carry out any of the stipulations, purposes, prices, rates or orders made in furtherance of such conspiracy, shall, on conviction, be punished by a fine of not less than one hundred dollars nor more than five thousand dollars, and by imprisonment in the penitentiary not less than one year nor more than ten years, or, in the judgment of the court, by either such fine or such imprisonment. § 4. The persons designed by this act to be effected hereby are those who own, control or manufacture the output of any particular article of merchandise mentioned herein: Provided, however, that the provisions of this act shall not apply to agricultural products or live stock while in the possession of the producer or raiser. § 5. That any person or persons, or corporation, that may be injured or damaged by any such arrangement, contract, agreement, trust or combination, described in section one of this act, may sue for and recover in any court of competent jurisdiction, in this State, of any person, persons, or corporation, operating such trust or combination, the full consideration or sum paid by him or them for any goods, wares, merchandise or articles, the sale of which is controlled by such combination or trust. § 6. That it shall be the duty of the judges of the circuit court of this State to specially instruct the grand juries as to the provisions of this act. § 7. That all laws and parts of laws in conflict with the provisions of this act be and the same are hereby repealed.

§ **193. Iowa Anti-Pool and Trust Law.**—The statute of Iowa, relating to trusts and monopolies, is entitled, "An act for the punishment of pools, trusts, combinations and conspiracies, and as to evidence in such cases." It was approved May 6th, 1890, and is, as follows: Be it enacted by the General Assembly of the State of Iowa: § 1. If any corporation, organized under the laws of this or any other State or country, for transacting or conducting any kind of business in this State, or any partnership or individual or other association of persons whosoever, shall create, enter into, or become a member of, or a party to, any trust, agreement, combination, confederation or understanding with any other corporation, partnership, individual, or any person or association of persons, to regulate or fix the price of any article of merchandise or commodity, or shall enter into, become a member of, or party to, any pool, agreement, contract, combination or confederation to fix or limit the amount or quantity of any article, commodity or merchandise to be manufactured, raised, produced or sold in this State, shall be deemed and adjudged guilty of a conspiracy to defraud, and be subject to indictment and punishment as provided in this act. § 2. It shall not be lawful for any corporation to issue or to own trust certificates, or for any corporation, agent, officer or employes, or the directors or stockholders of any corporation, to enter into any combination, contract or agreement with any person or persons, corporation or corporations, or with any stockholder or director thereof, the purpose and effect of which combination, contract or agreement shall be to place the management or control of such combination or combinations, or the manufactured product thereof, in the hands of any trustee or trustees, with the intent to limit or fix the price or lessen the production and sale of any article of commerce, use or consumption, or to prevent, restrict or diminish the manufacture or output of any such article. § 3. If a corporation or a company, firm or association shall be found guilty of a violation of this act, it shall be punished by a fine of not less than one per cent. of the capital stock of such corporation or amount invested in such company, firm or association, and not to exceed twenty per cent. of such capital stock or amount invested. Any president, manager, director or other officer, or agent or receiver, of any corporation, company, firm or association, or any member of any company, firm or association, or any individual found guilty of a violation of the first section of this act, shall be punished by a fine of not less than five hundred dollars, nor to exceed five thousand dollars, and, in addition thereto, may be imprisoned in the county jail not to exceed one year. § 4. Any contract or agreement in violation of any provisions of the preceding sections of this act shall be absolutely void. § 5. Any purchaser of any article or commodity from any individual, company or corporation transacting business contrary to any provision of the preceding sections of this act shall not be liable for the price or payment of such article or commodity, and may plead this act as a defense to any suit for such price or payment. § 6. Any corporation, created or organized by or under the laws of this State, which shall violate any provision of the preceding sections of this act, shall thereby forfeit its corporate right and franchises, and its corporate existence shall thereupon cease and determine, as provided in this section, and it shall be the duty of the secretary of state, after the passage of this act, to address to the president, secretary or treasurer of each incorporated company doing business in this State a letter of inquiry as to whether the said corporation has merged all or any part of its business or interest in or with any trust, combination or association of persons or stockholders, as named in the preceding provisions of this act, and to require an answer, under oath, of the president, secretary, treasurer or any director of said company; a form of affidavit prescribed by the secretary of state shall be enclosed in said letter of inquiry, and, on refusal to make oath in answer to said inquiry, the secretary of state shall immediately cause a certified statement of the facts to be filed in the office of the attorney-general of the State, who shall proceed or direct such proceedings, by any county attorney in the State, to commence an action in the district court of any county in the State of competent jurisdiction. When said proceedings are instituted they shall be conducted as ordinary law actions, triable by a court or jury on the final decision of the same,—should the defendant be found guilty of a violation of any of the provisions of this act, said court shall render a judgment and order a revocation of the charter of said company as a penalty for the violation or violations of which the said company shall be found guilty, and the secretary of state shall make publication of such revocation in four newspapers in general circulation in the four largest cities in the State. § 7. It shall be the duty of the secretary of state upon satisfactory evidence that any company or association of persons, duly incorporated and operating under the laws of this State, have entered into any trust, combination or association, as provided in the preceding provisions of this act, to give notice to such corporation that unless they withdraw from and sever all business connection with said trust, combination or association, their charter will be revoked at the expiration of thirty days from date of such notice. § 8. It shall be the duty of the prosecuting attorneys in their respective jurisdictions, and the attorney-general, to enforce the foregoing provisions of this act, and any prosecuting attorney, or the attorney-general, securing a conviction, under the provisions of this act, shall be entitled, in addition to such fee or salary as by law he is allowed for such prosecution, to one-fifth of the fine recovered. When the attorney-general and prosecuting attorney act in conjunction in the prosecution of any case, under the provisions of this act, they shall be entitled to one-fourth of the fine recovered, which they shall divide equally between them, where there is no agreement to the contrary, and it shall be the duty of the grand jury to inquire into and ascertain if there exist any pools, trusts, combinations within their respective counties. § 9. Chapter 84, Acts of the 22d General Assembly and all acts or parts of acts in conflict with the provisions of this act are hereby repealed. § 10. Whereas, great injustice is being done to the people of this State by the formation of trusts and trust companies, therefore an emergency exists, and this act shall take effect and be in force from and after its passage and publication, as required by law, in the Iowa State Register and Des Moines Leader, newspapers published in Des Moines, Iowa.

§ **194. Kansas Law Prohibiting Trusts.**—The anti-trust law of Kansas is a statute of 1897. It is entitled "An act defining and prohibiting trusts, providing procedure to enforce the provisions of this act, and providing penalties for violations of the provisions of this act." This act was approved March 8th, 1897. It is, as follows: Be it enacted by the legislature of the State of Kansas: § 1. A trust is a combination of capital, skill or acts, by two or more persons, firms, corporations or associations of persons, or either two or more of them, for either, any or all of the following purposes: *First.* To create or carry out restrictions in trade or commerce, or aids to commerce, or to carry out restrictions in the full and free pursuit of any business authorized or permitted by the laws of this State. *Second.* To increase or reduce the price of merchandise, produce or commodities, or to control the cost or rate of insurance. *Third.* To prevent competition in the manufacture, making, transportation, sale or purchase of merchandise, produce or commodities, or to prevent competition in aids to commerce. *Fourth.* To fix any standard or figure, whereby its price to the public shall be, in any manner controlled or established, any article or commodity of merchandise, produce or commerce intended for sale, use or consumption in this State. *Fifth.* To make or enter into, or execute or carry out, any contract, obligation or agreement of any kind or description by which they shall bind, or have to bind, themselves not to sell, manufacture, dispose of, or transport any article or commodity, or article of trade, use, merchandise, commerce or consumption below a common standard figure or by which they shall agree, in any manner, to keep the price of such article, commodity or transportation at a fixed or graded figure, or by which they shall, in any manner, establish or settle the price of any article or commodity, or transportation, between them or themselves and others, to preclude a free and unrestricted competition among themselves or others in transportation, sale or manufacture of any such article or commodity, or by which they shall agree to pool, combine or unite any interest they may have in connection with the manufacture, sale or transportation of any such article or commodity, that its price may, in any manner, be affected. And any such combinations are hereby declared to be against public policy, unlawful and void. § 2. All persons, companies or corporations, within this State, are hereby denied the right to form or to be in any manner interested, either directly or indirectly, as principal, agent, representative, consignee or otherwise in any trust, as defined in section one of this act. § 3. Any corporation, holding a charter, under the laws of the State of Kansas, which shall violate any of the provisions of this act, shall thereby forfeit its charter and franchise, and its corporate existence shall cease and determine. And any stockholder, director, officer, agent, representative or consignee of any such corporation shall be subject to the penalties herein prescribed. § 4. For a violation of any of the provisions of this act by any corporation, or any of its officers or agents mentioned herein, it shall be the duty of the attorney-general of the State, or county attorney of any county in which said violation may occur, or either of them, upon his own motion, to institute an action in any court in this State having jurisdiction thereof, for the forfeiture of the charter, rights and franchise of such corporation, and the dissolution of its corporate existence. § 5. Every person, company or corporation, within or without this State, their officers, agents, representatives or consignees, violating any of the provisions of this act, within this State, are hereby denied the right, and are hereby prohibited from doing any business within this State, and all persons, companies and corporations, their officers, agents, representatives and consignees, within this State, are hereby denied the right to handle the goods of, or in any manner deal with, directly or indirectly, any such person, company or corporation, their officers, agents, representatives or consignees, and it shall be the duty of the attorney-general, and the county attorney of any county in the State where any violation of this act be committed, or either of them, to enforce the provisions of this section by injunction or other proceeding; and all persons, companies and corporations, their officers, agents, representatives or consignees, violating any of the provisions of this section, either directly or indirectly, or of abetting or aiding, either directly or indirectly, in any violation of any provisions of this section, shall be deemed guilty of a misdemeanor, and shall be fined not less than one hundred dollars nor more than one thousand dollars, and confined in jail not less than thirty days nor more than six months, and shall forfeit not less than one hundred dollats for each and every day such violation may continue, which may be recovered in the name of the State of Kansas in any court of competent jurisdiction. § 6. Each and every person, company or corporation, their officers, agents, representatives or consignees, who, either directly or indirectly, violate any of the provisions of this act shall be deemed guilty of a misdemeanor, and, on conviction thereof, shall be subject to a fine of not less than one hundred dollars nor more than one thousand dollars, and shall be imprisoned not less than thirty days nor more than six months, and, in addition thereto, for each and every day thereafter that such violation shall be committed or continued, forfeit and pay the sum of one hundred dollars, which may be recovered in the name of the State of Kansas, in any county where the offense is committed or where either of the offenders reside, and it shall be the duty of the attorney-general of the State, or the county attorney of any county in the State, in which said violation shall occur, or either of them, to prosecute and enforce the provisions of this act. § 7. Any contract or agreement in violation of any of the provisions of this act shall be absolutely void and not enforceable in any of the courts of this State, and when any civil action shall be commenced in any court of this State, it shall be lawful to plead, in defense thereof, that the plaintiff or any other person interested in the prosecution of the case is at the time or has within one year next preceding the date of the commencement of any such action, been guilty either as principal, agent, representative or consignee, directly or indirectly, of a violation of any of the provisions of this act, or that the cause of action grows out of any business transaction in violation of this act. § 8. That any person, firm, company or corporation that may be damaged by any such agreement, trusts or combinations described in sections one and two of this act, may sue for and recover in any court of competent jurisdiction in this State, of any person, company or corporation, operating such trust or combination, such damages as they have sustained, together with a reasonable attorney fee. § 9. It shall be the duty of the attorney-general of the State, and the county attorneys in their respective counties, to diligently prosecute any and all persons violating any of the provisions of this act, and it shall be the duty of all State and county officials, having notice and knowledge of any violation of the provisions of this act, to notify the county attorneys of their respective counties, and the attorney-general of the State, of the fact of such violation, and to furnish them with the names of any witnesses by whom such violations can be proved; if any such officer or officers shall fail to comply with the provisions of this section he shall, upon conviction, be fined in any sum not less than one hundred dollars nor more than one thousand dollars, and such a conviction shall be a forfeiture of the office held by such person, and the court before whom such conviction is had shall, in addition to the imposition of the fine aforesaid, order and adjudge the forfeiture of his said office. § 10. The several district courts of this State, and the judges thereof, shall have jurisdiction, and it shall be their duty, upon good cause shown and upon written application of the county attorney or the attorney-general, to cause to be issued by the clerk of said court, subpœnas for such witnesses as may be named in the application of a county attorney or the attorney-general, and to cause the same to be served by the sheriff of the county where such subpœna is issued; and such witnesses shall be compelled to appear before such court or judge, at the time and place set forth in the subpœna, and shall be compelled to testify as to any knowledge they may have of the violations of any of the provisions of this act. And any witness who fails or refuses to attend and testify shall be punished as for contempt, as provided by law. Any person subpœnaed and examined shall not be liable to criminal prosecution for any violation of this act about which he may testify. Neither shall the evidence of any such witness be used against him in any criminal proceeding. The evidence of all witnesses so subpœnaed shall be taken down by the reporter of said court, and shall be transcribed and placed in the hands of the county attorney or the attorney-general, and he shall in the proper courts at once prosecute such violator or violators of this act, as the testimony so taken shall disclose. Witnesses subpœnaed, as provided for in this section, shall be compelled to attend from any county in the State. § 11. Nothing in this chapter shall be held or construed to affect any action or prosecution which is now pending, under the provisions of any law now in existence in this State. § 12. This act shall take effect and be in force from and after its publication in the official State paper.

§ 195. Kentucky Law Prohibiting Pools, Trusts and Conspiracies.—The anti-trust and monopoly statute of Kentucky is entitled, "An act to prevent the establishment of pools, trusts and conspiracies, and to provide punishments therefor." It was approved May 20th, 1890, and is, as follows: Be it enacted by the General Assembly of the Commonwealth of Kentucky: § 1. That if any corporation, under the laws of Kentucky, or under the laws of any other State or county, for transacting or conducting any kind of business in this State, or any partnership company, firm or individual, or other association of persons, shall create, establish, organize or enter into, or become a member of, or a party to, or in any way interested in any pool, trust, combine, agreement, confederation or understanding with any other corporation, partnership, individual or person, or association of persons, for the purpose of regulating or controlling or fixing the price of any merchandise, manufactured articles or property of any kind, or shall enter into, become a member of, or party to, or in any way interested in any pool, agreement, contract, understanding, combination or confederation, having for its object the fixing, or in any way limiting the amount or quantity of any article of property, commodity or merchandise to be produced or manufactured, mined, bought or sold, shall be deemed guilty of the crime of conspiracy, and punished therefor, as provided in the subsequent sections of this act. § 2. It shall not be lawful for any corporation to issue or to own, have or sell any trust certificates or stocks, or for any corporation's agent, officer or employe, agent or director, or any corporation to enter into, either verbally or in writing, any combination, contract, agreement or understanding with any person or persons, corporation or corporations, or with any director, agent or officer thereof, the purpose or effect of which combination, contract, agreement or understanding would be to place the management, control or any part of the business of such combination or association, or the manufactured product thereof, in the hands or under the control, in whole or in part, of any trustee or trustees, or agents or any person whatever, with the intent or to have the effect to limit, fix, establish or change the price of the production or sale of any article of property or of commerce, or to prevent, restrict, or in any way diminish the manufacture or output of any such article or property. § 3. If any corporation, company, firm, partnership or person, or association of persons, shall, by court of competent jurisdiction, be found guilty of a violation of any of the provisions of this act, such guilty party shall be punished by a fine of not less than five hundred dollars, and not more than five thousand dollars. Any president, manager, director or other officer or agent, or receiver of any corporation, company, firm, partnership, or any corporation, company, firm, or association, or member of any corporation, firm or association, or any member of any company, firm or other association, or any individual found, by a court of competent jurisdiction, guilty of any violation of this act, shall be punished by a fine of not less than five hundred dollars nor more than five thousand dollars, or may be imprisoned in the county jail not less than six months nor more than twelve months, or may be both so fined and imprisoned in the discretion of the court or jury trying the case. § 4. Any contract or agreement or understanding in violation of the provisions of the preceding sections of this act shall be null and void; and any purchasers of property or article, or of any commodity, from any individual, firm, company or corporation transacting business contrary to the preceding sections of this act, shall not be liable for the price or payment of such article or commodity or property, and may plead and rely on this act as a complete defense to any suit for such price or payment. § 5. If any corporation created or organized by or under the laws of this State shall be indicted and convicted for any violation of any of the provisions of this act, such indictment, trial and conviction in any court of competent jurisdiction shall have the effect to forfeit the charter of such corporation without any further proceedings on the subject of the forfeiture of its charter, but any corporation whose charter is so forfeited shall have the right of appeal, as is provided in other cases, and the filing of the board, as is required by law, shall suspend the judgment of forfeiture until same is passed upon by the court to which the case is appealed. § 6. It shall be the duty of the circuit judges, and other judges of similar jurisdiction in this State, to give the provisions of this act in charge to the grand juries at each term of their courts. § 7. The provisions of the code of practice regulating appeals in other cases shall apply to appeals under this act, and this act shall take effect and be in force from and after its passage.

§ 196. Louisiana Law for the Prohibition of Trusts and Combinations in Restraint of Trade.—The anti-trust law of Louisiana is entitled "An act to prevent trusts or combinations intended to restrain trade or to control the market value of merchandise, produce or commodities, and to provide for penalties and punishment of persons, corporations, firms and associations of persons connected with them, and to promote free competition in the State of Louisiana." This law was passed in 1892, and became operative July 7th of that year. The law is as follows: § 1. Be it enacted by the General Assembly of the State of Louisiana, that after the passage of this act it shall be unlawful for any individual, firm, company, corporation or association to enter into, continue or maintain any combination, agreement or arrangement of any kind, expressed or implied, with any other individual, firm, company, association or corporation for any of the following purposes: First, to create or carry out restrictions in trade. Second, to limit or reduce the production or increase or reduce the price of merchandise, produce or commodities. Third, to prevent competition in manufacture, making, transportation, sale or purchase of merchandise, produce or commodities. Fourth, to fix at any standard or figure, whereby its price shall be in any manner controlled or established, any article of merchandise, produce, commodity or commerce intended for consumption in this State, Fifth, to make or enter into, or execute, or carry out any contract, obligation or agreement of any kind or description, by which they shall bind, or have bound, themselves not to sell, dispose of, or transport any article, or commodity, or article of trade, use, merchandise, commerce or consumption below a common standard figure, or by which they shall agree in any manner to keep the price of such article at a fixed or graduated figure, or by which they shall in any manner establish or settle the price of any article or commodity, or transportation between them or themselves and others to preclude a free and unrestricted competition among themselves, or others, in the sale or transportation of any such article or commodity, or by which they shall agree to pool, combine or unite any interest they may have in connection with the sale or transportation of any such article or commodity that its price might in any manner be affected. § 2. Be it further enacted, etc., that any corporation holding a charter under the laws of the State of Louisiana, which shall be convicted of a violation of the provisions of this act, shall thereby forfeit its rights and franchises, and its corporate existence shall cease and determine, and it shall be the duty of the attorney-general, of his own motion, and without leave or orders of any court or judge, to institute an action in the name of the State of Louisiana for the forfeiture of such rights and franchises and the dissolution of such corporate existence. § 3. Be it further enacted, etc., that every foreign corporation, or any corporation organized under or pursuant to the laws of any State, who shall be convicted of a violation of the provisions of this act, is hereby denied the right and prohibited from doing any business within this State, and it shall be the duty of the attorney-general to enforce this provision by injunction or other proceedings in the name of the State of Louisiana. § 4. Be it further enacted, etc., that any violation of either or all the provisions of this act shall be, and is, hereby declared a conspiracy against trade, and any person who may be or may become engaged in any such conspiracy, or take part therein, or aid or advise in its commission, or who shall, as principal, manager, director or agent, knowingly carry out any of the stipulations, purposes, prices, rates or orders thereunder or in pursuance thereof, shall be punished by fine not less than one hundred dollars nor more than one thousand dollars, and by imprisonment in the penitentiary not less than six months nor more than one year, or by either such fine or imprisonment, in the discretion of the court. It shall be the duty of the district attorneys in their respective jurisdictions, and the attorney-general, to enforce this provision, and any district attorney of any parish securing a conviction under this provision shall be entitled to such fee or salary as by law he is allowed for such persecution. § 5. Be it further enacted, etc., that in any indictment for an offense named in this act, it is sufficient to state the purposes or effects of the trust or combination that the accused was a member of, acted with, or in pursuance of it, without giving its name or description, or how, when or where it was created, provided that no contract or agreement or arrangement which does not include, or which cannot be held to include a stipulation between the parties to share in the profits of any such contract, agreement or arrangement, or which contract, agreement or arrangement does not provide for, or does not contemplate, a profit or pool to be divided between the parties to such contract, agreement or arrangement, shall be held or construed to be in violation of the provision of this act. § 6. Be it further enacted, etc., that in prosecutions under this act it shall not be necessary to prove who constitute all the members belonging to the trust or combination. § 7. Be it further enacted, etc., that any contract or agreement in violation of the provisions of this act shall be absolutely void. § 8. Be it further enacted, etc., that the provisions of this act shall not apply to agricultural products or live stock while in the hands of the producer or raiser, nor be so construed as to affect any combination or confederation of laborers for the purpose of procuring an increase of their wages or redress of grievances. § 9. Be it further enacted, etc., that this act shall take effect from and after its passage, and that all laws and parts of laws conflicting with same are hereby repealed.

§ **197. Maine Anti-Trust Law.**—The anti-trust statute of the State of Maine is entitled "An act to prevent such formation of trusts, combination of business firms, incorporated or unincorporated, companies, or association of persons or stockholders, as may be contrary to public policy." This act was approved March 7, 1889, and is, as follows: Be it enacted by the Senate and House of Representatives in legislature assembled, as follows: § 1. It shall be unlawful for any firm or incorporated company, or any number of firms or incorporated companies, or any unincorporated company, or association of persons or stockholders, organized for the purpose of manufacturing, producing, refining or mining any article or product which enters into general use and consumption by the people, to form or organize any trust, or to enter into any combination of firms, incorporated or unincorporated companies, or association of stockholders, or to delegate to any one or more board or boards of trustees or directors the power to conduct and direct the business of the whole number of firms, corporations, companies or associations which may have or which may propose to form a trust, combination or association inconsistent with the provisions of this section and contrary to public policy. § 2. No certificate of stock, or other evidence of interest, in any trust, combination or association, as named in section one of this act, shall have legal recognition in any court in this State, and any deed to real estate given by any person, firm or corporation, for the purpose of becoming interested in such trust, combination or association, or any mortgage given by the latter to the seller, as well as all certificates growing out of such transaction, shall be void. § 3. Any incorporated company now operating under the laws of this State, and which at the date of the passage of this act may be interested in any trust, combination or association, named in section one of this act, or any firm, incorporated or unincorporated company, or association of persons or stockholders, who shall enter into or become interested in such trust, combination or association, after the passage of this act, shall be deemed guilty of a misdemeanor, and be subject to a fine of not less than five nor more than ten thousand dollars: Provided, that nothing in this section shall be so construed as to apply to such incorporated companies as shall, within ninety days from the date of the passage of this act, withdraw from and sever all connections with such trust, combination or association. § 4. It shall be the duty of the secretary of state, as soon as may be after the passage of this act, to forward to the president, secretary or treasurer, of each incorporated company, organized for the purpose of manufacturing, producing, refining or mining any article or product which enters into general use and consumption by the people, and doing business within this State, a copy of this act, and, also, a letter of inquiry as to whether said corporation has merged all or any part of its business or interests in or with any trust, combination or association of persons, or stockholders, as named in section one of this act, and to require an answer, under oath, of the president, secretary, treasurer or directors of said company; a form of affidavit, together with questions to be answered, shall be prescribed by the secretary of state, and forwarded with said letter, and on neglect or refusal to make answers, under oath, to such questions for the term of ninety days from the date of this act, the secretary of state shall notify the attorney-general, whose duty it shall be forthwith to file an information in the nature of a writ of *quo warranto*, with the Supreme Judicial Court, against said corporation, and the court may, upon hearing and proof of such neglect or refusal, decree the dissolution of said corporation, and its corporate rights and powers shall be terminated.

§ **198. Michigan Anti-Trust Act.**—The anti-trust statute of Michigan is entitled, "An act declaring certain contracts, agreements, understandings and combinations unlawful, and to provide punishments for those who shall enter into the same or do any act in performance thereof." This statute became a law July 1st, 1889, and is, as follows: § 1. The people of the State of Michigan enact that all contracts, agreements, understandings and combinations made, entered into, or knowingly assented to by and between any parties capable of making a contract or agreement, which would be valid at law or in equity, the purpose or object or intent of which shall be to limit, control, or in any manner to restrict or regulate the amount of production or the quantity of any article or commodity to be raised or produced by mining, manufacture, agriculture or any other branch of business or labor, or to enhance, control or regulate the market price thereof, or in any manner to prevent or restrict free competition in the production or sale of any article or commodity, shall be utterly illegal and void, and every such contract, agreement, understanding and combination shall constitute a criminal conspiracy, and every person, who, for himself, personally, or as a member or in the name of a partnership, or as a member, agent or officer of a corporation, or of any association for business purposes of any kind, who shall enter into or knowingly consent to any such void and illegal contract, agreement, understanding or combination, shall be deemed a party to such conspiracy. And all parties so offending shall, on conviction thereof, be punished by a fine of not less than fifty dollars nor more than three hundred dollars, or by imprisonment in the county jail not more than six months, or by both such fine and imprisonment, at the discretion of the court. And the prosecution for offenses under this section may be instituted and the trial had in any county where any of the conspirators became parties to such conspiracy, or in which any one of the conspirators shall reside: Provided, however, that this section shall in no manner invalidate or affect contracts for what is known and recognized at common law and in equity as contracts for the "good will of a trade or business," but all such contracts shall be left to stand upon the same terms and within the same limitations, recognized at common law and in equity. § 2. Every contract, agreement, understanding and combination declared void and illegal by the first section of this act shall be equally void and illegal within this State, whether made and entered into within or without this State. § 3. The carrying into effect, in whole or in part, of any such illegal contract, agreement, understanding or combination, as mentioned in the first section of this act, and every act which shall be done for that purpose by any of the parties, or through their agency or the agency of any one of them, shall constitute a misdemeanor, and, on conviction, the offenders shall be punished by imprisonment in the State prison not more than one year, or in the county jail not more than six months, or by a fine not less than one hundred dollars nor more than five hundred dollars, or by both such fine and imprisonment, in the discretion of the court. § 4. Any corporation, now or hereafter, organized under the laws of this State, which shall enter into any contract, agreement, understanding or combination, declared illegal and criminal by the first section of this act, or shall do any act towards or for the purpose of carrying the same into effect, in whole or in part, and who shall not, within thirty days from the time when this act shall take effect, withdraw its assent thereto and repudiate the same, and file in the office of the secretary of state such refusal and repudiation, under its corporate seal, shall forfeit its charter and all its rights and franchise thereunder. § 5. It shall be the duty of the attorney-general, upon his own relation or upon the relation of any private person, whenever he shall have good reasons to believe that the same can be established by proof, to file an information in the nature of a *quo warranto*, against any corporation offending against any of the provisions of this act; and, thereupon, the same proceedings shall be had, as provided by chapter 298, of Howell's Annotated Statutes, relating to proceedings by information in the nature of *quo warranto*, against corporations offending against any of the provisions of the act, or acts creating, altering or renewing such corporations, and in other cases. § 6. The provisions of this act shall not apply to agricultural products or live stock, while in the hands of the producer or raiser, nor to the services of laborers or artisans, who are formed into societies or organizations for the benefit and protection of their members. § 7. It shall be the duty of the secretary of state to cause this act to be published for four successive weeks in some daily paper in each of the cities of Lansing, Detroit, Grand Rapids and Marquette, commencing within ten days after this act shall take effect, and he shall also within the same time cause to be mailed to each of the corporations, whose articles of association are on file in his office, a printed copy of this act, with a notice calling special attention thereto. Approved July 1st, 1889.

§ 199. Minnesota Law to Prohibit Pools and Trusts.— The anti-monopoly and trust statute of Minnesota is entitled, "An act to prohibit pools and trusts in the State of Minnesota." It was approved April 20th, 1891, and is, as follows: Be it enacted by the legislature of the State of Minnesota: § 1. If any corporation, organized under the laws of this State, or any other State or country, for transacting or conducting any kind of business in this State, or any partnership or individual shall create, enter into, become a member of, or a party to, any pool, trust, agreement, combination or confederation with any other corporation, partnership or individual to regulate or fix the price of oil, lumber, coal, grain, flour, provisions or any other commodity or article whatever, or shall create, enter into, become a member of, or a party to, any pool, agreement, combination or confederation to fix or limit the amount or quantity of any commodity or article to be manufactured, mined, produced or sold in this State, shall be deemed guilty of a conspiracy to defraud, and be subject to indictment. § 2. Any person or corporation found guilty of a violation of this act shall be punished by a fine of not less than one hundred ($100) dollars nor to exceed five thousand ($5,000) dollars. § 3. Upon the trial of an indictment against a corporation or a co-partnership for a violation of the first section of this act, all officers and agents of such corporation or co-partnership shall be competent witnesses against the defendant on trial, and such officers and agents may be compelled to testify against such defendant, and produce all books and papers in his custody or under his control, pertinent to the issue in such trial, and shall not be excused from answering any such questions or from producing any books or papers, because the same might tend to criminate such witness; but nothing to which such witness shall testify and no books or papers produced by him shall in any manner be used against him in any suit, civil or criminal, to which he is a party. § 4. All acts and parts of acts in conflict with this act be and the same are hereby repealed. § 5. This act shall take effect and be in force from and after its passage.

§ 200. Mississippi Law Prohibiting Trusts and Combines.—The original act relating to this subject is a part of the "Annotated Code of the General Statute Laws of the State of Mississippi." This code was adopted by the legislature at its regular session in 1892. An amendment to this act was approved March 11th, 1896. As amended, the statute is, as follows, the sections being the sections of the code: § 4437. A trust and combine is a combination, contract, understanding or agreement, express or implied, between two or more persons, corporations, or firms or associations of persons, or between one or more of either, with one or more of the others. (*a*) In restraint of trade; (*b*) to limit, increase or reduce the price of a commodity; (*c*) to limit, increase or reduce the production or output of a commodity; (*d*) intended to hinder competition in the production, importation, manufacture, transportation, sale or purchase of a commodity; (*e*) to engross or forestall a commodity; (*f*) to issue, own or hold the certificates of stock of any trust or combine; (*g*) to place the control, to any extent, of business, or of the products or earnings thereof, in the power of trustees, by whatever name called; (*h*) by which any other person than themselves, their proper officers, agents and employes shall, or shall have, the power to, dictate or control the management of business; or (*i*) to unite or pool interests in the importation, manufacture, production, transportation or price of a commodity, and is inimical to the public welfare, unlawful and a criminal conspiracy. But this shall not apply to the associations of those engaged in husbandry in their dealings with commodities in the hands of the producer, nor to the societies of artisans, employes and laborers, formed for the benefit and protection of their members. § 4438. Every contract or agreement, to enter into or pursue any trust and combine, and every contract or agreement, made by another with any trust and combine, or with any member of a trust and combine, for any purpose relative to the business of such trust and combine, is void, and cannot be enforced in any court. § 4439. Every corporation which shall enter into, be concerned in or share the profit or loss of any trust and combine shall forfeit its charter and franchise, and, if a foreign corporation, shall forfeit its right to do business in this State. § 4440. The producer and owner of any commodity, whose cost or price is affected by any unlawful trust or combine, may recover the sum of five hundred dollars and all actual damages, and he may maintain his action therefor against one or more of the parties to the trust or combine, their attorneys, officers or agents, and that whether or not all the parties to the trust and combine be known, or whether or not the trust and combine were made or shall exist in this State. This remedy is also extended and granted to any person whose cost or price of service is affected, or who in any other way is injured or damaged by any unlawful trust or combine. In all cases for the recovery of this penalty, evidence that the cost of any commodity, or that the price of any service was intended to be unlawfully affected by any trust or combine, shall be conclusive proof that such trust and combine did affect the cost of such commodity or the price of such service. The above penalty and damages may also be recovered by any affected or injured person from any railroad, express, telegraph, telephone or other transportation company which may be a party to any unlawful trust or combine, or which, because of any unlawful trust or combine, may refuse to transmit any message or transport any commodity from one place in this State to another. § 4441. If any person, corporation, firm or association of persons shall combine with any other person, corporation, firm or association of persons, or if either of them combine with one or more of the other, to prevent, by pooling, any or either of said persons, corporations, firms or association of persons from separately or individually bidding for the performance of a public work for the State, or any county, municipality or levee board thereof, or if any person, corporation, firm or association of persons shall prevent, by persuasion or reward, any other person, corporation, firm or association of persons, or any one or more of them, from bidding for the performance of such public work, they and each of them shall be guilty of a misdemeanor, and shall be fined not less than twenty-five dollars nor more than one thousand dollars. § 4442. All sums of money to be paid on any contract on behalf of the State, or any county, municipality or levee board thereof, when the provisions of the last section have been violated, shall not be collectible, nor shall the same be paid by any officer or board having the payment thereof. The constitution of the State contains the following provisions, viz.: § 198. The legislature shall enact laws to prevent all trusts, combinations, contracts and agreements inimical to the public welfare.

§ **201. Missouri Anti-Trust Act.**—The anti-trust law of Missouri was enacted in 1891, and revised in 1895 and again in 1897. It is entitled "An act providing for the punishment of pools, trusts and conspiracies to control prices, and as to evidence and prosecution in such cases. The original act was approved April 2, 1891; the first revision was approved Aprill 11, 1895, and the second revision March 24, 1897. As amended, the act is as follows: Be it enacted by the General Assembly of the State of Missouri as follows: § 1. Any corporation organized under the laws of this or any other State or country, for transacting or conducting any kind of business in this State, or which does transact or conduct any kind of business in this State, or any partnership or individual, or other association of persons whatsoever, who shall create, enter into, become a member of, or a party to, any pool, trust, agreement, combination, confederation or understanding with any other corporation, partnership, individual, or any other person or association of persons, to regulate or fix the price of any article of manufacture, mechanism, merchandise, commodity, convenience, repair, any product of mining, or any article or thing whatsoever, or the price or premium to be paid for insuring property against loss or damage by fire, lightning or storm, or to maintain said price when so regulated or fixed, or shall enter into, become a member of, or a party to, any pool, agreement, contract, combination or confederation to fix or limit the amount or quantity of any article of manufacture, mechanism, merchandise commodity, convenience, repair, any product of mining, or any article or thing whatsoever, or the price or premium to be paid for insuring property against loss or damage by fire, lightning or storm, shall be deemed and adjudged guilty of a conspiracy to defraud, and be subject to penalties as provided in this act: Provided, however, that the provisions of this section shall not apply to agreements of fire insurance companies, or their agents, or boards of fire underwriters, to regulate the price or premium to be paid for insuring property against loss or damage by fire, lightning or storm in cities in this State which now have or which may hereafter acquire a population of one hundred thousand inhabitants or more; and, provided, further, that if such insurance companies or their agents, or the board of fire underwriters, doing business in any such city shall combine in such city, either directly or indirectly, or agree or attempt to agree, directly or indirectly, to fix or regulate the price or premium to be paid for insuring property located wholly outside of such city against loss or damage by fire, lightning or storm, such company so violating the provisions of this act, either by itself, its agents or by any such board of underwriters, shall be taken and deemed to have forfeited its right to do business in this State, and shall become liable to all the penalties and forfeitures provided for by the provisions of this act. § 1*a*. That from and after the passage of this act all arrangements, contracts, agreements or combinations, between persons or corporations, or between persons or any association of persons and corporations, designed or made with a view to lessen, or which tend to lessen, full and free competition in the importation, manufacture or sale of an article, product or commodity in this State, and all arrangements, combinations, contracts or agreements, whereby, or under the terms of which, it is proposed, stipulated, provided, agreed or understood that any person, association of persons or corporations, doing business in this State, shall deal in, sell or offer for sale in this State any particular or specified article, product or commodity, and shall not, during the continuance or existence of any such arrangement, combination, contract or agreement, deal in, sell or offer for sale in this State, any competing article, product or commodity, are hereby declared to be against public policy, unlawful and void; and any person, association of persons or corporations, becoming a party to any such arrangement, contract, agreement or combination, shall be deemed and adjudged guilty of a conspiracy to defraud, and be subject to the penalties provided for in the act of which this act is amendatory. § 2. It shall not be lawful for any corporation to issue or to own trust certificates, or for any corporation, agent, officer or employe, or the directors or stockholders of any corporation, to enter into any combination, contract or agreement with any person or persons, corporation or corporations, or with any stockholder or director thereof, the purpose and effect of which combination, contract or agreement shall be to place the management or control of such combinations or the manufactured product thereof in the hands of any trustee or trustees, with the intent to limit or fix the price or lessen the production and sale of any article of commerce, use or consumption, or to prevent, restrict or diminish the manufacture or output of any such article. § 3. Any corporation or company, individual, firm or association violating any of the provisions of this act shall forfeit not less than five dollars nor more than one hundred dollars for each day it shall continue to do so, to be recovered by an action in the name of the State at the relation of the attorney-general, circuit or prosecuting attorney,—moneys thus recovered to go into the county school fund of the county in which the cause accrues, and in the city of St. Louis into the school fund of said city. § 4. Any contract or agreement in violation of any provision of the preceding sections of this act shall be absolutely void. § 5. Any purchaser of any article or commodity from any individual, company or corporation transacting business contrary to any provision of the preceding sections of this act shall not be liable for the price or payment of such article or commodity, and may plead this act as a defense to any suit for such price or payment. § 6. Any corporation, created or organized by or under the laws of this State, which shall violate any provisions of the preceding sections of this act, shall thereby forfeit its corporate rights and franchises; and its corporate existence shall, upon proper proof being made thereof in any court of competent jurisdiction in this State, be by the court declared forfeited, void and of non-effect, and shall thereupon cease and determine; and any corporation, created or organized by or under the laws of any other State or country, which shall violate any provisions of the preceding sections of this act, shall thereby forfeit its right and privilege thereafter to do any business in this State, and upon proper proof being made thereof in any court of competent jurisdiction in this State, its right and privilege to do business in this State shall be declared forfeited; and in all proceedings to have such forfeiture declared, proof that any person, who has been acting as the agent of such foreign corporation in transacting its business in this State, has been, while acting as such agent, and in the name, behalf or interest of such foreign corporation, violating any provision of the preceding section of this act, shall be received as *prima facia* proof of the act of the corporation itself; and it shall be the duty of the clerk of said court to certify the decree thereof to the secretary of state, and if it be an insurance company, also to the superintendent of the insurance department, who shall take notice and be governed thereby as to the corporate powers and rights of said corporation. § *6a*. That whenever the corporate rights and franchises of any corporation, organized under the laws of this State, have been declared forfeited by the judgment of a court of competent jurisdiction for any violation of the provisions of this act, or of the act of which this act is amendatory; and whenever the right and privilege of any corporation, organized under the laws or any other State or country, to do business in this State, has been declared forfeited by the judgment of a court of competent jurisdiction for any violations of the provisions of this act, or of the act of which this act is amendatory, it shall thereafter be unlawful for any person, association of persons or corporation to deal in, sell or offer for sale in this State any article, product or commodity made, produced or manufactured, in whole or in part, by any corporation whose rights, franchises or privileges have been so declared to be forfeited; and the foregoing provisions of this section are hereby made applicable in all respects to the successor or assigns of any corporation whose rights, franchises or privileges have been so forfeited. Any person violating the provisions of this section is hereby declared to be guilty of a felony, and upon conviction shall be punished by imprisonment in the penitentiary for a term not exceeding three years, or by imprisonment in the county jail for a term not exceeding one year, or by a fine not less than one hundred dollars nor more than one thousand dollars, or by both such fine and jail imprisonment: Provided, that no statement made by any person in any affidavit made under the provisions of sections seven and eight of the act of which this act is amendatory shall be competent as evidence against such person in any criminal prosecutions brought under this section. § 7. It shall be the duty of secretary of the state, on or about the first day of July of each year, to address to the president, secretary or treasurer of each incorporated company doing business in this State, a letter of inquiry as to whether the said corporation has all or any part of its business or interest in or with any trust, combination or association of persons or stockholders, as named in the preceding provisions of this act, and to require an answer, under oath, of the president, secretary or treasurer, or any director of said company. A form of affidavit shall be enclosed in said letter of inquiry, as follows:

AFFIDAVIT.

STATE OF MISSOURI, }
County of .... } ss.

I, ———, do solemnly swear that I am the——— (president, secretary [treasurer] or director) of the corporation known and styled ———, duly incorporated under the laws of———, on the———day of———18—, and now transacting or conducting business in the State of Missouri, and that I am duly authorized to represent said corporation in the making of this affidavit, and I do further solemnly swear that the said———, known and styled as aforesaid, has not, since the———day of——— (naming the day upon which this act takes effect), created, entered into or became a member of, or a party to, and was not on ———day———, nor any day since that date, and is not now a member of, or a party to, any pool, trust, agreement, combination, confederation or understanding with any other corporation, partnership, individual, or any other person or association of persons, to regulate or fix the price of any article of manufacture, mechanism, merchandise, commodity, convenience, repair, any product of mining, or article or thing whatsoever, or the price or premium to be paid for insuring property against loss or damage by fire, lightning or storm; and that it has not entered into or become a member of, or a party to, any pool, trust, agreement, contract, combination or confederation to fix or limit the amount or quantity of any article of manufacture, mechanism, merchandise, commodity, convenience, repair, any product of mining or any article or thing whatsoever, or the price or premium to be paid for insuring property against loss or damage by fire, lightning or storm; and that it has not issued, and does not own any trust certificates; and for any corporation, agent, officer or employe, or for the directors or stockholders of any corporation, has not entered into and is not now in any combination, contract or agreement with any person or persons, corporation or corporations, or with any stockholders or directors thereof, the purpose and effect of which said combination, contract or agreement would be to place the management or control of such combination or combinations, or the manufactured product thereof, in the hands of any trustee or trustees, with the intent to limit or fix the price or lessen the production and sale of any article of commerce, use or consumption, or to prevent, restrict or diminish the manufacture or output of any article; and that it has not made or entered into any arrangement, contract or agreement with any person, association of persons or corporation designed to lessen, or which tend to lessen, full and free competition in the importation, manufacture or sale of any article, product or commodity in this State, or under the terms of which it is proposed, stipulated, provided, agreed or understood that any particular or specified article, product or commodity shall be dealt in, sold or offered for sale in this State to the exclusion, in whole or in part, of any competing article, product or commodity.

———

[President, secretary, treasurer or director.]

Subscribed and sworn to before me, a———, within and for the county of———, this———day of———, 18—.

[SEAL] ———

And on refusal to make oath in answer to said inquiry, or on failure to do so within thirty days from the mailing thereof, the secretary of state shall certify said fact to the prosecuting attorney of the county (the circuit attorney in the city of St. Louis) wherein said corporation is located, and it shall be the duty of such prosecuting or circuit attorney, at the earliest practicable moment, in the name of the State, and at the relation of said prosecuting or circuit attorney, to proceed against such corporation for the recovery of the money forfeit, provided for in this act, and also for the forfeiture of its charter or its certificate of incorporation, or its right and privilege to do business in this State. § 8. It shall be the duty of the secretary of state, at any time, upon satisfactory evidence that any company or association of persons, duly incorporated under the laws of this State, has entered into any trust, combination or association, in violation of the preceding sections of this act, to demand that it shall make the affidavit, as above set forth in this act, as to the conduct of its business. In case of failure of compliance on the part of the corporation, then the same procedure shall ensue as is provided in section seven of this act: Provided, that no corporation, firm, association or individual shall be subject to any criminal prosecution by reason of anything truthfully disclosed by the affidavit required by this act, or truthfully disclosed in any testimony elicited in the execution thereof. § 9. It shall be the duty of the attorney-general, the circuit attorney of the city of St. Louis and the prosecuting attorney of each county, respectively, to enforce the provisions of this act. The attorney-general, the circuit or prosecuting attorneys shall institute and conduct all suits begun in the circuit courts, and, upon appeal, the attorney-general shall prosecute said suits in the Supreme Court and courts of appeals. As compensation for his services in this behalf the attorney-general shall be entitled to his actual expenses incurred in the prosecution of such suits, to be paid by the defendant or defendants, when judgment is rendered for the State. The circuit and prosecuting attorneys shall receive for their compensation one-fourth of the penalty collected. § 10. In all suits instituted under this act, to forfeit the charter of corporations or to forfeit the right of a corporation to do business in this State, where a judgment of forfeiture is obtained and the cause is not appealed to the supreme court or courts of appeals, the circuit court rendering such judgment shall allow the circuit or prosecuting attorney a fee of not less than twenty-five dollars nor more than five hundred dollars, to be paid out of the assets of said corporation, and when the attorney-general takes part in said prosecution he shall be entitled to his actual expense, to be paid in like manner. § 11. It is hereby made the duty of all county officers in the State to furnish to the secretary of state any information which he may request of them, to enable him the more fully to execute the duties imposed upon him by this act, and for such services the said county officers shall be paid by their respective counties, upon allowance by the county court, such fees as would accrue for like services for the county. § 12. Chapter 128, Revised Statutes 1889, entitled "Pools and Trusts," is hereby repealed.

§ 202. Montana Statute Against Monopolies and Trusts.—The anti-trust and monopoly legislation of Montana is found in the Annotated Code of 1895. That portion of the statute relating to this subject is, as follows: The sections are the sections of the code. § 321. Every person, corporation, stock company or association of persons in this State who, directly or indirectly, combine or form what is known as a trust, or make any contract with any person or persons, corporations or stock companies, foreign or domestic, through their stockholders, directors, officers, or in any manner whatever, for the purpose of fixing the price or regulating the production of any article of commerce, or of the product of the soil for consumption by the people, or to create or carry out any restriction in trade, to limit productions, or increase or reduce the price of merchandise or commodities, or to prevent competition in merchandise or commodities, or to fix a standard or figure whereby the price of any article of merchandise, commerce or produce, intended for sale, use or consumption, will be in any way controlled, or to create a monopoly in the manufacture, sale or transportation of any such article, or to enter into an obligation by which they shall bind others or themselves not to manufacture, sell or transport any such article below a common standard or figure, or by which they agree to keep such article or transportation at a fixed or graduated figure, or by which they settle the price of such article so as to preclude unrestricted competition, is punishable by imprisonment in the State prison not exceeding five years, or by fine not exceeding ten thousand dollars, or both. Every corporation violating the provisions of this section forfeits to the State all its property and franchises, and, in case of a foreign corporation, it is prohibited from carrying on business in the State. § 325. The provisions of this chapter do not apply to any arrangement, agreement or combination between laborers made with the object of lessening the number of hours of labor or increasing wages, nor to persons engaged in horticulture or agriculture, with a view of enhancing the price of their products.

§ 203. Nebraska Statute Against Trusts and Conspiracies Against Trade and Business.—The legislation of Nebraska relating to this subject consists of the statute of 1897. This statute repeals the previous statute,—chapter xci*a*, entitled "Trusts" of the Compiled Statutes of Nebraska for the year 1895,—and, as a substitute, enacts the law of 1897. This statute was passed April 8th of that year. It is, as follows: A bill for an act to define trusts and conspiracies against trade and business, declaring the same unlawful and void, and providing means for the suppression of the same and remedies for persons injured thereby, and to provide punishment for violations of this act, and to repeal chapter ninety-one *a* (91*a*), entitled "Trusts" of the Compiled Statutes of Nebraska for the year 1895. Be it enacted by the legislature of the State of Nebraska: § 1. That a trust is a combination of capital, skill or acts by any person or persons to fix the price of any article or commodity of trade, use or merchandise, with the intent to prevent others from conducting or carrying on the same business or selling or trafficking in the same article, use or merchandise, or a combination of capital, skill or acts by two or more persons or by two or more of them for either, any or all of the following purposes: 1. To create or carry out restrictions in trade. 2. To limit or reduce the production or increase or reduce the price of merchandise or commodities. 3. To prevent competition in insurance, either life, fire, accident or any other kind, or in manufacture, making, constructing, transportation, sale or purchase of merchandise, produce or commodities. 4. To fix at any standard or figure whereby its price to the public shall be in any manner controlled or established upon any article of merchandise, produce or manufacture of any kind intended for sale, use or consumption in this State; to establish any pretended agency whereby the sale of any such article, commodity, merchandise or product shall be covered up, concealed or made to appear to be for the original vendor, for a like purpose or purposes, and to enable such original vendor, producer or manufacturer to control the wholesale or retail price of any such article of merchandise, product or commodity after the title to the same shall have passed from such vendor or manufacturer. 5. To make or enter into, carry on or carry out any contract, obligation or agreement of any kind or description by which they shall bind or have heretofore bound themselves not to sell, dispose of, traffic in or transport any article of merchandise or commodity, or article of trade, product, use, merchandise, consumption or commerce, below a common standard figure, card or list price, or by which they shall agree in any manner to keep the price of such article, product, commodity or transportation at a fixed or graduated figure or price, or by which they shall in any manner establish or settle the price of any article of merchandise, commodity, or of insurance, fire, life or accident, or transportation between them or between themselves and others, or with the intent to preclude or the tendency of which is to prevent or preclude a free and unrestricted competition among themselves or others or the people generally in the production, sale, traffic or transportation of any such article of merchandise, product or commodity, or conducting a like business, or by which they shall agree to pool, combine or unite any interest they may have in connection with the sale, production or transportation of any such article of merchandise, product or commodity, or the carrying on of any such business that its price might in any manner be affected thereby. § 2. That any and all acts by any person or persons carrying on, creating or attempting to create, either directly or indirectly, a trust as defined in section one (1) of this act are hereby declared to be a conspiracy against trade and business and unlawful, and any person who may be or may become engaged in any such conspiracy, or take part therein, or aid or advise, in its commission, or who shall as principal, manager, director, agent, servant or employe, or in any other capacity, knowingly aid or advise, or attempt to carry out or carry out any of the stipulations, purposes, prices, rates, orders thereunder or in pursuance thereof, shall be deemed guilty of a misdemeanor, and upon conviction thereof shall be punished by a fine of not less than twenty-five dollars, nor more than five thousand dollars. § 3. That any corporation, organized under the laws of this State, which violates any of the provisions of this act shall thereby forfeit its charter and franchise, and its corporate existence shall thereupon cease and determine. And for a violation of any of the provisions of this act by any corporation it shall be the duty of the attorney-general of the State, or county attorney, within his county, upon his own motion, to institute suit or *quo warranto* proceedings in any county in this State, in which such corporation was organized or is engaged in transacting business, for the forfeiture of its charter rights and franchise, and the dissolution of its corporate existence. There shall be taxed against the defendant, as part of the cost in any such suit of proceeding, upon the forfeiture of its charter and franchise, as provided herein, a fee for the services rendered by the county attorney, a sum not less than one hundred dollars ($100) and not more than five hundred dollars ($500), to be fixed by the court rendering the judgment. § 4. Every foreign corporation or person, not a resident of this State, violating any of the provisions of this act, is hereby denied the right and prohibited from doing any business within this State; and it shall be the duty of the attorney-general and each county attorney within his county to enforce this provision, by injunction or other proper proceeding, in any county in which such foreign corporation or non-resident person does business, in the name of the State on his relation. And for services rendered by the county attorney, in any such suit or proceedings, the court rendering judgment shall allow a reasonable sum to be taxed against the defendant as part of the costs in case judgment is rendered against the defendant. For the purpose of obtaining service upon any foreign corporation or non-resident person in any suit or proceedings brought, as provided in this act, it shall be sufficient to serve a summons upon any person in any county within the State who may be the agent of said foreign corporation or non-resident person for the purpose of soliciting business or transacting or doing business for said corporation or non-resident person at the time when summons is issued upon petition filed against said corporation or non-resident person or when summons is served on such agent. § 5. In any indictment or information for any offense named in this act it shall be sufficient to state the purpose and effects of the trust or combination in a general way, and that the accused was a member of, aided or advised, or acted with or in pursuance of such trust or combination without giving its name or description, or how, where or when it was created. § 6. In prosecutions under this act it shall be sufficient to prove that a trust or combination, as defined herein or under the common law, exists, and that the defendant belonged to it or acted for or in connection with it, or aided or advised such trust or combination, or attempted to, or did fully carry out any of the stipulations, purposes, prices, rates or orders of any person connected therewith, and it shall not be necessary to make any proof of all the members belonging to such trust, combination or conspiracy, or to prove or produce any article of agreement or any written instrument on which it may have been based, or when, where or how such trust, combination or conspiracy was formed or that it was evidenced by any written instrument, or came into existence by any agreement of any kind or character, whether in parol or written. § 7. Prosecutions may be brought by any person in the name of the State of Nebraska against any person or persons violating any of the provisions of this act, and it shall be the duty of all county attorneys, in their respective counties, to prosecute all criminal suits on behalf of the State arising under the provisions of this act, and there shall be taxed by the court a fee for the county attorney of not less than twenty-five dollars ($25) nor more than one hundred dollars ($100) as services for trying said suit, and same shall be taxed as part of the costs against the defendant or defendants. § 8. That any contract or agreement, in violation of the provisions of this act, shall be absolutely void and not enforceable either in law or equity. § 9. Nothing herein contained shall be construed to prevent any assemblies or associations of laboring men from passing and adopting such regulations as they may think proper, in reference to wages and the compensation of labor, and such assemblies and associations shall retain, and there is hereby reserved to them the rights and privileges now accorded to them by law, anything herein contained to the contrary notwithstanding. § 10. Any purchaser of any article, commodity, matter or thing purchased or contracted for within or without this State from any person, firm, corporation or association of persons, or of two or more of them, transacting business contrary to any provision of the preceding sections of this act, shall not be liable for the price or payment of such article, commodity, matter or thing, and may plead this act as a defense to any suit for such price or payment. § 11. Any person who shall be injured in his business, employment or property by any other person, firm, association or corporation by reason of anything forbidden or declared to be unlawful by this act, may have his right of action and sue therefor in any court of competent jurisdiction, and he shall recover the damages by him sustained, and the cost of suit together with a reasonable attorney's fee, to be fixed by the court in every case of recovery, which attorney's fee shall be taxed and collected as part of the costs in the case. § 12. In any action brought under any of the provisions of this act the court before whom the same shall be pending may compel any person or persons, partnership, company, association or corporation so proceeded against, or any of the members of any such partnership or corporation, or any director, officer, receiver, trustee, agent, employe or clerk of them, or either of them, to attend, appear and testify in such suit or proceeding, and may compel the production of the books and papers of any such person, persons, partnership, company, association or corporation party to any such proceeding. No person shall be excused from attending and testifying, or producing books and papers, in any prosecution under this act, for the reason that the testimony, documentary or otherwise, required of him, may tend to criminate him, or subject him to a penalty or forfeiture, but no person shall be prosecuted or subject to any penalty or forfeiture for or on account of any transaction, matter or thing concerning which he may testify or produce evidence, documentary or otherwise, in any prosecution under the provisions of this act: Provided, that no person so testifying shall be exempt from prosecution for perjury committed in so testifying. § 13. That the word "person" or "persons," whenever used in this act, shall be deemed to include firm, firms, corporation, corporations, partnerships, co-partnerships and associations existing under, permitted or authorized by the laws of the United States, this State or any other State, or the laws of any foreign country or territory of the United States. § 14. That chapter ninety-one *a* (91*a*), entitled "Trusts" of the Compiled Statutes of Nebraska for the year 1895, be and the same is hereby repealed.

§ 204. New Mexico Law Declaring Trust Combinations Illegal.—The statute of New Mexico for declaring trusts illegal is entitled "An act declaring certain trusts, pools and combinations illegal, and providing for the punishment thereof." It was approved February 4th, 1891, and is, as follows: Be it enacted by the legislative assembly of the territory of New Mexico: § 1. Every contract or combination between individuals, associations or corporations, having for its object or which shall operate to restrict trade or commerce, or control the quantity, price or exchange of any article of manufacture or product of the soil or mine, is hereby declared to be illegal. Every person, whether as individual or agent, or officer or stockholder, of any corporation or association, who shall make any such contract or engage in any such combinations, shall be deemed guilty of a misdemeanor, and on conviction thereof shall be punished by a fine not exceeding one thousand dollars nor less than one hundred dollars, and by imprisonment at hard labor not exceeding one year, or until such fine has been paid. § 2. Every person who shall monopolize, or attempt to monopolize, or combine or conspire with any other person or persons to monopolize any part of the trade or commerce of this territory, shall be deemed guilty of a misdemeanor, and on conviction thereof shall be punished by a fine not exceeding one thousand dollars, or by imprisonment not exceeding one year, or by both said punishments, in the discretion of the court. § 3. All contracts and agreements in violation of sections one and two of this act shall be void, and any purchaser of any commodity from any individual, corporation or association transacting business in violation of this act shall be liable for the payment for such commodity. § 4. This act shall take effect and be in force from and after its passage and publication three times in the Daily New Mexican.

§ **205. New York Law to Prevent Monopolies.**—The anti-monopoly law of New York is "An act to prevent monopolies in articles or commodities of common use, and to prohibit restraints of trade and commerce, providing penalties for violations of the provisions of this act, and procedure to enable the attorney-general to secure testimony in relation thereto." This act became a law May 7th, 1897, and is, as follows: The people of the State of New York, represented in senate and assembly, do enact as follows: § 1. Every contract, agreement, arrangement or combination, whereby a monopoly in the manufacture, production or sale in this State of any article or commodity of common use is or may be created, established or maintained, or whereby competition in this State in the supply or price of any such article or commodity is or may be restrained or prevented, or whereby for the purpose of creating, establishing or maintaining a monopoly within this State of the manufacture, production or sale of any such article or commodity the free pursuit in this State of any lawful business, trade or occupation, is or may be restricted or prevented, is hereby declared to be against public policy, illegal and void. § 2. Every person or corporation, or any officer or agent thereof, who shall make, or attempt to make, or enter into, any such contract, agreement, arrangement or combination, or who, within this State, shall do any act pursuant thereto, or in, toward or for the consummation thereof, wherever the same may have been made, is guilty of a misdemeanor, and on conviction thereof shall, if a natural person, be punished by a fine not exceeding five thousand dollars, or by imprisonment for not longer than one year, or by both such fine and imprisonment; and if a corporation, by a fine of not exceeding five thousand dollars. § 3. The attorney-general may bring an action in the name and in behalf of the people of the State against any person, trustee, director, manager, or other officer or agent of a corporation, or against a corporation, foreign or domestic, to restrain and prevent the doing in this State of any act herein declared to be illegal, or any act in, toward or for the making or consummation of any contract, agreement, arrangement or combination herein prohibited wherever the same may have been made. § 4. The provisions of article one of title three of chapter nine of the code of civil procedure, relating to the application for an order for the examination of witnesses before the commencement of an action and the conduct of such examination shall apply, so far as practicable, to an action or proceeding by the attorney-general instituted pursuant to this chapter; and for the purpose of determining whether an action or proceeding should be commenced hereunder, the attorney-general may examine and procure the testimony of witnesses in the manner herein prescribed. § 5. Whenever the attorney-generel deems it necessary or proper to procure testimony before beginning any action or proceeding under this chapter, he may present to any justice of the supreme court an application in writing for an order directing such persons as the attorney-general may require to appear before a justice of the supreme court, or a referee designated in such order, and answer such relevant and material questions as may be put to them, concerning any alleged illegal contract, arrangement, agreement or combination, in violation of this chapter, if it appears to the satisfaction of the justice of the supreme court to whom the application for an order is made that such an application is necessary, then such order shall be granted. Such orders shall be granted without notice, unless notice is required to be given by the justice of the supreme court to whom the application is made, in which event an order to show cause why such application should not be granted shall be made containing such preliminary injunction or stay as may appear to said justice to be proper or expedient, and shall specify the time when and place where the witnesses are required to appear, and such examination shall be held either in the city of Albany or in the judicial district in which the witness resides or in which the principal office within this State of the corporation affected is located. The justice or referee may adjourn such examination from time to time and witnesses must attend accordingly. § 6. The order for such examination must be signed by the justice making it, and the service of a copy thereof, with an indorsement by the attorney-general, signed by him, to the effect that the person named therein is required to appear and be examined at the time and place, and before the justice or referee specified in such indorsement, shall be sufficient notice for the attendance of witnesses, such indorsements may contain a clause requiring such person to produce on such examination all books, papers and documents in his possession, or under his control, relating to the subject of such examination. The order shall be served upon the person named in the indorsement aforesaid by showing him the original order, and delivering to and leaving with him, at the same time, a copy thereof, indorsed as above provided, and by paying or tendering to him the fee allowed by law to witnesses subpœnaed to attend trial of civil actions in a court of record in this State. § 7. The testimony of each witness must be subscribed by him, and all testimony taken by such justice, or referee appointed, must be certified and delivered to the attorney-general at the close of the examination. The testimony given by a witness in a proceeding or examination under this act shall not be given in evidence against him in any criminal action or proceeding, nor shall any criminal action or proceeding be brought against such witness on account of the testimony so given by him, nor shall any person be excused from answering any questions that may be put to him on the ground that it may tend to convict him of a violation of the provisions of this act. § 8. A referee appointed, as provided in this act, possesses all the powers and is subject to all the duties of a referee appointed under section ten hundred and eighteen of the code of civil procedure, so far as practicable, and may punish for contempt a witness duly served, as prescribed in this act, for non-attendance or refusal to be sworn or to testify, or to produce books, papers and documents, according to the direction of the indorsement aforesaid, in the same manner and to the same extent as a referee appointed to hear, try and determine an issue of fact or of law. § 9. Chapter seven hundred and sixteen of the laws of eighteen hundred and ninety-three and chap ter two hundred and sixty-seven of the laws of eighteen hundred and ninety-six are hereby repealed. § 10. This act shall take effect immediately.

§ **206. North Carolina Law for the Prohibition of Trusts.**—The statute of this State for the prohibition of trusts is entitled "An act to prohibit trusts in the State of North Carolina, and to provide for the punishment of persons connected with them." It was ratified March 11th, 1889, and is, as follows: The General Assembly of North Carolina do enact: § 1. That all combinations and trusts, as defined by this act, are unlawful, dangerous to the liberty of the people and are hereby forbidden to be formed or carried on in this State. § 2. That a trust is an arrangement, understanding or agreement, either private or public, entered into by two or more persons or corporations for the purpose of increasing or reducing the price of the shares of stock of any company or corporation, or of any class of products, materials or manufactured articles beyond the price that would be fixed by the natural demand for or the supply of such shares, products, materials or manufactured articles; and any attempt to carry out such purpose shall be evidence that such arrangement, understanding or agreement exists. § 3. That any person, company or corporation who shall form, or attempt to form, a trust in this State, or the agent or representative of any trust in any State or county, who shall attempt to carry on operations in this State, shall be guilty of a misdemeanor, and upon conviction may be fined not more than ten thousand dollars, or may be imprisoned not more than ten years for each offense. § 4. That any person, company or corporation who enters into an arrangement, understanding or agreement not to mine, manufacture, buy, sell or transport more than a certain specified amount of any goods, products or commodities within a specified time, will have violated section three of this act, and will be liable to indictment therefor; and any person, company or corporation who gives bond or makes a forfeit of any kind not to break such arrangement, understanding or agreement, shall be guilty of a misdemeanor, and on conviction thereof shall be fined or imprisoned, or both, in the discretion of the court. § 5. That any merchant, broker, manufacturer or dealers in raw materials of any kind, or the agent of such persons, who shall sell any particular class of goods, raw materials or manufactured articles, for less than actual cost for the purpose of breaking down competitors, shall be guilty of a misdemeanor, and upon conviction may be fined or imprisoned, or both, in the discretion of the court: Provided, that nothing contained in this act shall operate or be construed so as to forbid or prevent any person or persons who desire and intend to purchase any article or commodity for his or their own use or consumption, from combining or otherwise lawfully acting so as to protect or help themselves from imposition in the cost or purchase price of such articles or commodities as they or either of them may design and intend to use or consume. § 6. That this act shall be in full force and effect from and after the first day of May of the year one thousand eight hundred and eighty-nine.

§ 207. North Dakota Law Declaring Certain Trusts and Combinations Unlawful.—The statute of North Dakota relating to this subject is entitled "An act to declare unlawful and void all arrangements, contracts, agreements, trusts or combinations, made with a view to lessen, or which tend to lessen, free competition in the importation or sale of articles imported into this State, or in the manufacture or sale of articles of domestic growth or of domestic raw material, to declare unlawful and void all arrangements, contracts, agreements, trusts or combinations between persons or corporations designed, or which tend to advance, reduce or control the price of such product or article to producer or consumer of any such product or article, to provide for forfeiture of the charter and franchise of any corporation organized under the laws of this State, violating any of the provisions of this act; to prohibit every foreign corporation violating any of the provisions of this act from doing business in this State; to require the attorney-general of this State to institute legal proceedings against any such corporations violating the provisions of this act, and to enforce the penalties prescribed; to prescribe penalties for any violation of this act; to authorize any person or corporation damaged by any such trust, agreement or combination, to sue for the recovery of such damage, and for other purposes." This act was approved March 9th, 1897, and is, as follows: Be it enacted by the Legislative Assembly of the State of North Dakota: § 1. That all arrangements, contracts, agreements, trusts or combinations between persons or corporations made with a view to lessen, or which tend to lessen, full and free competition in the importation or sale of articles imported into this State, or in the manufacture or sale of articles of domestic growth, or of domestic raw material, and all arrangements, contracts, agreements, trusts or combinations between persons or corporations, designed or which tend to advance, reduce or control the price or the cost to the producer or to the consumer of any such product or articles, are hereby declared to be against public policy, unlawful and void. § 2. That any corporation chartered under the laws of this State, which shall violate any of the provisions of this act, shall thereby forfeit its charter and its franchise, and its corporate existence shall thereupon cease and determine. Every foreign corporation which shall violate any of the provisions of this act is hereby denied the right to do, and is prohibited from doing business in this State. It is hereby made the duty of the attorney-general of this State to enforce this provision by due process of law. § 3. That any violation of the provisions of this act shall be deemed, and is hereby declared to be destructive of full and free competition, and a conspiracy against trade, and any person or persons who may engage n any such conspiracy, or who shall, as principal, manager, director or agent, or in any other capacity, knowingly carry out any of the stipulations, purposes, prices, rates or orders made in furtherance of such conspiracy, shall, on conviction, be punished by a fine of not less than one hundred dollars nor more than five thousand dollars, and by imprisonment in the penitentiary not less than one year nor more than ten years, or, in the judgment of the court, by either such fine or such imprisonment. § 4. That any person or persons, or corporation that may be injured or damaged by any such arrangement, contract, agreement, trust or combination, described in section one of this act, may sue for and recover in any court of competent jurisdiction in this State, or any person, persons or corporations operating such trusts or combinations, the full consideration or sum paid by him or them for any goods, wares, merchandise or articles, the sale of which is controlled by any such combination or trust. § 5. That it shall be the duty of the judges of the district courts of this State specially to instruct the grand juries as to the provisions of this act.

§ 208. Oklahoma Law to Prevent Combinations in Restraint of Trade.—The anti-trust legislation is a statute entitled "An act to prevent combinations in restraint of trade." It became a law December 25th, 1890, and is, as follows: Be it enacted by the legislative assembly of the territory of Oklahoma: § 1. If any individual, firm, partnership, or any association of persons whatsoever, shall create, enter into, become a member of, or a party to, any pool, trust, agreement, combination or understanding with any other individual, firm, partnership or association of persons whatsoever, to regulate or fix the price of, or prevent or restrict the competition in the sale of provisions, feed, fuel, lumber, or other building materials, articles of merchandise or other commodity, they shall be deemed guilty of a misdemeanor, and upon conviction thereof shall be fined not less than fifty nor more that five hundred dollars. § 2. It shall not be lawful for any corporation organized under the laws of this territory, or organized under the laws of any other territory or State, and doing business in this territory, to enter into any combination, contract, trust, pool or agreement with any other corporation or corporations, or with any individual, firm, partnership or association of persons whatsoever, for the purpose of regulating or fixing the price of, or preventing or restricting competition in the sale of provisions, feed, fuel, lumber or other building materials, articles of merchandise or other commodity, including the fixing of the rate of interest, any president, manager, director, agent, receiver or other officer of any such corporation violating the provisions of this section, shall be deemed guilty of a misdemeanor, and upon conviction thereof shall be fined not less than fifty nor more than five hundred dollars, for the first offense, and upon a second conviction shall be fined a sum equal to twice the amount of the first fine, and such corporation shall forfeit its corporate right and franchise, and its corporate existence in this territory shall thereupon cease and determine. § 3. Any person purchasing provisions, feed, material, articles of merchandise, or any commodity from any individual, firm, partnership or corporation, transacting business in violation of the provisions of this act, such person so purchasing shall not be liable for the price or payment of any such article or commodity, and may plead this act as a defense in any suit for price or payment. In any civil action brought under the provisions of this section the court before whom such suit shall be pending may compel the plaintiff to testify, but if the plaintiff be a corporation then the court may compel any officer, agent or employe of such corporation to attend, appear and testify, or compel the production of any contract or papers in evidence in such civil action: Provided, the evidence so obtained shall not be used in any criminal prosecution against the person so testifying except in a criminal prosecution for perjury committed in giving such testimony. § 4. Any person who shall have purchased from any individual, firm, partnership or corporation, doing business in violation of the provisions of this act, any provisions, feed, fuel, lumber or other building material, articles of merchandise or other commodity, and paid for the same, may maintain a civil action to recover the full amount of damages sustained in consequence of any such violation of the provisions of this act, together with a reasonable attorney's fee, to be fixed by the court, which attorney's fee shall be taxed and collected as part of the costs in such case. In any civil action, brought under the provisions of this section, the court before whom such suit be pending may compel the defendant to testify; but if the defendant be a corporation, then the court may compel any officer, agent or employe of such corporation to attend, appear and testify, or compel the production of any contract or paper, as evidence in such civil action: Provided, the evidence so obtained shall not be used in any criminal action against the person so testifying except in a criminal prosecution for perjury committed in giving such testimony. § 5. It shall be the duty of the prosecuting attorneys, in their respective counties, to enforce the foregoing provisions of this act, and any prosecuting attorney securing a conviction, under the provisions of this act, shall be entitled, in addition to such fee or salary, as by law he is allowed for such prosecution, to one-fifth of the fine received.

§ 209. South Carolina Prohibition of Trusts and Combinations.—The anti-trust legislation of South Carolina is of very recent date. It consists of "An act to prohibit trusts and combinations and to provide penalties," approved February 25th, 1897. The act is, as follows: § 1. Be it enacted by the General Assembly of the State of South Carolina that from and after the passage of this act all arrangements, contracts, agreements, trusts or combinations, between two or more persons, as individuals, firms or corporations, made with a view to lessen, or which tend to lessen, full and free competition in the importation or sale of articles imported into this State, or in the manufacture or sale of articles of domestic growth or of domestic raw material, and all arrangements, contracts, agreements, trusts or combinations, between persons or corporations, designed or which tend to advance, reduce or control the price or the cost to the producer or to the consumer of any such product or article, are hereby declared to be against public policy, unlawful and void. § 2. Whenever complaint is made upon sufficient affidavit or affidavits, showing a *prima facie* case of violation of the provisions of the first section of this act by any corporation, domestic or foreign, it shall be the duty of the attorney-general to begin an action against such domestic corporation to forfeit its charter, and in case such violation shall be established, the court shall adjudge the charter of such corporation to be forfeited, and such corporation shall be dissolved, and its charter shall cease and determine; and in the case of such showing as to a foreign corporation, an action shall be begun by the attorney-general in said court against such corporation to determine the truth of such charge; and in case such charge shall be considered established, the effect of the judgment of the court shall be to deny to such corporation the recognition of its corporate existence in any court of law or equity in this State. But nothing in this section shall be construed to affect any right of action then existing against said corporation. § 3. Any violation of the provisions of this act shall be deemed, and is hereby declared to be, destructive of full and free competition and a conspiracy against trade, and any person or persons who may engage in any such conspiracy, or, who shall, as principal, manager, director or agent, or in any other capacity, knowingly carry out any of the stipulations, purposes, prices, rates or orders made in furtherance of such conspiracy shall on conviction be punished by a fine of not less than one hundred dollars nor more than five hundred dollars, and by imprisonment in the penitentiary not less than six months nor more than ten years, or, in the judgment of the court, by either such fine or such imprisonment. § 4. That any person or persons, or corporation, that may be injured or damaged by any such arrangement, contract, agreement, trust or combination, described in section one of this act, may sue for and recover, in any court of competent jurisdiction in this State, of any person, persons or corporation operating such trust or combination the full consideration or sum paid by him or them for any goods, wares, merchandise or articles, the sale of which is controlled by such combination or trust. § 5. That any and all persons may be compelled to testify in any action or prosecution under this act: Provided, that such testimony shall not be used in any other action or prosecution against such witness or witnesses, and such witness or witnesses shall forever be exempt from any prosecution for the act or acts concerning which he or they testify. § 6. Nothing contained in this act shall be taken or construed to apply to any person or persons acting in the discharge of official duties under the laws of this State. § 7. All acts in conflict with this act be and the same are hereby repealed.

§ **210. South Dakota.**—The latest legislation of South Dakota relating to monopolies and industrial trusts, is entitled "An act to enforce section twenty, of article seventeen, of the constitution of the State of South Dakota." The act was approved March 1st, 1897, and is as follows: Be it enacted by the legislature of the State of South Dakota: 1. That within the meaning of this act, a trust or a monopoly is a combination of capital, skill, or acts of two or more persons, firms, corporations or associations of persons; first, to create or carry out restrictions in trade; second, to limit the production, or to increase or reduce the price of commodities; third, to prevent competition in the manufacture, transportation, sale or purchase of merchandise, produce or commodities; fourth, to fix any standard or figure whereby the price to the public shall be in any manner established or controlled, provided that nothing in this act shall be construed so as to include labor organizations. 2. That it shall be unlawful for any incorporated company, co-partnership or association of persons in this State, directly or otherwise, to fix prices, limit the production or regulate the transportation of any product or commodity, so as to obstruct, or delay or prevent competition in such production or transportation, or limit transportation of commodities, or to fix prices therefor. 3. That it shall be unlawful for any incorporated company, co-partnership or association of persons in any other State, to directly or otherwise combine, or make any contract, with any incorporated company, co-partnership or association of persons in this State to combine or make any contract to fix prices, limit the production of commodity, or regulate the transportation, directly or otherwise, of any product or commodity so as to obstruct or prevent competition, or limit transportation or to fix prices therefor. 4. Any person or persons, officers or servants of any company, co-partnership or association of persons, convicted of violating any provisions of this act, shall be deemed guilty of a misdemeanor, and upon conviction thereof, for the first offense, shall be fined not less than one thousand dollars, nor more than five thousand dollars, and upon conviction for the second offense, not less than five thousand dollars nor more than ten thousand dollars. 5. All fines recovered under this act shall be paid one-half to the person or persons aggrieved, and the other half shall be paid into the county treasury of the county in which the conviction may be made, to the credit of the general county fund of said county. 6. It shall be the special duty of the State's attorney of each county in the State, upon the affidavit of any person or persons aggrieved showing that any person or persons has violated any provision of this act, to make complaint and cause the arrest of such person or persons, and to prosecute him or them to conviction, if proved to be guilty, and it shall be the duty of the attorney-general of the State, upon the request of any State's attorney for any county, to aid in the prosecution of actions under this act. 7. That all acts, or parts of acts, in conflict with this act are hereby repealed.

§ 211. **Tennessee Law to Prohibit Conspiracies and Trusts.**—The first statute enacted by the legislature of Tennessee on this subject is entitled, "An act to prevent conspiracies and formation of trusts against legitimate trade and commerce, and to suppress illegal combinations against the same." It was approved April 6th, 1889, and is, as follows: § 1. Be it enacted by the General Assembly of the State of Tennessee that it shall not be lawful for any person or persons, or associations of persons or any corporation in this State, or doing business in this State, to form or agree to, or to conspire to form any trust, pool, or corner or combination, or any other arrangement or device, in or about any article of legitimate traffic, the production or manufacture or sale of such article that may injuriously affect, and for the purpose of injuriously affecting the legitimate trade and commerce of the country, or to limit the supply or production of said articles, whereby the price of such produce or manufactured articles or other articles of legitimate trade may be unduly depressed and put down, or unduly raised or increased, for the purpose of speculation, either by pooling or purchasing said articles for the purpose of withdrawing them from market to destroy legitimate competition, or to create a monopoly or corner in the same, or to produce an undue demand for the same, and that to unduly raise the price of said articles, or by throwing the same on the market when so accumulated or purchased, for the purpose of creating an undue depression in the price of such article, and by such means to destroy or limit legitimate competition in the production, manufacture or sale of such articles, as by any other device or arrangement for such purpose. All such agreements, trusts, pools, corners and combinations are hereby prohibited:

Provided, nothing herein contained shall be construed to prevent or interfere with parties engaged in legitimate trade and speculation. § 2. Be it further enacted that any person or persons or corporation violating the first section of this act, for the first offense, shall, on conviction, pay a fine of not less than two hundred and fifty dollars, and for the second offense a fine of not less than five hundred dollars, and the attorney-general, for each conviction, shall have a taxed fee of fifty dollars, and shall have, in addition, fifty per cent. of the money actually received on such fine, and he shall prosecute all such cases, *ex officio*, without any other prosecutor, and the courts shall give this act in charge, and the grand jury shall have full inquisitorial power in such cases. § 3. Be it further enacted that no contract made by any person or persons, or incorporations, whereby to carry out, or agree to carry out, any of the agreements or combinations enumerated in and prohibited in the foregoing act shall be enforced in any of the courts of this State, whether the same be made by citizens of this or any other State. § 4. Be it further enacted that any corporation, created or incorporated by or under the laws of this State, which violates any provisions of this act, shall thereby forfeit its corporate rights and franchises, and its corporate existence shall thereupon cease and determine, and it shall be the duty of the attorney-general of the State, of their own motion and without leave or order of any court or judge, to institute an action in behalf of the people and in the name of the State for the forfeiture of such rights and franchise, and the dissolution of such corporate existence, or any citizen of the State may institute such suit by proceedings in a court of chancery in the name of the State, and said corporations may be enjoined from violation of this act, pending such proceedings: Provided such citizen may not begin such proceedings without giving security for cost in such cases. This law was followed in 1891 by a statute which is supplementary to it. It is entitled, "An act to declare unlawful all trusts, pools, contracts, arrangements and combinations in the restraint of trade, production, manufacture or sale, to fix the liability of and punish persons and corporations concerned therein." This act was approved March 30th, 1891, and is, as follows: § 1. Be it enacted by the General Assembly of the State of Tennessee that all trusts, pools, contracts, arrangements or combinations now existing or hereafter made with a view or which tend to prevent full and free competition in the production, manufacture or sale of any article of domestic growth, production or manufacture, or in the importation or sale of any article of domestic growth, production or manufacture, or in the importation or sale of any article growed, produced or manufactured in any other State or country, or which are designated or tend to fix, regulate, limit or reduce the price of any article of growth, production or manufacture, or which are designed or tend in a way to create a monopoly, are hereby declared to be unlawful, against public policy and void. § 2. Be it further enacted that all persons, entering into or continuing in any trust, pool, contract, arrangement, agreement or combination, either in his own account or as agent or attorney for another, or as an officer, agent or stockholder of any corporation, or in any capacity whatever, shall be deemed guilty of a felony, and on conviction thereof shall be punished by a fine of not less than five hundred ($500) dollars nor more than five thousand ($5,000) dollars, and imprisonment in the penitentiary not less than one (1) year nor more than five (5) years. § 3. Be it further enacted that all persons and corporations, and the officers and the stockholders of all corporations that shall become or continue to be members of, or in any way connected with, or concerned in any such trust, contract, agreement or combination, shall be jointly and severally liable to pay all the debts, obligations and liabilities of each and every person and corporation that may become or continue a member thereof, connected therewith or concerned therein, as fully as if all were partners in the creation of such debts, obligations and liabilities. § 4. Be it further enacted that if any corporation, organized under the laws of this State, or any officer or stockholder thereof, as such, shall become or continue to be a member of any such trust, pool, contract, agreement, arrangement or combination, its charter shall become and be hereby forfeited, and it shall be the duty of the attorney-general of the county where the same is located, or having its principal office, to bring suit against such corporation in the circuit court of such county to have its said charter declared forfeited for that reason, and to wind up the same under the order of such courts. § 5. Be it further enacted that where action at law or suit in equity shall be commenced in any court of this State it shall be lawful in the defense thereof to plead in bar or in abatement of the action that the plaintiff or any other person or corporation interested in the prosecution of the action is a member or connected with and the cause of action grows out of some business or transaction with such trust, pool, contract, agreement, arrangement or combination, as described in the first section of this act. § 6. Be it further enacted that any person or corporation injured or damaged by any such trust, pool, contract, agreement, arrangement or combination may sue and recover fines in any court of competent jurisdiction double the amount of damages suffered by such person or corporation. § 7. Be it further enacted that upon the trial of any civil action against any corporation, person or co-partnership for a violation of any section of this act all officers, stockholders and agents of such corporation, person or co-partnership shall be competent witnesses against the defendant as such on trial, and such officers, stockholders and agents may be compelled to testify against such defendant, and produce all books and papers in their custody or control pertinent to the issues in such action at or before the time of trial, and shall not be excused from producing any books or papers, because the same might tend to criminate such witnesses, but nothing which such witness shall testify to and no books or papers produced by him shall in any manner be used against him in any criminal action to which he is a party. § 8. Be it further enacted that all acts and part of acts of the General Assembly of the State of Tennessee in conflict with this act be and the same are hereby repealed. § 9. Be it further enacted that this act take effect from and after its passage, the public welfare requiring it.

§ **212. Texas Law for the Suppression of Trusts and the Promotion of Free Competition.**—The original statute enacted by the legislature of the State of Texas was approved March 30th, 1889. It was entitled, "An act to define trusts, provide for penalties and punishment of corporations, persons, firms and associations of persons connected with them and to promote free competition in the State of Texas, and to repeal all laws and parts of laws in conflict with this act." In 1895 this act was amended. The amendment took effect April 30th, 1895. As amended the statute is, as follows: § 1. Be it enacted by the legislature of the State of Texas that a trust is a combination of capital, skill or acts by two or more persons, firms, corporations or association of persons, or either two or more of them, for either, any or all of the following purposes: 1. To create or carry out restrictions in trade or commerce, or aids to commerce, or to create or carry out restrictions in the full and free pursuit of any business authorized or permitted by the laws of this State. 2. To increase or reduce the price of merchandise, produce or commodities. 3. To prevent competition in manufacture, making, transportation, sale or purchase of merchandise, produce or commodities, or to prevent competition in aids to commerce. 4. To fix at any standard or figure, whereby its price to the public shall be in any manner controlled or established, any article or commodity of merchandise, produce or commerce intended for sale, use or consumption in this State. 5. To make or enter into or execute or carry out any contract, obligation or agreement of any kind or description by which they shall bind or have bound themselves not to sell, dispose of or transport any article or commodity, or article of trade, use, merchandise, commerce or consumption below a common standard figure, or by which they shall agree in any manner to keep the price of such article, commodity or transportation at a fixed or graded figure, or by which they shall in any manner establish or settle the price of any article or commodity or transportation between them or themselves and others to preclude a free and unrestricted competition among themselves or others in the sale or transportation of any such article or commodity, or by which they shall agree to pool, combine or unite any interest they may have in connection with the sale or transportation of any such article or commodity that its price might in any manner be affected. § 2. That any corporation holding a charter under the laws of the State of Texas which shall violate any of the provisions of this act shall thereby forfeit its charter and franchise, and its corporate existence shall cease and determine. § 3. For a violation of any of the provisions of this act by any corporation mentioned herein it shall be the duty of the attorney-general or district attorney, or either of them, upon his own motion and without leave or order of any court or judge, to institute suit or *quo warranto* proceedings in Travis county, at Austin, or at the county seat of any county in the State where such corporation exists, does business or may have a domicile, for the forfeiture of its charter rights and franchise and the dissolution of its corporate existence. § 4. Every foreign corporation violating any of the provisions of this act is hereby denied the right and prohibited from doing any business within this State, and it shall be the duty of the attorney-general to enforce this provision by injunction or other proper proceedings in the district court of Travis county, in the name of the State of Texas. § 5. That the provisions of chapter 48, general laws of this State, approved July 9th, 1879, to prescribe the remedy and regulate the proceedings by *quo warranto*, etc., shall, except in so far as they may conflict herewith, govern and control the proceedings when instituted to forfeit any charter under this act. § 6. If any person shall be or may become engaged in any combination of capital, skill or acts by two or more persons, firms, corporations or association of persons, or of either, two or more of them, for either, any or all of the following purposes: 1. To create or carry out restrictions in trade or commerce, or aids to commerce, or to create or carry out restrictions in the full and free pursuit of any business authorized or permitted by the laws of this State. 2. To increase or reduce the price of merchandise, produce or commodities. 3. To prevent competition in manufacture, making, transportation, sale or purchase of merchandise, produce or commodities, or to prevent competition in aids to commerce. 4. To fix at any standard or figure, whereby its price to the public shall be in any manner controlled or established, any article or commodity of merchandise, produce or commerce intended for sale, use or consumption in this State. 5. To make or enter into or execute or carry out any contract, obligation or agreement of any kind or description by which they shall bind or have bound themselves not to sell, dispose of or transport any article or commodity, or article of trade, use, merchandise, commerce or consumption below a common standard figure, or by which they shall agree in any manner to keep the price of such article, commodity or transportation at a fixed or graduated figure, or by which they shall in any manner establish or settle the price of any article or commodity or transportation between them or themselves and others to preclude a free and unrestricted competition among themselves and others in the sale or transportation of any such article or commodity, or by which they shall agree to pool, combine or unite any interest they may have in connection with the sale or transportation of any such article or commodity that its prices may in any manner be affected, or aid or advise in the creation or carrying out of any such combination, or who shall, as principal, manager, director, agent, servant or employe, or in any other capacity, knowingly carry out any of the stipulations, purposes, prices, rates, directions, conditions or orders of such combination, shall be punished by a fine of not less than fifty nor more than five thousand dollars, and by imprisonment in the penitentiary not less than one nor more than ten years, or by either such fine or imprisonment. Each day during a violation of this provision shall constitute a separate offense. § 7. In any indictment for an offense named in this act it is sufficient to state the effects or purposes of the trust or combination, and that the accused was a member of, acted with or in pursuance of it, without giving its name or description, or how, when or where it was created. § 8. In prosecutions under this act it shall be sufficient to prove that a trust or combination, as defined herein, exists, and that the defendant belonged to it or acted for or in connection with it, without proving all the members belonging to it or proving or producing any article of agreement or any written instrument on which it may have been based, or that it was evidenced by any written instrument at all. The character of the trust or combination alleged may be established by proof of its general reputation as such. § 9. Persons out of the State may commit and be liable to indictment and conviction for committing any of the offenses enumerated in this act, which do not in their commission necessarily require a personal presence in this State, the object being to reach and punish all persons offending against its provisions, whether within or without the State. § 10. Each and every firm, person, corporation or association of persons who shall in any manner violate any of the provisions of this act shall for each and every day that such violation shall be committed or continued forfeit and pay the sum of fifty dollars, which may be recovered in the name of the State of Texas in any county where the offense is committed, or where either of the offenders reside, or in Travis county, and it shall be the duty of the attorney-general or the district or county attorney to prosecute for and recover the same. § 11. That any contract or agreement in violation of the provisions of this act shall be absolutely void and not enforceable either in law or equity. § 12. That the provisions hereof shall be held cumulative of each other and of all other laws in any way affecting them now in force in this State: Provided, this act shall not be held to apply to live stock and agricultural products in the hands of the producer or raiser, nor shall it be understood or construed to prevent the organization of laborers for the purpose of maintaining any standard of wages. § 13. That nothing in this act shall be held or construed to affect or destroy any rights which may have accrued or to affect the right of the State to recover penalties or to affect the right of the State to forfeit charters of domestic corporations and prohibit foreign corporations from doing business in this State, or affect the right of the State to maintain prosecutions for violations thereof, under any law of this State relating to trusts, for acts heretofore done. § 14. Any court, officer or tribunal, having jurisdiction of the offense defined in this act, or any district or county attorney or grand jury may subpœna persons and compel their attendance as witnesses to testify as to the violation of any of the provisions of the foregoing sections. Any person so summoned and examined shall not be liable to prosecution for any violation of said sections about which he may testify fully and without reservation. § 15. All laws or parts of laws in conflict with this act are hereby repealed. § 16. Whereas the people of this State are without an adequate remedy against trust, therefore an emergency and imperative public necessity exists requiring that the constitutional rule which requires that all bill shall be read on three several days be suspended, and it is so enacted.

§ **213. Utah Law Prohibiting Pools and Trusts.**—The legislature of the State of Utah, relating to pools and trusts, consists of, "An act prohibiting and providing for the punishment of persons, co-partnerships, associations and corporations forming pools, trusts, combinations or conspiracies to affect or control the price of professional services or to affect or control the price, or limit or lessen the production, manufacture, consumption, use or sale of any article or commerce, manufacture or product of the soil, means for the suppression of such evils and remedies for persons injured thereby." This act was approved March 9th, 1896, and is, as follows: Be it enacted by the legislature of the State of Utah: § 1. Any combination by persons, having for its object or effect the controlling of the prices of any professional services, any products of the soil, or of any article of manufacture or commerce, or the cost of exchange or transportation, is prohibited and hereby declared unlawful. Any persons who shall violate the foregoing provisions shall be subject to prosecution and punishment as hereinafter provided. § 2. If any person or association of persons shall create, enter into, become a member of, or a party to, any pool, trust, agreement, combination, confederation or understanding with any other person or persons to regulate or fix the price of any article of merchandise or commodity, or shall enter into, become a member of, or a party to, any pool, trust, agreement, contract, combination or confederation to fix or limit the amount or quantity of any article, commodity or merchandise to be manufactured, mined, produced or sold in this State, such person or persons shall be deemed and adjudged guilty of a conspiracy to defraud, and be subject to punishment as hereinafter provided. § 3. It shall not be lawful for any corporation to issue or to own trust certificates, or for any corporation, agent, officer or employe, or the directors or stockholders of any corporation, to enter into any combination, contract or agreement with any person or persons, the purpose and effect of which combination, contract or agreement shall be to place the management or control of such combination or combinations, or the manufactured product thereof, in the hand of any trustee or trustees, with the intent to limit or fix the price or lessen the production and sale of any article of commerce, use or consumption, or to prevent, restrict or diminish the manufacture or output of any such article, or to monopolize any part of the trade or commerce within this State. § 4. If a corporation, a company, a firm or association shall be found guilty of a violation of this act it shall be punished by a fine in any sum not less than one hundred dollars nor more than two thousand dollars for the first offense; and for the second offense not less than five hundred dollars nor more than five thousand dollars; and for the third offense not less than five thousand dollars nor more than ten thousand dollars; and for every subsequent offense shall be liable to a fine of fifteen thousand dollars. § 5. Any president, manager, director or other officer, agent or receiver of any corporation, company, firm or association, or any member of any company, firm or association or any individual, found guilty of a violation of this act may be punished by a fine of not less than one hundred dollars nor to exceed one thousand dollars, or by confinement in the county jail not to exceed one year, or both, in the discretion of the court before which such conviction may be had. § 6. Any contract or agreement in violation of any provision of the preceding sections of this act shall be absolutely void. § 7. Any corporation created or organized by or under the laws of this State, which shall violate any of the provisions of the preceding sections of this act, shall thereby forfeit its corporate right and franchise, and its corporate existence shall thereupon cease and determine. § 8. It shall be the duty of the secretary of state, upon satisfactory evidence that any corporation or association of persons, incorporated or operating under the laws of this State, have entered into any trust, combination or association, as provided in the preceding provisions of this act, to give notice to such corporation that unless they withdraw from and sever all business connections with said trust, combination or association, their corporate right and franchise will be revoked at the expiration of thirty days from the date of such notice. § 9. At the expiration of the thirty days mentioned in the last preceding section, the secretary of state shall cause a certified statement of the facts to be filed in the office of the attorney-general of the State, who shall procure or direct such proceedings by any county attorney in the State, to commence an action in the district court of any county in the State of competent jurisdiction, to forfeit and revoke the corporate right and franchise of such corporation. When such proceedings are instituted they shall be conducted as orderly law actions, triable by court or jury. On the final decision of the same, should the defendant be found guilty of a violation of any of the provisions of this act said court shall render a judgment, and order a revocation of the charter, corporate rights and franchises of said corporation as a penalty for the violation or violations of which the said corporation shall be found guilty, and the secretary of state shall thereupon make publication of such revocation in four newspapers in general circulation in four of the largest cities of the State. § 10. In case any person or persons shall do, cause to be done or permit to be done any act, matter or thing in this act, prohibited or declared to be unlawful, such person or persons shall be liable to the person or persons injured thereby for treble the amount of damages sustained in consequence of any such violation of the provisions of this act. § 11. The words "person" or "persons," wherever used in this act, shall be deemed to include corporations, companies and associations existing under or authorized by the laws of either the United States or any of the territories, any State or any foreign country.

§ 214. **Washington Law Forbidding Trusts and Monopolies.**—Section 22d, of article XII., of the constitution of the State of Washington, provides that monopolies and trusts shall never be allowed in this State, and no incorporated company, co-partnership or association of persons in this State shall, directly or indirectly, combine or make any contract with any other incorporated company, foreign or domestic, through their stockholders or the trustees or assignees of such stockholders, or with any co-partnership or association of persons, or in any manner whatever, for the purpose of fixing the price or limiting the production or regulating the transportation of any product or commodity. The legislature shall pass laws for the enforcement of this section by adequate penalties, and, in case of incorporated companies, if necessary for that purpose, may declare a forfeiture of their charter. The legislation for the enforcement of this provision is included in a statute, entitled, "An act to regulate the sale of farm, dairy, orchard or garden produce on commission." This act was approved March 21st, 1895, and is, as follows: The section here given is the section of chapter CXLVIII. of the Session

Laws of Washington for 1885: § 5. It shall be unlawful for persons engaged in the business of commission merchants to enter into any combination, conspiracy or pool for the purpose of artificially raising or depressing the market prices of any farm, dairy, orchard or garden produce, or of excluding from the market the produce of any particular locality,—grown or manufactured by any person.

§ 215. **Wisconsin Statute Prohibiting Trusts and Combinations in Restraint of Trade.**—The law of Wisconsin on this subject is entitled, "An act to prevent corporations organized under the laws of this State from entering into any combination, conspiracy, trust, agreement or contract intended to operate in restraint of any lawful trade or commerce carried on in this State." This act was approved April 27th, 1897, and is, as follows: The people of the State of Wisconsin, represented in senate and assembly, do enact, as follows: § 1. Corporations organized under the laws of this State are prohibited from entering into any combination, conspiracy, trust, pool, agreement or contract intended to restrain or prevent competition in the supply or price of any article or commodity in general use in this State, or constituting a subject of trade or commerce therein, or to control the price of any such article or commodity, to regulate or fix the price thereof, to limit or fix the amount or quantity thereof to be manufactured, mined, produced or sold in this State, or to fix any standard or figure by which its price to the public shall be in any manner controlled or established. § 2. Whenever the attorney-general of this State shall be notified or shall have reason to believe that any corporation, organized under the laws of this State, has violated any provision of section one of this act, it shall be his duty forthwith to address to any such corporation, or to any director or officer thereof, such inquiries as he may deem necessary for the purpose of determining whether or not such corporation has violated any provisions of section one of this act, and it shall be the duty of such corporation, director or officer thereof, so addressed, to promptly and fully answer in writing, under oath, such inquiries, and in case such corporation, or director or officer thereof, shall fail or neglect to do so within sixty days from the receipt of such inquiries, unless such time is extended in writing by the attorney-general, it shall be the duty of the attorney-general to proceed against such corporation, as hereinafter provided. § 3. In case of the failure or neglect of any corporation, organized under the laws of this State, or of any director or officer of such corporation, to answer such inquiries, as hereinbefore provided, such failure or neglect is hereby declared to be a forfeiture of the charter of such corporation, and it is hereby made the duty of the attorney-general on leave granted by the supreme court of this State, upon cause shown, to bring an action for the purpose of vacating the charter and annulling the existence of such corporation. § 4. No person shall be excused from answering any of the inquiries herein provided for, nor excused from attending and testifying, nor from producing any books, papers, contracts, agreements or documents in obedience to a subpœna issued by any lawful authority in any case or proceeding based upon or growing out of any alleged violation of any of the provisions of this chapter, or of any law of this State in regard to trusts, monopolies or illegal combinations, on the ground of or for the reason that the answer, testimony, evidence, documentary or otherwise, required of him, may tend to criminate him, or subject him to a penalty or forfeiture, but no person shall be prosecuted or subjected to any penalty or forfeiture for or on account of any transaction, matter or thing concerning which he may answer, testify or produce evidence, documentary or otherwise, in obedience to any request under this chapter, or any subpœna, or either of them, in any case or proceeding, except that the charter of any corporation may be vacated and its corporate existence annulled, as hereinbefore provided, and except further, that no person testifying in any case or proceeding aforesaid shall be exempt from prosecution and punishment for perjury committed in so testifying. § 5. This act shall take effect and be in force from and after its passage and publication.

CHAPTER XIV.

REMEDIES BY QUO WARRANTO AND INJUNCTION.

§ 216. Introductory.
217. The Writ of Quo Warranto.
218. The Subject Continued.
219. Ground of Proceedings against Monopolies and Industrial Combinations.
220. What Courts have Jurisdiction.
221. Who may File an Information.
222. Pleadings and Averments.
223. Judgment under Proceedings in Quo Warranto.
224. Application of the Rule to Illegal Combinations.
225. Remedy by Injunction.
226. The Subject Continued.
227. Punishment for Contempt.

§ **216. Introductory.**—From the preceding chapter it will be seen that constitutional and statutory remedies against monopolies and illegal combinations have been provided by the Federal government and by more than two-thirds of the States. In other States the courts have granted relief of an extraordinary character by *quo warranto* and injunction. Though certain phases of the law remain in a degree unsettled, some progress has been made during recent years, and the present trend is in the direction of granting full and adequate relief in this manner. The object of this chapter is to present some illustrations of the remedies of this character.

§ **217. The Writ of Quo Warranto.**—The origin of the writ of *quo warranto* is traceable to a very early period of English jurisprudence. The earliest case that has been cited is that of Darley v. The Queen, in A. D. 1198.[1] During the centuries which followed it came into frequent

[1] Darlay v. The Queen, 12 Cl. & Fin. 520.

use, and was sometimes used to strengthen the power of the crown at the expense of the barons. But where these encroachments had been in a degree restrained by statute, ambitious princes resorted to the original writ of *quo warranto*. Both the original writ and the information in the nature of the writ were remedies of the crown, and though they were not infrequently abused they have always been recognized as the proper remedies for the abuse or for the usurpation of franchises.[1] This writ is defined by

[1] "In times of feudal barbarity which accompanied and followed, for many years, the overgrown power of the nobles, there was constant occasion to apply the corrective of the *quo warranto*. It was the only effectual remedy, even if it could be called a remedy in itself; for monopolies had become so numerous, and so fortified by interest and power, that the application of the writ depended in greater measure on the personal character of the prince, than moral submission to the law. This was especially so, when the writ was brought to bear upon manorial claims residing in the hands of the barons or lords, either temporal or spiritual. Looking at Keilwey's report of cases in Eyre, in time of the memorable king, Richard the Third, fol. 137 to 152, one would be led to believe that a good deal of his reign was devoted to this sort of judicial contest with his nobles. Indeed, his predecessor, Edward the First, had found single writs too slow; and caused a statute to be passed under which his noblemen were called by proclamation and obliged to come by squadrons before his immediate court or his justices in Eyre, whenever they entered the county. 2 Reeves' Hist. 220, Dubl. ed. 1787; Com. Dig. Quo Warranto (C. 2): Crabb's History of the Engl. Law, 174, 175. This bearing too much the appearance of plunder, another statute was passed somewhat moderating the proceeding, and bringing it back to about the common law course. 2 Reeves' Hist. ed., before cited, 221; Crabb, *ut supra*. This is the statute on which Sir Edward Coke has furnished us with a labored commentary in his 2 Inst. 294. Still, as appears from the history of the times, the writ continued to be a very common resort, and to have been almost avowedly used to strengthen the crown at the expense of the barons. It was sometimes extended even to lands, though Coke shows that its proper office respected franchises only. Pursued in such a spirit, it may be true that the consequences claimed were occasionally severe and disproportioned to the offenses alleged. The pursuit being also sometimes more stringent, and sometimes more lax, when the case of the city of London came to be argued, it is not surprising that authorities should be found conflicting on the question whether you could go merely for correcting some particular abuse, or claim a forfeiture of the whole franchise on that ground. Several distinct franchises, though in the same hand, might be sev-

Blackstone, as follows: "A writ of *quo warranto* is in the nature of a writ of right, for the king, against him who claims or usurps any office, franchise or liberty, to inquire by what authority he supports his claim, in order to determine the right. It lies, also, in case of non-user or long neglect of a franchise, of misuser or abuse of it, being a writ commanding the defendant to show by what warrant he exercises such a franchise, having never had any

ered by judgment; and the extending of the writ to land must have increased the confusion, this being so easily divisible from the incidental prescriptive franchise. Judgments must, therefore, often have been given in the same cause, for the king in respect to the latter, leaving the former still in the hands of the subject. The instance put in argument, that, for the abuse of a tenant by the commission of waste, the landlord shall recover only the place wasted, finds an answer in the divisible nature of the subject. The difficulty was probably increased by the crown many times suing merely to cut off an extravagant claim made in respect to a single franchise, being willing to leave the acknowledged franchise untouched, even in cases where total forfeiture might have been claimed. The question will be found to have been a great deal examined in the case of the city of London by Finch, solicitor-general, 3 Harg. St. Tr. 549, 550, for the crown; by Sir George Treby, recorder of the city, *contra*, *Id.* 565, to 567, and by Sir Robert Sawyer, *Id.* 579. The latter said that, to forfeit the toll illegally taken is idle; it is no punishment, for they never had any right to it. They can only be punished by taking away their acknowledged rights. *Vide*, also, Comyn's Dig. Franch. (G. 3.) Some of the distinctions depending on the divisible character of the subject are noticed in Viner's Abr. Franch. (E.) Other pertinent rules are then laid down: 'A man has franchises and uses more than he ought, this is a forfeiture; but if 'he uses less, this is finable.' *Pl.* 1. He who has fair to hold two days, and holds it three days, forfeits the whole fair. So where a man has market to hold the Saturday, and he holds it another day.' *Pl.* 3, *marg. and Pl. 3.* 'If a lord refuses to do a thing according to his franchise, or does contrary to his franchise, or misuses it, by himself, his bailiff or deputy, or non-uses the franchise, the franchise shall be reseized. *Pl.* 7. He puts several abuses in respect to prisoners in jails held within a franchise or liberty, viz.: groundless detention, or repeated escapes, as a reason of forfeiting the whole liberty. *Pl.* 4, 10. So oppression arising from gross ignorance of the judge as to the nature of the crime, or his usurpation by repeatedly issuing a *capias* where he has jurisdiction of summons only, or for inflicting illegal punishment. *Pl.* 13, 15, 16. So of non-feasance,— as if the lord having liberty of jurisdiction, refuses to attend the justices of assize in person or by deputy; and so the not having able grant of it, or having forfeited it by neglect or abuse. This was originally returnable before the king's justices at Westminster, but afterwards only before the justices in Eyre, by virtue of the statutes of *quo warranto;* but since those justices have given place to the king's temporary commissioners of Assize, the judges in the several circuits, this branch of the statutes hath lost its effect: and writs of *quo warranto* must now be prosecuted and determined before the king's justices at Westminister. And in case of judgment for the defendant, he shall have an allowance of his franchise; but in case of judgment for the king, for that the party is entitled to no such franchise, or hath disused

officers, judicial and ministerial, with proper instruments of punishment, or omitting legal punishments after conviction. *Pl.* 8. 13. He winds up with the general remark of Lord Holt, which I before cited from 12 Mod. 271. Under the same title (A) *pl.* 3. he lays down what must be a very general if not an universal rule, that franchises cannot be divided if they are entire. To all the cases put he cites the authorities. In Earl of Shrewbury's Case, 9 Rep. 50, much of the doctrine as noticed in Viner, is summed up and what acts of non-feasance shall operate as a forfeiture is examined with reference to the nature of the franchise. In Baggs' Case, 11 Rep. 98, it is said of misfeasance and non-feasance, that in order to found a proceeding for forfeiture, there must be an act or such neglect as is tantamount; and an instance of the last is a game keeper, and game being killed in consequence of his negligence. There he shall lose his office. The ancient authorities when looked into on the point of divisibility, and applied to a corporation, must now all be received subject to the city of London. There the taking of an illegal toll was held sufficient to work a total forfeiture of the city charter, with its thousand franchises. *Vide*, a summary of that case, 2 Show. 263 to 279, marg. page and note (*t*). Lond. ed. 1794. The entire roll is given in 6 Harg. St. Tr. App. 15 to 39, including at the last page judgment of general and absolute seizure. The corporate abuse which is to work a forfeiture, therefore, need not be of any particular measure or extent. The writ and information were known remedies; and in the historical sketch already given, will be seen to have been sometimes pushed beyond their proper bearing against the subject. So far they should be taken with grains of allowance. Sometimes, however, they were unreasonably narrowed in the hands of weak princes, but they have been steadily recognized as in general of most salutary effect in favor of the commonwealth, and in a view to this have been sustained by the courts as important remedies, in nature of right." Cowen, J., in People v. Bristol & Rensselaerville Turnpike Co., 23 Wend. 222, 240.

or abused it, the franchise is either seized into the king's hands, to be granted out again to whomsoever he shall please; or if be not such a franchise as may subsist in the hands of the crown, there is merely judgment of *ouster*, to turn out the party who usurped it. The judgment on a writ of *quo warranto* is final and conclusive, even against the crown, which, together with the length of its process, probably occasioned that disuse into which it is now fallen, and introduced a more modern method of prosecution, by *information*, filed in the court of the king's bench by the attorney-general, in the nature of a writ of *quo warranto;* wherein the process is speedier, and the judgment not quite so decisive. This is properly a criminal method of prosecution, as well to punish the usurper by a fine for the usurpation of the franchise as to oust him, or to seize it for the crown; but hath long been applied to the mere purposes of trying the civil right, seizing the franchise or ousting the wrongful possessor; the fine being nominal only."[1]

§ **218. The Subject Continued.**—The following statement of the office of an information in the nature of a *quo warranto* and of the conditions which justify a judgment of forfeiture in *quo warranto* proceedings, by Mr. Justice Michell, in The State v. The Minnesota Thresher Manufacturing Company, is very clear and comprehensive: "It is proper in this connection to consider briefly the second principal question referred to at the outset, viz.: the office of an information in the nature of *quo warranto*, and what will amount to such a misuser of corporate franchises as to justify a judgment of forfeiture in such proceedings. And right here it is important to keep in mind certain distinctions which it seems to us counsel for relator has over-

[1] 3 Blackstone's Commentaries, 262. See also State v. Real Estate Bank, 5 Ark. 595; s. c., 41 Am. Dec. 109; People v. Manhattan Co., 9 Wend. 351; Reg. v. Archdall, 3 N. & P. 696; s. c., 8 A. & E. 281; State v. Ashley, 1 Ark. 279; Com. v. Small, 26 Pa. St. 31; Rex v. Trinity House, Sid. 86; Lindsey v. Attorney-General, 33 Miss. 509; State v. Paul, 5 Stew. & P. (Ala.) 40; Com. v. Murray, 11 S. & R. 73; s. c., 14 Am. Dec. 614; State v. Portland, etc. R. Co., 58 N. H. 113; Rex v. Williams, 1 Burr. 402. See also 9 Anne, chap. 20.

looked. And, first, these special proceedings upon information must not be confounded with a civil action, under Gen. Stat. 1878, chap. 79. Although, in a general sense, the two may be termed 'concurrent remedies,' yet it is undoubtedly true that the office or function of the latter has been enlarged somewhat beyond that of a common law *quo warranto* information. In some jurisdictions, as formerly with us, the civil action is the only remedy. But while *quo warranto* having been revived in this State, we have now the two remedies, yet the office of the writ of *quo warranto* ought not to be extended beyond what it was at common law. The remedy by civil action is more in accordance with the ordinary mode of judicial procedure in determining property rights; and ought to be pursued except in those special or exceptional cases where the public interests seem to demand a more speedy or summary mode of procedure than by action in the district court. The common law *quo warranto* information, as we have it to-day, is substantially as left by the changes and modifications made by the statute of 9 Anne, chap. 20. The scope of the remedy furnished by it is to forfeit the franchises of a corporation for misuser or non-user. It is, therefore, necessary, in order to secure a judicial forfeiture of the respondent's charter to show a misuser of its franchise justifying such a forfeiture; and, as already remarked, the object being to protect the public, and not to redress private grievances, the misuser must be such as to work or threaten a substantial injury to the public, or such as to amount to a violation of the fundamental condition of the contract by which the franchise was granted, and thus defeat the purpose of the grant; and ordinarily the wrong or evil must be one remediable in no other form of judicial proceeding. Courts always proceed with great caution in declaring a forfeiture of franchise, and require the prosecutor seeking the forfeiture to bring the case clearly within the rules of law entitling him to exact so severe a penalty. It is also necessary to notice the distinction frequently overlooked between *franchises* and *powers*. The definition of a 'franchise,' given by Finch, adopted by Blackstone, and accepted by every authority since, is 'a royal privilege or branch of the king's prerogative, subsisting in the hands of a subject.' To a franchise the right possessed must be such as cannot be excused without the express permission of the sovereign power, —a privilege or immunity of a public nature which cannot be legally exercised without legislative grant. It follows that the right, whether existing in a natural or artificial person, to carry on any particular business, is not necessarily or usually a franchise. The kinds of business which corporations, organized either under title 2, chap. 34, or under the Act of 1873 are authorized to carry on are powers, but not franchises, because it is a right possessed by all citizens who choose to engage in it without any legislative grant. The only franchise which such corporation possess is the general franchise to be or exist as a corporate entity. Hence, if they engage in any business not authorized by the statute, it is *ultra vires*, or in excess of their powers, but not a usurpation of franchise not granted nor necessarily a misuser of those granted. Acts in excess of power may undoubtedly be carried so far as to amount to a misuser of the franchise to be a corporation and a ground for its forfeiture. How far it must go to amount to this the courts have wisely never attempted to define, except in very general terms, preferring the safer course of adopting a gradual process of judicial inclusion and exclusion as the cases arise. But we think it may be safely stated as the general consensus of the authorities that, to constitute a misuser of the corporate franchise, such as to warrant its forfeiture, the *ultra vires* acts must be so substantial and continued as to amount to a clear violation of the condition upon which the franchise was granted, and so derange or destroy the business of the corporation that it no longer fulfills the end for which it was created. But, in case of excess of powers, it is only where some public mischief is done or threatened that the State, by the attorney-general, should interfere. If, as between the company and its stockholders, there is a wrongful application of the capital, or an illegal incurring of liabilities, it is for the stockholders to complain. If the company is entering contracts *ultra vires*, to the prejudice of persons outside the corporation, such as creditors, it is for such persons to take steps to protect their interests. The mere fact that acts are *ultra vires* is not necessarily a ground for interference by the State, especially by *quo warranto*, to forfeit the corporate franchises. It should also be borne in mind that acts *ultra vires* may justify interference on the part of the State by injunction to prohibit a continuance of the excess of powers, which would not be sufficient ground for a forfeiture in proceedings in *quo warranto*, and hence many of the numerous authorities cited by relator, being of that class, are not entirely in point here."[1]

[1] State v. Minnesota Thresher Mfg. Co., 40 Minn. 213, 224. "The code rules of pleading do not apply to proceedings in the nature of *quo warranto*. Pleading in such cases is governed by the rules in force at the time of the adoption of the code. At common law, unaided by statute, double pleading was not allowable: and as the proceeding by information, in the nature of *quo warranto*, was regarded in England as a criminal prosecution, as well to punish the usurper by fine for the usurpation of the franchise, as to oust him or seize it for the crown, such proceeding was held not to be embraced in the statute of 4 Anne, chap. 16, § 4, allowing defendants to plead more than one plea. Cole on Criminal Informations, 112, 113, 129; Rex v. Newland, Sayres, 96; Rex v. Leigh, 4 Burr. 2146. In New York, the same view has been taken as to the nature of the proceedings. People v. President, etc. Manhattan Co., 9 Wend. 337, and note to People v. Richardson, 4 Cow. 113; People v. Jones, 18 Wend. 604. But in this State the proceeding has been divested of its criminal character, and is treated by the statute merely in the nature of a civil proceeding. No punishment is authorized to be inflicted by fine or otherwise, except where the party is adjudged guilty of contempt in disobeying the order of the court." State v. McDaniel, 22 Ohio St. 354, 361. The jurisdiction and power of the courts was not affected by the provision of the Code of Procedure (§ 428), abolishing the writ of *quo warranto* and proceedings by information in the nature thereof; it is only the form of the proceeding that was done away with. The remedies theretofore had in those forms may now be obtained by civil action. People v. Hall, 80 N. Y. 117. "A writ of *quo warranto* is not a writ of right. Even our Act of Assembly of June 14, 1836, recognizes this. * * * Before the Act of 1836, informations in the nature of *quo warranto*, at the instance of a private relator were always required to be with leave

§ 219. Ground of Proceedings Against Monopolies and Industrial Combinations.—Judgment against a corporation under proceedings in *quo warranto* is an extreme penalty. It is a death sentence, and is pronounced only where the action complained of is clearly in violation of the terms of its charter. The rule by which the courts are governed is stated by Mr. Justice Finch, with great clearness and force, in the case of The People v. The North River Sugar Refining Company, as follows: "The judgment sought against the defendant is one of corporate

of the court, and leave was not granted except on application of a competent relator. No one was held competent who had not a sufficient interest to warrant his interference, and our statute has made no change in this particular. Its second section gives to courts of common pleas concurrent jurisdiction with the supreme court in five classes of cases. The first three relate to municipal and other corporate offices, and the act provided that, in any such case, the writ might be issued upon the suggestion of the attorney-general or his deputy in the respective county, or of any person or persons desiring to prosecute the same. The other two classes relate to usurpations of corporate rights or forfeitures of corporate privileges. As the act was reported by the commissioners to revise the Civil Code, it was drawn so as to provide that writs in such cases should be granted only upon the suggestion of the attorney-general or his deputy. The legislature, however, altered the provision, and enacted that writs in these cases, as in the others, might be issued upon the suggestion of any person or persons desiring to prosecute the same. But the statute of 9 Anne allowed information at the relation of any person desiring to sue or prosecute them, and under that statute the rule was that a private relator must have an interest. Our act which substantially incorporates the provision of the British statute has received the same construction. This court has construed the words 'any person or persons desiring to prosecute the same' to mean any person who has an interest to be affected. They do not give a private relator the writ in a case of public right involving no individual grievance. This was ruled in Commonwealth v. Allegheny Bridge Company, 20 Pa. St. 185, in Murphy v. Farmers' Bank, 20 Pa. St. 415, and Commonwealth v. Railroad Co., 20 Pa. St. 518. And it is to be observed that the legislature has placed all five classes of cases enumerated in the act on the same footing in this particular. If a private relator cannot sue out a writ to enforce a forfeiture without having an interest, the statute gives him no greater right when he complains of usurpation of a county or township office." Commonwealth v. Cluley, 56 Pa. St. 270; s. c., 94 Am. Dec. 75, 76. "A *quo warranto* information is a criminal proceeding only in name and in form, in its nature it is death. The State, which created, asks us to destroy; and the penalty invoked represents the extreme rigor of the law. Its infliction must rest upon grave cause, and be warranted by material misconduct. The life of a corporation is indeed less than that of the humblest citizen, and yet it envelopes great accumulations of property, moves and carries in large volume the business and enterprise of the people, and may not be destroyed without clear and abundant reason. That would be true even if the legislature should debate the destruction of the corporate life by repeal of the corporate charter; but it is beyond dispute where the State summons the offender before its judicial tribunals and submits its complaint to their judgment and review. By that process it assumes the burden of establishing the charges which it has made and must show us warrant in the facts for the relief which it seeks. Two of the charges preferred in the complaint have dropped out of sight. They were of little importance, and have been prudently dismissed from the inquiry for that reason; and we are left to consider the one grave and serious accusation to which alone the proofs and

purely a civil proceeding. See 2 Kyd. on Corp. 439: The King v. Francis, 2 T. R. 484. In the language used in The King v. The Mayor, etc. of Cambridge, cited in 2 Kyd. on Corp. 483, the corporation is called upon to answer to no crime or offense, but only touching its liberties. The primary and only material object of the proceedings is not the infliction of pains or penalties as in criminal proceedings, but to deprive the individual members of the supposed corporation of privileges they claim to enjoy above the lot of citizens in general. The fine inflicted on a conviction is merely nominal. It is so immaterial a part of the proceedings, that the books on the subject of corporations have almost lost sight of it. The conclusion of the judgment, it is true, is said to be with a *capias pro fine*. But this is more the form than the substance of the judgment as in all civil actions founded on tort: for when the proceedings are by writ of *quo warranto*, the conclusion of the judgment is, that the defendants be in mercy, etc., as in civil actions founded on contract. 2 Kyd. on Corp. 409. The fine authorized by the Act of 1819, p. 156, to be inflicted in *quo warranto* informations, is not embraced by this case, as that act extends only to usurpations of office. So, that, with us, the fine may be very properly left out of the case: and then the proceedings are so conclusively of a civil nature as to form no colorable pretense for this constitutional objection." State Bank v. State, 1 Blackf. 267, 272.

argument have been directed. That accusation is adequate to the purpose for which it was framed, but upon two conditions, which dictate the line of inquiry and limit the area of discussion. It appears to be settled that the State, as prosecutor, must show on the part of the corporation accused some sin against the law of its being which has produced, or tends to produce, injury to the public. The transgression must not be merely formal or incidental, but material and serious, and such as to harm or menace the public welfare; for the State does not concern itself with the quarrels of private litigants. It furnishes for them sufficient courts and remedies, but intervenes as a party only where some public interest requires its action. Corporations may, and often do, exceed their authority where only private rights are affected. When these are adjusted all mischief ends and all harm is averted. But where the transgression has a wider scope and threatens the welfare of the people, they may summon the offender to answer for the abuse of its franchise or the violation of its corporate duty. The code of civil procedure authorizes an action for that purpose when the corporation has 'violated any provision of law whereby it has forfeited its charter or become liable to be dissolved by the abuse of its powers.' In Thompson v. People the ground of forfeiture was tersely described as 'some misdemeanor in the trust injurious to the public;' and as recently as the case of Leslie v. Lorillard we said, 'in the granting of charters the legislature is presumed to have had in view the public interest; and public policy is concerned in the restriction of corporations within chartered limits; and a departure therefrom is only deemed excusable where it cannot result in prejudice to the public.' "[1]

[1] People v. North River Sugar Refining Co., 121 N. Y. 582, 608. See also People v. Bristol, 23 Wend. 235; Ches., etc. Co. v. Baltimore, etc. R. Co., 4 Gill & J. 1; Leslie v. Lorillard, 110 N. Y. 531; s. c., 18 N. E. Rep. 363. Where all, or a majority of the stockholders composing a corporation, do an act which is designed to affect the property and business of the company, and which, through the control their members give them over the selection and

§ 220. What Courts Have Jurisdiction.—It is well established that in the absence of legislation on this subject the common law courts have exclusive jurisdiction in all cases relating to the forfeiture of franchises. A bill in equity will not lie for the purpose of determining whether a corporation was organized in a legal manner where this power has not been specifically conferred by legislative enactment. In that class of States in which the distinction

conduct of the corporate agencies, does affect the property and business of the company, in the same manner as if it had been a formal resolution of its board of directors, and the act so done is *ultra vires* of the corporation and against public policy, and was done in their individual capacities for the purpose of concealing their real purpose and object, the act should be regarded as the act of the corporation; and, to prevent the abuse of corporate power, may be challenged as such by the State in a proceeding in *quo warranto*. State *ex rel.* v. Standard Oil Co., 49 Ohio St. 137. "The trust, then, being repugnent to public policy and illegal, it is impossible to see why the same is not true of the corporation which succeeds to it and takes its place. The control exercised over the distillery business of the country,—over production and prices,—and the virtual monopoly formerly held by the trust, are in no degree changed or relaxed, but the methods and purposes of the trust are perpetuated and carried out with the same persistance and vigor as before the organization of the corporation. There is no magic in a corporate organization which can purge the trust scheme of its illegality, and it remains as essentially opposed to the principles of sound public policy as when the trust was in existence. It was illegal before and is illegal still, and for the same reasons. But it is urged that the defendant, by its charter, is authorized to purchase and own distillery property, and that there is no limit placed upon the amount of property which it may thus acquire. By its certificate of organization it is authorized to engage in a general distillery business in Illinois and elsewhere, and to own the property necessary for that purpose. It should be remembered that grants of powers in corporate charters are to be construed strictly, and that what is not clearly given is, by implication, denied. The defendant is authorized to own such property as is necessary for carrying on its distillery business, and no more. Its power to acquire and hold property is limited to that purpose, and it has no power, by its charter, to enter upon a scheme of getting into its hands and under its control all, or substantially all, the distillery plants and the distillery business of the country, for the purpose of controlling production and prices, of crushing out competition, and of establishing a virtual monopoly in that business. Such purposes are foreign to the powers granted by the charter. Acquisitions of property to such between law and equity has been abolished, a petition in which the relator sets forth a cause of forfeiture will be sustained, if supported by adequate proof. The granting of a writ of *quo warranto* is the exercise of an original jurisdiction, hence where the supreme court of a State is vested with appellate jurisdiction only, it has no power to issue such a writ. But where the constitution of a State invests the supreme court with original jurisdiction in such "remedial cases," as may be prescribed by statute, such power is held to include proceedings in *quo warranto*, In many of the States the supreme court will decline to issue this suit. In the case of The State *ex rel.* McIlhaney v. Stewart, before the Supreme Court of Missouri, Mr. Justice Napton, in delivering the opinion of the court, said: "There is no doubt that this court is mainly intended by the constitution as an appellate tribunal. In some instances original jurisdiction has been given to it, but chiefly with a view to enable it to exercise more effectually its superintending control over inferior courts. Its power in proceedings in *quo warranto* seems to be a departure from the general policy evinced in the construction of the court. Whether this jurisdiction was designed to extend to that class of information which, under the English statutes, had become essentially civil actions, commenced and conducted in the name of a public officer, but really for the mere ascertainment and settlement of private rights, is a question which might justify some hesitation and consideration, if it were necessary now to determine it. The legislature, it is certain, has furnished this court with none of the machinery

extent and for such purpose do not come within the authority to own the property necessary for the purpose of carrying on a general distillery business. In acquiring distillery properties in the manner and for the purposes shown by the information, the defendant has not only misused and abused the powers granted by its charter, but has usurped and exercised powers not conferred by, but which are wholly foreign to, that instrument. it has thus rendered itself liable to prosecution by the State by *quo warranto*, and we are of the opinion that upon the facts shown by the information the judgment of ouster is clearly warranted." Distilling and Cattle Feeding Co. v. The People, 156 Ill. 448, 491.

for trying issues in fact, and in practice such trials are altogether without precedent. These informations are attended with all the forms, and must progress through all the stages incident to any other writ. There are pleas and demurrers, issues in law and in fact, trials by jury, motions for new trials in arrest of judgment and writs of error. The issue of fact by the common law must be tried in the county where the franchise is situated. If such a proceeding is entertained by this court, it must be conducted solely according to the forms of the common law, for neither the statute of W. & M. nor of Anne is in force here; nor does our own statute apply to the supreme court, but is exclusively confined to the circuit courts."[1] In New Jersey the same rule

[1] State v. Stewart, 32 Mo. 379, 384. "As the information in this case was filed at the relation of a private person, and as it further appears from the pleadings in the cause that the relation and respondent are rival claimants for the office of register of the city of Lexington, and that the proceeding is, therefore, nothing more than a contest over the title to said office, we are of opinion that the writ of *quo warranto* has been improvidently issued, and the proceeding will, therefore, be dismissed. We see nothing in the circumstances of this case of such an exceptional nature as to induce us to depart from our long established custom to decline original cognizance of causes of this character. State *ex rel.* Young v. Buskirk, 43 Mo. 111, and cases there cited. They can be tried with much less expense and inconvenience by the inferior tribunals having jurisdiction thereof, and the condition of our docket is not such as to invite accessions thereto by the unnecessary exercise of our original jurisdiction." State v. Claggett, 73 Mo. 388. The supreme court is strictly an appellate tribunal, and has no original jurisdiction except in cases of *habeas corpus;* and consequently is not empowered to issue a writ of *quo warranto*, for the purpose of inquiring by what authority a person exercises the duties of a collector of the foreign license tax. People v. Attorney-General, 1 Cal. 85. "In People v. Perry (79 Cal. 106), we said: '*Quo warranto* was a case at law; it afforded the legal remedy for the usurpation of an office, and we think this court retains jurisdiction of the case, notwithstanding the legislature may have changed the procedure, enlarged the remedy, and given it a new name. To hold otherwise, would be to admit a power in the legislature to abridge our jurisdiction, and take from parties the right of appeal, by the easy device of a change of procedure, in many cases, where the right and jurisdiction are unquestioned.' Jurisdiction in this class of cases having been conferred on the superior court by the constitution, such jurisdiction could not be taken away or abridged by the legisla-

is maintained. In a leading case, the court said: "It is an established principle of the law concerning corporations that the charter of a corporation will not be declared to be forfeited, for misuse or abuse of its powers, except in a proceeding instituted directly for that purpose, by the government granting the charter. In such matters the courts will never act on the relation of any individual, and the reason is that the matter is one which concerns the State alone. The State may exact the forfeiture or waive it, as may seem best to it for the public interests. The question whether a corporation has forfeited its franchises or not is one over which the common law courts have exclusive jurisdiction, and over which this court has no control whatever in the absence of legislations."[1] In Minnesota it has been held that the

ture, and a statute existing at the time the constitution was adopted conferring jurisdiction on some other tribunal was superseded by such constitutional provision, so far, at least, as it could be held to have conferred exclusive jurisdiction upon such tribunal. Haight v. Gay, 8 Cal. 300; s. c., 48 Am. Dec. 323; Montrose v. State, 61 Miss. 429; High on Extraordinary Legal Remedies, § 615." People v. Bingham, 82 Cal. 238, 242. The supreme court of this State is limited in its powers to the decision of such questions as properly arise in the due course of law, in a judicial proceeding within its jurisdiction. Hence, in a proceeding in *quo warranto* to try the title of persons to an office, held under the provision of an act of the General Assembly, when its validity is questioned, it is only such provisions of said act as affect the title to the office, that are properly before the court for its judicial settlement. State v. Baughman, 38 Ohio St. 455. The legality of the organization or formation of a corporate body, such as a drainage district and its right to perform corporate acts or functions when it is a *de facto* corporation, cannot be questioned by bill in chancery. The proper remedy to test the legality of a corporation, and its power to perform certain acts assumed by it, is by information in the nature of a *quo warranto*. Kergivin v. Drainage Commissioners, 115 Ill. 347.

[1] Jersey City Gas Light Co. v. Consumers' Gas Co., 40 N. J. Eq. 427, 431. The remedy by information in the nature of *quo warranto*, though criminal in form, is in effect a civil proceeding. A statute abolishing the common law proceeding by information in the nature of *quo warranto*, and authorizing an action to be brought in cases in which that remedy was applicable, makes the proceeding a civil action for the enforcement of a civil right, subject to removal from State courts to the courts of the United States when other circumstances permit. Proceedings by a State against a corporation created under its own laws, in the

supreme court has jurisdiction by *quo warranto* to enforce the forfeiture of the charter of a corporation.[1] In the decision in this case, the court said: "In this case the jurisdiction of this court to issue writs of *quo warranto* is for

nature of *quo warranto* for the abondonment, relinquishment and surrender of its powers to another corporation with which it has been consolidated under a law of the United States, and proceedings against the directors of said consolidated company for usurping the powers of such State corporation are, when in the form of civil actions, suits arising under the laws of the United States, within the meaning of the acts regulating the removal of causes. When a suit brought by a State in one of its own courts against a corporation amenable to its own process, to try the right of the corporation to exercise corporate powers within the territorial limits of the State, presents a case arising under the laws of the United States, it may be removed to the Circuit Court of the United States, if other jurisdictional conditions exist. In view of the practical construction put upon the constitution by Congress and the courts in the statutes and decisions, the court is unwilling to say that it is not within the power of Congress to grant to inferior courts of the United States jurisdiction in cases where the supreme court has been vested by the constitution with original jurisdiction. Ames v. Kansas, 111 U. S. 449.

[1] State v. St. Paul & Sioux City Ry. Co., 35 Minn. 222. The right of the supreme court to issue the writ of *quo warranto* is recognized in general terms by our statutes,—the occasions are left to be determined by common law rules. And by those rules, it is apparent the writ is the appropriate mode in which to try any alleged usurpation of offices, or franchises inconsistent with the State sovereignty. State v. Boston, etc. R. R. Co., 25 Vt. 433. "Original jurisdiction in proceedings in *quo warranto* is conferred upon the supreme court by the constitution of the State. (Const. Art. 3, § 3.) And this jurisdiction so conferred is just what was understood to be *quo warranto* jurisdiction at the time when the constitution was adopted. As throwing light upon the last proposition, see Leavenworth Co. v. Miller, 7 Kan. 502; The State v. W. W. Ry. Co., 34 Wis. 197. This jurisdiction cannot be abolished, or increased, or diminished, by the legislature. The State v. Allen, 5 Kan. 213; Graham v. Cowgill, 13 Kan. 114; State v. Graham, 13 Kan. 136. Of course, the legislature has the power indirectly to affect the exercise of this jurisdiction, as it has the power directly or indirectly to affect almost every other matter or thing coming within the purview of the constitution. It may increase or diminish, or create or destroy any particular instances in which this jurisdiction may be exercised; but it cannot increase, or diminish, or abolish, or destroy the jurisdiction itself. Thus it may create additional offices, or additional grounds for forfeiture, and thereby increase the number of instances in which the court may exercise its jurisdiction; or it may abolish some of the offices

the first time brought in question. The act conferring on the court the power 'to issue the writ' was passed in 1876. The constitution (§ 2, art. 6), prescribes that the court shall have 'original jurisdiction in such remedial cases as may be prescribed by law, and appellate jurisdiction in all cases, both in law and in equity, but there shall be no trial by jury in said court.' It is evident that the term 'remedial cases' has here but a limited signification, and cannot extend to all remedies for wrongs; for a very important part of the machinery to administer such remedies in most cases, to-wit, the jury, is withheld from the court. It has been the understanding of the court, as we think from the beginning, and we think also of the bar, as it evidently has been of the legislature, that the cases intended by the term 'remedial cases' are those where the remedy is afforded summarily, through certain extraordinary writs, such as prohibition, *mandamus*, *certiorari* and *quo warranto*, any greater or less extensive meaning could hardly be given to the term without making it so indefinite as to make it difficult to say what it means. We are satisfied that is the sense in which the term was used in the constitution. Taking that to be the meaning, the grant of power by the legislature to the court in cases of *quo warranto* is ample and unlimited. There is nothing in the suggestion of respondent that the legislature did not intend to vest the power, or that if so, it ought not to be exercised in cases where the statute furnishes some other adequate mode of reaching the same result, as is furnished, in cases falling within the scope of the writ of *quo warranto*, by chapters 76, 79, Gen. Stat. 1878. Those chapters were in force

already existing, or some of the grounds for forfeiture already existing, and thereby diminish the number of instances in which the court may exercise its jurisdiction. In this way it may really create or destroy instances in which the jurisdiction may be exercised. But within these limitations whenever a proper case arises for the exercise of *quo warranto* jurisdiction, as *quo warranto* jurisdiction was understood and known at the time of the adoption of the constitution, this court may take jurisdiction of the case and determine the same, whatever may be the enactments of the legislature upon the subject." State v. Wilson, 30 Kan. 661, 665.

when the Act of 1876 was passed, and of course the legislature, in passing that act, must have intended that the court should have, and also should, in proper cases, exercise jurisdiction by *quo warranto*, notwithstanding the provisions of those chapters. As between the remedy in this court by *quo warranto* and that by action in the district court, it is for the attorney-general, to whom the interests of the State in such cases are intrusted, to determine which he will pursue."[1]

§ 221. **Who May File an Information.**—The misuse or the non-use of its franchise by a corporation is an offense against the public. Theoretically, at least, a franchise is granted as a public benefit. In accepting a franchise a corporation assumes certain public obligations, and it forfeits its franchise only as these obligations are not discharged. The public there is the party to bring a suit for the forfeiture of a franchise, and the public can act in such a case only through the attorney-general. A private citizen will not have leave to file an information unless he has some special ground of complaint. In order to obtain such permission he must have some cause of complaint that is not common to other citizens similarly situated. But when individuals and not the public are affected by the abuse of a franchise, a private person may obtain leave of the court to file an information. The court has power to grant or refuse such a motion in the case of a private citizen, but the attorney-general or a prosecuting attorney may institute *quo warranto* proceedings, *virtute officii*, and without the permission of the court.[2] In some of the States there are

[1] State v. St. Paul & Sioux City Ry. Co., 35 Minn. 222.

[2] Commonwealth v. Lexington, etc. Turnpike, 6 B. Mon. 397; Commonwealth v. Union Ins. Co., 5 Mass. 230; Houston v. Neuse River, etc. Co., 8 Jones. 476; Commonwealth v. Burrell, 7 Pa. St. 34; Harrison v. Greaves, 59 Miss. 453; State v. McConnell, 3 Lea, 332; Gibbs v. Somers' Point, 49 N. J. L. 515; Patterson v. Hubbs, 65 N. Car. 119; Wright v. Allen, 2 Tex. 158; State v. Schneirle, 5 Rich. 299; State v. Dehesseline, 1 McCord, 52; Cleary v. Dehesseline, 1 McCord, 35; People v. Dernille, 15 Mich. 164; State v. Haumer, 42 N. J. L. 435; State v. Jenkins, 25 Mo. 484; Churchill v. Walker, 68 Ga. 681; Barnum v. Gilman, 27 Minn. 466; State v. Bieler, 87 Ind.

statutes authorizing any person who has an interest in the corporation to request the attorney-general or other prosecuting officer to institute proceedings, and in case of his re-

320; State v. London, 91 Ind. 351; Miller v. Palermo, 12 Kan. 14; Demarest v. Wickham, 63 N. Y. 320; Robinson v. Jones, 14 Fla. 256; State v. Stein, 13 Neb. 529; State v. Tipton, 109 Ind. 73; Commonwealth v. McCarter, 98 Pa. St. 604. "In England, the attorney-general could file *quo warranto* and other informations at his discretion. But in practice he seldom did so except where the prerogatives of the crown were specially concerned. Where the interests of individuals were intermingled with those of the crown, the master of the crown office in Kings' Bench was the usual officer to exhibit informations. In the exercise of this function he stood in a relation to individuals similar to that of the attorney-general to the crown. Cole on Informations, 110; Goddard v. Smithett, 3 Gray, 116. But in 1693, Statute of 4 and 5, Wand., M., chap. 18, relating to trespasses and batteries and other misdemeanors, was passed, for the purpose, as Mr. Justice Wilmot says, in Rex v. Marsdon, 3 Burr. 1817: 'To prevent the master of the crown office from vexing and oppressing the subject, or without sufficient ground and foundation; so that the act was made to check and control the power of the master of the crown office; not to give him a right to exercise a power which he never exercised before; quite the contrary.' After this act, the master of the crown office could not file an information without leave. This statute has been shown to govern *quo warranto* informations by the master of the crown office, the filing of which by that officer was not introduced but only regulated by the statute of 9 Anne. Cole on Informations, 126. This act required the relator's name to be mentioned in the information, and this, and the previous act of W. & M. requiring the person at whose suggestion the suit had been instituted, to give an undertaking for costs, should prosecution fail, gave rise to the practice of filing *quo warranto* informations, entitled on the relation of private persons,— the relator being altogether the creature of statute. Ang. & Ames on Corp. § 733; Cole on Informations, 127. But an information against a corporation as a body, to annul its corporate existence, could not be filed by the master of the crown office. Such informations were filed by the attorney-general; and leave was not required,—he was the sole judge of the propriety of filing the information. The law requiring leave of the court before an information could be filed, applied only to the master of the crown office. Rex v. Carmarthen, 2 Burr. 869; Murphy v. Farmers' Bank, 20 Pa. St. 415; Commonwealth v. Turnpike Co., 6 B. Mon. 397. With us, the filing of *quo warranto* information, the several district attorneys possess the powers as well as those usually exercised by the attorney-general, as by the master of the crown office; but the statute preserves, with few exceptions, the distinction between actions by them, acting *ex officio* in the former capacity, and *ex relatione* in the Attorney-General v. Railroad Co.,

9 Vroom. 282; The State v. Stewart, 32 Mo. 379. Our statute limits the power of the district attorney, acting *ex officio*, in requiring him to get leave. But when leave has been granted, the discretionary power of the court has been expended. The State v. Brown, 5 R. I. 6. The district attorney is the law officer of the State, within the limits of his district, with the powers, in the absence of statutory regulation, of the attorney-general at common law. Constitution of Oregon, art. 7, § 17. Therefore, when, as in the case before us, the district attorney files a *quo warranto* information in a distinctly State action, he has as much the sole control over it as the attorney-general would have in a like case at common law. A relator cannot be a party to the proceeding,—is a mere stranger,—and if his name is put in the information, it is surplusage. Rex v. Williams, 1 Burr. 408; The People v. The Trustees of Geneva College, 5 Wend. 219. The reason is plain the State, out of its sovereign power, has created the corporation for the purposes declared in its charter, and the same power must preside at its dissolution. The State may waive the forfeiture of the charter, and its power to do so, acting through its attorney, cannot be controlled by the court. State v. McConnell, 3 Lea (Tenn.), 339; Commonwealth v. Union Insurance Co., 5 Mass. 232; The People v. Attorney-General, 22 Barb. 117; The People v. Tobacco Co., 42 How. Pr. 162; The People v. Fairchild, 8 Hun. 334; s. c., 67 N. Y. 334." State v. Douglas Co. Road Co., 10 Ore. 198, 200. The attorney-general has the right, in the name and behalf of the commonwealth, at his own discretion, to file an information against one usurping a public office, the court has no authority to grant or to withhold leave to file it, and the mention of relators in the information is mere surplusage, which does not affect the validity of the information, or the form of the judgment to be rendered thereon. Commonwealth v. Allen, 128 Mass. 308. "There is no doubt about the jurisdiction of the circuit court. It is an information filed by the prosecuting attorney *ex officio*. Informations filed by the attorney-general or prosecuting attorney, *ex officio*, may be filed without leave, as a matter of course. Information by either officer, at the relation of an individual, must be filed by leave of court. State *ex rel.* Stewart v. McIlhany, 32 Mo. 382; State *ex rel.* v. Hequembourg, 38 Mo. 535; State *ex rel.* v. Vail, 53 Mo. 97; State *ex rel.* v. Townley, 56 Mo. 107." State v. Boyd, 84 Mo. 198, 201. "It was objected on behalf of the defendants that they should not be put to answer this information, because it was filed without leave of the court. The objection, however, is not well taken. When facts exist which, in the opinion of the attorney-general, call for a *quo warranto* information, he has the right to present it, without leave asked of any one. In that respect he represents the sovereignty, whose attorney he is. Such a power existed unquestionably at common law, and neither the statute of 9 Anne, nor our own statute, in any way abridged it. Before 9 Anne *quo warranto* informations were filed either by the attorney-general or solicitor-general *ex officio*, or by an officer of the court under the direction of the court, at the instance of the party concerned. Such officer, in

fusal such person may act directly or in person.[1] In Colorado it has been held that a complaint filed by a private citizen for the dissolution of a corporation under the code provisions relating to "actions for the usurpation of an office or franchise," alleging that the district attorney refused the to bring suit, but stating no other or different interest of the relator in the result than that common to every citizen, is insufficient to support the action, and a demurrer thereto for such cause may be properly sustained. The general rule is that prosecutions for wrongs done to the public must be instituted by the State, through its properly authorized agents, while an individual can sue only for injuries peculiarly affecting himself.[2] In Illinois it has been held that if a public wrong is done by the abuse of a franchise, and no private injury appears, a proceeding by *quo warranto* must be by the public prosecutor or other authorized agent of the State, and a private citizen cannot in such case have the aid of this extraordinary remedy. But in cases affecting only private rights, and which merely affect the administration of corporate functions, and not the existence of the corporation, the court may interpose upon proper showing. The attorney-general or State's attorney, if the information affects public rights only, may act at the instance of any individual who may furnish him the requisite proofs to authorize him to act, whom he may name relator, but he must act in his official capacity, under a sense of official duty, and not merely lend his name for the use of a

the Kings' Bench, was the master of the crown office. The statute of 9 Anne merely regulated the practice in some cases of this latter class, requiring the parties concerned to be named as relators and to become responsible for costs, etc. Our statute substitutes the attorney-general for this master of the crown office and extends the range of the act; but in such case the attorney-general is only nominally a party,—a mere officer of he court,—subject to its control; he is not there as attorney-general, exercising in the cause that power which such officer had at common law, and which he still wields when he appears *ex officio*. Attorney-General v. Delaware, etc. R. R. Co., 38 N. J. L. 282, 286.

[1] People v. Grand River Bridge Co., 13 Colo. 11; s. c., 21 Pac. Rep. 898.

[2] People v. Grand River Bridge Co., 13 Colo. 11; s. c., 21 Pac. Rep. 898.

private party.[1] In the case of Murphy v. The Farmers' Bank of Schuylkill County of Pennsylvania, the court said: "The authorities show that they do not give a private relator the writ of *quo warranto* in a case of public prerogative involving no individual grievance. On this point the authorities are full, direct and harmonious. The usurpation of an office, established by the constitution, under color of an executive appointment, and the abuse of a public franchise under color of a legislative grant, are public wrongs, and not private injuries, and the remedy by *quo warranto*, in this court at least, must be on the suggestion of the attorney-general, or some authorized agent of the commonwealth. For the authorities I refer myself to those cited in the argument of the respondent's counsel. They establish this as the uniform construction in questions involving the existence of a corporation. In questions involving merely the administration of corporate functions, or duties which touch only individual rights, such as the election of officers, admission of a corporate officer or member, and the like, the writ may issue at the suit of the attorney-general, or of any person or persons desiring to prosecute the same. * * * These are general views which harmonize with the doctrine of the cases, and, therefore, whilst I recognize the right of any relator to have a *quo warranto* in the supreme court who is desirous to prosecute the same to redress any private grievance that falls within that remedy, I deny the right of any party except the attorney-general or other officer of the commonwealth to sue for it to dissolve a corporation."[2]

§ 222. **Pleadings and Averments.**—A proceeding by information in *quo warranto*, though it still retains its original form as a criminal process, is now regarded in nearly all the States as a civil remedy for the determination of civil rights. No uniform system has been adopted, but in ordinary cases it is not necessary for the relator to allege

[1] The People v. North Chicago Railway Co., 88 Ill. 537.

[2] Murphy v. Farmers' Bank, 20 Pa. St. 415, 418.

and prove his title to the thing in controversy.[1] At present the weight of authority favors the rule that where an information is filed against a corporation by its corporate name, and process is issued and served upon it by that

[1] People v. Clark, 4 Cow. 95; State v. Com. Bank, 10 Ohio, 535. "The demurrer to the information filed by the solicitor-general rests upon the ground: first, that it does not follow the application, but enlarges the same. We do not understand that the officer of the State who is required *ex officio* to prepare the information and make out the declaration on which the State, *ex relatione* of the relators, rests its case is narrowed to the rigid rule of strictly following the petition of the relators. He may amplify and enlarge the facts and the prayer, not going out of the substantial subject-matter complained of before the judge and the judgment granting the prayer and directing the information filed. Secondly, it alleges that, even with the original petition or application, the two together make no case for the writ or judgment of ouster. It will be seen above that we differ from the learned counsel for plaintiffs in error, because we hold that the petition alone makes a sufficient case." Whelchel v. State, 76 Ga. 644, 648. The code rules of pleading do not apply to proceedings in the nature of *quo warranto*. Pleading in such cases is governed by the rules in force at the time of the adoption of the code. At common law, unaided by statute, double pleading was not allowable; and as the proceeding by information, in the nature of *quo warranto*, was regarded in England as a criminal prosecution, as well to punish the usurper by fine for the usurpation of the franchise, as to oust him or seize it for the crown, such proceeding was held not to be embraced in the statute of 4 Anne, chap. 16, § 4, allowing defendants to plead to more than one plea. Cole on Criminal Information, 112, 113, 129; Rex v. Newland, Sayres, 96; Rex v. Leigh, 4 Burr. 2146. * * * But in this State the proceeding has been divested of its criminal character, and is treated by the statute merely in the nature of a civil proceeding. No punishment is authorized to be inflicted by fine or otherwise, except where the party is adjudged guilty of contempt in disobeying the order of the court." State v. McDaniel, 22 Ohio St. 354, 360. "In proceedings by information in the nature of *quo warranto*, the range of inquiry is limited to the charges in the information; and matter set up by way of plea is only material in so far as it shows warrant in law for the exercise of the authority alleged in the information to be usurped. State v. City of Cincinnati, 23 Ohio St. 445, 465. A plea is a sufficeint response to an information in the nature of a *quo warranto*, if it sets up facts showing a right to exercise the office or franchise alleged to have been usurped. Where a statute prescribes a qualification for exercising an office or franchise, the plea need not be framed in the words of the law. It is sufficient if the facts set up show clearly the right. State *ex rel.* v. Jones, 16 Fla. 306. "In Mud

name, its legal existence as a corporation is thereby admitted. Where the corporation appears and makes answer by its corporate name, it is not competent for the State, by

Creek Draining Co. v. State, 43 Ind. 236, the court says: 'This first paragraph was clearly bad. It is not against certain persons claiming to be a corporation, but against the corporation by its corporate name. It is brought into court as a corporation to answer on allegation that it is not and never was a corporation. When a corporation is brought into court by its corporate name, its existence is thereby admitted.' In this case the corporation being made a party, its existence is admitted. It must follow, therefore, that there is no cause of action stated as against it. But there are other defendants sued jointly with it, and charged with having jointly with such corporation usurped the rights of a corporation, etc. There is no question made in the record or in the briefs as to misjoinder of these parties. But we are clear that the people cannot bring both a corporation and the individuals who compose it before the court, by information in the nature of *quo warranto*, and claim the non-existence of the corporation thus brought before the court, and that the other defendants jointly with it are claiming to be and exercise the rights and privileges of such corporation. To permit such a course would be subversive of all rules of pleading. If we are right in the position taken, that by suing the corporation as such its existence is admitted, this is an end of the matter, so far as this count of the complaint is concerned, for the reason that the whole force of its applications, as against the individual defendants, rests upon the sole ground that no such corporation exists. If the complaint can be defended on the ground that it admits that such a corporation once existed, but has ceased to exist, it is open to the objection made to it that it does not state the facts showing how and by what means it has ceased to exist. We are of the opinion that it would be sufficient, in an action against individuals charging that they are wrongfully claiming to act as a corporation, to allege, in general terms, that there never was such a corporation. In such case, the allegation that there never was such a corporation covers the whole ground. Nothing can be added to this general statement, which is itself an allegation of a fact. We are equally clear that where the existence of the corporation is expressly averred, or is admitted, it is not sufficient to allege that it has ceased to exist. The facts showing that its existence has terminated must be set forth. And if the claim is, that the corporation is acting as such, but the proceedings under which it is acting are defective, the facts showing that it is so claiming to act, and the defects claimed to exist should be set out specifically.'' People v. Stanford, 77 Cal. 360, 364. See also State v. Kupferle, 44 Mo. 154; State v. Beecher, 15 Ohio, 723; People v. Bartlett, 6 Wend. 422; Rex v. Leigh, 4 Burr. 2143; People v. Maynom, 5 Mich. 146; State v. Gleason, 12 Fla. 265; Thompson v. People, 23 Wend. 538.

replication, to deny the corporate existence of the defendant. If the franchise is to be brought into the question, the proceedings should be against the individuals who have usurped it. Where the charge is that of an unlawful use of a franchise by a corporation, the information should be against the corporation, but if the charge is that of usurping the rights and privileges of a corporation, it should be directed against the individuals who have committed the offense. If the corporation has no legal existence, the parties who are setting up the claim are the offenders and not the alleged corporation.[1] In a recent and leading case in Illi nois, the modern rule is stated by the court, as follows: "The tendency of the courts in modern times being to regard an information in the nature of a *quo warranto* in the light of a civil remedy, invoked for the determination of civil rights, although still retaining its criminal form and some of the incidents of criminal proceedings, the better doctrine now is that the pleadings should conform, as far as possible, to the general principles and rules which govern in ordinary civil actions. And this is especially so in this State in view of section 10 of our Practice Act, which provides that in cases of this character it shall be sufficient to summon the defendant to appear and answer the plaintiff in an action of *quo warranto*, and that the issues shall be made up by answering, pleading or demurring to the petition, as in other cases. It has been repeatedly held in this State that in proceedings of this character the defendant must

[1] Draining Co. v. State, 43 Ind. 236; People v. Stanford, 77 Cal. 360; s. c., 19 Pac. Rep. 694; State v. Gas Light & Coke Co., 18 Ohio St. 262; Commercial Bank v. State, 6 Sm. & M. 599. The information having been filed by the attorney-general, under the Act of May 1, 1852, against the defendant, by its corporate name, charging a usurpation of certain corporate franchises, and process having been issued and served accordingly, and the defendant having appeared and pleaded in a corporate capacity, setting up its charter, etc., it is not competent for the State, by replication, to deny the corporate existence of the defendant. When the franchise to be a corporation is intended to be drawn in question, the proceeding should, under our statutes, be against the individuals who usurp such franchise. State v. Cincinnati Gas Light & Coke Co., 18 Ohio St. 262.

either disclaim or justify. If he disclaims, the people are at once entitled to judgment; and if he justifies he must set out his title specially."[1]

§ 223. Judgment Under Proceedings in Quo Warranto.—In England a distinction is recognized between a judgment of ouster and a judgment of seizure.[2] The distinction of the English courts appears to have been recognized in this country at an early period.[3] In a leading case,

[1] Distilling & Cattle Feeding Co. v. People, 156 Ill. 448, 482.

[2] Smith's Case, 4 Mod. 53; Rex v. City of London, 3 Hay. Towns. St. Tr. 545; 1 Blackstone's Commentaries, 485.

[3] People v. Bartlett, 6 Wend. 422; People v. Rensselaer, etc. R. Co., 15 Wend. 113. "It is certain, however, that the dissolution of a corporation is effected by a seizure of its franchises, although the franchises themselves are not thereby destroyed, for they exist in the hands of the State and may be afterwards granted to the same or other individuals, in the same manner in which they were originally granted. But the existence of the corporation is terminated. It being so completely lost that it can have no power over nor connection with anything in existence; of course it can no longer be considered as the owner or possessor of lands or goods, rights or credits. But it does not follow that those lands and goods, rights and credits necessarily fall into the hands of the State; much less that they are proper objects to be included in the terms of the judgment. There are but two grounds on which it can be contended, that the corporate effects fall into the hands of the State: First, as a forfeiture for abusing the franchises; or, secondly, for the want of an owner by the dissolution of the corporation. When we examine the first of these grounds, we find nothing in the books to support an idea, that the abuse of corporate franchises occasions a forfeiture of lands or goods, rights or credits, or in fact, occasions any other forfeiture but the franchise themselves. The consequence of a breach of the implied condition on which their liberties were granted, was not that they should forfeit their property or possession if they abused their franchises, but only that they should forfeit the franchises. That which comes out of the hands of the king, is the proper subject of forfeiture; the king, by the seizure, resuming what originally flowed from his bounty. Authorities leading to this conclusion are numerous. See the cases cited in 2 Bac. 32, and in The King v. Emery, 2 T. R. 515. For the forfeiture is the same for non-user, when no property has been held or rights exercised, as for misuser or abuser, after the possession of much property and the exercise of extensive rights and credits; and the judgment is the same in both cases. Consequently, the judgment could not direct a seizure of the corporate possessions as a forfeiture for the violation of the charter. Nor is the second ground,—that the property falls to the State

before the Supreme Court of Judicature of the State of New York, the rule is stated, as follows: "Whenever individuals or a corporation shall be found guilty, either of usurping or intruding into any office or franchise, or of unlawfully holding, judgment of ouster shall be rendered, and a fine may be imposed; but when the proceeding is against a corporation, and a conviction ensues for misuser, non-user or surrender, judgment of ouster and of dissolution shall be rendered; which is equivalent to judgment of seizure at common law. If, therefore, the information in this case had for its object to oust the defendants from acting as a corporation, and to test the fact of their incorporation, it should have been filed against individuals; if the object was to effect the dissolution of a corporation which had had an actual existence, or to oust such corporation of some franchise which it unlawfully exercised, then the information is correctly filed against the corporation. The distinction is well exemplified by Sir Robert Sawyer, in The King v. The City of London.[1] He says the rule is this: 'When it clearly appears to the court that a liberty is usurped by wrong and upon no title, judgment only of ouster shall be entered. But

for the want of an owner, on the dissolution of the corporation,—more tenable as a foundation on which to sustain this judgment. For the ownership of the corporation does not cease until its dissolution. And whether it is dissolved by the judgment of seizure or not, until the State has execution on that judgment, is not here very material. For if the corporation is dissolved by the judgment, the judgment must be regularly entered, and have its full effect, before the dissolution takes place; and it is not till then that the property can be said to be without an owner. The loss of the property to the corporation is a consequence of the judgment; and it is a contradiction of the first principles of reason,—a complete reversal of effect and cause,—to make such loss of property a part of the judgment. That which cannot exist until after judgment, can never be the subject-matter on which the judgment is given. But the better opinion seems to be, that the corporation is not dissolved by the judgment of seizure; but that it exists until the franchises are seized by execution on that judgment. See 2 Kyd. on Corp. 409, 410, and the authorities there cited. Consequently, the last shadow of a support for this judgment on this ground must vanish." Holman, J., in State Bank v. State, 1 Blackf. 267, 280.

[1] King v. City of London, 2 T. R. 522.

when it appears that a liberty has been granted, but has been misused, judgment of seizure into the king's hands shall be given.' The reason is given: that which came from the king is returned there by seizure; but that which never came from him, but was usurped, shall be declared null and void. Judgment of ouster is rendered against individuals for unlawfully assuming to be a corporation. It is rendered against corporations for exercising a franchise not authorized by their charter. In such case the corporation is ousted of such franchise, but not of being a corporation. Judgment of seizure is given against a corporation for a forfeiture of its corporate privileges. The information in this case is, therefore, not the proper proceeding to call in question the corporate existence of the defendant; but in so far as it seeks to oust the defendants from the exercise of any franchise not granted to them it is appropriate. When, therefore, an information is filed under the revised statutes against a corporation by its corporate name, the existence of the corporation is admitted, or rather that it once had a legal existence."[1] In Massachusetts the rule has been stated, as follows: "Upon an information in the nature of a *quo warranto*, which in our practice has superseded the ancient writ of *quo warranto*, the judgment may be, that the franchise usurped be seized into the sovereigns hands, if it be one which the sovereign can repossess and enjoy, or it may be a judgment of ouster. In this commonwealth, in the case of a business corporation, where the object of the information is merely to declare the charter forfeited and to exclude the corporation from the right to further exercise its franchises, a judgment of ouster is appropriate, strictly and technically a judgment either of seizure or of ouster, probably does not dissolve the corporation, but it at least suspends the right to exercise its franchises."[2]

[1] People v. Rensselaer & Sar. R. R. Co., 15 Wend. 113; s. c., 30 Am. Dec. 33, 37.

[2] Campbell v. Talbott, 132 Mass. 174, 177. See also Rex v. Mayor of London, 1 Show. 274, 280; Rex v. Mayor & Aldermen of Hertford, 1 Ld. Raym. 426; s. c., 3 Salk. 374; Attorney-General v. Salem, 103 Mass. 138.

§ 224. Application of the Rule to Illegal Combinations.—In a recent and leading case in Nebraska we have the following illustration of the application of this rule in cases of this character: "The findings in this case, to which no objections are made, clearly show that the object of the distilling company in entering into the illegal combination was to destroy competition and create a monopoly, not only by limiting the production of alcohol, but by dismantling as many distilleries as the trust saw fit, absolutely prevent the manufacture of the article except in the few establishments controlled by the trust, and thus it would be enabled to control prices, prevent production, and create a monopoly of the most offensive character. Any contract entered into with such an object in view is, under the laws of this State, null and void, and the conveyance from the distilling company to the trust was in contravention of the authority conferred by the statutes on that company in excess of the powers granted by its charter, and against public policy and void, and no title passed by such conveyance. Since the bringing of this action the trust has endeavored to transfer the title of the property, and its attorney, after making an elaborate and able argument in its favor in this court, announced that he withdrew from the case. The court, however, cannot permit the trust thus to evade the law. If it can dismantle the property, it will, in part at least, have accomplished its illegal purpose. The property is within the jurisdiction of the court, and it is the duty of the court to make such disposition of it as the ends of justice may require. As there has been an abuse of the corporate franchise, it will be dissolved and annulled."[1]

[1] State v. Nebraska Distilling Co., 29 Neb. 700, 719. The Gas Trust Company mentioned was incorporated under the general law for two purposes, as expressed in its articles of association: First, for the purpose of erecting and operating gas works for the manufacture and sale of gas in Chicago and other places in this State; and, second, "to purchase and hold or sell the capital stock, or purchase or lease or operate the property, plant, good will, rights and franchises of any gas company or companies, in Chicago or elsewhere," etc. The company sought to exercise the powers claimed under the second clause only, and for that purpose bought a majority of

§ 225. Remedy by Injunction.—As we have seen, information by *quo warranto* is the usual process where there is an appeal to an extraordinary remedy, but there are cases where an injunction will issue. In the case of the United States v. The Trans-Missouri Freight Association, it was held that the fourth section of the act,—referring to the Federal Anti-Trust Act of July 2d, 1890,—invests the government with full power and authority to bring such a suit as this; and if the facts alleged are proved, an injunction should issue.[1] In the opinion in this case the rule is set forth by Mr. Justice Peckham, as follows: "It is also argued that the United States have no standing in court to maintain this bill; that they have no pecuniary interest in the result of the litigation, or in the question to be decided by the court. We think the fourth section of the act invests the government with full power and authority to bring such an action as this, and if the facts be proved, an injunction should issue. Congress having the control of interstate commerce, has also the duty of protecting it, and it is entirely competent for that body to give the remedy by injunction as more efficient than any other civil remedy."[2]

the shares of all the stock of all the gas companies in Chicago, being four in number, whereby it might have the control of all the gas companies in the city, and thus destroy competition and monopolize the gas business: *Held*, that the corporation so formed was not for a lawful purpose, and that all acts done by it toward the accomplishment of such object were illegal and void. People v. Chicago Gas Trust Co., 130 Ill. 268.

[1] United States v. Trans-Missouri Freight Association, 166 U. S. 290.

[2] United States v. Trans-Missouri Freight Association, 166 U. S. 290, 343. "We need not inquire how far, or under what circumstances, considerations of public policy and of the general interests of the State may affect the right of a corporation to discontinue the business for which it was created, and to surrender to another corporation its property and the conduct of such business. We do decide that such a surrender of the property, and, so far as possible, of the functions, of a corporation, in order that, which it is still to continue in existence, its business may be carried on by another corporation, to which such transfer is made, would violate the rights of a non-assenting stockholder arising from the contract implied, if not expressed, in the creation of such an organization; and he would be entitled to have such acts restrained by injunction. Stewart v. Erie & Western Trans. Co., 17 Minn. 348; Cook,

The leading authorities cited in this opinion is that of the decision of this court in the case of *In re* Debs. The opinion in this case is referred to as a full and able discussion of the rule. In that opinion the rule is stated, as follows: "Is there no other alternative than the use of force on the part of the executive authorities whenever obstructions arise to the freedom of interstate commerce or the transportation of the mails? Is the army the only instrument by which

Stocks, §§ 667, 668; 1 Mor. Priv. Corp. §§ 413, 416; Black v. Delaware, etc. Canal Co., 24 N. J. Eq. 455; Zabriskie v. Hackensack & N. Y. R. Co., 18 N. J. Eq. 178; Abbott v. Am. Hard Rubber Co., 33 Barb. 578; Middlesex R. Co. v. Boston & Chelsea R. Co., 115 Mass. 347. In the absence of express provisions to the contrary, it is to be considered as the law concerning business corporations that their affairs are to be managed in the interest of their stockholders, and by directors or agents appointed by them. Small v. Minneapolis Electro Matrix Co., 45 Minn. 264, 267. See also Central R. R. Co. v. Collins, 40 Ga. 582. "It is well settled that where a corporate excess of power tends to the public injury or to defeat public policy it may be restrained in equity at his suit. In Attorney-General v. Delaware & Bound Brook R. R. Co., 12 C. E. Green, 631, 633, in pronouncing the opinion of the court of errors and appeals, Mr. Justice Dixon said: 'In equity, as in the law court, the attorney-general has the right, in cases where the property of the sovereign or interests of the public are directly concerned, to institute suit by what may be called civil information for their protection. The State is not left without redress in its own court, because no private citizen chooses to encounter the difficulty of defending it, but has appointed this high public officer, on whom it has cast the responsibility, and to whom, therefore, it has given the right of appearing in its behalf and invoking the judgment of the court on such question of public moment.' Professor Pomeroy, in his work on Equity Jurisprudence, § 1093, states the rule in this language: 'When the managing body are doing, or are about to do, an *ultra vires* act of such a nature as to produce public mischief, the attorney-general, as the representative of the public and of the government, may maintain an equitable suit for preventive relief.' It appears that the attorney-general has the election in his discretion whether, in cases of excess in corporate powers, he will proceed at law to forfeit the charter and franchises or apply in equity for a restraint of the excess. Both tribunals are open to him. The right of appeal to equity does not depend upon the inadequacy of the legal remedy. This subject is stated by Chief Justice Ryan, in Attorney-General v. Railroad Companies, 35 Wis. 524, in this way: 'The equitable jurisdiction precludes the objection that there is an adequate remedy at law. It admits the remedy at law, but administers its own remedy in prefrights of the public can be enforced and the peace of the nation preserved? Grant that any public nuisance may be forcibly abated, either at the instance of the authorities or by any individual suffering private damage therefrom, the existence of this right of forcible abatement is not inconsistent with, nor does it destroy, the right of appeal in an orderly way to the courts for a judicial determination, and

erence when the State seeks it in preference. It seems to proceed on the presumption that it may better serve the public interest to restrain a corporation than to permit it by penal remedies or to forfeit its charter: and that, on that view, the proper officers of the State should have an election of remedies. And we may as well say, in this connection, that the jurisdiction to entertain these informations is wholly independent of an adequate remedy at law; and that were that otherwise we could not consider the informations in the nature of a *quo warranto*, pending in this court against these defendants, as an adequate remedy at law, which could be a substitute for or bar to the injunction asked. Judgment of ouster on those informations might not only be of far more grave consequence to the defendants, but might be far less beneficial to the State, and less accordant with its policy, and altogether less equitable and proper than the injunction sought to restrain the defendants from doing what is alleged to work a forfeiture of their charters.' There has been some disagreement among the cases as to whether an injunction will issue at the instance of the attorney-general to restrain every excess of corporate power or whether before it issues, actual threatened injury must be manifest. The argument which sustains the first class of cases is that every excess of corporate power violates the contract with the government, and thereby invades public and governmental rights. The law deems such invasion to be a public injury. An apt illustration is to be found in the case of Thomas v. West Jersey R. R. Co., 101 U. S. 71, where there was an authorized lease of a railroad. The supreme court there held, that the franchises and powers granted to a railway company are designed to be exercised by it for the public good, and this purpose enters into the consideration for the grant any contract therefore, by which the corporation disables itself to perform those duties to the public, or attempts to absolve itself from their obligation, without the consent of the State, is a violation of its contract with the State and tends to the public injury. The argument to sustain the other class of cases is that a court of equity should not move upon mere legal intendment, but should be satisfied of a real, substantial public injury which demands the writ of injunction in the due protection of the public. In the use at least, of a preliminary injunction, the latter class of cases appears to be the better founded in fitness and reason, for if there be no present emergency to be met why may not an exercise of their powers, by writ of injunction and otherwise, to accomplish the same result. In Stamford v. Stamford Horse Railroad Co.,[1] an injunction was asked by the borough to restrain the company from laying down its track in a street of the borough. The right of the borough to forcibly remove the track was insisted upon as a ground for questioning the jurisdiction of a court of equity, but the court sustained the injunction, adding: 'And none the less so because of its right to remove the track by force. As a rule, injunctions are denied to those who have adequate remedy at law, where the choice is between the ordinary and the extraordinary processes of law, and the former are sufficient, the rule will not permit the use of the latter. In some cases of nuisance, and in some cases of trespass, the law permits an individual to abate the one and prevent the other by force, because such permission is necessary to the complete protection of property and person. When the choice is between redress or prevention of injury by force and by peaceful process, the law is well pleased if the individual will consent to waive his right to the use of force and await its action. Therefore, as between force and the extraordinary writ of injunction, the rule will permit the latter.' "[2]

the injunction be reserved until final hearing? The authorities upon this subject are numerous. The following, among them, appear to me to best exhibit the contrariety of opinion that I have stated: Green's Brice's Ultra Vires (2d ed.), 708; Attorney-General v. Shrewsbury Bridge Co., L. R. 21 Ch. D. 752; Attorney-General v. Cockermough Local Board, L. R. 18 Eq. Cas. 172; Attorney-General v. Gt. Eastern Ry. Co., L. R. 11 Ch. D. 449; Attorney-General v. Gt. Northern Ry. Co., 1 Drew. & S. 184; s. c., 6 Jur. (N. S.) 1006; Attorney-General v. Railroads, 35 Wis. 525. The last cited case collects almost all the authority upon this subject." Stockton v. Central R. R. Co., 50 N. J. Eq. 52, 78. See also Cincinnati, New Orleans, etc. Ry. v. Interstate Commerce Commission, 162 U. S. 184; Texas & Pacific Ry. v. Interstate Commerce Commission, 162 U. S. 197.

[1] Stamford v. Stamford Horse Railroad Co., 56 Conn. 381.

[2] *In re* Debs, 158 U. S. 564, 582. See also Attorney-General v. Johnson, 2 Wils. Ch. 87; Attorney-General v. Forbes, 2 Myl. & Cr. 123; Attorney-General v. Terry, L. R. 9 Ch. App. 423; Attorney-General v. Birmingham, 4 Kay & J. 528; People v. Miner, 2 Lans. 396; People v. Ferry Co., 68 N.

§ **226. The Subject Continued.**—The right to bring a suit for an injunction under the Federal Anti-Trust Act of July 2d, 1890, is limited to the government. It is conferred by the act only on the government, and it has been held that it cannot be exercised in private suits. In the case of Greer, Mills & Co. v. Stoller,[1] before the Circuit Court for

Y. 71; Davis v. Mayor, etc., 14 N. Y. 526; People v. Vanderbilt, 28 N. Y. 396; s. c., 26 N. Y. 287; Attorney-General v. Hunter, 1 Dev. Eq. 12; State v. Dayton & S. E. R. Co., 36 Ohio St. 434; People v. St. Louis, 5 Gilman, 351; Gilbert v. Canal, etc. Co., 8 N. J. Eq. 495.

[1] Greer, Mills & Co. v. Stoller, 77 Fed. Rep. 1. The statute against unlawful restraints and monopolies (Act 1890, 26 St. p. 209) does not authorize the bringing of injunction suits or suits in equity by any parties except the government. Blindell v. Hagan, 54 Fed. Rep. 40. "The demurrer challenges the jurisdiction of this court to maintain, under the act in question, a bill in equity filed by a private individual and his solicitor. It is clear that the right to maintain such a suit is not expressly conferred by the act. Indeed, such right is, by implication, denied,—first, because a private person is given (section 7) the right to maintain an action at law; and, second, the district attorneys of the United States under the direction of the attorney-general (section 4) are charged with the duty of commencing suits in equity. If it were the intention of the law makers to vest in every irresponsible individual, who may deem himself aggrieved, the right to invoke the drastic and far reaching remedies conferred by the act, is it not reasonable to suppose that they would have said so in unambiguous terms? The first three sections are penal statutes. They give no civil remedy. Section 4, vests the right to institute proceedings in equity in the district-attorneys of the United States, and, together with section 5, prescribes the procedure in such suits. Section 6, provides for the seizure and forfeiture to the United States of property illegally owned under the provisions of the act. So far, then, the act is a public act providing no private remedy. If it ended with section 6 there would probably be no pretense that it sanctioned a suit like the one at bar. What follows, however, in no way strengthens the complainant's position. The only section which gives a private remedy is the seventh, which is, as follows: 'Any person who shall be injured in his business or property by any other person or corporation by reason of any thing forbidden or declared to be unlawful by this act, may sue therefor in any circuit court of the United States in the district in which the defendant resides or is found, without respect to the amount in controversy, and shall recover three fold the damages by him sustained, and the costs of suit including a reasonable attorneys fee.' But for this section no private person would have any standing in court, and as the only right conferred by it is the right to

the Western District of Missouri, it was held that a bill by members of a business exchange to enjoin the board of directors from enforcing against them certain by-laws of the association, on the ground that the same are illegal as being in restraint of trade and commerce, cannot be based upon the "anti-trust law" of July 2d, 1890 (26 Stat. 209); for the right given by section four thereof, to bring suits for injunction, is limited to suits instituted on behalf of the government. Therefore, the authority given by section five, to bring in non-residents of the district, cannot be availed of in private suits, and the court can acquire no jurisdiction over them.

§ 227. **Punishment for Contempt.**—The violation of an injunction is a contempt of court, and may be punished as such. Where the court has authority to issue an injunction it has power to enforce its decree by an appropriate penalty. In the case *In re Debs*, the rule is stated by the court, as follows: "The power of a court to make an order carries with it the equal power to punish for a disobedience of that order, and the inquiry as to the question of disobedience has been from time immemorial the special function of the court. And this is no technical rule. In order that a court may compel obedience to its orders it must have the right to inquire whether there has been any disobedience thereof. To submit the question of disobedience to another tribunal, be it a jury or another court, would operate to deprive the proceeding of half its efficiency. In the case of Yates,[1] Chancellor Kent, then Chief Justice of the Supreme Court of the State of New York, said: 'In the case of The Earl of Shaftesbury,[2] who was imprisoned by the House of Lords for "high contempts committed against it," and brought into the King's Bench, the court

sue for damages in a court of law, it follows that the point presented by the demurrer is well founded." Pidcock v. Harrington, 64 Fed. Rep. 821, 822.

[1] In the case of J. V. N. Yates, 4 Johns. 314, 369.

[2] In the case of the Earl of Shaftesbury, 2 St. Trials, 615; s. c., 1 Mod. 144.

held that they had no authority to judge of the contempt, and remanded the prisoner. The court in that case seem to have laid down a principle from which they never have departed, and which is essential to the due administration of justice. This principle that every court, at least of the superior kind, in which great confidence is placed, must be *the sole judge*, in the last resort, of contempts arising therein, is more explicitly defined and more emphatically enforced in the two subsequent cases of The Queen v. Paty and others,[1] and of The King v. Crosby.'[2] And again, on page 371, 'Mr. Justice Blackstone pursued the same train of observation, and declared that all courts, by which he meant to include the two houses of Parliament, and the courts of Westminister Hall, could have no control in matters of contempt. That the sole adjudication of contempts, and the punishment thereof, belonged exclusively, and without interfering, to each respective court.' In Watson v. Williams,[3] it was said: 'The power to fine and imprison for contempt, from the earliest history of jurisprudence, has been regarded as a necessary incident and attribute of a court, without which it would no more exist than without a judge. It is a power inherent in all courts of record and co-existing with them by the wise provisions of the common law. A court without the power effectually to protect itself against the assaults of the lawless, or to enforce its orders, judgments or decrees against the recusant parties before it, would be a disgrace to the legislation, and a stigma upon the age which invented it.' In Cartwright's Case,[4] we find this language: 'The summary power to commit and punish for contempt tending to obstruct or degrade the administration of justice is inherent in courts of chancery and other superior courts, as essential to the execution of their powers, and to the maintenance of their authority,

[1] Queen v. Paty. 2 Ld. Raym. 1105.

[2] King v. Crosby. 3 Wils. 188; s. c., 2 Bl. Rep. 754.

[3] Watson v. Williams, 36 Miss. 331, 341.

[4] Cartwright's Case. 114 Mass. 230, 238.

and is part of the law of the land, within the meaning of Magna Charter and of the twelfth article of our Declaration of Rights.' "[1]

[1] *In re* Debs. 158 U. S. 564, 594. "The contention of these parties is, that they were entitled to a trial by jury on the question as to whether they were guilty or not of the contempt charged upon them, and because they did not have this trial by jury they say that they were deprived of their liberty without due process of law within the meaning of the Fourteenth Amendment to the Constitution of the United States. If it has ever been understood that proceedings according to the common law for contempt of court have been subject to the right of trial by jury, we have been unable to find any instance of it. It has always been one of the attributes,— one of the powers necessarily incident to a court of justice,— that it should have this power of vindicating its dignity, of enforcing its orders, of protecting itself from insult without the necessity of calling upon a jury to assist it in the exercise of this power." Eilenbecker v. Plymouth County, 134 U. S. 31, 36. See also United States v. Hudson, 7 Cranch, 32; Anderson v. Dunn, 6 Wheat. 204; *Ex parte* Robinson, 19 Wall. 505; Mugler v. Kansas, 123 U. S. 623, 672; *Ex parte* Terry, 128 U. S. 289; Interstate Commerce Commission v. Brunson, 154 U. S. 447, 488.

CHAPTER XV.

STATUTORY REGULATION OF RATES OF TRANSPORTATION.

§ 228. Introductory.
229. Statutory Enactments Subject to Judicial Investigation.
230. Right of Railroad Corporations to Legal Protection.
§ 231. Right of Railway Companies to Discriminate in Rates of Transportation.
232. Rule for Determining what are Reasonable Rates.

§ 228. **Introductory.**—It is now well settled that a State legislature has the power to regulate the rates of transportation of persons and property by railways, subject to its authority, unless it has parted with its inherent right by a special contract with a railway corporation in granting its charter. But this power is not absolute. It is subject to certain constitutional and legal limitations. A legislature has power to protect the people of a State by prohibiting the collection of unjust and oppressive rates of transportation, but it may not itself act the part of an oppressor by compelling a railway company to carry persons or property at a rate so low as to deprive it of a fair compensation for the use of its property, and thus practically to deprive it of the capital invested by it, without due process of law and without consideration. Statutory regulations of railway charges must not be in contravention of the constitutional rights of railway corporations, and they must be within the bounds of justice and reason. The recent decision of the Supreme Court of the United States in the leading and very important case of Smyth v. Ames, presents a number of points which involve a new application of legal principles, and which are of special interest and importance.

§ 229. **Statutory Enactments Subject to Judicial Investigation.**—So far as relates to questions of legality, the enactments of legislatures are subject to investigation by the courts. While a legislature may fix the rates of transportation by railways, subject to its authority, it must not exceed its powers in that direction, and the question of the extent of its powers is a matter for judicial investigation and decision. In the case of Smyth v. Ames, it was held by the Supreme Court of the United States that a suit against individuals for the purpose of preventing them, as officers of a State, from enforcing an unconstitutional statute to the injury of plaintiff's rights, is not a suit against the State, within the meaning of the Eleventh Amendment to the Federal Constitution. While rates for the transportation of persons and property within the limits of a State are, primarily, for its determination, the question whether they are so unreasonably low as to deprive the carrier of its property without such compensation as the constitution secures, and, therefore, without due process of law, cannot be so conclusively determined by the legislature of the State, or by regulations adopted under its authority, that the matter may not become the subject of judicial inquiry.[1]

[1] Smyth v. Ames, 18 Sup. Ct. Rep. 418. "The adequacy or inadequacy of a remedy at law for the protection of the rights of one entitled upon any ground to invoke the powers of a Federal court, is not to be conclusively determined by the statutes of the particular State in which the suit may be brought. One who is entitled to sue in the Federal court may invoke its jurisdiction in equity whenever the established principles and rules of equity permit such a suit in that court; and he cannot be deprived of that right by reason of his being allowed to sue at law in a State court in the same cause of action. It is true that an enlargement of equitable rights, arising from the statutes of a State, may be administered by the circuit courts of the United States. Case of Broderick's Will, 21 Wall. 503, 520; Holland v. Challen, 110 U. S. 1524; s. c., 3 Sup. Ct. Rep. 495; Dick v. Foraker, 155 U. S. 404, 415; s. c., 15 Sup. Ct. Rep. 124; Barden v. Improvement Co., 157 U. S. 327, 330; s. c., 15 Sup. Ct. Rep. 650; Rich v. Braxton, 158 U. S. 375, 405; s. c., 15 Sup. Ct. Rep. 1006

§ 230. Right of Railroad Corporations to Legal Protection.—In organizing themselves into a corporation for the construction and operation of a railway, individuals do not lose their rights as citizens. As a corporation, no less than as individuals, they have an unquestionable right to the equal protection of the law. As a railway corporation, to all legal intents and purposes, is a person, and as the law knows nothing of distinctions of classes among persons, a railway corporation has the same right as an individual to legal protection. In the leading case of Smyth v. Ames, it was held that a railroad corporation is a person, within the meaning of the Fourteenth Amendment declaring that no

But if the case, in its essence, be one cognizable in equity, the plaintiff,—the required value being in dispute,—may invoke the equity powers of the proper circuit court of the United States, whenever jurisdiction attaches by reason of diverse citizenship, or upon any other ground of Federal jurisdiction. Payne v. Hook, 7 Wall. 425, 430; McConihay v. Wright, 121 U. S. 201, 205; s. c., 7 Sup. Ct. Rep. 940. A party, by going into a National court, does not, this court has said, lose any right or appropriate remedy of which he might have availed himself in the State courts of the same locality; that the wise policy of the constitution gives him a choice of tribunals. Davis v. Gray, 16 Wall. 203, 221; Cowley v. Railroad Co., 159 U. S. 569, 583; s. c., 16 Sup. Ct. Rep. 127. So, whenever a citizen of a State can go into the courts of a State to defend his property against the illegal acts of its officers, a citizen of another State may invoke the jurisdiction of the Federal courts to maintain a like defense. A State cannot tie up a citizen of another State, having property rights within its territory, invaded by unauthorized acts of its own officers, to suits for redress in its own courts. Regan v. Trust Co., 154 U. S. 362, 391; s. c., 14 Sup. Ct. Rep. 1047; Mississippi Mill v. Cohn, 150 U. S. 202, 204; s. c., 14 Sup. Ct. Rep. 75; Cowles v. Mercer Co., 7 Wall. 118; Lincoln Co. v. Luning, 133 U. S. 529; s. c., 10 Sup. Ct. Rep. 363; Scott v. Neely, 140 U. S. 106; s. c., 11 Sup. Ct. Rep. 712; Chicot Co. v. Sherwood, 148 U. S. 529; s. c., 13 Sup. Ct. Rep. 695; Cates v. Allen, 149 U. S. 451; s. c., 13 Sup. Ct. Rep. 883, 977. It is the settled doctrine of this court that a suit against individuals for the purpose of preventing them, as officers of a State, from enforcing an unconstitutional enactment to the injury of the rights of the plaintiff, is not a suit against the State within the meaning of that amendment. Pennoyer v. McConnaughy, 140 U. S. 1, 10; s. c., 11 Sup. Ct. Rep. 699; *In re* Tyler, 149 U. S. 164, 190; s. c., 13 Sup. Ct. Rep. 785; Scott v. Donald, 165 U. S. 58, 68; s. c., 17 Sup. Ct. Rep. 265; Tindal v. Wesley, 167 U. S. 204, 220; s. c., 17 Sup. Ct. Rep. 770." Harlan, J., in Smyth v. Ames, 18 Sup. Ct. Rep. 418, 423.

State shall deprive any person of property without due process of law, nor deny to any person within its jurisdiction the equal protection of the law. A State enactment, or regulations made under the authority thereof, establishing rates for the transportation of persons or property by railroads, that will not admit of the carrier earning such compensation as, under all the circumstances, is just to it and to the public, would deprive such carrier of its property without due process of law and deny to it the equal protection of the laws, and would, therefore, be repugnant to the Fourteenth Amendment to the Constitution of the United States.[1] In the opinion in this case the court said: "By the fourteenth amendment it is provided that no State shall deprive any person of property without due process of law, nor deny to any person within its jurisdiction the equal protection of the laws. That corporations are persons within the meaning of this amendment, is now settled.[2] What

[1] Smyth v. Ames, 18 Sup. Ct. Rep. 418.

[2] Santa Clara Co. v. So. Pac. R. Co., 118 U. S. 394, 396; s. c., 6 Sup. Ct. Rep. 1132; Railroad Co. v. Gibbes, 142 U. S. 386, 391; s. c., 12 Sup. Ct. Rep. 255; Railway Co. v. Ellis, 165 U. S. 150, 154; s. c., 17 Sup. Ct. Rep. 255. "Railroad Commission Cases, 116 U. S. 307, 325, 331; s. c., 6 Sup. Ct. Rep. 334, 348, 349, 388, 391, 1191. This principle was recognized in Dow v. Beidelman, 125 U. S. 680, 689; s. c., 8 Sup. Ct. Rep. 1028, and has been re-affirmed in other cases. In Banking Co. v. Smith, 128 U. S. 174, 179; s. c., 9 Sup. Ct. Rep. 47, it was said that the power of the State to prescribe the charges of a railroad company for the carriage of persons and merchandise within its limits,—in the absence of any provision in the charter of the company constituting a contract, vesting it with authority over those matters,—was 'subject to the limitation that the carriage is not required without reward, or upon conditions amounting to the taking of property for public use without just compensation; and that what is done does not amount to a regulation of foreign or interstate commerce.' In Chicago, M. & St. P. Ry. Co. v. Minnesota, 134 U. S. 418, 458; s. c., 10 Sup. Ct. Rep. 462, 702, it was said: 'If the company is deprived of the power of charging reasonable rates for the use of its property, and such deprivation takes place in the absence of an investigation by judicial machinery, it is deprived of the lawful use of its property, and thus, in substance and effect, of the property itself, without due process of law, and in violation of the constitution of the United States; and in so far as it is thus injured, while other persons are permitted to receive reasonable profits upon their invested capital,

amounts to deprivation of property without due process of law, or what is a denial of the equal protection of the laws, is often difficult to determine, especially when the question relates to the property of a quasi public corporation, and the extent to which it may be subjected to public control. But this court, speaking by Chief Justice Waite, has said that while the State has power to fix the charges by railroad companies for the transportation of persons and property within its own jurisdiction, unless restrained by a valid contract, or unless what is done amounts to a regulation of foreign or interstate commerce, such power is not without limit; and that 'under pretense of regulating fares and freights, the State cannot require a railroad corporation to carry persons or property without reward, neither can it do that which in law amounts to the taking of private property for public use without just compensation or without due process of law.' "[1]

§ 231. Right of Railway Companies to Discriminate in Rates of Transportation.—It is now held by the highest authority that where lines of railroad extend through more than one State, the management is not bound to make uniform rates of transportation. It may have one rate for domestic or local business, and another and a different rate

the company is deprived of the equal protection of the laws.' In Railway Co. v. Wellman, 143 U. S. 339, 344; s. c., 12 Sup. Ct. Rep. 400, the court, in answer to the suggestion that the legislature had no authority to prescribe maximum rates for railroad transportation, said that 'the legislature has power to fix rates, and the extent of judicial interference is protection against unreasonable rates.' In Budd v. New York, 143 U. S. 517; s. c., 12 Sup. Ct. Rep. 468, the court, while sustaining the power of New York by statute to regulate charges to be exacted at grain elevators and warehouses in that State, took care to state, as a result of former decisions, that such power was not one 'to destroy or a power to compel, the doing of the services without reward, or to take private property for public use without just compensation or without due process of law.' See also Regan v. Trust Co., 154 U. S. 362, 399; s. c., 14 Sup. Ct. Rep. 1047; Railway Co. v. Gill, 156 U. S. 649, 657; s. c., 15 Sup. Ct. Rep. 484; Road Co. v. Sanford, 164 U. S. 578, 584, 594, 595, 597; s. c., 17 Sup. Ct. Rep. 198; Chicago, B. & Q. R. Co. v. City of Chicago, 166 U. S. 226, 241; s. c., 17 Sup. Ct. 581."

[1] Smyth v. Ames, 18 Sup. Ct. Rep. 418.

for through traffic for the same distance and over the same line. While it may not discriminate in their charges against the people of any one State, they are not necessarily bound to give absolutely the same rates to the people of all the States; for the kind and amount of business, the cost thereof, the cost of construction and maintenance are factors which determine largely the question of rates, and these vary materially in different States. When a State undertakes to prescribe maximum rates for local business done by an interstate carrier, it must do so with reference exclusively to what is just and reasonable as between the carrier and the public, in respect of domestic business alone; and interstate business cannot be made to bear losses resulting from the rates prescribed for local business.[1] In the opinion in the case here cited, the court said: "In our judgment it must be held that the reasonableness or unreasonableness of rates, prescribed by a State for the transportation of persons and property wholly within its limits, must be determined without reference to the interstate business done by the carrier, or to the profits derived from it. The State cannot justify unreasonably low rates for domestic transportation, considered alone upon the ground that the carrier is earning large profits on its interstate business, over which, so far as rates are concerned, the State has no control. Nor can the carrier justify unreasonably high rates on domestic business upon the ground that it will be able only in that way to meet losses on its interstate business. So far as rates of transportation are concerned, domestic business should not be made to bear the losses on interstate business, nor the latter the losses on domestic business. It is only rates for the transportation of persons and property between points within the State that the State can prescribe; and when it undertakes to prescribe rates not to be exceeded by the carrier, it must do so with reference exclusively to what is just and reasonable, as between the carrier and the public in respect of domestic business. The argument that a railroad line is an entirety; that its

[1] Smyth v. Ames, 18 Sup. Ct. Rep. 418.

income goes into, and its expenses are provided for out of, a common fund, and that its capitalization is on its entire line within and without the State, can have no application when the State is without authority over rates on the entire line, and can only deal with local rates and make such regulations as are necessary to give just compensation on local business."[1]

§ 232. **Rule for Determining what are Reasonable Rates.**—The management of a railway corporation has power to fix the rates of transportation of both persons and property. It may determine what charges shall be made, not only on through traffic, but also on domestic or local business. But while this right is unquestionable, it is not absolute. It must be exercised in accordance with justice and reason. It can lawfully make only fair and reasonable rates. The rule on this point involves some difficulty of application, but it is a rule that the courts undertake to enforce. Railway corporations will be held responsible for a fair and reasonable discharge of their obligations in this direction. In the recent leading case of Smyth v. Ames, the Supreme Court of the United States laid down a rule by which courts will be governed in determining what is reasonable and just in the fixing of rates of transportation. In that case it was held that if a railroad company has bonded its property for an amount that exceeds its fair value, or if its capitalization is largely fictitious, it may not impose upon the public the burden of increased rates necessary to realize profits on this fictitious capitalization, but the basis of all calculations as to the reasonableness of rates must be the fair value of the property used by the company for the convenience of the public. In ascertaining this value, the original cost of construction, the amount expended in permanent improvements, the amount and market value of its bonds and stocks, the present as compared with the original cost of construction, the probable earning capacity of the property under particular rates, prescribed by statute, and

[1] Smyth v. Ames, 18 Sup. Ct. Rep. 418, 432.

the sum required to meet operating expenses, are all matters for consideration, and are to be given such weight as may be just and right in each case.[1] In the opinion on this point the court said: "A corporation maintaining a public highway, although it owns the property which it employs for accomplishing public objects, must be held to have accepted its rights, privileges and franchises subject to the condition that the government creating it or the government within whose limits it conducts its business, may, by legislation, protect the people against unreasonable charges for the services rendered by it. It cannot be assumed that any railroad corporation, accepting franchises, rights and privileges at the hands of the public, ever supposed that it acquired, or that it was intended to grant to it, the power to construct a public highway, simply for its own benefit without regard to the rights of the public. But it is equally true that the corporation performing such public services, and the people financially interested in its business and affairs, have rights that may not be invaded by legislative enactments in disregard of the fundamental guaranties for the protection of property. The corporation may not be required to use its property for the benefit of the public without receiving just compensation for the services rendered by it. How such compensation may be ascertained, and what are the necessary elements in such an inquiry, will always be an embarrassing question. As said in the case last cited, 'Each case must depend upon its special facts, and when a court, without assuming itself to prescribe rates, is required to determine whether the rates prescribed by the legislature for a corporation controlling a public highway are, as an entirety, so unjust as to destroy the value of its property for all the purposes for which it was acquired, its duty is to take into consideration the interests both of the public and of the owner of the property, together with all other circumstances that are fairly to be considered in determining whether the legislature has, under the guise of regulating rates, exceeded its constitutional au-

[1] Smyth v. Ames, 18 Sup. Ct. Rep. 418.

thority, and practically deprived the owner of property without due process of law. * * * The utmost that any corporation operating a public highway can rightfully demand at the hands of the legislature, when exerting its general powers, is that it receive what, under all the circumstances, is just compensation for the use of its property, and will be just both to it and to the public.'[1] We hold, however, that the basis of all calculations as to the reasonableness of rates to be charged by a corporation maintaining a highway under legislative sanction, must be the fair value of the property being used by it for the convenience of the public. And in order to ascertain that value the original cost of construction, the amount expended in permanent improvements, the amount and market value of its bonds and stocks, the present as compared with the original cost of construction, the probable earning capacity of the property under particular rates prescribed by statute, and the sum required to meet operating expenses, are all matters for consideration, and are to be given such weight as may be just and right in each case. We do not say that there may not be other matters to be regarded in estimating the value of the property. What the company is entitled to ask is a fair return upon the value of that which it employs for the public convenience. On the other hand, what the public is entitled to demand is that no more be exacted from it for the use of a public highway, than the services rendered by it are reasonably worth.'"[2]

[1] Turnpike Co. v. Sanford, 164 U. S. 578, 596, 597; s. c., 17 Sup. Ct. Rep. 198.

[2] Smyth v. Ames, 18 Sup. Ct. Rep. 418, 433.

CHAPTER XVI.

CONCLUDING REFLECTIONS.

The drawing of this treatise to a close is suggestive of some reflections on the general subject of modern trust combinations. Indeed, one can hardly study the law of monopolies and trusts without receiving a very deep and lively impression of the vast and increasing importance of the subject. So extensive and strong has this conviction become that the literature of the subject, in its general aspects, has already become a library.[1] The aggregation of capital, with

[1] Some conception of the immense mass of this literature can be gathered from "The Bibliography of Commercial Trusts,—Law Literature of Trust Combinations, Monopolies, etc.," prepared by William H. Winters, Librarian of the New York Law Institute in 1890. The work shows great ability and research. The amount of literature on the subject since would make a mass much greater. The following is the result of Mr. Winters' labor. At the close we attach some articles appearing in the leading periodicals since that time:

Adams (Geo. H.), The "Trusts" and the Civil Code; pamphlet, New York, 1888. (8 pp.)

Beach (Charles F., Jr.), Facts about Trusts; pamphlet, New York, 1889. (12 pp.)

——— Railway Federation; the Proposed Railway Trusts; pamphlet, New York, 1890. (20 pp.)

Dodd (S. C. T.), Combinations; Their Uses and Abuses; with a History of the Standard Oil Trust; pamphlet, New York, 1888. (46 pp.)

——— Statement of Pending Legislation and its Consequences; pamphlet, New York, 1888. (25 pp.)

——— Combinations and Competition; an address delivered before the Merchants' Association of Boston, Jan. 8, 1889; pamphlet, New York, 1889 (17 pp.); 5 Railway & Corp. L. Jour. (1887) 97, 100.

——— Authorities on Combinations; pamphlet, New York, 1889. (4 pp.)

Sullivan (A. S.), Address at the laying of the corner stone of the new building of the Consolidated a view to the creating of a practical monopoly, is the prominent feature of the industrial conditions of the present. The closing decades of the century will go into history as the trust period, as the time at which the trust took form and

Stock Exchange in New York City, Sept. 8, 1887. Stock Exchange Annual Rep. 1888, pp. 120, 123.

Sumner (Wm. G.). Good Sense on the Trust Question—N. Y. Independent, 1888.

Thurber (F. B.). Combination Competition; pamphlet. New York, 1888 (12 pp.): 5 Railway & Corp. L. Jour. (1889) 20, 24.

Wiman (Erastus). The Waste of Competition: pamphlet. New York, 1889. (8 pp.)

Bugaboo of Trusts—A. Carnegie, 148 No. Amer. Rev. (1889) 141, 150.

Bugbear of Trusts—Henry Wood. 5 Forum (1888), 584, 590.

Commercial "Trusts" in Rome—A. H. Marsh, 8 Can. L. Times (1888), 299, 300; 23 Am. L. Rev. (1889) 261; 13 N. J. Law Jour. (1890) 28.

Competition and the Trusts—George Iles, 34 Pop. Sci. Mo. (1889) 619, 630.

Dangerous Trusts—W. M. Rapsher. 146 No. Am. Rev. (1888) 509, 514.

Development of the Whiskey Trust—J. W. Jenks, 4 Pol. Sci. Quar. (1889) 296, 319.

Difference in Trusts—5 Railway & Corp. L. Jour. (1889) 455, 456: Amer. Grocer. March 27, 1889.

Economic and Social Aspect of Trusts—Geo. Gunton, 3 Pol. Sci. Quar. (1888) 385, 408.

Economic Effects of Combinations—Age of Steel, Jan. 5, 1889.

Facts about Trusts—Charles F. Beach, Jr., 8 Forum (1889), 61, 72: also pamphlet, New York, 1889. (12 pp.)

Gunton's Apology of Trusts—Nation, Feb. 7, 1889.

History of Trusts — James F. Minturn, 3 Belford's Magazine (1889), 61, 66.

Industrial Trusts—18 American, Phil. (1889) 246.

List of the Syndicates of the World—Handel's Museum (1888), Wien, Austria.

Morality of Trusts—66 Sat. Review, London (1888), 609.

Pepper Trust of Germany—Karl Braun, 97 Verteljahrschrift fur Volksw.

Railway Trusts — 5 Railway & Corp. L. Jour. (1889) 165; 6 *Ib.* (1889) 61, 101, 201.

——— Beach (Charles F., Jr.). Railway Federation; pamphlet, New York, 1890. (20 pp.)

——— Bonham (John M.). Railway Secrecy and Trusts, 12 Mo. New York, 1890. (138 pp.)

——— McCook's (John J.), Proposed Railway "Trust"—5 Railway & Corp. L. Jour. (1889) 165, 166: 6 *Ib.* (1889) 201, 202: N. Y. Star. Jan. 12, 1890.

——— Proceedings of Conferences of Railway and Bank Presidents, New York City, Jan. 8, 10, 1889; pamphlet, New York, 1889 (96 pp.): 5 Railway & Corp. L. Jour. (1889) 165, 166.

——— History of the "Gentlemen's Agreement," N. Y. Star, Jan 12, 1890.

See *infra* Voting Trusts.

Standard Oil Company—Camden

assumed its gigantic proportions. The massing of capital and of business organizations has created a revolution in the business of the country. One of the effects of this change is a large increase in the productiveness of capital

(J. N.), 136 No. Amer. Rev. (1883) pp. 181, 190.

——— Dodd (S. C. T.), pamphlet, New York, 1888. (46 pp.)

——— Hudson (J. F.), — Railways and the Republic (1886), pp. 67, 106.

——— Lloyd (H. D.), — 47 Atlantic, Mo. (1881), pp. 317, 334.

——— Welch (J. C.),—136 No. Amer. Rev. (1883), pp. 191, 200.

——— Trust Agreement,—N. Y. World. Feb. 28, 1888; N. Y. Senate Doc. No. 55 (1888), pp. 455. 466, Cook's Trust (2d ed.), pp. 78. 89.

——— By-Laws of the Trustees, —Cook on Trusts (2d ed.). pp. 90, 94.

——— Brief History of its Methods and Influence; pamphlet, New York, 1887. (23 pp.)

——— List of Corporations, — Cook on Trusts. 2d ed. (1888), pp. 107, 110.

——— Railway Discrimination in favor of,—1 Int. Commerce Com. Rep. (1888) 503; s. c., 1 Int. Com. Rep. (1888) 722.

——— Secret Rebates, — Report of testimony in the case of Taylor v. Oil Co. (1879), pp. 661, 737.

See *infra* Legislative Reports.

Sugar Refineries Company's Deed—3 Pol. Sci. Quar. (1888) 611, 617; N. Y. Senate Rep. (1888), No. 50, pp. 644, 651; Cook on Trusts (2d ed.) (1888), pp. 94, 105; Sugar Trust Case on Appeal (1890), pp. 3, 12.

Syndicates; Trusts and Corners—E. M. Clerke, 21 Dublin Rev. (1889) 353, 377; 6 Railway & Corp. L. Jour. (1889) 241, 250.

The Monopoly Trust — London Railway News, Feb. 18, 1888, 3 Railway & Corp. L. Jour. (1888) 315, 317.

The Trust Company Fancy—67 Sat. Review (1889), 247, 248.

Trusts, The New Juggernaut—E. Willett, 7 Drake's Magazine, 1889.

Trusts According to Official Investigation — E. B. Andrews, 3 Quar. Journal of Econ. (1889) 117, 152.

Trusts and How to Deal With Them — Chautauquau, Feb. No. 1890.

Trusts and Syndicates; Copper (France), Salt Union (England), etc.—66 Chamber's Jour. (1889) 33, 36.

Trusts in America—61 London Spectator (1888), 1253.

Trusts in Germany — No. 106 Rep. U. S. Consuls (1889), pp. 271, 275; 48 Nation (1889), 462.

Voting Trusts — 5 Railway & Corp. L. Jour. (1889) 597; Cook on Stock and Stockholders (1889), pp. 533, 534; 19 Abb. N. C. (1888), Note of Cases, p. 448; 84 Ala. (1888) 608; 6 Pa. Co. Ct. Rep. (1889) 193; 7 Railway & Corp. L. Jour. (1890) 87.

——— The Atchison—6 Railway & Corp. L. Jour. (1889), 501; Beach (Charles F., Jr.), 7 *Ib.* (1890) 21, 22.

——— The Reading—N. Y. Star, Jan. 11, 1890, 7 Railway & Corp. L. Jour. (1890) 87; 47 Leg. Int. (1890) 26.

What Shall be Done with Trusts —M. I. Swift, 10 Andover Rev.

thus employed, while the profits of the small producer and dealer are proportionately diminished. In very numerous instances it converts the man who has been engaged in business on his own account into a laborer or other em-

(1888) 109, 127: pamphlet, reprint, 18 pp.

A Tyrant Trust — N. Y. Eve. World, June 28, 1889.

After the Trust: Views of S. C. T. Dodd, John R. Dos Passos, John E. Parsons, etc.—N. Y. Mail and Express, Feb. 1, 1890.

American Cotton Oil Trust, How a Million was Lost—N. Y. Evening Post, Sept. 2, 1889.

——— List of Corporations, Cook on Trusts (2d ed.) (1888), pp. 111, 113.

American Cotton Oil Trust Secrets — N. Y. Times, Feb. 15, 1890.

An Old Trust, 1579. Independent, June 13, 1889.

Book Trust (A)—N. Y. Mail and Express, Feb. 7, 1890; N. Y. World, March 7, 1890.

Butchers, Envelope, Milk, Oil and Rubber Trusts (The)—N. Y. Times, Feb. 24, 29, 1888.

Chicago Gas Trust—N. Y. Daily Times, Jan. 4, 1888; 5 Railway & Corp. L. Jour. (1889) 536.

Coffin-Makers and Undertakers' Trust — Industrial Journal, Feb. 1889.

Defense of Trusts — S. C. T. Dodd, N. Y. Tribune, Feb. 2, 1890.

Effect of Trust Combinations—N. Y. Comm. Bull. Advertiser, April 1, 1889.

Farmers' Trust of the Northwest — N. Y. Comm. Advertiser, March 26, 1888.

Ferry Syndicate of New York City—N. Y. Star, Feb. 20, 1890.

Foes of Competition — N. Y. Daily Times, Feb. 20, Feb. 27, March 19, 1888; N. Y. Daily World, Feb. 21, 1888.

Frenzy for Trusts—N. Y. Evening Sun, June 27, 1889.

How Fortunes are Made; Combination as a Fortune Getter. Erastus Winan — N. Y. Tribune, Dec. 5, 1889.

Lead Trust Secrets—N. Y. Herald, Feb. 6, 1890.

Power of Trusts — Public Opinion, March 1, 1890.

Striking at Trusts — Congressional Legislation—N. Y. Tribune, Feb. 21, 1890; N. Y. Sun, March 1, 1890.

The Law Defied—N. Y. Daily Times, Nov. 21, 1887.

Trusts and Syndicates — Edinburg Scotsman, Feb. 5, 1889.

Report of the Speeches at the Banquet of the Merchants' Association, Boston, Jan. 8, 1889.

Boston Journal, Jan. 9, 1889; pamphlet report, Boston, 1889. (80 pp.)

Report of the Addresses to the Plymouth League: subject, "Trusts"— Brooklyn Eagle, Feb. 7, 1889.

Proceedings of Conferences between Presidents of Railroad Lines and Representatives of Banking Houses, held at New York City, Jan. 8, 10, 1889; pamphlet, New York, 1889 (96 pp.); 5 Railway & Corp. L. Jour. (1889) 165, 166.

Acts Illegal by General Law—Freeman's Note of Cases, 8 Amer. St. Rep. (1889) 191, 193.

Anti-Combine Acts — 25 Can. Law Jour. (1889) 417, 418; 9 London Pump Court (1889), 31, 32.

ploye of the trust. But this is not a desirable change. It is not for the public weal. In its tendency to degrade that great middle class of our people, which constitutes the strength and stability of our political institutions, to the

Car Trust Securities — 8 Amer. Bar Assoc. Rep. (1885) 277, 322; 140 Mass. Rep. (1886) 346; 29 Fed. Rep. (1887) 410; 36 *Ib.* (1889) 520.

Cost-Book Mining Companies— 11 County Court Chron. 50; 10 Law Rep. Q. B. (1874) 7.

Share Trusts — 70 London Law Times (1880), 94, 95.

Statutory Enactments Against "Trusts"—28 Cent. L. Jour. (1889) 533, 534.

Stock Trusts for the Control of Corporations — Austin Abbott's Note of Cases, 19 Abb. N. C. (1888) 448, 466.

Syndicates and Pools — Austin Abbott's Note of Cases, 16 Abb. N. C. (1886) 380, 394.

The Commercial "Trusts" in Rome—8 Can. L. Times (1888), 299, 300; 23 Amer. Law Rev. (1889) 261; 13 N. J. Law Jour. 189.

The So-Called "Trusts"—21 Am. L. Rev. (1887) 976, 979.

Competition and Combination— 11 London Law Mag. (1834) 143, 180; 51 London Law Times 1871), 81; 3 Albany L. Jour. (1871) 405, 406; 2 Andover Rev. (1885) 455; 20 Am. L. Rev. (1886) 194, 216; 21 Irish Law Times (1887), 499, 516, 526; 4 Railway & Corp. L. Jour. (1888) 145, 241; 20 Week. L. Bull. (1888) 320, 321; 22 Am. L. Rev. (1888) 873, 889; 5 Railway & Corp L. Jour. (1889) 20, 24; 6 *Ib.* (1889) 121, 124; 24 London Law Jour. (1889) 430, 431; 25 Can. Law Jour. (1889) 417, 418; 9 London Pump Court (1889), 31, 32.

——— Condition of the Law as to Combinations—Austin Abbott, 23 Am. L. Rev. (1889) 755, 758.

——— Constitutional and Statutory Provisions Affecting Combinations — Robt. Desty's Note of Cases. 1 Lawy. Rep. Ann. (1888) 849, 852.

——— Adams (H. C.), Relation of the State to Industrial Action— Amer. Econ. Assoc. Publ. (1887) No. 6.

Alexander (E. P.), Pools and Combinations, Railway Practice, (1887), pp. 23, 60.

Coquelin (Chas.), Competition, 1 Lalor's Cyclo. Pol. Sci. (1881). pp. 642, 683.

Farrer (T. H.), The State in Its Relation to Trade, 1, 12 Mo. London, 1883.

Greenhood (Elisha), Doctrine of Public Policy (1886), pp. 642, 683.

Hadley (A. T.), Railroad Transportation (1886), pp. 63, 99.

Holtzendorff (Fr. von), Rechtslexikon (1881), Band II, s. 795.

Hudson (J. F.), Railways and the Republic (1886), pp. 287, 315.

Sedgwick (Henry), Political Economy (1883), Book II, chap. X.

Swann (John), Combinations and Pools, Hints to Investors (1886), pp. 44, 55.

Limits of Competition—John B. Clark, 2 Pol. Sci. Quar. (1887), pp. 45, 61.

Modern Competition—62 Frazer Mag. 767.

Modern Feudalism — Jas. F. Hudson, 144 No. Am. Rev. (1887) 277, 290.

Persistence of Competition—F.

position of employes, it is in a high degree prejudicial to the public welfare. It materially detracts from the power and glory of the nation. The introduction of a system of business that is adapted to increase the wealth of a small

H. Giddings, 2 Pol. Sci. Quar. (1887) 62, 78.

Public Business Management—A. T. Hadley, 3 Pol. Sci. Quar. (1888) 572, 591.

Selfishness in Competition—C. A. Gripps, National Rev., 1889.

Criminal Conspiracies and Combinations—10 Wash. L. Rep. (1882) 353, 369, 401, 433, 449, 481, 497; 16 Cent. L. Jour. (1883) 39; 21 Irish L. Times (1887), 499, 516, 526.

——— Wright (R. S.), Law of Criminal Conspiracies, Amer. Ed., 8 vo., Philadelphia, 1887.

——— N. Y. Penal Code, Sec. 168, subd. 6.

——— N. Y. Rev. Stats. vol. 2 (1st ed.), pp. 691, 692.

Combination: Is it a Crime?—A. Morgan, 33 Pop. Sci. Mo. (1888) 42, 54.

Conspiracy or Business-like Selfishness—23 London Law Jour. (1888) 513, 514; 30 Sollicitor's Journal (1886), 197, 198; Desty's Note of Cases, 2 Lawry. Rep. Ann. (1889) 33, 34.

Conspiracy Prosecutions and Conspiracy Laws of New Netherland, New York, etc.,—Chas. F. Peck, vol. 9, N. Y. Assembly Doc. 1888, No. 68, pp. 563, 700.

Baker (Chas. W.), Monopolies and the People, 12 mo., New York, 1890 (263 pp.).

Bonham (John M.), Industrial Liberty, 8 vo., New York, 1888, pp. 96, 221.

Cloud (D. C.), Monopolies and the People: Railway and Bank Monopolies, etc. (3d ed.), 8 vo., Davenport, 1873 (514 pp.).

Monopolies and Combinations—Barry (W.), 7 Forum, 424; Bruce (E. C.), 35 Lippincott Mag. 433; Godson (Richard), Law of Patents (1st ed.), p. 42; Hadley (A. T.), 1 Quar. J. of Econ. 28; Hess (J. S.), 30 Ref. Quar. Rev. 450; Hudson (J. F.), 144 No. Am. Rev. 277; Sterne (Simon), 2 Lalor Cyclo. of Pol. Sci. 890.

Agreements Creating Monopolies — Desty (Robt.), Notes of Cases, 11 Fed. Rep. (1882) 632, 634; 1 Lawry. Rep. Ann. (1888), 458, 849; 2 *Ib.* (1889) 33, 34; 4 *Ib.* (1889) 154, 157; Wharton (Fr.), Note of Cases, 11 Fed. Rep. (1882) 10, 14; Smith's Lead. Cas. vol. 1 (8th Amer. ed.), 777, 783; Notes of Cases, 92 Am. Dec. (1887) 763; 18 Pac. Rep. (1888) 391; 9 So. East. Rep. (1889), 422; 7 N. Y. Supl. (1889) 415; 22 N. E. Rep. (1890) 798.

Corporations and Monopolies—E. L. Godkin, 18 Nation (1874), 359, 360.

Effect of Monopolies on Value—A. L. Bolles, 117 No. Am. Rev. (1873) 319.

History of a Monopoly: Trinity House Corporation—W. M. Gattie, 45 Fortnightly Rev. (N. S.) (1889) 490, 500.

Industrial Monopolies — T. H. Farrer, Quart. Rev. Oct., 1870.

Jobs in Cities — Ferd. Seeger; pamphlet, N. Y., 1886. (16 pp.)

Lords of Industry—H. D. Lloyd, 138 No. Am. Rev. (1884) 535, 553.

Monopoly in Business—40 Mo. Rel. Mag. 202.

Municipal Ordinances Creating a

class, while it diminishes the resources of the mass of the people, is a national evil. The prosperity and elevation of the people of the land as a whole is essential to the highest measure of national prosperity and greatness. The multiplying of his millions and the corresponding increase of his power is not a personal benefit to the millionaire, and the corresponding contraction of the pecuniary resources of the

Monopoly — 34 Am. Dec. (1882) 637, 638.

New Jersey Monopolies; Camden and Amboy Co., etc.,—104 No. Am. Rev. (1867) 428, 476.

Regulation of Monopolies—A. T. Hadley, Railw. Gazette, 1890; 7 Railway & Corp. L. Jour. (1890) 59, 60.

Remedies for the Evils of Monopolies—8 West. Jur. (1874) 511, 519.

Story of a Great Monopoly; The Standard Oil Co.,—H. D. Lloyd, 47 Atlantic, Mo. (1881) 317, 334.

The Spirit of Monopoly—3 Am. L. Jour. (N. S.) (1850) 283, 286.

The Telegraph Monopoly — Richard T. Ely, 149 No. Am. Rev. (1889) 44, 53.

Consolidation of Corporations— Elliott (C. B.), 17 West. Jur. (1883) 345, 359; Elliott (C. B.), 17 Cent. L. Jour. (1883) 382, 383; 6 N. J. Law Jour. (1883) 360, 363; Freeman (A. C.), 79 Am. Dec. (1886) 422, 428; Desty (Robt.). 2 Lawy. Rep. Ann. (1889) 726, 728.

Amalgamation of Companies— 43 London Law Times (1867), 209, 210; 17 Solicitor's Journal (1873), 362, 364.

Forfeiture of Corporate Franchises—Abbott (Austin), 22 Abb. N. C. (1889) 210, 227; Black (H. C.) 21 Cent. L. Jour. (1883) 432, 435; Freeman (A. C.), 5 Am. State Rep. (1889) 803, 807; 8 *Ib.* (1889) 179, 202; Ingersoll (C. J.), 5 Dem. Rev. 99; Redfield (I. F.), 13 Am. L. Reg. (N. S.) (1874) 185, 190; Redfield (I. F.), 5 Am L. Reg. (N. S.) (1866) 577, 588.

Corporations—*Ultra Vires* Contracts—Aiddle (Arth.). 11 Cent. L. Jour. (1880) 81, 101; Holmes (O. W., Jr.), 5 Am. L. Rev. (1871), 272, 290; Tiedeman (C. G.), 21 Cent. L. Jour. (1885) 210, 213.

Corporations Entering into Partnership—3 Cent. L. Jour. (1876) 668, 669; 15 Fed. Rep.. Note of Cases (1883) 667, 678; 71 Am. Dec. (1886) 681; 8 S. W. Rep. (1888) 396; McKinney's Note of Cases, 20 Am. & Eng. Corp. Cas. (1888) 485, 486; 3 No. of Cases (1888), 58, 59; 4 No. of Cases (1889), 1, 3.

Points for Petitioners in *Re* Grant *et al.* on a hearing before Hon. Chas. Tabor, Attorney-General; pamphlet, N. Y., 1888. (9 pp.)

Petitions and Answers with Opinion of the Attorney-General, Hon. Chas. F. Tabor, in the Matter of Grant *et al.*, U. S. House of Rep. Doc. No. 3112 (1888), pp. 200, 209.

Crain (T. C. T.), Points for Petitioners, etc.; pamphlet, New York, 1888. (24 pp.)

Hawes (G. P.), Argument in the Matter of the Proposed Legislation Relative to Trusts; pamphlet, New York, 1888. (32 pp.)

Pryor (Roger A.), Substance of an Argument before the Legislative Committee of the State of middle and lower classes means the diminishing of their happiness and well being and, in consequence, of their value to the State as citizens. The tendency and the effect are altogether evil.

This evil is attracting the attention of wise and far-seeing statesmen and, as well, of the thoughtful patriot and

New York; pamphlet, New York, 1888. (14 pp.)

Case of The People v. North River Sugar Refining Co., Supreme Court Circuit—Brief of Hon. Roger A. Pryor; pamphlet, New York, 1888. (39 pp.)

——— Reply of Hon. Roger A. Pryor; pamphlet, New York, 1888. (9 pp.)

——— Additional Brief for Plaintiff by the Attorney-General and Roger A. Pryor; pamphlet, New York, 1889. (42 pp.)

——— Brief for Appellant by John E. Parsons; pamphlet, New York, 1889. (18 pp.)

——— Brief for Defendant by Hon. Chas. P. Daly; pamphlet, New York, 1889. (24 pp.)

——— Argument for Defendants by James C. Carter; pamphlet, New York, 1889 (62 pp.); reprint of the same; pamphlet. (67 pp.)

——— Opinion of Hon. Geo. C. Barrett, with Briefs of Counsel, 22 Abb. N. C. (1889) 164; 19 N. Y. State Rep. 853; 16 N. Y. Civ. Proc. Rep. 1; 22 Am. & Eng. Corp. Cas. 511; 5 Railway & Corp. L. Jour. 56; 3 N. Y. Supl. 401; 2 Lawy. Rep. Ann. 33.

——— Judge Barrett and the Newspapers, 5 Railway & Corp. L. Jour. (1889) 53, 54.

——— Supreme Court, General Term—Appellant's Brief; pamphlet, 1889. (74 pp.)

——— ——— Respondent's Brief; pamphlet, 1889. (74 pp.)

——— ——— Case on Appeal from Judgment; pamphlet, 1889 (111 pp.)

——— ——— Opinion of Hon. Chas. Daniels, 7 N. Y. Supl. (1889) 406; 27 N. Y. State Rep. 282; 5 Lawy. Rep. Ann. 386; 2 N. Y. Law Jour. 1505, 1508; 36 N. Y. Daily Reg. 726.

——— Court of Appeals Decision, 1890.

——— Sugar Trust Injunction—23 Abb. N. C. (1889) 314; 2 N. Y. Law Jour. (1890) 2155.

——— ——— Commonwealth Refining Company Incorporation — Conn. Special Acts, 1889, p. 1095.

——— ——— Effect of Judge O'Brien's Decision, N. Y. Herald, Feb. 16, 1890.

The following are more recent articles:

The Pool and the Trust, William L. Royall, 3 Virginia Law Register, July and August, 1897.

Trusts and Monopolies, Jackson Guy, 1 Virginia Law Register, 709.

Trusts and Monopolies—Reply, John Hunter, Jr., 2 Virginia Law Register, 160.

Boycotting, Its Legal Phase, D. H. Pingrey, 38 Cent. L. Jour. 427.

Boycotting, Charles A. Dickson, 37 Cent. L. Jour. 166.

Unfair Competition, Oliver R. Mitchell, 10 Harvard Law Review, 275.

"Monopoly" under the National Anti-Trust Act, William F. Dana, 7 Harvard Law Review, 338.

philanthropist. The following well considered thoughts are from an article in a popular law periodical:

"We have heard much of the dangers of corporations in late years; but, while our publicists had hardly whetted their swords to meet this question, we are confronted with a new monster a thousand times more terrible. Every student knows how corporations have grown from a monastic institution to the predominance they now occupy in the business world; but American ingenuity has invented a legal machine which may swallow a hundred corporations or a hundred thousand individuals; and then with the corporate irresponsibility, their united power be stored, like a dynamo, in portable compass, and wielded by one or two

Trusts, The Present Legal Status of. S. C. T. Dodd, 7 Harvard Law Review, 157.

Constitutionality of the Sherman Anti-Trust Act of 1890, as interpreted by the United States Supreme Court in the case of the Trans-Missouri Traffic Association, William D. Guthrie, 11 Harvard Law Review, 80.

The Trust, an Economic Evolution, Charles F. Beach, Jr., 2 Northwestern Law Review, 127.

The Doctrine of Lumley v. Wagner, Ernest C. C. Frith, 13 Law Quarterly Review, 306.

Pooling Contracts and Public Policy, Charles W. Willard, 31 American Law Review, 236.

The Sugar Trust Cases; A Legal Comedy of Errors, Joseph Wheless, 31 American Law Review, 560.

A Newspaper Trust, Thomas W. Brown, 31 American Law Review, 569.

The Relation of the Police Power of the States to the Commerce Power of the Nation, Address Charles Carroll Bonney, before Illinois State Bar Association, Jan. 28, 1891, American Law Review, March, 1891.

Federal Power to Regulate Interstate Commerce and the Police Powers of the States, Herbert B. Shoemaker, 29 American Law Review, 59.

How to Deal with Trusts, 29 American Law Review, 284.

Strikes and Trusts. Address of U. M. Rose, before American Bar Association, August 31, 1893, at Milwaukee, 27 American Law Review.

Legality of Trust Combinations, Louis Bosoit, Jr., 30 American Law Register, 751.

The Case of the Trans-Missouri Freight Association, George Stuart Patterson, 36 American Law Register and Review, 307.

The Law of Labor and Trade, Address P. C. Knox, before Pennsylvania Bar Association, 36 American Law Register and Review, 417.

Legal Side of the Strike Question, Ardemus Stewart, 33 American Law Register and Review, 609.

Protest against Administering Criminal Law by Injunction, A.—The Debs Case, William Draper Lewis, 33 American Law Register and Review, 879.

men. Not even amenable to the restraints or corporation law, these 'trusts' may realize the Satanic ambition,—infinite and irresponsible power free of check or conscience. Corporations are bad enough; it is ever of the defects of the historical growth of law that the conditions which attend the birth of a legal idea so infinitely differ from those that make possible its greatest development; but the trust is to the corporation what the mitrailleuse is to a blunderbus."[1]

It is a ground of encouragement that our legislators are awakening to the necessity and to the vital importance of repressive legislation. While a few of the States are, apparently, in a state of hopeless bondage to the trust, a large majority of them have recently enacted very wholesome laws for the suppression or the regulation of this evil, and it may be believed that other States will follow the good example.[2] In any honest and well directed efforts of this character legislators ought to have the hearty and earnest support, not only of the legal profession but, as well, of all good citizens. But when this is accomplished it will remain that the remedy for this evil is not in the good laws secured so much as in the fearless and honest enforcement of the law. In most of the States it is already true that what is needed is not a change in the law already on the statute books, but the enforcement of the law as it now stands. "If the wit of man has brought into existence this new thing, this Frankenstein, surely the wit of man will also prove equal to the task of determining how it shall be rendered amenable to the law of the land and the public good."[3]

To every loyal American it is a matter of congratulation and of national pride that in regard to this evil we are so far in advance of our cousins across the water. Not only our legislation, but the decisions of our courts are, by a long

[1] F. J. Stimson, 1 Harvard Law Review, 132.

[2] More than two-thirds of the States have Anti-Trust Statutes. See Chap. XIII.

[3] Amasa M. Eaton, in 4 Hart. Law Review, p.

stride, in advance of those of the British Empire. In England and in her dependences the trust has essentially full sway. The strong are permitted to oppress the weak and to rob the public almost without restraint. If the evil has not attained the same proportions in England that it has in this country the difference must be attributed to some other cause than the excellence of her legislation or the decisions of her courts.

INDEX.

[The references are to sections.]

A.

ANTI-MONOPOLY ACT.
statute of Georgia. 120.

ANTI-TRUST ACT.
law of Michigan. 198.
statute of Missouri. 201.

ANTI-TRUST LAW.
statute of Maine. 197.
statute of South Dakota. 210.

ANTI-TRUST LEGISLATION.
introductory. 183.
federal anti-trust act. 184.
Alabama insurance act. 185.
Arkansas anti-trust act. 186.
California cattle trust. 187.
Delaware life insurance law. 188.
Florida legislation relating to trusts and monopolies. 189.
Georgia anti-monopoly act. 190.
Illinois act prohibiting pools, trusts and combines. 191.
Indiana anti-trust act. 192.
Iowa anti-pool and trust law. 193.
Kansas law prohibiting trusts. 194.
Kentucky law prohibiting pools, trusts and conspiracies. 195.
Louisiana law for the prohibition of trusts and combinations in restraint of trade. 196.
Maine anti-trust law. 197.
Michigan anti-trust act. 198.
Minnesota law to prohibit pools and trusts. 199.
Mississippi law prohibiting trusts and combines. 200.
Missouri anti-trust act. 201.
Montana statute against monopolies and trusts. 202.
Nebraska statute against trusts and conspiracies against trade and business. 203.
New Mexico law declaring trust combinations illegal. 204.

[The references are to sections.]

ANTI-TRUST LEGISLATION—Continued.
New York law to prevent monopolies, 205.
North Carolina law for the prohibition of trusts, 206.
North Dakota law declaring certain trusts and combinations unlawful, 207.
Oklahoma law to prevent combinations in restraint of trade, 208.
South Carolina prohibition of trusts and combinations, 209.
South Dakota anti-trust law, 210.
Tennessee law to prohibit conspiracies and trusts, 211.
Texas law for the suppression of trusts and the promotion of true competition, 212.
Law of Utah prohibiting pools and trusts, 213.
Washington law forbidding trusts and monopolies, 214.
Wisconsin statute prohibiting trusts and combinations in restraint of trade, 215.

B.

BADGERING,
the offense abolished, 9.
SEE INTRODUCTION.

BAKING BUSINESS,
power of the State to regulate the manufacture of bread, 144.
SEE THE POWER TO REGULATE PRIVATE CORPORATIONS.

C.

CATTLE TRUST,
California, 187.

COMBINATIONS IN RESTRAINT OF TRADE. SEE RESTRAINT OF TRADE.
law of Oklahoma to prevent, 208.

COMBINATIONS OF RAILWAY COMPANIES,
subject to certain public obligations, 148.
privileges of railway corporations, 148.
granted for the benefit of the public, 148.
rule stated by Supreme Court of the United States, 148.
the rule in New York, 148.
for suppression of competition, 149.
illegal and void, 149.
pooling by railway companies. 149.
in contravention of public policy and void. 149.
the rule in Indiana and in Connecticut, 149.
the leading case before the United States Supreme Court, 150.
principle stated by Peckham, Justice, 150.
purchase of competing lines, 151.
object to create a monopoly, 151.
when illegal and void. 151.
the rule in Texas and in New Jersey, 151.

[The references are to sections.]

COMBINATIONS OF RAILWAY COMPANIES—Continued.
lease of competing lines, 152.
when such leases will be upheld, 152.
provisions of charter granting such privileges strictly construed, 152.
the rule in Nebraska, 152.
consolidation of parallel lines, 153.
illegal at law, 153.
subject to statutory regulations, 153.
the leading case, 153.
general power to consolidate, 153.
liability to abrogation, when, 153.
may be treated as a license, 153.
the principle expounded, 153.
free competition essential to the security of the public, 153.
the law in Minnesota, 153.
indirect consolidation not sustained, 154.
decision of the Supreme Court of the United States, 154.
rule in case of traffic arrangement, 155.
governed by rule relating to parallel lines, 155.
decision of federal court, 155.
the rule in Pennsylvania, 155.
depot grounds, admission to, 156.
question not definitely determined, 156.
not permitted to discriminate, 156.
may make reasonable regulations, 156.
cannot admit one and exclude another, 156 and n.
general powers of railway corporations, 157.
must be granted by charter and legal rules, 157.
railway companies *quasi* public corporations, 157.
stockholders in railway corporations, 157.
not bound by acts of directory outside of ordinary business, 157.
private interests subordinate to public interests, 157.

COMMON CARRIERS. See Public Policy.
obligations of, as affected by strikes, 109.
when responsible for delays, 109.
the English rule, 109.

COMPETING RAILWAY LINES,
purchase of, when illegal and void, 151.
See Combinations of Railway Companies.

CONSPIRACIES AND TRUSTS.
law of Tennessee to prohibit, 211.

CONSPIRACIES IN RESTRAINT OF TRADE.
present formidable proportions a recent growth, 77.
an attempt to avoid the penalties of the trust, 77.
legislative remedies, 77.

[The references are to sections.]

CONSPIRACIES IN RESTRAINT OF TRADE—Continued.
conspiracy defined, 78 and n.
the gist of the offense, 78.
the New Jersey rule, 78.
rule in Maryland, 78.
the English doctrine, 79.
more tolerant than the American rule, 79.
conspiracy by a corporation, 80.
action against, maintainable, 80.
corporations responsible for, 80.
combinations to monopolize a particular branch of business a conspiracy, 81.
contracts relating to such combinations illegal and void, 81.
decisions of State courts in regard to such combinations not uniform, 81.
the rule in Pennsylvania, 81.
the rule in Wisconsin, 81.
in Illinois, in Minnesota, in Texas, 81.
combinations for regulating prices, 82.
such combinations a conspiracy in restraint of trade, 82.
the rule in Ohio, 82.
in Illinois, in Massachusetts, 82 and n.
conspiracies under federal anti-trust act, 83 and n.
combination to prevent competition at a judicial sale, 84.
rule in England, 84.
rule in New York, 84.
the Illinois doctrine, 84.
when such combinations become a conspiracy, 84.
conspiracy for severing the relation of a minister to his congregation, 86.
indictment for, 87.
particular offense must be definitely charged, 87.
must aver the criminality of the act or of the means employed, 87.
law relating to, fixed by statute, 88.
the law in Illinois, 88.
the Texas statute, Act of 1889, 88.

CONTRACTS IN CONTRAVENTION OF LAW. SEE PUBLIC POLICY.

CONTRACTS IN RESTRAINT OF TRADE. SEE RESTRAINT OF TRADE.
general principle on which held illegal, 36.
injurious to the parties, 36.
public deprived of valuable services, 36.
discourages industry and enterprise, 36.
prevents competition, 36.
fosters the evils of monopolies, 36.

[The references are to sections.]

CONTRACTS IN RESTRAINT OF TRADE—Continued.
rule early established in England, 36.
still the doctrine of England and American courts, 36.
general rule relating to contracts, 37.
what contract will be upheld, 37.
courts inclined to leniency, 37.
rule stated by Justice Bradley, 37.
doctrine modified by circumstances, 37 and n.
rule stated by Justice Bronson, 37.
the rule in England, 38 and n.
modification of English rule, 38.
Maxim-Nordenfeldt case, 38 and n.
partially distinguished from general restraint, 39.
limitations in respect to mode and execution, 39.
limitations in respect to persons or places, 39.
limitations of area, 39.
questions of consideration, 40.
contracts without consideration invalid, 40.
question whether bargain was judicious not to be considered, 40.
limitations of time, 41.
the rule stated, 41 and n.
Lord Smith's exposition, 41.
contract in general restraint not rendered valid by limitation in time, 42.
void if restraint unreasonable, 42.
rule stated by Justice Black, 42 and n.
territorial limitations, 43.
without such limitations, illegal and void, 43.
all the circumstances of the case to be considered, 43.
rule in California, 43.
rule in Alabama, 43.
rule stated by the Supreme Court of the United States, 43.
modification of the rule by some of the State courts, 44.
the leading case, 44.
rule stated by Justice Andrews, 44.
rule stated by Sir George Jessell, 44.
rule in Wisconsin, 44.
territorial limits determined, 45.
rule in Michigan, 45.
rule in Connecticut, 45.
validity of, as affected by their reasonableness, 46.
question of validity the question of reasonableness, 46.
reasonableness determined by circumstances, 46.
what is held unreasonable, 46 and n.
the rule in New Jersey, 46.
when invalid by statute reasonableness not considered, 46.
opinion of Justice Peckham, 46.
divisibility of illegal contract, 47.
when only partially illegal, may be divided, 47.

[The references are to sections.]

CONTRACTS IN RESTRAINT OF TRADE—Continued.
the rule in England, 47.
rule in Massachusetts, 47 and n. and 48 and n.
rule in Indiana, 48.
limitations in conveyances, 49.
stipulations of use for or against a specified purpose upheld, 49.
rule in New York, 49 and n.
restrictions upon the right to sell liquor upheld, 50 and n.
rule in Michigan, 50.
rule in Kentucky, 50.
grantee restrained by the terms of the conveyance, 51.
contracts relating to trade secrets, 52.
ground of the rule, 52.
rule relating to proprietary medicines. 52.
the rule in New York, 52.
restraint by patents, 53.
rule of the Federal courts, 53.
English rule, 53.
the rule in Massachusetts, 53.
when contracts relating to patents will not be upheld, 54.
the rule in Wisconsin, 54 and n.
rule applicable to sale of trade-marks, 55.
the rule in Georgia, 55.
restraint in contract relating to publications, 56.
the rule in Massachusetts, 56.
rule in England, 56 and n.

CONTRACTS RELATING TO PROFESSIONS AND TRADES,
contract not to continue the practice of, 57.
consideration essential, 57.
restraint must be reasonable, 57.
the English rule sustained in this country, 57 and n.
various statements of the rule, 57.
sale of physician's practice, 58.
ground on which contract is upheld, 58.
what is sufficiently definite, 58.
doctrine of limitation in time not definitely established, 59.
where restraint granted larger than necessary, contract void, 59.
professional skill not vendible, 59.
contract indefinite in time may be valid, 59 and n.
the rule as applied to attorneys, 60.
the rule in England, 60.
the rule as applied to dentists, 61.
validity of contract determined by its reasonableness, 61.
the doctrine as held in Connecticut, 61 and n.
exclusive sale of teeth, 61 and n.
application of the rule to the profession of teaching, 62.
the rule in Georgia, 62 and n.
restraint upon the services of artists and actors, 63.

CONTRACTS RELATING TO PROFESSIONS AND TRADES—Continued.
the general rule applicable, 63.
the rule in England. 63.
the rule in Maryland. 63.
the doctrine as applied to trades and other occupations. 64.
the rule in England. 64 and n.
the rule in Ohio. in Maine and in New York. 64.
the rule as applied to traveling salesmen. 65.
the English rule. 65 and n.
constraint of trade as a limited partnership. 66.
subject to partnership rules. 66.
rule in South Carolina. 66.

PROFESSIONS AND TRADES. SEE CONTRACTS RELATING TO PROFESSIONS AND TRADES.

CONTRACTS RELATING TO RESTRICTIONS IN BUSINESS.
subject to general principles governing restraint of trade. 67.
contract for exclusive business privilege. 68.
must relate to a single individual or association. 68.
such contract not a monopoly. 68 and n.
rule in Illinois. 68.
rule in New York. 68.
contracts relating to a particular article. 69.
not in restraint of trade and enforceable. 69.
when grantor retains an interest in the business. 70.
when such contract will be held void. 70 and n.
sale of good will. 71.
when such sale will be upheld. 71.
part of the assets of a business. 71.
good will defined by Justice Story. 71.
contracts in restraint of trade not regarded with favor. 72.
rule in Massachusetts. 72.
doctrine in New York. 72.
doctrine in Alabama. 72.
in Ohio. 72.
value of good will, how determined. 73.
rule in North Carolina. 73.
agreement not to buy or sell a particular article. 74.
when such agreement will be upheld. 74.
where no consideration. contract void. 74.
the rule in New York. 74.
agreement to maintain prices. 75.
such agreements a monopoly and void. 75.
the English rule, 75.
the rule in Kentucky. 75.
common law rule modified by statutes. 76.
the California statute. 76.
the rule in Texas. 76.

[The references are to sections.]

CORNERING THE MARKET. SEE THE CREATING OF A CORNER.

COVENANT NOT TO CONVEY LAND TO A CHINAMAN. SEE PUBLIC POLICY.

CREATING OF A CORNER,
the modern idea, 89.
how it differs from the early engrossing, or forestalling, 89 and n.
the corner defined, 90.
the rule in Illinois stated, 90.
option, 91.
nature of, 91.
puts and calls explained, 91.
when an optional contract is a wager and void, 91.
common law doctrine modified, 92.
the law in England, 92.
the rule in Michigan, 92.
the creation of a corner in necessaries, 93.
distinction between different commodities, 93.
the rule in Illinois, 93.
corner in stocks, 94.
"tying up of stocks," what, 94.
"squeeze in the market," what, 94.
where contracts for future delivery are sustained, 95.
must be a *bona fide* transaction, 95.
when contracts are sustained, 95.
when a contract is gambling in part it is wholly void, 95.
the rule in Wisconsin, 95.
how far a contract of this character will be sustained, 95.
the rule in Illinois, 95.
rule of the federal courts, 95.
rights and liabilities of third parties, 96.
legal position same as that of principals, 96.
the rule stated, 96 and n.
statutory prohibitions, 97.
statute of Illinois, 97.
followed by other States, 97.

D.

DEPOT GROUNDS,
admission to, 156.
question not definitely determined, 156.
not permitted to discriminate, 156.
SEE COMBINATIONS OF RAILWAY COMPANIES.

DIAMOND MATCH COMPANY,
held in contravention of public policy and void, 165.
SEE INDUSTRIAL TRUSTS.

[The references are to sections.]

E.

ENGROSSING. SEE INDUSTRIAL TRUSTS.

F.

FEDERAL ANTI-TRUST ACT.
an act to protect trade and commerce against unlawful restraints and monopolies. 184.
the strike as a violation of, 110.

FORESTALLING. SEE ORIGIN OF INDUSTRIAL TRUSTS.

I.

INDUSTRIAL TRUSTS.
the term indefinite. 158.
how employed. 158.
the primary design. 158.
how organized. 158.
legal title to stock. 158.
how held. 158.
business of. 158.
how conducted. 158.
directors. 158.
how chosen. 158.
classification of. 159.
first class. 159.
how organized. 159.
second class. 159.
how organized. 159.
third class. 159.
how constituted, 159.
title. both legal and equitable. 159.
how held. 159.
object of combination. 159.
how far legal. 160.
on what legality depends. 160.
trusts of first class. 160.
prominent examples. 160.
Standard Oil Trust. 160.
held in contravention of public policy and illegal. 160.
opinion of Justice Minshall. 160.
the North River Sugar Refining Company. 161.
object of the refiners in the combination. 161.
how organized. 161.
law expounded by Justice Finch. 162.
the car trust. 162.
described by Allen. Justice. 162 and n.

[The references are to sections.]

INDUSTRIAL TRUSTS—Continued.
trusts of second class, 163.
legality of, 163.
Ohio Gas Trust Company, 163.
how organized, 163.
object of the organization, 163.
the rule in Illinois, 163.
purpose illegal, 163.
rule in England not in accordance with American decisions, 164.
one limited company as shareholder in another, 164.
decision in *In re* Barnard's Banking Company, 164 and n.
rule stated by Lord Justice Selwin, 164.
trusts of third class, 165.
trusts of third class defined, 165.
object of this class of trusts, 165.
legality of this class of trusts, 165.
the leading case, 165.
Diamond Match Company, 165.
in contravention of public policy and void, 165.
rule stated, 166.
importance of the subject, Chap. XVI.
bibliography of the industrial trust, Chap XVI.
effects of the introduction of this method of business, Chap. XVI.
dangers of the system, Chap. XVI.

INDUSTRIAL TRUSTS, ORIGIN AND PROGRESS OF,
a recent development, 1.
idea not new, 1.
understood by the ancient Hebrews, 1.
motives and objects of, not new, 1.
present proportions not possible at an earlier period, 1.
origin of the term, 2.
Standard Oil Trust, what, 2.
joint stock companies as trusts, 2.
a corporation as trustee of a trust, 2.
a wider significance, 3.
prices maintained how, 3.
trust arrangements, what, 3.
some early illustrations, 4.
plans for suppressing trust combinations, 4.
the term in its latest usage, 3.
object to control prices, 3.
edict of Zeno, 4.
early legislation in England, 4.
regrating, early act against, 4.
forestalling, what, 4.
penalties of violating forestalling act, 4.
engrossing, what, 4.

[The references are to sections.]

INDUSTRIAL TRUSTS, ORIGIN AND PROGRESS OF—Continued.
the trust illegal, 13.
on what grounds, 13.
power of trust combinations, 13.

INJUNCTION.
remedy by, 225.
SEE REMEDIES BY QUO WARRANTO AND INJUNCTION.

INSURANCE COMPANIES,
combinations of, prohibited by statute, 181.
Alabama insurance act, 185.
Delaware life insurance law, 188.
SEE TRUST COMBINATIONS.

L.

LABOR ORGANIZATIONS,
combinations for increasing or maintaining wages, 12.
legal methods of obtaining redress, 12.

LAUNDRY BUSINESS,
may be regulated by legislative enactment, 145.
SEE THE POWER TO REGULATE PRIVATE CORPORATIONS.

LEASE OF COMPETING LINES OF RAILWAYS.
where lease will be upheld, 152.
SEE COMBINATIONS OF RAILWAY LINES.

M.

MONOPOLIES.
early English, 5.
Lord Coke's definition, 5.
early English statute relating to, 6.
the doctrine modified, 7.
vigor relaxed, 6.
Lord Kenyon's rule, 6.
the leading case, 7.
historical review, 8.
Lord Justice Bowen's discussion, 8.
early decisions, 8.
general and partial restraint of trade, 8.
New York law to prevent, 205.

MONOPOLIES AND INDUSTRIAL COMBINATIONS.
ground of proceeding against, 219.

MONOPOLIES AND TRUSTS.
Montana statute against, 202.

MONOPOLIES FROM MUNICIPAL GRANTS AND CONTRACTS.
monopoly, 117.
the original idea of, 117.

[The references are to sections.]

MONOPOLIES FROM MUNICIAPL GRANTS AND CONTRACTS—Continued.
exclusive privilege not necessarily a monopoly, 117.
grant of exclusive privilege a contract, 117.
grant of special privileges, 117 and n.
grant to a street railway, 117 and n.
grant of exclusive privilege not an invasion of the private rights of a citizen, 117.
grant which enables the grantee to create a monopoly illegal and void, 117.
limitation of exclusive privilege, 118.
duty of government to maintain highways, 117 and n.
ferries parts of highways, 117 and n.
perpetual franchise, 118.
municipal authorities not authorized to grant, 118.
duration of grant to be determined by circumstances, 118.
the rule explained, 118.
statutory regulations, 119.
the rule in Texas, in Montana and in Michigan, 119.
the rule in Georgia, 119.
the foregoing rule not sustained in all the States, 120.
the rule in Connecticut, 120.
sustained in New Hampshire, 120.
rule in Iowa, 120.
special privileges not favored in equity, 121.
public prejudice not a rule in equity, 121.
monopoly in street railways, 122.
power of municipal corporations to grant, 122.
power of the legislature, 122.
in what manner exercised, 122.
nothing presumed in favor of such grant, 122.
grant of monopoly by municipal corporations illegal and void, 122.
exceptions to the rule, 122.
the rule in New York, 122.
rule of the federal courts, 122.
rule in Louisiana, 122.
power of municipal corporations fixed by statute, 122.
construction of statute, 122.
the rule in New York, 122.
exclusive gas privilege, 123.
may be a practical monopoly, 123.
city government may act directly, 123.
the rule in Louisiana, 123.
prohibition of laws impairing the obligation of a contract, 123.
the privilege of supplying a city with water, 124.
power of municipal corporation determined by its charter, 124.
the rule in New Jersey and in Georgia, 124.
contract between two corporations, 124.
powers of a committee of a municipal corporation, 125.

[The references are to sections.]

MONOPOLIES FROM MUNICIPAL GRANTS AND CONTRACTS—Continued.
city government may be enjoined from carrying out an illegal contract, 125.
rule in Minnesota, 125.
exclusive privilege of erecting a toll bridge or of establishing a ferry, 126.
rule in England, 126.
rule of the federal courts, 126.
power of the State, 126.
rights of individuals, 126.
not strictly a monopoly, 126.
rule in Texas, 126.
rule where a river is a State boundary, 127.
the grant relates to landing, not to the water, 127.
not a federal power, 127.
power of a legislature, 127.
power of a State legislature to impose a license tax, 128.
rule in Kansas, 129.
market franchise, 130.
power of legislature to grant, 130.
rule not uniform, 130.
leading case in Michigan, 130.
rule in Iowa, 130.
exclusive privilege may be granted, 131.
rule in Louisiana, 131.
public power defined, 131.
legislative and business power distinguished, 132.
rule in Indiana, 132.

MONOPOLIES AND STREET RAILWAYS. SEE MONOPOLIES FROM MUNICIPAL GRANTS AND CONTRACTS.

MONOPOLIES UNDER PATENTS.
a patent an essential monopoly, 174.
SEE TRUST COMBINATIONS.

MUNICIPAL GRANTS AND CONTRACTS. SEE MONOPOLIES FROM MUNICIPAL GRANTS AND CONTRACTS.

O.

OPTIONAL CONTRACTS. SEE THE CREATING OF A CORNER.

P.

PARALLEL RAILWAY LINES.
consolidation of, illegal at law, but subject to statutory regulations, 153.
SEE COMBINATIONS OF RAILWAY COMPANIES.

[The references are to sections.]

PATENTED PROPERTY,
power of government to regulate, 143.
SEE THE POWER TO REGULATE PRIVATE CORPORATIONS.

PICKETING. SEE TRADES UNIONS AND LABOR ORGANIZATIONS.

POOLING BY RAILWAY COMPANIES,
in contravention of public policy and void, 170.
SEE TRUST COMBINATIONS.

POOLING OF PRODUCTS,
in contravention of public policy, and void, 172.
SEE TRUST COMBINATIONS.

POOLING OF STOCKS,
not necessarily illegal, 171.
SEE TRUST COMBINATIONS.

POOLS AND TRUSTS,
Minnesota law to prohibit, 199.
law of Utah prohibiting, 213.

POOLS, TRUSTS AND CONSPIRACIES,
law of Kentucky prohibiting, 195.

PRIVATE CORPORATIONS,
the power to regulate. SEE THE POWER TO REGULATE PRIVATE CORPORATIONS.

POWER TO REGULATE PRIVATE CORPORATIONS,
power of the government to regulate, 133.
the leading Illinois case, 133.
the usage in England, 133.
office of statutes in relation to this subject, 133.
private corporations constituted for the benefit of the public, 133.
power of government to regulate the business of a railway company, 134 and n.
property and employment of a railway corporation a public use, 134.
the rule in Wisconsin, 134 and n.
the rule in Georgia. 134 and n.
power of the legislature not lost by non-user, 135.
rule stated by Supreme Court of the United States, 135.
power to act through a commission, 136.
rule of the Supreme Court of the United States, 136.
power to assess damages. 137.
responsibility of railway company for negligence of officers or agents, 137.
power of legislature to prescribe the mode of enforcing penalties 137.
warehouses and warehousing, 138.
power of legislature to regulate, 138.
not affected by the limitation of the powers of congress, 138

[The references are to sections.]

POWER TO REGULATE PRIVATE CORPORATIONS—Continued.
the leading case in Illinois, 138.
the law in New York, 138.
subject to statutory regulations, 139.
the rule in Illinois, 139.
telegraph companies, 140.
legal *status* analogous to that of common carriers, 140.
power of legislature to regulate, 140.
the rule in New York, 140.
the rule in Vermont, 140.
the rule in Virginia, 140.
when subject to congressional control, 141.
decision of the Supreme Court of the United States, 141.
application of the law to the telephone business, 142.
patented property, 143.
power of the government to regulate, 143.
decision in Indiana, 143.
the baking business, 144.
power of the State to regulate the manufacture of bread, 144.
the leading case, 144.
the principle expounded, 144.
the laundry business, 145.
may be regulated by legislative enactment, 145.
right implied in municipal powers, 145.
the charter of a corporation a contract, 146.
may be protected from future legislative control, 146.
legislation may bind itself not to interfere with traffic rates, 146.
immunity from governmental control never presumed, 146.
a business *juris publici* distinguished from a business *juris privati*, 147.
a private business not affected by a public use, by any enlargement of operations, 147.
rule stated by Key, Justice, 147.

PUBLIC POLICY.
origin of the doctrine, 14.
the leading case, 14.
difficulty of applying the rule, 14.
English opinions, 14.
general recognition of the principles involved, 14.
liability to misapplication, 14.
opinion of Lord St. Leonards, 14 and note.
"an unruly horse," 14.
view of Chief Justice Wilmot, 14.
doctrine modified by recent decisions, 14.
the doctrine defined, 15.
construction of rule not uniform, 15.
indicated by constitutional and statutory enactments and decisions of courts, 15.

[The references are to sections.]

PUBLIC POLICY—Continued.
maxim on which the rule is based, 15.
Mr. Story's explanation, 15 and n.
the rule in New Jersey, 15.
statement of rule by Justice Peckham, 15.
contracts not invalidated by change of, 16.
contracts *contra bonos mores* opposed to, 17.
rule of the civil law, 17.
upheld by the common law, 17.
propagation opposed to, 17.
doctrine based on christianity, 17.
contracts for influencing legislation opposed to and not enforceable, 18.
the rule in New York, 18.
public stations a trust, 18.
American theory, 18.
effort to influence legislation in contravention of public policy, in what sense, 19.
ground of the rule prohibiting it, 19.
lobbying contracts. 20.
not *per se* illegal. 20.
services in procuring legislation 20.
not presumed to be illegal, 20.
where the services of an attorney may be employed, 20.
services in influencing public officials, 21.
agreements for, opposed to public policy and void, 21.
personal influence in this direction not vendible. 21.
rule of public policy in Kentucky, 21.
an agent may be employed to negotiate a government contract, 21.
services in procuring appointments to public offices, 22.
agreements pertaining to, not enforceable, 22.
principle on which the rule is based, 22.
sale of a vote and of personal influence opposed to, 22.
exception to the rule, 23.
withdrawal of opposing candidate for public office, 24.
agreements pertaining thereto not enforceable, 24.
void at common law. 24.
grounds of the rule. 24 and n.
services in procuring a pardon, 25.
contracts relating to, not enforceable, 25.
services which are in violation of public duty. 26.
agreements relating to, illegal and void, 26.
covenant not to convey land to a Chinaman, 26.
in contravention of treaty with China, and void, 26.
services in opposing a public enterprise, 27.
contracts relating to, opposed to public policy and void, 27, 28.
location of a railroad station not salable, 28.
may not limit their power to locate, 28.

[The references are to sections.]

PUBLIC POLICY—Continued.
duty of company to regard the public interest, 28.
common carriers, 29.
employment of a public obligation, 29.
when a private carrier, 29.
relation to his customer, 29.
the rule in New York, 29.
stipulation against liability, how far legal, 29.
the rule in England, 29.
the rule of Supreme Court of the United States not upheld in New York, 30.
in that State carrier may limit his liability, 30.
in Missouri, New York rule sustained, 30.
in some States common law rule upheld, 30.
contracts in contravention of law, 31.
illegal and void, 31.
the rule in England, 31.
services in influencing the administration of justice, 32.
covenants relating to it illegal and void, 32.
ground of the rule, 32.
rule in relation to fees of justices of the peace, 32.
offer to perform the duties of an office for less than legal fees, 32.
changing the officers of a corporations, 33.
cannot be made a matter of bargain and sale, 33.
the relation that of trust and confidence, 33.
ground of the rule, 33.
renouncing an executorship, 34.
covenant for, illegal and void, 34.
the principle stated, 34.
the rule applies to administrators, 34.
rule in Ireland, 34.
assignment of salary by public officers, 35.
illegal and void, 35.
ground of illegality, 35.

Q.

QUO WARRANTO. SEE REMEDIES BY QUO WARRANTO AND INJUNCTION.

R.

RAILWAY COMPANIES.
combinations of, for the suppression of competition, 149.
SEE COMBINATIONS OF RAILWAY COMPANIES.
RAILWAY STATIONS.
location of, not salable, 28.
may not limit their power to locate, 28.
duty of company to regard the public interest, 28.

[The references are to sections.]

REASONABLENESS IN RESTRAINT OF TRADE. SEE CONTRACTS IN RESTRAINT OF TRADE.

REBATES IN FREIGHT BILLS,
in some States not illegal, 179.
SEE TRUST COMBINATIONS.

REGRATING. SEE ORIGIN OF INDUSTRIAL TRUSTS.

REMEDIES BY QUO WARRANTO AND INJUNCTION,
extraordinary relief by *quo warranto* and injunction, 216.
certain phrases of the law still unsettled, 216.
direction of the present trend, 216.
writ of *quo warranto*, origin of, 217.
earliest case cited, 217.
defined by Blackstone, 217 and n.
office of an information in the nature of a *quo warranto*, 218.
conditions of a judgment of forfeiture in, 218.
statement by Justice Mitchell, 218.
what constitutes a misuser, 218.
monopolies and industrial combinations, 219.
ground of proceedings against, 219.
judgment under *quo warranto* an extreme remedy, 219.
rule stated by Justice Finch, 219.
what courts have jurisdiction, 220.
where the distinction between law and equity has been abolished, 220.
granting of writ the exercise of an original jurisdiction, 220.
where the supreme court of a State may be invested with original jurisdiction in such cases, 220.
jurisdiction of the court defended, 220.
who may file an information, 221.
misuser or non-user of franchise an offense, 221.
a franchise a public benefit, 221.
public may bring suit for forfeiture of franchise, 221.
must act through attorney-general, 221.
the court may refuse the motion of a private citizen, 221.
attorney-general or prosecuting attorney may institute proceedings without permission of court, 221.
rule in Colorado, 221.
the general rule, 221.
rule in Pennsylvania, 221.
pleadings and averments, 222.
proceeding by information in *quo warranto* a civil remedy, 222.
no uniform system, 222.
present tendency of the courts, 222.
provisions of Illinois practice act, 222.
proceedings in *quo warranto*, 223.
judgment under, 223.
judgment of ouster and judgment of seizure, 223.

[The references are to sections.]

REMEDIES BY QUO WARRANTO AND INJUNCTION—Continued.
distinction of English courts recognized in the United States. 223.
rule in New York. 223.
the rule in Massachusetts. 223.
application of rule to illegal combinations. 224.
leading Nebraska case. 224 and n.
remedy by injunction. 225.
cases where an injunction will issue. 225.
the leading case. 225.
the rule stated. 225 and n.
rule stated in *In re* Debs. 325 and n.
when an injunction will be denied. 225.
injunction under federal anti-trust act. 226.
punishment for contempt. 227.
violation of injunction contempt. 227.
the rule in regard to contempt of court. 227.
rule stated in the Debs case. 227.
rule in Massachusetts. 227.

RENOUNCING AN EXECUTORSHIP. SEE PUBLIC POLICY.

RESTRAINT OF TRADE. SEE CONTRACTS IN RESTRAINT OF TRADE.
general and partial. 8.
reasons for favoring partial restraint. 8.
adequacy of consideration. 8.
when unlimited prohibition is held void. 8.
modern doctrine sustained by popular sentiment. 9.
common law modified by statute. 9.
offense of badgering, etc., abolished. 9.
prohibition must be reasonable. 9.
combinations by workmen and by employees. 9.
American doctrine. 10.
English rule accepted only in part. 10.
court will inquire whether restraint is reasonable. 10.
legality determined by reasonableness. 10.
statutory enactments. 10.
rule established by federal statute. 10.
railway companies subject to general rule. 10.
the Sugar Trust case. 11 and n.
anti-trust laws. 11.
right of the States to enact. 11.
adverse contention. 11.
labor organizations. 12.
combinations for increasing or maintaining wages. 12.
legal methods of obtaining redress. 12.

S.

SPECIAL PRIVILEGES, GRANT OF. SEE MONOPOLIES FROM MUNICIPAL GRANTS AND CONTRACTS.

[The references are to sections.]

STATUTORY REGULATION OF RATES OF TRANSPORTATION,
power of legislature to regulate rates of transportation, 228.
power not absolute, 228.
must respect constitutional rights, 228.
recent decision of Supreme Court of the United States, 228.
statutory enactments subject to judicial investigation, 229.
carrier not to be deprived of property without compensation, 229.
right of railway corporation to legal protection, 230.
members of railway corporations do not lose their rights as citizens, 230.
to all legal intents and purposes a railway corporation is a person, 230.
has the same right to protection as an individual, 230.
power of the State to fix rates of transportation not unlimited, 230.
cannot require railway companies to carry persons or property without consideration, 230.
when a railway company is not bound to make uniform rates, 231.
may have one rate for local and another for through traffic, 231.
local rates must be determined by local business, 231.
through rates not to bear losses on local business, 231.
legislation can fix only local rates, 231.
rates must be reasonable, 231.
rules for determining reasonableness of rates, 232.
what to be considered in fixing value, 232.
each case to be determined by itself, 232.
railway corporation entitled to fair compensation for use of its property, 232.
the public entitled to reasonable protection, 232.

STRIKE AND LOCKOUT. SEE TRADES UNIONS AND LABOR ORGANIZATIONS.

T.

THE BOYCOTT. SEE TRADES UNIONS AND LABOR ORGANIZATIONS.
TELEGRAPH COMPANIES,
legal *status* of, 140.
SEE THE POWER TO REGULATE PRIVATE CORPORATIONS.

TELEPHONE COMPANIES,
application of the law governing telegraph companies to, 142.
SEE THE POWER TO REGULATE PRIVATE CORPORATIONS.

TRADE-MARKS,
restraint in sale of, 55.
SEE CONTRACTS IN RESTRAINT OF TRADE.

TRADES UNIONS AND LABOR ORGANIZATIONS,
law relating to, of recent origin, 98.
first American case, 98.

[The references are to sections.]

TRADES UNIONS AND LABOR ORGANIZATIONS—Continued.
when combinations of this character are held criminal. 98 and n.
general theory of the decisions. 98.
the strike and the lockout. 99.
the terms explained, 99.
nature of legislation in regard to such combinations. 99.
what they may and may not attempt to do. 99.
the object of the strike. 99.
the lockout. 99.
an act of employers corresponding to the strike by laborers. 99.
lockout by employees. 99.
the strike as a conspiracy. 100.
when combinations of this character become illegal. 100.
the law stated. 100.
general principle on which the decisions are based. 101.
where a strike will be upheld. 102.
English and early American decisions. 102.
modification of the rule. 102.
what renders the strike an offense. 102.
the rule of the federal courts. 102.
rights of the parties. 102.
the rule in relation to receivers and railroads, 102.
where a lockout will be sustained. 103.
rights of the parties. 103.
right of employees to combine. 104.
the rule in England. 104.
where lockout lawful. 103.
what constitutes a lockout. 103.
the English rule upheld in Pennsylvania. 104.
the boycott. 105.
the boycott defined. 105.
object of the boycott. 105.
origin of the boycott. 105.
historical notice. 105.
nature of the offense. 106.
the rule in England. 106.
the rule in Virginia. 106.
the rule in Connecticut. 106.
picketing. 107.
the device explained. 107.
the English rule. 107.
the principle on which the American rule is based. 107.
the rule in New York. 107.
blacklisting. 108.
the term explained. 108.
the object of the device. 108.
the law stated. 108.
law in North Dakota. 108.
the Indiana statute. 108.

[The references are to sections.]

TRADES UNIONS AND LABOR ORGANIZATIONS—Continued.
common carriers,
obligations of, as affected by strikes, 109.
the English rule, 109.
the law in Illinois, 109.
rule in Texas, 109.
the strike as a violation of the federal anti-trust act, 110.
rule of the federal courts, 110.
the strike in restraint of interstate commerce, 110 and n.
relation of trades unions to a receiver, 111.
the authority of a receiver, 111.
a representative of the court, 111.
interruption in the transportation of mails, 112.
powers of the general government relating thereto, 112.
how far the executive branch of the government may exercise this power, 112.
appeal to the courts, 112.
ruling of the Supreme Court of the United States, 112.
contracts between employers and trades unions, 113.
terms and conditions of service may be fixed by contract, 113.
the English rule, 113.
sustained by American courts, 113.
the rule in New York, 113.
remedy by civil action, 114.
action against third parties, 114.
the law in Massachusetts, 114.
remedy by injunction, 115.
the rule in Massachusetts, 115.
decision of the federal court, 115.
statutory regulations, 116.
statutes of the States not uniform, 116.

TRUST COMBINATIONS,
designed to conform to the law, 167.
object of such combinations, 167.
illegality of, not affected by change of methods, 167.
purpose and scope of federal legislation in regard to, 168.
act of July 2, 1890, 168.
leading case, 168 and n.
anti-trust act construed by Justice Peckham, 169 and n.
application of the act to railways, 169 and n.
pooling by railroads, 170.
in contravention of public policy and void, 170.
the pool explained, 170.
in England not illegal, 170 and n.
American decisions not in entire harmony, 170 and n.
tendency to a more rigid enforcement of American doctrine, 170.
leading case in Pennsylvania, 170.
opinion of Justice Agnew, 170.

[The references are to sections.]

TRUST COMBINATIONS—Continued.
pooling of stocks, 171.
not necessarily illegal, 171.
leading case in New York, 171.
pooling of products, 172.
in contravention of public policy and void, 172.
the rule in Ohio, 172.
combination to control the price of an article in common use, 173.
a conspiracy and void, 173.
followed by overt acts a misdemeanor, 173.
monopoly under a patent, 174.
a patent an essential monopoly, 174.
confers exclusive privileges, 174.
patent not an infringement of the rights of another, 174.
not created by a combination, 174.
a patent not a permission to enter into an illegal combination, 175.
leading case, 175.
the voting trust, 176.
legality determined the object and the circumstances, 176.
not essentially illegal, 176.
the law in Massachusetts, 176.
presumption that the end in view vitiates the act, 176.
the principle expounded, 176.
the rule in Ohio, 177.
the rule in New York, 177.
where a voting trust will not be upheld, 178.
the rule in New York, 178.
rebates on freight bills, 179.
in some States not illegal, 179.
leading case, 179.
law in Indiana, 179.
the rule in Pennsylvania, 179.
in some States void at common law, 180.
rule in Illinois, 180.
combinations of insurance companies, 181.
in some States prohibited by statute, 181.
rule in Kansas, 181.
rule in Texas, 81.
right of parties under trust combinations, 182.
illegal contract not enforced, 182.
members of trust combinations not protected, 182.
rule in New York, 182.
legal position of receiver, 182.
the general rule, 182.
the rule in Illinois, 182.
law of New Mexico declaring illegal, 204.

[The references are to sections.]

TRUST COMBINATIONS—Continued.
Louisiana law for the prohibition of, 196.
North Dakota law declaring certain, unlawful, 207.
statute of South Carolina prohibiting, 209.

TRUSTS AND COMBINATIONS IN RESTRAINT OF TRADE,
law of Louisiana prohibiting, 196.
Wisconsin statute prohibiting, 215.

TRUSTS AND COMBINES,
Mississippi law prohibiting, 200.
Illinois act prohibiting, 191.

TRUSTS AND CONSPIRACIES,
Nebraska statute against, 203.

TRUSTS AND MONOPOLIES,
Florida legislation relating to, 189.
law of Washington forbidding, 214.

V.

VOTING TRUSTS,
not essentially illegal, 176.
legality determined by objects and circumstances, 176.
SEE TRUST COMBINATIONS.

W.

WAREHOUSES AND WAREHOUSING, PUBLIC.
power of legislature to regulate, 138.